CHILTON'S™

CHRYSLER

CARAVAN/VOYAGER/TOWN & COUNTRY 1996-99 REPAIR MANUAL

PUBLISHED BY **W. G. NICHOLS, INC.**

Manufactured in USA

1020 Andrew Drive
West Chester, PA 19380
ISBN 0-8019-9115-3
Library of Congress Catalog Card No. 99-072302
1234567890 8765432109

www.chiltonsonline.com

Contents

Contents

See last page for information on additional titles

SAFETY NOTICE

Proper service and repair procedures are vital to the safe, reliable operation of all motor vehicles, as well as the personal safety of those performing repairs. This manual outlines procedures for servicing and repairing vehicles using safe, effective methods. The procedures contain many NOTES, CAUTIONS and WARNINGS which should be followed, along with standard procedures to eliminate the possibility of personal injury or improper service which could damage the vehicle or compromise its safety.

It is important to note that repair procedures and techniques, tools and parts for servicing motor vehicles, as well as the skill and experience of the individual performing the work vary widely. It is not possible to anticipate all of the conceivable ways or conditions under which vehicles may be serviced, or to provide cautions as to all possible hazards that may result. Standard and accepted safety precautions and equipment should be used when handling toxic or flammable fluids, and safety goggles or other protection should be used during cutting, grinding, chiseling, prying, or any other process that can cause material removal or projectiles.

Some procedures require the use of tools specially designed for a specific purpose. Before substituting another tool or procedure, you must be completely satisfied that neither your personal safety, nor the performance of the vehicle will be endangered.

Although information in this manual is based on industry sources and is complete as possible at the time of publication, the possibility exists that some car manufacturers made later changes which could not be included here. While striving for total accuracy, Chilton cannot assume responsibility for any errors, changes or omissions that may occur in the compilation of this data.

PART NUMBERS

Part numbers listed in this reference are not recommendations by Chilton for any product brand name. They are references that can be used with interchange manuals and aftermarket supplier catalogs to locate each brand supplier's discrete part number.

SPECIAL TOOLS

Special tools are recommended by the vehicle manufacturer to perform their specific job. Use has been kept to a minimum, but where absolutely necessary, they are referred to in the text by the part number of the tool manufacturer. These tools can be purchased, under the appropriate part number, from your local dealer or regional distributor, or an equivalent tool can be purchased locally from a tool supplier or parts outlet. Before substituting any tool for the one recommended, read the SAFETY NOTICE at the top of this page.

ACKNOWLEDGMENTS

NP/Chilton expresses appreciation to Chrysler Corporation for their generous assistance.

A special thanks to the fine companies who supported the production of this book. Hand tools, supplied by Craftsman, were used during all phases of vehicle teardown and photography. Many of the fine specialty tools used in procedures were provided courtesy of Lisle Corporation. Lincoln Automotive Products has provided their industrial shop equipment including jacks, engine stands and shop presses. A Rotary lift, the largest automobile lift manufacturer in the world offering the biggest variety of surface and inground lifts available, was also used.

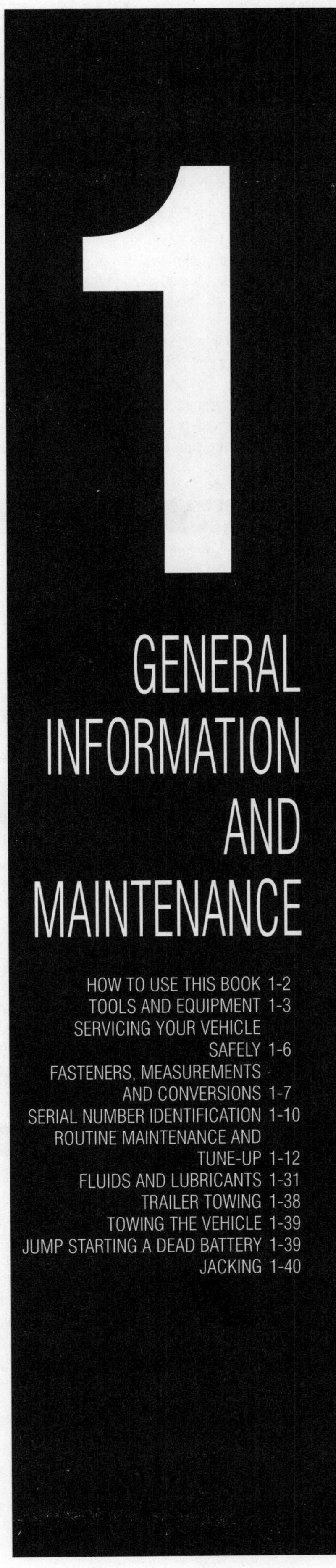
1
GENERAL INFORMATION AND MAINTENANCE

HOW TO USE THIS BOOK

Chilton's Total Car Care manual for the 1996–99 Chrysler Town & Country, Dodge Caravan and Plymouth Voyager minivan is intended to help you learn more about the inner workings of your vehicle while saving you money on its upkeep and operation.

The beginning of the book will likely be referred to the most, since that is where you will find information for maintenance and tune-up. The other sections deal with the more complex systems of your vehicle. Operating systems from engine through brakes are covered to the extent that the average do-it-yourselfer becomes mechanically involved. This book will not explain such things as rebuilding a differential for the simple reason that the expertise required and the investment in special tools make this task uneconomical. It will, however, give you detailed instructions to help you change your own brake pads and shoes, replace spark plugs, and perform many more jobs that can save you money, give you personal satisfaction and help you avoid expensive problems.

A secondary purpose of this book is a reference for owners who want to understand their vehicle and/or their mechanics better. In this case, no tools at all are required.

Where to Begin

Before removing any bolts, read through the entire procedure. This will give you the overall view of what tools and supplies will be required. There is nothing more frustrating than having to walk to the bus stop on Monday morning because you were short one bolt on Sunday afternoon. So read ahead and plan ahead. Each operation should be approached logically and all procedures thoroughly understood before attempting any work.

All sections contain adjustments, maintenance, removal and installation procedures, and in some cases, repair or overhaul procedures. When repair is not considered practical, we tell you how to remove the part and then how to install the new or rebuilt replacement. In this way, you at least save labor costs. "Backyard" repair of some components is just not practical.

Avoiding Trouble

Many procedures in this book require you to "label and disconnect . . . " a group of lines, hoses or wires. Don't be lulled into thinking you can remember where everything goes—you won't. If you hook up vacuum or fuel lines incorrectly, the vehicle may run poorly, if at all. If you hook up electrical wiring incorrectly, you may instantly learn a very expensive lesson.

You don't need to know the official or engineering name for each hose or line. A piece of masking tape on the hose and a piece on its fitting will allow you to assign your own label such as the letter A or a short name. As long as you remember your own code, the lines can be reconnected by matching similar letters or names. Do remember that tape will dissolve in gasoline or other fluids; if a component is to be washed or cleaned, use another method of identification. A permanent felt-tipped marker or a metal scribe can be very handy for marking metal parts. Remove any tape or paper labels after assembly.

Maintenance or Repair?

It's necessary to mention the difference between maintenance and repair. Maintenance includes routine inspections, adjustments, and replacement of parts which show signs of normal wear. Maintenance compensates for wear or deterioration. Repair implies that something has broken or is not working. A need for repair is often caused by lack of maintenance. Example: draining and refilling the automatic transmission fluid is maintenance recommended by the manufacturer at specific mileage intervals. Failure to do this can shorten the life of the transmission/transaxle, requiring very expensive repairs. While no maintenance program can prevent items from breaking or wearing out, a general rule can be stated: MAINTENANCE IS CHEAPER THAN REPAIR.

Two basic mechanic's rules should be mentioned here. First, whenever the left side of the vehicle or engine is referred to, it is meant to specify the driver's side. Conversely, the right side of the vehicle means the passenger's side. Second, screws and bolts are removed by turning counterclockwise, and tightened by turning clockwise unless specifically noted.

Safety is always the most important rule. Constantly be aware of the dangers involved in working on an automobile and take the proper precautions. See the information in this section regarding SERVICING YOUR VEHICLE SAFELY and the SAFETY NOTICE on the acknowledgment page.

Avoiding the Most Common Mistakes

Pay attention to the instructions provided. There are 3 common mistakes in mechanical work:

1. Incorrect order of assembly, disassembly or adjustment. When taking something apart or putting it together, performing steps in the wrong order usually just costs you extra time; however, it CAN break something. Read the entire procedure before beginning disassembly. Perform everything in the order in which the instructions say you should, even if you can't immediately see a reason for it. When you're taking apart something that is very intricate, you might want to draw a picture of how it looks when assembled at one point in order to make sure you get everything back in its proper position. We will supply exploded views whenever possible. When making adjustments, perform them in the proper order. One adjustment possibly will affect another.
2. Overtorquing (or undertorquing). While it is more common for overtorquing to cause damage, undertorquing may allow a fastener to vibrate loose causing serious damage. Especially when dealing with aluminum parts, pay attention to torque specifications and utilize a torque wrench in assembly. If a torque figure is not available, remember that if you are using the right tool to perform the job, you will probably not have to strain yourself to get a fastener tight enough. The pitch of most threads is so slight that the tension you put on the wrench will be multiplied many times in actual force on what you are tightening. A good example of how critical torque is can be seen in the case of spark plug installation, especially where you are putting the plug into an aluminum cylinder head. Too little torque can fail to crush the gasket, causing leakage of combustion gases and consequent overheating of the plug and engine parts. Too much torque can damage the threads or distort the plug, changing the spark gap.

   There are many commercial products available for ensuring that fasteners won't come loose, even if they are not torqued just right (a very common brand is Loctite®). If you're worried about getting something together tight enough to hold, but loose enough to avoid mechanical damage during assembly, one of these products might offer substantial insurance. Before choosing a threadlocking compound, read the label on the package and make sure the product is compatible with the materials, fluids, etc. involved.
3. Crossthreading. This occurs when a part such as a bolt is screwed into a nut or casting at the wrong angle and forced. Crossthreading is more likely to occur if access is difficult. It helps to clean and lubricate fasteners, then to start threading the bolt, spark plug, etc. with your fingers. If you encounter resistance, unscrew the part and start over again at a different angle until it can be inserted and turned several times without much effort. Keep in mind that many parts, especially spark plugs, have tapered threads, so that gentle turning will automatically bring the part you're threading to the proper angle. Don't put a wrench on the part until it's been tightened a couple of turns by hand. If you suddenly encounter resistance, and the part has not seated fully, don't force it. Pull it back out to make sure it's clean and threading properly.

Be sure to take your time and be patient, and always plan ahead. Allow yourself ample time to perform repairs and maintenance. You may find maintaining your car a satisfying and enjoyable experience.

TOOLS AND EQUIPMENT

See Figures 1 thru 15

Naturally, without the proper tools and equipment it is impossible to properly service your vehicle. It would also be virtually impossible to catalog every tool that you would need to perform all of the operations in this book. Of course, It would be unwise for the amateur to rush out and buy an expensive set of tools on the theory that he/she may need one or more of them at some time.

The best approach is to proceed slowly, gathering a good quality set of those tools that are used most frequently. Don't be misled by the low cost of bargain tools. It is far better to spend a little more for better quality. Forged wrenches, 6 or 12-point sockets and fine tooth ratchets are by far preferable to their less expensive counterparts. As any good mechanic can tell you, there are few worse experiences than trying to work on a vehicle with bad tools. Your monetary savings will be far outweighed by frustration and mangled knuckles.

Begin accumulating those tools that are used most frequently: those associated with routine maintenance and tune-up. In addition to the normal assortment of screwdrivers and pliers, you should have the following tools:

- Wrenches/sockets and combination open end/box end wrenches in sizes from 1/8–3/4 in. or 3–19mm, as well as a 13/16 in. or 5/8 in. spark plug socket (depending on plug type).

➡ If possible, buy various length socket drive extensions. Universal-joint and wobble extensions can be extremely useful, but be careful when using them, as they can change the amount of torque applied to the socket.

- Jackstands for support.
- Oil filter wrench.
- Spout or funnel for pouring fluids.
- Grease gun for chassis lubrication (unless your vehicle is not equipped with any grease fittings—for details, please refer to information on Fluids and Lubricants, later in this section).
- Hydrometer for checking the battery (unless equipped with a sealed, maintenance-free battery).

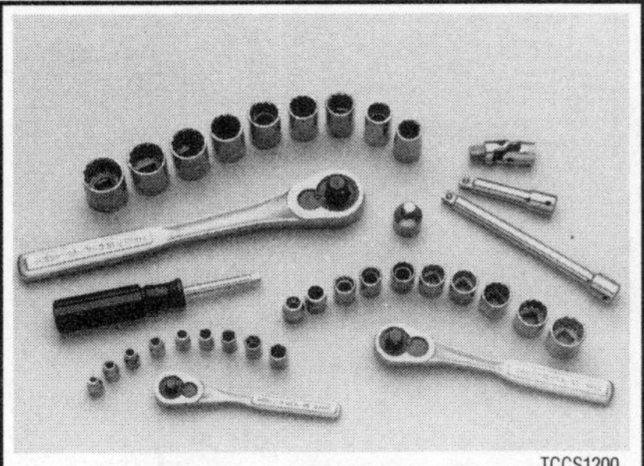

TCCS1200

Fig. 1 All but the most basic procedures will require an assortment of ratchets and sockets

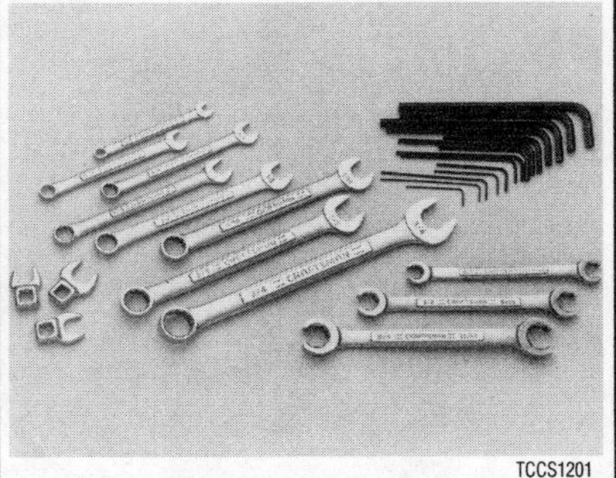

TCCS1201

Fig. 2 In addition to ratchets, a good set of wrenches and hex keys will be necessary

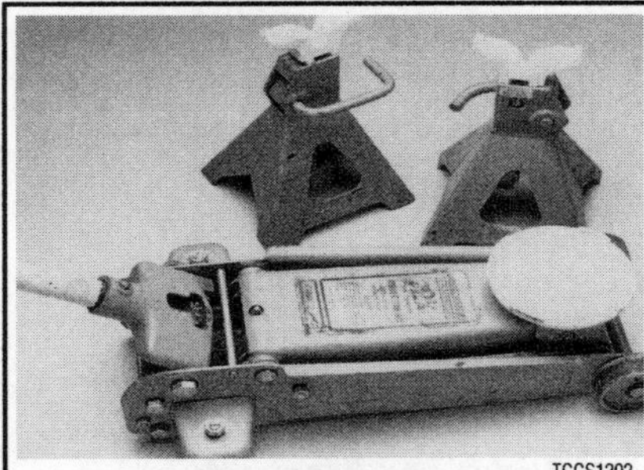

TCCS1202

Fig. 3 A hydraulic floor jack and a set of jackstands are essential for lifting and supporting the vehicle

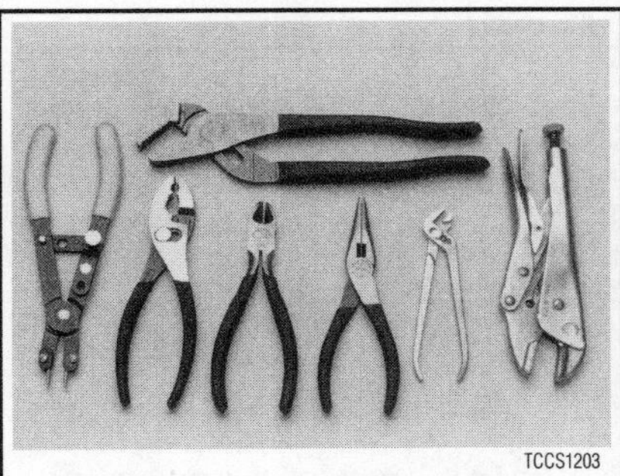

TCCS1203

Fig. 4 An assortment of pliers, grippers and cutters will be handy for old rusted parts and stripped bolt heads

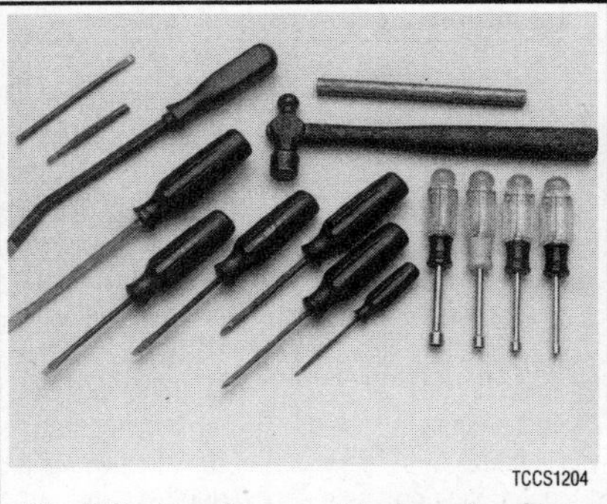

TCCS1204

Fig. 5 Various drivers, chisels and prybars are great tools to have in your toolbox

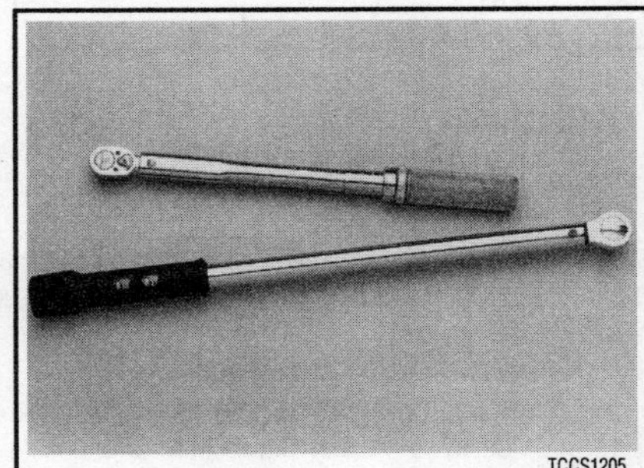

TCCS1205

Fig. 6 Many repairs will require the use of a torque wrench to assure the components are properly fastened

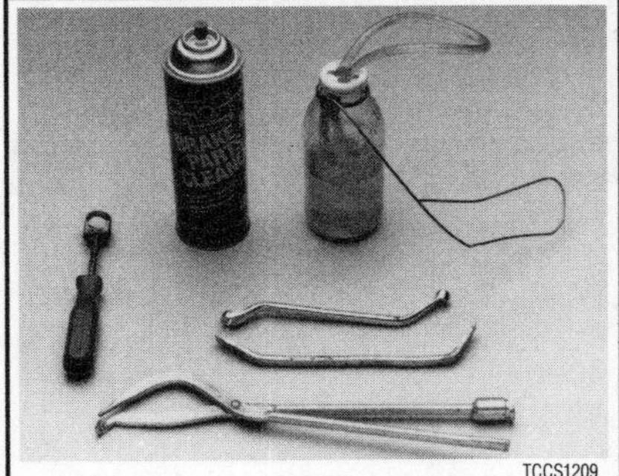

TCCS1209

Fig. 7 Although not always necessary, using specialized brake tools will save time

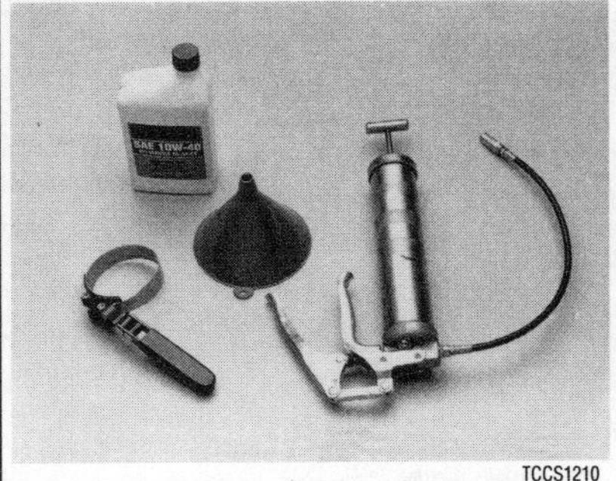

TCCS1210

Fig. 8 A few inexpensive lubrication tools will make maintenance easier

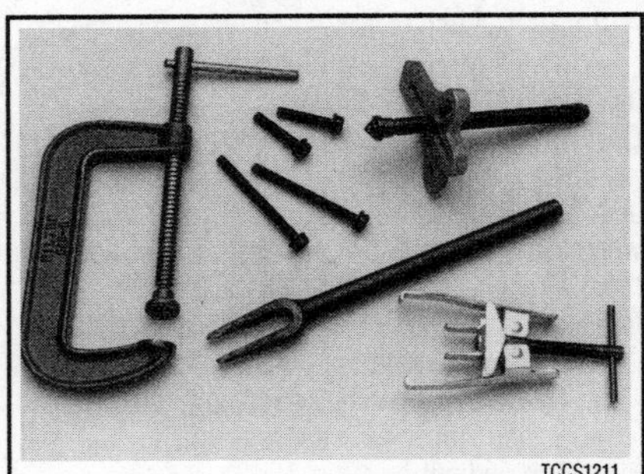

TCCS1211

Fig. 9 Various pullers, clamps and separator tools are needed for many larger, more complicated repairs

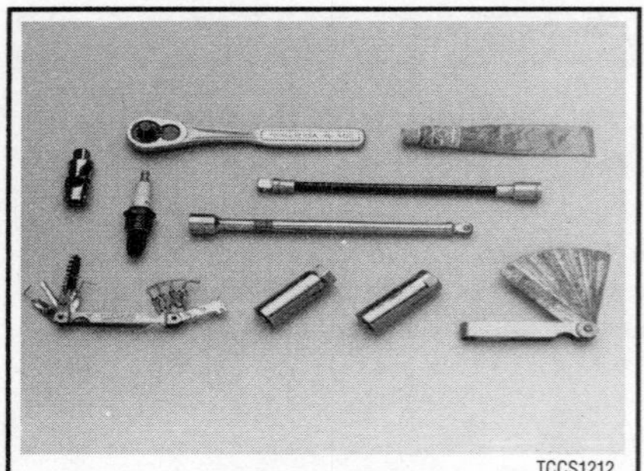
TCCS1212

Fig. 10 A variety of tools and gauges should be used for spark plug gapping and installation

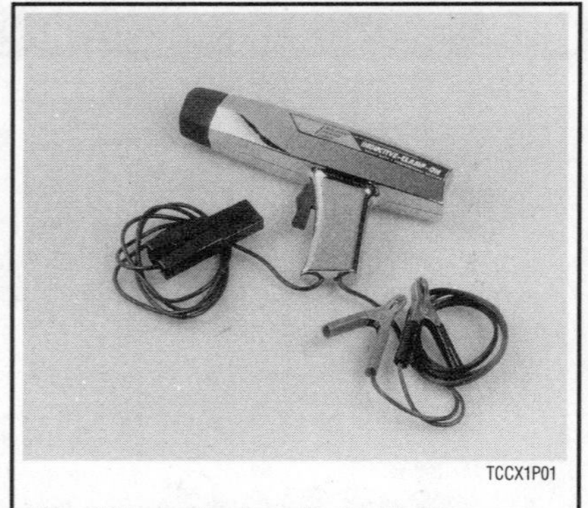
TCCX1P01

Fig. 11 Inductive type timing light

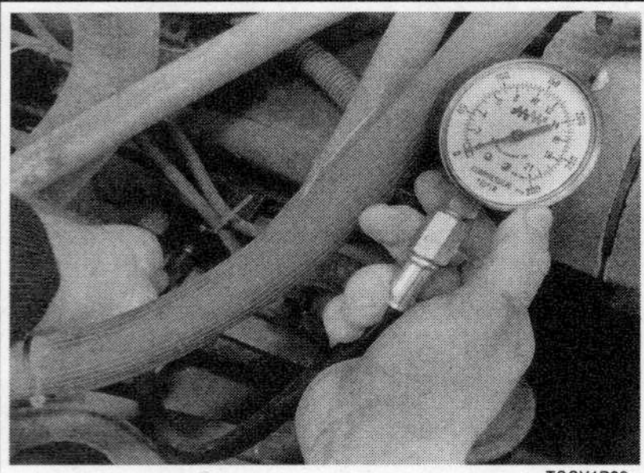
TCCX1P02

Fig. 12 A screw-in type compression gauge is recommended for compression testing

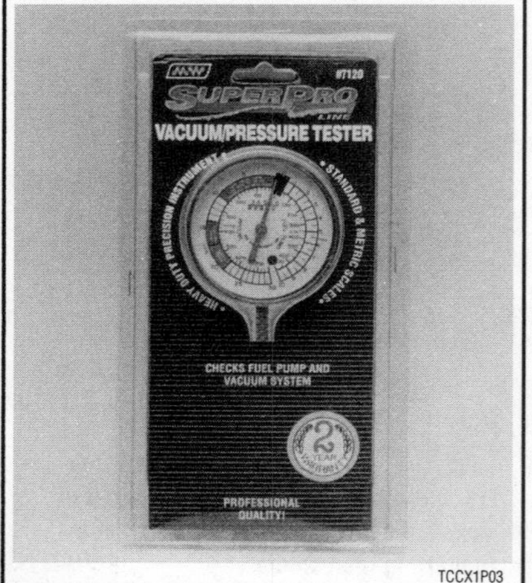

TCCX1P03

Fig. 13 A vacuum/pressure tester is necessary for many testing procedures

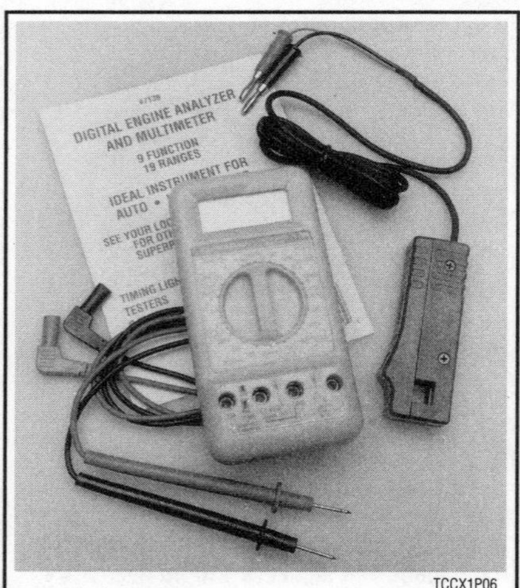

TCCX1P06

Fig. 14 Most modern automotive multimeters incorporate many helpful features

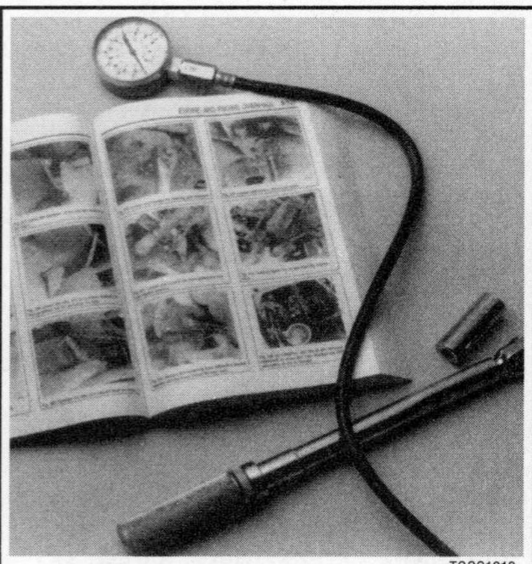
TCCS1213

Fig. 15 Proper information is vital, so always have a Chilton Total Car Care manual handy

- A container for draining oil and other fluids.
- Rags for wiping up the inevitable mess.

In addition to the above items there are several others that are not absolutely necessary, but handy to have around. These include Oil Dry® (or an equivalent oil absorbent gravel—such as cat litter) and the usual supply of lubricants, antifreeze and fluids, although these can be purchased as needed. This is a basic list for routine maintenance, but only your personal needs and desire can accurately determine your list of tools.

After performing a few projects on the vehicle, you'll be amazed at the other tools and non-tools on your workbench. Some useful household items are: a large turkey baster or siphon, empty coffee cans and ice trays (to store parts), ball of twine, electrical tape for wiring, small rolls of colored tape for tagging lines or hoses, markers and pens, a note pad, golf tees (for plugging vacuum lines), metal coat hangers or a roll of mechanic's wire (to hold things out of the way), dental pick or similar long, pointed probe, a strong magnet, and a small mirror (to see into recesses and under manifolds).

A more advanced set of tools, suitable for tune-up work, can be drawn up easily. While the tools are slightly more sophisticated, they need not be outrageously expensive. There are several inexpensive tach/dwell meters on the market that are every bit as good for the average mechanic as a professional model. Just be sure that it goes to a least 1200–1500 rpm on the tach scale and that it works on 4, 6 and 8-cylinder engines. The key to these purchases is to make them with an eye towards adaptability and wide range. A basic list of tune-up tools could include:

- Tach/dwell meter.
- Spark plug wrench and gapping tool.
- Feeler gauges for valve adjustment.
- Timing light.

The choice of a timing light should be made carefully. A light which works on the DC current supplied by the vehicle's battery is the best choice; it should have a xenon tube for brightness. On any vehicle with an electronic ignition system, a timing light with an inductive pickup that clamps around the No. 1 spark plug cable is preferred.

In addition to these basic tools, there are several other tools and gauges you may find useful. These include:

- Compression gauge. The screw-in type is slower to use, but eliminates the possibility of a faulty reading due to escaping pressure.
- Manifold vacuum gauge.
- 12V test light.
- A combination volt/ohmmeter
- Induction Ammeter. This is used for determining whether or not there is current in a wire. These are handy for use if a wire is broken somewhere in a wiring harness.

As a final note, you will probably find a torque wrench necessary for all but the most basic work. The beam type models are perfectly adequate, although the newer click types (breakaway) are easier to use. The click type torque wrenches tend to be more expensive. Also keep in mind that all types of torque wrenches should be periodically checked and/or recalibrated. You will have to decide for yourself which better fits your pocketbook, and purpose.

Special Tools

Normally, the use of special factory tools is avoided for repair procedures, since these are not readily available for the do-it-yourself mechanic. When it is possible to perform the job with more commonly available tools, it will be pointed out, but occasionally, a special tool was designed to perform a specific function and should be used. Before substituting another tool, you should be convinced that neither your safety nor the performance of the vehicle will be compromised.

Special tools can usually be purchased from an automotive parts store or from your dealer. In some cases special tools may be available directly from the tool manufacturer.

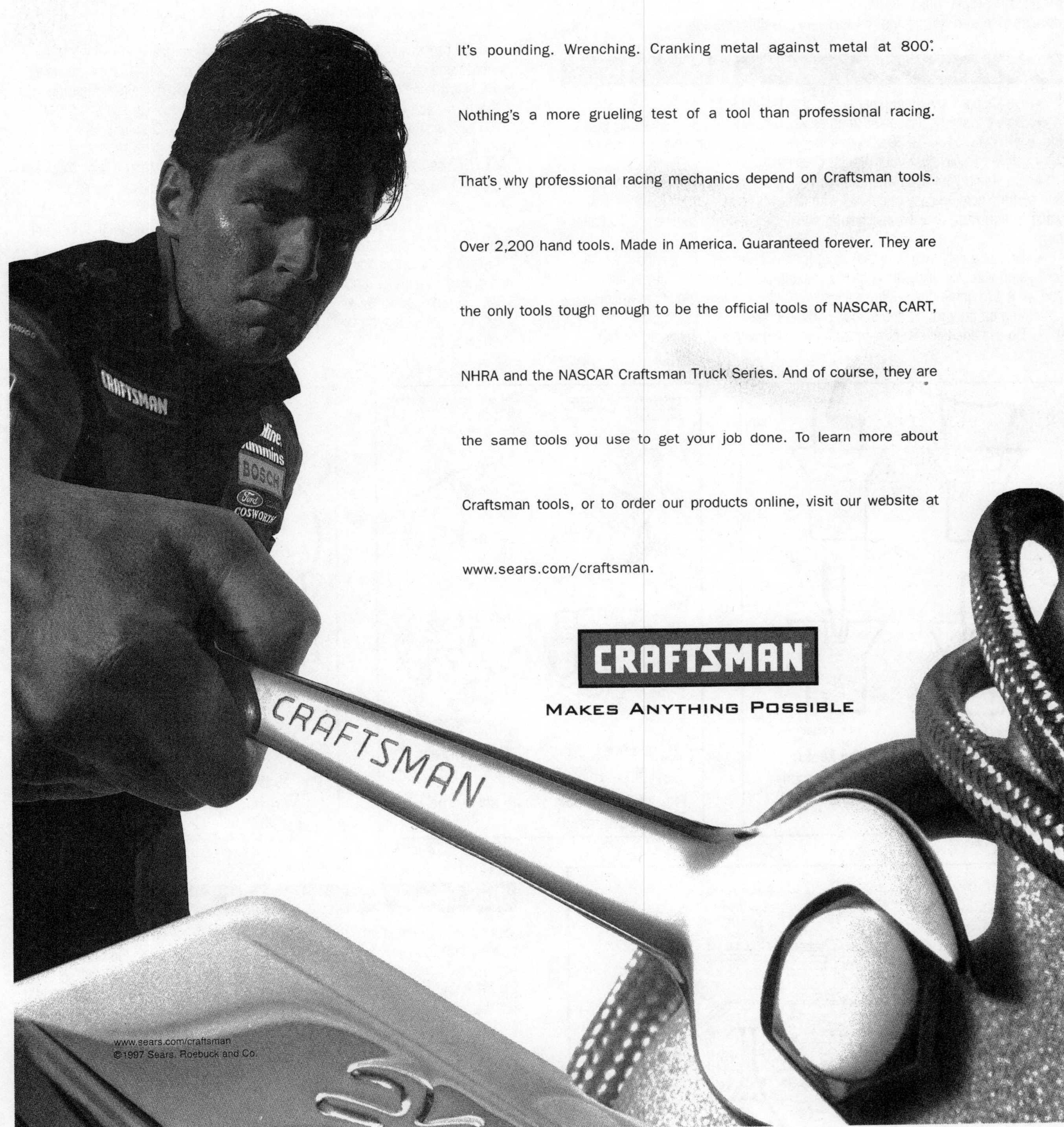
It's pounding. Wrenching. Cranking metal against metal at 800°. Nothing's a more grueling test of a tool than professional racing. That's why professional racing mechanics depend on Craftsman tools. Over 2,200 hand tools. Made in America. Guaranteed forever. They are the only tools tough enough to be the official tools of NASCAR, CART, NHRA and the NASCAR Craftsman Truck Series. And of course, they are the same tools you use to get your job done. To learn more about Craftsman tools, or to order our products online, visit our website at www.sears.com/craftsman.
CRAFTSMAN
MAKES ANYTHING POSSIBLE
CRAFTSMAN
BOSCH
COSWORTH
CRAFTSMAN
www.sears.com/craftsman
©1997 Sears, Roebuck and Co.

TCCA1AC1

SERVICING YOUR VEHICLE SAFELY

▸ See Figures 16, 17, 18 and 19

It is virtually impossible to anticipate all of the hazards involved with automotive maintenance and service, but care and common sense will prevent most accidents.

The rules of safety for mechanics range from "don't smoke around gasoline," to "use the proper tool(s) for the job." The trick to avoiding injuries is to develop safe work habits and to take every possible precaution.

Do's

- Do keep a fire extinguisher and first aid kit handy.
- Do wear safety glasses or goggles when cutting, drilling, grinding or prying, even if you have 20–20 vision. If you wear glasses for the sake of vision, wear safety goggles over your regular glasses.
- Do shield your eyes whenever you work around the battery. Batteries contain sulfuric acid. In case of contact with the eyes or skin, flush the area with water or a mixture of water and baking soda, then seek immediate medical attention.
- Do use safety stands (jackstands) for any undervehicle service. Jacks are for raising vehicles; jackstands are for making sure the vehicle stays raised until you want it to come down. Whenever the vehicle is raised, block the wheels remaining on the ground and set the parking brake.
- Do use adequate ventilation when working with any chemicals or hazardous materials. Like carbon monoxide, the asbestos dust resulting from some brake lining wear can be hazardous in sufficient quantities.
- Do disconnect the negative battery cable when working on the electrical system. The secondary ignition system contains EXTREMELY HIGH VOLTAGE. In some cases it can even exceed 50,000 volts.
- Do follow manufacturer's directions whenever working with potentially hazardous materials. Most chemicals and fluids are poisonous if taken internally.
- Do properly maintain your tools. Loose hammerheads, mushroomed punches and chisels, frayed or poorly grounded electrical cords, excessively worn screwdrivers, spread wrenches (open end), cracked sockets, slipping ratchets, or faulty droplight sockets can cause accidents.
- Likewise, keep your tools clean; a greasy wrench can slip off a bolt head, ruining the bolt and often harming your knuckles in the process.
- Do use the proper size and type of tool for the job at hand. Do select a wrench or socket that fits the nut or bolt. The wrench or socket should sit straight, not cocked.
- Do, when possible, pull on a wrench handle rather than push on it, and adjust your stance to prevent a fall.
- Do be sure that adjustable wrenches are tightly closed on the nut or bolt and pulled so that the force is on the side of the fixed jaw.
- Do strike squarely with a hammer; avoid glancing blows.
- Do set the parking brake and block the drive wheels if the work requires a running engine.

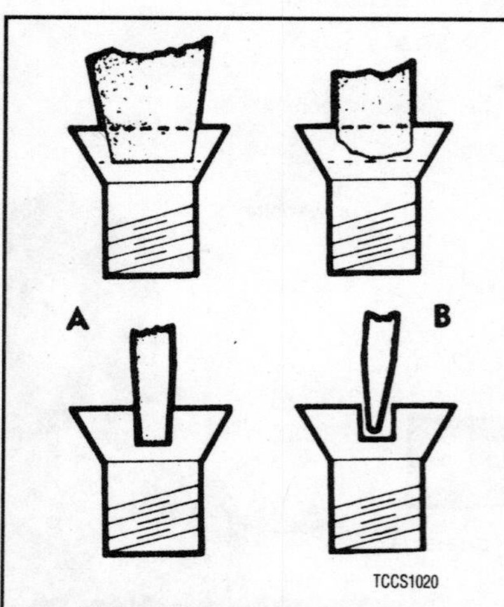

Fig. 16 Screwdrivers should be kept in good condition to prevent injury or damage which could result if the blade slips from the screw

Fig. 17 Power tools should always be properly grounded

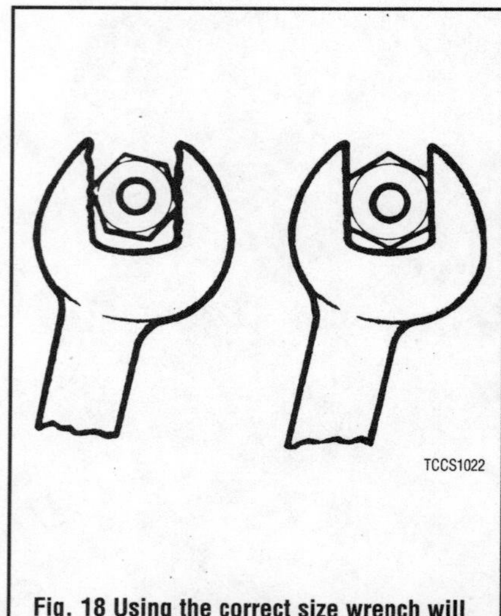

Fig. 18 Using the correct size wrench will help prevent the possibility of rounding off a nut

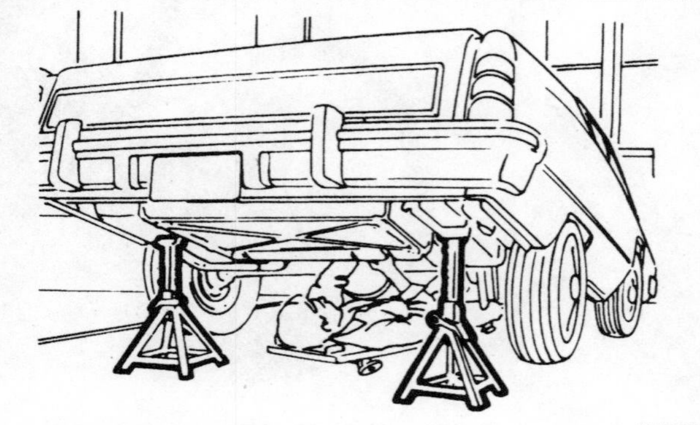

Fig. 19 NEVER work under a vehicle unless it is supported using safety stands (jackstands)

Don'ts

- Don't run the engine in a garage or anywhere else without proper ventilation—EVER! Carbon monoxide is poisonous; it takes a long time to leave the human body and you can build up a deadly supply of it in your system by simply breathing in a little every day. You may not realize you are slowly poisoning yourself. Always use power vents, windows, fans and/or open the garage door.
- Don't work around moving parts while wearing loose clothing. Short sleeves are much safer than long, loose sleeves. Hard-toed shoes with neoprene soles protect your toes and give a better grip on slippery surfaces. Jewelry such as watches, fancy belt buckles, beads or body adornment of any kind is not safe working around a vehicle. Long hair should be tied back under a hat or cap.
- Don't use pockets for toolboxes. A fall or bump can drive a screwdriver deep into your body. Even a rag hanging from your back pocket can wrap around a spinning shaft or fan.
- Don't smoke when working around gasoline, cleaning solvent or other flammable material.

• Don't smoke when working around the battery. When the battery is being charged, it gives off explosive hydrogen gas.

• Don't use gasoline to wash your hands; there are excellent soaps available. Gasoline contains dangerous additives which can enter the body through a cut or through your pores. Gasoline also removes all the natural oils from the skin so that bone dry hands will suck up oil and grease.

• Don't service the air conditioning system unless you are equipped with the necessary tools and training. When liquid or compressed gas refrigerant is released to atmospheric pressure it will absorb heat from whatever it contacts. This will chill or freeze anything it touches.

• Don't use screwdrivers for anything other than driving screws! A screwdriver used as an prying tool can snap when you least expect it, causing injuries. At the very least, you'll ruin a good screwdriver.

• Don't use an emergency jack (that little ratchet, scissors, or pantograph jack supplied with the vehicle) for anything other than changing a flat! These jacks are only intended for emergency use out on the road; they are NOT designed as a maintenance tool. If you are serious about maintaining your vehicle yourself, invest in a hydraulic floor jack of at least a 1½ ton capacity, and at least two sturdy jackstands.

FASTENERS, MEASUREMENTS AND CONVERSIONS

Bolts, Nuts and Other Threaded Retainers

See Figures 20, 21, 22 and 23

Although there are a great variety of fasteners found in the modern car or truck, the most commonly used retainer is the threaded fastener (nuts, bolts, screws, studs, etc.). Most threaded retainers may be reused, provided that they are not damaged in use or during the repair. Some retainers (such as stretch bolts or torque prevailing nuts) are designed to deform when tightened or in use and should not be reinstalled.

Whenever possible, we will note any special retainers which should be replaced during a procedure. But you should always inspect the condition of a retainer when it is removed and replace any that show signs of damage. Check all threads for rust or corrosion which can increase the torque necessary to achieve the desired clamp load for which that fastener was originally selected. Additionally, be sure that the driver surface of the fastener has not been compromised by rounding or other damage. In some cases a driver surface may become only partially rounded, allowing the driver to catch in only one direction. In many of these occurrences, a fastener may be installed and tightened, but the driver would not be able to grip and loosen the fastener again. (This could lead to frustration down the line should that component ever need to be disassembled again).

If you must replace a fastener, whether due to design or damage, you must ALWAYS be sure to use the proper replacement. In all cases, a retainer of the

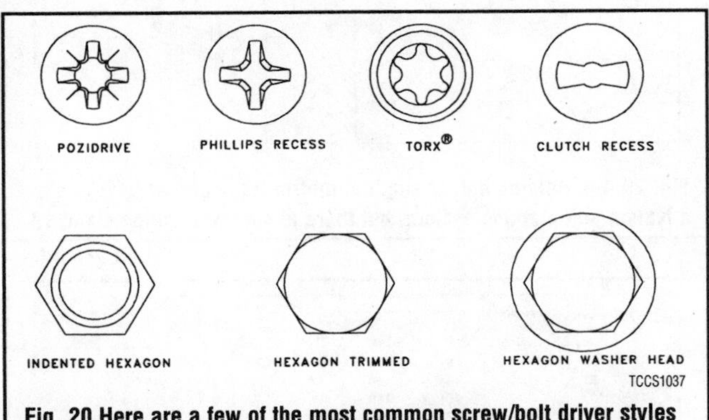

Fig. 20 Here are a few of the most common screw/bolt driver styles

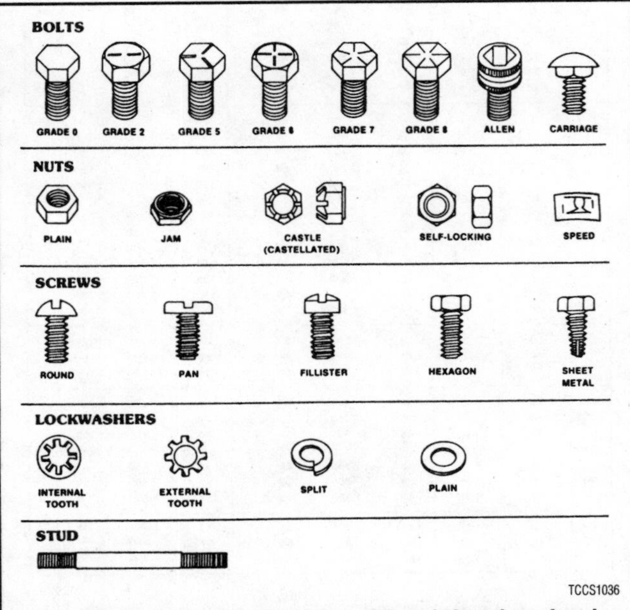

Fig. 21 There are many different types of threaded retainers found on vehicles

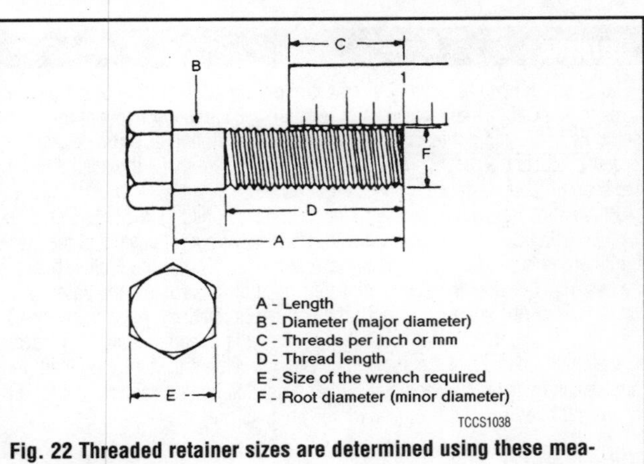

Fig. 22 Threaded retainer sizes are determined using these measurements

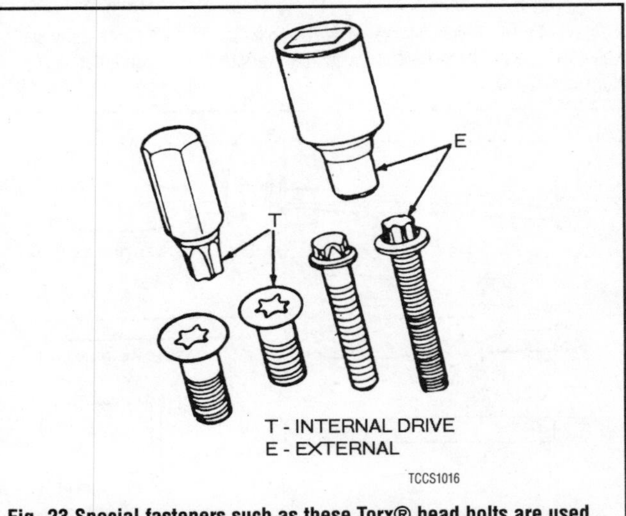

Fig. 23 Special fasteners such as these Torx® head bolts are used by manufacturers to discourage people from working on vehicles without the proper tools

same design, material and strength should be used. Markings on the heads of most bolts will help determine the proper strength of the fastener. The same material, thread and pitch must be selected to assure proper installation and safe operation of the vehicle afterwards.

Thread gauges are available to help measure a bolt or stud's thread. Most automotive and hardware stores keep gauges available to help you select the proper size. In a pinch, you can use another nut or bolt for a thread gauge. If the bolt you are replacing is not too badly damaged, you can select a match by finding another bolt which will thread in its place. If you find a nut which threads properly onto the damaged bolt, then use that nut to help select the replacement bolt. If however, the bolt you are replacing is so badly damaged (broken or drilled out) that its threads cannot be used as a gauge, you might start by looking for another bolt (from the same assembly or a similar location on your vehicle) which will thread into the damaged bolt's mounting. If so, the other bolt can be used to select a nut; the nut can then be used to select the replacement bolt.

In all cases, be absolutely sure you have selected the proper replacement. Don't be shy, you can always ask the store clerk for help.

✱✱ WARNING

Be aware that when you find a bolt with damaged threads, you may also find the nut or drilled hole it was threaded into has also been damaged. If this is the case, you may have to drill and tap the hole, replace the nut or otherwise repair the threads. NEVER try to force a replacement bolt to fit into the damaged threads.

Torque

Torque is defined as the measurement of resistance to turning or rotating. It tends to twist a body about an axis of rotation. A common example of this would be tightening a threaded retainer such as a nut, bolt or screw. Measuring torque is one of the most common ways to help assure that a threaded retainer has been properly fastened.

When tightening a threaded fastener, torque is applied in three distinct areas, the head, the bearing surface and the clamp load. About 50 percent of the measured torque is used in overcoming bearing friction. This is the friction between the bearing surface of the bolt head, screw head or nut face and the base material or washer (the surface on which the fastener is rotating). Approximately 40 percent of the applied torque is used in overcoming thread friction. This leaves only about 10 percent of the applied torque to develop a useful clamp load (the force which holds a joint together). This means that friction can account for as much as 90 percent of the applied torque on a fastener.

TORQUE WRENCHES

➧ See Figures 24, 25 and 26

In most applications, a torque wrench can be used to assure proper installation of a fastener. Torque wrenches come in various designs and most automotive supply stores will carry a variety to suit your needs. A torque wrench should be used any time we supply a specific torque value for a fastener. A torque wrench can also be used if you are following the general guidelines in the accompanying charts. Keep in mind that because there is no worldwide standardization of fasteners, the charts are a general guideline and should be used

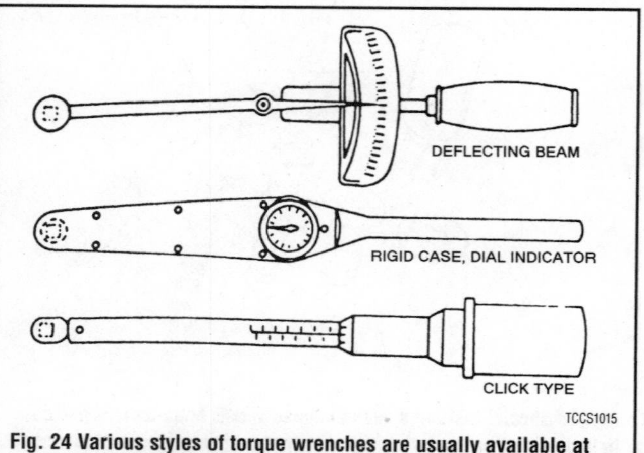

Fig. 24 Various styles of torque wrenches are usually available at your local automotive supply store

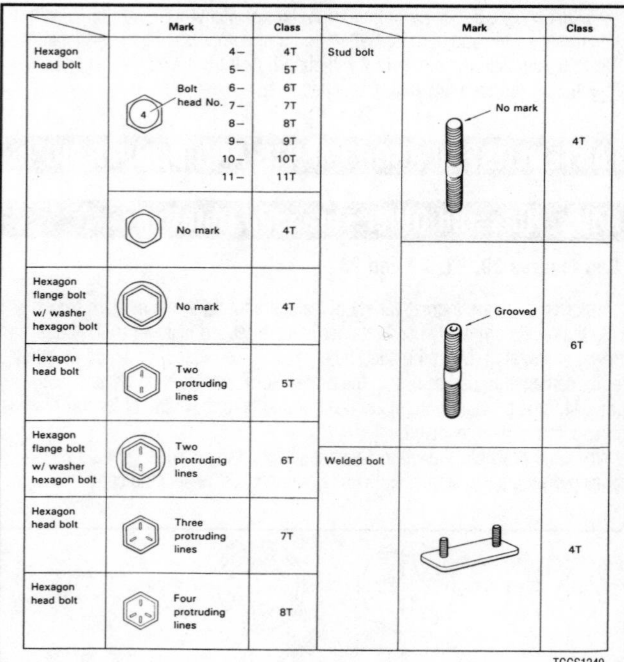

	Mark	Class
Hexagon head bolt	Bolt head No. 4– 5– 6– 7– 8– 9– 10– 11–	4T 5T 6T 7T 8T 9T 10T 11T
	No mark	4T
Hexagon flange bolt w/ washer hexagon bolt	No mark	4T
Hexagon head bolt	Two protruding lines	5T
Hexagon flange bolt w/ washer hexagon bolt	Two protruding lines	6T
Hexagon head bolt	Three protruding lines	7T
Hexagon head bolt	Four protruding lines	8T
Stud bolt	No mark	4T
	Grooved	6T
Welded bolt		4T

TCCS1240

Fig. 25 Determining bolt strength of metric fasteners—NOTE: this is a typical bolt marking system, but there is not a worldwide standard

Class	Diameter mm	Pitch mm	Specified torque: Hexagon head bolt N·m	kgf·cm	ft·lbf	Hexagon flange bolt N·m	kgf·cm	ft·lbf
4T	6	1	5	55	48 in.·lbf	6	60	52 in.·lbf
	8	1.25	12.5	130	9	14	145	10
	10	1.25	26	260	19	29	290	21
	12	1.25	47	480	35	53	540	39
	14	1.5	74	760	55	84	850	61
	16	1.5	115	1,150	83	–	–	–
5T	6	1	6.5	65	56 in.·lbf	7.5	75	65 in.·lbf
	8	1.25	15.5	160	12	17.5	175	13
	10	1.25	32	330	24	36	360	26
	12	1.25	59	600	43	65	670	48
	14	1.5	91	930	67	100	1,050	76
	16	1.5	140	1,400	101	–	–	–
6T	6	1	8	80	69 in.·lbf	9	90	78 in.·lbf
	8	1.25	19	195	14	21	210	15
	10	1.25	39	400	29	44	440	32
	12	1.25	71	730	53	80	810	59
	14	1.5	110	1,100	80	125	1,250	90
	16	1.5	170	1,750	127	–	–	–
7T	6	1	10.5	110	8	12	120	9
	8	1.25	25	260	19	28	290	21
	10	1.25	52	530	38	58	590	43
	12	1.25	95	970	70	105	1,050	76
	14	1.5	145	1,500	108	165	1,700	123
	16	1.5	230	2,300	166	–	–	–
8T	8	1.25	29	300	22	33	330	24
	10	1.25	61	620	45	68	690	50
	12	1.25	110	1,100	80	120	1,250	90
9T	8	1.25	34	340	25	37	380	27
	10	1.25	70	710	51	78	790	57
	12	1.25	125	1,300	94	140	1,450	105
10T	8	1.25	38	390	28	42	430	31
	10	1.25	78	800	58	88	890	64
	12	1.25	140	1,450	105	155	1,600	116
11T	8	1.25	42	430	31	47	480	35
	10	1.25	87	890	64	97	990	72
	12	1.25	155	1,600	116	175	1,800	130

TCCS1241

Fig. 26 Typical bolt torques for metric fasteners—WARNING: use only as a guide

with caution. Again, the general rule of "if you are using the right tool for the job, you should not have to strain to tighten a fastener" applies here.

Beam Type

➧ See Figure 27

The beam type torque wrench is one of the most popular types. It consists of a pointer attached to the head that runs the length of the flexible beam (shaft) to a scale located near the handle. As the wrench is pulled, the beam bends and the pointer indicates the torque using the scale.

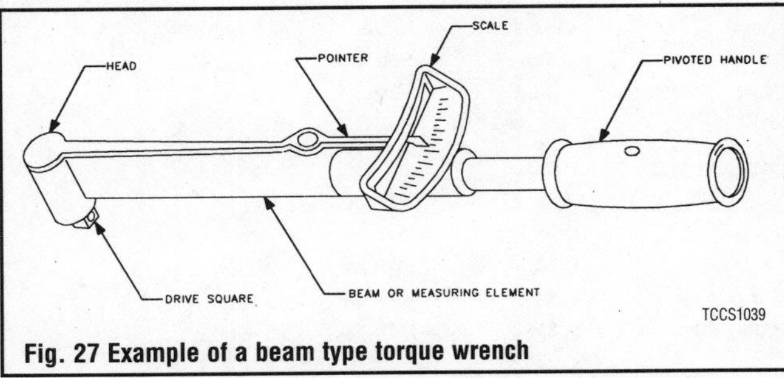

Fig. 27 Example of a beam type torque wrench

Click (Breakaway) Type

➧ See Figure 28

Another popular design of torque wrench is the click type. To use the click type wrench you pre-adjust it to a torque setting. Once the torque is reached, the wrench has a reflex signaling feature that causes a momentary breakaway of the torque wrench body, sending an impulse to the operator's hand.

Pivot Head Type

➧ See Figures 28 and 29

Some torque wrenches (usually of the click type) may be equipped with a pivot head which can allow it to be used in areas of limited access. BUT, it must be used properly. To hold a pivot head wrench, grasp the handle lightly, and as you pull on the handle, it should be floated on the pivot point. If the handle comes in contact with the yoke extension during the process of pulling, there is a very good chance the torque readings will be inaccurate because this could alter the wrench loading point. The design of the handle is usually such as to make it inconvenient to deliberately misuse the wrench.

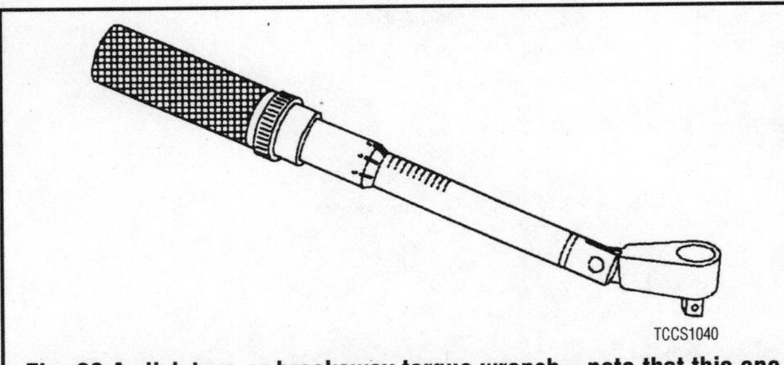

Fig. 28 A click type or breakaway torque wrench—note that this one has a pivoting head

➡ It should be mentioned that the use of any U-joint, wobble or extension will have an effect on the torque readings, no matter what type of wrench you are using. For the most accurate readings, install the socket directly on the wrench driver. If necessary, straight extensions (which hold a socket directly under the wrench driver) will have the least effect on the torque reading. Avoid any extension that alters the length of the wrench from the handle to the head/driving point (such as a crow's foot). U-joint or wobble extensions can greatly affect the readings; avoid their use at all times.

Rigid Case (Direct Reading)

➧ See Figure 30

A rigid case or direct reading torque wrench is equipped with a dial indicator to show torque values. One advantage of these wrenches is that they can be held at any position on the wrench without affecting accuracy. These wrenches are often preferred because they tend to be compact, easy to read and have a great degree of accuracy.

TORQUE ANGLE METERS

➧ See Figure 31

Because the frictional characteristics of each fastener or threaded hole will vary, clamp loads which are based strictly on torque will vary as well. In most applications, this variance is not significant enough to cause worry. But, in certain applications, a manufacturer's engineers may determine that more precise clamp loads are necessary (such is the case with many aluminum cylinder heads). In these cases, a torque angle method of installation would be specified. When installing fasteners which are torque angle tightened, a predetermined seating torque and standard torque wrench are usually used first to remove any compliance from the joint. The fastener is then tightened the specified additional portion of a turn measured in degrees. A torque angle gauge (mechanical protractor) is used for these applications.

Standard and Metric Measurements

➧ See Figure 32

Throughout this manual, specifications are given to help you determine the condition of various components on your vehicle, or to assist you in their installation. Some of the most common measurements include length (in. or cm/mm), torque (ft. lbs., inch lbs. or Nm) and pressure (psi, in. Hg, kPa or mm Hg). In most cases, we strive to provide the proper measurement as determined by the manufacturer's engineers.

Though, in some cases, that value may not be conveniently measured with what is available in your toolbox. Luckily, many of the measuring devices which

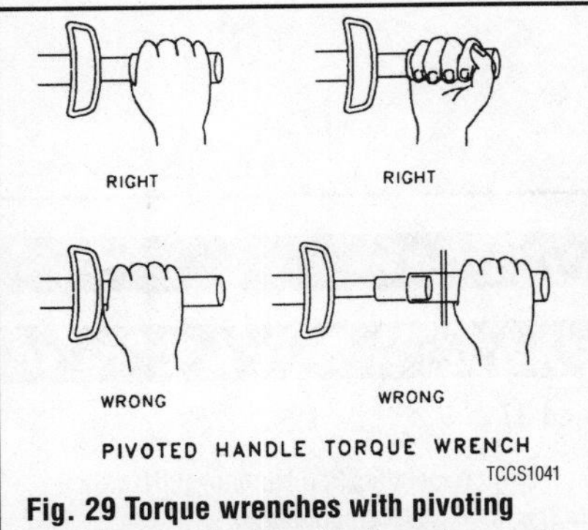

Fig. 29 Torque wrenches with pivoting heads must be grasped and used properly to prevent an incorrect reading

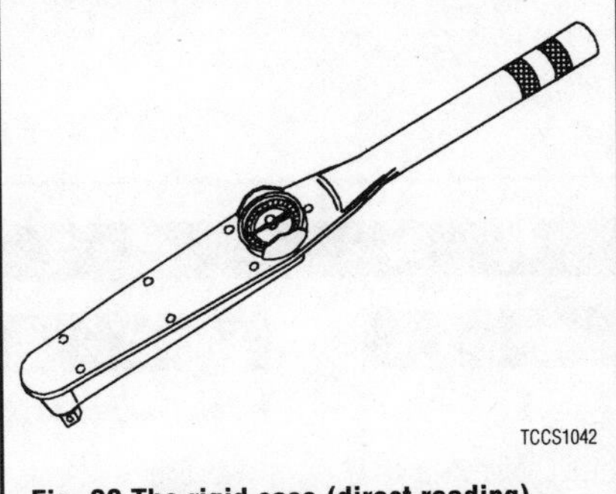

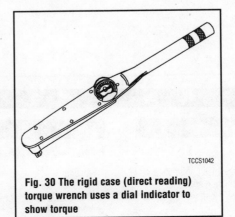

Fig. 30 The rigid case (direct reading) torque wrench uses a dial indicator to show torque

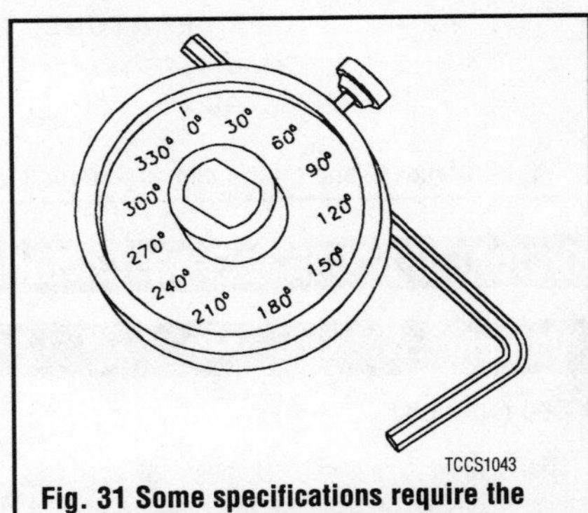

Fig. 31 Some specifications require the use of a torque angle meter (mechanical protractor)

are available today will have two scales so the Standard or Metric measurements may easily be taken. If any of the various measuring tools which are available to you do not contain the same scale as listed in the specifications, use the accompanying conversion factors to determine the proper value.

The conversion factor chart is used by taking the given specification and multiplying it by the necessary conversion factor. For instance, looking at the first line, if you have a measurement in inches such as "free-play should be 2 in." but your ruler reads only in millimeters, multiply 2 in. by the conversion factor of 25.4 to get the metric equivalent of 50.8mm. Likewise, if the specification was given only in a Metric measurement, for example in Newton Meters (Nm), then look at the center column first. If the measurement is 100 Nm, multiply it by the conversion factor of 0.738 to get 73.8 ft. lbs.

CONVERSION FACTORS

LENGTH–DISTANCE				
Inches (in.)	x 25.4	= Millimeters (mm)	x .0394	= Inches
Feet (ft.)	x .305	= Meters (m)	x 3.281	= Feet
Miles	x 1.609	= Kilometers (km)	x .0621	= Miles
VOLUME				
Cubic Inches (in3)	x 16.387	= Cubic Centimeters	x .061	= in3
IMP Pints (IMP pt.)	x .568	= Liters (L)	x 1.76	= IMP pt.
IMP Quarts (IMP qt.)	x 1.137	= Liters (L)	x .88	= IMP qt.
IMP Gallons (IMP gal.)	x 4.546	= Liters (L)	x .22	= IMP gal.
IMP Quarts (IMP qt.)	x 1.201	= US Quarts (US qt.)	x .833	= IMP qt.
IMP Gallons (IMP gal.)	x 1.201	= US Gallons (US gal.)	x .833	= IMP gal.
Fl. Ounces	x 29.573	= Milliliters	x .034	= Ounces
US Pints (US pt.)	x .473	= Liters (L)	x 2.113	= Pints
US Quarts (US qt.)	x .946	= Liters (L)	x 1.057	= Quarts
US Gallons (US gal.)	x 3.785	= Liters (L)	x .264	= Gallons
MASS–WEIGHT				
Ounces (oz.)	x 28.35	= Grams (g)	x .035	= Ounces
Pounds (lb.)	x .454	= Kilograms (kg)	x 2.205	= Pounds
PRESSURE				
Pounds Per Sq. In. (psi)	x 6.895	= Kilopascals (kPa)	x .145	= psi
Inches of Mercury (Hg)	x .4912	= psi	x 2.036	= Hg
Inches of Mercury (Hg)	x 3.377	= Kilopascals (kPa)	x .2961	= Hg
Inches of Water (H_2O)	x .07355	= Inches of Mercury	x 13.783	= H_2O
Inches of Water (H_2O)	x .03613	= psi	x 27.684	= H_2O
Inches of Water (H_2O)	x .248	= Kilopascals (kPa)	x 4.026	= H_2O
TORQUE				
Pounds–Force Inches (in–lb)	x .113	= Newton Meters (N·m)	x 8.85	= in–lb
Pounds–Force Feet (ft–lb)	x 1.356	= Newton Meters (N·m)	x .738	= ft–lb
VELOCITY				
Miles Per Hour (MPH)	x 1.609	= Kilometers Per Hour (KPH)	x .621	= MPH
POWER				
Horsepower (Hp)	x .745	= Kilowatts	x 1.34	= Horsepower
FUEL CONSUMPTION*				
Miles Per Gallon IMP (MPG)	x .354	= Kilometers Per Liter (Km/L)		
Kilometers Per Liter (Km/L)	x 2.352	= IMP MPG		
Miles Per Gallon US (MPG)	x .425	= Kilometers Per Liter (Km/L)		
Kilometers Per Liter (Km/L)	x 2.352	= US MPG		

*It is common to covert from miles per gallon (mpg) to liters/100 kilometers (1/100 km), where mpg (IMP) x 1/100 km = 282 and mpg (US) x 1/100 km = 235.

TEMPERATURE

Degree Fahrenheit (°F)	= (°C x 1.8) + 32
Degree Celsius (°C)	= (°F – 32) x .56

TCCS1044

Fig. 32 Standard and metric conversion factors chart

SERIAL NUMBER IDENTIFICATION

Vehicle

See Figure 33

The Vehicle Identification Number (VIN) consists of seventeen numbers and letters embossed on a plate which provides special information about the vehicle. The VIN can be viewed through the windshield on the upper left corner of the instrument panel, next to the windshield pillar.

Engine

See Figures 34, 35, 36 and 37

All engine assemblies carry an Engine Identification Number (EIN) which must be referenced when ordering engine replacement parts.

On 1996 2.4L engines, the EIN is located on the left rear of the engine block, behind the starter motor.

ENGINE AND VEHICLE IDENTIFICATION CHART

Engine						
Code	Liters	Cu. In. (cc)	Cyl.	Fuel Sys.	Engine Type	Eng. Mfg.
B	2.4	148 (2429)	I4	SMFI	DOHC	Chrysler
3	3.0	181 (2972)	V6	SMFI	SOHC	Mitsubishi
R	3.3	201 (3300)	V6	SMFI	OHV	Chrysler
L	3.8	231 (3785)	V6	SMFI	OHV	Chrysler

Model Year	
Code	Year
T	1996
V	1997
W	1998
X	1999

SMFI - Sequential Multi-port Fuel Injection
DOHC - Double Overhead Camshaft
SOHC - Single Overhead Camshaft
OHV - Overhead Valve

91151C01

GENERAL ENGINE SPECIFICATIONS

Year	Model	Engine Displacement Liters (cc)	Engine ID/VIN	Fuel System Type	Net Horsepower @ rpm	Net Torque @ rpm (ft. lbs.)	Bore x Stroke (in.)	Com-pression Ratio	Oil Pressure (psi @ rpm)
1996	Caravan	2.4 (2429)	B	SMFI	150@5200	167@4000	3.44x3.98	9.4:1	25-80@3000
	Caravan	3.0 (2972)	3	SMFI	143@5000	170@2800	3.59x2.99	8.9:1	35-75@3000
	Caravan	3.3 (3300)	R	SMFI	162@4800	194@3600	3.66x3.19	8.9:1	30-80@3000
	Caravan	3.8 (3785)	L	SMFI	162@4400	213@3300	3.78x3.43	8.9:1	30-80@3000
	Town & Country	3.3 (3300)	R	SMFI	162@4800	194@3600	3.66x3.19	8.9:1	30-80@3000
	Town & Country	3.8 (3785)	L	SMFI	162@4400	213@3300	3.78x3.43	8.9:1	30-80@3000
	Voyager	2.4 (2429)	B	SMFI	150@5200	167@4000	3.44x3.98	9.4:1	25-80@3000
	Voyager	3.0 (2972)	3	SMFI	143@5000	170@2800	3.59x2.99	8.9:1	35-75@3000
	Voyager	3.3 (3300)	R	SMFI	162@4800	194@3600	3.66x3.19	8.9:1	30-80@3000
	Voyager	3.8 (3785)	L	SMFI	162@4400	213@3300	3.78x3.43	8.9:1	30-80@3000
1997	Caravan	2.4 (2429)	B	SMFI	150@5200	167@4000	3.44x3.98	9.4:1	25-80@3000
	Caravan	3.0 (2972)	3	SMFI	143@5000	176@4000	3.59x2.99	8.9:1	35-75@3000
	Caravan	3.3 (3300)	R	SMFI	162@4800	203@3250	3.66x3.19	8.9:1	30-80@3000
	Caravan	3.8 (3785)	L	SMFI	162@4400	227@3100	3.78x3.43	8.9:1	30-80@3000
	Town & Country	3.3 (3300)	R	SMFI	162@4800	203@3250	3.66x3.19	8.9:1	30-80@3000
	Town & Country	3.8 (3785)	L	SMFI	162@4400	227@3100	3.78x3.43	8.9:1	30-80@3000
	Voyager	2.4 (2429)	B	SMFI	150@5200	167@4000	3.44x3.98	9.4:1	25-80@3000
	Voyager	3.0 (2972)	3	SMFI	143@5000	176@4000	3.59x2.99	8.9:1	35-75@3000
	Voyager	3.3 (3300)	R	SMFI	162@4800	203@3250	3.66x3.19	8.9:1	30-80@3000
	Voyager	3.8 (3785)	L	SMFI	162@4400	227@3100	3.78x3.43	8.9:1	30-80@3000
1998	Caravan	2.4 (2429)	B	SMFI	150@5200	167@4000	3.44x3.98	9.4:1	25-80@3000
	Caravan	3.0 (2972)	3	SMFI	150@5200	176@4000	3.59x2.99	8.9:1	45-75@3000
	Caravan	3.3 (3300)	R	SMFI	158@4850	203@3250	3.66x3.19	8.9:1	30-80@3000
	Caravan	3.8 (3785)	L	SMFI	180@4400	240@3200	3.78x3.43	9.6:1	30-80@3000
	Town & Country	3.3 (3300)	R	SMFI	158@4850	203@3250	3.66x3.19	8.9:1	30-80@3000
	Town & Country	3.8 (3785)	L	SMFI	180@4400	240@3200	3.78x3.43	9.6:1	30-80@3000
	Voyager	2.4 (2429)	B	SMFI	150@5200	167@4000	3.44x3.98	9.4:1	25-80@3000
	Voyager	3.0 (2972)	3	SMFI	150@5200	176@4000	3.59x2.99	8.9:1	45-75@3000
	Voyager	3.3 (3300)	R	SMFI	158@4850	203@3250	3.66x3.19	8.9:1	30-80@3000
	Voyager	3.8 (3785)	L	SMFI	180@4400	240@3200	3.78x3.43	9.6:1	30-80@3000
1999	Caravan	2.4 (2429)	B	SMFI	150@5200	167@4000	3.44x3.98	9.4:1	25-80@3000
	Caravan	3.0 (2972)	3	SMFI	150@5200	176@4000	3.59x2.99	8.9:1	45-75@3000
	Caravan	3.3 (3300)	R	SMFI	158@4850	203@3250	3.66x3.19	8.9:1	30-80@3000
	Caravan	3.8 (3785)	L	SMFI	180@4400	240@3200	3.78x3.43	9.6:1	30-80@3000
	Town & Country	3.3 (3300)	R	SMFI	158@4850	203@3250	3.66x3.19	8.9:1	30-80@3000
	Town & Country	3.8 (3785)	L	SMFI	180@4400	240@3200	3.78x3.43	9.6:1	30-80@3000
	Voyager	2.4 (2429)	B	SMFI	150@5200	167@4000	3.44x3.98	9.4:1	25-80@3000
	Voyager	3.0 (2972)	3	SMFI	150@5200	176@4000	3.59x2.99	8.9:1	45-75@3000
	Voyager	3.3 (3300)	R	SMFI	158@4850	203@3250	3.66x3.19	8.9:1	30-80@3000
	Voyager	3.8 (3785)	L	SMFI	180@4400	240@3200	3.78x3.43	9.6:1	30-80@3000

SMFI - Sequential Multi-port Fuel Injection

91151C02

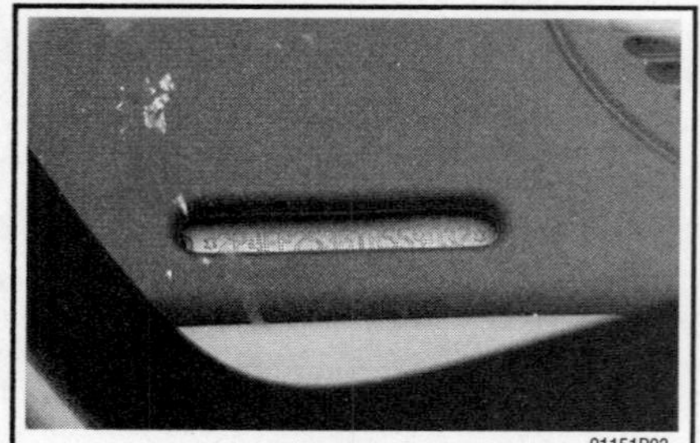

91151P03

Fig. 33 The VIN is located on the upper left corner of the instrument panel, next to the windshield pillar

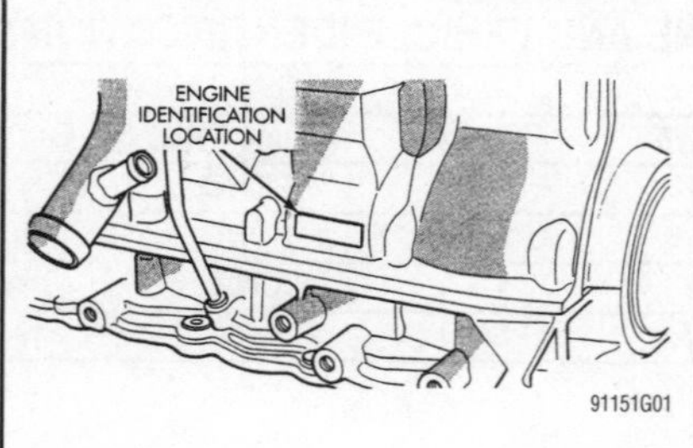

Fig. 34 EIN location on the 2.4L engine for 1996

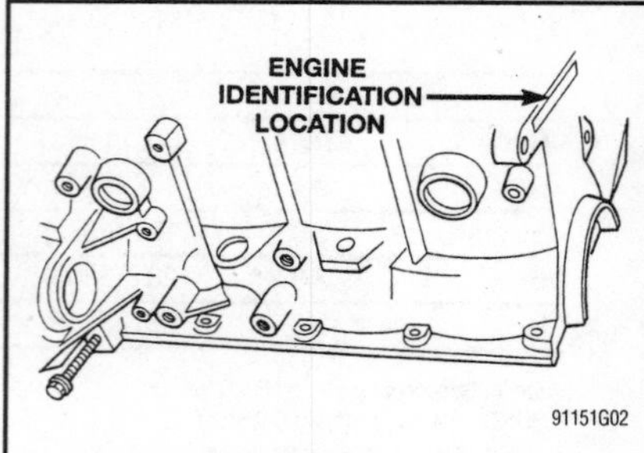

Fig. 35 EIN location on the 2.4L engine for 1997–99

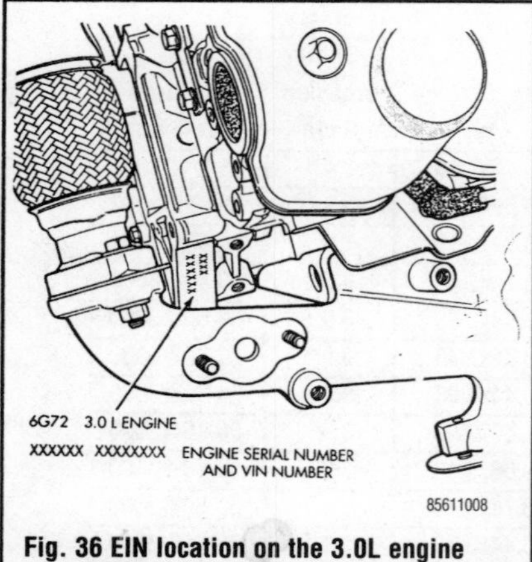

Fig. 36 EIN location on the 3.0L engine

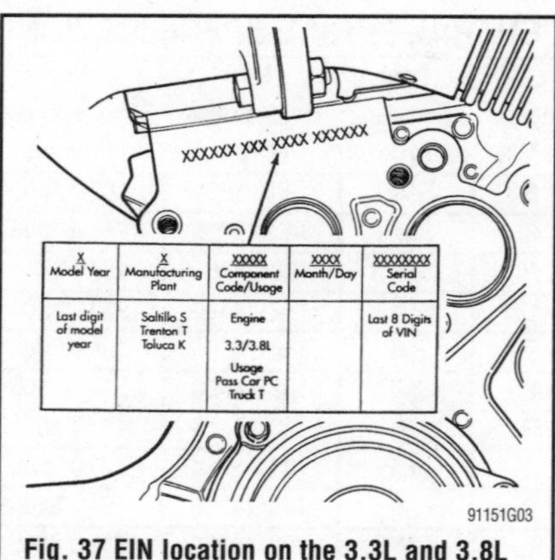

X Model Year	X Manufacturing Plant	XXXXX Component Code/Usage	XXXX Month/Day	XXXXXXXX Serial Code
Last digit of model year	Saltillo S Trenton T Toluca K	Engine 3.3/3.8L Usage Pass Car PC Truck T		Last 8 Digits of VIN

Fig. 37 EIN location on the 3.3L and 3.8L engines

SOLENOID ASSEMBLY

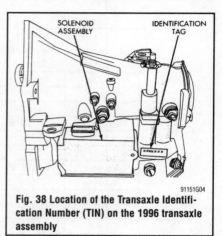

IDENTIFICATION TAG

91151G04

Fig. 38 Location of the Transaxle Identification Number (TIN) on the 1996 transaxle assembly

On 1997–99 2.4L engines, the EIN is located on the rear of the engine block, directly under the cylinder head. On the 3.0L, 3.3L and 3.8L engines, the EIN is located on the rear face of the engine block, just below the cylinder head.

Transaxle

See Figures 38 and 39

On 1996 vehicles, the Transaxle Identification Number (TIN) is printed on a label that is located on the transaxle housing, next to the solenoid assembly.

On 1997–99 vehicles, the TIN is printed on a bar-code label that is located on the left upper transaxle housing.

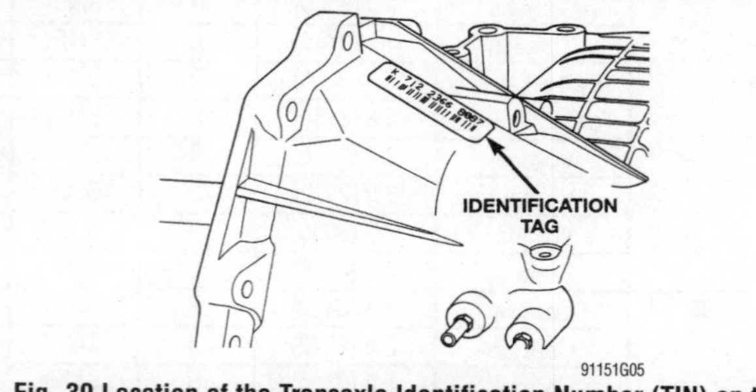

Fig. 39 Location of the Transaxle Identification Number (TIN) on the 1997–99 transaxle assembly

ROUTINE MAINTENANCE AND TUNE-UP

Proper maintenance and tune-up is the key to long and trouble-free vehicle life, and the work can yield its own rewards. Studies have shown that a properly tuned and maintained vehicle can achieve better gas mileage than an out-of-tune vehicle. As a conscientious owner and driver, set aside a Saturday morning, say once a month, to check or replace items which could cause major problems later. Keep your own personal log to jot down which services you performed, how much the parts cost you, the date, and the exact odometer reading at the time. Keep all receipts for such items as engine oil and filters, so that they may be referred to in case of related problems or to determine operating expenses. As a do-it-yourselfer, these receipts are the only proof you have that the required maintenance was performed. In the event of a warranty problem, these receipts will be invaluable.

The literature provided with your vehicle when it was originally delivered includes the factory recommended maintenance schedule. If you no longer have this literature, replacement copies are usually available from the dealer. A maintenance schedule is provided later in this section, in case you do not have the factory literature.

Air Cleaner (Element)

REMOVAL & INSTALLATION

See Figures 40 thru 47

1. Remove the 2 retaining bolts to the air inlet resonator, using a 10mm socket.
2. Disconnect the hose at the side of the air inlet resonator.
3. Using a 10mm socket, remove the bolt mounting the air cleaner to the radiator crossmember.
4. Loosen the hose clamp, then disconnect the air inlet hose to the throttle body.
5. Lift the air inlet resonator/filter housing assembly straight up out of the engine compartment.
6. Loosen the clamps securing the air cleaner housing halves together.
7. Remove the air cleaner filter element.

UNDERHOOD COMPONENT LOCATIONS—3.0L ENGINE

1. Windshield wiper blades
2. Accessory drive belt routing diagram
3. Power steering fluid level reservoir
4. Accessory drive belt
5. Master cylinder/brake fluid reservoir
6. Battery
7. Automatic transmission fluid level dipstick
8. PCV valve
9. Windshield washer fluid reservoir
10. Coolant recovery container
11. Upper radiator hose
12. Timing belt
13. Distributor cap and rotor (spark plug wires lead to spark plugs)
14. Engine oil fill cap
15. Engine oil level dipstick
16. Radiator pressure cap

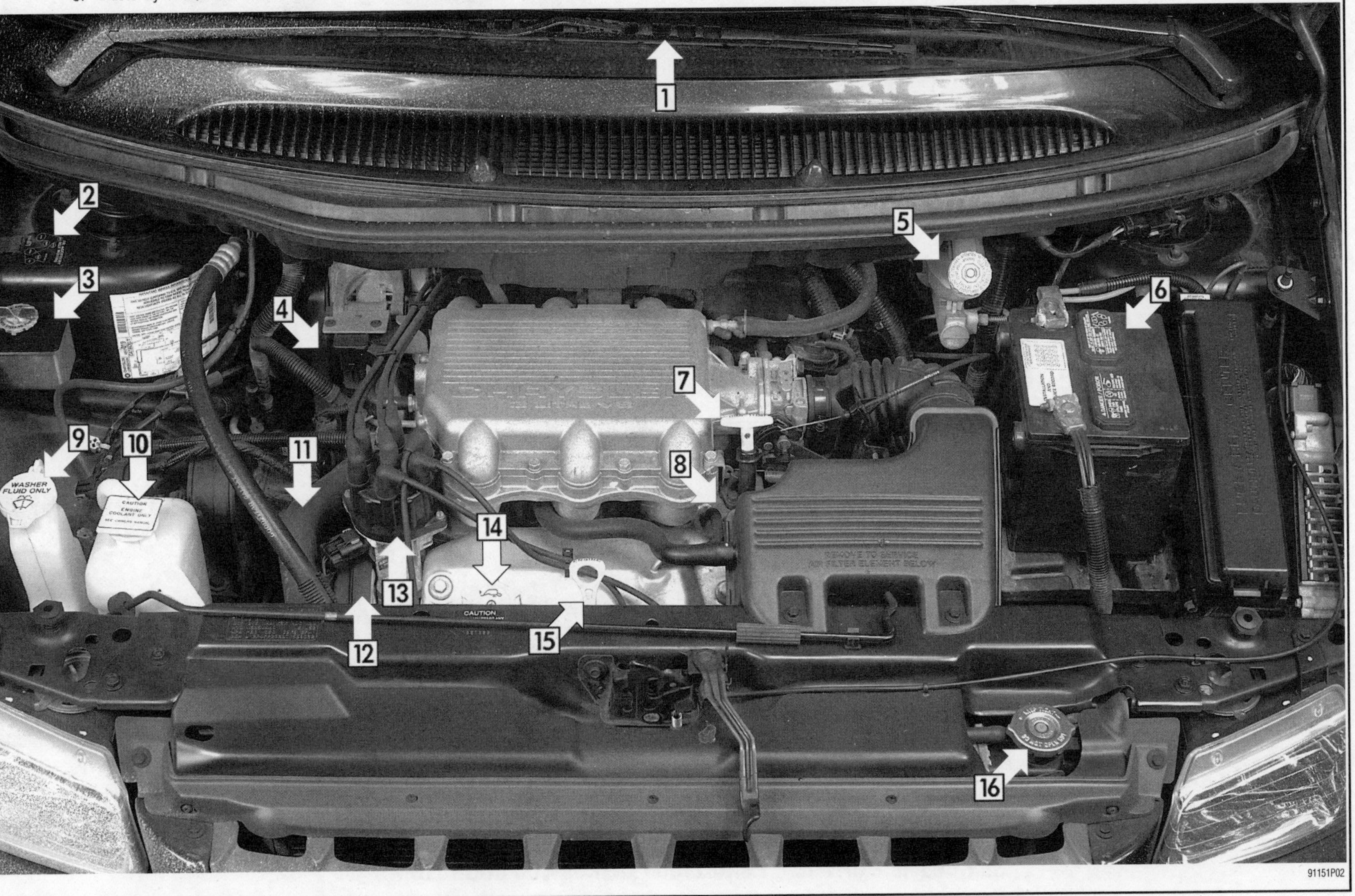

UNDERHOOD COMPONENT LOCATIONS—3.3L AND 3.8L ENGINES

1. Windshield wiper blades
2. Accessory drive belt routing diagram
3. Power steering fluid reservoir
4. Accessory drive belt
5. Master cylinder/brake fluid reservoir
6. Battery
7. Automatic transmission fluid level dipstick
8. PCV valve
9. Windshield washer fluid reservoir
10. Coolant recovery container
11. Upper radiator hose
12. Engine oil fill cap
13. Spark plug wires (lead to spark plugs)
14. Air inlet resonator/air cleaner filter housing assembly
15. Engine oil level dipstick
16. Radiator pressure cap

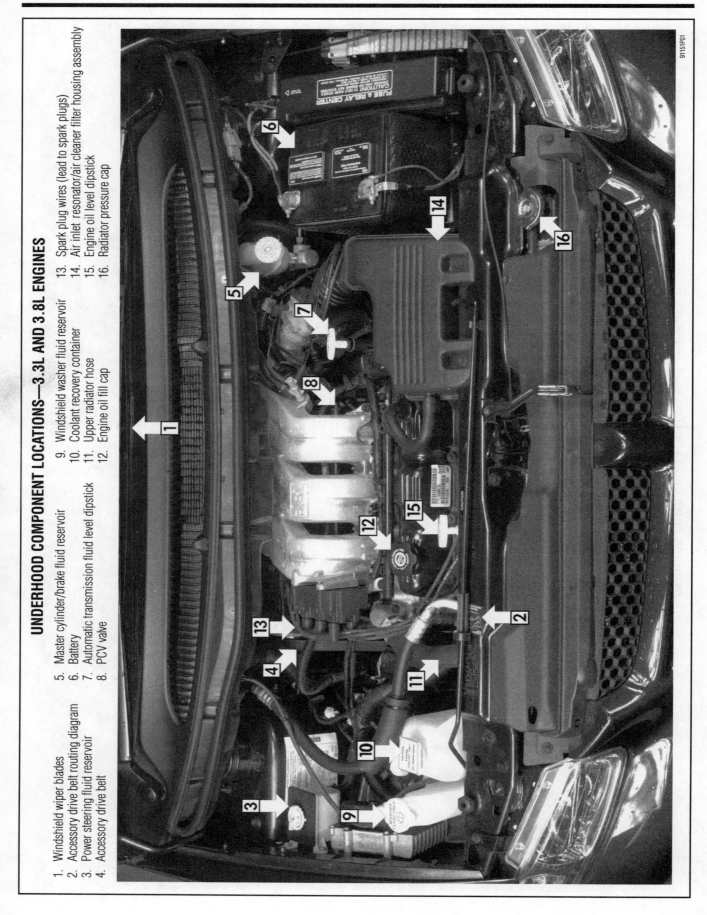

91151P01

To install:

8. Install a new air cleaner filter element.
9. Join the air cleaner housing halves together and secure with the housing clamps.
10. Install the air inlet resonator/filter housing assembly into the engine compartment. Be sure that the 2 dowels on the bottom of the filter housing mount into the two holes at the bottom of the engine compartment.
11. Connect the air inlet hose to the throttle body and tighten the hose clamp.
12. Install and tighten the air cleaner-to-radiator crossmember mounting bolt.
13. Connect the rubber hose to the side of the air inlet resonator.
14. Install and tighten the air inlet resonator retaining bolts.

Fuel Filter

REMOVAL & INSTALLATION

See Figures 48, 49, 50, 51 and 52

CAUTION

The fuel injection system remains under pressure, even after the engine has been turned OFF. The fuel system pressure must be relieved before disconnecting any fuel lines. Failure to do so may result in fire and/or personal injury.

The fuel delivery system uses quick-connect fittings. The fuel filter mounts to the top of the fuel tank.

1. Properly relieve the fuel system pressure.
2. Disconnect the negative battery cable.
3. Raise and safely support the vehicle.
4. Place a drain pan underneath the fuel filter to catch any spilling fuel that will result from disconnecting the fuel lines.

It may be necessary to support the weight of the fuel tank with a block of wood and a floor jack. Once this is accomplished, loosen, but

Fig. 40 Remove the 2 air inlet resonator mounting bolts

Fig. 41 Pull off the rubber hose from the side of the air inlet resonator

Fig. 42 Remove the air cleaner-to-radiator crossmember mounting bolt

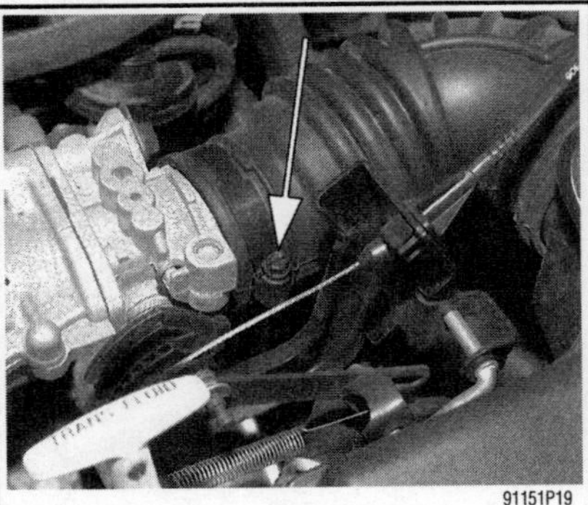

Fig. 43 Loosen the hose clamp . . .

Fig. 44 . . . then separate the air inlet resonator hose from the throttle body

Fig. 45 Remove the air inlet resonator/filter housing assembly from the vehicle

Fig. 46 Loosen the clamps around the air cleaner housing . . .

Fig. 47 . . . then remove the air cleaner filter element from the housing

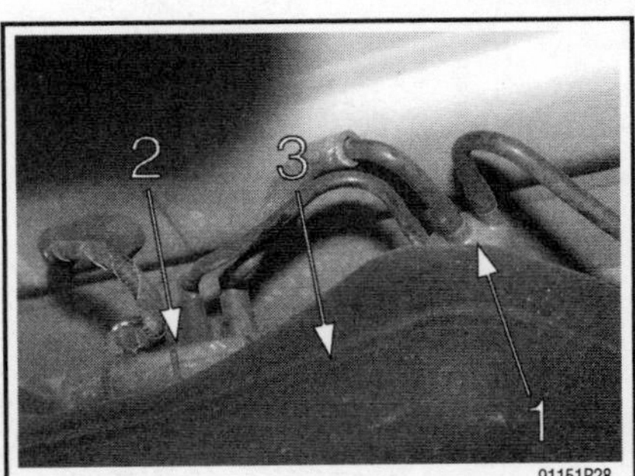

Fig. 48 The fuel filter (1) is mounted next to the fuel pump module (2), on top of the fuel tank (3)

do not remove, the fuel tank strap bolts. Allow the fuel tank to lower just enough to access the fuel line fittings at the fuel pump module.

5. Locate the fuel filter in its mounting on top of the fuel tank. Detach the quick-connect fittings from the chassis fuel supply tube and fuel pump module by squeezing the quick-connect fitting retainer tabs together and pulling the fitting assembly away from the fuel line nipple. The retainer will remain on the fuel tube.
6. Remove the fuel filter mounting bolt and remove the fuel filter from the fuel tank.

To install:

7. Install the fuel filter on the top of the fuel tank and tighten the mounting bolt.

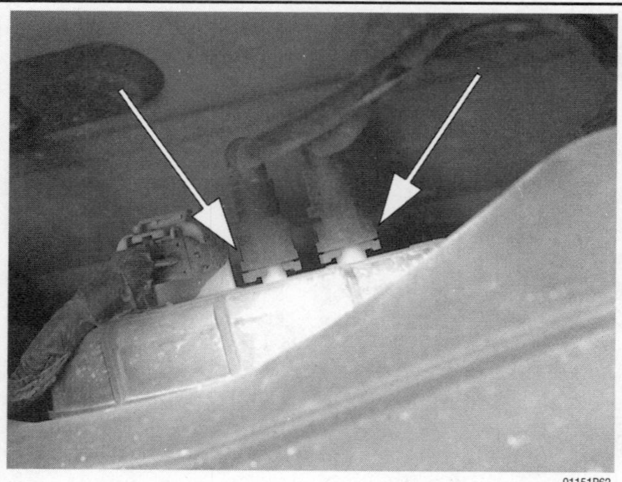

Fig. 49 Disengage the fuel line quick-connect fittings from the fuel pump module

8. The fuel supply tube (to chassis fuel line), return tube (to pump module) and fuel supply (to fuel filter) tube are permanently attached to the fuel filter. The quick-connect fitting ends of the fuel supply and return tubes are of different sizes.
9. Apply a light coating of 30W engine oil to the nipples of the fuel filter.
10. Push the quick-connect fitting over the fuel line until the retainer seats and clicks into place. Be sure the retainer tabs have locked into the case of the fitting.
11. If necessary, raise the fuel tank and tighten the fuel tank strap bolts.
12. Lower the vehicle. Start the engine and check for leaks.

PCV Valve

REMOVAL & INSTALLATION

2.4L, 3.3L and 3.8L Engines

See Figures 53 and 54

1. With the engine **OFF**, clean PCV valve area with a suitable solvent.
2. Remove the PCV valve from the mounting grommet or vent valve hose.
3. Disconnect the other end of the PCV valve from the vacuum hose.
4. Examine the vacuum hose and replace if the hose is cracked, broken or dried out. Always check the vent hose for clogging. If clogged, replace or clean as necessary.
5. Install a new PCV valve into the hose and install into mounting grommet or vent valve hose.

3.0L Engine

See Figures 55, 56 and 57

1. With the engine **OFF**, clean PCV valve area with a suitable solvent.
2. Remove the PCV valve vacuum hose.
3. Using a 15mm box wrench, loosen, then remove, the PCV valve from the intake manifold.
4. Examine the vacuum hose and replace if the hose is cracked, broken or dried out. If clogged, replace or clean as necessary.

Fig. 50 Be sure to place a drain pan underneath the filter line fittings to catch all fuel spillage

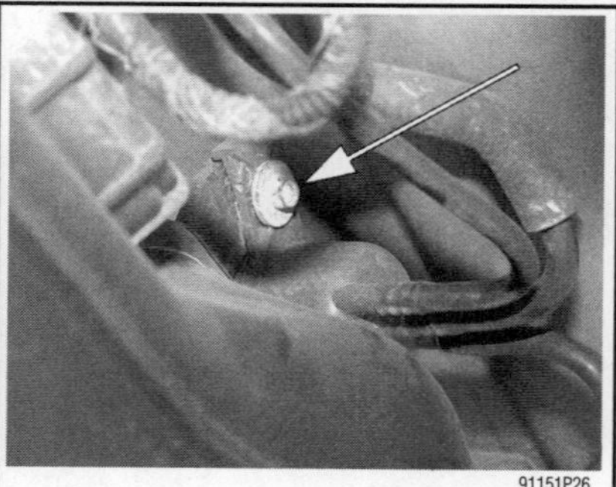

Fig. 51 Using a 10mm socket, remove the fuel filter mounting bolt . . .

Fig. 52 . . . then remove the fuel filter from the top of the fuel tank

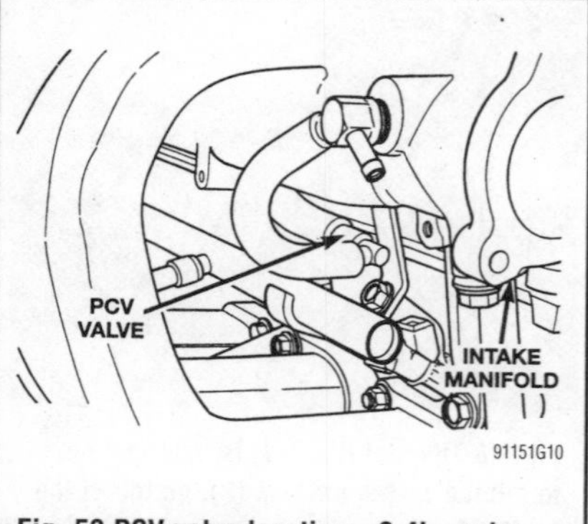

Fig. 53 PCV valve location—2.4L engine

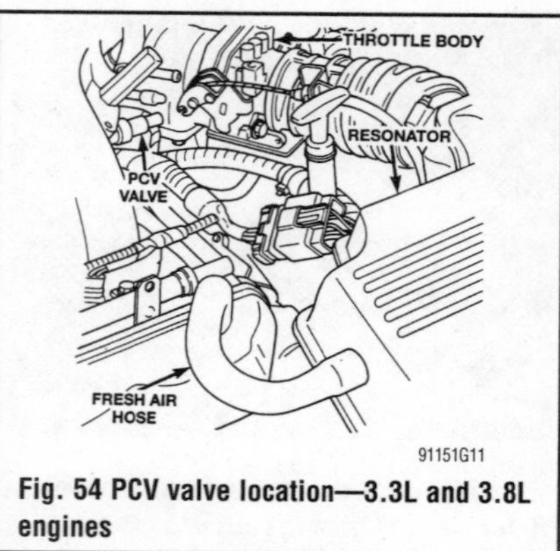

Fig. 54 PCV valve location—3.3L and 3.8L engines

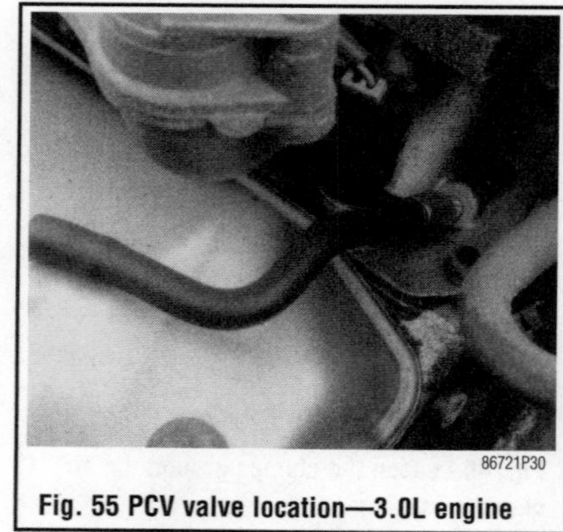

Fig. 55 PCV valve location—3.0L engine

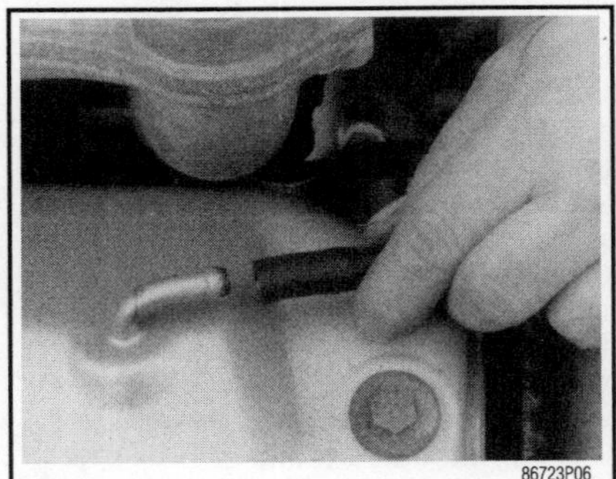
86723P06

Fig. 56 Remove the PCV valve vacuum hose

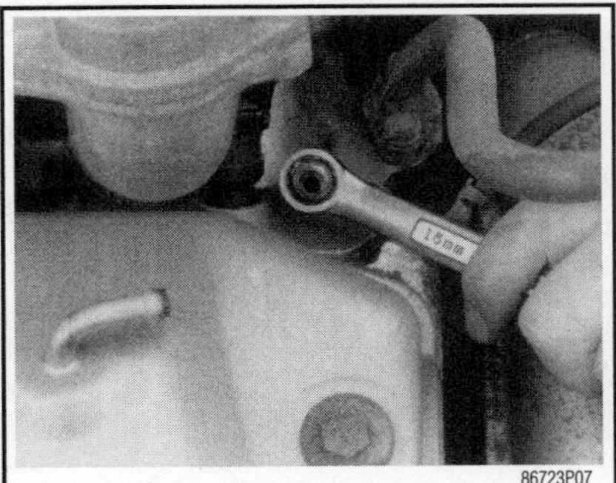
86723P07

Fig. 57 Using a box wrench, remove the PCV valve

91151P33

Fig. 58 Underbody location of the evaporative canister

5. Install a new PCV valve into the intake manifold and connect the vacuum hose.

Evaporative Canister

See Figure 58

All vehicles are equipped with a sealed, maintenance free charcoal canister, located underneath the driver's seat, mounted to the chassis frame. Fuel vapors are temporarily held in the canister until they can be drawn into the intake manifold and burned in the engine.

SERVICING

Periodic inspection of the vent hoses is required. Replace any hoses that are cracked, torn or become hard. Use only fuel resistant hose if replacement becomes necessary.

Battery

PRECAUTIONS

Always use caution when working on or near the battery. Never allow a tool to bridge the gap between the negative and positive battery terminals. Also, be careful not to allow a tool to provide a ground between the positive cable/terminal and any metal component on the vehicle. Either of these conditions will cause a short circuit, leading to sparks and possible personal injury.

Do not smoke, have an open flame or create sparks near a battery; the gases contained in the battery are very explosive and, if ignited, could cause severe injury or death.

All batteries, regardless of type, should be carefully secured by a battery hold-down device. If this is not done, the battery terminals or casing may crack from stress applied to the battery during vehicle operation. A battery which is not secured may allow acid to leak out, making it discharge faster; such leaking corrosive acid can also eat away at components under the hood.

Always visually inspect the battery case for cracks, leakage and corrosion. A white corrosive substance on the battery case or on nearby components would indicate a leaking or cracked battery. If the battery is cracked, it should be replaced immediately.

GENERAL MAINTENANCE

See Figure 59

A battery that is not sealed must be checked periodically for electrolyte level. You cannot add water to a sealed maintenance-free battery (though not all maintenance-free batteries are sealed); however, a sealed battery must also be checked for proper electrolyte level, as indicated by the color of the built-in hydrometer "eye."

Always keep the battery cables and terminals free of corrosion. Check these components about once a year. Refer to the removal, installation and cleaning procedures outlined in this section.

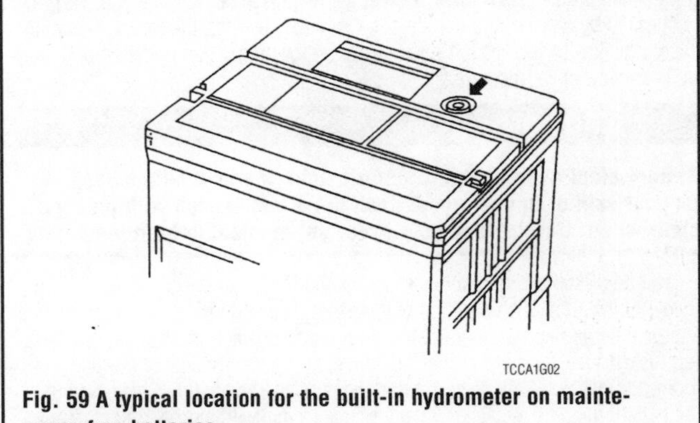
TCCA1G02

Fig. 59 A typical location for the built-in hydrometer on maintenance-free batteries

Keep the top of the battery clean, as a film of dirt can help completely discharge a battery that is not used for long periods. A solution of baking soda and water may be used for cleaning, but be careful to flush this off with clear water. DO NOT let any of the solution into the filler holes. Baking soda neutralizes battery acid and will de-activate a battery cell.

Batteries in vehicles which are not operated on a regular basis can fall victim to parasitic loads (small current drains which are constantly drawing current from the battery). Normal parasitic loads may drain a battery on a vehicle that is in storage and not used for 6–8 weeks. Vehicles that have additional accessories such as a cellular phone, an alarm system or other devices that increase parasitic load may discharge a battery sooner. If the vehicle is to be stored for 6–8 weeks in a secure area and the alarm system, if present, is not necessary, the negative battery cable should be disconnected at the onset of storage to protect the battery charge.

Remember that constantly discharging and recharging will shorten battery life. Take care not to allow a battery to be needlessly discharged.

BATTERY FLUID

Check the battery electrolyte level at least once a month, or more often in hot weather or during periods of extended vehicle operation. On non-sealed batteries, the level can be checked either through the case on translucent batteries or by removing the cell caps on opaque-cased types. The electrolyte level in each cell should be kept filled to the split ring inside each cell, or the line marked on the outside of the case.

If the level is low, add only distilled water through the opening until the level is correct. Each cell is separate from the others, so each must be checked and filled individually. Distilled water should be used, because the chemicals and minerals found in most drinking water are harmful to the battery and could significantly shorten its life.

If water is added in freezing weather, the vehicle should be driven several miles to allow the water to mix with the electrolyte. Otherwise, the battery could freeze.

Although some maintenance-free batteries have removable cell caps for access to the electrolyte, the electrolyte condition and level on all sealed maintenance-free batteries must be checked using the built-in hydrometer "eye." The exact type of eye varies between battery manufacturers, but most apply a sticker to the battery itself explaining the possible readings. When in doubt, refer to the battery manufacturer's instructions to interpret battery condition using the built-in hydrometer.

➡ **Although the readings from built-in hydrometers found in sealed batteries may vary, a green eye usually indicates a properly charged battery with sufficient fluid level. A dark eye is normally an indicator of a battery with sufficient fluid, but one which may be low in charge. And a light or yellow eye is usually an indication that electrolyte supply has dropped below the necessary level for battery (and hydrometer) operation. In this last case, sealed batteries with an insufficient electrolyte level must usually be discarded.**

Checking the Specific Gravity

▶ **See Figures 60, 61 and 62**

A hydrometer is required to check the specific gravity on all batteries that are not maintenance-free. On batteries that are maintenance-free, the specific gravity is checked by observing the built-in hydrometer "eye" on the top of the battery case. Check with your battery's manufacturer for proper interpretation of its built-in hydrometer readings.

⁂ CAUTION

Battery electrolyte contains sulfuric acid. If you should splash any on your skin or in your eyes, flush the affected area with plenty of clear water. If it lands in your eyes, get medical help immediately.

The fluid (sulfuric acid solution) contained in the battery cells will tell you many things about the condition of the battery. Because the cell plates must be kept submerged below the fluid level in order to operate, maintaining the fluid level is extremely important. And, because the specific gravity of the acid is an indication of electrical charge, testing the fluid can be an aid in determining if the battery must be replaced. A battery in a vehicle with a properly operating charging system should require little maintenance, but careful, periodic inspection should reveal problems before they leave you stranded.

As stated earlier, the specific gravity of a battery's electrolyte level can be used as an indication of battery charge. At least once a year, check the specific gravity of the battery. It should be between 1.20 and 1.26 on the gravity scale. Most auto supply stores carry a variety of inexpensive battery testing hydrometers. These can be used on any non-sealed battery to test the specific gravity in each cell.

The battery testing hydrometer has a squeeze bulb at one end and a nozzle at the other. Battery electrolyte is sucked into the hydrometer until the float is lifted from its seat. The specific gravity is then read by noting the position of the float. If gravity is low in one or more cells, the battery should be slowly charged and checked again to see if the gravity has come up. Generally, if after charging, the specific gravity between any two cells varies more than 50 points (0.50), the battery should be replaced, as it can no longer produce sufficient voltage to guarantee proper operation.

CABLES

▶ **See Figures 63, 64, 65, 66 and 67**

Once a year (or as necessary), the battery terminals and the cable clamps should be cleaned. Loosen the clamps and remove the cables, negative cable first. On batteries with posts on top, the use of a puller specially made for this purpose is recommended. These are inexpensive and available in most auto parts stores.

Clean the cable clamps and the battery terminal with a wire brush, until all corrosion, grease, etc., is removed and the metal is shiny. It is especially important to clean the inside of the clamp thoroughly (an old knife is useful here), since a small deposit of foreign material or oxidation there will prevent a sound electrical connection and inhibit either starting or charging. Special tools are available for cleaning these parts. It is also a good idea to apply some dielectric grease to the terminal, as this will aid in the prevention of corrosion.

After the clamps and terminals are clean, reinstall the cables, negative cable last; DO NOT hammer the clamps onto battery posts. Tighten the clamps

TCCA1P07

Fig. 60 On non-maintenance-free batteries, the fluid level can be checked through the case on translucent models; the cell caps must be removed on other models

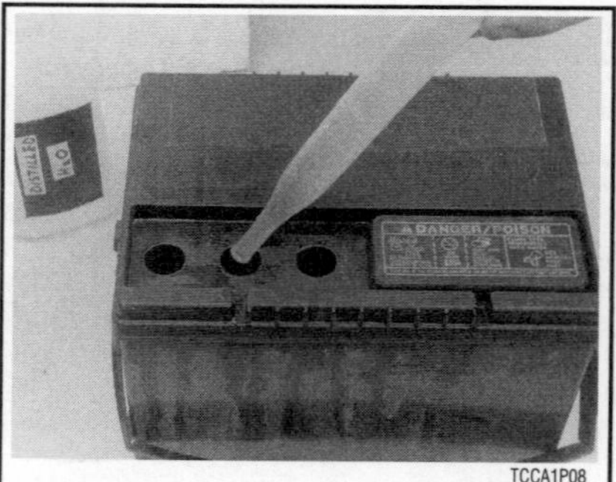

TCCA1P08

Fig. 61 If the fluid level is low, add only distilled water through the opening until the level is correct

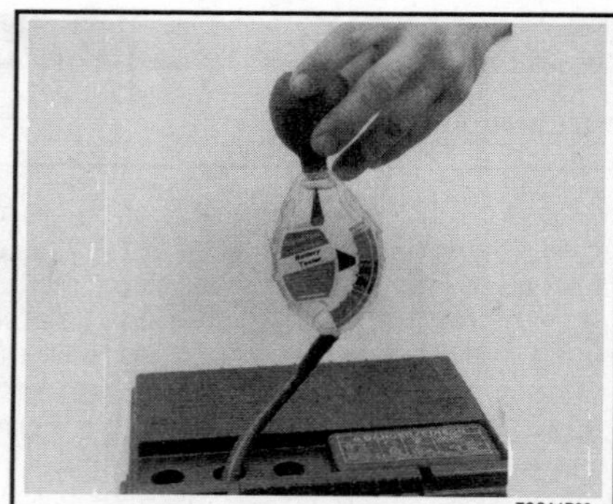

TCCA1P09

Fig. 62 Check the specific gravity of the battery's electrolyte with a hydrometer

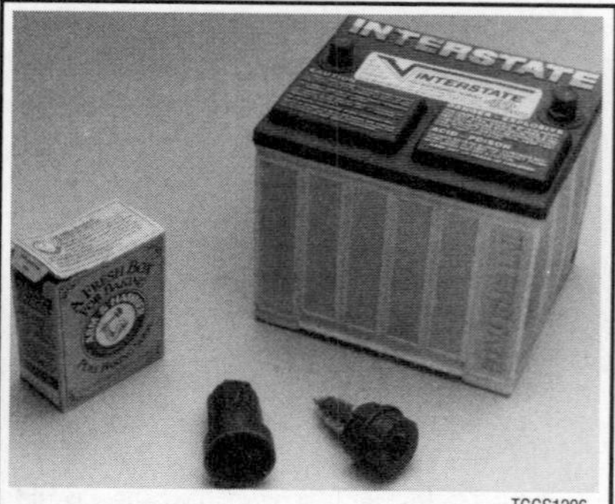

TCCS1206

Fig. 63 Maintenance is performed with household items and with special tools like this post cleaner

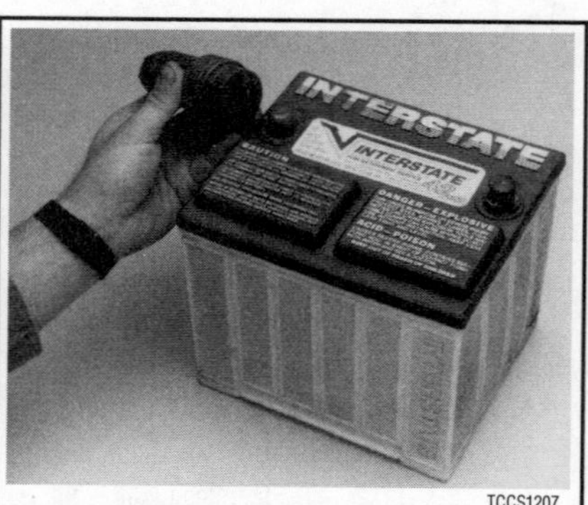

TCCS1207

Fig. 64 The underside of this special battery tool has a wire brush to clean post terminals

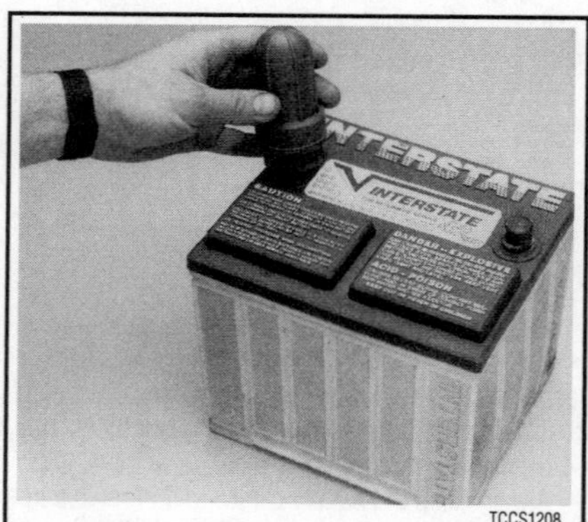

TCCS1208

Fig. 65 Place the tool over the battery posts and twist to clean until the metal is shiny

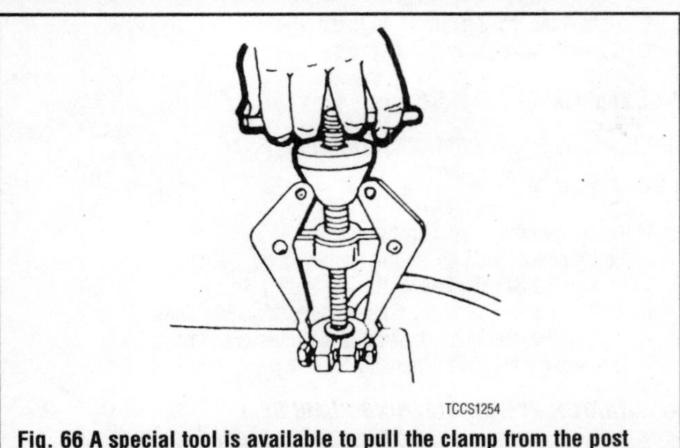

TCCS1254

Fig. 66 A special tool is available to pull the clamp from the post

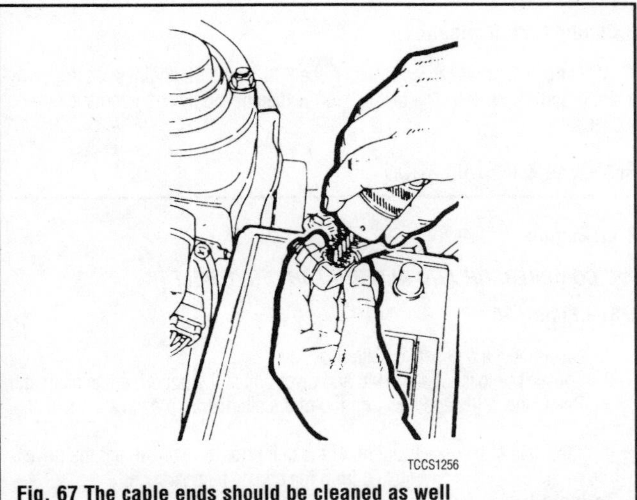

TCCS1256

Fig. 67 The cable ends should be cleaned as well

securely, but do not distort them. Give the clamps and terminals a thin external coating of grease after installation, to retard corrosion.

Check the cables at the same time that the terminals are cleaned. If the cable insulation is cracked or broken, or if the ends are frayed, the cable should be replaced with a new cable of the same length and gauge.

CHARGING

***** CAUTION**

The chemical reaction which takes place in all batteries generates explosive hydrogen gas. A spark can cause the battery to explode and splash acid. To avoid serious personal injury, be sure there is proper ventilation and take appropriate fire safety precautions when connecting, disconnecting, or charging a battery and when using jumper cables.

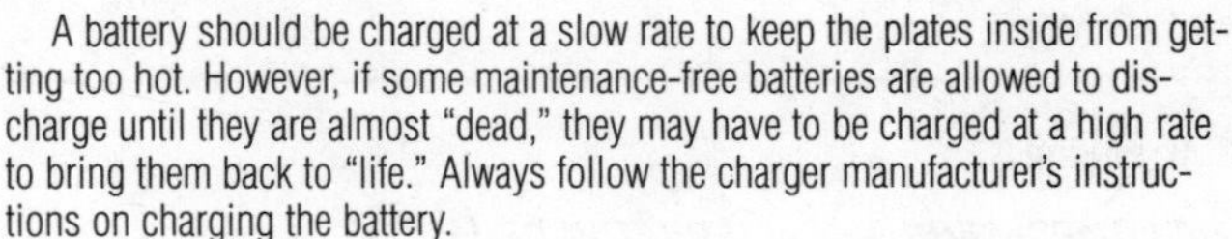

A battery should be charged at a slow rate to keep the plates inside from getting too hot. However, if some maintenance-free batteries are allowed to discharge until they are almost "dead," they may have to be charged at a high rate to bring them back to "life." Always follow the charger manufacturer's instructions on charging the battery.

REPLACEMENT

When it becomes necessary to replace the battery, select one with an amperage rating equal to or greater than the battery originally installed. Deterioration and just plain aging of the battery cables, starter motor, and associated wires makes the battery's job harder in successive years. The slow increase in electrical resistance over time makes it prudent to install a new battery with a greater capacity than the old.

Belts

INSPECTION

➧ See Figures 68, 69, 70, 71 and 72

Inspect the belts for signs of glazing or cracking. A glazed belt will be perfectly smooth from slippage, while a good belt will have a slight texture of fabric visible. Cracks will usually start at the inner edge of the belt and run outward. All worn or damaged drive belts should be replaced immediately. It is best to replace all drive belts at one time, as a preventive maintenance measure, during this service operation.

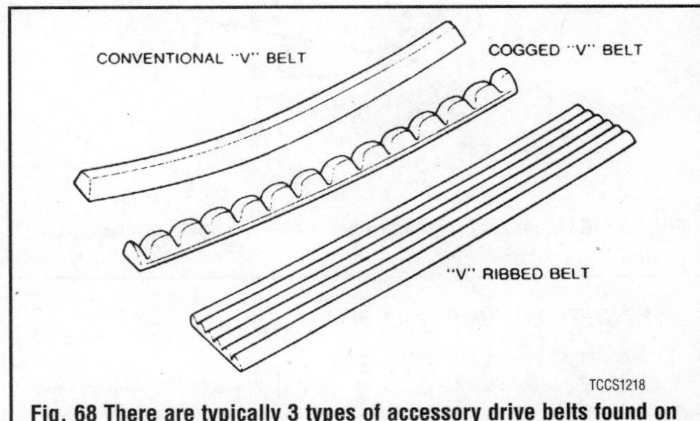

TCCS1218

Fig. 68 There are typically 3 types of accessory drive belts found on vehicles today

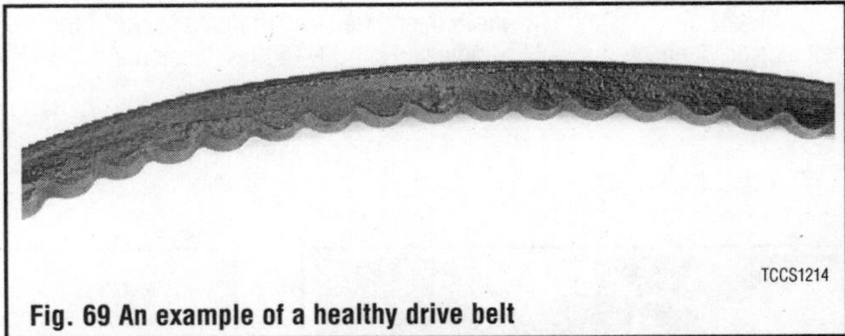

TCCS1214

Fig. 69 An example of a healthy drive belt

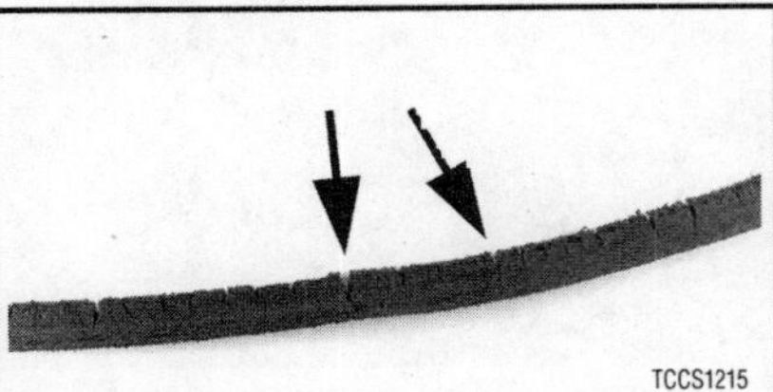

TCCS1215

Fig. 70 Deep cracks in this belt will cause flex, building up heat that will eventually lead to belt failure

TCCS1216

Fig. 71 The cover of this belt is worn, exposing the critical reinforcing cords to excessive wear

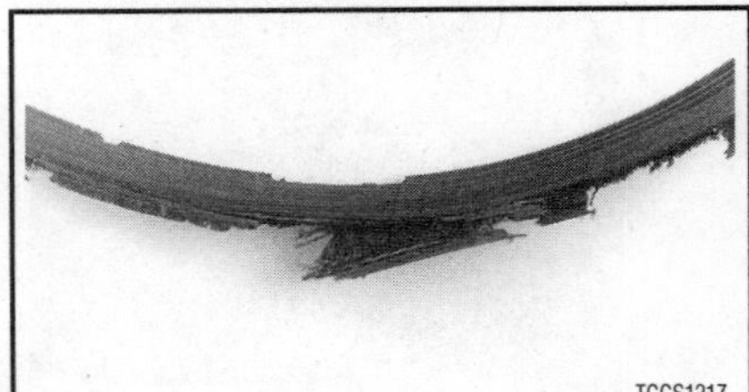

TCCS1217

Fig. 72 Installing too wide a belt can result in serious belt wear and/or breakage

ADJUSTMENT

2.4L Engine

A/C COMPRESSOR AND ALTERNATOR DRIVE BELT

See Figure 73

1. Disconnect the negative battery cable.
2. Loosen the locknut at the top and pivot bolt at the bottom of the alternator.
3. Adjust the belt by rotating the adjusting bolt until the correct tension is reached. A new belt should be adjusted to 130–150 lbs. tension. A used belt should be adjusted to 80–90 lbs. tension.
4. After the belt is properly adjusted, tighten the pivot bolt and locknut to 40 ft. lbs. (54 Nm).
5. Connect the negative battery cable.

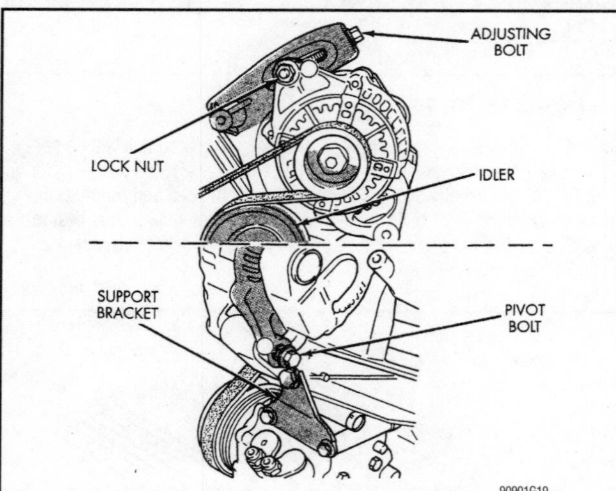

Fig. 73 A/C compressor and alternator belt adjustment on the 2.4L engine

POWER STEERING PUMP DRIVE BELT

1. Disconnect the negative battery cable.
2. From above the vehicle, loosen the locking nuts at the top of the power steering pump.
3. Raise and safely support the front of the vehicle securely on jackstands.
4. From underneath the vehicle, loosen the pivot bolt at the bottom of the power steering pump.
5. Rotate the adjusting bolt above the power steering pump to adjust the belt tension. A new belt should be adjusted to 130–150 lbs. tension. A used belt should be adjusted to 80–90 lbs. tension.
6. After the belt is adjusted properly, tighten the pivot bolt to 40 ft. lbs. (54 Nm).
7. Lower the vehicle.
8. Tighten the locking nuts to 40 ft. lbs. (54 Nm).
9. Connect the negative battery cable.

3.0L Engines

AIR CONDITIONING COMPRESSOR BELT

See Figure 74

1. Disconnect the negative battery cable.
2. Loosen the locknut on the idler pulley.
3. Loosen the adjuster bolt on the idler pulley.
4. Adjust to specification by tightening the adjusting screw.
5. Tighten the idler pulley locknut to 40 ft. lbs. (55 Nm).
6. Connect the negative battery cable.

ALTERNATOR/POWER STEERING PUMP BELT

The alternator/power steering pump belt is provided with a dynamic tensioner to maintain proper belt tension.

3.3L and 3.8L Engines

All of the belt driven accessories on the 3.3L and 3.8L engines are driven by a single serpentine belt. The belt tension is maintained by am automatic tensioner.

REMOVAL & INSTALLATION

2.4L Engine

A/C COMPRESSOR AND ALTERNATOR DRIVE BELT

See Figure 75

1. Disconnect the negative battery cable.
2. Loosen the locknut at the top and pivot bolt at the bottom of the alternator.
3. Rotate the adjuster screw , on top of the alternator, to decrease the belt tension.
4. Take note of the exact routing of the belt prior to removal. Lift the drive belt from the pulleys and remove it from the engine compartment.

To install:

5. Position the replacement belt around the pulleys, making sure the belt routing is correct.
6. Adjust the belt by rotating the adjusting bolt until the correct tension is reached. Refer to the procedure earlier in this section for belt adjustment.
7. After the belt is installed and/or properly adjusted, tighten the pivot bolt and locknut to 40 ft. lbs. (54 Nm).
8. Connect the negative battery cable.

POWER STEERING PUMP DRIVE BELT

See Figure 75

1. Disconnect the negative battery cable.
2. From above the vehicle, loosen the locking nuts at the top of the power steering pump.
3. Raise and safely support the front of the vehicle securely on jackstands.

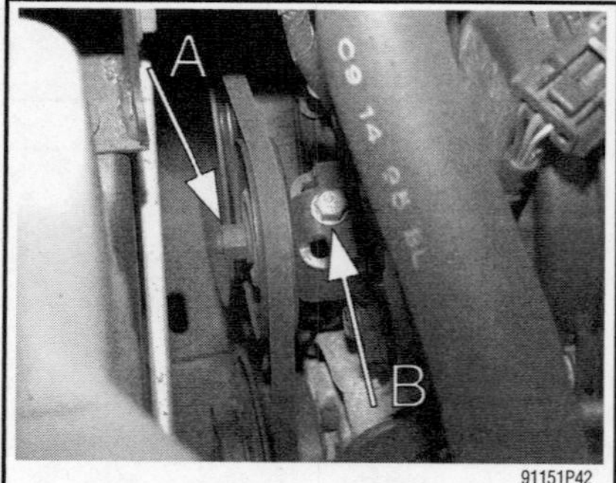

Fig. 74 Air conditioning compressor belt locknut (A) and adjuster bolt (B) location

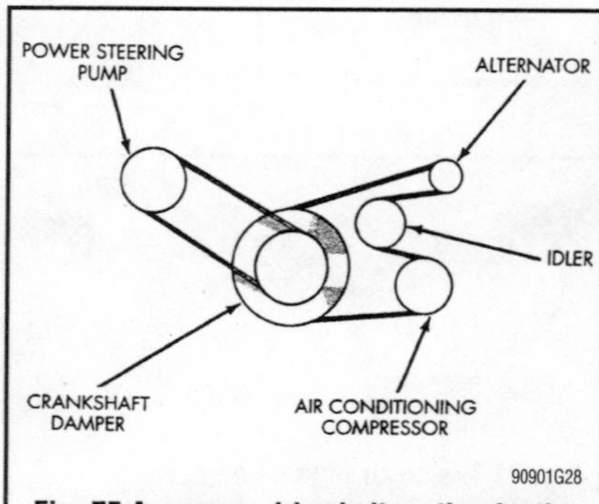

Fig. 75 Accessory drive belt routing for the 2.4L engine

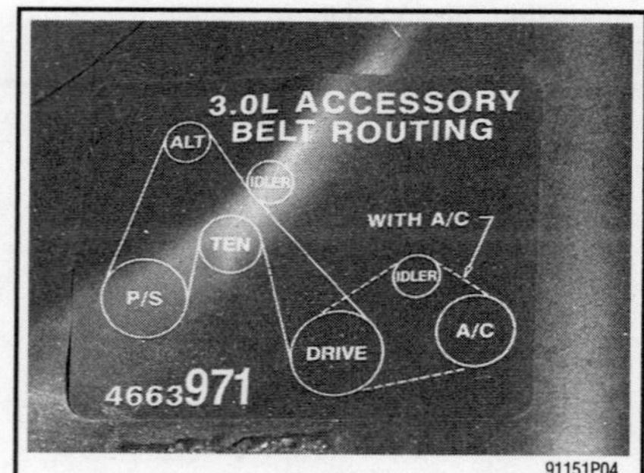

Fig. 76 Accessory drive belt routing for the 3.0L engine. The roting diagram can be found in the engine compartment

4. From underneath the vehicle, loosen the pivot bolt at the bottom of the power steering pump.
5. Loosen the adjusting bolt above the power steering pump. With the tension released, remove the drive belt.

To install:

6. Install the drive belt around the crankshaft and power steering pump pulleys.
7. Rotate the adjusting bolt clockwise to adjust the belt tension. Refer to the procedure earlier in this section for belt adjustment.
8. After the belt is installed and/or adjusted properly, tighten the pivot bolt to 40 ft. lbs. (54 Nm).
9. Lower the vehicle.
10. Tighten the locking nuts to 40 ft. lbs. (54 Nm).
11. Connect the negative battery cable.

3.0L Engines

AIR CONDITIONING COMPRESSOR BELT

See Figures 74 and 76

1. Disconnect the negative battery cable.
2. Loosen the locknut on the idler pulley.
3. Loosen the adjuster bolt on the idler pulley.
4. Remove the belt and install a replacement.
5. Adjust to specification by tightening the adjusting screw.
6. Tighten the idler pulley locknut to 40 ft. lbs. (55 Nm).
7. Connect the negative battery cable.

ALTERNATOR/POWER STEERING PUMP BELT

See Figures 76 and 77

The alternator/power steering pump belt is provided with a dynamic tensioner to maintain proper belt tension.

1. Disconnect the negative battery cable.
2. Raise the front of the vehicle and safely support it with jackstands.
3. Remove the right front splash shield.
4. Release tension by rotating the tensioner clockwise.
5. Remove the belt and install a replacement.
6. Proper belt tension is maintain by the dynamic tension.
7. Install the right front splash shield. Lower the front of the vehicle.
8. Connect the negative battery cable.

3.3L and 3.8L Engines

ACCESSORY DRIVE BELT

See Figure 78

All of the belt driven accessories on the 3.3L and 3.8L engines are driven by a single serpentine belt. The belt tension is maintained by am automatic tensioner.

1. Disconnect the negative battery cable.
2. Raise the front of the vehicle and safely support it with jackstands.
3. Remove the right front splash shield.
4. Release tension by rotating the tensioner clockwise.
5. Remove the belt and install a replacement.
6. Proper belt tension is maintain by the dynamic tension.
7. Install the right front splash shield. Lower the front of the vehicle.
8. Connect the negative battery cable.

Timing Belts

SERVICING

The 2.4L and 3.0L engines utilize a timing belt to drive the camshaft from the crankshaft's turning motion and to maintain proper valve timing. Some manufacturers schedule periodic timing belt replacement to assure optimum engine performance, to make sure the motorist is never stranded should the belt break (as the engine will stop instantly) and for some (manufacturers with interference motors), to prevent the possibility of severe internal engine damage should the belt break.

The 2.4L engine is listed as an interference motor (a motor whose valves will contact the pistons if the camshaft was rotated separately from the crankshaft), however, the 3.0L engine is not listed as an interference motor. In any case, the first 2 reasons for periodic replacement still apply. You will have to decide for yourself if the peace of mind offered by a new belt is worth it on higher mileage engines. Chrysler recommends replacing the timing belt on the 2.4L engine at 120,000 miles (192,000 km) and the 3.0L engine at 60,000 miles (96,000 km).

➡ **For inspection and/or replacement information of the timing belt, refer to Section 3.**

Whether or not you decide to replace it, you would be wise to check it periodically to make sure it has not become damaged or worn. Generally speaking, a severely worn belt may cause engine performance to drop dramatically, but a damaged belt (which could give out suddenly) may not give as much warning. In general, any time the engine timing cover(s) is (are) removed you should inspect the belt for premature parting, severe cracks or missing teeth.

Hoses

CAUTION

The vehicles covered in this book are equipped with an electric cooling fan. Be sure to disengage the negative battery cable, or fan motor wiring harness connector before replacing any radiator/heater hose. The fan may come on, under certain circumstances, even though the ignition is OFF.

REMOVAL & INSTALLATION

See Figures 79, 80, 81 and 82

Inspect the condition of the radiator and heater hoses periodically. Early spring and at the beginning of the fall or winter, when you are performing other maintenance, are good times. Make sure the engine and cooling system are cold. Visually inspect for cracking, rotting or collapsed hoses, replace as neces-

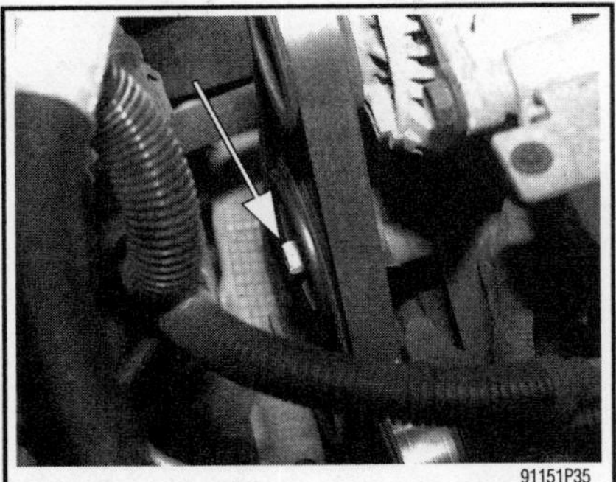

Fig. 77 Alternator/power steering pump belt tensioner bolt location

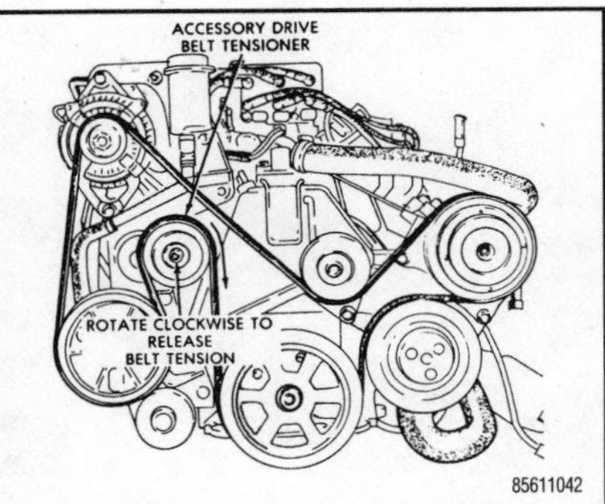

Fig. 78 Accessory drive belt adjustment—3.3L and 3.8L engines

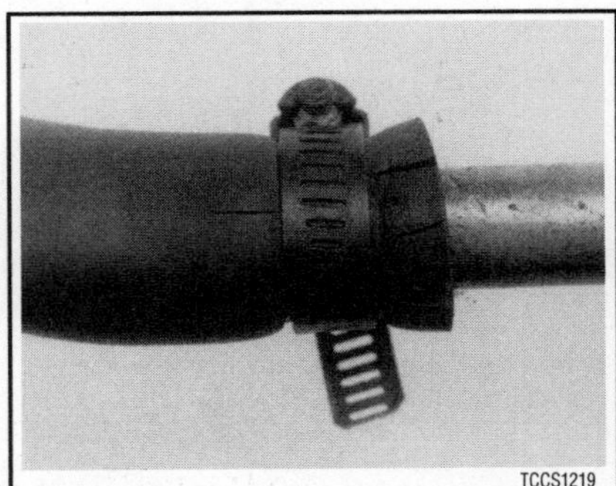

Fig. 79 The cracks developing along this hose are a result of age-related hardening

TCCS1220
Fig. 80 A hose clamp that is too tight can cause older hoses to separate and tear on either side of the clamp

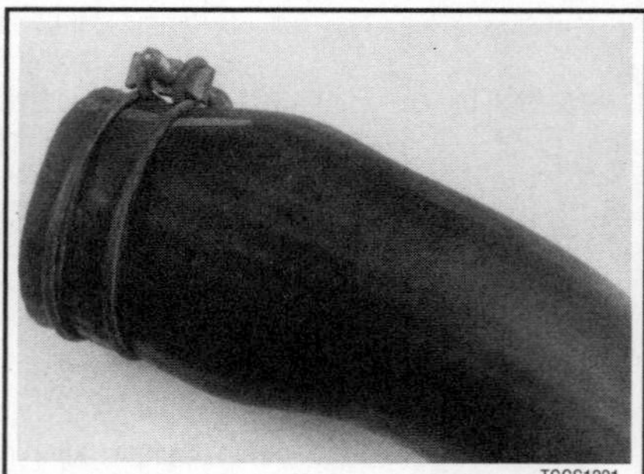
TCCS1221
Fig. 81 A soft spongy hose (identifiable by the swollen section) will eventually burst and should be replaced

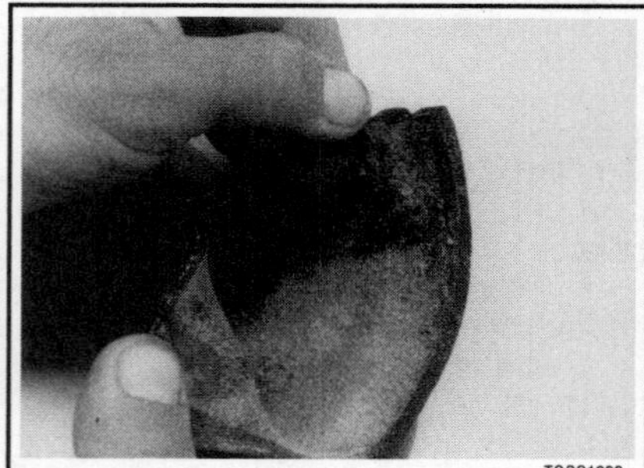
TCCS1222
Fig. 82 Hoses are likely to deteriorate from the inside if the cooling system is not periodically flushed

sary. Run your hand along the length of the hose. If a weak or swollen spot is noted when squeezing the hose wall, replace the hose.

1. Drain the cooling system into a suitable container (if the coolant is to be reused).

CAUTION

When draining the coolant, keep in mind that cats and dogs are attracted by ethylene glycol antifreeze, and are quite likely to drink any that is left in an uncovered container or in puddles on the ground. This will prove fatal in sufficient quantity. Always drain the coolant into a sealable container. Coolant should be reused unless it is contaminated or several years old.

2. Loosen the hose clamps at each end of the hose that requires replacement.
3. Twist, pull and slide the hose off the radiator, water pump, thermostat or heater connection.
4. Clean the hose mounting connections. Position the hose clamps on the new hose.
5. Coat the connection surfaces with a water resistant sealer and slide the hose into position. Make sure the hose clamps are located beyond the raised bead of the connector (if equipped) and centered in the clamping area of the connection.
6. Tighten the clamps to 20–30 inch lbs. (2–3 Nm). Do not overtighten.
7. Fill the cooling system.
8. Start the engine and allow it to reach normal operating temperature. Check for leaks.

CV-Boots

INSPECTION

See Figures 83 and 84

The CV (Constant Velocity) boots should be checked for damage each time the oil is changed and any other time the vehicle is raised for service. These boots keep water, grime, dirt and other damaging matter from entering the CV-joints. Any of these could cause early CV-joint failure which can be expensive to repair. Heavy grease thrown around the inside of the front wheel(s) and on the brake caliper/drum can be an indication of a torn boot. Thoroughly check the boots for missing clamps and tears. If the boot is damaged, it should be replaced immediately. Please refer to Section 7 for procedures.

Spark Plugs

See Figure 85

A typical spark plug consists of a metal shell surrounding a ceramic insulator. A metal electrode extends downward through the center of the insulator and protrudes a small distance. Located at the end of the plug and attached to the side of the outer metal shell is the side electrode. The side electrode bends in at a 90° angle so that its tip is just past and parallel to the tip of the center electrode. The distance between these two electrodes (measured in thousandths of an inch or hundredths of a millimeter) is called the spark plug gap.

The spark plug does not produce a spark, but instead provides a gap across which the current can arc. The coil produces anywhere from 20,000 to 50,000 volts (depending on the type and application) which travels through the wires to the spark plugs. The current passes along the center electrode and jumps the gap to the side electrode, and in doing so, ignites the air/fuel mixture in the combustion chamber.

SPARK PLUG HEAT RANGE

See Figure 86

Spark plug heat range is the ability of the plug to dissipate heat. The longer the insulator (or the farther it extends into the engine), the hotter the plug will operate; the shorter the insulator (the closer the electrode is to the block's cooling passages) the cooler it will operate. A plug that absorbs little heat and remains too cool will quickly accumulate deposits of oil and carbon since it is not hot enough to burn them off. This leads to plug fouling and consequently to misfiring. A plug that absorbs too much heat will have no deposits but, due to the excessive heat, the electrodes will burn away quickly and might possibly lead to preignition or

TCCS1011
Fig. 83 CV-Boots must be inspected periodically for damage

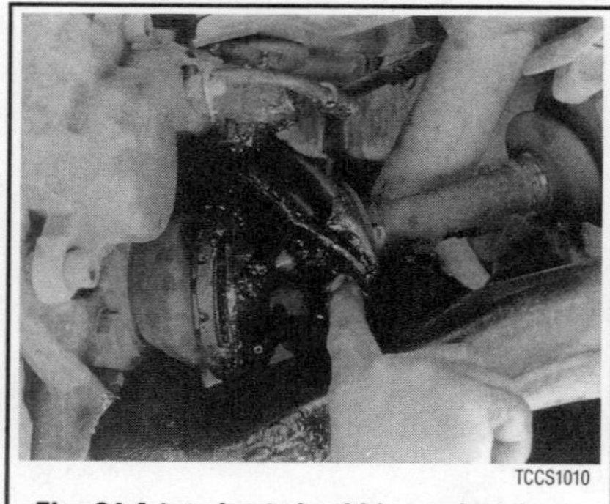
TCCS1010
Fig. 84 A torn boot should be replaced immediately

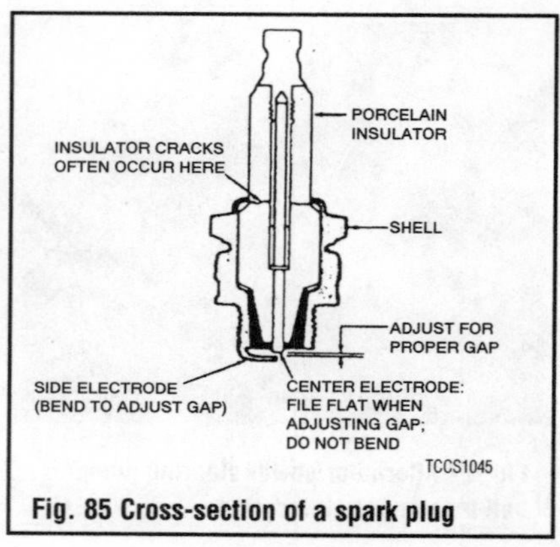

TCCS1045
Fig. 85 Cross-section of a spark plug

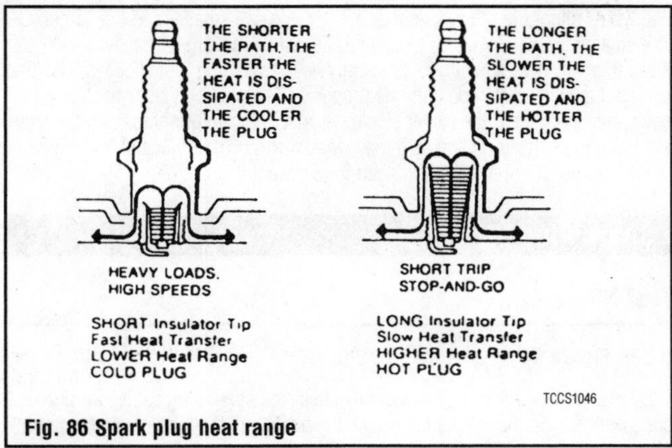

Fig. 86 Spark plug heat range

other ignition problems. Preignition takes place when plug tips get so hot that they glow sufficiently to ignite the air/fuel mixture before the actual spark occurs. This early ignition will usually cause a pinging during low speeds and heavy loads.

The general rule of thumb for choosing the correct heat range when picking a spark plug is: if most of your driving is long distance, high speed travel, use a colder plug; if most of your driving is stop and go, use a hotter plug. Original equipment plugs are generally a good compromise between the 2 styles and most people never have the need to change their plugs from the factory-recommended heat range.

REMOVAL & INSTALLATION

See Figures 87, 88 and 89

A set of spark plugs usually requires replacement after about 20,000–30,000 miles (32,000–48,000 km), depending on your style of driving. In normal operation plug gap increases about 0.001 in. (0.025mm) for every 2500 miles (4000 km). As the gap increases, the plug's voltage requirement also increases. It requires a greater voltage to jump the wider gap and about two to three times as much voltage to fire the plug at high speeds than at idle. The improved air/fuel ratio control of modern fuel injection combined with the higher voltage output of modern ignition systems will often allow an engine to run significantly longer on a set of standard spark plugs, but keep in mind that efficiency will drop as the gap widens (along with fuel economy and power).

When you're removing spark plugs, work on one at a time. Don't start by removing the plug wires all at once, because, unless you number them, they may become mixed up. Take a minute before you begin and number the wires with tape.

1. Disconnect the negative battery cable, and if the vehicle has been run recently, allow the engine to thoroughly cool.

➡ When removing the spark plugs on the V-6 engine only on the firewall side, it may be necessary to remove the windshield wiper/motor module assembly from the vehicle. This will allow more room to work between the engine and the engine compartment firewall. Refer to Section 6 for removal procedures

2. On V-6 models only, remove the windshield wiper/motor module assembly from the vehicle for access to the spark plugs on the firewall side.
3. Carefully twist the spark plug wire boot to loosen it, then pull upward and remove the boot from the plug. Be sure to pull on the boot and not on the wire, otherwise the connector located inside the boot may become separated.
4. Using compressed air, blow any water or debris from the spark plug well to assure that no harmful contaminants are allowed to enter the combustion chamber when the spark plug is removed. If compressed air is not available, use a rag or a brush to clean the area.

➡ Remove the spark plugs when the engine is cold, if possible, to prevent damage to the threads. If removal of the plugs is difficult, apply a few drops of penetrating oil or silicone spray to the area around the base of the plug, and allow it a few minutes to work.

5. Using a spark plug socket that is equipped with a rubber insert to properly hold the plug, turn the spark plug counterclockwise to loosen and remove the spark plug from the bore.

WARNING

Be sure not to use a flexible extension on the socket. Use of a flexible extension may allow a shear force to be applied to the plug. A shear force could break the plug off in the cylinder head, leading to costly and frustrating repairs.

To install:

6. Inspect the spark plug boot for tears or damage. If a damaged boot is found, the spark plug wire must be replaced.
7. Using a wire feeler gauge, check and adjust the spark plug gap. When using a gauge, the proper size should pass between the electrodes with a slight drag. The next larger size should not be able to pass while the next smaller size should pass freely.
8. Carefully thread the plug into the bore by hand. If resistance is felt before the plug is almost completely threaded, back the plug out and begin threading again. In small, hard to reach areas, an old spark plug wire and boot could be used as a threading tool. The boot will hold the plug while you twist the end of the wire and the wire is supple enough to twist before it would allow the plug to crossthread.

WARNING

Do not use the spark plug socket to thread the plugs. Always carefully thread the plug by hand or using an old plug wire to prevent the possibility of crossthreading and damaging the cylinder head bore.

9. Carefully tighten the spark plug. If the plug you are installing is equipped with a crush washer, seat the plug, then tighten about ¼ turn to crush the washer. If you are installing a tapered seat plug, tighten the plug to specifications provided by the vehicle or plug manufacturer.
10. Apply a small amount of silicone dielectric compound to the end of the spark plug lead or inside the spark plug boot to prevent sticking, then install the boot to the spark plug and push until it clicks into place. The click may be felt or heard, then gently pull back on the boot to assure proper contact.

Fig. 87 Hold the spark plug boot firmly, while giving it a slight ½ twist in each direction before pulling it off of the spark plug

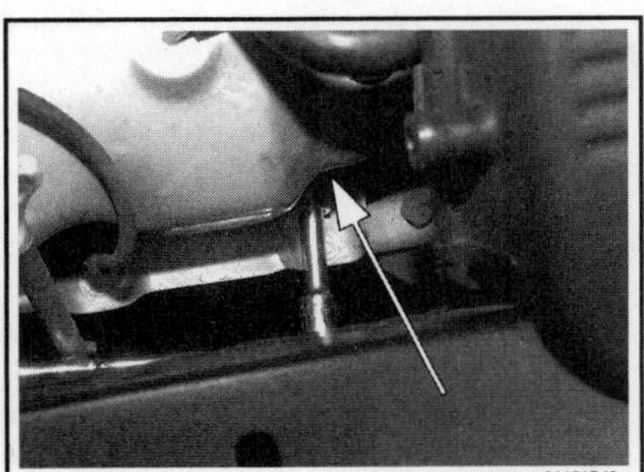

Fig. 88 Once all dirt is removed from around the spark plug, carefully loosen and remove the plug

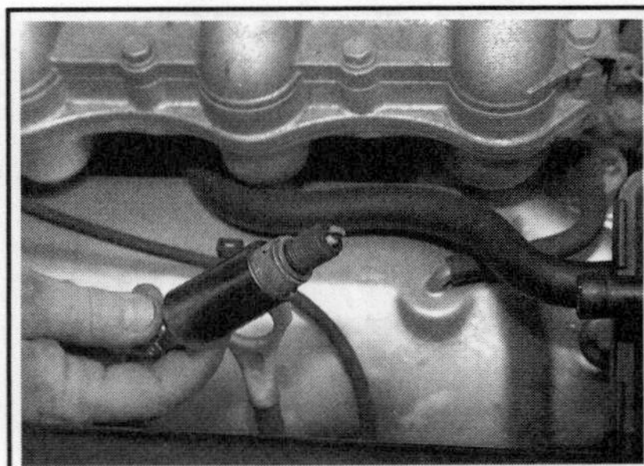

Fig. 89 Pull the used spark plug out of the cylinder head once it is completely loosened

INSPECTION & GAPPING

See Figures 90, 91, 92, 93 and 94

Check the plugs for deposits and wear. If they are not going to be replaced, clean the plugs thoroughly. Remember that any kind of deposit will decrease the efficiency of the plug. Plugs can be cleaned on a spark plug cleaning machine, which can sometimes be found in service stations, or you can do an acceptable job of cleaning with a stiff brush. If the plugs are cleaned, the electrodes must be filed flat. Use an ignition points file, not an emery board or the like, which will leave deposits. The electrodes must be filed perfectly flat with sharp edges; rounded edges reduce the spark plug voltage by as much as 50%.

Check spark plug gap before installation. The ground electrode (the L-shaped one connected to the body of the plug) must be parallel to the center electrode and the specified size wire gauge (please refer to the Tune-Up Specifications chart for details) must pass between the electrodes with a slight drag.

➡ NEVER adjust the gap on a used platinum type spark plug.

Always check the gap on new plugs as they are not always set correctly at the factory. Do not use a flat feeler gauge when measuring the gap on a used plug, because the reading may be inaccurate. A round-wire type gapping tool is the best way to check the gap. The correct gauge should pass through the electrode gap with a slight drag. If you're in doubt, try one size smaller and one larger. The smaller gauge should go through easily, while the larger one shouldn't go through at all. Wire gapping tools usually have a bending tool attached. Use that to adjust the side electrode until the proper distance is obtained. Absolutely never attempt to bend the center electrode. Also, be careful not to bend the side electrode too far or too often as it may weaken and break off within the engine, requiring removal of the cylinder head to retrieve it.

Spark Plug Wires

TESTING

See Figure 95

At every tune-up/inspection, visually check the spark plug cables for burns cuts, or breaks in the insulation. Check the boots and the nipples on the distributor cap and/or coil. Replace any damaged wiring.

Every 50,000 miles (80,000 Km) or 60 months, the resistance of the wires should be checked with an ohmmeter. Wires with excessive resistance will cause misfiring, and may make the engine difficult to start in damp weather.

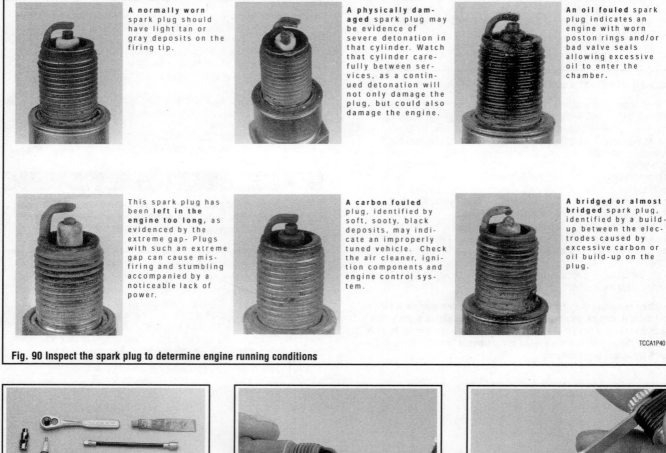

A normally worn spark plug should have light tan or gray deposits on the firing tip.

A physically damaged spark plug may be evidence of severe detonation in that cylinder. Watch that cylinder carefully between services, as a continued detonation will not only damage the plug, but could also damage the engine.

An oil fouled spark plug indicates an engine with worn poston rings and/or bad valve seals allowing excessive oil to enter the chamber.

This spark plug has been **left in the engine too long**, as evidenced by the extreme gap- Plugs with such an extreme gap can cause misfiring and stumbling accompanied by a noticeable lack of power.

A carbon fouled plug, identified by soft, sooty, black deposits, may indicate an improperly tuned vehicle. Check the air cleaner, ignition components and engine control system.

A bridged or almost bridged spark plug, identified by a build-up between the electrodes caused by excessive carbon or oil build-up on the plug.

TCCA1P40

Fig. 90 Inspect the spark plug to determine engine running conditions

TCCS1212

Fig. 91 A variety of tools and gauges are needed for spark plug service

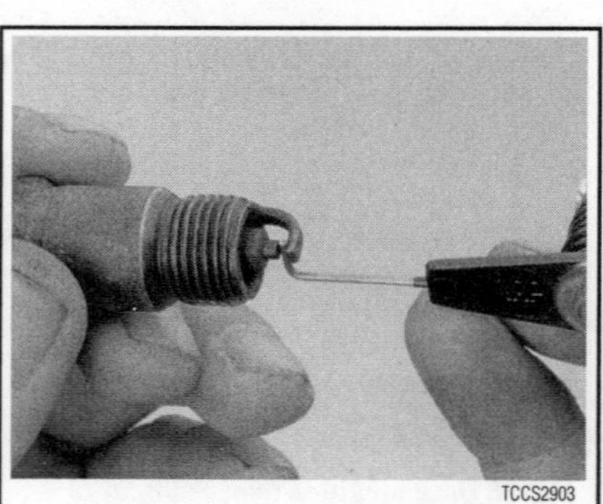

TCCS2903

Fig. 92 Checking the spark plug gap with a feeler gauge

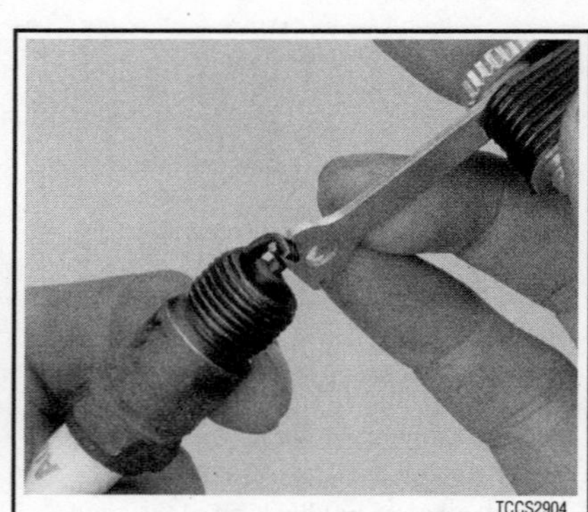

TCCS2904

Fig. 93 Adjusting the spark plug gap

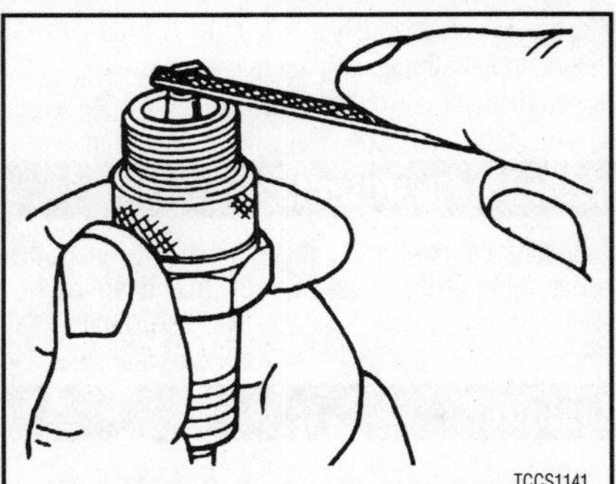
TCCS1141

Fig. 94 If the standard plug is in good condition, the electrode may be filed flat—WARNING: do not file platinum plugs

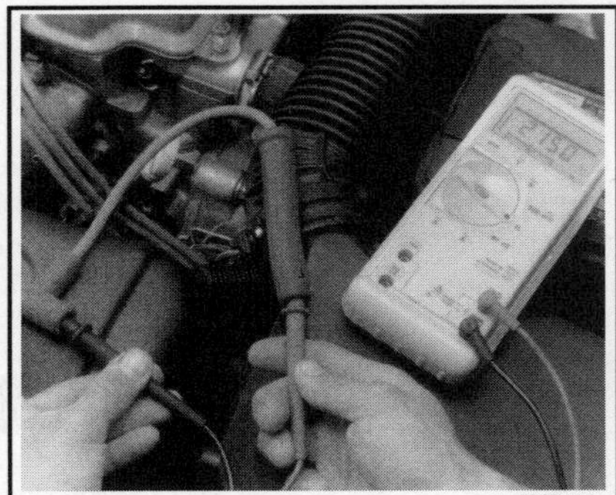
TCCS1009

Fig. 95 Checking individual plug wire resistance with a digital ohmmeter

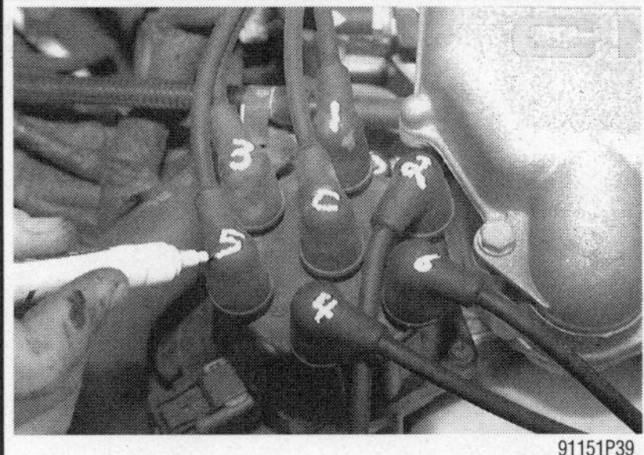
91151P39

Fig. 96 If the wires are being removed, or at least disconnected from the distributor cap, always matchmark each wire to its correct terminal

To check resistance, disconnect the spark plug wire from the plug and ignition coil or distributor, then use an ohmmeter to measure the resistance.

For 2.4L engines, the resistance should be as follows:

- Cables #1 and #4: 4,200 ohms
- Cables #2 and #3: 3,200 ohms

For 3.0L engines, the resistance should be as follows:

- Cable #1: 14,000 ohms
- Cable #2: 10,400 ohms
- Cable #3: 14,900 ohms
- Cable #4: 11,500 ohms
- Cable #5: 17,500 ohms
- Cable #6: 10,300 ohms
- Coil lead: 11,100 ohms

For 3.3L and 3.8L engines, the resistance should be as follows:

- Cable #1: 18,500 ohms
- Cable #2: 15,500 ohms
- Cable #3: 20,400 ohms
- Cable #4: 21,200 ohms
- Cable #5: 27,700 ohms
- Cable #6: 26,700 ohms

If resistance falls outside of specifications, the cable(s) should be replaced with new ones.

REMOVAL & INSTALLATION

See Figures 87 and 96

➡As the spark plug wires must be routed and connected properly, if all of the wires must be disconnected from the spark plugs or from the ignition coil pack/distributor at the same time, be sure to tag or mark the wires to assure proper reconnection.

When installing a new set of spark plug wires, replace the wires one at a time so there will be no mix-up. Start by replacing the longest cable first. Twist the boot of the spark plug wire ½ turn in each direction before pulling if off. Install the boot firmly over the spark plug. Route the wire exactly the same as the original. Insert the nipple firmly onto the tower on the ignition coil or distributor, if equipped. Be sure to apply silicone dielectric compound to the spark plug wire boots and tower connectors prior to installation.

➡ For easier access, it may be necessary to remove the windshield wiper/motor module assembly from the vehicle. This will allow more room to work between the engine and the engine compartment firewall. Refer to Section 6 for removal procedures.

Distributor Cap and Rotor

➡Only the ignition system of the 3.0L engine utilizes a distributor.

REMOVAL & INSTALLATION

See Figures 96, 97, 98 and 99

1. Disconnect the negative battery cable.
2. Loosen the distributor cap retaining screws.
3. Remove the distributor cap.
4. Using an 8mm socket, loosen the setscrew securing the rotor to the distributor shaft.
5. Remove the rotor.

Light deposits on the terminals can be scraped cleaned with a knife, heavy deposits or scaling will require cap replacement.

Wash the cap with a solution of warm water and mild detergent, scrub with a soft brush and dry with a clean soft cloth to remove dirt and grease.

6. If cap replacement is necessary, take notice of the cap installed position in relationship to the distributor assembly.
7. Number each plug wire so that the correct wire goes on the proper cap terminal when replaced. This can be done with pieces of adhesive tape.

➡ Do not pull plug wires from distributor cap, they must first be released from inside of cap.

8. Install the rotor onto the distributor shaft and tighten the 8mm setscrew.

91151P31

Fig. 97 After loosening the 2 retaining screws, lift the distributor cap off of the distributor

91151P25

Fig. 98 Loosen the setscrew that holds the rotor onto the distributor shaft . . .

91151P13

Fig. 99 . . . then pull the rottor straight up to remove from the distributor

9. Position the replacement cap on the distributor assembly, and tighten the distributor cap retaining screws.
10. Push the wire terminals firmly to properly seat the wires into the cap.
11. Connect the negative battery cable.

INSPECTION

Inspect the inside of the distributor cap for spark flash over (burnt tracks on cap or terminals), center carbon button wear or cracking, and worn terminals. Inspect the rotor for cracks, excessive wear or burn marks and sufficient spring tension of the spring-to-cap carbon button terminal. Clean light deposits, replace the rotor if scaled or burnt heavily. Replace the cap and/or rotor if any of these problems are present or suspected.

Ignition Timing

GENERAL INFORMATION

All vehicles covered by this manual are equipped with a "fixed" ignition system. This means that ignition timing is controlled by the Powertrain Control Module (PCM) and is not adjustable.

Valve Lash

ADJUSTMENT

2.4L And 3.0L Engines

These engines are equipped with hydraulic auto lash adjusters. The auto lash adjusters automatically control valve lash. No adjustment is necessary.

3.3L And 3.8L Engines

These engines are equipped with hydraulic valve lifters. The function of the hydraulic valve lifter is to maintain zero valve lash during the entire valve opening and closing process; any lash is instantaneously taken up by hydraulic action. Proper adjustment is maintained automatically by hydraulic pressure in the valves, therefore, valve lash adjustment is not possible.

Idle Speed and Mixture Adjustments

Idle speed and mixture for all engines, covered by this manual, are electronically controlled by a computerized fuel injection system. Adjustments are neither necessary nor possible.

Air Conditioning System

SYSTEM SERVICE & REPAIR

➡ **It is recommended that the A/C system be serviced by an EPA Section 609 certified automotive technician utilizing a refrigerant recovery/recycling machine.**

The do-it-yourselfer should not service his/her own vehicle's A/C system for many reasons, including legal concerns, personal injury, environmental damage and cost. The following are some of the reasons why you may decide not to service your own vehicle's A/C system.

According to the U.S. Clean Air Act, it is a federal crime to service or repair (involving the refrigerant) a Motor Vehicle Air Conditioning (MVAC) system for money without being EPA certified. It is also illegal to vent R-134a refrigerant into the atmosphere.

State and/or local laws may be more strict than the federal regulations, so be sure to check with your state and/or local authorities for further information. For further federal information on the legality of servicing your A/C system, call the EPA Stratospheric Ozone Hotline.

➡ **Federal law dictates that a fine of up to $25,000 may be levied on people convicted of venting refrigerant into the atmosphere. Additionally, the EPA may pay up to $10,000 for information or services leading to a criminal conviction of the violation of these laws.**

When servicing an A/C system you run the risk of handling or coming in contact with refrigerant, which may result in skin or eye irritation or frostbite.

ENGINE TUNE-UP SPECIFICATIONS

Year	Engine ID/VIN	Engine Displacement Liters (cc)	Spark Plugs Gap (in.)	Ignition Timing (deg.) MT	Ignition Timing (deg.) AT	Fuel Pump (psi)	Idle Speed (rpm) MT	Idle Speed (rpm) AT	Valve Clearance In.	Valve Clearance Ex.
1996	B	2.4 (2429)	0.050	—	①	49	—	②	HYD	HYD
	3	3.0 (2972)	0.035	—	①	48	—	②	HYD	HYD
	R	3.3 (3300)	0.050	—	①	49	—	②	HYD	HYD
	L	3.8 (3785)	0.050	—	①	49	—	②	HYD	HYD
1997	B	2.4 (2429)	0.048-0.053	—	①	49	—	②	HYD	HYD
	3	3.0 (2972)	0.039-0.044	—	①	48	—	②	HYD	HYD
	R	3.3 (3300)	0.048-0.053	—	①	49	—	②	HYD	HYD
	L	3.8 (3785)	0.048-0.053	—	①	49	—	②	HYD	HYD
1998	B	2.4 (2429)	0.048-0.053	—	①	49	—	②	HYD	HYD
	3	3.0 (2972)	0.039-0.044	—	①	48	—	②	HYD	HYD
	R	3.3 (3300)	0.048-0.053	—	①	55	—	②	HYD	HYD
	L	3.8 (3785)	0.048-0.053	—	①	49	—	②	HYD	HYD
1999	B	2.4 (2429)	0.048-0.053	—	①	49	—	②	HYD	HYD
	3	3.0 (2972)	0.039-0.044	—	①	48	—	②	HYD	HYD
	R	3.3 (3300)	0.048-0.053	—	①	55	—	②	HYD	HYD
	L	3.8 (3785)	0.048-0.053	—	①	49	—	②	HYD	HYD

NOTE: The Vehicle Emission Control Information label often reflects specification changes made during production. The label figures must be used if they differ from those in this chart.

HYD - Hydraulic

① Ignition timing is regulated by the Powertrain Control Module (PCM), and cannot be adjusted.

② Refer to the Vehicle Emission Control Information (VECI) label for correct specification.

91151C03

Although low in toxicity (due to chemical stability), inhalation of concentrated refrigerant fumes is dangerous and can result in death; cases of fatal cardiac arrhythmia have been reported in people accidentally subjected to high levels of refrigerant. Some early symptoms include loss of concentration and drowsiness.

Also, refrigerants can decompose at high temperatures (near gas heaters or open flame), which may result in hydrofluoric acid, hydrochloric acid and phosgene (a fatal nerve gas).

R-134a refrigerant is a greenhouse gas which, if allowed to vent into the atmosphere, will contribute to global warming (the Greenhouse Effect).

It is usually more economically feasible to have a certified MVAC automotive technician perform A/C system service to your vehicle. While it is illegal to service an A/C system without the proper equipment, the home mechanic would have to purchase an expensive refrigerant recovery/recycling machine to service his/her own vehicle.

PREVENTIVE MAINTENANCE

Although the A/C system should not be serviced by the do-it-yourselfer, preventive maintenance can be practiced and A/C system inspections can be performed to help maintain the efficiency of the vehicle's A/C system. For preventive maintenance, perform the following:

- The easiest and most important preventive maintenance for your A/C system is to be sure that it is used on a regular basis. Running the system for five minutes each month (no matter what the season) will help ensure that the seals and all internal components remain lubricated.

➡ Some newer vehicles automatically operate the A/C system compressor whenever the windshield defroster is activated. When running, the compressor lubricates the A/C system components; therefore, the A/C system would not need to be operated each month.

- In order to prevent heater core freeze-up during A/C operation, it is necessary to maintain a proper antifreeze protection. Use a hand-held coolant tester (hydrometer) to periodically check the condition of the antifreeze in your engine's cooling system.

➡ Antifreeze should not be used longer than the manufacturer specifies.

- For efficient operation of an air conditioned vehicle's cooling system, the radiator cap should have a holding pressure which meets manufacturer's specifications. A cap which fails to hold these pressures should be replaced.
- Any obstruction of or damage to the condenser configuration will restrict air flow which is essential to its efficient operation. It is, therefore, a good rule to keep this unit clean and in proper physical shape.

➡ Bug screens which are mounted in front of the condenser (unless they are original equipment) are regarded as obstructions.

- The condensation drain tube expels any water, which accumulates on the bottom of the evaporator housing, into the engine compartment. If this tube is obstructed, the air conditioning performance can be restricted and condensation buildup can spill over onto the vehicle's floor.

SYSTEM INSPECTION

Although the A/C system should not be serviced by the do-it-yourselfer, preventive maintenance can be practiced and A/C system inspections can be performed to help maintain the efficiency of the vehicle's A/C system. For A/C system inspection, perform the following:

The easiest and often most important check for the air conditioning system consists of a visual inspection of the system components. Visually inspect the air conditioning system for refrigerant leaks, damaged compressor clutch, abnormal compressor drive belt tension and/or condition, plugged evaporator drain tube, blocked condenser fins, disconnected or broken wires, blown fuses, corroded connections and poor insulation.

A refrigerant leak will usually appear as an oily residue at the leakage point in the system. The oily residue soon picks up dust or dirt particles from the surrounding air and appears greasy. Through time, this will build up and appear to be a heavy dirt impregnated grease.

For a thorough visual and operational inspection, check the following:

- Check the surface of the radiator and condenser for dirt, leaves or other material which might block air flow.
- Check for kinks in hoses and lines. Check the system for leaks.
- Make sure the drive belt is properly tensioned. When the air conditioning is operating, make sure the drive belt is free of noise or slippage.
- Make sure the blower motor operates at all appropriate positions, then check for distribution of the air from all outlets with the blower on **HIGH** or **MAX**.

➡ Keep in mind that under conditions of high humidity, air discharged from the A/C vents may not feel as cold as expected, even if the system is working properly. This is because vaporized moisture in humid air retains heat more effectively than dry air, thereby making humid air more difficult to cool.

- Make sure the air passage selection lever is operating correctly. Start the engine and warm it to normal operating temperature, then make sure the temperature selection lever is operating correctly.

Windshield Wiper (Elements)

ELEMENT (REFILL) CARE & REPLACEMENT

See Figures 100 thru 109

For maximum effectiveness and longest element life, the windshield and wiper blades should be kept clean. Dirt, tree sap, road tar and so on will cause streaking, smearing and blade deterioration if left on the glass. It is advisable to wash the windshield carefully with a commercial glass cleaner at least once a month. Wipe off the rubber blades with the wet rag afterwards. Do not attempt to move wipers across the windshield by hand; damage to the motor and drive mechanism will result.

To inspect and/or replace the wiper blade elements, place the wiper switch in the **LOW** speed position and the ignition switch in the **ACC** position. When the wiper blades are approximately vertical on the windshield, turn the ignition switch to **OFF**.

Examine the wiper blade elements. If they are found to be cracked, broken or torn, they should be replaced immediately. Replacement intervals will vary with usage, although ozone deterioration usually limits element life to about one year. If the wiper pattern is smeared or streaked, or if the blade chatters across the glass, the elements should be replaced. It is easiest and most sensible to replace the elements in pairs.

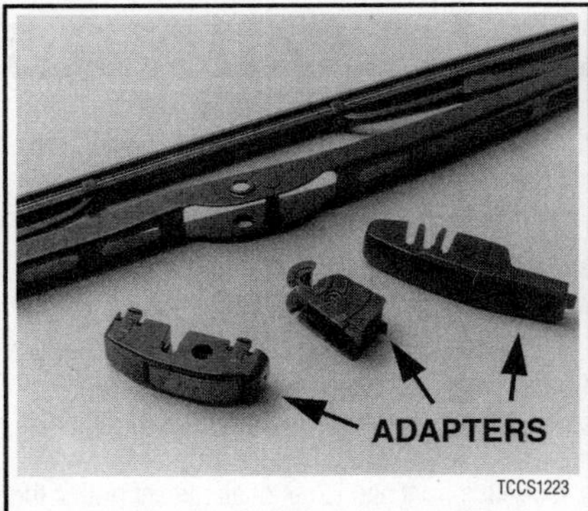

Fig. 100 Bosch® wiper blade and fit kit

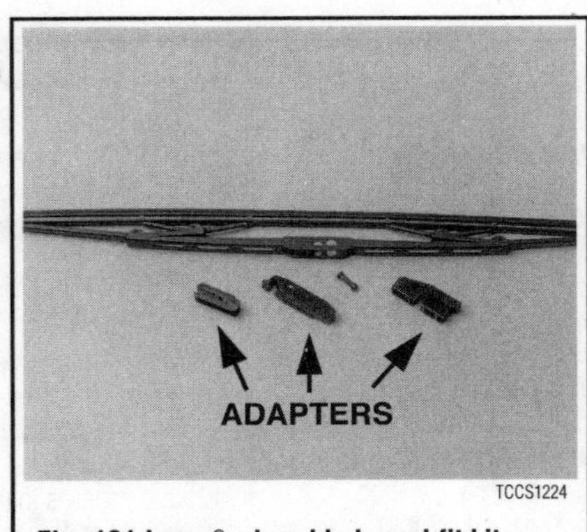

Fig. 101 Lexor® wiper blade and fit kit

Fig. 102 Pylon® wiper blade and adapter

TCCS1226
Fig. 103 Trico® wiper blade and fit kit

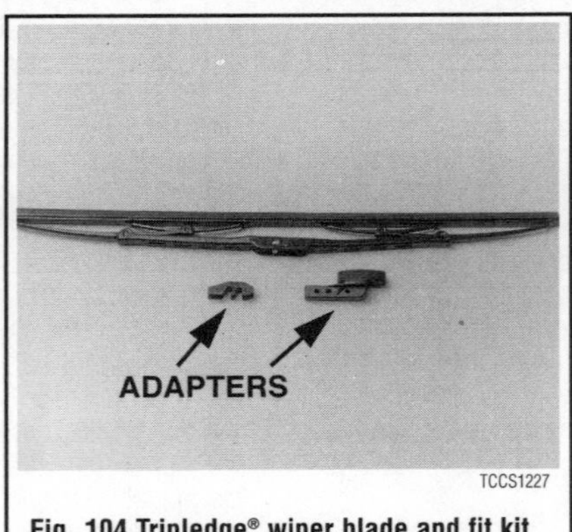

TCCS1227
Fig. 104 Tripledge® wiper blade and fit kit

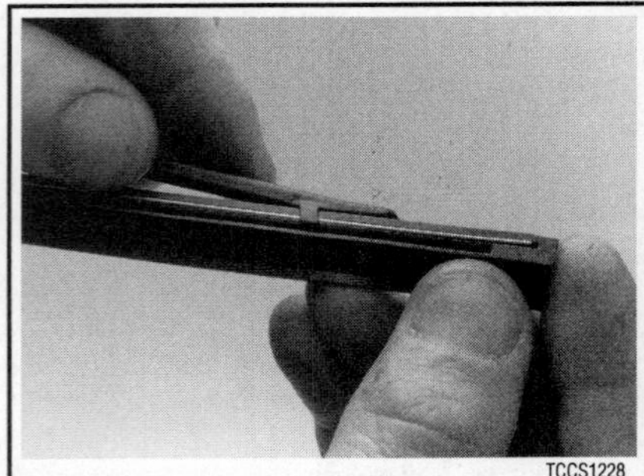
TCCS1228
Fig. 105 To remove and install a Lexor® wiper blade refill, slip out the old insert and slide in a new one

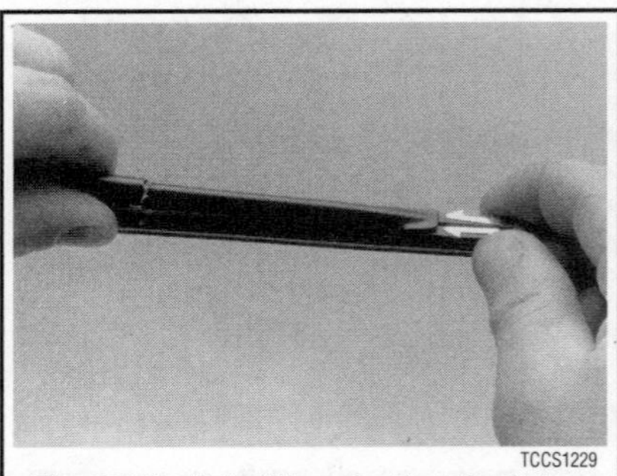
TCCS1229
Fig. 106 On Pylon® inserts, the clip at the end has to be removed prior to sliding the insert off

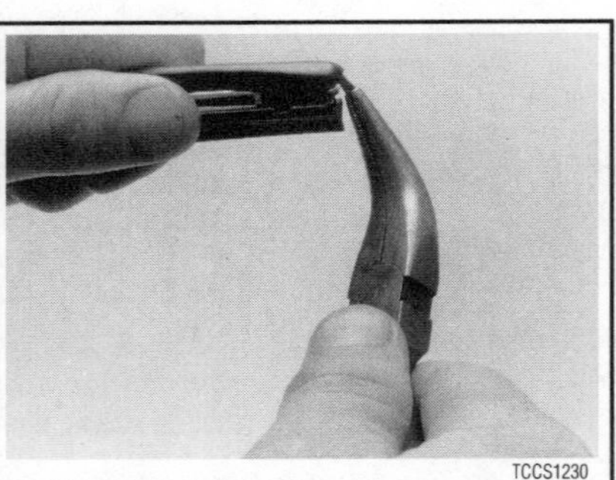
TCCS1230
Fig. 107 On Trico® wiper blades, the tab at the end of the blade must be turned up . . .

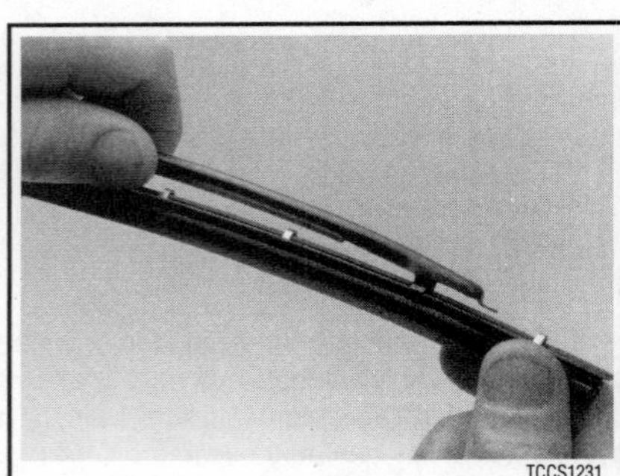
TCCS1231
Fig. 108 . . . then the insert can be removed. After installing the replacement insert, bend the tab back

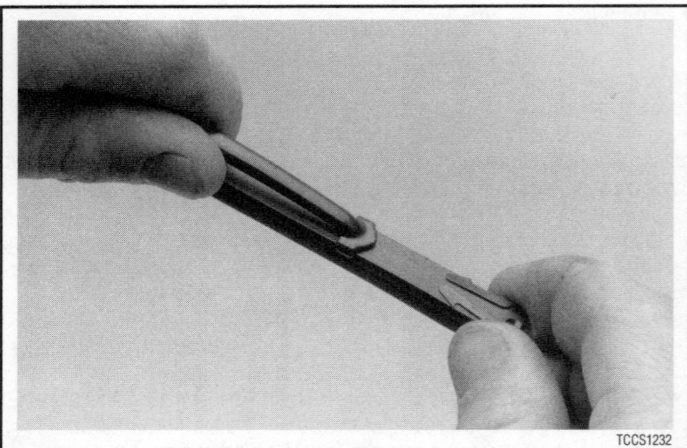
TCCS1232
Fig. 109 The Tripledge® wiper blade insert is removed and installed using a securing clip

If your vehicle is equipped with aftermarket blades, there are several different types of refills and your vehicle might have any kind. Aftermarket blades and arms rarely use the exact same type blade or refill as the original equipment. Here are some typical aftermarket blades; not all may be available for your vehicle:

The Anco® type uses a release button that is pushed down to allow the refill to slide out of the yoke jaws. The new refill slides back into the frame and locks in place.

Some Trico® refills are removed by locating where the metal backing strip or the refill is wider. Insert a small screwdriver blade between the frame and metal backing strip. Press down to release the refill from the retaining tab.

Other types of Trico® refills have two metal tabs which are unlocked by squeezing them together. The rubber filler can then be withdrawn from the frame jaws. A new refill is installed by inserting the refill into the front frame jaws and sliding it rearward to engage the remaining frame jaws. There are usually four jaws; be certain when installing that the refill is engaged in all of them. At the end of its travel, the tabs will lock into place on the front jaws of the wiper blade frame.

Another type of refill is made from polycarbonate. The refill has a simple locking device at one end which flexes downward out of the groove into which the jaws of the holder fit, allowing easy release. By sliding the new refill through all the jaws and pushing through the slight resistance when it reaches the end of its travel, the refill will lock into position.

To replace the Tridon® refill, it is necessary to remove the wiper blade. This refill has a plastic backing strip with a notch about 1 in. (25mm) from the end. Hold the blade (frame) on a hard surface so that the frame is tightly bowed. Grip the tip of the backing strip and pull up while twisting counterclockwise. The backing strip will snap out of the retaining tab. Do this for the remaining tabs until the refill is free of the blade. The length of these refills is molded into the end and they should be replaced with identical types.

Regardless of the type of refill used, be sure to follow the part manufacturer's instructions closely. Make sure that all of the frame jaws are engaged as the refill is pushed into place and locked. If the metal blade holder and frame are allowed to touch the glass during wiper operation, the glass will be scratched.

Tires and Wheels

Common sense and good driving habits will afford maximum tire life. Fast starts, sudden stops and hard cornering are hard on tires and will shorten their useful life span. Make sure that you don't overload the vehicle or run with incorrect pressure in the tires. Both of these practices will increase tread wear.

➡ **For optimum tire life, keep the tires properly inflated, rotate them often and have the wheel alignment checked periodically.**

Inspect your tires frequently. Be especially careful to watch for bubbles in the tread or sidewall, deep cuts or underinflation. Replace any tires with bubbles in the sidewall. If cuts are so deep that they penetrate to the cords, discard the tire. Any cut in the sidewall of a radial tire renders it unsafe. Also look for uneven tread wear patterns that may indicate the front end is out of alignment or that the tires are out of balance.

TIRE ROTATION

➧ See Figures 110 and 111

Tires must be rotated periodically to equalize wear patterns that vary with a tire's position on the vehicle. Tires will also wear in an uneven way as the front steering/suspension system wears to the point where the alignment should be reset.

Rotating the tires will ensure maximum life for the tires as a set, so you will not have to discard a tire early due to wear on only part of the tread. Regular rotation is required to equalize wear.

When rotating "unidirectional tires," make sure that they always roll in the same direction. This means that a tire used on the left side of the vehicle must not be switched to the right side and vice-versa. Such tires should only be rotated front-to-rear or rear-to-front, while always remaining on the same side of the vehicle. These tires are marked on the sidewall as to the direction of rotation; observe the marks when reinstalling the tire(s).

Some styled or "mag" wheels may have different offsets front to rear. In these cases, the rear wheels must not be used up front and vice-versa. Furthermore, if these wheels are equipped with unidirectional tires, they cannot be rotated unless the tire is remounted for the proper direction of rotation.

➡ The compact or space-saver spare is strictly for emergency use. It must never be included in the tire rotation or placed on the vehicle for everyday use.

TIRE DESIGN

➧ See Figure 112

For maximum satisfaction, tires should be used in sets of four. Mixing of different types (radial, bias-belted, fiberglass belted) must be avoided. In most cases, the vehicle manufacturer has designated a type of tire on which the vehicle will perform best. Your first choice when replacing tires should be to use the same type of tire that the manufacturer recommends.

When radial tires are used, tire sizes and wheel diameters should be selected to maintain ground clearance and tire load capacity equivalent to the original specified tire. Radial tires should always be used in sets of four.

⁂ CAUTION

Radial tires should never be used on only the front axle.

When selecting tires, pay attention to the original size as marked on the tire. Most tires are described using an industry size code sometimes referred to as P-Metric. This allows the exact identification of the tire specifications, regardless of the manufacturer. If selecting a different tire size or brand, remember to check the installed tire for any sign of interference with the body or suspension while the vehicle is stopping, turning sharply or heavily loaded.

Snow Tires

Good radial tires can produce a big advantage in slippery weather, but in snow, a street radial tire does not have sufficient tread to provide traction and control. The small grooves of a street tire quickly pack with snow and the tire behaves like a billiard ball on a marble floor. The more open, chunky tread of a snow tire will self-clean as the tire turns, providing much better grip on snowy surfaces.

To satisfy municipalities requiring snow tires during weather emergencies, most snow tires carry either an M + S designation after the tire size stamped on the sidewall, or the designation "all-season." In general, no change in tire size is necessary when buying snow tires.

Most manufacturers strongly recommend the use of 4 snow tires on their vehicles for reasons of stability. If snow tires are fitted only to the drive wheels, the opposite end of the vehicle may become very unstable when braking or turning on slippery surfaces. This instability can lead to unpleasant endings if the driver can't counteract the slide in time.

Note that snow tires, whether 2 or 4, will affect vehicle handling in all non-snow situations. The stiffer, heavier snow tires will noticeably change the turning and braking characteristics of the vehicle. Once the snow tires are installed, you must re-learn the behavior of the vehicle and drive accordingly.

➡ Consider buying extra wheels on which to mount the snow tires. Once done, the "snow wheels" can be installed and removed as needed. This eliminates the potential damage to tires or wheels from seasonal removal and installation. Even if your vehicle has styled wheels, see if inexpensive steel wheels are available. Although the look of the vehicle will change, the expensive wheels will be protected from salt, curb hits and pothole damage.

TIRE STORAGE

If they are mounted on wheels, store the tires at proper inflation pressure. All tires should be kept in a cool, dry place. If they are stored in the garage or basement, do not let them stand on a concrete floor; set them on strips of wood, a mat or a large stack of newspaper. Keeping them away from direct moisture is of paramount importance. Tires should not be stored upright, but in a flat position.

INFLATION & INSPECTION

➧ See Figures 113 thru 120

The importance of proper tire inflation cannot be overemphasized. A tire employs air as part of its structure. It is designed around the supporting strength of the air at a specified pressure. For this reason, improper inflation drastically reduces the tire's ability to perform as intended. A tire will lose some air in day-to-day use; having to add a few pounds of air periodically is not necessarily a sign of a leaking tire.

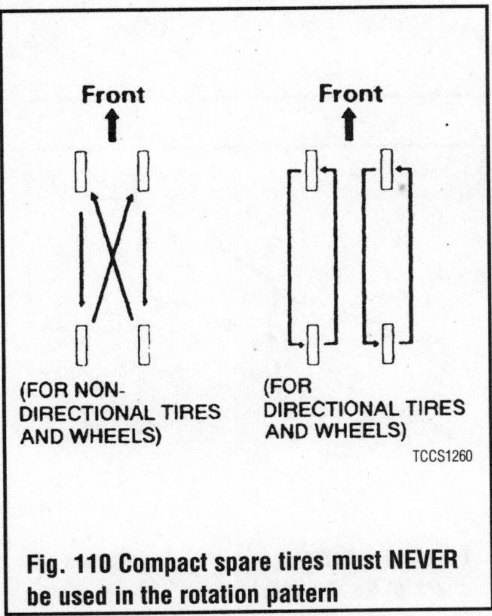

Fig. 110 Compact spare tires must NEVER be used in the rotation pattern

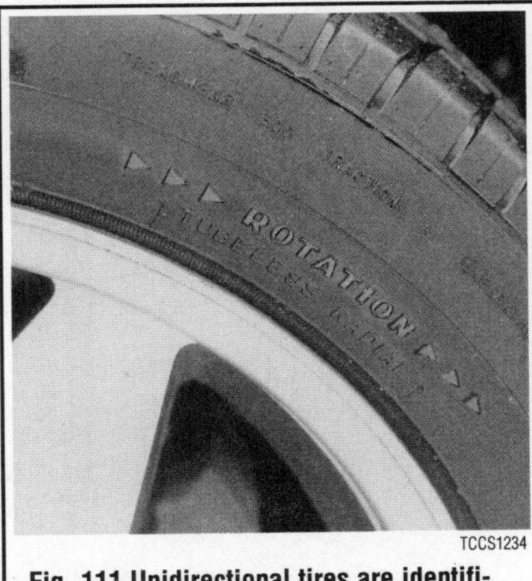

Fig. 111 Unidirectional tires are identifiable by sidewall arrows and/or the word "rotation"

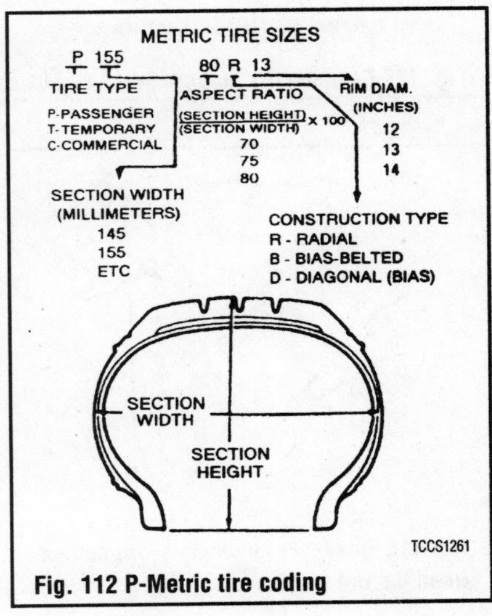

Fig. 112 P-Metric tire coding

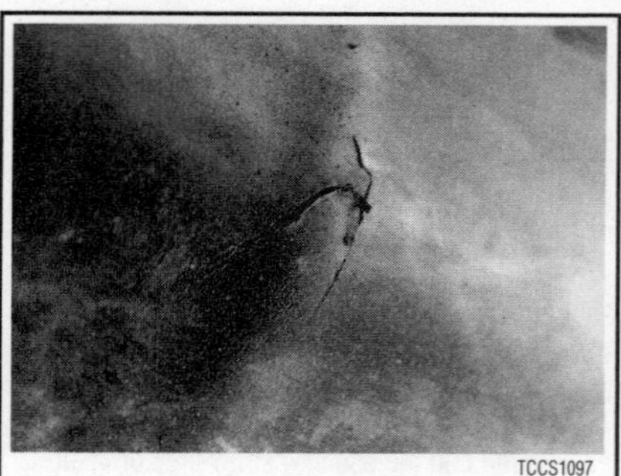

Fig. 113 Tires should be checked frequently for any sign of puncture or damage

Fig. 114 Tires with deep cuts, or cuts which bulge, should be replaced immediately

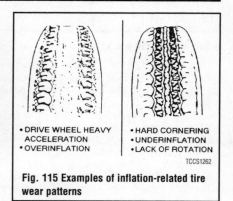

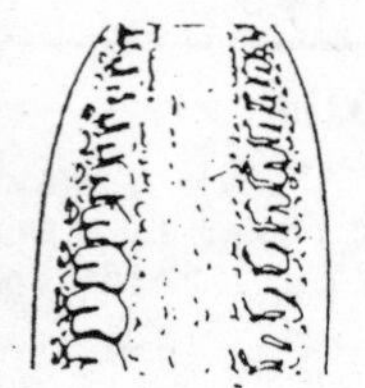

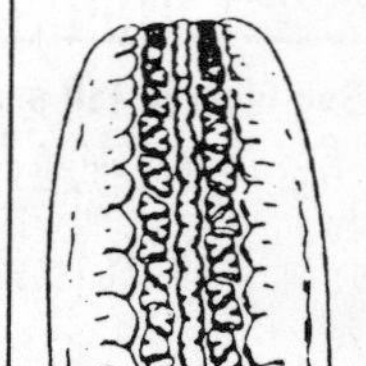

Fig. 115 Examples of inflation-related tire wear patterns

Two items should be a permanent fixture in every glove compartment: an accurate tire pressure gauge and a tread depth gauge. Check the tire pressure (including the spare) regularly with a pocket type gauge. Too often, the gauge on the end of the air hose at your corner garage is not accurate because it suffers too much abuse. Always check tire pressure when the tires are cold, as pressure increases with temperature. If you must move the vehicle to check the tire inflation, do not drive more than a mile before checking. A cold tire is generally one that has not been driven for more than three hours.

A plate or sticker is normally provided somewhere in the vehicle (door post, hood, tailgate or trunk lid) which shows the proper pressure for the tires. Never counteract excessive pressure build-up by bleeding off air pressure (letting some air out). This will cause the tire to run hotter and wear quicker.

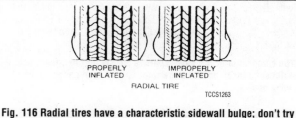

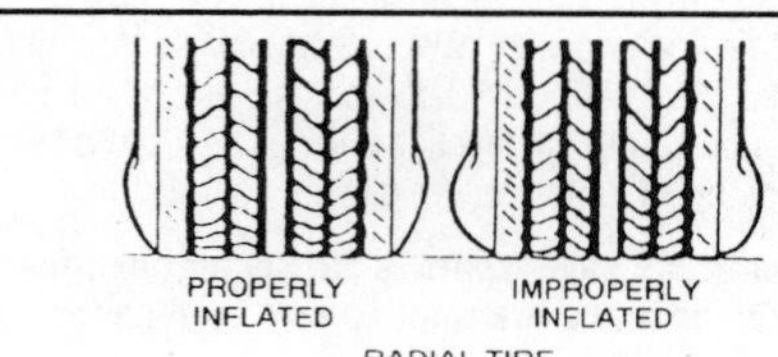

Fig. 116 Radial tires have a characteristic sidewall bulge; don't try to measure pressure by looking at the tire. Use a quality air pressure gauge

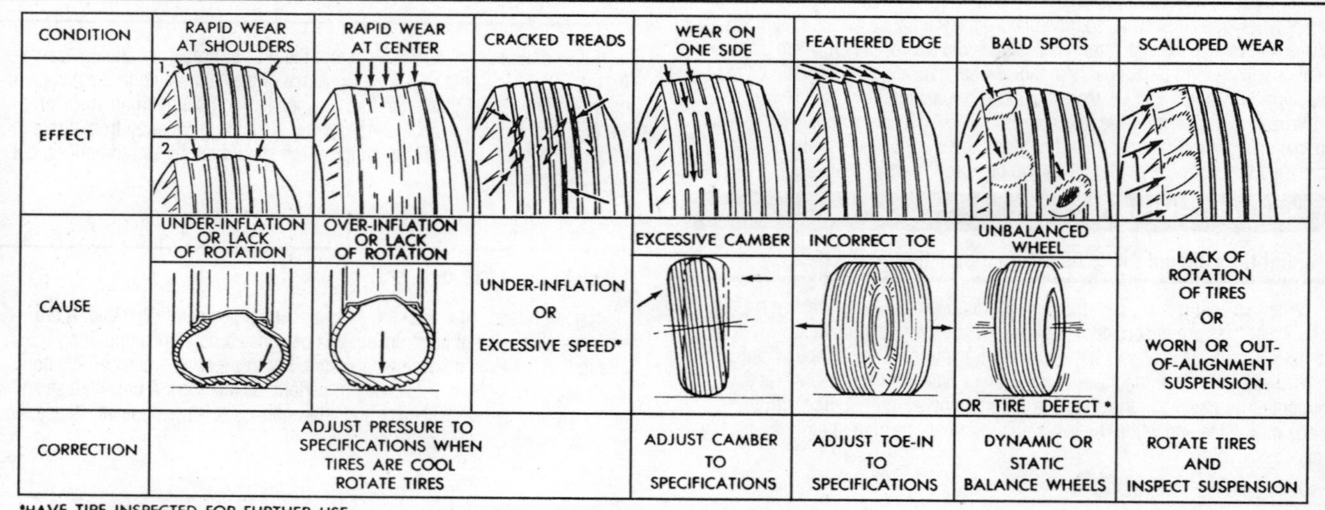

CONDITION	RAPID WEAR AT SHOULDERS	RAPID WEAR AT CENTER	CRACKED TREADS	WEAR ON ONE SIDE	FEATHERED EDGE	BALD SPOTS	SCALLOPED WEAR
EFFECT	1. 2.						
CAUSE	UNDER-INFLATION OR LACK OF ROTATION	OVER-INFLATION OR LACK OF ROTATION	UNDER-INFLATION OR EXCESSIVE SPEED*	EXCESSIVE CAMBER	INCORRECT TOE	UNBALANCED WHEEL OR TIRE DEFECT*	LACK OF ROTATION OF TIRES OR WORN OR OUT-OF-ALIGNMENT SUSPENSION.
CORRECTION	ADJUST PRESSURE TO SPECIFICATIONS WHEN TIRES ARE COOL ROTATE TIRES			ADJUST CAMBER TO SPECIFICATIONS	ADJUST TOE-IN TO SPECIFICATIONS	DYNAMIC OR STATIC BALANCE WHEELS	ROTATE TIRES AND INSPECT SUSPENSION

*HAVE TIRE INSPECTED FOR FURTHER USE.

TCCS1267

Fig. 117 Common tire wear patterns and causes

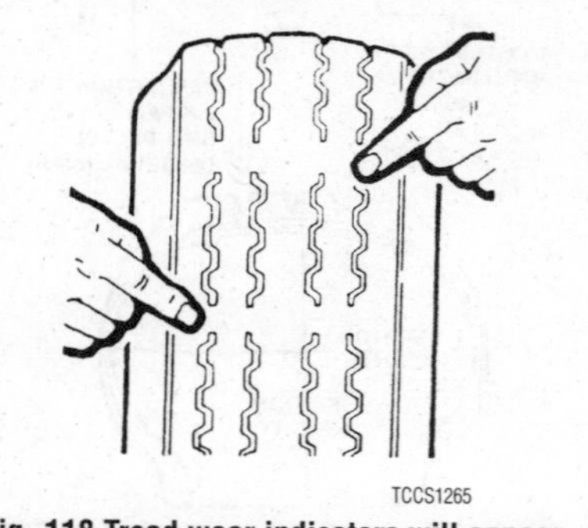

Fig. 118 Tread wear indicators will appear when the tire is worn

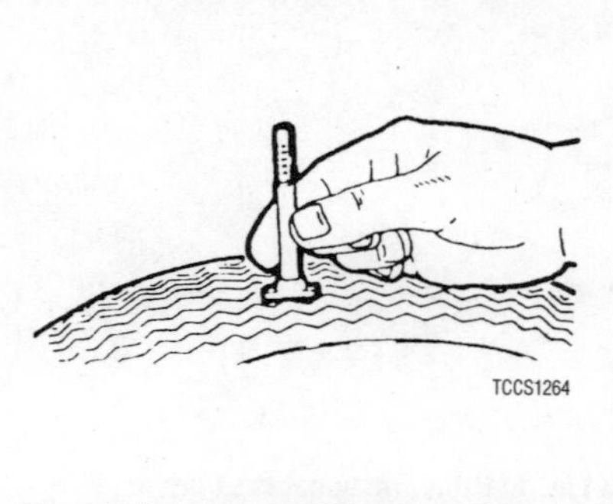

Fig. 119 Accurate tread depth indicators are inexpensive and handy

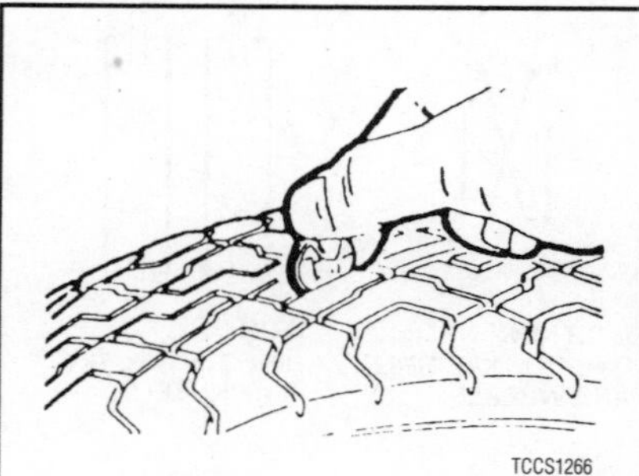

Fig. 120 A penny works well for a quick check of tread depth

CAUTION

Never exceed the maximum tire pressure embossed on the tire! This is the pressure to be used when the tire is at maximum loading, but it is rarely the correct pressure for everyday driving. Consult the owner's manual or the tire pressure sticker for the correct tire pressure.

Once you've maintained the correct tire pressures for several weeks, you'll be familiar with the vehicle's braking and handling personality. Slight adjustments in tire pressures can fine-tune these characteristics, but never change the cold pressure specification by more than 2 psi. A slightly softer tire pressure will give a softer ride but also yield lower fuel mileage. A slightly harder tire will give crisper dry road handling but can cause skidding on wet surfaces. Unless you're fully attuned to the vehicle, stick to the recommended inflation pressures.

All tires made since 1968 have built-in tread wear indicator bars that show up as ½ in. (13mm) wide smooth bands across the tire when ¹⁄₁₆ in. (1.5mm) of tread remains. The appearance of tread wear indicators means that the tires should be replaced. In fact, many states have laws prohibiting the use of tires with less than this amount of tread.

You can check your own tread depth with an inexpensive gauge or by using a Lincoln head penny. Slip the Lincoln penny (with Lincoln's head upside-down) into several tread grooves. If you can see the top of Lincoln's head in 2 adjacent grooves, the tire has less than ¹⁄₁₆ in. (1.5mm) tread left and should be replaced. You can measure snow tires in the same manner by using the "tails" side of the Lincoln penny. If you can see the top of the Lincoln memorial, it's time to replace the snow tire(s).

CARE OF SPECIAL WHEELS

If you have invested money in magnesium, aluminum alloy or sport wheels, special precautions should be taken to make sure your investment is not wasted and that your special wheels look good for the life of the vehicle.

Special wheels are easily damaged and/or scratched. Occasionally check the rims for cracking, impact damage or air leaks. If any of these are found, replace the wheel. But in order to prevent this type of damage and the costly replacement of a special wheel, observe the following precautions:

- Use extra care not to damage the wheels during removal, installation, balancing, etc. After removal of the wheels from the vehicle, place them on a mat or other protective surface. If they are to be stored for any length of time, support them on strips of wood. Never store tires and wheels upright; the tread may develop flat spots.
- When driving, watch for hazards; it doesn't take much to crack a wheel.
- When washing, use a mild soap or non-abrasive dish detergent (keeping in mind that detergent tends to remove wax). Avoid cleansers with abrasives or the use of hard brushes. There are many cleaners and polishes for special wheels.
- If possible, remove the wheels during the winter. Salt and sand used for snow removal can severely damage the finish of a wheel.
- Make certain the recommended lug nut torque is never exceeded or the wheel may crack. Never use snow chains on special wheels; severe scratching will occur.

FLUIDS AND LUBRICANTS

Fluid Disposal

Used fluids such as engine oil, transmission fluid, antifreeze and brake fluid are hazardous wastes and must be disposed of properly. Before draining any fluids, consult with your local authorities; in many areas, waste oil, antifreeze, etc. is being accepted as a part of recycling programs. A number of service stations and auto parts stores are also accepting waste fluids for recycling.

Be sure of the recycling center's policies before draining any fluids, as many will not accept different fluids that have been mixed together.

Fuel and Engine Oil Recommendations

➡Some fuel additives contain chemicals that can damage the catalytic converter and/or oxygen sensor. Read all of the labels carefully before using any additive in the engine or fuel system.

All Town & Country, Caravan and Voyager models are designed to run on unleaded fuel. The use of a leaded fuel in a vehicle requiring unleaded fuel will plug the catalytic converter and render it inoperative. It will also increase exhaust backpressure to the point where engine output will be severely reduced. The minimum octane rating of the unleaded fuel being used must be at least 87, which usually means regular unleaded, but some high performance engines may require higher ratings. Fuel should be selected for the brand and octane which performs best with your engine. Judge a gasoline by its ability to prevent pinging, its engine starting capabilities (cold and hot) and general all weather performance.

As far as the octane rating is concerned, refer to the General Engine Specifications chart earlier in this section to find your engine and its compression ratio. If the compression ratio is 9.0:1 or lower, a regular grade of unleaded gasoline can be used in most cases. If the compression ratio is higher than 9.0:1, use a premium grade of unleaded fuel.

The use of a fuel too low in octane (a measure of anti-knock quality) will result in spark knock. Since many factors such as altitude, terrain, air temperature and humidity affect operating efficiency, knocking may result even though the recommended fuel is being used. If persistent knocking occurs, it may be necessary to switch to a higher grade of fuel. Continuous or heavy knocking may result in engine damage.

➡ Your engine's fuel requirement can change with time, mainly due to carbon build-up, which will, in turn, change the compression ratio. If your engine pings, knocks or diesels (runs with the ignition OFF) switch to a higher grade of fuel. Sometimes, just changing brands will cure the problem.

OIL

➧ See Figures 121 and 122

The Society Of Automotive Engineer (SAE) grade number indicates the viscosity of the engine oil and, thus, its ability to lubricate at a given temperature. The lower the SAE grade number, the lighter the oil; the lower the viscosity, the easier it is to crank the engine in cold weather. Oil viscosities should be chosen from those oils recommended for the lowest anticipated temperatures during the oil change interval. With the proper viscosity, you will be assured of easy cold starting and sufficient engine protection.

Multi-viscosity oils (5W-30, 10W-30, etc.) offer the important advantage of being adaptable to temperature extremes. They allow easy starting at low temperatures, yet they give good protection at high speeds and engine temperatures. This is a decided advantage in changeable climates or in long distance driving.

The American Petroleum Institute (API) designation indicates the classification of engine oil used under certain given operating conditions. Only oil designated for Service SH, or the latest superseding oil grade, should be used. Oils of the SH type perform a variety of functions inside the engine in addition to their basic function as a lubricant. Through a balanced system of metallic deter-

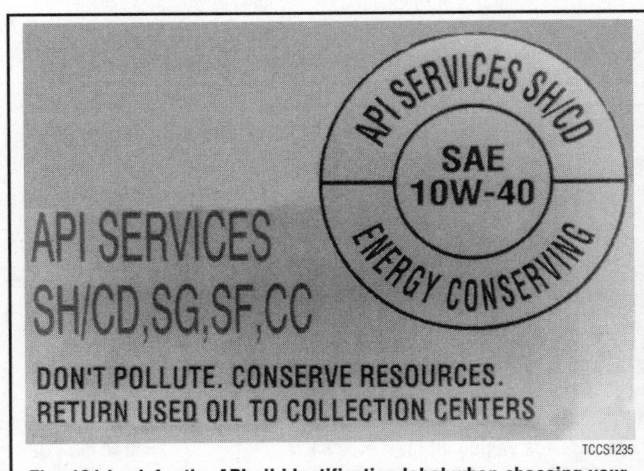

Fig. 121 Look for the API oil identification label when choosing your engine oil

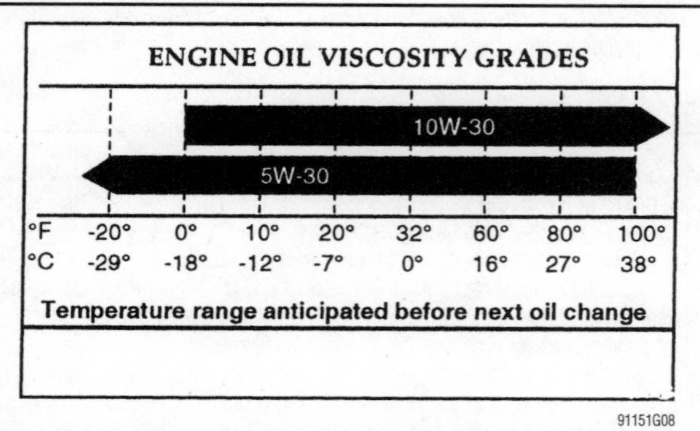

Fig. 122 Recommended SAE engine oil viscosity grades for gasoline engines

gents and polymeric dispersants, engine oil prevents the formation of high and low temperature deposits and also keeps sludge and particles of dirt in suspension. Acids, particularly sulfuric acid, as well as other byproducts of combustion, are neutralized. Both the SAE grade number and the API designation can be found on the side of the oil bottle.

Synthetic Oils

There are excellent synthetic and fuel-efficient oils available that, under the right circumstances, can help provide better fuel mileage and better engine protection. However, these advantages come at a price, which can be significantly more than the price per quart of conventional motor oils.

Before pouring any synthetic oils into your vehicle's engine, you should consider the condition of the engine and the type of driving you do. It is also wise to check the vehicle manufacturer's position on synthetic oils.

Generally, it is best to avoid the use of synthetic oil in both brand new and older, high mileage engines. New engines require a proper break-in, and the synthetics are so slippery that they can impede this; most manufacturers recommend that you wait at least 5,000 miles (8,000 km) before switching to a synthetic oil. Conversely, older engines which have worn parts tend to lose more oil; synthetics will slip past worn parts more readily than regular oil. If your car already leaks oil, (due to worn parts or bad seals/gaskets), it may leak more with a synthetic inside.

Consider your type of driving. If most of your accumulated mileage is on the highway at higher, steadier speeds, a synthetic oil will reduce friction and probably help deliver better fuel mileage. Under such ideal highway conditions, the oil change interval can be extended, as long as the oil filter can continue to operate effectively for the extended life of the oil. If the filter can't do its job for this extended period, dirt and sludge will build up in your engine's crankcase, sump, oil pump and lines, no matter what type of oil is used. If using synthetic oil in this manner, you should continue to change the oil filter at the recommended intervals.

Cars used under harder, stop-and-go, short hop circumstances should always be serviced more frequently; for these cars, synthetic oil may not be a wise investment. Because of the necessary shorter change interval needed for this type of driving, you cannot take advantage of the long recommended change interval of most synthetic oils.

Engine

OIL LEVEL CHECK

See Figures 123, 124 and 125

The engine oil level is checked with the dipstick which is located on the radiator side of the engine.

➡ The oil should be checked before the engine is started or five minutes after the engine has shut OFF. This gives the oil time to drain back to the oil pan and prevents an inaccurate oil level reading.

Remove the dipstick from the tube, wipe it clean, and insert it back into the tube. Remove it again and observe the oil level. It should be maintained within the **FULL** (or **MAX**) mark on the dipstick.

➡ Do not overfill the crankcase. This will cause oil aeration and loss of oil pressure.

OIL & FILTER CHANGE

See Figures 126 thru 134

CAUTION

The EPA warns that prolonged contact with used engine oil may cause a number of skin disorders, including cancer! You should make every effort to minimize your exposure to used engine oil. Protective gloves should be worn when changing the oil. Wash your hands and any other exposed skin areas as soon as possible after exposure to used engine oil. Soap and water, or waterless hand cleaner should be used.

The manufacturer's recommended oil change interval is 7500 miles (12,000 km) under normal operating conditions. We recommend an oil change interval of 3000–3500 miles (4800–5600 km) under normal conditions; more frequently under severe conditions such as when the average trip is less than 4 miles (6 km), the engine is operated for extended periods at idle or low speed, when towing a trailer or operating in dusty areas.

In addition, we recommend that the filter be replaced EVERY time the oil is changed.

➡ Please be considerate of the environment. Dispose of waste oil properly by taking it to a service station, municipal facility or recycling center.

1. Run the engine until it reaches normal operating temperature. Then turn the engine **OFF**.
2. Remove the oil filler cap.
3. Raise and safely support the front of the vehicle using jackstands.
4. Slide a drain pan of at least 5 quarts (4.7 liters) capacity under the oil pan. Wipe the drain plug and surrounding area clean using an old rag.

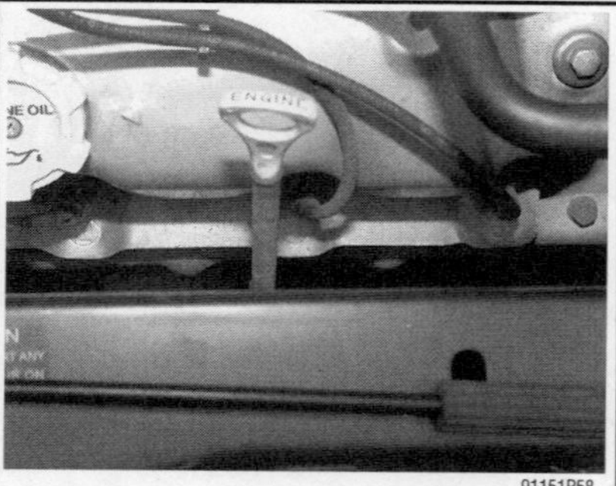

91151P58
Fig. 123 The engine oil level dipstick is located in the front of the engine compartment, on the radiator side of the engine

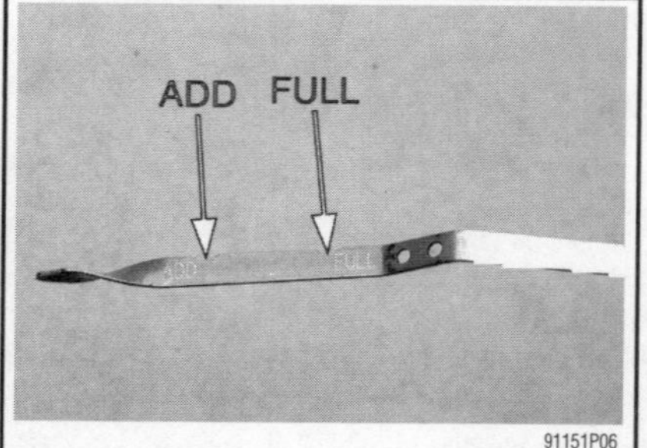

91151P06
Fig. 124 Always maintain the engine oil level to the FULL mark. If the level drops down to, or below the ADD mark, top it off to the FULL mark with 1 quart of oil

91151P10
Fig. 125 For easier filling and to avoid spilling, always use a funnel when adding engine oil

5. Loosen the drain plug using a 17mm socket or a box wrench. Turn the plug out by hand, use a rag, if necessary, to shield your fingers from the hot oil. By keeping an inward pressure on the plug as you unscrew it, oil won't escape past the threads and you can remove it without being burned by hot oil. Quickly withdraw the plug and move your hands out of the way, but be careful not to drop the plug into the drain pan, as fishing it out can be an unpleasant mess. Allow the oil to drain completely.

6. Examine the condition of the drain plug for thread damage or stretching, then examine the plug gasket for cracks or wear. Replace the drain plug, if damaged. However, it is usually recommended that the drain plug gasket be replaced.

7. Install the drain plug and gasket. Tighten the drain plug to 20 ft. lbs. (27 Nm) on 2.4L and 3.3L/3.8L engines or 29 ft. lbs. (39 Nm) on 3.0L engines. Do not overtighten the plug.

8. Move the drain pan under the oil filter. Use a strap-type or end cap-type wrench to loosen the oil filter. Cover your hand with a rag, if necessary, and spin the filter off by hand, but turn it slowly.

➡ **Be careful when removing the oil filter, because the filter contains about 1 quart of hot, dirty oil.**

9. Empty the old oil filter into the drain pan, then properly dispose of the filter.

10. Using a clean shop towel, wipe off the filter adapter on the engine block. Be sure the towel does not leave any lint which could clog an oil passage.

11. Coat the rubber gasket and pour some fresh oil into the new filter before installation; this will lubricate the engine quicker during initial startup. Spin the filter onto the adapter by hand until it contacts the mounting surface, then tighten it an additional ½–¾ turn. Do NOT overtighten the filter.

12. Carefully lower the vehicle.

13. Refill the crankcase with the correct amount of fresh engine oil. Please refer to the Capacities chart later in this section.

14. Install the oil filler cap.

15. Check the oil level on the dipstick. It is normal for the level to be a bit

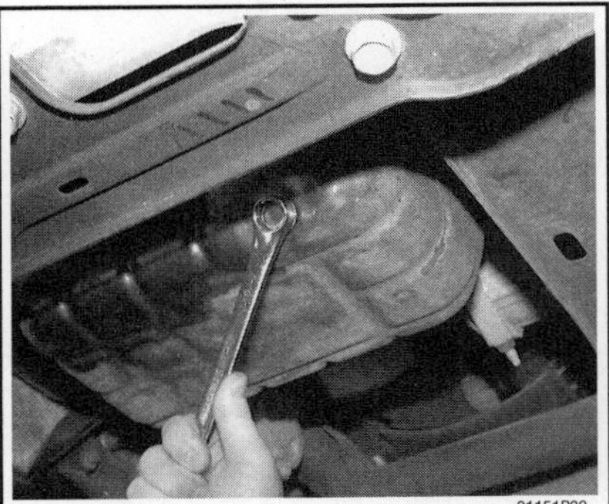

91151P32

Fig. 126 After placing a drain pan in correct position, loosen the oil pan drain plug

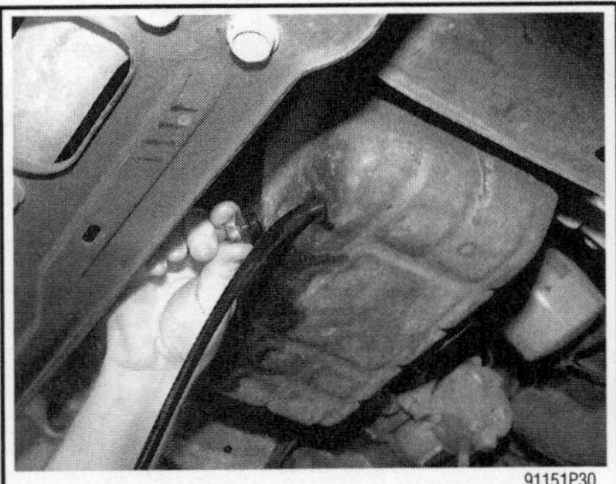

91151P30

Fig. 127 Remove the plug and allow the oil to drain until it stops dripping. Be careful not to drop the plug into the pan

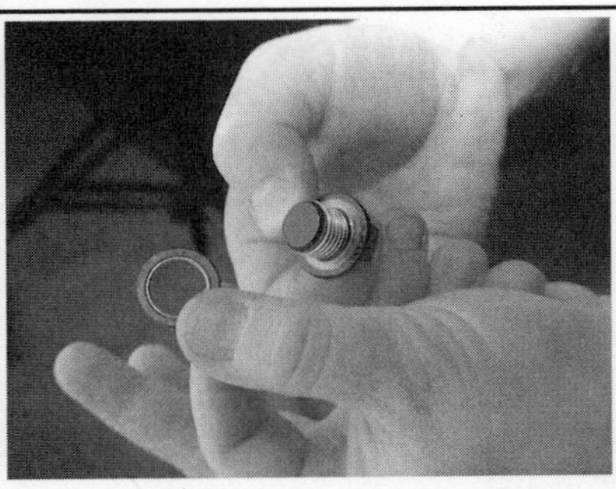

91151P36

Fig. 128 Replace the drain plug gasket. The drain plug must always be installed with a gasket

91151P34

Fig. 129 This illustrates why it is recommended to replace the used oil pan drain plug gasket after it is removed. The used one usually becomes flattened out and distorted

91151P40

Fig. 130 Loosen the filter using a strap-type oil filter wrench

91151P37

Fig. 131 After rotating the filter off, always keep the opening of the filter straight up to prevent any of the old oil, still contained in the filter, from spilling out

91151P46

Fig. 132 Always check the filter adapter surface once the old filter is removed. The filter mounting gasket may have remained stuck to the surface. Be sure to clean the contact surface as well

TCCS1901

Fig. 133 Before installing a new oil filter, lightly coat the rubber gasket with clean engine oil

91151P45

Fig. 134 Pour some fresh oil into the new filter before installation to lubricate the engine quicker during initial start-up

above the full mark until the engine is run and the new filter is filled with oil. Start the engine and allow it to idle for a few minutes.

WARNING

Do not run the engine above idle speed until it has built up oil pressure, as indicated when the oil light goes out.

16. Shut off the engine and allow the oil to flow back to the crankcase for a minute, then recheck the oil level. Check around the filter and drain plug for any leaks, and correct as necessary.

When you have finished this job, you will notice that you now possess four or five quarts of dirty oil. The best thing to do is to pour it into plastic jugs, such as milk or old antifreeze containers. Then, locate a service station or automotive parts store where you can pour it into their used oil tank for recycling.

Improperly disposing of used motor oil not only pollutes the environment, it violates federal law. Dispose of waste oil properly.

Automatic Transaxle

FLUID RECOMMENDATIONS

All automatic transaxles use ATF PLUS 3 Type 7176 automatic transaxle fluid. Under normal operating conditions, periodic fluid changes are not required. If the vehicle is operating under severe operating conditions change the fluid and filter every 15,000 miles.

LEVEL CHECK

See Figures 135, 136 and 137

When checking the fluid level, the condition of the fluid should be observed. If severe darkening of the fluid and a strong odor are present, the fluid, filter and pan gasket (RTV sealant) should be changed and watched closely for the next few hundred miles. If the fresh fluid also turns color, the vehicle should be taken to a qualified service center.

1. Make sure the vehicle is on level ground. The engine should be at normal operating temperatures, if possible, and be idling for at least 60 seconds.
2. Apply the parking brake, start the engine and move the gear selector through each position. Place the selector in the PARK position.
3. Remove the dipstick and determine if the fluid is warm or hot.
4. Wipe the dipstick clean and reinsert until fully seated. Remove and take note of the fluid level.
5. If the fluid is hot (approximately 180°F / 82°C), the reading should be in the crosshatched area marked **HOT**.

91151P12

Fig. 135 Removing the automatic transaxle fluid level dipstick

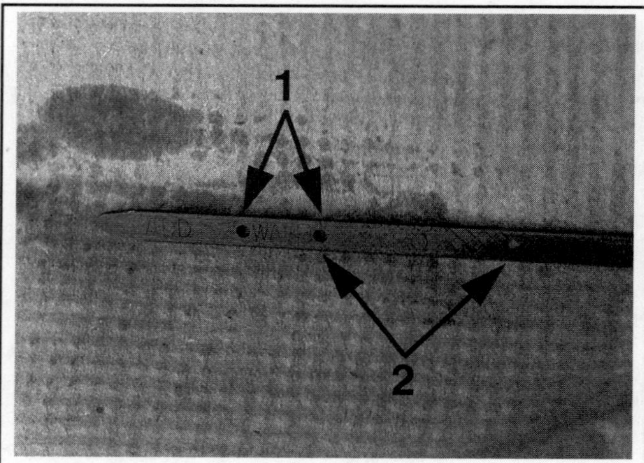

90901P09

Fig. 136 If the fluid is warm, the level should be within the lower two holes of the dipstick (1). If the fluid is hot, the reading should be within the two upper holes of the dipstick (2)

6. If the fluid is warm (85–125°F / 29–52°C), the fluid level should be in the area marked **WARM**.
7. If the fluid level checks low, add enough fluid (ATF PLUS 3) through the fill tube, to bring the level within the marks appropriate for average temperature of the fluid.
8. Insert the dipstick and recheck the level. Make sure the dipstick is fully seated to prevent dirt from entering. Do not overfill the transaxle.

PAN & FILTER SERVICE

See Figures 138 thru 148

Filter replacement is recommended when the fluid is changed.

1. Raise and support the front of the vehicle on jackstands.
2. Place a suitable container that will hold at least four quarts of fluid under the oil pan.
3. Using a 10mm socket, loosen all of the pan bolts slightly, then remove all of the pan bolts except for two bolts at each end of the pan.
4. Continue backing off the two pan bolts at the lower end of the pan, creating a "hinge" effect that will enable the fluid to drain from the pan at a less "sloppy" rate. If the fluid drains to "sloppy", you will find yourself taking a shower in ATF. If necessary, tap the oil pan at one corner to break it loose from the transaxle, allowing the fluid to drain. As the fluid starts to drain, unfasten the bolts around the point where the fluid is draining to increase the flow.
5. When the bulk of the fluid has drained, remove the oil pan. Clean the dirt from the pan and magnet.
6. Remove RTV sealant or gasket material from the pan and case mounting surfaces.
7. Using size T25 Torx® bit, loosen the mounting screws, then remove the filter and filter O-ring or gasket from the bottom of the valve body.

To install:

8. Install a new filter and gasket. Tighten the mounting screw to 40 inch lbs. (5 Nm).
9. Apply an unbroken bead ⅛ inch thick of RTV sealant to the mounting flange of the oil pan. Install the oil pan to the transaxle. Tighten the mounting bolts to 165 inch lbs. (19 Nm).
10. Lower the vehicle.
11. Pour four quarts of ATF PLUS 3 Type 7176 fluid through the dipstick fill tube, using a funnel. Start the engine and allow it to idle for at least 1 minute. Then, with parking and service brakes applied, move the gear selector through the various positions ending up in the **PARK** or **NEUTRAL** position.
12. Add sufficient fluid, if necessary, to bring the level to ⅛ in. (3mm) below the **ADD** mark.
13. Check the fluid level after engine and transaxle have reached the normal operating temperature. The level should be within the **HOT** range on the dipstick.

Always make sure that the dipstick is fully seated in its tube to prevent dirt from entering the transaxle.

91151P11

Fig. 137 Using a funnel, add the necessary amount of fluid to the automatic transaxle

91151P51

Fig. 138 Loosen, then remove all the transaxle pan bolts except for two bolts at each end of the pan

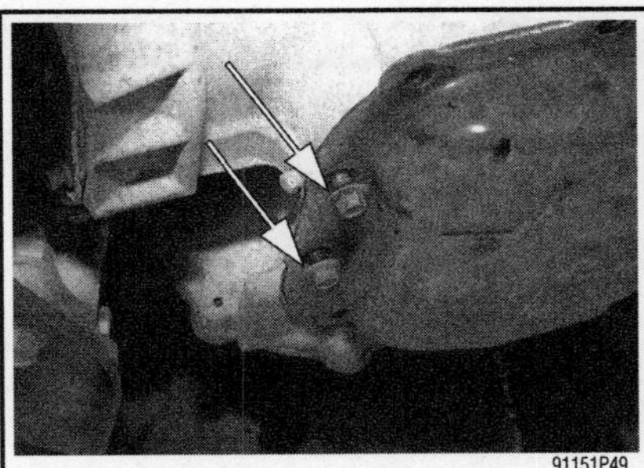
91151P49

Fig. 139 Back of the two bolts at the lower part of the pan, allowing the pan to separate from the transaxle case slightly, allowing fluid to drain

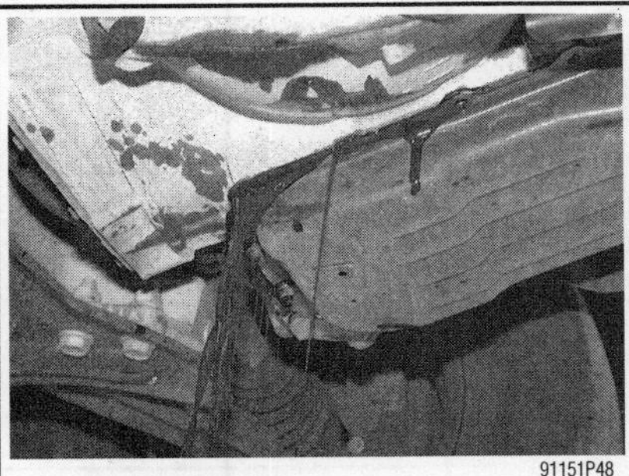
91151P48

Fig. 140 After tapping the pan loose, allow the pan to hang slightly, enabling the fluid to drain into a suitable container

91151P47

Fig. 141 After the fluid has fully drained, remove the remaining bolts and then the pan

91151P57

Fig. 142 Always clean the oil pan magnet of all metallic shavings and dirt

91151P54

Fig. 143 Clean the mounting flange of the oil pan of all old sealant (or gasket material) using an appropriate scraping tool

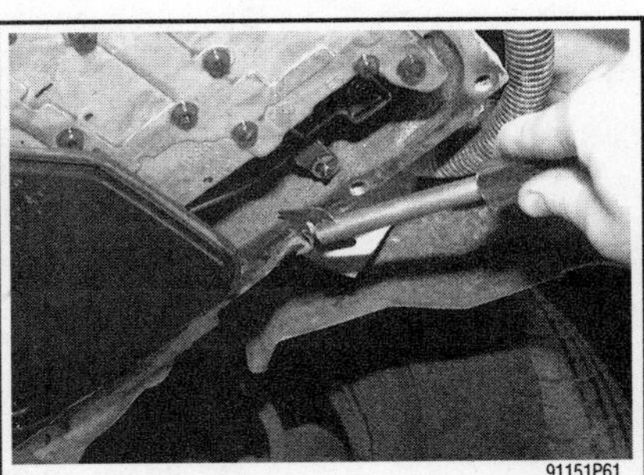
91151P61

Fig. 144 Clean the mounting flange of the transaxle case of all old sealant (or gasket material) using an appropriate surface scraping tool

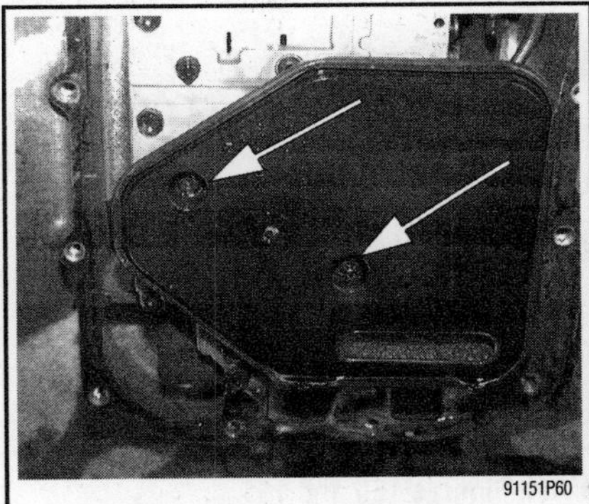
91151P60

Fig. 145 Remove the two fluid filter mounting screws . . .

91151P56

Fig. 146 . . . then remove the transaxle fluid filter . . .

91151P55

Fig. 147 . . . as well as the rubber gasket (or O-ring) between the filter and valve body

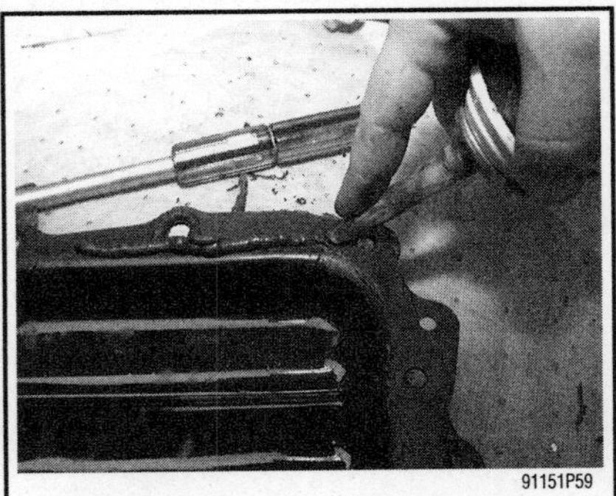
91151P59

Fig. 148 Applying a bead of RTV sealant to the oil pan

Power Transfer Unit (PTU)

On models with All Wheel Drive (AWD), a power transfer unit is used that is connected to the transaxle. This unit is separate from the other drive train components.

FLUID RECOMMENDATION

Chrysler recommends the use of Multi-purpose Gear Oil SAE 80W–90, meeting API specification GL-5. The module is full when the fluid level is at the bottom of the filler hole opening.

LEVEL CHECK

▶ See Figure 149

The Power Transfer Unit fluid level can only be checked and topped off, if necessary, but it cannot be drained and refilled. To check, remove the fill plug and place your finger in the hole. The fluid level should be to the bottom of the fill plug hole.

DRAIN & REFILL

The PTU cannot be serviced. If fluid leakage is detected, the unit must be disassembled and the seals replaced.

Drive Line Module

On models with All Wheel Dive (AWD), the rear wheels are driven by shafts from the Drive Line Module. This module serves as the rear drive axle.

As well as containing the rear differential, this module contains a set of overrunning clutches in their own case. This clutch assembly serves to control differences in drive line speed and traction.

FLUID RECOMMENDATION

Drive Line Module

Chrysler recommends the use of a Multi-purpose Gear Oil SAE 80W–90, meeting API specification GL-5. The module is full when the fluid level is at the bottom of the filler hole opening.

Overrunning Clutch

Chrysler recommends the use of Mopar® ATF+2 type 7176 or equivalent. The oil level should be full to the bottom of the oil filler hole opening.

LEVEL CHECK

▶ See Figures 150 and 151

The Drive Line Module/Overrunning Clutch fluid level can only be checked and topped off, if necessary, but it cannot be drained and refilled. To check, remove the fill plug and place your finger in the hole. The fluid level should be to the bottom of the fill plug hole.

DRAIN & REFILL

The Drive Line Module cannot be serviced. If fluid leakage is detected, the unit must be disassembled and the seals replaced.

Cooling System

FLUID RECOMMENDATION

A 50/50 mixture of water and a high-quality ethylene glycol type antifreeze that is safe for use in aluminum components is recommended. The 50/50 mixture offers protection to –37°F (–40°C). If additional cold weather protection is necessary a concentration of no more than 70% antifreeze may be used.

LEVEL CHECK

▶ See Figure 152

All vehicles are equipped with a transparent coolant reserve container. A minimum and maximum level mark are provided for a quick visual check of the coolant level.

1. Run the engine until normal operating temperature is reached.
2. Open the hood and observe the level of the coolant in the reserve.
3. Fluid level should be between the two lines. Add coolant, if necessary, through the fill cap of the reserve tank.

DRAIN & REFILL

▶ See Figures 153 and 154

⁂ CAUTION

When draining the coolant, keep in mind that cats and dogs are attracted by ethylene glycol antifreeze, and are quite likely to drink any that is left in an uncovered container or in puddles on the ground. This will prove fatal in sufficient quantity. Always drain the coolant into a sealable container. Coolant should be reused unless it is contaminated or several years old.

1. Without removing the radiator pressure cap and the system not under pressure, turn the engine **OFF**, then raise and safely support the vehicle on jackstands.
2. Place a drain pan underneath the radiator drain hose and open the radiator draincock located on the lower left side of the radiator.
3. The coolant recovery/reserve container should empty out first, then remove the radiator pressure cap.

➡ Removal of the coolant sensor on the 2.4L engine is required because the thermostat does not have an air bleed vent. Removal of the sensor allows an air bleed for coolant to drain from the engine block.

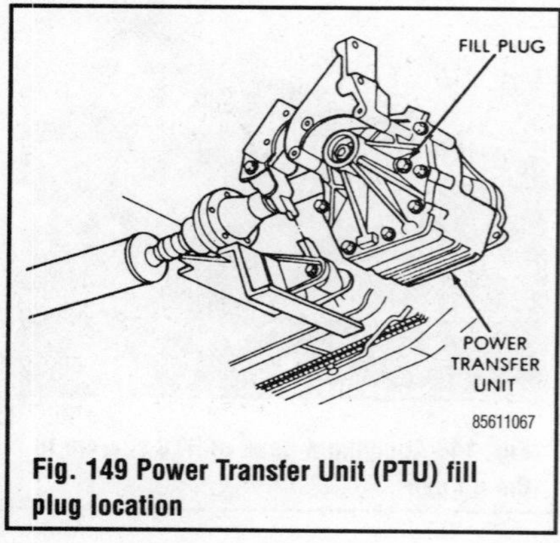

Fig. 149 Power Transfer Unit (PTU) fill plug location

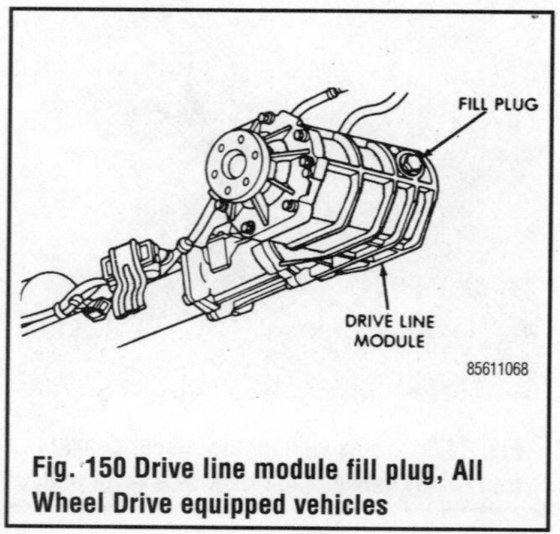

Fig. 150 Drive line module fill plug, All Wheel Drive equipped vehicles

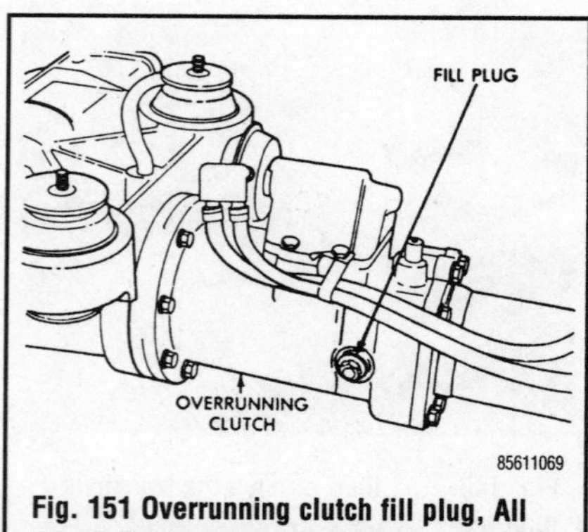

Fig. 151 Overrunning clutch fill plug, All Wheel Drive equipped vehicles

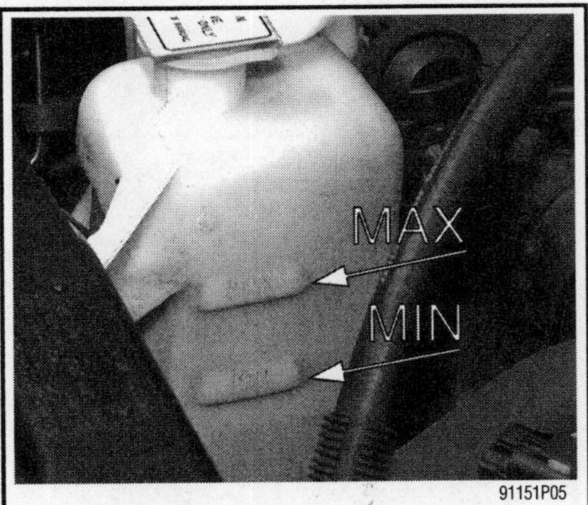

Fig. 152 Check the coolant level through the reserve tank

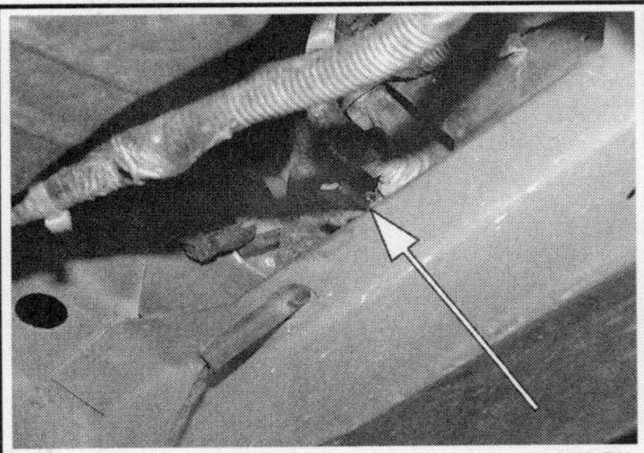

Fig. 153 After placing a drain pan underneath the drain hose, open up the radiator draincock and allow the cooling system to drain

Fig. 154 Fill the coolant recovery/reserve container with a 50/50 mixture of ethylene glycol type antifreeze and water

4. To vent the engine, remove the coolant temperature sensor located above the water outlet housing on the 2.4L engine, or loosen the air bleed vent screw located on the thermostat housing on 3.0L, 3.3L and 3.8L engines.
5. Fill the system with a 50/50 mixture of clean ethylene glycol antifreeze and water until the system is full.
6. When coolant reaches the coolant sensor opening on the 2.4L engine, install the sensor, then continue filling up the system until it is full.

**** WARNING**

Be careful not to spill coolant on the alternator or drive belts.

7. Fill the coolant recovery/reserve container with a 50/50 mixture of clean ethylene glycol antifreeze and water until it reaches the **MAX** mark.
8. It may be necessary to add coolant to the recovery/reserve container after 3–4 warm up/cool down cycles to maintain the coolant level between the **MIN** and **MAX** marks. This will remove any trapped air from the system.

FLUSHING & CLEANING THE SYSTEM

1. Drain the cooling system and refill with clean water only.
2. Install the radiator cap, then start the engine.
3. Allow it to run until the upper radiator hose is hot.
4. Stop the engine and drain the system.
5. If the water is dirty, refill the system, run the engine, then drain the system again. Continue to do this until the water drains clear.
6. After the water drains clear, refill the system with a 50/50 mixture of clean antifreeze and water.

Brake Master Cylinder

FLUID RECOMMENDATION

Use only a DOT 3 approved type brake fluid in your vehicle. Always use fresh fluid when servicing or refilling the brake system.

LEVEL CHECK

➧ See Figures 155, 156 and 157

The fluid level in the reservoir of the master cylinder should be maintained up to the top of the **"FULL"** mark on the side of the reservoir. Clean the cap and surrounding area of the reservoir before opening, to prevent possible contamination. Add the necessary fluid to maintain a proper level. A drop in the fluid level should be expected as the brake pads and shoes wear. However, if an unusual amount of fluid is required, check for system leaks.

Power Steering Pump

FLUID RECOMMENDATIONS

Power steering fluid such as Mopar Power Steering Fluid (Part Number 4318055) or equivalent should be used. Only petroleum fluids formulated for minimum effect on the rubber hoses should be added. Do not use automatic transaxle fluid.

**** CAUTION**

Check the power steering fluid level with engine off, to avoid injury from moving parts.

LEVEL CHECK

➧ See Figures 158, 159 and 160

1. Wipe off the power steering pump reservoir cap with a cloth before removal.
2. A dipstick is built into the cover. Remove the reservoir cover cap and wipe the dipstick with a cloth.
3. Reinstall the dipstick and check the level indicated.
4. Add fluid as necessary, but do not overfill.

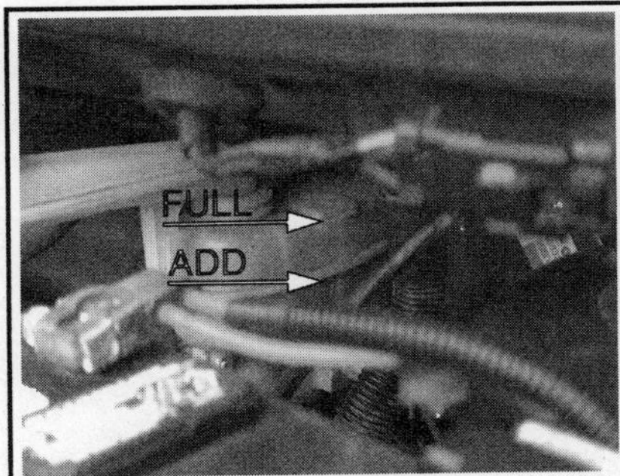

Fig. 155 Check the master cylinder fluid level

Fig. 156 To prevent any dirt from entering the system, always clean the reservoir cap and surrounding area

Fig. 157 If necessary, use a funnel with a long nozzle when adding brake fluid to the reservoir

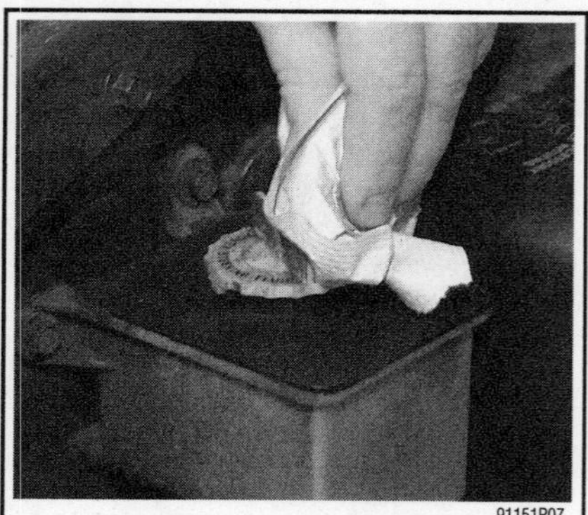

91151P07

Fig. 158 Before removing the reservoir dipstick, wipe the cap and surrounding area clean of any debris

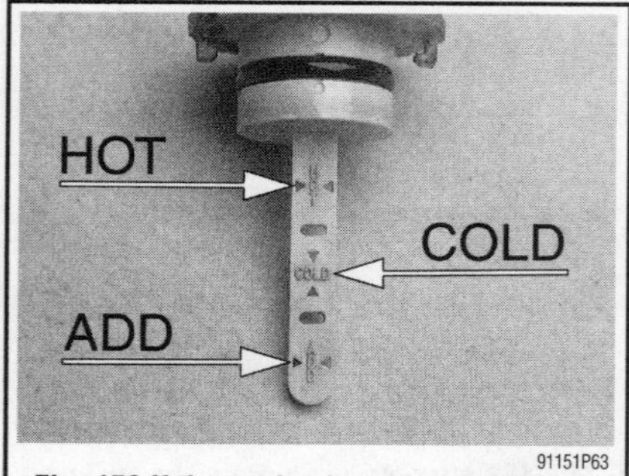

91151P63

Fig. 159 If the engine is cold, the fluid level should reach the COLD mark. If the engine is hot, the level should reach the HOT mark. If the fluid measures to the ADD mark, add fluid accordingly

91151P08

Fig. 160 Adding fluid to the power steering reservoir

Chassis Greasing

The front suspension and tie rod end ball joints, on all Chrysler minivans, are permanently lubricated/sealed units. No regular/periodic maintenance is required for these components.

Body Lubrication and Maintenance

The following body parts and mechanisms should be lubricated periodically at all pivot and sliding points. Use the lubricant specified;

Engine Oil:

- Door Hinge pin and pivot contact area.
- Hood Hinges
- Liftgate Hinges
- Sliding Door at center hinge pivot.

White Spray Lube:

- Door check straps
- Parking Brake Mechanisms
- Liftgate Latches
- Liftgate Prop Pivots
- Cup holders/Ash tray slides
- Front Seat tracks
- Sliding Door rear latch striker shaft and wedge

Multi-purpose Lubricant (Water Resistant):

- Sliding Door: center and upper tracks, and the open position striker spring

Multi-purpose Grease, NLGI Grade 2:

- Hood Latch: release mechanism and safety catch/pivot and sliding contact areas

Mopar Lock Cylinder Lubricant, P/N4318084 (or equivalent):

- All External Lock Cylinders

Wheel Bearings

All Chrysler minivans covered in this book are equipped with sealed hub and bearing assemblies. The hub and bearing assembly is non-serviceable. If the assembly is damaged, the complete unit must be replaced. Refer to Section 8 for the hub and bearing removal and installation procedure.

TRAILER TOWING

General Recommendations

Your vehicle was primarily designed to carry passengers and cargo. It is important to remember that towing a trailer will place additional loads on your vehicle's engine, drive train, steering, braking and other systems. However, if you decide to tow a trailer, using the proper equipment is a must.

Local laws may require specific equipment such as trailer brakes or fender mounted mirrors. Check your local laws.

Trailer Weight

The weight of the trailer is the most important factor. A good weight-to-horsepower ratio is about 35:1, 35 lbs. of Gross Combined Weight (GCW) for every horsepower your engine develops. Multiply the engine's rated horsepower by 35 and subtract the weight of the vehicle passengers and luggage. The number remaining is the approximate ideal maximum weight you should tow, although a numerically higher axle ratio can help compensate for heavier weight.

Hitch (Tongue) Weight

▶ See Figure 161

Calculate the hitch weight in order to select a proper hitch. The weight of the hitch is usually 9–11% of the trailer gross weight and should be measured with the trailer loaded. Hitches fall into various categories: those that mount on the frame and rear bumper, the bolt-on type, or the weld-on distribution type used for larger trailers. Axle mounted or clamp-on bumper hitches should never be used.

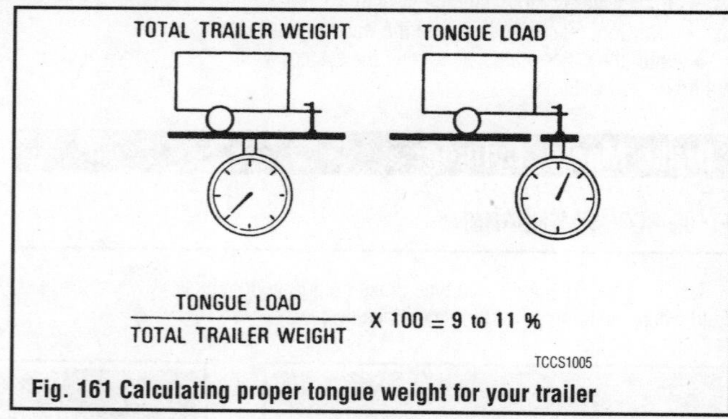

TCCS1005

Fig. 161 Calculating proper tongue weight for your trailer

Check the gross weight rating of your trailer. Tongue weight is usually figured as 10% of gross trailer weight. Therefore, a trailer with a maximum gross weight of 2000 lbs. will have a maximum tongue weight of 200 lbs. Class I trailers fall into this category. Class II trailers are those with a gross weight rating of 2000–3000 lbs., while Class III trailers fall into the 3500–6000 lbs. category. Class IV trailers are those over 6000 lbs. and are for use with fifth wheel trucks, only.

When you've determined the hitch that you'll need, follow the manufacturer's installation instructions, exactly, especially when it comes to fastener torques. The hitch will be subjected to a lot of stress and good hitches come with hardened bolts. Never substitute an inferior bolt for a hardened bolt.

Engine

One of the most common, if not THE most common, problems associated with trailer towing is engine overheating. If you have a cooling system without an expansion tank, you'll definitely need to get an aftermarket expansion tank kit, preferably one with at least a 2 quart capacity. These kits are easily installed on the radiator's overflow hose, and come with a pressure cap designed for expansion tanks.

Aftermarket engine oil coolers are helpful for prolonging engine oil life and reducing overall engine temperatures. Both of these factors increase engine life. While not absolutely necessary in towing Class I and some Class II trailers, they are recommended for heavier Class II and all Class III towing. Engine oil cooler systems usually consist of an adapter, screwed on in place of the oil filter, a remote filter mounting and a multi-tube, finned heat exchanger, which is mounted in front of the radiator or air conditioning condenser.

Transaxle

An automatic transaxle is usually recommended for trailer towing. Modern automatics have proven reliable and, of course, easy to operate, in trailer towing. The increased load of a trailer, however, causes an increase in the temperature of the automatic transaxle fluid. Heat is the worst enemy of an automatic transaxle. As the temperature of the fluid increases, the life of the fluid decreases.

It is essential, therefore, that you install an automatic transaxle cooler. The cooler, which consists of a multi-tube, finned heat exchanger, is usually installed in front of the radiator or air conditioning compressor, and hooked inline with the transaxle cooler tank inlet line. Follow the cooler manufacturer's installation instructions.

Select a cooler of at least adequate capacity, based upon the combined gross weights of the vehicle and trailer.

Cooler manufacturers recommend that you use an aftermarket cooler in addition to, and not instead of, the present cooling tank in your radiator. If you do want to use it in place of the radiator cooling tank, get a cooler at least two sizes larger than normally necessary.

➡ **A transaxle cooler can, sometimes, cause slow or harsh shifting in the transaxle during cold weather, until the fluid has a chance to come up to normal operating temperature. Some coolers can be purchased with or retrofitted with a temperature bypass valve which will allow fluid flow through the cooler only when the fluid has reached above a certain operating temperature.**

Handling a Trailer

Towing a trailer with ease and safety requires a certain amount of experience. It's a good idea to learn the feel of a trailer by practicing turning, stopping and backing in an open area such as an empty parking lot.

TOWING THE VEHICLE

♦ **See Figure 162**

The vehicle can be towed from either the front or rear. If the vehicle is towed from the front make sure the parking brake is completely released.

The steering wheel must be unlocked and clamped in a straight ahead position.

**** WARNING**

Do not use the steering column lock to secure front wheel position for towing.

These vehicles may be towed on the drive wheels at speeds not to exceed 25 mph (40 km/h) for a period of 15 miles (24 km).

**** WARNING**

If this requirement cannot be met the drive front wheels must be placed on a dolly. Also, if the transaxle is damaged, the vehicle should not be pulled on the drive wheels, use a dolly or flatbed.

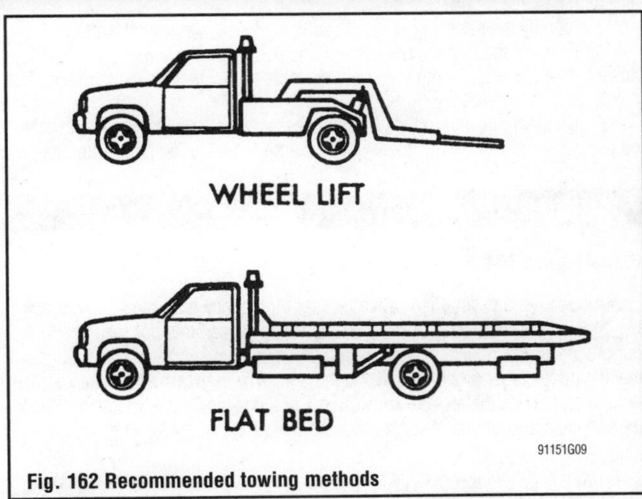

Fig. 162 Recommended towing methods

JUMP STARTING A DEAD BATTERY

♦ **See Figure 163**

Whenever a vehicle is jump started, precautions must be followed in order to prevent the possibility of personal injury. Remember that batteries contain a small amount of explosive hydrogen gas which is a by-product of battery charging. Sparks should always be avoided when working around batteries, especially when attaching jumper cables. To minimize the possibility of accidental sparks, follow the procedure carefully.

**** CAUTION**

NEVER hook the batteries up in a series circuit or the entire electrical system will go up in smoke, including the starter!

Jump Starting Precautions

- Be sure that both batteries are of the same voltage. Vehicles covered by this manual and most vehicles on the road today utilize a 12 volt charging system.

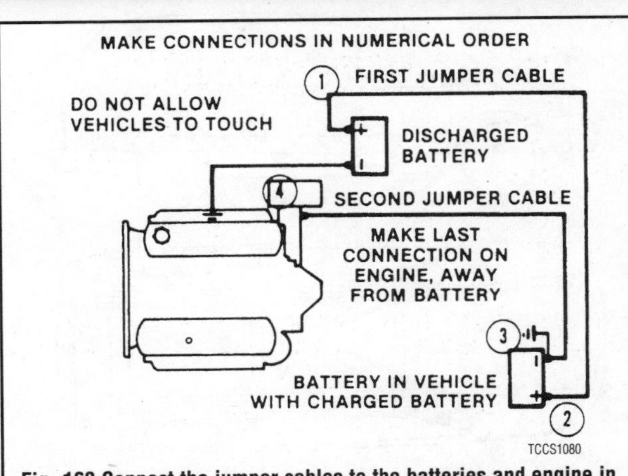

Fig. 163 Connect the jumper cables to the batteries and engine in the order shown

• Be sure that both batteries are of the same polarity (have the same terminal, in most cases NEGATIVE grounded).
• Be sure that the vehicles are not touching or a short could occur.
• On serviceable batteries, be sure the vent cap holes are not obstructed.
• Do not smoke or allow sparks anywhere near the batteries.
• In cold weather, make sure the battery electrolyte is not frozen. This can occur more readily in a battery that has been in a state of discharge.
• Do not allow electrolyte to contact your skin or clothing.

Jump Starting Procedure

1. Make sure that the voltages of the 2 batteries are the same. Most batteries and charging systems are of the 12 volt variety.
2. Pull the jumping vehicle (with the good battery) into a position so the jumper cables can reach the dead battery and that vehicle's engine. Make sure that the vehicles do NOT touch.
3. Place the transmissions of both vehicles in **Neutral** (MT) or **P** (AT), as applicable, then firmly set their parking brakes.

➡ If necessary for safety reasons, the hazard lights on both vehicles may be operated throughout the entire procedure without significantly increasing the difficulty of jumping the dead battery.

4. Turn all lights and accessories OFF on both vehicles. Make sure the ignition switches on both vehicles are turned to the **OFF** position.
5. Cover the battery cell caps with a rag, but do not cover the terminals.
6. Make sure the terminals on both batteries are clean and free of corrosion or proper electrical connection will be impeded. If necessary, clean the battery terminals before proceeding.
7. Identify the positive (+) and negative (-) terminals on both batteries.
8. Connect the first jumper cable to the positive (+) terminal of the dead battery, then connect the other end of that cable to the positive (+) terminal of the booster (good) battery.
9. Connect one end of the other jumper cable to the negative (-) terminal on the booster battery and the final cable clamp to an engine bolt head, alternator bracket or other solid, metallic point on the engine with the dead battery. Try to pick a ground on the engine that is positioned away from the battery in order to minimize the possibility of the 2 clamps touching should one loosen during the procedure. DO NOT connect this clamp to the negative (-) terminal of the bad battery.

✲✲ CAUTION

Be very careful to keep the jumper cables away from moving parts (cooling fan, belts, etc.) on both engines.

10. Check to make sure that the cables are routed away from any moving parts, then start the donor vehicle's engine. Run the engine at moderate speed for several minutes to allow the dead battery a chance to receive some initial charge.
11. With the donor vehicle's engine still running slightly above idle, try to start the vehicle with the dead battery. Crank the engine for no more than 10 seconds at a time and let the starter cool for at least 20 seconds between tries. If the vehicle does not start in 3 tries, it is likely that something else is also wrong or that the battery needs additional time to charge.
12. Once the vehicle is started, allow it to run at idle for a few seconds to make sure that it is operating properly.
13. Turn ON the headlights, heater blower and, if equipped, the rear defroster of both vehicles in order to reduce the severity of voltage spikes and subsequent risk of damage to the vehicles' electrical systems when the cables are disconnected. This step is especially important to any vehicle equipped with computer control modules.
14. Carefully disconnect the cables in the reverse order of connection. Start with the negative cable that is attached to the engine ground, then the negative cable on the donor battery. Disconnect the positive cable from the donor battery and finally, disconnect the positive cable from the formerly dead battery. Be careful when disconnecting the cables from the positive terminals not to allow the alligator clips to touch any metal on either vehicle or a short and sparks will occur.

JACKING

➧ See Figure 164

Your vehicle was supplied with a jack for emergency road repairs. This jack is fine for changing a flat tire or other short term procedures not requiring you to go beneath the vehicle. If it is used in an emergency situation, carefully follow the instructions provided either with the jack or in your owner's manual. Do not attempt to use the jack on any portions of the vehicle other than specified by the vehicle manufacturer. Always block the diagonally opposite wheel when using a jack.

A more convenient way of jacking is the use of a garage or floor jack. You may use the floor jack to raise the front of the vehicle with the jack placed under the torque box section of the frame rail just behind the front wheel. The rear of the vehicle is raised by the floor jack by placing the jack underneath the body reinforced pinch weld, located just ahead of the rear wheel.

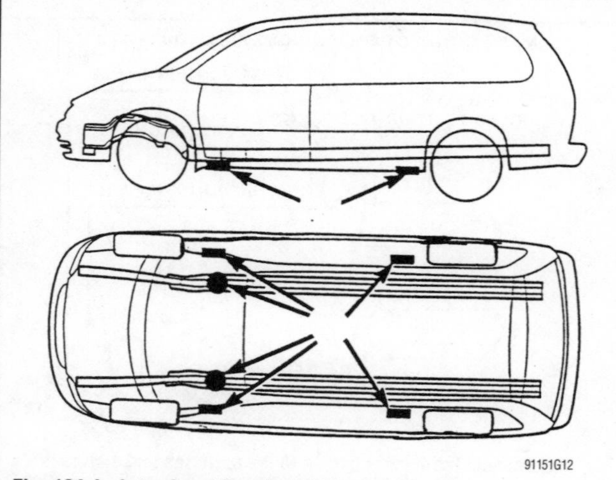

Fig. 164 Jackstand and floor jack lifting locations

Never place the jack under the radiator, engine or transmission components. Severe and expensive damage will result when the jack is raised. Additionally, never jack under the floorpan or bodywork; the metal will deform.

Whenever you plan to work under the vehicle, you must support it on jackstands or ramps. Never use cinder blocks or stacks of wood to support the vehicle, even if you're only going to be under it for a few minutes. Never crawl under the vehicle when it is supported only by the tire-changing jack or other floor jack.

➡ Always position a block of wood or small rubber pad on top of the jack or jackstand to protect the lifting point's finish when lifting or supporting the vehicle.

Small hydraulic, screw, or scissors jacks are satisfactory for raising the vehicle. Drive-on trestles or ramps are also a handy and safe way to both raise and support the vehicle. Be careful though, some ramps may be too steep to drive your vehicle onto without scraping the front bottom panels. Never support the vehicle on any suspension member, front crossmember (unless specifically instructed to do so by a repair manual) or by an underbody panel.

Jacking Precautions

The following safety points cannot be overemphasized:

• Always block the opposite wheel or wheels to keep the vehicle from rolling off the jack.
• When raising the front of the vehicle, firmly apply the parking brake.
• When the drive wheels are to remain on the ground, leave the vehicle in gear to help prevent it from rolling.
• Always use jackstands to support the vehicle when you are working underneath. Place the stands beneath the vehicle's jacking brackets. Before climbing underneath, rock the vehicle a bit to make sure it is firmly supported.

NORMAL MAINTENANCE INTERVALS

TO BE SERVICED	TYPE OF SERVICE	VEHICLE MILEAGE INTERVAL (x1000)																
		7.5	15	22.5	30	37.5	45	52.5	60	67.5	75	82.5	90	97.5	100	105	112.5	120
Engine oil	R	✓	✓	✓	✓	✓	✓	✓	✓	✓	✓	✓	✓	✓		✓	✓	✓
Engine oil filter	R	✓	✓	✓	✓	✓	✓	✓	✓	✓	✓	✓	✓	✓		✓	✓	✓
Accessory drive belt(s)	S/I		✓		✓		✓		✓		✓		✓			✓		✓
Brake pads and linings	S/I			✓			✓			✓			✓				✓	
Engine air cleaner and filter	R				✓				✓				✓					✓
Spark plugs (2.4L & 3.0L only)	R				✓				✓				✓					✓
Tie rod ends and boot seals	S/I				✓				✓				✓					✓
Engine coolant	R						✓				✓					✓		
Spark plug wires (2.4L & 3.0L only)	R								✓									✓
PCV valve	S/I								✓				✓					✓
Timing belt (3.0L engine)	S/I								✓				✓					✓
Spark plugs (3.3L & 3.8L only)	R														✓			
Spark plug wires (3.3L & 3.8L only)	R														✓			
Timing belt (2.4L engine)	R																	✓
Exhaust system	S/I	✓	✓	✓	✓	✓	✓	✓	✓	✓	✓	✓	✓	✓		✓	✓	✓
Brake hoses	S/I	✓	✓	✓	✓	✓	✓	✓	✓	✓	✓	✓	✓	✓		✓	✓	✓
CV-joints and front suspension	S/I	✓	✓	✓	✓	✓	✓	✓	✓	✓	✓	✓	✓	✓		✓	✓	✓
Coolant level, hoses and clamps	S/I	✓	✓	✓	✓	✓	✓	✓	✓	✓	✓	✓	✓	✓		✓	✓	✓

R - Replace S/I - Inspect and service, if needed

91151C04

SEVERE MAINTENANCE INTERVALS

TO BE SERVICED	TYPE OF SERVICE	VEHICLE MILEAGE INTERVAL (x1000) 3	6	9	12	15	18	21	24	27	30	33	36	39	42	45	48	51	54	57	60
Engine oil	R	✓	✓	✓	✓	✓	✓	✓	✓	✓	✓	✓	✓	✓	✓	✓	✓	✓	✓	✓	✓
Engine oil filter	R	✓	✓	✓	✓	✓	✓	✓	✓	✓	✓	✓	✓	✓	✓	✓	✓	✓	✓	✓	✓
Brake pads and linings	S/I			✓			✓			✓			✓			✓			✓		
Engine air cleaner filter	S/I					✓					✓					✓					✓
Transaxle fluid and filter	R					✓					✓					✓					✓
Transaxle band (if equipped)	A					✓					✓					✓					✓
AWD power transfer unit fluid	R					✓					✓					✓					✓
Accessory drive belt(s)	S/I					✓					✓					✓					✓
AWD overrunning clutch and rear carrier fluid	R							✓							✓						
PCV valve	S/I										✓										✓
Spark plugs (2.4L & 3.0L only)	R										✓										✓
Tie rod ends and boot seals	S/I										✓										✓
Engine coolant	R																	✓			
Spark plug wires (2.4L & 3.0L only)	R																				✓
Timing belt (3.0L engine)	S/I																				✓
Exhaust system	S/I	✓	✓	✓	✓	✓	✓	✓	✓	✓	✓	✓	✓	✓	✓	✓	✓	✓	✓	✓	✓
Brake hoses	S/I	✓	✓	✓	✓	✓	✓	✓	✓	✓	✓	✓	✓	✓	✓	✓	✓	✓	✓	✓	✓
CV-joints and front suspension	S/I	✓	✓	✓	✓	✓	✓	✓	✓	✓	✓	✓	✓	✓	✓	✓	✓	✓	✓	✓	✓
Coolant level, hoses and clamps	R	✓	✓	✓	✓	✓	✓	✓	✓	✓	✓	✓	✓	✓	✓	✓	✓	✓	✓	✓	✓

R - Replace S/I - Inspect and service, if needed A - Adjust

FREQUENT OPERATION MAINTENANCE (SEVERE SERVICE)

If a vehicle is operated under any of the following conditions it is considered severe service, and you should use this chart:

- **Towing a trailer or using a camper or car-top carrier.**
- **Repeated short trips of less than 5 miles in temperatures below freezing, or trips of less than 10 miles in any temperature.**
- **Extensive idling or low-speed driving for long distances as in heavy commercial use, such as delivery, taxi or police cars.**
- **Operating on rough, muddy or salt-covered roads.**
- **Operating on unpaved or dusty roads.**
- **Driving in extremely hot (over 90°) conditions.**

91151C05

CAPACITIES

Year	Model	Engine ID/VIN	Engine Displacement Liters (cc)	Engine Oil with Filter (qts.)	Transmission (pts.) 4-Spd	5-Spd	Auto.	Transfer Case (pts.)	Drive Axle Front (pts.)	Rear (pts.)	Fuel Tank (gal.)	Cooling System (qts.)
1996	Caravan	B	2.4 (2429)	4.5	—	—	18.0 ①	—	—	—	20.0	9.5
	Caravan	3	3.0 (2972)	4.5	—	—	18.0 ①	—	—	—	20.0	10.5
	Caravan	R	3.3 (3300)	4.5	—	—	18.0 ①	2.4	—	4.0 ④	③	10.5
	Caravan	L	3.8 (3785)	4.5	—	—	18.0 ①	2.4	—	4.0 ④	③	10.5
	Town & Country	R	3.3 (3300)	4.5	—	—	18.2 ①	NA	NA	NA	20.0	10.5
	Town & Country	L	3.8 (3785)	4.5	—	—	18.2 ①	NA	NA	NA	20.0	10.5
	Voyager	B	2.4 (2429)	4.5	—	—	8.0 ②	—	—	—	20.0	9.5
	Voyager	3	3.0 (2972)	4.5	—	—	8.0 ②	—	—	—	20.0	10.5
	Voyager	R	3.3 (3300)	4.5	—	—	8.0 ②	—	—	—	20.0	10.5
	Voyager	L	3.8 (3785)	4.5	—	—	8.0 ②	—	—	4.0 ④	20.0	10.5
1997	Caravan	B	2.4 (2429)	4.5	—	—	8.0 ②	—	—	4.0 ④	20.0	9.5
	Caravan	3	3.0 (2972)	4.5	—	—	8.0 ②	—	—	4.0 ④	20.0	10.5
	Caravan	R	3.3 (3300)	4.5	—	—	8.0 ②	—	—	4.0 ④	20.0	10.5
	Caravan	L	3.8 (3785)	4.5	—	—	8.0 ②	—	—	4.0 ④	20.0	10.5
	Town & Country	R	3.3 (3300)	4.5	—	—	8.0 ②	—	—	4.0 ④	20.0	10.5
	Town & Country	L	3.8 (3785)	4.5	—	—	8.0 ②	—	—	4.0 ④	20.0	10.5
	Voyager	B	2.4 (2429)	4.5	—	—	8.0 ②	—	—	4.0 ④	20.0	9.5
	Voyager	3	3.0 (2972)	4.5	—	—	8.0 ②	—	—	4.0 ④	20.0	10.5
	Voyager	R	3.3 (3300)	4.5	—	—	8.0 ②	—	—	4.0 ④	20.0	10.5
	Voyager	L	3.8 (3785)	4.5	—	—	8.0 ②	—	—	4.0 ④	20.0	10.5
1998	Caravan	B	2.4 (2429)	4.5	—	—	8.0 ②	—	—	4.0 ④	20.0	9.5
	Caravan	3	3.0 (2972)	4.5	—	—	8.0 ②	—	—	4.0 ④	20.0	10.5
	Caravan	R	3.3 (3300)	4.5	—	—	8.0 ②	—	—	4.0 ④	20.0	10.5
	Caravan	L	3.8 (3785)	4.5	—	—	8.0 ②	—	—	4.0 ④	20.0	10.5
	Town & Country	R	3.3 (3300)	4.5	—	—	8.0 ②	—	—	4.0 ④	20.0	10.5
	Town & Country	L	3.8 (3785)	4.5	—	—	8.0 ②	—	—	4.0 ④	20.0	10.5
	Voyager	B	2.4 (2429)	4.5	—	—	8.0 ②	—	—	4.0 ④	20.0	9.5
	Voyager	3	3.0 (2972)	4.5	—	—	8.0 ②	—	—	4.0 ④	20.0	10.5
	Voyager	R	3.3 (3300)	4.5	—	—	8.0 ②	—	—	4.0 ④	20.0	10.5
	Voyager	L	3.8 (3785)	4.5	—	—	8.0 ②	—	—	4.0 ④	20.0	10.5
1999	Caravan	B	2.4 (2429)	4.5	—	—	8.0 ②	—	—	4.0 ④	20.0	9.5
	Caravan	3	3.0 (2972)	4.5	—	—	8.0 ②	—	—	4.0 ④	20.0	10.5
	Caravan	R	3.3 (3300)	4.5	—	—	8.0 ②	—	—	4.0 ④	20.0	10.5
	Caravan	L	3.8 (3785)	4.5	—	—	8.0 ②	—	—	4.0 ④	20.0	10.5
	Town & Country	R	3.3 (3300)	4.5	—	—	8.0 ②	—	—	4.0 ④	20.0	10.5
	Town & Country	L	3.8 (3785)	4.5	—	—	8.0 ②	—	—	4.0 ④	20.0	10.5
	Voyager	B	2.4 (2429)	4.5	—	—	8.0 ②	—	—	4.0 ④	20.0	9.5
	Voyager	3	3.0 (2972)	4.5	—	—	8.0 ②	—	—	4.0 ④	20.0	10.5
	Voyager	R	3.3 (3300)	4.5	—	—	8.0 ②	—	—	4.0 ④	20.0	10.5
	Voyager	L	3.8 (3785)	4.5	—	—	8.0 ②	—	—	4.0 ④	20.0	10.5

NOTE: All capacities are approximate. Add fluid gradually and check to be sure a proper fluid level is obtained.

① Overhaul fill capacity with torque converter empty

② 31TH overhaul fill capacity with torque converter empty: 17.0
41TE overhaul fill capacity with torque converter empty: 18.2

③ FWD: 20.0 gals.
AWD: 18.0 gals.

④ Overrunning clutch: 0.75 pts.

91151C06

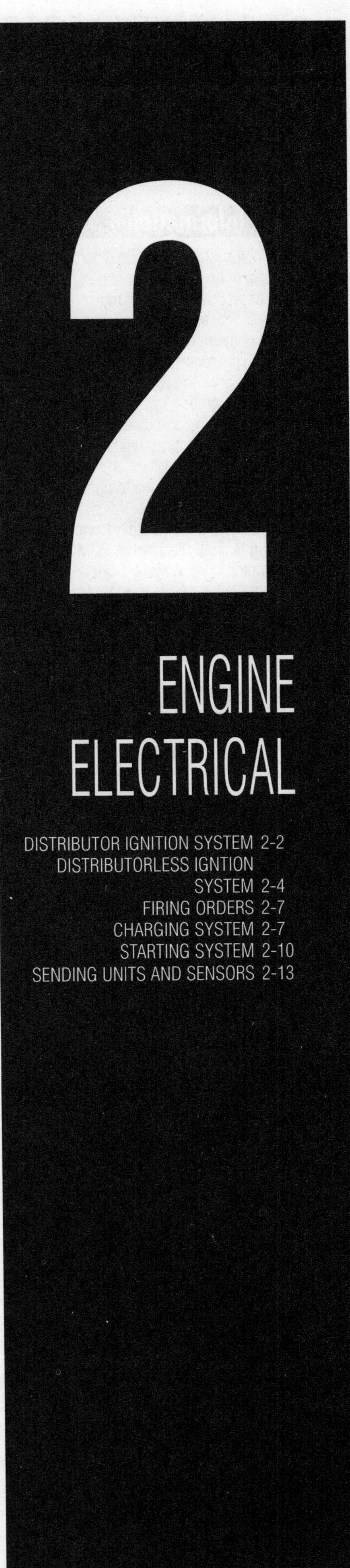

2 ENGINE ELECTRICAL

DISTRIBUTOR IGNITION SYSTEM

➡For information on understanding electricity and troubleshooting electrical circuits, please refer to Section 6 of this manual.

General Information

The distributor ignition system differs from the conventional breaker points system in form only; its function is exactly the same: to supply a spark to the spark plugs at precisely the right moment to ignite the compressed air/fuel mixture in the cylinders and create mechanical movement.

The 3.0L engine utilizes a distributor, crankshaft sensor and ignition coil. The system's main components are the distributor, distributor pickup, camshaft signal, crankshaft signal and ignition coil.

The distributor ignition system has timing controlled by the Powertrain Control Module (PCM). The standard reference ignition timing data for the engine operating conditions are programmed in the memory of the PCM. The engine conditions (rpm, load and temperature) are detected by various sensors. Based on these sensor signals and the ignition timing data, a signal is sent to interrupt the primary current at the power transistor. The ignition coil is activated and a spark sent through the distributor, down the spark plug wires to the spark plugs. Ignition timing is controlled by the PCM for optimum performance.

The distributor ignition system can be identified by looking for the presence of a distributor (with spark plug wires connecting the distributor cap to the spark plugs). If no distributor is found, it can be assumed that the engine uses a distributorless ignition system. Coverage of the distributorless ignition system is found later in this section.

Diagnosis and Testing

SPARK PLUG CABLE TEST

⁂ WARNING

Before beginning this test, be sure to wear rubber gloves and rubber-soled shoes for safety.

1. One at a time, disengage each spark plug wire with the engine idling to check whether the engine's performance changes or not.
2. If the performance does not change, check the resistance of each spark plug and wire. Refer to Section 1 for checking the resistance of the spark plug wires.

SECONDARY SPARK TEST

➧ See Figures 1 and 2

1. Remove a spark plug from the engine. Examine the spark plug for cracks in its insulation and replace if necessary.
2. Connect the spark plug to its spark plug wire.
3. Ground the spark plug's outer electrode to the engine (touch the spark plug's metal body to the engine block or other piece of metal on the vehicle).
4. Crank the engine and look for spark across the electrodes of the spark plug.
5. If a strong blue spark exists across the plug electrode, the ignition system is functioning properly.
6. Repeat the test for the remaining cylinders. If one or more tests indicate irregular, weak or no spark, refer to the coil test.
7. If spark does not exist, remove the distributor cap and ensure that the rotor is turning when the engine is cranked.

Adjustments

All adjustments of the ignition system are controlled by the Powertrain Control Module (PCM) for optimum performance. No manual adjustments are possible.

Ignition Coil

TESTING

➧ See Figure 3

1. Remove the coil wire from the distributor cap. Using non-conductive ignition pliers, hold the end of the wire about ¼ in. (6mm) away from a good engine ground point.
2. Have a helper crank the engine. Check for a spark between the coil wire end and the ground point.
3. If there is a spark, it must be constant and bright blue in color.
4. Continue to crank the engine. Slowly move the wire away from the ground point. If arching at the coil tower occurs, replace the coil.
5. If the spark is good and no arcing at the coil tower occurs, the ignition system is producing the necessary high secondary voltage.
6. Check to make sure that the voltage is getting to the spark plugs. Inspect the distributor cap, rotor, spark plug wires and spark plugs.
7. If all of the components check okay, the ignition system is probably not the reason why the engine does not start.
8. Check the fuel system and engine mechanical items, such as the timing belt.

REMOVAL & INSTALLATION

➧ See Figures 4, 5, 6, 7 and 8

➡The ignition coil is located at the back of the intake manifold.

1. Disconnect the negative battery cable.
2. If necessary, remove the windshield wiper/motor module assembly. Refer to Section 6 for this procedure.
3. Disengage the wiring harness connector from the ignition coil.
4. Disconnect the ignition wire from the coil.
5. Remove the coil mounting bracket bolts, then remove the coil and mounting bracket assembly from the vehicle.
6. The ignition coil can be separated from the mounting bracket.

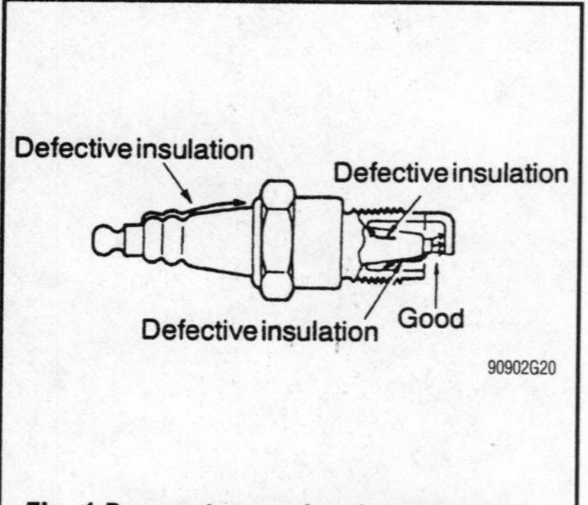

Fig. 1 Be sure to examine the spark plug insulation carefully before testing

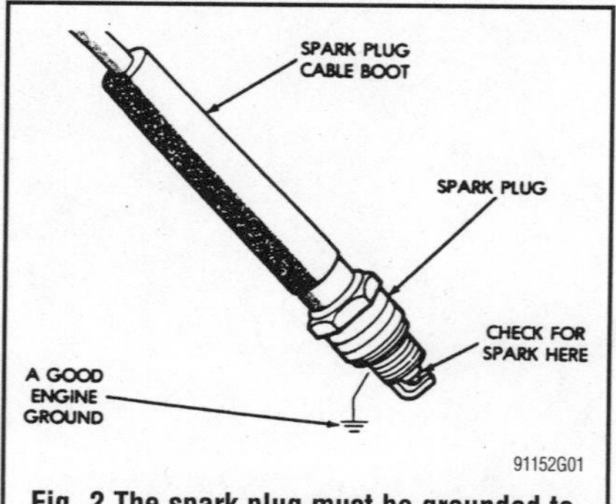

Fig. 2 The spark plug must be grounded to a metal part of the vehicle, such as the engine block

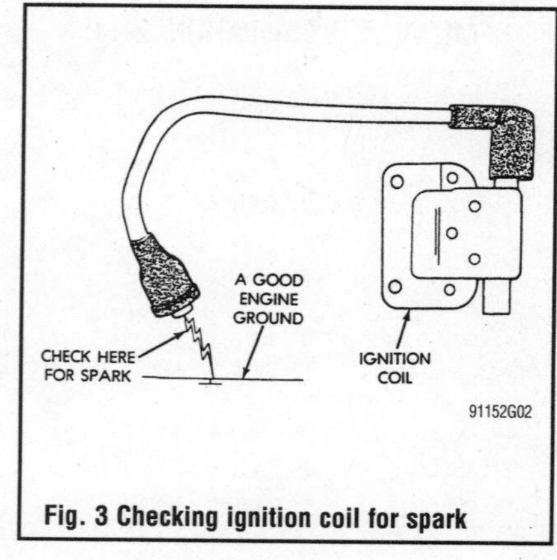

Fig. 3 Checking ignition coil for spark

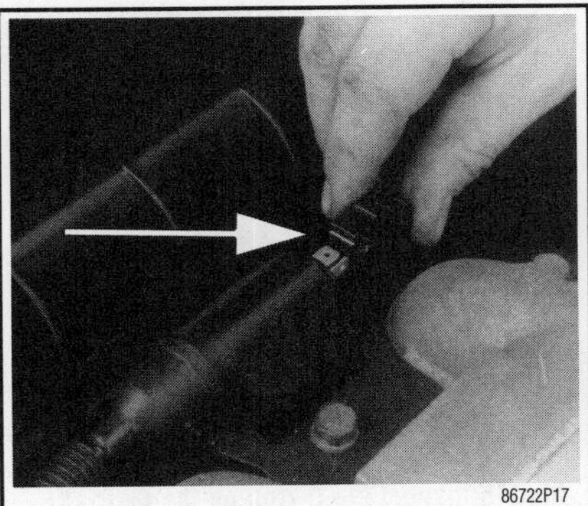
86722P17

Fig. 4 Unplug the engine wiring harness connector from the ignition coil . . .

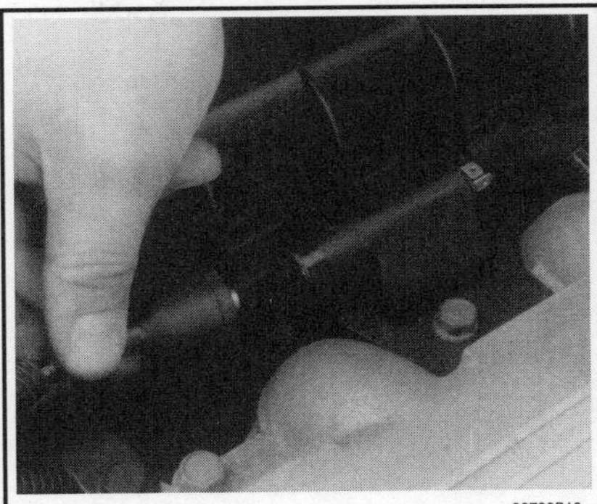
86722P18

Fig. 5 . . . then disconnect the coil-to-distributor wire at the ignition coil

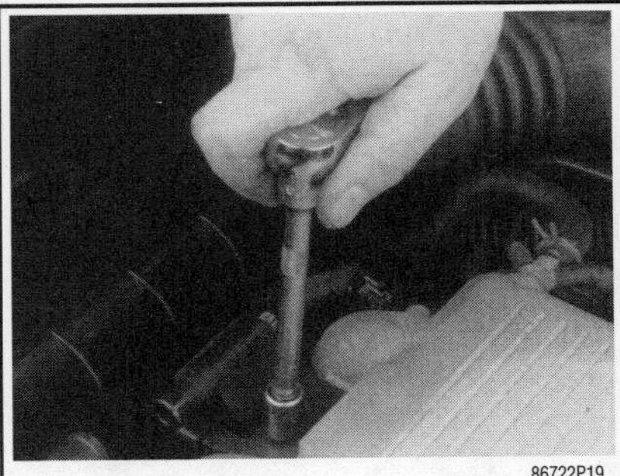
86722P19

Fig. 6 Loosen and remove the top mounting bolt from the ignition coil mounting bracket . . .

86722P20

Fig. 7 . . . then remove the 2 lower ignition coil mounting bracket bolts

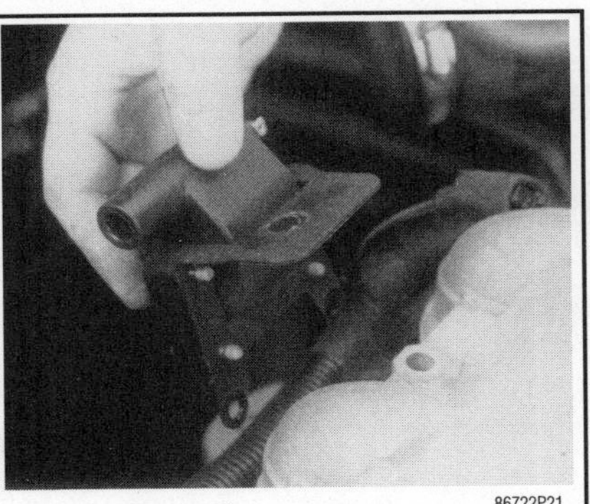
86722P21

Fig. 8 Remove the ignition coil and mounting bracket together from the engine

86722P01

Fig. 9 After detaching the electrical connector from the distributor, loosen the two distributor cap hold-down screws . . .

To install:

7. If separated, loosely mount the ignition coil to the mounting bracket.
8. Loosely install the coil and mounting bracket assembly to the intake manifold. Tighten the coil mounting bracket-to-intake manifold bolts to 115 inch lbs. (13 Nm) and the ignition coil-to-mounting bracket fasteners to 96 inch lbs. (10 Nm).
9. Connect the ignition wire to the coil.
10. Engage the wiring harness connector to the ignition coil.
11. If removed, install the windshield wiper/motor module assembly.
12. Connect the negative battery cable.

Distributor

➡The following procedure only applies to the 3.0L engine. Only the 3.0L engine uses a distributor, the other engines utilize a Distributorless Ignition System (DIS).

REMOVAL

See Figures 9 thru 15

1. Disconnect the negative battery cable.
2. Detach the electrical connector from the distributor.
3. Remove the distributor cap.
4. Mark the position of the rotor in relation to the distributor housing on the intake manifold and mark the position of the distributor housing in relation to the engine. It is a good idea to take the time to turn the crankshaft to TDC No. 1 cylinder, compression stroke (firing position). This aligns the distributor rotor with the No. 1 spark plug tower in the distributor cap. This is a good reference point and makes installation easier.
5. Remove the distributor hold-down bolt.
6. Carefully lift the distributor from the engine. The shaft will rotate slightly when the drive gear disengages as the distributor is removed.

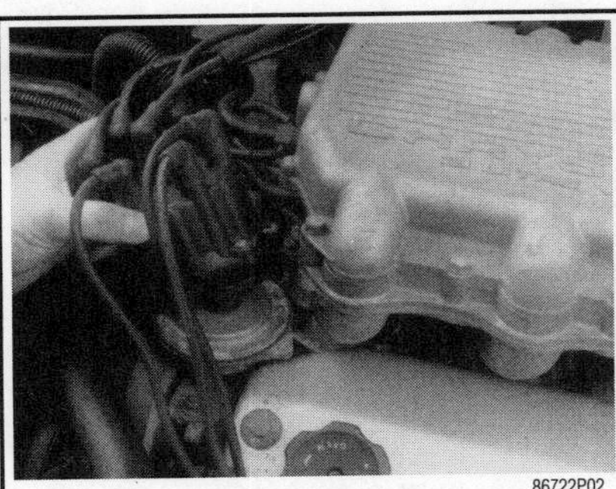
86722P02

Fig. 10 . . . then lift the distributor cap off its base, the spark plug wires need not be removed

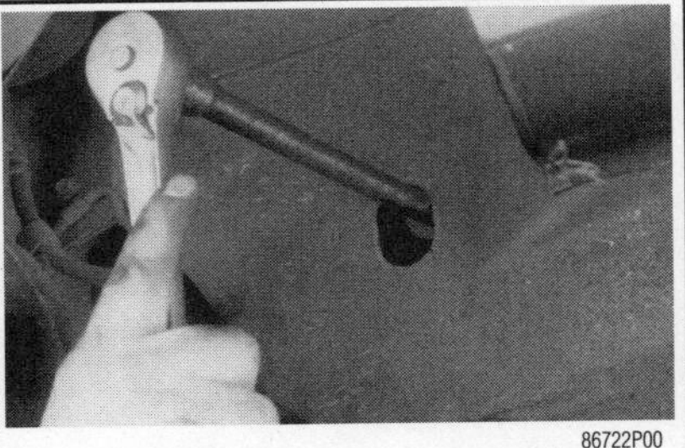
86722P00

Fig. 11 If placing the No. 1 piston at top dead center, remove the splash shield's access plug and use a ratchet and extension to turn the crankshaft while an assistant holds a finger over the spark plug hole

86722P04

Fig. 12 Mark the rotor position once it is pointing at the intake manifold

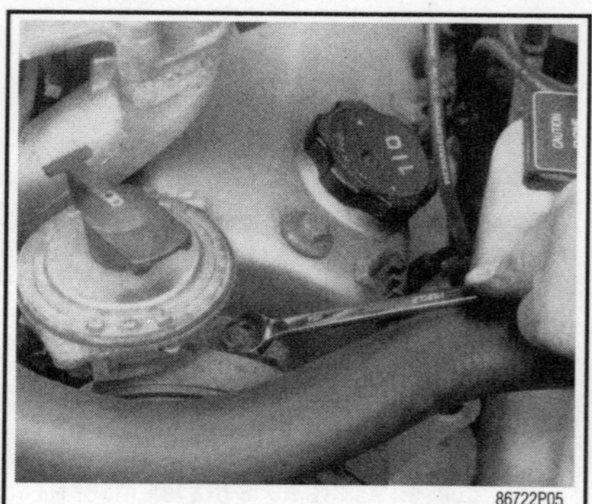
86722P05

Fig. 13 Loosen and remove the distributor hold-down nut and bracket

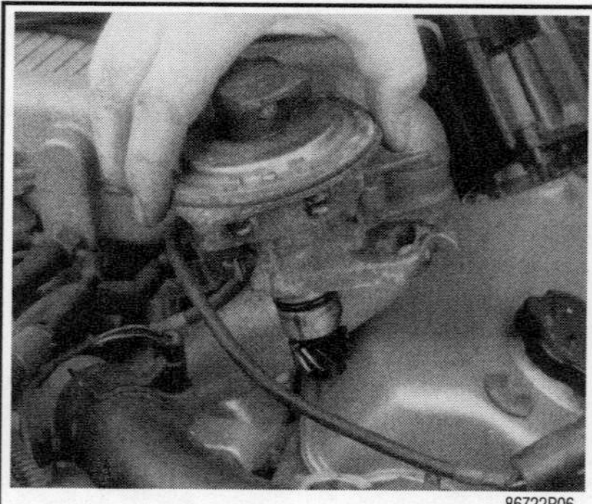
86722P06

Fig. 14 Gently pull the distributor up and out of the engine block

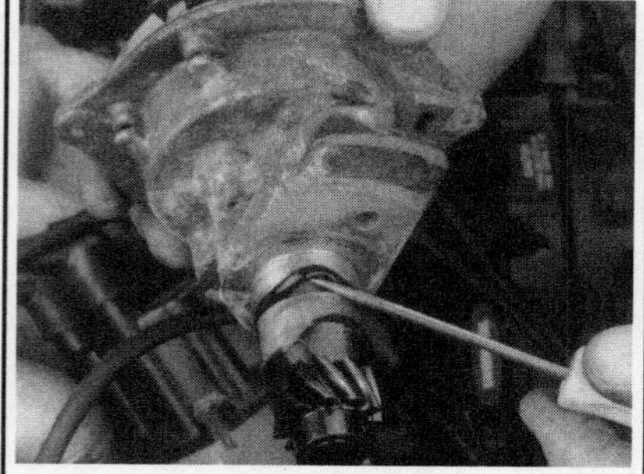
86722P07

Fig. 15 Inspect the O-ring on the distributor shaft and replace with a new one if any damage is evident

INSTALLATION

Timing Not Disturbed

1. Lower the distributor into the engine, aligning the marks made during removal. Be sure the O-ring is properly seated on the distributor. Replace the O-ring with a new one if it is cracked or nicked.

➡**Be sure the distributor drive is engaged with the gear on the camshaft.**

2. Install the distributor cap.
3. Tighten the hold-down bolt.
4. Reattach the electrical connector to the distributor.
5. Reconnect the negative battery cable.
6. Check, and if necessary, adjust the ignition timing.

Timing Disturbed

➧ **See Figure 11**

1. Remove the spark plug from No. 1 cylinder. Place a finger over the spark plug hole.
2. Rotate the crankshaft in the normal direction of rotation, until compression is felt at the spark plug hole (air will leak out of the plug hole past your finger).
3. Continue rotating the crankshaft until the No. 1 piston is at the top of the compression stroke.
4. Install the distributor so that the distributor housing is fully seated when the rotor points to the No. 1 spark plug terminal on the distributor cap.
5. Install the distributor cap.
6. Tighten the hold-down bolt. Reattach the electrical connector to the distributor.
7. Check, and if necessary, adjust the ignition timing.

Crankshaft and Camshaft Position Sensors

Refer to Electronic Engine Controls in Section 4 for information on servicing the position sensors.

DISTRIBUTORLESS IGNITION SYSTEM

General Information

➧ **See Figures 16, 17 and 18**

The distributorless ignition system is referred to as the Direct Ignition System (DIS). This system's three main components are the coil pack, crankshaft sensor, and camshaft sensor. The crankshaft and camshaft sensors are Hall effect devices.

The ignition system is regulated by the Powertrain Control Module (PCM). The PCM supplies battery voltage to the ignition coil through the Auto Shutdown (ASD) relay. The PCM also controls the ground circuit for the ignition coil. By switching the ground path for the coil on and off, the PCM adjusts the ignition timing to meet changing engine operating conditions.

During the crank/start, period the PCM advances ignition timing a set amount. During engine operation, the amount of spark advance provided by the PCM is determined by these input factors:

- Intake air temperature
- Coolant temperature
- Engine RPM
- Available manifold vacuum
- Knock sensor

The PCM also regulates the fuel injection system.

The camshaft position sensor provides fuel injection synchronization and cylinder identification information. The sensor generates pulses that serve as input to the PCM. The PCM interprets the camshaft position sensor input (along with the crankshaft position sensor input) to determine crankshaft position. The PCM uses the crankshaft position sensor input to determine injector sequence and ignition timing.

The camshaft position sensor is mounted to the rear of the cylinder head on the 2.4L engine and mounted in the front timing case cover on the 3.3L/3.8L engines.

On the 2.4L engine, a target magnet attaches to the rear of the camshaft and indexes to the correct position. The target magnet has four different poles arranged in an asymmetrical pattern. As the target magnet rotates, the camshaft position sensor recognizes the change in polarity. The sensor switches from high (5 volts) to low (0.3 volts) as the target magnet rotates. When the north pole of the target magnet passes under the sensor, the output switches high. The sensor output switches low when the south pole of the target magnet passes underneath.

The PCM uses the camshaft position sensor to determine injector sequence. The PCM determines ignition timing from the crankshaft position sensor. Once the crankshaft position has been determined, the PCM begins energizing the injectors in sequence.

The crankshaft position sensor is mounted to the engine block behind the alternator, just above the oil filter. The second crankshaft counterweight has machined into it two sets of four timing reference notches, including a 60 degree signature notch. From the crankshaft position sensor input, the PCM determines engine speed and crankshaft angle (position). The notches generate pulses front high to low in the crankshaft position sensor output voltage. When a metal portion of the counterweight aligns with the crankshaft position sensor, the sensor output voltage goes low (less than 0.5 volts). When a notch aligns with the sensor, voltage goes high (5.0 volts). As a group of notches pass under the sensor, the output voltage switches from low (metal) to high (notch), then back to low.

From the frequency of the output voltage pulses, the PCM calculates engine speed. The width of the pulses represent the amount of time the output voltage stays high before switching back to low. The period of time the voltage stays high before returning to low is called a pulse width. The faster the engine is operating, the smaller the pulse width.

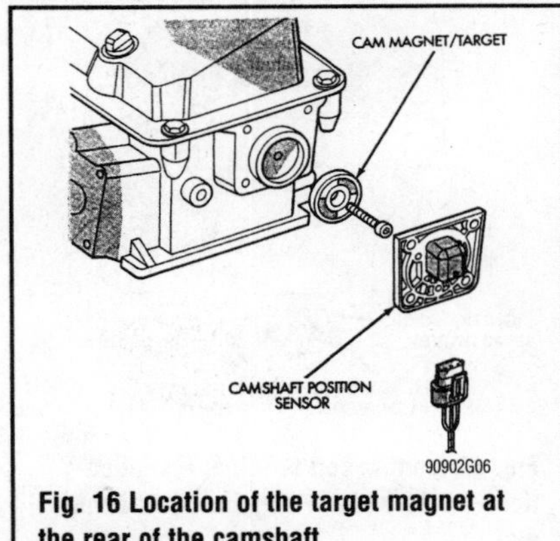

Fig. 16 Location of the target magnet at the rear of the camshaft

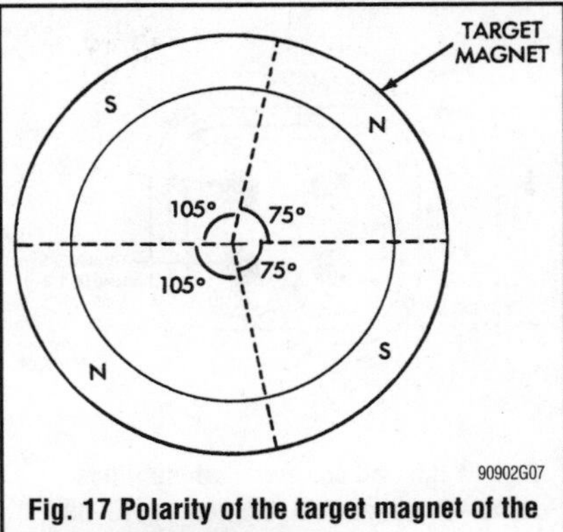

Fig. 17 Polarity of the target magnet of the camshaft position sensor

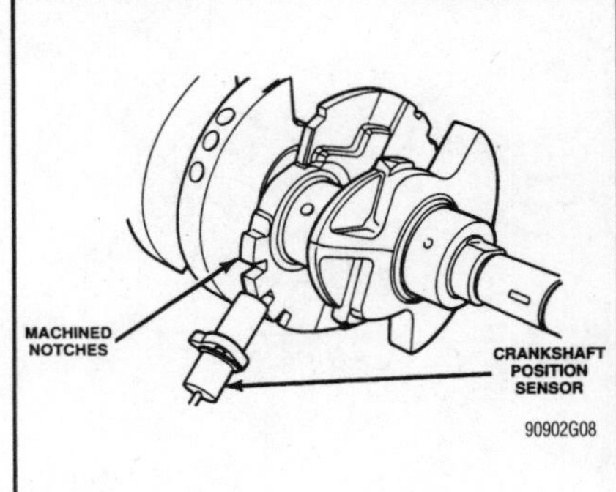

Fig. 18 Timing reference notches for the crankshaft position sensor

By counting the pulses and referencing the pulse from the 60 degree signature notch, the PCM calculates crankshaft angle (position). In each group of timing reference notches, the first notch represents 69 degrees Before Top Dead Center (BTDC). The second notch represents 49 degrees BTDC. The third notch represents 29 degrees. The last notch in each set represents 9 degrees BTDC.

The timing reference notches are machined at 20 degree increments. From the voltage pulse-width, the PCM tells the difference between the timing reference notches and the 60 degree reference notches. The 60 degree signature notch produces a longer pulse-width than the smaller timing reference notches. If the camshaft position sensor input switches from high to low when the 60 degree signature notch passes under the crankshaft position sensor, the PCM knows cylinder No. 1 is the next cylinder at TDC.

The ignition coil assembly consists of 2 coils molded together. The assembly is mounted on top of the engine. The number of each coil appears on the front of the coil pack.

High tension leads route to each cylinder from the coil. The coil fires two spark plugs every power stroke; one plug is the cylinder under compression, the other cylinder fires on the exhaust stroke. The PCM determines which of the coils to charge and fire at the correct time. The coil's low primary resistance allows the PCM to fully charge the coil for each firing.

Diagnosis and Testing

To test the ignition system, perform the test procedures in a particular sequence. Start with the secondary spark test, commence to the coil test (located under the coil procedures later in this section) and, finally, perform the failure-to-start test. Performing the tests in this order will narrow down the ignition system problem in the easiest manner.

SECONDARY SPARK TEST

➧ See Figure 2

CAUTION

The Direct Ignition System generates approximately 40,000 volts. Personal injury could result from contact with this system.

Since the coil pack contains independent coils in the assembly, each coil must be checked individually. Cylinders 1 and 4, and 2 and 3 are grouped together on the 2.4L engine and cylinders 1\4, 2\5 and 3\6 are grouped together on the 3.3L and 3.8L engines.

1. Remove the cable from the No. 1 spark plug, then insert a clean spark plug into the spark plug boot.

➡Due to the high secondary voltage and risk of electrical shock, it is advisable to wrap a thick, dry cloth around the boot before grasping it.

WARNING

Spark plug wire damage may occur if the spark plug is moved more than 1/4 inch (6mm) away from the engine ground.

2. Ground the plug to the engine (touch the spark plug metal body to the engine block or other piece of metal on the car).
3. Crank the engine and look for a strong, blue spark across the electrodes of the spark plug.
4. Repeat the test for the remaining cylinders. If there is no spark during all cylinder tests, refer to the failure-to-start test. If one or more tests indicate irregular, weak or no spark, refer to the coil test.

FAILURE-TO-START TEST

➧ See Figures 19, 20, 21 and 22

Before proceeding with this test, refer to the testing procedures for the ignition coil, later in this section.

1. Using a Digital Volt/Ohmmeter (DVOM) measure the voltage from the negative (-) battery terminal to the positive (+) battery terminal. The voltage should be at least 12.66 volts. This amount of voltage is necessary for an accurate inspection of the system.
2. Detach the ignition coil harness connector.
3. Connect a suitable test light to the B+ (battery voltage) terminal of the ignition coil electrical connector and ground. The B+ (battery voltage) wire for the DIS coil is dark green with an orange tracer. Do not spread the terminal with the test light probe.
4. Turn the ignition key to the **ON** position. The test light should flash ON and then OFF. Leave the ignition key **ON**.

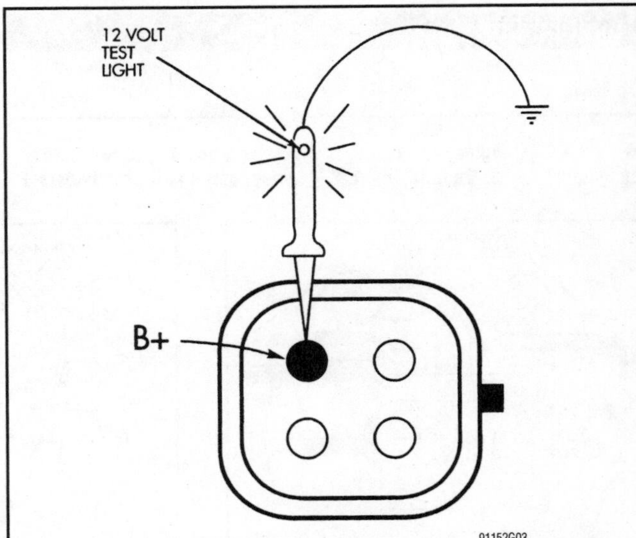

Fig. 19 Connect a suitable test light to the B+ (battery voltage) terminal (or ASD relay output terminal) of the ignition coil electrical connector and ground

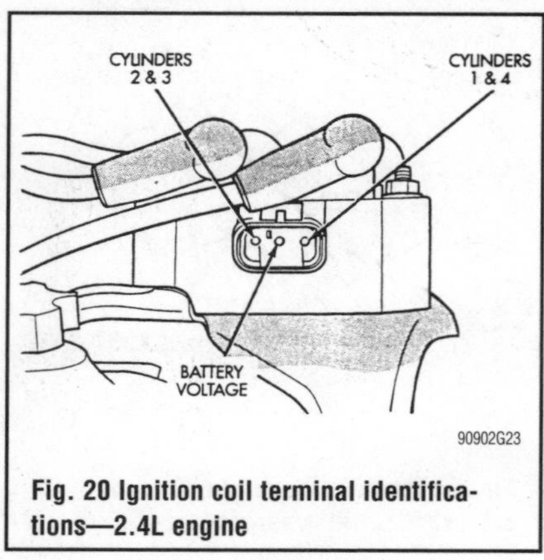

Fig. 20 Ignition coil terminal identifications—2.4L engine

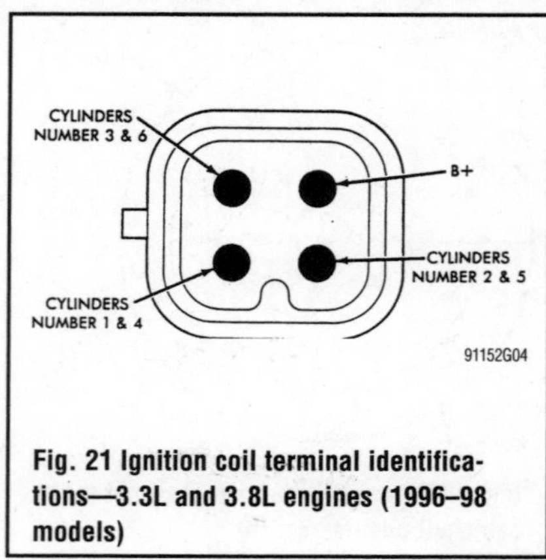

Fig. 21 Ignition coil terminal identifications—3.3L and 3.8L engines (1996–98 models)

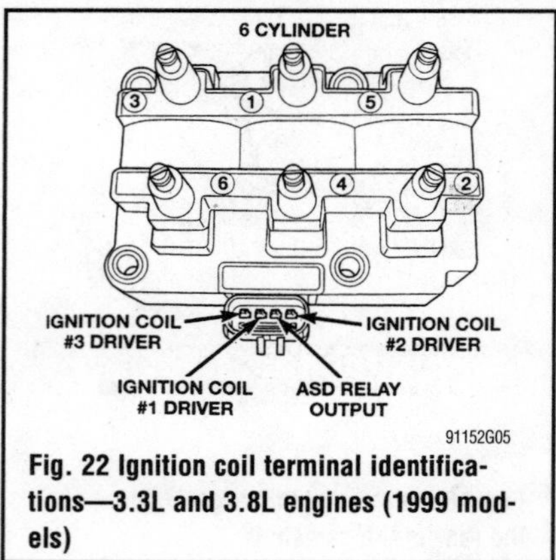

Fig. 22 Ignition coil terminal identifications—3.3L and 3.8L engines (1999 models)

a. If the test light flashes momentarily, the PCM grounded the ASD relay. Proceed to the next step.

b. If the test light did not flash, the ASD relay did not energize. This is caused by either the relay or one of the relay circuits.

5. Crank the engine. (If the key was placed in the **OFF** position in Step 4, turn the key to the **ON** position before cranking. Wait for the test light to flash once, then crank the engine).

a. If the test light momentarily flashes during cranking, the PCM is not receiving a crankshaft position sensor signal. Use a DRB or equivalent scan tool to test the sensor and related circuitry.

b. If the test light did not flash during cranking, unplug the crankshaft position sensor connector. Turn the ignition key to the **OFF** position. Turn the key to the **ON** position, wait for the test light to momentarily flash once, then crank the engine. If the test light momentarily flashes, the crankshaft position sensor is shorted and must be replaced. If the light did not flash when the engine was cranked, the cause of the no-start condition is in either the crankshaft or camshaft position sensor 8-volt supply circuit, or the camshaft position sensor output or ground circuits. Use a DRB or equivalent scan tool to test the camshaft position sensor and related circuitry.

Adjustments

All adjustments in the ignition system are controlled by the Powertrain Control Module (PCM) for optimum performance. No adjustments are possible.

Ignition Coil Pack

TESTING

➡On the 2.4L engine, coil one fires cylinders 1 and 4, coil two fires cylinders 2 and 3. On 3.3L and 3.8L engines, coil one fires cylinders 1 and 4, coil two fires cylinders 2 and 5, coil three fires cylinders 3 and 6. Each coil tower is labeled with the number of the corresponding cylinder.

Primary Coil Resistance Test

➧ See Figures 20, 21 and 22

1. Unplug the electrical connector from the ignition coil pack.
2. Measure the primary resistance of each coil. At the coil, connect an ohmmeter between the B+ pin and the pin corresponding to the cylinders in question.
3. The resistance on the primary side of each coil should be 0.45–0.65 ohms at 70°–80°F (21°–27°C).
4. A coil that has not been allowed to cool off, would result in an inaccurate measurement. Replace the coil if not within specifications.

Secondary Coil Resistance Test

➧ See Figure 23

1. Disconnect the spark plug wires from the secondary towers of the ignition coil.
2. Use an ohmmeter to measure the secondary resistance of the coil between the towers of each individual coil pack.
3. The secondary resistance should be 7,000–15,800 ohms on 1996–98 vehicles and 10,900–14,700 ohms on 1999 vehicles. If resistance is not within specifications, the coil must be replaced.

REMOVAL & INSTALLATION

➧ See Figures 24 and 25

1. Disconnect the negative battery cable.
2. Label and disconnect the spark plug wires from each of the coil pack towers.

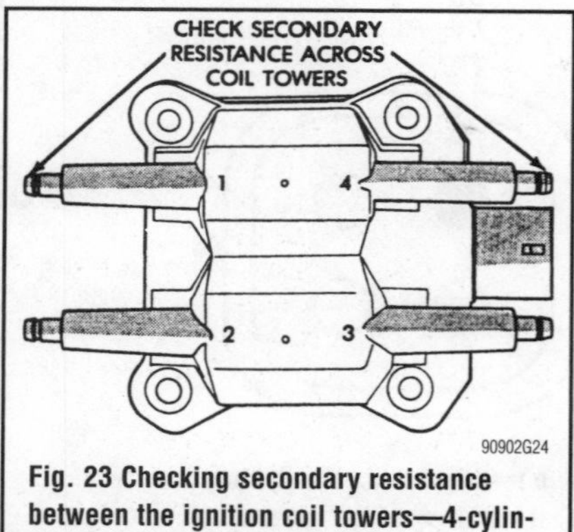

Fig. 23 Checking secondary resistance between the ignition coil towers—4-cylinder shown, 6-cylinder similar

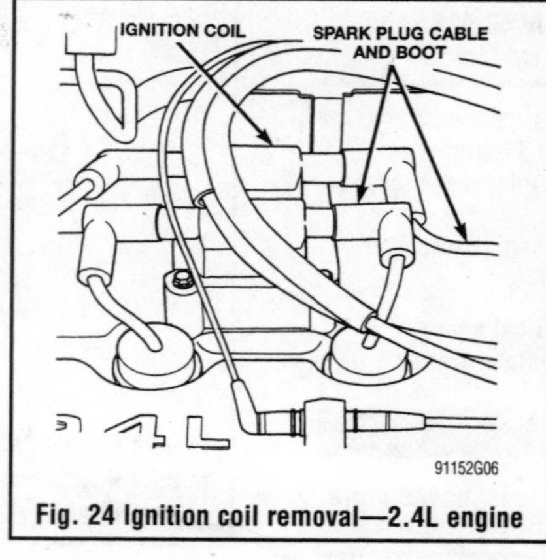

Fig. 24 Ignition coil removal—2.4L engine

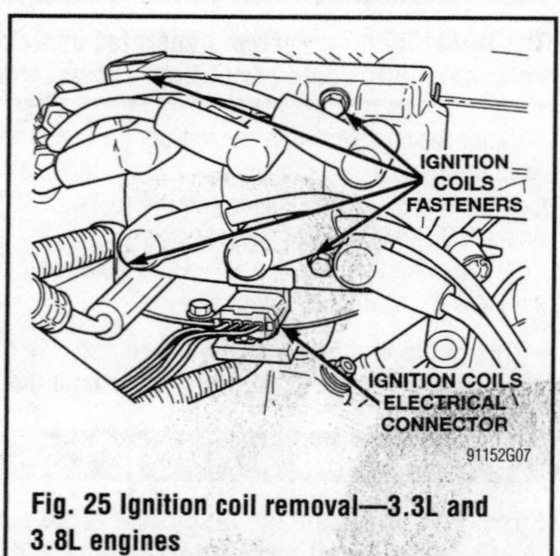

Fig. 25 Ignition coil removal—3.3L and 3.8L engines

3. Disengage the electrical connector from the ignition coil pack.
4. Remove the coil pack mounting fasteners.
5. Remove the coil pack from the vehicle. If equipped, remove the coil pack from the mounting bracket.

To install:

6. Place the coil pack into position on top of the engine valve cover, or mounting bracket, if equipped.
7. Install and tighten the coil pack mounting fasteners to 9 ft. lbs. (12 Nm).
8. Plug in the electrical connector to the ignition coil pack.
9. Connect each spark plug wire to each corresponding coil pack tower. The coil pack towers are numbered with the correct cylinder identification. Be sure that the spark plug wires snap firmly onto each coil tower.
10. Connect the negative battery cable.

Crankshaft and Camshaft Position Sensors

Refer to Electronic Engine Controls in Section 4 for information on servicing the position sensors.

FIRING ORDERS

See Figures 26, 27 and 28

To avoid confusion, remove and tag the spark plug wires one at a time, for replacement.

If a distributor is not keyed for installation with only one orientation, it could have been removed previously and rewired. The resultant wiring would hold the correct firing order, but could change the relative placement of the plug towers in relation to the engine. For this reason it is imperative that you label all wires before disconnecting any of them. Also, before removal, compare the current wiring with the accompanying illustrations. If the current wiring does not match, make notes in your book to reflect how your engine is wired.

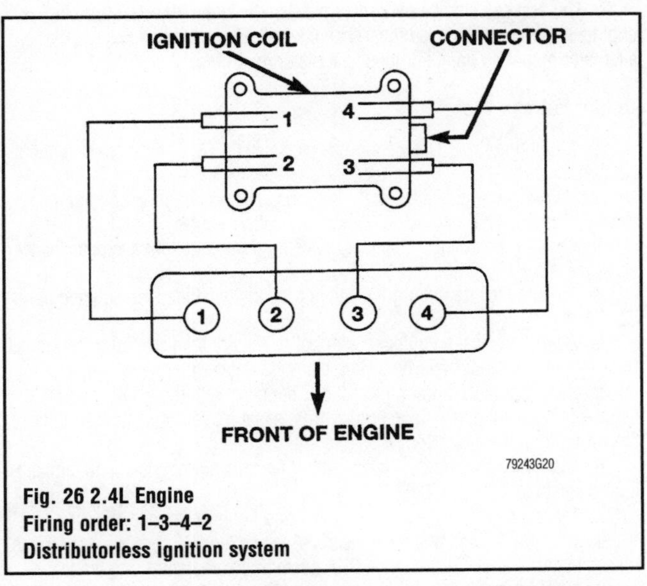

Fig. 26 2.4L Engine
Firing order: 1–3–4–2
Distributorless ignition system

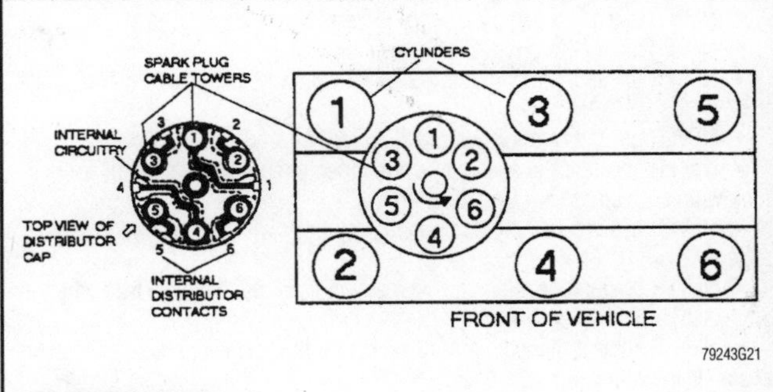

Fig. 27 3.0L Engine
Firing order: 1–2–3–4–5–6
Distributor rotation: Counterclockwise

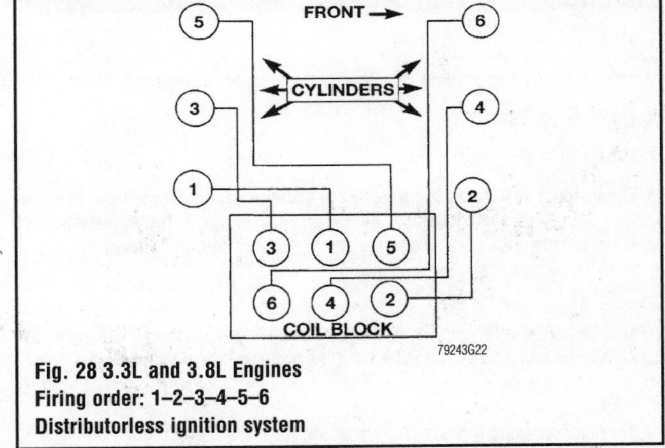

Fig. 28 3.3L and 3.8L Engines
Firing order: 1–2–3–4–5–6
Distributorless ignition system

CHARGING SYSTEM

General Information

The charging system is a negative (-) ground system which consists of an alternator, a regulator within the Powertrain Control Module (PCM), ignition switch, charge indicator lamp, battery, circuit protection and wiring connecting the components.

The alternator is belt-driven from the engine. Energy is supplied from the alternator to the rotating field through brushes to slip-rings. The slip-rings are mounted on the rotor shaft and are connected to the field coil. This energy supplied to the rotating field from the battery is called excitation current and is used to initially energize the field to begin the generation of electricity. Once the alternator starts to generate electricity, the excitation current comes from its own output, rather than from the battery.

The alternator produces power in the form of alternating current. The alternating current is rectified by diodes into direct current. The direct current is used to charge the battery and power the rest of the electrical system. When the ignition key is turned **ON**, current flows from the battery, through the charging system indicator light on the instrument panel, to the voltage regulator in the PCM, and to the alternator. Since the alternator is not producing any current, the alternator warning light comes on. When the engine is started, the alternator begins to produce current and turns the alternator light off.

As the alternator turns and produces current, the current is divided in two ways: charging the battery and powering the electrical components of the vehicle. Part of the current is returned to the alternator to enable it to increase its output. In this situation, the alternator is receiving current from the battery and from itself. A voltage regulator is wired into the current supply to the alternator to prevent it from receiving too much current, which would cause it to overproduce current. Conversely, if the voltage regulator does not allow the alternator to receive enough current, the battery will not be fully charged and will eventually go dead.

The battery is connected to the alternator at all times, whether the ignition key is turned **ON** or **OFF**. If the battery were shorted to ground, the alternator would also be shorted. This would damage the alternator. To prevent this, circuit protection (usually in the form of a fuse link) is installed in the wiring between the battery and the alternator. If the battery is shorted, the circuit protection will protect the alternator.

Alternator Precautions

Several precautions must be observed with alternator equipped vehicles to avoid damage to the unit.

- ALWAYS observe proper polarity of the battery connections; be especially careful when jump starting the car. Reversing the battery connections may result in damage to the one-way rectifiers.
- ALWAYS remove the battery or, at least, disconnect the cables while charging.
- ALWAYS match and/or consider the polarity of the battery, alternator and regulator before making any electrical connections within the system.
- ALWAYS disconnect the battery ground terminal while repairing or replacing any electrical components.
- NEVER use a fast battery charger to jump start a dead battery.
- NEVER attempt to polarize an alternator.
- NEVER use test lights of more than 12 volts when checking diode continuity.
- NEVER ground or short out the alternator or regulator terminals.
- NEVER separate the alternator on an open circuit. Make sure all connections within the circuit are clean and tight.
- NEVER use arc welding equipment on the car with the alternator connected.
- NEVER operate the alternator with any of its or the battery's lead wires disconnected.
- NEVER subject the alternator to excessive heat or dampness (for instance, steam cleaning the engine).
- When utilizing a booster battery as a starting aid, always connect the positive to positive terminals and the negative terminal from the booster battery to a good engine ground on the vehicle being started.

Alternator

TESTING

Voltage Drop Test

➧ See Figure 29

➡These tests will show the amount of voltage drop across the alternator output wire from the alternator output (B+) terminal to the battery positive post. They will also show the amount of voltage drop from the ground (-) terminal on the alternator.

A voltmeter with a 0–18 volt DC scale should be used for these tests. By repositioning the voltmeter test leads, the point of high resistance (voltage drop) can easily be found. Test points on the alternator can be reached by removing the windshield wiper/motor module assembly. Refer to Section 6 to remove this component.

1. Before starting the test, make sure the battery is in good condition and is fully charged. Check the conditions of the battery cables.
2. Start the engine, let it warm up to normal operating temperatures, then turn the engine **OFF**.
3. Connect an engine tachometer, following the manufacturer's directions.

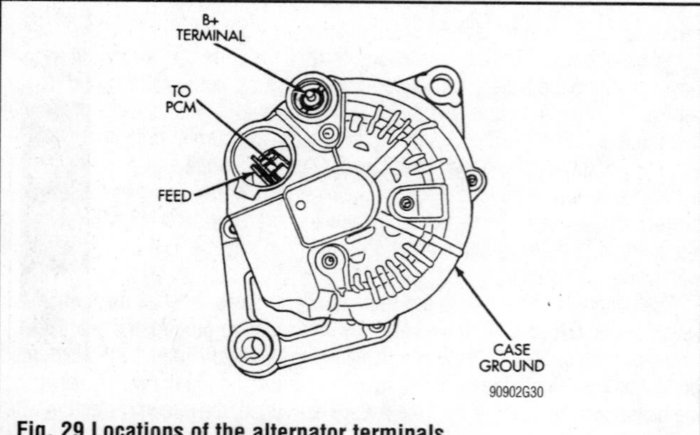

Fig. 29 Locations of the alternator terminals

4. Make sure the parking brake is fully engaged.
5. Start the engine, then place the blower on HIGH, and turn on the high beam headlamps and rear window defogger.
6. Bring the engine speed up to 2,400 rpm and hold it there.
7. To test the positive (+) circuitry, perform the following:
   a. Touch the negative (-) lead of the voltmeter directly to the positive battery post.
   b. Touch the positive (+) lead of the voltmeter to the B+ output terminal stud on the alternator case (NOT the terminal mounting nut). The voltage should be no higher than 0.6 volt. If the voltage is higher than 0.6 volt, touch the test lead to the terminal mounting stud nut, and then to the wiring connector. If the voltage is now below 0.6 volt, look for dirty, loose or poor connections at this point. Also inspect the condition of the alternator output wire-to-battery bullet connector. A voltage drop test may be performed at each negative (-) ground connection in this circuit to locate the excessive resistance.
8. To test the negative (-) ground circuitry, perform the following:
   a. Touch the positive (+) lead of the voltmeter directly to the negative battery post.
   b. Touch the negative lead of the voltmeter to the alternator case (NOT the terminal mounting nut). The voltage should be no higher than 0.3 volt. If the voltage is higher than 0.3 volt, touch the test lead to the alternator case, and then to the engine block. If the voltage is now below 0.3 volt, look for dirty, loose or poor connections at this point. A voltage drop test may be performed at each connection in this circuit to locate excessive resistance.
9. This test can also be performed between the alternator case and the engine. If the test voltage is higher than 0.3 volt, check for corrosion at the alternator mounting points or loose alternator mounting.

Output Voltage Test

1. Determine if any Diagnostic Trouble Codes (DTC'S) exist, as outlined in Section 4.
2. Before starting the test, make sure the battery is in good condition and is fully charged. Check the conditions of the battery cables.
3. Perform the voltage drop test to ensure clean and tight alternator/battery electrical connections.
4. Be sure the alternator drive belt is properly tensioned, as outlined in Section 1.
5. A volt/amp tester equipped with both a battery load control (carbon pile rheostat) and an inductive-type pickup clamp (ammeter probe) will be used for this test. Make sure to follow all directions supplied with the tester. If you are using a tester equipped with an inductive-type clamp, you don't have to remove the wiring from the alternator.
6. Start the engine and let it run until it reaches normal operating temperature, then shut the engine **OFF**.
7. Make sure all electrical accessories and lights are turned OFF.
8. Connect the volt/amp tester leads to the battery. Be sure the carbon pile rheostat control is in the **OPEN** or **OFF** position before connecting the leads.
9. Connect the inductive clamp (ammeter probe), following the instructions supplied with the test equipment.
10. If a volt/amp tester is not equipped with an engine tachometer, connect a separate tachometer to the engine.
11. Fully engage the parking brake.
12. Start the engine, then bring the engine speed up to 2,500 rpm.

✲✲ WARNING

This load test must be performed within 15 seconds to prevent damage to the test equipment!

13. With the engine speed held at 2,500 rpm, slowly adjust the rheostat control (load) on the tester to get the highest amperage reading. Do not let the voltage drop below 12 volts. Record the reading.

➡On certain brands of test equipment, this load will be applied automatically. Be sure to read the operating manual supplied with the test equipment before performing the test.

14. The ammeter reading must meet the minimum test amps specification of 86 amps.
15. Rotate the load control to the OFF position.

16. Continue holding the engine speed at 2,500 rpm. If the Electronic Voltage Regulator (EVR) circuitry is OK, the amperage should drop below 15–20 amps. With all of the electrical accessories and vehicle lighting off, this could take several minutes of engine operation.

17. After the procedure is complete, remove the volt/amp tester.

REMOVAL & INSTALLATION

2.4L Engine

➧ See Figure 30

1. Disconnect the negative battery cable.
2. Remove the accessory drive belt.
3. Unplug the push-in field wire connector from behind the alternator.
4. Remove the B+ nut and wire from behind the alternator.
5. Remove the nut securing the top of the alternator to the adjuster bolt (a.k.a T-bolt).
6. Remove the alternator pivot nut and bolt, located below the alternator.
7. Remove the alternator from the vehicle.

To install:

8. Install the alternator into position on the vehicle's engine.
9. Install, but do not tighten, the alternator pivot nut and bolt.
10. Install the nut securing the top of the alternator to the adjuster bolt.
11. Connect the B+ wire and tighten the retaining nut to 75 inch lbs. (9 Nm).
12. Plug in the push-in field wire connector onto the back of the alternator.
13. Install the accessory drive belt. Be sure the drive belt is correctly routed on the engine and correctly seated on all of the pulleys, especially the alternator.
14. Adjust the drive belt and tighten the adjuster/locking bolt to 40 ft. lbs. (54 Nm).
15. Tighten the pivot bolt to 40 ft. lbs. (54 Nm).
16. Reconnect the negative battery cable.
17. Verify the charging rate of the alternator.

3.0L Engine

➧ See Figures 31, 32, 33, 34 and 35

1. Disconnect the negative battery cable.
2. Remove the windshield wiper/motor module assembly. Refer to Section 6 for this procedure.
3. Remove the accessory drive belt from the alternator.
4. Remove the bolt securing the top of the alternator to the mounting bracket.
5. Remove the bolt securing the bottom of the alternator to the lower pivot bracket.
6. While holding the alternator, unplug the push-in field wire connector from behind the alternator.
7. While holding the alternator, remove the B+ nut and wire from behind the alternator.
8. Remove the alternator from the vehicle.

To install:

9. Hold the alternator in position near the mounting bracket, then connect the B+ wire and tighten the retaining nut to 75 inch lbs. (9 Nm).
10. Plug in the push-in field wire connector onto the back of the alternator.
11. Place the alternator into position on the mounting bracket, then install the bolt securing the bottom of the alternator to the lower pivot bracket.
12. Install the bolt securing the top of the alternator to the mounting bracket. Tighten the upper and lower alternator bolts to 40 ft. lbs. (54 Nm).
13. Install the accessory drive belt. Be sure the drive belt is correctly routed on the engine and correctly seated on all of the pulleys.
14. Install the windshield wiper/motor module assembly.
15. Reconnect the negative battery cable.
16. Verify the charging rate of the alternator.

3.3L and 3.8L Engines

➧ See Figures 36, 37 and 38

1. Disconnect the negative battery cable.
2. Remove the windshield wiper/motor module assembly. Refer to Section 6 for this procedure.

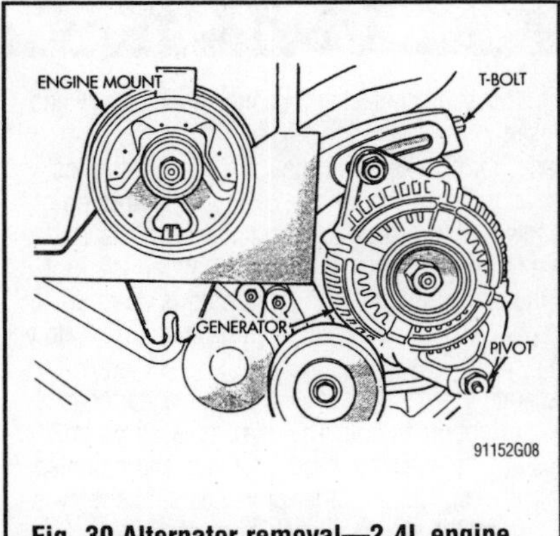

Fig. 30 Alternator removal—2.4L engine

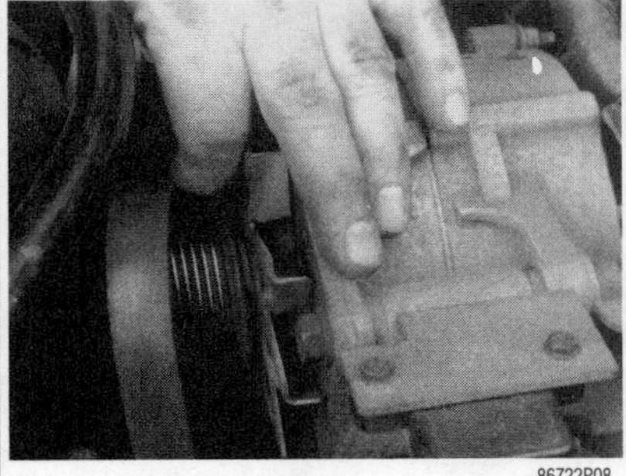

Fig. 31 Rotate the accessory drive belt tensioner clockwise, and slip the belt off of the pulley . . .

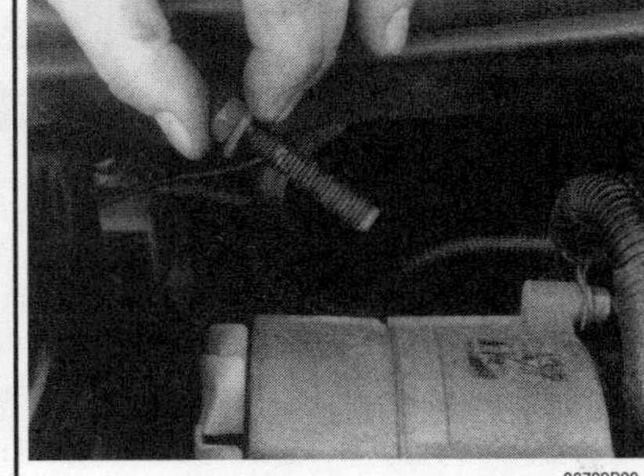

Fig. 32 . . . then remove the bolt securing the top of the alternator to the bracket . . .

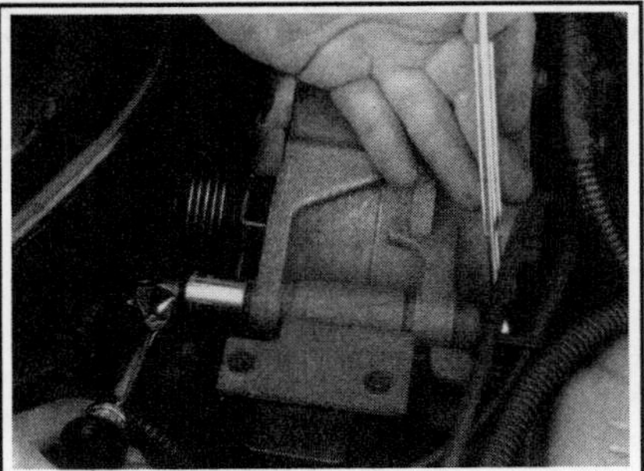

Fig. 33 . . . as well as the bottom bolt securing the alternator to the lower pivot bracket

Fig. 34 With both mounting bolts removed, lift and rotate the alternator to access the wiring harness

Fig. 35 Disconnect the wiring from behind the alternator

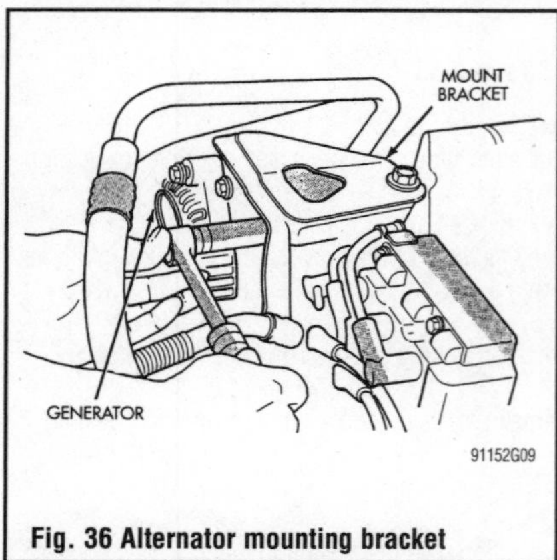

Fig. 36 Alternator mounting bracket

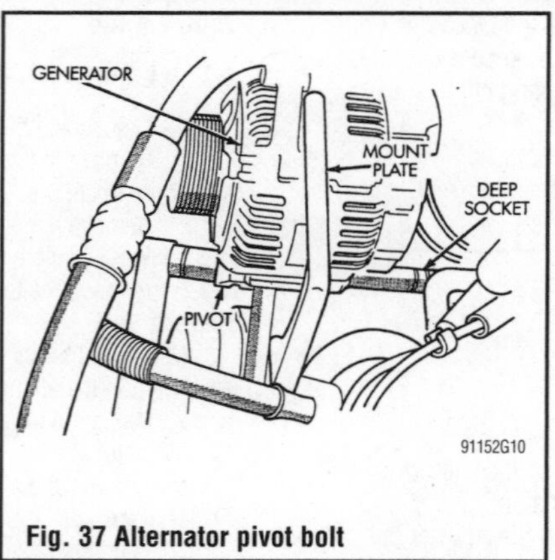

Fig. 37 Alternator pivot bolt

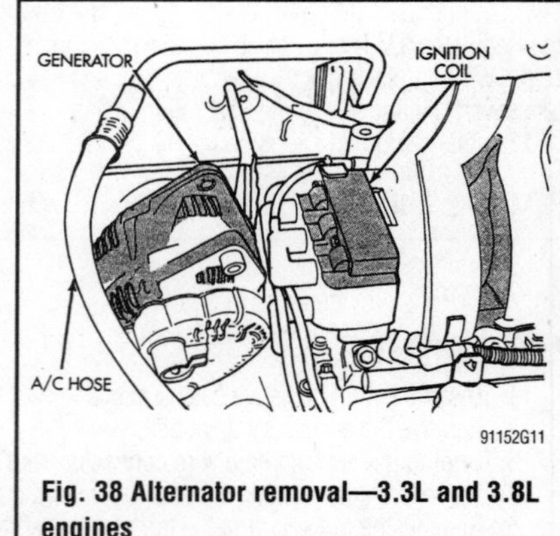

Fig. 38 Alternator removal—3.3L and 3.8L engines

3. Remove the accessory drive belt.
4. Remove the bolt securing the top of the alternator mounting bracket to the engine air intake plenum.
5. Remove the bolts securing the outside of the alternator mounting bracket to the alternator mounting plate.
6. Remove the bolt securing the top of the alternator to the mounting bracket.
7. Remove the alternator mounting bracket from the vehicle.
8. Rotate the alternator toward the dash panel.
9. Unplug the push-in field wire connector from behind the alternator.
10. Remove the B+ nut and wire from behind the alternator.
11. Remove the bolt securing the bottom of the alternator to the lower pivot bracket.
12. Remove the alternator from the vehicle.

To install:

13. Install the alternator into position on the vehicle's engine.
14. Install the bolt securing the bottom of the alternator to the lower pivot bracket.
15. Connect the B+ wire and tighten the retaining nut to 75 inch lbs. (9 Nm).
16. Plug in the push-in field wire connector onto the back of the alternator.
17. Rotate the alternator forward away from the dash panel.
18. Install the alternator mounting bracket in position on the vehicle.
19. Install the bolt to secure the top of the alternator to the mounting bracket.
20. Install the bolts to secure the outside of the alternator mounting bracket to the alternator mounting plate.
21. Install the bolt to secure the top of the alternator mounting bracket to the engine air intake plenum.
22. Tighten all of the alternator mounting bolts to 40 ft. lbs. (54 Nm).
23. Install the accessory drive belt. Be sure the drive belt is correctly routed on the engine and correctly seated on all of the pulleys.
24. Install the windshield wiper/motor module assembly.
25. Reconnect the negative battery cable.
26. Verify the charging rate of the alternator.

STARTING SYSTEM

General Information

The battery and starting motor are linked by very heavy electrical cables designed to minimize resistance to the flow of current. Generally, the major power supply cable that leaves the battery goes directly to the starter, while other electrical system needs are supplied by a smaller cable. During starter operation, power flows from the battery to the starter and is grounded through the vehicle's frame/body or engine and the battery's negative ground strap.

The starter is a specially designed, direct current electric motor capable of producing a great amount of power for its size. One thing that allows the motor to produce a great deal of power is its tremendous rotating speed. It drives the engine through a tiny pinion gear (attached to the starter's armature), which drives the very large flywheel ring gear at a greatly reduced speed. Another factor allowing it to produce so much power is that only intermittent operation is required of it. Thus, little allowance for air circulation is necessary, and the windings can be built into a very small space.

The starter solenoid is a magnetic device which employs the small current supplied by the start circuit of the ignition switch. This magnetic action moves a plunger which mechanically engages the starter and closes the heavy switch connecting it to the battery. The starting switch circuit usually consists of the starting switch contained within the ignition switch, a neutral safety switch or clutch pedal switch, and the wiring necessary to connect these in series with the starter solenoid or relay.

The pinion, a small gear, is mounted to a one-way drive clutch. This clutch is splined to the starter armature shaft. When the ignition switch is moved to the **START** position, the solenoid plunger slides the pinion toward the flywheel ring gear via a collar and spring. If the teeth on the pinion and flywheel match properly, the pinion will engage the flywheel immediately. If the gear teeth butt one another, the spring will be compressed and will force the gears to mesh as soon as the starter turns far enough to allow them to do so. As the solenoid plunger reaches the end of its travel, it closes the contacts that connect the battery and starter, then the engine is cranked.

As soon as the engine starts, the flywheel ring gear begins turning fast enough to drive the pinion at an extremely high rate of speed. At this point, the one-way clutch begins allowing the pinion to spin faster than the starter shaft so that the starter will not operate at excessive speed. When the ignition switch is released from the starter position, the solenoid is de-energized, and a spring pulls the gear out of mesh, interrupting the current flow to the starter.

Some starters employ a separate relay, mounted away from the starter, to switch the motor and solenoid current on and off. The relay replaces the solenoid electrical switch, but does not eliminate the need for a solenoid mounted on the starter used to mechanically engage the starter drive gears. The relay is used to reduce the amount of current the starting switch must carry.

Starter

TESTING

Testing Preparation

Before commencing with the starting system diagnostics, verify:

- The battery posts/terminals are clean.
- The alternator drive belt tension and condition is correct.
- The battery state-of-charge is correct.
- The battery cable connections at the starter and engine block are clean and free from corrosion.
- The wiring harness connectors and terminals are clean and free from corrosion.
- The circuit is properly grounded.

Starter Feed Circuit

➧ **See Figures 39 and 40**

✲✲ CAUTION

The ignition and fuel systems must be disabled to prevent engine start while performing the tests.

1. Connect a volt-ampere tester to the battery terminals. Refer to the operating instructions provided with the tester.
2. Disable the ignition and fuel systems by disconnecting the Automatic Shutdown (ASD) relay, located in the Power Distribution Center (PDC) in the engine compartment.
3. Verify that all lights and accessories are **OFF**, and the transaxle shift selector is in **PARK**. Set the parking brake.
4. Rotate and hold the ignition switch in the **START** position. Observe the volt-ampere tester:
   - If the voltage reads above 9.6 volts, and the amperage draw reads above 280 amps, check for engine seizing or a faulty starter, then go to the starter feed circuit resistance test.
   - If the voltage reads 12.4 volts or greater and the amperage reads 0–10 amps, check for corroded cables and/or bad connections.
   - If the voltage reads below 9.6 volts and the amperage draw reads above 300 amps, the trouble is within the starter.

✲✲ WARNING

Do not overheat the starter motor or draw the battery voltage below 9.6 volts during cranking operations.

5. After the starting system problems have been corrected, verify the battery's state of charge, and charge the battery if necessary. Disconnect all of the testing equipment and connect the ASD relay. Start the vehicle several times to assure the problem was corrected.

Starter Feed Circuit Resistance

➧ **See Figures 41, 42, 43 and 44**

The following test will require a voltmeter, which is capable of accuracy to within 0.1 volt.

✲✲ CAUTION

The ignition and fuel systems must be disabled to prevent engine start while performing the tests.

1. Disable the ignition and fuel systems by disconnecting the Automatic Shutdown (ASD) relay, located in the Power Distribution Center (PDC) in the engine compartment.
2. With all wiring harnesses and components properly connected, perform the following:
   a. Connect the negative (-) lead of the voltmeter to the negative battery post, and the positive (+) lead to the negative battery cable clamp. Rotate and hold the ignition switch in the **START** position. Observe the voltmeter. If voltage is detected, correct the poor contact between the cable clamp and battery post.
   b. Connect the positive (+) lead of the voltmeter to the positive battery post, and the negative (-) lead to the positive battery cable clamp. Rotate and hold the ignition switch key in the **START** position while observing the voltmeter. If voltage is detected, correct the poor contact between the cable clamp and battery post.
   c. Connect the negative lead of the voltmeter to the negative (-) battery terminal, and the positive lead to the engine block near the battery cable attaching point. Rotate and hold the ignition switch in the **START** position. If the voltage reads above 0.2 volt, correct the poor contact at the ground cable attaching point. If the voltage reading is still above 0.2 volt after correcting the poor contact, replace the negative ground cable with a new one.
   d. Connect the positive (+) voltmeter lead to the starter motor housing and the negative (-) lead to the negative battery terminal. Hold the ignition

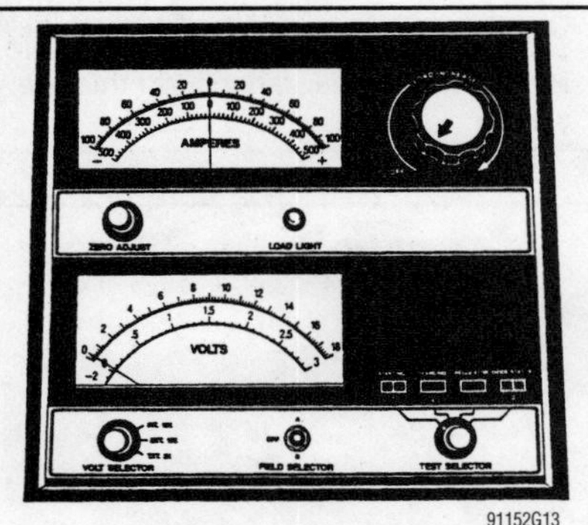

Fig. 39 This is the type of volt-ampere tester required for this type of testing

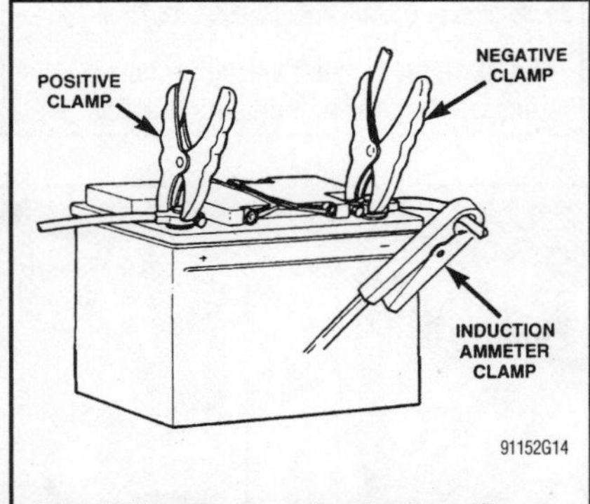

Fig. 40 Proper connection for the volt-ampere tester

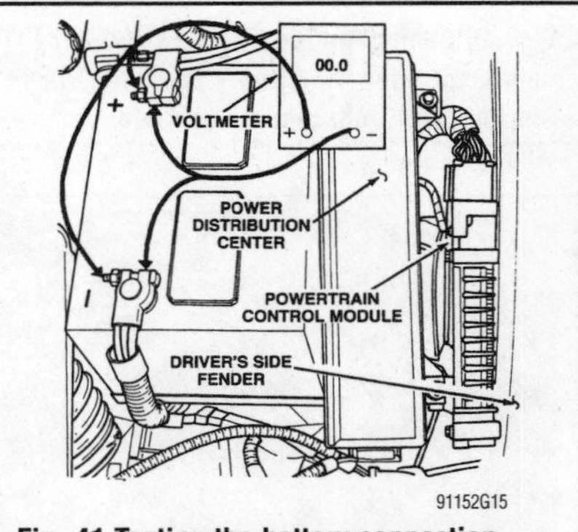

Fig. 41 Testing the battery connection resistance

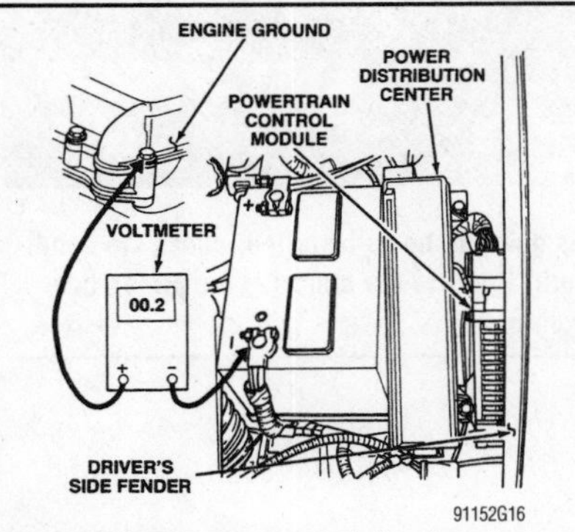

Fig. 42 Testing the ground circuit resistance

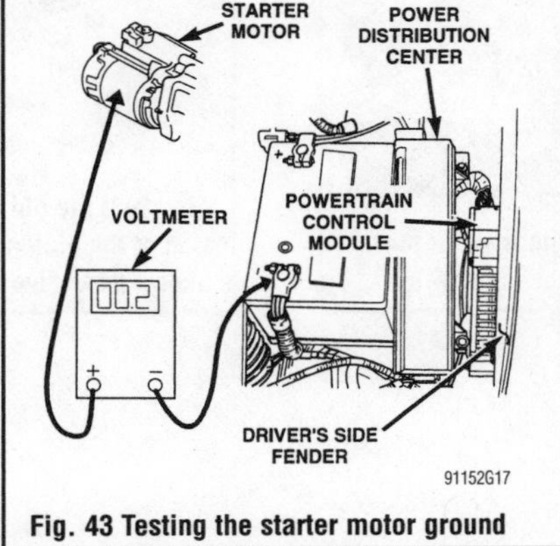

Fig. 43 Testing the starter motor ground

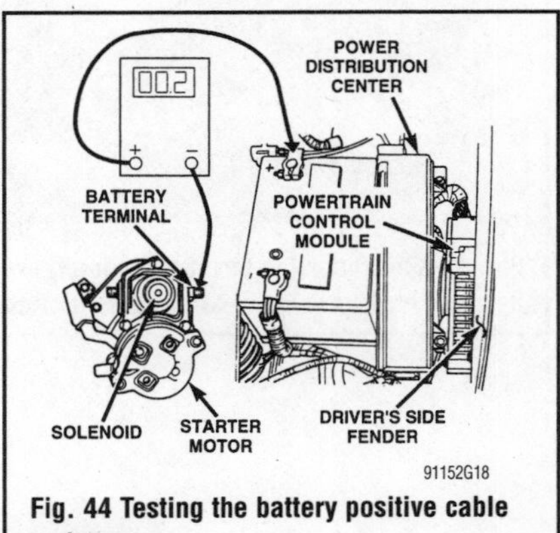

Fig. 44 Testing the battery positive cable resistance

switch key in the **START** position. If the voltage reads above 0.2 volt, correct the poor starter to engine ground.

e. Connect the positive (+) voltmeter lead to the positive battery terminal, and the negative lead to the battery cable terminal on the starter solenoid. Rotate and hold the ignition key in the **START** position. If the voltage reads above 0.2 volt, correct the poor contact at the battery cable to the solenoid connection. If the reading is still above 0.2 volt after correcting the poor contact, replace the positive battery cable with a new one.

f. If the resistance tests did not detect feed circuit failures, replace the starter motor.

REMOVAL & INSTALLATION

See Figures 45, 46, 47, 48 and 49

1. Disconnect the negative battery cable.
2. Raise and safely support the front of the vehicle securely on jackstands.
3. Disengage the solenoid wiring connector from the terminal. This connection may be held in place by a retaining nut, or it could be a push-in connector.
4. Remove the B+ nut and wire from the starter motor terminal.
5. Remove the starter motor-to-transaxle bellhousing mounting bolts.
6. Remove the starter from the vehicle. If equipped, remove the starter motor spacer.

To install:

7. If equipped, hold the starter motor spacer in position.
8. Install the starter motor into position on the vehicle.
9. Install the starter motor-to-transaxle bellhousing mounting bolts. Tighten the mounting bolts to 40 ft. lbs. (54 Nm).
10. Engage the solenoid wiring connector onto the starter terminal.
11. Connect the B+ wire and tighten the retaining nut to 90 inch lbs. (10 Nm).
12. Lower the vehicle.
13. Connect the negative battery cable.
14. Verify starter motor operation.

RELAY REPLACEMENT

The starter relay is located in the Power Distribution Center (PDC) in the engine compartment. Refer to the underside of the PDC cover for starter relay location.

To remove the relay from the vehicle, simply grasp the relay and firmly pull straight up to disengage from the PDC.

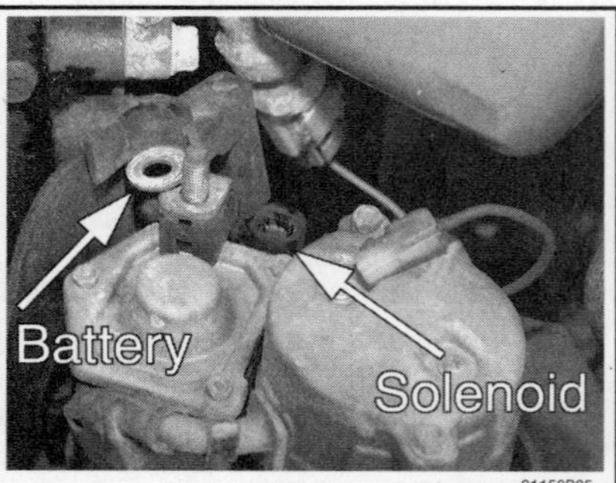

Fig. 45 Disengage the solenoid wiring connector, then the battery positive (B+) nut and wire from the starter motor

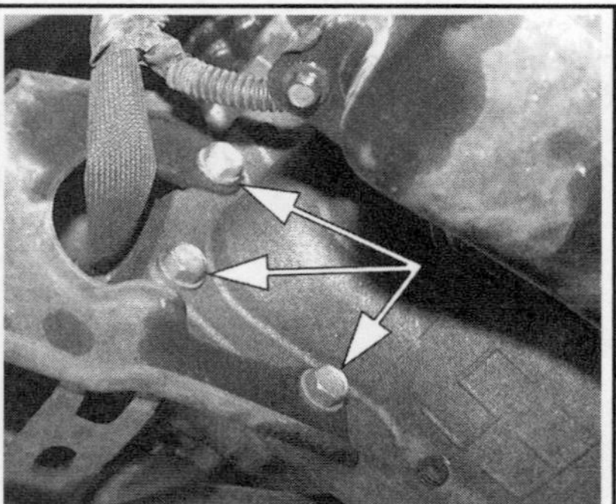

Fig. 46 Remove the 3 starter motor-to-transaxle bellhousing mounting bolts

Fig. 47 Remove the starter motor from the vehicle

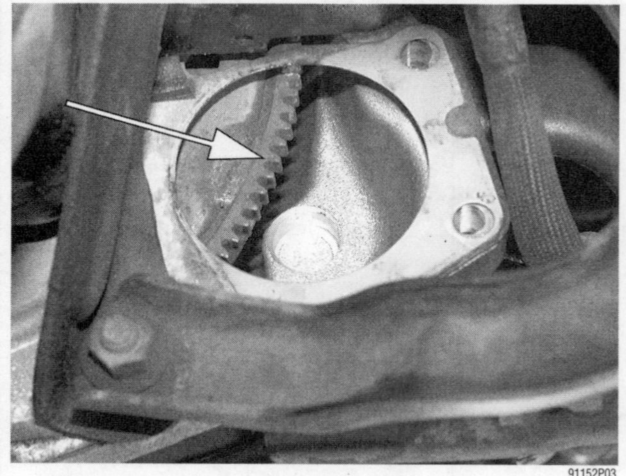

Fig. 48 After removing the starter motor, examine the teeth of the flywheel for excessive wear or damage. Repair if necessary

Fig. 49 If the old starter is going to be re-installed, check the condition of the pinion gear teeth. Replace the starter if the pinion gear shows excessive wear or damage

SENDING UNITS AND SENSORS

➡This section describes the operating principles of sending units, warning lights and gauges. Sensors which provide information to the Electronic Control Module (ECM) are covered in Section 4 of this manual.

Instrument panels contain a number of indicating devices (gauges and warning lights). These devices are composed of two separate components. One is the sending unit, mounted on the engine or other remote part of the vehicle, and the other is the actual gauge or light in the instrument panel.

Several types of sending units exist, however most can be characterized as being either a pressure type or a resistance type. Pressure type sending units convert liquid pressure into an electrical signal which is sent to the gauge. Resistance type sending units are most often used to measure temperature and use variable resistance to control the current flow back to the indicating device. Both types of sending units are connected in series by a wire to the battery (through the ignition switch). When the ignition is turned **ON**, current flows from the battery through the indicating device and on to the sending unit.

Coolant Temperature Sensor

The coolant temperature information is conveyed to the instrument panel, through the PCM, from the Engine Coolant Temperature (ECT) sensor. To test and remove the sensor, refer to Section 4. To test the gauge, perform the following testing procedure.

TESTING

1. With the ignition switch in the **OFF** position, initiate the instrument cluster self-diagnostics by pressing the **TRIP** and **RESET** buttons.
2. While holding the **TRIP** and **RESET** buttons, turn the ignition key to the **ON** position.
3. Continue to hold the **TRIP** and **RESET** buttons until the word "CODE" appears in the odometer windows (approximately 5 seconds) then release the buttons.
4. If a problem exists, the system will display Diagnostic Trouble Codes (DTC's). If no problems exist, the code 999 (End of Codes) will momentarily appear.
5. If the needle of the gauge does not move, replace the main cluster circuit board. If the needle of the gauge moves erratically, replace the cluster dial assembly. If the temperature gauge is reading inaccurately, use a DRB®, or equivalent scan tool to check the gauge calibration and adjust it if necessary.
6. If fault code 110 is displayed, replace the main cluster circuit board, check the gauge calibration using a DRB®, or equivalent scan tool, then repeat the self diagnostic procedure. If the test is okay, then stop, however, if it is not okay, replace the dial assembly.
7. If fault code 111 is displayed, check the gauge calibration and adjust, if necessary. Install the cluster assembly and retest. If the test is okay, then stop, however, if it is not okay, replace the main cluster circuit board. Check the gauge calibration and retest. If not okay, replace the dial assembly.

Temperature Gauge Calibration Points

- First Mark—Cold {C}
- Second Mark—Low Normal
- Third Mark—High Normal
- Fourth Mark—Hot {H}

Instrument Cluster Diagnostic Trouble Code (DTC) Table

- Code 110—Memory Fault In Cluster
- Code 111—Calibration Fault In Cluster
- Code 905—No CCD BUS Messages From Transmission Control Module (TCM)
- Code 920—No CCD Messages From Body Control Module (BCM)
- Code 921—Odometer Fault From BCM
- Code 940—No CCD BUS Messages From Powertrain Control Module (PCM)
- Code 999—End Of Codes

Oil Pressure Switch

TESTING

▸ See Figures 50, 51, 52, 53 and 54

The low oil pressure warning lamp will illuminate when the ignition switch is turned to the **ON** position without the engine running. The lamp also illuminates

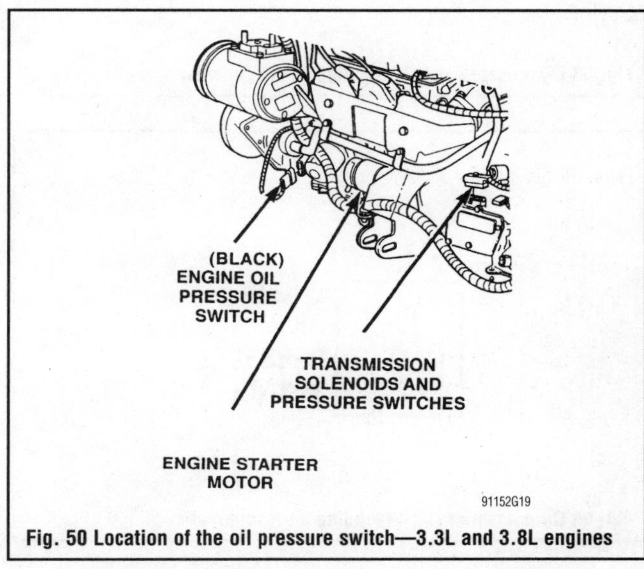

Fig. 50 Location of the oil pressure switch—3.3L and 3.8L engines

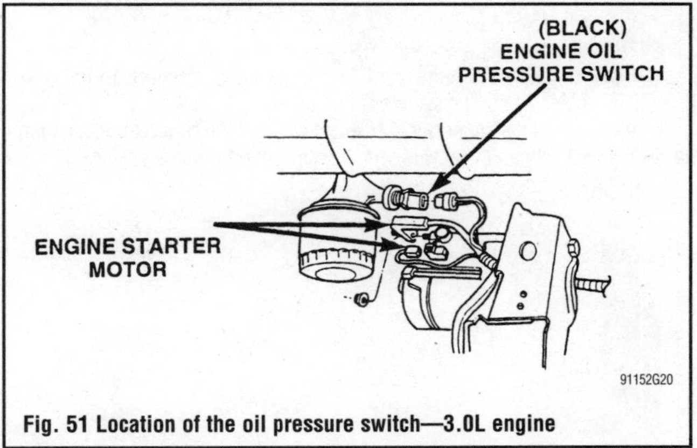

Fig. 51 Location of the oil pressure switch—3.0L engine

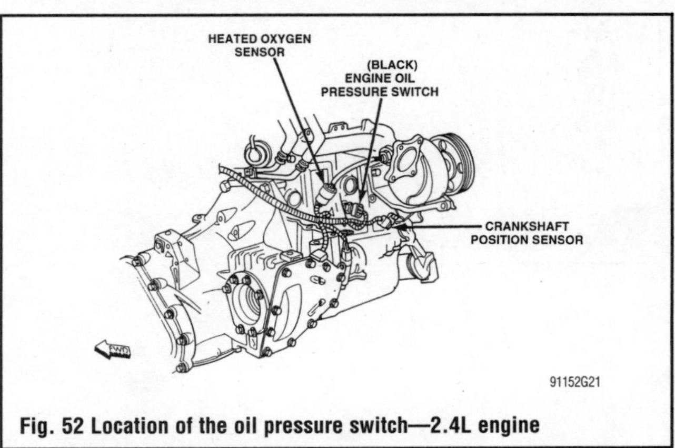

Fig. 52 Location of the oil pressure switch—2.4L engine

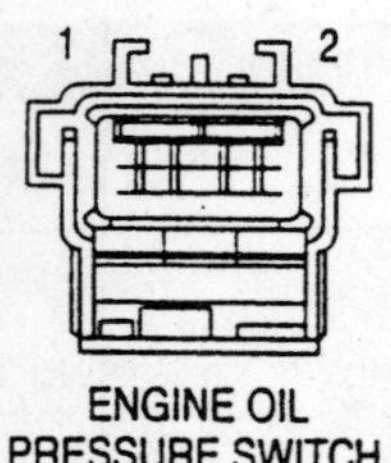

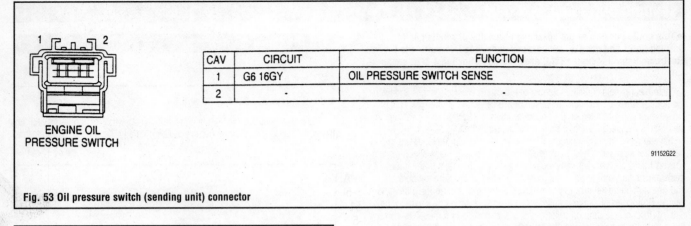

CAV	CIRCUIT	FUNCTION
1	G6 16GY	OIL PRESSURE SWITCH SENSE
2	-	-

91152G22

Fig. 53 Oil pressure switch (sending unit) connector

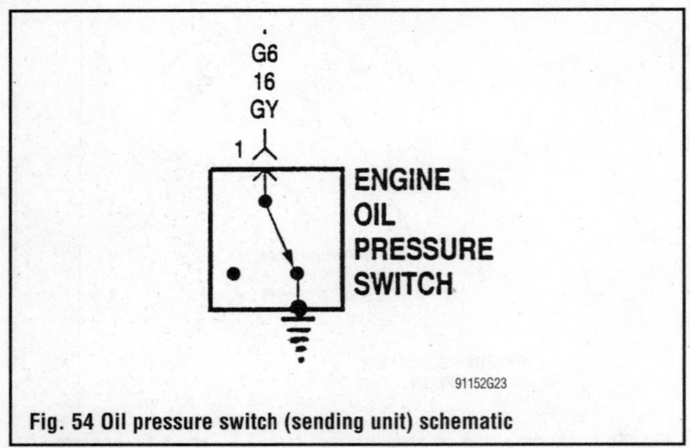

Fig. 54 Oil pressure switch (sending unit) schematic

if the engine oil pressure drops below a safe oil pressure level. To test the system, perform the following:

1. Turn the ignition switch to the **ON** position.
2. If the lamp does not light, check for a broken or disconnected wire around the engine and oil pressure sending unit switch.
3. If the wire at the connector checks out OK, pull the connector loose from the switch and, with a jumper wire, ground the connector to the engine.
4. With the ignition switch turned to the **ON** position, check the warning lamp. If the lamp still fails to light, check for a burned out lamp or disconnected socket in the instrument cluster.

REMOVAL & INSTALLATION

See Figures 50, 51 and 52

On the 2.4L engine, the oil pressure switch is located on the side of the engine block facing the firewall. On the 3.0L engine, the oil pressure switch is located on the oil filter adapter housing, next to the starter motor. On the 3.3L and 3.8L engines, the oil pressure switch is located next to the oil filter.

1. Locate the oil pressure sending unit on the engine.
2. Disconnect the negative battery cable.
3. Disconnect the pressure switch electrical harness.
4. Using a pressure switch socket, deep-well socket or wrench, loosen and remove the pressure switch from the engine.

To install:

5. Install the pressure switch into the engine and tighten securely.
6. Attach the electrical connector to the switch.
7. Connect the negative battery cable.
8. Start the engine, allow it to reach operating temperature and check for leaks.
9. Check for proper oil pressure switch operation.

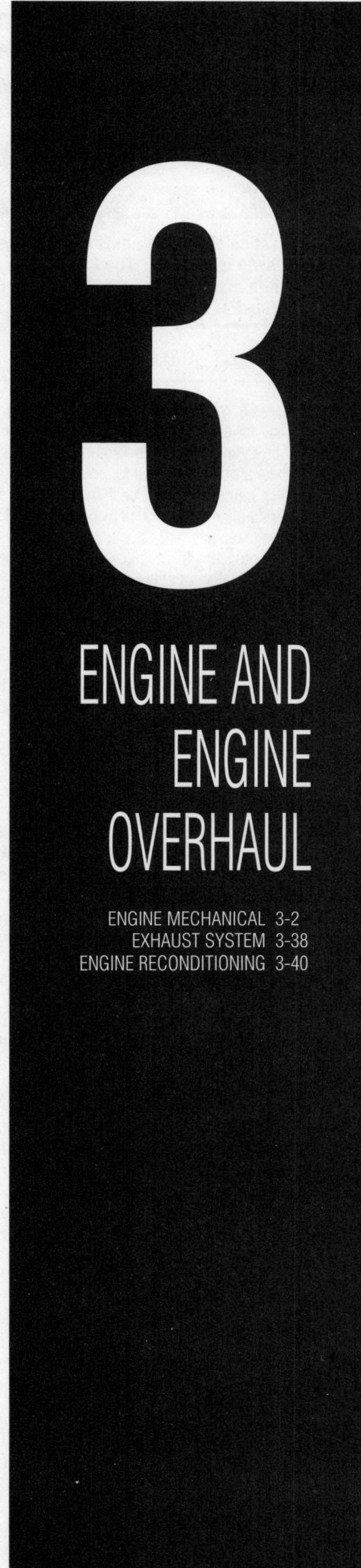

3
ENGINE AND ENGINE OVERHAUL
ENGINE MECHANICAL 3-2
EXHAUST SYSTEM 3-38
ENGINE RECONDITIONING 3-40

ENGINE MECHANICAL

Engine

CAUTION

The fuel injection system remains under pressure, even after the engine has been turned OFF. The fuel system pressure must be relieved before disconnecting any fuel lines. Failure to do so may result in fire and/or personal injury.

REMOVAL & INSTALLATION

In the process of removing the engine, you will come across a number of steps which call for the removal of a separate component or system, such as "disconnect the exhaust system" or "remove the radiator." In most instances, a detailed removal procedure can be found elsewhere in this manual.

It is virtually impossible to list each individual wire and hose which must be disconnected, simply because so many different model and engine combinations have been manufactured. Careful observation and common sense are the best possible approaches to any repair procedure.

Removal and installation of the engine can be made easier if you follow these basic points:

- If you have to drain any of the fluids, use a suitable container.
- Always tag any wires or hoses and, if possible, the components they came from before disconnecting them.
- Because there are so many bolts and fasteners involved, store and label the retainers from components separately in muffin pans, jars or coffee cans. This will prevent confusion during installation.
- After unbolting the transmission or transaxle, always make sure it is properly supported.
- If it is necessary to disconnect the air conditioning system, have this service performed by a qualified technician using a recovery/recycling station. If the system does not have to be disconnected, unbolt the compressor and set it aside.
- When unbolting the engine mounts, always make sure the engine is properly supported. When removing the engine, make sure that any lifting devices are properly attached to the engine. It is recommended that if your engine is supplied with lifting hooks, your lifting apparatus be attached to them.
- Lift the engine from its compartment slowly, checking that no hoses, wires or other components are still connected.
- After the engine is clear of the compartment, place it on an engine stand or workbench.
- After the engine has been removed, you can perform a partial or full teardown of the engine using the procedures outlined in this manual.

1. Properly relieve the fuel system pressure.
2. Disconnect the battery cables from the battery, negative cable first.
3. Detach the fuel line-to-fuel rail quick-disconnect fittings by squeezing the retainer tabs together and pulling back on the fitting.
4. Scribe the hood hinge outlines on the hood and remove the hood.
5. Remove the wiper arm and blade assemblies.
6. Remove the cowl cover from the vehicle.
7. Detach the positive lock on the wiper unit electrical connector.
8. Detach the wiper unit electrical connector from the engine compartment wiring harness.
9. Disconnect the windshield washer hose from the hose coupling inside the wiper unit.
10. Remove the drain tubes from the bottom of the wiper unit.
11. Remove the sound absorbers from the ends of the wiper unit.
12. Remove the attaching nuts securing the wiper unit to the lower windshield fence.
13. Remove the attaching bolts securing the wiper unit to the dash panel.
14. Raise the wiper unit from the weld-studs on the lower windshield fence and remove the wiper unit from the vehicle.
15. Remove the air cleaner assembly and related hoses.
16. Remove the battery cover, battery, battery tray and integral vacuum reservoir from the vehicle.
17. If equipped, block off the rear heater to the rear heater unit.
18. Drain the cooling system. Remove the upper and lower radiator hoses from the radiator.
19. Disconnect and plug the heater hoses from the engine.
20. Remove the radiator and cooling fan assembly.
21. Disconnect the transaxle shift linkage.
22. Disconnect the throttle body linkage and all vacuum hoses to the throttle body.
23. Remove accessory drive belts.
24. Remove the air conditioner compressor from the engine and mounting brackets. Keep the A/C compressor hoses connected. Position the assembly aside and secure out of the way.
25. Detach the wiring harness connector to the alternator.
26. Remove the alternator.
27. Raise and safely support the vehicle. Remove the right and left halfshaft assemblies.
28. Disconnect the starter motor wiring and remove the starter motor.
29. Drain the engine oil and remove the oil filter.
30. Remove the right and left fender inner splash shields.
31. Disconnect the exhaust pipe from the exhaust manifold.
32. Remove the front motor mount and mount bracket as an assembly.
33. Remove the rear transaxle motor mount and bracket.
34. Remove the power steering pump and mounting bracket assembly from the engine.
35. Detach, label and remove the wiring harness and connectors from the front of the engine.
36. Remove bending braces.
37. Remove the transaxle case inspection cover.
38. Mark the flexplate-to-torque converter location.
39. Remove the bolts that mount the converter to the flexplate. Attach a small C-clamp to the front bottom of the converter housing to prevent the converter from falling out of the transaxle, if necessary.
40. Lower the vehicle to the ground.
41. Disconnect the engine ground straps.
42. Attach an engine lifting hoist to the engine.
43. Remove the right engine mount assembly and left transaxle mount throughbolt.
44. Using the engine hoist, raise the engine and transaxle assembly slowly out of the vehicle. Separate the engine and transaxle. Secure the engine on an engine stand.

To install:

45. Attach the transaxle to the engine assembly.
46. With the hoist attached to the engine/transaxle assembly, lower the engine/transaxle into the engine compartment.
47. Align the engine and transaxle motor mounts to their attaching points. Install the right engine and left transaxle mount bolts.
48. Remove the engine hoist.
49. Install bending braces.
50. Install the alternator.
51. Install and reattach the wiring harness connectors on the front of the engine.
52. Install the air conditioning compressor to the engine.
53. Install the power steering pump and mounting bracket to the engine.
54. Install accessory drive belts and adjust to the proper tension, if necessary.
55. Raise and safely support the vehicle.
56. Remove the C-clamp from the torque converter housing, if utilized.
57. Align the flexplate and torque converter with the marks made previously.
58. Install the converter-to-flexplate mounting bolts. Tighten them to 55 ft. lbs. (75 Nm).
59. Install the transaxle case lower inspection cover.
60. Install right and left halfshaft assemblies.
61. Install the engine and transaxle mount and bracket assemblies.
62. Install the exhaust system to the exhaust manifolds.
63. Install the left and right fender inner splash shields.
64. Install the starter assembly and reconnect the starter motor wiring.
65. Reconnect the automatic transaxle shift linkage.
66. Lower the vehicle.
67. Reattach the fuel line quick-disconnect fitting to the fuel rail.
68. Reconnect the cooling system heater hoses to the engine.
69. Unblock the heater hoses to the rear heater unit, if equipped.
70. Secure the engine ground straps.

71. Reattach the engine and throttle body vacuum connections and wiring harness connectors.
72. Reconnect the throttle body linkage.
73. Install the radiator, cooling fan and shroud assembly.
74. Reconnect the upper and lower radiator hoses.
75. Install the battery tray, battery and battery cover into the vehicle.
76. Install the air cleaner assembly and hoses.
77. Install a new engine oil filter. Fill the crankcase to the proper oil level with the correct type of clean engine oil.
78. Refill the cooling system to the proper level with a 50/50 mixture of clean ethylene glycol antifreeze and water.
79. Install the wiper unit into the vehicle engine compartment, making sure the wiper unit is installed properly over the weld-studs on the lower windshield fence. Install and tighten the attaching nuts to the weld-studs.
80. Install and tighten the attaching bolts securing the wiper unit to the dash panel.
81. Install the sound absorbers to each end of the wiper unit.
82. Install the drain tubes to the bottom of the wiper unit and reconnect the windshield washer hose to the hose coupling inside the wiper unit.
83. Reattach the wiper unit wiring connector to the engine wiring harness.
84. Place the cowl cover onto the vehicle. Reconnect the right side windshield washer hose to the right washer nozzle located on the underside of the cowl cover.
85. Engage the retainers that secure the cowl cover to the front fender edge.
86. Install and tighten the wing nuts that secure the front of the cowl cover to the wiper module.
87. Engage the quarter turn fasteners that secure the outer ends of the cowl cover to the wiper module.
88. Install and tighten the bolts that hold the lower area of the cowl cover to the wiper module.
89. Reconnect the positive battery cable, then the negative battery cable and verify that the wiper motor and wiper linkage are in the PARK position.
90. Install the wiper arm in the correct position over the wiper arm pivot. Align the wiper arm positions as follows:
   a. Left arm should be no closer than 2.5 in. (65mm) from the lower edge of the windshield.
   b. Right arm should be no closer than 1.5 in. (40mm) from the lower edge of the windshield.
91. Install the wiper arm-to-wiper arm pivot retaining nut and tighten to 26 ft. lbs. (35 Nm).
92. Push down the wiper arm cap cover and engage the clip that secures the outside end of the cover to the wiper arm.
93. Operate the windshield wipers and ensure they work and park properly.
94. Adjust linkages.
95. Install the hood.
96. Ensure all electrical connections, cables, hoses, vacuum and fuel lines have been attached.
97. Start the engine and run until normal operating temperature is indicated. Check for leaks. Road test the vehicle.

Rocker Arm (Valve) Cover

REMOVAL & INSTALLATION

2.4L Engine

➧ **See Figure 1**

1. Disconnect the negative battery cable.
2. Label and disconnect the spark plug wires. Remove the ignition coil pack, as described in Section 2.
3. Remove the ground strap from the valve cover.
4. Disconnect the PCV and breather hoses.
5. Remove the valve cover retaining bolts.
6. Remove the valve cover from the engine.

To install:

➡**Before installing the valve cover, clean the valve cover-to-cylinder head mating surfaces. Inspect the spark plug well seals for swelling or cracking, and replace if necessary.**

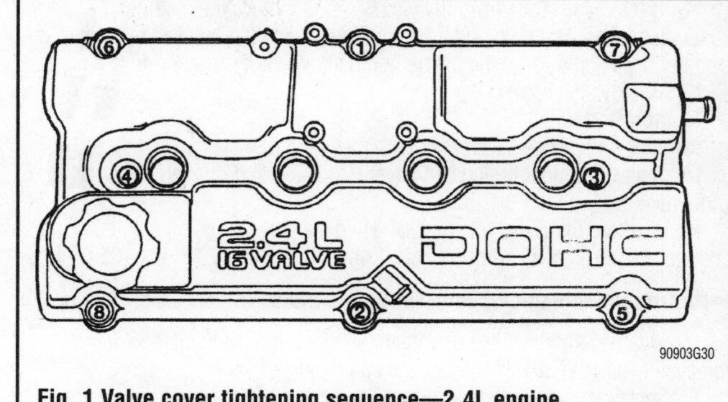

Fig. 1 Valve cover tightening sequence—2.4L engine

7. Install the new valve cover gasket.
8. Apply MOPAR® Silicone Rubber Adhesive Sealant or equivalent at the camshaft cap corners and at the top edge of the ½ round seal.
9. Place the valve cover into position on top of the cylinder head. Tighten the valve cover retaining bolts in the correct sequence as illustrated. Use the 3-step tightening sequence as follows:
   a. 40 inch lbs. (4.5 Nm)
   b. 80 inch lbs. (9 Nm)
   c. 105 inch lbs. (12 Nm)
10. Connect the PCV and breather hoses.
11. Install the coil pack assembly, as described in Section 2.
12. Connect the spark plug wires. Follow the labels to assure correct plug wire connections.
13. Attach the ground strap to the valve cover.
14. Connect the negative battery cable.

3.0L Engine

➧ **See Figure 2**

1. Properly relieve the fuel system pressure.
2. Disconnect the negative battery cable. Drain the cooling system.
3. Remove the accessory drive belts and the air conditioning compressor from its mount and support it aside. Remove the alternator and power steering pump from the brackets and move them aside.
4. Raise the vehicle and support safely. Remove the right front wheel and the right inner splash shield.
5. Remove the crankshaft pulleys and the torsional damper.
6. Lower the vehicle. Using a floor jack and a block of wood positioned under the oil pan, raise the engine slightly. Remove the engine mount bracket from the timing cover end of the engine.
7. Remove the timing belt covers.
8. Remove the timing belt as described in the unit repair section in the beginning of this manual.
9. Hold the camshaft sprocket using a suitable tool and remove the camshaft sprocket retaining bolt. Remove the sprocket and the inner timing belt cover (left bank) and/or alternator bracket (right bank).
10. Label and disconnect the spark plug wires from the spark plugs.

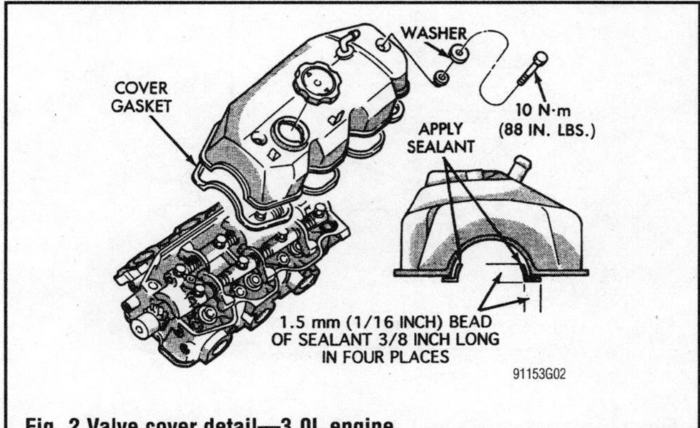

Fig. 2 Valve cover detail—3.0L engine

11. If removing the left (front) cylinder head, remove the distributor cap and spark plug wires. Mark the position of the rotor and distributor in relation to the cylinder head and remove the distributor. Remove the distributor drive adapter.
12. Remove the valve cover.

To install:

13. Install the valve cover.
14. Install the inner timing belt cover (left bank) and/or alternator bracket (right bank).
15. Position the camshaft sprocket. Hold the sprocket using a suitable tool and install the camshaft sprocket bolt. Tighten the bolt to 70 ft. lbs. (95 Nm).

➡Be sure the timing belt sprocket timing marks are aligned.

16. If removed, install the distributor, aligning the marks made during removal. Install the distributor cap and spark plug wires.
17. Install the timing belt.
18. Install the timing belt covers and the engine support bracket.
19. Install the torsional damper and tighten the bolt to 112 ft. lbs. (151 Nm). Install the crankshaft pulleys.
20. Install the inner splash shield and the right front wheel. Tighten the wheel lug nuts to 95 ft. lbs. (129 Nm). Lower the vehicle.
21. Install the alternator, power steering pump and air conditioning compressor.
22. Install the accessory drive belts and adjust to the proper tension.
23. Refill the cooling system. Since coolant can contaminate the engine oil when a cylinder head is removed, an oil and filter change is recommended.
24. Reconnect the negative battery cable.
25. Start the engine and check for leaks. Check the ignition timing.

3.3L and 3.8L Engines

➧ See Figure 3

1. Properly relieve the fuel system pressure.
2. Disconnect the negative battery cable and drain the cooling system.
3. Remove the intake manifold with the throttle body.
4. Disconnect the coil wires, sending unit wire, heater hoses and bypass hose.
5. Remove the closed ventilation system, evaporation control system and cylinder head cover(s).
6. Clean all gasket mating surfaces.

To install:

7. Install the valve cover with a new gasket. Tighten the valve cover bolts to 105 inch lbs. (12 Nm). Install the exhaust manifold crossover pipe. Tighten the bolts to 20 ft. lbs. (27 Nm) and the nuts to 15 ft. lbs. (20 Nm).
8. Install the closed ventilation system and the evaporation control system.
9. Reconnect the coil wires, sending unit wire, heater hoses and bypass hose.
10. Ensure all wiring connections, cables, hoses, vacuum and fuel lines have been reattached.
11. Refill the cooling system to the correct level.
12. Reconnect the negative battery cable. Start the engine and check for leaks.

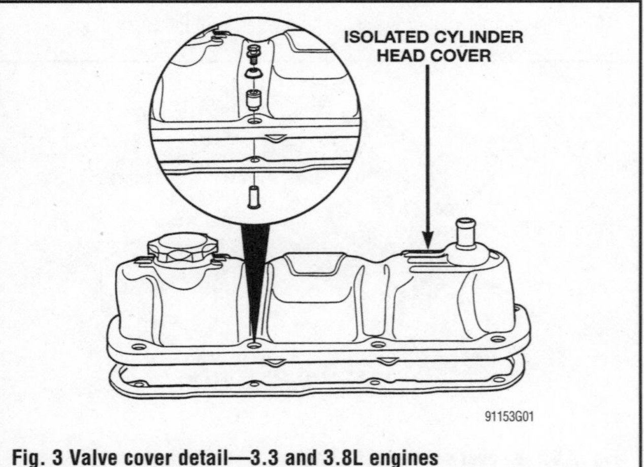

Fig. 3 Valve cover detail—3.3 and 3.8L engines

Rocker Arm/Shafts

REMOVAL & INSTALLATION

3.0L Engine

➧ See Figures 4, 5 and 6

The rocker arms and shafts are retained by the camshaft bearing journal caps. Four shafts are used, one for each intake and exhaust rocker arm assembly on each cylinder head. The hollow shafts provide a duct for lubricating oil from the cylinder head to the valve mechanisms. The rocker arms are lightweight die-cast with roller-type followers operating against the camshaft. The valve actuating end of the rocker arms are machined to retain hydraulic lash adjusters, eliminating valve lash adjustment.

1. Disconnect the negative battery cable. Disconnect and label the spark plug wires.
2. Remove the air cleaner assembly. Remove the accessory drive belts, and detach the vacuum connections.
3. Remove the valve cover.
4. Before removing the rocker arm shaft assembly, a function check can be made of the auto lash adjusters. Use the following procedure:

➡The auto lash adjusters are precision units installed in machined openings in the valve actuating ends of the rocker arms. Do not disassemble the auto lash adjusters.

a. Check the adjusters for free-play by inserting a small wire through the air bleed hole in the rocker arm.
b. VERY LIGHTLY push the auto adjuster check ball down.
c. While lightly holding the check ball down, move the rocker arm up and down to check for free-play. If there is no free-play, replace the adjuster.

5. Install Lash Adjuster Retainers MD998443 or equivalent, on the rocker arms.
6. Loosen all the camshaft bearing cap bolts. Do not remove the bolts from bearing caps. Remove the rocker arms, rocker shafts and bearing caps as an assembly.
7. Remove the bolts from the camshaft bearing caps and remove the rocker shafts and arms. Keep all parts in order. Note the way the rocker shaft, rocker arms, bearing caps and springs are mounted. The rocker arm shaft on the intake side has a 3mm diameter oil passage hole from the cylinder head. The exhaust side does not have this oil passage.
8. Inspect the rocker arm mounting area and rocker for damage. Replace if worn or heavily damaged. Check oil passages for clogging and clean, if necessary.

To install:

9. Lubricate the rocker arms and shafts with clean engine oil prior to installation.
10. Identify No. 1 bearing cap, (No. 1 and No. 4 caps are similar). Install the

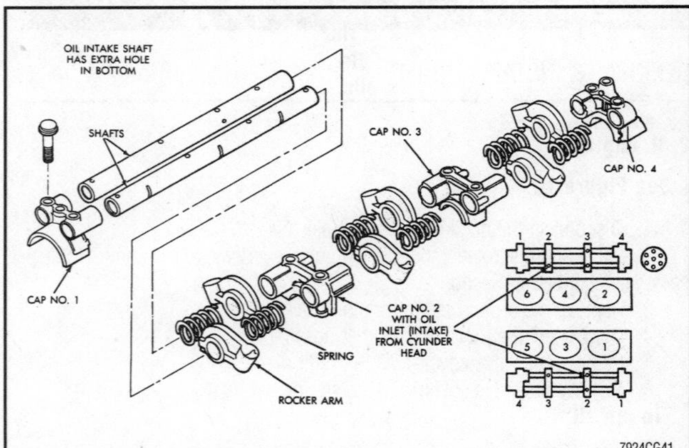

Fig. 4 Exploded view of the rocker arms and shafts. Install cap No. 2 in the correct position on the oil hole—3.0L engine

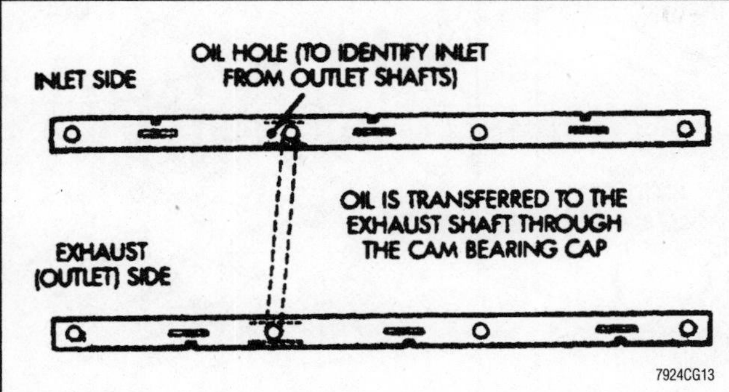

Fig. 5 Be sure to install the rocker arm shaft with the oil hole on the intake side of the head—3.0L engine

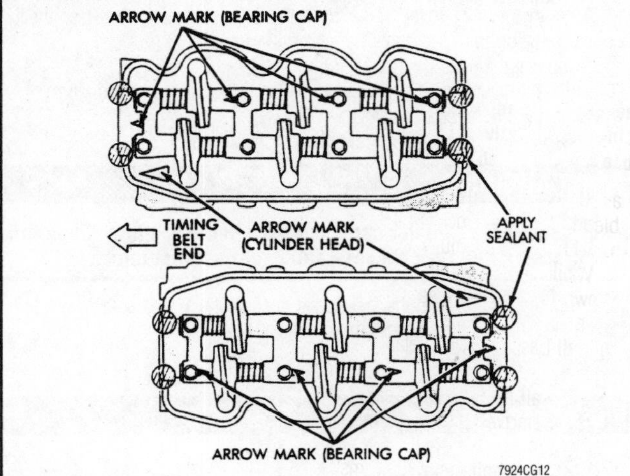

Fig. 6 Apply silicone sealant to the cylinder head in the areas indicated—3.0L engine

rocker shafts into the bearing cap with notches in proper position. Insert the attaching bolts to retain assembly.

11. Install the rocker arms, springs and bearing caps on shafts in numerical sequence.
12. Align the camshaft bearing caps with arrows (depending on the cylinder bank).
13. Install the bolts in No. 4 cap to retain assembly.
14. Apply silicone rubber sealant at bearing cap ends.
15. Install the rocker arm shaft assembly.

➡**Be sure the arrow mark on the bearing caps and the arrow mark on the cylinder heads are in the same direction. The direction of arrow marks on the front and rear assemblies are opposite to each other.**

16. Tighten the bearing caps bolts to 85 inch lbs. (10 Nm) in the following order:
    a. No. 3 cap
    b. No. 2 cap
    c. No. 1 cap
    d. No. 4 cap
17. Repeat the previous step, increasing torque to 180 inch lbs. (20 Nm).
18. Remove the lash adjuster retainers.
19. Install the distributor drive adapter, if removed.
20. Install the valve cover. Tighten the valve cover retaining bolts to 88 inch lbs. (10 Nm).
21. Reattach all vacuum connections. Install the accessory drive belts and adjust to the proper tension.
22. Install air cleaner assembly. Reconnect the spark plug wires.
23. Reconnect the negative battery cable. Run the engine and check for leaks and proper engine operation.

3.3L and 3.8L Engines

➧ **See Figure 7**

1. Disconnect the negative battery cable.
2. Remove the upper intake manifold assembly. Disconnect and label the spark plug wires.
3. Disconnect the closed ventilation system.
4. Remove the rocker arm cover and gasket.
5. Remove the four rocker shaft retaining bolts and retainers.
6. Remove the rocker arms and shaft assembly.
7. If disassembling the rocker shaft, be sure to identify all components so they can be reinstalled in their original locations.
8. Inspect the rocker arms and shafts for wear and/or damage; replace components as necessary.
9. If necessary, remove the pushrods. Identify each pushrod as it is removed, so it can be reinstalled in its original location.
10. Inspect the pushrods for wear and/or damage. Roll each pushrod on a flat surface to check for a bent condition. Replace pushrods as necessary.

To install:

11. If removed, install the pushrods in their proper locations. Lubricate the pushrod ends with clean engine oil, prior to installation. Be sure the pushrods are seated in the lifters.
12. Lubricate the rocker arms and shafts with clean engine oil, prior to installation.
13. If the rocker shaft was disassembled, reassemble making sure all components are installed in their original locations.

➡**The rocker arm shaft should be tightened slowly, starting with the center bolts. Allow 20 minutes, for tappet bleed down after installation, before engine operation.**

14. Install the rocker arm and shaft assembly, using the four retainers. Be sure the pushrods are seated in the rocker arms. Tighten the retaining bolts to 250 inch lbs. (28 Nm).
15. Install the rocker cover with a new gasket. Be sure the cover gasket mating surface is clean and smooth. Tighten the rocker cover retaining bolts to 105 inch lbs. (12 Nm).
16. Install the crankcase ventilation components and reconnect the spark plug wires.
17. Install the upper intake manifold assembly. Reconnect the negative battery cable.
18. Run the engine and check for leaks and proper engine operation.

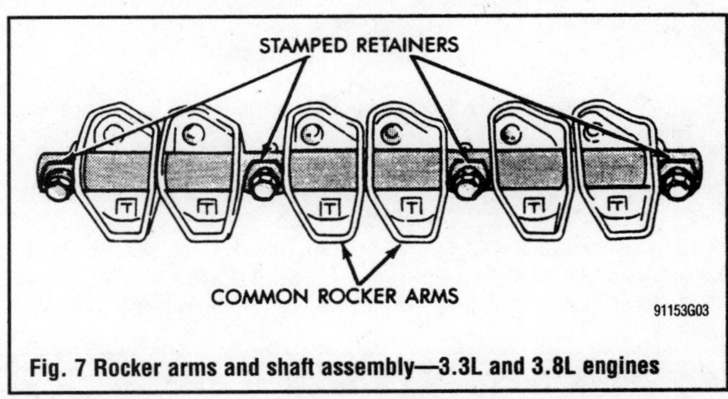

Fig. 7 Rocker arms and shaft assembly—3.3L and 3.8L engines

Thermostat

REMOVAL & INSTALLATION

2.4L Engine

➧ **See Figure 8**

1. Disconnect the negative battery cable.
2. Place a large drain pan under the radiator drain plug. Allow the cooling system to sufficiently cool down before opening the drain plug to avoid personal injury. Drain the coolant to below the thermostat level.
3. Disconnect the upper radiator hose at the thermostat housing.

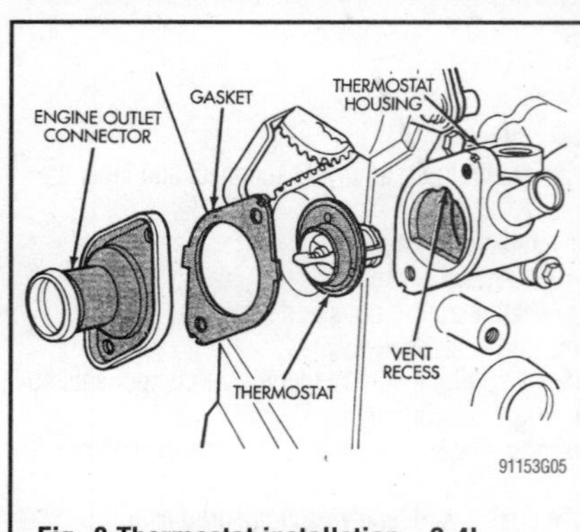

Fig. 8 Thermostat installation—2.4L engine

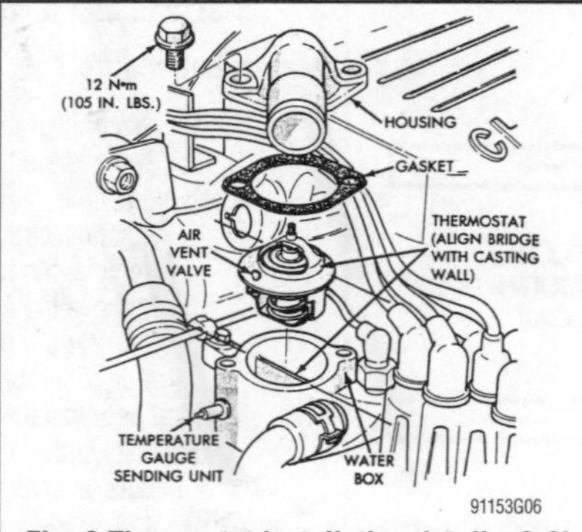

Fig. 9 Thermostat installation detail—3.0L engine

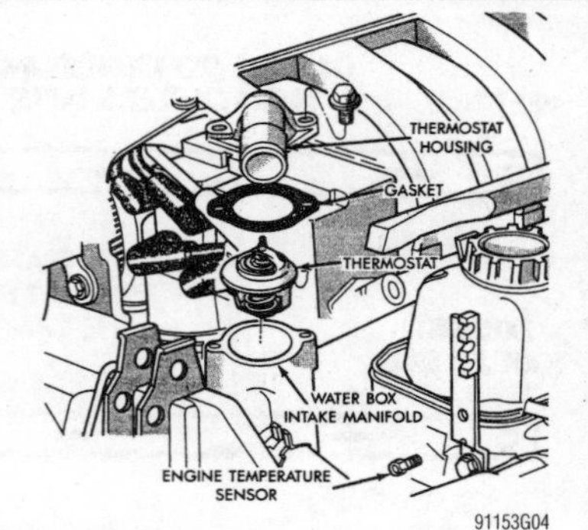

Fig. 10 Thermostat installation detail—3.3L and 3.8L engines

4. Remove the thermostat housing bolts and coolant outlet connector of the thermostat housing.
5. Remove the thermostat assembly from the vehicle and discard. Discard the old thermostat gasket.

To install:

6. Clean all gasket mating surfaces.
7. Install the new thermostat in the correct position. If equipped, align the air bleed valve on top of thermostat to the vent recess in the water box (engine side) of the thermostat housing.
8. Dip the new new gasket in clean water and install on the water box surface of the thermostat housing.
9. Install the thermostat housing over the gasket and thermostat, making sure the thermostat is in correct position.
10. Install the thermostat housing bolts and torque to 20 ft. lbs. (28 Nm).
11. Reconnect the radiator hose. Tighten the radiator hose clamp.
12. Connect the negative battery cable.
13. Fill and bleed the engine cooling system.
14. Pressure test for leaks.

3.0L, 3.3L and 3.8L Engines

See Figures 9 thru 15

1. Disconnect the negative battery cable.
2. Place a drain pan under the radiator drain and drain the cooling system to just below the thermostat level. Close the drain.
3. Remove the upper radiator hose from the thermostat housing, then remove the housing.
4. Remove the thermostat and discard the gasket.

To install:

5. Clean the housing mating surfaces.
6. Dip the new gasket in clean water and place it on the water box surface.
7. Center the thermostat on the gasket, in the water box.
8. Make certain the bolt threads are clean. Threaded bolt holes exposed to coolant are subject to corrosion and should be cleaned with a small wire brush or correct size thread-cutting tap. Install the housing, making sure the thermostat is still in the recess, and tighten the retaining bolts to 105 inch lbs. (12 Nm) for 3.0L engine or to 21 ft. lbs. (28 Nm) for 3.3L and 3.8L engines. Reconnect the upper radiator hose and tighten the hose clamp.
9. Connect the negative battery cable.
10. Fill and bleed the engine cooling system with a clean 50/50 mixture of ethylene glycol antifreeze and water.
11. Make sure the radiator is full and start the vehicle.

CAUTION

Do not remove the radiator cap once the vehicle is warm. Coolant is under pressure and may cause scalding or personal injury.

12. Run the vehicle until the thermostat opens. Check the coolant level in the overflow tank and fill if necessary.
13. Pressure test for leaks.

Intake Manifold

REMOVAL & INSTALLATION

CAUTION

The fuel injection system remains under pressure even after the engine has been turned OFF. The fuel system pressure must be relieved before disconnecting any fuel lines. Failure to do so may result in fire and/or personal injury.

2.4L Engine

See Figure 16

The 2.4L engine intake manifold is a long branch design made of cast aluminum. It is attached to the cylinder head with eight fasteners.

Fig. 11 Remove the radiator hose from the waterneck by loosening the hose clamp . . .

Fig. 12 . . . then loosen and remove the waterneck housing retaining bolts

Fig. 13 Lift the waterneck housing off of the lower intake manifold, then . . .

86723P00

Fig. 14 . . . remove the thermostat out of its mounting flange

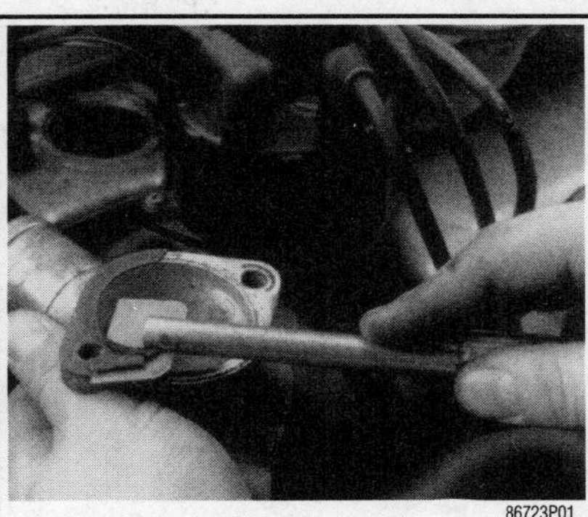
86723P01

Fig. 15 Make sure to clean the waterneck before installation

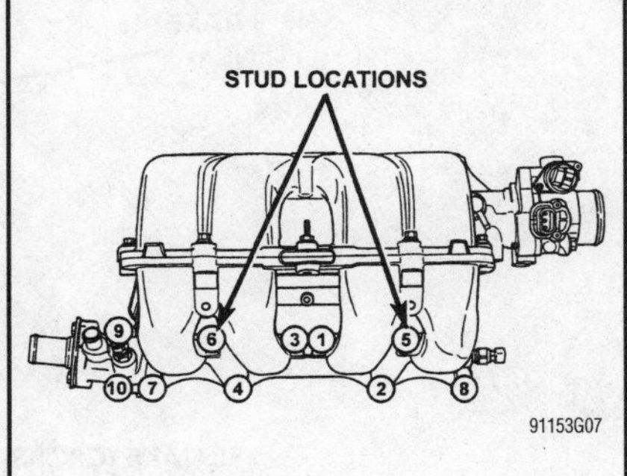

Fig. 16 Lower intake manifold mounting points—2.4L engine

1. Properly relieve the fuel system pressure.
2. Disconnect the negative battery cable.
3. Disconnect the air cleaner inlet hose from the throttle body.
4. Disconnect the throttle cable and speed control cable (if equipped) from the throttle lever and cable bracket. The cable(s) can be removed from the bracket by compressing the retaining tabs.
5. Detach the Idle Air Control (IAC) motor and Throttle Position Sensor (TPS) wiring connectors on the throttle body.
6. Disconnect the vacuum hoses from the intake plenum fittings.
7. Detach the electrical connectors from the Manifold Absolute Pressure (MAP) and Intake Air Temperature (IAT) sensors.
8. Detach the fuel line quick-disconnect fitting from the chassis fuel line tube by squeezing the retainer tabs together and pulling the fitting assembly from the fuel tube nipple. The retainer will remain on the fuel tube. Use shop towels to catch any spilled fuel.
9. Remove the EGR tube and gasket at the EGR valve.
10. Drain the cooling system and remove the accessory drive belt.
11. If necessary, remove the alternator mounting bracket.
12. Remove the mounting bolts that secure the bottom of the intake support bracket.
13. Remove the eight intake manifold fasteners and washers. Remove the intake manifold from the engine.

To install:

14. Thoroughly clean all parts. Check the mating surfaces for cracks or distortion.
15. Install a new intake manifold gasket and position the manifold on the cylinder head. Install and tighten the fasteners to 200 inch lbs. (23 Nm) starting from the center and working outward in both directions.
16. Install the mounting bolt that secures the bottom of the intake support bracket, and install the alternator mounting bracket (if removed).
17. Install the accessory drive belt and adjust to the proper tension.
18. Install the EGR gasket and tube to the EGR valve.
19. Inspect the quick-disconnect fittings for damage and repair as required. Lightly lube the fuel line tube with clean 30W engine oil. Reconnect the fuel hose quick-disconnect fitting to the chassis fuel tube. Push the quick-disconnect fitting onto the chassis fuel tube until it clicks into place. Check the connection by pulling on the fitting to insure it is locked in position.
20. Reconnect the MAP and IAT air temperature sensor wiring connectors.
21. Reconnect the vacuum hoses to the intake plenum fittings.
22. Reattach the IAC motor and TPS wiring connectors.
23. Install the throttle cables into the throttle cable bracket. Be sure to engage the retaining tabs.
24. Reconnect the throttle cable and speed control cable (if equipped) to the throttle lever.
25. Install the air cleaner inlet hose to the throttle body.
26. Refill the cooling system with a 50/50 mixture of clean, ethylene glycol antifreeze and water to the proper level.
27. Reconnect the negative battery cable.
28. Run the engine and check for leaks and proper operation.

3.0L Engine

See Figures 17 thru 34

1. Properly relieve the fuel system pressure.
2. Disconnect the negative battery cable.
3. Drain the cooling system.
4. Remove the air cleaner-to-throttle body hose.
5. Remove the throttle cable and transaxle kickdown cable.
6. Remove the Automatic Idle Speed (AIS) motor and Throttle Position Sensor (TPS) electrical connectors from the throttle body. Detach the vacuum connections from throttle body.
7. Remove the PCV and brake booster hoses from the air intake plenum.
8. Remove the ignition coil from the intake plenum.
9. Remove the EGR tube from the intake plenum (if equipped).
10. Remove the electrical connection from the coolant temperature sensor.
11. Remove the vacuum connection from the fuel pressure regulator.
12. Remove the air intake connection from the air intake plenum. Remove the fuel hose-to-fuel rail connections.
13. Remove the air intake plenum-to-manifold bolts (8), and remove the air intake plenum and gasket.

**** WARNING**

Whenever the air intake plenum is removed, cover the intake manifold properly to keep objects from entering the cylinder head.

14. Label and disconnect the fuel injector wiring harness from the engine wiring harness.
15. Disconnect the vacuum hose from the fuel rail, then remove the pressure regulator attaching bolts and remove the pressure regulator from the rail.
16. Remove the fuel rail attaching bolts and remove the fuel rail.
17. Remove the radiator hose from the thermostat housing and the heater hose from the pipe.
18. Remove the intake manifold attaching nuts and washers, and remove the intake manifold.
19. Clean the gasket material from the cylinder head and manifold gasket surface. Check for cracks or damaged mounting surfaces.

To install:

20. Install a new gasket on the intake surface of the cylinder head and install the intake manifold.
21. Install the intake manifold washers and nuts. Tighten the intake manifold attaching nuts, in sequence, to 15 ft. lbs. (20 Nm).
22. Clean the injectors and lubricate the injector O-rings with a drop of clean engine oil.
23. Place the tip of each injector into their ports. Push the assembly into place until the injectors are seated in their ports.
24. Install the fuel rail attaching bolts and tighten to 115 inch lbs. (13 Nm).
25. Install the fuel supply and return tube hold-down bolt and the vacuum crossover tube hold-down bolt. Tighten to 95 inch lbs. (11 Nm).
26. Connect the injector wiring harness to the engine wiring harness.

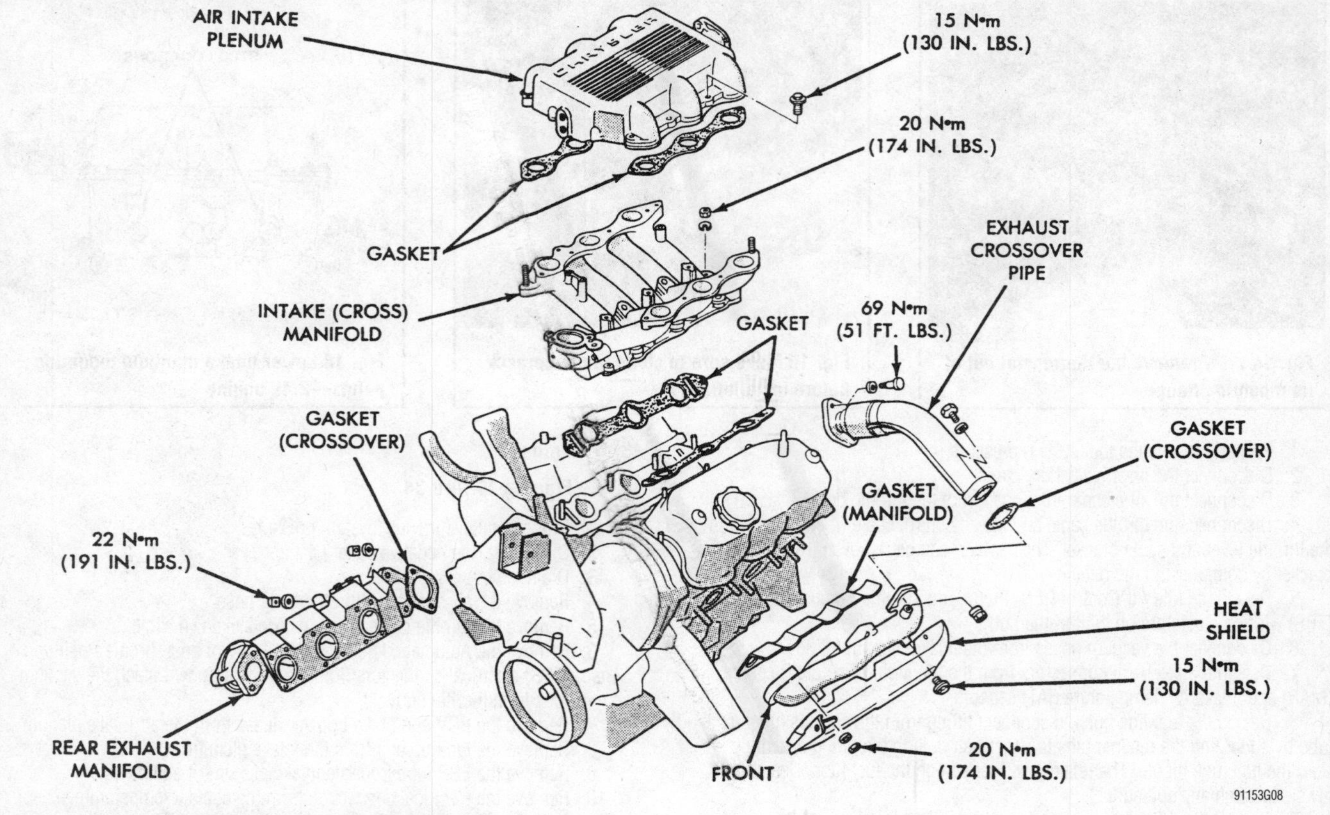

AIR INTAKE PLENUM
15 N•m (130 IN. LBS.)
20 N•m (174 IN. LBS.)
GASKET
EXHAUST CROSSOVER PIPE
INTAKE (CROSS) MANIFOLD
GASKET
69 N•m (51 FT. LBS.)
GASKET (CROSSOVER)
GASKET (CROSSOVER)
GASKET (MANIFOLD)
22 N•m (191 IN. LBS.)
HEAT SHIELD
15 N•m (130 IN. LBS.)
REAR EXHAUST MANIFOLD
FRONT
20 N•m (174 IN. LBS.)
91153G08

Fig. 17 3.0L intake and exhaust manifold exploded view

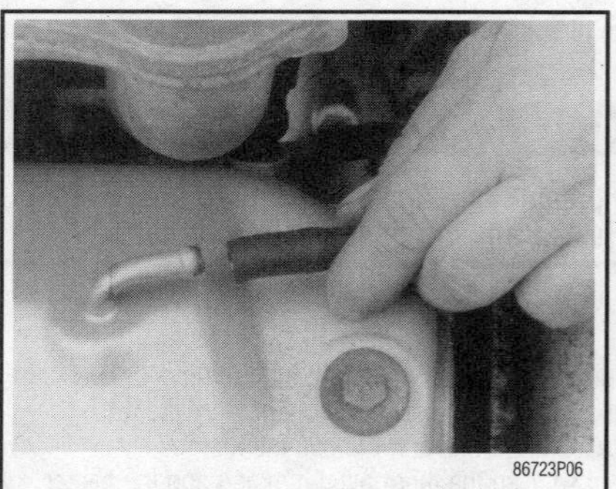
86723P06

Fig. 18 First, label and remove the PCV valve hose from the rocker arm cover and valve . . .

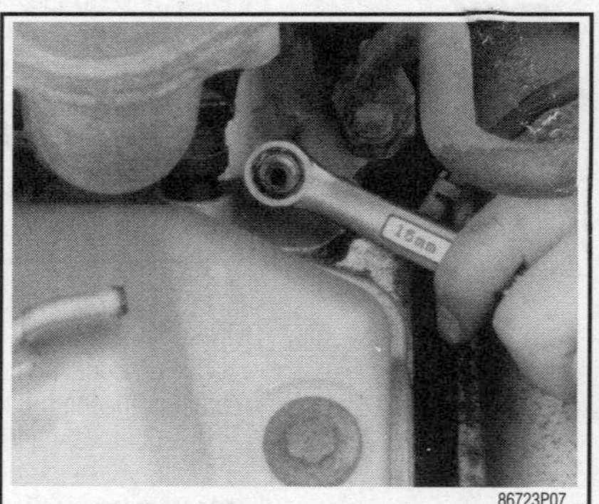
86723P07

Fig. 19 . . . then unbolt the PCV valve from the lower intake manifold

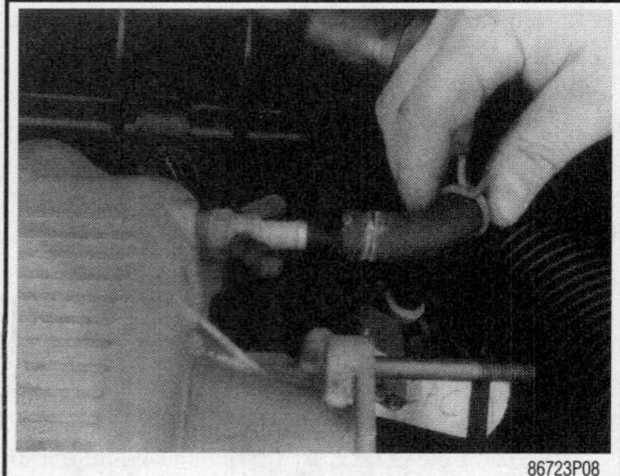
86723P08

Fig. 20 After removing the throttle body, disconnect any residual vacuum lines from the manifold plenum

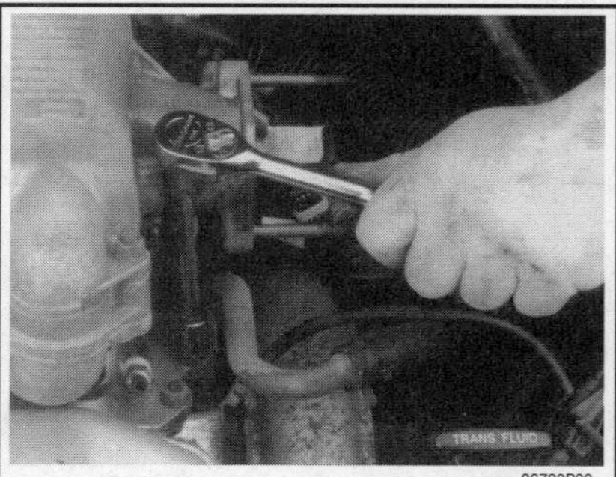

86723P09

Fig. 21 Loosen and remove the EGR tube flange-to-lower intake manifold mounting bolts . . .

86723P10

Fig. 22 . . . and remove the EGR tube itself from the intake manifold

86723P12

Fig. 23 Remove and label the vacuum hose from the front of the upper intake manifold plenum . . .

86723P22

Fig. 24 . . . then label and remove any electrical wires and connectors from the lower manifold

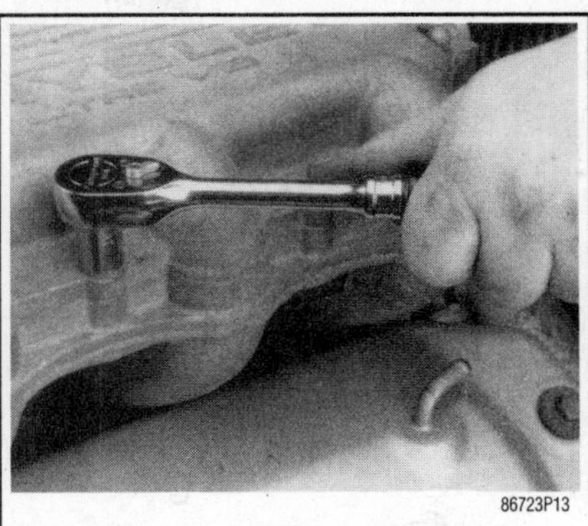
86723P13

Fig. 25 Loosen and remove the upper-to-lower manifold fasteners . . .

86723P14

Fig. 26 . . . then lift the upper intake manifold plenum from the lower manifold

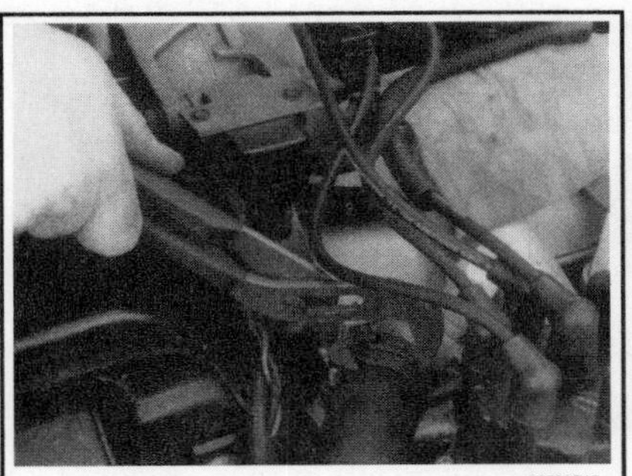
86723P15

Fig. 27 Disconnect the radiator-to-water-neck coolant hose from the waterneck and . . .

86723P17

Fig. 28 . . . disconnect the smaller coolant hose from the water box

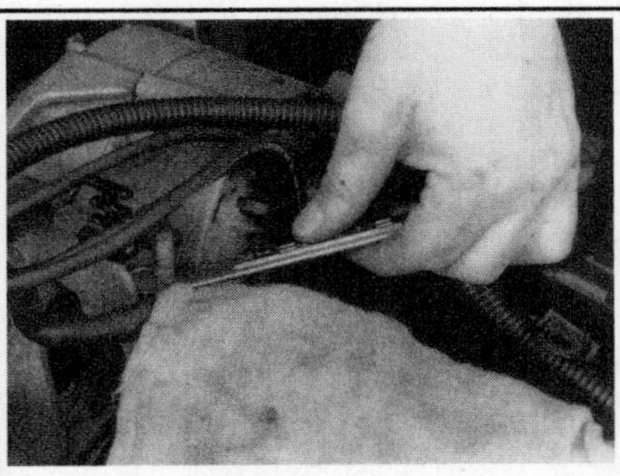
86723P19

Fig. 29 Loosen and remove the relay bracket-to-lower intake manifold attaching nut, . . .

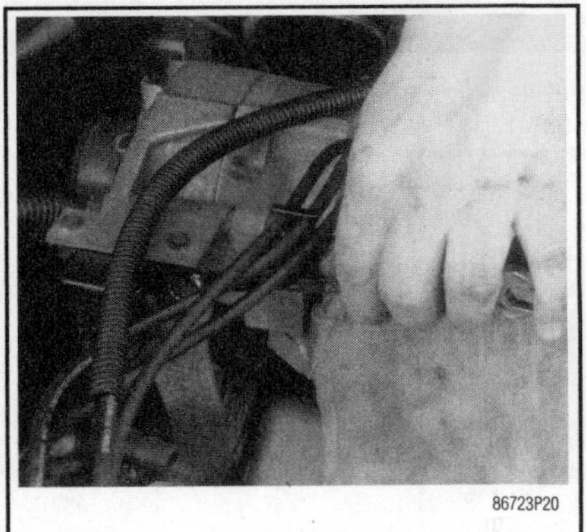
86723P20

Fig. 30 . . . unscrew the bolt and . . .

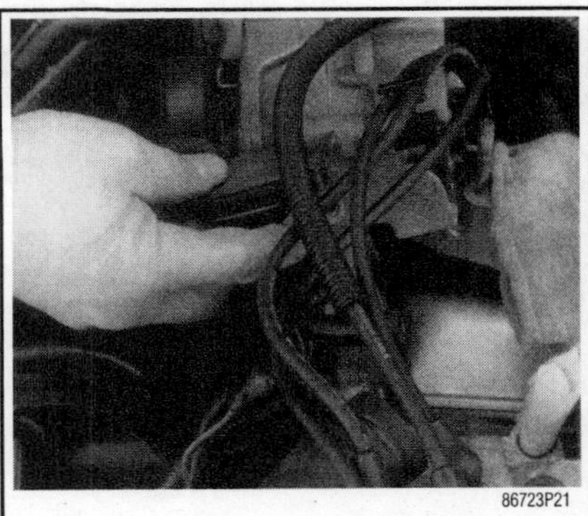
86723P21

Fig. 31 . . . remove the relay and bracket from the engine

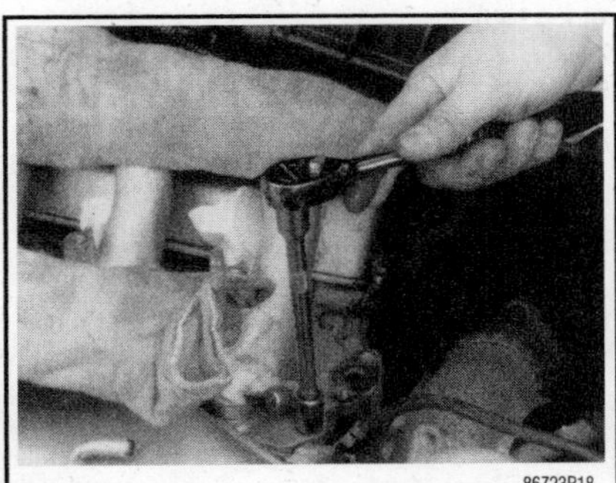
86723P18

Fig. 32 Remove the remaining lower intake manifold mounting bolts, then lift the manifold off of the engine

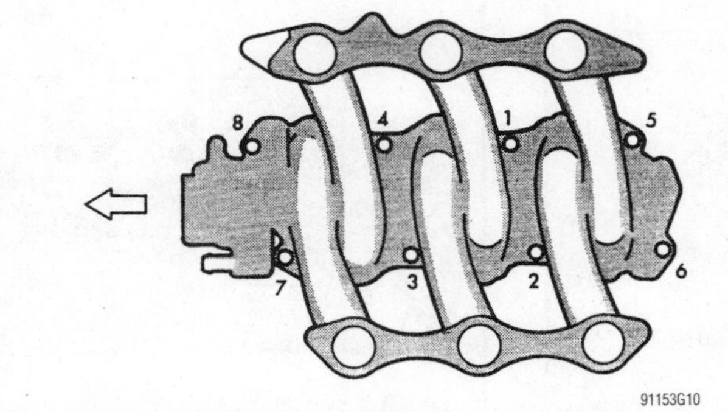

91153G10

Fig. 33 Tighten the intake manifold bolts in the correct sequence to prevent vacuum leaks—3.0L engine

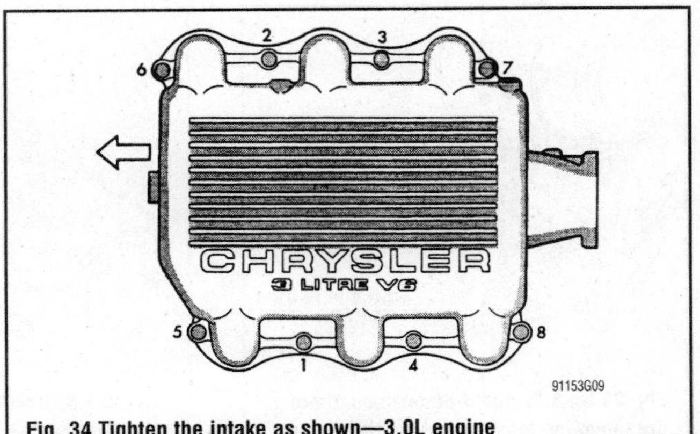

91153G09

Fig. 34 Tighten the intake as shown—3.0L engine

27. Remove the covering from the intake manifold.
28. Position the intake manifold gasket, beaded side up, on the intake manifold.
29. Place the air intake plenum in position. Install the attaching bolts and tighten, in sequence, to 115 inch lbs. (13 Nm).
30. Connect the fuel line to the fuel rail. Tighten the clamps to 10 inch lbs. (1 Nm).
31. Connect the vacuum hoses to the intake plenum.
32. Connect the electrical connection to the coolant temperature sensor.
33. Connect the EGR tube flange to the intake plenum (if equipped) and tighten to 15 ft. lbs. (20 Nm).
34. Reconnect the PCV hose and the brake booster supply hose to the intake plenum.
35. Reconnect the automatic idle speed control motor and TPS electrical connectors.
36. Connect the throttle body vacuum hoses and electrical connections.
37. Install the throttle cable and transaxle kickdown linkage.
38. Install the air inlet hose assembly.
39. Install the radiator and heater hose.
40. Refill the cooling system with a 50/50 mixture of clean, ethylene glycol antifreeze and water to the proper level.
41. Reconnect the negative battery cable. An engine oil and filter change is recommended.
42. Run the vehicle until it reaches operating temperature and check the cooling system, fuel system and engine for fuel, oil or coolant leaks.

3.3L and 3.8L Engines

See Figures 35, 36 and 37

1. Properly relieve the fuel system pressure.
2. Disconnect the negative battery cable.
3. Remove the wiper arm and blade assemblies.
4. Remove the cowl cover from the vehicle.
5. Open the hood. Detach the positive lock on the wiper unit electrical connector.
6. Detach the wiper unit electrical connector from the engine compartment wiring harness.
7. Disconnect the windshield washer hose from the hose coupling inside the wiper unit.
8. Remove the drain tubes from the bottom of the wiper unit.
9. Remove the sound absorbers from the ends of the wiper unit.
10. Remove the attaching nuts securing the wiper unit to the lower windshield fence.
11. Remove the attaching bolts securing the wiper unit to the dash panel.
12. Raise up the wiper unit from the from the weld-studs on the lower windshield fence and remove the wiper unit from the vehicle.
13. Drain the cooling system.
14. If equipped, remove the intake manifold cover.
15. Disconnect the air inlet resonator-to-throttle body hose assembly.
16. Disconnect the throttle cable and remove the wiring harness from the cable bracket.
17. Remove the Automatic Idle Speed (AIS) motor and Throttle Position Sensor (TPS) wiring connectors from the throttle body.
18. Remove the vacuum hose harness from the throttle body.
19. Remove the PCV and brake booster hoses from the air intake plenum.
20. Remove the EGR tube flange and the vacuum harness connectors from the intake plenum.
21. If equipped, detach the charge temperature sensor electrical connector. Remove the vacuum harness connectors from the intake plenum.
22. Remove the cylinder head-to-intake plenum strut.
23. Detach the MAP sensor wiring connector. Remove the engine mounted ground strap.
24. Remove the fuel hose quick-disconnect fittings from the fuel rail by pulling back on the fitting while pushing in the plastic ring. This may require the use of an open end wrench to push in the plastic ring. Be sure to plug the open fuel lines to prevent system contamination. Wrap a shop towel around the fuel hoses to absorb any fuel spill.
25. Remove the DIS coils and the alternator bracket to intake manifold bolt.
26. Remove the alternator wiring harness from the back of the upper intake manifold plenum.
27. Remove the attaching bolts and remove the upper intake manifold. Cover the intake manifold openings to prevent foreign material from entering the engine.
28. Remove the fuel tube retainer bracket bolt and fuel rail attaching bolts. Spread the retainer bracket to allow for clearance when removing the fuel tube.
29. Detach the cam sensor and coolant temperature sensor connectors.
30. Remove the injector wiring clip from the intake manifold water tube.
31. Remove the fuel rail. Be careful not to damage the fuel injector O-rings.
32. Remove the upper radiator hose, bypass hose and rear intake manifold hose.
33. Remove the intake manifold bolts and remove the manifold from the engine.
34. Remove the intake manifold seal retaining bolts and remove the manifold gasket.
35. Clean out any clogged end water passages and fuel runners.

To install:

36. Clean and dry all gasket mating surfaces.
37. Place a bead of approximately 1/4 in. (6mm) diameter of silicone sealant onto each of the four manifold-to-cylinder head gasket corners.

CAUTION

The intake manifold gasket is made of very thin material and could cause personal injury. Handle with care.

38. Carefully install the intake manifold gasket and tighten the end seal retainer bolts to 105 inch lbs. (12 Nm).
39. Install the intake manifold and eight retaining bolts and tighten to 10 inch lbs. (1 Nm). Then tighten the bolts, in sequence, to 200 inch lbs. (22 Nm).
40. When the bolts are tightened, inspect the seals to ensure that they have not become dislodged.
41. Lubricate the injector O-rings with clean oil to ease installation. Put the tip of each injector into its port and place the fuel rail in position. Install the fuel rail mounting bolts and tighten to 200 inch lbs. (22 Nm).
42. Install the fuel tube retaining bracket bolt. Tighten the bolt to 35 inch lbs. (4 Nm).

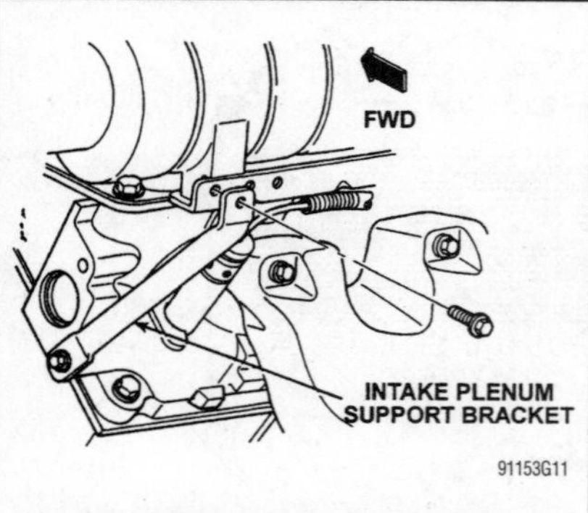

Fig. 35 On 3.3L and 3.8L engines, there are mounting brackets behind the plenum

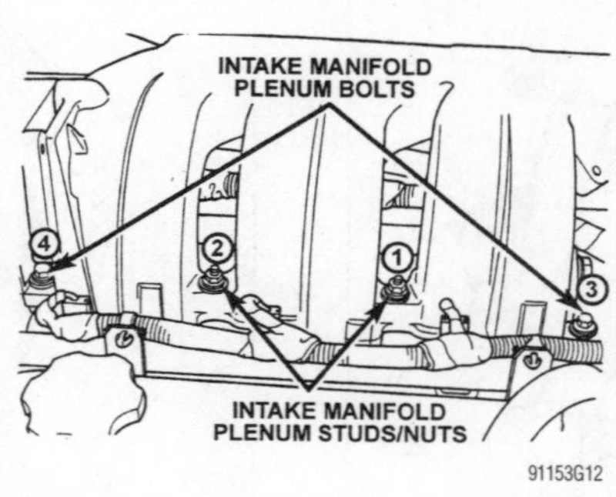

Fig. 36 3.3L and 3.8L plenum-to-manifold attachment detail

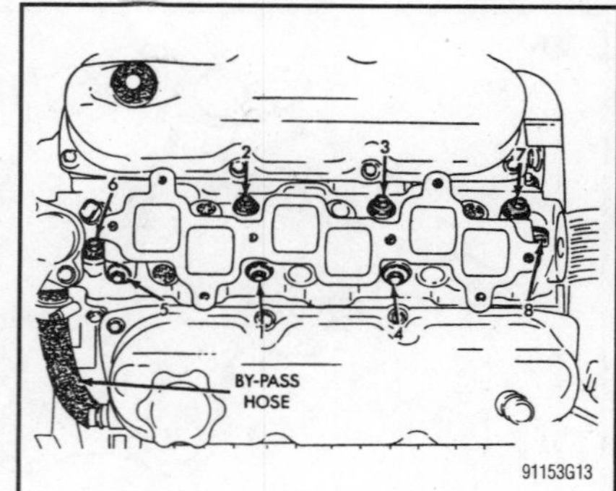

Fig. 37 Intake manifold removal—3.3L and 3.8L engines

43. Connect the cam, coolant temperature and engine temperature sensors if equipped.
44. Install the upper intake manifold with a new intake manifold gasket. Install the bolts only finger-tight. Install the alternator bracket to intake manifold bolt and the cylinder head to intake manifold strut bolts. Tighten the intake manifold mounting bolts to 250 inch lbs. (28 Nm) starting from the middle and working outward.
45. Tighten the alternator bracket and cylinder head-to-intake manifold strut bolts to 40 ft. lbs. (54 Nm).
46. Connect the alternator wiring harness to the alternator and to the rear of the intake manifold.
47. Reconnect the ground strap and MAP sensor connectors.
48. Reconnect the intake plenum vacuum harness.
49. Install a new gasket and connect the EGR tube to the intake manifold. Tighten the retaining fasteners to 200 inch lbs. (22 Nm).
50. Clip the wiring harness into the throttle cable bracket hole. Reconnect the Throttle Position Sensor (TPS) and Automatic Idle Speed (AIS) control motor wiring connectors.
51. Reconnect the throttle body vacuum harness and install the ignition coils. Tighten the ignition coil fasteners to 105 inch lbs. (12 Nm).
52. Lightly lubricate the ends of the fuel lines with clean, 30W engine oil. Reconnect the fuel hoses to the rail. Push the fittings in until they click in place. Pull back on the quick-disconnect fittings to ensure that the fuel lines are securely locked in place.
53. Reconnect the throttle cable.
54. Reconnect the fuel injector wiring harness.
55. Install the air inlet resonator to throttle body hose assembly.
56. If equipped, install the intake manifold cover.
57. Install the wiper unit into the vehicle engine compartment. Be sure the wiper unit is installed properly over the weld-studs on the lower windshield fence. Install and tighten the attaching nuts to the weld-studs.
58. Install and tighten the attaching bolts securing the wiper unit to the dash panel.
59. Install the sound absorbers to each end of the wiper unit.
60. Install the drain tubes to the bottom of the wiper unit and reconnect the windshield washer hose to the hose coupling inside the wiper unit.
61. Reconnect the wiper unit wiring connector to the engine wiring harness.
62. Place the cowl cover onto the vehicle. Reconnect the right side windshield washer hose to the right
washer nozzle located on the underside of the cowl cover.
63. Engage the retainers that secure the cowl cover to the front fender edge.
64. Install and tighten the wing nuts that secure the front of the cowl cover to the wiper module.
65. Engage the quarter turn fasteners that secure the outer ends of the cowl cover to the wiper module.
66. Install and tighten the bolts that hold the lower area of the cowl cover to the wiper module.
67. Reconnect the negative battery cable and verify that the wiper motor and wiper linkage are in the PARK position.
68. Install the wiper arm in correct position over the wiper arm pivot.
69. Install the wiper arm-to-wiper arm pivot retaining nut and tighten to 26 ft. lbs. (35 Nm).
70. Push down the wiper arm cap cover and engage the clip that secures the outside end of the cover to the wiper arm.
71. Reconnect the negative battery cable.
72. Operate the windshield wipers and ensure they work and park properly.
73. Refill the cooling system with a 50/50 mixture of clean, ethylene glycol antifreeze and water. Bleed the cooling system.
74. Start the engine. Check for leaks and proper engine operation.

Exhaust Manifold

REMOVAL & INSTALLATION

2.4L Engine

➧ **See Figure 38**

1. Disconnect the negative battery cable.
2. Raise and safely support the vehicle.

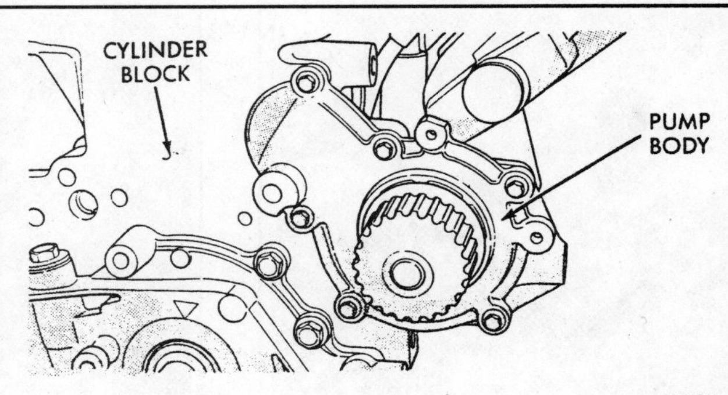

Fig. 38 Tighten the exhaust manifold bolts in the sequence shown to prevent exhaust leaks—2.4L engine (Removal should be in reverse order)

3. Disconnect the exhaust pipe from the exhaust manifold at the flex joint. Apply penetrating oil on the exhaust manifold-to-exhaust pipe flange bolts to aid in removal. It may be necessary to remove the entire exhaust system.
4. Detach the oxygen sensor wiring connector at the rear of the exhaust manifold.
5. Remove the eight manifold attaching bolts and remove the manifold from the cylinder head.

To install:

6. Thoroughly clean all parts. Discard the gasket (if equipped) and clean all gasket surfaces of the manifold and cylinder head. Test the manifold gasket surface for flatness with a straightedge and feeler gauge. The surface must be flat within 0.006 inches per foot (0.15mm per 30cm) of manifold length. Inspect the manifold for cracks or distortion. Replace if necessary.
7. Install the manifold to the vehicle with a new gasket. DO NOT APPLY SEALER.
8. Install the eight manifold bolts and tighten, starting at the center and working outward in both directions, to 17 ft. lbs. (23 Nm).
9. Reconnect the oxygen sensor wiring connector.
10. Reconnect the exhaust pipe to the exhaust manifold and tighten the fasteners to 20 ft. lbs. (28 Nm).
11. Reconnect the negative battery cable. Start the engine and allow it to idle while inspecting the manifold for exhaust leaks.

3.0L Engine

➧ **See Figures 17 and 39 thru 46**

1. Disconnect the negative battery cable. Raise and safely support the vehicle.
2. Disconnect the exhaust pipe from the rear exhaust manifold, at the flex joint.
3. Remove the rear exhaust manifold heat shield.
4. Remove the rear exhaust manifold-to-cylinder head nuts and remove the exhaust manifold.
5. Remove the crossover pipe-to-exhaust manifold attaching bolts.
6. Lower the vehicle and remove the heat shield from the front exhaust manifold.
7. Remove the bolts fastening the crossover pipe to the front exhaust manifold. Remove the front exhaust manifold-to-cylinder head nuts and remove the exhaust manifold.
8. Clean the gasket mounting surfaces. Inspect the manifolds for cracks, flatness and/or damage.

To install:

➡Install the gasket with the numbers 1–3–5 embossed on the top on the rear bank and those with the numbers 2–4–6 on the front (radiator side) bank.

9. Raise and safely support the vehicle.
10. Install the new gasket and rear exhaust manifold to the cylinder head. Install and tighten the rear exhaust manifold-to-cylinder head nuts to 175 inch lbs. (20 Nm).

91153P53

Fig. 39 To remove an exhaust manifold, unbolt the heat shield . . .

91153P50

Fig. 40 . . . and remove it to access the manifold fasteners

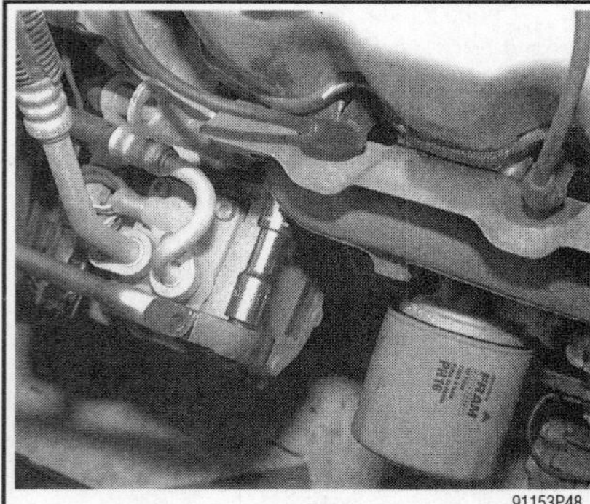
91153P48

Fig. 41 Use an extension if necessary to access the manifold fasteners

91153P49

Fig. 42 In addition to removing the exhaust pipe from the manifold, be sure to remove the crossover pipe-to-exhaust manifold fasteners

91153P44

Fig. 43 With everything unfastened, the manifold can be removed from the cylinder head

91153P46

Fig. 44 Always use a new gasket to prevent leakage (Note how the exhaust manifold gasket doubles as a heat shield)

11. Attach the exhaust pipe to the exhaust manifold and tighten the shoulder bolts to 20 ft. lbs. (28 Nm)
12. Attach the crossover pipe to the exhaust manifold and tighten the bolts to 51 ft. lbs. (69 Nm).
13. Install the rear exhaust manifold heat shield and tighten the heat shield mounting fasteners to 130 inch lbs. (15 Nm).
14. Connect the EGR tube to the rear manifold, if removed, and reconnect the oxygen sensor.
15. Lower the vehicle.
16. Install the front exhaust manifold and attach the exhaust crossover pipe. Tighten the bolts to 51 ft. lbs. (69 Nm).
17. Install the front exhaust manifold heat shield and tighten the bolts to 130 inch lbs. (15 Nm).
18. Reconnect the negative battery cable. Start the engine and check for exhaust leaks.

3.3L and 3.8L Engines

See Figures 47, 48 and 49

1. Disconnect the negative battery cable.
2. Remove the accessory drive belt.
3. Remove the alternator.
4. Raise and safely support the vehicle.
5. Disconnect the exhaust pipe from the rear exhaust manifold at the flex joint.
6. Separate the EGR tube from the exhaust manifold and disconnect the oxygen sensor.
7. Remove the alternator/power steering support strut.
8. Remove the crossover pipe attaching bolts to the rear exhaust manifold.
9. Remove the rear exhaust manifold heat shield.

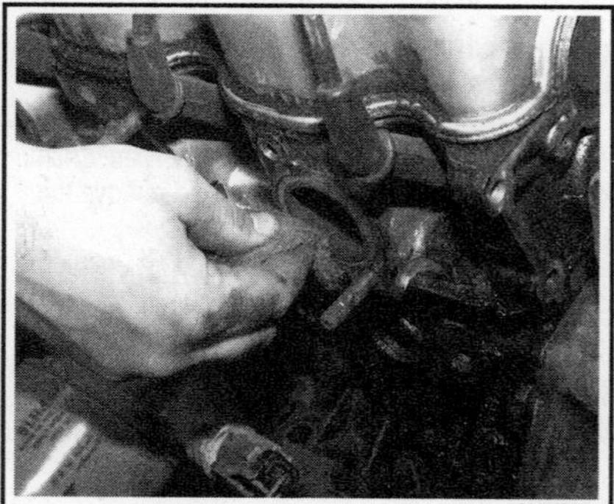
91153P42

Fig. 45 Before installing the exhaust manifold, clean both the cylinder head . . .

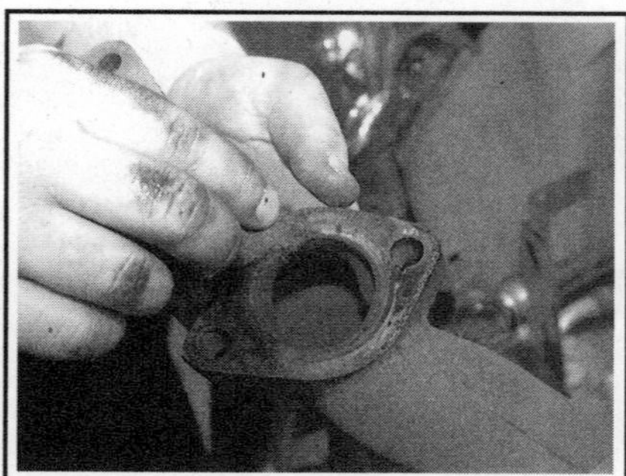
91153P41

Fig. 46 . . . and manifold mating surfaces, to ensure a clean surface for the new gaskets to seal properly

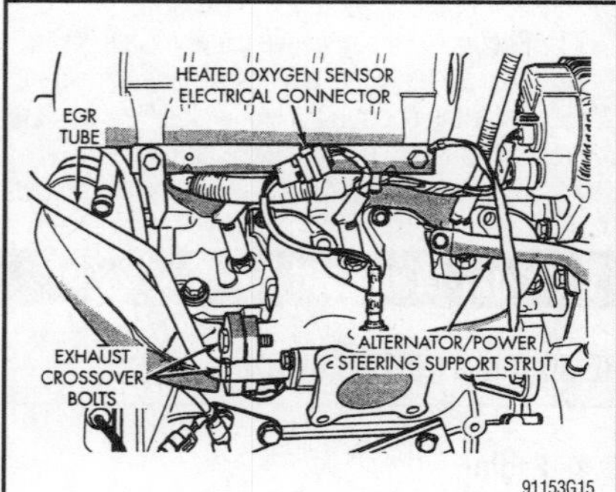

91153G15

Fig. 47 Rear exhaust manifold mounting detail—3.3 and 3.8L engines

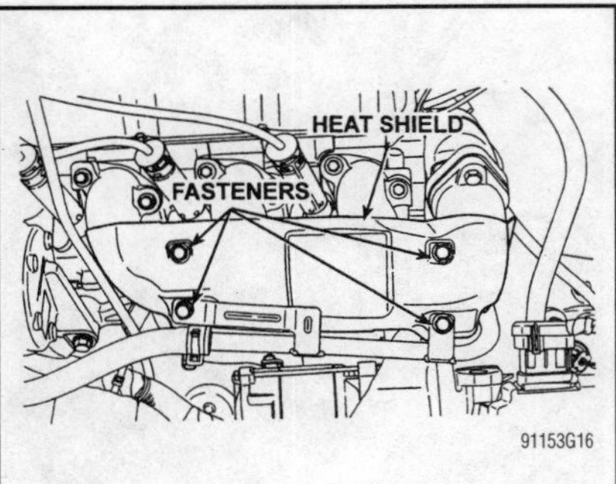

Fig. 48 Front exhaust manifold mounting detail—3.3 and 3.8L engines

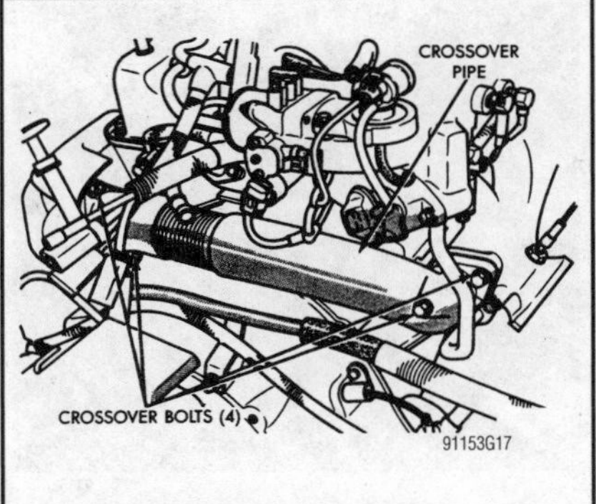

Fig. 49 Crossover pipe mounting detail—3.3 and 3.8L engines

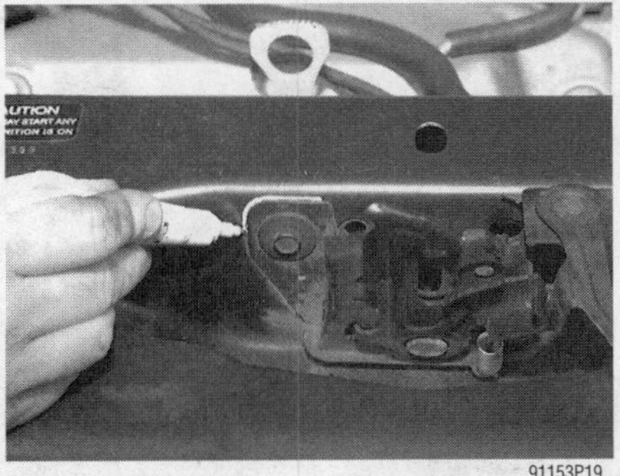

Fig. 50 Before removing the hood latch, mark it's location on the crossmember with a paint marker or other tool

10. Remove the rear manifold-to-cylinder head nuts, then remove the rear manifold.
11. Lower the vehicle and remove the front exhaust manifold heat shield.
12. Remove the front exhaust manifold crossover pipe bolts.
13. Remove the front manifold-to-cylinder head nuts, then remove the front exhaust manifold.
14. Clean the mounting surfaces. Inspect the manifolds for cracks or other damage. With a straightedge and feeler gauge, check for flatness. Standard is 0.004 in. (0.1mm) with 0.008 in. (0.2mm) out-of-flatness the service limit. If distorted beyond these specifications, replace the manifold.

To install:

15. Raise and safely support the vehicle.
16. Install the new gasket and rear manifold. Tighten the manifold-to-cylinder head nuts to 17 ft. lbs. (23 Nm).
17. Install the rear exhaust manifold heat shield. Tighten the heat shield mounting fasteners to 17 ft. lbs. (23 Nm).
18. Install the alternator unit.
19. Connect the exhaust pipe to the exhaust manifold and tighten the bolt to 20 ft. lbs. (28 Nm).
20. Connect the crossover pipe to the rear manifold and tighten the bolts to 25 ft. lbs. (33 Nm).
21. Connect the oxygen sensor.
22. Connect the EGR tube to the exhaust manifold and install the alternator/power steering support strut.
23. Lower the vehicle.
24. Install the new gasket and front exhaust manifold to the cylinder head. Tighten the exhaust manifold-to-cylinder head nuts to 17 ft. lbs. (23 Nm).
25. Connect the crossover pipe to the front manifold.
26. Install the front manifold heat shield. Tighten the heat shield mounting fasteners to 200 inch lbs. (23 Nm).
27. Install the accessory drive belt.
28. Reconnect the negative battery cable.
29. Start the engine and check for exhaust leaks.

Radiator

REMOVAL & INSTALLATION

▸ See Figures 50 thru 61

1. Disconnect the negative battery cable.

✱✱ CAUTION

Do not remove the radiator cap or drain with the cooling system hot and under pressure or serious personal injury can occur from hot pressurized coolant.

2. Place a drain pan under the radiator drain. Open the radiator drain plug and allow the coolant to drain.
3. Remove the air intake resonator from the air cleaner assembly.
4. Remove the Coolant Recovery System (CRS) overflow tank filler neck hose.
5. Disconnect the cooling fan electrical connector located on the left side of the cooling fan module.
6. Remove the CRS overflow tank mounting screw from the upper radiator crossmember.
7. Remove the upper radiator-to-crossmember mounting screws.
8. If equipped, disconnect the engine block heater wiring connector.
9. Remove the upper radiator crossmember.
10. Remove the entire air cleaner assembly.
11. Disconnect and plug the automatic transaxle oil cooler lines from the radiator.
12. Disconnect the upper and lower radiator hoses from the radiator. Remove the lower radiator hose clip from the cooling fan module.
13. Remove the A/C condenser mounting fasteners and separate the A/C condenser from the radiator. Be sure the condenser is supported in position.

Fig. 51 Once the hood latch is match-marked, remove it from the crossmember (without disconnecting the cable) and set it aside

Fig. 52 Remove the grill extension . . .

Fig. 53 . . . and the upper radiator-to-crossmember bolts, then . . .

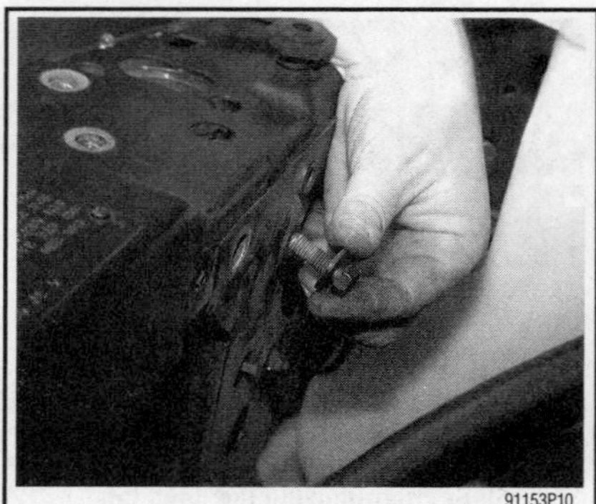
91153P10
Fig. 54 . . . unbolt the crossmember . . .

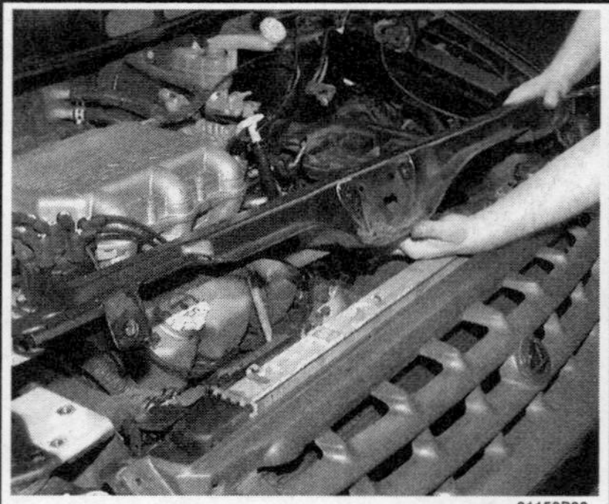
91153P08
Fig. 55 . . . and lift it from the front of the vehicle

91153P29
Fig. 56 Spring-type hose clamps can be removed with pliers

91153P35
Fig. 57 Worm-type hose clamps can be removed with a screwdriver, or in some cases, a small socket

91153P34
Fig. 58 Special tools are available to make removing hoses from connections easier

91153P33
Fig. 59 To avoid spilling residual coolant, it's a good idea to plug the radiator connections and hoses

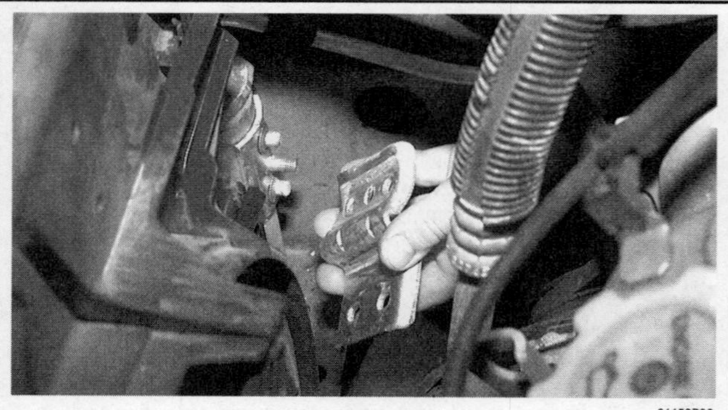
91153P36
Fig. 60 Unbolt the lower radiator mounting brackets

91153P28
Fig. 61 Once all of the components are removed or set aside, the radiator can be removed from the vehicle

14. Remove the A/C filter/drier mounting bracket, 2 mounting bolts to the cooling fan module and 2 mounting nuts to the filter/drier. Remove the mounting bracket.
15. Carefully lift the radiator out of the engine compartment. Be careful not to damage the radiator cooling fins or water tubes during removal.

To install:

16. Be sure the air seals are properly positioned before installation of the radiator. Lower the radiator into position and seat the radiator with the rubber isolators into the mounting holes provided.
17. Install the A/C filter/drier and mounting bracket onto the cooling fan module. Install the bracket mounting fasteners.
18. Install the A/C condenser to the radiator.
19. Unplug and connect the transaxle oil cooler lines to the radiator.
20. Connect the upper and lower radiator hoses to the radiator.
21. Connect the CRS overflow tank filler neck hose to the radiator.
22. Reconnect the cooling fan motor electrical connector.
23. Install the entire air cleaner assembly.
24. Install the upper radiator crossmember.
25. Install the upper radiator mounting screws and torque to 105 inch lbs. (12 Nm).
26. Reconnect the engine block heater electrical connector, if equipped.
27. Install the CRS overflow tank mounting screw to the upper radiator crossmember. Torque the screw to 18 inch lbs. (2 Nm).
28. Install the air intake resonator.
29. Refill the cooling system with a 50/50 mixture of clean, fresh ethylene glycol antifreeze and water to the proper level.
30. Reconnect the negative battery cable.
31. Start the engine and run until it reaches normal operating temperature, then check the coolant level and the automatic transmission fluid level. Add fluids, if necessary.

Electric Cooling Fan

REMOVAL & INSTALLATION

See Figures 50 thru 55, and 62, 63, 64

The electric cooling fan assembly cannot be disassembled. If the fan is warped, cracked or otherwise damaged, it must be replaced as an assembly.

1. Disconnect the negative battery cable.
2. Raise and safely support the vehicle.
3. Remove the radiator outlet hose from the radiator hose retaining clip and remove the retaining clip from the shroud.
4. If equipped, remove the lower auxiliary transaxle cooler lines from the retaining clips on the cooling fan module shroud.
5. Lower the vehicle.
6. Remove the entire air cleaner assembly and the air intake resonator.
7. Disconnect the fan motor electrical connector(s).
8. Remove the Coolant Recovery System (CRS) mounting screw from the upper radiator crossmember.
9. Disconnect the mounts to the upper radiator from the radiator crossmember.
10. Remove the upper radiator crossmember.
11. Remove the cooling fan module mounting screws.
12. If equipped, remove the upper auxiliary transaxle cooler lines from the retaining clips on the cooling fan module shroud.
13. Disconnect and plug the transaxle oil cooler line from the radiator fitting on the lower left side.
14. Raise and safely support the vehicle.
15. Remove the filter/drier, cooling fan module and radiator mounting bolts located on the lower right of the cooling fan module.
16. Lower the vehicle. Remove the upper cooling fan module-to-radiator retaining clips.
17. Remove the cooling fan module from the vehicle.

To install:

18. Install the cooling fan module assembly into the retaining clips of the radiator.
19. Install the upper cooling fan module-to-radiator retaining clips.
20. Raise and safely support the vehicle.
21. Install the filter/drier, cooling fan module and radiator mounting bolts located on the lower right of the cooling fan module.
22. Lower the vehicle. Reconnect the transaxle cooler line to the radiator fitting on the lower left side.
23. If equipped, install the upper auxiliary transaxle cooler lines to the retaining clips on the cooling fan module shroud.
24. Install the cooling fan module retaining screws and torque to 105 inch lbs. (12 Nm).
25. Install the entire air cleaner assembly.
26. Install the upper radiator crossmember and connect the upper radiator mounts to the crossmember. Torque the mounting fasteners to 105 inch lbs. (12 Nm).
27. Install the Coolant Recovery System (CRS) mounting screw to the upper radiator crossmember. Torque the mounting screw to 18 inch lbs. (2 Nm).
28. Reconnect the fan motor electrical connector.
29. Install the air intake resonator to the air cleaner assembly.
30. Raise and safely support the vehicle.
31. If equipped, install the lower auxiliary transaxle cooler lines to the retaining clips on the cooling fan module shroud.
32. Install the radiator outlet hose retainer clip to the fan module shroud.
33. Install the radiator outlet hose to the retaining clip. Lower the vehicle.
34. Reconnect the negative battery cable. Run the engine and check for proper cooling fan operation when the engine reaches operating temperature.

TESTING

When diagnosing an inoperative cooling fan it may be necessary to use a diagnostic scan tool to monitor engine coolant temperature and the engine control computer.

1. Perform a visual inspection of the cooling fan. If the fan does not turn with ease, the fan motor is seized and needs to be replaced.
2. Check all the fuses and fusible links related to the cooling fan circuit.
3. Check the integrity of the electrical connections related to the cooling fan circuit.
4. Check the cooling fan motor.
5. Check the relays associated with the cooling fan circuit.
6. Using a scan tool, determine if the engine control computer is calling for the fan to activate.

Cooling Fan Motor

1. Disconnect the negative battery cable.
2. Disengage the cooling fan motor connector.
3. Identify and label the ground and the power terminals of the cooling fan connector using the wiring diagrams provided.
4. Using jumper leads with a fuse in series, apply battery voltage to the appropriate terminals of the cooling fan.

CAUTION

Keep away from the fan blades when performing this procedure.

5. The cooling fan should operate. If not, replace the cooling fan.

If the cooling fan functions properly during this test, proceed to the cooling fan relay test.

Cooling Fan Relay

See Figure 65

1. Turn the ignition **OFF**.
2. Remove the relay.
3. Locate the two terminals on the relay, which are connected to the coil windings. Check the relay coil for continuity. Connect the common meter lead to terminal 85 and positive meter lead to terminal 86. There should be continuity. If not, replace the relay.

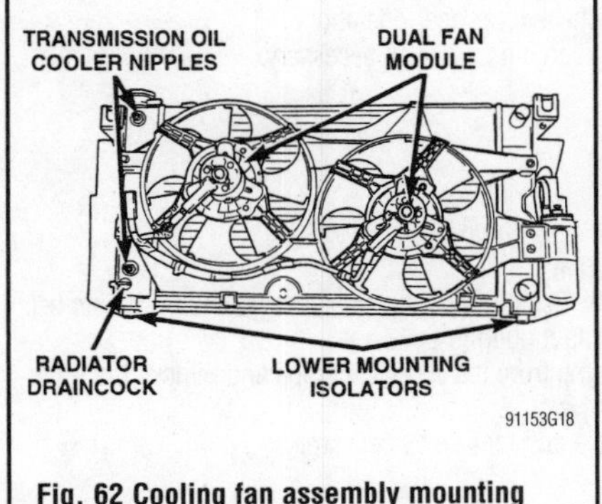

Fig. 62 Cooling fan assembly mounting points

Fig. 63 Unplug the connectors that supply power to the cooling fan

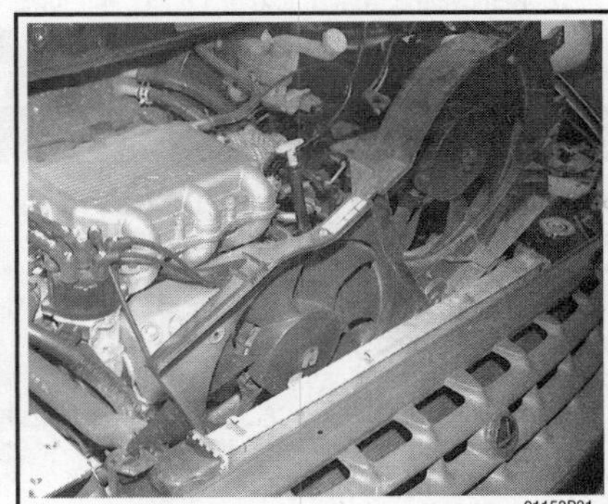

Fig. 64 Removing the cooling fan assembly

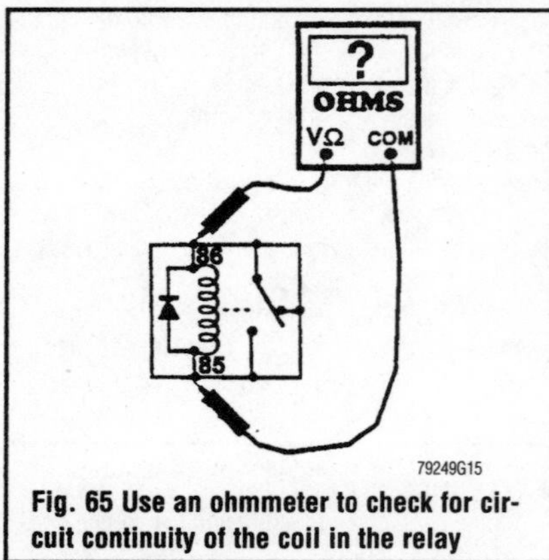

Fig. 65 Use an ohmmeter to check for circuit continuity of the coil in the relay

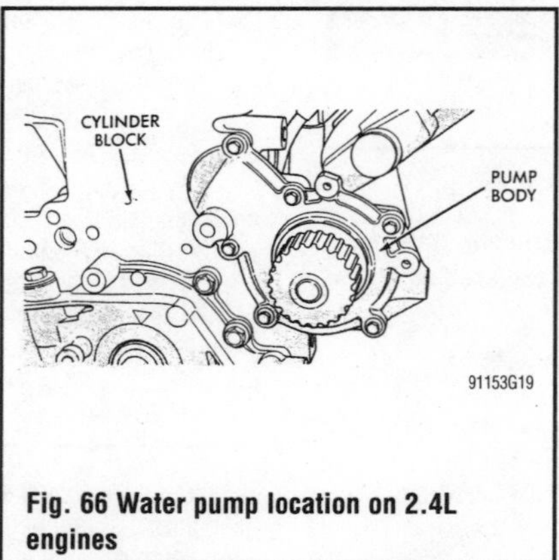

Fig. 66 Water pump location on 2.4L engines

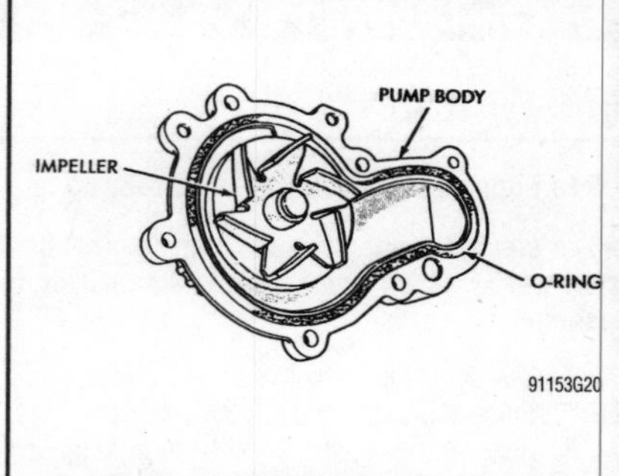

Fig. 67 When installing the pump, make sure that the O-ring is fully seated inside the groove

4. Check the operation of the internal relay contacts.

a. Connect the meter leads to terminals 30 and 87. Meter polarity does not matter for this step.

b. Apply positive battery voltage to terminal 86 and ground to terminal 85. The relay should click as the contacts are drawn toward the coil and the meter should indicate continuity. Replace the relay if your results are different.

If the relay functions properly during this test, inspect the coolant temperature sensor and the cooling fan system wiring for defects.

Water Pump

REMOVAL & INSTALLATION

2.4L Engine

➧ See Figures 66 and 67

1. Disconnect the negative battery cable.

➡This procedure requires removing the engine timing belt and the auto-tensioner. The factory specifies that the timing marks should always be aligned before removing the timing belt. Set the piston in the No. 1 cylinder to TDC on the compression stroke. This should align all timing marks on the crankshaft sprocket and both camshaft sprockets.

2. Raise and safely support the vehicle.
3. Remove the right inner splash shield.
4. Remove the accessory drive belts.
5. Place a drain pan under the radiator drain plug. Drain the cooling system.
6. Support the engine and remove the right motor mount.
7. Remove the power steering pump mounting bracket bolts and place the pump/bracket assembly off to one side. Do not disconnect the power steering fluid lines.
8. Remove the right engine mount bracket.
9. Remove the front timing belt upper and lower covers.
10. Loosen the timing belt tensioner bolts and remove the belt tensioner and timing belt.

✲✲ WARNING

With the timing belt removed, DO NOT rotate the camshaft or crankshaft or damage to the engine could occur.

11. Remove the camshaft sprockets. With the timing belt removed, remove both camshaft sprocket bolts. Do not allow the camshafts to turn when the camshaft sprockets are being removed.
12. Remove the rear timing belt cover to access the water pump.
13. Remove the water pump attaching bolts.
14. Remove the water pump.

To install:

15. Thoroughly clean all parts. Replace the water pump if there are any cracks, signs of coolant leakage from the shaft seal, loose or rough turning bearing, damaged impeller or sprocket, or the sprocket flange is loose or damaged.
16. Clean all sealing surfaces. Install a new rubber O-ring into the water pump O-ring groove.

➡Be sure the O-ring is properly seated in the water pump groove before tightening the bolts. An improperly located O-ring may cause damage to the O-ring and cause a coolant leak.

17. Install the water pump to the engine and tighten the bolts to 105 inch lbs. (12 Nm).
18. Pressurize the cooling system to 15 psi (103 kPa) and check for leaks. If okay, release the pressure and continue the assembly process.
19. Install the rear timing belt cover.
20. Install the camshaft sprockets and tighten the attaching bolts to 75 ft. lbs. (101 Nm). To maintain timing mark alignment, DO NOT allow the camshafts to turn while the sprocket bolts are being tightened.

✲✲ WARNING

Do not attempt to compress the tensioner plunger with the tensioner assembly installed in the engine. This will cause damage to the tensioner and other related components. The tensioner MUST be compressed in a vise.

21. Install the timing belt tensioner and timing belt. Be sure to properly tension the timing belt.
22. Install the front upper and lower timing belt covers.
23. Install the right engine mount bracket and engine mount.
24. Install the crankshaft damper and tighten the center bolt to 105 ft. lbs. (142 Nm).
25. Install the right inner splash shield.
26. Lower the vehicle.
27. Install the power steering pump bracket and power steering pump. Tighten the bracket mounting bolts to 40 ft. lbs. (54 Nm).
28. Install and adjust the drive belts.
29. Refill the cooling system using a 50/50 mixture of water and ethylene glycol antifreeze. Bleed the cooling system.
30. Start the engine and check for proper operation.
31. Check and top off the cooling system, if necessary.

3.0L Engine

➧ See Figure 68

1. Disconnect the negative battery cable.
2. Drain the cooling system.
3. Remove the drive belts. Remove the timing belt covers and the timing belt.
4. Remove the water pump mounting bolts.
5. Separate the water pump from the water inlet pipe and remove the water pump.
6. Inspect the water pump and replace as necessary.

To install:

7. Clean all gasket and O-ring surfaces on the water pump and water pipe inlet tube.

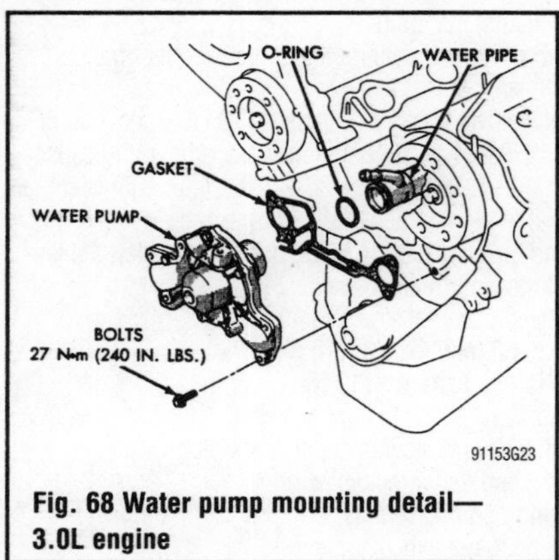

Fig. 68 Water pump mounting detail—3.0L engine

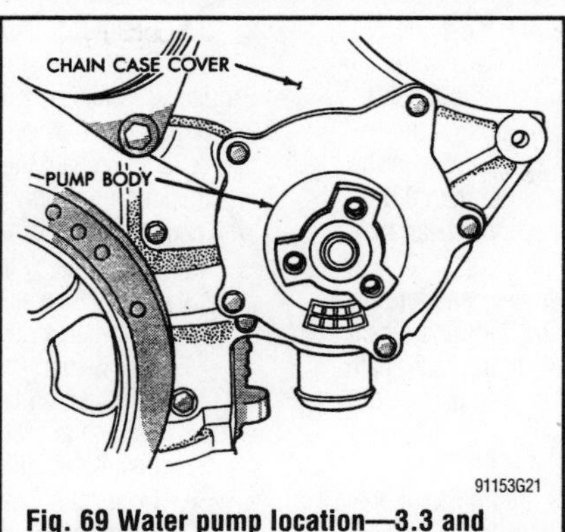

Fig. 69 Water pump location—3.3 and 3.8L engines

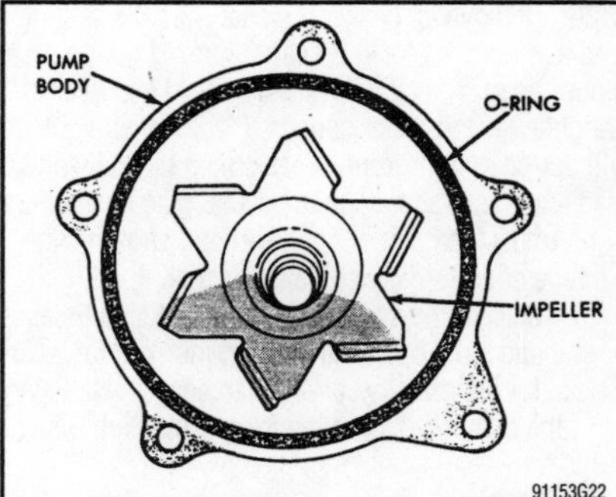

Fig. 70 When installing the pump, make sure that the O-ring is properly seated in the groove in the pump body

8. Wet a new O-ring with water and install it on the water inlet pipe.
9. Install a new gasket on the water pump.
10. Install the pump inlet opening over the water pipe and press until the pipe is completely inserted into the pump housing.
11. Install the water pump-to-block mounting bolts and tighten to 20 ft. lbs. (27 Nm).
12. Install the timing belt and timing belt covers. Install and adjust the drive belts.
13. Reconnect the negative battery cable. Fill the cooling system to the proper level with a 50/50 mixture of clean, ethylene glycol antifreeze and water.
14. Run the engine and check for leaks. Top off the coolant level, if necessary.

3.3L and 3.8L Engines

➧ See Figures 69 and 70

1. Disconnect the negative battery cable.
2. Drain the cooling system.
3. Remove the serpentine belt.
4. Raise and safely support the vehicle. Remove the right front wheel and lower fender shield.
5. Remove the water pump pulley.
6. Remove the five mounting bolts and remove the pump from the engine.
7. Discard the O-ring. Clean the O-ring sealing surface and inspect the water pump for damage, cracks, seal leaks, and loose or rough turning bearings.

To install:

8. Install a new O-ring into the water pump groove. Install the pump onto the engine. Tighten the mounting bolts to 108 inch lbs. (12 Nm).
9. Install the water pump pulley. Tighten the water pump pulley bolts to 20 ft. lbs. (28 Nm).
10. Install the fender shield and wheel. Tighten the wheel lug nuts, in sequence, to 95 ft. lbs. (129 Nm). Lower the vehicle.
11. Install the serpentine belt.
12. Refill the cooling system to the correct level with a 50/50 mixture of clean, ethylene glycol antifreeze and water. Bleed the cooling system.
13. Reconnect the negative battery cable, run the vehicle until the thermostat opens, fill the overflow tank and check for leaks.
14. Once the vehicle has cooled, recheck the coolant level.

Cylinder Head

REMOVAL & INSTALLATION

CAUTION

The fuel injection system remains under pressure, even after the engine has been turned OFF. The fuel system pressure must be relieved before disconnecting any fuel lines. Failure to do so may result in fire and/or personal injury.

2.4L Engine

➧ See Figure 71

1. Properly relieve the fuel system pressure.
2. Disconnect the negative battery cable.
3. Place a large drain pan under the radiator drain plug. Open up the drain plug and drain the cooling system.
4. Remove the air cleaner assembly and disconnect all vacuum lines, electrical wiring and fuel lines from the throttle body.
5. Disconnect the throttle linkage.
6. Remove the accessory drive belts.
7. Disconnect the power brake vacuum hose from the intake manifold.
8. Raise and safely support the vehicle. Disconnect the exhaust pipe from the exhaust manifold.
9. Lower the vehicle as required to remove the power steering pump. Do not disconnect the fluid lines. Set the pump aside.
10. Label the spark plug wires for correct installation. Detach the coil pack wiring connector and remove the coil pack and spark plug wires from the engine.
11. Detach the cam sensor and fuel injector wiring connectors.
12. Remove the timing belt covers, timing belt and camshaft sprockets.
13. Remove the timing belt idler pulley and rear timing belt cover.
14. Remove the cylinder head cover mounting fasteners and cylinder head cover. Remove the ground strap.
15. Identify the camshafts, if they are to be reused, for later installation. The camshafts are not interchangeable. Remove the camshaft bearing caps and the camshafts.
16. Remove the camshaft followers. Any components that are to be reused must be installed in their original locations. Use care to identify and mark the positions of any removed valvetrain components so they may be reinstalled correctly.
17. Remove the intake and exhaust manifolds.
18. Remove the cylinder head bolts.
19. Remove the cylinder head from the vehicle, using care not to damage the aluminum gasket surfaces.

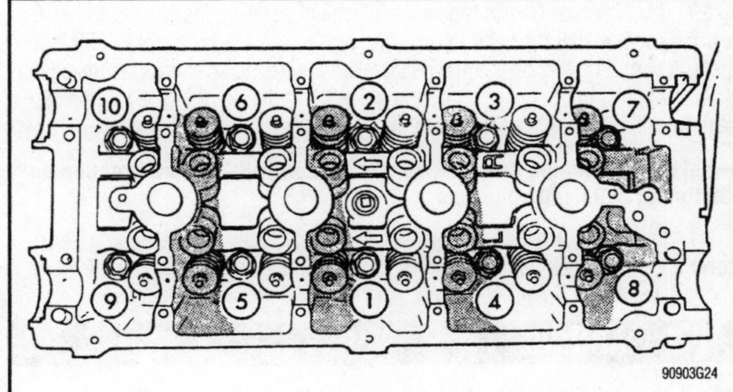

Fig. 71 Cylinder head bolt tightening sequence—2.4L engine

20. Remove all gasket material from the sealing surfaces of the cylinder head and engine block. Be careful not to gouge or scratch the surface of the aluminum head. The cylinder head should be checked for warpage using a good straightedge and feeler gauges. Place the straightedge on the bottom of the cylinder head from front to back, then try to insert the feeler gauge between the head and the straightedge in several places. If a feeler gauge larger than 0.004 in. (0.1mm) fits between the head and straightedge, take the cylinder head to a machine shop for service before installing it.

21. Inspect the camshaft bearing oil feed holes in the cylinder head for clogging. Inspect the camshaft bearing journals for wear or scoring. Check the cam surface for abnormal wear and damage. A visible worn groove in the roller path or on the cam lobes is cause for replacement. Valve service may be performed at this time.

To install:

22. Clean all parts well. Note that the cylinder head bolts are tightened using a new procedure. The cylinder head bolts should be checked carefully BEFORE reuse. If the threads are necked down the bolts should be replaced with new bolts. Necking can be checked by holding a steel scale or straightedge against the threads. If all the threads do not contact the scale, the bolt should be replaced. New cylinder head bolts are recommended for any engine rebuild, especially if known that the engine has been disassembled before.

23. Be sure both the top of the engine block and the bottom of the cylinder head are clean. Install a new gasket making sure all holes align with the openings in the engine block. Carefully set the cylinder head in place.

24. Apply clean engine oil to the threads and under the heads of the bolts. Install the bolts and tighten them in sequence using the following four substeps:

a. Tighten all bolts to 25 ft. lbs. (34 Nm).
b. Tighten all bolts to 50 ft. lbs. (68 Nm).
c. Tighten all bolts again to 50 ft. lbs. (68 Nm).

➡Do not use a torque wrench for the fourth step.

d. Tighten all bolts an additional ¼ turn.

25. The camshaft end-play should be checked using the following procedure:

a. Oil the camshaft journals and install the camshaft WITHOUT the cam follower assemblies. Install the rear cam caps and tighten them to 250 inch lbs. (28 Nm).
b. Carefully push the camshaft as far rearward as it will go.
c. Set up a dial indicator to bear against the front of the camshaft (the sprocket end). Zero the indicator.
d. Move the camshaft forward as far as it will go. Read the dial indicator. End-play specification is 0.002–0.010 in. (0.05–0.15mm).

26. When satisfied with the fit and condition of the camshafts, remove the camshafts for installation of the cam followers.

27. Lubricate the camshaft followers with clean engine oil. Install the cam followers in their original positions on the hydraulic adjuster and valve stem.

⁂ WARNING

Be sure none of the pistons are at Top Dead Center (TDC) when installing the camshafts.

28. Lubricate the camshaft bearing journals and cam followers with clean engine oil and install the camshafts. Install right and left camshaft bearing caps No. 2 through No. 5 and right side No. 6. Tighten the M6 fasteners to 105 inch lbs. (12 Nm) in sequence.

29. Apply Mopar Gasket Maker or equivalent sealer to the No. 1 and No. 6 bearing caps. Install the bearing caps and tighten the M8 fasteners to 250 inch lbs. (28 Nm). The end caps must be installed before the seals may be installed.

30. Apply a light coating of clean engine oil to the lip of the new camshaft seal. Install the camshaft seal until it fits flush with the cylinder head.

➡Refer to the timing belt Unit Repair Section (URS) for information on the timing belts and sprockets.

31. Install the camshaft sprockets, if removed. Install the rear timing belt cover and timing belt using care to be sure all timing marks are properly aligned. Install the timing belt cover.

⁂ WARNING

Verify that all timing marks are correct. If the timing belt or sprockets are incorrectly installed, engine damage will occur. Take time to be sure all timing marks are correctly aligned.

32. Install the intake and exhaust manifolds.

33. Clean the cylinder head cover and cylinder head gasket rails (mating surfaces). Make certain the rails are flat.

34. Install new cylinder head cover gaskets. Use care; DO NOT allow oil or solvents to contact the timing belt as they can deteriorate the rubber and cause tooth skipping. Apply Mopar Silicone Rubber Adhesive Sealant, or equivalent, at the camshaft cap corners and at the top edge of the ½ round seal.

35. Install the cylinder head cover assembly to the head and tighten the fasteners in sequence using the following three substeps:

a. Tighten all cylinder head cover fasteners to 40 inch lbs. (4.5 Nm).
b. Tighten all fasteners to 80 inch lbs. (9 Nm).
c. Tighten all fasteners to 105 inch lbs. (12 Nm).

36. Install the ground strap.

37. Install the ignition coil pack and reconnect the spark plug wiring.

38. Connect the cam sensor and fuel injectors' wiring.

39. Install the power steering pump assembly.

40. Connect the exhaust pipe to the exhaust manifold.

41. Connect all vacuum lines and remaining wiring. Connect the throttle linkage and fuel lines.

42. Install and adjust the accessory drive belts.

43. Refill the cooling system. An oil and filter change is recommended since coolant can enter the oil system when a head is removed.

44. Connect the remaining air ducting. Connect the negative battery cable and test run the vehicle. Check for leaks and for proper operation.

3.0L Engine

➧ See Figures 72 thru 80

1. Properly relieve the fuel system pressure.

2. Disconnect the negative battery cable. Drain the cooling system.

3. Remove the accessory drive belts and the air conditioning compressor from its mount and support it aside. Remove the alternator and power steering pump from the brackets and move them aside.

4. Raise the vehicle and support safely. Remove the right front wheel and the right inner splash shield.

5. Remove the crankshaft pulleys and the torsional damper.

6. Lower the vehicle. Using a floor jack and a block of wood positioned under the oil pan, raise the engine slightly. Remove the engine mount bracket from the timing cover end of the engine.

7. Remove the timing belt covers.

8. Remove the timing belt as described in the unit repair section in the beginning of this manual.

9. Hold the camshaft sprocket using a suitable tool and remove the camshaft sprocket retaining bolt. Remove the sprocket and the inner timing belt cover (left bank) and/or alternator bracket (right bank).

10. Label and disconnect the spark plug wires from the spark plugs.

11. If removing the left (front) cylinder head, remove the distributor cap and spark plug wires. Mark the position of the rotor and distributor in relation to the cylinder head and remove the distributor. Remove the distributor drive adapter.

12. Remove the valve cover.

13. Install the auto lash adjuster retainers on the rocker arms. Remove the camshaft bearing cap-to-cylinder head bolts (do not remove the bolts from the assembly). Remove the rocker arms, rocker shafts and bearing caps as an assembly. Remove the camshaft from the cylinder head.

14. Remove the intake manifold assembly.

15. Remove the exhaust manifold and crossover pipe.

16. Remove the cylinder head bolts starting from the outside and working inward. Remove the cylinder head from the engine.

17. Clean the gasket mounting surfaces and check the head gasket surface for leaks, damage or warpage; the maximum warpage allowed is 0.008 in. (0.20mm).

To install:

18. Clean all parts well. Install the new cylinder head gasket over the dowels on the engine block.

19. Install the cylinder head on the engine block and tighten the 10mm Allen cylinder head bolts in sequence, using three even steps, to 80 ft. lbs. (108 Nm).

20. Install the intake and exhaust manifolds.

21. Lubricate the camshaft with clean engine oil and install on the cylinder head.

22. Apply silicone sealant to the cylinder head at the front and rear cam

Fig. 72 A breaker bar should be used to loosen the cylinder head bolts

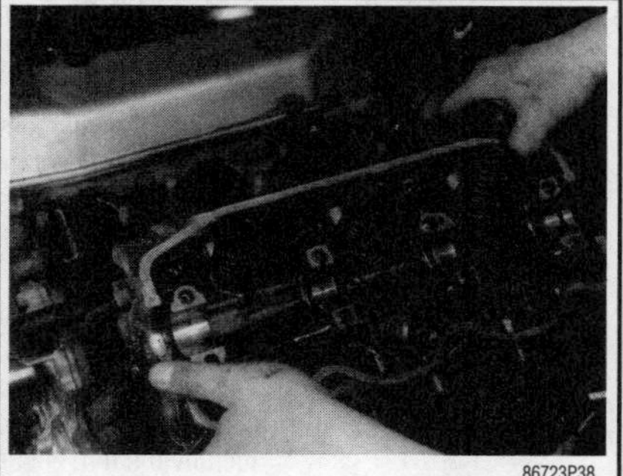

Fig. 73 After the cylinder head bolts are removed in the proper sequence, lift the cylinder heads from the engine block

Fig. 74 Clean the cylinder head mating surfaces before installation

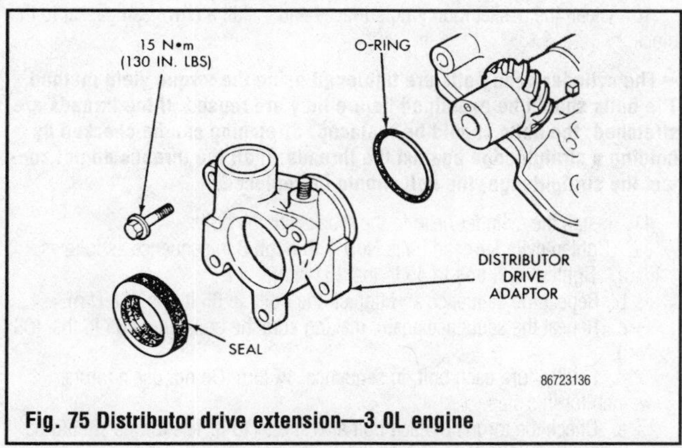

Fig. 75 Distributor drive extension—3.0L engine

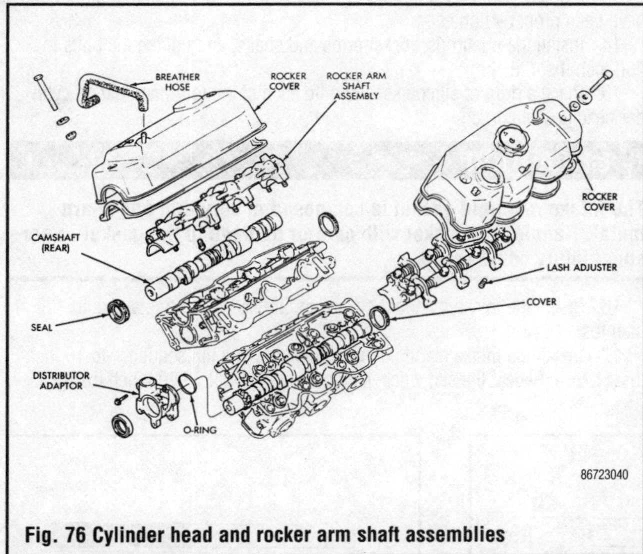

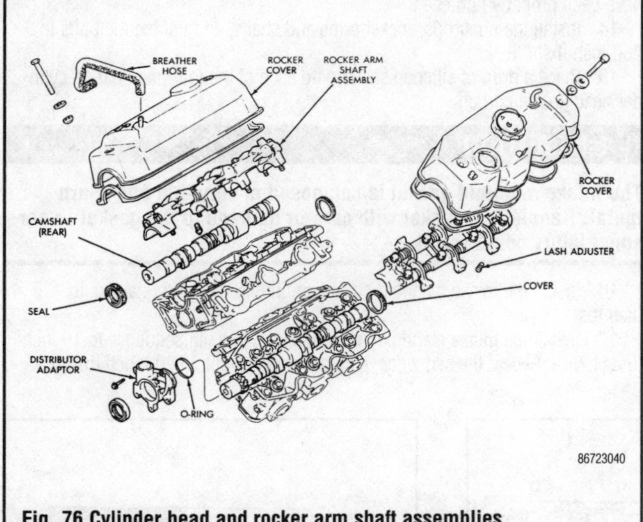

Fig. 76 Cylinder head and rocker arm shaft assemblies

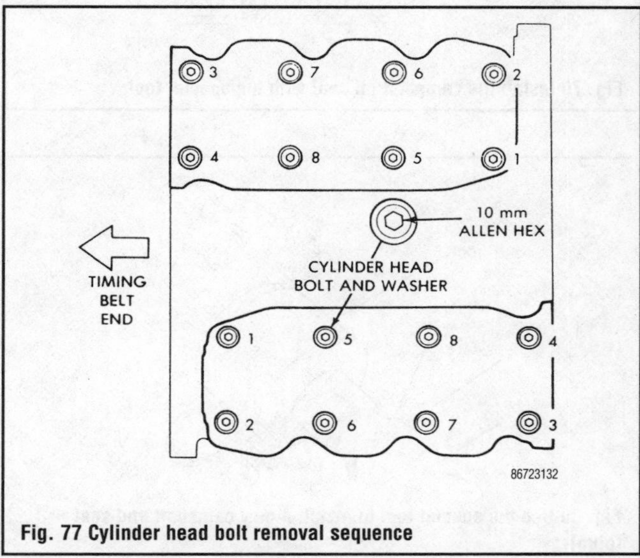

Fig. 77 Cylinder head bolt removal sequence

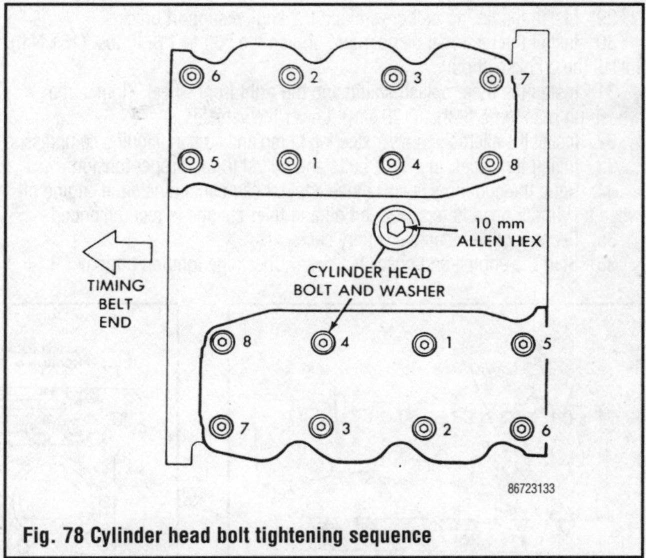

Fig. 78 Cylinder head bolt tightening sequence

bearing cap contact areas. Install the rocker arm shaft assembly and tighten the bearing cap bolts to 85 inch lbs. (10 Nm) in the following sequence: No. 3, No. 2, No. 1 and No. 4. Retighten to 180 inch lbs. (20 Nm) in the same sequence.

23. If removed, install the distributor drive adapter. Install a new camshaft seal.

24. Install the valve cover.

25. Install the inner timing belt cover (left bank) and/or alternator bracket (right bank).

26. Position the camshaft sprocket. Hold the sprocket using a suitable tool and install the camshaft sprocket bolt. Tighten the bolt to 70 ft. lbs. (95 Nm).

➡Be sure the timing belt sprocket timing marks are aligned.

27. If removed, install the distributor, aligning the marks made during removal. Install the distributor cap and spark plug wires.

28. Install the timing belt.

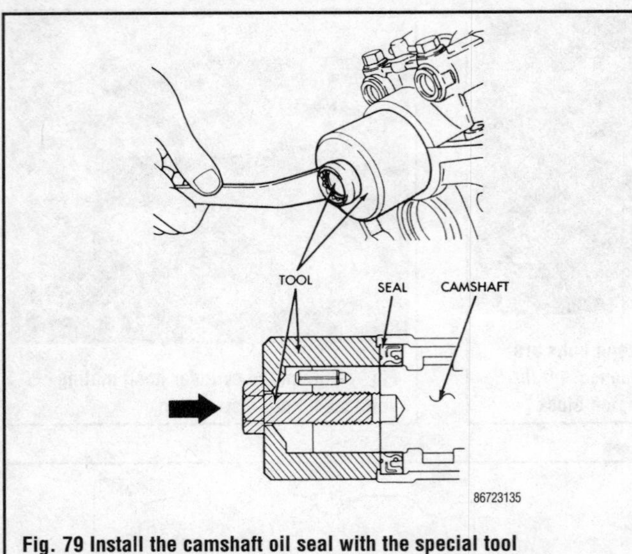

Fig. 79 Install the camshaft oil seal with the special tool

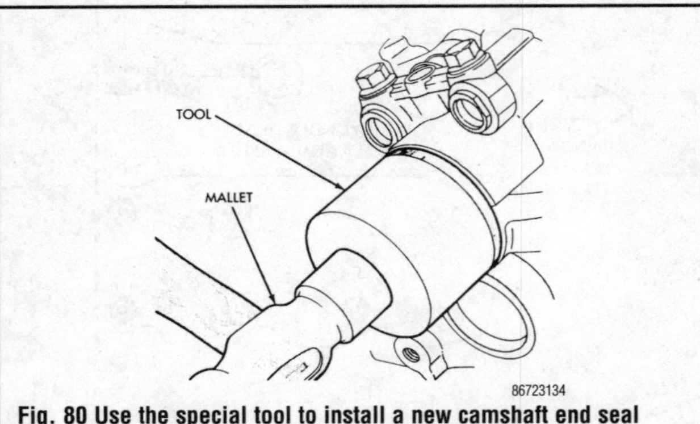

Fig. 80 Use the special tool to install a new camshaft end seal (plug)

29. Install the timing belt covers and the engine support bracket.
30. Install the torsional damper and tighten the bolt to 112 ft. lbs. (151 Nm). Install the crankshaft pulleys.
31. Install the inner splash shield and the right front wheel. Tighten the wheel lug nuts to 95 ft. lbs. (129 Nm). Lower the vehicle.
32. Install the alternator, power steering pump and air conditioning compressor.
33. Install the accessory drive belts and adjust to the proper tension.
34. Refill the cooling system. Since coolant can contaminate the engine oil when a cylinder head is removed, an oil and filter change is recommended.
35. Reconnect the negative battery cable.
36. Start the engine and check for leaks. Check the ignition timing.

3.3L and 3.8L Engines

➧ See Figures 81, 82, 83 and 84

1. Properly relieve the fuel system pressure.
2. Disconnect the negative battery cable and drain the cooling system.
3. Remove the intake manifold with the throttle body.
4. Disconnect the coil wires, sending unit wire, heater hoses and bypass hose.
5. Remove the closed ventilation system, evaporation control system and cylinder head cover(s).
6. Remove the exhaust manifold(s).
7. Remove the rocker arm and shaft assemblies. Remove the pushrods and identify them to ensure installation in their original positions.
8. Loosen the cylinder head bolts in the reverse order of the torque sequence. Remove the cylinder head bolts and remove the cylinder head(s) from the block.
9. Clean all gasket mating surfaces.

To install:

10. Clean the gasket mounting surfaces and install a new head gasket to the block.

➡The cylinder head bolts are tightened using the torque yield method. The bolts should be examined before they are reused. If the threads are stretched, the bolts should be replaced. Stretching can be checked by holding a straightedge against the threads. If all the threads do not contact the straightedge, the bolt should be replaced.

11. Install the cylinder head to the block with the bolts.
12. Tighten cylinder head bolts Nos. 1 through 8 in sequence as follows:
    a. Tighten each bolt to 45 ft. lbs. (61 Nm).
    b. Repeat the sequence and tighten the bolts to 65 ft. lbs. (88 Nm).
    c. Repeat the sequence again, making sure the bolts are at 65 ft. lbs. (88 Nm).
    d. Finally, turn each bolt, in sequence, ¼ turn. Do not use a torque wrench for this step.
    e. Check the torque of each bolt after the ¼ turn. The torque should be over 90 ft. lbs. (122 Nm). If not, replace the bolt.
13. Tighten head bolt No. 9 to 25 ft. lbs. (33 Nm) after the other eight bolts have been properly tightened.
14. Install the pushrods, rocker arms and shafts, and tighten the bolts to 250 inch lbs. (28 Nm).
15. Place a drop of silicone sealer onto each of the four manifold-to-cylinder head gasket corners.

⁂ CAUTION

The intake manifold gasket is composed of very thin and sharp metal. Handle this gasket with care or damage to the gasket or personal injury could result.

16. Install the intake manifold gasket and tighten the end retainers to 105 inch lbs. (12 Nm).
17. Install the intake manifold and tighten the bolts in sequence to 10 inch lbs. (1 Nm). Repeat the sequence, increasing the torque to 200 inch lbs. (22

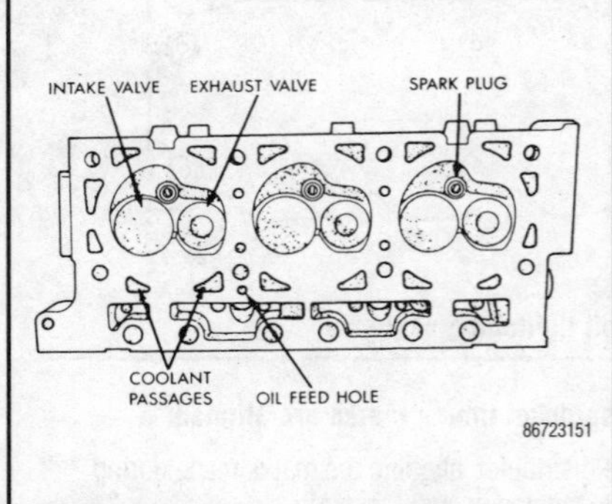

Fig. 81 Cylinder head assembly—3.3L and 3.8L engines

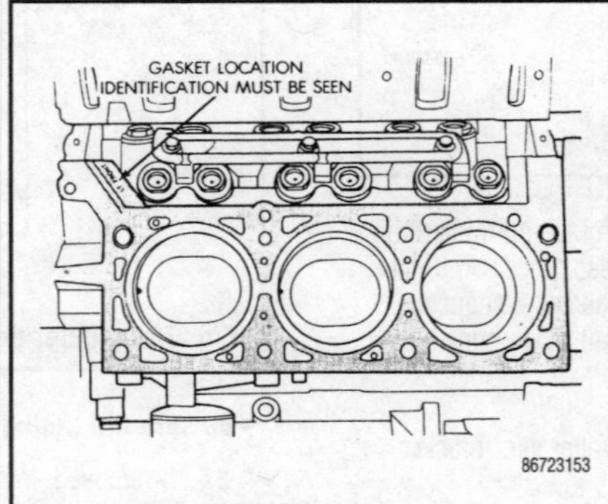

Fig. 82 Cylinder head gasket installation—3.3L and 3.8L engines

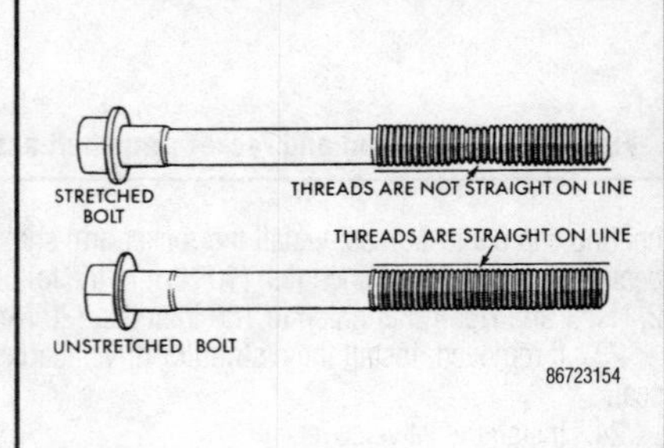

Fig. 83 Checking the cylinder head mounting bolts for stretching (necking)—3.3L and 3.8L engines

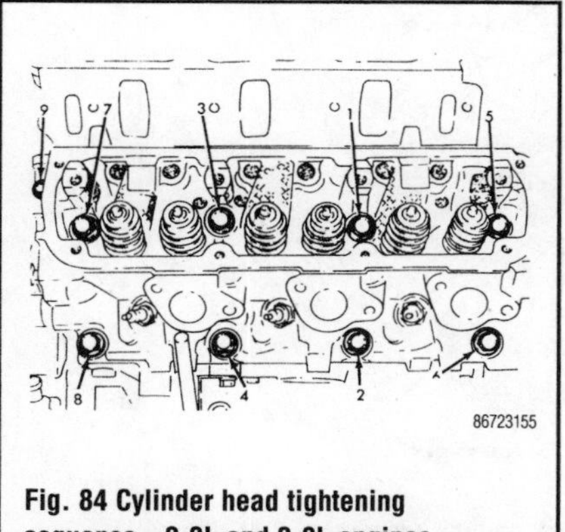
86723155

Fig. 84 Cylinder head tightening sequence—3.3L and 3.8L engines

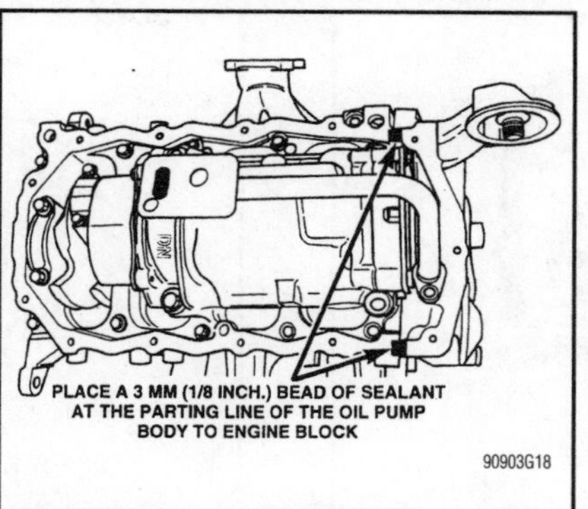
PLACE A 3 MM (1/8 INCH.) BEAD OF SEALANT AT THE PARTING LINE OF THE OIL PUMP BODY TO ENGINE BLOCK
90903G18

Fig. 85 Oil pan sealant application—2.4L engine

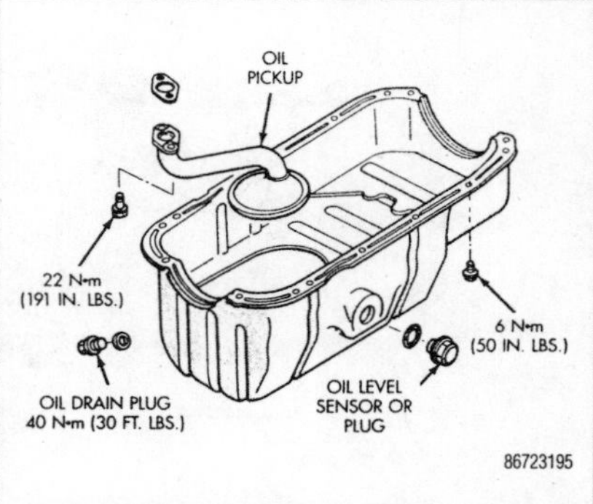

Fig. 86 Oil pan and related components—3.0L engines, except Premier and Monaco

Nm). Recheck each bolt, making sure it is at 200 inch lbs. (22 Nm) of torque. As the bolts are tightened, inspect the seals to ensure that they have not become dislodged.

18. Install the valve cover with a new gasket. Tighten the valve cover bolts to 105 inch lbs. (12 Nm). Install the exhaust manifold and crossover pipe. Tighten the bolts to 20 ft. lbs. (27 Nm) and the nuts to 15 ft. lbs. (20 Nm).
19. Install the closed ventilation system and the evaporation control system.
20. Reconnect the coil wires, sending unit wire, heater hoses and bypass hose.
21. Ensure all wiring connections, cables, hoses, vacuum and fuel lines have been reattached.
22. Refill the cooling system to the correct level. Coolant can contaminate the engine oil when performing cylinder head service. An oil and filter change is recommended.
23. Reconnect the negative battery cable. Start the engine and check for leaks.

Oil Pan

REMOVAL & INSTALLATION

2.4L Engine

▸ See Figure 85

1. Disconnect the negative battery cable.
2. Raise and safely support the vehicle.
3. Drain the engine oil.
4. Remove the oil pan attaching bolts.
5. Remove the oil pan.
6. Thoroughly clean the inside of the oil pan. Clean the gasket mating surfaces of the oil pan and engine block.

To install:

7. Using a suitable gasket sealant, apply a ⅛ in. (3mm) bead at the oil pump-to-engine block parting line.
8. Install the new oil pan gasket.
9. Install the oil pan to the engine.
10. Tighten the oil pan attaching bolts to 105 inch lbs. (12 Nm).
11. Install the oil pan drain plug and gasket. Tighten the drain plug to 25 ft. lbs. (34 Nm).
12. Lower the vehicle.
13. Fill the engine with the correct type of clean engine oil to the proper level.
14. Reconnect the negative battery cable. Start the engine and check for leaks.

3.0L Engine

▸ See Figures 86, 87 and 88

1. Disconnect the negative battery cable.
2. Raise and safely support the vehicle.
3. Drain the engine oil.
4. Remove the oil pan attaching bolts and remove the oil pan.

To install:

5. Thoroughly clean the inside of the oil pan. Clean the oil pan and engine block gasket mating surfaces.
6. Apply RTV sealant to the oil pan.
7. Install the oil pan, then tighten the bolts in sequence to 50 inch lbs. (6 Nm).
8. Install the oil pan drain plug and tighten to 30 ft. lbs. (40 Nm).
9. Lower the vehicle.
10. Refill the engine with the proper type and quantity of oil.
11. Connect the negative battery cable.
12. Start the engine and check for leaks. After the engine has been turned **OFF**, check the oil level and top off, if necessary.

3.3L and 3.8L Engines

▸ See Figures 89 and 90

1. Disconnect the negative battery cable. Remove the engine oil dipstick.
2. Raise the vehicle and support safely.

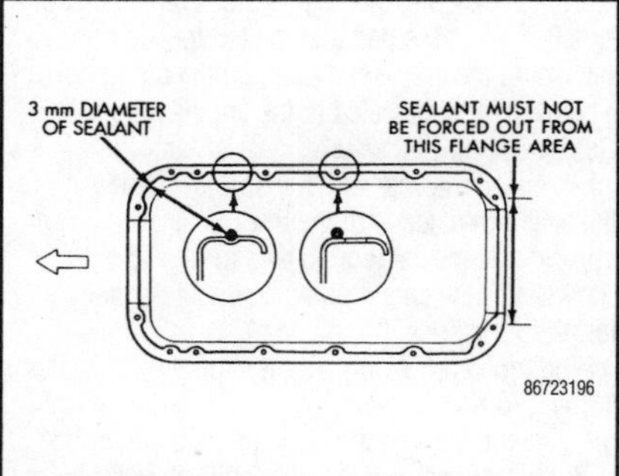
3 mm DIAMETER OF SEALANT
SEALANT MUST NOT BE FORCED OUT FROM THIS FLANGE AREA
86723196

Fig. 87 Make certain that the silicone sealant is applied as shown in the illustration

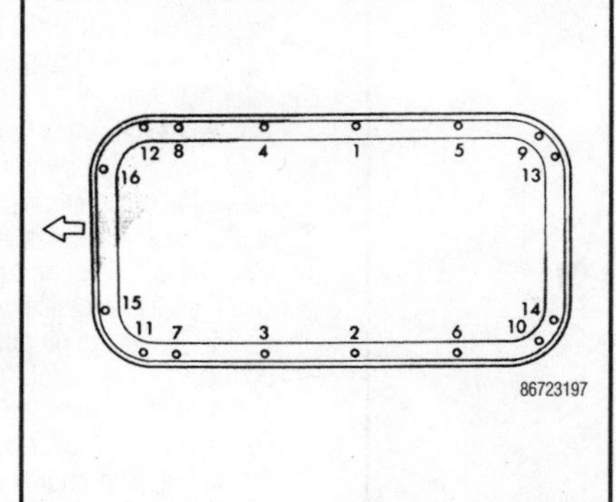
86723197

Fig. 88 Oil pan bolt tightening sequence

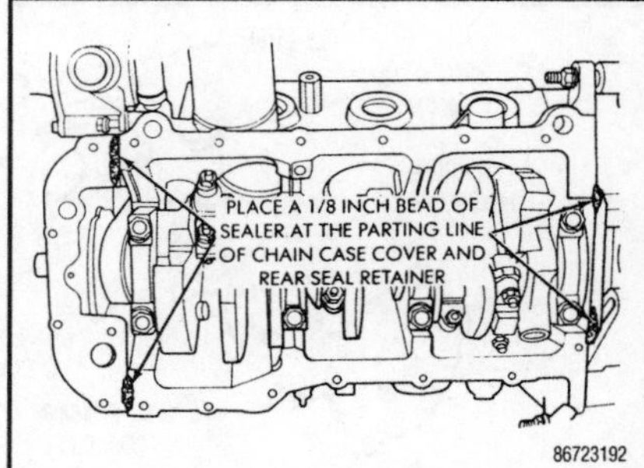
PLACE A 1/8 INCH BEAD OF SEALER AT THE PARTING LINE OF CHAIN CASE COVER AND REAR SEAL RETAINER
86723192

Fig. 89 Oil pan sealing using Mopar® silicone rubber adhesive sealant—3.3L and 3.8L engines

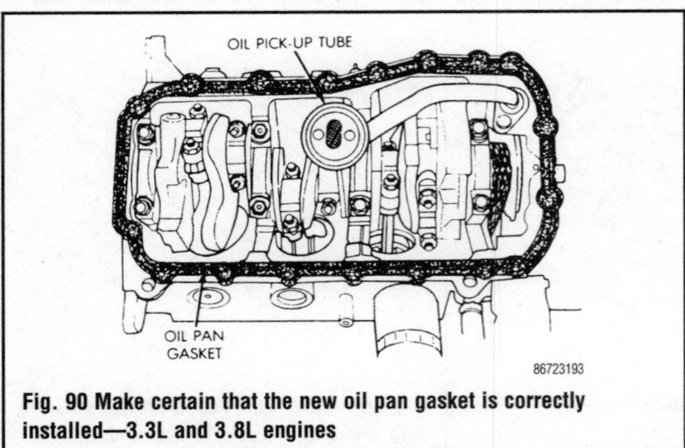

Fig. 90 Make certain that the new oil pan gasket is correctly installed—3.3L and 3.8L engines

3. Remove the torque converter bolt access cover, if equipped.
4. Drain the engine oil.
5. Remove the oil pan retaining bolts and remove the oil pan and gasket.

To install:

6. Thoroughly clean the inside of the oil pan. Thoroughly clean and dry all sealing surfaces, bolts and bolt holes.
7. Apply a 1/8 in. (3mm) bead of silicone sealer to the chain cover-to-block mating seam and the rear main seal retainer-to-block seam.
8. Install a new oil pan gasket and install the oil pan to the engine.
9. Install the retaining bolts and tighten to 105 inch lbs. (12 Nm).
10. Install the oil pan drain plug and tighten to 25 ft. lbs. (34 Nm).
11. Install the torque converter bolt access cover, if equipped. Lower the vehicle.
12. Install the oil dipstick. Refill the engine with the proper type and quantity of oil.
13. Reconnect the negative battery cable. Start the engine and check for leaks. After the engine has been turned **OFF**, check the oil level and top off, if necessary.

Oil Pump

REMOVAL & INSTALLATION

2.4L Engine

➧ **See Figures 91 and 92**

1. Disconnect the negative battery cable.
2. Raise and safely support the vehicle.
3. Drain the engine oil and the engine coolant into suitable containers.
4. Lower the vehicle.
5. Remove the accessory drive belts, as required.
6. Take up the weight of the engine with an engine support tool and remove the right engine mount and bracket. Be sure the engine is safely supported.
7. Remove the timing belt cover.

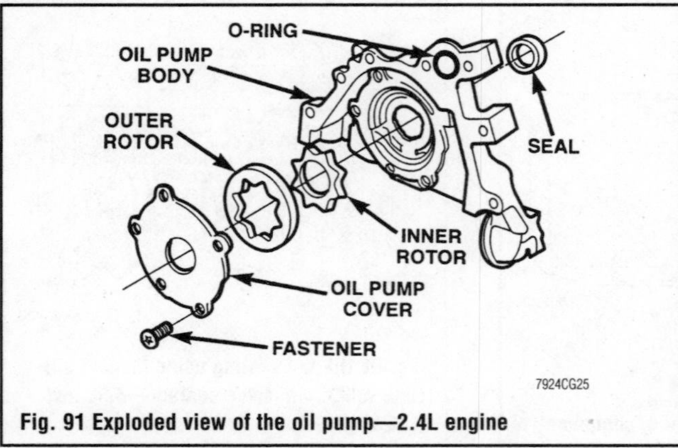

Fig. 91 Exploded view of the oil pump—2.4L engine

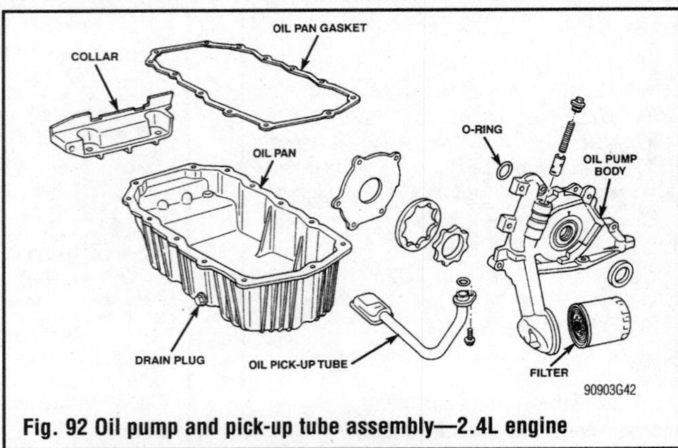

Fig. 92 Oil pump and pick-up tube assembly—2.4L engine

8. Loosen the timing belt tensioner bolts and remove the tensioner and the timing belt.
9. Raise and safely support the vehicle.
10. Remove the oil pan assembly. Remove the oil pump pick-up tube and O-ring.
11. Using a suitable puller, remove the crankshaft damper from the front of the crankshaft.
12. Using a suitable puller, draw the crankshaft sprocket from the front of the crankshaft.
13. Loosen the oil pump bolts and remove. Take note of the location of each bolt for reassembly. Remove the oil pump from the face of the engine block. If necessary, tap lightly with a soft face mallet. Use care working with light alloy parts.
14. To remove the relief valve from the pump body, unscrew threaded plug, then pull out the spring and valve. Note the order of the parts' removal.

To install:

15. Clean all parts well for inspection. Remove the bolts holding the back cover to the pump body. Remove the pump rotors. The mating surface of the oil pump should be smooth. Replace the pump cover if scratched or grooved.
16. The pump should be checked for wear by carefully measuring the components.

➡If oil pressure is low and the pump is within specifications, inspect for worn engine bearings or other reasons for oil pressure loss.

17. Clean all oil pump parts in suitable solvent before assembly. Assemble the pump with new parts as required. **Install the inner rotor with the chamfer facing the cast iron oil pump cover (back of the pump)**. Tighten the cover bolts to 105 inch lbs. (12 Nm).
18. Install the relief valve first, then the spring, gasket and cover cap into the pump body. Note that installing the spring first will seriously damage the engine. The relief valve goes in first. Tighten the cover cap to 40 ft. lbs. (55 Nm).
19. Prime the oil pump before installation by filling the rotor cavity with clean engine oil.
20. Insert a new oil ring seal in the oil pump counterbore on the pump body discharge passage. Apply Mopar Gasket Maker or equivalent anaerobic type gasket sealer, to the oil pump body flange. This material cures in the absence of air when squeezed between two flat machined metal surfaces. For this reason, the mating surfaces of both the pump body and the engine block must be spotlessly clean so all air will be expelled when the parts are bolted together and tightened. Install the pump slowly onto the crankshaft aligning the oil pump rotor flats with the flats on the crankshaft until seated to the engine block. Tighten the fasteners to 20 ft. lbs. (28 Nm).
21. Install a new front oil seal. Install the seal with the spring side towards the inside of the engine. Tap the seal into place until flush with the cover.
22. Install the crankshaft sprocket. A special tool is used to draw the sprocket onto the end of the crankshaft. Use care if using a substitute tool.
23. Raise and safely support the vehicle.
24. Install the oil pump pick-up tube and O-ring. Tighten the oil pump pick-up tube mounting bolt to 20 ft. lbs. (28 Nm).
25. Thoroughly clean the oil pan and be sure the gasket rails are in good condition. Use Mopar Silicone Rubber Adhesive Sealant or equivalent sealer at the oil pump-to-engine block parting line. Use a new oil pan gasket, install the oil pan and tighten the 13 oil pan bolts to 105 inch lbs. (12 Nm).
26. Install a new oil filter.

27. Lower the vehicle.
28. Install the timing belt and covers using the recommended procedures. Use care to be sure all valve timing marks are aligned. This is most important. Failure to properly align the timing marks will result in severe engine damage.
29. Install the crankshaft damper. A special tool making use of a 12mm x 1.75 x 150mm bolt is used to draw the crankshaft damper onto the end of the crankshaft. Use care if using substitute tools. Tighten the center bolt to 105 ft. lbs. (142 Nm).
30. Install the accessory drive belts, as required. Adjust the accessory drive belts to the proper tension.
31. Install the engine mount and bracket, as required. Remove the engine support fixture from the vehicle.
32. Refill the engine with the correct type and amount of fresh, clean engine oil. Refill the cooling system with a 50/50 mixture of clean, ethylene glycol antifreeze and water.
33. Test run the vehicle to check for leaks. An oil pressure gauge should be installed to verify proper engine oil pressure.

3.0L Engine

See Figure 93

The oil pump assembly is mounted at the front of the crankshaft. The oil pump housing also retains the front crankshaft oil seal. Since the timing belt must be removed to access the front cover, care must be taken. It is good practice to set the engine up to TDC No. 1 cylinder firing position. Verify that all timing marks on the crankshaft and camshaft sprockets are properly aligned before removing the timing belt. This serves as a point of reference for all work that follows. Valve timing is most important and engine damage will result if the work is incorrect.

1. Disconnect the negative battery cable.
2. Remove the accessory drive belts.
3. Remove the air conditioning compressor from the mounting bracket and lay it aside, if equipped. Remove the compressor mounting bracket and adjustable drive belt tensioner from the engine.
4. Remove the power steering pump/alternator belt tensioner mounting bolt and remove the tensioner.
5. Remove the power steering pump mounting bracket bolts, rear support locknut and set the power steering pump aside.
6. Raise and safely support the vehicle.
7. Drain the engine oil into a suitable container.
8. Remove the right inner fender inner shield.
9. Remove the crankshaft drive pulley bolt, drive pulley and torsional damper. Lower the vehicle.
10. Place a floor jack under the engine. Separate the engine mount insulator from the engine mount bracket.
11. Raise the engine slightly and remove the engine mount bracket.
12. Remove the timing belt cover and timing belt.
13. Remove the crankshaft sprocket.
14. Remove the five oil pump mounting bolts, then remove the oil pump assembly. Mark the mounting bolts for proper installation during reassembly.
15. Remove the front crankshaft oil seal from the oil pump cover.

To install:

16. Clean all parts well for inspection. Remove the bolts holding the rear cover to the oil pump body. Remove the pump rotors. The mating surface of the oil pump should be smooth. Replace the pump cover if scratched or grooved.

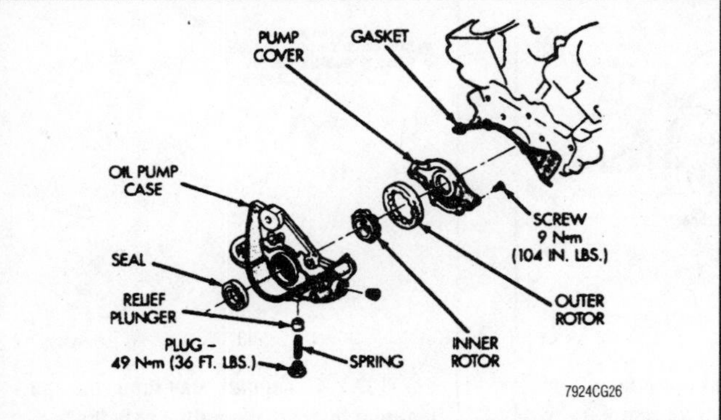

Fig. 93 Exploded view of the oil pump assembly—3.0L engine

17. The pump should be checked for wear by carefully measuring the components.

➡If oil pressure is low and the pump is within specifications, inspect for worn engine bearings or other reasons for oil pressure loss.

18. Clean all oil pump parts in suitable solvent before assembly. Assemble the pump with new parts as required.
19. Clean the oil pump and engine block gasket surfaces thoroughly.
20. Position a new gasket on the pump assembly and install on the cylinder block. Be sure the correct length bolts are in their proper locations and tighten all bolts to 11 ft. lbs. (15 Nm).
21. Install a new front crankshaft oil seal into the oil pump using Seal Installer tool MD-998717 or an equivalent seal driver tool.
22. Install the crankshaft sprocket and timing belt. Recheck the engine timing marks.
23. Install the timing belt covers. Tighten the timing belt cover fasteners to 10 ft. lbs. (14 Nm).
24. Raise the engine slightly and install the engine mount bracket. Install the engine mount insulator into the engine mount bracket.
25. Install the torsional damper, crankshaft drive pulley and drive pulley bolt. Tighten to 112 ft. lbs. (151 Nm).
26. Install the right fender inner splash shield. Lower the vehicle.
27. Install the power steering mount bracket and power steering pump.
28. Install the power steering/alternator belt tensioner.
29. Install the air conditioning adjustable drive belt tensioner and mounting bracket. Tighten the mounting bolts to 40 ft. lbs. (54 Nm).
30. Install the air conditioning compressor. Tighten the compressor mounting bolts to 40 ft. lbs. (54 Nm).
31. Install the accessory drive belts and adjust to the proper tension.
32. Reconnect the negative battery cable.
33. Refill the crankcase with the correct amount of clean engine oil and start the engine. Check for leaks.
34. Check engine oil pressure.

3.3L and 3.8L Engines

See Figures 94, 95, 96 and 97

1. Disconnect the negative battery cable. Remove the dipstick. Drain the cooling system.
2. Raise the vehicle and support safely. Support the engine and remove the right side engine mount.
3. Drain the oil and remove the oil pan.
4. Remove the oil pick-up tube. Remove the transaxle inspection cover, if necessary.
5. Remove the timing chain case cover.
6. Disassemble the oil pump as required.

To install:

7. Clean all parts well for inspection. Remove the bolts holding the back cover to the pump body. Remove the pump rotors. The mating surface of the oil pump should be smooth. Replace the pump cover if scratched or grooved.
8. The pump should be checked for wear by carefully measuring the components.

➡If oil pressure is low and the pump is within specifications, inspect for worn engine bearings or other reasons for oil pressure loss.

9. Clean all oil pump parts in suitable solvent before assembly. Assemble the pump with new parts as required. **Install the inner rotor with the chamfer facing the cast iron oil pump cover (back of the pump).** Tighten the cover bolts to 105 inch lbs. (12 Nm).
10. Install the relief valve first, then the spring, then the cover cap into the pump body. Note that installing the spring first will seriously damage the engine. The relief valve goes in first.
11. Prime the oil pump by filling the rotor cavity with fresh oil and turning the rotors until oil comes out the pressure port. Repeat a few times until no air bubbles are present.
12. Install the chain case cover. Tighten the timing chain case cover bolts as follows:
    a. M8 x 1.25—20 ft. lbs. (27 Nm)
    b. M10 x 1.5—40 ft. lbs. (54 Nm)
13. Clean out the oil pick-up or replace as required. Replace the oil pick-up O-ring and install the pick-up to the pump. Tighten the pick-up tube retaining bolt to 250 inch lbs. (28 Nm).

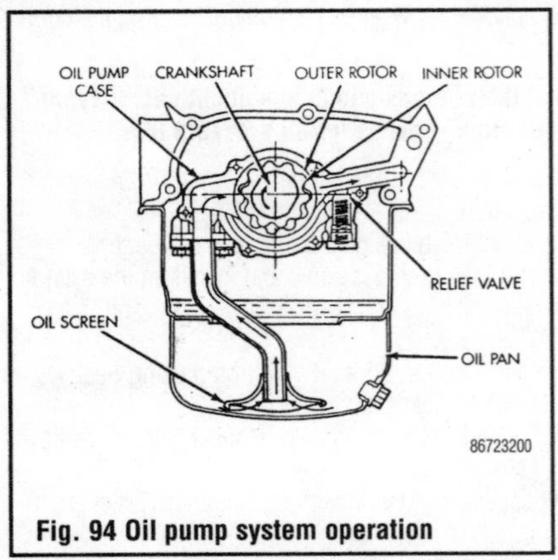

Fig. 94 Oil pump system operation

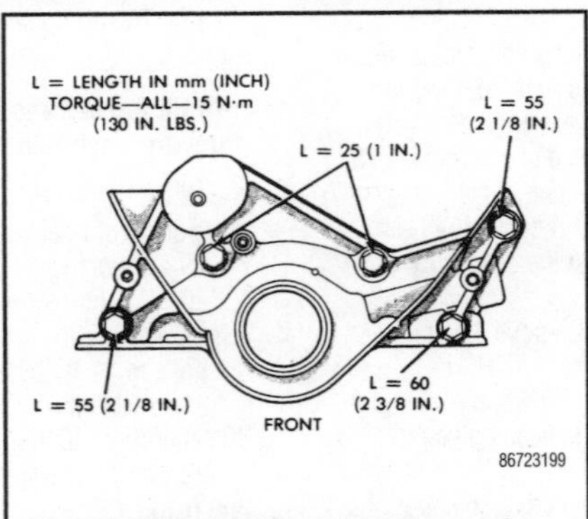

Fig. 95 Oil pump assembly and mounting bolt lengths

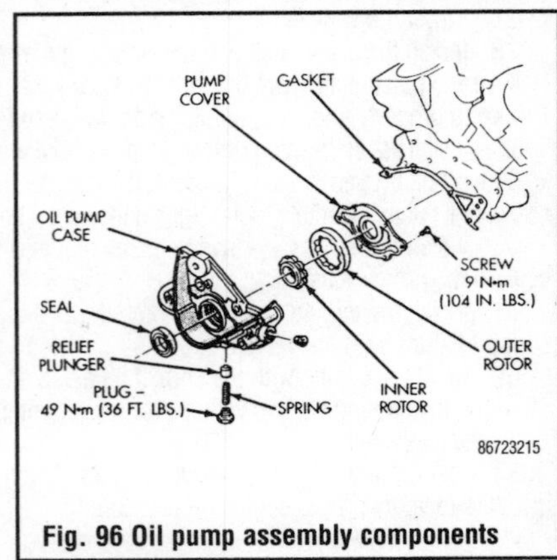

Fig. 96 Oil pump assembly components

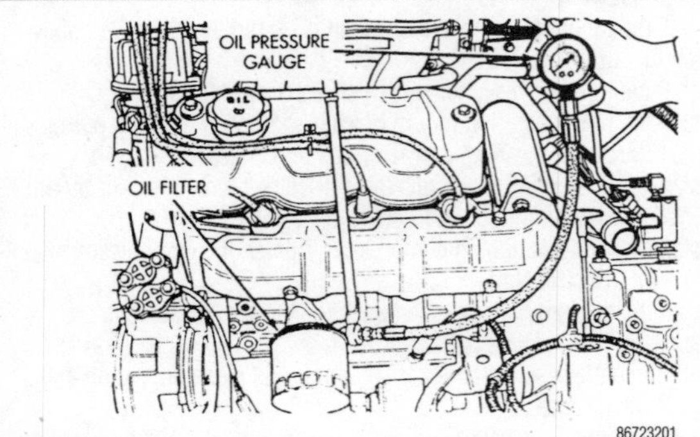

Fig. 97 Checking the oil pump pressure after installation is complete

14. Install the oil pan. Install the right side engine mount.
15. Lower the vehicle. Install the dipstick. Refill the engine with the proper amount of oil.
16. Refill the cooling system to the proper level.
17. Reconnect the negative battery cable and start the engine.
18. Check the area for leaks and check the oil pressure.

Crankshaft Damper

REMOVAL & INSTALLATION

See Figures 98 thru 103

1. Disconnect the negative battery cable.
2. Raise and safely support the vehicle. Remove the right side wheel and tire assembly.

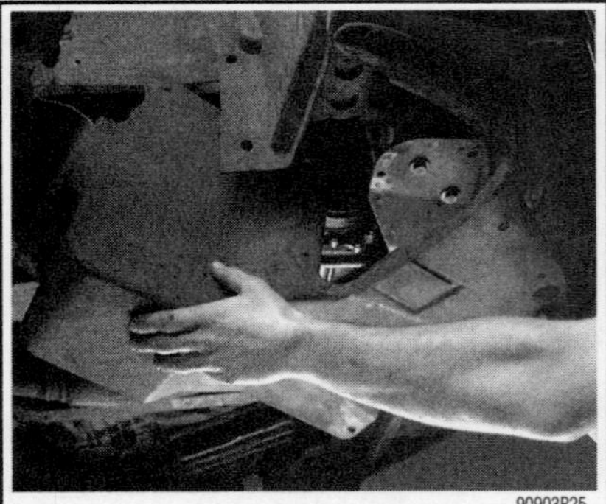

Fig. 98 Remove the right side inner fender splash shield

Fig. 99 From below the vehicle, remove the accessory drive belts

Fig. 100 Remove the crankshaft damper center bolt and washer

Fig. 101 The pulley usually slides off of the crankshaft

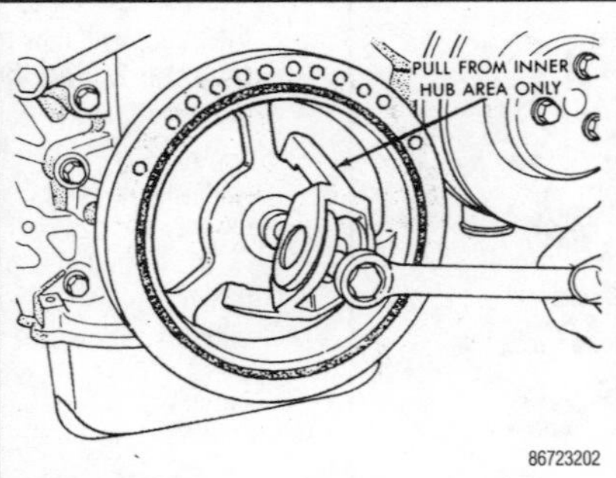

Fig. 102 If a puller is used, sure to pull on the inner hub area only—3.3L and 3.8L engines

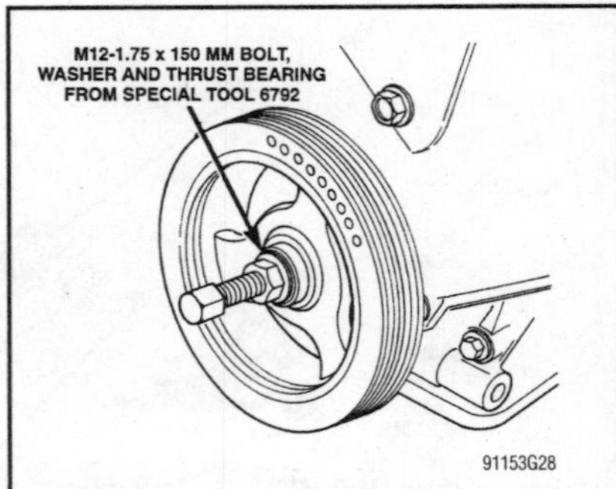

Fig. 103 2.4L engines may require a special tool to press the pulley onto the crankshaft

3. Remove the right inner splash shield.
4. Remove the accessory drive belts.
5. Break the crankshaft damper bolt loose, but do not remove it.
6. Remove the crankshaft damper. If necessary, attach a suitable 3-jawed puller to the crankshaft damper, then tighten the center bolt and remove the damper bolt and damper.

To install:

7. Install the crankshaft damper. It may be necessary to install the crankshaft damper using an M12-1.75 x 150mm bolt, washer, thrust bearing and nut from the crankshaft damper installation tool kit 6792 or equivalent.
8. Install the crankshaft damper bolt and tighten to the following specifications:
   - 2.4L engine—100 ft. lbs. (135 Nm).
   - 3.0L engine—100 ft. lbs. (135 Nm)
   - 3.3L and 3.8L engines—40 ft. lbs. (54 Nm)
9. Install the accessory drive belts.
10. Install the right inner splash shield. Install the right side wheel and tire assembly.
11. Carefully lower the vehicle, then connect the negative battery cable.

Front Crankshaft Seal

REMOVAL AND INSTALLATION

2.4L Engine

➧ See Figures 104, 105, 106 and 107

The timing belt must be removed for this procedure. Use care that all timing marks are aligned after installation or the engine will become damaged.

1. Disconnect the negative battery cable.
2. Remove the accessory drive belts.
3. Raise and safely support the vehicle. Drain the engine oil.
4. Remove the crankshaft damper/pulley using a jaw puller tool.
5. Remove the timing belt cover and timing belt.

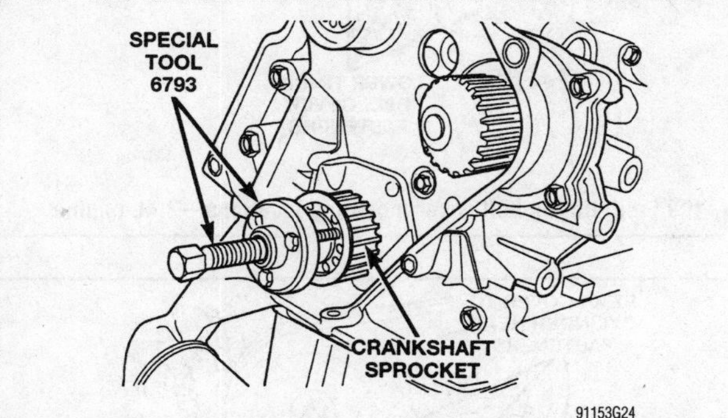

Fig. 104 To replace the front crankshaft seal on 2.4L engines, the crankshaft sprocket must be removed with a puller

6. Remove the crankshaft timing belt sprocket using tool No. 6793 or equivalent.

✻✻ WARNING

Do not nick the seal surface of the crankshaft or the seal bore.

7. Remove the front crankshaft seal using tool No. 6771 or equivalent seal puller. Be careful not to damage the seal contact area of the crankshaft.

To install:

8. Apply a light coating of clean engine oil to the lip of the new oil seal. Install the new front crankshaft oil seal using oil seal installer tool No. 6780-1 or equivalent. Install the new oil seal into the opening with the seal spring facing the inside of the engine. Be sure the oil seal is installed flush with the front cover.
9. Install the crankshaft timing belt sprocket using tool No. 6792.

➡Be sure the word "FRONT" on the timing belt sprocket is facing you.

10. Install the timing belt and timing belt cover.
11. Install the crankshaft damper/pulley onto the crankshaft. Use thrust bearing/washer and 12M-1.75 x 150mm bolt from special tool No. 6792. Install the crankshaft damper/pulley retaining bolt and torque to 105 ft. lbs. (142 Nm).
12. Lower the vehicle.
13. Install the accessory drive belts. Adjust the belts to the proper tension.
14. Refill the engine with the correct amount of clean engine oil.
15. Reconnect the negative battery cable. Start the engine and check for leaks.

3.0L Engine

1. Disconnect the negative battery cable.
2. Remove the accessory drive belts.
3. Remove the air conditioning compressor from the mounting bracket and lay it aside, if equipped. Remove the compressor mounting bracket and adjustable drive belt tensioner from the engine.
4. Remove the power steering pump/alternator belt tensioner mounting bolt and remove the tensioner.
5. Remove the power steering pump mounting bracket bolts, rear support lock nut and set the power steering pump aside.
6. Raise and safely support the vehicle.
7. Drain the engine oil into a suitable container.
8. Remove the right inner fender inner splash shield.
9. Remove the crankshaft drive pulley bolt, drive pulley and torsional damper. Lower the vehicle.
10. Place a floor jack under the engine. Separate the engine mount insulator from the engine mount bracket.
11. Raise the engine slightly and remove the engine mount bracket.
12. Remove the timing belt cover and timing belt.
13. Remove the crankshaft sprocket.
14. Remove the oil pump mounting bolts (5), and remove the oil pump assembly. Mark the mounting bolts for proper installation during reassembly.
15. Remove the front crankshaft oil seal from the oil pump cover using a suitable seal removal tool.

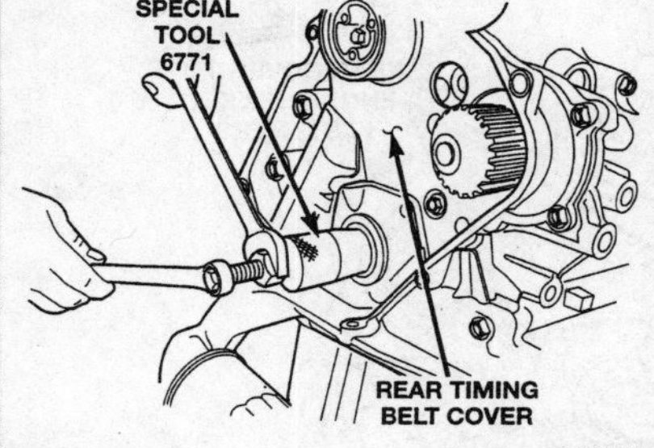

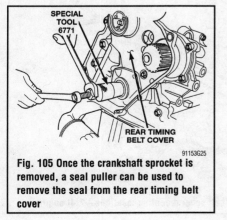

Fig. 105 Once the crankshaft sprocket is removed, a seal puller can be used to remove the seal from the rear timing belt cover

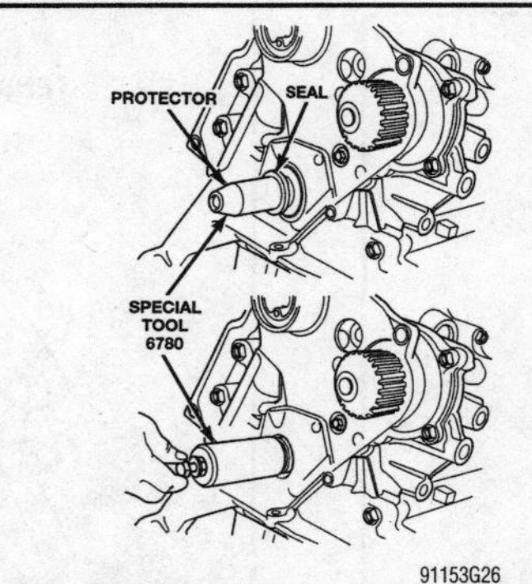

Fig. 106 Installing the new seal with the special tool

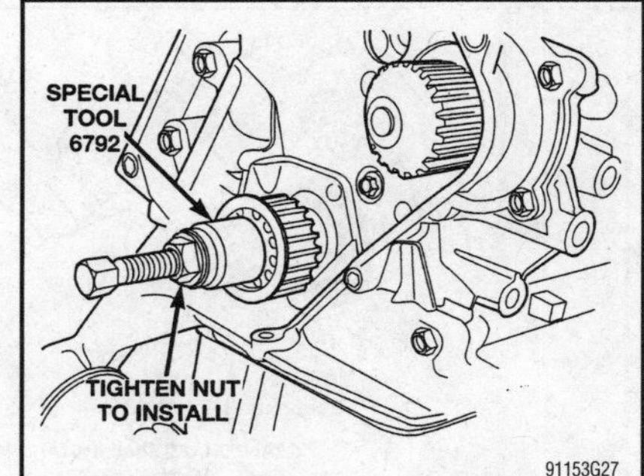

Fig. 107 Once the new seal is installed, the crankshaft pulley is pressed onto the crankshaft with a special tool

To install:

16. Clean the oil pump and engine block gasket surfaces thoroughly.
17. Position a new gasket on the pump assembly and install on the cylinder block. Make sure the correct length bolts are in their proper locations and torque all bolts to 11 ft. lbs. (15 Nm).
18. Install a new front crankshaft oil seal into the oil pump using seal installer tool MD-998717 or equivalent seal driver tool.
19. Install the crankshaft sprocket and timing belt. Recheck engine timing marks.
20. Install the timing belt covers. Torque the timing belt cover fasteners to 10 ft. lbs. (14 Nm).
21. Raise the engine slightly and install the engine mount bracket. Install the engine mount insulator into the engine mount bracket.
22. Install the torsional damper, crankshaft drive pulley and drive pulley bolt. Torque to 112 ft. lbs. (151 Nm).
23. Install the right fender inner splash shield. Lower the vehicle.
24. Install the power steering mount bracket and power steering pump.
25. Install the power steering/alternator belt tensioner.
26. Install the air conditioning adjustable drive belt tensioner and mounting bracket. Torque the mounting bolts to 40 ft. lbs. (54 Nm).
27. Install the air conditioning compressor. Torque the compressor mounting bolts to 40 ft. lbs. (54 Nm).
28. Install the accessory drive belts and adjust to the proper tension.
29. Reconnect the negative battery cable.
30. Refill the crankcase with the correct amount of clean engine oil and start the engine. Check for leaks.

3.3L and 3.8L Engines

➧ **See Figure 108**

1. Disconnect the negative battery cable.
2. Raise the vehicle and support safely.
3. Remove the right front wheel and the splash shield.
4. Remove the accessory drive belt.
5. Remove the crankshaft pulley bolt and remove the pulley using a suitable puller.
6. Remove the crankshaft oil seal from the cover using crankshaft seal removal tool C-4991 or equivalent. Be careful not to damage the crankshaft seal surface of the front timing chain cover.

To install:

7. Lubricate the lip of the new crankshaft oil seal with clean engine oil.
8. Use tool C-4992 or equivalent seal driver, to install the new crankshaft oil seal.
9. Install the crankshaft pulley using a bolt approximately 5.9 in. long and thrust bearing and washer plate. Make sure the pulley bottoms out on the crankshaft seal diameter. Install the bolt and torque to 40 ft. lbs. (54 Nm).
10. Install the accessory drive belt.
11. Install the inner splash shield and the wheel. Torque the wheel lug nuts, in a star pattern, to 95 ft. lbs. (129 Nm).
12. Lower the vehicle.
13. Reconnect the negative battery cable. Check the engine oil level; add oil as necessary.
14. Start the engine and check for leaks.

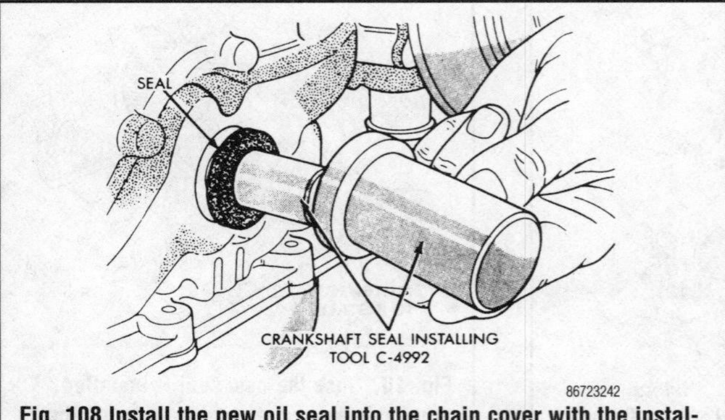

Fig. 108 Install the new oil seal into the chain cover with the installation tool as shown

Timing Belt Cover

REMOVAL & INSTALLATION

2.4L Engine

➧ **See Figures 109 and 110**

1. Disconnect the negative battery cable.
2. Remove the right inner splash shield.
3. Remove the accessory drive belts.
4. Remove the crankshaft damper.
5. Remove the right engine mount.
6. Place a floor jack under the engine to support it while the engine mount is removed.
7. Remove the engine mount bracket.
8. Remove the timing belt cover.

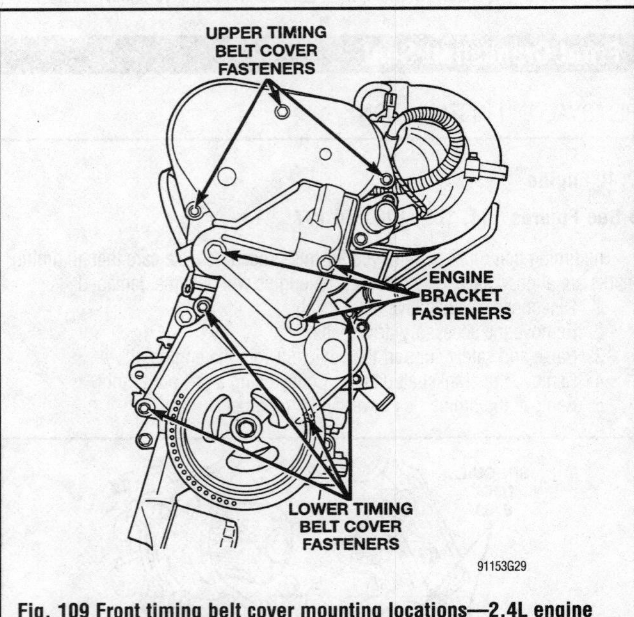

Fig. 109 Front timing belt cover mounting locations—2.4L engine

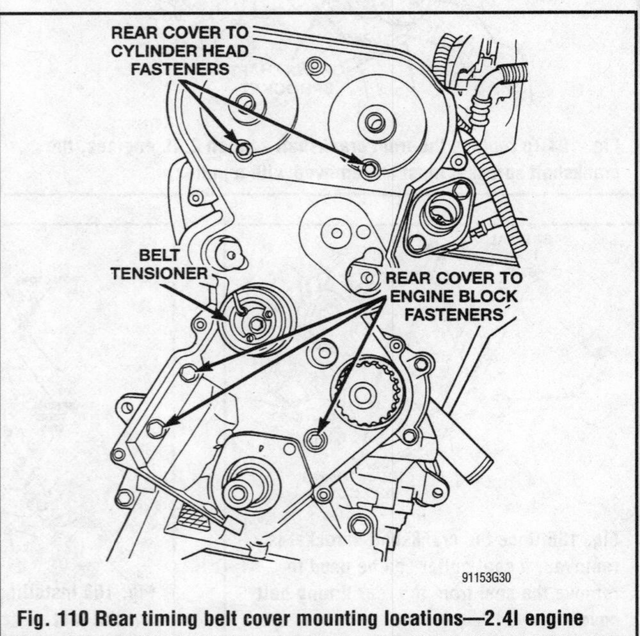

Fig. 110 Rear timing belt cover mounting locations—2.4l engine

To install:

9. Install the timing belt cover.
10. Install the engine mount bracket.
11. Install the right engine mount.
12. Remove the floor jack from under the vehicle.
13. Install the crankshaft damper.
14. Install the accessory drive belts and adjust to the proper tension.
15. Install the right inner splash shield.
16. Reconnect the negative battery cable.

3.0L Engine

➧ **See Figure 111**

1. Disconnect the negative battery cable.
2. Remove the accessory drive belts. Remove the engine mount insulator from the engine support bracket.
3. Remove the engine support bracket. Remove the crankshaft pulleys and torsional damper. Remove the timing belt covers.

To install:

4. Install the timing belt covers. Install the engine support bracket. Tighten the support bracket mounting bolts to 35 ft. lbs. (47 Nm).
5. Install the engine mount insulator, torsional damper and crankshaft pulleys.
6. Install the accessory drive belts and adjust them to the proper tension.
7. Reconnect the negative battery cable.

Timing Chain Cover

REMOVAL & INSTALLATION

3.3L and 3.8L Engines

➧ **See Figures 112, 113, 114 and 115**

1. If removing the timing chain, turn the crankshaft and position the engine so the No. 1 piston is at TDC on the compression stroke (firing position).
2. Disconnect the negative battery cable. Drain the engine coolant.
3. Support the engine with a floor jack and remove the right engine mount.
4. Raise and safely support the vehicle. Drain the engine oil.
5. Remove the oil pan and oil pump pick-up tube. If necessary, remove the transaxle inspection cover.
6. Remove the right front wheel and inner fender splash shield.
7. Remove the accessory drive belt.
8. Remove the air conditioning compressor and set aside. Remove A/C compressor mounting bracket.
9. Remove the crankshaft pulley bolt and remove the pulley using a suitable puller.
10. Remove the idler pulley from the engine bracket and remove the bracket.
11. Remove the cam sensor from the timing chain cover.

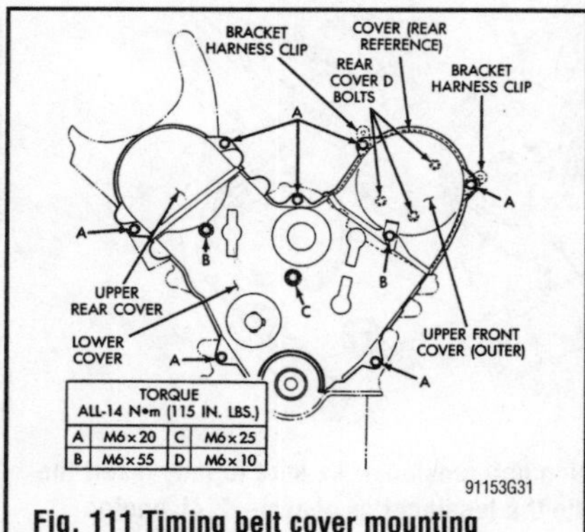

Fig. 111 Timing belt cover mounting detail—3.0L engine

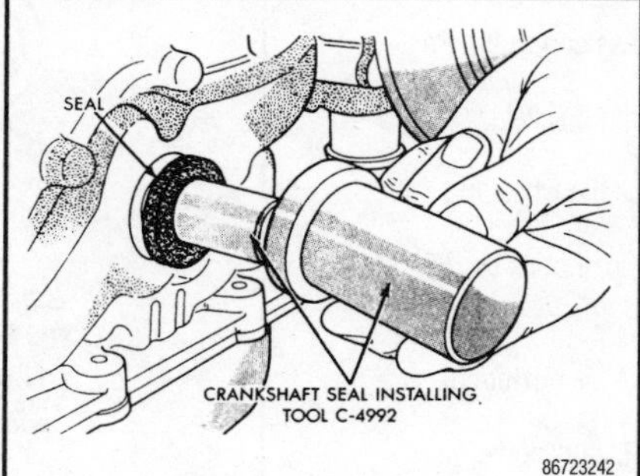

Fig. 112 Install the new oil seal with the installation tool C-4992—3.3L and 3.8L engines

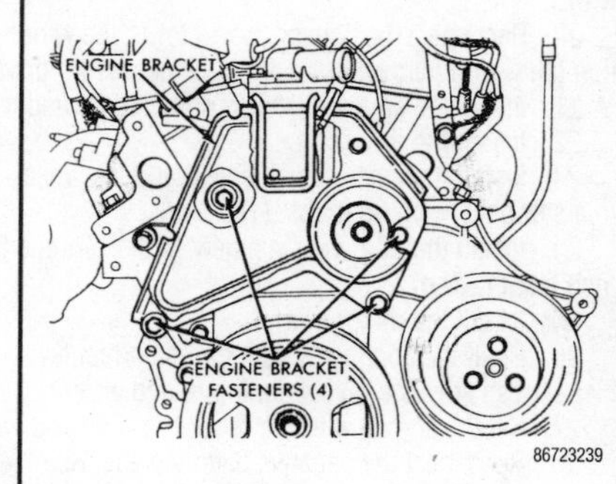

Fig. 113 Remove these four engine bracket fasteners—3.3L and 3.8L engines

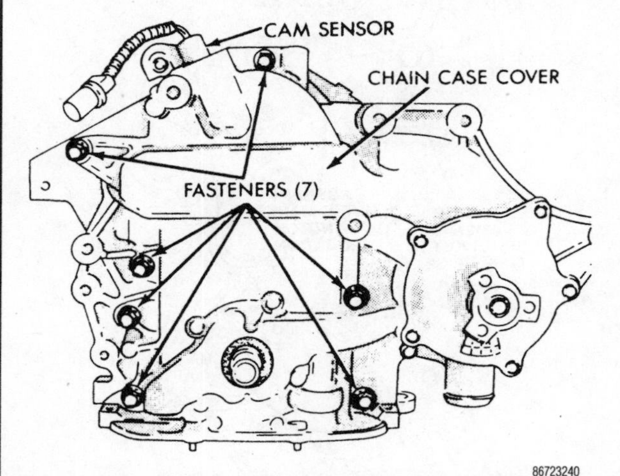

Fig. 114 To remove the timing chain cover loosen the seven fasteners—3.3L and 3.8L engines

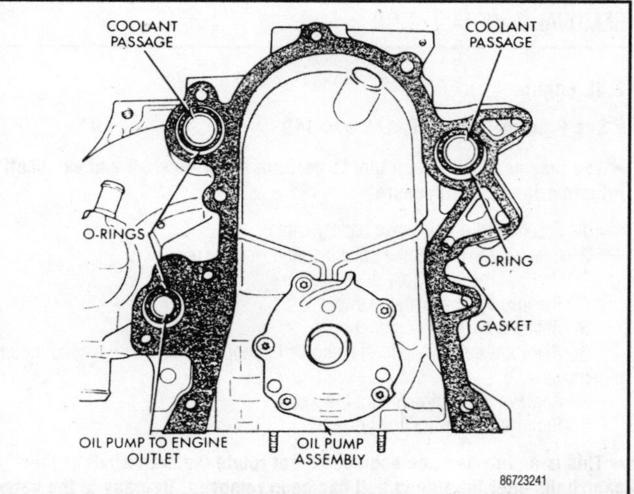

Fig. 115 Timing chain case cover gaskets and O-rings—3.3L and 3.8L engines

12. Unbolt and remove the timing chain cover from the engine. Make sure the oil pump inner rotor does not fall out.
13. Remove the crankshaft oil seal from the cover. The seal must be removed from the cover when installing to ensure proper oil pump engagement. The seal is installed from the front AFTER the timing chain front cover is completely installed as outlined below.

To install:

14. Using a new gasket, install the timing chain cover to the engine. DO NOT adhere the new gasket to the cover. Make sure the lower edge of the gasket is flush to 0.020 in. (0.50mm) past the lower edge of the cover.
15. If necessary, rotate the crankshaft so the oil pump drive flats are vertical and position the oil pump rotor so its mating flats are in the same position. Make certain that the oil pump is engaged onto the crankshaft before proceeding, or severe engine damage will result. Install the attaching bolts and torque to 20 ft. lbs. (27 Nm).
16. Use tool C-4992 or equivalent seal driver to install the crankshaft oil seal.
17. Install the crankshaft pulley.
18. Install the engine bracket and torque the bolts to 40 ft. lbs. (54 Nm). Install the idler pulley to the engine bracket.
19. Install the cam sensor, first clean off the old spacer from the sensor face completely. Inspect the O-ring for damage and replace if necessary. A new spacer must be attached to the cam sensor, prior to installation. If a new spacer is not used, engine performance will be affected. Oil the O-ring lightly and push the sensor into its bore in the timing case cover until contact is made with the cam timing sprocket. Hold in this position and tighten it to 108 inch lbs. (12 Nm).
20. Reconnect the sensor connector to the wiring harness connector. Position the wiring harness away from the accessory drive belt.
21. Install the air conditioning compressor and mounting bracket.
22. Install the drive belt.
23. Install the inner splash shield and the wheel. Torque the wheel lug nuts, in a star pattern, to 95 ft. lbs. (129 Nm).
24. Install the oil pan with a new gasket. Torque the oil pan bolts to 105 inch lbs. (12 Nm).
25. Install the motor mount.
26. Refill the cooling system to the correct level with a 50/50 mixture of clean, fresh ethylene glycol antifreeze and water.
27. Fill the engine with the proper amount and type of clean engine oil.
28. Reconnect the negative battery cable. Road test the vehicle and check for leaks.

Timing Belt and Sprockets

REMOVAL & INSTALLATION

2.4L Engine

See Figures 116, 117, 118 and 119

You may need DRB scan tool to perform the crankshaft and camshaft relearn alignment procedure.

1. Disconnect the negative battery cable.
2. Remove the right inner splash shield.
3. Remove the accessory drive belts.
4. Remove the crankshaft damper.
5. Remove the right engine mount.
6. Place a floor jack under the engine to support it while the engine mount is removed.
7. Remove the engine mount bracket.
8. Remove the timing belt cover.

This is an interference engine. Do not rotate the crankshaft or the camshafts after the timing belt has been removed. Damage to the valve components may occur. Before removing the timing belt, always align the timing marks.

9. Align the timing marks of the timing belt sprockets to the timing marks on the rear timing belt cover and oil pump cover. Loosen the timing belt tensioner bolts.
10. Remove the timing belt and the tensioner.

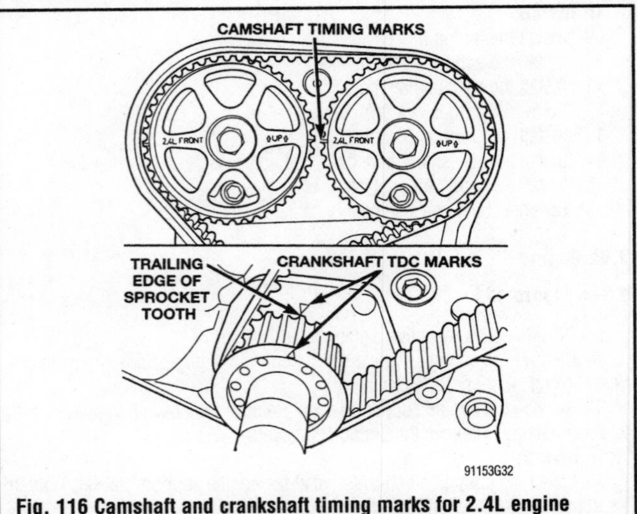

Fig. 116 Camshaft and crankshaft timing marks for 2.4L engine

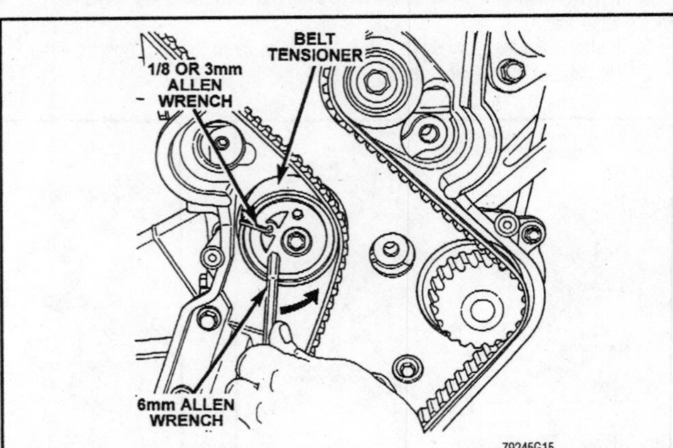

Fig. 117 To lock the timing belt tensioner, be sure to fully insert the smaller Allen wrench into the tensioner as shown—2.4L engine

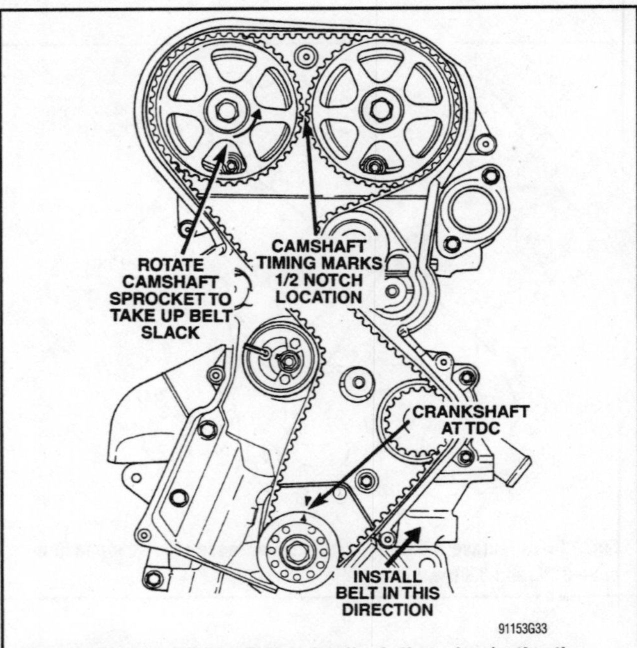

Fig. 118 Timing belt installation detail—2.4L engine (notice the camshaft alignment)

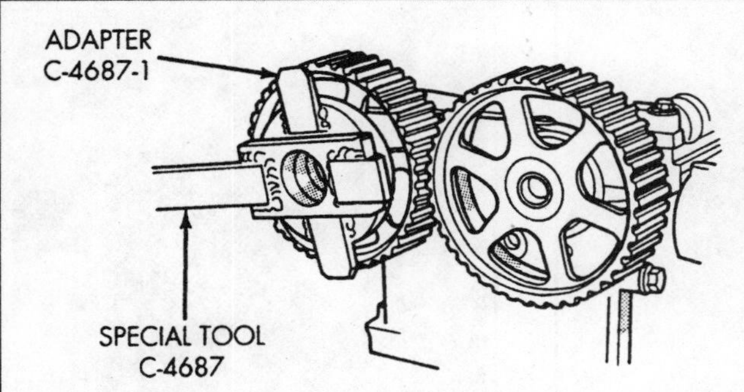

Fig. 119 The upper sprockets should be held in place with the special tool for removal and installation

11. If necessary, remove the camshaft timing belt sprockets.
12. If necessary, remove the crankshaft timing belt sprocket using removal tool No. 6793 or equivalent.
13. Place the tensioner into a soft-jawed vise to compress the tensioner.
14. After compressing the tensioner, insert a pin (5⁄64 in. Allen wrench will also work) into the plunger side hole to retain the plunger until installation.

To install:

15. If necessary, using tool No. 6792 or equivalent, to install the crankshaft timing belt sprocket onto the crankshaft.
16. If necessary, install the camshaft sprockets onto the camshafts. Install and tighten the camshaft sprocket bolts to 75 ft. lbs. (101 Nm).
17. Set the crankshaft sprocket to Top Dead Center (TDC) by aligning the notch on the sprocket with the arrow on the oil pump housing.
18. Set the camshafts to align the timing marks on the sprockets.
19. Move the crankshaft to ½ notch before TDC.
20. Install the timing belt starting at the crankshaft, then around the water pump sprocket, idler pulley, camshaft sprockets and around the tensioner pulley.
21. Move the crankshaft sprocket to TDC to take up the belt slack.
22. Install the tensioner on the engine block but do not tighten.
23. Using a torque wrench on the tensioner pulley, apply 250 inch lbs.(28 Nm) of torque to the tensioner pulley.
24. With torque being applied to the tensioner pulley, move the tensioner up against the tensioner pulley bracket and tighten the fasteners to 23 ft. lbs.(31 Nm).
25. Remove the tensioner plunger pin, the tension is correct when the plunger pin can be removed and reinserted easily.

✻✻ WARNING

If any binding is felt when adjusting the timing belt tension by turning the crankshaft, STOP turning the engine, because the pistons may be hitting the valves.

26. Rotate the crankshaft two revolutions and recheck the timing marks. Wait several minutes and then recheck that the plunger pin can easily be removed and installed.
27. Install the front timing belt cover.
28. Install the engine mount bracket.
29. Install the right engine mount.
30. Remove the floor jack from under the vehicle.
31. Install the crankshaft damper and tighten it to 105 ft. lbs. (142 Nm).
32. Install the accessory drive belts and adjust to the proper tension.
33. Install the right inner splash shield.
34. Reconnect the negative battery cable.
35. Perform the crankshaft and camshaft relearn alignment procedure using the DRB scan tool or equivalent.

3.0L Engine

See Figures 120 thru 128

The timing belt can be inspected by removing the upper front outer timing belt cover.

Working on any engine (especially overhead camshaft engines) requires much care be given to valve timing. It is good practice to set the engine up at TDC No. 1 cylinder firing position before beginning work. Verify that all timing marks on the crankshaft and camshaft sprockets are properly aligned before removing the timing belt and starting camshaft service. This serves as a point of reference for all work that follows. Valve timing is very important and engine damage will result if the work is incorrect.

1. Disconnect the negative battery cable.
2. Remove the accessory drive belts. Remove the engine mount insulator from the engine support bracket.

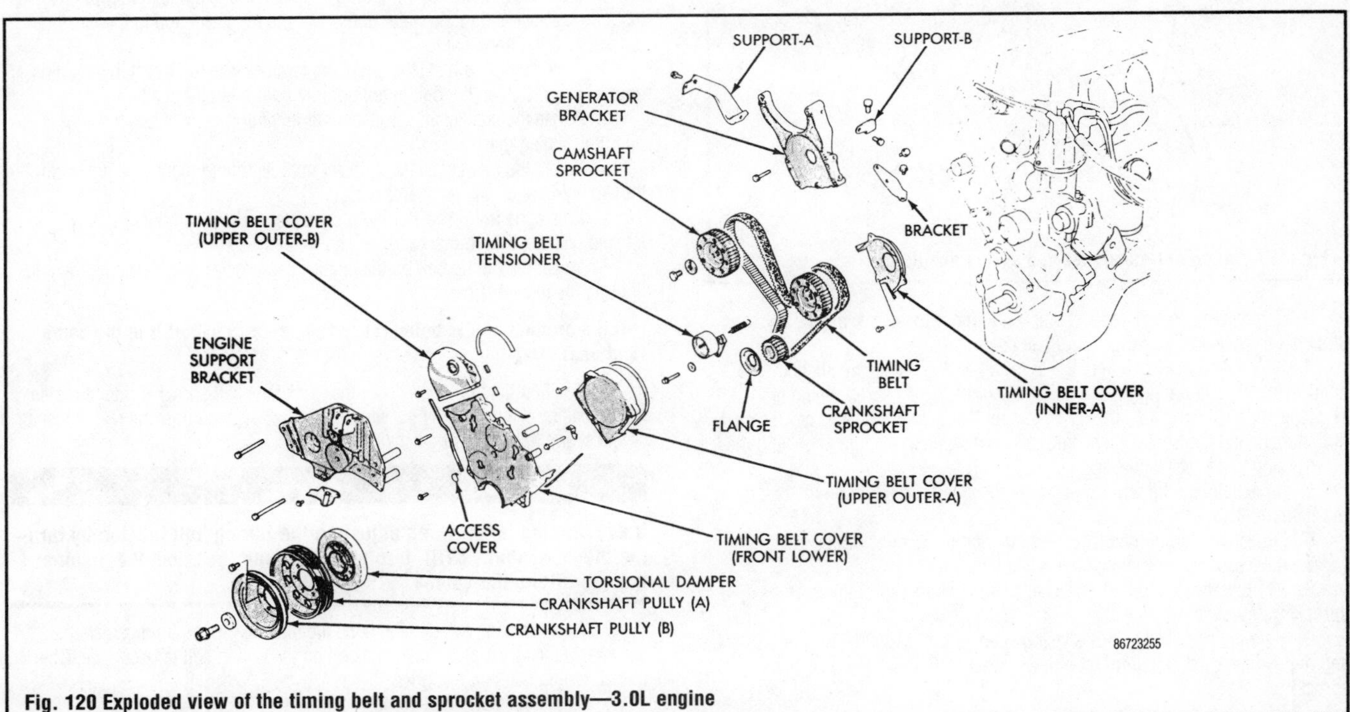

Fig. 120 Exploded view of the timing belt and sprocket assembly—3.0L engine

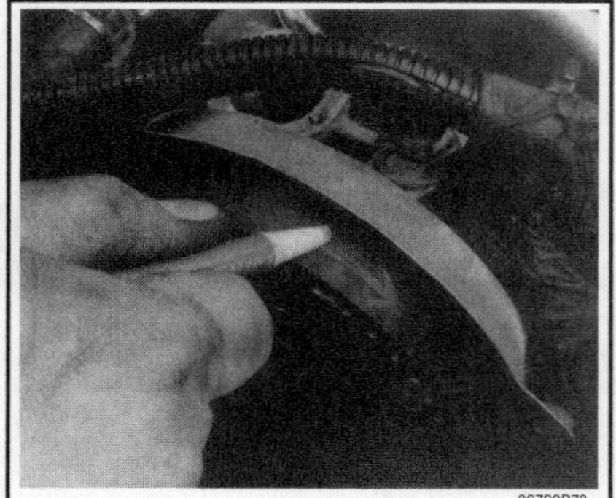
86723P72

Fig. 121 Mark the direction of travel for the timing belt for correct installation

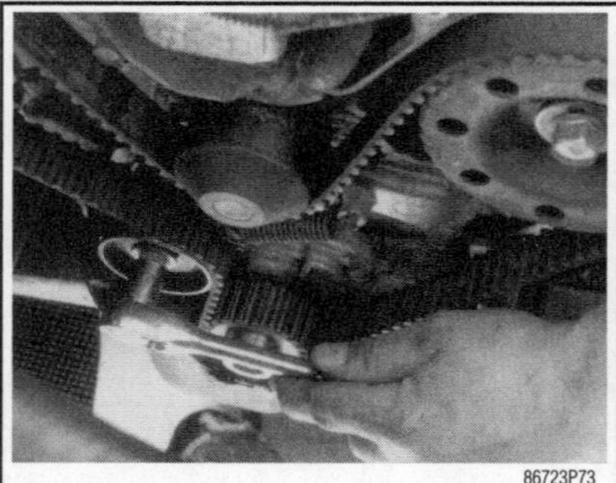
86723P73

Fig. 122 Turn the center tensioner pulley bolt until the timing belt has enough slack . . .

86723P74

Fig. 123 . . . then slide the timing belt off of the camshaft sprockets

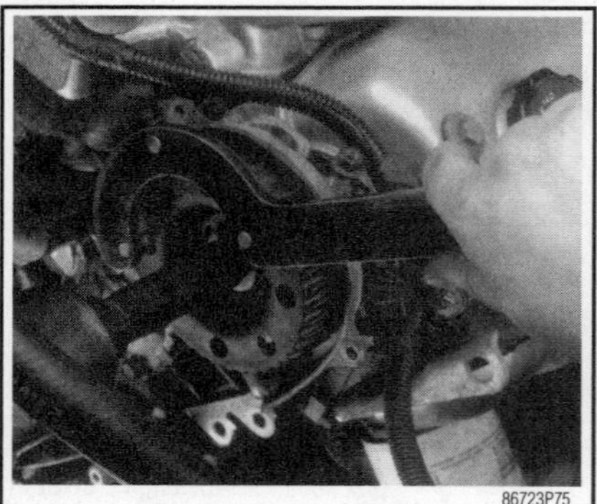
86723P75

Fig. 124 Rent or borrow the special tool to hold the camshaft sprockets steady . . .

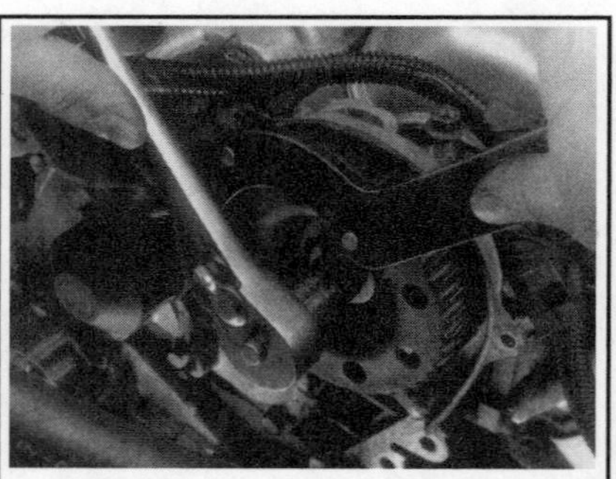
86723P76

Fig. 125 . . . while loosening the center retaining bolt on the camshaft pulley, then . . .

86723P77

Fig. 126 . . . remove the camshaft sprocket from the end of the camshaft

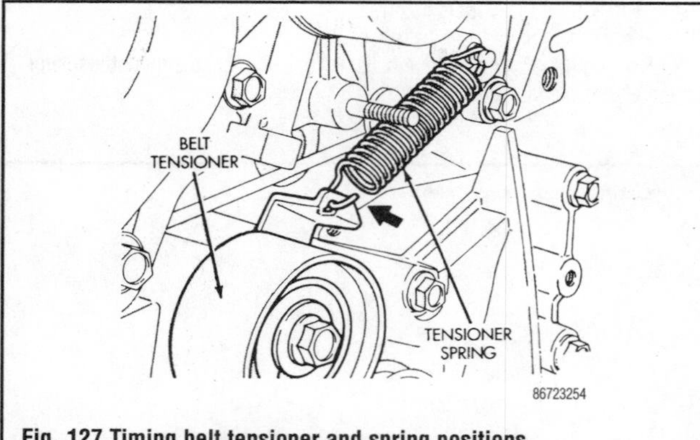

Fig. 127 Timing belt tensioner and spring positions

3. Remove the engine support bracket. Remove the crankshaft pulleys and torsional damper. Remove the timing belt covers.

4. Rotate the crankshaft until the sprocket timing marks are aligned. The crankshaft sprocket timing mark should align with the oil pump timing mark. The rear camshaft sprocket timing mark should align with the generator bracket timing mark and the front camshaft sprocket timing mark should align with the inner timing belt cover timing mark.

5. If the belt is to be reused, mark the direction of rotation on the belt for installation reference.

6. Loosen the timing belt tensioner bolt and remove the timing belt.

7. If necessary, remove the timing belt tensioner.

8. Remove the crankshaft sprocket flange shield and crankshaft sprocket.

9. Hold the camshaft sprocket using spanner tool MB990775 or equivalent, and remove the camshaft sprocket bolt and washer. Remove the camshaft sprocket.

To install:

10. Install the camshaft sprocket on the camshaft with the retaining bolt and washer. Hold the camshaft sprocket using spanner tool MB990775 or equivalent, and tighten the bolt to 70 ft. lbs. (95 Nm).

11. Install the crankshaft sprocket.

12. If removed, install the timing belt tensioner and tensioner spring. Hook the spring upper end to the water pump pin and the lower end to the tensioner bracket with the hook out.

13. Turn the timing belt tensioner counterclockwise full travel in the adjustment slot and tighten the bolt to temporarily hold it in this position.

14. Rotate the crankshaft sprocket until its timing mark is aligned with the oil pump timing mark.

15. Rotate the rear camshaft sprocket until its timing mark is aligned with the timing mark on the generator bracket.

16. Rotate the front (radiator side) camshaft sprocket until its mark is aligned with the timing mark on the inner timing belt cover.

17. Install the timing belt on the crankshaft sprocket while keeping the belt tight on the tension side.

➡If the original belt is being reused, be sure to install it in the same rotational direction.

18. Position the timing belt over the front camshaft sprocket (radiator side). Next, position the belt under the water pump pulley, then over the rear camshaft sprocket and finally over the tensioner.

⁂ WARNING

If any binding is felt when adjusting the timing belt tension by turning the crankshaft, STOP turning the engine, because the pistons may be hitting the valves.

19. Apply rotating force in the opposite direction to the front camshaft sprocket (radiator side) to create tension on the timing belt tension side. Check that all timing marks are aligned.

20. Install the crankshaft sprocket flange.

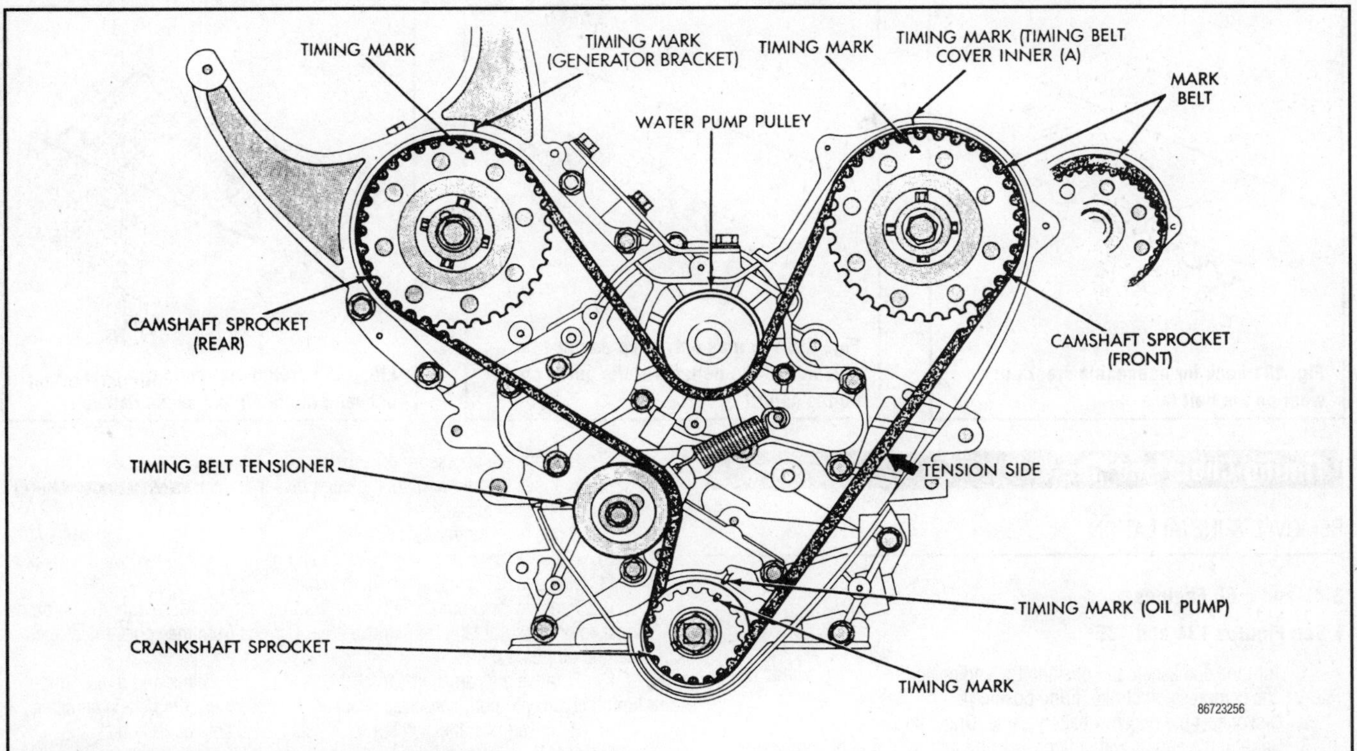

Fig. 128 Timing belt routing and timing mark locations

21. Loosen the tensioner bolt and allow the tensioner spring to tension the belt.
22. Rotate the crankshaft two full turns in a clockwise direction. Turn the crankshaft smoothly and in a clockwise direction only.
23. Again line up the timing marks. If all marks are aligned, tighten the tensioner bolt to 250 inch lbs. (28 Nm). Otherwise repeat the installation procedure.
24. Install the timing belt covers. Install the engine support bracket. Tighten the support bracket mounting bolts to 35 ft. lbs. (47 Nm).
25. Install the engine mount insulator, torsional damper and crankshaft pulleys. Tighten the crankshaft pulley bolt to 112 ft. lbs. (151 Nm).
26. Install the accessory drive belts and adjust them to the proper tension.
27. Reconnect the negative battery cable.
28. Run the engine and check for proper operation. Road test the vehicle.

INSPECTION

See Figures 129, 130, 131, 132 and 133

WARNING

Timing belt maintenance is extremely important! All Neon models utilize an interference-type, non-free-wheeling engine. If the timing belt breaks, the valves in the cylinder head may strike the pistons, causing potentially serious (also time-consuming and expensive) engine damage. The recommended replacement interval for the timing belt is 102,000 miles (163,000km), or sooner.

You would be wise to check the belt periodically to make sure it has not become damaged or worn. Generally speaking, a severely worn belt may cause engine performance to drop dramatically, but a damaged belt (which could give out suddenly) may not give as much warning. In general, any time the engine timing cover(s) is(are) removed you should inspect the belt for premature parting, severe cracks or missing teeth. Also, an access plug or cover is provided in the upper portion of the timing cover so that camshaft timing can be checked without cover removal. If timing is found to be off, cover removal and further belt inspection or replacement is necessary.

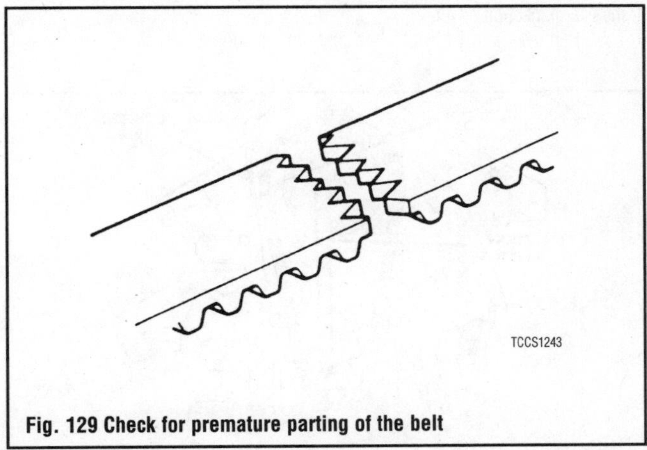

Fig. 129 Check for premature parting of the belt

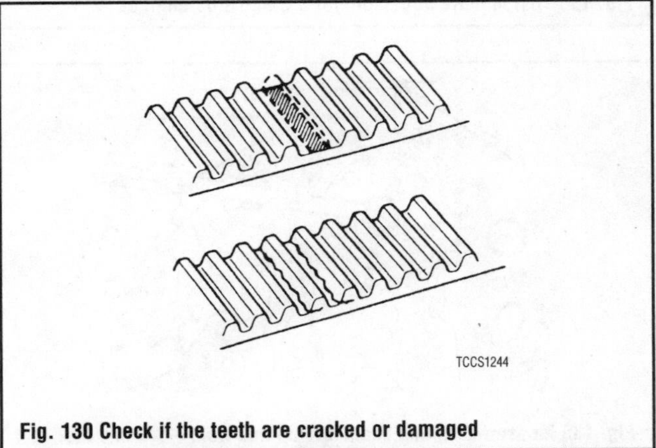

Fig. 130 Check if the teeth are cracked or damaged

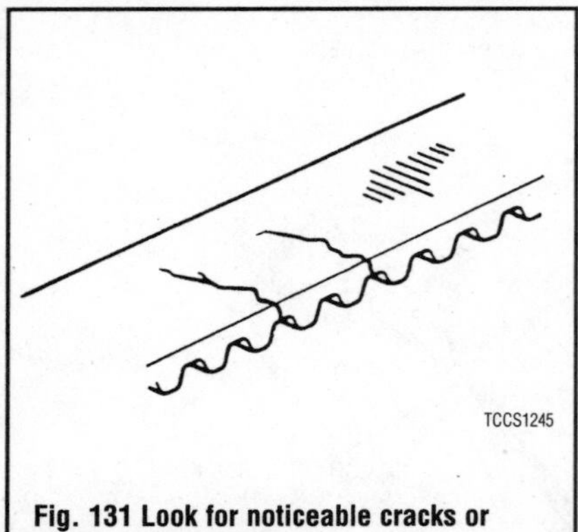

Fig. 131 Look for noticeable cracks or wear on the belt face

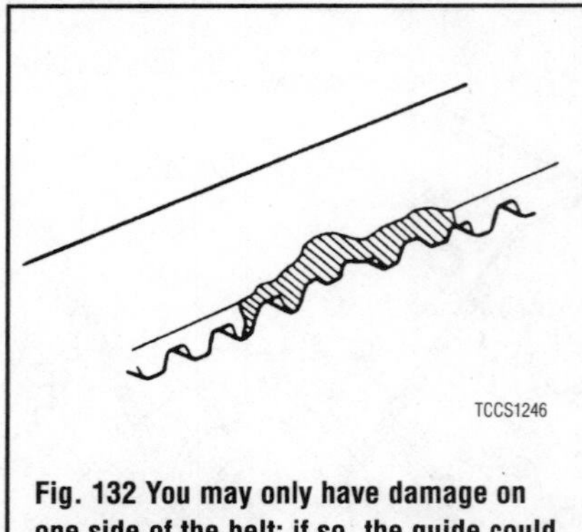

Fig. 132 You may only have damage on one side of the belt; if so, the guide could be the culprit

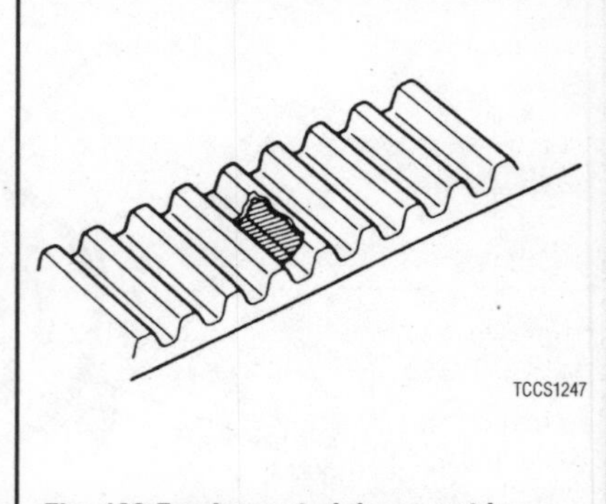

Fig. 133 Foreign materials can get in between the teeth and cause damage

Timing Chain and Gears

REMOVAL & INSTALLATION

3.3L and 3.8L Engines

➧ **See Figures 134 and 135**

1. Turn the crankshaft and position the engine so the No. 1 piston is at TDC on the compression stroke (firing position).
2. Disconnect the negative battery cable. Drain the coolant.
3. Support the engine with a floor jack and remove the right engine mount.
4. Raise and safely support the vehicle. Drain the engine oil.
5. Remove the oil pan and oil pump pick-up tube. If necessary, remove the transaxle inspection cover.
6. Remove the right front wheel and inner fender splash shield.

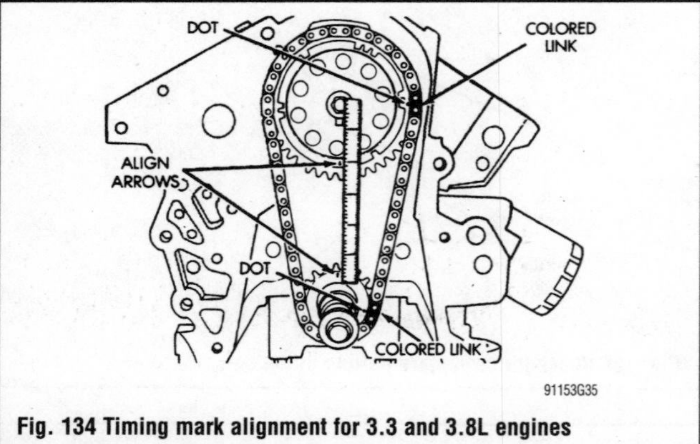

Fig. 134 Timing mark alignment for 3.3 and 3.8L engines

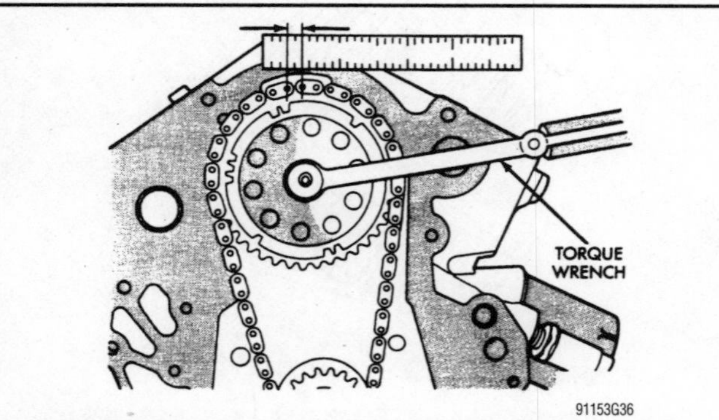

Fig. 135 Measuring timing chain stretch and wear—3.3 and 3.8L engines

7. Remove the accessory drive belt.
8. Remove the air conditioning compressor and set aside. Remove A/C compressor mounting bracket.
9. Remove the crankshaft pulley.
10. Remove the idler pulley from the engine bracket and remove the bracket.
11. Remove the camshaft position sensor.
12. Remove the timing chain cover from the engine. Make sure the oil pump inner rotor does not fall out. Remove the 3 O-rings from the coolant passages and the oil pump outlet.
13. Remove the camshaft sprocket attaching cup washer and remove the timing chain with both sprockets attached. Remove the timing chain snubber.
14. Remove the crankshaft sprocket using a suitable puller tool.

To install:

15. Assemble the timing chain and sprockets.
16. Turn the crankshaft and camshaft to line up with the key way locations of the sprockets.
17. Slide both sprockets over their respective shafts and use a straightedge to confirm alignment.
18. Install the cup washer and camshaft bolt. Torque the bolt to 40 ft. lbs. (54 Nm).
19. Check camshaft end-play. The specification with a new plate is 0.005–0.012 in. (0.0127–0.304mm) and 0.012 in. (0.310mm) maximum with a used plate. Replace the thrust plate if not within specifications.
20. Install the timing chain snubber.
21. Clean all parts well. Thoroughly clean and dry the gasket mating surfaces. Install new O-rings to the block.
22. Remove the crankshaft oil seal from the cover. The seal must be removed from the cover when installing to ensure proper oil pump engagement. The seal is installed from the front AFTER the timing chain front cover is completely installed as outlined below.
23. Using a new gasket, install the chain case cover to the engine. DO NOT adhere the new gasket to the cover. Make sure the lower edge of the gasket is flush to 0.020 in. (0.50mm) past the lower edge of the cover.
24. If necessary, rotate the crankshaft so the oil pump drive flats are vertical and position the oil pump rotor so its mating flats are in the same position. Make certain that the oil pump is engaged onto the crankshaft before proceeding, or severe engine damage will result. Install the attaching bolts and torque to 20 ft. lbs. (27 Nm).
25. Use tool C-4992 or equivalent seal driver to install the crankshaft oil seal.
26. Install the crankshaft pulley using a bolt approximately 6 in. (150mm) long and thrust bearing and washer plate. Make sure the pulley bottoms out on the crankshaft seal diameter. Install the bolt and torque to 40 ft. lbs. (54 Nm).
27. Install the engine bracket and torque the bolts to 40 ft. lbs. (54 Nm). Install the idler pulley to the engine bracket.
28. Install the camshaft position sensor.
29. Install the air conditioning compressor and mounting bracket.
30. Install the drive belt.
31. Install the inner splash shield and the wheel. Torque the wheel lug nuts, in a star pattern, to 95 ft. lbs. (129 Nm).
32. Install the oil pan.
33. Install the motor mount.
34. Refill the cooling system to the correct level with a 50/50 mixture of clean, fresh ethylene glycol antifreeze and water.

35. Fill the engine with the proper amount and type of clean engine oil.
36. Reconnect the negative battery cable. Road test the vehicle and check for leaks.

Camshaft, Bearings and Lifters

REMOVAL & INSTALLATION

✱✱ CAUTION

The fuel injection system remains under pressure, even after the engine has been turned OFF. The fuel system pressure must be relieved before disconnecting any fuel lines. Failure to do so may result in fire and/or personal injury.

2.4L Engine

See Figures 136, 137, 138 and 139

This engine uses a Dual Over Head Camshaft (DOHC) 4-valves per cylinder crossflow aluminum cylinder head. The valves are actuated by roller cam followers which pivot on stationary hydraulic valve lash adjusters. Care must be taken to ensure all valve timing marks align after cylinder head and valvetrain service.

1. Properly relieve the fuel system pressure.
2. Disconnect the negative battery cable.
3. Label and disconnect the spark plug wires from the spark plugs.
4. Remove the ignition coil pack and spark plug wires.
5. Remove the cylinder head cover retaining fasteners and remove the cylinder head cover from the cylinder head. Discard the old cylinder head cover gasket.
6. Remove the ground strap.
7. Remove the timing belt covers, timing belt and camshaft sprockets.
8. Take note that the camshaft bearing caps are numbered for correct location during installation. Remove the outer bearing caps first.

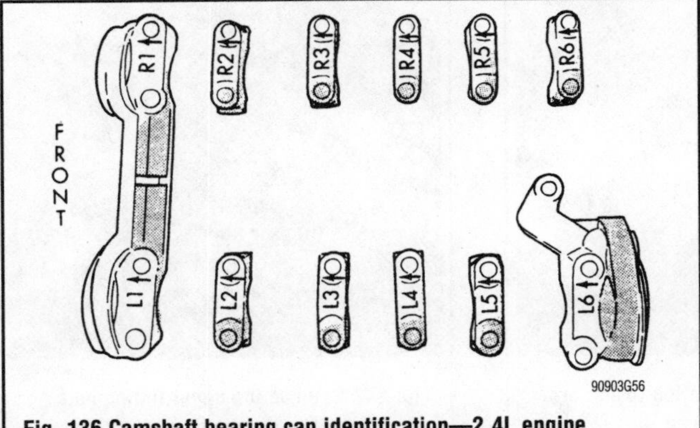

Fig. 136 Camshaft bearing cap identification—2.4L engine

9. Loosen, but do not remove, the camshaft bearing cap retaining fasteners in the correct sequence. Perform this step on one camshaft at a time.
10. Tag the camshafts for intake and exhaust, if they are to be reused, for later installation. The camshafts are not interchangeable. Remove the camshaft bearing caps and the camshafts.
11. Remove the camshaft followers. Any components that are to be reused must be installed in their original locations. Use care to identify and mark the positions of any removed valvetrain components so they may be reinstalled correctly.
12. Inspect the camshaft bearing oil feed holes in the cylinder head for clogging. Inspect the camshaft bearing journals for wear or scoring. Check the cam surface for abnormal wear and damage. A visible worn groove in the roller path or on the cam lobes is cause for replacement.

To install:

13. Thoroughly clean the camshafts and related parts.
14. The camshaft end-play should be checked using the following procedure:
    a. Oil the camshaft journals and install the camshaft **WITHOUT** the cam follower assemblies. Install the rear cam caps and tighten to 250 inch lbs. (28 Nm).
    b. Carefully push the camshaft as far rearward as it will go.
    c. Set up a dial indicator to bear against the front of the camshaft (the sprocket end). Zero the indicator.
    d. Move the camshaft forward as far as it will go. Read the dial indicator. End-play specification is 0.002–0.010 in. (0.05–0.15mm).
    e. If excessive end-play is present, inspect the cylinder head and camshaft for wear; replace if necessary.
15. If satisfied with the fit and condition of the camshafts, remove the camshafts for installation of the cam followers.
16. The hydraulic valve lash adjusters are inside the roller cam followers. Ensure they are clean, well-lubricated with clean engine oil and properly positioned. Install the cam followers in their original positions on the hydraulic lash adjuster and valve stem.

✱✱ WARNING

To avoid valve-to-piston contact, be sure NONE of the pistons are at Top Dead Center (TDC) when installing the camshafts.

17. Lubricate the camshaft bearing journals and cam followers with clean engine oil and install the camshafts. Install right and left camshaft bearing caps No. 2 through No. 5 and right side No. 6. Tighten the M6 fasteners to 105 inch lbs. (12 Nm) in correct sequence.
18. Apply Mopar® Gasket Maker or equivalent sealer to the No. 1 and left side No. 6 bearing caps. Install the bearing caps and tighten the M8 fasteners to 250 inch lbs. (28 Nm). The end caps must be installed before the seals may be installed.
19. Install the camshaft end seals.
20. Install the camshaft sprockets, if removed. Install the timing belt using care to be sure all timing marks are properly aligned. Install the timing belt covers.

✱✱ WARNING

Verify that all timing marks are correct. If the timing belt or sprockets are incorrectly installed, engine damage will occur. Take time to be sure all timing marks are correctly aligned.

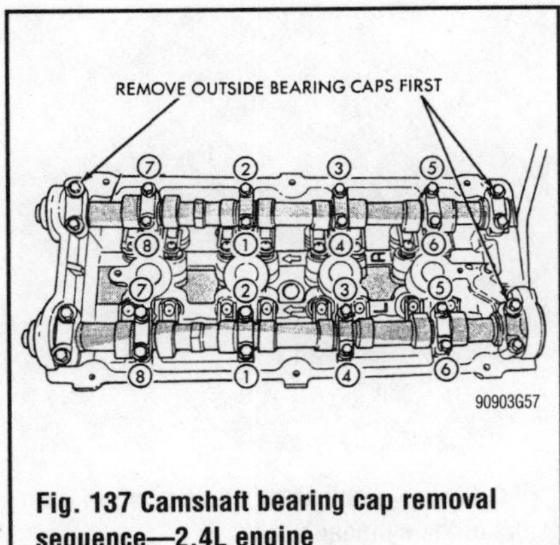

Fig. 137 Camshaft bearing cap removal sequence—2.4L engine

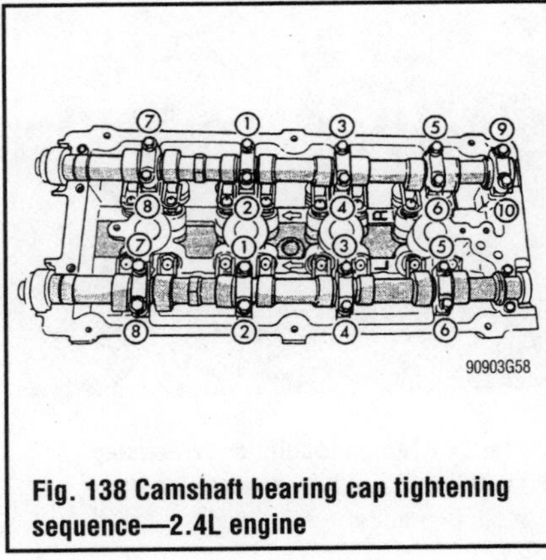

Fig. 138 Camshaft bearing cap tightening sequence—2.4L engine

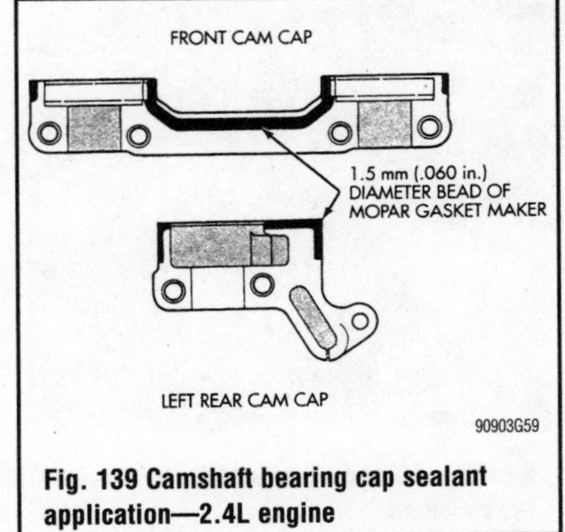

Fig. 139 Camshaft bearing cap sealant application—2.4L engine

21. Clean the cylinder head cover and cylinder head gasket rails (mating surfaces). Make certain the rails are flat.

22. Install new cylinder head cover gaskets. Use care; DO NOT allow oil or solvents to contact the timing belt as they can deteriorate the rubber and cause tooth skipping. Apply Mopar Silicone Rubber Adhesive Sealant, or equivalent, at the camshaft cap corners and at the top edge of the ½ round seal.

➡Inspect the spark plug well seals for cracking and/or swelling, and replace if necessary.

23. Install the cylinder head cover assembly to the head and tighten the fasteners in sequence using the following three substeps:

a. Tighten all cylinder head cover fasteners to 40 inch lbs. (4.5 Nm).
b. Tighten all fasteners to 80 inch lbs. (9 Nm).
c. Tighten all fasteners to 105 inch lbs. (12 Nm).

24. Install the ignition coil pack and connect the spark plug wiring to the correct spark plugs. Tighten the coil pack retaining fasteners to 105 inch lbs. (12 Nm).

25. Reconnect the ground strap.

26. Ensure all vacuum lines and remaining wiring have been reconnected.

➡To remove any dirt particles that may have fallen in the engine, an oil and filter change is recommended.

27. Connect the negative battery cable and test run the vehicle. Check for leaks and for proper operation.

3.0L Engine

➧ See Figures 140 thru 153

Working on any engine, but especially overhead camshaft engines, requires much care be given to valve timing. It is good practice to set the engine up at TDC No. 1 cylinder firing position. Verify that all timing marks on the crankshaft and camshaft sprockets are properly aligned before removing the timing belt and beginning camshaft service. This serves as a point of reference for all work that follows. Valve timing is very important and engine damage will result if the work is incorrect.

1. Disconnect the negative battery cable.
2. Remove the air cleaner assembly. Disconnect and label the spark plug wires.
3. Remove the accessory drive belts, if necessary.
4. Move away any wiring harnesses for easier access to the rear valve cover. Disconnect and label any vacuum hoses required for easier removal of the valve covers.
5. Remove the valve covers from the vehicle.
6. Remove the timing belt. Remove the camshaft timing belt sprockets.
7. Install auto lash adjuster retainers MD998443 or equivalent on the rocker arms.
8. If removing the right side (front) camshaft, remove the distributor adapter.
9. Remove the camshaft bearing caps, but do not remove the bolts from the caps.
10. Remove the rocker arms, rocker shafts and bearing caps, as an assembly.

➡Use care not to mix rocker arms and shafts. The oil holes are different in the shafts and each must be returned to its original location or the engine overhead will not be lubricated.

11. Remove the camshaft from the cylinder head.
12. Inspect the bearing journals on the camshaft, cylinder head and bearing caps.

To install:

13. Clean all parts well. Pay particular attention to the oil feed holes in the cylinder head, checking for clogging. If the camshafts are to be reused, check with a micrometer. Measure the cam height and replace if out of limit. Standard value is 1.624 in. (41.25mm) and wear limit is 1.604 in. (40.75mm).
14. Lubricate the camshaft journals and camshaft with clean engine oil and install the camshaft in the cylinder head.
15. Align the camshaft bearing caps with the arrow mark (depending on cylinder numbers) and in numerical order.
16. Apply sealer at the ends of the bearing caps and install the assembly.
17. Tighten the bearing cap bolts, in the following sequence: No. 3, No. 2, No. 1 and No. 4 to 85 inch lbs. (10 Nm).
18. Repeat the sequence, increasing torque to 180 inch lbs. (20 Nm).
19. Install the distributor adapter, if it was removed.

86723P78

Fig. 140 After the timing belt and camshaft sprocket are removed, loosen the rocker arm hold-down bolts . . .

86723P79

Fig. 141 . . .then remove the rocker arm cover from the cylinder head

86723P80

Fig. 142 Remove the upper timing belt rear cover rétaining bolts . . .

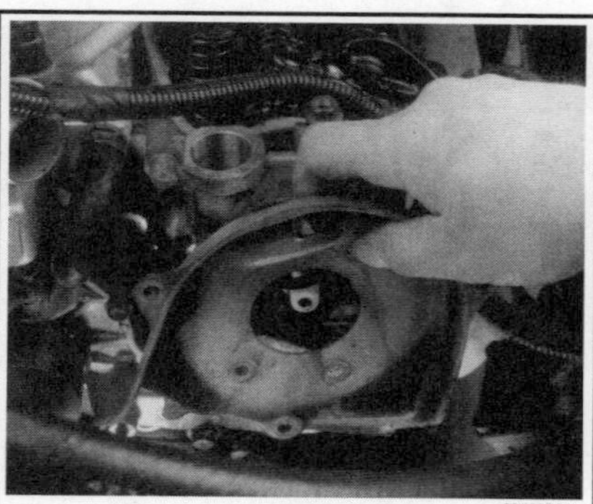

86723P81

Fig. 143 . . . and lift the rear cover from the camshaft

86723P82

Fig. 144 The distributor drive housing must be removed by unscrewing the mounting bolts . . .

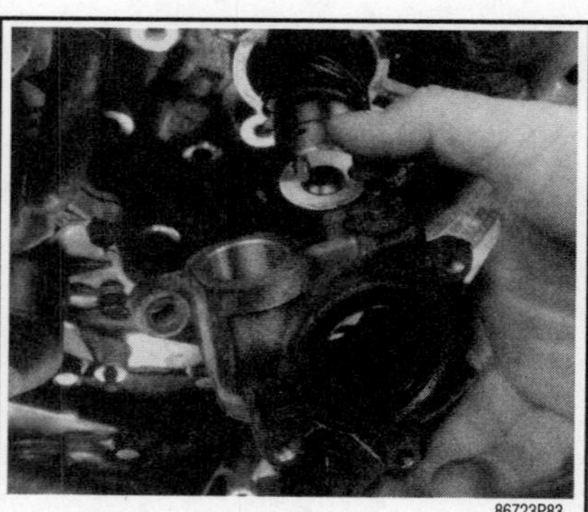

86723P83

Fig. 145 . . . and simply pulling off of the end of the cylinder head

Fig. 146 Make sure to remove the used O-ring and install a new one on the drive housing for assembly

Fig. 147 Completely loosen the rocker arm shaft hold-down bolts

Fig. 148 Lift the rocker arm shaft assembly off of the cylinder head (do not lose the lash adjusters)

Fig. 149 Lift the camshaft out of the cylinder head

Fig. 150 Make sure to remove and discard the used rear and front camshaft seals

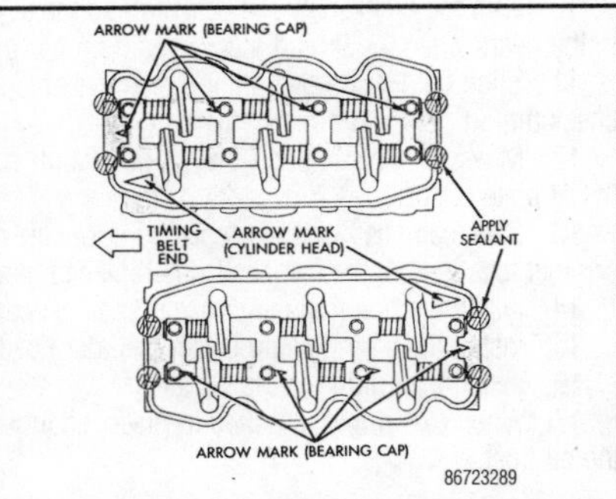

Fig. 151 When installing the rocker shafts make sure the arrows point in the same direction as the arrows on the cylinder heads

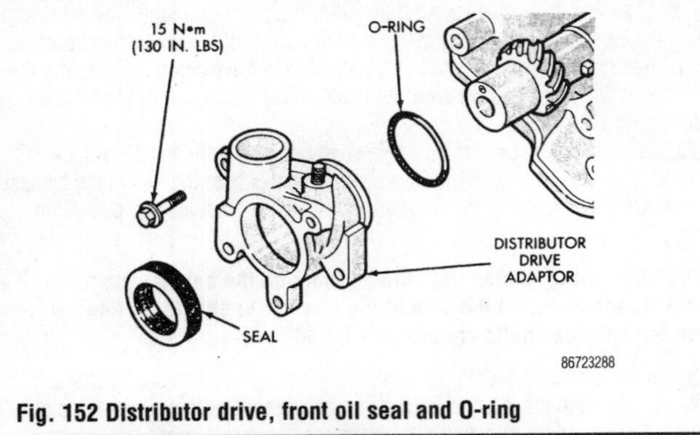

Fig. 152 Distributor drive, front oil seal and O-ring

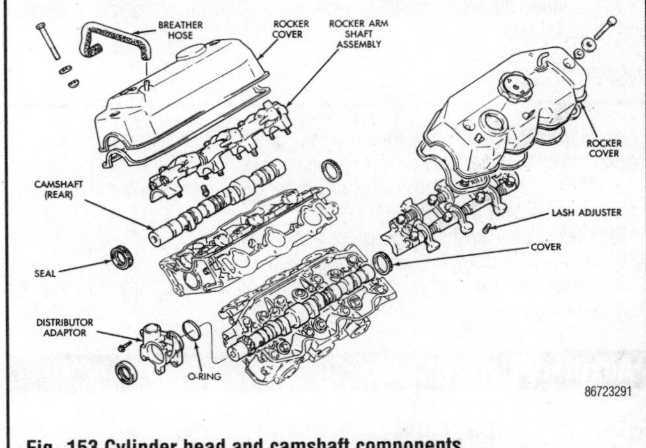

Fig. 153 Cylinder head and camshaft components

20. Remove the lash adjuster retainers. Install the camshaft timing belt sprockets and timing belt.
21. Install the valve covers and new gaskets. Tighten the valve cover retaining bolts to 88 inch lbs. (10 Nm).
22. Reconnect all vacuum hoses that were removed during the removal procedure. Be sure they are all reconnected to the correct vacuum lines.
23. Position the wiring harnesses back to their original locations. Install the accessory drive belts and adjust to the proper tension.
24. Reconnect the spark plug wires to the correct spark plugs.
25. Install the air cleaner assembly. Reconnect the negative battery cable.
26. Run the engine and check for leaks and proper engine operation.

3.3L And 3.8L Engines

See Figure 154

1. Relieve the fuel system pressure. Disconnect the negative battery cable.
2. Remove the engine from the vehicle. Remove the intake manifold, cylinder heads, timing chain cover and timing chain from the engine.
3. Remove the rocker arm and shaft assemblies.
4. Label and remove the pushrod and lifters.
5. Remove the camshaft thrust plate.
6. Install a long bolt into the front of the camshaft to facilitate its removal. Remove the camshaft being careful not to damage the cam bearings with the cam lobes.

To install:

7. Install the camshaft to within 2 in. of its final installation position.
8. Install the camshaft thrust plate and two bolts. Tighten the bolts to 10 ft. lbs. (12 Nm).
9. Place both camshaft and crankshaft gears on the bench with the timing marks on the exact imaginary center line through both gear bores as they are installed on the engine. Place the timing chain around both sprockets.

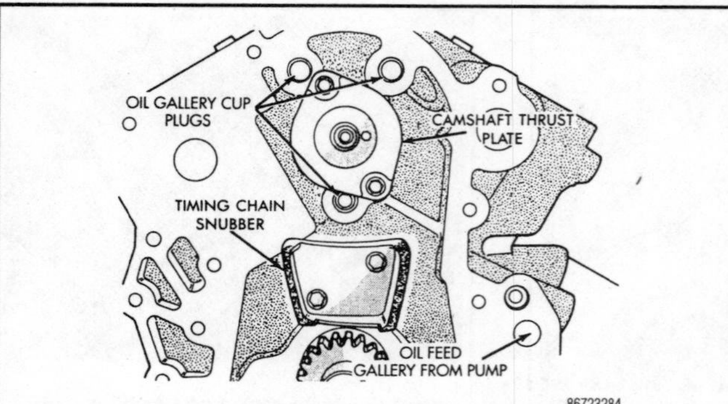

Fig. 154 The camshaft is held in place by thrust plate retained by two bolts—3.3L and 3.8L engines

10. Turn the crankshaft and camshaft so the keys line up with the key ways in the gears when the timing marks are in proper position.
11. Slide both gears over their respective shafts and use a straight edge to check timing mark alignment.
12. Measure camshaft end-play. If not within specifications, replace the thrust plate.
13. If the camshaft was not replaced, lubricate and install the lifters in their original locations. If the camshaft was replaced, new lifters must be used.
14. Install the pushrods and rocker shaft assemblies.
15. Install the timing chain cover, cylinder heads and intake manifold.
16. Install the engine in the vehicle.
17. When everything is bolted in place, change the engine oil and replace the oil filter.

➡If the camshaft or lifters have been replaced, add 1 pint of Mopar crankcase conditioner, or equivalent when replenishing the oil to aid in break in. This mixture should be left in the engine for a minimum of 500 miles and drained at the next normal oil change.

18. Fill the radiator with coolant.
19. Connect the negative battery cable, set all adjustments to specifications and check for leaks.

INSPECTION

1. Inspect the camshaft bearing journals for wear or damage.2. Inspect the cylinder head and check oil return holes.
3. Check the tooth surface of the distributor drive gear teeth of the right camshaft for wear or damage.
4. Check both camshaft surfaces for wear or damage.
5. Remove the distributor drive adaptor seal.
6. Check camshaft lobe height and replace if out of limit. Standard value is 1.61 in. (41mm).

Auxiliary (Idler) Shaft

REMOVAL & INSTALLATION

2.4L Engine

▸ See Figures 155, 156 and 157

The 2.4L engine is equipped with 2 balance shafts installed in a carrier mounted to the lower crankcase. These balance shafts interconnect through gears to rotate in opposite directions. The gears are powered by a short, crankshaft-driven chain and rotate at 2 times the speed of the crankshaft. This will counterbalance certain reciprocating masses of the engine.

An oil passage from the No. 1 main bearing cap through the balance shaft carrier support leg provides lubrication to the balance shafts. This passage directly supplies engine oil to the front bearings and internal machined passages in the shafts that routes engine oil from the front to the rear shaft bearing journals.

Please note that this procedure requires removal of the timing belt. Valve train timing is critical to engine performance and to prevent engine damage. Work carefully and verify all timing marks as the engine is reassembled.

1. Disconnect the negative battery cable.
2. Remove the accessory drive belts. Refer to Section 1.
3. Remove the timing belt covers and timing belt, as outlined earlier in this section.
4. Raise and safely support the vehicle.
5. Place a large drain pan under the oil pan drain plug and drain the engine oil.
6. Remove the oil pump and oil pan.
7. Remove the balance shaft drive chain cover.
8. Remove the drive chain guide and drive chain tensioner.
9. Remove the gear cover retaining stud (double ended to also mount the drive chain guide).
10. Remove the balance shaft gear and chain sprocket retaining screws.
11. Remove the drive chain and chain sprocket assembly by using 2 prybars to work the sprocket back and forth until it is removed from the crankshaft.
12. Remove the gear cover and balance shafts.
13. Remove the 4 balance shaft carrier-to-crankcase mounting bolts, then separate the carrier from the engine bedplate.

To install:

14. Install the balance shafts into the carrier and place the carrier into proper position against the engine bedplate. Install and tighten the 4 mounting bolts to 40 ft. lbs. (54 Nm).
15. Rotate the balance shafts until both balance shaft keyways are pointed up parallel to the vertical centerline of the engine.
16. Reinstall the short hub drive gear onto the sprocket driven balance shaft and the long hub gear onto the chain driven shaft. Once the gears are installed onto the shafts, the gear and balance shaft keyways must be up, and gear alignment dots properly meshed.
17. Reinstall the gear cover and retaining stud fastener. Tighten the double ended retaining stud fastener to 105 inch lbs. (12 Nm).
18. Reinstall the drive chain's crankshaft sprocket. Be sure to align the flat on the sprocket to the flat on the crankshaft, with the sprocket facing front.
19. Rotate the crankshaft until the No. 1 cylinder is at Top Dead Center (TDC). The timing marks on the chain sprocket should align with the parting line on the left side of No. 1 main bearing cap.
20. Place the drive chain around the crankshaft sprocket so the nickel plated link of the chain is on the No. 1 cylinder timing mark of the crankshaft sprocket.
21. Reinstall the balance shaft sprocket into the drive chain. Be sure the timing mark on the balance shaft sprocket (yellow dot) lines up with lower nickel plated link on the chain.
22. With the keyways of the balance shaft pointing up in the 12 o'clock position, slide the balance shaft drive chain sprocket onto the end of the balance shaft. If necessary to allow for clearance, the balance shaft may be pushed in slightly.

➡The lower nickel plated link, timing mark on the balance shaft sprocket, and arrow on the side of the gear cover should all line up when the balance shafts are properly timed.

23. If the sprockets are timed correctly, install the balance shaft bolts and tighten to 250 inch lbs. (28 Nm). It may be necessary to place a wooden block between the crankcase and crankshaft counterbalance to prevent crankshaft and gear rotation.

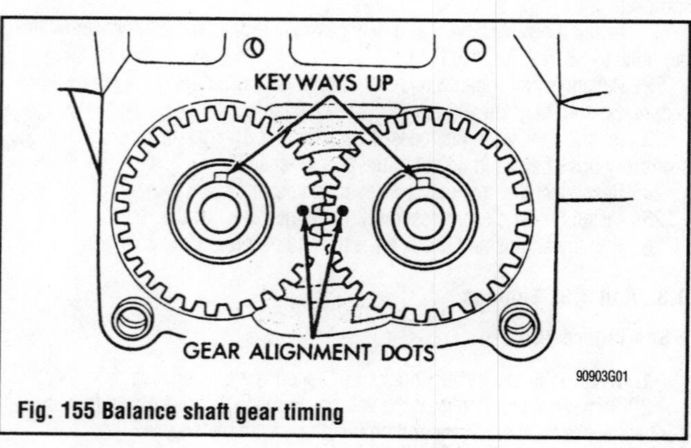

Fig. 155 Balance shaft gear timing

24. Install the drive chain tensioner, but keep it loose at this point.

25. Position the drive chain guide onto the double ended stud fastener. Be sure the tab on the guide fits into the slot on the gear cover. Install the nut/washer assembly and tighten to 105 inch lbs. (12 Nm).

26. Place a shim 0.039 in. x 2.75 in. (1mm x 70mm) long between the tensioner and chain. Push the tensioner and shim up against the chain. Apply pressure of 5.5–6.6 lbs. directly behind the adjustment slot to take up the slack. Be sure the chain makes shoe radius contact.

27. With the pressure applied, tighten the top tensioner adjustment bolt first, then the lower pivot bolt. Tighten the bolts to 105 inch lbs. (12 Nm). Remove the shim after tightening the bolts.

28. Install the chain cover and tighten the screws to 105 inch lbs. (12 Nm).

29. Install oil pump and oil pan.

30. Install the oil pan drain plug and gasket. Tighten the drain plug to 25 ft. lbs. (34 Nm).

31. Lower the vehicle.

32. Install the timing belt and timing belt covers, as described earlier in this section. It is very important that all valve timing marks align properly, or engine damage will result.

33. Install the accessory drive belts, and adjust as necessary.

34. Refill the engine with new, clean engine oil to the proper level. An oil filter change is also recommended.

35. Reconnect the negative battery cable. Start the engine and check for leaks.

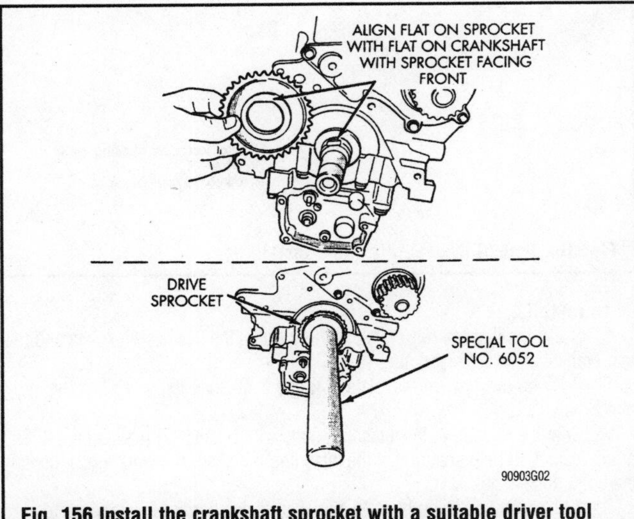

Fig. 156 Install the crankshaft sprocket with a suitable driver tool

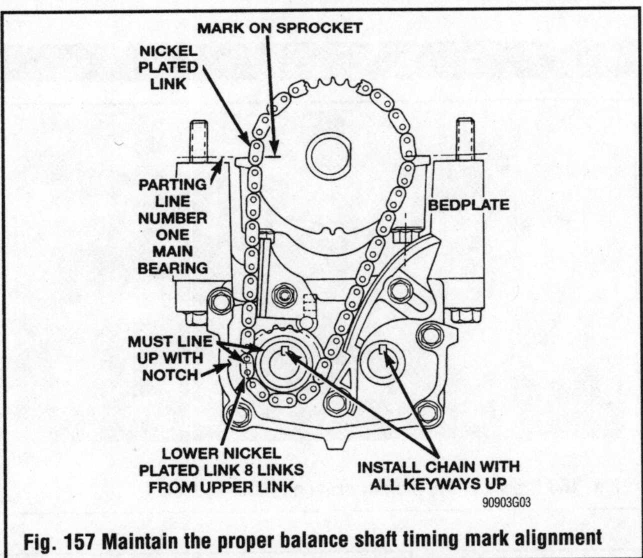

Fig. 157 Maintain the proper balance shaft timing mark alignment

Rear Main Seal

REMOVAL & INSTALLATION

See Figures 158, 159, 160 and 161

1. Disconnect the negative battery cable.
2. Remove the transaxle.
3. Remove the flexplate from the crankshaft.

WARNING

Do not let the prytool damage the sealing surface of the crankshaft, or an oil leak may result.

4. Carefully pry the oil seal out of the bore with a flat-bladed prytool.

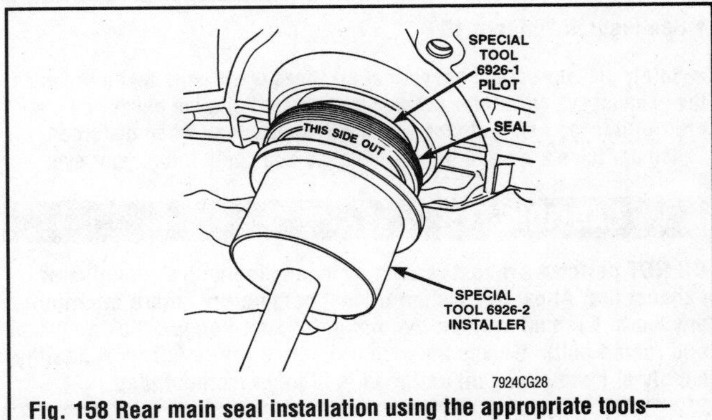

Fig. 158 Rear main seal installation using the appropriate tools—2.4L engine

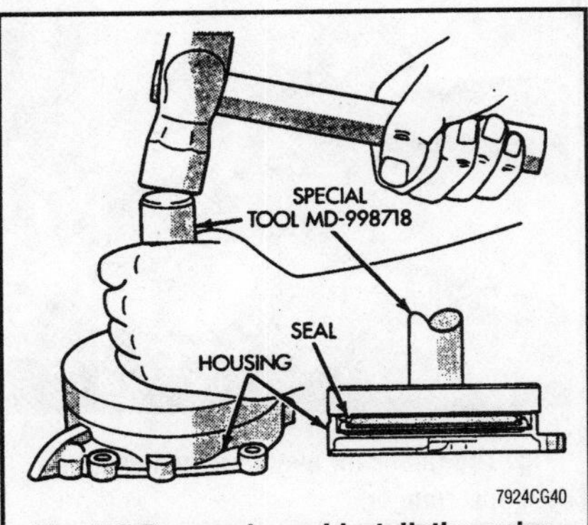

Fig. 159 Rear main seal installation using the appropriate tools—3.0L engine

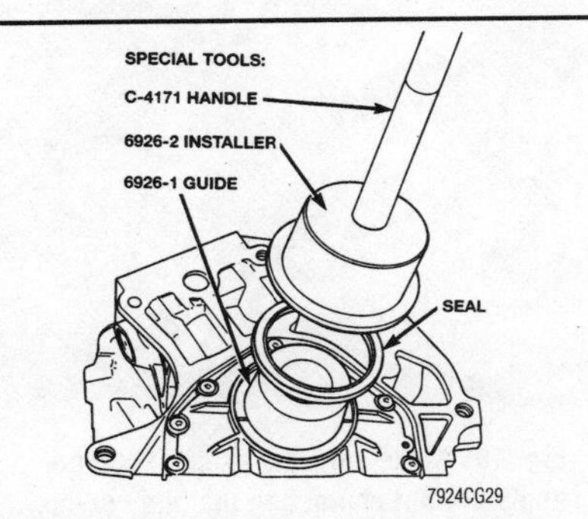

Fig. 160 Install the rear main seal using the appropriate seal driver—3.3 and 3.8L engines

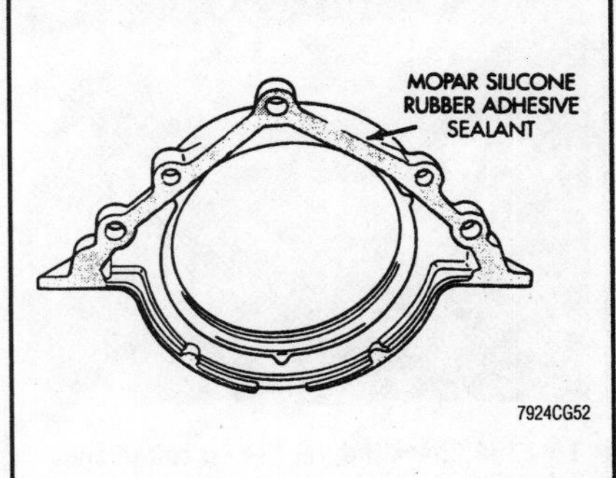

Fig. 161 Apply silicone sealant to the seal retainer before installation—3.0l engine

To install:

WARNING

To prevent seal damage, remove any burrs or scratches on the edge of the crankshaft with 400 grit sandpaper before installing the seal.

5. Install the seal using the appropriate seal installation tool.
6. Install the flexplate and the transaxle assembly.

Flywheel/Flexplate

REMOVAL & INSTALLATION

See Figure 162

The most common reason to replace the flexplate is broken teeth on the starter ring gear. On automatic transaxle vehicles, the torque converter actually forms part of the flywheel. It is bolted to a thin flexplate which, in turn, is bolted to the crankshaft. The flexplate also serves as the ring gear with which the starter pinion engages in engine cranking. The flexplate occasionally cracks; the teeth on the ring gear may also break, especially if the starter is often engaged while the pinion is still spinning. The torque converter and flexplate are separated, so the converter and transaxle can be removed together.

1. Remove the transaxle from the vehicle. For more information, refer to Section 7.
2. Support the flywheel in a secure manner.
3. Matchmark the flywheel/flexplate to the rear flange of the crankshaft.
4. Remove the attaching bolts and pull the flywheel/flexplate from the crankshaft.

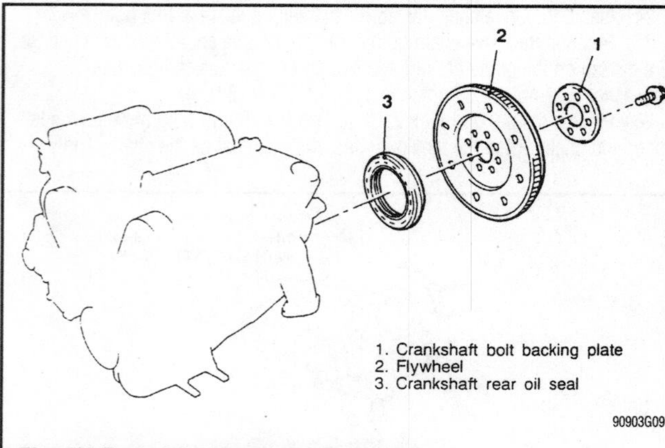

Fig. 162 Typical flywheel/flexplate installation

To install:

5. Clean the flywheel/flexplate attaching bolts, the flywheel/flexplate and the rear crankshaft mounting flange.
6. Position the flywheel/flexplate onto the crankshaft flange so that the matchmarks align.
7. Coat the threads of the attaching bolts with Loctite® Thread Locker 271, or equivalent, to help ensure that the attaching bolts will not work loose. Install the bolts finger-tight.
8. Tighten the attaching bolts in a crisscross fashion in 3 even steps to 68–70 ft. lbs. (92–95 Nm).
9. Install the transaxle, as described in Section 7.

EXHAUST SYSTEM

Inspection

See Figures 163 thru 169

Safety glasses should be worn at all times when working on or near the exhaust system. Older exhaust systems will almost always be covered with loose rust particles which will shower you when disturbed. These particles are more than a nuisance and could injure your eye.

CAUTION

DO NOT perform exhaust repairs or inspection with the engine or exhaust hot. Allow the system to cool completely before attempting any work. Exhaust systems are noted for sharp edges, flaking metal and rusted bolts. Gloves and eye protection are required. A healthy supply of penetrating oil and rags is highly recommended.

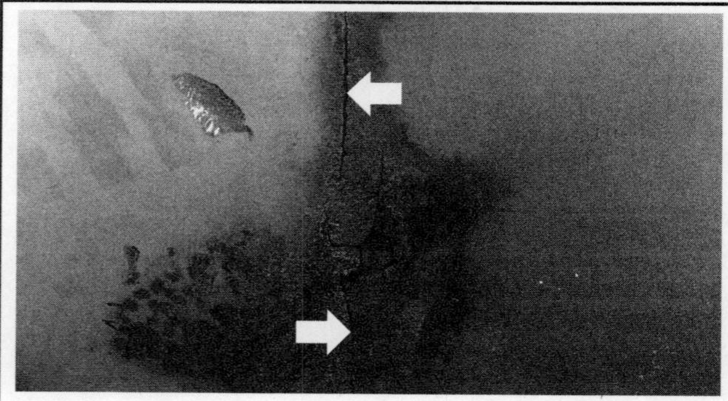

Fig. 163 Cracks in the muffler are a guaranteed leak

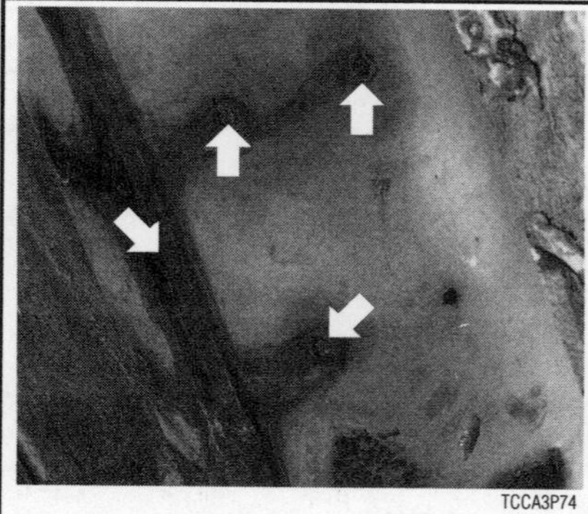

Fig. 164 Check the muffler for rotted spot welds and seams

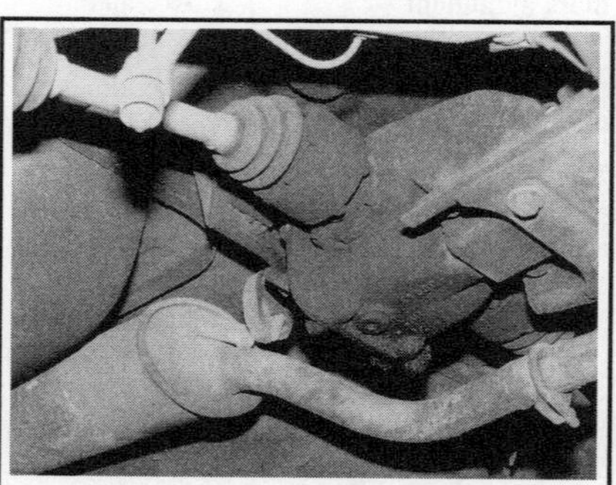

Fig. 165 Make sure the exhaust components are not contacting the body or suspension

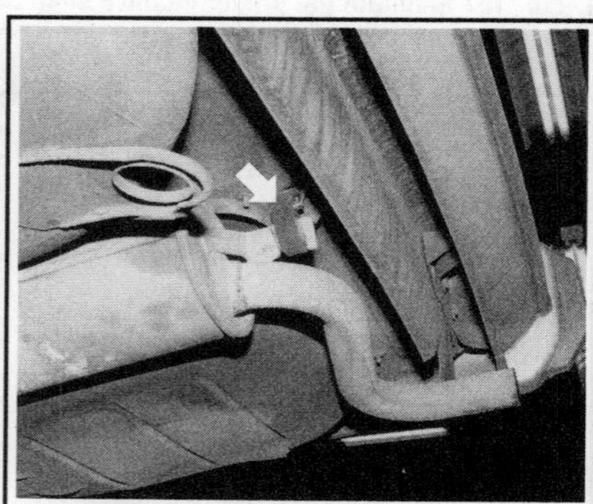

Fig. 166 Check for overstretched or torn exhaust hangers

TCCA3P75

Fig. 167 Example of a badly deteriorated exhaust pipe

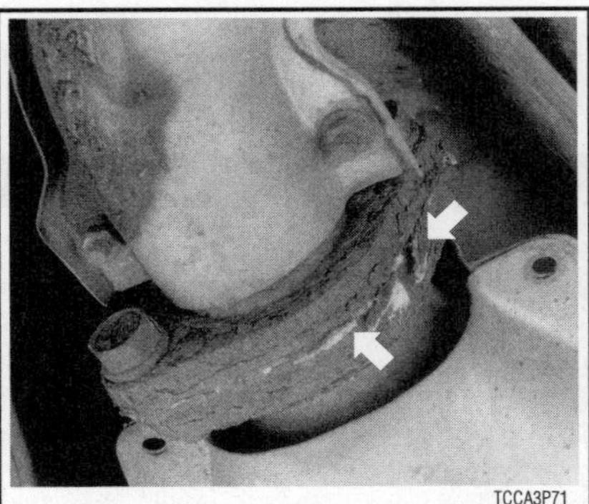
TCCA3P71

Fig. 168 Inspect flanges for gaskets that have deteriorated and need replacement

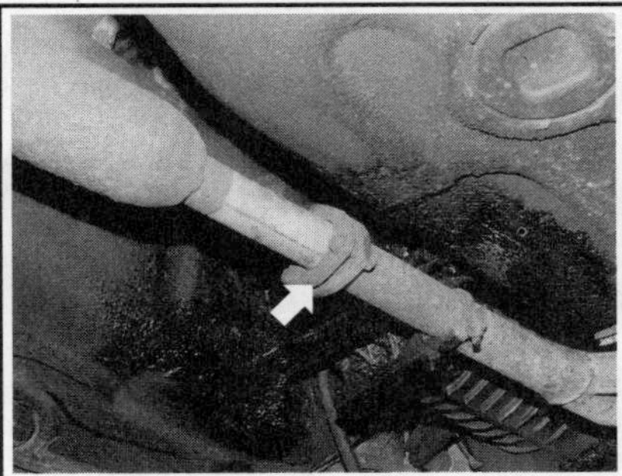
TCCA3P76

Fig. 169 Some systems, like this one, use large O-rings (doughnuts) in between the flanges

Your vehicle must be raised and supported safely to inspect the exhaust system properly. By placing 4 safety stands under the vehicle for support should provide enough room for you to slide under the vehicle and inspect the system completely. Start the inspection at the exhaust manifold or turbocharger pipe where the header pipe is attached and work your way to the back of the vehicle. On dual exhaust systems, remember to inspect both sides of the vehicle. Check the complete exhaust system for open seams, holes loose connections, or other deterioration which could permit exhaust fumes to seep into the passenger compartment. Inspect all mounting brackets and hangers for deterioration, some models may have rubber O-rings that can be overstretched and non-supportive. These components will need to be replaced if found. It has always been a practice to use a pointed tool to poke up into the exhaust system where the deterioration spots are to see whether or not they crumble. Some models may have heat shield covering certain parts of the exhaust system, it will be necessary to remove these shields to have the exhaust visible for inspection also.

REPLACEMENT

▶ See Figure 170

There are basically two types of exhaust systems. One is the flange type where the component ends are attached with bolts and a gasket in-between. The other exhaust system is the slip joint type. These components slip into one another using clamps to retain them together.

✱✱ CAUTION

Allow the exhaust system to cool sufficiently before spraying a solvent exhaust fasteners. Some solvents are highly flammable and could ignite when sprayed on hot exhaust components.

Before removing any component of the exhaust system, ALWAYS squirt a liquid rust dissolving agent onto the fasteners for ease of removal. A lot of knuckle skin will be saved by following this rule. It may even be wise to spray the fasteners and allow them to sit overnight.

Flange Type

▶ See Figure 171

✱✱ CAUTION

Do NOT perform exhaust repairs or inspection with the engine or exhaust hot. Allow the system to cool completely before attempting any work. Exhaust systems are noted for sharp edges, flaking metal and rusted bolts. Gloves and eye protection are required. A healthy supply of penetrating oil and rags is highly recommended. Never spray liquid rust dissolving agent onto a hot exhaust component.

Before removing any component on a flange type system, ALWAYS squirt a liquid rust dissolving agent onto the fasteners for ease of removal. Start by unbolting the exhaust piece at both ends (if required). When unbolting the headpipe from the manifold, make sure that the bolts are free before trying to remove them. if you snap a stud in the exhaust manifold, the stud will have to be removed with a bolt extractor, which often means removal of the manifold itself. Next, disconnect the component from the mounting; slight twisting and turning may be required to remove the component completely from the vehicle. You may need to tap on the component with a rubber mallet to loosen the component. If all else fails, use a hacksaw to separate the parts. An oxy-acetylene cutting torch may be faster but the sparks are DANGEROUS near the fuel tank, and at the very least, accidents could happen, resulting in damage to the under-car parts, not to mention yourself.

Slip Joint Type

▶ See Figure 172

Before removing any component on the slip joint type exhaust system, ALWAYS squirt a liquid rust dissolving agent onto the fasteners for ease of removal. Start by unbolting the exhaust piece at both ends (if required). When unbolting the headpipe from the manifold, make sure that the bolts are free

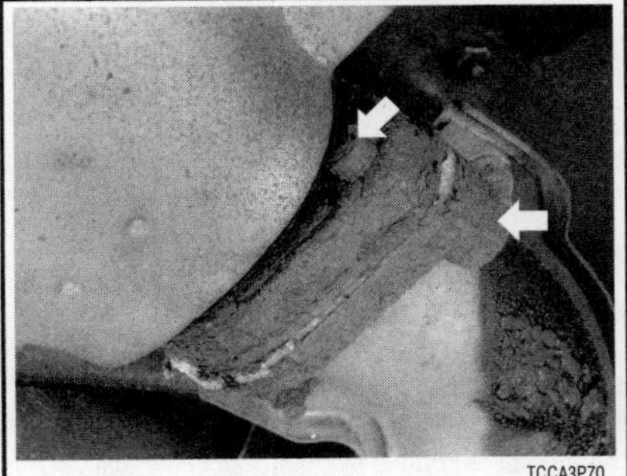
TCCA3P70

Fig. 170 Nuts and bolts will be extremely difficult to remove when deteriorated with rust

TCCA3P72

Fig. 171 Example of a flange type exhaust system joint

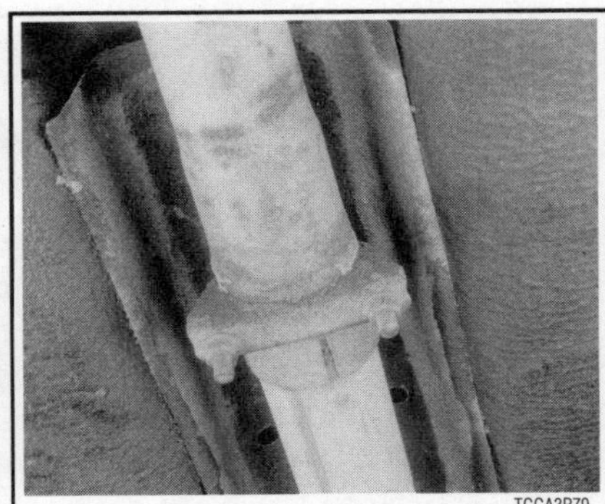
TCCA3P79

Fig. 172 Example of a common slip joint type system

before trying to remove them. if you snap a stud in the exhaust manifold, the stud will have to be removed with a bolt extractor, which often means removal of the manifold itself. Next, remove the mounting U-bolts from around the exhaust pipe you are extracting from the vehicle. Don't be surprised if the U-bolts break while removing the nuts. Loosen the exhaust pipe from any mounting brackets retaining it to the floor pan and separate the components.

ENGINE RECONDITIONING

Determining Engine Condition

Anything that generates heat and/or friction will eventually burn or wear out (for example, a light bulb generates heat, therefore its life span is limited). With this in mind, a running engine generates tremendous amounts of both; friction is encountered by the moving and rotating parts inside the engine and heat is created by friction and combustion of the fuel. However, the engine has systems designed to help reduce the effects of heat and friction and provide added longevity. The oiling system reduces the amount of friction encountered by the moving parts inside the engine, while the cooling system reduces heat created by friction and combustion. If either system is not maintained, a break-down will be inevitable. Therefore, you can see how regular maintenance can affect the service life of your vehicle. If you do not drain, flush and refill your cooling system at the proper intervals, deposits will begin to accumulate in the radiator, thereby reducing the amount of heat it can extract from the coolant. The same applies to your oil and filter; if it is not changed often enough it becomes laden with contaminates and is unable to properly lubricate the engine. This increases friction and wear.

There are a number of methods for evaluating the condition of your engine. A compression test can reveal the condition of your pistons, piston rings, cylinder bores, head gasket(s), valves and valve seats. An oil pressure test can warn you of possible engine bearing, or oil pump failures. Excessive oil consumption, evidence of oil in the engine air intake area and/or bluish smoke from the tailpipe may indicate worn piston rings, worn valve guides and/or valve seals. As a general rule, an engine that uses no more than one quart of oil every 1000 miles is in good condition. Engines that use one quart of oil or more in less than 1000 miles should first be checked for oil leaks. If any oil leaks are present, have them fixed before determining how much oil is consumed by the engine, especially if blue smoke is not visible at the tailpipe.

COMPRESSION TEST

➧ See Figure 173

A noticeable lack of engine power, excessive oil consumption and/or poor fuel mileage measured over an extended period are all indicators of internal engine wear. Worn piston rings, scored or worn cylinder bores, blown head gaskets, sticking or burnt valves, and worn valve seats are all possible culprits. A check of each cylinder's compression will help locate the problem.

➡A screw-in type compression gauge is more accurate than the type you simply hold against the spark plug hole. Although it takes slightly longer to use, it's worth the effort to obtain a more accurate reading.

1. Make sure that the proper amount and viscosity of engine oil is in the crankcase, then ensure the battery is fully charged.
2. Warm-up the engine to normal operating temperature, then shut the engine **OFF**.
3. Disable the ignition system.

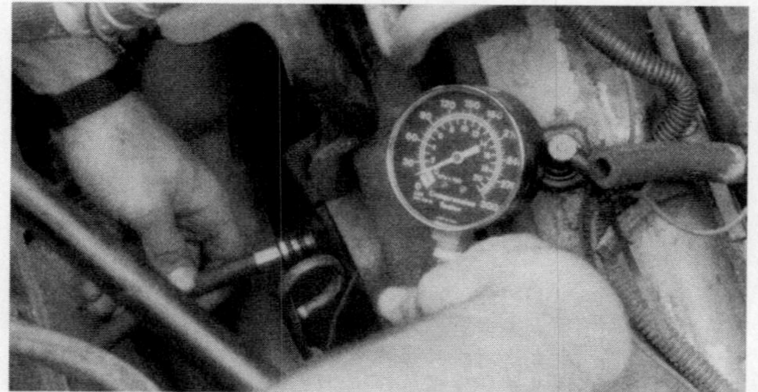

TCCS3801

Fig. 173 A screw-in type compression gauge is more accurate and easier to use without an assistant

4. Label and disconnect all of the spark plug wires from the plugs.
5. Thoroughly clean the cylinder head area around the spark plug ports, then remove the spark plugs.
6. Set the throttle plate to the fully open (wide-open throttle) position. You can block the accelerator linkage open for this, or you can have an assistant fully depress the accelerator pedal.
7. Install a screw-in type compression gauge into the No. 1 spark plug hole until the fitting is snug.

**** WARNING**

Be careful not to crossthread the spark plug hole.

8. According to the tool manufacturer's instructions, connect a remote starting switch to the starting circuit.
9. With the ignition switch in the **OFF** position, use the remote starting switch to crank the engine through at least five compression strokes (approximately 5 seconds of cranking) and record the highest reading on the gauge.
10. Repeat the test on each cylinder, cranking the engine approximately the same number of compression strokes and/or time as the first.
11. Compare the highest readings from each cylinder to that of the others. The indicated compression pressures are considered within specifications if the lowest reading cylinder is within 75 percent of the pressure recorded for the highest reading cylinder. For example, if your highest reading cylinder pressure was 150 psi (1034 kPa), then 75 percent of that would be 113 psi (779 kPa). So the lowest reading cylinder should be no less than 113 psi (779 kPa).
12. If a cylinder exhibits an unusually low compression reading, pour a tablespoon of clean engine oil into the cylinder through the spark plug hole and repeat the compression test. If the compression rises after adding oil, it means that the cylinder's piston rings and/or cylinder bore are damaged or worn. If the pressure remains low, the valves may not be seating properly (a valve job is needed), or the head gasket may be blown near that cylinder. If compression in any two adjacent cylinders is low, and if the addition of oil doesn't help raise compression, there is leakage past the head gasket. Oil and coolant in the combustion chamber, combined with blue or constant white smoke from the tailpipe, are symptoms of this problem. However, don't be alarmed by the normal white smoke emitted from the tailpipe during engine warm-up or from cold weather driving. There may be evidence of water droplets on the engine dipstick and/or oil droplets in the cooling system if a head gasket is blown.

OIL PRESSURE TEST

Check for proper oil pressure at the sending unit passage with an externally mounted mechanical oil pressure gauge (as opposed to relying on a factory installed dash-mounted gauge). A tachometer may also be needed, as some specifications may require running the engine at a specific rpm.

1. With the engine cold, locate and remove the oil pressure sending unit.
2. Following the manufacturer's instructions, connect a mechanical oil pressure gauge and, if necessary, a tachometer to the engine.
3. Start the engine and allow it to idle.
4. Check the oil pressure reading when cold and record the number. You may need to run the engine at a specified rpm, so check the specifications.
5. Run the engine until normal operating temperature is reached (upper radiator hose will feel warm).
6. Check the oil pressure reading again with the engine hot and record the number. Turn the engine **OFF**.
7. Compare your hot oil pressure reading to that given in the chart. If the reading is low, check the cold pressure reading against the chart. If the cold pressure is well above the specification, and the hot reading was lower than the specification, you may have the wrong viscosity oil in the engine. Change the oil, making sure to use the proper grade and quantity, then repeat the test.

Low oil pressure readings could be attributed to internal component wear, pump related problems, a low oil level, or oil viscosity that is too low. High oil pressure readings could be caused by an overfilled crankcase, too high of an oil viscosity or a faulty pressure relief valve.

Buy or Rebuild?

Now that you have determined that your engine is worn out, you must make some decisions. The question of whether or not an engine is worth rebuilding is largely a subjective matter and one of personal worth. Is the engine a popular one, or is it an obsolete model? Are parts available? Will it get acceptable gas mileage once it is rebuilt? Is the car it's being put into worth keeping? Would it be less expensive to buy a new engine, have your engine rebuilt by a pro, rebuild it yourself or buy a used engine from a salvage yard? Or would it be simpler and less expensive to buy another car? If you have considered all these matters and more, and have still decided to rebuild the engine, then it is time to decide how you will rebuild it.

➡The editors at Chilton feel that most engine machining should be performed by a professional machine shop. Don't think of it as wasting money, rather, as an assurance that the job has been done right the first time. There are many expensive and specialized tools required to perform such tasks as boring and honing an engine block or having a valve job done on a cylinder head. Even inspecting the parts requires expensive micrometers and gauges to properly measure wear and clearances. Also, a machine shop can deliver to you clean, and ready to assemble parts, saving you time and aggravation. Your maximum savings will come from performing the removal, disassembly, assembly and installation of the engine and purchasing or renting only the tools required to perform the above tasks. Depending on the particular circumstances, you may save 40 to 60 percent of the cost doing these yourself.

A complete rebuild or overhaul of an engine involves replacing all of the moving parts (pistons, rods, crankshaft, camshaft, etc.) with new ones and machining the non-moving wearing surfaces of the block and heads. Unfortunately, this may not be cost effective. For instance, your crankshaft may have been damaged or worn, but it can be machined undersize for a minimal fee.

So, as you can see, you can replace everything inside the engine, but, it is wiser to replace only those parts which are really needed, and, if possible, repair the more expensive ones. Later in this section, we will break the engine down into its two main components: the cylinder head and the engine block. We will discuss each component, and the recommended parts to replace during a rebuild on each.

Engine Overhaul Tips

Most engine overhaul procedures are fairly standard. In addition to specific parts replacement procedures and specifications for your individual engine, this section is also a guide to acceptable rebuilding procedures. Examples of standard rebuilding practice are given and should be used along with specific details concerning your particular engine.

Competent and accurate machine shop services will ensure maximum performance, reliability and engine life. In most instances it is more profitable for the do-it-yourself mechanic to remove, clean and inspect the component, buy the necessary parts and deliver these to a shop for actual machine work.

Much of the assembly work (crankshaft, bearings, piston rods, and other components) is well within the scope of the do-it-yourself mechanic's tools and abilities. You will have to decide for yourself the depth of involvement you desire in an engine repair or rebuild.

TOOLS

The tools required for an engine overhaul or parts replacement will depend on the depth of your involvement. With a few exceptions, they will be the tools found in a mechanic's tool kit (see Section 1 of this manual). More in-depth work will require some or all of the following:

- A dial indicator (reading in thousandths) mounted on a universal base
- Micrometers and telescope gauges
- Jaw and screw-type pullers
- Scraper
- Valve spring compressor
- Ring groove cleaner
- Piston ring expander and compressor
- Ridge reamer
- Cylinder hone or glaze breaker
- Plastigage®
- Engine stand

The use of most of these tools is illustrated in this section. Many can be rented for a one-time use from a local parts jobber or tool supply house specializing in automotive work.

Occasionally, the use of special tools is called for. See the information on Special Tools and the Safety Notice in the front of this book before substituting another tool.

OVERHAUL TIPS

Aluminum has become extremely popular for use in engines, due to its low weight. Observe the following precautions when handling aluminum parts:

- Never hot tank aluminum parts (the caustic hot tank solution will eat the aluminum.
- Remove all aluminum parts (identification tag, etc.) from engine parts prior to the tanking.
- Always coat threads lightly with engine oil or anti-seize compounds before installation, to prevent seizure.
- Never overtighten bolts or spark plugs especially in aluminum threads.

When assembling the engine, any parts that will be exposed to frictional contact must be prelubed to provide lubrication at initial start-up. Any product specifically formulated for this purpose can be used, but engine oil is not recommended as a prelube in most cases.

When semi-permanent (locked, but removable) installation of bolts or nuts is desired, threads should be cleaned and coated with Loctite• or another similar, commercial non-hardening sealant.

CLEANING

See Figures 174, 175, 176 and 177

Before the engine and its components are inspected, they must be thoroughly cleaned. You will need to remove any engine varnish, oil sludge and/or carbon deposits from all of the components to insure an accurate inspection. A crack in the engine block or cylinder head can easily become overlooked if hidden by a layer of sludge or carbon.

Most of the cleaning process can be carried out with common hand tools and readily available solvents or solutions. Carbon deposits can be chipped away using a hammer and a hard wooden chisel. Old gasket material and varnish or sludge can usually be removed using a scraper and/or cleaning solvent. Extremely stubborn deposits may require the use of a power drill with a wire brush. If using a wire brush, use extreme care around any critical machined surfaces (such as the gasket surfaces, bearing saddles, cylinder bores, etc.). USE OF A WIRE BRUSH IS NOT RECOMMENDED ON ANY ALUMINUM COMPONENTS. Always follow any safety recommendations given by the manufacturer of the tool and/or solvent. You should always wear eye protection during any cleaning process involving scraping, chipping or spraying of solvents.

An alternative to the mess and hassle of cleaning the parts yourself is to drop them off at a local garage or machine shop. They will, more than likely, have the necessary equipment to properly clean all of the parts for a nominal fee.

CAUTION

Always wear eye protection during any cleaning process involving scraping, chipping or spraying of solvents.

Remove any oil galley plugs, freeze plugs and/or pressed-in bearings and carefully wash and degrease all of the engine components including the fasteners and bolts. Small parts such as the valves, springs, etc., should be placed in a metal basket and allowed to soak. Use pipe cleaner type brushes, and clean all passageways in the components. Use a ring expander and remove the rings from the pistons. Clean the piston ring grooves with a special tool or a piece of broken ring. Scrape the carbon off of the top of the piston. You should never use a wire brush on the pistons. After preparing all of the piston assemblies in this manner, wash and degrease them again.

WARNING

Use extreme care when cleaning around the cylinder head valve seats. A mistake or slip may cost you a new seat.

When cleaning the cylinder head, remove carbon from the combustion chamber with the valves installed. This will avoid damaging the valve seats.

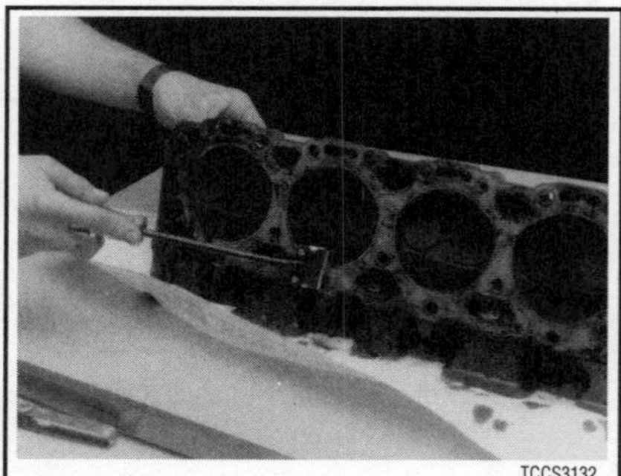
TCCS3132

Fig. 174 Use a gasket scraper to remove the old gasket material from the mating surfaces

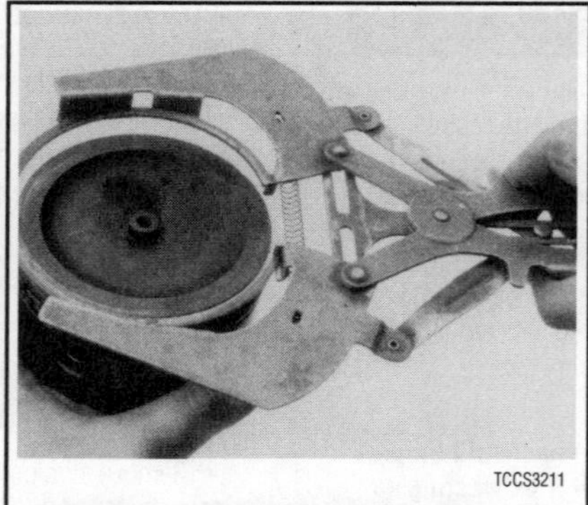
TCCS3211

Fig. 175 Use a ring expander tool to remove the piston rings

TCCS3208

Fig. 176 Clean the piston ring grooves using a ring groove cleaner tool, or . . .

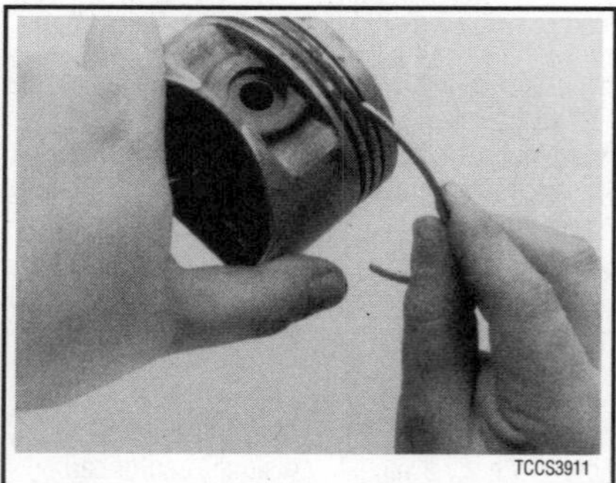
TCCS3911

Fig. 177 . . . use a piece of an old ring to clean the grooves. Be careful, the ring can be quite sharp

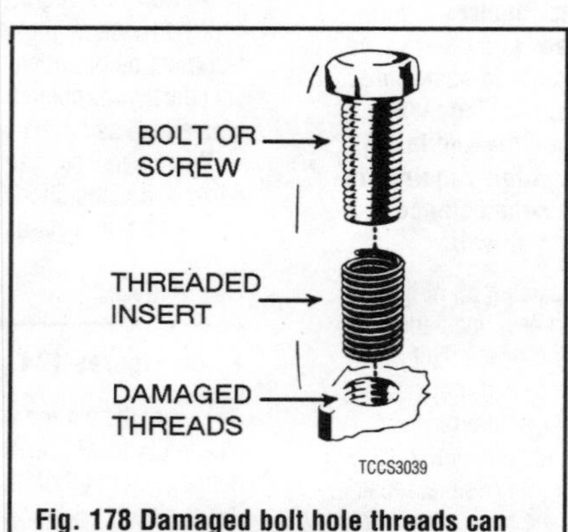

TCCS3039

Fig. 178 Damaged bolt hole threads can be replaced with thread repair inserts

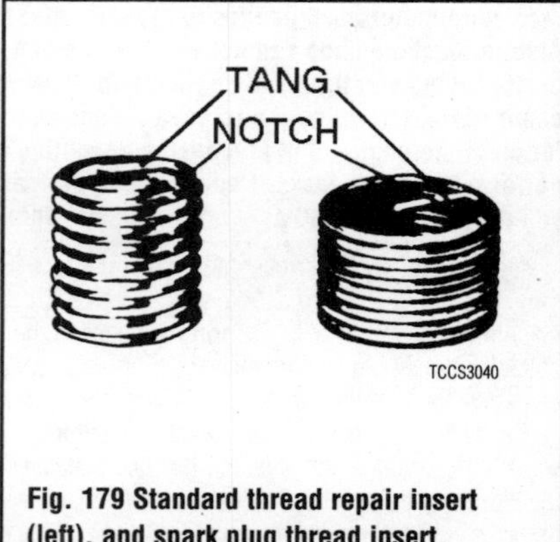

TCCS3040

Fig. 179 Standard thread repair insert (left), and spark plug thread insert

REPAIRING DAMAGED THREADS

See Figures 178, 179, 180, 181 and 182

Several methods of repairing damaged threads are available. Heli-Coil® (shown here), Keenserts® and Microdot® are among the most widely used. All involve basically the same principle—drilling out stripped threads, tapping the hole and installing a prewound insert—making welding, plugging and oversize fasteners unnecessary.

Two types of thread repair inserts are usually supplied: a standard type for most inch coarse, inch fine, metric course and metric fine thread sizes and a spark lug type to fit most spark plug port sizes. Consult the individual tool manufacturer's catalog to determine exact applications. Typical thread repair kits will contain a selection of prewound threaded inserts, a tap (corresponding to the outside diameter threads of the insert) and an installation tool. Spark plug inserts usually differ because they require a tap equipped with pilot threads and a combined reamer/tap section. Most manufacturers also supply blister-packed thread repair inserts separately in addition to a master kit containing a variety of taps and inserts plus installation tools.

Before attempting to repair a threaded hole, remove any snapped, broken or damaged bolts or studs. Penetrating oil can be used to free frozen threads. The offending item can usually be removed with locking pliers or using a screw/stud extractor. After the hole is clear, the thread can be repaired, as shown in the series of accompanying illustrations and in the kit manufacturer's instructions.

Engine Preparation

To properly rebuild an engine, you must first remove it from the vehicle, then disassemble and diagnose it. Ideally you should place your engine on an engine stand. This affords you the best access to the engine components. Follow the manufacturer's directions for using the stand with your particular engine. Remove the flywheel or flexplate before installing the engine to the stand.

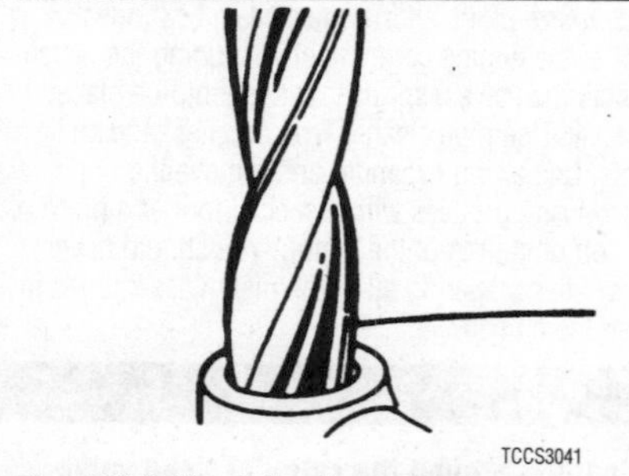
TCCS3041

Fig. 180 Drill out the damaged threads with the specified size bit. Be sure to drill completely through the hole or to the bottom of a blind hole

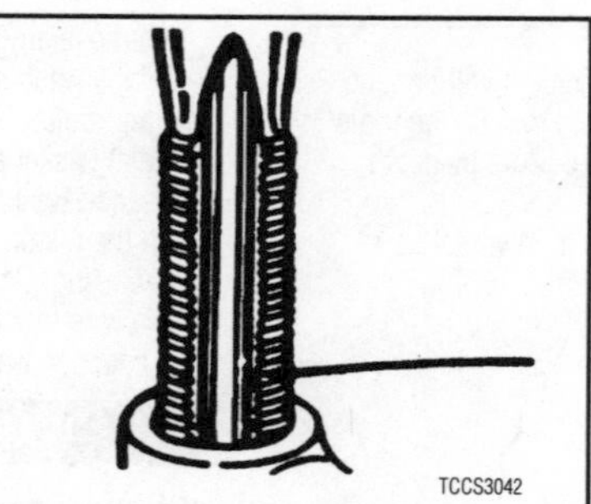
TCCS3042

Fig. 181 Using the kit, tap the hole in order to receive the thread insert. Keep the tap well oiled and back it out frequently to avoid clogging the threads

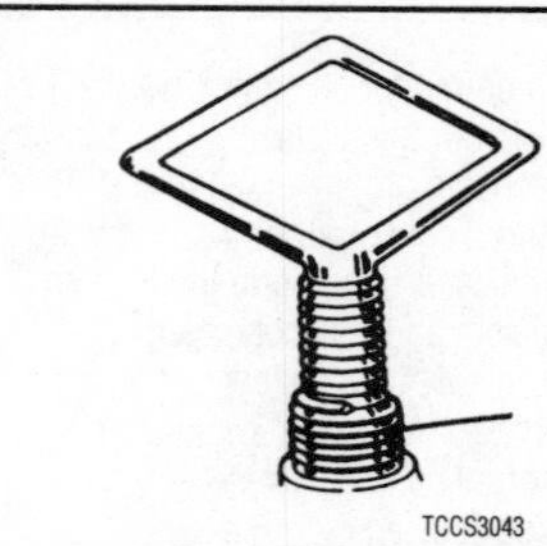
TCCS3043

Fig. 182 Screw the insert onto the installer tool until the tang engages the slot. Thread the insert into the hole until it is ¼–½ turn below the top surface, then remove the tool and break off the tang using a punch

Now that you have the engine on a stand, and assuming that you have drained the oil and coolant from the engine, it's time to strip it of all but the necessary components. Before you start disassembling the engine, you may want to take a moment to draw some pictures, or fabricate some labels or containers to mark the locations of various components and the bolts and/or studs which fasten them. Modern day engines use a lot of little brackets and clips which hold wiring harnesses and such, and these holders are often mounted on studs and/or bolts that can be easily mixed up. The manufacturer spent a lot of time and money designing your vehicle, and they wouldn't have wasted any of it by haphazardly placing brackets, clips or fasteners on the vehicle. If it's present when you disassemble it, put it back when you assemble, you will regret not remembering that little bracket which holds a wire harness out of the path of a rotating part.

You should begin by unbolting any accessories still attached to the engine, such as the water pump, power steering pump, alternator, etc. Then, unfasten any manifolds (intake or exhaust) which were not removed during the engine removal procedure. Finally, remove any covers remaining on the engine such as the rocker arm, front or timing cover and oil pan. Some front covers may require the vibration damper and/or crank pulley to be removed beforehand. The idea is to reduce the engine to the bare necessities (cylinder head(s), valve train, engine block, crankshaft, pistons and connecting rods), plus any other `in block' components such as oil pumps, balance shafts and auxiliary shafts.

Finally, remove the cylinder head(s) from the engine block and carefully place on a bench. Disassembly instructions for each component follow later in this section.

Cylinder Head

There are two basic types of cylinder heads used on today's automobiles: the Overhead Valve (OHV) and the Overhead Camshaft (OHC). Of the four different engines covered in this book, the 3.3L and 3.8L engines are of the overhead valve type, while the 2.4L and 3.0L engines are of the overhead camshaft type. The latter can also be broken down into two subgroups: the Single Overhead Camshaft (SOHC), which is the 3.0L engine, and the Dual Overhead Camshaft (DOHC), which is the 2.4L engine. Generally, if there is only a single camshaft on a head, it is just referred to as an OHC head. Also, an engine with an OHV cylinder head is also known as a pushrod engine.

Most cylinder heads these days are made of an aluminum alloy due to its light weight, durability and heat transfer qualities. However, cast iron was the material of choice in the past, and is still used on many vehicles today. Whether made from aluminum or iron, all cylinder heads have valves and seats. Some use two valves per cylinder, while the more hi-tech engines will utilize a multi-valve configuration using 3, 4 and even 5 valves per cylinder. When the valve contacts the seat, it does so on precision machined surfaces, which seals the combustion chamber. All cylinder heads have a valve guide for each valve. The guide centers the valve to the seat and allows it to move up and down within it. The clearance between the valve and guide can be critical. Too much clearance and the engine may consume oil, lose vacuum and/or damage the seat. Too little, and the valve can stick in the guide causing the engine to run poorly if at all, and possibly causing severe damage. The last component all cylinder heads have are valve springs. The spring holds the valve against its seat. It also returns the valve to this position when the valve has been opened by the valve train or camshaft. The spring is fastened to the valve by a retainer and valve locks (sometimes called keepers). Aluminum heads will also have a valve spring shim to keep the spring from wearing away the aluminum.

An ideal method of rebuilding the cylinder head would involve replacing all of the valves, guides, seats, springs, etc. with new ones. However, depending on how the engine was maintained, often this is not necessary. A major cause of valve, guide and seat wear is an improperly tuned engine. An engine that is running too rich, will often wash the lubricating oil out of the guide with gasoline, causing it to wear rapidly. Conversely, an engine which is running too lean will place higher combustion temperatures on the valves and seats allowing them to wear or even burn. Springs fall victim to the driving habits of the individual. A driver who often runs the engine rpm to the redline will wear out or break the springs faster then one that stays well below it. Unfortunately, mileage takes it toll on all of the parts. Generally, the valves, guides, springs and seats in a cylinder head can be machined and re-used, saving you money. However, if a valve is burnt, it may be wise to replace all of the valves, since they were all operating in the same environment. The same goes for any other component on the cylinder head. Think of it as an insurance policy against future problems related to that component.

Unfortunately, the only way to find out which components need replacing, is to disassemble and carefully check each piece. After the cylinder head(s) are disassembled, thoroughly clean all of the components.

DISASSEMBLY

OHV Heads (3.3L/3.8L Engines)

See Figures 183 thru 188

Before disassembling the cylinder head, you may want to fabricate some containers to hold the various parts, as some of them can be quite small (such as keepers) and easily lost. Also keeping yourself and the components organized will aid in assembly and reduce confusion. Where possible, try to maintain a components original location; this is especially important if there is not going to be any machine work performed on the components.

1. If you haven't already removed the rocker arms and/or shafts, do so now.
2. Position the head so that the springs are easily accessed.
3. Use a valve spring compressor tool, and relieve spring tension from the retainer.

Due to engine varnish, the retainer may stick to the valve locks. A gentle tap with a hammer may help to break it loose.

4. Remove the valve locks from the valve tip and/or retainer. A small magnet may help in removing the locks.
5. Lift the valve spring, tool and all, off of the valve stem.
6. If equipped, remove the valve seal. If the seal is difficult to remove with the valve in place, try removing the valve first, then the seal. Follow the steps below for valve removal.
7. Position the head to allow access for withdrawing the valve.

Cylinder heads that have seen a lot of miles and/or abuse may have mushroomed the valve lock grove and/or tip, causing difficulty in removal of the valve. If this has happened, use a metal file to carefully remove the high spots around the lock grooves and/or tip. Only file it enough to allow removal.

TCCS3137

Fig. 183 When removing an OHV valve spring, use a compressor tool to relieve the tension from the retainer

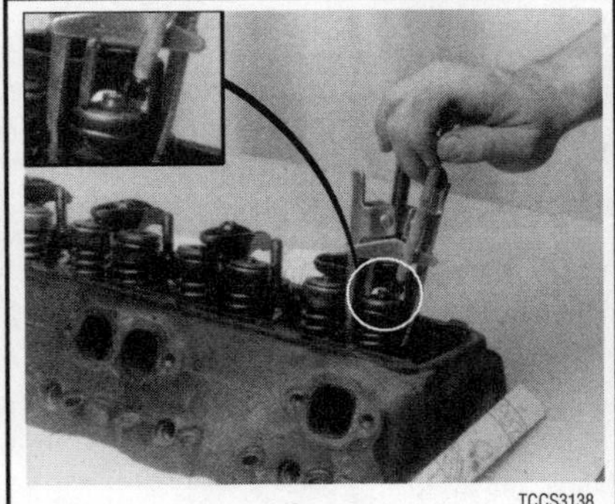
TCCS3138

Fig. 184 A small magnet will help in removal of the valve locks

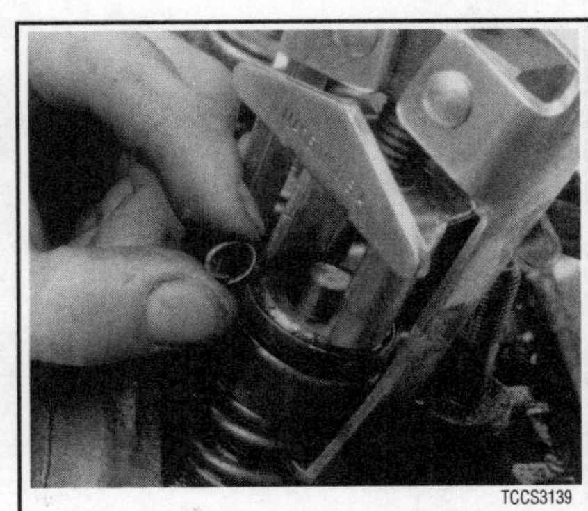
TCCS3139

Fig. 185 Be careful not to lose the small valve locks (keepers)

TCCS3140

Fig. 186 Remove the valve seal from the valve stem—O-ring type seal shown

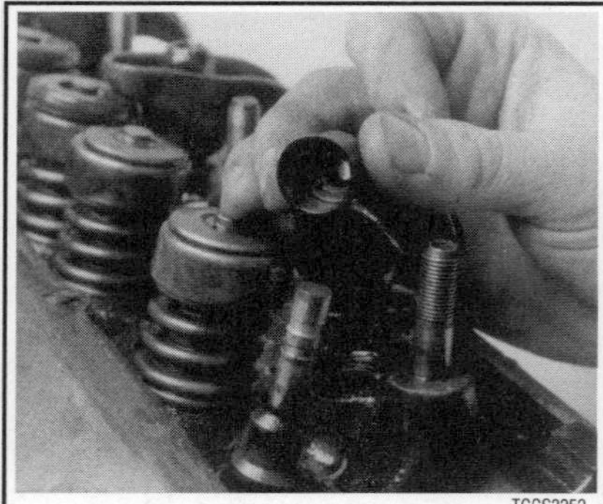
TCCS3252

Fig. 187 Removing an umbrella/positive type seal

TCCS3141

Fig. 188 Invert the cylinder head and withdraw the valve from the valve guide bore

8. Remove the valve from the cylinder head.
9. If equipped, remove the valve spring shim. A small magnetic tool or screwdriver will aid in removal.
10. Repeat Steps 3 though 9 until all of the valves have been removed.

OHC Heads (2.4L and 3.0L Engines)

▶ See Figures 189 and 190

Whether it is a single or dual overhead camshaft cylinder head, the disassembly procedure is relatively unchanged. One aspect to pay attention to is careful labeling of the parts on the dual camshaft cylinder head. There will be an intake camshaft and followers as well as an exhaust camshaft and followers and they must be labeled as such. In some cases, the components are identical and could easily be installed incorrectly. DO NOT MIX THEM UP! Determining which is which is very simple; the intake camshaft and components are on the same side of the head as was the intake manifold. Conversely, the exhaust camshaft and components are on the same side of the head as was the exhaust manifold.

TCCA3P54

Fig. 189 Exploded view of a valve, seal, spring, retainer and locks from an OHC cylinder head

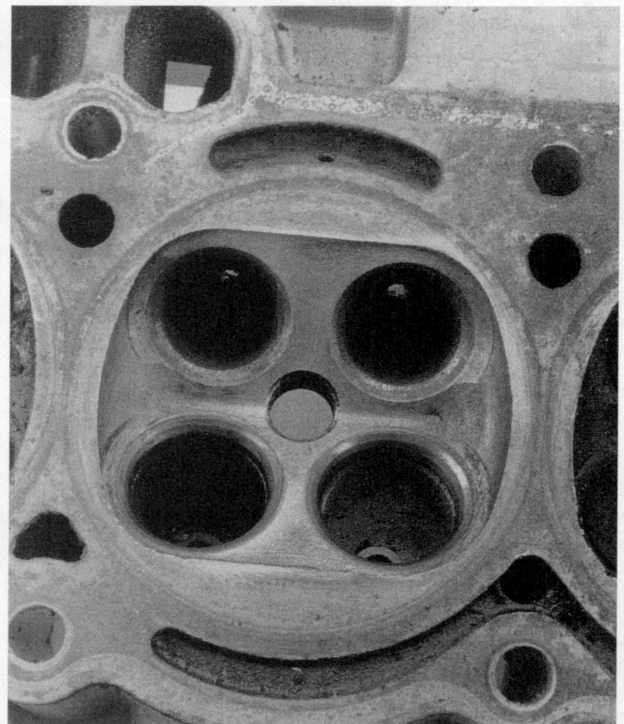
TCCA3P62

Fig. 190 Example of a multi-valve cylinder head. Note how it has 2 intake and 2 exhaust valve ports

CUP TYPE CAMSHAFT FOLLOWERS

▶ See Figures 191, 192 and 193

Most cylinder heads with cup type camshaft followers will have the valve spring, retainer and locks recessed within the follower's bore. You will need a C-clamp style valve spring compressor tool, an OHC spring removal tool (or equivalent) and a small magnet to disassemble the head.

1. If not already removed, remove the camshaft(s) and/or followers. Mark their positions for assembly.
2. Position the cylinder head to allow use of a C-clamp style valve spring compressor tool.

➡It is preferred to position the cylinder head gasket surface facing you with the valve springs facing the opposite direction and the head laying horizontal.

3. With the OHC spring removal adapter tool positioned inside of the fol-

TCCA3P51

Fig. 191 C-clamp type spring compressor and an OHC spring removal tool (center) for cup type followers

TCCA3P63

Fig. 192 Most cup type follower cylinder heads retain the camshaft using bolt-on bearing caps

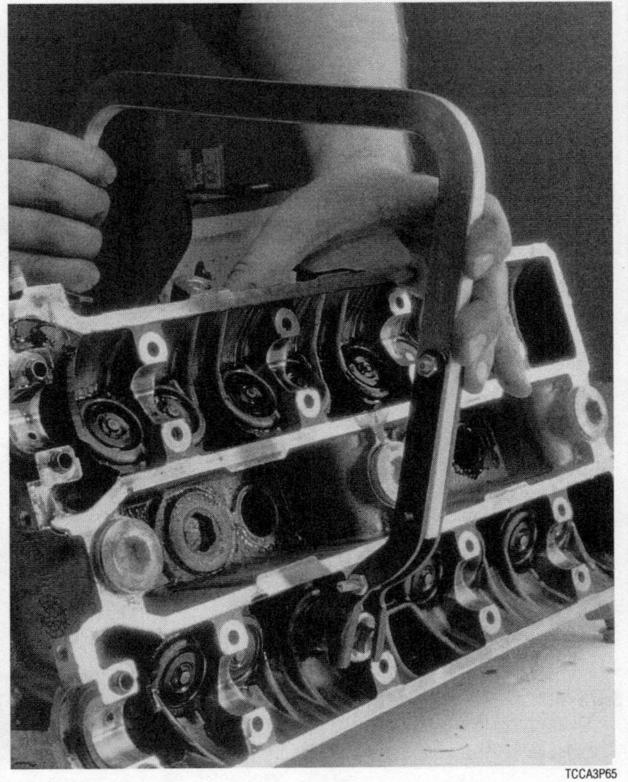

TCCA3P65

Fig. 193 Position the OHC spring tool in the follower bore, then compress the spring with a C-clamp type tool

lower bore, compress the valve spring using the C-clamp style valve spring compressor.

4. Remove the valve locks. A small magnetic tool or screwdriver will aid in removal.
5. Release the compressor tool and remove the spring assembly.
6. Withdraw the valve from the cylinder head.
7. If equipped, remove the valve seal.

➡Special valve seal removal tools are available. Regular or needlenose type pliers, if used with care, will work just as well. If using ordinary pliers, be sure not to damage the follower bore. The follower and its bore are machined to close tolerances and any damage to the bore will effect this relationship.

8. If equipped, remove the valve spring shim. A small magnetic tool or screwdriver will aid in removal.
9. Repeat Steps 3 through 8 until all of the valves have been removed.

ROCKER ARM TYPE CAMSHAFT FOLLOWERS

➧ See Figures 194 thru 202

Most cylinder heads with rocker arm-type camshaft followers are easily disassembled using a standard valve spring compressor. However, certain models may not have enough open space around the spring for the standard tool and may require you to use a C-clamp style compressor tool instead.

1. If not already removed, remove the rocker arms and/or shafts and the camshaft. If applicable, also remove the hydraulic lash adjusters. Mark their positions for assembly.
2. Position the cylinder head to allow access to the valve spring.
3. Use a valve spring compressor tool to relieve the spring tension from the retainer.

➡Due to engine varnish, the retainer may stick to the valve locks. A gentle tap with a hammer may help to break it loose.

TCCA3P53

Fig. 194 Example of the shaft mounted rocker arms on some OHC heads

TCCA3P61

Fig. 195 Another example of the rocker arm type OHC head. This model uses a follower under the camshaft

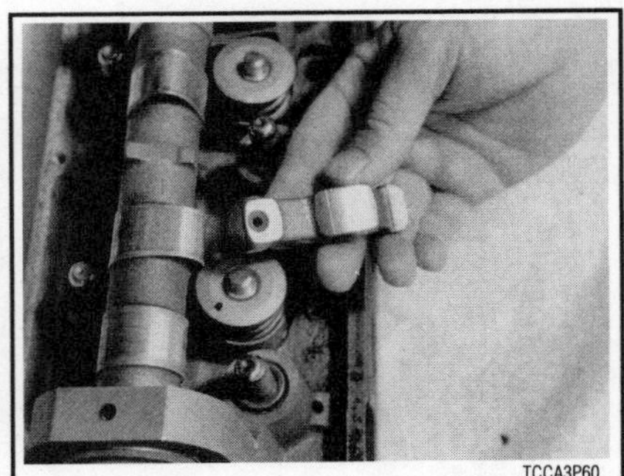

TCCA3P60

Fig. 196 Before the camshaft can be removed, all of the followers must first be removed . . .

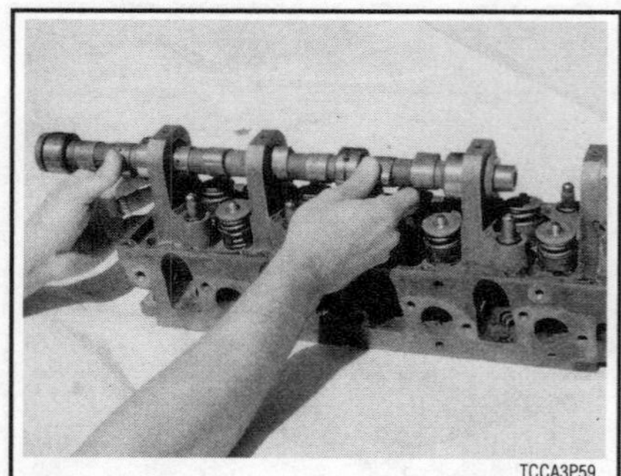

Fig. 197 . . . then the camshaft can be removed by sliding it out (shown), or unbolting a bearing cap (not shown)

Fig. 198 Compress the valve spring . . .

Fig. 199 . . . then remove the valve locks from the valve stem and spring retainer

Fig. 200 Remove the valve spring and retainer from the cylinder head

Fig. 201 Remove the valve seal from the guide. Some gentle prying or pliers may help to remove stubborn ones

Fig. 202 All aluminum and some cast iron heads will have these valve spring shims. Remove all of them as well

4. Remove the valve locks from the valve tip and/or retainer. A small magnet may help in removing the small locks.
5. Lift the valve spring, tool and all, off of the valve stem.
6. If equipped, remove the valve seal. If the seal is difficult to remove with the valve in place, try removing the valve first, then the seal. Follow the steps below for valve removal.
7. Position the head to allow access for withdrawing the valve.

➡Cylinder heads that have seen a lot of miles and/or abuse may have mushroomed the valve lock grove and/or tip, causing difficulty in removal of the valve. If this has happened, use a metal file to carefully remove the high spots around the lock grooves and/or tip. Only file it enough to allow removal.

8. Remove the valve from the cylinder head.
9. If equipped, remove the valve spring shim. A small magnetic tool or screwdriver will aid in removal.
10. Repeat Steps 3 though 9 until all of the valves have been removed.

INSPECTION

Now that all of the cylinder head components are clean, it's time to inspect them for wear and/or damage. To accurately inspect them, you will need some specialized tools:

- A 0–1 in. micrometer for the valves
- A dial indicator or inside diameter gauge for the valve guides
- A spring pressure test gauge

If you do not have access to the proper tools, you may want to bring the components to a shop that does.

Valves

➧ See Figures 203 and 204

The first thing to inspect are the valve heads. Look closely at the head, margin and face for any cracks, excessive wear or burning. The margin is the best place to look for burning. It should have a squared edge with an even width all around the diameter. When a valve burns, the margin will look melted and the edges rounded. Also inspect the valve head for any signs of tulipping. This will show as a lifting of the edges or dishing in the center of the head and will usually not occur to all of the valves. All of the heads should look the same, any that seem dished more than others are probably bad. Next, inspect the valve lock grooves and valve tips. Check for any burrs around the lock grooves, especially if you had to file them to remove the valve. Valve tips should appear flat, although slight rounding with high mileage engines is normal. Slightly worn valve tips will need to be machined flat. Last, measure the valve stem diameter with the micrometer. Measure the area that rides within the guide, especially towards the tip where most of the wear occurs. Take several measurements along its length and compare them to each other. Wear should be even along the length with little to no taper. If no minimum diameter is given in the specifications, then the stem should not read more than 0.001 in. (0.025mm) below the unworn area of the valve stem. Any valves that fail these inspections should be replaced.

Springs, Retainers and Valve Locks

➧ See Figures 205 and 206

The first thing to check is the most obvious, broken springs. Next check the free length and squareness of each spring. If applicable, insure to distinguish between intake and exhaust springs. Use a ruler and/or carpenter's square to measure the length. A carpenter's square should be used to check the springs for squareness. If a spring pressure test gauge is available, check each springs rating and compare to the specifications chart. Check the readings against the specifications given. Any springs that fail these inspections should be replaced.

The spring retainers rarely need replacing, however they should still be checked as a precaution. Inspect the spring mating surface and the valve lock retention area for any signs of excessive wear. Also check for any signs of cracking. Replace any retainers that are questionable.

Valve locks should be inspected for excessive wear on the outside contact area as well as on the inner notched surface. Any locks which appear worn or broken and its respective valve should be replaced.

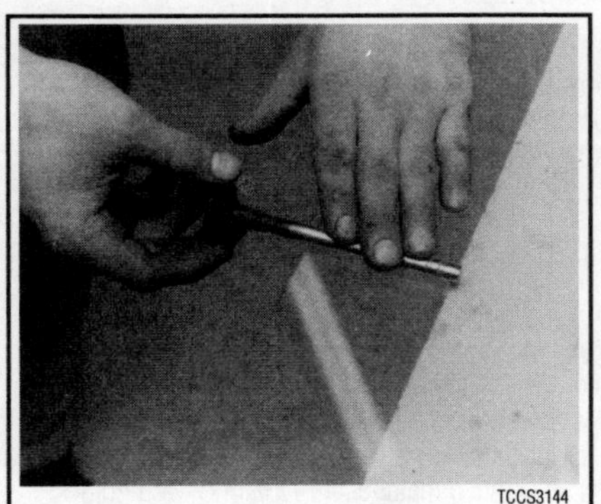
TCCS3144

Fig. 203 Valve stems may be rolled on a flat surface to check for bends

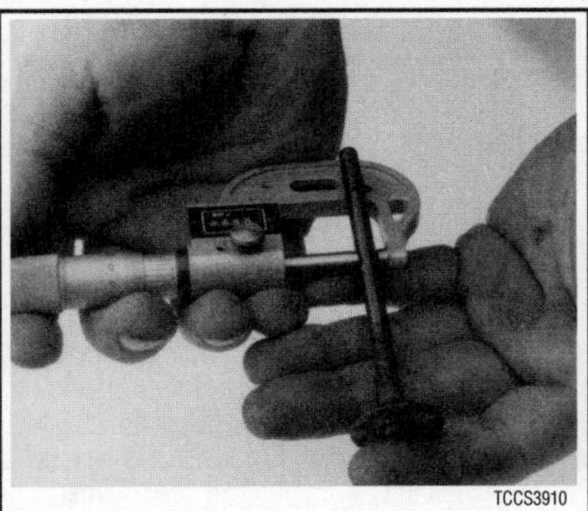
TCCS3910

Fig. 204 Use a micrometer to check the valve stem diameter

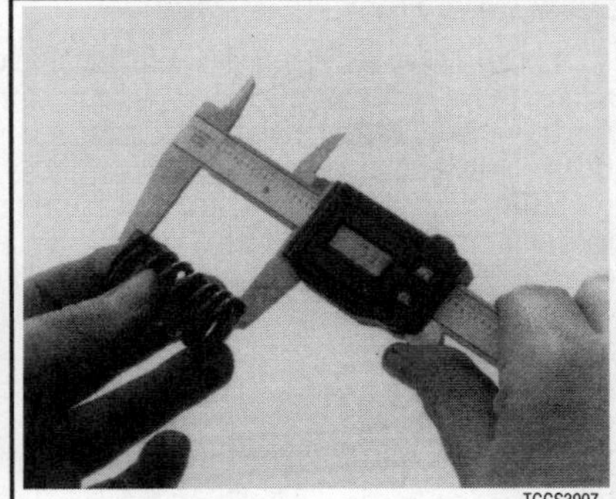
TCCS3907

Fig. 205 Use a caliper to check the valve spring free-length

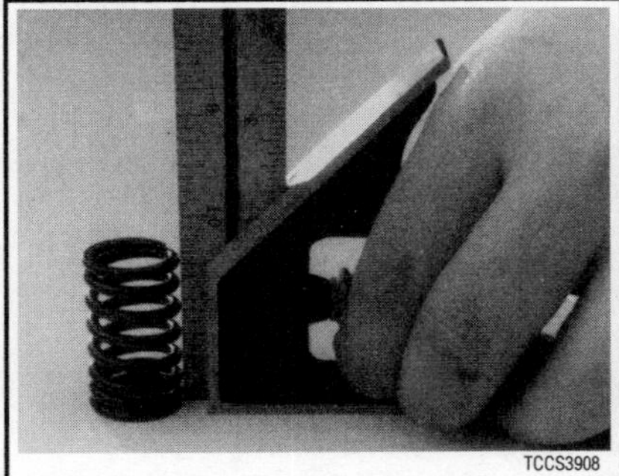
TCCS3908

Fig. 206 Check the valve spring for squareness on a flat surface; a carpenter's square can be used

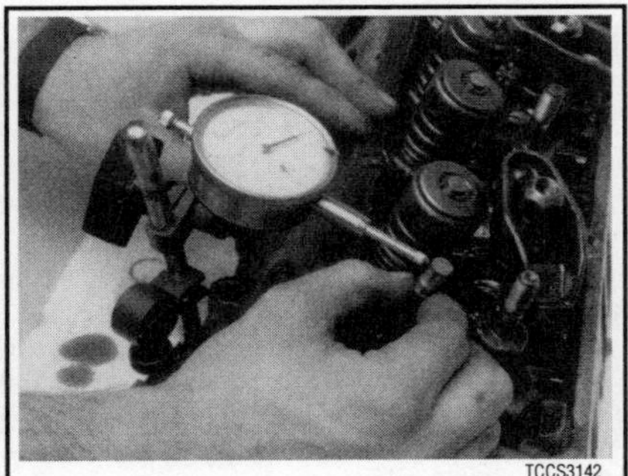
TCCS3142

Fig. 207 A dial gauge may be used to check valve stem-to-guide clearance; read the gauge while moving the valve stem

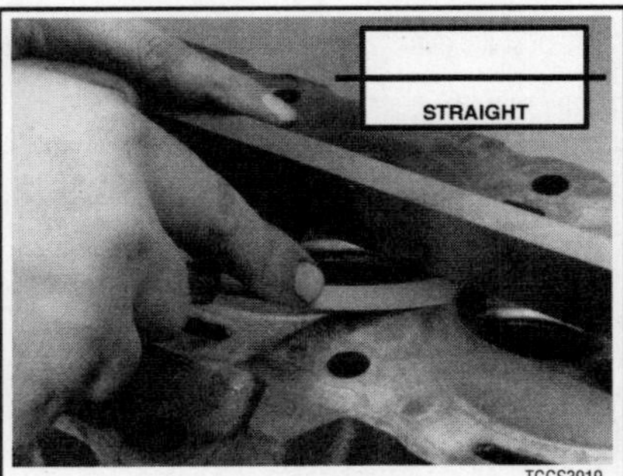

TCCS3919

Fig. 208 Check the head for flatness across the center of the head surface using a straightedge and feeler gauge

Cylinder Head

There are several things to check on the cylinder head: valve guides, seats, cylinder head surface flatness, cracks and physical damage.

VALVE GUIDES

See Figure 207

Now that you know the valves are good, you can use them to check the guides, although a new valve, if available, is preferred. Before you measure anything, look at the guides carefully and inspect them for any cracks, chips or breakage. Also if the guide is a removable style (as in most aluminum heads), check them for any looseness or evidence of movement. All of the guides should appear to be at the same height from the spring seat. If any seem lower (or higher) from another, the guide has moved. Mount a dial indicator onto the spring side of the cylinder head. Lightly oil the valve stem and insert it into the cylinder head. Position the dial indicator against the valve stem near the tip and zero the gauge. Grasp the valve stem and wiggle towards and away from the dial indicator and observe the readings. Mount the dial indicator 90 degrees from the initial point and zero the gauge and again take a reading. Compare the two readings for a out of round condition. Check the readings against the specifications given. An Inside Diameter (I.D.) gauge designed for valve guides will give you an accurate valve guide bore measurement. If the I.D. gauge is used, compare the readings with the specifications given. Any guides that fail these inspections should be replaced or machined.

VALVE SEATS

A visual inspection of the valve seats should show a slightly worn and pitted surface where the valve face contacts the seat. Inspect the seat carefully for severe pitting or cracks. Also, a seat that is badly worn will be recessed into the cylinder head. A severely worn or recessed seat may need to be replaced. All cracked seats must be replaced. A seat concentricity gauge, if available, should be used to check the seat run-out. If run-out exceeds specifications the seat must be machined (if no specification is given use 0.002 in. or 0.051mm).

CYLINDER HEAD SURFACE FLATNESS

See Figures 208 and 209

After you have cleaned the gasket surface of the cylinder head of any old gasket material, check the head for flatness.

Place a straightedge across the gasket surface. Using feeler gauges, determine the clearance at the center of the straightedge and across the cylinder head at several points. Check along the centerline and diagonally on the head surface. If the warpage exceeds 0.003 in. (0.076mm) within a 6.0 in. (15.2cm) span, or 0.006 in. (0.152mm) over the total length of the head, the cylinder head must be resurfaced. After resurfacing the heads of a V-type engine, the intake manifold flange surface should be checked, and if necessary, milled proportionally to allow for the change in its mounting position.

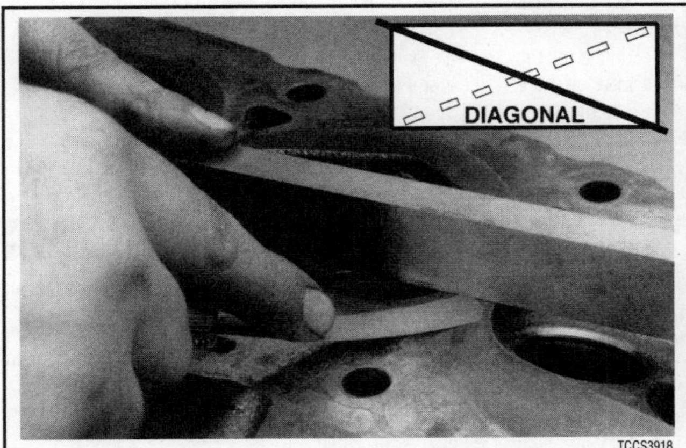

TCCS3918

Fig. 209 Checks should also be made along both diagonals of the head surface

CRACKS AND PHYSICAL DAMAGE

Generally, cracks are limited to the combustion chamber, however, it is not uncommon for the head to crack in a spark plug hole, port, outside of the head or in the valve spring/rocker arm area. The first area to inspect is always the hottest: the exhaust seat/port area.

A visual inspection should be performed, but just because you don't see a crack does not mean it is not there. Some more reliable methods for inspecting for cracks include Magnaflux®, a magnetic process or Zyglo®, a dye penetrant. Magnaflux® is used only on ferrous metal (cast iron) heads. Zyglo® uses a spray on fluorescent mixture along with a black light to reveal the cracks. It is strongly recommended to have your cylinder head checked professionally for cracks, especially if the engine was known to have overheated and/or leaked or consumed coolant. Contact a local shop for availability and pricing of these services.

Physical damage is usually very evident. For example, a broken mounting ear from dropping the head or a bent or broken stud and/or bolt. All of these defects should be fixed or, if unrepairable, the head should be replaced.

Camshaft and Followers

Inspect the camshaft(s) and followers as described earlier in this section.

REFINISHING & REPAIRING

Many of the procedures given for refinishing and repairing the cylinder head components must be performed by a machine shop. Certain steps, if the inspected part is not worn, can be performed yourself inexpensively. However, you spent a lot of time and effort so far, why risk trying to save a couple bucks if you might have to do it all over again?

Valves

Any valves that were not replaced should be refaced and the tips ground flat. Unless you have access to a valve grinding machine, this should be done by a machine shop. If the valves are in extremely good condition, as well as the valve seats and guides, they may be lapped in without performing machine work.

It is a recommended practice to lap the valves even after machine work has been performed and/or new valves have been purchased. This insures a positive seal between the valve and seat.

LAPPING THE VALVES

➡Before lapping the valves to the seats, read the rest of the cylinder head section to insure that any related parts are in acceptable enough condition to continue.

➡Before any valve seat machining and/or lapping can be performed, the guides must be within factory recommended specifications.

1. Invert the cylinder head.
2. Lightly lubricate the valve stems and insert them into the cylinder head in their numbered order.
3. Raise the valve from the seat and apply a small amount of fine lapping compound to the seat.
4. Moisten the suction head of a hand-lapping tool and attach it to the head of the valve.
5. Rotate the tool between the palms of both hands, changing the position of the valve on the valve seat and lifting the tool often to prevent grooving.
6. Lap the valve until a smooth, polished circle is evident on the valve and seat.
7. Remove the tool and the valve. Wipe away all traces of the grinding compound and store the valve to maintain its lapped location.

⁂ WARNING

Do not get the valves out of order after they have been lapped. They must be put back with the same valve seat with which they were lapped.

Springs, Retainers and Valve Locks

There is no repair or refinishing possible with the springs, retainers and valve locks. If they are found to be worn or defective, they must be replaced with new (or known good) parts.

Cylinder Head

Most refinishing procedures dealing with the cylinder head must be performed by a machine shop. Read the sections below and review your inspection data to determine whether or not machining is necessary.

VALVE GUIDE

➡If any machining or replacements are made to the valve guides, the seats must be machined.

Unless the valve guides need machining or replacing, the only service to perform is to thoroughly clean them of any dirt or oil residue.

There are only two types of valve guides used on automobile engines: the replaceable-type (all aluminum heads) and the cast-in integral-type (most cast iron heads). There are four recommended methods for repairing worn guides.

- Knurling
- Inserts
- Reaming oversize
- Replacing

Knurling is a process in which metal is displaced and raised, thereby reducing clearance, giving a true center, and providing oil control. It is the least expensive way of repairing the valve guides. However, it is not necessarily the best, and in some cases, a knurled valve guide will not stand up for more than a short time. It requires a special knurlizer and precision reaming tools to obtain proper clearances. It would not be cost effective to purchase these tools, unless you plan on rebuilding several of the same cylinder head.

Installing a guide insert involves machining the guide to accept a bronze insert. One style is the coil-type which is installed into a threaded guide. Another is the thin-walled insert where the guide is reamed oversize to accept a split-sleeve insert. After the insert is installed, a special tool is then run through the guide to expand the insert, locking it to the guide. The insert is then reamed to the standard size for proper valve clearance.

Reaming for oversize valves restores normal clearances and provides a true valve seat. Most cast-in type guides can be reamed to accept an valve with an oversize stem. The cost factor for this can become quite high as you will need to purchase the reamer and new, oversize stem valves for all guides which were reamed. Oversizes are generally 0.003 to 0.030 in. (0.076 to 0.762mm), with 0.015 in. (0.381mm) being the most common.

To replace cast-in type valve guides, they must be drilled out, then reamed to accept replacement guides. This must be done on a fixture which will allow centering and leveling off of the original valve seat or guide, otherwise a serious guide-to-seat misalignment may occur making it impossible to properly machine the seat.

Replaceable-type guides are pressed into the cylinder head. A hammer and a stepped drift or punch may be used to install and remove the guides. Before removing the guides, measure the protrusion on the spring side of the head and record it for installation. Use the stepped drift to hammer out the old guide from the combustion chamber side of the head. When installing, determine whether or not the guide also seals a water jacket in the head, and if it does, use the recommended sealing agent. If there is no water jacket, grease the valve guide and its bore. Use the stepped drift, and hammer the new guide into the cylinder head from the spring side of the cylinder head. A stack of washers the same thickness as the measured protrusion may help the installation process.

VALVE SEATS

➡Before any valve seat machining can be performed, the guides must be within factory recommended specifications.

➡If any machining or replacements were made to the valve guides, the seats must be machined.

If the seats are in good condition, the valves can be lapped to the seats, and the cylinder head assembled. See the valves section for instructions on lapping.

If the valve seats are worn, cracked or damaged, they must be serviced by a machine shop. The valve seat must be perfectly centered to the valve guide, which requires very accurate machining.

CYLINDER HEAD SURFACE

If the cylinder head is warped, it must be machined flat. If the warpage is extremely severe, the head may need to be replaced. In some instances, it may be possible to straighten a warped head enough to allow machining. In either case, contact a professional machine shop for service.

➡Any OHC cylinder head that shows excessive warpage should have the camshaft bearing journals align bored after the cylinder head has been resurfaced.

✲✲✲ WARNING

Failure to align bore the camshaft bearing journals could result in severe engine damage including but not limited to: valve and piston damage, connecting rod damage, camshaft and/or crankshaft breakage.

CRACKS AND PHYSICAL DAMAGE

Certain cracks can be repaired in both cast iron and aluminum heads. For cast iron, a tapered threaded insert is installed along the length of the crack. Aluminum can also use the tapered inserts, however welding is the preferred method. Some physical damage can be repaired through brazing or welding. Contact a machine shop to get expert advice for your particular dilemma.

ASSEMBLY

The first step for any assembly job is to have a clean area in which to work. Next, thoroughly clean all of the parts and components that are to be assembled. Finally, place all of the components onto a suitable work space and, if necessary, arrange the parts to their respective positions.

OHV Engines (3.3L/3.8L Engines)

1. Lightly lubricate the valve stems and insert all of the valves into the cylinder head. If possible, maintain their original locations.
2. If equipped, install any valve spring shims which were removed.
3. If equipped, install the new valve seals, keeping the following in mind:
   - If the valve seal presses over the guide, lightly lubricate the outer guide surfaces.
   - If the seal is an O-ring type, it is installed just after compressing the spring but before the valve locks.
4. Place the valve spring and retainer over the stem.
5. Position the spring compressor tool and compress the spring.
6. Assemble the valve locks to the stem.
7. Relieve the spring pressure slowly and insure that neither valve lock becomes dislodged by the retainer.
8. Remove the spring compressor tool.
9. Repeat Steps 2 through 8 until all of the springs have been installed.

OHC Engines (2.4L and 3.0L Engines)

➧ See Figure 210

CUP TYPE CAMSHAFT FOLLOWERS

To install the springs, retainers and valve locks on heads which have these components recessed into the camshaft follower's bore, you will need a small screwdriver-type tool, some clean white grease and a lot of patience. You will also need the C-clamp style spring compressor and the OHC tool used to disassemble the head.

1. Lightly lubricate the valve stems and insert all of the valves into the cylinder head. If possible, maintain their original locations.
2. If equipped, install any valve spring shims which were removed.
3. If equipped, install the new valve seals, keeping the following in mind:
   - If the valve seal presses over the guide, lightly lubricate the outer guide surfaces.
   - If the seal is an O-ring type, it is installed just after compressing the spring but before the valve locks.
4. Place the valve spring and retainer over the stem.
5. Position the spring compressor and the OHC tool, then compress the spring.
6. Using a small screwdriver as a spatula, fill the valve stem side of the lock with white grease. Use the excess grease on the screwdriver to fasten the lock to the driver.
7. Carefully install the valve lock, which is stuck to the end of the screwdriver, to the valve stem then press on it with the screwdriver until the grease squeezes out. The valve lock should now be stuck to the stem.

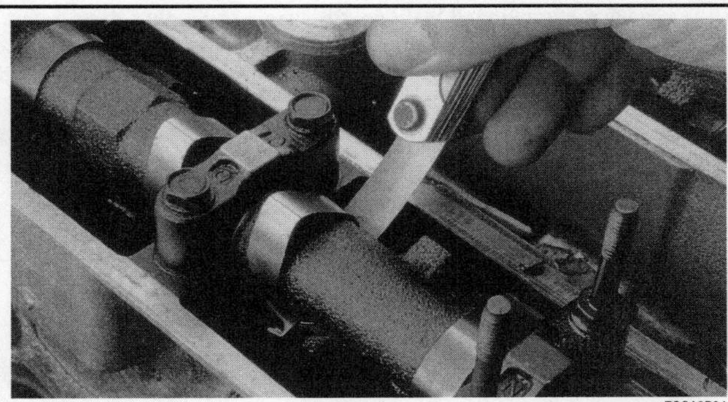
TCCA3P64

Fig. 210 Once assembled, check the valve clearance and correct as needed

8. Repeat Steps 6 and 7 for the remaining valve lock.
9. Relieve the spring pressure slowly and insure that neither valve lock becomes dislodged by the retainer.
10. Remove the spring compressor tool.
11. Repeat Steps 2 through 10 until all of the springs have been installed.
12. Install the followers, camshaft(s) and any other components that were removed for disassembly.

ROCKER ARM TYPE CAMSHAFT FOLLOWERS

1. Lightly lubricate the valve stems and insert all of the valves into the cylinder head. If possible, maintain their original locations.
2. If equipped, install any valve spring shims which were removed.
3. If equipped, install the new valve seals, keeping the following in mind:
   - If the valve seal presses over the guide, lightly lubricate the outer guide surfaces.
   - If the seal is an O-ring type, it is installed just after compressing the spring but before the valve locks.
4. Place the valve spring and retainer over the stem.
5. Position the spring compressor tool and compress the spring.
6. Assemble the valve locks to the stem.
7. Relieve the spring pressure slowly and insure that neither valve lock becomes dislodged by the retainer.
8. Remove the spring compressor tool.
9. Repeat Steps 2 through 8 until all of the springs have been installed.
10. Install the camshaft(s), rockers, shafts and any other components that were removed for disassembly.

Engine Block

GENERAL INFORMATION

A thorough overhaul or rebuild of an engine block would include replacing the pistons, rings, bearings, timing belt/chain assembly and oil pump. For OHV engines also include a new camshaft and lifters. The block would then have the cylinders bored and honed oversize (or if using removable cylinder sleeves, new sleeves installed) and the crankshaft would be cut undersize to provide new wearing surfaces and perfect clearances. However, your particular engine may not have everything worn out. What if only the piston rings have worn out and the clearances on everything else are still within factory specifications? Well, you could just replace the rings and put it back together, but this would be a very rare example. Chances are, if one component in your engine is worn, other components are sure to follow, and soon. At the very least, you should always replace the rings, bearings and oil pump. This is what is commonly called a "freshen up".

Cylinder Ridge Removal

Because the top piston ring does not travel to the very top of the cylinder, a ridge is built up between the end of the travel and the top of the cylinder bore.

Pushing the piston and connecting rod assembly past the ridge can be difficult, and damage to the piston ring lands could occur. If the ridge is not removed before installing a new piston or not removed at all, piston ring breakage and piston damage may occur.

➡It is always recommended that you remove any cylinder ridges before removing the piston and connecting rod assemblies. If you know that new pistons are going to be installed and the engine block will be bored oversize, you may be able to forego this step. However, some ridges may actually prevent the assemblies from being removed, necessitating its removal.

There are several different types of ridge reamers on the market, none of which are inexpensive. Unless a great deal of engine rebuilding is anticipated, borrow or rent a reamer.

1. Turn the crankshaft until the piston is at the bottom of its travel.
2. Cover the head of the piston with a rag.
3. Follow the tool manufacturers instructions and cut away the ridge, exercising extreme care to avoid cutting too deeply.
4. Remove the ridge reamer, the rag and as many of the cuttings as possible. Continue until all of the cylinder ridges have been removed.

DISASSEMBLY

See Figures 211 and 212

The engine disassembly instructions following assume that you have the engine mounted on an engine stand. If not, it is easiest to disassemble the engine on a bench or the floor with it resting on the bell housing or transmission mounting surface. You must be able to access the connecting rod fasteners and turn the crankshaft during disassembly. Also, all engine covers (timing, front, side, oil pan, whatever) should have already been removed. Engines which are seized or locked up may not be able to be completely disassembled, and a core (salvage yard) engine should be purchased.

Pushrod Engines

If not done during the cylinder head removal, remove the pushrods and lifters, keeping them in order for assembly. Remove the timing gears and/or timing chain assembly, then remove the oil pump drive assembly and withdraw the camshaft from the engine block. Remove the oil pick-up and pump assembly. If equipped, remove any balance or auxiliary shafts. If necessary, remove the cylinder ridge from the top of the bore. See the cylinder ridge removal procedure earlier in this section.

OHC Engines (2.4L and 3.0L Engines)

If not done during the cylinder head removal, remove the timing chain/belt and/or gear/sprocket assembly. Remove the oil pick-up and pump assembly and, if necessary, the pump drive. If equipped, remove any balance or auxiliary shafts. If necessary, remove the cylinder ridge from the top of the bore. See the cylinder ridge removal procedure earlier in this section.

All Engines

Rotate the engine over so that the crankshaft is exposed. Use a number punch or scribe and mark each connecting rod with its respective cylinder number. The cylinder closest to the front of the engine is always number 1. However, depending on the engine placement, the front of the engine could either be the flywheel or damper/pulley end. Generally the front of the engine faces the front of the vehicle. Use a number punch or scribe and also mark the main bearing caps from front to rear with the front most cap being number 1 (if there are five caps, mark them 1 through 5, front to rear).

TCCS3803

Fig. 211 Place rubber hose over the connecting rod studs to protect the crankshaft and cylinder bores from damage

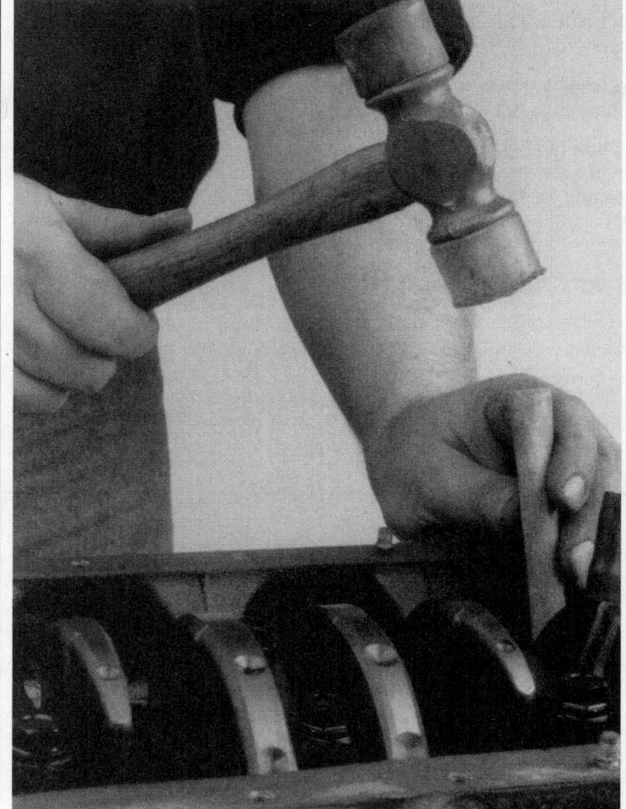

TCCS3804

Fig. 212 Carefully tap the piston out of the bore using a wooden dowel

✲✲ WARNING

Take special care when pushing the connecting rod up from the crankshaft because the sharp threads of the rod bolts/studs will score the crankshaft journal. Insure that special plastic caps are installed over them, or cut two pieces of rubber hose to do the same.

Again, rotate the engine, this time to position the number one cylinder bore (head surface) up. Turn the crankshaft until the number one piston is at the bottom of its travel, this should allow the maximum access to its connecting rod. Remove the number one connecting rods fasteners and cap and place two lengths of rubber hose over the rod bolts/studs to protect the crankshaft from damage. Using a sturdy wooden dowel and a hammer, push the connecting rod up about 1 in. (25mm) from the crankshaft and remove the upper bearing insert. Continue pushing or tapping the connecting rod up until the piston rings are out of the cylinder bore. Remove the piston and rod by hand, put the upper half of the bearing insert back into the rod, install the cap with its bearing insert installed, and hand-tighten the cap fasteners. If the parts are kept in order in this manner, they will not get lost and you will be able to tell which bearings came form what cylinder if any problems are discovered and diagnosis is necessary. Remove all the other piston assemblies in the same manner. On V-style engines, remove all of the pistons from one bank, then reposition the engine with the other cylinder bank head surface up, and remove that banks piston assemblies.

The only remaining component in the engine block should now be the crankshaft. Loosen the main bearing caps evenly until the fasteners can be turned by hand, then remove them and the caps. Remove the crankshaft from the engine block. Thoroughly clean all of the components.

INSPECTION

Now that the engine block and all of its components are clean, it's time to inspect them for wear and/or damage. To accurately inspect them, you will need some specialized tools:

- Two or three separate micrometers to measure the pistons and crankshaft journals
- A dial indicator
- Telescoping gauges for the cylinder bores
- A rod alignment fixture to check for bent connecting rods

If you do not have access to the proper tools, you may want to bring the components to a shop that does.

Generally, you shouldn't expect cracks in the engine block or its components unless it was known to leak, consume or mix engine fluids, it was severely overheated, or there was evidence of bad bearings and/or crankshaft damage. A visual inspection should be performed on all of the components, but just because you don't see a crack does not mean it is not there. Some more reliable methods for inspecting for cracks include Magnaflux®, a magnetic process or Zyglo®, a dye penetrant. Magnaflux® is used only on ferrous metal (cast iron). Zyglo® uses a spray on fluorescent mixture along with a black light to reveal the cracks. It is strongly recommended to have your engine block checked professionally for cracks, especially if the engine was known to have overheated and/or leaked or consumed coolant. Contact a local shop for availability and pricing of these services.

Engine Block

ENGINE BLOCK BEARING ALIGNMENT

Remove the main bearing caps and, if still installed, the main bearing inserts. Inspect all of the main bearing saddles and caps for damage, burrs or high spots. If damage is found, and it is caused from a spun main bearing, the block will need to be align-bored or, if severe enough, replacement. Any burrs or high spots should be carefully removed with a metal file.

Place a straightedge on the bearing saddles, in the engine block, along the centerline of the crankshaft. If any clearance exists between the straightedge and the saddles, the block must be align-bored.

Align-boring consists of machining the main bearing saddles and caps by means of a flycutter that runs through the bearing saddles.

DECK FLATNESS

The top of the engine block where the cylinder head mounts is called the deck. Insure that the deck surface is clean of dirt, carbon deposits and old gasket material. Place a straightedge across the surface of the deck along its centerline and, using feeler gauges, check the clearance along several points. Repeat the checking procedure with the straightedge placed along both diagonals of the deck surface. If the reading exceeds 0.003 in. (0.076mm) within a 6.0 in. (15.2cm) span, or 0.006 in. (0.152mm) over the total length of the deck, it must be machined.

CYLINDER BORES

➧ **See Figure 213**

The cylinder bores house the pistons and are slightly larger than the pistons themselves. A common piston-to-bore clearance is 0.0015–0.0025 in. (0.0381mm–0.0635mm). Inspect and measure the cylinder bores. The bore should be checked for out-of-roundness, taper and size. The results of this inspection will determine whether the cylinder can be used in its existing size and condition, or a rebore to the next oversize is required (or in the case of removable sleeves, have replacements installed).

The amount of cylinder wall wear is always greater at the top of the cylinder than at the bottom. This wear is known as taper. Any cylinder that has a taper of 0.0012 in. (0.305mm) or more, must be rebored. Measurements are taken at a number of positions in each cylinder: at the top, middle and bottom and at two points at each position; that is, at a point 90 degrees from the crankshaft centerline, as well as a point parallel to the crankshaft centerline. The measurements are made with either a special dial indicator or a telescopic gauge and micrometer. If the necessary precision tools to check the bore are not available, take the block to a machine shop and have them mike it. Also if you don't have the tools to check the cylinder bores, chances are you will not have the necessary devices to check the pistons, connecting rods and crankshaft. Take these components with you and save yourself an extra trip.

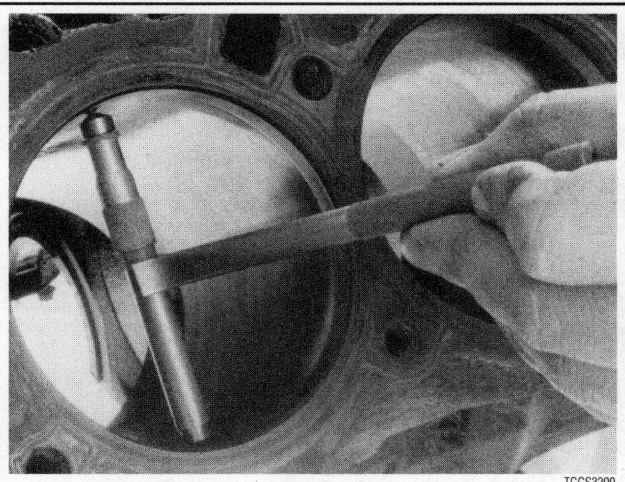

TCCS3209

Fig. 213 Use a telescoping gauge to measure the cylinder bore diameter—take several readings within the same bore

For our procedures, we will use a telescopic gauge and a micrometer. You will need one of each, with a measuring range which covers your cylinder bore size.

1. Position the telescopic gauge in the cylinder bore, loosen the gauges lock and allow it to expand.

➡Your first two readings will be at the top of the cylinder bore, then proceed to the middle and finally the bottom, making a total of six measurements.

2. Hold the gauge square in the bore, 90 degrees from the crankshaft centerline, and gently tighten the lock. Tilt the gauge back to remove it from the bore.
3. Measure the gauge with the micrometer and record the reading.
4. Again, hold the gauge square in the bore, this time parallel to the crankshaft centerline, and gently tighten the lock. Again, you will tilt the gauge back to remove it from the bore.
5. Measure the gauge with the micrometer and record this reading. The difference between these two readings is the out-of-round measurement of the cylinder.
6. Repeat steps 1 through 5, each time going to the next lower position, until you reach the bottom of the cylinder. Then go to the next cylinder, and continue until all of the cylinders have been measured.

The difference between these measurements will tell you all about the wear in your cylinders. The measurements which were taken 90 degrees from the crankshaft centerline will always reflect the most wear. That is because at this position is where the engine power presses the piston against the cylinder bore the hardest. This is known as thrust wear. Take your top, 90 degree measurement and compare it to your bottom, 90 degree measurement. The difference between them is the taper. When you measure your pistons, you will compare these readings to your piston sizes and determine piston-to-wall clearance.

Crankshaft

Inspect the crankshaft for visible signs of wear or damage. All of the journals should be perfectly round and smooth. Slight scores are normal for a used crankshaft, but you should hardly feel them with your fingernail. When measuring the crankshaft with a micrometer, you will take readings at the front and rear of each journal, then turn the micrometer 90 degrees and take two more readings, front and rear. The difference between the front-to-rear readings is the journal taper and the first-to-90 degree reading is the out-of-round measurement. Generally, there should be no taper or out-of-roundness found, however, up to 0.0005 in. (0.0127mm) for either can be overlooked. Also, the readings should fall within the factory specifications for journal diameters.

If the crankshaft journals fall within specifications, it is recommended that it be polished before being returned to service. Polishing the crankshaft insures that any minor burrs or high spots are smoothed, thereby reducing the chance of scoring the new bearings.

Pistons and Connecting Rods

PISTONS

➧ See Figure 214

The piston should be visually inspected for any signs of cracking or burning (caused by hot spots or detonation), and scuffing or excessive wear on the skirts. The wrist pin attaches the piston to the connecting rod. The piston should move freely on the wrist pin, both sliding and pivoting. Grasp the connecting rod securely, or mount it in a vise, and try to rock the piston back and forth along the centerline of the wrist pin. There should not be any excessive play evident between the piston and the pin. If there are C-clips retaining the pin in the piston then you have wrist pin bushings in the rods. There should not be any excessive play between the wrist pin and the rod bushing. Normal clearance for the wrist pin is approx. 0.001–0.002 in. (0.025mm–0.051mm).

Use a micrometer and measure the diameter of the piston, perpendicular to the wrist pin, on the skirt. Compare the reading to its original cylinder measurement obtained earlier. The difference between the two readings is the piston-to-wall clearance. If the clearance is within specifications, the piston may be used as is. If the piston is out of specification, but the bore is not, you will need a new piston. If both are out of specification, you will need the cylinder rebored and oversize pistons installed. Generally if two or more pistons/bores are out of specification, it is best to rebore the entire block and purchase a complete set of oversize pistons.

CONNECTING ROD

You should have the connecting rod checked for straightness at a machine shop. If the connecting rod is bent, it will unevenly wear the bearing and piston, as well as place greater stress on these components. Any bent or twisted connecting rods must be replaced. If the rods are straight and the wrist pin clearance is within specifications, then only the bearing end of the rod need be checked. Place the connecting rod into a vice, with the bearing inserts in place, install the cap to the rod and torque the fasteners to specifications. Use a telescoping gauge and carefully measure the inside diameter of the bearings. Compare this reading to the rods original crankshaft journal diameter measurement. The difference is the oil clearance. If the oil clearance is not within specifications, install new bearings in the rod and take another measurement. If the clearance is still out of specifications, and the crankshaft is not, the rod will need to be reconditioned by a machine shop.

➥You can also use Plastigage® to check the bearing clearances. The assembling section has complete instructions on its use.

Camshaft

Inspect the camshaft and lifters/followers as described earlier in this section.

Bearings

All of the engine bearings should be visually inspected for wear and/or damage. The bearing should look evenly worn all around with no deep scores or pits. If the bearing is severely worn, scored, pitted or heat blued, then the bearing, and the components that use it, should be brought to a machine shop for inspection. Full-circle bearings (used on most camshafts, auxiliary shafts, balance shafts, etc.) require specialized tools for removal and installation, and should be brought to a machine shop for service.

Oil Pump

➥The oil pump is responsible for providing constant lubrication to the whole engine and so it is recommended that a new oil pump be installed when rebuilding the engine.

Completely disassemble the oil pump and thoroughly clean all of the components. Inspect the oil pump gears and housing for wear and/or damage. Insure that the pressure relief valve operates properly and there is no binding or sticking due to varnish or debris. If all of the parts are in proper working condition, lubricate the gears and relief valve, and assemble the pump.

REFINISHING

➧ See Figure 215

Almost all engine block refinishing must be performed by a machine shop. If the cylinders are not to be rebored, then the cylinder glaze can be removed with a ball hone. When removing cylinder glaze with a ball hone, use a light or penetrating type oil to lubricate the hone. Do not allow the hone to run dry as this may cause excessive scoring of the cylinder bores and wear on the hone. If new pistons are required, they will need to be installed to the connecting rods. This should be performed by a machine shop as the pistons must be installed in the correct relationship to the rod or engine damage can occur.

Pistons and Connecting Rods

➧ See Figure 216

Only pistons with the wrist pin retained by C-clips are serviceable by the home-mechanic. Press fit pistons require special presses and/or heaters to remove/install the connecting rod and should only be performed by a machine shop.

All pistons will have a mark indicating the direction to the front of the engine and the must be installed into the engine in that manner. Usually it is a notch or arrow on the top of the piston, or it may be the letter F cast or stamped into the piston.

C-CLIP TYPE PISTONS

1. Note the location of the forward mark on the piston and mark the connecting rod in relation.
2. Remove the C-clips from the piston and withdraw the wrist pin.

➥Varnish build-up or C-clip groove burrs may increase the difficulty of removing the wrist pin. If necessary, use a punch or drift to carefully tap the wrist pin out.

3. Insure that the wrist pin bushing in the connecting rod is usable, and lubricate it with assembly lube.
4. Remove the wrist pin from the new piston and lubricate the pin bores on the piston.
5. Align the forward marks on the piston and the connecting rod and install the wrist pin.

TCCS3210

Fig. 214 Measure the piston's outer diameter, perpendicular to the wrist pin, with a micrometer

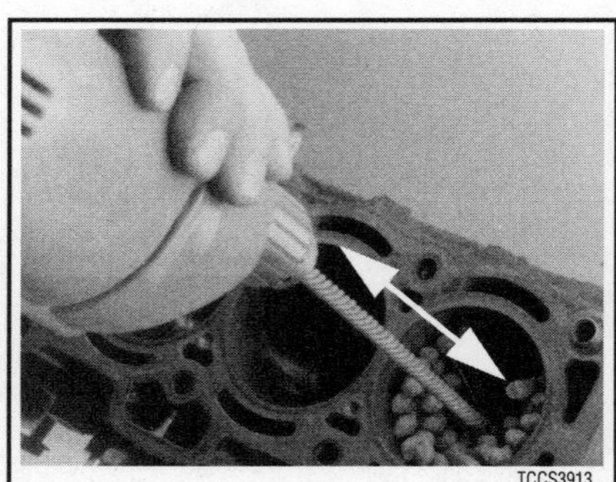

TCCS3913

Fig. 215 Use a ball type cylinder hone to remove any glaze and provide a new surface for seating the piston rings

TCCS3814

Fig. 216 Most pistons are marked to indicate positioning in the engine (usually a mark means the side facing the front)

6. The new C-clips will have a flat and a rounded side to them. Install both C-clips with the flat side facing out.

7. Repeat all of the steps for each piston being replaced.

ASSEMBLY

Before you begin assembling the engine, first give yourself a clean, dirt free work area. Next, clean every engine component again. The key to a good assembly is cleanliness.

Mount the engine block into the engine stand and wash it one last time using water and detergent (dishwashing detergent works well). While washing it, scrub the cylinder bores with a soft bristle brush and thoroughly clean all of the oil passages. Completely dry the engine and spray the entire assembly down with an anti-rust solution such as WD-40® or similar product. Take a clean lint-free rag and wipe up any excess anti-rust solution from the bores, bearing saddles, etc. Repeat the final cleaning process on the crankshaft. Replace any freeze or oil galley plugs which were removed during disassembly.

Crankshaft

➧ See Figures 217, 218, 219 and 220

1. Remove the main bearing inserts from the block and bearing caps.
2. If the crankshaft main bearing journals have been refinished to a definite undersize, install the correct undersize bearing. Be sure that the bearing inserts and bearing bores are clean. Foreign material under inserts will distort bearing and cause failure.
3. Place the upper main bearing inserts in bores with tang in slot.

➡The oil holes in the bearing inserts must be aligned with the oil holes in the cylinder block.

4. Install the lower main bearing inserts in bearing caps.
5. Clean the mating surfaces of block and rear main bearing cap.
6. Carefully lower the crankshaft into place. Be careful not to damage bearing surfaces.
7. Check the clearance of each main bearing by using the following procedure:
   a. Place a piece of Plastigage® or its equivalent, on bearing surface across full width of bearing cap and about 1/4 in. off center.
   b. Install cap and tighten bolts to specifications. Do not turn crankshaft while Plastigage® is in place.
   c. Remove the cap. Using the supplied Plastigage® scale, check width of Plastigage® at widest point to get maximum clearance. Difference between readings is taper of journal.
   d. If clearance exceeds specified limits, try a 0.001 in. or 0.002 in. undersize bearing in combination with the standard bearing. Bearing clearance must be within specified limits. If standard and 0.002 in. undersize bearing does not bring clearance within desired limits, refinish crankshaft journal, then install undersize bearings.
8. After the bearings have been fitted, apply a light coat of engine oil to the journals and bearings. Install the rear main bearing cap. Install all bearing caps except the thrust bearing cap. Be sure that main bearing caps are installed in original locations. Tighten the bearing cap bolts to specifications.
9. Install the thrust bearing cap with bolts finger-tight.
10. Pry the crankshaft forward against the thrust surface of upper half of bearing.
11. Hold the crankshaft forward and pry the thrust bearing cap to the rear. This aligns the thrust surfaces of both halves of the bearing.
12. Retain the forward pressure on the crankshaft. Tighten the cap bolts to specifications.
13. Measure the crankshaft end-play as follows:
   a. Mount a dial gauge to the engine block and position the tip of the gauge to read from the crankshaft end.
   b. Carefully pry the crankshaft toward the rear of the engine and hold it there while you zero the gauge.
   c. Carefully pry the crankshaft toward the front of the engine and read the gauge.
   d. Confirm that the reading is within specifications. If not, install a new

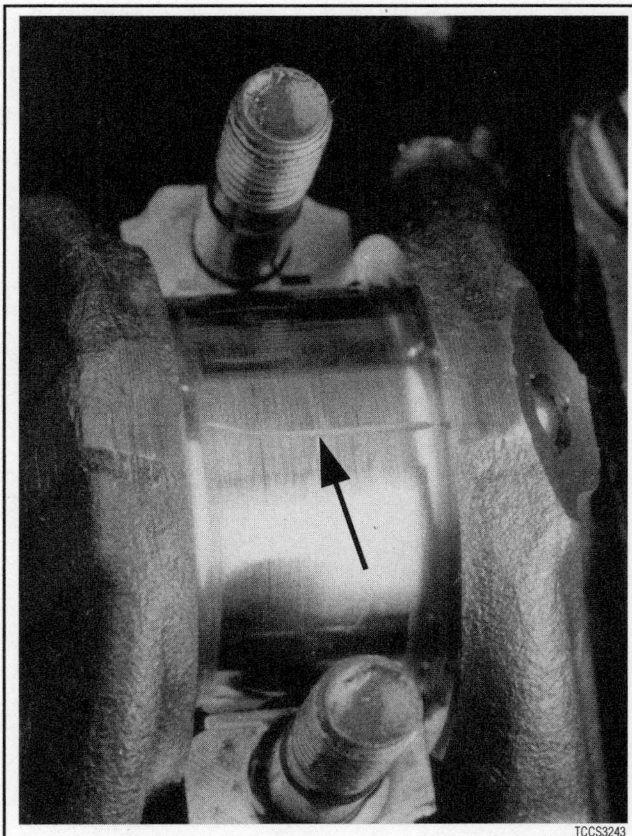

TCCS3243

Fig. 217 Apply a strip of gauging material to the bearing journal, then install and torque the cap

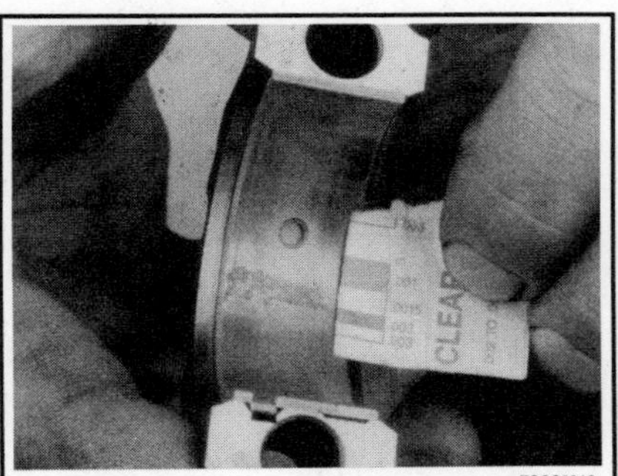

TCCS3912

Fig. 218 After the cap is removed again, use the scale supplied with the gauging material to check the clearance

TCCS3805

Fig. 219 A dial gauge may be used to check crankshaft end-play

TCCS3806

Fig. 220 Carefully pry the crankshaft back and forth while reading the dial gauge for end-play

thrust bearing and repeat the procedure. If the reading is still out of specifications with a new bearing, have a machine shop inspect the thrust surfaces of the crankshaft, and if possible, repair it.

14. Install the rear main seal.
15. Rotate the crankshaft so as to position the first rod journal to the bottom of its stroke.

Pistons and Connecting Rods

See Figures 221, 222, 223 and 224

1. Before installing the piston/connecting rod assembly, oil the pistons, piston rings and the cylinder walls with light engine oil. Install connecting rod bolt protectors or rubber hose onto the connecting rod bolts/studs. Also perform the following:
   a. Select the proper ring set for the size cylinder bore.
   b. Position the ring in the bore in which it is going to be used.
   c. Push the ring down into the bore area where normal ring wear is not encountered.
   d. Use the head of the piston to position the ring in the bore so that the ring is square with the cylinder wall. Use caution to avoid damage to the ring or cylinder bore.
   e. Measure the gap between the ends of the ring with a feeler gauge. Ring gap in a worn cylinder is normally greater than specification. If the ring gap is greater than the specified limits, try an oversize ring set.
   f. Check the ring side clearance of the compression rings with a feeler gauge inserted between the ring and its lower land according to specification. The gauge should slide freely around the entire ring circumference without binding. Any wear that occurs will form a step at the inner portion of the lower land. If the lower lands have high steps, the piston should be replaced.

TCCS3923

Fig. 221 Checking the piston ring-to-ring groove side clearance using the ring and a feeler gauge

2. Unless new pistons are installed, be sure to install the pistons in the cylinders from which they were removed. The numbers on the connecting rod and bearing cap must be on the same side when installed in the cylinder bore. If a connecting rod is ever transposed from one engine or cylinder to another, new bearings should be fitted and the connecting rod should be numbered to correspond with the new cylinder number. The notch on the piston head goes toward the front of the engine.
3. Install all of the rod bearing inserts into the rods and caps.
4. Install the rings to the pistons. Install the oil control ring first, then the second compression ring and finally the top compression ring. Use a piston ring expander tool to aid in installation and to help reduce the chance of breakage.
5. Make sure the ring gaps are properly spaced around the circumference of the piston. Fit a piston ring compressor around the piston and slide the piston and connecting rod assembly down into the cylinder bore, pushing it in with the wooden hammer handle. Push the piston down until it is only slightly below the top of the cylinder bore. Guide the connecting rod onto the crankshaft bearing journal carefully, to avoid damaging the crankshaft.
6. Check the bearing clearance of all the rod bearings, fitting them to the crankshaft bearing journals. Follow the procedure in the crankshaft installation above.
7. After the bearings have been fitted, apply a light coating of assembly oil to the journals and bearings.
8. Turn the crankshaft until the appropriate bearing journal is at the bottom of its stroke, then push the piston assembly all the way down until the connecting rod bearing seats on the crankshaft journal. Be careful not to allow the bearing cap screws to strike the crankshaft bearing journals and damage them.
9. After the piston and connecting rod assemblies have been installed, check the connecting rod side clearance on each crankshaft journal.
10. On the 2.4L engine only, install the balance shafts and carrier assembly.
11. Prime and install the oil pump and the oil pump intake tube.

OHV Engines (3.3L/3.8L Engines)

CAMSHAFT, LIFTERS AND TIMING ASSEMBLY

1. Install the camshaft.
2. Install the lifters/followers into their bores.
3. Install the timing gears/chain assembly.

CYLINDER HEAD(S)

1. Install the cylinder head(s) using new gaskets.
2. Assemble the rest of the valve train (pushrods and rocker arms and/or shafts).

OHC Engines (2.4L and 3.0L Engines)

CYLINDER HEAD(S)

1. Install the cylinder head(s) using new gaskets.
2. Install the timing sprockets/gears and the belt/chain assemblies.

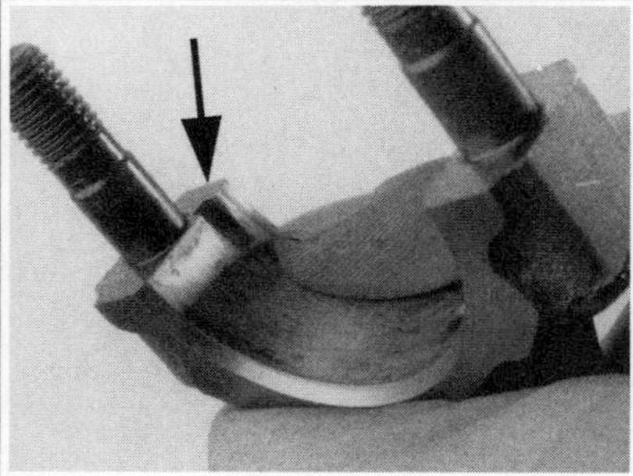

TCCS3917

Fig. 222 The notch on the side of the bearing cap matches the tang on the bearing insert

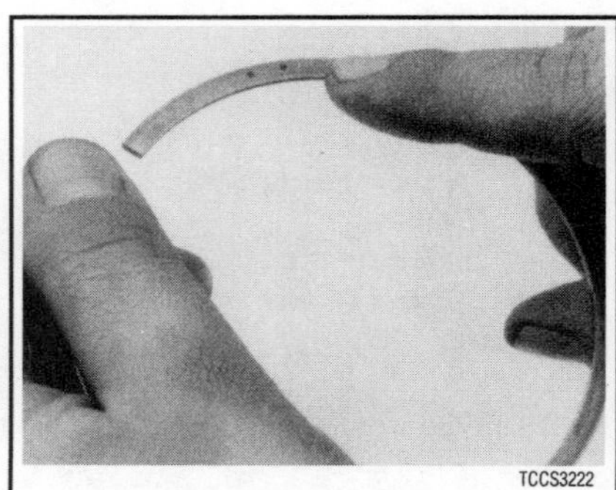

TCCS3222

Fig. 223 Most rings are marked to show which side of the ring should face up when installed to the piston

TCCS3914

Fig. 224 Install the piston and rod assembly into the block using a ring compressor and the handle of a hammer

Engine Covers and Components

Install the timing cover(s) and oil pan. Refer to your notes and drawings made prior to disassembly and install all of the components that were removed. Install the engine into the vehicle.

Engine Start-up and Break-in

STARTING THE ENGINE

Now that the engine is installed and every wire and hose is properly connected, go back and double check that all coolant and vacuum hoses are connected. Check that your oil drain plug is installed and properly tightened. If not already done, install a new oil filter onto the engine. Fill the crankcase with the proper amount and grade of engine oil. Fill the cooling system with a 50/50 mixture of coolant/water.

1. Connect the vehicle battery.
2. Start the engine. Keep your eye on your oil pressure indicator; if it does not indicate oil pressure within 10 seconds of starting, turn the vehicle off.

***** WARNING**

Damage to the engine can result if it is allowed to run with no oil pressure. Check the engine oil level to make sure that it is full. Check for any leaks and if found, repair the leaks before continuing. If there is still no indication of oil pressure, you may need to prime the system.

3. Confirm that there are no fluid leaks (oil or other).
4. Allow the engine to reach normal operating temperature (the upper radiator hose will be hot to the touch).
5. At this point you can perform any necessary checks or adjustments, such as checking the ignition timing.
6. Install any remaining components or body panels which were removed.

BREAKING IT IN

Make the first miles on the new engine, easy ones. Vary the speed but do not accelerate hard. Most importantly, do not lug the engine, and avoid sustained high speeds until at least 100 miles. Check the engine oil and coolant levels frequently. Expect the engine to use a little oil until the rings seat. Change the oil and filter at 500 miles, 1500 miles, then every 3000 miles past that.

KEEP IT MAINTAINED

Now that you have just gone through all of that hard work, keep yourself from doing it all over again by thoroughly maintaining it. Not that you may not have maintained it before, heck you could have had one to two hundred thousand miles on it before doing this. However, you may have bought the vehicle used, and the previous owner did not keep up on maintenance. Which is why you just went through all of that hard work. See?

2.4L DOHC ENGINE MECHANICAL SPECIFICATIONS

Description	English Specifications	Metric Specifications
Engine	In-line OHV, DOHC	
Number of cylinders	4	
Bore	3.445 in.	87.5mm
Stroke	3.976 in.	101mm
Piston displacement	121.8 cu. in.	1,996 cm (cubed)
Compression ratio	9.4:1	
Displacement	148 cubic inches	2.4 liters
Firing order	1-3-4-2	
Compression pressure	170-225 psi	1172-1551 kPa
Maximum variation between cylinders	25%	
Lubrication	Pressure feed-full flow filtration (crankshaft driven pump)	
Cylinder block		
Cylinder bore diameter	3.4446-3.4452 in.	87.4924-87.5076mm
Out-of-round (max.)	0.002 in.	0.051mm
Taper (max.)	0.002 in.	0.051mm
Pistons		
Piston clearance A	0.0009-0.0022 in.	0.024-0.057mm
Weight	11.85-12.20 oz.	332-346 grams
Top land clearance (diametrical)	0.024-0.026 in.	0.614-0.664mm
Piston length	2.374 in.	60.30mm
Piston ring groove depth		
No. 1	0.182-0.188 in.	4.640-4.784 in.
No. 2	0.180-0.185 in.	4.575-4.719mm
No. 3	0.161-0.166 in.	4.097-4.236mm
Piston pin clearance in piston	0.0001-0.0007 in.	0.005-0.018mm
Piston pin in rod (interference)	0.0007-0.0017 in.	0.018-0.043mm
Piston pin diameter	0.8660-0.8662 in.	21.998-22.003mm
Piston pin length	2.864-2.883 in.	72.75-73.25mm
End-play	None	
Piston ring gap		
Top compression ring	0.0098-0.020 in.	0.25-0.51mm
2nd compression ring	0.009-0.018 in.	0.023-0.48mm
Oil control (steel) ring	0.0098-0.025 in.	0.25-0.64mm
Piston ring side clearance		
Top and 2nd compression ring	0.0011-0.0031 in.	0.030-0.080mm
Oil control (pack) ring	0.0004-0.0070 in.	0.012-0.178mm
Piston ring width		
Compression rings	0.057-0.059 in.	1.47-1.50mm
Oil control (pack) ring	0.107-0.1133 in.	2.72-2.88mm
Connecting rod		
Connecting rod bearing clearance	0.0009-0.0027 in.	0.025-0.071mm
Connecting rod piston pin bore diameter	0.8252-0.8260 in.	20.96-20.98mm
Connecting rod large end bore diameter	2.0868-2.0863 in.	53.007-52.993mm
Connecting rod side clearance	0.0051-0.0150 in.	0.013-0.0150mm

91153C01

2.4L DOHC ENGINE MECHANICAL SPECIFICATIONS

Description	English Specifications	Metric Specifications
Crankshaft		
Connecting rod journal diameter	1.967-1.9685 in.	49.984-50.000mm
Out-of-round (max.)	0.0001 in.	0.0035mm
Taper (max.)	0.0001 in.	0.0038mm
Main bearing diametrical clearance		
No's. 1-5	0.0007-0.0023 in.	0.018-0.058mm
End-play	0.0035-0.0094 in.	0.09-0.24mm
Main bearing journals		
Diameter	2.361-2.3625 in.	59.992-60.008mm
Out-of-round (max.)	0.0001 in.	0.0035mm
Taper (max.)	0.0001 in.	0.0038mm
Hydraulic lash adjuster body diameter	0.626-0.6264 in.	15.901-15.913mm
Hydraulic lash adjuster plunger minimum travel (dry)	0.118 in.	3.0mm
Camshaft		
Bearing bore diameters		
No's. 1-6	1.024-1.025 in.	26.020-26.041mm
Diametrical bearing clearance	0.0027-0.003 in.	0.069-0.071mm
End-play	0.0019-0.0066 in.	0.050-0.170mm
Bearing journal diameter		
No's. 1-6	1.021-1.022 in.	25.951-25.970mm
Lift (zero lash)		
Intake	0.324 in.	8.25mm
Exhaust	0.256 in.	6.25mm
Valve timing		
Intake valve		
Closes (ABDC)	51°	
Opens (BTDC)	1°	
Duration	232°	
Exhaust valve		
Close (ATDC)	8°	
Opens (BBDC)	52°	
Duration	240°	
Valve overlap	9°	
Cylinder head		
Material	Cast aluminum	
Gasket thickness (compressed)	0.045 in.	1.15mm
Valve seat		
Angle	45°	
Run-out (max.)	0.002 in.	0.050mm
Width (finish)		
Intake	0.035-0.051 in.	0.9-1.3mm
Exhaust	0.035-0.051 in.	0.91.3mm
Guide bore diameter (std.)	0.4330-0.4338 in.	11.0-11.02mm
Finish guide bore ID	0.235-0.236 in.	5.975-6.000mm

91153C02

2.4L DOHC ENGINE MECHANICAL SPECIFICATIONS

Description	English Specifications	Metric Specifications
Valves		
Face angle	44 1/2—45°	
Head diameter		
Intake	1.364-1.375 in.	34.67-34.93mm
Exhaust	1.195-1.205 in.	30.37-30.63mm
Length (overall)		
Intake	4.439-4.461 in.	112.76-113.32mm
Exhaust	4.314-4.334 in.	109.59-110.09mm
Valve margin		
Intake	0.050-0.063 in.	1.285-1.615mm
Exhaust	0.038-0.051 in.	0.985-1.315mm
Valve stem tip height		
Intake	1.891 in.	48.04mm
Exhaust	1.889 in.	47.99mm
Stem diameter		
Intake	0.234-0.234 in.	5.934-5.952mm
Exhaust	0.233-0.233 in.	5.906-5.924mm
Stem-to-guide clearance		
Intake	0.0018-0.0025 in.	0.048-0.066mm
Exhaust	0.0029-0.0037 in.	0.0736-0.094mm
Maximum stem-to-guide clearance		
Intake	0.010 in.	0.025mm
Exhaust	0.010 in.	0.025mm
Valve springs		
Free length (approx.)	1.905 in.	48.4mm
Spring tension		
Valve closed	71.48-80.48 lbs. @1.496 in.	318-358 N @ 38.0mm
Valve open	129-144 @ 1.172 in.	577-637 N @ 29.5mm
Number of coils	7.82	
Wire diameter	0.151 in.	3.86mm
Installed spring height	1.496 in.	38mm
Oil pump		
Oil pump clearance over rotors (max.)	0.004 in.	0.10mm
Oil pump cover out-of-flatness (max.)	0.001 in.	0.025mm
Oil pump inner rotor's thickness (min.)	0.370 in.	9.40mm
Oil pump outer rotor clearance (max.)	0.015 in.	0.39mm
Oil pump outer rotor diameter (min.)	3.148 in.	79.95mm
Oil pump outer rotor thickness (min.)	0.370 in.	9.40mm
Oil pump tip clearance between rotors (max.)	0.008 in.	0.20mm
Oil pressure		
At curb idle speed B	4 psi	25 kPa
At 3000 rpm	25-80 psi	170-550 kPa

A Measured at 9/16 inch (14mm) from bottom of skirt

B If pressure reads zero at curb idle, do not run engine at 3000 rpm

BTDC: Before Top Dead Center

BBDC: Before Bottom Dead Center

ABDC: After Bottom Dead Center

ATDC: After Top Dead Center

Max: Maximum

Min: Minimum

91153C03

3.0L SOHC ENGINE MECHANICAL SPECIFICATIONS

Description	English Specifications	Metric Specifications
Engine	V-type OHV, SOHC	
Number of cylinders	6	
Bore	3.587 in.	91.1mm
Stroke	2.992 in.	76mm
Compression ratio	8.85:1	
Displacement	181 cubic inches	3.0 liters
Firing order	1-2-3-4-5-6	
Compression pressure	178 psi	1227 kPa
Maximum variation between cylinders	25%	
Cylinder block		
Cylinder bore diameter	3.587 in.	91.1mm
Top surface flatness	0.002 in.	0.05mm
Grinding limit of top surface (including cyl. head)	0.008 in.	0.2mm
Pistons		
Piston clearance	0.0012-0.002 in.	0.03-0.05mm
Piston ring gap		
Top compression ring	0.012-0.018 in.	0.30-0.45mm
2nd compression ring	0.018-0.024 in.	0.45-0.60mm
Oil control (steel) ring	0.008-0.024 in.	0.20-0.60mm
Piston ring side clearance		
Top compression ring	0.0012-0.0028 in.	0.030-0.070mm
2nd compression ring	0.0004-0.0070 in.	0.012-0.178mm
Connecting rod		
Connecting rod bearing clearance	0.0007-0.0014 in.	0.018-0.036mm
Length center-to-center	5.547-5.551 in.	140.9-141.0mm
Parallelism-twist	0.0019 in.	0.05mm
Torsion	0.004 in.	0.10mm
Connecting rod side clearance	0.004-0.010 in.	0.018-0.036mm
Crankshaft		
Connecting rod journal diameter	1.967-1.9685 in.	49.984-50.000mm
Out-of-round (max.)	0.001 in.	0.03mm
Taper (max.)	0.0002 in.	0.005mm
Main and rod bearing clearance	0.0007-0.0014 in.	0.018-0.036mm
Main bearing journal diameter	2.361-2.3625 in.	59.992-60.008mm
End-play	0.002-0.010 in.	0.05-0.25mm
Cylinder head		
Valve seat		
Angle	44°-44°.3'	
Contact width		
Intake	0.035-0.051 in.	0.9-1.3mm
Exhaust	0.035-0.051 in.	0.91.3mm
Guide bore diameter (std.)	0.313-0.314 in.	7.95-7.98mm

91153C04

3.0L SOHC ENGINE MECHANICAL SPECIFICATIONS

Description	English Specifications	Metric Specifications
Valves		
Face angle	45°-45° 30'	
Head diameter		
Intake	1.915-1.925 in.	48.64-48.90mm
Exhaust	1.575-1.585 in.	40.01-40.26mm
Length (overall)		
Intake	4.055 in.	103mm
Exhaust	4.043 in.	102.7mm
Valve margin		
Intake	0.047 in.	1.2mm
Exhaust	0.079 in.	2mm
Valve stem tip height		
Intake	1.929 in.	49.02mm
Exhaust	1.929 in.	49.02mm
Stem diameter		
Intake	0.313-0.314 in.	7.960-7.975mm
Exhaust	0.312-0.3125 in.	7.930-7.950mm
Stem-to-guide clearance		
Intake	0.001-0.002 in.	0.03-0.06mm
Exhaust	0.0019-0.003 in.	0.05-0.09mm
Valve springs		
Free length (approx.)	1.960 in.	49.8mm
Loaded hieght	1.59 in. @73 lbs.	40.4mm @33kg
Oil pump		
Oil pump clearance over rotors (max.)	0.003 in.	0.077mm
Oil pump cover out-of-flatness (max.)	0.003 in.	0.076mm
Oil pump inner rotor's thickness (min.)	0.744 in.	18.92mm
Oil pump outer rotor clearance (max.)	0.007 in.	0.19mm
Oil pump outer rotor diameter (min.)	3.246 in.	82.45mm
Oil pump outer rotor thickness (min.)	0.744 in.	18.92mm
Oil pump tip clearance between rotors (max.)	0.0068 in.	0.150mm
Oil pressure		
At curb idle speed A	10 psi	68.9 kPa
At 3000 rpm	45-75 psi	310-517 kPa

A If pressure reads zero at curb idle, do not run engine at 3000 rpm

Max: Maximum

Min: Minimum

91153C05

3.3L OHV ENGINE MECHANICAL SPECIFICATIONS

Description	English Specifications	Metric Specifications
Engine	V-type OHV	
Number of cylinders	6	
Bore	3.66 in.	93.0mm
Stroke	3.188 in.	81mm
Piston displacement	121.8 cu. in.	1,996 cm (cubed)
Compression ratio	8.9:1	
Displacement	201 cubic inches	3.3 liters
Firing order	1-2-3-4-5-6	
Cylinder block		
Cylinder bore diameter	3.66 in.	93mm
Out-of-round (max.)	0.003 in.	0.076mm
Taper (max.)	0.002 in.	0.051mm
Pistons		
Piston clearance A	0.001-0.0022 in.	0.025-0.057mm
Piston pin clearance in piston @70°	0.0002-0.0007 in.	0.006-0.019mm
Piston pin in rod	interference	
Piston pin diameter	0.9009 in.	22.88mm
Piston pin length	2.648-2.667 in.	67.25-67.75mm
Piston ring gap		
Top compression ring	0.0118-0.0217 in.	0.30-0.55mm
2nd compression ring	0.0118-0.0217 in.	0.30-0.55mm
Oil control (steel) ring	0.0098-0.0394 in.	0.25-1.00mm
Piston ring side clearance		
Top and 2nd compression ring	0.0012-0.0037 in.	0.030-0.095mm
Oil control (pack) ring	0.0005-0.0089 in.	0.014-0.226mm
Piston ring width		
Compression rings	0.0575-0.0591 in.	1.46-1.50mm
Oil control (pack) ring	0.0201 in.	0.510mm
Connecting rod		
Connecting rod bearing clearance	0.00075-0.0026 in.	0.019-0.065mm
Connecting rod side clearance	0.005-0.015 in.	0.127-0.381mm
Crankshaft		
Connecting rod journal diameter	2.124-2.125 in.	53.950-53.975mm
Main bearing diametrical clearance		
No's. 1-4	0.0023-0.0043 in.	0.011-0.059mm
End-play	0.0036-0.0095 in.	0.09-0.24mm
Main bearing journals		
Diameter	2.5195-2.5202 in.	63.993-64.013mm
Out-of-round (max.)	0.001 in.	0.025mm
Taper (max.)	0.001 in.	0.025mm
Camshaft		
Diametrical bearing clearance	0.001-0.004 in.	0.025-0.101mm
End-play	0.005-0.012 in.	0.127-0.304mm

91153C06

3.3L OHV ENGINE MECHANICAL SPECIFICATIONS

Description	English Specifications	Metric Specifications
Valve timing		
Intake valve		
Closes (BTDC)	58°	
Opens	2°	
Duration	240°	
Exhaust valve		
Close (ATDC)	12°	
Opens (BBDC)	48°	
Duration	240°	
Valve overlap	14°	
Cylinder head		
Gasket thickness (compressed)	0.070 in.	1.78mm
Valve seat		
Angle	45°-45.5°	
Run-out (max.)	0.003 in.	0.0762mm
Width (finish)		
Intake	0.069-0.088 in.	1.75-2.25mm
Exhaust	0.057-0.078 in.	1.50-2.00mm
Guide bore diameter (std.)	0.314-0.315 in.	7.975-8.00mm
Valves		
Face angle	44.5° (intake) 45° (exhaust)	
Head diameter		
Intake	1.79 in.	45.5mm
Exhaust	1.476 in.	37.5mm
Length (overall)		
Intake	5.000-5.041 in.	127.005-128.036mm
Exhaust	5.032-5.058 in.	127.825-128.465
Valve stem tip height		
Intake	1.950-2.018 in.	49.541-51.271mm
Exhaust	1.950-2.018 in.	49.541-51.271mm
Stem diameter		
Intake	0.312-0.313 in.	7.935-7.953mm
Exhaust	0.3112-0.3119 in.	7.906-7.924mm
Stem-to-guide clearance		
Intake	0.001-0.003 in.	0.025-0.095mm
Exhaust	0.002-0.006 in.	0.051-0.175mm
Maximum stem-to-guide clearance		
Intake	0.010 in.	0.025mm
Exhaust	0.414 in.	0.016mm
Valve springs		
Free length (approx.)	1.909 in.	48.5mm
Spring tension		
Valve closed	95-100 lbs. @1.57 in.	
Valve open	207-229 @ 1.169 in.	
Installed spring height	1.622-1.681 in.	41.2-42.7mm

91153C07

3.3L OHV ENGINE MECHANICAL SPECIFICATIONS

Description	English Specifications	Metric Specifications
Oil pump		
Oil pump clearance over rotors (max.)	0.004 in.	0.10mm
Oil pump cover out-of-flatness (max.)	0.001 in.	0.025mm
Oil pump inner rotor's thickness (min.)	0.301 in.	7.64mm
Oil pump outer rotor clearance (min.)	0.015 in.	0.39mm
Oil pump outer rotor diameter (min.)	3.148 in.	79.95mm
Oil pump outer rotor thickness (min.)	0.301 in.	7.64mm
Oil pump tip clearance between rotors (max.)	0.008 in.	0.20mm
Oil pressure		
At curb idle speed B	5 psi	34.47 kPa
At 3000 rpm	30-80 psi	205-551 kPa

A Measured at size location

B If pressure reads zero at curb idle, do not run engine at 3000 rpm

BTDC: Before Top Dead Center

BBDC: Before Bottom Dead Center

ABDC: After Bottom Dead Center

ATDC: After Top Dead Center

Max: Maximum

Min: Minimum

91153C08

3.8L OHV ENGINE MECHANICAL SPECIFICATIONS

Description	English Specifications	Metric Specifications
Engine	V-type OHV	
Number of cylinders	6	
Bore	3.779 in.	96.0mm
Stroke	3.425 in.	87mm
Piston displacement	121.8 cu. in.	1,996 cm (cubed)
Compression ratio	9.6:1	
Displacement	231 cubic inches	3.8 liters
Firing order	1-2-3-4-5-6	
Cylinder block		
Cylinder bore diameter	3.779 in.	96mm
Out-of-round (max.)	0.003 in.	0.076mm
Taper (max.)	0.002 in.	0.051mm
Pistons		
Piston clearance A	0.001-0.0022 in.	0.025-0.057mm
Piston pin clearance in piston @70°	0.0002-0.0007 in.	0.006-0.019mm
Piston pin in rod	interference	
Piston pin diameter	0.9009 in.	22.88mm
Piston pin length	2.805-2.824 in.	71.25-71.75mm
Piston ring gap		
Top compression ring	0.0118-0.0217 in.	0.30-0.55mm
2nd compression ring	0.0118-0.0217 in.	0.30-0.55mm
Oil control (steel) ring	0.0098-0.0394 in.	0.25-1.00mm
Piston ring side clearance		
Top and 2nd compression ring	0.0012-0.0037 in.	0.030-0.095mm
Oil control (pack) ring	0.0005-0.0089 in.	0.014-0.226mm
Piston ring width		
Compression rings	0.0575-0.0591 in.	1.46-1.50mm
Oil control (pack) ring	0.0201 in.	0.510mm
Connecting rod		
Connecting rod bearing clearance	0.00075-0.0026 in.	0.019-0.065mm
Connecting rod side clearance	0.005-0.015 in.	0.127-0.381mm
Crankshaft		
Connecting rod journal diameter	2.124-2.125 in.	53.950-53.975mm
Main bearing diametrical clearance		
No's. 1-4	0.0023-0.0043 in.	0.011-0.059mm
End-play	0.0036-0.0095 in.	0.09-0.24mm
Main bearing journals		
Diameter	2.5195-2.5202 in.	63.993-64.013mm
Out-of-round (max.)	0.001 in.	0.025mm
Taper (max.)	0.001 in.	0.025mm
Camshaft		
Diametrical bearing clearance	0.001-0.004 in.	0.025-0.101mm
End-play	0.005-0.012 in.	0.127-0.304mm

91153C09

3.8L OHV ENGINE MECHANICAL SPECIFICATIONS

Description	English Specifications	Metric Specifications
Valve timing		
Intake valve		
Closes (BTDC)	58°	
Opens	2°	
Duration	240°	
Exhaust valve		
Close (ATDC)	12°	
Opens (BBDC)	48°	
Duration	240°	
Valve overlap	14°	
Cylinder head		
Gasket thickness (compressed)	0.070 in.	1.78mm
Valve seat		
Angle	45°-45.5°	
Run-out (max.)	0.003 in.	0.0762mm
Width (finish)		
Intake	0.069-0.088 in.	1.75-2.25mm
Exhaust	0.057-0.078 in.	1.50-2.00mm
Guide bore diameter (std.)	0.314-0.315 in.	7.975-8.00mm
Valves		
Face angle	44.5° (intake) 45° (exhaust)	
Head diameter		
Intake	1.79 in.	45.5mm
Exhaust	1.476 in.	37.5mm
Length (overall)		
Intake	5.000-5.041 in.	127.005-128.036mm
Exhaust	5.032-5.058 in.	127.825-128.465
Valve stem tip height		
Intake	1.950-2.018 in.	49.541-51.271mm
Exhaust	1.950-2.018 in.	49.541-51.271mm
Stem diameter		
Intake	0.312-0.313 in.	7.935-7.953mm
Exhaust	0.3112-0.3119 in.	7.906-7.924mm
Stem-to-guide clearance		
Intake	0.001-0.003 in.	0.025-0.095mm
Exhaust	0.002-0.006 in.	0.051-0.175mm
Maximum stem-to-guide clearance		
Intake	0.010 in.	0.025mm
Exhaust	0.414 in.	0.016mm
Valve springs		
Free length (approx.)	1.909 in.	48.5mm
Spring tension		
Valve closed	95-100 lbs. @1.57 in.	
Valve open	207-229 @ 1.169 in.	
Installed spring height	1.622-1.681 in.	41.2-42.7mm

91153C10

3.8L OHV ENGINE MECHANICAL SPECIFICATIONS

Description	English Specifications	Metric Specifications
Oil pump		
Oil pump clearance over rotors (max.)	0.004 in.	0.10mm
Oil pump cover out-of-flatness (max.)	0.001 in.	0.025mm
Oil pump inner rotor's thickness (min.)	0.301 in.	7.64mm
Oil pump outer rotor clearance (min.)	0.015 in.	0.39mm
Oil pump outer rotor diameter (min.)	3.148 in.	79.95mm
Oil pump outer rotor thickness (min.)	0.301 in.	7.64mm
Oil pump tip clearance between rotors (max.)	0.008 in.	0.20mm
Oil pressure		
At curb idle speed B	5 psi	34.47 kPa
At 3000 rpm	30-80 psi	205-551 kPa

A Measured at size location

B If pressure reads zero at curb idle, do not run engine at 3000 rpm

BTDC: Before Top Dead Center

BBDC: Before Bottom Dead Center

ABDC: After Bottom Dead Center

ATDC: After Top Dead Center

Max: Maximum

Min: Minimum

91153C11

TORQUE SPECIFICATIONS—2.4L ENGINES

DESCRIPTION	TORQUE
Balance Shaft Carrier to Block	
Bolts	54 N·m (40 ft. lbs.)
Balance Shaft Gear Cover	
Double Ended Fastener	12 N·m (105 in. lbs.)
Balance Shaft Sprockets	
Bolts	28 N·m (250 in. lbs.)
Balance Shaft Chain Tensioner	
Bolts	12 N·m (105 in. lbs.)
Balance Shaft Carrier Cover	
Fasteners	12 N·m (105 in. lbs.)
Camshaft Sensor Pick Up	
Bolts	27 N·m (20 ft. lbs.)
Timing Belt Cover	
Outer to Inner Attaching Bolts M6	4.5 N·m (40 in. lbs.)
Inner Cover to Head/Oil Pump Bolts M6	12 N·m (105 in. lbs.)
Camshaft Sprocket	
Bolt	101 N·m (75 ft. lbs.)
Connecting Rod Cap	
Bolts	27 N·m (20 ft. lbs.) Plus 1/4 Turn
Crankshaft Main Bearing Cap/Bedplate	
M8 Bedplate Bolts	34 N·m (250 in. lbs.)
Main Cap Bolts M11	41 N·m (30 ft. lbs.) Plus 1/4 Turn
Crankshaft Damper	
Bolt	135 N·m (100 ft. lbs.)
Cylinder Head	
Bolts	Refer To Cylinder Head Installation
Cylinder Head Cover	
Bolts	12 N·m (105 in. lbs.)
Engine Mount Bracket	
Bolts	61 N·m (45 ft. lbs.)
Engine Mount—Front and Rear	
Through Bolt	61 N·m (45 ft. lbs.)
Exhaust Manifold to Cylinder Head	
Bolts	23 N·m (200 in. lbs.)
Exhaust Manifold Heat Shield	
Bolts	12 N·m (105 in. lbs.)
Front Torque Bracket—2.0/2.4L Engine	
Bolts	33 N·m (24 ft. lbs.)
Front Torque Bracket Strut—2.0/2.4L Engine	
Long Bolts	110 N·m (80 ft. lbs.)
Short Bolt	61 N·m (45 ft. lbs.)
Intake Manifold	
Bolts	27 N·m (20 ft. lbs.)
Oil Filter	
Filter	20 N·m (15 ft. lbs.)
Oil Pan	
Oil Pan Bolts	12 N·m (105 in. lbs.)
Drain Plug	27 N·m (20 ft. lbs.)
Oil Pump Attaching	
Bolts	28 N·m (250 in. lbs.)
Oil Pump Cover Fastener	12 N·m (105 in. lbs.)
Oil Pump Pick-up Tube Bolt	28 N·m (250 in. lbs.)
Oil Pump Relief Valve Cap	41 N·m (30 ft. lbs.)
Rear Torque Bracket	
Bolts	110 N·m (80 ft. lbs.)
Spark Plugs	
Plugs	28 N·m (20 ft. lbs.)
Thermostat Housing	
Bolts	23 N·m (200 in lbs.)
Timing Belt Tensioner Assembly	
Bolts	61 N·m (45 ft. lbs.)
Water Pump Mounting	
Bolts	12 N·m (105 in. lbs.)

91153C12

TORQUE SPECIFICATIONS—3.0L ENGINES

DESCRIPTION	TORQUE
Camshaft Bearing Cap	
Bolts	Refer to procedure outlined in this section.
Camshaft Sensor Pick Up	
Bolts	27 N·m (20 ft. lbs.)
Timing Belt Cover	
Outer to Inner Attaching Bolts	4.5 N·m (40 in. lbs.)
Inner Cover to Head/Oil Pump Bolts	12 N·m (105 in. lbs.)
Camshaft Sprocket	
Bolt	95 N·m (70 ft. lbs.)
Connecting Rod Cap	
Bolts	27 N·m (20 ft. lbs.) Plus 1/4 Turn
Oil Pan	
Oil Pan Bolts	12 N·m (105 in. lbs.)
Drain Plug	39 N·m (29 ft. lbs.)
Oil Pump Attaching	
Bolts	15 N·m (130 in. lbs.)
Oil Pump Cover Fastener	9 N·m (104 in. lbs.)
Oil Pump Pick-up Tube Bolt	28 N·m (250 in. lbs.)
Oil Pump Relief Valve Cap	49 N·m (36 ft. lbs.)
Spark Plugs	
Plugs	28 N·m (20 ft. lbs.)
Thermostat Housing	
Bolts	23 N·m (200 in lbs.)
Timing Belt Tensioner	
Bolt	28 N·m (20 ft. lbs.)
Timing Belt Tensioner Pulley Assembly	
Bolt	41 N·m (30 ft. lbs.)
Water Pump Mounting	
Bolts	12 N·m (105 in. lbs.)

DESCRIPTION	TORQUE
Crankshaft Main Bearing Cap/Bedplate	
M8 Bedplate Bolts	34 N·m (250 in. lbs.)
M11 Main Cap Bolts	41 N·m (30 ft. lbs.) Plus 1/4 Turn
Crankshaft Vibration Damper	
Bolt	135 N·m (100 ft. lbs.)
Cylinder Head	
Bolts	Refer To Cylinder Head Installation
Cylinder Head Cover	
Bolts	12 N·m (105 in. lbs.)
Engine Mount Bracket	
Bolts	41 N·m (30 ft. lbs.)
Engine Mount—Front and Rear	
Through Bolt	61 N·m (45 ft. lbs.)
Exhaust Manifold to Cylinder Head	
Bolts	22 N·m (191 in. lbs.)
Exhaust Manifold Crossover	
Bolts	69 N·m (51 ft. lbs.)
Exhaust Manifold Heat Shield	
Bolts	15 N·m (130 in. lbs.)
Intake Manifold Plenum—Upper	
Bolts	15 N·m (130 in. lbs.)
Intake Manifold—Lower	
Bolts	20 N·m (174 in. lbs.)
Oil Filter to Engine Block Adapter	
Bolts	55 N·m (40 ft. lbs.)
Oil Filter	
Filter	20 N·m (15 ft. lbs.)

91153C13

TORQUE SPECIFICATIONS—3.3L AND 3.8L ENGINES

DESCRIPTION	TORQUE
A/C Compressor Mounting	
Compressor Bracket to Water Pump Bolt	41 N·m (30 ft. lbs.)
Compressor to Bracket Bolt	68 N·m (50 ft. lbs.)
Compressor Support Bolt	41 N·m (30 ft. lbs.)
Camshaft Sprocket	
Bolt	54 N·m (40 ft. lbs.)
Camshaft Thrust Plate	
Bolt	12 N·m (105 in. lbs.)
Connecting Rod	
Nut	54 N·m (40 ft. lbs.) +¼ Turn
Crankshaft Damper Pulley to Crankshaft	
Bolt	54 N·m (40 ft. lbs.)
Cylinder Head	
Bolts	Refer to Cylinder Head Removal and Installation Procedure in this Section
Cylinder Head Cover	
Bolts	12 N·m (105 in. lbs.)
Exhaust Manifold	
Bolts	23 N·m (200 in. lbs.)
Exhaust Crossover Pipe Flange	
Fasteners	33 N·m (25 ft. lbs.)
Generator Mounting	
Adjusting Strap Bolt	23 N·m (200 in. lbs.)
Adjusting Strap Mounting Bolt	41 N·m (30 ft. lbs.)
Bracket Bolt	41 N·m (30 ft. lbs.)
Pivot Nut	41 N·m (30 ft. lbs.)
Intake Manifold	
Bolts	23 N·m (200 in. lbs.)
Intake Manifold Gasket Retaining	
Screws	12 N·m (105 in. lbs.)
Intake Manifold Plenum	
Bolts	28 N·m (250 in. lbs.)
Main Bearing Cap	
Bolts	41 N·m (30 ft. lbs.) +¼ Turn
Oil Filter Attaching	
Nipple	41 N·m (30 ft. lbs.)
Oil Pan	
Bolts	12 N·m (105 in. lbs.)
Drain Plug	27 N·m (20 ft. lbs.)
Level Sensor Plug	41 N·m (30 ft. lbs.)
Oil Pressure Gauge Sending Unit	7 N·m (60 in. lbs.)
Oil Pump	
Cover Bolts	12 N·m (105 in. lbs.)
Pick-up Tube Bolt	28 N·m (250 in. lbs.)
Rocker Shaft Bracket	
Bolts	28 N·m (250 in. lbs.)
Spark Plug	27 N·m (20 ft. lbs.)
Starter Mounting	
Bolt	68 N·m (50 ft. lbs.)
Strut—Intake Manifold to Cylinder Head	
Bolt	54 N·m (40 ft. lbs.)
Tappet Retainer Yoke	
Bolt	12 N·m (105 in. lbs.)
Temperature Gauge Sending Unit	7 N·m (60 in. lbs.)
Timing Chain Case Cover	
Bolt–M8 × 1.25	27 N·m (20 ft. lbs.)
Bolt–M10 × 1.5	54 N·m (40 ft. lbs.)
Water Pump to Chain Case Cover	
Bolts	12 N·m (105 in. lbs.)

91153C14

USING A VACUUM GAUGE

White needle = steady needle ***Dark needle = drifting needle***

The vacuum gauge is one of the most useful and easy-to-use diagnostic tools. It is inexpensive, easy to hook up, and provides valuable information about the condition of your engine.

Indication: Normal engine in good condition

Gauge reading: Steady, from 17–22 in./Hg.

Indication: Sticking valve or ignition miss

Gauge reading: Needle fluctuates from 15–20 in./Hg. at idle

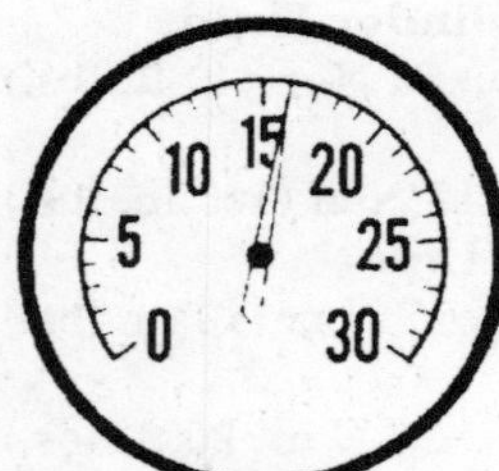

Indication: Late ignition or valve timing, low compression, stuck throttle valve, leaking carburetor or manifold gasket.

Gauge reading: Low (15–20 in./Hg.) but steady

Indication: Improper carburetor adjustment, or minor intake leak at carburetor or manifold

NOTE: Bad fuel injector O-rings may also cause this reading.

Gauge reading: Drifting needle

Indication: Weak valve springs, worn valve stem guides, or leaky cylinder head gasket (vibrating excessively at all speeds).

NOTE: A plugged catalytic converter may also cause this reading.

Gauge reading: Needle fluctuates as engine speed increases

Indication: Burnt valve or improper valve clearance. The needle will drop when the defective valve operates.

Gauge reading: Steady needle, but drops regularly

Indication: Choked muffler or obstruction in system. Speed up the engine. Choked muffler will exhibit a slow drop of vacuum to zero.

Gauge reading: Gradual drop in reading at idle

Indication: Worn valve guides

Gauge reading: Needle vibrates excessively at idle, but steadies as engine speed increases

TCCS3C01

4 DRIVEABILITY AND EMISSIONS CONTROLS

AUTOMOTIVE EMISSIONS

Before emission controls were mandated on internal combustion engines, other sources of engine pollutants were discovered along with the exhaust emissions. It was determined that engine combustion exhaust produced approximately 60 percent of the total emission pollutants, fuel evaporation from the fuel tank and carburetor vents produced 20 percent, with the final 20 percent being produced through the crankcase as a by-product of the combustion process.

Exhaust Gases

The exhaust gases emitted into the atmosphere are a combination of burned and unburned fuel. To understand the exhaust emission and its composition, we must review some basic chemistry.

When the air/fuel mixture is introduced into the engine, we are mixing air, composed of nitrogen (78 percent), oxygen (21 percent) and other gases (1 percent) with the fuel, which is 100 percent hydrocarbons (HC), in a semi-controlled ratio. As the combustion process is accomplished, power is produced to move the vehicle while the heat of combustion is transferred to the cooling system. The exhaust gases are then composed of nitrogen, a diatomic gas (N_2), the same as was introduced in the engine, carbon dioxide (CO_2), the same gas that is used in beverage carbonation, and water vapor (H_2O). The nitrogen (N_2), for the most part, passes through the engine unchanged, while the oxygen (O_2) reacts (burns) with the hydrocarbons (HC) and produces the carbon dioxide (CO_2) and the water vapors (H_2O). If this chemical process would be the only process to take place, the exhaust emissions would be harmless. However, during the combustion process, other compounds are formed which are considered dangerous. These pollutants are hydrocarbons (HC), carbon monoxide (CO), oxides of nitrogen (NOx) oxides of sulfur (SOx) and engine particulates.

HYDROCARBONS

Hydrocarbons (HC) are essentially fuel which was not burned during the combustion process or which has escaped into the atmosphere through fuel evaporation. The main sources of incomplete combustion are rich air/fuel mixtures, low engine temperatures and improper spark timing. The main sources of hydrocarbon emission through fuel evaporation on most vehicles used to be the vehicle's fuel tank and carburetor float bowl.

To reduce combustion hydrocarbon emission, engine modifications were made to minimize dead space and surface area in the combustion chamber. In addition, the air/fuel mixture was made more lean through the improved control which feedback carburetion and fuel injection offers and by the addition of external controls to aid in further combustion of the hydrocarbons outside the engine. Two such methods were the addition of air injection systems, to inject fresh air into the exhaust manifolds and the installation of catalytic converters, units that are able to burn traces of hydrocarbons without affecting the internal combustion process or fuel economy.

To control hydrocarbon emissions through fuel evaporation, modifications were made to the fuel tank to allow storage of the fuel vapors during periods of engine shut-down. Modifications were also made to the air intake system so that at specific times during engine operation, these vapors may be purged and burned by blending them with the air/fuel mixture.

CARBON MONOXIDE

Carbon monoxide is formed when not enough oxygen is present during the combustion process to convert carbon (C) to carbon dioxide (CO_2). An increase in the carbon monoxide (CO) emission is normally accompanied by an increase in the hydrocarbon (HC) emission because of the lack of oxygen to completely burn all of the fuel mixture.

Carbon monoxide (CO) also increases the rate at which the photo chemical smog is formed by speeding up the conversion of nitric oxide (NO) to nitrogen dioxide (NO_2). To accomplish this, carbon monoxide (CO) combines with oxygen (O_2) and nitric oxide (NO) to produce carbon dioxide (CO_2) and nitrogen dioxide (NO_2). ($CO + O_2 + NO = CO_2 + NO_2$).

The dangers of carbon monoxide, which is an odorless and colorless toxic gas are many. When carbon monoxide is inhaled into the lungs and passed into the blood stream, oxygen is replaced by the carbon monoxide in the red blood cells, causing a reduction in the amount of oxygen supplied to the many parts of the body. This lack of oxygen causes headaches, lack of coordination, reduced mental alertness and, should the carbon monoxide concentration be high enough, death could result.

NITROGEN

Normally, nitrogen is an inert gas. When heated to approximately 2500°F (1371°C) through the combustion process, this gas becomes active and causes an increase in the nitric oxide (NO) emission.

Oxides of nitrogen (NOx) are composed of approximately 97–98 percent nitric oxide (NO). Nitric oxide is a colorless gas but when it is passed into the atmosphere, it combines with oxygen and forms nitrogen dioxide (NO_2). The nitrogen dioxide then combines with chemically active hydrocarbons (HC) and when in the presence of sunlight, causes the formation of photo-chemical smog.

Ozone

To further complicate matters, some of the nitrogen dioxide (NO_2) is broken apart by the sunlight to form nitric oxide and oxygen. (NO_2+ sunlight = NO + O). This single atom of oxygen then combines with diatomic (meaning 2 atoms) oxygen (O_2) to form ozone (O_3). Ozone is one of the smells associated with smog. It has a pungent and offensive odor, irritates the eyes and lung tissues, affects the growth of plant life and causes rapid deterioration of rubber products. Ozone can be formed by sunlight as well as electrical discharge into the air.

The most common discharge area on the automobile engine is the secondary ignition electrical system, especially when inferior quality spark plug cables are used. As the surge of high voltage is routed through the secondary cable, the circuit builds up an electrical field around the wire, which acts upon the oxygen in the surrounding air to form the ozone. The faint glow along the cable with the engine running that may be visible on a dark night, is called the "corona discharge." It is the result of the electrical field passing from a high along the cable, to a low in the surrounding air, which forms the ozone gas. The combination of corona and ozone has been a major cause of cable deterioration. Recently, different and better quality insulating materials have lengthened the life of the electrical cables.

Although ozone at ground level can be harmful, ozone is beneficial to the earth's inhabitants. By having a concentrated ozone layer called the "ozonosphere," between 10 and 20 miles (16–32 km) up in the atmosphere, much of the ultra violet radiation from the sun's rays are absorbed and screened. If this ozone layer were not present, much of the earth's surface would be burned, dried and unfit for human life.

OXIDES OF SULFUR

Oxides of sulfur (SOx) were initially ignored in the exhaust system emissions, since the sulfur content of gasoline as a fuel is less than 1⁄10 of 1 percent. Because of this small amount, it was felt that it contributed very little to the overall pollution problem. However, because of the difficulty in solving the sulfur emissions in industrial pollution and the introduction of catalytic converters to automobile exhaust systems, a change was mandated. The automobile exhaust system, when equipped with a catalytic converter, changes the sulfur dioxide (SO_2) into sulfur trioxide (SO_3).

When this combines with water vapors (H_2O), a sulfuric acid mist (H_2SO_4) is formed and is a very difficult pollutant to handle since it is extremely corrosive. This sulfuric acid mist that is formed, is the same mist that rises from the vents of an automobile battery when an active chemical reaction takes place within the battery cells.

When a large concentration of vehicles equipped with catalytic converters are operating in an area, this acid mist may rise and be distributed over a large ground area causing land, plant, crop, paint and building damage.

PARTICULATE MATTER

A certain amount of particulate matter is present in the burning of any fuel, with carbon constituting the largest percentage of the particulates. In gasoline, the remaining particulates are the burned remains of the various other compounds used in its manufacture. When a gasoline engine is in good internal condition, the particulate emissions are low but as the engine wears internally, the particulate emissions increase. By visually inspecting the tail pipe emissions, a determination can be made as to where an engine defect may exist. An engine with light gray or blue smoke emitting from the tail pipe normally indicates an increase in the oil consumption through burning due to internal engine wear. Black smoke would indicate a defective fuel delivery system, causing the engine to operate in a rich mode. Regardless of the color of the smoke, the internal part of the engine or the fuel delivery system should be repaired to prevent excess particulate emissions.

Diesel and turbine engines emit a darkened plume of smoke from the exhaust system because of the type of fuel used. Emission control regulations are mandated for this type of emission and more stringent measures are being used to prevent excess emission of the particulate matter. Electronic components are being introduced to control the injection of the fuel at precisely the proper time of piston travel, to achieve the optimum in fuel ignition and fuel usage. Other particulate after-burning components are being tested to achieve a cleaner emission.

Good grades of engine lubricating oils should be used, which meet the manufacturer's specification. Cut-rate oils can contribute to the particulate emission problem because of their low flash or ignition temperature point. Such oils burn prematurely during the combustion process causing emission of particulate matter.

The cooling system is an important factor in the reduction of particulate matter. The optimum combustion will occur, with the cooling system operating at a temperature specified by the manufacturer. The cooling system must be maintained in the same manner as the engine oiling system, as each system is required to perform properly in order for the engine to operate efficiently for a long time.

Crankcase Emissions

Crankcase emissions are made up of water, acids, unburned fuel, oil fumes and particulates. These emissions are classified as hydrocarbons (HC) and are formed by the small amount of unburned, compressed air/fuel mixture entering the crankcase from the combustion area (between the cylinder walls and piston rings) during the compression and power strokes. The head of the compression and combustion help to form the remaining crankcase emissions.

Since the first engines, crankcase emissions were allowed into the atmosphere through a road draft tube, mounted on the lower side of the engine block. Fresh air came in through an open oil filler cap or breather. The air passed through the crankcase mixing with blow-by gases. The motion of the vehicle and the air blowing past the open end of the road draft tube caused a low pressure area (vacuum) at the end of the tube. Crankcase emissions were simply drawn out of the road draft tube into the air.

To control the crankcase emission, the road draft tube was deleted. A hose and/or tubing was routed from the crankcase to the intake manifold so the blow-by emission could be burned with the air/fuel mixture. However, it was found that intake manifold vacuum, used to draw the crankcase emissions into the manifold, would vary in strength at the wrong time and not allow the proper emission flow. A regulating valve was needed to control the flow of air through the crankcase.

Testing, showed the removal of the blow-by gases from the crankcase as quickly as possible, was most important to the longevity of the engine. Should large accumulations of blow-by gases remain and condense, dilution of the engine oil would occur to form water, soots, resins, acids and lead salts, resulting in the formation of sludge and varnishes. This condensation of the blow-by gases occurs more frequently on vehicles used in numerous starting and stopping conditions, excessive idling and when the engine is not allowed to attain normal operating temperature through short runs.

Evaporative Emissions

Gasoline fuel is a major source of pollution, before and after it is burned in the automobile engine. From the time the fuel is refined, stored, pumped and transported, again stored until it is pumped into the fuel tank of the vehicle, the gasoline gives off unburned hydrocarbons (HC) into the atmosphere. Through the redesign of storage areas and venting systems, the pollution factor was diminished, but not eliminated, from the refinery standpoint. However, the automobile still remained the primary source of vaporized, unburned hydrocarbon (HC) emissions.

Fuel pumped from an underground storage tank is cool but when exposed to a warmer ambient temperature, will expand. Before controls were mandated, an owner might fill the fuel tank with fuel from an underground storage tank and park the vehicle for some time in warm area, such as a parking lot. As the fuel would warm, it would expand and should no provisions or area be provided for the expansion, the fuel would spill out of the filler neck and onto the ground, causing hydrocarbon (HC) pollution and creating a severe fire hazard. To correct this condition, the vehicle manufacturers added overflow plumbing and/or gasoline tanks with built in expansion areas or domes.

However, this did not control the fuel vapor emission from the fuel tank. It was determined that most of the fuel evaporation occurred when the vehicle was stationary and the engine not operating. Most vehicles carry 5–25 gallons (19–95 liters) of gasoline. Should a large concentration of vehicles be parked in one area, such as a large parking lot, excessive fuel vapor emissions would take place, increasing as the temperature increases.

To prevent the vapor emission from escaping into the atmosphere, the fuel systems were designed to trap the vapors while the vehicle is stationary, by sealing the system from the atmosphere. A storage system is used to collect and hold the fuel vapors from the carburetor (if equipped) and the fuel tank when the engine is not operating. When the engine is started, the storage system is then purged of the fuel vapors, which are drawn into the engine and burned with the air/fuel mixture.

EMISSION CONTROLS

Crankcase Ventilation System

OPERATION

Crankcase vapors and piston blow-by from the engine is removed by intake manifold vacuum. The engine emissions pass through the PCV valve into the intake manifold where they become part of the calibrated air-fuel mixture. They are burned and expelled with the exhaust gases. When the engine cannot supply enough vapor or blow-by gases, make up air is provided by the air cleaner. In this system, fresh air does not enter the crankcase.

Positive Crankcase Ventilation (PCV) Valve

See Figures 1, 2 and 3

The PCV valve contains a spring loaded plunger. Based on intake manifold vacuum, this plunger meters the amount of crankcase vapors routed into the combustion chamber. The spring will seat the plunger when the engine is not operating or during engine backfire, which will prevent vapors from flowing through the valve.

High intake manifold vacuum is present when the engine is idling or cruising. During these times, the vacuum is strong enough to completely compress the spring, moving the plunger to the top of the valve which allows minimal vapor flow through the valve.

Maximum vapor flow through the PCV valve is produced during periods of moderate manifold vacuum, when the plunger is only partially pulled away from the inlet.

COMPONENT TESTING

See Figure 4

CAUTION

ALWAYS block the drive wheels and apply the parking brake any time you are performing a test or adjustment in which the engine must be running!

1. With the engine idling, remove the PCV valve from its attaching point. If the valve is not obstructed, a hissing noise will be heard as air passes through the valve. Also, a strong vacuum should be felt when you place your finger over the valve inlet.
2. Turn the engine **OFF**. Remove the PCV valve from its attaching point, then shake the valve. The valve is OK if a rattling noise is heard as the valve is shaken.

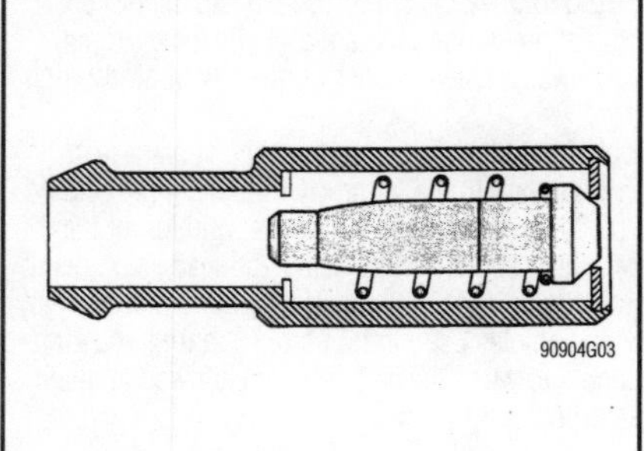

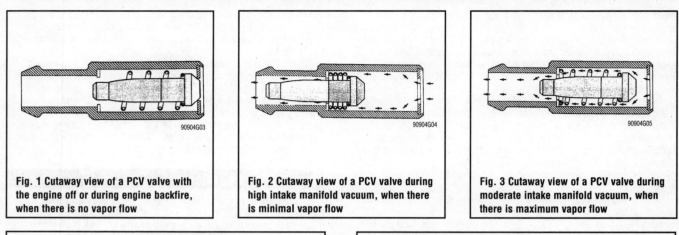

Fig. 1 Cutaway view of a PCV valve with the engine off or during engine backfire, when there is no vapor flow

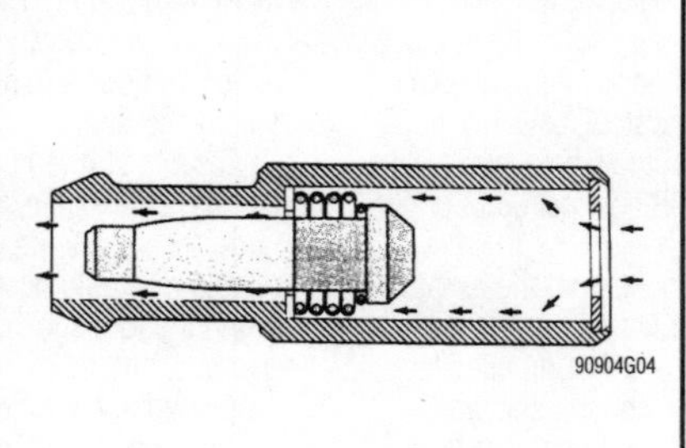

Fig. 2 Cutaway view of a PCV valve during high intake manifold vacuum, when there is minimal vapor flow

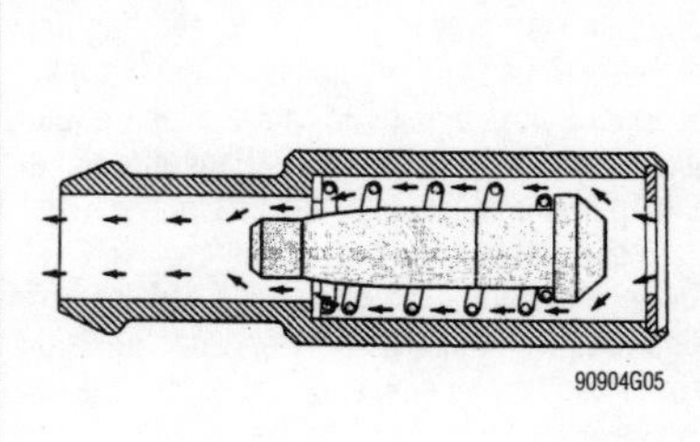

Fig. 3 Cutaway view of a PCV valve during moderate intake manifold vacuum, when there is maximum vapor flow

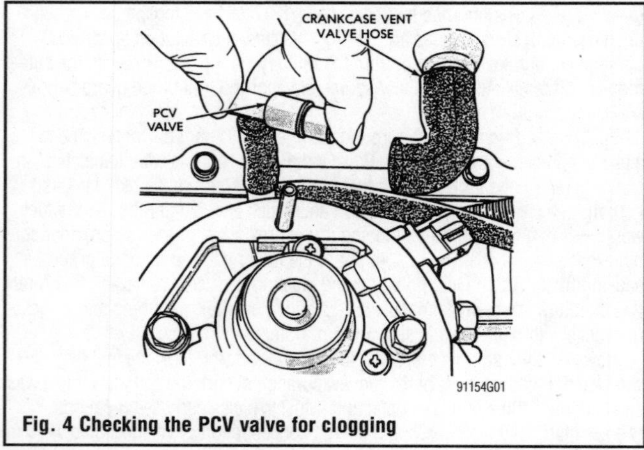

Fig. 4 Checking the PCV valve for clogging

3. If any of the previous tests fail, replace the PCV valve and/or hose and retest the system. Do not try to clean and reuse the old PCV valve. It should be replaced with a new one.

REMOVAL & INSTALLATION

For PCV valve removal and installation procedures, refer to Section 1 of this manual.

Evaporative Emission Controls

OPERATION

See Figure 5

The evaporation control system prevents the emission of fuel tank vapors into the atmosphere. When fuel evaporates in the fuel tank, the vapors pass through vent hoses or tubes to a charcoal filled evaporative canister. This canister holds the vapors temporarily. The Powertrain Control Module (PCM) allows intake manifold vacuum to draw vapors into the combustion chambers during certain operating conditions.

➡The evaporative system utilizes specially manufactured hoses. If they are in need of replacement, use only fuel resistant hoses.

All engines utilize a duty cycle purge system. The PCM controls vapor flow by operating the duty cycle EVAP purge solenoid. The evaporation control system is made up of the following components:

Crankcase Vent Filter

All engines use filtered air to vent the crankcase. The filtered air is drawn through the resonator assembly located between the air cleaner and the throttle body.

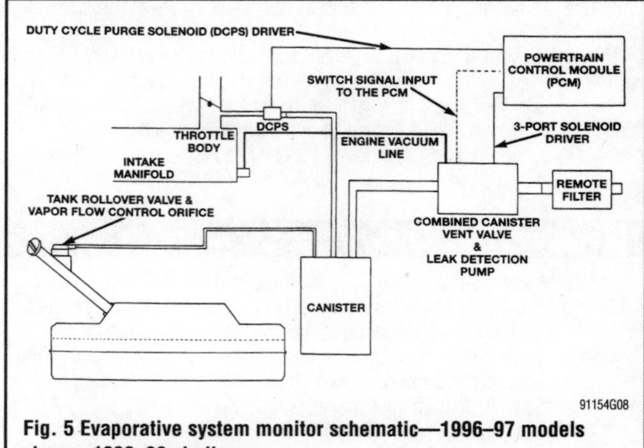

Fig. 5 Evaporative system monitor schematic—1996–97 models shown, 1998–99 similar

Pressure Relief/Rollover Valve

All Chrysler minivans are equipped with rollover valve(s). The rollover valve is a safety device which prevents fuel flow through the fuel tank vent valve hoses, should the vehicle roll over in an accident. The rollover valve is located on top of the fuel tank. In order to access the rollover valve, the fuel tank must be removed; however, the valve is not a serviceable component.

EVAP Canister

See Figure 6

All vehicles use a sealed, maintenance-free evaporative (EVAP) canister. Fuel tank pressure vents into the canister. The canister temporarily holds the fuel vapors until intake manifold vacuum draws them into the combustion chamber. The canister proportional purge solenoid allows the canister to be purged at predetermined intervals and engine conditions.

On all Chrysler minivans, the canister mounts to the vehicle frame underneath the driver's seat. There is no scheduled maintenance interval for the charcoal canister.

Duty Cycle EVAP Canister Purge Solenoid

See Figure 7

All 1996–97 Chrysler minivans come equipped with a Duty Cycle Evap Canister Purge solenoid. The Duty Cycle EVAP Canister Purge solenoid regulates the rate of vapor flow from the EVAP canister to the throttle body. The PCM operates the solenoid. During the cold start warm-up period and the hot start time delay, the PCM does not energize the solenoid. When de-energized, no vapors are purged. The PCM de-energizes the solenoid during open loop operation.

The engine enters closed loop operation after it reaches a specific temperature and the time delay ends. During closed loop operation, the PCM energizes

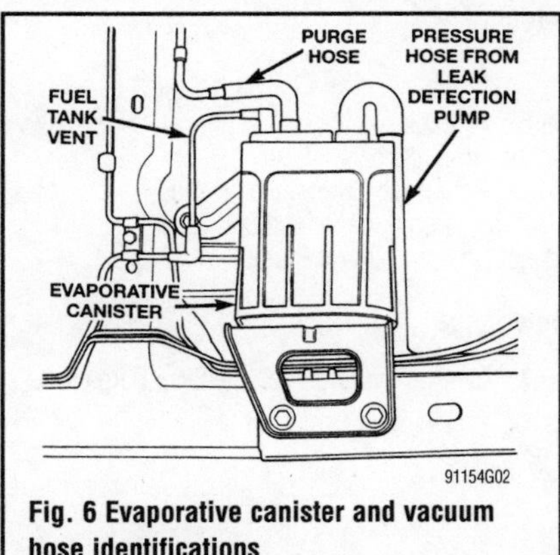

Fig. 6 Evaporative canister and vacuum hose identifications

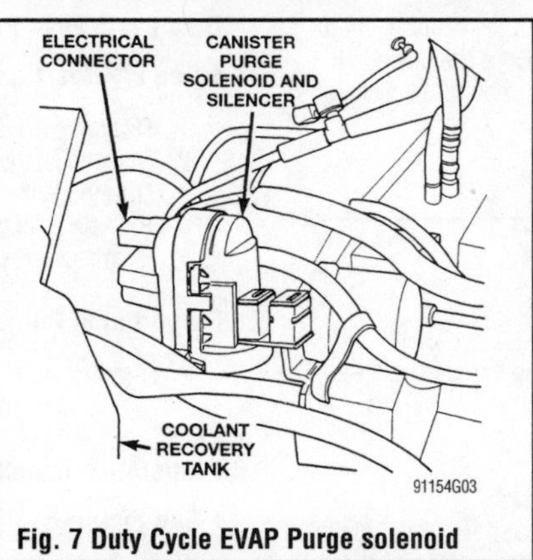

Fig. 7 Duty Cycle EVAP Purge solenoid

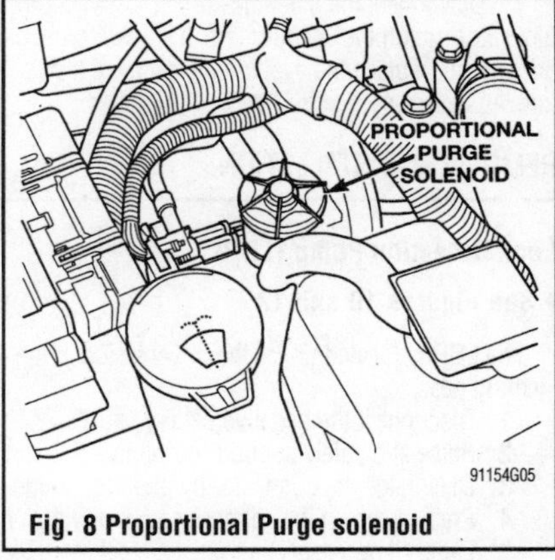

Fig. 8 Proportional Purge solenoid

and de-energizes the solenoid about 5–10 times per second, depending upon operating conditions. The PCM varies the vapor flow rate by changing the solenoid pulse width. Pulse width is the amount of time the solenoid energizes. The PCM adjusts solenoid pulse width based on engine operating conditions.

The solenoid is mounted on a bracket, located on the right engine mount. The solenoid will not operate properly unless it is installed with the electrical connector at the top.

Proportional Purge Solenoid

➧ See Figure 8

All 1998–99 Chrysler minivans come equipped with a Proportional Purge solenoid. The solenoid regulates the rate of vapor flow from the EVAP canister to the throttle body. The PCM operates the solenoid. During the cold start warm-up period and the hot start time delay, the PCM does not energize the solenoid. When de-energized, no vapors are purged.

The solenoid operates at a frequency of 200 Hz and is controlled by an engine controller circuit that senses the current being applied to the solenoid, then adjusts that same current to achieve the desired purge flow. The proportional purge solenoid controls the purge rate of the fuel vapors from the EVAP canister and fuel tank to the engine intake manifold.

Pressure Vacuum Filler Cap

➧ See Figure 9

A pressure vacuum relief cap is used to seal the fuel tank. Tightening the cap on the fuel filler tube creates a seal between them. The relief valves in the cap are a safety feature which prevent possible excessive pressure or vacuum in the fuel tank. Excessive fuel tank pressure could be caused by a malfunction in the system or damage to the vent lines.

When the cap is removed, the seal is broken and fuel tank pressure is relieved. If the filler cap ever needs to be replaced, make sure to get the correct part.

Leak Detection Pump

➧ See Figure 10

All Chrysler minivans utilize a leak detection pump, which is a device used to find leaks in the evaporative emission system. The pump has a 3-port solenoid, a pump that contains a switch, a spring loaded canister vent valve seal, 2 check valves and a spring/diaphragm.

COMPONENT TESTING

Evaporative System Check

➧ See Figures 5, 6 and 11

1. Before beginning the check, inspect all connectors for a clean, tight fit.
2. Start the engine and allow it to reach normal operating temperatures.
3. Inspect the throttle body-to-evaporative emission solenoid vacuum line. Check for vacuum leaks or restrictions. If the vacuum line is damaged, replace or repair as necessary. If the line is OK, proceed with the test.
4. Check the vacuum line running from the evaporative solenoid to the canister for damage or restriction. If the vacuum line is damaged, replace or repair as necessary. If the line is OK, proceed with the test.

➡Allow the engine to idle for 2 minutes after reaching normal operating temperature.

5. Disconnect the canister-to-solenoid vacuum line from the solenoid. Is the evaporative solenoid allowing vacuum to cycle through intermittently at a steady rate? If not, replace the evaporative solenoid. If so, proceed with the test.

➡During the next steps, do NOT use more than 5 psi of air pressure.

6. Turn the ignition key to the **OFF** position. Attempt to blow air through the vacuum line that goes to the canister. Do the canister and vacuum line allow air to pass? If so, the purge solenoid and hoses are OK. If not, proceed with the test.

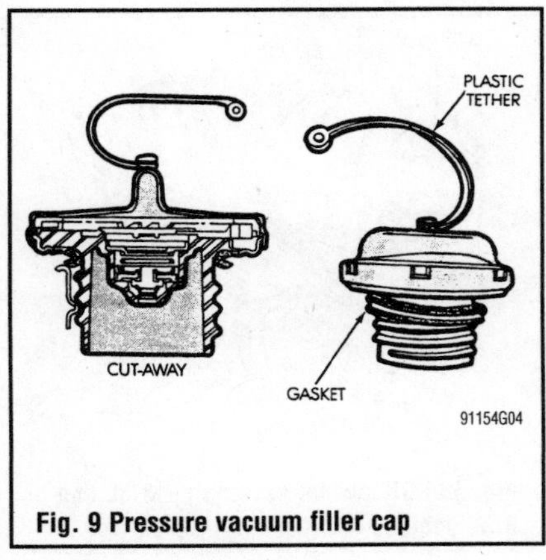

Fig. 9 Pressure vacuum filler cap

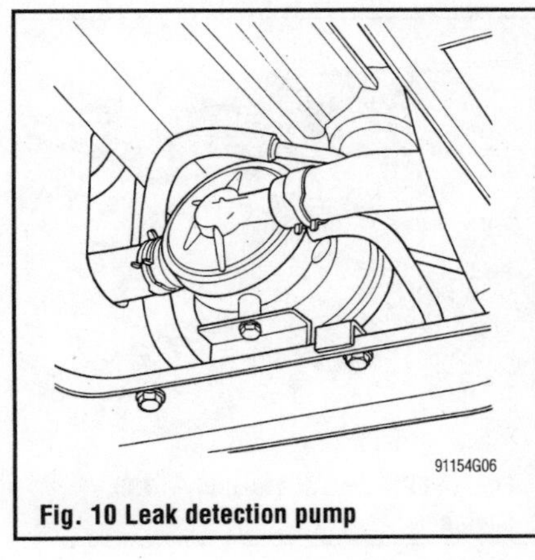

Fig. 10 Leak detection pump

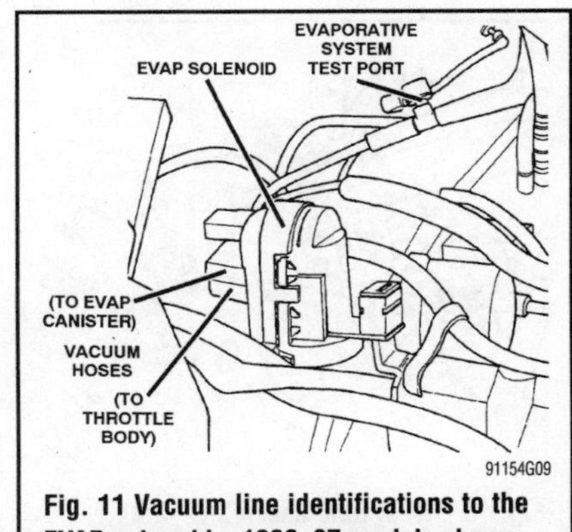

Fig. 11 Vacuum line identifications to the EVAP solenoid—1996–97 models shown

7. Disconnect the solenoid-to-canister vacuum line from the canister. Try to blow air through the vacuum line that goes to the canister. Does the line let air pass? If so, replace the evaporative canister. If not, repair or replace the vacuum line, as necessary.

REMOVAL & INSTALLATION

Leak Detection Pump (LDP)

➧ See Figures 10 and 12

The LDP is located under the driver's side in the cast cradle underneath the steering gear.

1. Disconnect the negative battery cable.
2. Raise and safely support the vehicle.
3. Disengage the connector by pushing on the locking tab.
4. Press down on the connector latch and pull the connector from the pump.
5. Label (if necessary) and disconnect the hoses from the pump.
6. Remove the bolts that secure the LDP and bracket to the cradle.
7. Remove the bracket from the LDP.

To install:

8. Install the LDP to the bracket.
9. Install the LDP and bracket to the cradle. Tighten the mounting bolts to 85–125 inch lbs. (10–14 Nm).

➡Before installing hoses to the LDP, make sure they are not cracked, split or damaged in any way. If a hose leaks, it will cause the CHECK ENGINE light to illuminate.

10. Connect the hoses to the LDP.
11. Plug the wiring harness connector to the LDP and push the connector locking tab into place.
12. Lower the vehicle.
13. Connect the negative battery cable.
14. Using the DRB, or equivalent, scan tool, verify the proper operation of the LDP.

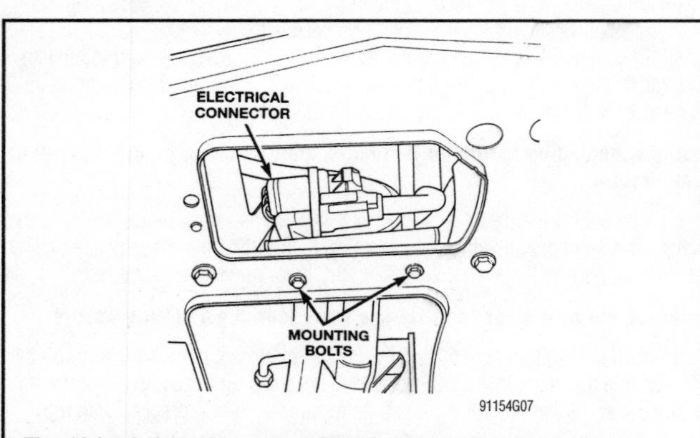

Fig. 12 Leak detection pump wiring harness connector lock

Duty Cycle Evap Purge Solenoid

➧ See Figures 1 and 3

1. Disconnect the negative battery cable.
2. Disconnect the vacuum hose from the solenoid.
3. Disengage the wiring harness connector from the solenoid.
4. Pull the solenoid up to remove it from the mounting bracket.
5. Installation is the reverse of the removal procedures.

Proportional Purge Solenoid Valve

Refer to the same procedure for removal of the Duty Cycle Evap Purge solenoid.

Evaporative Canister

➧ See Figure 6

1. Disconnect the negative battery cable.
2. Raise and safely support the vehicle.
3. Tag and disconnect the vacuum lines from the evaporative canister.
4. Push the locking tab on the electrical connector to unlock and disengage the connector.
5. Unfasten the retaining nuts, then remove the canister from the mounting bracket.

To install:

6. Install the evaporative canister to the bracket, then secure with the retaining nuts.
7. Attach the electrical connector to the pump, then push the locking tab to lock the connector in place.
8. Connect the vacuum lines to the canister, as tagged during removal.
9. Carefully lower the vehicle.
10. Connect the negative battery cable.

Exhaust Gas Recirculation System

OPERATION

➧ See Figures 13, 14, 15 and 16

The Exhaust Gas Recirculation (EGR) system reduces oxides of Nitrogen (NOx) in the engine exhaust and helps prevent detonation (engine knock). Under normal operating conditions, engine cylinder temperature can reach over 3000°F (1649°C). The formation of NOx increases proportionally with combustion temperature. To reduce the emission of these oxides, cylinder temperature must be lowered. The system allows a predetermined amount of hot exhaust gas to recirculate and dilute the incoming air/fuel mixture. The diluted mixture lowers temperatures during combustion. The EGR system consists of the following components:

- EGR tube
- EGR valve
- Electric EGR Transducer (EET)
- Connecting hoses

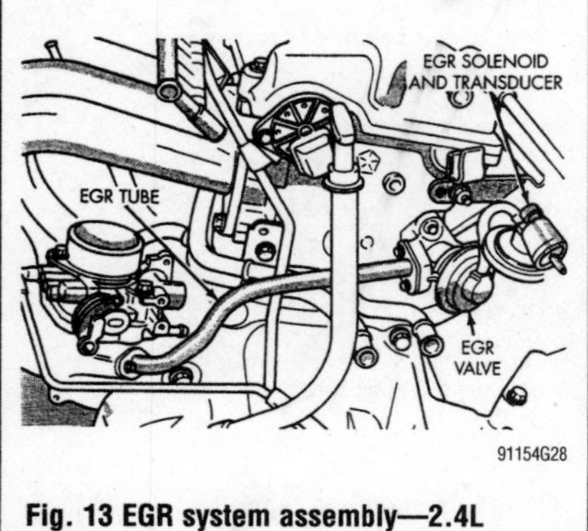

Fig. 13 EGR system assembly—2.4L engine

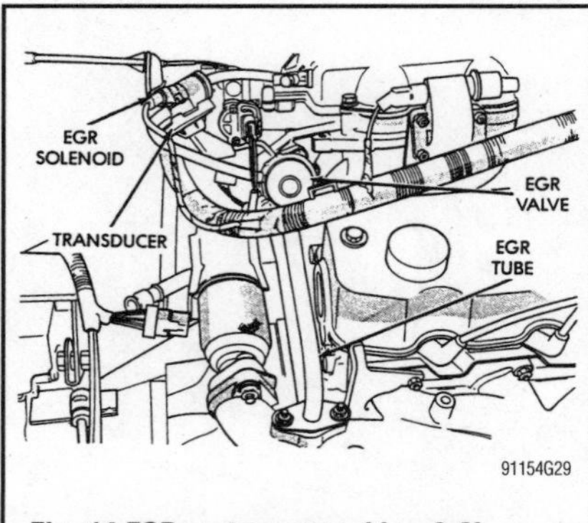

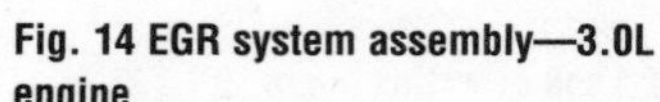

Fig. 14 EGR system assembly—3.0L engine

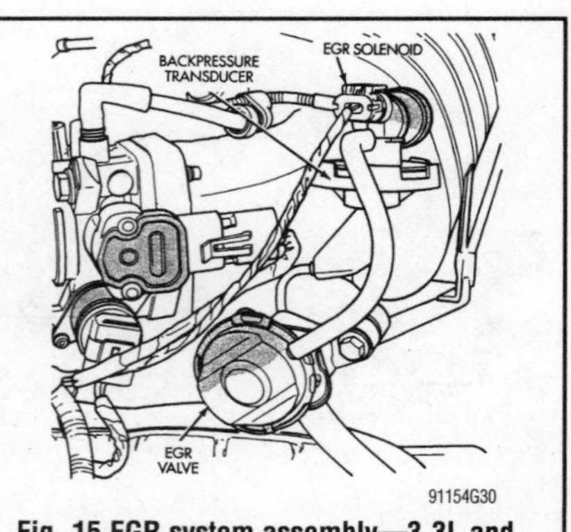

Fig. 15 EGR system assembly—3.3L and 3.8L engines

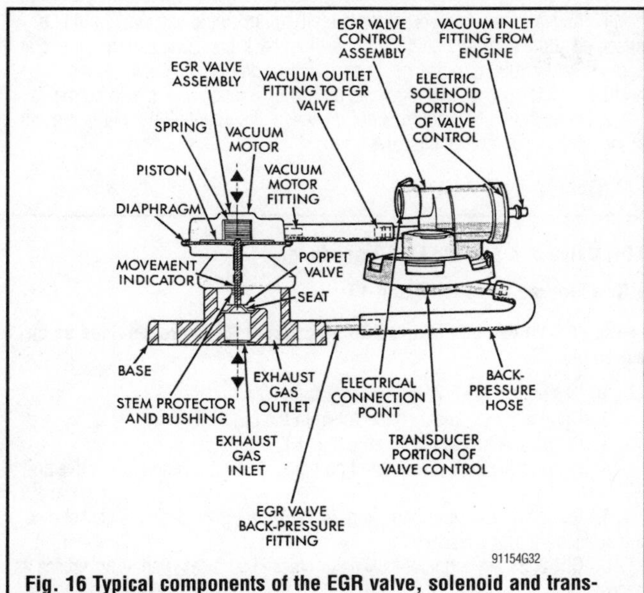

Fig. 16 Typical components of the EGR valve, solenoid and transducer assembly

The electric EGR transducer contains an electrically operated solenoid and a backpressure transducer. The Powertrain Control Module (PCM) operates the solenoid, determining when to energize the solenoid. Exhaust system backpressure controls the transducer.

When the PCM energizes the solenoid, vacuum doesn't reach the transducer. Vacuum flows to the transducer when the PCM de-energizes the solenoid. When exhaust system backpressure becomes high enough, it fully closes a bleed valve in the transducer. When the PCM de-energizes the solenoid and backpressure closes the transducer bleed valve, vacuum flows through the transducer to operate the EGR valve.

De-engergizing the solenoid, but not fully closing the transducer bleed hole (because of low backpressure), varies the strength of vacuum applied to the EGR valve. Varying the strength of the vacuum changes the amount of EGR supplied to the engine. This provides the correct amount of exhaust gas recirculation for different operating conditions. This system does not allow EGR at idle.

COMPONENT TESTING

EGR System On-Board Diagnostics

See Figure 16

The PCM performs an on-board diagnostic check of the EGR system. The diagnostic system uses the electric EGR transducer for the system tests.

The check activates only during certain conditions. When the conditions are met, the PCM energizes the transducer solenoid to disable the EGR system. The PCM checks for a change in the heated oxygen sensor signal. If the air/fuel ratio goes lean, the PCM will try to enrich the mixture. The PCM records a Diagnostic Trouble Code (DTC) if the EGR system is not operating properly. After registering a DTC, the PCM turns on the Check Engine lamp (malfunction indicator) after 2 consecutive trips. There are 2 types of failures sensed by the PCM; a short or open in the circuit, or a mechanical failure or loss of vacuum. The Malfunction Indicator Lamp (MIL) denotes the need for service.

If you find a problem indicated by the MIL and a DTC is set, first check for proper operation of the EGR system. If the system tests properly, check the system using Chrysler's DRB® or equivalent scan tool. Make sure to follow all of the instructions included with the scan tool.

EGR System Test

CAUTION

ALWAYS block the drive wheels and apply the parking brake anytime you are performing a test or adjustment in which the engine must be running.

1996 VEHICLES

See Figure 16

A failed or malfunctioning EGR system can cause engine spark knock, hesitation or sags, rough idle, stalling and/or increased emissions. To make sure the EGR system is operating properly, all passages and moving parts must be clean of deposits that could cause plugging or sticking. Make sure the hoses don't leak and replace any components that do leak.

Check the hose connections between the throttle body, intake manifold, EGR solenoid and transducer, and the EGR valve. Replace any hardened, cracked, melted or leaking hoses. Repair or replace faulty connectors.

1. Check the EGR control system and EGR valve with the engine fully warmed up and running with the engine coolant temperature at 150°F or over. With the transmission in Neutral and the throttle closed, allow the engine to idle for about 70 seconds.
2. Abruptly accelerate the engine to about 2,000 rpm, but NOT over 3,000 rpm. The EGR valve stem should move when accelerating the engine.
3. Repeat the test a few times to confirm movement. If the valve stem moves, the EGR system is operating properly. If the stem doesn't move, then the EGR system is not operating properly.
4. Disconnect and plug the vacuum hose from the EGR valve.

1997–99 VEHICLES

See Figure 16

1. Check the condition of all EGR system hoses and tubes for leaks, blockage, cracks, kinks or hardening. Repair or replace them as necessary before beginning the test.
2. Make sure the hoses at both the EGR valve and EGR valve control are connected properly, and that the electrical connector is firmly attached at the valve control.
3. To check EGR system operation, connect a DRB® or equivalent scan tool to the 16-way data link connector. (The data link connector is located on the lower edge of the instrument panel, near the steering column.) Make sure to follow all of the manufacturer's instructions when connecting the scan tool and testing the EGR system.
4. After checking the system with the scan tool, proceed to the remaining EGR valve control tests.

EGR Gas Flow Test

See Figure 16

Use this test to see if exhaust gas is flowing through the EGR system. It can also be used to determine if the EGR tube is plugged, or the system passages in the intake or exhaust manifolds are plugged.

The engine must be started, running and at normal operating temperature for this test. This test is not to be used as a complete test of the EGR system, but in conjunction with the other system tests.

1. All engines are equipped with 2 fittings on the EGR valve. The upper fitting (located on the vacuum motor) supplies engine vacuum to a diaphragm within the EGR valve for valve operation. The lower fitting (located on the base of the EGR valve) is used to supply exhaust backpressure to the EGR valve control.
2. Disconnect the rubber hose from the vacuum motor fitting on top of the EGR valve vacuum motor.
3. Connect a hand-held vacuum pump to the vacuum motor fitting (top fitting).
4. Start the engine. Using the hand-held vacuum pump, slowly apply about 5 in. (17 kPa) of vacuum to the fitting on the EGR valve motor.
5. While applying a minimum 3 in. (10 kPa) of vacuum, and with the engine running at idle speed, the idle speed should drop or the engine may even stall, if the vacuum is applied quickly. This indicates that exhaust gas is flowing through the EGR tube between the intake and exhaust manifolds.
6. If the engine speed did not change, the EGR valve may be defective or the EGR tube may be plugged with carbon, or the passages in the intake and/or exhaust manifold may be plugged with carbon. Perform the following to see if the components are plugged:
   a. Remove the EGR valve from the engine, as outlined later in this section.
   b. Apply vacuum to the vacuum motor fitting and check the stem on the valve. If it's moving, the EGR valve is working properly and the problem is either a plugged EGR tube or plugged passages at the intake or exhaust manifolds (refer to the next step).

c. Remove the EGR tube between the intake and exhaust manifolds. Check and clean the EGR tube and its related openings on the manifolds.

7. Do not try to clean the EGR valve. If the valve shows evidence of heavy carbon build-up near the base, replace it.

EGR Valve Leakage Test

See Figure 16

If the engine will not idle, stalls while idling or the idle is rough or slow, the poppet valve, located at the base of the EGR valve, may be leaking in the closed position.

1. The engine should be **OFF** for the following test.
2. Disconnect the rubber hose from the fitting at the top (vacuum motor) side of the EGR valve, and perform the following:
   a. Connect a hand-held vacuum pump to this fitting.
   b. Apply 15 in. (51 kPa) of vacuum to the pump, then observe the gauge reading on the pump.
   c. If the vacuum falls off, the diaphragm in the EGR valve has ruptured.
   d. Replace the EGR valve, as outlined later in this section.

The EGR valve, valve control and attaching hoses are replaced as an assembly.

   e. Go on to the next step.
3. A small metal fitting (backpressure fitting) is located at the base of the EGR valve. A rubber backpressure hose connects it to the backpressure fitting on the EGR valve control. Disconnect this hose from the EGR valve fitting.
4. Remove the air cleaner inlet tube from the throttle body.
5. Using compressed air from an air nozzle with a rubber tip, apply about 50 psi (345 kPa) of regulated air to the metal backpressure fitting on the EGR valve.
6. By hand, open the throttle to the wide open position. Air should NOT be heard coming from the intake manifold while applying air pressure to the fitting.
7. If air CAN be heard coming from the intake manifold, the poppet valve is leaking at the bottom of the EGR valve. Replace the EGR valve.

EGR Valve Control (Transducer) Test

See Figure 16

The following procedures apply to testing the vacuum transducer portion of the valve. The electrical operation of the valve must be checked using the Chrysler DRB, or equivalent, scan tool. Be sure to follow the instructions that accompany the scan tool.

1. Disconnect the rubber back-pressure hose from the fitting at the bottom of the EGR valve.
2. Connect a hand-held vacuum pump to this fitting and apply 10 inches of vacuum. If the vacuum falls off, the valve diaphragm is leaking.
3. Replace the EGR valve assembly and continue with further testing.
4. Disconnect the rubber hose at the EGR valve vacuum inlet fitting and connect a vacuum gauge to this hose.
5. Start the engine and allow it to run until it has reached operating temperature. Hold the engine speed at approximately 1500 rpm while checking for steady engine vacuum (full manifold) at this hose.
6. If engine vacuum is not present, check the vacuum line to the engine and repair as necessary before continuing.
7. Reconnect the hose to the EGR valve vacuum inlet fitting, then disconnect the hose from the outlet fitting. Connect a vacuum gauge to this fitting.
8. Disengage the wiring harness connector from the valve control, which will then simulate an open circuit (no ground from the PCM) at the valve.
9. Start the engine and allow it to reach operating temperature. Hold the engine speed to approximately 2000 rpm while checking for steady engine vacuum (full manifold) at this fitting.

To allow full manifold vacuum to flow through the valve, exhaust back-pressure must be present at the valve. It must be high enough to hold the bleed valve in the transducer portion of the valve closed.

10. With the aid of an assistant, momentarily (1–2 seconds) hold a rag over the tailpipe opening to build up exhaust back-pressure while observing the vacuum gauge reading. Be sure to wear heavy gloves while doing this.

Do not cover the tailpipe opening for an extended period of time or damage to components or overheating could result.

11. As temporary back-pressure is built, full manifold vacuum should be observed at the vacuum outlet fitting. Without back-pressure, and the engine at approximately 2000 rpm, the gauge reading will be low. This low reading is normal. At idle speed, the gauge reading will be erratic. This is also normal.
12. If full manifold vacuum is not present at the outlet fitting, but is present at the inlet fitting, replace the valve.

REMOVAL & INSTALLATION

EGR Valve and Electric EGR Transducer

See Figures 13, 14, 15 and 17

The EGR valve and Electric EGR Transducer (EET) are serviced as an assembly.

1. Disconnect the negative battery cable.
2. Unplug the electrical connector from the EET.
3. Detach the vacuum hose from the EET.
4. Remove the EGR valve mounting bolts, then remove the EGR valve and EET.
5. Remove and discard the old gaskets. Thoroughly clean the gasket mating surfaces and/or passages.
6. Check for any signs of leakage or cracked surfaces. Repair or replace as necessary.

To install:

7. Using new gaskets, loosely install the EGR valve onto the intake manifold. Tighten the mounting bolts to 16 ft. lbs. (22 Nm).
8. Install the EET onto the mounting bracket.
9. Attach the electrical and vacuum hose connections to the EET.
10. Connect the negative battery cable.

EGR Tube

See Figures 13, 18 and 19

1. Disconnect the negative battery cable.
2. Remove the exhaust manifold-to-EGR tube flange fasteners. Be careful not to lose the gasket.
3. If necessary, remove the EGR valve nuts at the intake manifold. Be careful not to lose the gasket.
4. Remove the intake manifold-to-EGR tube flange fasteners. Be careful not to lose the gasket.
5. Remove the EGR tube.
6. Discard the old gaskets. Thoroughly clean the gasket mating surfaces and/or passages.
7. Check for any signs of leakage or cracked surfaces. Repair or replace as necessary.

To install:

8. Loosely install the EGR tube and fasteners, along with new gaskets, onto the intake and exhaust manifolds.
9. Tighten the EGR tube mounting fasteners to 16 ft. lbs. (22 Nm).
10. Connect the negative battery cable.

Fig. 17 Unplug the electrical connector from the transducer, then the vacuum hose

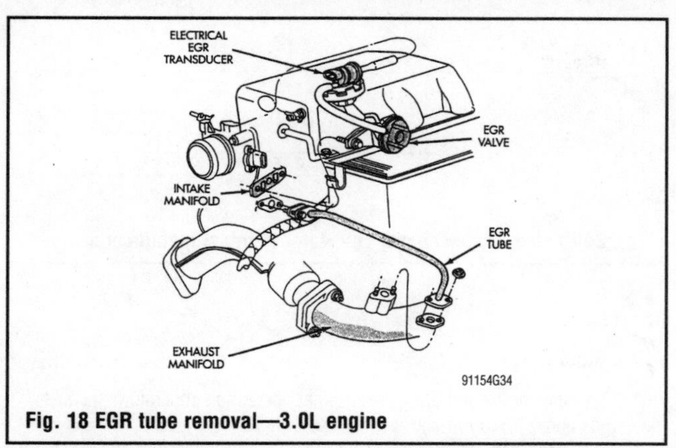

Fig. 18 EGR tube removal—3.0L engine

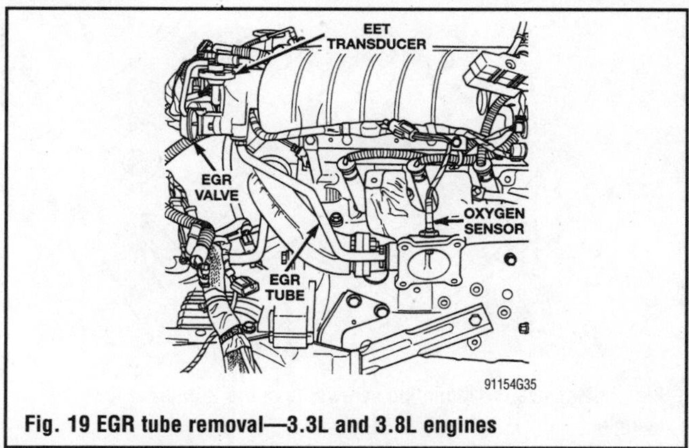

Fig. 19 EGR tube removal—3.3L and 3.8L engines

ELECTRONIC ENGINE CONTROLS

Powertrain Control Module (PCM)

OPERATION

The heart of the electronic control system, which is found on the vehicles covered by this manual, is a Powertrain Control Module (PCM). The Powertrain Control Module (PCM) is a digital computer containing a microprocessor. The PCM recieves input signals from various switches and sensors that are referred to as PCM inputs. Based on these inputs, the PCM adjusts various engine and vehicle operations through devices that are referred to as PCM outputs. It may also control the shift functions of the electronically controlled automatic transmission.

➡Care must be taken when handling these expensive components in order to protect them from damage. Carefully follow all instructions included with the replacement part. Avoid touching pins or connectors to prevent damage from static electricity.

Based on inputs it receives, the PCM adjusts fuel injector pulse width, idle speed, ignition spark advance, ignition coil dwell and EVAP canister purge operation. The PCM regulates the cooling fan, air conditioning and speed control systems. The PCM changes the alternator charge rate by adjusting the alternator field. The PCM also performs diagnostic functions.

✲✲ WARNING

To prevent the possibility of permanent control module damage, the ignition switch MUST always be OFF when disconnecting power from or reconnecting power to the module. This includes unplugging the module connector, disconnecting the negative battery cable, removing the module fuse or even attempting to jump start your dead battery using jumper cables.

The Automatic ShutDown (ASD) relay and fuel pump relay are mounted in the Power Distribution Center (PDC), but turned on and off by the PCM. The camshaft and crankshaft signals are sent to the PCM. If the PCM does not receive both signals within approximately one second of engine cranking, it deactivates the ASD and fuel pump relays. When these relays are deactivated, the power is shut off to the fuel injectors, ignition coils, fuel pump and heating element in each oxygen sensor.

The PCM contains a voltage converter that changes battery voltage to a regulated 8.0 volts. The 8.0 volts power the camshaft position sensor, crankshaft position sensor and vehicle speed sensor. The PCM also provides a 5.0 volt supply for the engine coolant temperature sensor, manifold absolute pressure sensor and throttle position sensor.

REMOVAL & INSTALLATION

➧ See Figures 20, 21, 22 and 23

1. Disconnect the negative battery cable first, then the positive battery cable.
2. Remove the two Power Distribution Center (PDC)-to-mounting bracket screws.
3. Remove the battery from the vehicle.
4. Turn the PDC toward the center of the vehicle to remove from the rear mounting bracket.
5. Push the PDC rearward to remove it from the front mounting bracket. Lay the PDC aside, allowing access to the Powertrain Control Module (PCM).
6. Disengage the two 40-way connectors from the PCM by squeezing the tabs on each side of the connector and pulling rearward.
7. Remove the 3 screws mounting the PCM to the inner fender.
8. Remove the PCM from the vehicle.

To install:

9. Install the PCM into the vehicle in the proper position and tighten the 3 mounting screws.

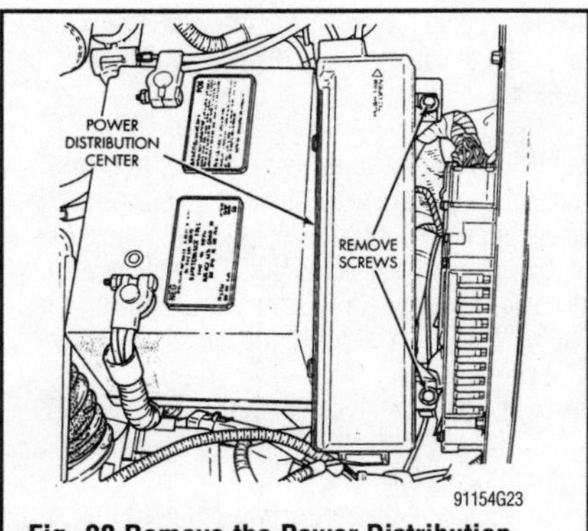

Fig. 20 Remove the Power Distribution Center (PDC) retaining screws

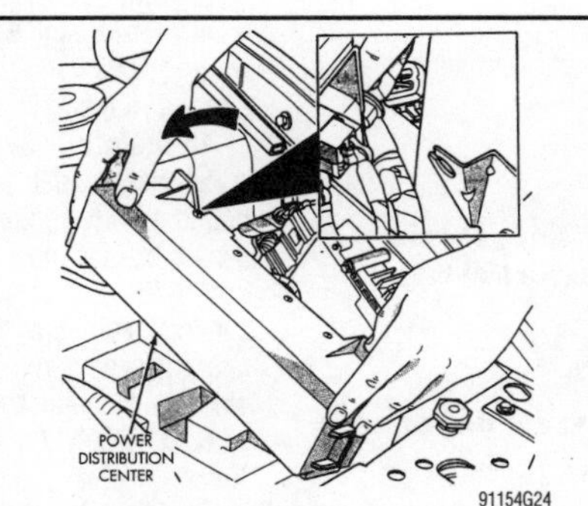

Fig. 21 Rotate the PDC toward the center of the vehicle to remove from the rear bracket

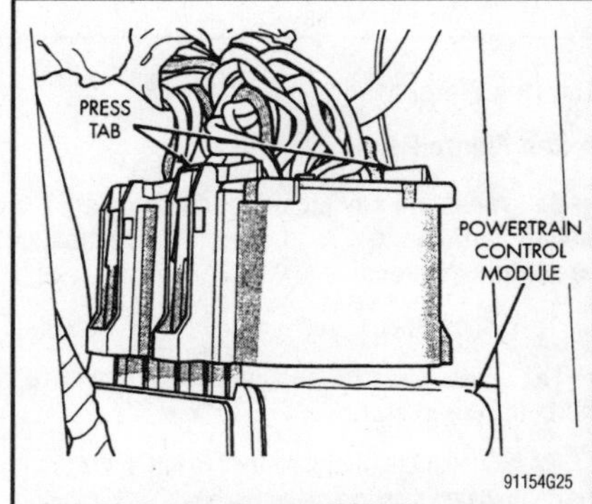

Fig. 22 Unplug the two PCM 40-way connectors

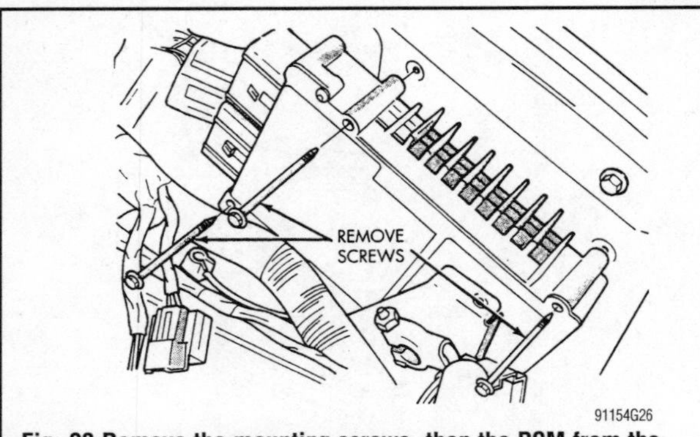

Fig. 23 Remove the mounting screws, then the PCM from the vehicle

10. Attach the two 40-way connectors to the PCM.
11. Install the PDC into its original position and secure with the 2 mounting screws.
12. Install the battery into the vehicle.
13. Connect the positive battery cable first, then connect the negative battery cable.

Heated Oxygen Sensor

OPERATION

As a vehicle accrues mileage, the catalytic converter deteriorates. The deterioration results in a less effective catalyst. To monitor catalytic converter deterioration, the fuel injection system uses two heated oxygen sensors: one which is upstream of the catalytic converter and one downstream of the converter.

The heated oxygen sensor, or HO2S sensor is usually located near the catalytic converter. It produces a voltage signal of 0.1–1.0 volts based on the amount of oxygen in the exhaust gas. When a low amount of oxygen is present (caused by a rich air/fuel mixture), the sensor produces a high voltage. When a high amount of oxygen is present (caused by a lean air/fuel mixture), the sensor produces a low voltage. Because an accurate voltage signal is only produced if the sensor temperature is above approximately 600°F (315°C), a fast acting heating element is built into its body.

The PCM uses the HO2S sensor voltage signal to constantly adjust the amount of fuel injected which keeps the engine at its peak efficiency.

The PCM compares the reading from the sensors to calculate the catalytic converter oxygen storage capacity and storage efficiency. The PCM also uses the upstream heated oxygen sensor input when adjusting the injector pulse width. When the catalytic converter efficiency drops below preset emission criteria, the PCM stores a Diagnostic Trouble Code (DTC) and illuminates the Malfunction Indicator Lamp (MIL).

The automatic shutdown relay supplies battery voltage to both of the heated oxygen sensors. The sensors have heating elements which reduce the amount of time it takes for the sensors to reach operating temperature.

TESTING

Heating Element

➧ See Figure 24

➡Before testing any electrical component, inspect the wiring and connectors for damage. Also wiggle the connectors to ensure a that they are firmly engaged.

1. Disconnect the electrical harness from each of the sensors.

➡The white wires in the sensor connector are the power and ground circuits for the heater.

2. Connect the ohmmeter test leads to the terminals of the white wires in the heated oxygen sensor connector.
3. Check the resistance of the sensor, if it is not within 4–7 ohms, replace the sensor.

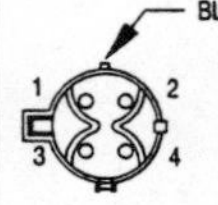

CAV	FUNCTION
1	GROUND
2	AUTOMATIC SHUT DOWN RELAY OUTPUT
3	SENSOR GROUND
4	HEATED OXYGEN SENSOE SIGNAL

91154G27

Fig. 24 Heated oxygen sensor connector terminal identifications

Sensor

➧ See Figure 24

1. Start the engine and bring it to normal operating temperature, then run the engine above 1200 rpm for two minutes.
2. Backprobe with a high impedance averaging voltmeter (set to the DC voltage scale) between the HO2S sensor signal wire and battery ground.
3. Verify that the sensor voltage fluctuates rapidly between 0.40–0.60 volts.
4. If the sensor voltage is stabilized at the middle of the specified range (approximately 0.45–0.55 volts) or if the voltage fluctuates very slowly between the specified range (HO2S signal crosses 0.5 volts less than 5 times in ten seconds), the sensor may be faulty.
5. If the sensor voltage stabilizes at either end of the specified range, the PCM is probably not able to compensate for a mechanical problem such as a vacuum leak. These types of mechanical problems will cause the sensor to report a constant lean or constant rich mixture. The mechanical problem will first have to be repaired and then the HO2S sensor test repeated.
6. Pull a vacuum hose located after the throttle plate. Voltage should drop to approximately 0.12 volts (while still fluctuating rapidly). This tests the ability of the sensor to detect a lean mixture condition. Reattach the vacuum hose.
7. Richen the mixture using a propane enrichment tool. Sensor voltage should rise to approximately 0.90 volts (while still fluctuating rapidly). This tests the ability of the sensor to detect a rich mixture condition.
8. If the sensor voltage is above or below the specified range, the sensor and/or the sensor wiring may be faulty. Check the wiring for any breaks, repair as necessary and repeat the test.
9. Further sensor operational testing requires the use of a special tester DRB scan tool or equivalent.

REMOVAL & INSTALLATION

Upstream Heated Oxygen Sensor

➧ See Figures 25, 26, 27 and 28

1. Disconnect the negative battery cable.

➡The upstream heated oxygen sensor is accessible from the top of the engine compartment, however, removal of the windshield wiper/motor module assembly is required.

2. Raise and safely support the vehicle, unless the sensor is going to be removed from the top of the engine compartment.
3. Unplug the upstream oxygen sensor connector.
4. Remove the sensor using a suitable oxygen sensor crow foot wrench or oxygen sensor socket. After removing the sensor, the exhaust manifold must be cleaned with an 18mm x 1.5 + 6E tap.

To install:

5. New oxygen sensors will be packaged with a special anti-seize compound already applied to the threads. If you are reinstalling the old sensor, the sensor threads must be coated with fresh anti-seize compound. You must use Loctite 771-64®, or equivalent, type of anti-seize compound. This is not a conventional anti-seize paste. The use of a regular compound may electrically insulator the sensor, rendering it inoperative. You must coat the threads with an electrically conductive anti-seize compound.
6. Carefully thread the sensor into the bore, then tighten to 20 ft. lbs. (27 Nm).
7. Attach the oxygen sensor electrical connector.
8. If raised, carefully lower the vehicle. If the sensor was removed from up top, install the windshield wiper/motor module assembly.
9. Connect the negative battery cable.

91154P27

Fig. 25 The oxygen sensor can be accessed from the top of the vehicle by removing the windshield wiper/motor module assembly

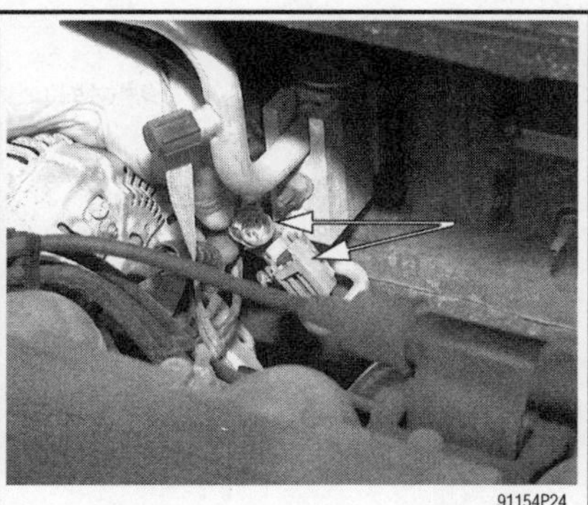
91154P24

Fig. 26 Locate the sensor connector and disengage

91154P23

Fig. 27 Using a special oxygen sensor socket tool, loosen the sensor . . .

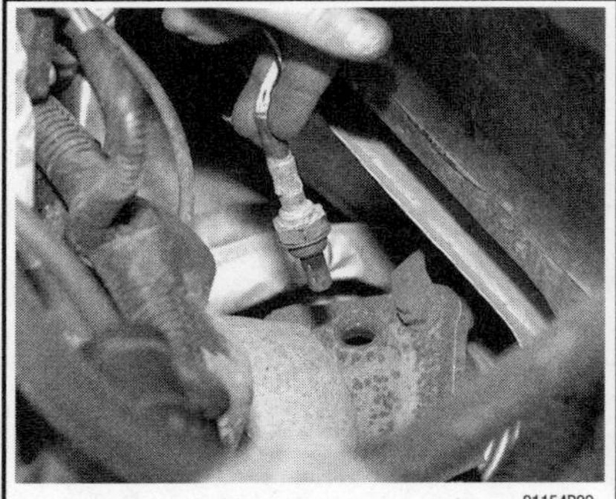
91154P22

Fig. 28 . . . then remove the heated oxygen sensor from the exhaust manifold

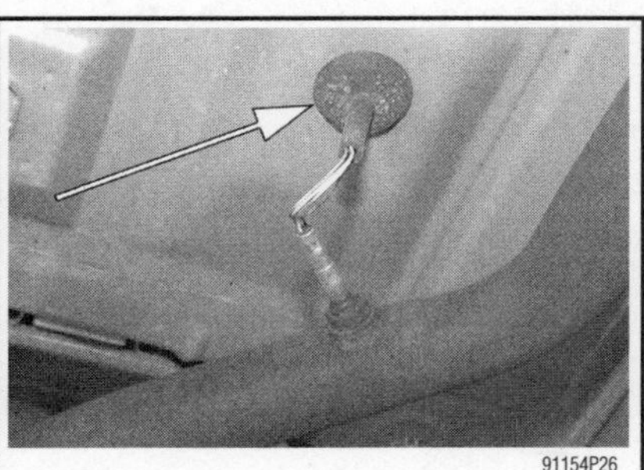
91154P26

Fig. 29 The downstream heated oxygen sensor is located under the vehicle. The sensor connector is on the other side of the rubber grommet

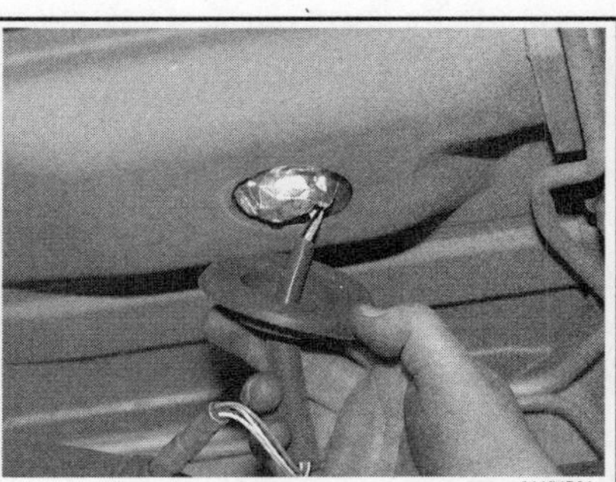
91154P21

Fig. 30 Pry out the grommet from the vehicle's floor and pull down the wiring harness connector . . .

Downstream Heated Oxygen Sensor

➧ See Figures 29, 30, 31, 32 and 33

1. Disconnect the negative battery cable.
2. Raise and safely support the vehicle.
3. Remove the grommet cover to expose the sensor connector.
4. Unplug the electrical connector from the downstream oxygen sensor by first pushing back the connector locking tab.
5. Remove the sensor using a suitable oxygen sensor crow foot wrench. After removing the sensor, the exhaust manifold must be cleaned with an 18mm x 1.5 + 6E tap.

To install:

6. New oxygen sensors will be packaged with a special anti-seize compound already applied to the threads. If you are reinstalling the old sensor, the sensor threads must be coated with fresh anti-seize compound. You must use Loctite 771-64®, or equivalent, type of anti-seize compound. This is not a conventional anti-seize paste. The use of a regular compound may electrically insulator the sensor, rendering it inoperative. You must coat the threads with an electrically conductive anti-seize compound.
7. Carefully thread the sensor into the bore, then tighten to 20 ft. lbs. (27 Nm).
8. Route the sensor electrical harness through the clips along the body.
9. Attach the oxygen sensor electrical connector.
10. Place the connector back into its original location and install the grommet cover.
11. Carefully lower the vehicle, then connect the negative battery cable.

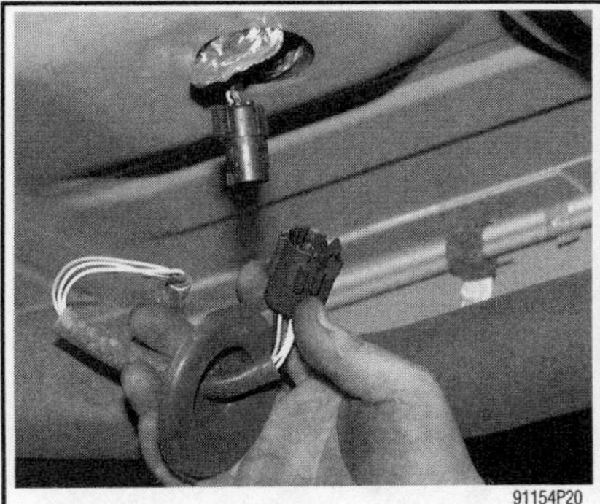
91154P20

Fig. 31 . . . then disengage the wiring harness connector

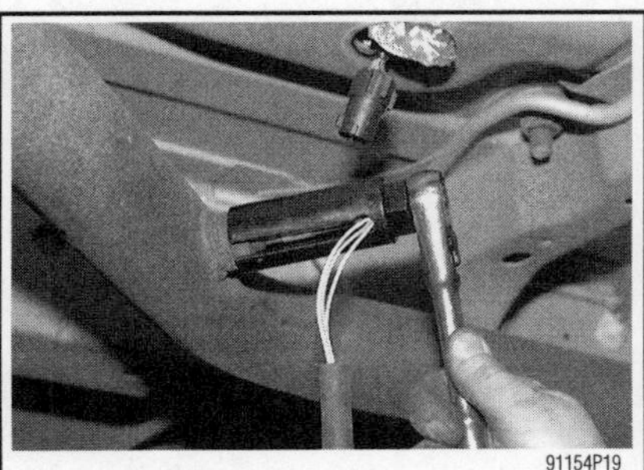
91154P19

Fig. 32 An easily accessible oxygen sensor such as this one can either be removed using a special oxygen sensor socket . . .

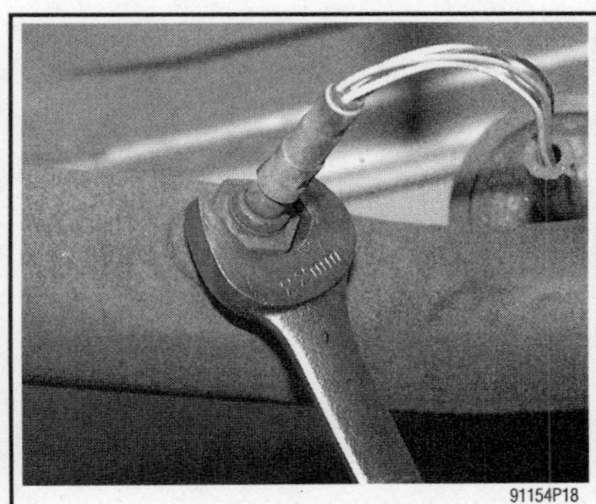
91154P18

Fig. 33 . . . or just a regular open end wrench

Idle Air Control (IAC) Motor

OPERATION

➧ See Figures 34, 35 and 36

The Idle Air Control (IAC) motor, attached to the side of the throttle body, is operated by the PCM. The PCM adjusts engine idle speed through the idle air control motor to compensate for load on the engine, or ambient conditions.

The throttle body has an air bypass passage that provides air for the engine during closed throttle idle. The idle air control motor pintle protrudes into the air bypass passage and regulates the air flow through it. The PCM adjusts the idle speed by moving the IAC motor pintle in and out of the bypass passage. The speed is based on various sensor and switch inputs received by the PCM. The inputs are from the throttle position sensor, crankshaft position sensor, coolant temperature sensor, as well as various switch operations (brake, park/neutral, air conditioning). Deceleration die out is also prevented by increasing airflow when the throttle is closed quickly after a driving condition.

TESTING

➧ See Figures 37 and 38

Visually check the connector, making sure it is properly attached and all of the terminals are straight, tight and free of corrosion.

You need to have access to a DRB® or equivalent scan tool to accurately test the Idle Air Control (IAC) motor and related circuits. Make sure to carefully follow all of the scan tool manufacturers directions when testing the IAC motor.

If you do not have access to a scan tool, this simple test should give you an indication if the circuit is working properly:

1. First attach a tachometer to the engine, then start the engine.
2. Observe the idle speed. Pull a vacuum hose (like the one leading from the brake booster to the intake manifold). The idle speed should rise, then fall as the IAC motor tries to compensate for the vacuum leak.
3. Reattach the vacuum hose. The idle should drop, then stabilize.
4. If the engine reacted as indicated, the circuit is probably OK.

REMOVAL & INSTALLATION

➧ See Figures 34, 35, 36 and 39

1. Disconnect the negative battery cable.
2. Detach the electrical connector from the IAC motor.
3. Unfasten the IAC motor mounting screws from the throttle body, then remove the motor from the throttle body. Make sure the O-ring is removed with the motor. Remove and discard the O-ring.

To install:

4. The new IAC motor has a new O-ring installed on it. Measure the pintle on the new IAC valve. If it is longer than 1 in. (25mm), it must be retracted using the Idle Air control Motor Open/Close test on the DRB® or equivalent scan tool. Note that the battery must be connected for this test.
5. If the old IAC motor is being installed, place a new O-ring on the motor.
6. Carefully plate the IAC motor into the throttle body and install the retaining screws. Tighten the screws to 17 inch lbs. (2 Nm).
7. Attach the electrical connector to the IAC motor.
8. Connect the negative battery cable.

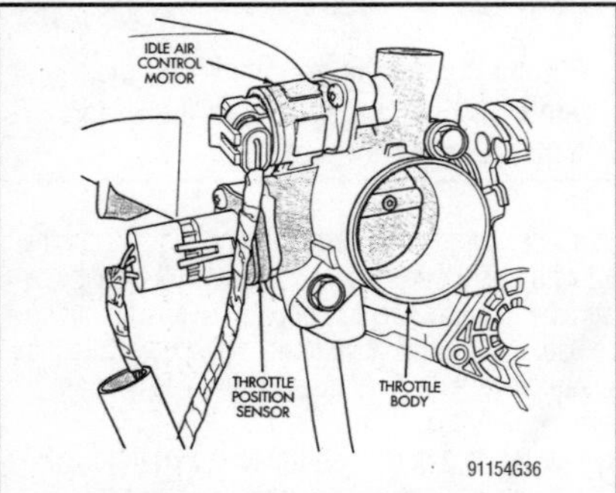

Fig. 34 The Idle Air Control (IAC) motor and Throttle Position Sensor (TPS) location on the throttle body—2.4L engine

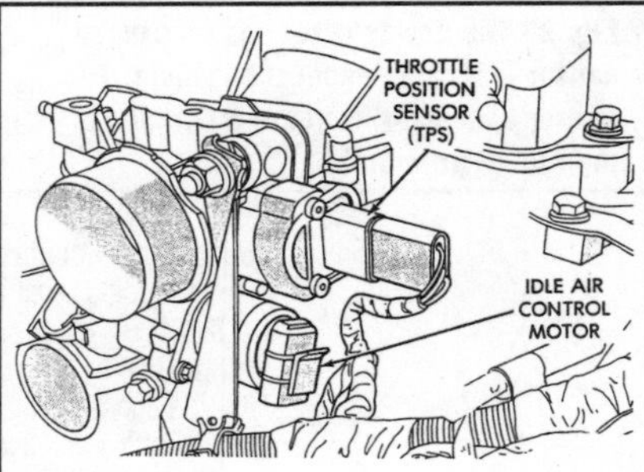

Fig. 35 The Idle Air Control (IAC) motor and Throttle Position Sensor (TPS) location on the throttle body—3.0L engine

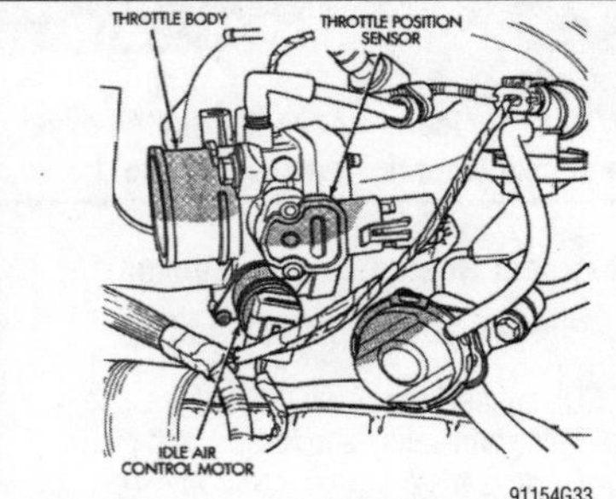

Fig. 36 The Idle Air Control (IAC) motor and Throttle Position Sensor (TPS) location on the throttle body—3.3L and 3.8L engines

Fig. 37 Connect a tachometer to the engine, then start the engine. Observe the idle speed . . .

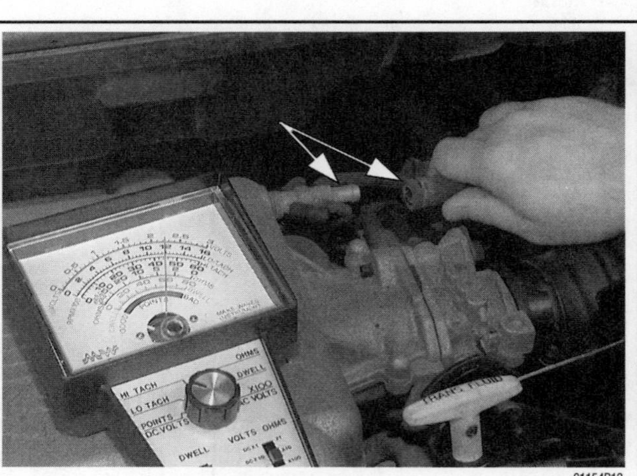

Fig. 38 . . . then, while observing the idle speed, disconnect a vacuum hose (such as brake booster-to-intake manifold). The IAC motor should compensate for the leak

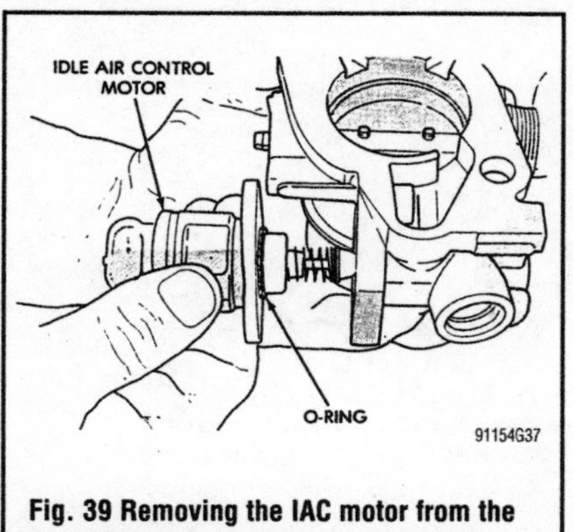

Fig. 39 Removing the IAC motor from the throttle body assembly

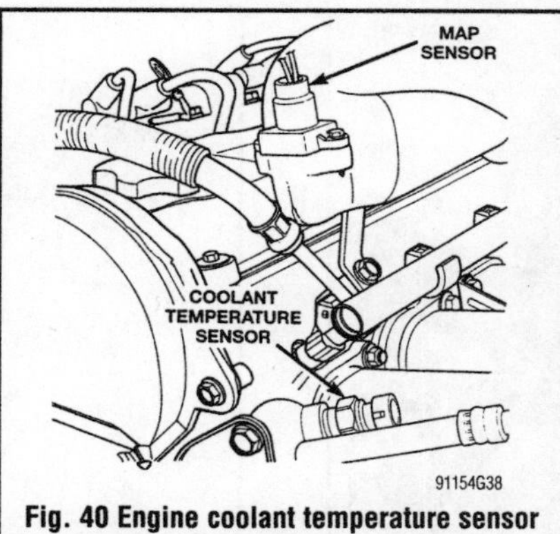

Fig. 40 Engine coolant temperature sensor location—2.4L engine

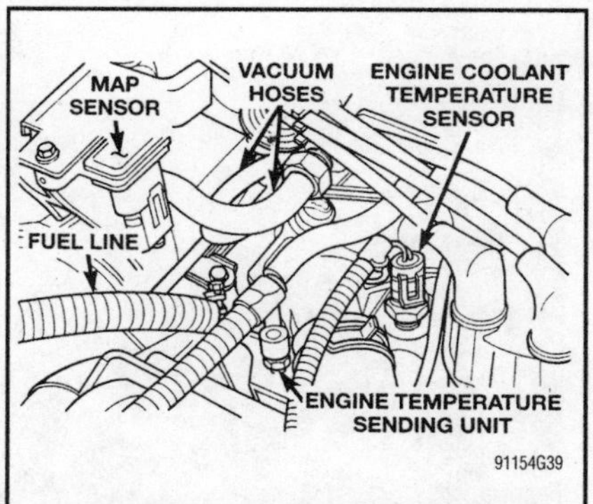

Fig. 41 Engine coolant temperature sensor location—3.0L engine

Coolant Temperature Sensor

OPERATION

➧ **See Figures 40, 41 and 42**

The engine coolant temperature sensor is a variable resistor with a range of -40°F–265°F (-5°C–129°C).

The engine coolant temperature sensor provides an input voltage to the PCM. As the coolant temperature varies, the sensor resistance changes resulting in a different input voltage to the PCM.

When the engine is cold, the PCM will demand slightly richer air/fuel mixtures and higher idle speeds until normal operating temperatures are reached.

The engine coolant temperature sensor is also utilized for control of the cooling fan.

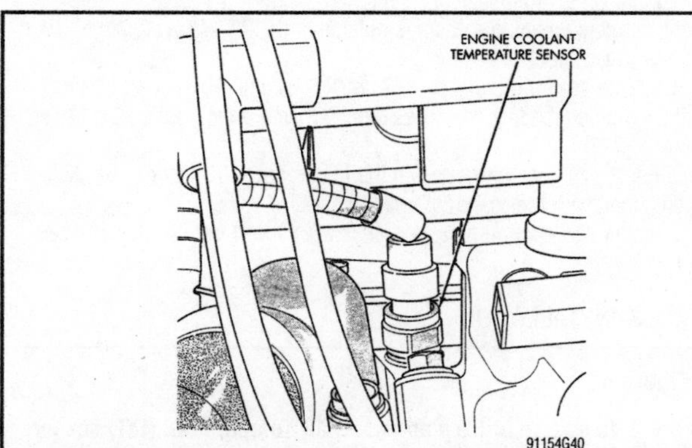

Fig. 42 Engine coolant temperature sensor location—3.3L and 3.8L engines

TESTING

➧ **See Figures 43, 44 and 45**

1. Turn the ignition switch to the **OFF** position.
2. Detach the coolant temperature sensor electrical connector.
3. Using a DVOM set to the ohms scale, connect one lead to terminal A and the other lead to terminal B of the coolant temperature sensor connector.
4. With the engine at normal operating temperature, approximaterly 200°F (93°C), the ohmmeter should read approximately 700–1000 ohms.
5. With the engine at room temperature, approximately 70°F (21°C), the ohmmeter should read approximately 7000–13,000 ohms.
6. If not within specifications, replace the engine coolant temperature sensor.
7. Test the resistance of the wiring harness between PCM terminal 26 and the sensor wiring harness connector. Also check for continuity between PCM connector terminal 43 and the sensor wiring harness connector. If the resistance measures greater than 1 ohm, repair the wiring harness as necessary.

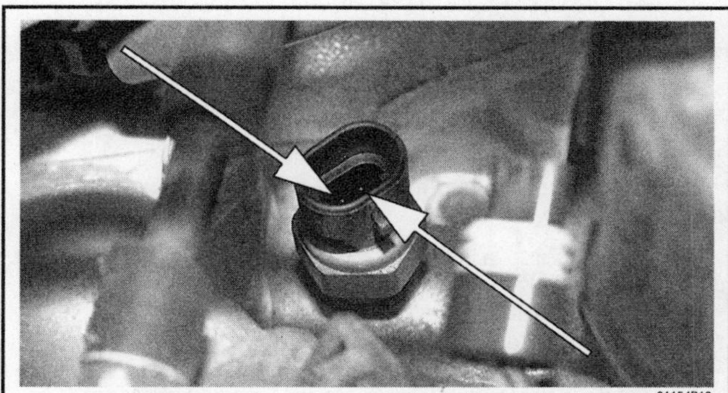

Fig. 43 Before testing the sensor, inspect the sensor terminals for damage or corrosion and replace if necessary

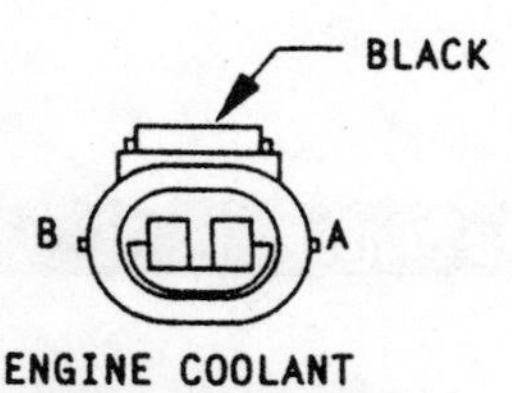

CAV	CIRCUIT	FUNCTION
A	K4 18BK/LB	SENSOR GROUND
B	K2 18TN/BK	ENGINE COOLANT TEMPERATURE SENSOR SIGNAL

91154G41

Fig. 44 Engine coolant temperature sensor connector terminal identifications

91154P11

Fig. 45 With the engine at normal operating temperature, the ohmmeter should read between 700–1000 ohms

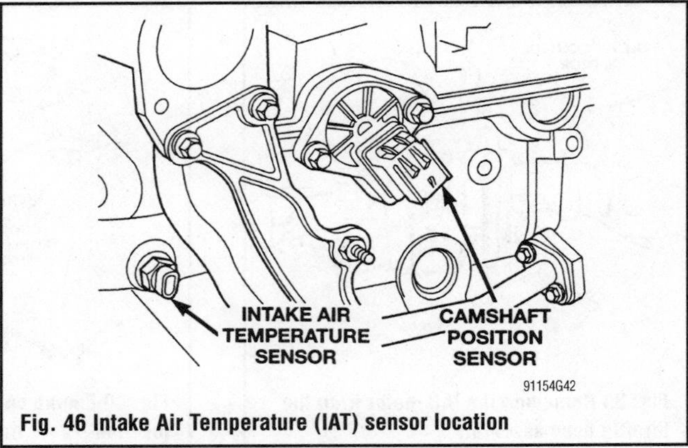

91154G42

Fig. 46 Intake Air Temperature (IAT) sensor location

REMOVAL & INSTALLATION

➧ **See Figures 40, 41 and 42**

On the 2.4L engine, the coolant temperature sensor threads into the top of the thermostat housing. On the 3.0L, 3.3L and 3.8L engines, the coolant temperature sensor is installed next to the thermostat housing.

⁂ CAUTION

Hot, pressurized coolant can cause injury by scalding. Cooling system must be partially drained before removing the coolant temperature sensor.

1. Locate the engine coolant temperature sensor on the engine.
2. Disconnect the negative battery cable.
3. Drain the engine coolant below the level of the sensor.
4. Disconnect the sensor electrical harness.
5. Using a deep-well socket or wrench, loosen and remove the sensor from the engine.

To install:

➡New coolant temperature sensors come with sealant already applied to the threads.

6. Install the sensor in the vehicle and tighten securely. Tighten the sensor to 60 inch lbs. (7 Nm).
7. Attach the electrical connector to the sensor.
8. Refill the cooling system.
9. Connect the negative battery cable.
10. Start the engine, allow it to reach operating temperature and check for leaks.
11. Check for proper sensor operation.

Intake Air Temperature (IAT) Sensor

➡Only the 2.4L engine is equipped with the Intake Air Temperature (IAT) sensor.

OPERATION

➧ **See Figure 46**

The IAT sensor threads into the intake manifold, where it measures the temperature of the intake air as it enters the engine. The sensor is a Negative Temperature Coefficient (NTC) thermistor-type sensor (resistance varies inversely with temperature). This means at high temperatures, resistance decreases and so the voltage will be low. At cold temperatures, the resistance is high and so the voltage will also be high. This allows the sensor to provide an analog voltage signal to the PCM. The PCM uses this signal to compensate for changes in air density due to temperature.

TESTING

➧ **See Figures 46 and 47**

1. Visually check the connector, making sure it is attached properly and all of the terminals are straight, tight and free of corrosion.
2. With the engine **OFF**, turn the ignition key to the **ON** position.

➡Do not allow more than 5 minutes delay between the next 2 steps.

3. Using a DRB, or equivalent scan tool, read the information on the Intake Air Temperature (IAT) sensor and record the reading.
4. Turn the ignition switch **OFF**.
5. Remove the IAT sensor.
6. Using a temperature probe, quickly measure intake temperature inside the sensor opening.
7. Replace the IAT sensor if the scan tool reading is NOT within 10° of the probe reading.
8. Using a DRB, or equivalent scan tool, read the IAT sensor voltage.
9. If the voltage reading measures outside of the 0.5–4.5 volt range, disengage the IAT sensor connector.
10. Using the scan tool, read the IAT sensor voltage.
11. If the voltage reading measures greater than 4 volts, replace the IAT sensor.
12. Connect a jumper wire between the IAT signal and sensor ground circuits, then, along with the scan tool, read the sensor voltage.
13. If the voltage reading measures less than 1 volt, replace the IAT sensor.

REMOVAL & INSTALLATION

➧ **See Figure 46**

➡Only the 2.4L engine utilizes an Intake Air Temperature (IAT) sensor.

1. Disconnect the negative battery cable.
2. Detach the electrical connector from the IAT sensor, which threads into the intake manifold plenum.
3. Remove the sensor from the vehicle.

To install:

4. Install the sensor into the intake manifold. Tighten the sensor to 20 ft. lbs. (28 Nm).
5. Attach the sensor electrical connector.
6. Connect the negative battery cable.

Manifold Absolute Pressure Sensor

OPERATION

➧ **See Figures 48, 49 and 50**

The PCM supplies 5 volts of direct current to the Manifold Absolute Pressure (MAP) sensor. The MAP sensor then converts the intake manifold pressure into voltage. The PCM monitors the MAP sensor output voltage. As vacuum

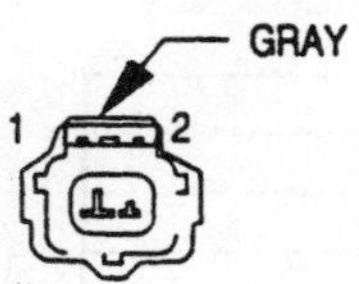

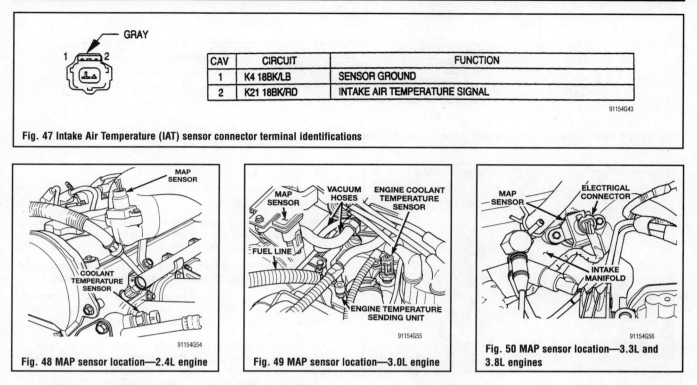

CAV	CIRCUIT	FUNCTION
1	K4 18BK/LB	SENSOR GROUND
2	K21 18BK/RD	INTAKE AIR TEMPERATURE SIGNAL

91154G43

Fig. 47 Intake Air Temperature (IAT) sensor connector terminal identifications

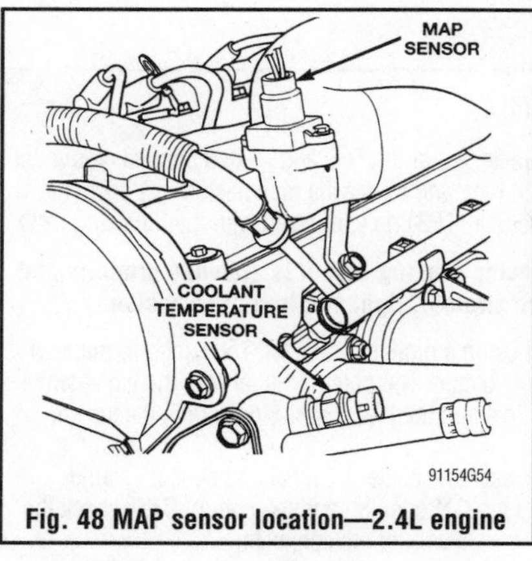

Fig. 48 MAP sensor location—2.4L engine

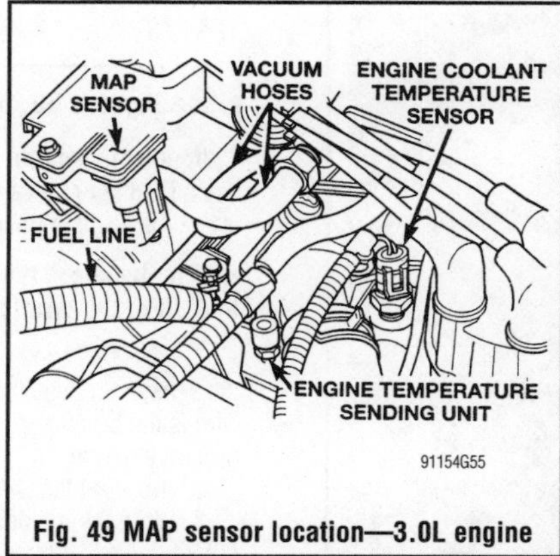

Fig. 49 MAP sensor location—3.0L engine

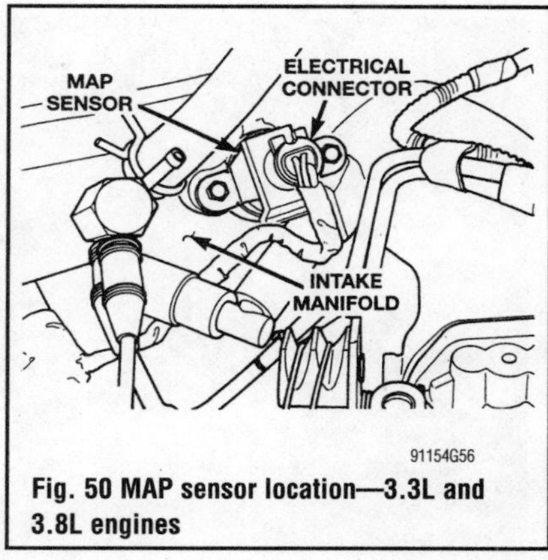

Fig. 50 MAP sensor location—3.3L and 3.8L engines

increases, the MAP sensor voltage decreases proportionately. Also, as vacuum decreases, the MAP sensor voltage increases proportionally.

With the ignition key **ON**, before the engine is started, the PCM determines atmospheric air pressure from the MAP sensor voltage. While the engine operates, the PCM figures out intake manifold pressure from the MAP sensor voltage. Based on the MAP sensor voltage and inputs from other sensors, the PCM adjusts spark advance and the air/fuel ratio. The MAP sensor is mounted to the intake manifold, near the throttle body inlet to the manifold. The sensor connects electrically to the PCM.

TESTING

See Figures 51, 52, 53 and 54

WARNING

When testing the MAP sensor, make sure the harness wires do not become damaged by the test meter probes.

1. Visually check the connector, making sure it is attached properly and that all of the terminals are straight, tight and free of corrosion.
2. Test the MAP sensor output voltage at the sensor connector between terminals B and C (2.4L, 3.3L and 3.8L engines), or A and B (3.0L engine).
3. With the ignition switch **ON** and the engine not running, the output voltage should be 4–5 volts. The voltage should fall to 1.5–2.1 volts with a hot, neutral idle speed condition. If OK, go to the next step. If not OK, go to Step 5.
4. Test the PCM terminal 36 for the same voltage described in the previous step to make sure the wire harness is OK. Repair as necessary.
5. Test the MAP sensor ground circuit at the sensor connector terminal A (2.4L, 3.3L and 3.8L engines) or C (3.0L engine) and PCM terminal 43. If OK, go to the next step. If not OK, repair as necessary.
6. Test the MAP sensor supply voltage between the sensor connector terminals A and B (2.4L, 3.3L and 3.8L engines) or A and C (3.0L engine) with the ignition key in the **ON** position. The voltage should be about 4.5–5.5 volts.
7. There should also be 4.5–5.5 volts at terminal 61 of the PCM. If OK, replace the MAP sensor.
8. If not, repair or replace the wire harness as required.

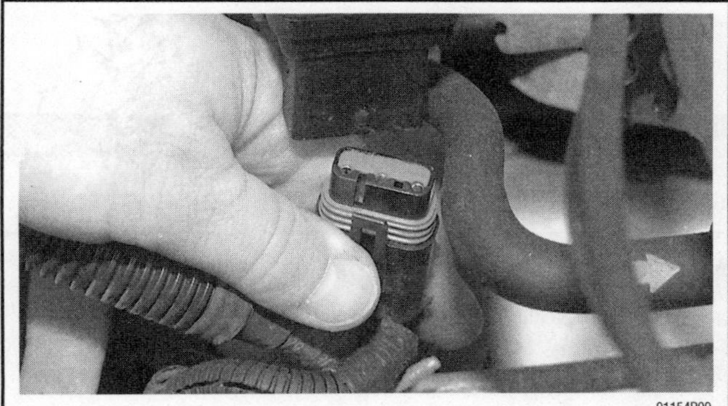

Fig. 51 Disengage the MAP sensor connector—3.0L engine shown

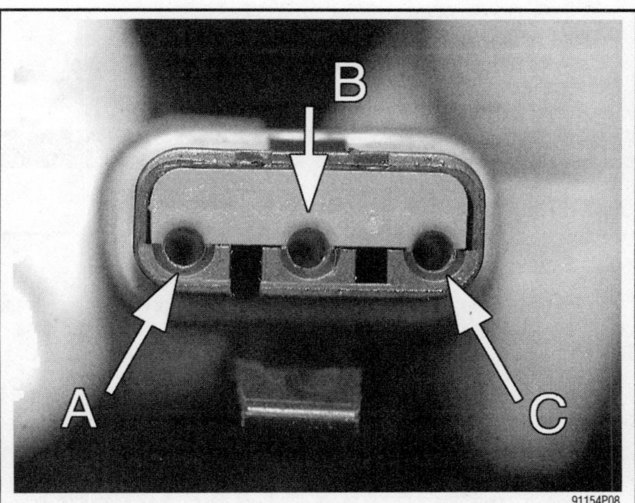

Fig. 52 MAP sensor connector terminal identifications: (A) 5-volt supply, (B) sensor signal, (C) ground—3.0L engine shown

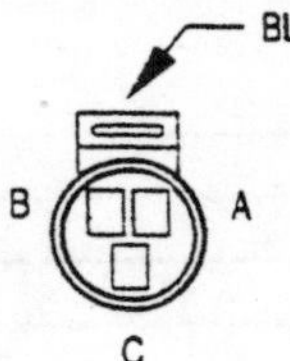

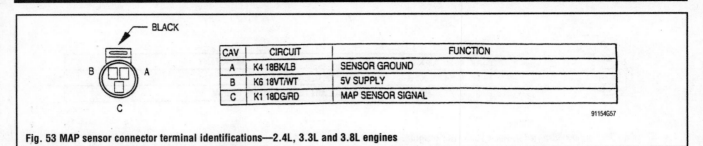

CAV	CIRCUIT	FUNCTION
A	K4 18BK/LB	SENSOR GROUND
B	K6 18VT/WT	5V SUPPLY
C	K1 18DG/RD	MAP SENSOR SIGNAL

91154G57

Fig. 53 MAP sensor connector terminal identifications—2.4L, 3.3L and 3.8L engines

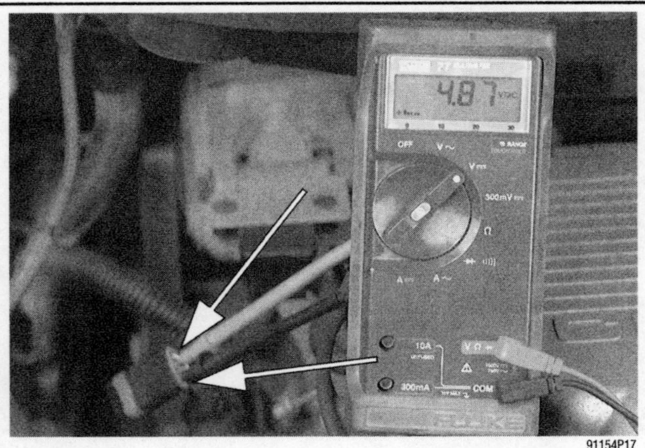

91154P17

Fig. 54 Using a digital volt-ohmmeter, test the MAP sensor voltage—3.0L engine shown

REMOVAL & INSTALLATION

See Figures 48, 49, 50 and 51

➡The MAP sensor is mounted on the intake manifold near the throttle body inlet to the manifold.

1. Disconnect the negative battery cable.
2. On the 3.0L engine only, disconnect the vacuum hose from the MAP sensor.
3. Detach the electrical connector from the MAP sensor.
4. Unfasten the mounting screws, then remove the MAP sensor from the vehicle.

To install:

5. Install the sensor onto the intake manifold and tighten the mounting screws to 35 inch lbs. (4 Nm).
6. Attach the sensor electrical connector.
7. On the 3.0L engine, connect the vacuum hose to the MAP sensor.
8. Connect the negative battery cable.

Throttle Position Sensor

OPERATION

See Figures 34, 35 and 36

The Throttle Position Sensor (TPS) is mounted to the side of the throttle body and connects to the throttle blade shaft. The TPS is a variable resistor that provides the PCM with an input signal (voltage). The signal represents throttle blade position. As the position of the throttle blade changes, the resistance of the TPS changes.

The PCM supplies about 5 volts of DC current to the TPS. The TPS output voltage (input signal to the PCM) represents throttle blade position. The TPS output voltage to the PCM varies from about 0.5 volt at idle to a maximum of 4.0 volts at wide open throttle.

Along with inputs from other sensors, the PCM uses the TPS input to determine current engine operating conditions. The PCM also adjusts fuel injector pulse width and ignition timing based on these inputs.

TESTING

See Figures 55, 56 and 57

In order to perform a complete test of the TPS and related circuits, you must use a DRB® or equivalent scan tool, and follow the manufacturer's directions. To check the Throttle Position Sensor (TPS) only, proceed with the following tests.

➡Visually check the connector, making sure it is attached properly and that all of the terminals are straight, tight and free of corrosion.

1. The TPS can be tested using a digital ohmmeter. The center terminal of the sensor supplies the output voltage. The outer terminal with the violet/white wire is the 5-volt supply terminal and the black/light blue wire is the sensor ground terminal.
2. Connect the DVOM between the center terminal and sensor ground.
3. With the ignition key to the **ON** position and the engine **OFF**, check the output voltage at the center terminal wire of the connector.
4. Check the output voltage at idle and at Wide Open Throttle (WOT):
   - For 1996 vehicles at idle, the TPS output voltage should be greater than 0.35 volt (0.4 volt for the 2.4L engine). At WOT, the output voltage should be less than 4.5 volts (3.8 volts for the 2.4L engine).
   - For 1997–99 vehicles at idle, the TPS output voltage should be about 0.38–1.20 volts. At WOT, the output voltage should be about 3.1–4.4 volts.
5. The output voltage should gradually increase as the throttle plate moves slowly from idle to WOT.
6. If voltage measures outside these values, replace the TPS.
7. Before replacing the TPS, check for spread terminals and also inspect the PCM connections.

REMOVAL & INSTALLATION

See Figures 34, 35, 36 and 58

1. Disconnect the negative battery cable.
2. Detach the electrical connector from the TPS.
3. Unfasten the mounting screws, then remove the TPS from the throttle body.

To install:

4. Install the TPS sensor onto the throttle shaft.
5. Install the sensor mounting screws and tighten to 17 inch lbs. (2 Nm).

➡After installing the TPS, the throttle plate should be closed. If the throttle plate is open, install the sensor on the other side of the tabs in the socket.

6. Attach the electrical connector to the TPS.
7. Connect the negative battery cable.

Camshaft Position Sensor

OPERATION

See Figures 59, 60 and 61

The camshaft position sensor (along with the crankshaft position sensor) provides inputs to the PCM to determine fuel injection synchronization and cylinder identification. From these inputs, the PCM determines crankshaft position.

The 3.0L engine is equipped with a camshaft driven mechanical distributor, which is equipped with an internal camshaft position (fuel sync) sensor.

CAV	CIRCUIT	FUNCTION
1	K4 18BK/LB	SENSOR GROUND
2	K22 18OR/DB	TPS SIGNAL
3	K6 18VT/WT	5 VOLT SUPPLY

91154G45

Fig. 55 Throttle Position Sensor (TPS) connector terminal identifications

Fig. 56 TPS output voltage should be greater than 0.35 volt (0.4 volt for the 2.4L engine)

Fig. 57 At WOT (Wide Open Throttle), the output voltage should be less than 4.5 volts (3.8 volts for the 2.4L engine)

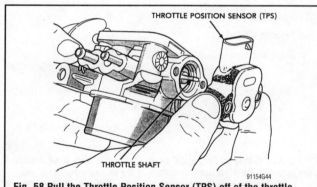

THROTTLE POSITION SENSOR (TPS)

THROTTLE SHAFT

91154G44

Fig. 58 Pull the Throttle Position Sensor (TPS) off of the throttle shaft

On the 2.4L engine, the camshaft position sensor mounts to the rear of the cylinder head. The sensor also serves as a thrust plate to control end-play of the camshaft.

On 3.3L and 3.8L engines, the camshaft position sensor mounts to the top of the timing case cover, in which the bottom of the sensor is positioned above the camshaft sprocket.

TESTING

See Figures 62 and 63

To test this sensor, you will need the use of an oscilloscope.

Visually check the connector, making sure it is attached properly and that all of the terminals are straight, tight and free of corrosion.

The output voltage of a properly operating camshaft position sensor switches from high (5.0 volts) to low (0.3 volts). By connecting an oscilloscope to the sensor output circuit, you can view the square wave pattern produced by the voltage swing.

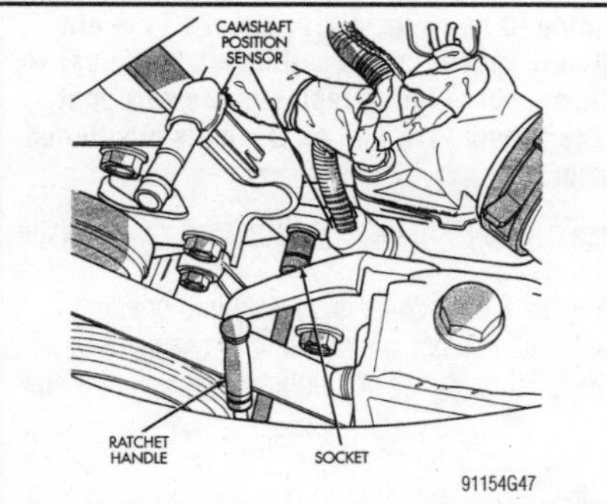

Fig. 59 Camshaft position sensor location/mounting bolt removal—3.3L and 3.8L engines

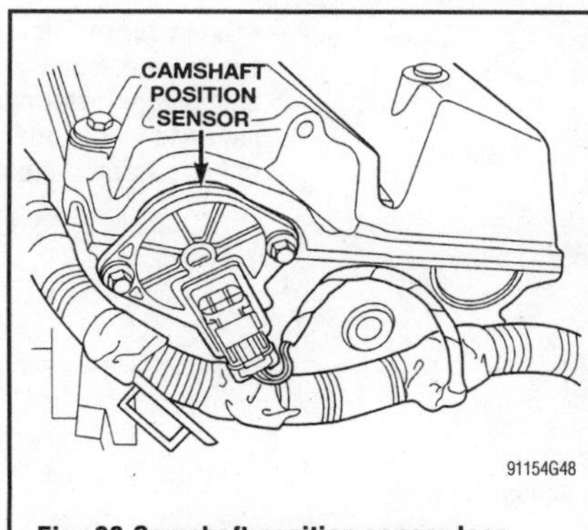

Fig. 60 Camshaft position sensor location—2.4L engine

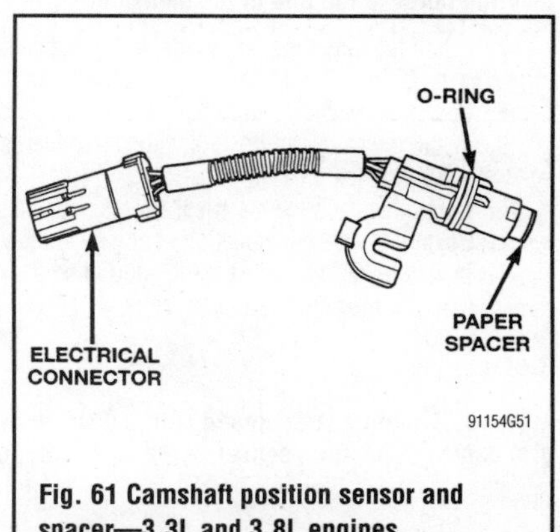

Fig. 61 Camshaft position sensor and spacer—3.3L and 3.8L engines

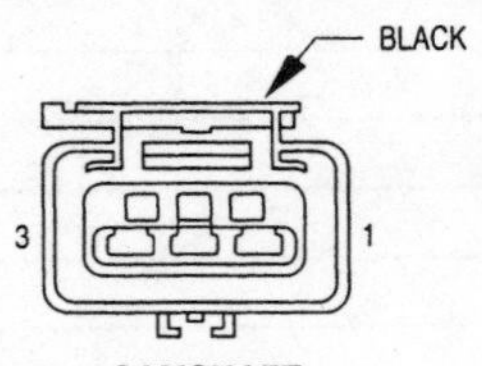

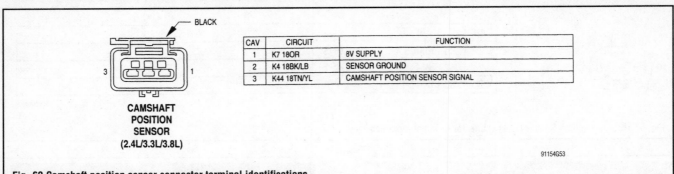

CAV	CIRCUIT	FUNCTION
1	K7 18OR	8V SUPPLY
2	K4 18BK/LB	SENSOR GROUND
3	K44 18TN/YL	CAMSHAFT POSITION SENSOR SIGNAL

91154G53

Fig. 62 Camshaft position sensor connector terminal identifications

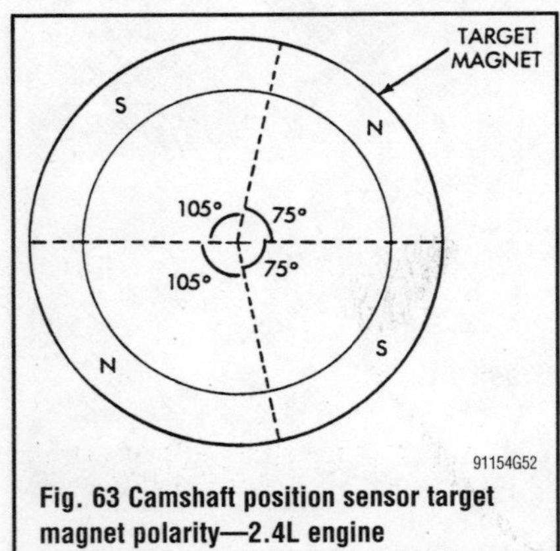

Fig. 63 Camshaft position sensor target magnet polarity—2.4L engine

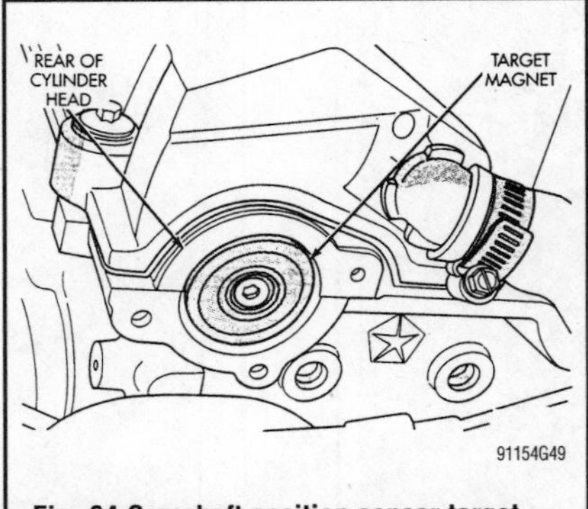

Fig. 64 Camshaft position sensor target magnet

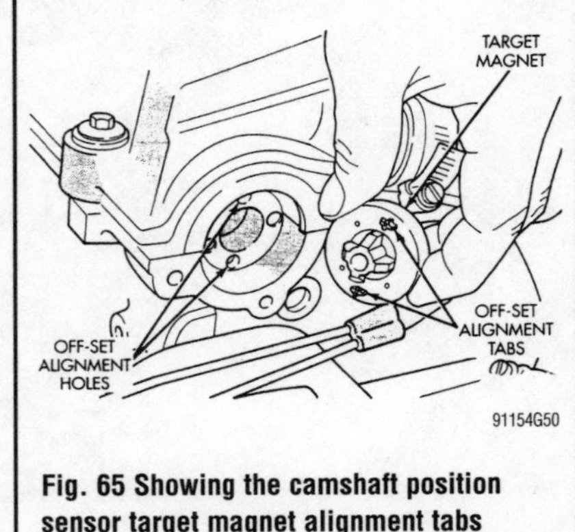

Fig. 65 Showing the camshaft position sensor target magnet alignment tabs

REMOVAL & INSTALLATION

2.4L Engine

➧ See Figures 60, 64 and 65

1. Disconnect the negative battery cable.
2. Disconnect the filtered air tube from the throttle body and air cleaner housing. Disconnect the air tube from the oil separator hose. Remove the filtered air tube.
3. Remove the air cleaner inlet tube from the vehicle.
4. Detach the electrical harness connector from the camshaft position sensor.
5. Unfasten the camshaft position sensor mounting screws, then remove the sensor.
6. Loosen the screw/bolt attaching the target magnet to the rear of the camshaft.

To install:

➡The target magnet has 2 locating dowels which fit into the machined locating holes in the end of the camshaft.

7. Install the target magnet in the end of the camshaft. Tighten the mounting screw to 50 inch lbs. (7 Nm).
8. Install a new O-ring onto the sensor.
9. Install the camshaft position sensor. Tighten the sensor mounting screws to 85 inch lbs. (10 Nm).
10. Carefully attach the electrical harness connector to the camshaft position sensor. Be careful, since installation at any angle may damage the pins.
11. Install the air cleaner inlet tube and filtered air tube.
12. Connect the negative battery cable.

3.0L Engine

➡The 3.0L engine is equipped with a distributor unit containing an integral camshaft position sensor. If the camshaft position sensor fails, the distributor assembly must be replaced. For distributor service, refer to Section 2.

3.3L and 3.8L Engines

➧ See Figures 59 and 61

1. Disconnect the negative battery cable.
2. Detach the electrical harness connector from the camshaft position sensor.
3. Unfasten the camshaft position sensor mounting bolt. There is a hole in the bracket for tool access to the sensor mounting bolt.
4. Rotate the sensor away from the engine block.
5. Pull the camshaft position sensor up out of the chain case cover. Do not pull on the sensor wire.

➡There is an O-ring on the sensor case. The O-ring may make removal of the sensor difficult. A light tap on top of the sensor prior to removal may reduce the force needed for removal. Inspect the O-ring for damage and replace if necessary.

To install:

➡If the sensor removed is going to be re-installed, clean off the old spacer on the sensor face. A new spacer must be attached to the sensor face before installation. If the sensor is being replaced, be sure that a paper spacer is attached to the sensor face and an O-ring is positioned in the groove of the new sensor.

6. Apply 1–2 drops of clean engine oil to the O-ring prior to installing the sensor.
7. Install the sensor into the chain case cover and rotate into position.
8. Push down on the sensor until contact is made with the camshaft gear. While holding the sensor in this position, install and tighten the mounting bolt to 10 ft. lbs. (14 Nm).
9. Attach the electrical harness connector to the camshaft position sensor.
10. Connect the negative battery cable.

Crankshaft Position Sensor

OPERATION

See Figures 66 and 67

The PCM determines what cylinder to fire from the crankshaft position sensor input and the camshaft position sensor input. On 4-cylinder engines, the second crankshaft counterweight has two sets of four timing reference notches, including a 60° signature notch. From the crankshaft position sensor input, the PCM determines engine speed and crankshaft angle (position). On 6-cylinder engines, this sensor is a Hall effect device that detects notches in the flexplate.

The notches generate pulses from high to low in the crankshaft position sensor output voltage. When a metal portion of the notches line up with the crankshaft position sensor, the sensor output voltage goes low (less than 0.5 volts). When a notch aligns with the sensor, voltage goes high (5.0 volts). As a group of notches pass under the sensor, the output voltage switches from low (metal) to high (notch), then back to low.

If available, an oscilloscope can display the square wave patterns of each voltage pulse. From the width of the output voltage pulses, the PCM calculates engine speed. The width of the pulses represent the amount of time the output voltage stays high before switching back to low. The period of time the sensor output voltage stays high before switching back to low is referred to as pulse width. The faster the engine is operating, the smaller the pulse width on the oscilloscope.

On 4-cylinder engines, the crankshaft position sensor is mounted to the engine block behind the alternator, just above the oil filter. On 6-cylinder engines, the crankshaft position sensor is mounted on the transaxle housing, above the vehicle speed sensor.

TESTING

See Figure 68

To test this sensor, you will need the use of an oscilloscope.

Visually check the connector, making sure it is attached properly and that all of the terminals are straight, tight and free of corrosion. Also inspect the notches in the crankshaft (4-cylinder) or flywheel (6-cylinder) for damage, and replace if necessary.

The output voltage of a properly operating crankshaft position sensor switches from high (5.0 volts) to low (0.3 volts). By connecting an oscilloscope to the sensor output circuit, you can view the square wave pattern produced by the voltage swing.

REMOVAL & INSTALLATION

See Figures 69, 70, 71, 72 and 73

On the 2.4L engine, the crankshaft position sensor is mounted to the engine block behind the alternator, just above the oil filter. On the 3.0L, 3.3L and 3.8L engines, the crankshaft position sensor is mounted on the transaxle housing, above the vehicle speed sensor.

1. Disconnect the negative battery cable.
2. Raise and safely support the vehicle.
3. Detach the crankshaft position sensor electrical connector.
4. Unfasten the sensor mounting screw, then remove the sensor from the vehicle by pulling it straight out.

To install:

If the sensor removed is going to be re-installed, clean off the old spacer on the sensor face. A new spacer must be attached to the sensor face before installation. If the sensor is being replaced, be sure that a paper spacer is attached to the sensor face.

5. Install sensor and push the sensor in until contact is made. While holding the sensor in this position, install and tighten the mounting bolt to 105 inch lbs. (12 Nm).
6. Attach the crankshaft position sensor electrical connector.
7. Lower the vehicle.
8. Connect the negative battery cable.

Knock Sensor

All engines covered in this book, except the 3.0L engine, utilize a knock sensor.

OPERATION

See Figures 74 and 75

The knock sensor is threaded into the side of the cylinder block, in front of the starter. When the knock sensor detects a knock in one of the cylinders, it

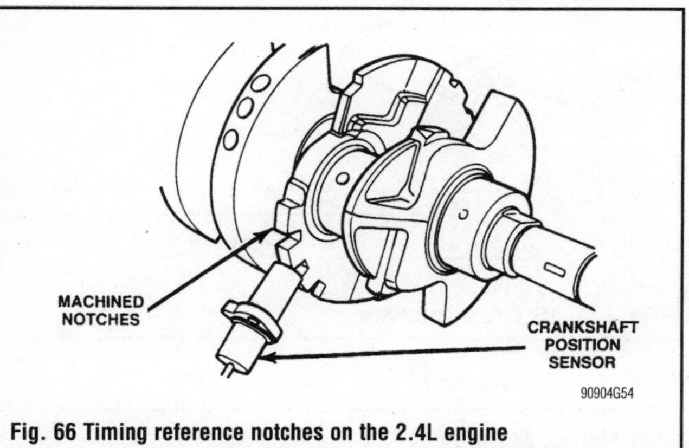

Fig. 66 Timing reference notches on the 2.4L engine

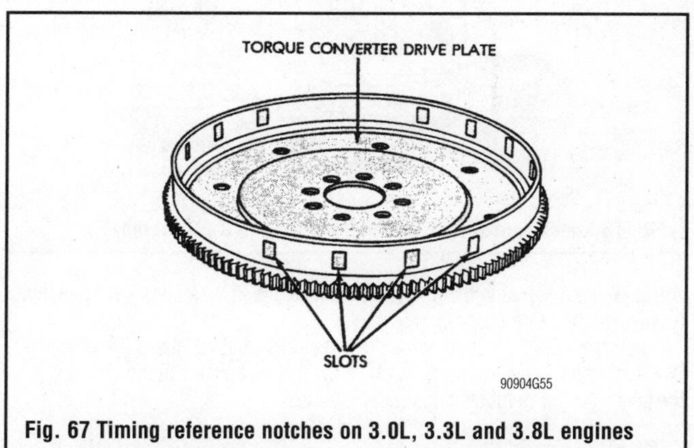

Fig. 67 Timing reference notches on 3.0L, 3.3L and 3.8L engines

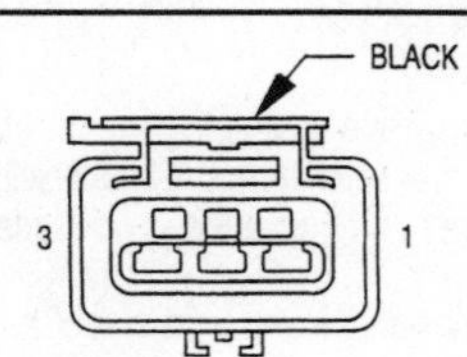

CAV	CIRCUIT	FUNCTION
1	K7 18OR	8V SUPPLY
2	K4 18BK/LB	SENSOR GROUND
3	K24 18GY/BK	CRANKSHAFT POSITION SENSOR SIGNAL

91154G19

Fig. 68 Crankshaft position sensor connector terminal identifications

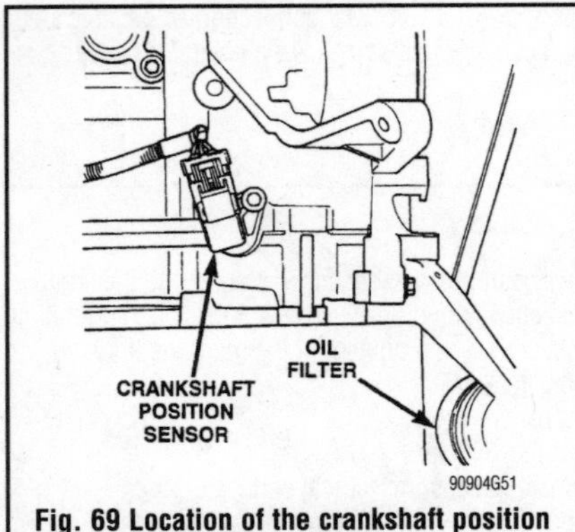

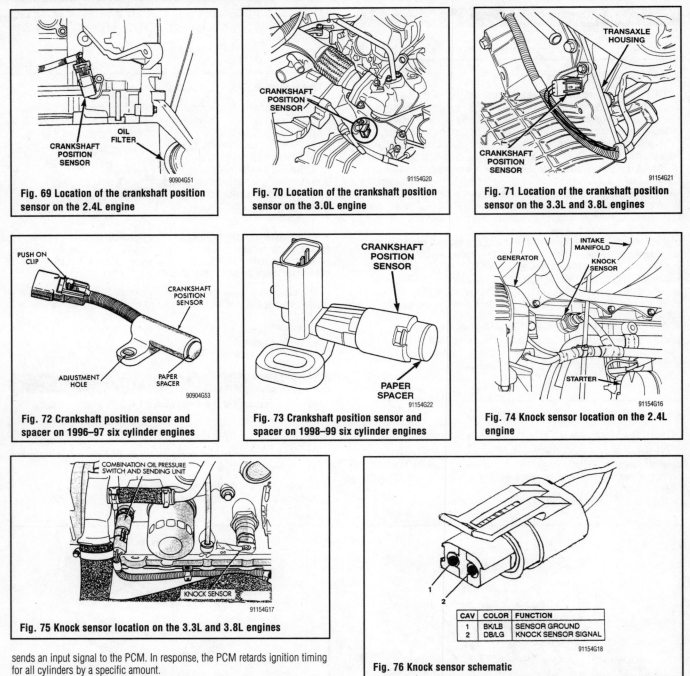

Fig. 69 Location of the crankshaft position sensor on the 2.4L engine

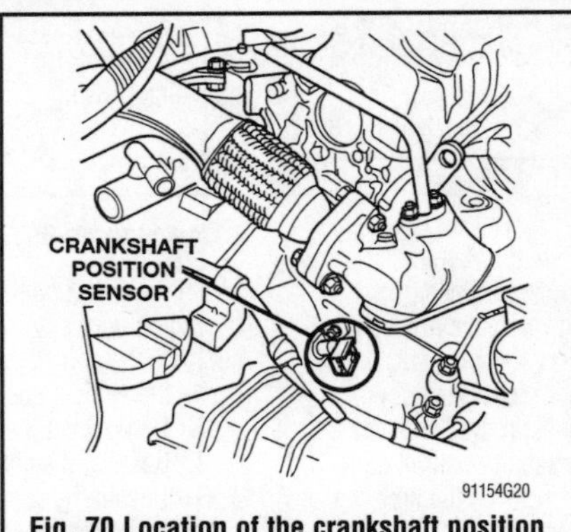

Fig. 70 Location of the crankshaft position sensor on the 3.0L engine

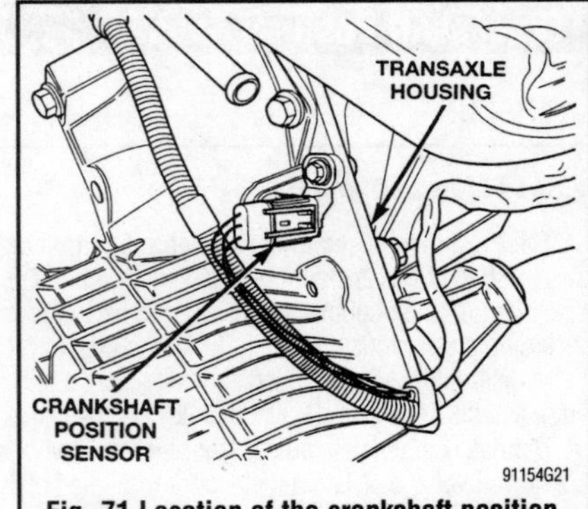

Fig. 71 Location of the crankshaft position sensor on the 3.3L and 3.8L engines

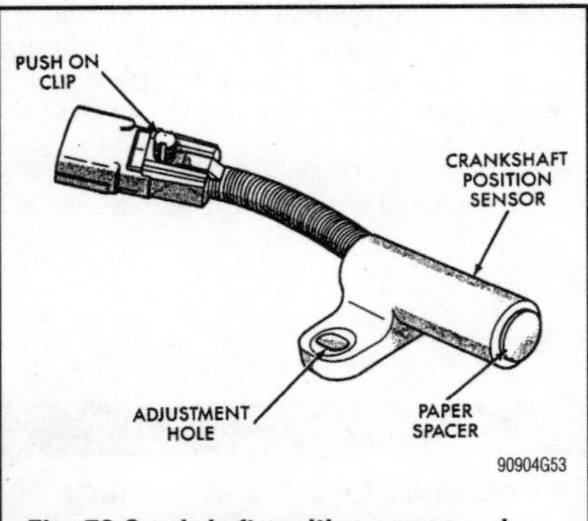

Fig. 72 Crankshaft position sensor and spacer on 1996–97 six cylinder engines

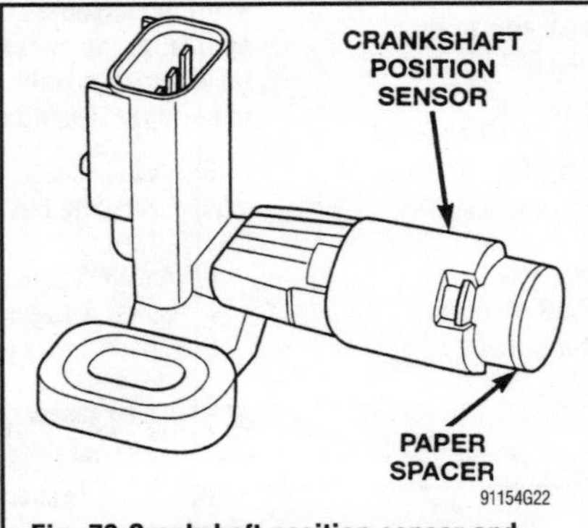

Fig. 73 Crankshaft position sensor and spacer on 1998–99 six cylinder engines

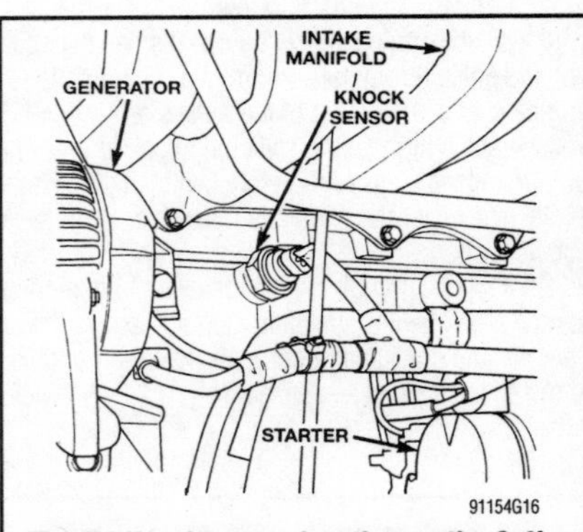

Fig. 74 Knock sensor location on the 2.4L engine

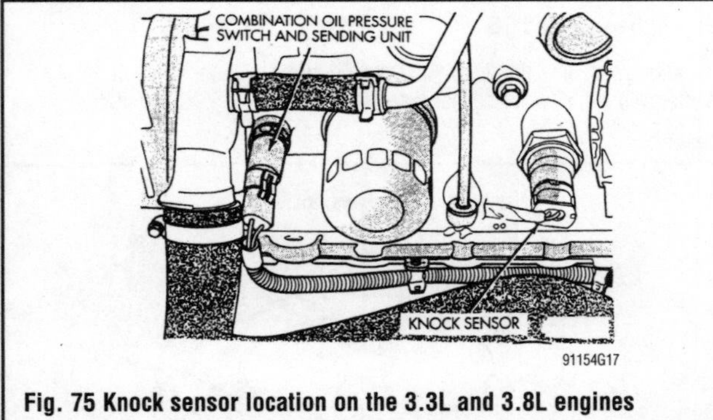

Fig. 75 Knock sensor location on the 3.3L and 3.8L engines

sends an input signal to the PCM. In response, the PCM retards ignition timing for all cylinders by a specific amount.

Knock sensors contain a piezoelectric material which sends an input signal (voltage) to the PCM. As the intensity of the engine knock vibration increases, the knock sensor output voltage also increases.

TESTING

➧ **See Figure 76**

Visually check the connector, making sure it is attached properly and that all of the terminals are straight, tight and free of corrosion.

A number of factors affect the engine knock sensor. A few of these are: ignition timing, cylinder pressure, fuel octane, etc. The knock sensor produces an AC voltage whose amplitude increases with the amount of engine knock. The knock sensor can be tested with a digital voltmeter. The knock sensor output voltage should measure between 80mV and 4 volts with the engine running between 576 and 2208 rpm. If the output falls outside of this range, a Diagnostic Trouble Code (DTC) will set.

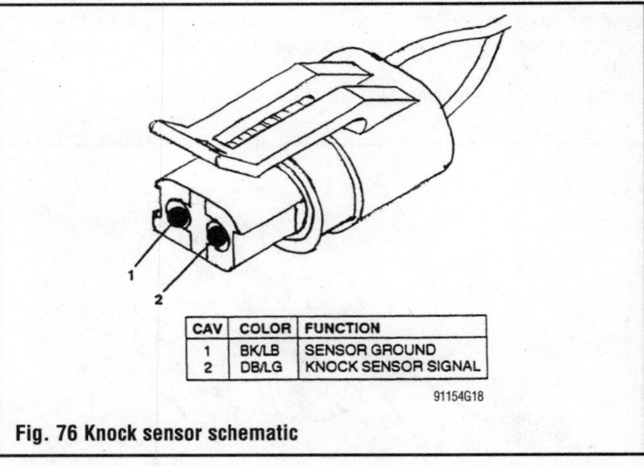

CAV	COLOR	FUNCTION
1	BK/LB	SENSOR GROUND
2	DB/LG	KNOCK SENSOR SIGNAL

Fig. 76 Knock sensor schematic

REMOVAL & INSTALLATION

➧ **See Figures 74 and 75**

➡ **The knock sensor is threaded into the side of the cylinder block, in front of the starter.**

1. Disconnect the negative battery cable.
2. Unplug the electrical connector from the knock sensor.
3. Use a crow's foot wrench to remove the knock sensor from the vehicle.

To install:

4. Install the sensor in the vehicle and tighten to 7 ft. lbs. (10 Nm). Make sure not to over or under-tighten the sensor, as is could adversely affect knock sensor performance, causing improper spark control.
5. Attach the knock sensor electrical connector.
6. Connect the negative battery cable.

COMPONENT LOCATIONS

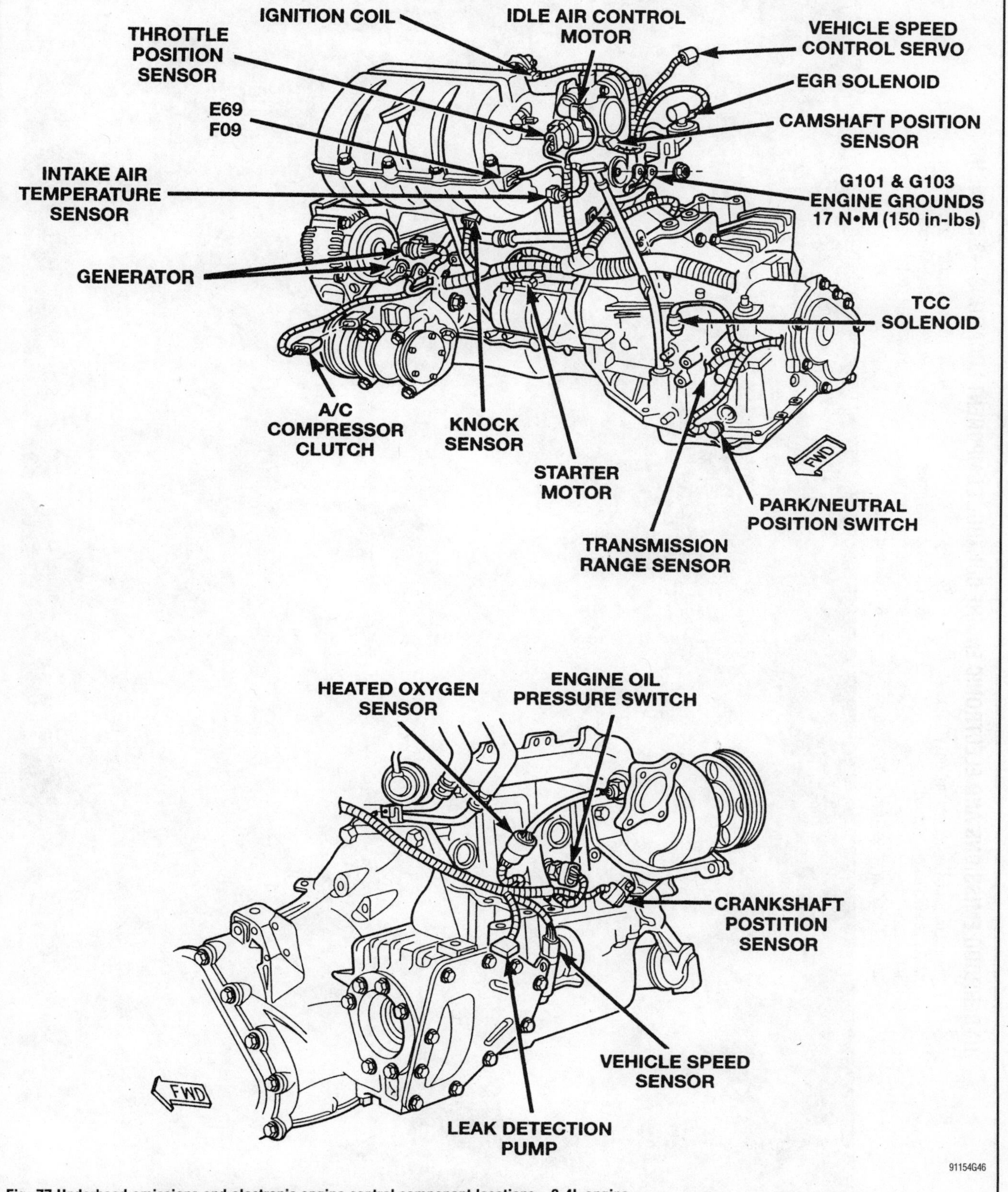

IGNITION COIL
IDLE AIR CONTROL MOTOR
THROTTLE POSITION SENSOR
VEHICLE SPEED CONTROL SERVO
EGR SOLENOID
E69
F09
CAMSHAFT POSITION SENSOR
INTAKE AIR TEMPERATURE SENSOR
G101 & G103 ENGINE GROUNDS 17 N•M (150 in-lbs)
GENERATOR
TCC SOLENOID
A/C COMPRESSOR CLUTCH
KNOCK SENSOR
STARTER MOTOR
FWD
PARK/NEUTRAL POSITION SWITCH
TRANSMISSION RANGE SENSOR
HEATED OXYGEN SENSOR
ENGINE OIL PRESSURE SWITCH
CRANKSHAFT POSTITION SENSOR
FWD
VEHICLE SPEED SENSOR
LEAK DETECTION PUMP
91154G46

Fig. 77 Underhood emissions and electronic engine control component locations—2.4L engine

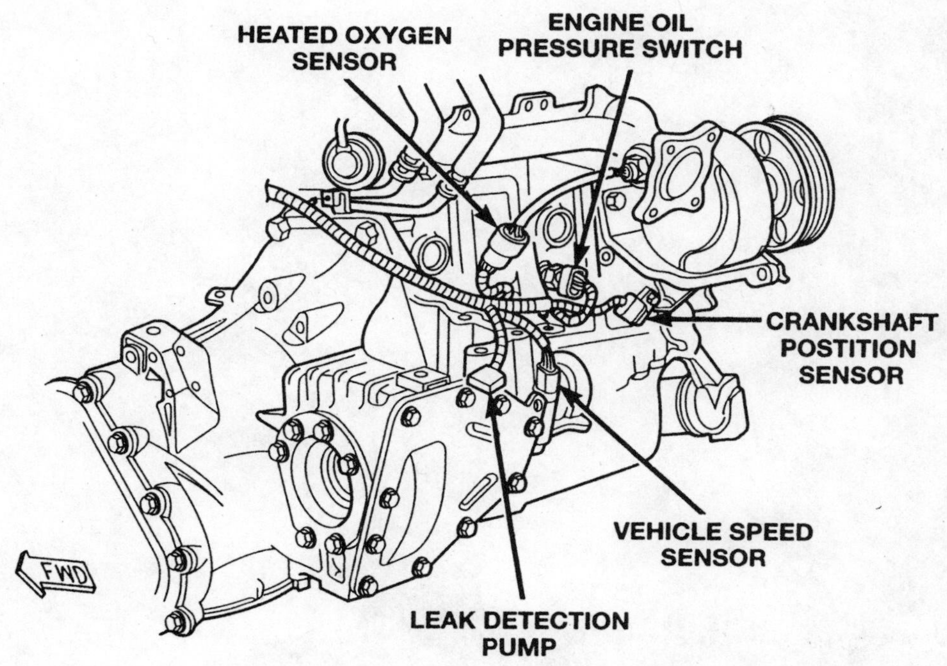

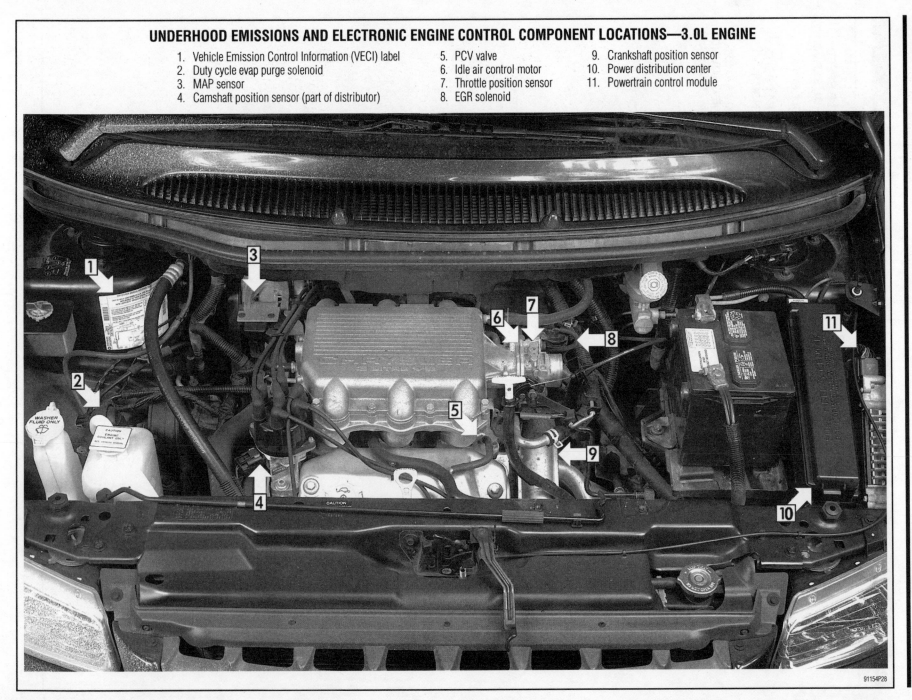

UNDERHOOD EMISSIONS AND ELECTRONIC ENGINE CONTROL COMPONENT LOCATIONS—3.0L ENGINE

1. Vehicle Emission Control Information (VECI) label
2. Duty cycle evap purge solenoid
3. MAP sensor
4. Camshaft position sensor (part of distributor)
5. PCV valve
6. Idle air control motor
7. Throttle position sensor
8. EGR solenoid
9. Crankshaft position sensor
10. Power distribution center
11. Powertrain control module

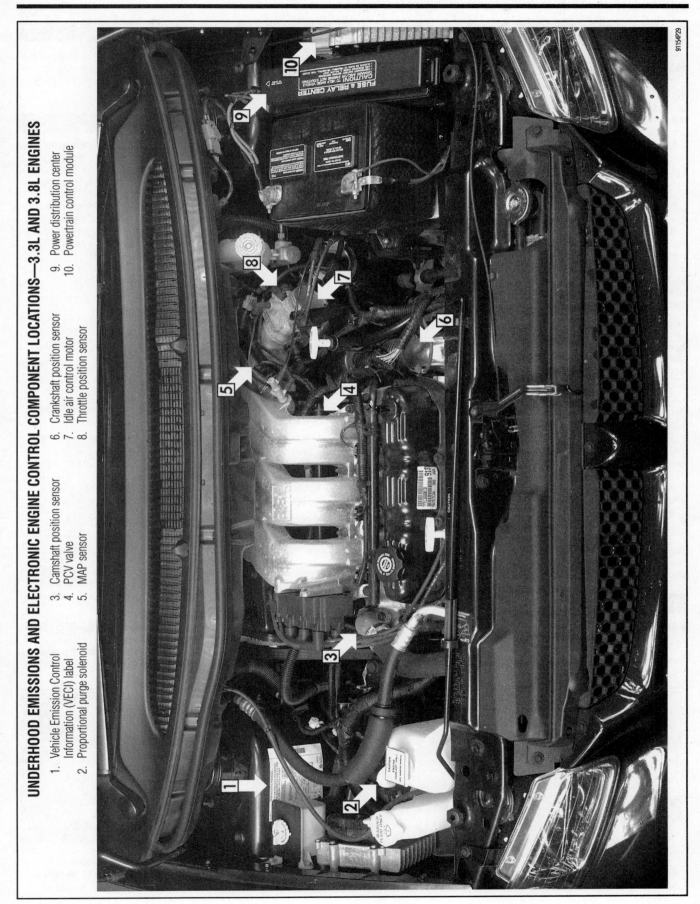

UNDERHOOD EMISSIONS AND ELECTRONIC ENGINE CONTROL COMPONENT LOCATIONS—3.3L AND 3.8L ENGINES

1. Vehicle Emission Control Information (VECI) label
2. Proportional purge solenoid
3. Camshaft position sensor
4. PCV valve
5. MAP sensor
6. Crankshaft position sensor
7. Idle air control motor
8. Throttle position sensor
9. Power distribution center
10. Powertrain control module

91154P29

TROUBLE CODES

General Information

The Powertrain Control Module (PCM) monitors many different circuits in the fuel injection, ignition, emissions and engine systems. If the PCM senses a problem with a monitored circuit often enough to indicate an actual problem, it will store a Diagnostic Trouble Code (DTC) in the PCM's memory. If the code is applicable to a non-emission related component or system, and the problem is repaired or ceases to exist, the PCM will cancel the code after 40 engine warm-up cycles. A DTC that affects emissions will light up the Malfunction Indicator Lamp (MIL).

Certain guidelines must be met before the PCM will store a code in its memory. The criteria might be a certain range of the engine rpm, engine temperature and/or input voltage to the PCM. The PCM may not store a DTC for a monitored circuit, even though a malfunction has occurred. This may happen because one of the DTC criteria for the circuit has not been met. For example, the DTC criteria may require the PCM to monitor the circuit only when the engine operates between 750–2,000 rpm. If the sensor's output circuit shorted to ground when the engine operated above 2,400 rpm, (with a result of 0 volt input to the PCM), then no DTC would be stored, since the engine condition occurred at an engine speed above the maximum threshold of 2,000 rpm. There are various operating conditions for which the PCM monitors and sets DTC's.

➡Various diagnostic procedures may actually cause a diagnostic monitor to set a DTC. For example, disconnecting a spark plug wire to perform a spark test may set the misfire code. When a repair is completed and verified, use Chryslers DRB® or equivalent scan tool to erase all DTC's, thereby shutting off the MIL.

As a functional test, the Malfunction Indicator Lamp (MIL) lights up at the ignition key **ON** position before engine cranking. Whenever the PCM sets a DTC that affects emissions, it lights up the MIL. If a problem is detected, the PCM sends a message to the instrument cluster, illuminating the lamp. The PCM will light up the MIL only for codes that affect vehicle emissions. The MIL stays on constantly when the PCM has entered Limp-In mode or has found a failed emission component or system. The MIL stays on until the DTC is erased.

The MIL will either flash or light up constantly when the PCM detects active engine misfire. Also, the PCM may reset (turn off) the MIL when one of the following conditions occur:

- PCM does not detect the malfunction for 3 successive trips (except misfire and fuel system monitors).
- PCM does not detect a malfunction while performing three consecutive engine misfire or fuel system tests. The PCM performs these tests while the engine is operating within 375 rpm of and within 10% of the load of the operating condition at which the problem was first detected.

Diagnostic Connector

➧ **See Figure 78**

The Data Link Connector (diagnostic connector), is a 16-pin connector located inside the vehicle, under the instrument panel, near the steering column. The diagnostic connector is used as a link between the DRB® or equivalent scan tool and the PCM. The PCM communicates with the scan tool through the data link receive and transmit circuits. You can attach the scan tool to the data link connector to access any stored DTC's.

Reading Codes

On all 1996–97 minivans, you can access the DTC's in the following two ways:

- The preferred and most accurate way of reading a DTC is by using Chrysler's DRB® or equivalent scan tool. The scan tool supplies detailed diagnostic information, which can be used for more accurate and specific diagnosis of the code.
- The second way of reading DTC's is by observing the 2-digit number displayed by the Malfunction Indicator Lamp (MIL). The MIL is shown on the instrument panel as the Check Engine lamp. This method should be used as a "quick test" only. You should always use a scan tool to get the most detailed information.

On all 1998–99 minivans, the only way to retrieve DTC's is by using a DRB® or equivalent scan tool.

➡Keep in mind that DTC's are the result of a system or circuit failure, but may not directly identify the failed component(s).

READING DTC'S USING A SCAN TOOL

1. Connect Chrysler's Diagnostic Readout Box (DRB) or equivalent scan tool to the data link (diagnostic) connector. This connector is located at the lower edge of the instrument panel, near the steering column.

➡Always make sure to follow the manufacturer's instructions when using a scan tool.

2. Turn the ignition switch **ON**, and access the "Read Fault" screen with the scan tool.
3. Record all of the DTC's and "freeze frame" information shown on the scan tool.
4. Once the repairs have been completed, erase the trouble codes. Once the codes have been erased, check that the scan tool displays "normal".

READING CODES USING MIL (CHECK ENGINE) LAMP

➧ **See Figures 79 and 80**

➡Be advised that the MIL, CHECK ENGINE, or SERVICE ENGINE SOON light can only perform a limited number of functions, and it is a good idea to have the system checked with a scan tool to double check the circuit function.

1. Within a period of 5 seconds, cycle the ignition key **ON—OFF—ON—OFF—ON**.
2. Count the number of times the MIL (check engine or service engine soon lamp) on the instrument panel flashes on and off. If it is not located at the bot-

91154P14

Fig. 78 Location of the Data Link Connector (DLC)

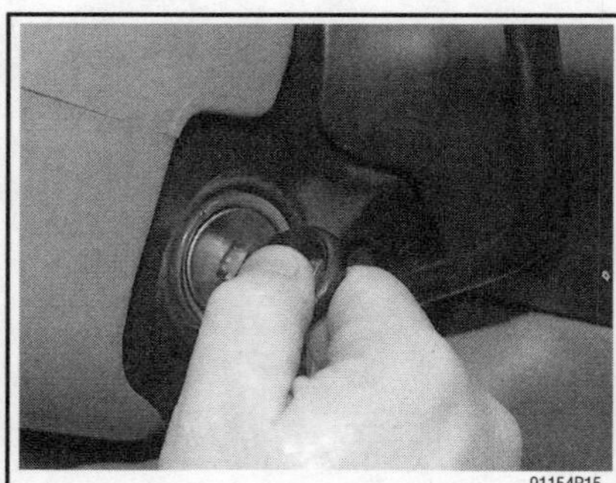

91154P15

Fig. 79 Within a 5 second period, cycle the ignition key ON—OFF—ON—OFF—ON . . .

91154P13

Fig. 80 . . . then count the number of times the SERVICE ENGINE SOON light on the instrument panel flashes on and off

tom of the instrument cluster, then it is located in the information center on the dashboard above the instrument cluster.

The number of flashes represents the trouble code. There is a short pause between the flashes representing the 1st and 2nd digits of the code. Longer pauses are used to separate individual 2-digit trouble codes.

An example of a flashed DTC is as follows:

- Lamp flashes 4 times, pauses, then flashes 6 more times. This denotes a DTC number 46.
- Lamp flashes 5 times, pauses, then flashes 5 more times. This indicates a DTC number 55. DTC 55 will always be the last code to be displayed.

Clearing Codes

Erase the DTC's with Chrysler's DRB® or equivalent scan tool, using the "Erase Trouble Code" data screen on the scan tool. Do NOT erase any DTC's until the malfunctions have been checked and repairs performed.

Code List

MIL CODES FOR 1996–97 MODELS

- **Code 11**—Intermittent loss of either camshaft or crankshaft position sensors.
- **Code 11**—Crankshaft position sensor target windows have too much variation.
- **Code 11**—No crank reference signal detected during engine cranking.
- **Code 12**—Direct battery input to PCM was disconnected within the last 50 Key-On cycles.
- **Code 13**—No variation in MAP sensor signal is detected or no difference is recognized between the engine MAP reading and the stored barometric pressure reading from start-up.
- **Code 14**—MAP sensor voltage too high or too low.
- **Code 15**—No vehicle speed sensor signal detected during road load conditions.
- **Code 17**—Closed loop temperature not reached—engine does not reach 50°F within 5 minutes with a vehicle speed signal.
- **Code 17**—Engine is cold too long—engine coolant temperature remains below normal operating temperature during vehicle travel; possible thermostat problem.
- **Code 21**—Oxygen sensor signal—neither rich or lean condition is detected from the oxygen sensor input.
- **Code 22**—Engine Coolant Temperature (ECT) sensor voltage too HIGH/LOW—ECT sensor input above or below the acceptable voltage limits.
- **Code 23**—Intake Air Temperature (IAT) sensor voltage HIGH/LOW—IAT sensor input above or below the acceptable voltage limits (2.4L engine only).
- **Code 24**—Throttle Position Sensor voltage does not agree with the MAP sensor.
- **Code 24**—TPS voltage above or below the acceptable voltage limits.
- **Code 25**—Idle Air Control (IAC) motor circuits—short or open detected in 1 or more of the IAC control circuits.
- **Code 25**—Target idle not reached—actual idle speed does not equal the target idle speed.
- **Code 27**—Fuel injector control circuit—fuel injector output driver does not respond properly to the control signal.
- **Code 31**—Evap purge solenoid circuit—an open or short detected in the duty cycle purge solenoid circuit.
- **Code 31**—Evap purge flow monitor failure—Insufficient or excessive vapor flow detected during evaporative emission system operation.
- **Code 31**—Evap leak monitor small leak detected—A small leak has been detected by the leak detection monitor.
- **Code 31**—Evap leak monitor large leak detected—leak detection monitor is unable to pressurize EVAP system, indicating a large leak.
- **Code 31**—Leak detection pump solenoid circuit—leak detection pump solenoid circuit fault (open or short).
- **Code 31**—Leak detection pump switch or mechanical fault—leak detection pump switch does not respond to input.
- **Code 31**—Evap leak monitor pinched hose found—plug or pinch found between purge solenoid and fuel tank.
- **Code 32**—Exhaust Gas Recirculation (EGR) system failure—required change in air/fuel ratio not detected during diagnostic test.
- **Code 32**—EGR solenoid circuit—open or short detected in the EGR transducer solenoid circuit.
- **Code 33**—Open or short detected in the A/C clutch relay circuit.
- **Code 33**—Air conditioner pressure sensor voltage too high—sensor input voltage is above 4.9 volts.
- **Code 33**—Air conditioner pressure sensor voltage too low—sensor input voltage is below 0.098 volt.
- **Code 34**—Speed control solenoid circuit—open or short detected in the speed control vacuum or vent solenoid circuits.
- **Code 35**—Radiator fan control relay circuit—open or short detected in the low speed radiator fan relay control circuit.
- **Code 37**—Torque converter clutch solenoid/Trans relay circuits—open or short detected in the torque converter part throttle unlock solenoid control circuit (2.4L engine w/31TH transmission and 3.0L engine only).
- **Code 37**—Torque converter clutch (no RPM drop at lockup)—relationship between engine speed and vehicle speed indicates no torque converter clutch engagement (automatic transmission only).
- **Code 37**—Park/Neutral switch stuck in PARK or in gear—incorrect input state detected for the P/N switch (automatic transmission only).
- **Code 41**—Alternator field not switching properly—open or short detected in the alternator field control circuit.
- **Code 42**—Autoshut-down (ASD) relay control circuit—open or short detected in the ASD relay circuit.
- **Code 42**—No ASD relay output voltage at the PCM—open condition detected in the ASD relay output circuit.
- **Code 42**—Fuel pump relay control circuit—open or short detected in the fuel pump relay control circuit.
- **Code 42**—Fuel level sending unit voltage too low—open circuit between PCM and fuel gauge sending unit.
- **Code 42**—Fuel level sending unit voltage too high—circuit shorted to voltage between PCM and fuel gauge sending unit.
- **Code 42**—No movement of the fuel level sending unit detected over miles.
- **Code 43**—Ignition coil #1, 2, or 3 primary circuits—peak primary circuit current not achieved within the maximum allowable dwell time.
- **Code 43**—Engine cylinder misfire—engine cylinder misfire detected in one or more cylinders.
- **Code 44**—Battery temperature sensor voltage too HIGH/LOW—battery temperature sensor input voltage above or below an acceptable range.
- **Code 45**—EATX controller DTC present—an automatic transmission input DTC has been set in the transmission controller.
- **Code 45**—Park/Neutral switch failure—incorrect input state detected for the park/neutral switch.
- **Code 46**—Charging system voltage too high—battery voltage sense input above target charging voltage during engine operation.
- **Code 47**—Charging system voltage too low—battery voltage sense input below target charging voltage during engine operation. Also, no significant change detected in battery voltage during active test of the alternator output circuit.
- **Code 51**—Fuel system lean—a lean air/fuel mixture has been indicated by an abnormally rich correction factor.
- **Code 52**—Fuel system rich—a rich air/fuel mixture has been indicated by an abnormally lean correction factor.
- **Code 53**—Internal controller failure or PCM failure SPI communications—PCM internal fault condition detected.
- **Code 54**—No cam signal at the PCM—No camshaft position sensor signal detected during engine cranking.
- **Code 55**—Completion of fault code display on Check Engine lamp.
- **Code 61**—Barometric pressure out of range (Key-On)—MAP sensor has a baro reading below an acceptable value.
- **Code 62**—PCM failure SRI mileage not stored—unsuccessful attempt to update EMR mileage in the PCM EEPROM.
- **Code 63**—PCM failure EEPROM write denied—unsuccessful attempt to write to an EEPROM location by the PCM.
- **Code 64**—Catalytic converter efficiency failure—catalyst efficiency below required level.
- **Code 64**—CNG system pressure too high—compressed natural gas pressure sensor reading above acceptable voltage (if equipped).
- **Code 65**—Brake switch sense circuit—No release of brake switch seen after too many accelerations or no brake switch activation seen on several DECELS to RESET (OMPH).

- **Code 66**—No CCD messages recieved from the Body Control Module (BCM) or the Transmission Control Module (TCM).
- **Code 71**—5 Volt supply output too low—5 volt output from the regulator does not meet minimum requirement.
- **Code 72**—Right rear (or just) catalyst efficiency failure—catalyst efficiency below required level.
- **Code 77**—Speed control power relay; or speed control 12V driver circuit—malfunction detected with power feed to speed control servo solenoids.

OBD-II CODES FOR 1996–99 MODELS

- **P0030**—O2 sensor heater relay circuit (bank no. 1, sensor no. 1)
- **P0036**—O2 sensor heater relay circuit (bank no. 1, sensor no. 2)
- **P0106**—Barometric pressure out of range (Key-On)—MAP sensor has a baro reading below an acceptable value.
- **P0107**—Manifold Absolute Pressure Sensor Circuit Low Input
- **P0108**—Manifold Absolute Pressure Sensor Circuit High Input
- **P0112**—Intake Air Temperature Sensor Circuit Low Input
- **P0113**—Intake Air Temperature Sensor Circuit High Input
- **P0116**—Rationality error detected in the Engine Coolant Temperature (ECT) sensor
- **P0117**—Engine Coolant Temperature Sensor Circuit Low Input
- **P0118**—Engine Coolant Temperature Sensor Circuit High Input
- **P0121**—Throttle Position Sensor voltage does not agree with MAP sensor
- **P0122**—Throttle Position Sensor voltage low input
- **P0123**—Throttle Position Sensor voltage high input
- **P0125**—Closed loop temperature not reached
- **P0128**—Closed Loop temperature not reached
- **P0131**—Right rear (or just) upstream O2 sensor voltage shorted to ground
- **P0132**—Right rear (or just) upstream O2 sensor shorted to voltage
- **P0133**—Right bank (or just) upstream O2 sensor circuit slow response
- **P0134**—Right rear (or just) upstream O2 sensor stays at center
- **P0135**—Right rear (or just) upstream O2 sensor heater failure
- **P0137**—Right rear (or just) downstream O2 sensor voltage shorted to ground
- **P0138**—Right rear (or just) downstream O2 sensor shorted to voltage
- **P0139**—Right rear (or just) downstream O2 sensor circuit slow response
- **P0140**—Right rear (or just) downstream O2 sensor stays at center
- **P0141**—Right rear (or just) downstream O2 sensor heater failure
- **P0143**—O2 sensor circuit shorted to ground (bank no. 1, sensor no. 3)
- **P0144**—O2 sensor circuit shorted to voltage (bank no. 1, sensor no. 3)
- **P0145**—O2 sensor circuit slow response (bank no. 1, sensor no. 3)
- **P0146**—O2 sensor stays at center (bank no. 1, sensor no. 3)
- **P0147**—O2 sensor heater failure (bank no. 1, sensor no. 3)
- **P0151**—O2 sensor circuit shorted to ground (bank no. 2, sensor no. 1)
- **P0152**—O2 sensor circuit shorted to voltage (bank no. 2, sensor no. 1)
- **P0153**—O2 sensor circuit slow response (bank no. 2, sensor no. 1)
- **P0154**—O2 sensor stays at center (bank no. 2, sensor no. 1)
- **P0155**—O2 sensor heater failure (bank no. 2, sensor no. 1)
- **P0157**—O2 sensor circuit shorted to ground (bank no. 2, sensor no. 2)
- **P0158**—O2 sensor circuit shorted to voltage (bank no. 2, sensor no. 2)
- **P0159**—O2 sensor circuit slow response (bank no. 2, sensor no. 2)
- **P0160**—O2 sensor stays at center (bank no. 2, sensor no. 2)
- **P0161**—O2 sensor heater failure (bank no. 2, sensor no. 2)
- **P0165**—Starter relay control circuit
- **P0171**—Fuel System Too Lean (bank no.1)
- **P0172**—Fuel System Too Rich (bank no. 1)
- **P0174**—Fuel System Too Lean (bank no. 2)
- **P0175**—Fuel System Too Rich (bank no. 2)
- **P0178**—Flex fuel sensor voltage too low (if equipped)
- **P0179**—Flex fuel sensor voltage too high (if equipped)
- **P0182**—CNG temperature sensor voltage too low (if equipped)
- **P0183**—CNG temperature sensor voltage too high (if equipped)
- **P0201**—Injector no. 1 Control Circuit
- **P0202**—Injector no. 2 Control Circuit
- **P0203**—Injector no. 3 Control Circuit
- **P0204**—Injector no. 4 Control Circuit
- **P0205**—Injector no. 5 Control Circuit
- **P0206**—Injector no. 6 Control Circuit
- **P0300**—Random/Multiple Cylinder Misfire Detected
- **P0301**—Cylinder no. 1—Misfire Detected
- **P0302**—Cylinder no. 2—Misfire Detected
- **P0303**—Cylinder no. 3—Misfire Detected
- **P0304**—Cylinder no. 4—Misfire Detected
- **P0305**—Cylinder no. 5—Misfire Detected
- **P0306**—Cylinder no. 6—Misfire Detected
- **P0320**—No Crank Reference Signal At PCM
- **P0325**—Knock sensor no. 1 circuit
- **P0330**—Knock sensor no. 2 circuit
- **P0340**—No Cam Signal at PCM
- **P0350**—Ignition coil draws too much current
- **P0351**—Ignition Coil no. 1 Primary Circuit
- **P0352**—Ignition Coil no. 2 Primary Circuit
- **P0353**—Ignition Coil no. 3 Primary Circuit
- **P0354**—Ignition Coil no. 4 Primary Circuit
- **P0355**—Ignition Coil no. 5 Primary Circuit
- **P0356**—Ignition Coil no. 6 Primary Circuit
- **P0401**—EGR system failure
- **P0403**—Open or short detected in the EGR solenoid circuit
- **P0404**—EGR position sensor rationality
- **P0405**—EGR position sensor voltage too low
- **P0406**—EGR position sensor voltage too high
- **P0412**—Secondary air solenoid circuit
- **P0420**—Catalyst system efficiency below threshold (bank no. 1)
- **P0432**—Main catalyst efficiency below threshold (bank no. 2)
- **P0441**—Evaporative Purge Flow Monitor Failure
- **P0442**—Evaporative Emission Control System Leak Detected (Small Leak)
- **P0443**—Evap Purge Solenoid Circuit
- **P0455**—Evaporative Emission Control System Leak Detected (Large Leak)
- **P0456**—Evaporative Emission Control System Leak Detected (Small Leak)
- **P0460**—Fuel level sender circuit malfunction
- **P0461**—Fuel level sender circuit range/performance
- **P0462**—Fuel level sending unit voltage too low
- **P0463**—Fuel level sending unit voltage too high
- **P0500**—No Vehicle Speed Sensor Signal
- **P0505**—Idle Air Control Motor Circuits
- **P0522**—Engine oil pressure sensor/switch voltage low
- **P0523**—Engine oil pressure sensor/switch voltage high
- **P0551**—Power steering switch failure
- **P0600**—PCM/Serial Communication Link Malfunction
- **P0601**—nternal Controller Failure
- **P0604**—Internal control module Random Access Memory (RAM) error
- **P0605**—Internal control module Read Only Memory (ROM) error
- **P0622**—Alternator field not switching properly
- **P0645**—A/C clutch relay circuit
- **P0700**—EATX controller DTC present
- **P0703**—Brake switch sense circuit/switch stuck pressed or released
- **P0711**—Transaxle temperature sensor shows no temperature rise after start-up
- **P0712**—Transaxle temperature sensor voltage too low
- **P0713**—Transaxle temperature sensor voltage too high
- **P0720**—Output speed sensor circuit malfunction
- **P0740**—Torque Converter Clutch, No RPM Drop At Lockup
- **P0743**—Torque Converter Clutch Solenoid/Trans. Relay Circuits
- **P0748**—Governor pressure solenoid control/transaxle relay circuits
- **P0751**—Overdrive switch pressed (LO) for more than 5 minutes
- **P0753**—Transaxle 3–4 shift solenoid/transaxle relay circuits
- **P0756**—AW4 shift solenoid B (2–3) functional failure
- **P0783**—3–4 shift solenoid, no RPM drop at lockup
- **P0801**—Reverse gear lockout circuit open or short
- **P1195**—O2 sensor slow during catalyst monitor (bank no. 1, sensor no. 1)
- **P1196**—O2 sensor slow during catalyst monitor (bank no. 2, sensor no. 1)
- **P1197**—O2 sensor slow during catalyst monitor (bank no. 1, sensor no. 2)
- **P1198**—Radiator temperature sensor voltage too high
- **P1199**—Radiator temperature sensor voltage too low
- **P1281**—Engine is cold too long
- **P1282**—Fuel pump relay control circuit
- **P1288**—Intake manifold short runner solenoid circuit
- **P1289**—Manifold tuning valve solenoid circuit
- **P1290**—CNG fuel system pressure too high (if equipped)
- **P1291**—No temperature rise seen from the intake heaters

- **P1292**—CNG pressure sensor voltage too high (if equipped)
- **P1293**—CNG pressure sensor voltage too low (if equipped)
- **P1294**—Target idle not reached
- **P1295**—No 5 volts to the throttle position sensor
- **P1296**—No 5 volts to the MAP sensor
- **P1297**—No Change In MAP From Start To Run
- **P1298**—Lean operation at wide open throttle
- **P1299**—Vacuum leak found (IAC fully seated)
- **P1388**—Auto ShutDown (ASD) relay control circuit
- **P1389**—No ASD relay output voltage at PCM
- **P1390**—Timing belt skipped 1 tooth or more
- **P1391**—Intermittent loss of CMP or CKP
- **P1398**—Misfire Adaptive Numerator At Limit
- **P1403**—Loss of 5 volt feed to the EGR position sensor
- **P1476**—Too little secondary air
- **P1477**—Too much secondary air
- **P1478**—Battery temperature sensor voltage out of limit
- **P1479**—Transmission fan relay circuit
- **P1481**—EATX RPM pulse generator signal for misfire detection does not correlate with expected value
- **P1482**—Catalyst temperature sensor circuit shorted low
- **P1483**—Catalyst temperature sensor circuit shorted high
- **P1484**—Catalytic converter overheat detected
- **P1486**—EVAP System Obstruction Found
- **P1487**—High speed radiator fan control relay circuit
- **P1488**—Auxiliary 5 volt supply output too low
- **P1489**—High speed fan control relay circuit
- **P1490**—Low speed fan control relay circuit
- **P1491**—Radiator fan control relay circuit
- **P1492**—Ambient/Battery Temp Sensor Voltage Too High
- **P1493**—Ambient/ Battery Temp Sensor Voltage Too Low
- **P1494**—Leak Detection Pump Pressure Switch Or Mechanical Fault
- **P1495**—Leak Detection Pump Solenoid Circuit
- **P1496**—5 Volt supply output too low
- **P1498**—High speed radiator fan ground control relay circuit
- **P1594**—Charging system voltage too high
- **P1595**—Speed control solenoid circuits
- **P1596**—Speed control switch always high
- **P1597**—Speed control switch always low
- **P1598**—A/C pressure sensor voltage too high
- **P1599**—A/C pressure sensor voltage too low
- **P1681**—No instrument panel cluster CCD/J1850 messages received
- **P1682**—Charging system voltage too low
- **P1683**—Speed control power relay; or speed control 12 volt driver circuit
- **P1684**—The battery has been disconnected within the last 50 starts
- **P1685**—Smart Key Immobilizer Module (SKIM) invalid key
- **P1686**—No SKIM BUS messages recieved
- **P1687**—No Mechanical Instrument Cluster (MIC) BUS message
- **P1695**—No CCD messages from the Body Control Module (BCM)
- **P1696**—PCM Failure EEPROM Write Denied
- **P1697**—PCM Failure SRI Mileage Not Stored
- **P1698**—PCM Failure EEPROM Write Denied
- **P1698**—No CCD messages from the Transmission or Body Control Module (TCM or BCM)
- **P1719**—Skip shift solenoid circuit
- **P1740**—Rationality error detected in the torque converter clutch solenoid or overdrive solenoid systems
- **P1756**—Governor pressure not equal to target @ 15–20 PSI (mid pressure malfunction)
- **P1757**—Governor pressure not equal to target @ 15–20 PSI (zero pressure malfunction)
- **P1762**—Governor pressure sensor offset voltage too low or high
- **P1763**—Governor pressure sensor voltage too high
- **P1764**—Governor pressure sensor voltage too low
- **P1765**—Trans. 12 volt supply relay control circuit
- **P1899**—P/N Switch Failure
- **P1899**—P/N switch stuck in PARK or in gear

VACUUM DIAGRAMS

Following are vacuum diagrams for most of the engine and emissions package combinations covered by this manual. Because vacuum circuits will vary based on various engine and vehicle options, always refer first to the vehicle emission control information label, if present. Should the label be missing, or should the vehicle be equipped with a different engine than the vehicle's original equipment, refer to the diagrams below for the same or similar configuration.

If you wish to obtain a replacement emissions label, most manufacturers make the labels available for purchase. The labels can usually be ordered from a local dealer.

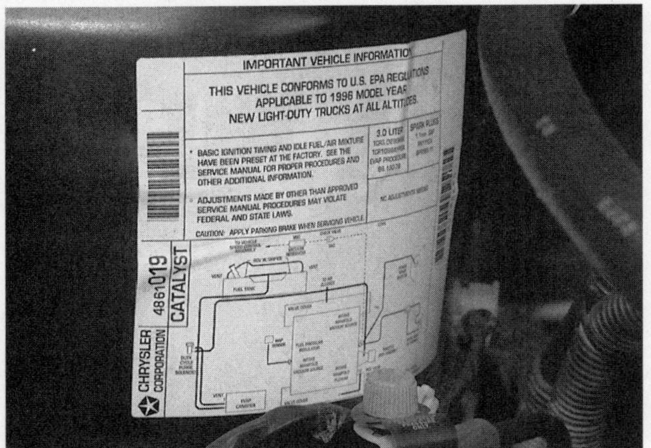

Fig. 81 The Vehicle Emission Control Information (VECI) label, located in the engine compartment, contains important emissions information

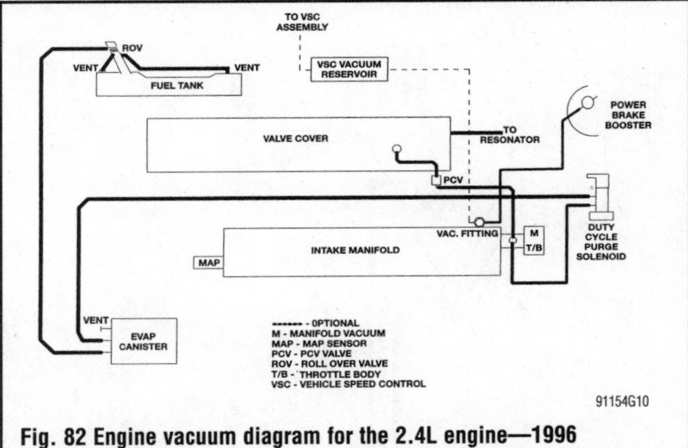

Fig. 82 Engine vacuum diagram for the 2.4L engine—1996

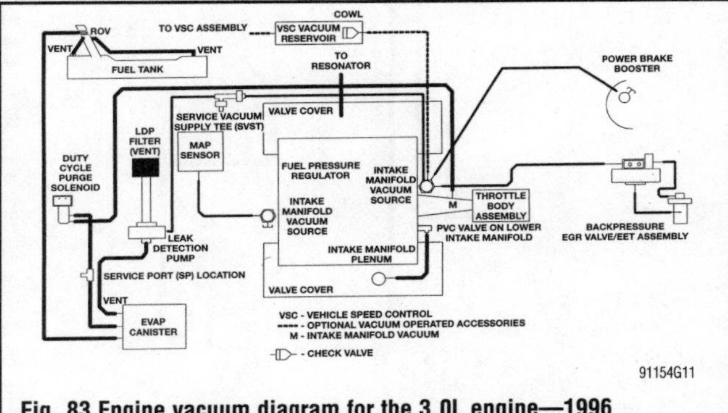

Fig. 83 Engine vacuum diagram for the 3.0L engine—1996

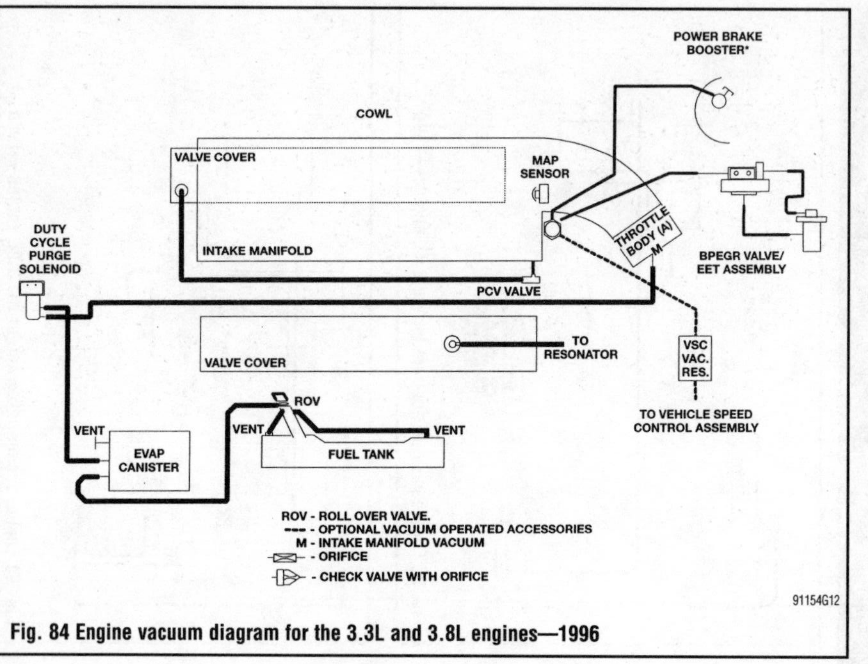

Fig. 84 Engine vacuum diagram for the 3.3L and 3.8L engines—1996

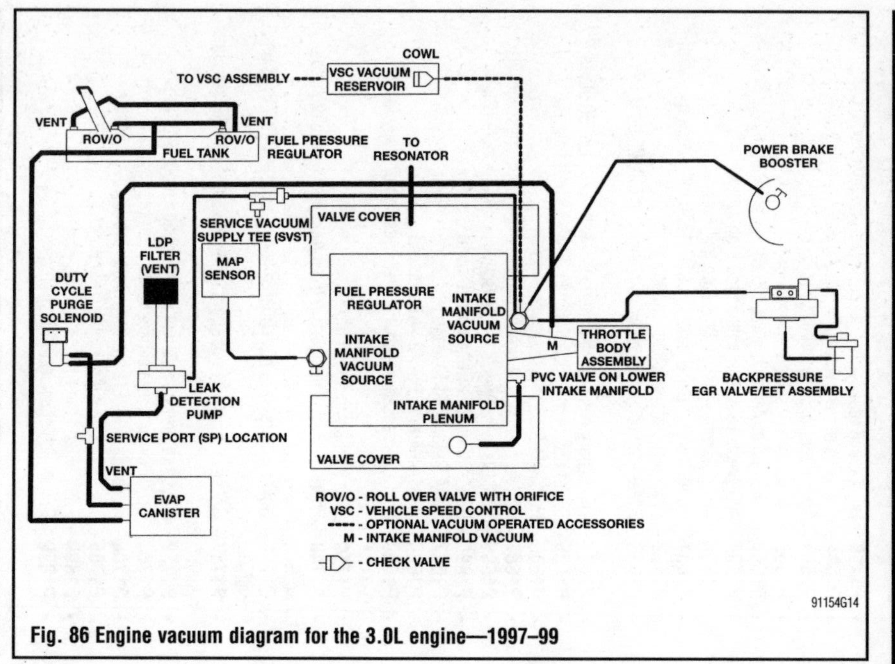

Fig. 86 Engine vacuum diagram for the 3.0L engine—1997–99

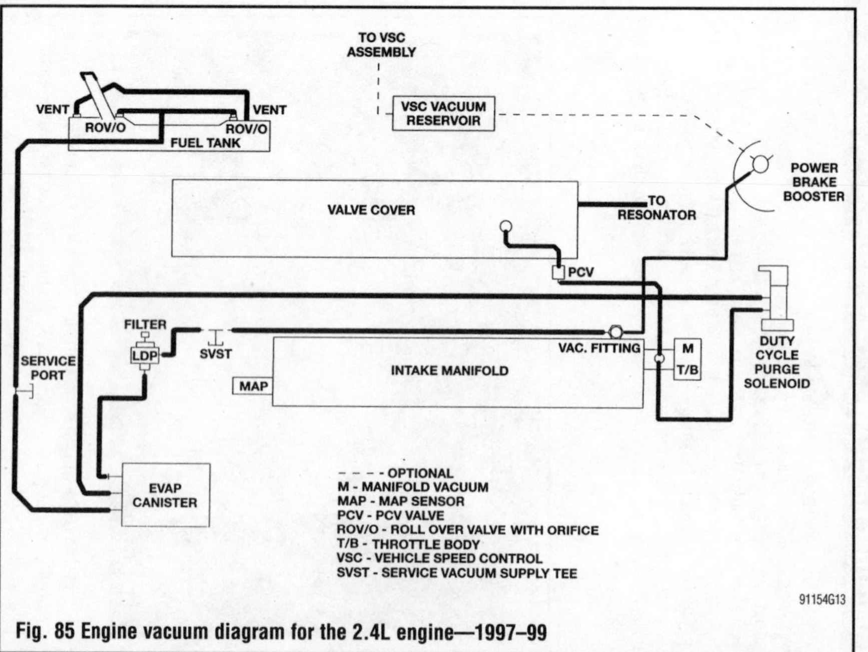

Fig. 85 Engine vacuum diagram for the 2.4L engine—1997–99

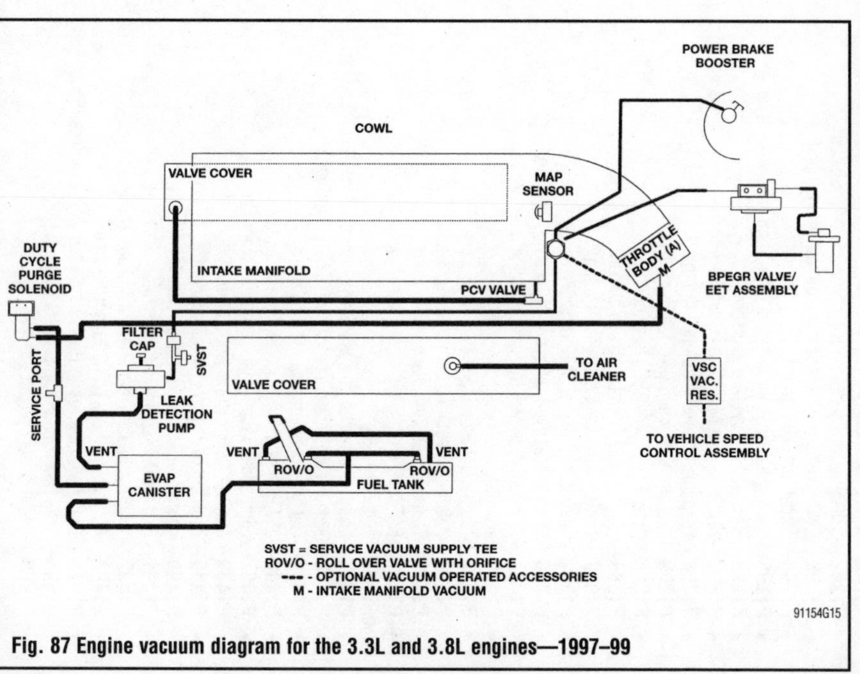

Fig. 87 Engine vacuum diagram for the 3.3L and 3.8L engines—1997–99

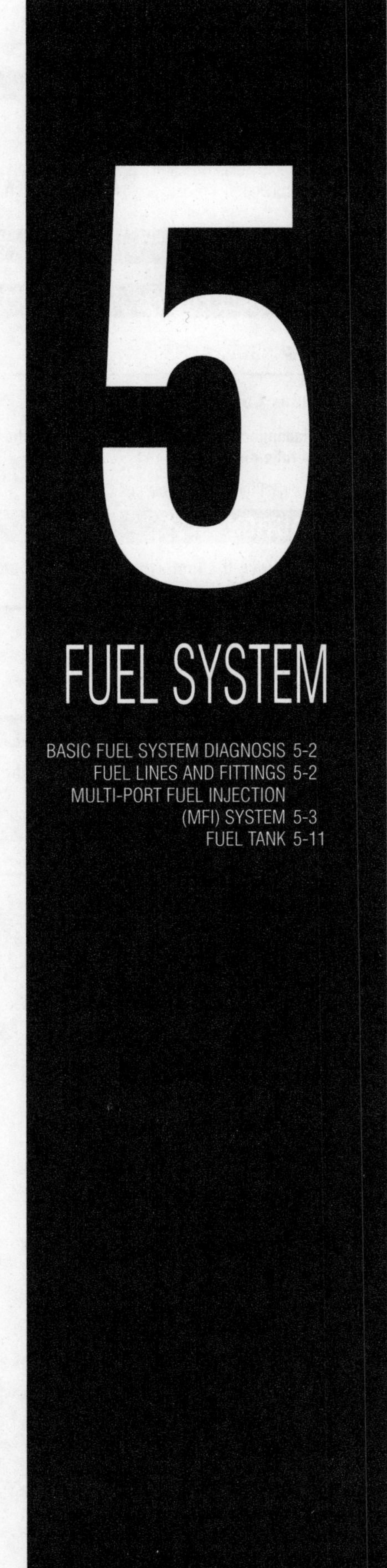

5 FUEL SYSTEM

BASIC FUEL SYSTEM DIAGNOSIS

When there is a problem starting or driving a vehicle, two of the most important checks involve the ignition and the fuel systems. The questions most mechanics attempt to answer first, "is there spark?" and "is there fuel?" will often lead to solving most basic problems. For ignition system diagnosis and testing, please refer to the information on engine electrical components and ignition systems found earlier in this manual. If the ignition system checks out (there is spark), then you must determine if the fuel system is operating properly (is there fuel?).

FUEL LINES AND FITTINGS

Quick-Connect Fittings

REMOVAL & INSTALLATION

See Figures 1 and 2

When disconnecting a quick-connect fitting, the retainer will remain on the fuel tube nipple.

1. Disconnect the negative battery cable.

CAUTION

You MUST relieve the fuel system pressure before disconnecting any quick-connect fittings.

2. Properly relieve the fuel system pressure, as outlined later in this section.
3. Squeeze the retainer tabs together and pull the fuel tube/quick-connect fitting assembly off of the fuel tube nipple. The retainer will remain on the tube.

To install:

WARNING

Never install a quick-connect fitting without the retainer being either on the fuel tube or already in the quick-connect fitting. In either case, make sure the retainer locks securely into the quick-connect fitting by firmly pulling on the fuel tube and fitting to ensure that it is fastened.

4. Using a clean, lint-free cloth, clean the fuel tube nipple and retainer.
5. Before connecting the fitting to the fuel tube, coat the tube nipple with clean 30-weight engine oil.
6. Push the quick-connect fitting over the fuel tube until the retainer seats and a click is heard.
7. The plastic quick-connect fitting has windows in the sides of the casing. When the fitting completely attaches to the fuel tube, the retainer locking ears and the fuel tube shoulder are visible in the windows. If they are not visible, the retainer was not installed properly. Do NOT count on the audible click to confirm a secure connection.
8. Use a DRB or equivalent scan tool to pressurize the fuel system and check for leaks.

Plastic Retainer Ring Type Fittings

This fitting is identified by the use of a full-round plastic retainer ring, usually black in color.

REMOVAL & INSTALLATION

See Figure 3

1. Perform the fuel pressure release procedure outlined in this section.

CAUTION

You MUST relieve the fuel system pressure before disconnecting any fittings.

2. Disconnect the negative battery cable.
3. Clean the fitting(s) of any dirt or foreign material before disconnecting.
4. To release the fuel system component from the plastic retainer ring type fitting, firmly push the fitting toward the component being serviced while firmly pushing the plastic retainer ring into the fitting. While the plastic ring is depressed, pull the fitting away from the component.

The plastic retainer ring must be pressed squarely into the fitting body. If the retainer is cocked during removal, it may be difficult to disconnect the fitting. To aid in removal, it may be necessary to use an open-end wrench on the shoulder of the plastic retainer ring.

5. After disconnection, the plastic retainer ring will remain with the fitting connector body.
6. Inspect the fitting connector body, plastic retainer ring and fuel system component for damage. Replace if necessary.

To install:

7. Using a clean, lint-free cloth, clean the fuel tube nipple and retainer.
8. Before connecting the fitting to the fuel tube, coat the tube nipple with clean 30-weight engine oil.
9. Push the fitting into the component being serviced until the retainer seats and a click is heard.
10. Make sure the retainer locks securely into the fitting by firmly pulling on the fuel tube and fitting to ensure that it is fastened.
11. Connect the negative battery cable.
12. Start the engine and check the system for leaks.

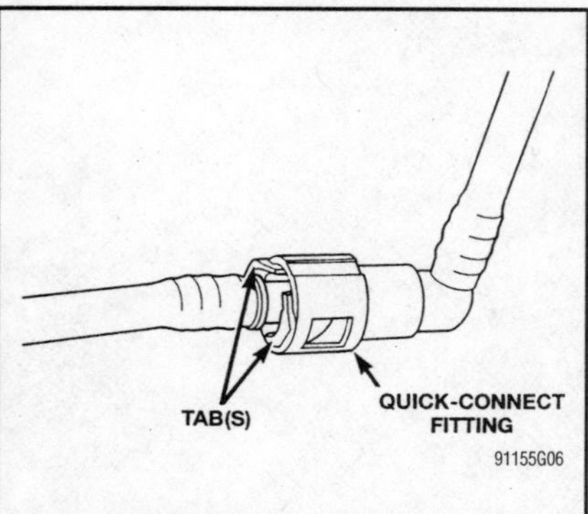

Fig. 1 Typical two-tab type quick-connect fitting

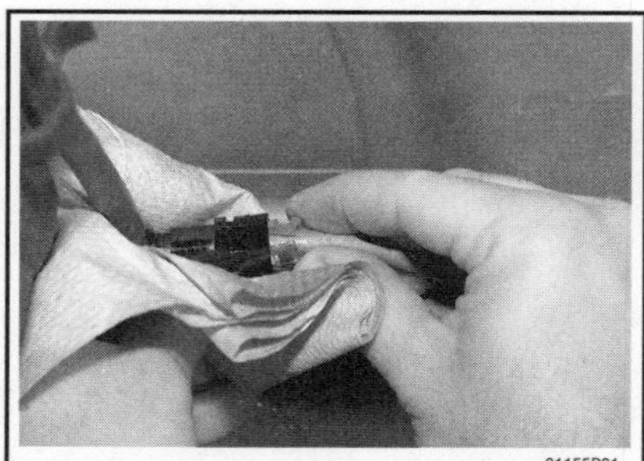

Fig. 2 Squeeze the retainer tabs together and pull the fuel tube/quick-connect fitting off of the fuel tube end. The retainer will remain on the tube

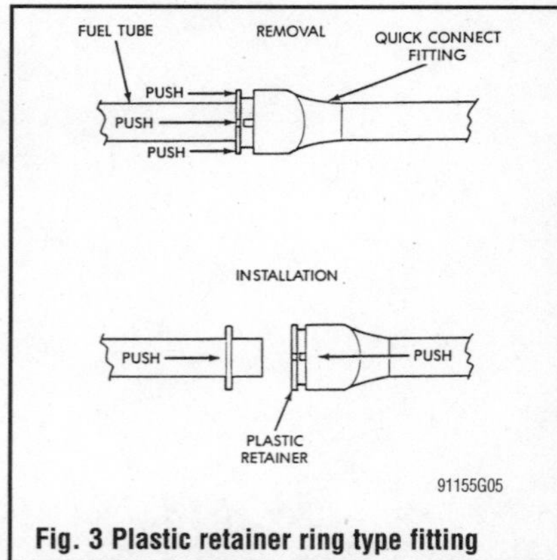

Fig. 3 Plastic retainer ring type fitting

MULTI-PORT FUEL INJECTION (MFI) SYSTEM

General Information

The Multi-port Fuel Injection (MFI) system is electronically controlled by the Powertrain Control Module (PCM), based on data from various sensors. The PCM controls the air/fuel ratio, fuel flow, idle speed and ignition timing.

Fuel is supplied to the injectors by an electric in-tank fuel pump and is distributed to the respective injectors via the main fuel pipe. The fuel pressure applied to the injector is constant and higher than the pressure in the intake manifold. The pressure is controlled by the fuel pressure regulator. All vehicles covered in this manual are equipped with a returnless fuel injection system.

When an electric current flows in the injector, the injector valve is fully opened to supply fuel. Since the fuel pressure is constant, the amount of the fuel injected from the injector into the manifold is increased or decreased in proportion to the time the electric current flows. Based on PCM signals, the injectors inject fuel to the cylinder manifold ports in firing order.

Air enters the air intake plenum or manifold through the throttle body. In the intake manifold, the air is mixed with the fuel from the injectors and is drawn into the cylinder. The air flow rate is controlled according to the degree of the throttle valve and the servo motor openings.

The system is monitored through a number of sensors which feed information on engine conditions and requirements to the PCM. The PCM calculates the injection time and rate according to the signals from the sensors.

Fuel System Service Precaution

Safety is an important factor when servicing the fuel system. Failure to conduct maintenance and repairs in a safe manner may result in serious personal injury. Maintenance and testing of the vehicle's fuel system components can be accomplished safely and effectively by adhering to the following rules and guidelines.

- To avoid the possibility of fire and personal injury, always disconnect the negative battery cable unless the repair or test procedure requires that battery voltage be applied.
- Always relieve the fuel system pressure prior to disconnecting any fuel system component (injector, fuel rail, pressure regulator, etc.), fitting or fuel line connection. Exercise extreme caution whenever relieving fuel system pressure to avoid exposing skin, face and eyes to fuel spray. Please be advised that fuel under pressure may penetrate the skin or any part of the body that it contacts.
- Always place a shop towel or cloth around the fitting or connection prior to loosening to absorb any excess fuel due to spillage. Ensure that all fuel spillage is quickly removed from engine surfaces. Ensure that all fuel soaked cloths or towels are deposited into a suitable waste container.
- Always keep a dry chemical (Class B) fire extinguisher near the work area.
- Do not allow fuel spray or fuel vapors to come into contact with a spark or open flame.
- Always use a backup wrench when loosening and tightening fuel line connection fittings. This will prevent unnecessary stress and torsion to fuel line piping. Always follow the proper torque specifications.
- Always replace worn fuel fitting O-rings. Do not substitute fuel hose where fuel pipe is installed.

Relieving Fuel System Pressure

RELIEVING

**** CAUTION**

The fuel injection system remains under pressure even after the engine has been turned OFF. The fuel system pressure must be relieved before disconnecting any fuel lines. Failure to do so may result in fire and/or personal injury.

2.4L, 3.3L and 3.8L Engines

See Figures 4, 5 and 6

➡The following procedure requires Fuel Pressure Release Hose C-4799–1 or equivalent. Fuel Gauge C-4799-B contains a hose to direct fuel into an approved container.

1. Disconnect the negative battery cable.
2. Remove the fuel tank filler cap to release the pressure in the fuel tank.
3. Remove the cap from the fuel pressure test port on the fuel rail.

**** CAUTION**

Always wear proper eye protection when relieving fuel system pressure. Do not allow fuel to spill on the intake or exhaust manifolds. Place shop towels under and around the pressure test port to absorb fuel when the pressure is released from the fuel rail.

4. Place the open end of Fuel Pressure Release Hose tool No. C-4799–1, or equivalent, into an approved gasoline container. Place a shop towel under the test port.
5. Connect the other end of the hose onto the fuel pressure test port, to relieve the system pressure.
6. After the fuel pressure has been released, remove the hose from the test port and install the cap.

3.0L Engine

1. Remove the fuel pump relay from the Power Distribution Center (PDC) located on the left side in the engine compartment. Location of the relay can be verified by the label located on the underside of the PDC cover.
2. Start the engine and allow it to run until it stalls.

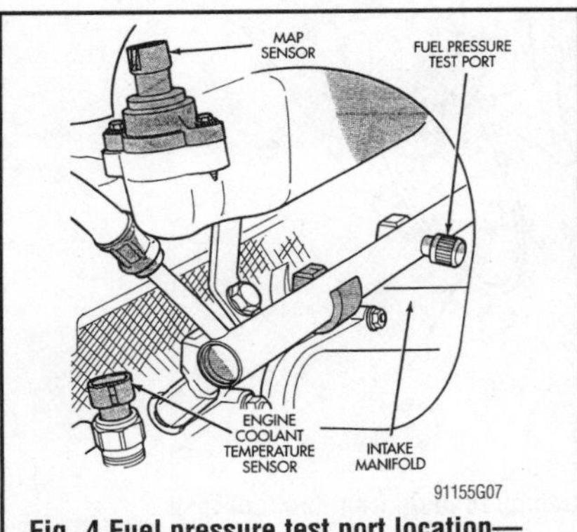

Fig. 4 Fuel pressure test port location—2.4L engine

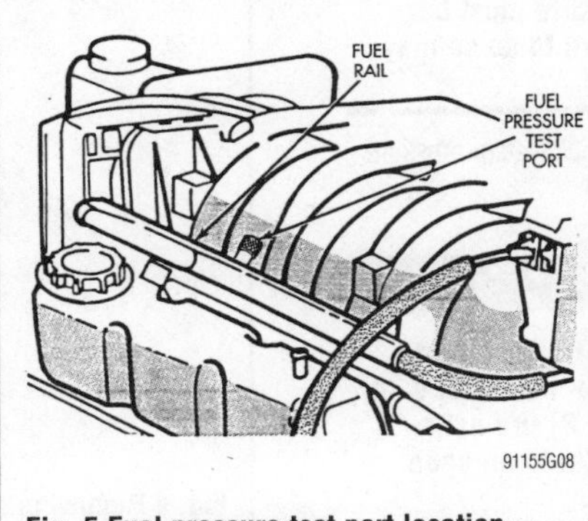

Fig. 5 Fuel pressure test port location—3.3L and 3.8L engines

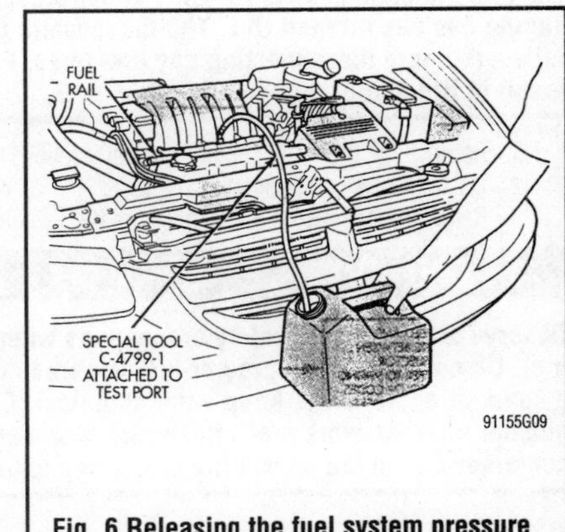

Fig. 6 Releasing the fuel system pressure

3. Continue to start the engine until it will no longer run.
4. Turn the ignition key to the **OFF** position.

⁂ WARNING

Steps 1–4 must be performed to relieve the pressurized fuel from within the fuel rail. Do NOT use the following steps to relieve this fuel pressure, as excessive fuel will be forced into a cylinder chamber.

5. Disconnect any fuel injector.
6. Connect one end of a jumper wire (18 gauge or smaller) to either injector terminal of the fuel injector harness connector (black connector located on fuel rail harness). Connect the other end of the jumper wire to the positive battery terminal.
7. Connect one end of a second jumper wire to the remaining (other) injector terminal.

⁂ WARNING

Do NOT supply power to the injector for more than four seconds or permanent damage to the injector will result.

8. Momentarily touch the other end of the second jumper wire to the negative battery terminal for **no more than four seconds**.
9. Place a shop rag or towel under the fuel line at the quick-disconnect fitting to the fuel rail.
10. Disconnect the negative battery cable. Squeeze the quick-disconnect fitting retainer tabs together and pull the fuel tube/quick-disconnect fitting assembly off the fuel tube nipple. The retainer will remain on the fuel tube.
11. Install the fuel pump relay into the PDC.
12. One or more Diagnostic Trouble Codes (DTC's) may have been stored in the PCM memory due to the removal of the fuel pump relay. Chrysler's Diagnostic Readout Box (DRB), or equivalent scan tool must be used to erase any DTC's.

Fuel Pump

REMOVAL & INSTALLATION

➧ See Figures 7 and 8

The in-tank fuel pump module contains the fuel pump and pressure regulator which adjusts fuel system pressure to approximately 49 psi. (338kPa). Voltage to the fuel pump is supplied through the fuel pump relay.

The fuel pump is serviced as part of the fuel pump module. The fuel pump module is installed in the top of the fuel tank and contains the electric fuel pump, fuel pump reservoir, inlet strainer, fuel gauge sending unit, fuel supply line and pressure regulator. The inlet strainer, fuel pressure regulator and level sensor are the only serviceable items. If the fuel pump requires service, replace the fuel pump module, using the following procedure:

⁂ CAUTION

The fuel injection system remains under pressure, even after the engine has been turned OFF. The fuel system pressure must be relieved before disconnecting any fuel lines. Failure to do so may result in fire and/or personal injury.

1. Remove the fuel filler cap and properly relieve the fuel system pressure.
2. Disconnect the negative battery cable.
3. Remove the fuel tank assembly from the vehicle.

⁂ CAUTION

Observe all applicable safety precautions when working around fuel. Do not allow fuel spray or fuel vapors to come in contact with a spark or open flame. Keep a dry chemical (Class B) fire extinguisher near the work area. Never drain or store fuel in an open container due to the possibility of fire or explosion.

4. Clean the top of the tank to remove any loose dirt.
5. Using special tool no. 6856 or equivalent, remove the fuel pump locknut by turning it counterclockwise.

⁂ CAUTION

The fuel reservoir of the fuel pump module does not empty out when the tank is drained. The fuel in the reservoir may spill out when the module is removed.

6. Remove the fuel pump and O-ring from the tank. Discard the O-ring.

To install:

7. Thoroughly clean all parts. Wipe the seal area of the tank clean. Place a new O-ring in position on the pump module.
8. While holding the fuel pump module in place install the locking ring and tighten to 43 ft. lbs. (58 Nm) using special tool no. 6856 or equivalent spanner-type tool.
9. Install the fuel tank assembly.
10. Reconnect the negative battery cable.
11. Fill the fuel tank with fuel. Install the fuel filler cap. Turn the ignition switch to the **ON** position to pressurize the system. Check the fuel system for leaks.

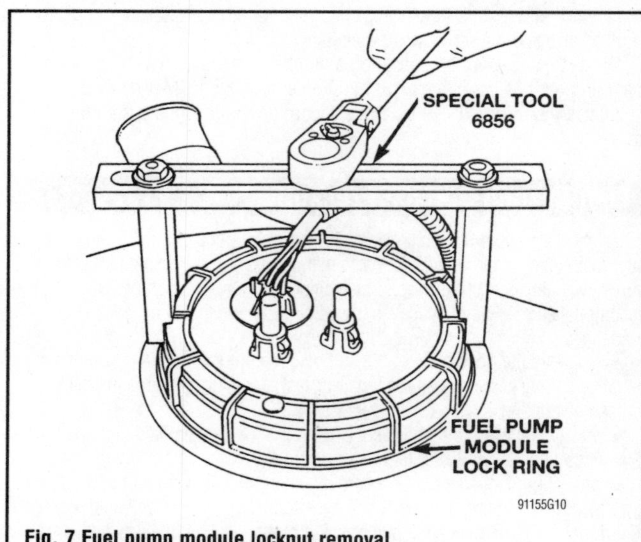

Fig. 7 Fuel pump module locknut removal

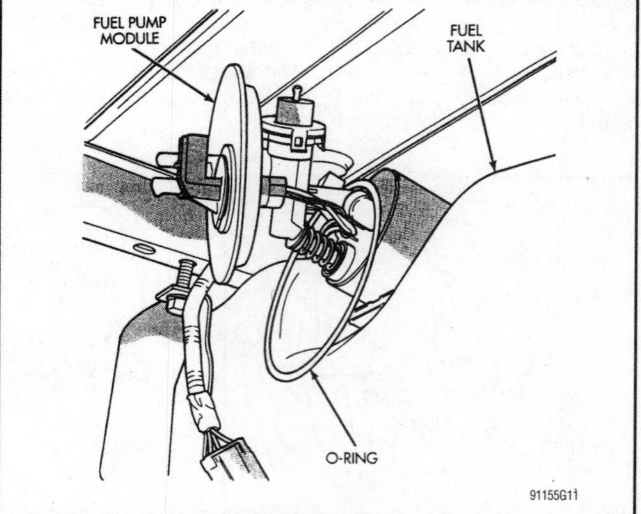

Fig. 8 Removing the fuel pump module from the fuel tank

TESTING

See Figures 4 and 5

➡Fuel system pressure testing requires the use of a DRB or equivalent scan tool.

The fuel pump operates at about 49 psi (338 kPa).

1. Release the fuel system pressure, as outlined earlier in this section.
2. On all 4-cylinder models, remove the cap from the fuel pressure test port on the fuel rail and connect a suitable fuel pressure gauge.
3. On the 6-cylinder models, disconnect the fuel supply hose at the engine. Refer to the quick-connect fitting disengagement procedure earlier in this section. Install fuel pressure test adapter 6539, or equivalent, between the fuel rail and fuel line. Connect a suitable fuel pressure gauge to the test port on the adapter.

➡ When using the ASD fuel system test, the ASD relay and fuel pump relay remain energized for 7 minutes or until the test is stopped, or until the ignition switch is turned to the OFF position.

4. Turn the ignition key to the **ON** position. Using the DRB or equivalent scan tool, access the ASD Fuel System Test. The ASD Fuel System Test will activate the fuel pump and pressurize the system. Note the gauge reading and compare with the following:
   - If the gauge reading equals approximately 49 psi (338 kPa), no further testing is required. If the pressure is not correct, record the reading.
   - If the fuel pressure is below specifications, check for a restricted fuel pump inlet strainer. If restricted, replace the inlet strainer. If not restricted, check for an incorrectly operating fuel filter, pressure regulator or fuel pump, and replace as necessary.
   - If the fuel pressure is above specifications (54 psi or higher), check for a kinked or restricted fuel supply line. If the line is not kinked or restricted, check for a restriction in the chassis fuel supply line or for a kinked or plugged fuel supply line. If none of the lines are restricted, replace the fuel pressure regulator.

Throttle Body

REMOVAL & INSTALLATION

See Figures 9 thru 19

1. Disconnect the negative battery cable.
2. Remove the air inlet-to-throttle body hose clamp.
3. Remove the 2 mounting screws and air inlet resonator.
4. Remove the throttle and speed control (if equipped) cables from the lever and bracket.
5. Disengage the electrical connectors from the Idle Air Control (IAC) motor and Throttle Position Sensor (TPS).
6. Disconnect the vacuum hoses from the throttle body.
7. Remove the throttle body mounting nuts.
8. Remove the throttle body assembly and mounting gasket.

To install:

9. Position the throttle body, along with a new mounting gasket, onto the intake manifold.
10. Install the mounting nuts and tighten to 18 ft. lbs. (25 Nm).
11. Connect the vacuum hoses to the throttle body.
12. Attach the IAC motor and TPS electrical connections to the throttle body.
13. Connect the throttle and speed control (if equipped) cables.
14. Install the air cleaner/inlet resonator assembly.
15. Connect the negative battery cable.

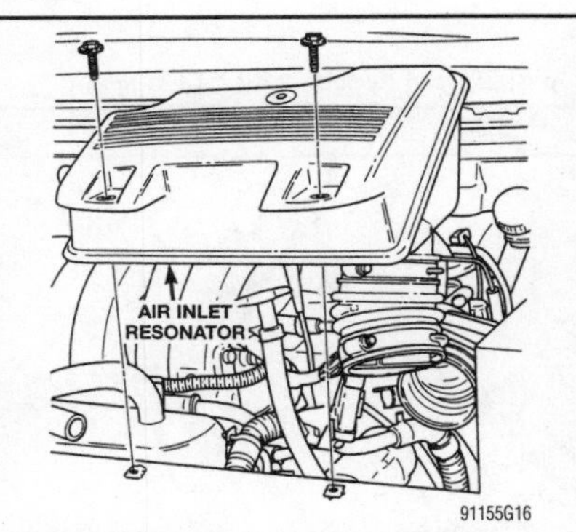

Fig. 9 Remove the air inlet resonator assembly

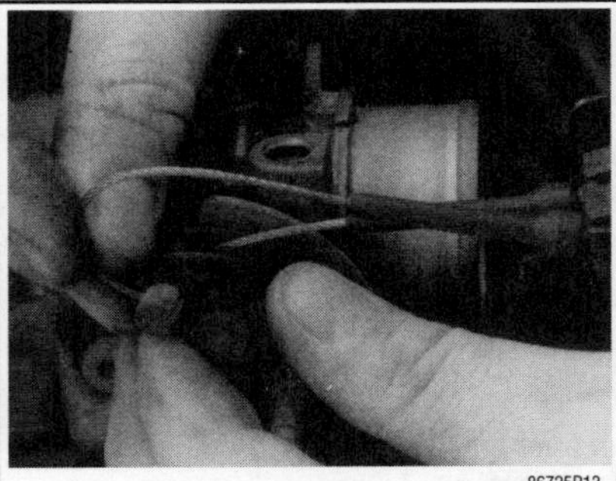

Fig. 10 Disconnect the throttle and speed control (if equipped) cables from the throttle lever

Fig. 11 Loosen the throttle cable bracket mounting nuts . . .

Fig. 12 . . . then remove the throttle cable bracket from the throttle body unit

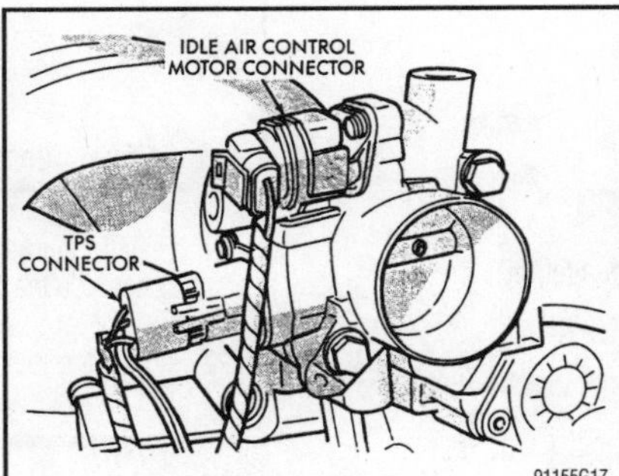

Fig. 13 Disengage the electrical connectors from the IAC motor and TPS—2.4L engine

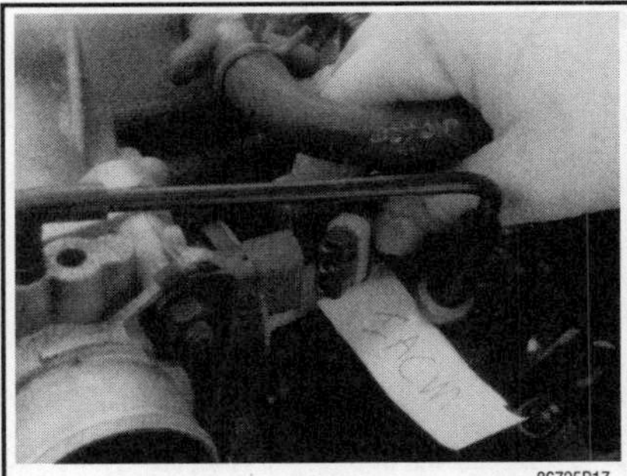

Fig. 14 Disengage the electrical connectors from the IAC motor and TPS—3.0L engine

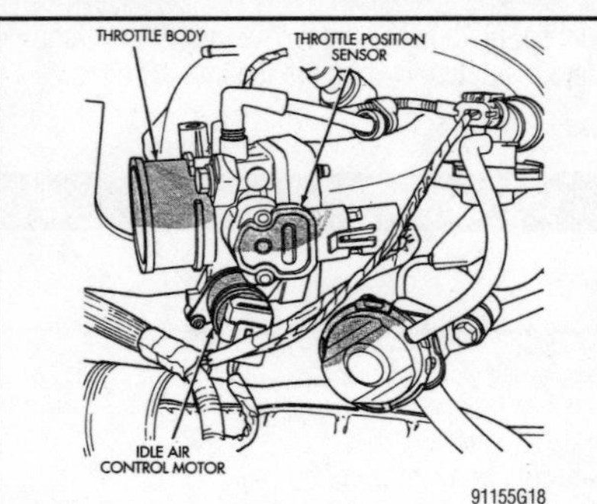

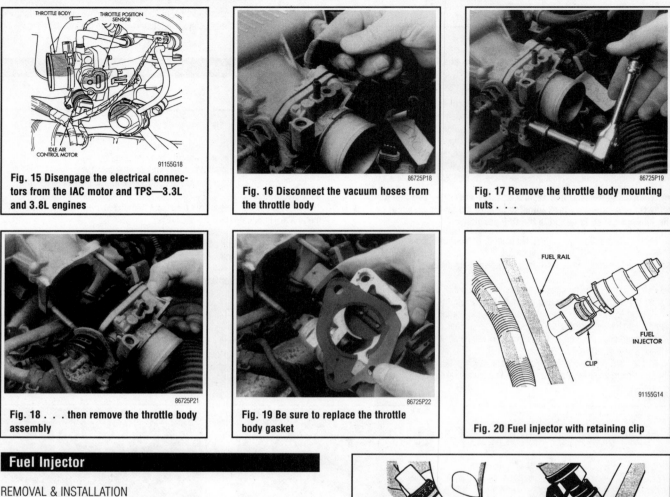

Fig. 15 Disengage the electrical connectors from the IAC motor and TPS—3.3L and 3.8L engines

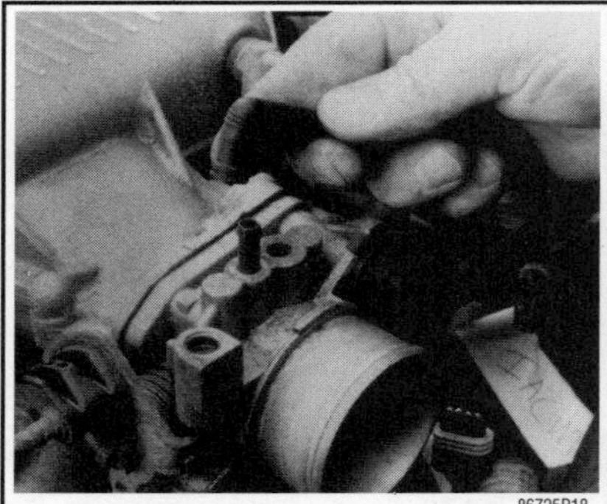

Fig. 16 Disconnect the vacuum hoses from the throttle body

Fig. 17 Remove the throttle body mounting nuts . . .

Fig. 18 . . . then remove the throttle body assembly

Fig. 19 Be sure to replace the throttle body gasket

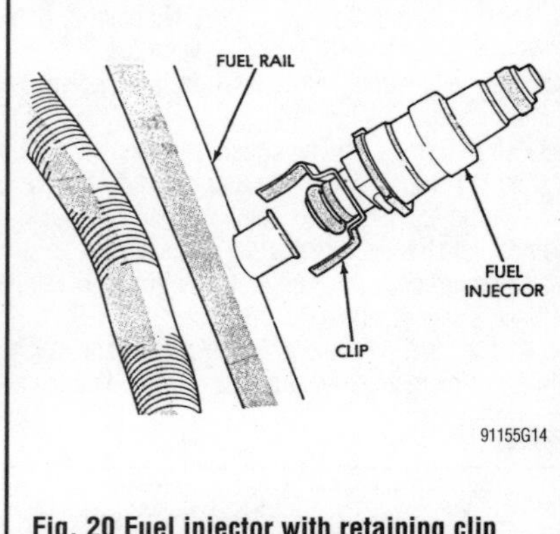

Fig. 20 Fuel injector with retaining clip

Fuel Injector

REMOVAL & INSTALLATION

CAUTION

Fuel injection systems remain under pressure, even after the engine has been turned OFF. The fuel system pressure must be relieved before disconnecting any fuel lines. Failure to do so may result in fire and/or personal injury.

Except 3.0L Engine

See Figures 20 and 21

1. Properly relieve the fuel system pressure.
2. Disconnect the negative battery cable.
3. Remove the fuel rail/injector assembly from the vehicle.
4. Position the fuel rail/injector assembly on a work bench or other working area that allows for easy access to the fuel injectors.
5. Rotate the fuel injector and pull the injector out of the fuel rail. The retaining clip will stay on the fuel injector.
6. Inspect the fuel injector O-ring for damage and replace, if necessary. If the injector is being reinstalled, place a protective cap over the injector tip to prevent damage.
7. Inspect the injector retaining clip and replace, if damaged.
8. Repeat for remaining injectors.

To install:

9. Before installing the injector into the fuel rail assembly, apply a light coating of clean engine oil to the O-ring on the fuel rail end of each injector. This will aid in the installation process.
10. Install the injector clip by sliding the open end into the top slot of the fuel injector. The edge of the reciever cup will slide into the side slots of the clip.

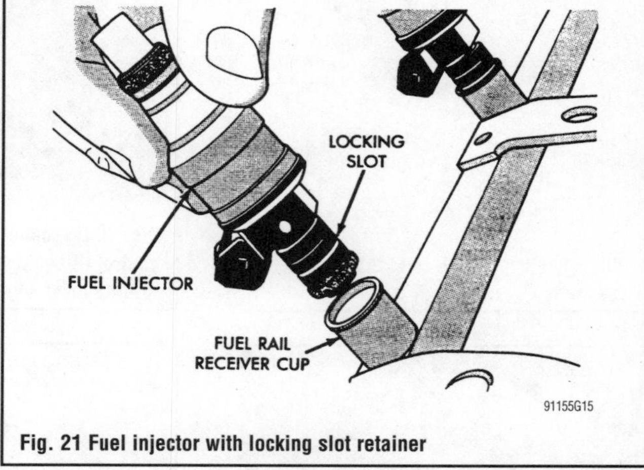

Fig. 21 Fuel injector with locking slot retainer

11. Install the injector top end into the reciever cap of the fuel rail. Be careful not to damage the fuel injector O-ring during installation.
12. Repeat for remaining injectors.
13. Install the fuel rail/injector assembly onto the engine.
14. Reconnect negative battery cable.

WARNING

When using the ASD Fuel System Test, the ASD relay and fuel pump relay remain energized for 7 minutes or until the test is stopped, or until the ignition switch is turned to the OFF position.

15. Turn the ignition key to the **ON** position and access the DRB scan tool ASD Fuel System Test to pressurize the fuel system. Check the fuel system for leaks.

3.0L Engine

➧ **See Figures 20 and 21**

The engine uses a sequential Multi-Port Electronic Fuel Injection (MPI) system. The MPI system uses fuel injectors positioned in the intake manifold with the nozzle ends directly above the intake port. The fuel rail assembly must be removed to service the injectors. The system pressure is approximately 48 psi. (330 Kpa). Perform the fuel pressure release procedure before attempting to service the fuel injectors.

1. Properly relieve the fuel system pressure.
2. Disconnect the negative battery cable.
3. Remove the fuel rail/injector assembly from the vehicle.
4. Position the fuel rail/injector assembly on a work bench or other working area that allows for easy access to the fuel injectors.
5. Remove the fuel injector retaining clip.
6. Remove the injector from the fuel rail by pulling the injector straight out of the fuel rail reciever cup.
7. Inspect the injector O-rings for damage and replace, as necessary. If the injector is being reinstalled, place a protective cap over the injector tip to prevent damage.
8. Inspect the injector retaining clip and replace, if damaged.
9. Repeat for remaining injectors.

To install:

10. Before installing the injector into the fuel rail assembly, apply a light coating of clean engine oil to the O-ring on the fuel rail end of each injector. This will aid in the installation process.
11. Install the injector top end into the reciever cap of the fuel rail. Be careful not to damage the fuel injector O-ring during installation.
12. Install the injector clip by sliding the open end into the top slot of the fuel injector. The edge of the reciever cup will slide into the side slots of the clip.
13. Repeat for remaining injectors.
14. Install the fuel rail/injector assembly onto the engine.
15. Reconnect negative battery cable.

✲✲ WARNING

When using the ASD Fuel System Test, the ASD relay and fuel pump relay remain energized for 7 minutes or until the test is stopped, or until the ignition switch is turned to the OFF position.

16. Turn the ignition key to the **ON** position and access the DRB scan tool ASD Fuel System Test to pressurize the fuel system. Check the fuel system for leaks.

TESTING

1. Unplug the injector electrical connector.
2. Using an ohmmeter, test the injector resistance across the injector terminals. The reading should be approximately 12 ohms at 68°F (20°C).
   a. If the resistance falls outside specifications, replace the faulty injector.
   b. If the resistance is within specifications, proceed with the testing.
3. Place a 12 volt test lamp across the injector's electrical connector terminals. Watch the test lamp while cranking the engine and compare with the following:
   a. If the test lamp does not flash, check the power feed and ground circuits between the PCM and the injector connector. Refer to the wiring diagrams in Section 6 for wire colors. If the circuits are faulty, repair them. If the circuits are OK, test the engine control system using the Chrysler DRB, or equivalent scan tool.
   b. If the test lamp flashes, proceed with the testing.
4. Check for fuel delivery at the suspect injector by removing the injector from the fuel rail and check for fuel and/or restrictions in the rail or injector fuel inlet. Compare your results with the following:
   a. If there is no fuel present at the injector, replace the plugged injector, or clean the restricted passage, as necessary.
   b. If there is fuel present at the injector, proceed with the testing.
5. With the injector removed from the fuel rail, connect a 12 volt source to one terminal on the injector connector and a ground wire to the other terminal. The injector should "click" each time the ground wire is connected and disconnected to and from the terminal.
6. If the injector "clicks," it is OK. If it does not "click," it must be replaced.

Fuel Rail (Charging) Assembly

REMOVAL & INSTALLATION

✲✲ CAUTION

Fuel injection systems remain under pressure, even after the engine has been turned OFF. The fuel system pressure must be relieved before disconnecting any fuel lines. Failure to do so may result in fire and/or personal injury.

2.4L Engine

➧ **See Figures 22, 23, 24, 25 and 26**

1. Properly relieve the fuel system pressure.
2. Disconnect the negative battery cable.
3. Disconnect the air inlet hose from the throttle body.
4. Disconnect the throttle cable and speed control cable (if equipped), from the throttle lever.
5. Compress the throttle cable retaining tabs and remove the throttle cables from the throttle bracket.
6. Disengage the electrical connectors from the Throttle Position Sensor (TPS) and Idle Air Control (IAC) motor.
7. Disconnect vacuum hoses from the fittings on the intake plenum.
8. Disengage electrical connectors from the Intake Air Temperature (IAT) sensor and MAP sensor.
9. Disconnect the fuel supply line from the fuel rail. This is a quick connect fitting. Squeeze the fitting retainer tabs together and pull the quick connect fitting assembly apart.

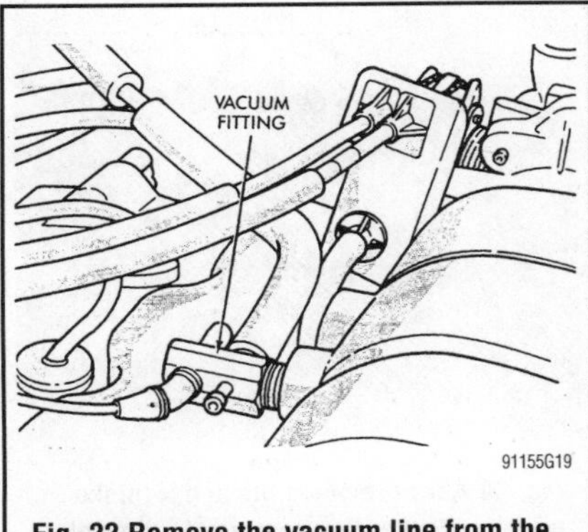

Fig. 22 Remove the vacuum line from the intake manifold

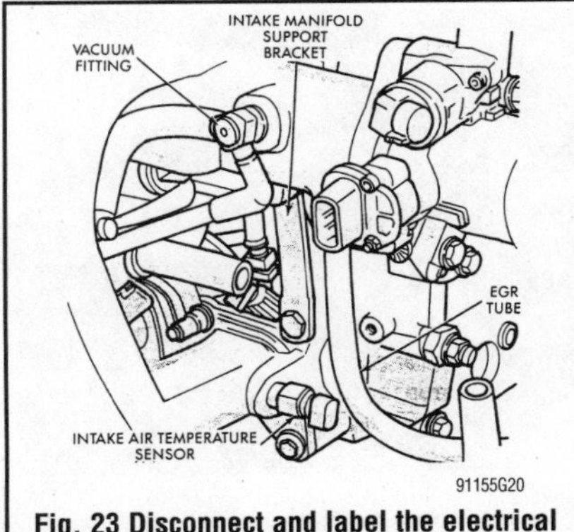

Fig. 23 Disconnect and label the electrical and vacuum connections

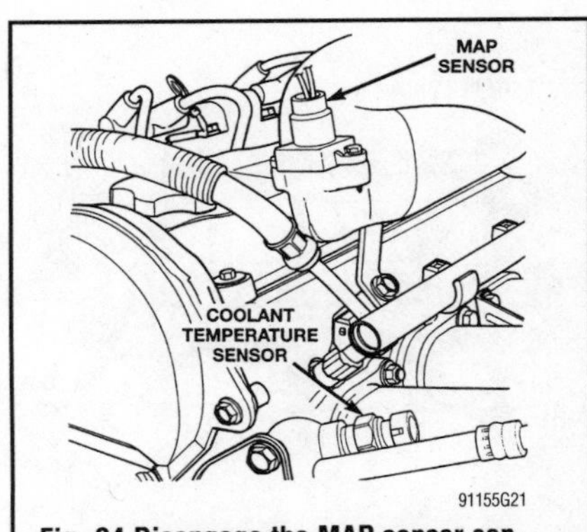

Fig. 24 Disengage the MAP sensor connector

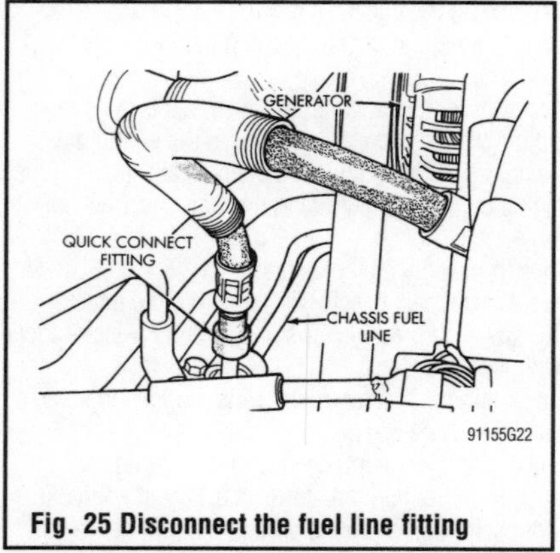

Fig. 25 Disconnect the fuel line fitting

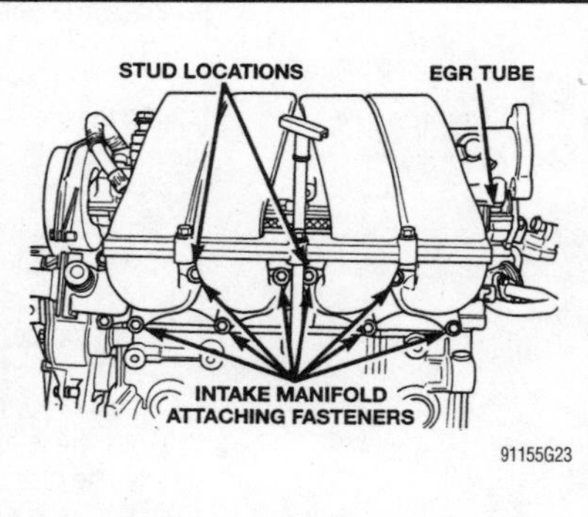

Fig. 26 Remove the intake manifold screws

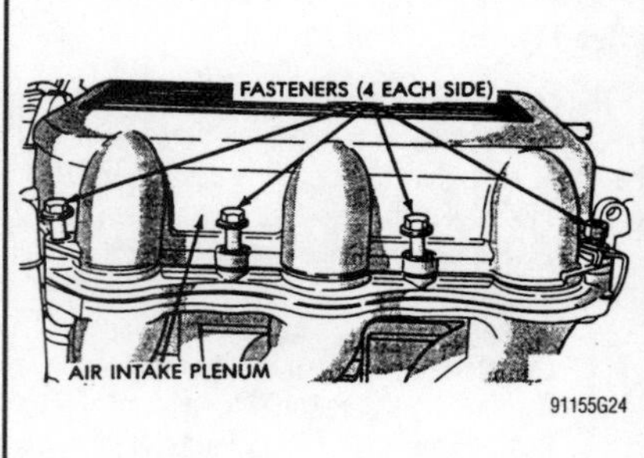

Fig. 27 Remove the air intake plenum-to-lower intake manifold mounting bolts

CAUTION

Wrap shop towels around the hose connection to catch any gasoline spillage.

10. Remove the bolt securing the bottom of the intake support bracket.
11. Remove the intake manifold mounting screws.
12. Disconnect the fuel injector electrical connectors.
13. Remove the fuel rail attaching screws.
14. Lift the fuel rail/injector assembly off the intake manifold. Be careful not to damage the injector O-rings during the removal from their ports. If they are damaged, replace them as necessary. Cover the fuel injector openings in the intake manifold.

To install:

15. Ensure that the fuel injector holes are clean.
16. Apply a light coating of clean engine oil to the O-ring on the nozzle end of each injector.
17. Insert the fuel injector nozzles into the openings in the intake manifold. Seat the injectors and tighten the fuel rail mounting screws to 16 ft. lbs. (22 Nm).
18. Reconnect the electrical connectors to the fuel injectors.
19. Install a new intake manifold gasket and position the intake manifold onto the engine.
20. Tighten the intake manifold mounting bolts, starting at the center of the manifold and working outward in both directions. Torque the mounting bolts to 17 ft. lbs. (23 Nm).
21. Lightly oil the tube end, then reconnect the fuel supply line quick connect fitting to the fuel rail. Be sure the quick connect fittings are fully engaged.
22. Install and tighten bolt that secures the bottom of the intake support bracket.
23. Attach the IAT sensor and MAP sensor electrical connectors.
24. Reconnect the vacuum lines to the intake plenum fittings.
25. Attach the IAC motor and TPS electrical connectors.
26. Secure the throttle cables into the cable bracket by engaging the retaining tabs.
27. Reconnect the throttle cable and speed control cable (if equipped) to the throttle lever.
28. Connect the air cleaner inlet hose to the throttle body.
29. Reconnect negative battery cable.

WARNING

When using the ASD Fuel System Test, the ASD relay and fuel pump relay remain energized for 7 minutes or until the test is stopped, or until the ignition switch is turned to the OFF position.

30. Turn the ignition key to the **ON** position and access the DRB scan tool ASD Fuel System Test to pressurize the fuel system. Check the fuel system for leaks.

3.0L Engine

See Figures 27 thru 32

The engine uses a sequential Multi-Port Electronic Fuel Injection (MPI) system. The MPI system uses fuel injectors positioned in the intake manifold with the nozzle ends directly above the intake port. The fuel rail assembly must be removed to service the injectors. The system pressure is approximately 48 psi (330 Kpa). Perform the fuel pressure release procedure before attempting to service the fuel injectors.

1. Properly relieve the fuel system pressure.
2. Disconnect the negative battery cable.
3. Remove the air inlet resonator assembly.
4. Remove the throttle cable.
5. Label and disengage the electrical connectors from the Idle Air Control (IAC) motor, Throttle Position Sensor (TPS) and Engine Coolant Temperature (ECT) sensor.
6. Label and disconnect the vacuum harness from the throttle body and the vacuum hoses from the air intake plenum.
7. Place a shop towel under the fuel hose connection to absorb any spilled fuel and disconnect the fuel hose from the fuel rail.

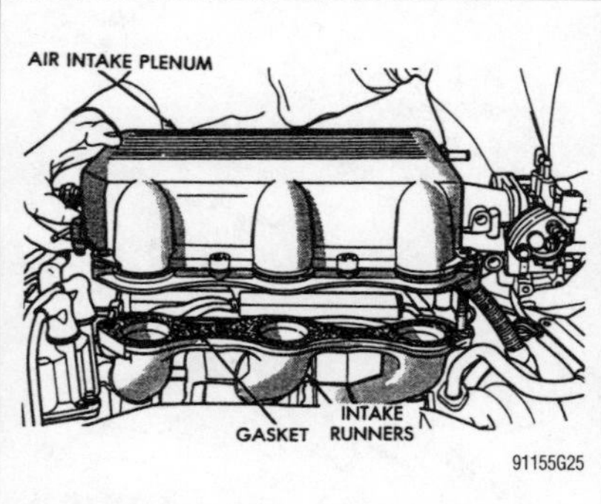

Fig. 28 Remove the air intake plenum (upper intake manifold)

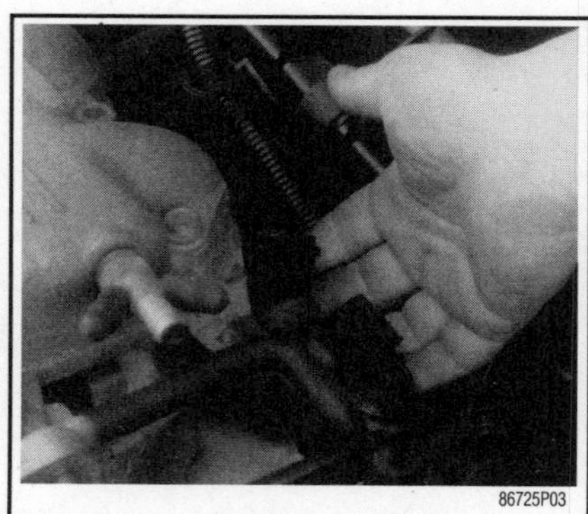

Fig. 29 Disconnect the fuel injector wiring harness from the engine wiring harness.

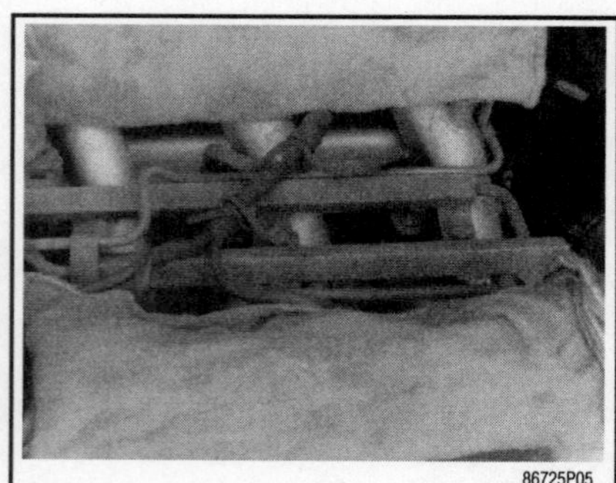

Fig. 30 After removing the upper intake manifold, cover the openings to prevent any dirt from entering

86725P09

Fig. 31 Remove the fuel rail retaining bolts . . .

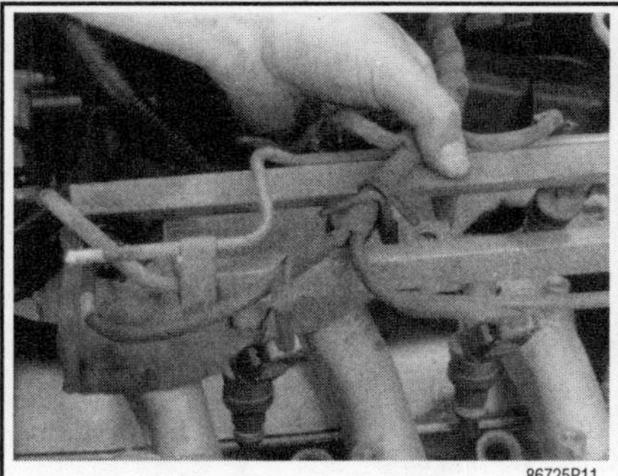
86725P11

Fig. 32 . . . then lift the fuel rail/injector assembly off the intake manifold. Be careful not to damage the fuel injector O-rings

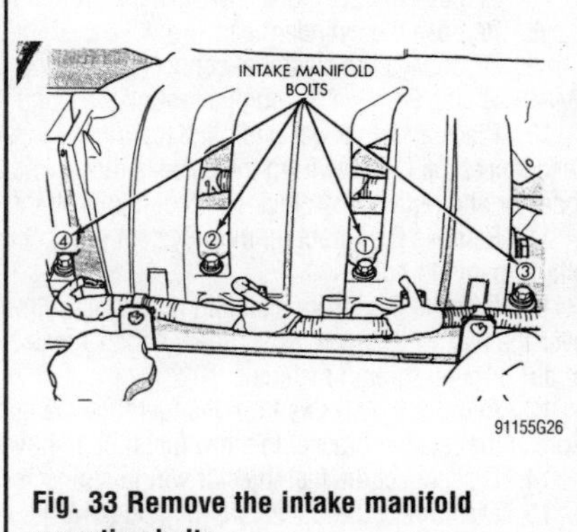

91155G26

Fig. 33 Remove the intake manifold mounting bolts

8. Disconnect the fuel injector wiring harness from the engine wiring harness.
9. Remove the intake plenum-to-intake manifold retaining bolts. Remove the ignition coil.
10. Remove the air intake plenum. Cover the the intake manifold to prevent the entrance of dirt or other foreign material.
11. Disconnect the fuel injector wiring harness from the engine wiring harness.
12. Remove the fuel rail retaining bolts. Lift the fuel rail/injector assembly off the intake manifold. Be careful not to damage the fuel injector O-rings.
13. Inspect the injector O-rings for damage and replace, as necessary.

To install:

14. Make sure the injectors are fully seated in the fuel rail and the clips are securely in place. Make sure the injector holes in the manifold are clean.
15. Lubricate the lower injector O-rings with clean engine oil. Start each injector into its hole and push the assembly into place until all injectors are fully seated.
16. Install the fuel rail retaining bolts and tighten to 115 inch lbs. (13 Nm).
17. Install the fuel supply and return tube hold-down bolt and the vacuum crossover tube hold-down bolt and tighten to 95 inch lbs. (10 Nm).
18. Attach the electrical connectors to the fuel injectors in correct order. Connect the fuel injector wiring harness to the engine harness.
19. Clean the intake manifold mating surfaces. Place the manifold gaskets, beaded sealer side up, on the lower manifold.
20. Place the air intake plenum in position and install the ignition coil. Install the retaining bolts and tighten to 115 inch lbs. (13 Nm).
21. Connect the fuel line to the fuel rail. Connect the vacuum line to the intake plenum.
22. Attach the electrical connectors to the ECT sensor, TPS and IAC motor.
23. Reconnect the PCV and power brake booster supply hose to the intake manifold.
24. Reconnect the vacuum vapor harness to the throttle body.
25. Install the throttle cable. Install the air inlet resonator.
26. Reconnect the negative battery cable.

**** WARNING**

When using the ASD Fuel System Test, the ASD relay and fuel pump relay remain energized for 7 minutes or until the test is stopped, or until the ignition switch is turned to the OFF position.

27. Turn the ignition key to the **ON** position and access the DRB scan tool ASD Fuel System Test to pressurize the fuel system. Check the fuel system for leaks.

3.3L and 3.8L Engines

See Figures 33, 34 and 35

The engines use a sequential Multi-Port Electronic Fuel Injection (MPI) system. The MPI system uses fuel injectors positioned in the intake manifold with the nozzle ends directly above the intake port. The fuel rail assembly must be removed to service the injectors. The system pressure is approximately 48 psi.

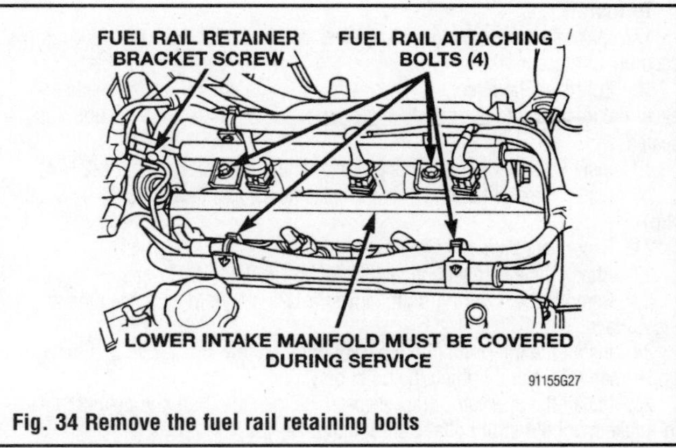

91155G27

Fig. 34 Remove the fuel rail retaining bolts

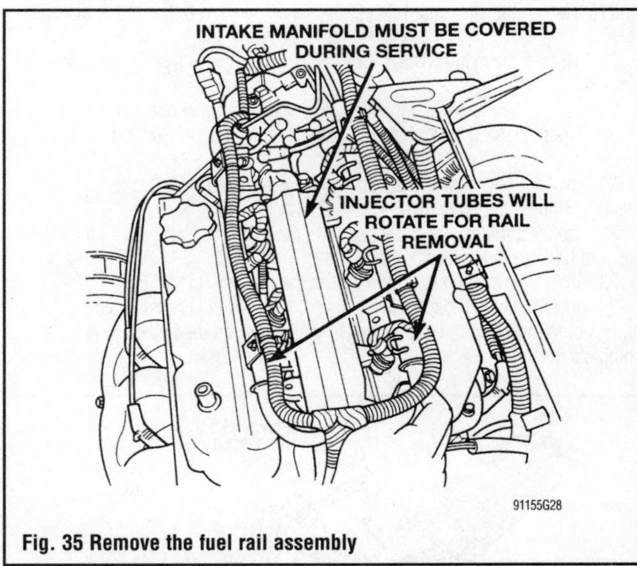

91155G28

Fig. 35 Remove the fuel rail assembly

(330 Kpa). Perform the fuel pressure release procedure before attempting to service the fuel injectors.

1. Properly relieve the fuel system pressure.
2. Disconnect the negative battery cable.
3. Remove the intake manifold cover.
4. Remove the air inlet resonator.
5. Disconnect the throttle cable and speed control cable (if equipped) from the throttle lever and cable bracket.
6. Disengage the Idle Air Control (IAC) motor and Throttle Position Sensor (TPS) electrical connectors. Tag and disconnect the vacuum hose harness from the throttle body and intake manifold.

7. Remove the EGR tube-to-intake manifold flange bolts.
8. Remove the cylinder head-to-intake plenum strut.
9. Disengage the electrical connector from the Manifold Absolute Pressure (MAP) sensor. Remove the engine mounted ground strap.
10. Place a shop towel under the fuel lines to catch any gasoline spillage. Disconnect the fuel line from the chassis tube by squeezing the retainer tabs together and pulling the quick-connect fitting off the fuel tube nipple.
11. Remove the Direct Ignition System (DIS) coils and alternator bracket-to-intake manifold bolt.
12. Remove the intake manifold mounting bolts and rotate the manifold back over the rear valve cover. Cover the the intake manifold to prevent the entrance of dirt or other foreign material.
13. Remove the screws from the fuel tube clamp and fuel rail retaining bolts. Spread the retainer bracket to allow fuel tube removal clearance.
14. Disconnect the fuel injector wiring connector from the fuel injector.
15. Disconnect the Camshaft Position (CMP) sensor and Engine Coolant Temperature (ECT) sensor. Remove the fuel rail.
16. Check the injector O-rings for damage and replace, as necessary.

To install:

17. Make sure the injectors are fully seated in the fuel rail and the clips are securely in place. Make sure the injector holes in the manifold are clean.
18. Lubricate the injector O-rings with clean engine oil. Install the tip of each fuel injector into their ports and push the assembly into place until fully seated.
19. Install the fuel rail mounting bolts and tighten to 16 ft. lbs. (22 Nm).
20. Install the fuel tube retaining bracket screw and tighten to 35 inch lbs. (4 Nm).
21. Reconnect the fuel injector wiring.
22. Attach the electrical connectors to the CMP and ECT sensors.
23. Remove the covering on the lower intake manifold and clean the mounting surface.
24. Install the intake manifold gasket onto the lower manifold and install the upper manifold. Hand tighten the bolts only.
25. Install the alternator bracket-to-intake manifold bolt and cylinder head-to-intake manifold strut bolts. Do not tighten.
26. Tighten the manifold bolts, in sequence, to 21 ft. lbs. (28 Nm).
27. Tighten the alternator bracket-to-intake manifold bolt to 40 ft. lbs. (54 Nm).
28. Tighten the cylinder head-to-intake manifold strut bolts to 40 ft. lbs. (54 Nm).
29. Attach the ground strap and MAP sensor electrical connector.
30. Connect the vacuum harness to the intake plenum. Connect the PCV hoses.
31. Install a new gasket and connect the EGR tube to the intake manifold plenum. Tighten the bolts to 16 ft. lbs. (22 Nm).
32. Connect the electrical connector to the TPS and IAC motor. Connect the vacuum harness to the throttle body.
33. Install the ignition coils and tighten the retainers to 105 inch lbs. (12 Nm).
34. Install the fuel hose quick-connect fittings to the chassis tubes. Push the fittings onto the tubes until they click in place. Pull on the fittings to ensure complete insertion.
35. Install the throttle cable and speed control cable, if equipped.
36. Install the air inlet resonator.
37. Reconnect the negative battery cable.

✲✲ WARNING

When using the ASD Fuel System Test, the ASD relay and fuel pump relay remain energized for 7 minutes or until the test is stopped, or until the ignition switch is turned to the OFF position.

38. Turn the ignition key to the **ON** position and access the DRB scan tool ASD Fuel System Test to pressurize the fuel system. Check the fuel system for leaks.

Fuel Pressure Regulator

REMOVAL & INSTALLATION

See Figures 36 and 37

The fuel pressure regulator is part of the fuel pump module. Remove the module from the fuel tank for access to the regulator.

1. Disconnect the negative battery cable.

✲✲ CAUTION

Observe all applicable safety precautions when working around fuel. Whenever servicing the fuel system, always work in a well ventilated area. Do not allow fuel spray or vapors to come in contact with a spark or open flame. Keep a dry chemical fire extinguisher near the work area. Always keep fuel in a container specifically designed for fuel storage; also, always properly seal fuel containers to avoid the possibility of fire or explosion.

2. Properly relieve the fuel system pressure, as described earlier in this section.
3. Remove the fuel pump module, as outlined earlier in this section.
4. Spread the tabs on the pressure regulator retainer.
5. Using a suitable prytool, carefully pry the regulator out of the housing.

➡Make sure both the upper and lower O-rings were removed with the regulator.

To install:

6. Lightly lubricate the O-rings with clean engine oil, then place them into the fuel pump module opening.
7. Push the regulator into the opening in the pump module.
8. Fold the tabs on the regulator retainer over the tabs on the housing.
9. Install the fuel pump module, as outlined earlier in this section.
10. Connect the negative battery cable.

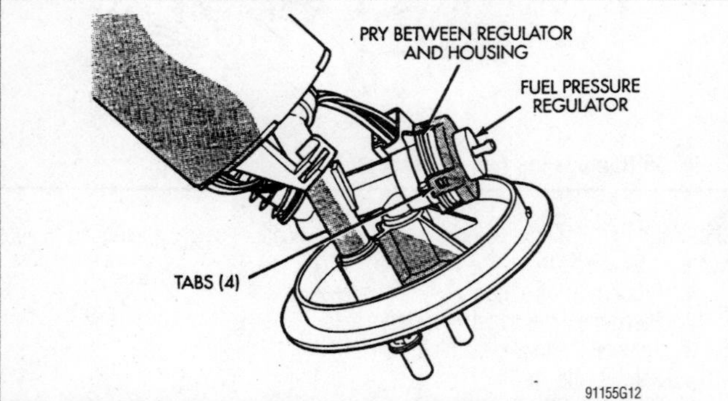

Fig. 36 Fuel pressure regulator location on the fuel pump module assembly

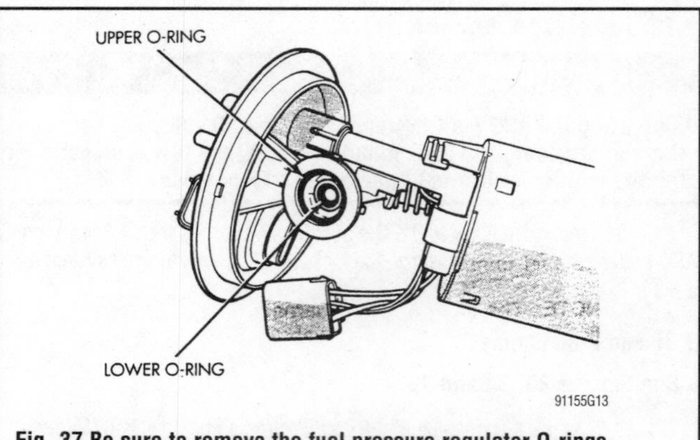

Fig. 37 Be sure to remove the fuel pressure regulator O-rings

FUEL TANK

Tank Assembly

REMOVAL & INSTALLATION

➧ See Figures 38 thru 43

**** CAUTION**

Observe all applicable safety precautions when working around fuel. Whenever servicing the fuel system, always work in a well ventilated area. Do not allow fuel spray or vapors to come in contact with a spark or open flame. Keep a dry chemical fire extinguisher near the work area. Always keep fuel in a container specifically designed for fuel storage; also, always properly seal fuel containers to avoid the possibility of fire or explosion.

1. Disconnect the negative battery cable.
2. Remove the fuel filler cap.
3. Properly relieve the fuel system pressure, as outlined earlier in this section.
4. Insert a fuel syphon hose into the fuel filler neck and push it into the fuel tank.
5. Drain the fuel tank dry into a proper holding tank or a properly labeled gasoline safety container.
6. Raise and safely support the vehicle.
7. Disconnect both the fuel filler and vent rubber hoses at the fuel tank.
8. Disconnect the supply lines from the: fuel pump module located on top of the fuel tank (1996), or the steel supply line (1997–99).
9. Slide the fuel pump module electrical connector lock to the unlock position, then push down on the retainer and pull the connector off of the module.
10. Place a transmission jack, or equivalent support fixture, under the fuel tank.

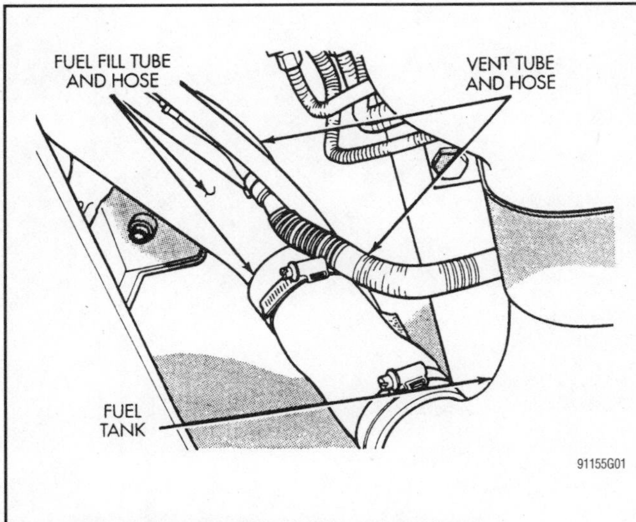

Fig. 38 Disconnect the fuel tank filler and vent hoses

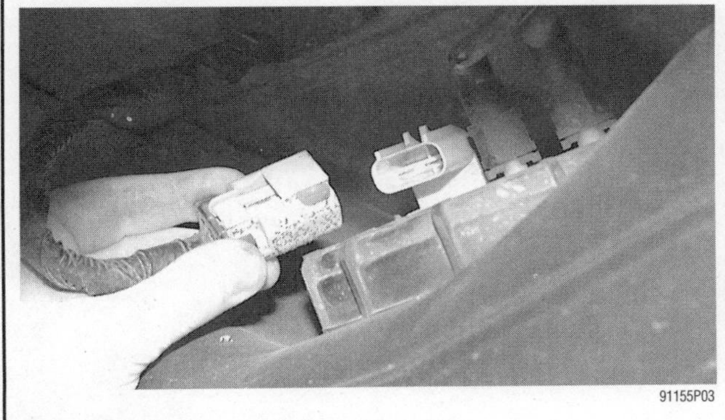

Fig. 39 Disengage the fuel pump connector . . .

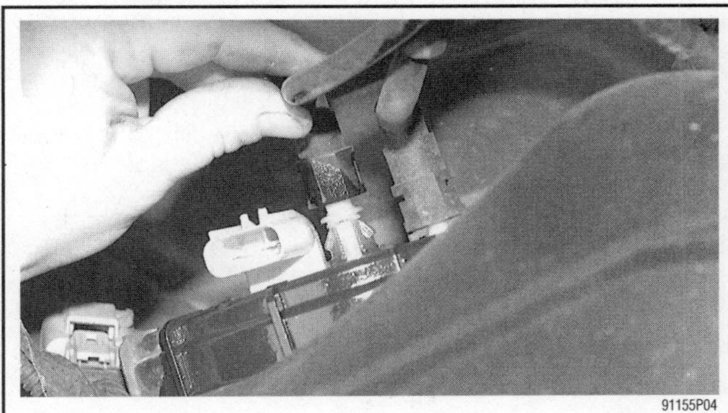

Fig. 40 . . . then disconnect the fuel line quick connect fittings

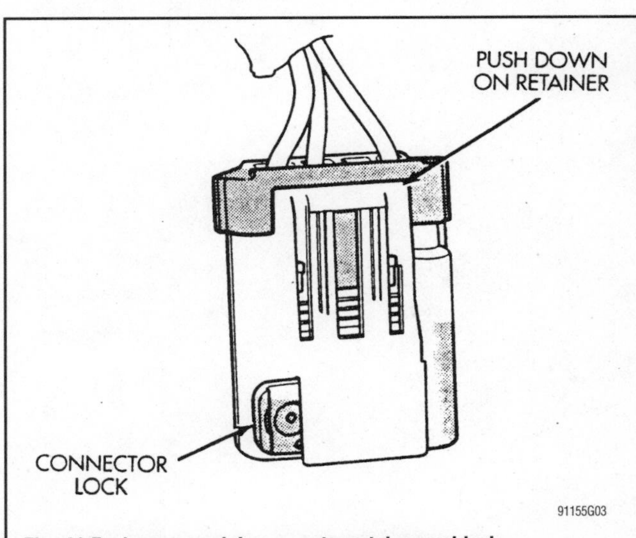

Fig. 41 Fuel pump module connector retainer and lock

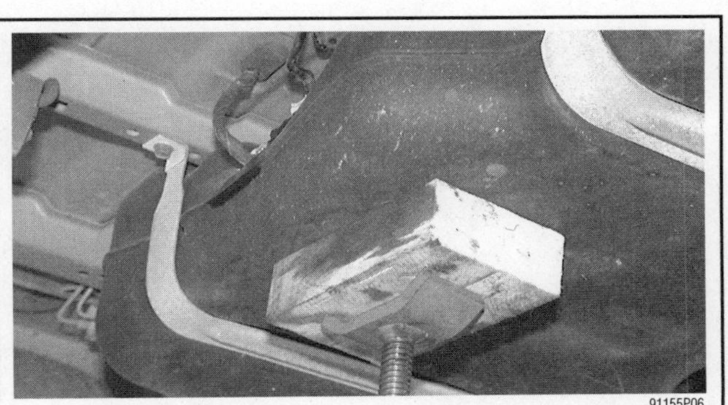

Fig. 42 With the tank supported by a transmission jack, or equivalent, remove the bolts and fuel tank mounting straps

11. With the tank supported by a transmission jack, or equivalent, remove the bolts and fuel tank mounting straps.

12. Lower the fuel tank slightly. Carefully remove the filler hose from the tank.

13. Lower the fuel tank. Disconnect the pressure relief/rollover valve hose at the front of the tank. Remove clamp, then remove the fuel filler tube vent hose. Remove the tank from the vehicle.

To install:

14. Position the fuel tank onto the transmission jack. Connect the pressure relief/rollover valve hose. Connect the fuel filler tube vent hose and replace the clamp.

15. Raise the tank into position and carefully work filler tube into the fuel tank. A light coating of clean engine oil on the tube end may be used to aid assembly.

16. Feed the filler vent line through the frame rail, being very careful not to cross the lines.

17. Tighten the fuel tank strap bolts to 40 ft. lbs. (54 Nm). Check to make sure that the tank straps are not twisted or bent. Remove the transmission jack.

18. Attach the fuel pump/module electrical connector and place the retainer in the locked position.

19. Lubricate the fuel line with clean 30W engine oil, then install the quick connect fitting. If necessary, refer to the quick-connect fitting information earlier in this section.

20. Carefully lower the vehicle.

21. Fill the fuel tank, install the filler cap, then connect the negative battery cable.

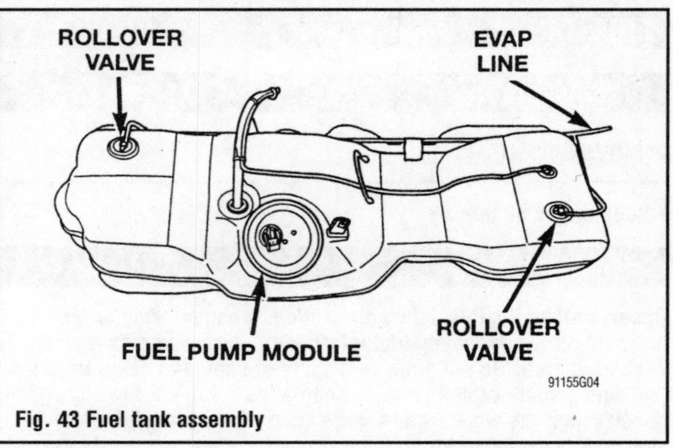

Fig. 43 Fuel tank assembly

⁂ CAUTION

When performing the ASD fuel system test, the ASD relay will remain energized for either 7 minutes, until the test is completed, or until the ignition switch is turned to the OFF position.

22. Pressurize the fuel system using the Chrysler DRB, or equivalent scan tool, to perform the ASD fuel system test. Check the fuel system for leaks.

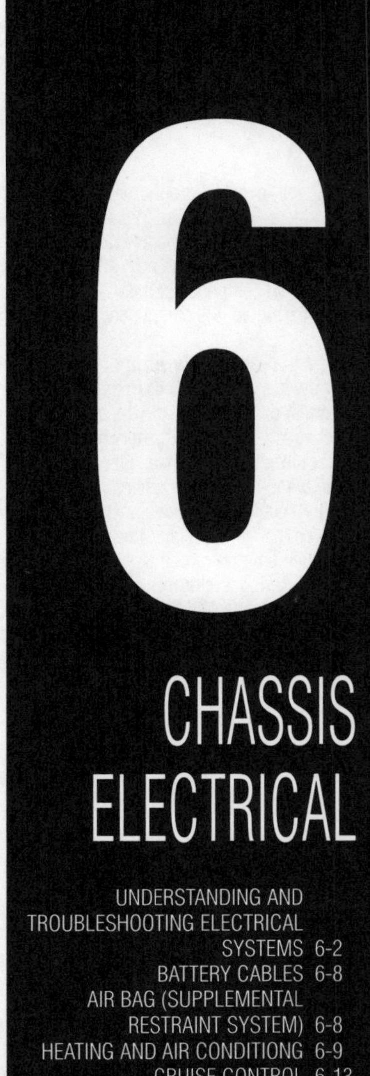

6 CHASSIS ELECTRICAL

UNDERSTANDING AND TROUBLESHOOTING ELECTRICAL SYSTEMS

Basic Electrical Theory

➧ See Figure 1

For any 12 volt, negative ground, electrical system to operate, the electricity must travel in a complete circuit. This simply means that current (power) from the positive (+) terminal of the battery must eventually return to the negative (–) terminal of the battery. Along the way, this current will travel through wires, fuses, switches and components. If, for any reason, the flow of current through the circuit is interrupted, the component fed by that circuit will cease to function properly.

Perhaps the easiest way to visualize a circuit is to think of connecting a light bulb (with two wires attached to it) to the battery—one wire attached to the negative (–) terminal of the battery and the other wire to the positive (+) terminal. With the two wires touching the battery terminals, the circuit would be complete and the light bulb would illuminate. Electricity would follow a path from the battery to the bulb and back to the battery. It's easy to see that with longer wires on our light bulb, it could be mounted anywhere. Further, one wire could be fitted with a switch so that the light could be turned on and off.

The normal automotive circuit differs from this simple example in two ways. First, instead of having a return wire from the bulb to the battery, the current travels through the frame of the vehicle. Since the negative (–) battery cable is attached to the frame (made of electrically conductive metal), the frame of the vehicle can serve as a ground wire to complete the circuit. Secondly, most automotive circuits contain multiple components which receive power from a single circuit. This lessens the amount of wire needed to power components on the vehicle.

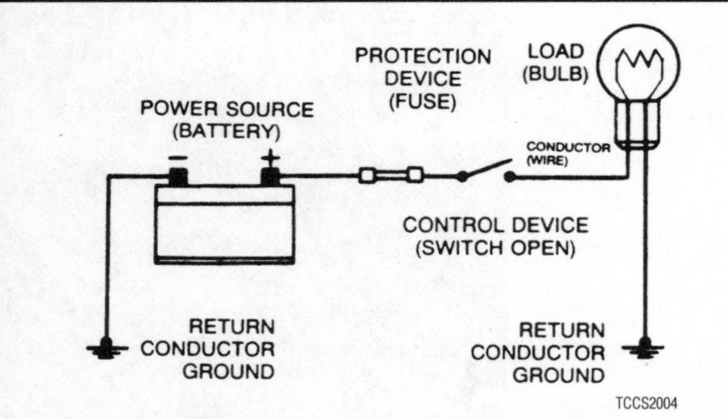

Fig. 1 This example illustrates a simple circuit. When the switch is closed, power from the positive (+) battery terminal flows through the fuse and the switch, and then to the light bulb. The light illuminates and the circuit is completed through the ground wire back to the negative (–) battery terminal. In reality, the two ground points shown in the illustration are attached to the metal frame of the vehicle, which completes the circuit back to the battery

HOW DOES ELECTRICITY WORK: THE WATER ANALOGY

Electricity is the flow of electrons—the subatomic particles that constitute the outer shell of an atom. Electrons spin in an orbit around the center core of an atom. The center core is comprised of protons (positive charge) and neutrons (neutral charge). Electrons have a negative charge and balance out the positive charge of the protons. When an outside force causes the number of electrons to unbalance the charge of the protons, the electrons will split off the atom and look for another atom to balance out. If this imbalance is kept up, electrons will continue to move and an electrical flow will exist.

Many people have been taught electrical theory using an analogy with water. In a comparison with water flowing through a pipe, the electrons would be the water and the wire is the pipe.

The flow of electricity can be measured much like the flow of water through a pipe. The unit of measurement used is amperes, frequently abbreviated as amps (a). You can compare amperage to the volume of water flowing through a pipe. When connected to a circuit, an ammeter will measure the actual amount of current flowing through the circuit. When relatively few electrons flow through a circuit, the amperage is low. When many electrons flow, the amperage is high.

Water pressure is measured in units such as pounds per square inch (psi); the electrical pressure is measured in units called volts (v). When a voltmeter is connected to a circuit, it is measuring the electrical pressure.

The actual flow of electricity depends not only on voltage and amperage, but also on the resistance of the circuit. The higher the resistance, the higher the force necessary to push the current through the circuit. The standard unit for measuring resistance is an ohm. Resistance in a circuit varies depending on the amount and type of components used in the circuit. The main factors which determine resistance are:

- Material—some materials have more resistance than others. Those with high resistance are said to be insulators. Rubber materials (or rubber-like plastics) are some of the most common insulators used in vehicles as they have a very high resistance to electricity. Very low resistance materials are said to be conductors. Copper wire is among the best conductors. Silver is actually a superior conductor to copper and is used in some relay contacts, but its high cost prohibits its use as common wiring. Most automotive wiring is made of copper.
- Size—the larger the wire size being used, the less resistance the wire will have. This is why components which use large amounts of electricity usually have large wires supplying current to them.
- Length—for a given thickness of wire, the longer the wire, the greater the resistance. The shorter the wire, the less the resistance. When determining the proper wire for a circuit, both size and length must be considered to design a circuit that can handle the current needs of the component.
- Temperature—with many materials, the higher the temperature, the greater the resistance (positive temperature coefficient). Some materials exhibit the opposite trait of lower resistance with higher temperatures (negative temperature coefficient). These principles are used in many of the sensors on the engine.

OHM'S LAW

There is a direct relationship between current, voltage and resistance. The relationship between current, voltage and resistance can be summed up by a statement known as Ohm's law.

Voltage (E) is equal to amperage (I) times resistance (R): $E=I \times R$

Other forms of the formula are $R=E/I$ and $I=E/R$

In each of these formulas, E is the voltage in volts, I is the current in amps and R is the resistance in ohms. The basic point to remember is that as the resistance of a circuit goes up, the amount of current that flows in the circuit will go down, if voltage remains the same.

The amount of work that the electricity can perform is expressed as power. The unit of power is the watt (w). The relationship between power, voltage and current is expressed as:

Power (w) is equal to amperage (I) times voltage (E): $W=I \times E$

This is only true for direct current (DC) circuits; The alternating current formula is a tad different, but since the electrical circuits in most vehicles are DC type, we need not get into AC circuit theory.

Electrical Components

POWER SOURCE

Power is supplied to the vehicle by two devices: The battery and the alternator. The battery supplies electrical power during starting or during periods when the current demand of the vehicle's electrical system exceeds the output capacity of the alternator. The alternator supplies electrical current when the engine is running. Just not does the alternator supply the current needs of the vehicle, but it recharges the battery.

The Battery

In most modern vehicles, the battery is a lead/acid electrochemical device consisting of six 2 volt subsections (cells) connected in series, so that the unit is capable of producing approximately 12 volts of electrical pressure. Each subsection consists of a series of positive and negative plates held a short distance apart in a solution of sulfuric acid and water.

The two types of plates are of dissimilar metals. This sets up a chemical reaction, and it is this reaction which produces current flow from the battery when its positive and negative terminals are connected to an electrical load. The power removed from the battery is replaced by the alternator, restoring the battery to its original chemical state.

The Alternator

On some vehicles there isn't an alternator, but a generator. The difference is that an alternator supplies alternating current which is then changed to direct current for use on the vehicle, while a generator produces direct current. Alternators tend to be more efficient and that is why they are used.

Alternators and generators are devices that consist of coils of wires wound together making big electromagnets. One group of coils spins within another set and the interaction of the magnetic fields causes a current to flow. This current is then drawn off the coils and fed into the vehicles electrical system.

GROUND

Two types of grounds are used in automotive electric circuits. Direct ground components are grounded to the frame through their mounting points. All other components use some sort of ground wire which is attached to the frame or chassis of the vehicle. The electrical current runs through the chassis of the vehicle and returns to the battery through the ground (–) cable; if you look, you'll see that the battery ground cable connects between the battery and the frame or chassis of the vehicle.

➡It should be noted that a good percentage of electrical problems can be traced to bad grounds.

PROTECTIVE DEVICES

➧ See Figure 2

It is possible for large surges of current to pass through the electrical system of your vehicle. If this surge of current were to reach the load in the circuit, the surge could burn it out or severely damage it. It can also overload the wiring, causing the harness to get hot and melt the insulation. To prevent this, fuses, circuit breakers and/or fusible links are connected into the supply wires of the electrical system. These items are nothing more than a built-in weak spot in the system. When an abnormal amount of current flows through the system, these protective devices work as follows to protect the circuit:

- Fuse—when an excessive electrical current passes through a fuse, the fuse "blows" (the conductor melts) and opens the circuit, preventing the passage of current.
- Circuit Breaker—a circuit breaker is basically a self-repairing fuse. It will open the circuit in the same fashion as a fuse, but when the surge subsides, the circuit breaker can be reset and does not need replacement.
- Fusible Link—a fusible link (fuse link or main link) is a short length of special, high temperature insulated wire that acts as a fuse. When an excessive electrical current passes through a fusible link, the thin gauge wire inside the link melts, creating an intentional open to protect the circuit. To repair the circuit, the link must be replaced. Some newer type fusible links are housed in plug-in modules, which are simply replaced like a fuse, while older type fusible links must be cut and spliced if they melt. Since this link is very early in the electrical path, it's the first place to look if nothing on the vehicle works, yet the battery seems to be charged and is properly connected.

⁂ CAUTION

Always replace fuses, circuit breakers and fusible links with identically rated components. Under no circumstances should a component of higher or lower amperage rating be substituted.

SWITCHES & RELAYS

➧ See Figures 3 and 4

Switches are used in electrical circuits to control the passage of current. The most common use is to open and close circuits between the battery and the various electric devices in the system. Switches are rated according to the amount of amperage they can handle. If a sufficient amperage rated switch is not used in a circuit, the switch could overload and cause damage.

Some electrical components which require a large amount of current to operate use a special switch called a relay. Since these circuits carry a large amount of current, the thickness of the wire in the circuit is also greater. If this large wire were connected from the load to the control switch, the switch would have to carry the high amperage load and the fairing or dash would be twice as large to accommodate the increased size of the wiring harness. To prevent these problems, a relay is used.

Relays are composed of a coil and a set of contacts. When the coil has a current passed though it, a magnetic field is formed and this field causes the contacts to move together, completing the circuit. Most relays are normally open, preventing current from passing through the circuit, but they can take any electrical form depending on the job they are intended to do. Relays can be considered "remote control switches." They allow a smaller current to operate devices that require higher amperages. When a small current operates the coil, a larger current is allowed to pass by the contacts. Some common circuits which may use relays are the horn, headlights, starter, electric fuel pump and other high draw ciruits.

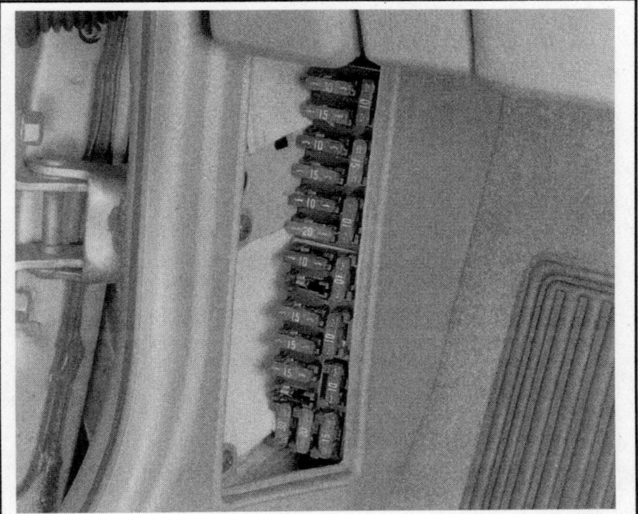

Fig. 2 Most vehicles use one or more fuse panels. This one is located on the driver's side kick panel

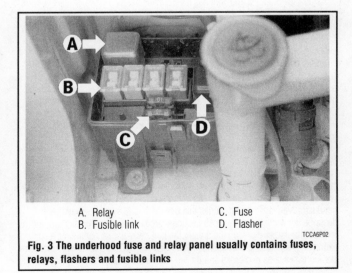

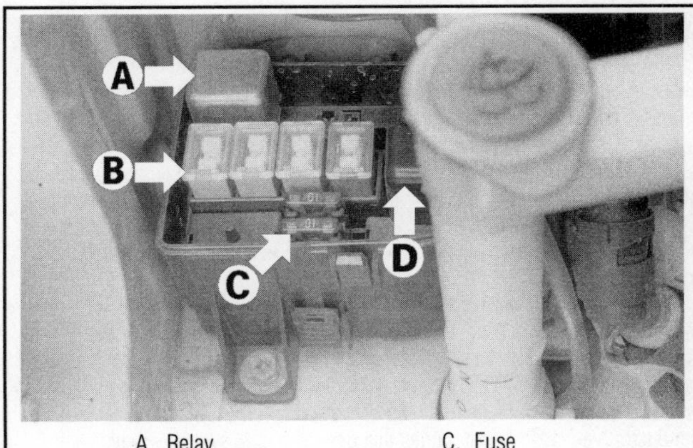

Fig. 3 The underhood fuse and relay panel usually contains fuses, relays, flashers and fusible links

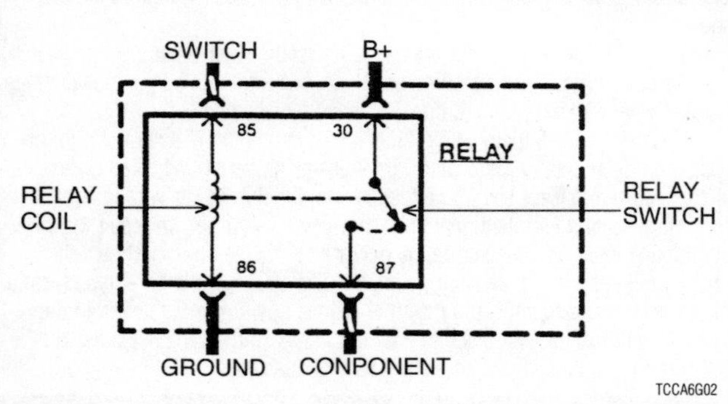

Fig. 4 Relays are composed of a coil and a switch. These two components are linked together so that when one operates, the other operates at the same time. The large wires in the circuit are connected from the battery to one side of the relay switch (B+) and from the opposite side of the relay switch to the load (component). Smaller wires are connected from the relay coil to the control switch for the circuit and from the opposite side of the relay coil to ground

LOAD

Every electrical circuit must include a "load" (something to use the electricity coming from the source). Without this load, the battery would attempt to deliver its entire power supply from one pole to another. This is called a "short circuit." All this electricity would take a short cut to ground and cause a great amount of damage to other components in the circuit by developing a tremendous amount of heat. This condition could develop sufficient heat to melt the insulation on all the surrounding wires and reduce a multiple wire cable to a lump of plastic and copper.

WIRING & HARNESSES

The average vehicle contains meters and meters of wiring, with hundreds of individual connections. To protect the many wires from damage and to keep them from becoming a confusing tangle, they are organized into bundles, enclosed in plastic or taped together and called wiring harnesses. Different harnesses serve different parts of the vehicle. Individual wires are color coded to help trace them through a harness where sections are hidden from view.

Automotive wiring or circuit conductors can be either single strand wire, multi-strand wire or printed circuitry. Single strand wire has a solid metal core and is usually used inside such components as alternators, motors, relays and other devices. Multi-strand wire has a core made of many small strands of wire twisted together into a single conductor. Most of the wiring in an automotive electrical system is made up of multi-strand wire, either as a single conductor or grouped together in a harness. All wiring is color coded on the insulator, either as a solid color or as a colored wire with an identification stripe. A printed circuit is a thin film of copper or other conductor that is printed on an insulator backing. Occasionally, a printed circuit is sandwiched between two sheets of plastic for more protection and flexibility. A complete printed circuit, consisting of conductors, insulating material and connectors for lamps or other components is called a printed circuit board. Printed circuitry is used in place of individual wires or harnesses in places where space is limited, such as behind instrument panels.

Since automotive electrical systems are very sensitive to changes in resistance, the selection of properly sized wires is critical when systems are repaired. A loose or corroded connection or a replacement wire that is too small for the circuit will add extra resistance and an additional voltage drop to the circuit.

The wire gauge number is an expression of the cross-section area of the conductor. Vehicles from countries that use the metric system will typically describe the wire size as its cross-sectional area in square millimeters. In this method, the larger the wire, the greater the number. Another common system for expressing wire size is the American Wire Gauge (AWG) system. As gauge number increases, area decreases and the wire becomes smaller. An 18 gauge wire is smaller than a 4 gauge wire. A wire with a higher gauge number will carry less current than a wire with a lower gauge number. Gauge wire size refers to the size of the strands of the conductor, not the size of the complete wire with insulator. It is possible, therefore, to have two wires of the same gauge with different diameters because one may have thicker insulation than the other.

It is essential to understand how a circuit works before trying to figure out why it doesn't. An electrical schematic shows the electrical current paths when a circuit is operating properly. Schematics break the entire electrical system down into individual circuits. In a schematic, usually no attempt is made to represent wiring and components as they physically appear on the vehicle; switches and other components are shown as simply as possible. Face views of harness connectors show the cavity or terminal locations in all multi-pin connectors to help locate test points.

CONNECTORS

▶ See Figures 5 and 6

Three types of connectors are commonly used in automotive applications—weatherproof, molded and hard shell.

- Weatherproof—these connectors are most commonly used where the connector is exposed to the elements. Terminals are protected against moisture and dirt by sealing rings which provide a weathertight seal. All repairs require the use of a special terminal and the tool required to service it. Unlike standard blade type terminals, these weatherproof terminals cannot be straightened once they are bent. Make certain that the connectors are properly seated and all of the sealing rings are in place when connecting leads.
- Molded—these connectors require complete replacement of the connector if found to be defective. This means splicing a new connector assembly into

Fig. 5 Hard shell (left) and weatherproof (right) connectors have replaceable terminals

Fig. 6 Weatherproof connectors are most commonly used in the engine compartment or where the connector is exposed to the elements

the harness. All splices should be soldered to insure proper contact. Use care when probing the connections or replacing terminals in them, as it is possible to create a short circuit between opposite terminals. If this happens to the wrong terminal pair, it is possible to damage certain components. Always use jumper wires between connectors for circuit checking and NEVER probe through weatherproof seals.

- Hard Shell—unlike molded connectors, the terminal contacts in hard-shell connectors can be replaced. Replacement usually involves the use of a special terminal removal tool that depresses the locking tangs (barbs) on the connector terminal and allows the connector to be removed from the rear of the shell. The connector shell should be replaced if it shows any evidence of burning, melting, cracks, or breaks. Replace individual terminals that are burnt, corroded, distorted or loose.

Test Equipment

Pinpointing the exact cause of trouble in an electrical circuit is most times accomplished by the use of special test equipment. The following describes different types of commonly used test equipment and briefly explains how to use them in diagnosis. In addition to the information covered below, the tool manufacturer's instructions booklet (provided with the tester) should be read and clearly understood before attempting any test procedures.

JUMPER WIRES

**** CAUTION**

Never use jumper wires made from a thinner gauge wire than the circuit being tested. If the jumper wire is of too small a gauge, it may overheat and possibly melt. Never use jumpers to bypass high resistance loads in a circuit. Bypassing resistances, in effect, creates a short circuit. This may, in turn, cause damage and fire. Jumper wires should only be used to bypass lengths of wire or to simulate switches.

Jumper wires are simple, yet extremely valuable, pieces of test equipment. They are basically test wires which are used to bypass sections of a circuit. Although jumper wires can be purchased, they are usually fabricated from lengths of standard automotive wire and whatever type of connector (alligator clip, spade connector or pin connector) that is required for the particular application being tested. In cramped, hard-to-reach areas, it is advisable to have insulated boots over the jumper wire terminals in order to prevent accidental grounding. It is also advisable to include a standard automotive fuse in any jumper wire. This is commonly referred to as a "fused jumper". By inserting an in-line fuse holder between a set of test leads, a fused jumper wire can be used for bypassing open circuits. Use a 5 amp fuse to provide protection against voltage spikes.

Jumper wires are used primarily to locate open electrical circuits, on either the ground (–) side of the circuit or on the power (+) side. If an electrical component fails to operate, connect the jumper wire between the component and a good ground. If the component operates only with the jumper installed, the ground circuit is open. If the ground circuit is good, but the component does not operate, the circuit between the power feed and component may be open. By moving the jumper wire successively back from the component toward the power source, you can isolate the area of the circuit where the open is located. When the component stops functioning, or the power is cut off, the open is in the segment of wire between the jumper and the point previously tested.

You can sometimes connect the jumper wire directly from the battery to the "hot" terminal of the component, but first make sure the component uses 12 volts in operation. Some electrical components, such as fuel injectors or sensors, are designed to operate on about 4 to 5 volts, and running 12 volts directly to these components will cause damage.

TEST LIGHTS

See Figure 7

The test light is used to check circuits and components while electrical current is flowing through them. It is used for voltage and ground tests. To use a 12 volt test light, connect the ground clip to a good ground and probe wherever necessary with the pick. The test light will illuminate when voltage is detected.

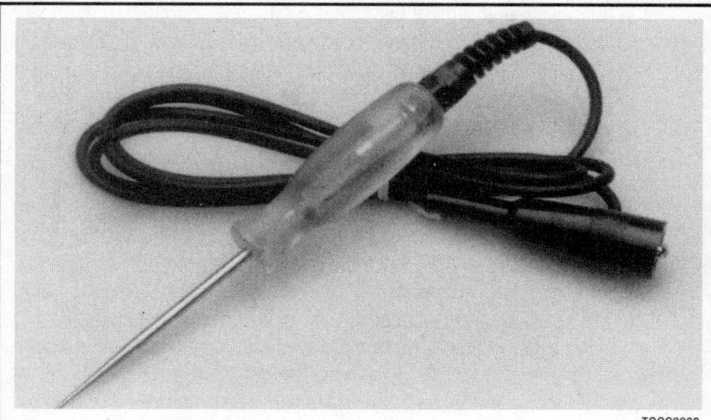
TCCS2006

Fig. 7 A 12 volt test light is used to detect the presence of voltage in a circuit

This does not necessarily mean that 12 volts (or any particular amount of voltage) is present; it only means that some voltage is present. It is advisable before using the test light to touch its ground clip and probe across the battery posts or terminals to make sure the light is operating properly.

**** WARNING**

Do not use a test light to probe electronic ignition, spark plug or coil wires. Never use a pick-type test light to probe wiring on computer controlled systems unless specifically instructed to do so. Any wire insulation that is pierced by the test light probe should be taped and sealed with silicone after testing.

Like the jumper wire, the 12 volt test light is used to isolate opens in circuits. But, whereas the jumper wire is used to bypass the open to operate the load, the 12 volt test light is used to locate the presence of voltage in a circuit. If the test light illuminates, there is power up to that point in the circuit; if the test light does not illuminate, there is an open circuit (no power). Move the test light in successive steps back toward the power source until the light in the handle illuminates. The open is between the probe and a point which was previously probed.

The self-powered test light is similar in design to the 12 volt test light, but contains a 1.5 volt penlight battery in the handle. It is most often used in place of a multimeter to check for open or short circuits when power is isolated from the circuit (continuity test).

The battery in a self-powered test light does not provide much current. A weak battery may not provide enough power to illuminate the test light even when a complete circuit is made (especially if there is high resistance in the circuit). Always make sure that the test battery is strong. To check the battery, briefly touch the ground clip to the probe; if the light glows brightly, the battery is strong enough for testing.

➡A self-powered test light should not be used on any computer controlled system or component. The small amount of electricity transmitted by the test light is enough to damage many electronic automotive components.

MULTIMETERS

Multimeters are an extremely useful tool for troubleshooting electrical problems. They can be purchased in either analog or digital form and have a price range to suit any budget. A multimeter is a voltmeter, ammeter and ohmmeter (along with other features) combined into one instrument. It is often used when testing solid state circuits because of its high input impedance (usually 10 megaohms or more). A brief description of the multimeter main test functions follows:

- Voltmeter—the voltmeter is used to measure voltage at any point in a circuit, or to measure the voltage drop across any part of a circuit. Voltmeters usually have various scales and a selector switch to allow the reading of different voltage ranges. The voltmeter has a positive and a negative lead. To avoid damage to the meter, always connect the negative lead to the negative (–) side of the circuit (to ground or nearest the ground side of the circuit) and connect the positive lead to the positive (+) side of the circuit (to the power source or the nearest power source). Note that the negative voltmeter lead will always be black and that the positive voltmeter will always be some color other than black (usually red).

- Ohmmeter—the ohmmeter is designed to read resistance (measured in ohms) in a circuit or component. Most ohmmeters will have a selector switch which permits the measurement of different ranges of resistance (usually the selector switch allows the multiplication of the meter reading by 10, 100, 1,000 and 10,000). Some ohmmeters are "auto-ranging" which means the meter itself will determine which scale to use. Since the meters are powered by an internal battery, the ohmmeter can be used like a self-powered test light. When the ohmmeter is connected, current from the ohmmeter flows through the circuit or component being tested. Since the ohmmeter's internal resistance and voltage are known values, the amount of current flow through the meter depends on the resistance of the circuit or component being tested. The ohmmeter can also be used to perform a continuity test for suspected open circuits. In using the meter for making continuity checks, do not be concerned with the actual resistance readings. Zero resistance, or any ohm reading, indicates continuity in the circuit. Infinite resistance indicates an opening in the circuit. A high resistance reading where there should be none indicates a problem in the circuit. Checks for short circuits are made in the same manner as checks for open circuits, except that the circuit must be isolated from both power and normal ground. Infinite resistance indicates no continuity, while zero resistance indicates a dead short.

**** WARNING**

Never use an ohmmeter to check the resistance of a component or wire while there is voltage applied to the circuit.

- Ammeter—an ammeter measures the amount of current flowing through a circuit in units called amperes or amps. At normal operating voltage, most circuits have a characteristic amount of amperes, called "current draw" which can be measured using an ammeter. By referring to a specified current draw rating, then measuring the amperes and comparing the two values, one can determine what is happening within the circuit to aid in diagnosis. An open circuit, for example, will not allow any current to flow, so the ammeter reading will be zero. A damaged component or circuit will have an increased current draw, so the reading will be high. The ammeter is always connected in series with the circuit being tested. All of the current that normally flows through the circuit must also flow through the ammeter; if there is any other path for the current to follow, the ammeter reading will not be accurate. The ammeter itself has very little resistance to current flow and, therefore, will not affect the circuit, but it will measure current draw only when the circuit is closed and electricity is flowing. Excessive current draw can blow fuses and drain the battery, while a reduced current draw can cause motors to run slowly, lights to dim and other components to not operate properly.

Troubleshooting Electrical Systems

When diagnosing a specific problem, organized troubleshooting is a must. The complexity of a modern automotive vehicle demands that you approach any problem in a logical, organized manner. There are certain troubleshooting techniques, however, which are standard:

- Establish when the problem occurs. Does the problem appear only under certain conditions? Were there any noises, odors or other unusual symptoms? Isolate the problem area. To do this, make some simple tests and observations, then eliminate the systems that are working properly. Check for obvious problems, such as broken wires and loose or dirty connections. Always check the obvious before assuming something complicated is the cause.
- Test for problems systematically to determine the cause once the problem area is isolated. Are all the components functioning properly? Is there power going to electrical switches and motors. Performing careful, systematic checks will often turn up most causes on the first inspection, without wasting time checking components that have little or no relationship to the problem.
- Test all repairs after the work is done to make sure that the problem is fixed. Some causes can be traced to more than one component, so a careful verification of repair work is important in order to pick up additional malfunctions that may cause a problem to reappear or a different problem to arise. A blown fuse, for example, is a simple problem that may require more than another fuse to repair. If you don't look for a problem that caused a fuse to blow, a shorted wire (for example) may go undetected.

Experience has shown that most problems tend to be the result of a fairly simple and obvious cause, such as loose or corroded connectors, bad grounds or damaged wire insulation which causes a short. This makes careful visual inspection of components during testing essential to quick and accurate troubleshooting.

Testing

OPEN CIRCUITS

See Figure 8

This test already assumes the existence of an open in the circuit and it is used to help locate the open portion.

1. Isolate the circuit from power and ground.
2. Connect the self-powered test light or ohmmeter ground clip to the ground side of the circuit and probe sections of the circuit sequentially.
3. If the light is out or there is infinite resistance, the open is between the probe and the circuit ground.
4. If the light is on or the meter shows continuity, the open is between the probe and the end of the circuit toward the power source.

SHORT CIRCUITS

Never use a self-powered test light to perform checks for opens or shorts when power is applied to the circuit under test. The test light can be damaged by outside power.

1. Isolate the circuit from power and ground.
2. Connect the self-powered test light or ohmmeter ground clip to a good ground and probe any easy-to-reach point in the circuit.
3. If the light comes on or there is continuity, there is a short somewhere in the circuit.

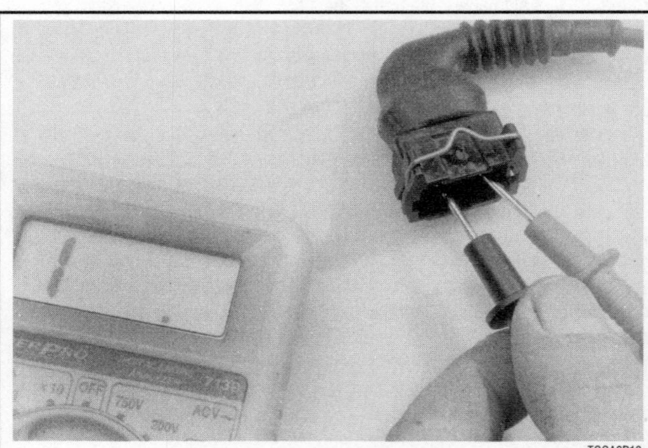

TCCA6P10

Fig. 8 The infinite reading on this multimeter indicates that the circuit is open

4. To isolate the short, probe a test point at either end of the isolated circuit (the light should be on or the meter should indicate continuity).

5. Leave the test light probe engaged and sequentially open connectors or switches, remove parts, etc. until the light goes out or continuity is broken.

6. When the light goes out, the short is between the last two circuit components which were opened.

VOLTAGE

This test determines voltage available from the battery and should be the first step in any electrical troubleshooting procedure after visual inspection. Many electrical problems, especially on computer controlled systems, can be caused by a low state of charge in the battery. Excessive corrosion at the battery cable terminals can cause poor contact that will prevent proper charging and full battery current flow.

1. Set the voltmeter selector switch to the 20V position.
2. Connect the multimeter negative lead to the battery's negative (–) post or terminal and the positive lead to the battery's positive (+) post or terminal.
3. Turn the ignition switch **ON** to provide a load.
4. A well charged battery should register over 12 volts. If the meter reads below 11.5 volts, the battery power may be insufficient to operate the electrical system properly.

VOLTAGE DROP

See Figure 9

When current flows through a load, the voltage beyond the load drops. This voltage drop is due to the resistance created by the load and also by small resistances created by corrosion at the connectors and damaged insulation on the wires. The maximum allowable voltage drop under load is critical, especially if there is more than one load in the circuit, since all voltage drops are cumulative.

1. Set the voltmeter selector switch to the 20 volt position.
2. Connect the multimeter negative lead to a good ground.
3. Operate the circuit and check the voltage prior to the first component (load).
4. There should be little or no voltage drop in the circuit prior to the first component. If a voltage drop exists, the wire or connectors in the circuit are suspect.
5. While operating the first component in the circuit, probe the ground side of the component with the positive meter lead and observe the voltage readings. A small voltage drop should be noticed. This voltage drop is caused by the resistance of the component.
6. Repeat the test for each component (load) down the circuit.
7. If a large voltage drop is noticed, the preceding component, wire or connector is suspect.

RESISTANCE

See Figures 10 and 11

WARNING

Never use an ohmmeter with power applied to the circuit. The ohmmeter is designed to operate on its own power supply. The normal 12 volt electrical system voltage could damage the meter!

1. Isolate the circuit from the vehicle's power source.
2. Ensure that the ignition key is **OFF** when disconnecting any components or the battery.
3. Where necessary, also isolate at least one side of the circuit to be checked, in order to avoid reading parallel resistances. Parallel circuit resistances will always give a lower reading than the actual resistance of either of the branches.
4. Connect the meter leads to both sides of the circuit (wire or component) and read the actual measured ohms on the meter scale. Make sure the selector switch is set to the proper ohm scale for the circuit being tested, to avoid misreading the ohmmeter test value.

Wire and Connector Repair

Almost anyone can replace damaged wires, as long as the proper tools and parts are available. Wire and terminals are available to fit almost any need. Even the specialized weatherproof, molded and hard shell connectors are now available from aftermarket suppliers.

Be sure the ends of all the wires are fitted with the proper terminal hardware and connectors. Wrapping a wire around a stud is never a permanent solution and will only cause trouble later. Replace wires one at a time to avoid confusion. Always route wires exactly the same as the factory.

If connector repair is necessary, only attempt it if you have the proper tools. Weatherproof and hard shell connectors require special tools to release the pins inside the connector. Attempting to repair these connectors with conventional hand tools will damage them.

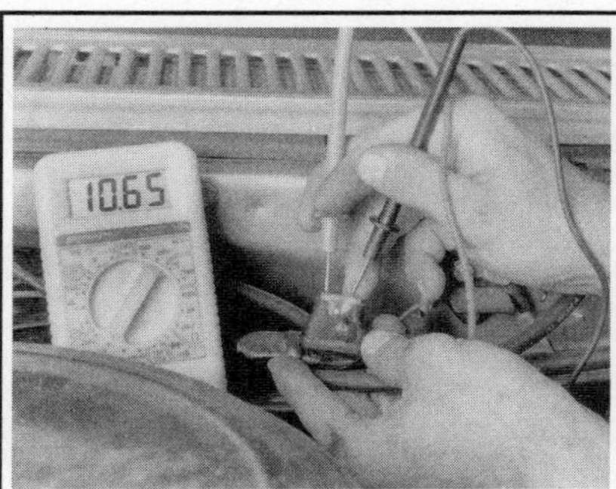

TCCA6P07

Fig. 9 This voltage drop test revealed high resistance (low voltage) in the circuit

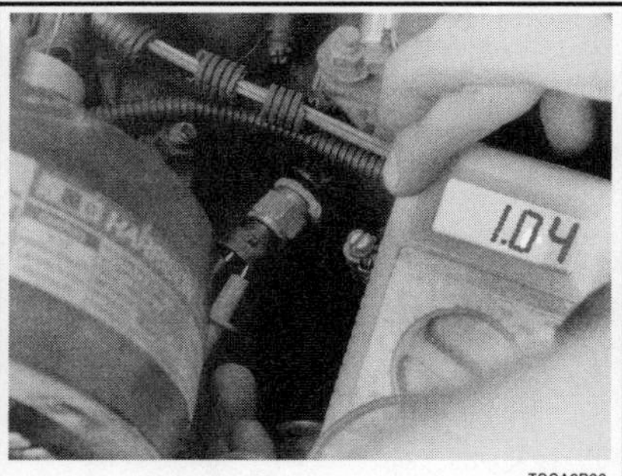

TCCA6P08

Fig. 10 Checking the resistance of a coolant temperature sensor with an ohmmeter. Reading is 1.04 kilohms

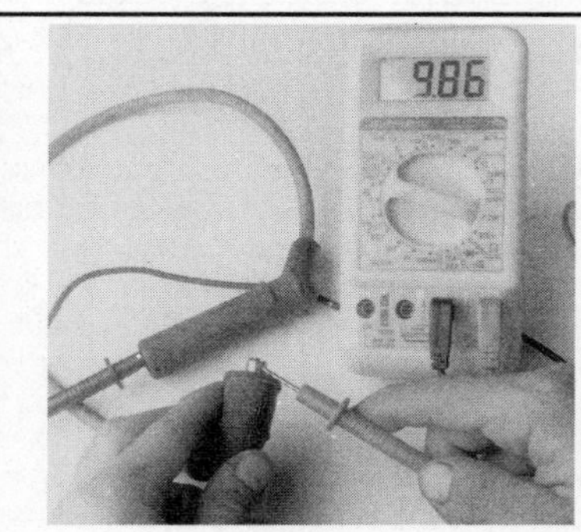

TCCA6P09

Fig. 11 Spark plug wires can be checked for excessive resistance using an ohmmeter

BATTERY CABLES

Disconnecting the Cables

➧ See Figure 12

When working on any electrical component on the vehicle, it is always a good idea to disconnect the negative (–) battery cable. This will prevent potential damage to many sensitive electrical components such as the Engine Control Module (ECM), radio, alternator, etc.

➡Any time you disengage the battery cables, it is recommended that you disconnect the negative (–) battery cable first. This will prevent your accidentally grounding the positive (+) terminal to the body of the vehicle when disconnecting it, thereby preventing damage to the above mentioned components.

Before you disconnect the cable(s), first turn the ignition to the **OFF** position. This will prevent a draw on the battery which could cause arcing (electricity trying to ground itself to the body of a vehicle, just like a spark plug jumping the gap) and, of course, damaging some components such as the alternator diodes.

When the battery cable(s) are reconnected (negative cable last), be sure to check that your lights, windshield wipers and other electrically operated safety components are all working correctly. If your vehicle contains an Electronically Tuned Radio (ETR), don't forget to also reset your radio stations. Ditto for the clock.

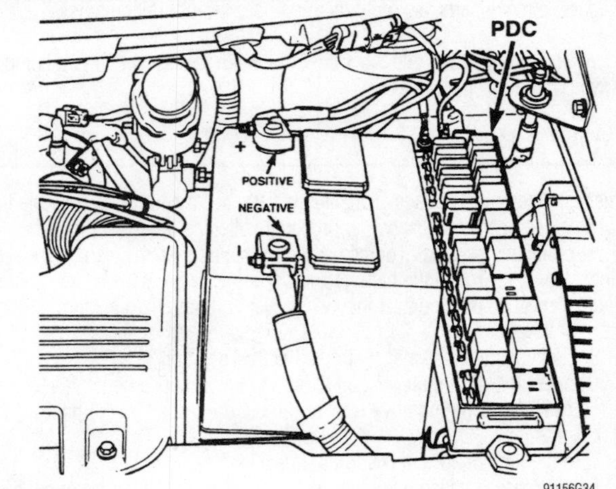

Fig. 12 Always disconnect the negative battery cable when servicing any electrical component on the vehicle

AIR BAG (SUPPLEMENTAL RESTRAINT SYSTEM)

General Information

The Supplemental Restraint System (SRS), found on all vehicles covered by this manual, is designed to be used along with the front seat belts to reduce the risk or amount of injury by deploying one or both air bags during certain frontal collisions.

The air bag system is made up of an Air bag Control Module (ACM), clockspring, air bag modules for the driver (in the steering wheel) and front passenger (right side instrument panel above the glove compartment), all system related wiring and an SRS warning lamp in the instrument cluster.

This SRS system only utilizes one impact sensor, which is an integral component of the ACM along with the energy reserve capacitor.

The SRS system is designed to deploy when in impact is severe enough to cause the ACM micro processor to send a signal that completes the electrical circuit to the driver and passenger's side air bags. The sensor is calibrated for the specific vehicle and reacts to the severity and direction of the impact.

SERVICE PRECAUTIONS

When working on the SRS or any components which require the removal of the air bag, adhere to all of these precautions to minimize the risks of personal injury or component damage:

- Before attempting to diagnose, remove or install the air bag system components, you must first detach and isolate the negative (–) battery cable. Failure to do so could result in accidental deployment and possible personal injury.
- When an undeployed air bag assembly is to be removed, after detaching the negative battery cable, allow the system capacitor to discharge for two minutes before commencing with the air bag system component removal.
- Place the inflator module (air bag unit) on a bench or other surface with the bag and trim cover facing up.
- When carrying a live inflator module, hold securely with both hands, and ensure that the bag and trim cover are pointed away from your body.
- Replace the air bag system components only with Mopar® specified replacement parts, or equivalent. Substitute parts may visually appear interchangeable, but internal differences may result in inferior occupant protection.
- The fasteners, screws, and bolts originally used for the SRS have special coatings and are specifically designed for the SRS. They must never be replaced with any substitutes. Anytime a new fastener is needed, replace with the correct fasteners provided in the service package or fasteners listed in the parts books.
- Never carry the inflator module by the wires or connector on the underside of the module.
- With the inflator module on the bench, never place anything on or close to the module which may be thrown in the event of an accidental deployment.
- SRS components should not be subjected to heat over 200°F (93°C), so remove the SRS control unit, air bag modules and clock spring before drying or baking the vehicle after painting.
- Never use an analog ohmmeter to test SRS components.

Handling a Live Air Bag Module

➧ See Figure 13

At no time should any source of electricity be permitted near the inflator on the back of the module. When carrying a live module, the trim cover should be pointed away from the body to minimize injury in the event of accidental deployment. In addition, if the module is placed on a bench or other surface, the plastic trim cover should be face up to minimize movement in case of accidental deployment.

When handling a steering column with an air bag module attached, never place the column on the floor or other surface with the steering wheel or module face down.

Handling a Deployed Air Bag Module

The vehicle interior may contain a very small amount of sodium hydroxide powder, a by-product of air bag deployment. Since this powder can irritate the

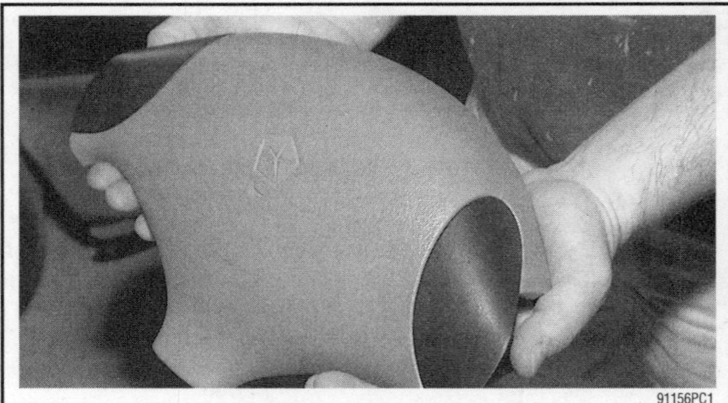

Fig. 13 Always hold a live air bag module away from your body as shown

skin, eyes, nose or throat, be sure to wear safety glasses, rubber gloves and long sleeves during cleanup.

If you find that the cleanup is irritating your skin, run cool water over the affected area. Also, if you experience nasal or throat irritation, exit the vehicle for fresh air until the irritation ceases. If irritation continues, see a physician.

Begin the cleanup by putting tape over the two air bag exhaust vents so that no additional powder will find its way into the vehicle interior. Then, remove the air bag(s) and air bag module(s) from the vehicle.

Use a vacuum cleaner to remove any residual powder from the vehicle interior. Work from the outside in so that you avoid kneeling or sitting in an uncleaned area.

Be sure to vacuum the heater and A/C outlets as well. In fact, it's a good idea to run the blower on low and to vacuum up any powder expelled from the plenum. You may need to vacuum the interior of the car a second time to recover all of the powder.

Check with the local authorities before disposing of the deployed bag and module in your trash.

After an air bag has been deployed, the air bag module and clockspring must be replaced because they cannot be reused. Other air bag system components should be replaced with new ones if damaged.

DISARMING THE SYSTEM

➧ See Figures 14 and 15

**** CAUTION**

The Supplemental Inflatable Restraint (SIR) system must be disarmed before working around the air bag or SIR wiring. Failure to do so may cause accidental deployment of the air bag, resulting in unnecessary SIR system repairs and/or personal injury.

1. Disconnect the negative battery cable. Isolate the battery cable by taping up any exposed metal areas of the cable. This will keep the cable from inadvertently contacting the battery and causing accidental deployment of the air bag.

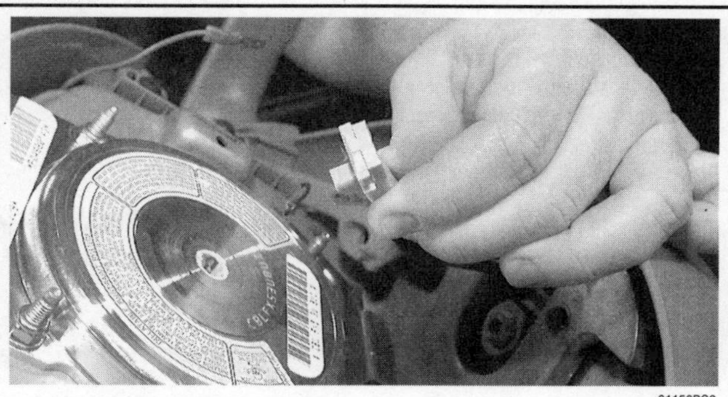

91156PC2

Fig. 14 Make ABSOLUTELY CERTAIN that the SIR system is disarmed before removing the airbag module from the vehicle

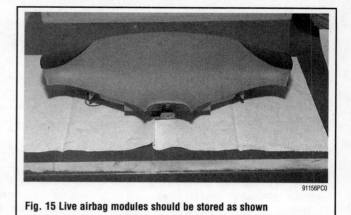

91156PC0

Fig. 15 Live airbag modules should be stored as shown

2. Allow the SIR system capacitor to discharge for at least two (2) minutes, before performing any removal procedures.
3. The air bag system is now disabled.

**** CAUTION**

When carrying a live air bag, be sure the bag and trim cover are pointed away from the body. In the unlikely event of an accidental deployment, the bag will then deploy with minimal chance of injury. When placing a live air bag on a bench or other surface, always face the bag and trim cover up, away from the surface. This will reduce the motion of the module if accidentally deployed.

ARMING THE SYSTEM

➡A DRB or equivalent scan tool is necessary to test the SRS after the system has been rearmed. If no scan tool is available, arm the system by simply removing the tape and reconnecting the negative battery cable.

If a scan tool is available, perform the following procedure:

1. Connect a DRB or equivalent scan tool to the Data Link Connector (DLC), located near the steering column and at the lower edge of the lower instrument panel.
2. Turn the ignition key to the **ON** position. Get out of the vehicle with the scan tool. Make sure you are using the latest version of the proper cartridge.
3. After making sure no one is in the vehicle, remove the tape, then reconnect the negative battery cable.
4. Read and record any stored Diagnostic Trouble Codes (DTCs). If any diagnostic trouble codes are recorded, take your vehicle to a reputable repair shop for diagnosis.
5. If there are no DTCs, and if the AIRBAG warning lamp either fails to light, with the ignition switch **ON**, or the light goes on and stays on, there is a system malfunction. If any of these conditions exist, you should take your vehicle to a reputable repair shop for diagnosis.

HEATING AND AIR CONDITIONING

Blower Motor

REMOVAL & INSTALLATION

**** CAUTION**

The Supplemental Inflatable Restraint (SIR) system must be disarmed before removing the blower motor assembly. Failure to do so may cause accidental deployment of the air bag, resulting in unnecessary SIR system repairs and/or personal injury.

Front Blower Motor

➧ See Figures 16, 17 and 18

1. Disconnect and isolate the negative battery cable, then wait 2 minutes before proceeding with the removal. This will effectively disable the air bag system preventing possible personal injury.
2. Remove the glove box from the instrument panel.
3. Remove the A/C-heater blower motor cover.
4. Disconnect the blower motor wiring connector.
5. Remove the blower motor wiring grommet and feed the wiring through the blower motor housing.
6. Remove the blower motor mounting screws.

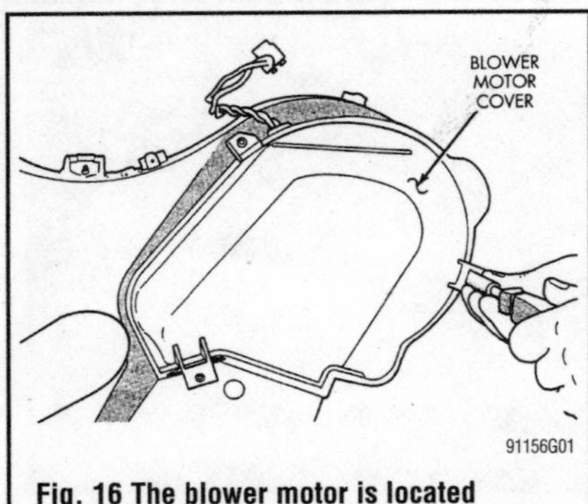

Fig. 16 The blower motor is located behind the glovebox, behind the blower motor cover

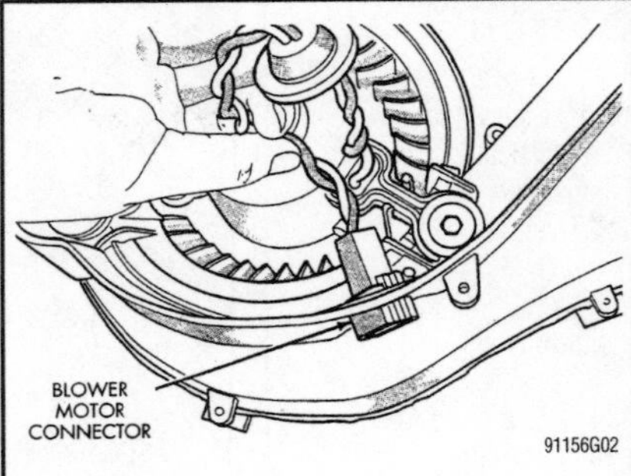

Fig. 17 Once the cover is removed, unplug the electrical connector and push it through the opening in the housing

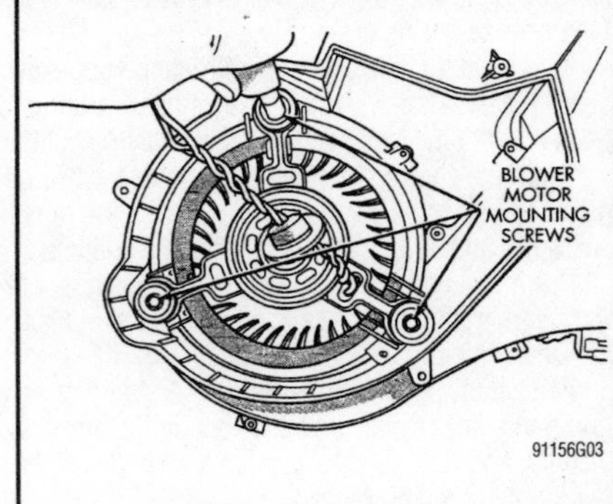

Fig. 18 The blower motor is secured to the housing with three small screws

7. Allow the blower motor assembly to drop downward to clear the instrument panel and remove from vehicle.

To install:

8. Place the blower motor assembly into position on the A/C-heater unit and tighten the mounting screws.
9. Route the blower motor wiring through the blower motor housing and seat the wiring grommet in the hole of the blower motor housing.
10. Reconnect the blower motor electrical connector.
11. Install the A/C-heater blower motor cover.
12. Install the glove box into the instrument panel.
13. Reconnect the negative battery cable. Check blower motor operation.

Rear Blower Motor

See Figures 19 and 20

1. Disconnect and isolate the negative battery cable.
2. Remove the right quarter trim panel as follows:
   a. Remove first rear seat. Remove the second rear seat, if equipped.
   b. Remove the sliding door sill plate.
   c. Remove the quarter trim bolster.
   d. Remove the upper C-pillar trim and D-pillar trim panel.
   e. Remove the first and second rear seat belt anchors.
   f. Remove the screws securing the quarter trim to quarter panel from the bolster area.
   g. Remove the screws securing the rear edge of the quarter trim to the support bracket.
   h. Carefully disengage the hidden clips securing the front of the quarter trim to the quarter panel just rearward of the sliding door opening.
   i. Disconnect the wiring harness connector from the accessory power outlet, if equipped.
   j. On long wheelbase wagons only, remove the quarter trim from the quarter panel and pull second rear seat belt through access hole.
   k. Pull first rear seat belt through the access hole.
   l. Remove the quarter trim panel from the vehicle.
3. Remove the 5 screws mounting the A/C-heater blower motor housing to the rear HVAC unit (one mounting screw located on evaporator cover).
4. Twist the blower motor out of scroll housing.
5. Disconnect the blower motor wiring connector.
6. Remove the blower motor from vehicle.

To install:

7. Install the blower motor unit into the vehicle.
8. Reconnect the blower motor wiring connector.
9. Secure the blower motor into scroll housing.
10. Install and tighten the 5 screws mounting the A/C-heater blower motor housing to the rear HVAC unit (one mounting screw located on evaporator cover).
11. Install the right quarter trim panel as follows:
   a. Install the quarter trim panel in position in the vehicle.
   b. Insert and pull the first rear seat belt through the access hole in quarter trim panel.
   c. On long wheelbase wagons only, insert and pull the second rear seat belt through access hole in quarter trim panel.
   d. Reconnect the wiring harness connector to the accessory power outlet, if equipped.
   e. Engage the hidden clips to secure the front of quarter trim to quarter panel rearward of sliding door opening.
   f. Install the retaining screws that secure the rear edge of quarter trim to support bracket.
   g. Install the retaining screws that secure the quarter trim to the quarter panel in bolster area.
   h. Install the second rear seat belt anchor (if equipped), and the first rear seat belt anchor.
   i. Install the D-pillar trim panel and upper C-pillar trim.
   j. Install the quarter trim bolster.
   k. Install the sliding door sill plate.
   l. Install the second rear seat, if equipped, and install the first rear seat.
12. Reconnect the negative battery cable. Check blower motor operation.

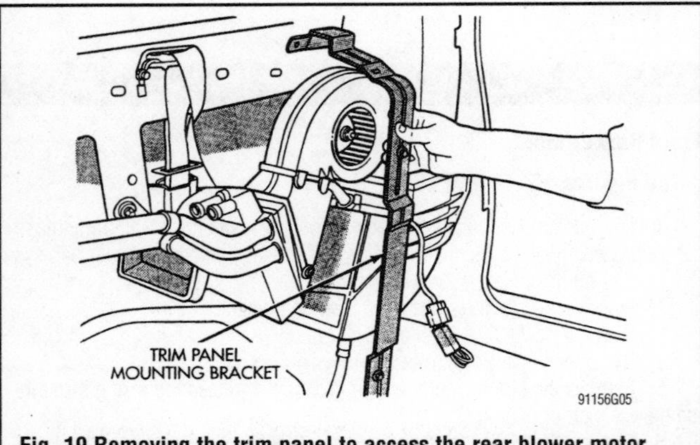

Fig. 19 Removing the trim panel to access the rear blower motor

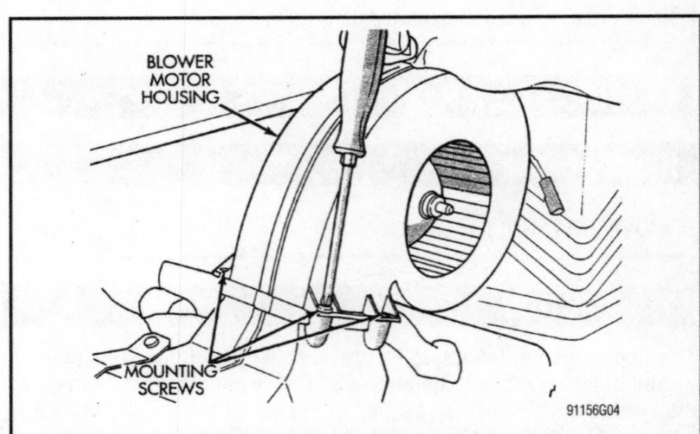

Fig. 20 The rear blower motor is held in place by four screws

Heater Core

REMOVAL & INSTALLATION

Front Heater Core

➧ See Figures 21, 22, 23, 24 and 25

1. Disconnect the negative battery cable.
2. Drain the cooling system.
3. Remove the left side lower steering column cover.
4. Place the steering wheel in the locked position, then remove the key.
5. Remove the air bag module.
6. Remove the steering wheel.
7. Remove the steering column assembly utilizing the following steps:
   a. Label and disengage the wiring harness connectors from the steering column.
   b. On the steering column shaft coupler, remove the safety pin, nut and pinch bolt.
   c. Separate the steering column shaft coupler from the shaft of the steering gear.
   d. Loosen, but do not remove, the 2 lower steering column mounting bracket nuts.
   e. Remove the 2 upper steering column mounting bracket nuts.
   f. Carefully remove the steering column assembly from the vehicle.
8. Remove the ABS module, bracket and wiring
9. Remove the instrument panel-to-body harness interconnect and bracket.
10. Located at the base of the steering shaft, remove the lower silencer boot.
11. Pinch off the heater lines located in the engine compartment.
12. Remove the cover from the heater core. Place some towels under the heater core tubes, then remove the heater core plate and tubes.
13. Depress the heater core retaining clips.
14. Pull up on the accelerator pedal and slide out the heater core.
15. Depress the brake pedal and remove the heater core from the HVAC housing.

To install:

16. Install the heater core into the HVAC housing. Install and tighten the retaining screws and engage the retaining clips.
17. Replace the heater core tube inlet O-rings. Install the heater core tube retaining plate screw and tighten to 18–36 inch lbs. (2–4 Nm).
18. Install the heater core cover.
19. Install the lower silencer boot to the base of the steering shaft.
20. Install the instrument panel-to-body harness interconnect and bracket.
21. Install the ABS module, bracket and wiring.
22. Install the steering column assembly into the vehicle.
23. Install the steering wheel and air bag module.
24. Install the left side lower steering column cover.
25. Un-pinch the heater lines in the engine compartment.
26. Connect the negative battery cable.
27. Fill the cooling system. Test the HVAC system for proper heating operation.

Rear Heater Core

➧ See Figures 26 and 27

1. Remove the lower right quarter trim panel.
2. Isolate and disconnect the lines from the heater core.
3. Remove the heater core retaining screws.
4. Carefully pull the heater core and tubes up and straight out of the unit.

To install:

5. Installation is the reverse of the removal procedure. However, it is also important to perform the following important steps.
6. Prefill the heater core before installation. If the heater core is empty and not prefilled, it is required to thermal cycle the vehicle twice. This is because the heater core is positioned higher than the radiator filler cap. Therefore, the heater core cannot gravity fill to level. To thermal cycle the vehicle, the system must be operated until the thermostat opens, then turned off and allowed to cool.

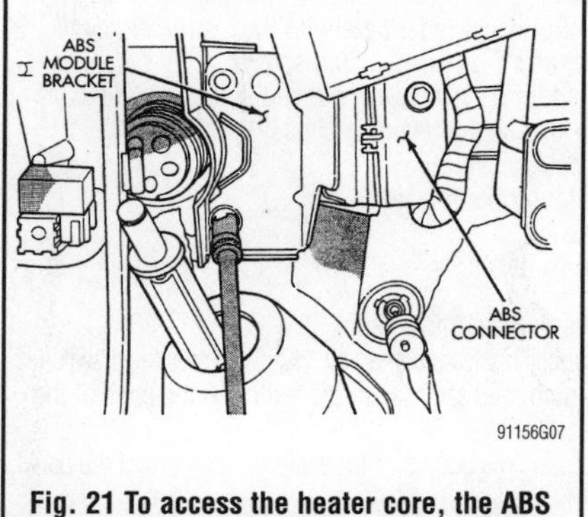

Fig. 21 To access the heater core, the ABS module and bracket needs to be removed

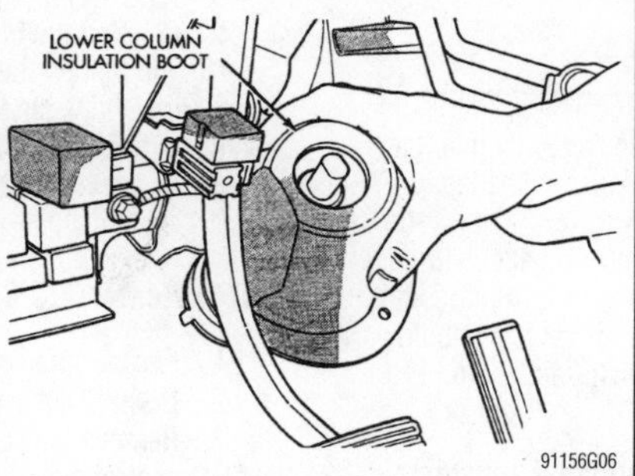

Fig. 22 After the steering column is removed and set aside, the insulation boot should be removed

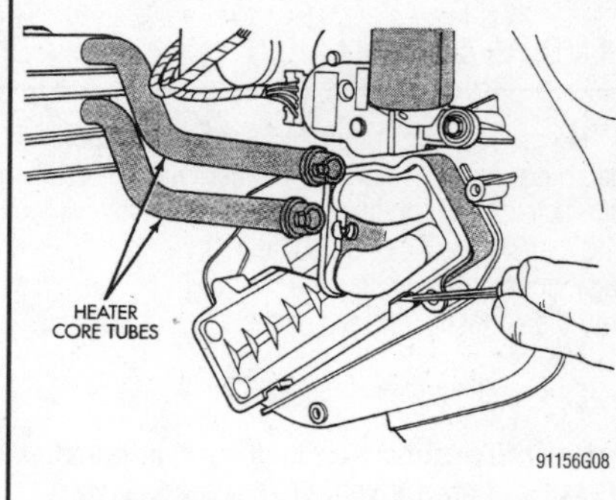

Fig. 23 After the heater core tubes are disconnected, depress the retaining clips . . .

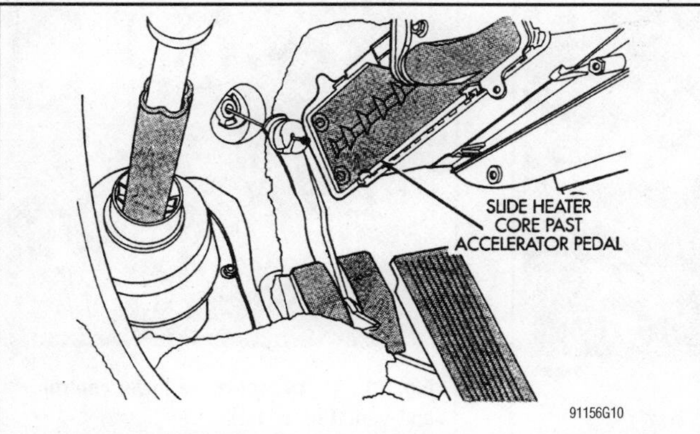

Fig. 24 . . . and slide it out, positioning the accelerator pedal . . .

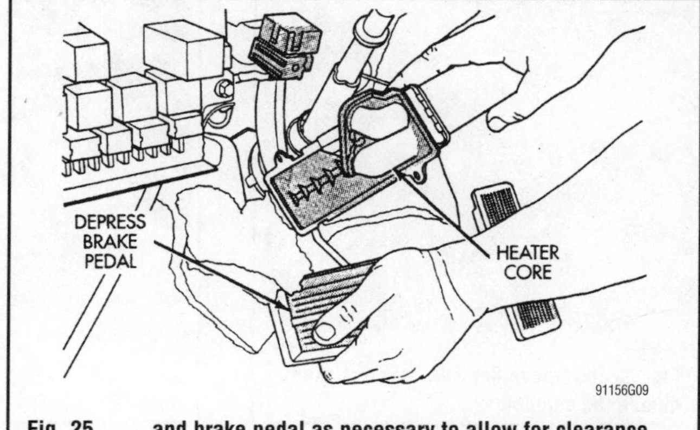

Fig. 25 . . . and brake pedal as necessary to allow for clearance

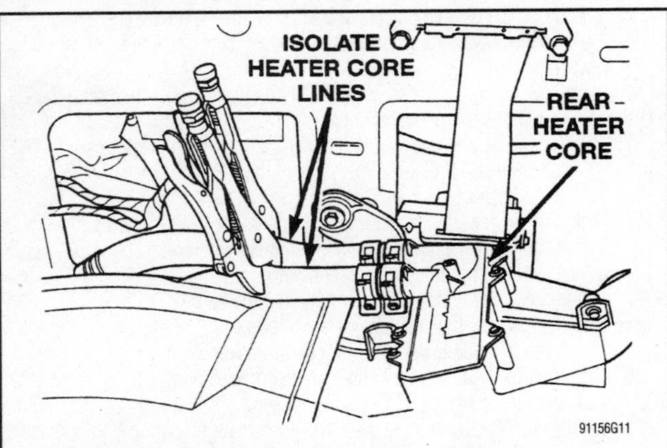

Fig. 26 Locking pliers can be used to prevent excess coolant spillage when removing the rear heater core

Fig. 27 Make sure to pre-fill the rear heater core before installation

7. To verify that the auxiliary unit is completely filled, utilize the following procedures:
   - Be sure that the vehicle is at room temperature.
   - The engine is brought up to operating temperature.
   - The front unit is OFF and the temperature slide is at the full HEAT position.
   - Engine is at idle.
   - Place the rear blower motor on the HIGH position.
   - Discharge air temperature, measured at the dual register located at the base of the C-pillar, is between 135°–145°F (57°–62°C).
8. Test the system for leaks and overall performance.

Air Conditioning Components

REMOVAL & INSTALLATION

Repair or service of air conditioning components is not covered by this manual, because of the risk of personal injury or death, and because of the legal ramifications of servicing these components without the proper EPA certification and experience. Cost, personal injury or death, environmental damage, and legal considerations (such as the fact that it is a federal crime to vent refrigerant into the atmosphere), dictate that the A/C components on your vehicle should be serviced only by a Motor Vehicle Air Conditioning (MVAC) trained, and EPA certified automotive technician.

➡Refer to Section 1 for additional information on additional considerations dealing with your vehicle's A/C system.

HVAC Control Panel

REMOVAL & INSTALLATION

Front Control Switch

➧ See Figures 28 thru 35

1. Disconnect the negative battery cable.
2. Pull the cup holder out, then remove the small plastic trim piece between the cup holder and the HVAC control panel/radio bezel.
3. Loosen the 2 lower and 2 upper mounting screws, then remove the HVAC control panel/radio bezel.
4. Disengage the wiring connectors from behind the HVAC control panel switches.

To install:

5. Plug the wiring connectors into the control panel switches.
6. Position the HVAC control panel/radio bezel into the instrument panel. Install and tighten the 2 upper and 2 lower mounting screws.
7. Install the small plastic trim piece between the cup holder and the control panel by firmly pushing in to engage the retaining clips.
8. Connect the negative battery cable.
9. Test the control panel for proper function.

Rear Heater-A/C Control Switch

1. Remove the HVAC control panel/radio bezel.
2. Disengage the wiring connectors from behind the HVAC control panel switches.
3. Remove the screw holding the rear heater-A/C switch to the back of the HVAC control panel/radio bezel.
4. Disengage the hook securing the bottom of the switch to the back of the panel.
5. Remove the switch.
6. Installation is the reverse of the removal procedure.

Fig. 28 To remove the HVAC control panel, detach the cup holder . . .

Fig. 29 . . . and the lower trim . . .

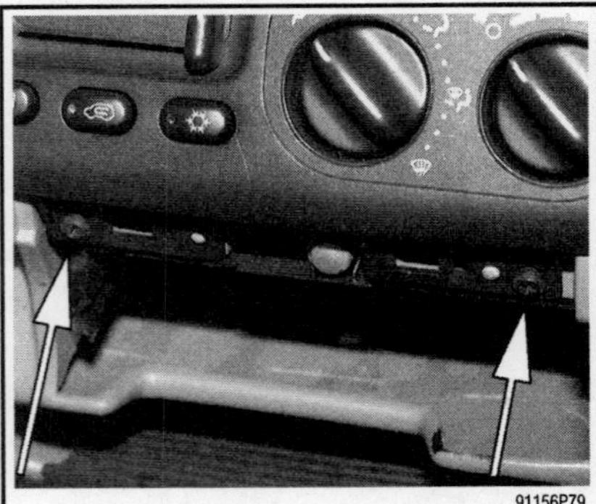

Fig. 30 . . . to access the lower control unit mounting screws

91156P90

Fig. 31 The upper mounting screws are above the radio

91156P78

Fig. 32 Once the screws are removed, unclip the light bulb from the cup holder bracket . . .

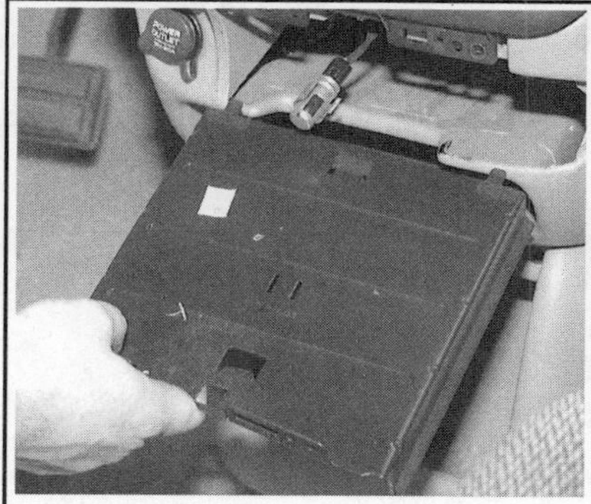

91156P91

Fig. 33 . . . and slide it out . . .

91156P89

Fig. 34 . . . to allow the control panel to be removed

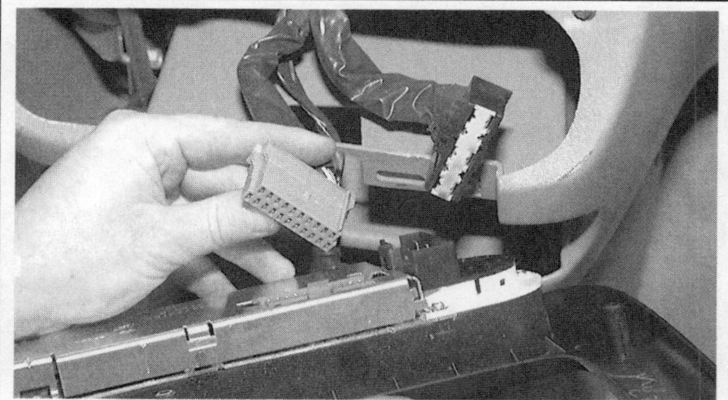

91156G88

Fig. 35 Once the unit is detached, unplug the electrical connectors

CRUISE CONTROL

Cruise control is a speed control system that maintains a desired vehicle speed under normal driving conditions. However, ascending or descending steep grades may cause variations in the selected speeds. On these vehicles, the speed control system is electrically controlled and vacuum operated. The electronic control is integrated in the Powertrain Control Module (PCM), located in the engine compartment.

The main parts of the cruise control system are the functional control switches, speed control servo, servo cable, PCM, vacuum reservoir and the release switches, including the dual function brake light switch.

The cruise control module assembly contains a low speed limit, which will prevent system engagement below 30 mph (50 km/h). The module is controlled by the functional switches, which are located on the steering wheel.

The cruise control can be manually disengaged by stepping on the brake pedal, depressing the OFF switch or the CANCEL switch. When this occurs, the cruise control system is electrically disengaged and the throttle is returned to the idle position.

CRUISE CONTROL TROUBLESHOOTING

Problem	*Possible Cause*
Will not hold proper speed	Incorrect cable adjustment
	Binding throttle linkage
	Leaking vacuum servo diaphragm
	Leaking vacuum tank
	Faulty vacuum or vent valve
	Faulty stepper motor
	Faulty transducer
	Faulty speed sensor
	Faulty cruise control module
Cruise intermittently cuts out	Clutch or brake switch adjustment too tight
	Short or open in the cruise control circuit
	Faulty transducer
	Faulty cruise control module
Vehicle surges	Kinked speedometer cable or casing
	Binding throttle linkage
	Faulty speed sensor
	Faulty cruise control module
Cruise control inoperative	Blown fuse
	Short or open in the cruise control circuit
	Faulty brake or clutch switch
	Leaking vacuum circuit
	Faulty cruise control switch
	Faulty stepper motor
	Faulty transducer
	Faulty speed sensor
	Faulty cruise control module

Note: Use this chart as a guide. Not all systems will use the components listed.

TCCA6C01

ENTERTAINMENT SYSTEMS

Radio Receiver/Amplifier/Tape Player/CD Player

REMOVAL & INSTALLATION

See Figures 36, 37, 38 and 39

1. Disconnect the negative battery cable.
2. Remove the HVAC control panel.
3. Remove the screws that secure the radio unit to the instrument panel.
4. Pull the radio rearward to gain access to the back of the radio.
5. Loosen the bolt, then remove the ground strap from behind the radio.
6. Unplug the radio antenna from behind the radio.
7. Unplug the wiring harness connector from the back of the radio. Then remove the radio from the vehicle.
8. Installation is the reverse of the removal procedure.

Speakers

REMOVAL & INSTALLATION

Instrument Panel Speakers

See Figures 40, 41 and 42

1. Disconnect the negative battery cable.
2. Remove the instrument panel top cover.
3. Remove the speaker mounting screws and lift the speaker.

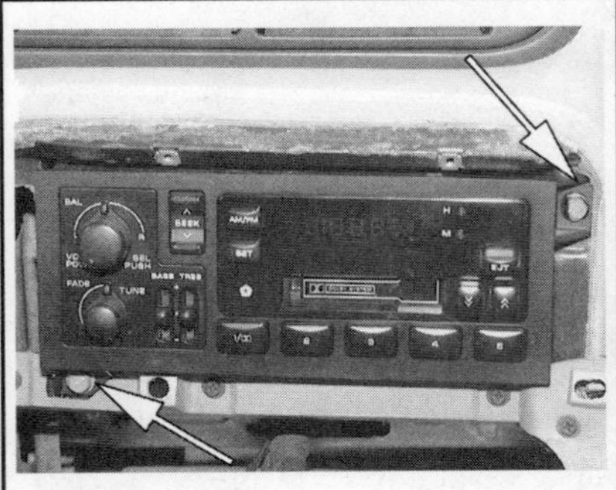

91156P87

Fig. 36 After the HVAC panel is removed, the radio mounting bolts can be accessed

91156P86

Fig. 37 Once the radio is unbolted, slide the radio forward . . .

91156P85

Fig. 38 . . . unplug the electrical connectors . . .

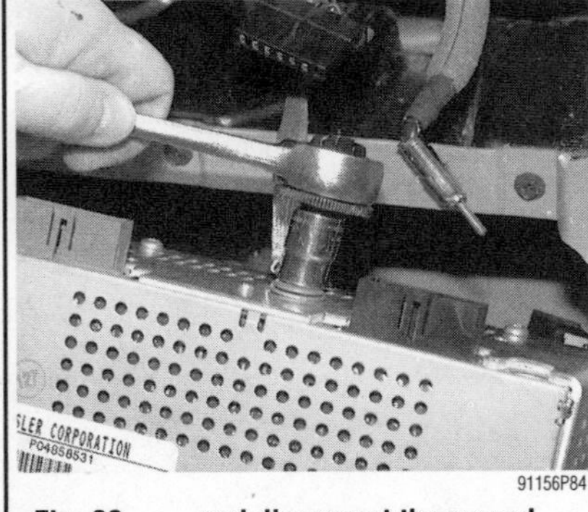

91156P84

Fig. 39 . . . and disconnect the ground strap

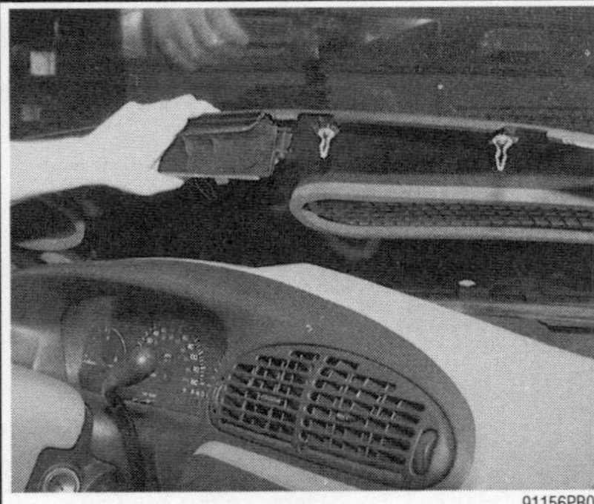

91156PB0

Fig. 40 To access the instrument panel speakers, remove the top cover

91156PB9

Fig. 41 After the instrument panel top cover is removed, remove the speaker mounting screws . . .

91156PB8

Fig. 42 . . . and unplug the wire connector

4. Disengage the wiring connector from under the speaker.
5. Remove the speaker from the vehicle.
6. Installation is the reverse of the removal procedure.

Door Mounted Speakers

See Figure 43

1. Disconnect the negative battery cable.
2. Remove the front interior door trim panel.
3. Remove the speaker mounting screws and move the speaker out of the mounting bracket.
4. Disengage the wiring connector from the back of the speaker.
5. Remove the speaker from the vehicle.
6. Installation is the reverse of the removal procedure.

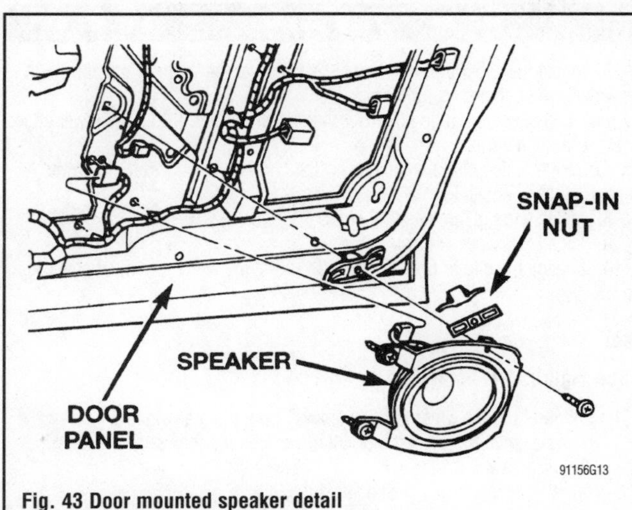

Fig. 43 Door mounted speaker detail

Quarter Panel Speaker

➧ See Figures 44, 45, 46 and 47

1. Disconnect the negative battery cable.
2. Remove the quarter trim bolster from the quarter trim panel.
3. Remove the speaker mounting screws and pull the speaker out of the inner quarter panel.
4. Disengage the wiring connector from the back of the speaker.
5. Remove the speaker from the vehicle.
6. Installation is the reverse of the removal procedure.

D-Pillar Speaker

➧ See Figure 48

1. Disconnect the negative battery cable.
2. Remove the D-pillar trim panel as necessary to gain access to the speaker.
3. Disengage the wiring connector from the back of the speaker.
4. Remove the speaker by sliding it out of the bracket by pushing on the magnet. The capacitor is wrapped with foam tape.
5. Remove the speaker from the vehicle.
6. Installation is the reverse of the removal procedure.

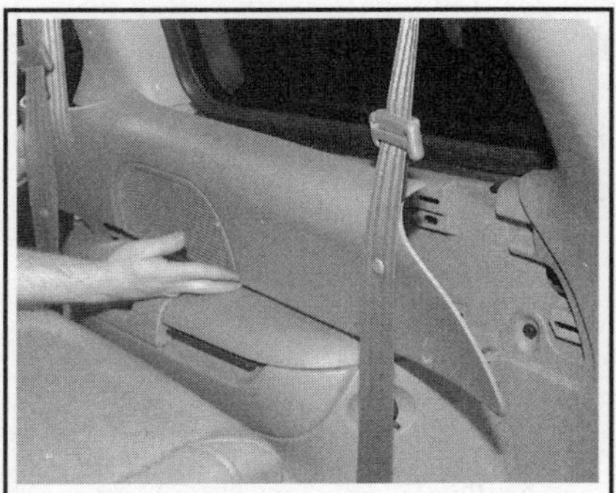

Fig. 44 To access the rear quarter panel speaker, remove the trim bolster

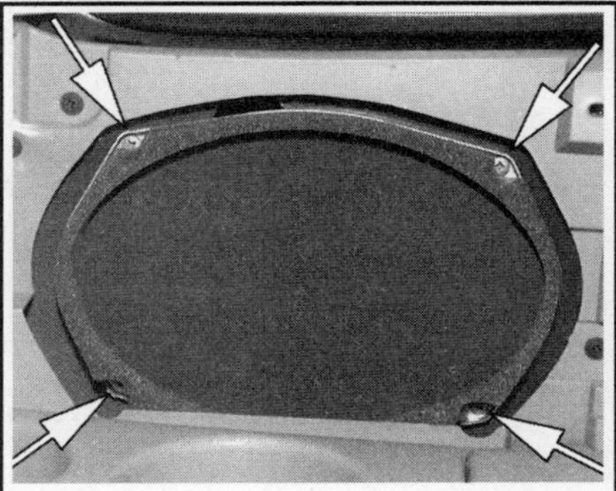

Fig. 45 The quarter panel speakers are retained by four screws

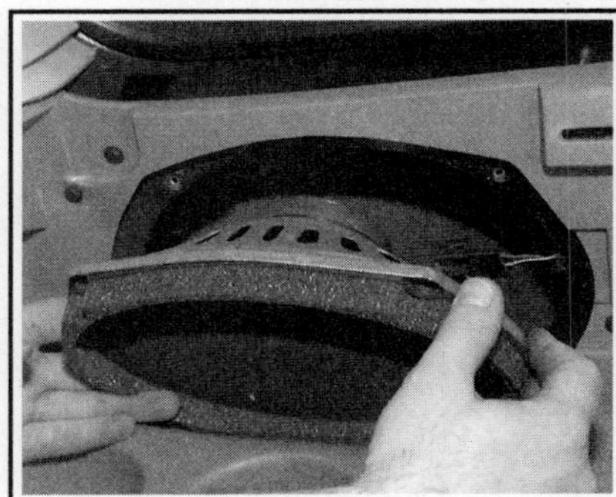

Fig. 46 Once the speaker screws are removed, pull the speaker out . . .

Fig. 47 . . . and disconnect the wire connector

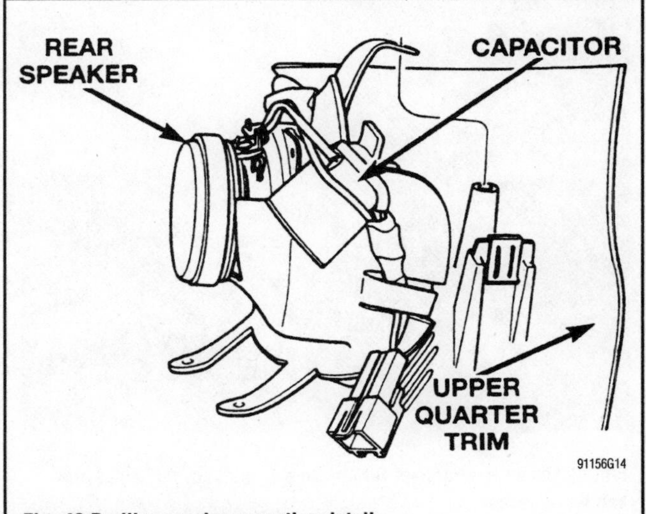

Fig. 48 D-pillar speaker mounting detail

WINDSHIELD WIPERS AND WASHERS

Windshield Wiper Blade and Arm

REMOVAL & INSTALLATION

Front

See Figures 49, 50, 51, 52 and 53

1. Disengage the clip holding the outside end of the wiper arm pivot cover to the wiper arm.
2. Lift the arm cap upward.
3. Remove the nut securing the wiper arm to the wiper pivot shaft.
4. Matchmark the position of the wiper arm to the pivot shaft to ensure correct installation.
5. Using a suitable 2-jaw puller tool, separate the wiper arm from the wiper pivot shaft.

To install:

6. Verify that the wiper motor and linkage are in the park position.
7. Install the wiper arm in correct position over the wiper arm pivot. Align the wiper arm positions as follows:
   a. Left side should be no closer than 2.5 in. (65mm) from the lower edge of the windshield.
   b. Right side should be no closer than 1.5 in. (40mm) from the lower edge of the windshield.
8. Install and tighten the pivot nut to 26 ft. lbs. (35 Nm).
9. Install the wiper arm cap cover.
10. Engage the clip to hold the outside end of the wiper arm pivot cover to the wiper arm.

Rear

See Figures 54, 55 and 56

1. Lift and hold the wiper arm/blade away from the rear window.
2. Using a small flat-bladed tool, lift upward on the lock securing the wiper arm to the wiper pivot shaft.
3. Allow the wiper arm to rest against the lock.
4. Remove the wiper arm from the pivot shaft.
5. Installation is the reverse of the removal procedure.

91156P49

Fig. 49 To access the front wiper blade, pivot back the cover . . .

91156P47

Fig. 50 . . . and remove the nut

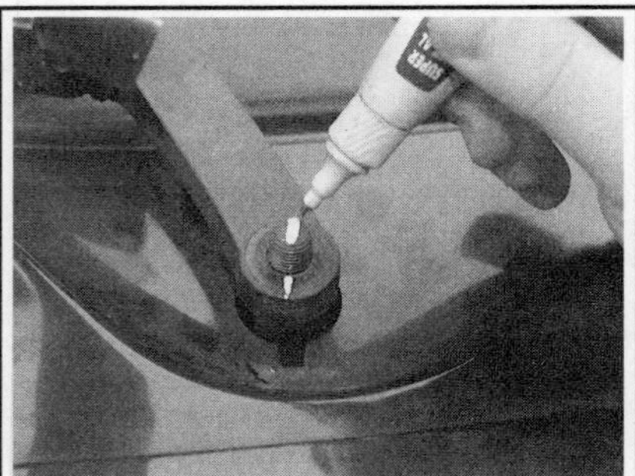
91156P53

Fig. 51 Once the nut is removed, use a paint marker to mark the relationship of the arm and pivot

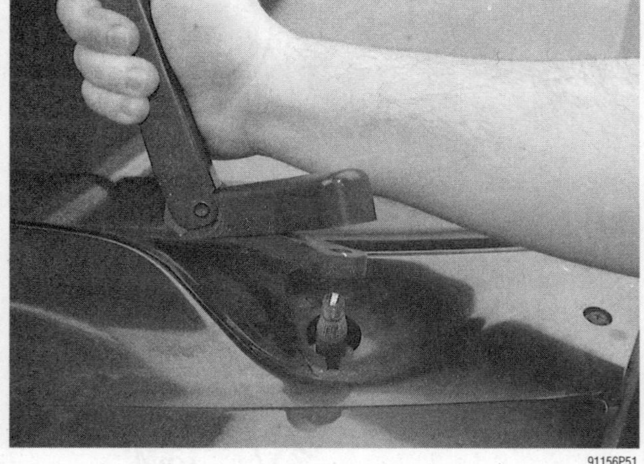
91156P51

Fig. 52 Once the arm/pivot relationship is marked, the wiper arm can be removed

91156P52

Fig. 53 Sometimes a puller may be required to remove the wiper arm

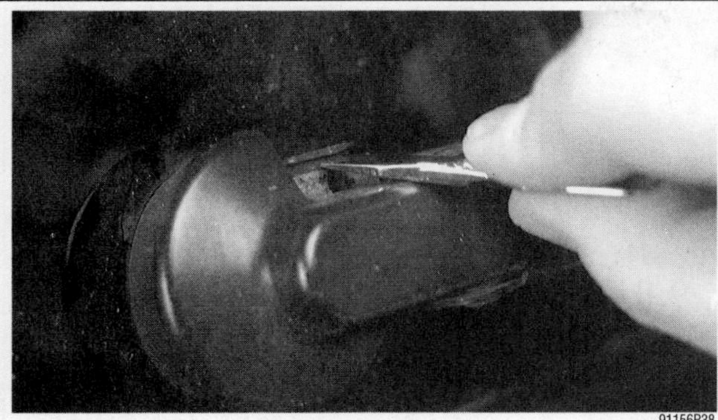

Fig. 54 Use a suitable tool to lift upward on the lock

Fig. 55 Once the lock is free, the wiper arm can be removed

Fig. 56 When installing the arm, make sure the wiper parks in the proper position

Windshield Wiper Motor

REMOVAL & INSTALLATION

Front

➧ **See Figures 57 thru 64**

1. Disconnect the negative battery cable.
2. Remove the wiper arm and blade assemblies.
3. Remove the cowl cover from the vehicle as follows:
   a. Close the hood to aid in the removal procedure.
   b. Remove the lower area cowl cover-to-wiper module mounting screws.
   c. Disengage the quarter turn fasteners securing the outer ends of the cowl cover to the wiper module.
   d. Open the hood.
   e. Remove the wing nuts securing the front of the cowl cover to the wiper module.
   f. Using a small flat bladed tool, disengage the retainers securing the cowl cover to the front fender edge.
   g. Raise up the cowl cover enough to gain access to the right side washer hose and disconnect from the right washer nozzle.
   h. Close the hood, but do not latch. Remove the cowl cover from the vehicle.
4. Open the hood. Disconnect the positive lock on the wiper unit electrical connector.
5. Disconnect the wiper unit electrical connector from the engine compartment wiring harness.
6. Disconnect the windshield washer hose from the hose coupling inside the wiper unit.
7. Remove the drain tubes from the bottom of the wiper unit.
8. Remove the sound absorbers from the ends of the wiper unit.
9. Remove the attaching nuts securing the wiper unit to the lower windshield fence.
10. Remove the attaching bolts securing the wiper unit to the dash panel.
11. Raise up the wiper unit from the from the weld-studs on the lower windshield fence and remove the wiper unit from the vehicle.
12. Place the wiper unit on a solid, level working surface. Remove the cowl cover brackets from the wiper unit.
13. Remove the attaching nuts securing the wiper linkage and wiper motor mount plate to the wiper unit.
14. Remove the wiper linkage from the wiper unit.
15. Disconnect the electrical connectors from the wiper motor.
16. Disconnect the wiper linkage from the wiper motor crank, but do NOT remove the crank from the wiper motor.
17. Remove the attaching bolts that secure the wiper motor to the mount plate and remove the wiper motor.

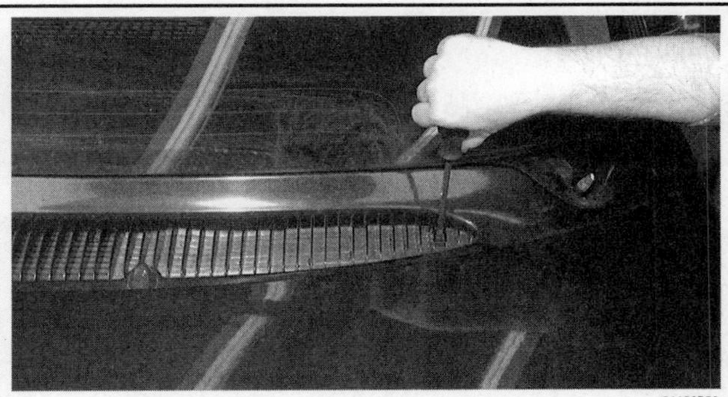

Fig. 57 To access the windshield wiper motor, the cowl cover must be removed

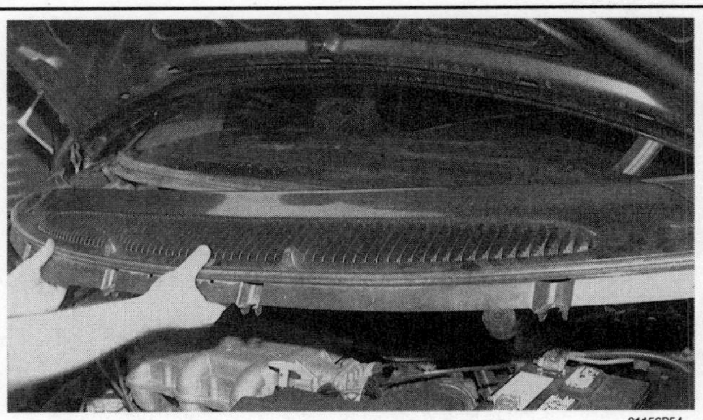

Fig. 58 With the hood open, remove the cowl cover

91156P64
Fig. 59 After the windshield washer hose and electrical connectors are unplugged, disconnect the wiper unit drain tubes

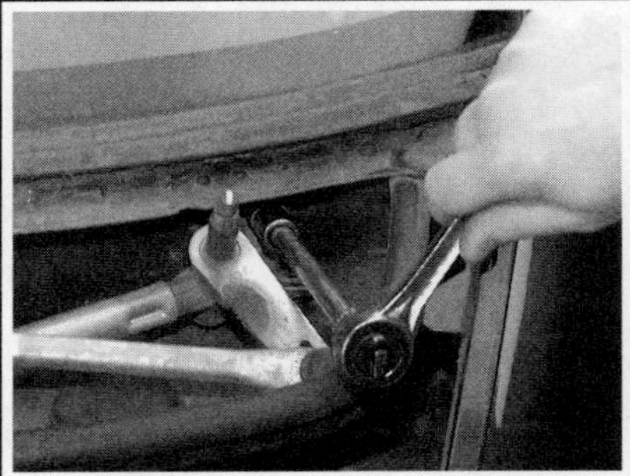
91156P65
Fig. 60 Once everything is disconnected from the wiper unit, remove the mounting bolts . . .

91156P63
Fig. 61 . . . and lift the wiper unit from the vehicle

91156P67
Fig. 62 Remove the wiper motor crank nut and mark the location as shown

91156P77
Fig. 63 If necessary, use a puller to remove the crank from the wiper motor shaft

91156P68
Fig. 64 Once the crank is removed from the wiper motor, unbolt it from the mount plate

To install:

18. Place the wiper motor onto the mounting plate and secure in position with the mounting bolts.
19. Install the wiper motor mount plate and wiper linkage into the wiper unit. Install and tighten the attaching nuts.
20. Install the cowl cover brackets onto the wiper unit and tighten the attaching nuts.
21. Reconnect the wiper motor electrical connectors.
22. Install the wiper unit into the vehicle engine compartment and be sure the wiper unit is installed properly over the weld-studs on the lower windshield fence. Install and tighten the attaching nuts to the weld-studs.
23. Install and tighten the attaching bolts securing the wiper unit to the dash panel.
24. Install the sound absorbers to each end of the wiper unit.
25. Install the drain tubes to the bottom of the wiper unit and reconnect the windshield washer hose to the hose coupling inside the wiper unit.
26. Reconnect the wiper unit wiring connector to the engine wiring harness.
27. Place the cowl cover onto the vehicle. Reconnect the right side windshield washer hose to the right washer nozzle located on the underside of the cowl cover.
28. Engage the retainers that secure the cowl cover to the front fender edge.
29. Install and tighten the wing nuts that secure the front of the cowl cover to the wiper module.
30. Engage the quarter turn fasteners that secure the outer ends of the cowl cover to the wiper module.
31. Install and tighten the screws that hold the lower area of the cowl cover to the wiper module.
32. Reconnect the negative battery cable and verify that the wiper motor and wiper linkage are in the **PARK** position.
33. Install the wiper arm and blade assemblies.
34. Operate the windshield wipers and check to make sure they work and park properly.

Rear

See Figures 65, 66, 67, 68 and 69

1. Disconnect the negative battery cable.
2. Remove the rear wiper arm.
3. Open the liftgate.
4. Remove the interior liftgate trim panel.
5. Disengage the wiring harness connector from the rear wiper motor.
6. Remove the rear wiper motor mounting screws.
7. Remove the rear wiper motor from the liftgate.
8. Installation is the reverse of the removal procedure.

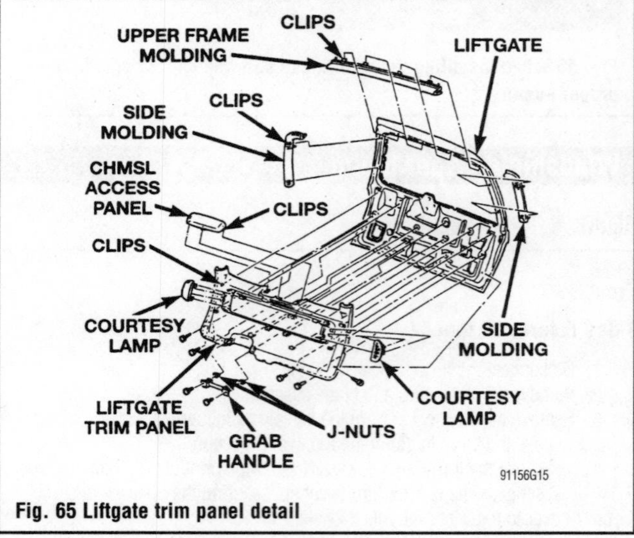

Fig. 65 Liftgate trim panel detail

91156P40

Fig. 66 To access the rear wiper motor, the liftgate trim panel must be removed

91156P39

Fig. 67 Unplug the electrical connector . . .

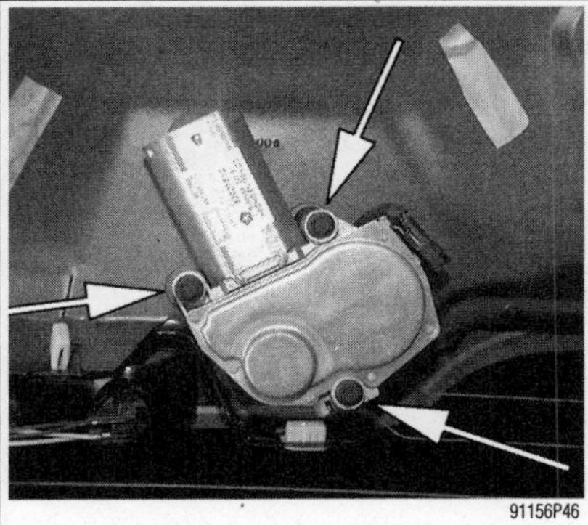
91156P46

Fig. 68 . . . remove the three bolts . . .

91156P45

Fig. 69 . . . and remove the wiper motor from the liftgate

Windshield Washer Pump Motor

REMOVAL & INSTALLATION

See Figure 70

1. Disconnect the negative battery cable.
2. Raise and safely support the front of the vehicle securely on jackstands.
3. Remove the right front wheel.
4. Remove the right front wheelhouse splash shield.
5. If the washer fluid bottle still has fluid in it, place a suitable drain pan underneath the hose connections.
6. Disengage the wiring connectors from the front windshield and rear window washer pump motors, fluid level sensor and the rear washer hose.
7. Disconnect the front washer hose at the front wiper unit in the engine compartment. The front hose will be removed with the washer bottle.
8. Allow the washer bottle to drain into the pan.
9. Remove the washer bottle-to-front fender support mounting screws.
10. Remove the washer bottle from the vehicle. The washer pump motors can now be removed from the washer bottle.
11. Installation is the reverse of the removal procedure.

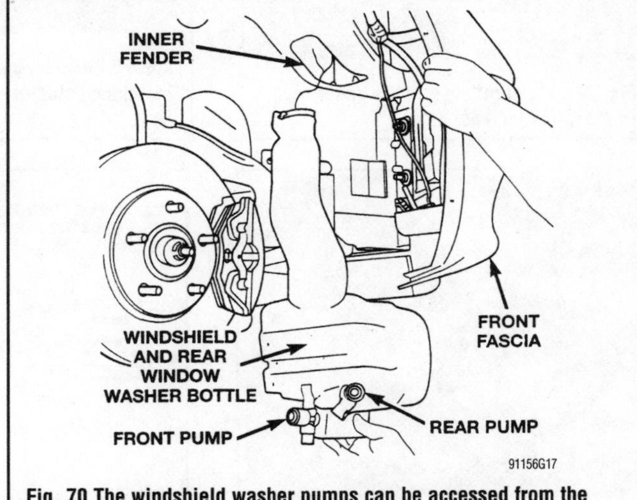

Fig. 70 The windshield washer pumps can be accessed from the right fenderwell

INSTRUMENTS AND SWITCHES

Instrument Cluster

REMOVAL & INSTALLATION

See Figures 71 thru 82

1. Disconnect the negative battery cable.

CAUTION

The models covered by this manual are equipped with a Supplemental Restraint System (SRS), which utilizes a driver and passenger side air bag. Whenever working near any of the SRS components, such as the impact sensors, the air bag module, steering column and instrument panel, disable the SRS, as described earlier in this section.

2. Disable the air bag system.
3. If equipped with a mechanical transmission range indicator, perform the following;
   a. Remove the lower steering column cover.
   b. Remove the knee blocker reinforcement panel from under the steering column.
   c. Remove the indicator cable loop.
   d. Remove the clip securing the gear shift cable end to the gear selector adapter.
   e. Pull the cable end from the gear selector.
4. Remove the instrument cluster bezel.
5. Remove the mounting screws securing the instrument cluster to the instrument panel.
6. Rotate the top of the cluster outward.
7. Disengage the wiring harness connectors from behind the cluster assembly.
8. Remove the instrument cluster from the vehicle. If equipped with a

91156PA7

Fig. 71 To access the instrument cluster mounting screws, remove the lower bezel . . .

91156PA5

Fig. 72 . . . and the driver's side end cap . . .

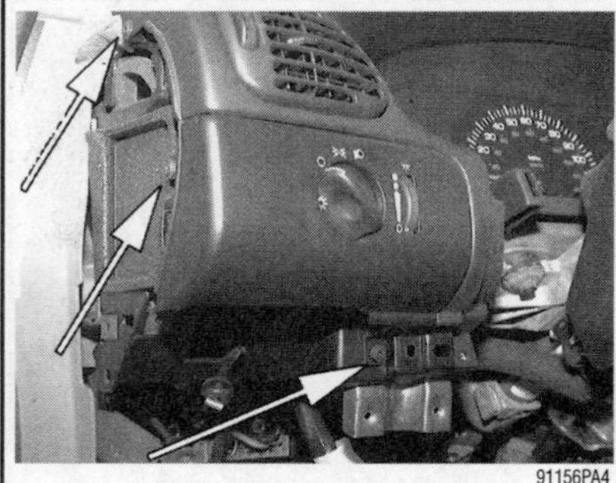

91156PA4

Fig. 73 . . . to access the upper trim bezel screws. After removing all of the screws . . .

91156PB3

Fig. 74 . . . carefully pull the upper bezel from the instrument panel

91156PB2

Fig. 75 Once the bezel is removed, the instrument cluster mounting screws can be removed (two on each side)

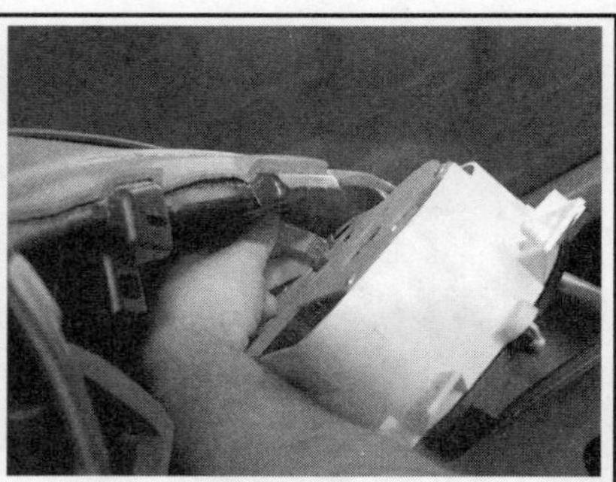

91156PB1

Fig. 76 After the mounting serews are removed, reach behind the cluster and unplug the electrical connectors . . .

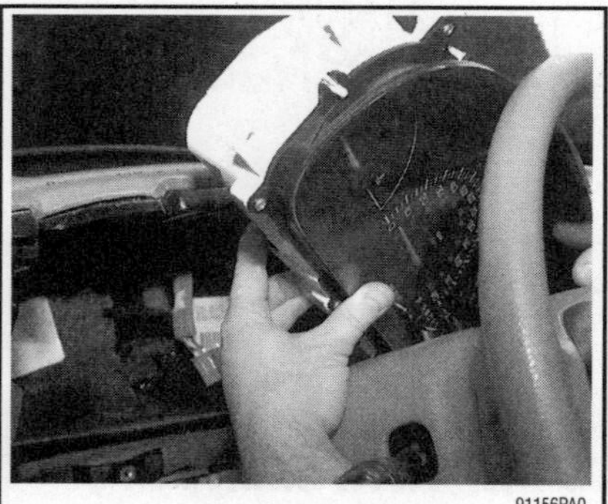

91156PA0

Fig. 77 . . . and remove the cluster from the instrument panel

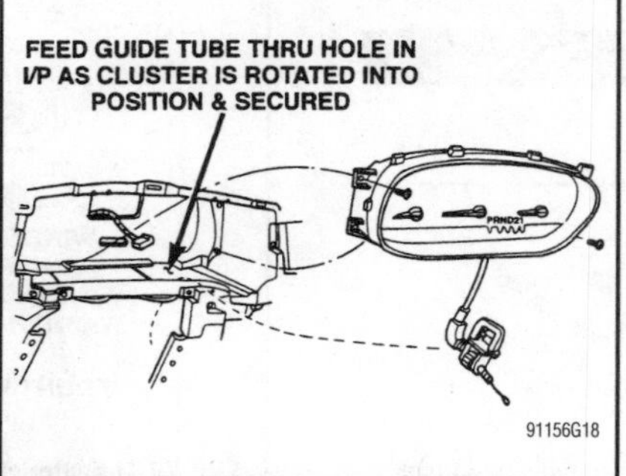
FEED GUIDE TUBE THRU HOLE IN I/P AS CLUSTER IS ROTATED INTO POSITION & SECURED

91156G18

Fig. 78 Instrument cluster mounting detail (models with a mechanical transmission range indicator)

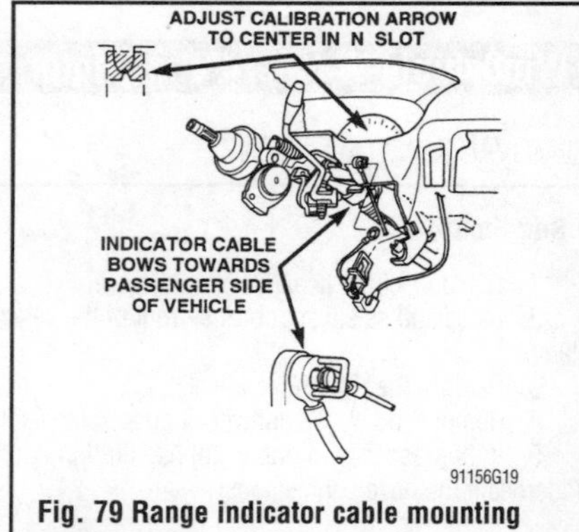
ADJUST CALIBRATION ARROW TO CENTER IN N SLOT
INDICATOR CABLE BOWS TOWARDS PASSENGER SIDE OF VEHICLE

91156G19

Fig. 79 Range indicator cable mounting detail

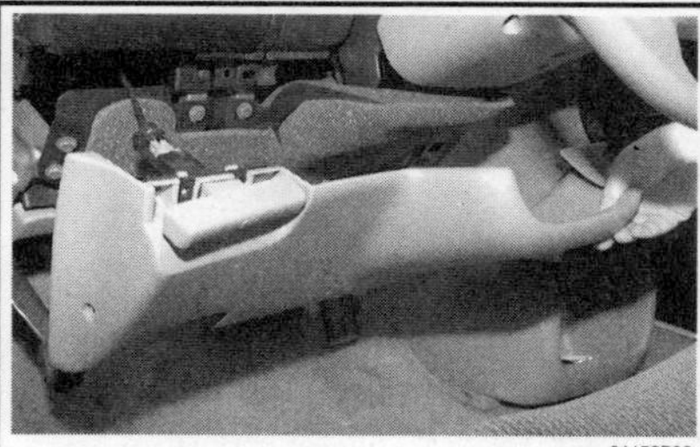

91156P96

Fig. 80 On models with a mechanical transmission range indicator, the cable must be accessed by removing the lower steering column cover. Remove the mounting fasteners, and lower the cover . . .

91156P93

Fig. 81 . . . disconnect the parking brake cable . . .

91156PA1

Fig. 82 and remove the reinforcement

mechanical transmission range indicator, carefully guide the range indicator cable and guide tube through the opening to avoid any possible damage.

To install:

9. If equipped with a mechanical transmission range indicator, verify the free travel of the range indicator cable from P to 1 by gently pulling on the cable, then relaxing the cable. Do NOT snap the cable once it is pulled.
10. Position the instrument cluster assembly into the instrument panel by leading the bottom of the cluster in first, plug in the wiring harness connector(s), and rotate upward. If equipped with a mechanical transmission range indicator, route the indicator cable and guide tube through the opening in the instrument panel.
11. Install and tighten the instrument cluster mounting screws.
12. Install the instrument cluster bezel.
13. If equipped with a mechanical transmission range indicator, install the indicator cable and guide tube. Install the cable retaining clips.
14. Install the knee blocker reinforcement panel.
15. Install the lower steering column cover.
16. Connect the negative battery cable.

Gauges

The gauges of the instrument cluster assembly are not individually replaceable. If any gauges require service or replacement, the entire cluster assembly must be replaced.

Rear Window Wiper Switch

The rear window wiper switch is an integral component of the HVAC control panel assembly. For removal and installation procedure, refer to the HVAC control panel removal earlier in this section.

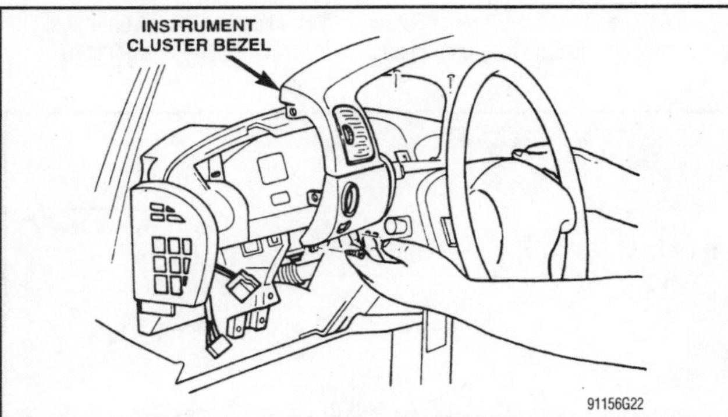

Fig. 83 The headlight switch is mounted on the instrument cluster bezel

Headlight Switch

REMOVAL & INSTALLATION

See Figures 83 and 84

1. Disconnect the negative battery cable.
2. Remove the instrument cluster bezel.
3. Disconnect the electrical connectors from the headlight switch and the power mirror switch.
4. Remove the mounting screws securing the headlight switch bezel to the instrument cluster bezel.
5. Remove the headlight switch bezel from the instrument cluster bezel.

To install:

6. Install the headlight switch bezel to the instrument cluster bezel and install the mounting screws.
7. Reconnect the electrical connectors to the power mirror switch and the headlight switch.
8. Install the instrument cluster bezel and headlight switch bezel to the instrument panel.
9. Reconnect the negative battery cable. Test the headlight switch for proper operation.

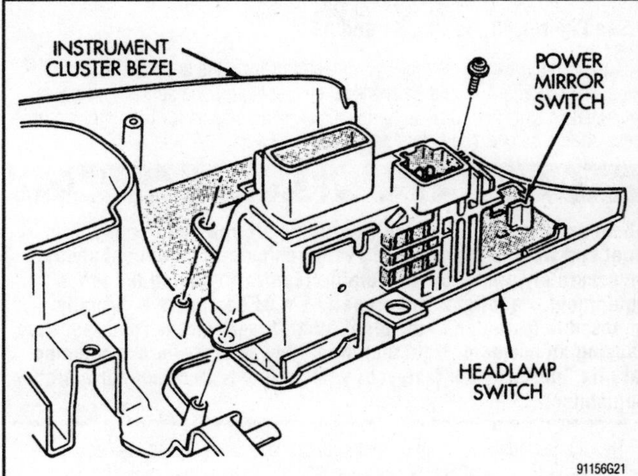

Fig. 84 To remove the headlight switch, remove the screws securing it to the instrument cluster bezel

LIGHTING

Headlights

REMOVAL & INSTALLATION

See Figures 85, 86 and 87

1. Disconnect the negative battery cable.
2. Rotate the bulb socket retaining ring counterclockwise and remove the ring.
3. Unplug the electrical connector from the rear of the bulb.
4. Pull the bulb out of the socket and replace the bulb.

To install:

WARNING

Do not touch the replacement bulb with your fingers. Oil contamination from your fingers will severely shorten the life of the bulb. If the bulb comes in contact with any oily surface, clean the bulb with rubbing alcohol.

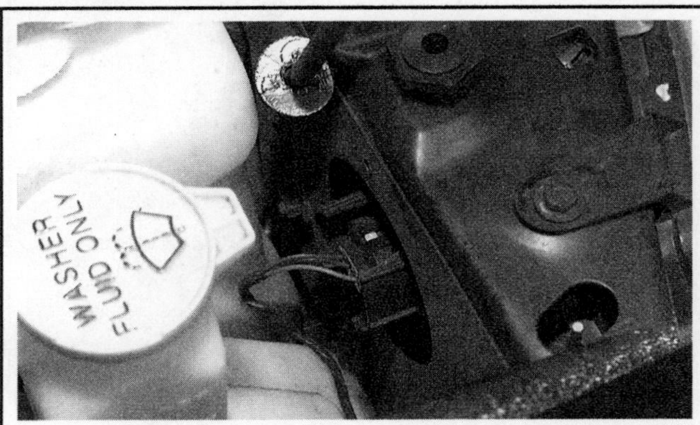

Fig. 85 The headlight bulbs can be accessed from the engine compartment, behind each headlight lens

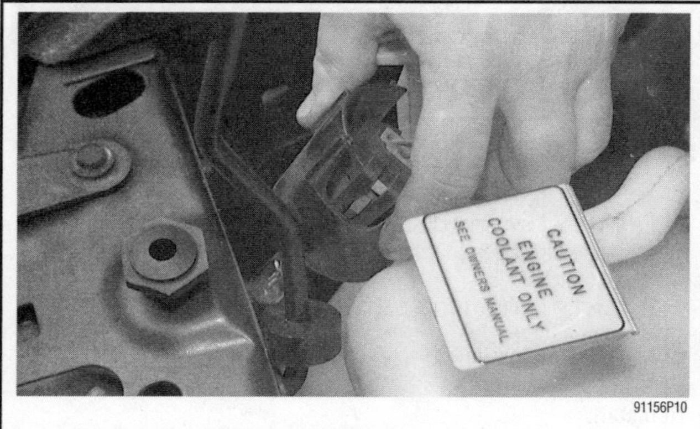

Fig. 86 Twist the bulb counter clockwise . . .

Fig. 87 . . . and unplug the electrical connector. DON'T touch the glass when installing the new bulb!

5. Install the bulb into the light housing and turn the retaining ring clockwise to secure the bulb.
6. Plug in the electrical connector.
7. Connect the negative battery cable.
8. Turn on the headlight to verify operation.

AIMING

See Figures 88, 89, 90, 91 and 92

The headlights must be properly aimed to provide the best, safest road illumination. The lights should be checked for proper aim and adjusted as necessary. Certain state and local authorities have requirements for headlight aiming; these should be checked before adjustment is made.

CAUTION

About once a year, when the headlights are replaced or any time front end work is performed on your vehicle, the headlight should be accurately aimed by a reputable repair shop using the proper equipment. Headlights not properly aimed can make it virtually impossible to see and may blind other drivers on the road, possibly causing an accident. Note that the following procedure is a temporary fix, until you can take your vehicle to a repair shop for a proper adjustment.

Headlight adjustment may be temporarily made using a wall, as described below, or on the rear of another vehicle. When adjusted, the lights should not glare in oncoming car or truck windshields, nor should they illuminate the passenger compartment of vehicles driving in front of you. These adjustments are rough and should always be fine-tuned by a repair shop which is equipped with headlight aiming tools. Improper adjustments may be both dangerous and illegal.

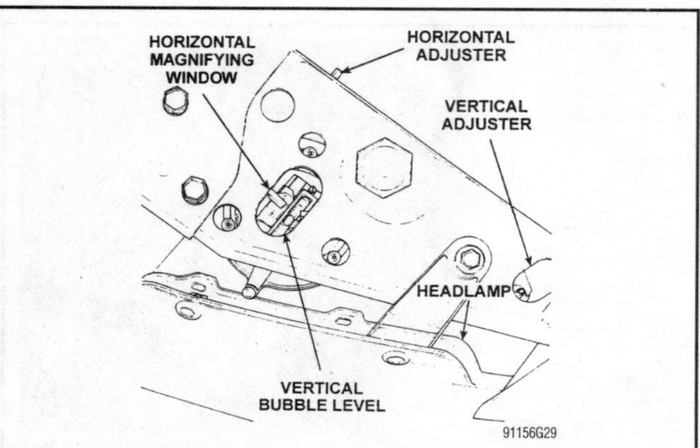

Fig. 88 The headlights are equipped with adjusters and a built in level to aid in proper aiming

Because the composite headlight assembly is bolted into position, no adjustment should be necessary or possible. Some applications, however, may be bolted to an adjuster plate or may be retained by adjusting screws. If so, follow this procedure when adjusting the lights, BUT always have the adjustment checked by a reputable shop.

Before removing the headlight bulb or disturbing the headlamp in any way, note the current settings in order to ease headlight adjustment upon reassembly. If the high or low beam setting of the old lamp still works, this can be done using the wall of a garage or a building:

1. Park the vehicle on a level surface, with the fuel tank full and with the vehicle empty of all extra cargo (unless normally carried). The vehicle should be facing a wall which is no less than 6 feet (1.8m) high and 12 feet (3.7m) wide. The front of the vehicle should be about 25 feet (7.6m) from the wall.
2. If aiming is to be performed outdoors, it is advisable to wait until dusk in order to properly see the headlight beams on the wall. If done in a garage,

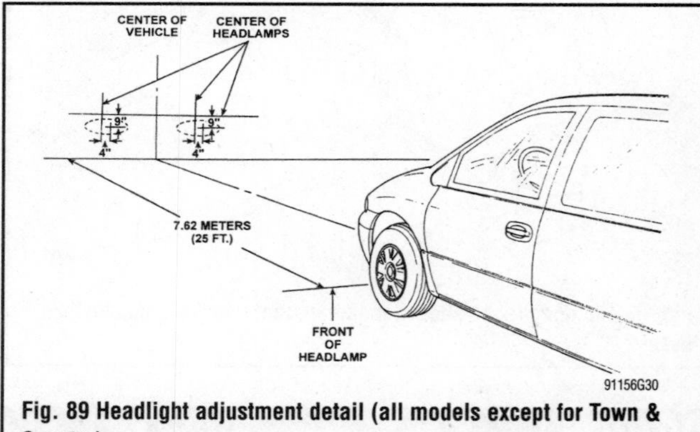

Fig. 89 Headlight adjustment detail (all models except for Town & Country)

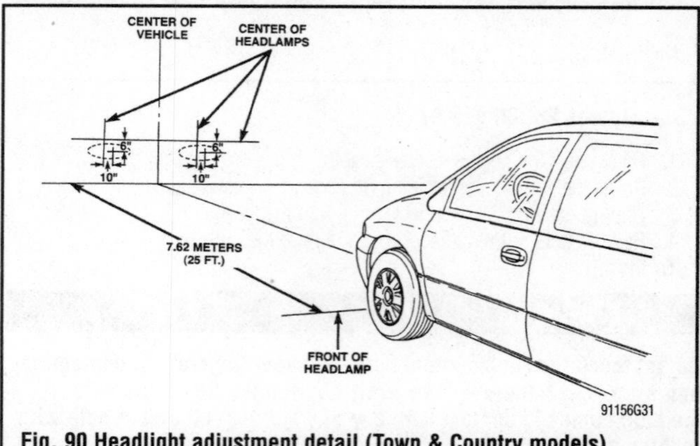

Fig. 90 Headlight adjustment detail (Town & Country models)

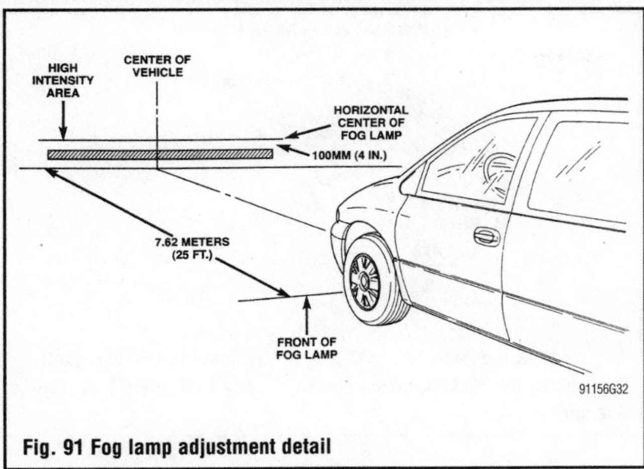

Fig. 91 Fog lamp adjustment detail

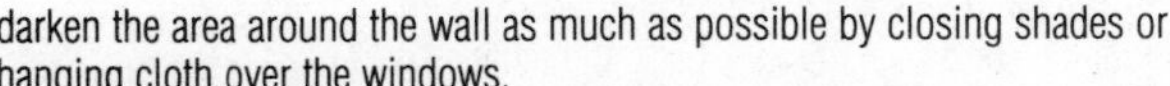

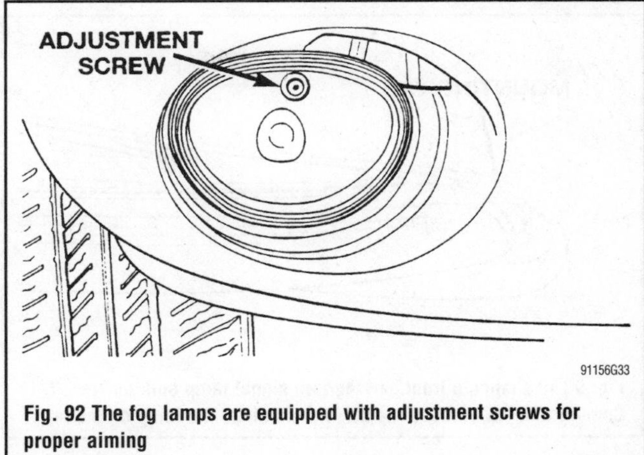

Fig. 92 The fog lamps are equipped with adjustment screws for proper aiming

darken the area around the wall as much as possible by closing shades or hanging cloth over the windows.

3. Turn the headlights **ON** and mark the wall at the center of each light's low beam, then switch on the brights and mark the center of each light's high beam. A short length of masking tape which is visible from the front of the vehicle may be used. Although marking all four positions is advisable, marking one position from each light should be sufficient.

4. If neither beam on one side is working, and if another like-sized vehicle is available, park the second one in the exact spot where the vehicle was and mark the beams using the same-side light. Then, switch the vehicles so the one to be aimed is back in the original spot. It must be parked no closer to or farther away from the wall than the second vehicle.

5. Perform any necessary repairs, but make sure the vehicle is not moved, or is returned to the exact spot from which the lights were marked. Turn the headlights **ON** and adjust the beams to match the marks on the wall.

6. Have the headlight adjustment checked as soon as possible by a reputable repair shop.

Signal and Marker Lights

REMOVAL & INSTALLATION

Front Parking and Turn Signal Lights

See Figures 93 thru 99

1. Disconnect the negative battery cable.
2. From under the front wheelhouse, remove the access cover behind the parking and turn signal lamp.

Fig. 93 The front parking and turn signal lights can be reached by removing the access cover in the wheelhouse

Fig. 94 To remove the cover, simply twist it counterclockwise

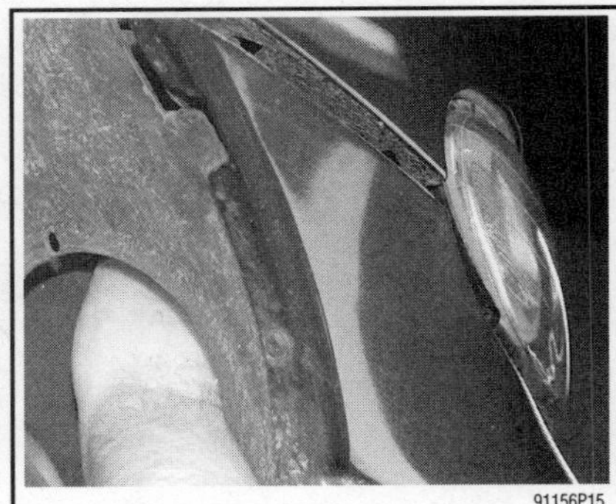

Fig. 95 Reach inside and twist the bulb socket out of the rear of the lens

Fig. 96 There is enough wire to pull the bulb and socket out of the wheelhouse slightly to make bulb replacement easier

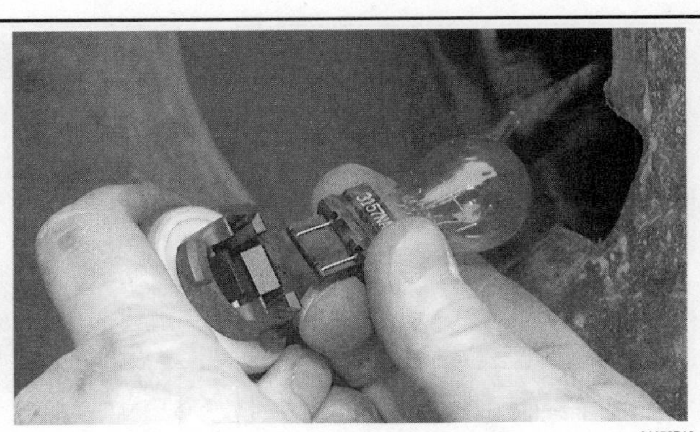

Fig. 97 The bulb pulls straight out of the socket

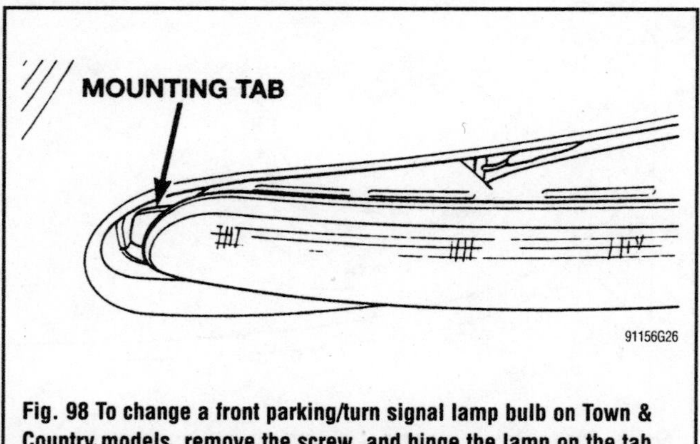

Fig. 98 To change a front parking/turn signal lamp bulb on Town & Country models, remove the screw, and hinge the lamp on the tab

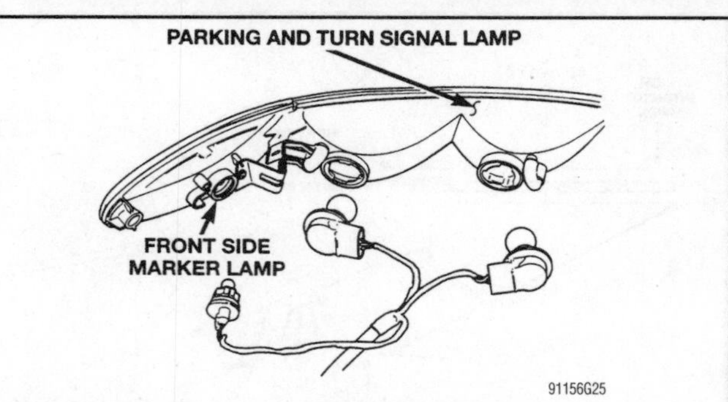

Fig. 99 With the lamp free of the facia, the bulbs can be accessed by twisting the sockets counterclockwise, and pulling the bulb from the socket

3. Through the access hole in the wheelhouse, rotate the parking and turn signal socket counterclockwise ¼ turn.
4. Pull the socket out from the back of the housing.
5. Pull the bulb straight out of the socket.
6. Replace the bulb.
7. Installation is the reverse of the removal procedure.
8. Verify light operation.

Front Side Marker Light (Town & Country)

▸ See Figure 100

1. Disconnect the negative battery cable.
2. Remove the retaining screw securing the side marker light housing to the front fascia.
3. Pull the side marker light housing away from the fascia.
4. Rotate the light socket counterclockwise ¼ turn.
5. Pull the socket out from the back of the housing.
6. Pull the bulb straight out of the socket.
7. Replace the bulb.
8. Installation is the reverse of the removal procedure.
9. Verify light operation.

Rear Turn Signal, Brake and Parking Lights

▸ See Figures 101, 102, 103, 104 and 105

1. Disconnect the negative battery cable.
2. Raise the liftgate.
3. Remove the 2 lamp assembly mounting screws.

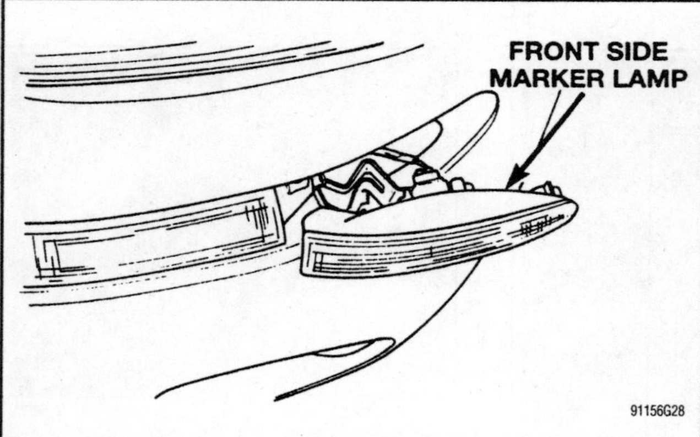

Fig. 100 The front side marker light bulb on Town & Country models can be accessed by removing the lamp from the facia

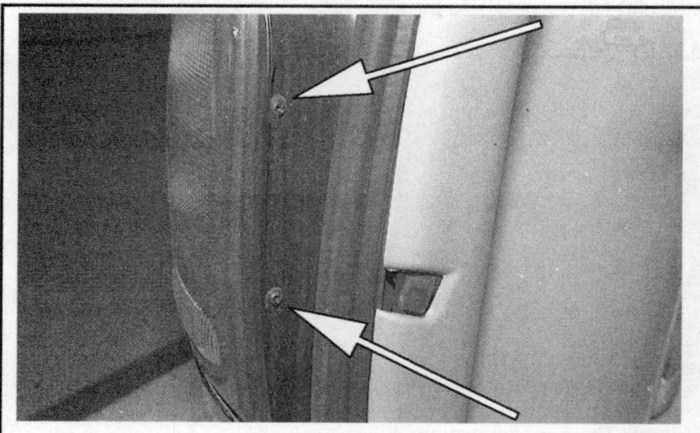

Fig. 101 The rear lamp assembly is held in place by two screws (arrows)

Fig. 102 Once the screws are removed, carefully pull the lamp assembly from the vehicle

Fig. 103 Twist the bulb socket counter-clockwise . . .

Fig. 104 . . . and remove it from the rear of the lens

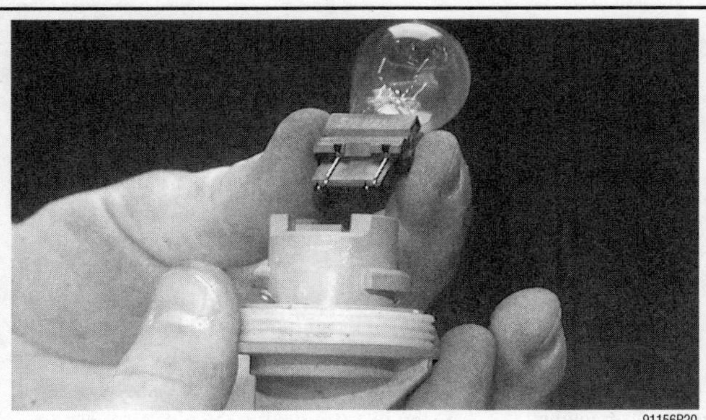

Fig. 105 The bulb simply pulls out of the socket

4. Rotate the lamp assembly outward and unhook it from the forward retainer.
5. Rotate the socket counterclockwise to remove it from the housing.
6. Remove the bulb by pulling it straight out of the socket.
7. Replace the bulb.
8. Installation is the reverse of the removal procedure.
9. Verify light operation.

High-mount Brake Light

See Figures 106, 107 and 108

1. Disconnect the negative battery cable.
2. Raise the liftgate.
3. Remove the center high mounted stop light trim cover. Use care to prevent damaging the trim panel.
4. Rotate the bulb socket counterclockwise to remove it from the light housing.
5. Pull the bulb straight out of the socket.
6. Replace the bulb.
7. Installation is the reverse of the removal procedure.
8. Verify light operation.

Dome Light

See Figures 109, 110 and 111

1. Disconnect the negative battery cable.
2. Insert a small, flat bladed prying tool between the dome light lens and the left side of the dome light body.
3. Disengage the left side of the dome light lens from the light body.
4. Pull the bulb from the socket.
5. Replace the bulb.
6. Installation is the reverse of the removal procedure.
7. Verify dome light operation.

Liftgate Courtesy Lamps

See Figures 112 thru 117

1. Disconnect the negative battery cable.
2. Insert a small, flat bladed prying tool between the lamp lens and trim panel. Pry out the assembly.
3. Insert a small, flat bladed prying tool between the lamp lens and the housing body.
4. Carefully depress the tabs retaining the lens to the body, then remove the lens.
5. Carefully press the lamp bulb contact toward the opposite contact.
6. Remove the bulb from the lamp body.
7. Replace the bulb.
8. Installation is the reverse of the removal procedure.
9. Verify light operation.

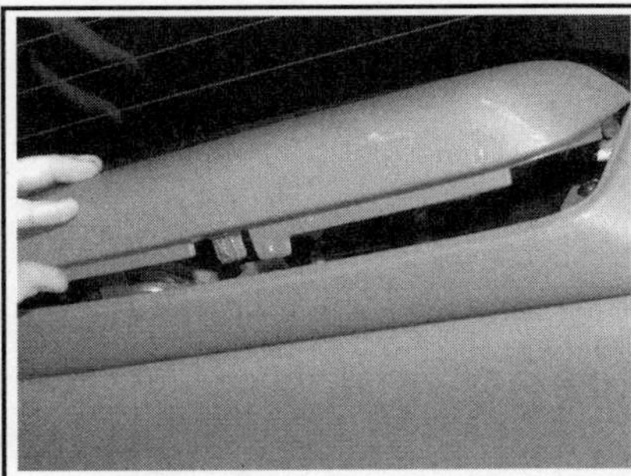

Fig. 106 To access the bulbs for the high-mount brake light, remove the cover on the inside of the liftgate

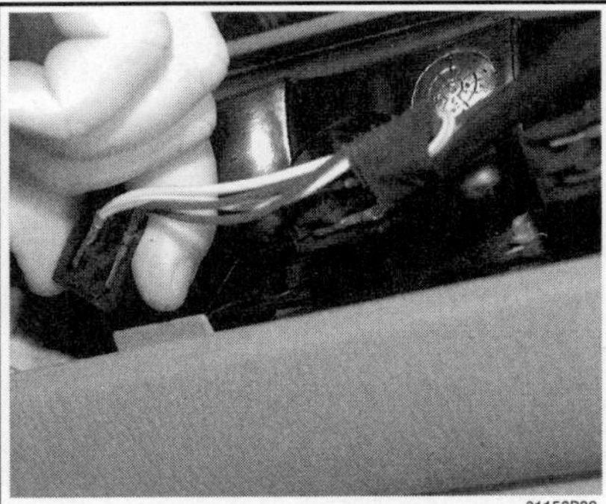

Fig. 107 The bulb sockets are removed by twisting them counterclockwise

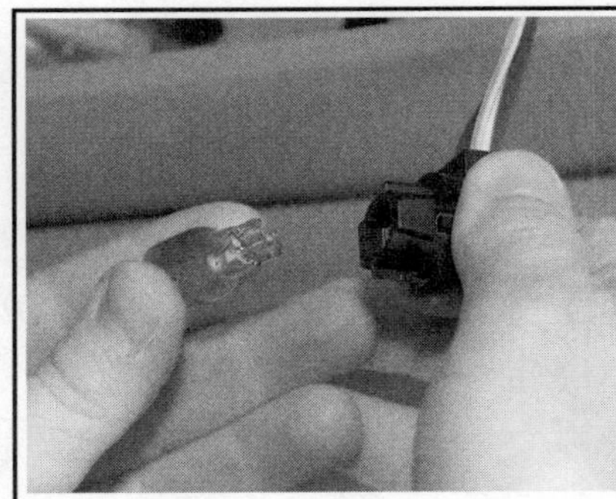

Fig. 108 the bulb pulls straight out of the socket

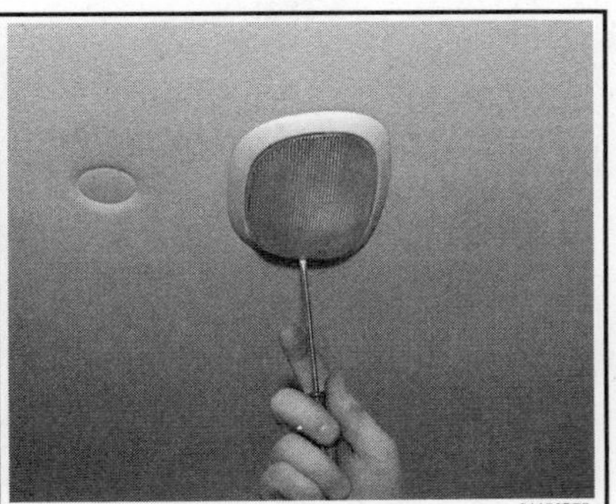

Fig. 109 Using a suitable tool, carefully pry the dome lens from the body

Fig. 110 The lens is hinged on the right side

Fig. 111 The bulb pulls straight out

91156P26

Fig. 112 Using a suitable tool, carefully pry the lens assembly from the liftgate

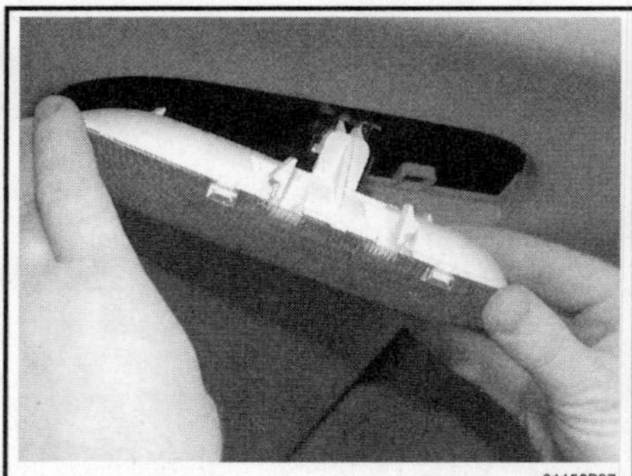
91156P27

Fig. 113 The lens is held in place by clips on the housing; be careful when removing it from the liftgate

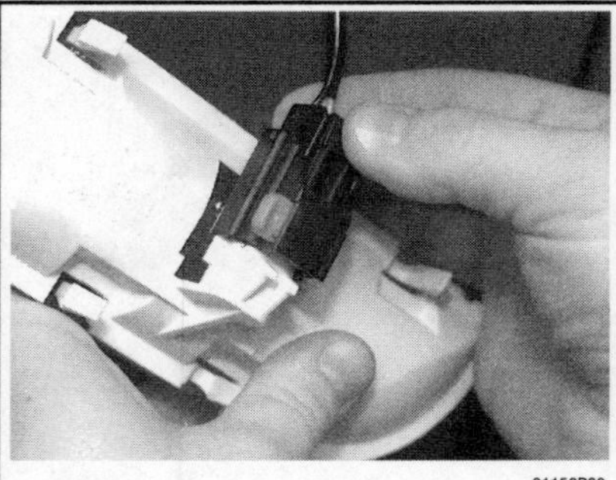
91156P29

Fig. 114 Once the lens assembly is free of the liftgate, unplug the electrical connector

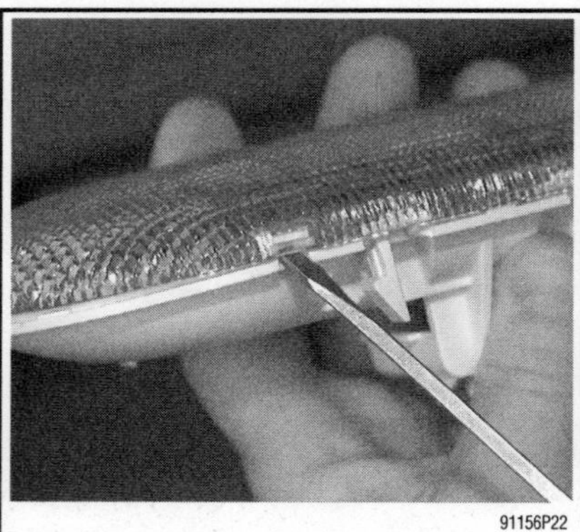
91156P22

Fig. 115 Using a suitable tool . . .

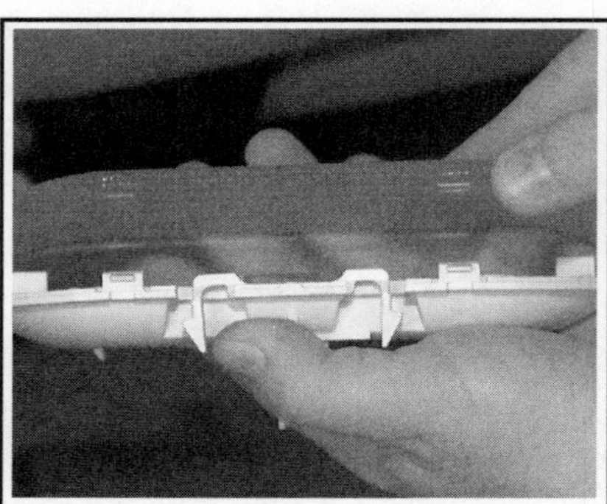
91156P23

Fig. 116 . . . carefully separate the lens . . .

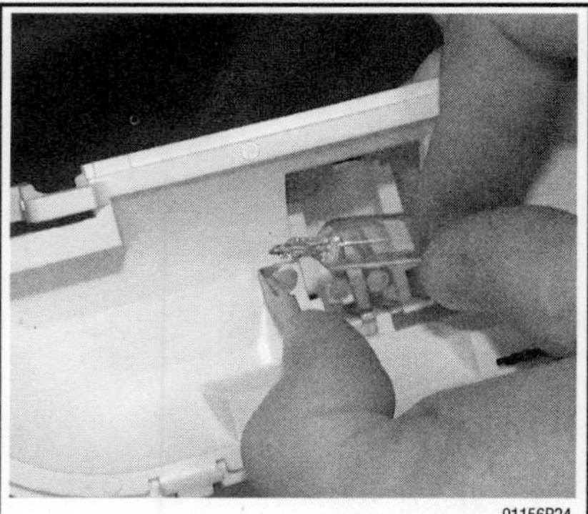
91156P24

Fig. 117 . . . and remove the bulb

Header Reading/Courtesy Lamp

See Figures 118, 119 and 120

1. Disconnect the negative battery cable.
2. Insert a small, flat bladed prying tool at the forward position between the reading/courtesy lamp lens and housing. Pry the lens out from the housing.
3. Insert a small, flat bladed prying tool between the lamp light shield and the lamp housing at the inboard rear corner of the light shield. Pry the shield out from the housing.
4. Carefully press forward lamp bulb contact toward the opposite contact and rotate. Remove the bulb.
5. Replace the bulb.
6. Installation is the reverse of the removal procedure.
7. Verify light operation.

License Plate Light

See Figures 121, 122 and 123

1. Disconnect the negative battery cable.
2. Remove the license plate lamp lens retaining screws.
3. Pull the license plate lamp lens from the liftgate.
4. Rotate the bulb socket 1/4 turn counterclockwise and pull out from the lamp lens.
5. Pull the bulb straight out of the socket.

To install:

6. Install the replacement bulb into the socket.
7. Install the bulb socket into the lens and lock it into place by rotating it 1/4 turn clockwise.
8. Place the license plate lamp lens into position on the liftgate.

91156P72

Fig. 118 Using a suitable tool, carefully pry the lens from the body

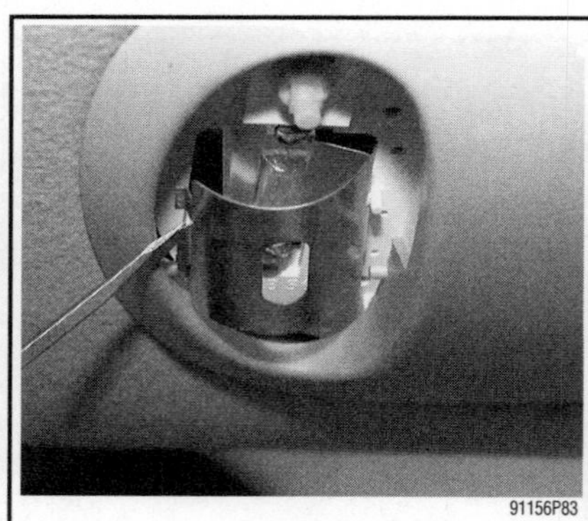
91156P83

Fig. 119 Then remove the shield . . .

91156P82

Fig. 120 . . . and disengage the bulb from the socket

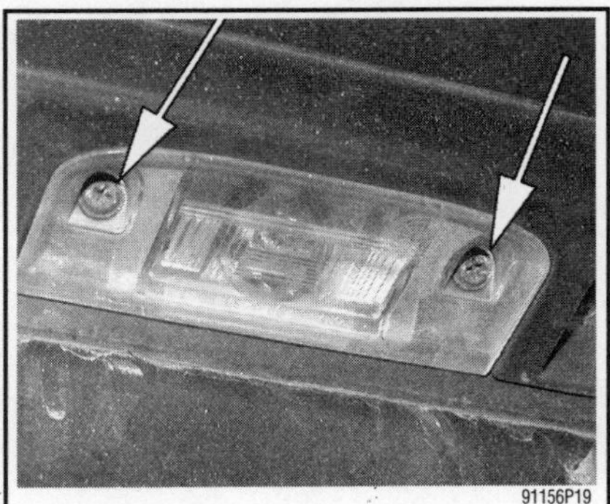

91156P19

Fig. 121 To change the rear license plate light, remove the screws . . .

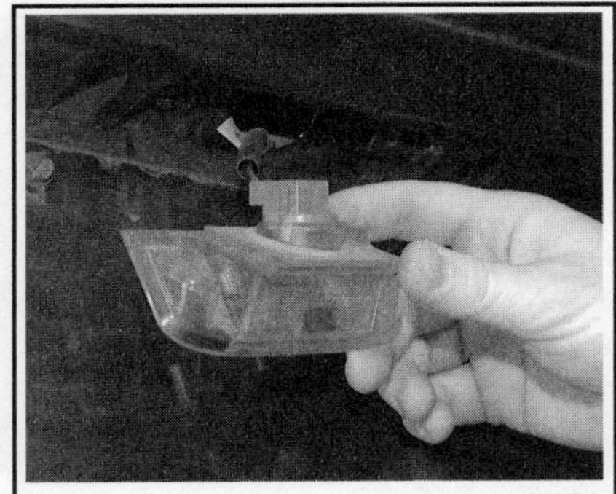

91156P18

Fig. 122 . . . and lower the lens. Twist the socket and pull it from the lens . . .

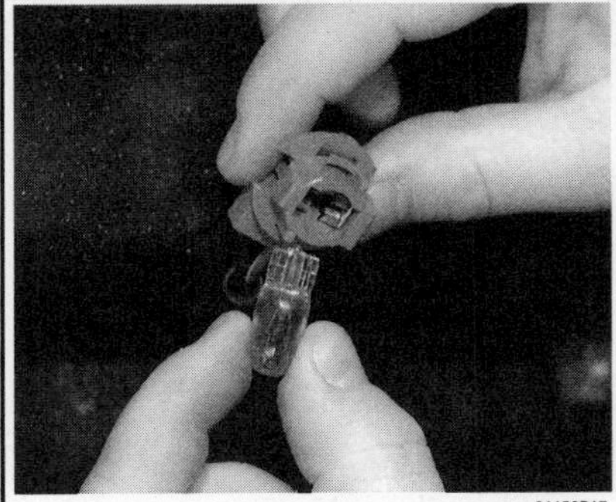

91156P17

Fig. 123 . . . and disengage the bulb from the socket

9. Install and tighten the license plate lamp lens retaining screws.
10. Connect the negative battery cable.
11. Verify license plate lamp operation.

Fog/Driving Lights

REMOVAL & INSTALLATION

Procedure A

See Figure 124

Procedure A applies to all 1996–97 minivan vehicles, as well as 1998 Voyager and Caravan only models, equipped with fog lights.

1. Disconnect the negative battery cable.
2. Remove the 2 screws securing the fog light to the bumper.
3. Pull the fog light housing out and unclip the back cover.
4. Disengage the wiring connector from the bulb.
5. Disengage the light bulb wire spring retainer and remove the bulb.

WARNING

Do not touch the replacement bulb with your fingers. Oil contamination from your fingers will severely shorten the life of the bulb. If the bulb comes in contact with any oily surface, clean the bulb with rubbing alcohol.

6. Installation is the reverse of the removal procedure.
7. Verify fog light operation.

Procedure B

See Figure 125

Procedure B applies to 1998 Town & Country models only, as well as all 1999 minivan vehicles, equipped with fog lights.

1. Disconnect the negative battery cable.
2. Reach around behind the front bumper fascia and remove the bulb by rotating it counterclockwise.
3. Disengage the wiring connector from the fog light bulb base.
4. Replace the bulb.

WARNING

Do not touch the replacement bulb with your fingers. Oil contamination from your fingers will severely shorten the life of the bulb. If the bulb comes in contact with any oily surface, clean the bulb with rubbing alcohol.

5. Installation is the reverse of the removal procedure.
6. Verify fog light operation.

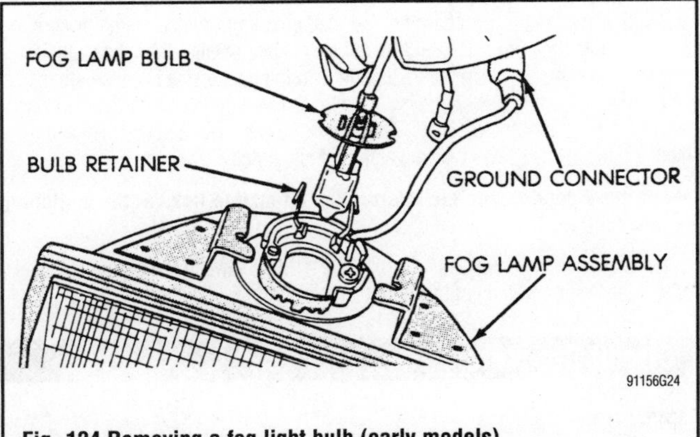

Fig. 124 Removing a fog light bulb (early models)

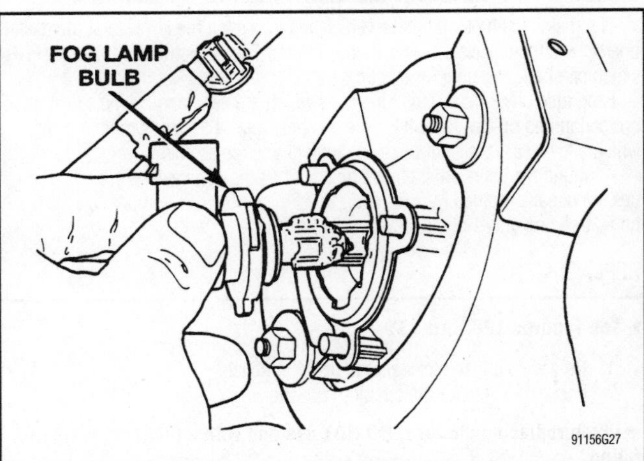

Fig. 125 Removing a fog light bulb (later Town & Country models)

REPLACEMENT LIGHT BULBS

LIGHT BULBS — Interior	Bulb Number
ABS	PC194
Airbag	PC194
Alarm Set (Security)	PC194
Brake System Warning Indicator	PC194
Center & Rear Dome Light	579
Center & Rear Reading Lamps	578
Cruise Indicator	PC194
Front Door Light	567
Door Open Indicator	PC194
Front Header Reading Lamps	567
Glove Box	194
High Beam Indicator	PC194
Instrument Cluster	PC194
Instrument Panel Bin (or Ash Tray if so equipped)	161
Liftgate Flood Lights	567
Liftgate Open Indicator	PC74
Oil Indicator, Low Fuel Indicator	PC194
Overhead Console Reading lamps	579
Seat Belt Indicator	PC74
Service Engine Soon Light	PC194
Temperature Indicator	PC194
Turn Signal Indicator	PC194
Underhood Light	579
Visor Vanity	6501966
Volts Indicator, Low Washer Fluid	PC74

NOTE: For lighted switches, see your dealer for replacement instructions.

All of the interior bulbs are glass wedge base or glass cartridge types. Aluminum base bulbs are not approved and should not be used for replacement.

LIGHT BULBS — Exterior	Bulb Number
Back-up, Tail, Stop, Turn Signal, & Sidemarker	3057
Center High-Mounted Stop Light	921
Fog Light	H3
Front Side marker, Park/Turn Signal	3157NA
Headlight	9007
License	168

91156GA1

TRAILER WIRING

Wiring the vehicle for towing is fairly easy. There are a number of good wiring kits available and these should be used, rather than trying to design your own.

All trailers will need brake lights and turn signals as well as tail lights and side marker lights. Most areas require extra marker lights for overwide trailers. Also, most areas have recently required back-up lights for trailers, and most trailer manufacturers have been building trailers with back-up lights for several years.

Additionally, some Class I, most Class II and just about all Class III and IV trailers will have electric brakes. Add to this number an accessories wire, to operate trailer internal equipment or to charge the trailer's battery, and you can have as many as seven wires in the harness.

Determine the equipment on your trailer and buy the wiring kit necessary. The kit will contain all the wires needed, plus a plug adapter set which includes the female plug, mounted on the bumper or hitch, and the male plug, wired into, or plugged into the trailer harness.

When installing the kit, follow the manufacturer's instructions. The color coding of the wires is usually standard throughout the industry. One point to note: some domestic vehicles, and most imported vehicles, have separate turn signals. On most domestic vehicles, the brake lights and rear turn signals operate with the same bulb. For those vehicles without separate turn signals, you can purchase an isolation unit so that the brake lights won't blink whenever the turn signals are operated.

One final point, the best kits are those with a spring loaded cover on the vehicle mounted socket. This cover prevents dirt and moisture from corroding the terminals. Never let the vehicle socket hang loosely; always mount it securely to the bumper or hitch.

CIRCUIT PROTECTION

Fuses

The main fuse block on these vehicles is located at the left side of the dashboard, behind an access panel. There is also a Power Distribution Center (PDC) which can be found under the hood.

Each fuse block uses miniature fuses which are designed for increased circuit protection and greater reliability. The compact fuse is a blade terminal design which allows easy pull-out/push-in removal and replacement.

Although the fuses are interchangeable, the amperage values are not. The values are usually molded in bold, color coded, easy to read numbers on the fuse body. Use only fuses of equal replacement valve.

REPLACEMENT

See Figures 126 thru 131

1. Remove the fuse block access panel or cover.
2. Locate the fuse for the circuit in question.

When replacing the fuse, DO NOT use one with a higher amperage rating.

3. Check the fuse by pulling it from the fuse block and observing the element. If it is broken, install a replacement fuse of the same amperage rating. If the fuse blows again, check the circuit for a short to ground or faulty device in the circuit protected by the fuse.
4. Continuity can also be checked with the fuse installed in the fuse block with the use of a test light connected across the 2 test points on the end of the fuse. If the test light lights, replace the fuse. Check the circuit for a short to ground or faulty device in the circuit which is protected by the fuse.

Fusible Links

In addition to circuit breakers and fuses, the wiring harness incorporates fusible links to protect the wiring. Links are used rather than a fuse, in wiring circuits that are not normally fused, such as the ignition circuit. The fusible links are color coded red in the charging and load circuits to match the color coding of the circuits they protect. Each link is four gauges smaller than the cable it protects, and is marked on the insulation with the gauge size because the insulation makes it appear heavier than it really is. The engine compartment wiring harness has several fusible links. The same size wire with a special Hypalon insulation must be used when replacing a fusible link.

For more details, see the information on fusible links at the beginning of this section.

On these vehicles, there is a fusible link placed between the output terminal of the alternator and the engine starter motor terminal.

Circuit Breakers

OPERATION

Circuit breakers differ from fuses in that they are reusable. Circuit breakers open when the flow of current exceeds a specified value and close after a few seconds when current flow returns to normal. Some of the circuits protected by circuit breakers include electric windows and power accessories. Circuit breakers are used in these applications due to the fact that they must operate at times under prolonged high current flow due to demand, even though there is not a malfunction in the circuit.

91156P76

Fig. 126 There are fuse panels located underneath the driver's side instrument panel . . .

91156P01

Fig. 127 . . . and in the engine compartment, next to the battery

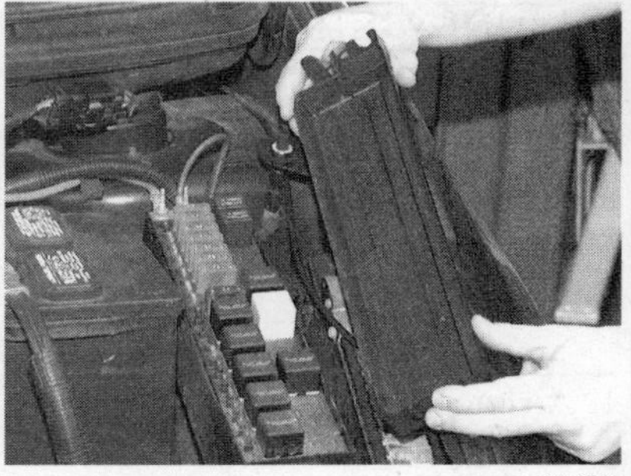
91156P02

Fig. 128 The fuse panel in the engine compartment is protected by a plastic cover

91156P03

Fig. 129 For the small-sized fuses, a puller tool should be used

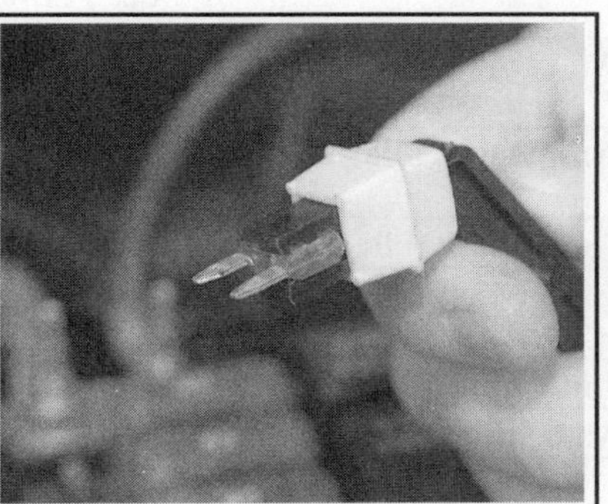
91156P04

Fig. 130 Note how the tool grabs the fuse, making removal and installation easier

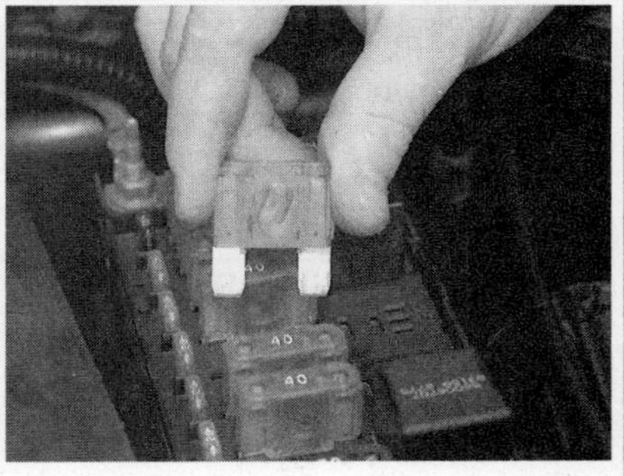
91156P05

Fig. 131 Maxi-fuses are removed easily by hand

There are 2 types of circuit breakers. The first type opens when high current flow is detected. A few seconds after the excessive current flow has been removed, the circuit breaker will close. If the high current flow is experienced again, the circuit will open again.

The second type is referred to as the Positive Temperature Coefficient (PTC) circuit breaker. When excessive current flow passes through the PTC circuit breaker, the circuit is not opened, but its resistance increases. As the device heats up with the increase in current flow, the resistance increases to the point where the circuit is effectively open. Unlike other circuit breakers, the PTC circuit breaker will not reset until the circuit is opened and voltage is removed from the terminals. Once the voltage is removed, the circuit breaker will not reset until the circuit is opened and voltage is removed from the terminals. Once the voltage is removed, the circuit breaker will re-close within a few seconds.

Various circuit breakers are located under the instrument panel. In order to gain access to these components, it may be necessary to first remove the underdash padding. Most of the circuit breakers are located in the power distribution center or the fuse panel. Replace the circuit breaker by unplugging the old one and plugging in the new one. Confirm proper circuit operation.

Flashers

REPLACEMENT

See Figure 132

Flashers are located either on the bottom of the fuse block or on a module under the dashboard (instrument panel). They are replaced by simply pulling them straight out. Note that the prongs are arranged in such a way that the flasher must be properly oriented before attempting to install it. Turn the flasher until the orientation of the prongs is correct and simply push it firmly in until the prongs are fully engaged.

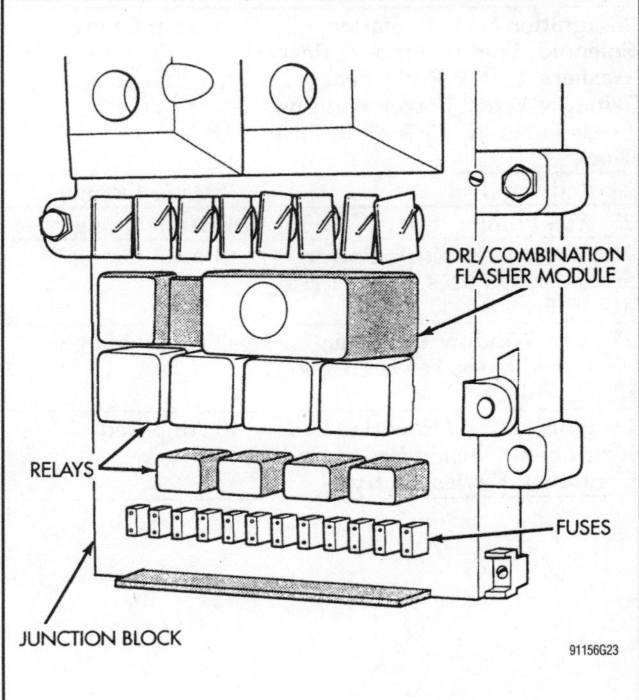

91156G23

Fig. 132 The flasher relay is located at the top of the junction block, which is underneath the driver's side of the instrument panel

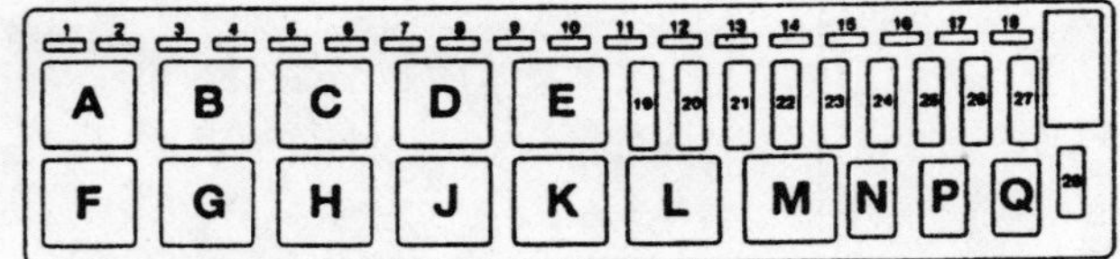

POWER DISTRIBUTION CENTER	
1. Airbag	10 Amp Mini Red
2. Airbag	10 Amp Mini Red
3. Open	
4. Headlight High - Left	10 Amp Mini Red
5. Headlight High - Right	10 Amp Mini Red
6. Headlight Low - Left, Fog Light - Left	15 Amp Mini Blue
7. Headlight Low - Right, Fog Light - Right	15 Amp Mini Blue
8. Cigarette Lighter, Accessory, Front Wiper De-Ice	20 Amp Mini Yellow
9. Horns	20 Amp Mini Yellow
10. Hazard Warning Flashers, Turn Signals	20 Amp Mini Yellow
11. A/C Clutch	15 Amp Mini Blue
12. ABS System	25 Amp Mini Natural

POWER DISTRIBUTION CENTER	
13. Stop Lights, Center High Mounted Stop Light	20 Amp Mini Yellow
14. Open	
15. Automatic Transmission Controller, Transmission Solenoids	20 Amp Mini Yellow
16. Fuel Pump, Engine Controller	20 Amp Mini Yellow
17. Engine, Generator	20 Amp Mini Yellow
18. Interior Lighting, Power Mirrors, Underhood Light	15 Amp Mini Blue
19. Wipers - Front	30 Amp Green
20. Open	
21. Blower Motor - Front	40 Amp Orange
22. Park Lights, License Light, Feeds Fuses #1, #4 & #6 In Fuse Block	40 Amp Orange

91156GA3

POWER DISTRIBUTION CENTER	
23. Ignition Switch, Starter Solenoid, Engine, Front & Rear Washers, Left & Right Rear Window Vents, Power Windows, Feeds Fuses #2, #3 & #8 In Fuse Block	40 Amp Orange
24. Radiator Fan	40 Amp Orange
25. ABS Pump	40 Amp Orange
26. Power Door Lock, Power Seats, Feeds Fuses #10, #11 & #12 In Fuse Block	40 Amp Orange
27. Rear Window Defroster, Heated Mirrors, Feeds Fuse #7 In Fuse Block	40 Amp Orange
28. Ignition Off Draw (I.O.D.), Instrument Cluster, Radio, Body Controller, Keyless Entry	10 Amp Red

91156GA4

POWER DISTRIBUTION CENTER	
A. Cigarette and Accessory	Relay
B. Front Wiper Hi/Lo	Relay
C. Front Wiper On	Relay
D. High Beam	Relay
E. Low Beam	Relay
F. Open	
G. Horn	Relay
H. A/C Clutch	Relay
J. Open	
K. Blower Motor	Relay
L. Starter	Relay
M. Park Lights	Relay
N. Automatic Transmission Controller Shutdown	Relay
P. Fuel Pump	Relay
Q. Auto Shutdown	Relay

91156GA5

INDEX OF WIRING DIAGRAMS

91156W01

SAMPLE DIAGRAM: HOW TO READ & INTERPRET WIRING DIAGRAMS

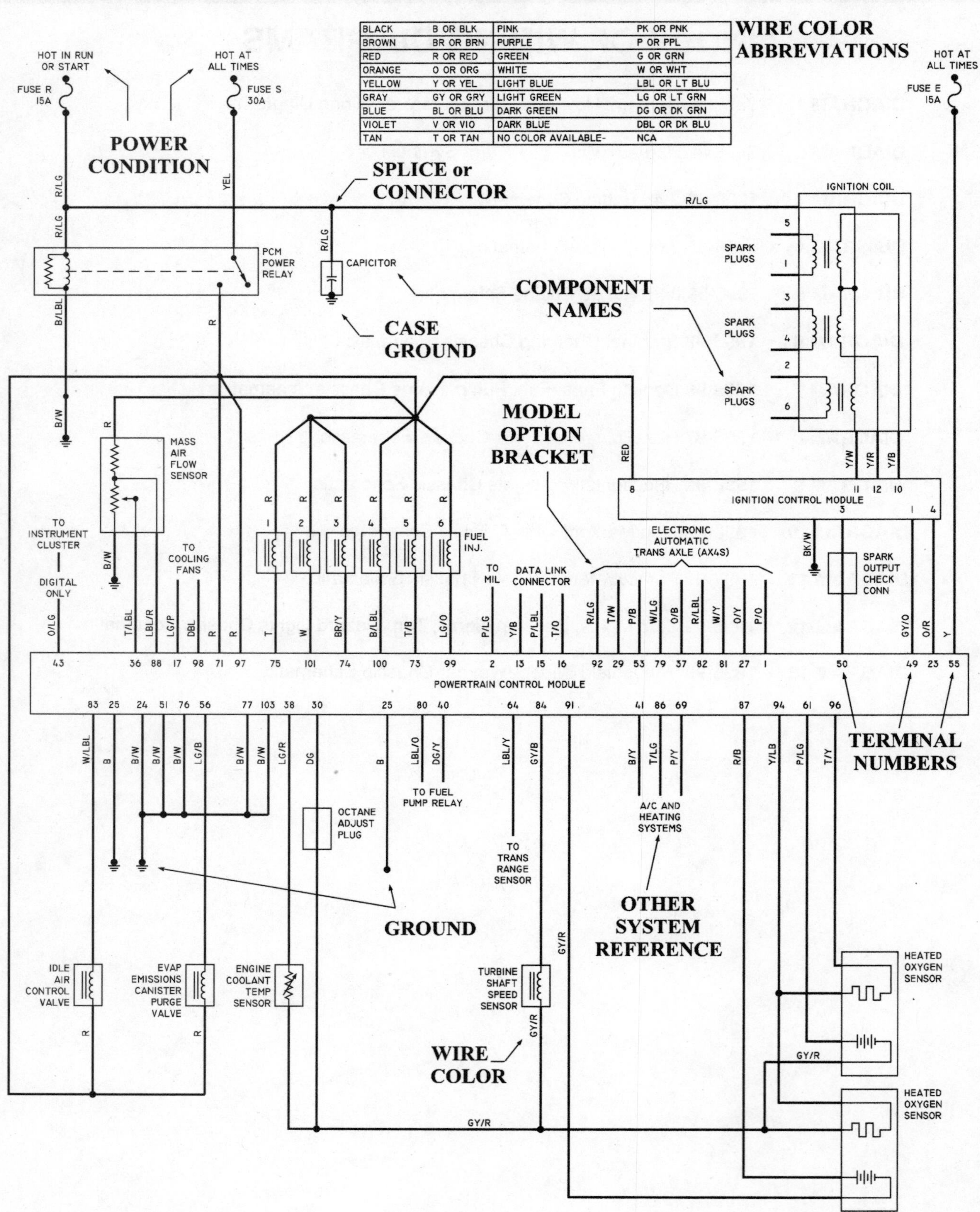

WIRE COLOR ABBREVIATIONS

BLACK	B OR BLK	PINK	PK OR PNK
BROWN	BR OR BRN	PURPLE	P OR PPL
RED	R OR RED	GREEN	G OR GRN
ORANGE	O OR ORG	WHITE	W OR WHT
YELLOW	Y OR YEL	LIGHT BLUE	LBL OR LT BLU
GRAY	GY OR GRY	LIGHT GREEN	LG OR LT GRN
BLUE	BL OR BLU	DARK GREEN	DG OR DK GRN
VIOLET	V OR VIO	DARK BLUE	DBL OR DK BLU
TAN	T OR TAN	NO COLOR AVAILABLE-	NCA

DIAGRAM 1

TCCA6W01

WIRING DIAGRAM SYMBOLS

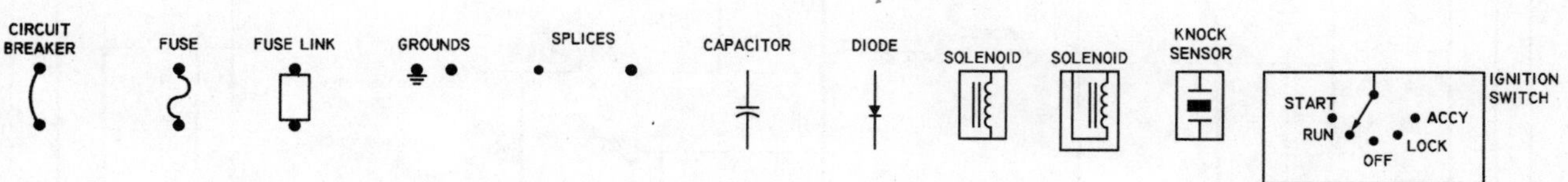

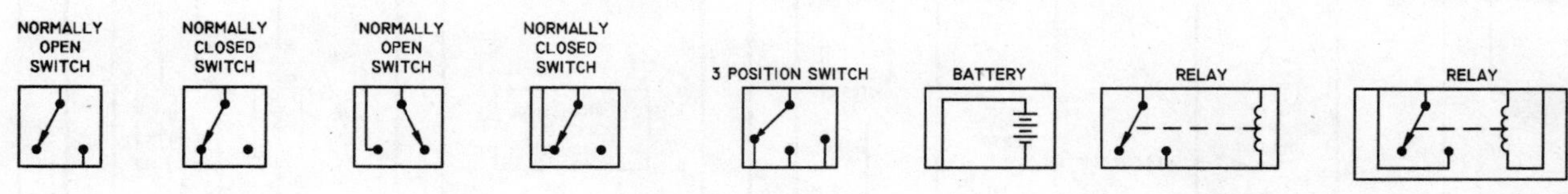

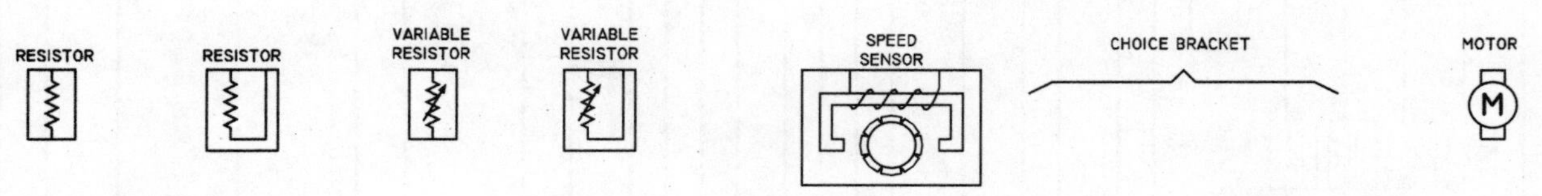

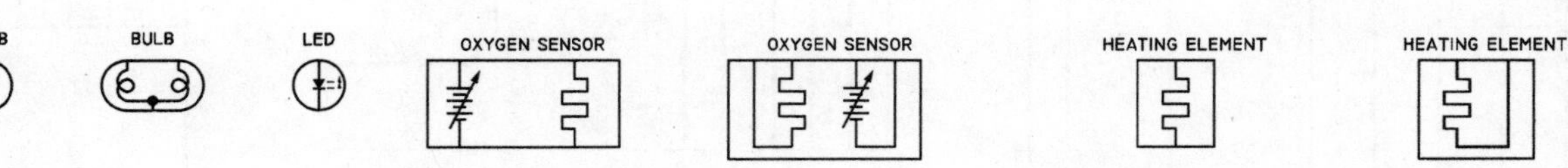

DIAGRAM 2

TCCA6W02

1996-99 2.4L ENGINE SCHEMATIC

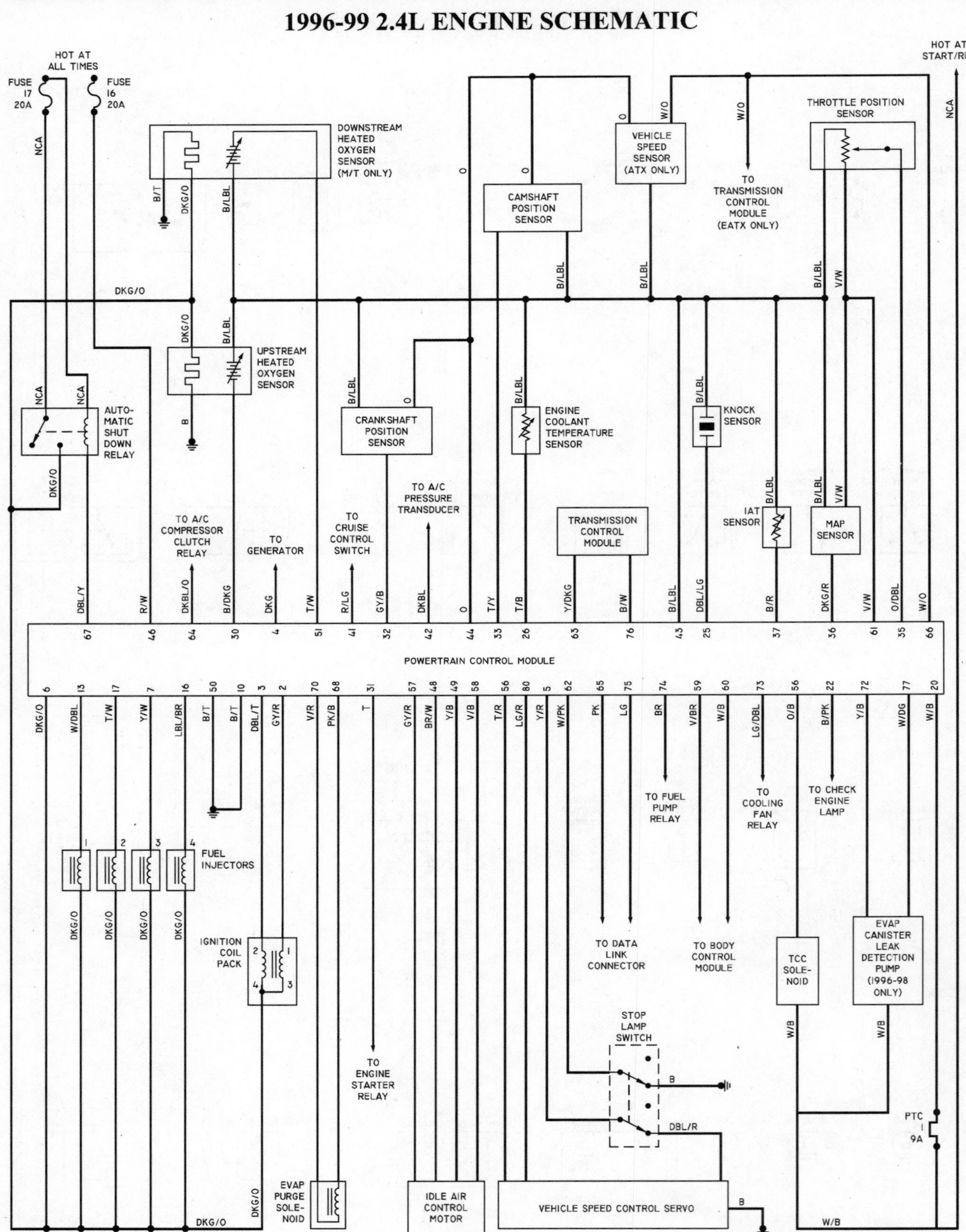

DIAGRAM 3

91156E01

1996-99 3.0L ENGINE SCHEMATIC

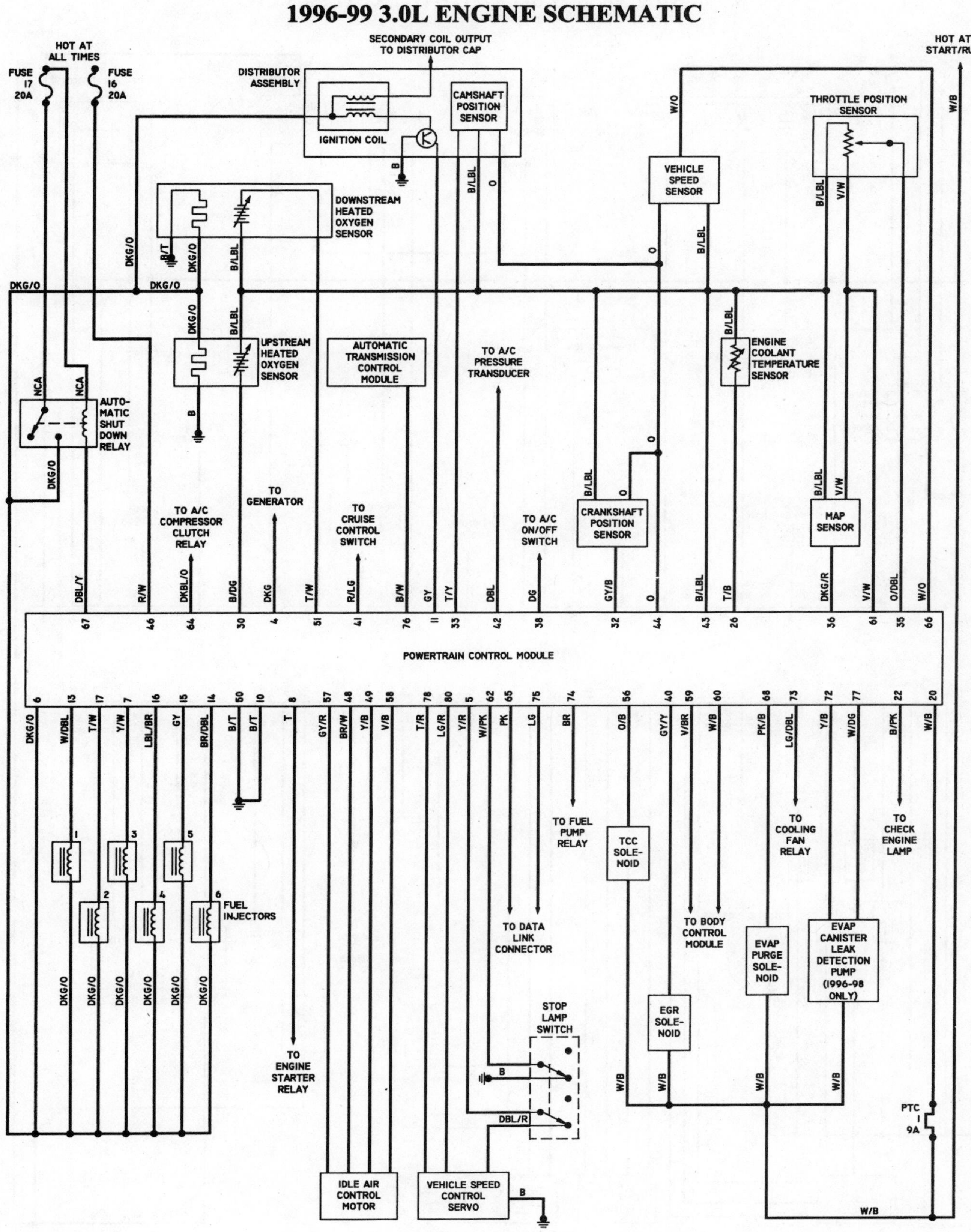

DIAGRAM 4

91156E02

1996-99 3.3L & 3.8L ENGINE SCHEMATIC

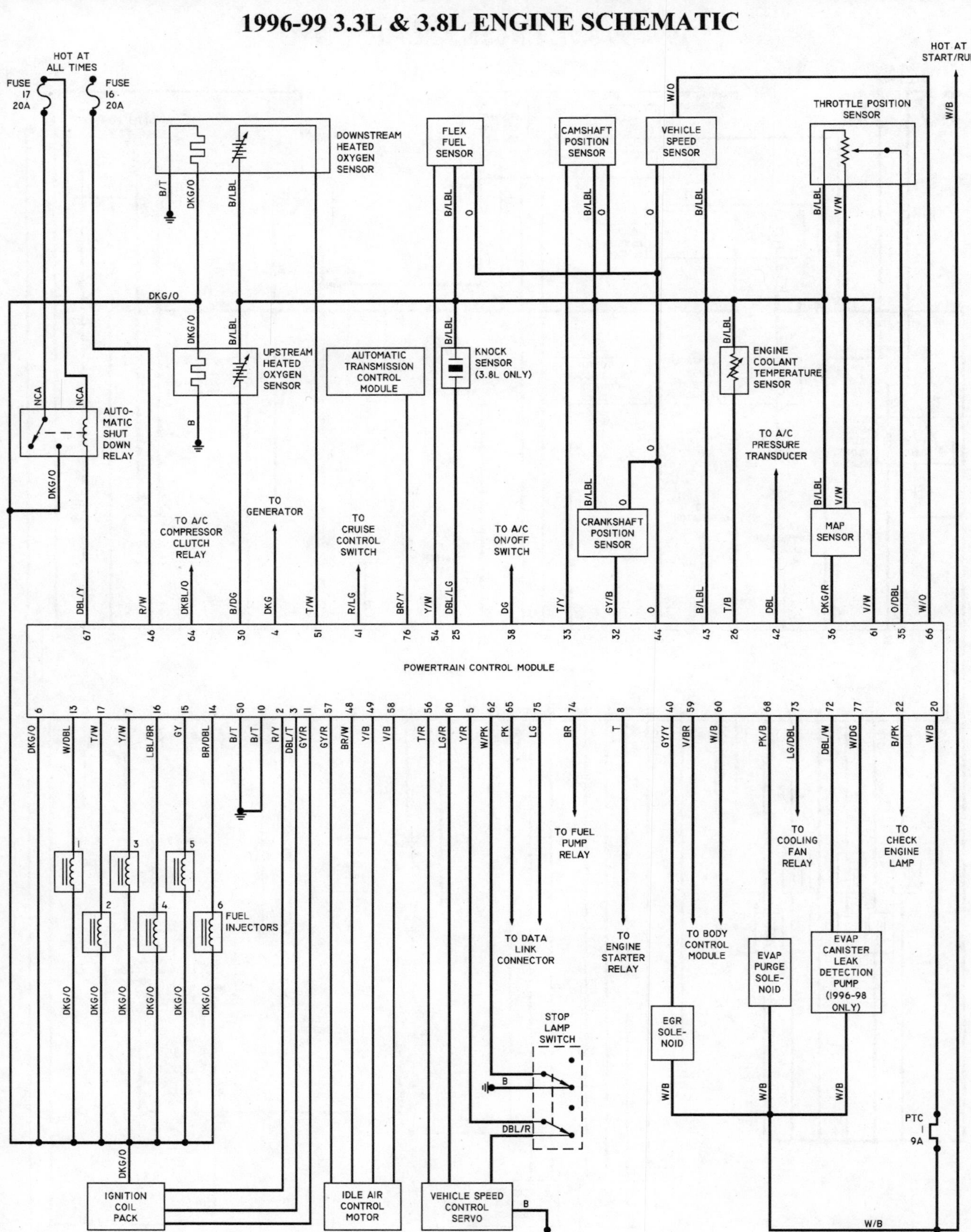

DIAGRAM 5

91156E03

1996-99 CHASSIS SCHEMATIC

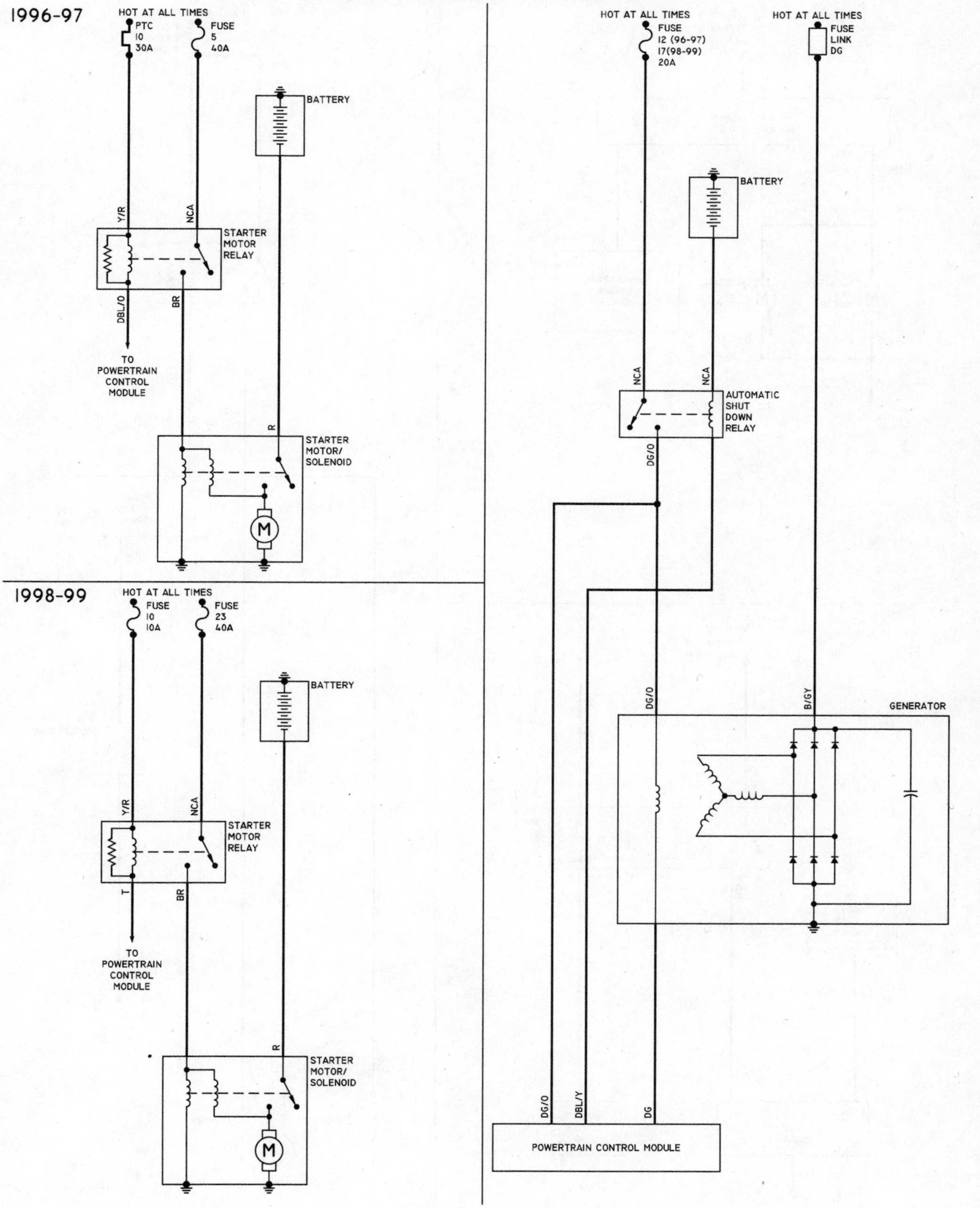

1996-97

HOT AT ALL TIMES
PTC
10
30A
FUSE
5
40A
BATTERY
Y/R
NCA
STARTER
MOTOR
RELAY
DBL/O
BR
TO
POWERTRAIN
CONTROL
MODULE
R
STARTER
MOTOR/
SOLENOID
M

1998-99

HOT AT ALL TIMES
FUSE
10
10A
FUSE
23
40A
BATTERY
Y/R
NCA
STARTER
MOTOR
RELAY
T
BR
TO
POWERTRAIN
CONTROL
MODULE
R
STARTER
MOTOR/
SOLENOID
M

HOT AT ALL TIMES
FUSE
12 (96-97)
17(98-99)
20A
HOT AT ALL TIMES
FUSE
LINK
DG
BATTERY
NCA
NCA
AUTOMATIC
SHUT
DOWN
RELAY
DG/O
DG/O
B/GY
GENERATOR
DG/O
DBL/Y
DG
POWERTRAIN CONTROL MODULE

DIAGRAM 6

91156B01

1996-99 CHASSIS SCHEMATIC

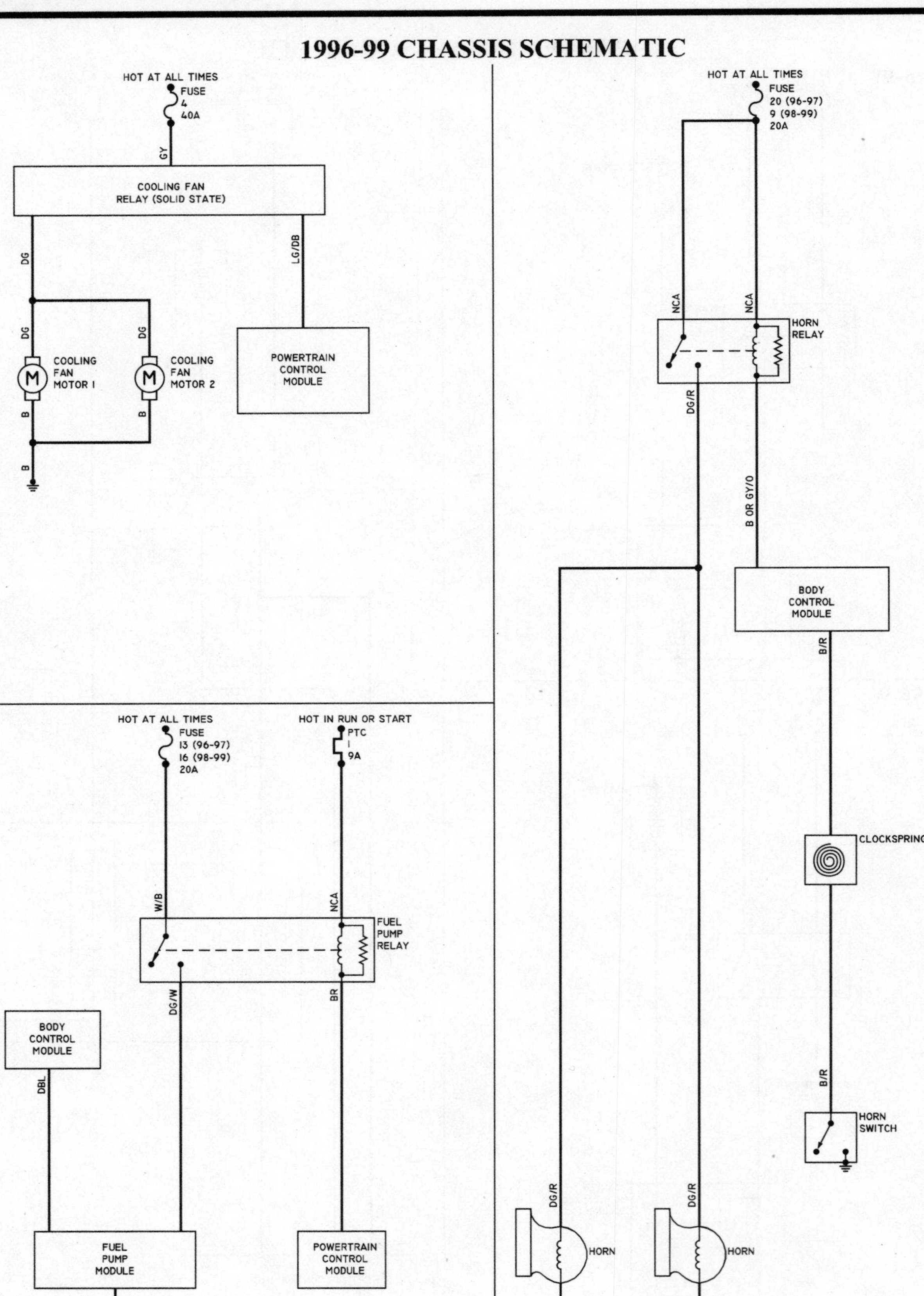

DIAGRAM 7

91156B02

1996-97 CHASSIS SCHEMATIC

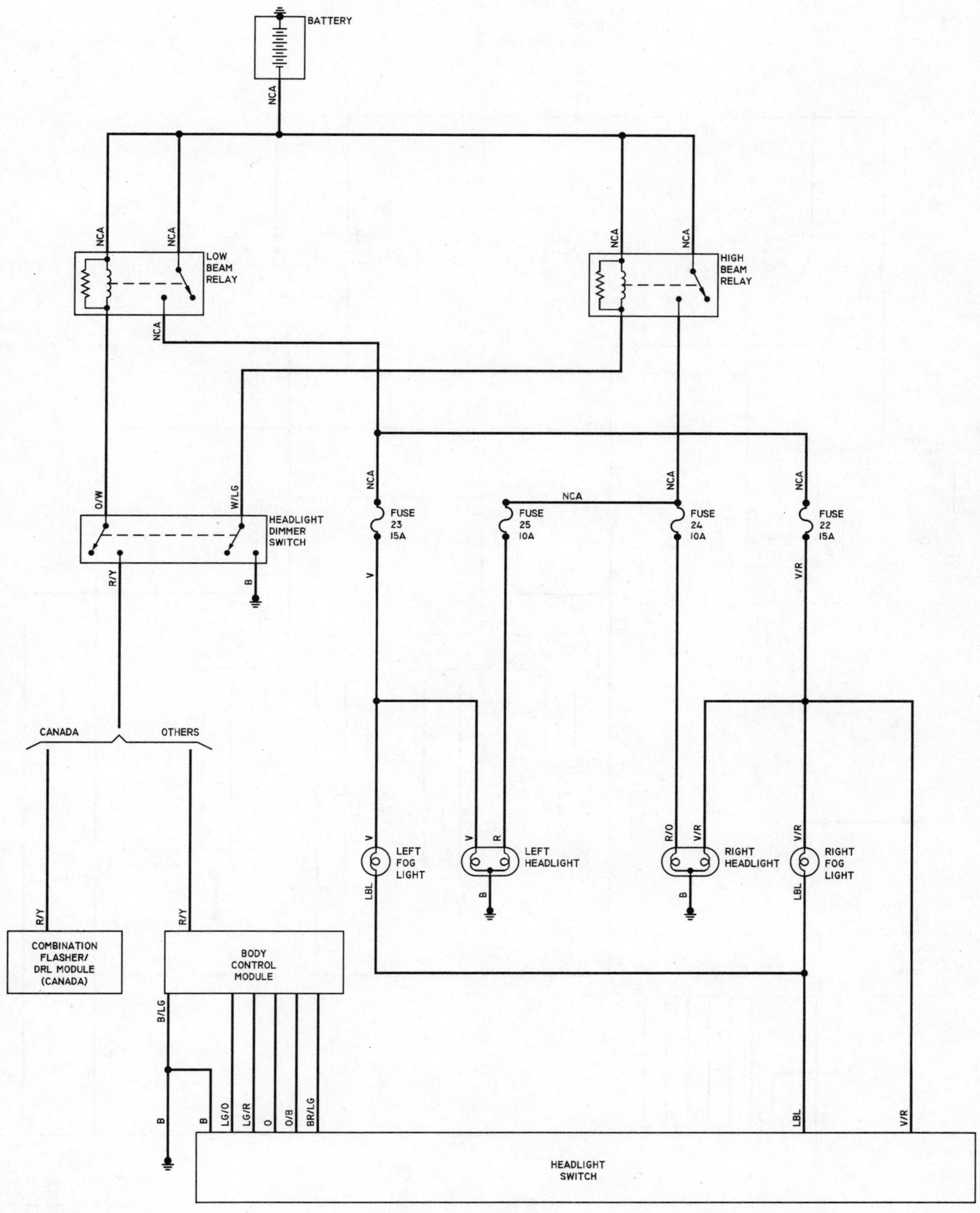

DIAGRAM 8

91156B03

1998-99 CHASSIS SCHEMATIC

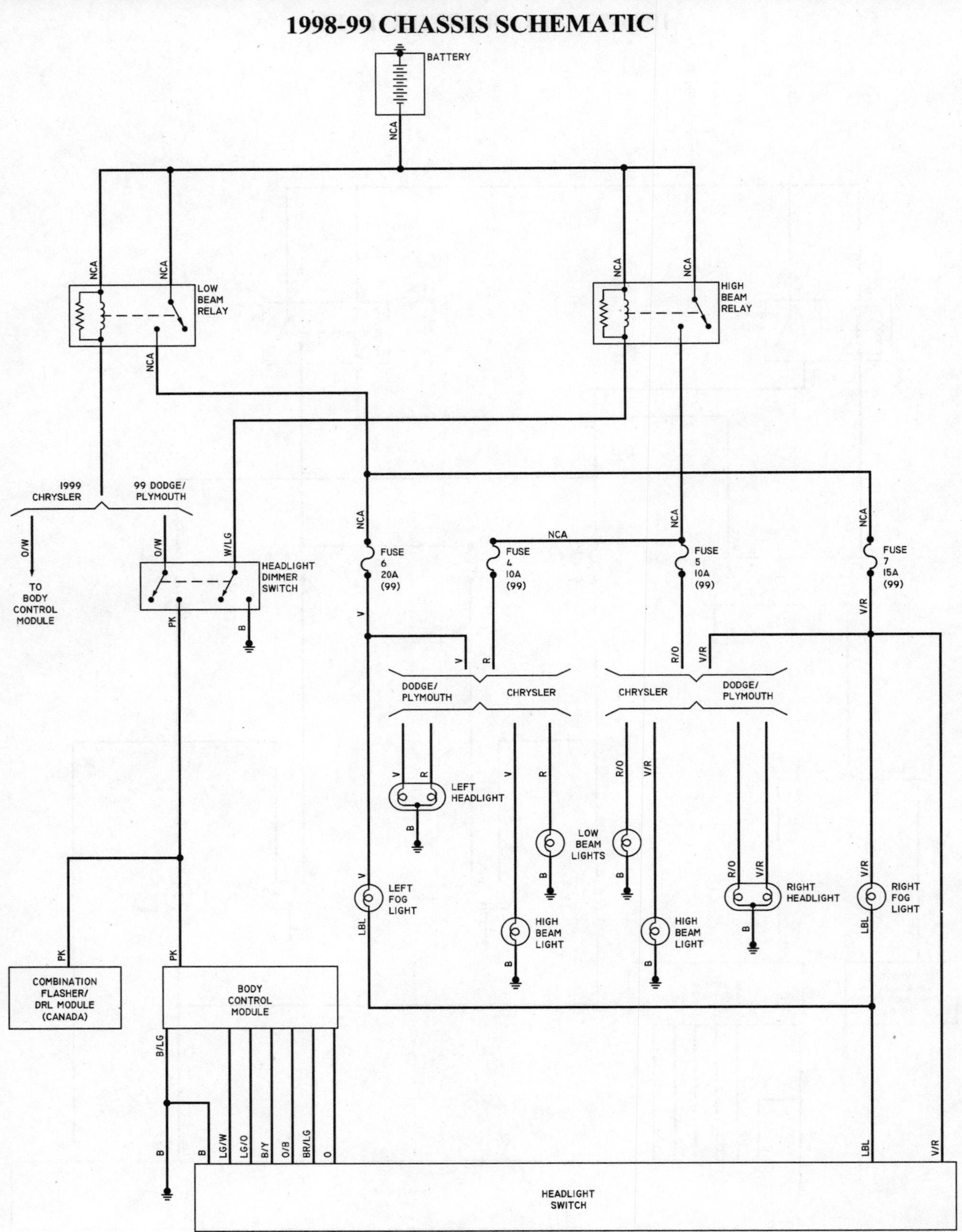

DIAGRAM 9

91156B07

1996 CHASSIS SCHEMATIC

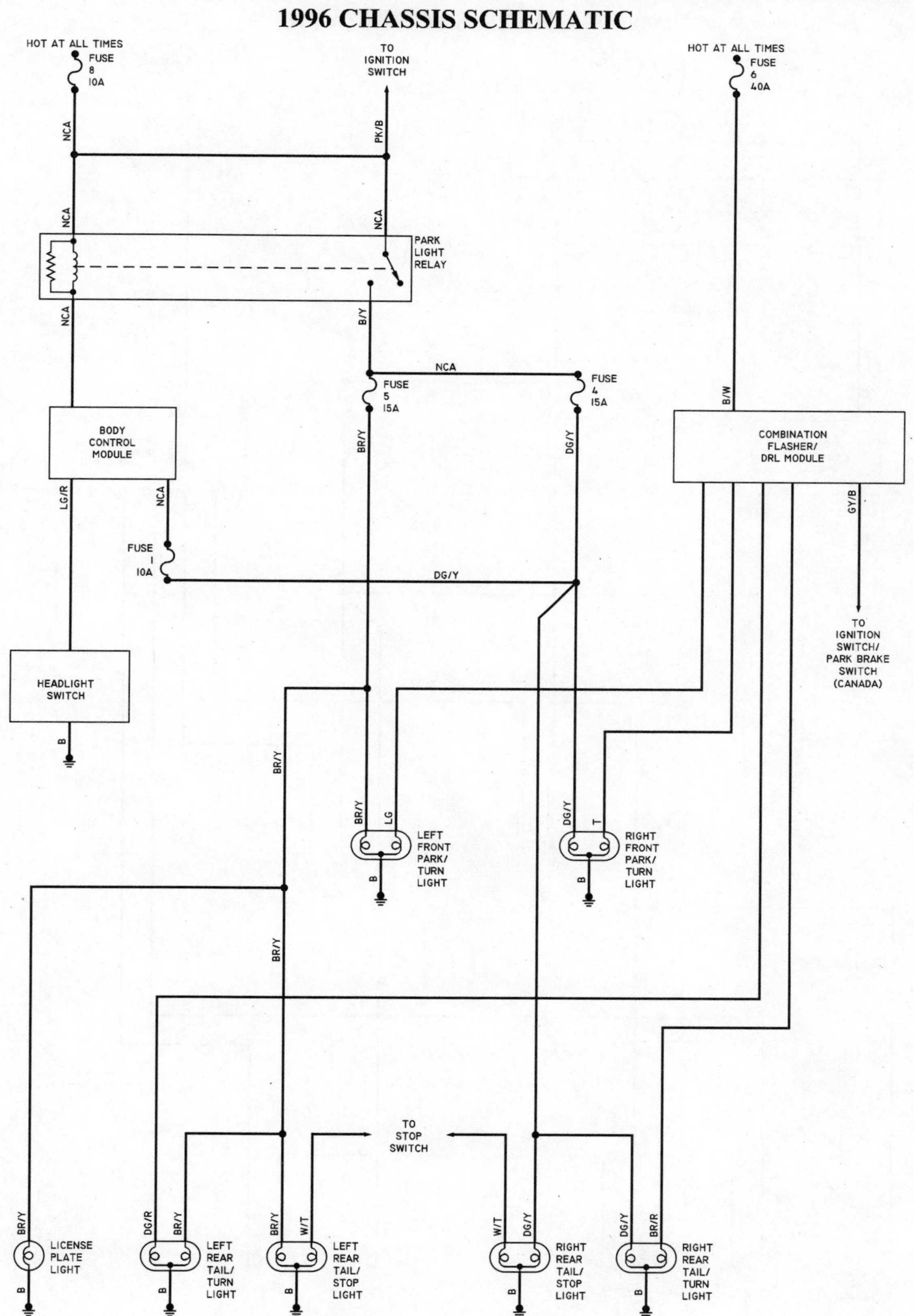

DIAGRAM 10

91156B08

1997-99 CHASSIS SCHEMATIC

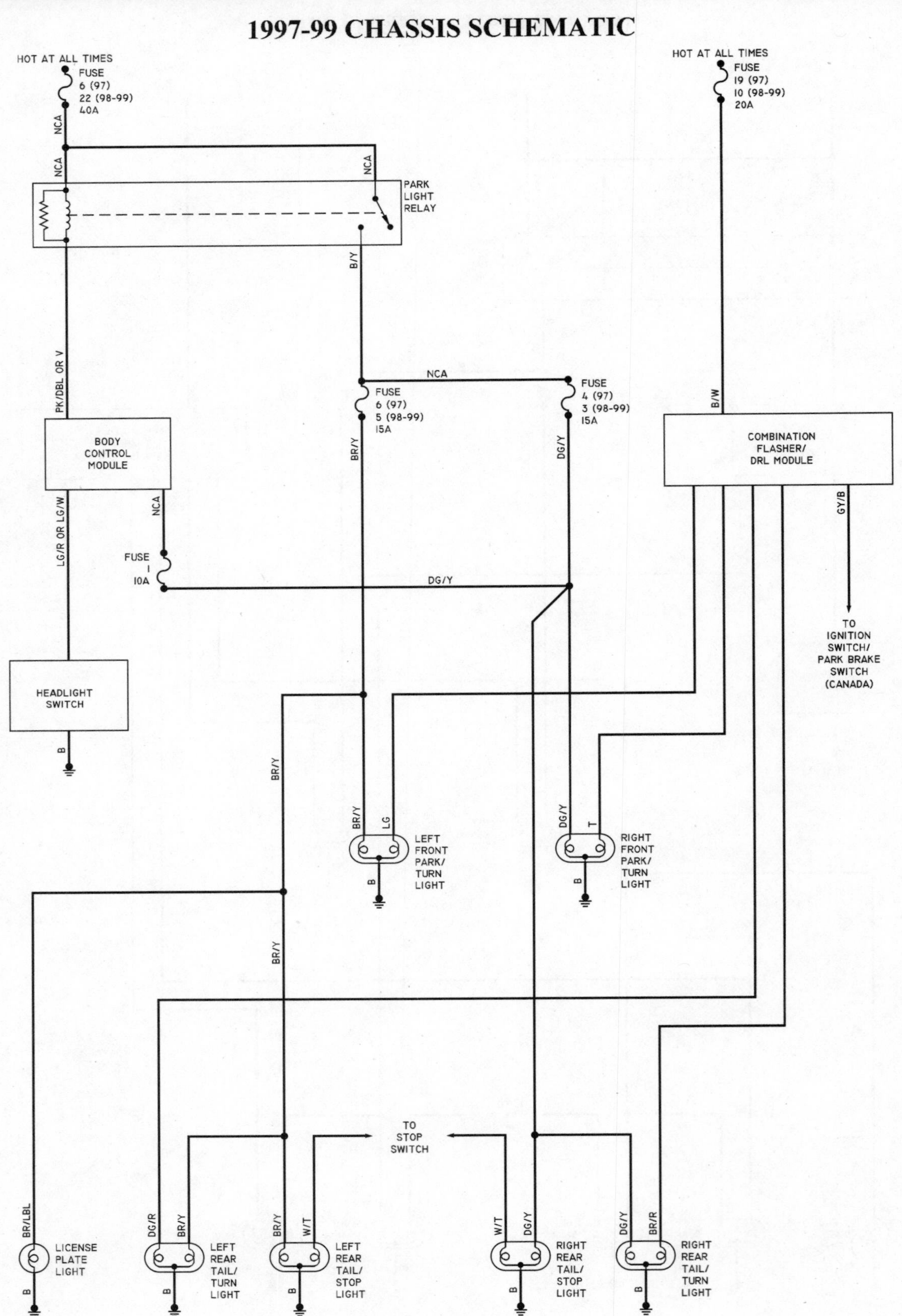

DIAGRAM 11

91156B04

1996-99 CHASSIS SCHEMATIC

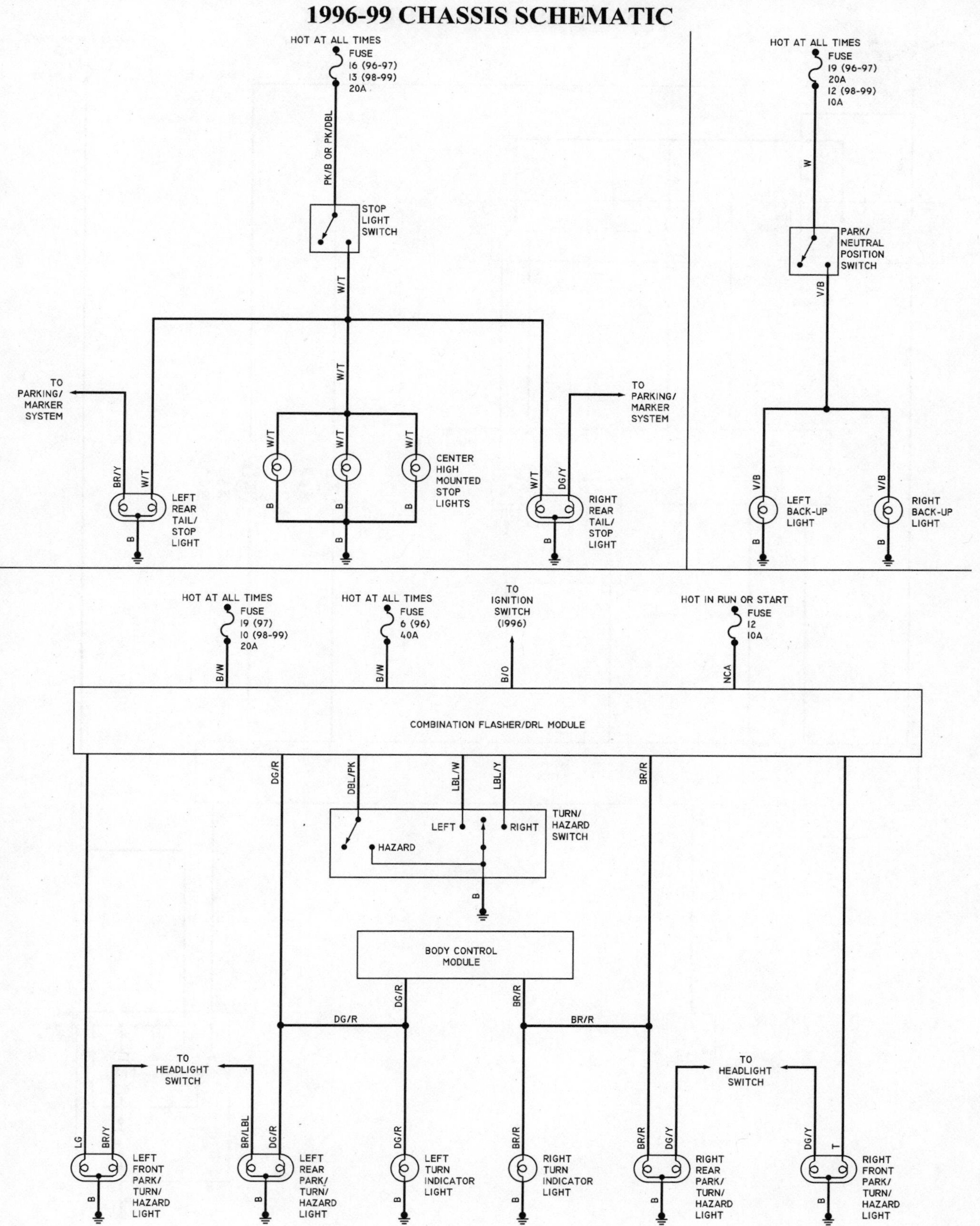

DIAGRAM 12

1996-99 CHASSIS SCHEMATIC

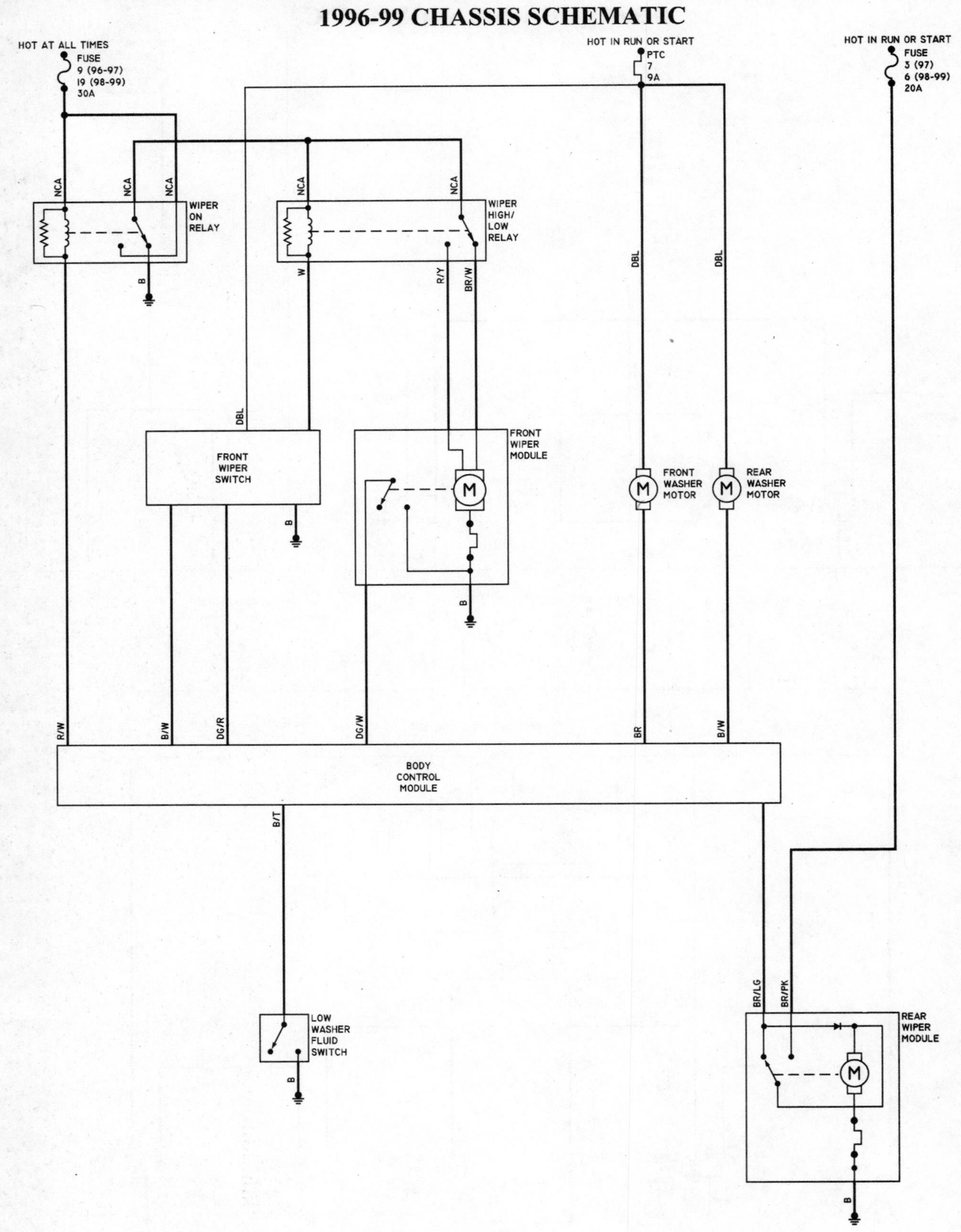

DIAGRAM 13

91156B06

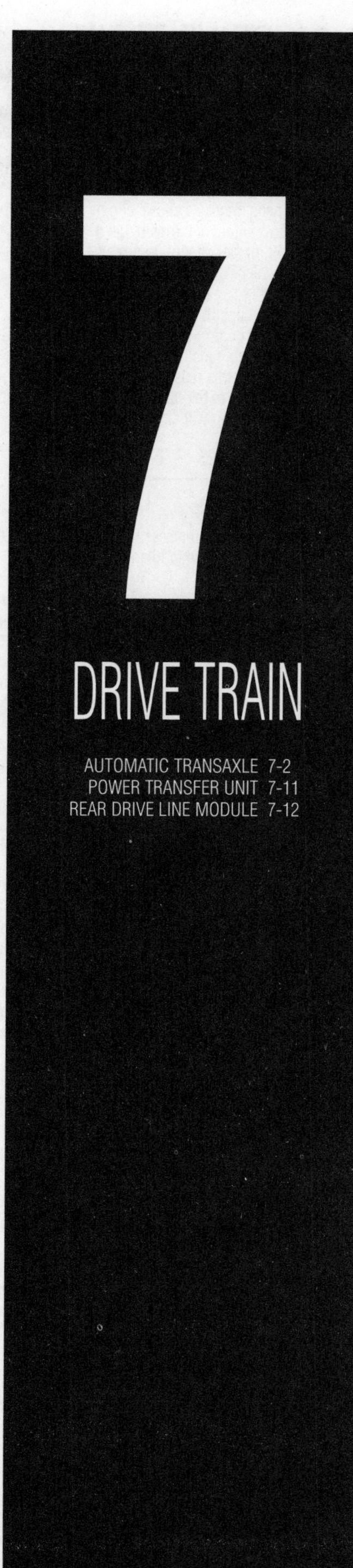

7 DRIVE TRAIN

AUTOMATIC TRANSAXLE

Understanding the Automatic Transaxle

The automatic transaxle allows engine torque and power to be transmitted to the front wheels within a narrow range of engine operating speeds. It will allow the engine to turn fast enough to produce plenty of power and torque at very low speeds, while keeping it at a sensible rpm at high vehicle speeds (and it does this job without driver assistance). The transaxle uses a light fluid as the medium for the transmission of power. This fluid also works in the operation of various hydraulic control circuits and as a lubricant. Because the transaxle fluid performs all of these functions, trouble within the unit can easily travel from one part to another. For this reason, and because of the complexity and unusual operating principles of the transaxle, a very sound understanding of the basic principles of operation will simplify troubleshooting.

TORQUE CONVERTER

See Figure 1

The torque converter replaces the conventional clutch. It has three functions:

1. It allows the engine to idle with the vehicle at a standstill, even with the transaxle in gear.
2. It allows the transaxle to shift from range-to-range smoothly, without requiring that the driver close the throttle during the shift.
3. It multiplies engine torque to an increasing extent as vehicle speed drops and throttle opening is increased. This has the effect of making the transaxle more responsive and reduces the amount of shifting required.

The torque converter is a metal case which is shaped like a sphere that has been flattened on opposite sides. It is bolted to the rear end of the engine's crankshaft. Generally, the entire metal case rotates at engine speed and serves as the engine's flywheel.The case contains three sets of blades. One set is attached directly to the case. This set forms the torus or pump. Another set is directly connected to the output shaft, and forms the turbine. The third set is mounted on a hub which, in turn, is mounted on a stationary shaft through a one-way clutch. This third set is known as the stator.A pump, which is driven by the converter hub at engine speed, keeps the torque converter full of transaxle fluid at all times. Fluid flows continuously through the unit to provide cooling.Under low speed acceleration, the torque converter functions as follows:

The torus is turning faster than the turbine. It picks up fluid at the center of the converter and, through centrifugal force, slings it outward. Since the outer edge of the converter moves faster than the portions at the center, the fluid picks up speed.The fluid then enters the outer edge of the turbine blades. It then travels back toward the center of the converter case along the turbine blades. In impinging upon the turbine blades, the fluid loses the energy picked up in the torus.If the fluid was now returned directly into the torus, both halves of the converter would have to turn at approximately the same speed at all times, and torque input and output would both be the same.In flowing through the torus and turbine, the fluid picks up two types of flow, or flow in two separate directions. It flows through the turbine blades, and it spins with the engine. The stator, whose blades are stationary when the vehicle is being accelerated at low speeds, converts one type of flow into another. Instead of allowing the fluid to flow straight back into the torus, the stator's curved blades turn the fluid almost 90° toward the direction of rotation of the engine. Thus the fluid does not flow as fast toward the torus, but is already spinning when the torus picks it up. This has the effect of allowing the torus to turn much faster than the turbine. This difference in speed may be compared to the difference in speed between the smaller and larger gears in any gear train. The result is that engine power output is higher, and engine torque is multiplied.As the speed of the turbine increases, the fluid spins faster and faster in the direction of engine rotation. As a result, the ability of the stator to redirect the fluid flow is reduced. Under cruising conditions, the stator is eventually forced to rotate on its one-way clutch in the direction of engine rotation. Under these conditions, the torque converter begins to behave almost like a solid shaft, with the torus and turbine speeds being almost equal.

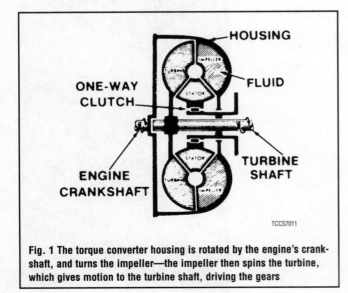

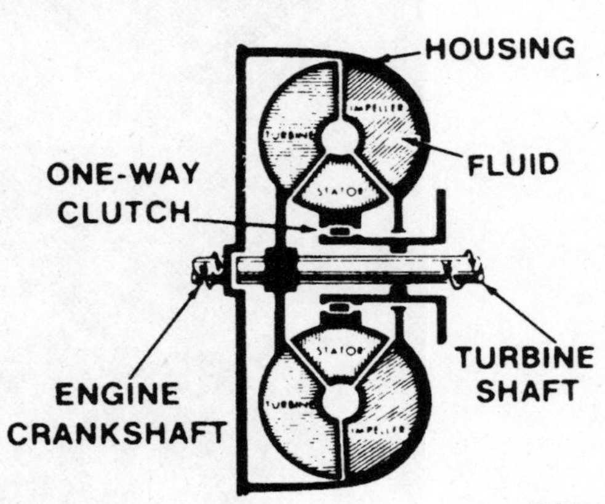

HOUSING
FLUID
ONE-WAY CLUTCH
TURBINE SHAFT
ENGINE CRANKSHAFT
TCCS7011

Fig. 1 The torque converter housing is rotated by the engine's crankshaft, and turns the impeller—the impeller then spins the turbine, which gives motion to the turbine shaft, driving the gears

PLANETARY GEARBOX

See Figures 2, 3 and 4

The ability of the torque converter to multiply engine torque is limited. Also, the unit tends to be more efficient when the turbine is rotating at relatively high speeds. Therefore, a planetary gearbox is used to carry the power output of the turbine to the driveshaft.

Planetary gears function very similarly to conventional transmission gears. However, their construction is different in that three elements make up one gear system, and, in that all three elements are different from one another. The three

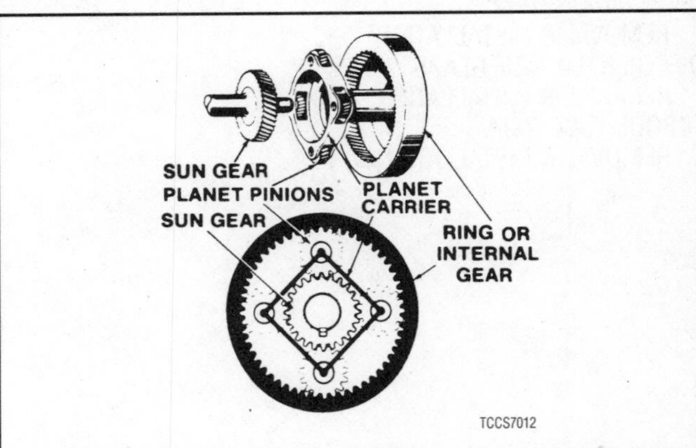

Fig. 2 Planetary gears work in a similar fashion to manual transmission gears, but are composed of three parts

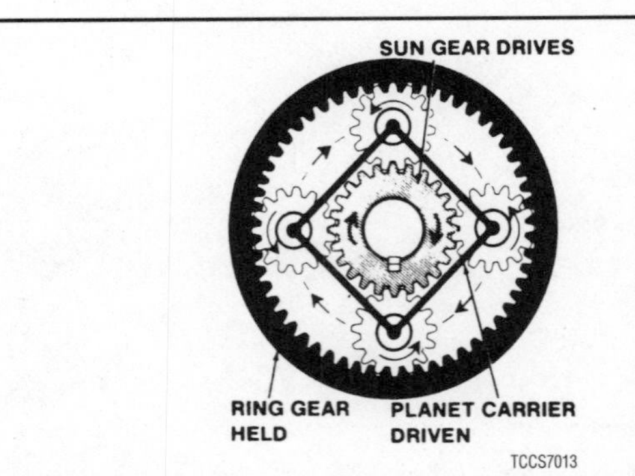

Fig. 3 Planetary gears in the maximum reduction (low) range. The ring gear is held and a lower gear ratio is obtained

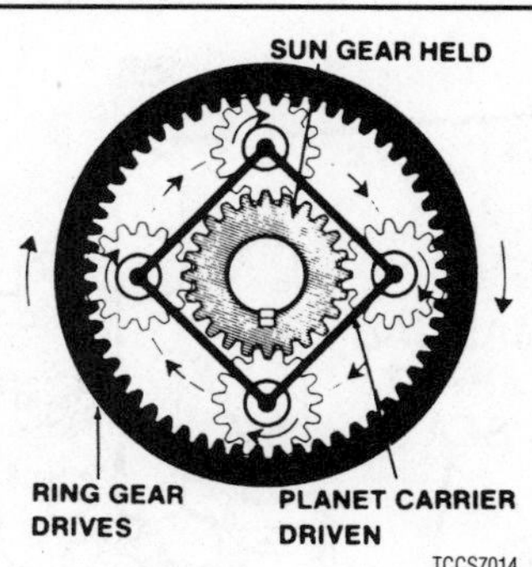

Fig. 4 Planetary gears in the minimum reduction (drive) range. The ring gear is allowed to revolve, providing a higher gear ratio

elements are: an outer gear that is shaped like a hoop, with teeth cut into the inner surface; a sun gear, mounted on a shaft and located at the very center of the outer gear; and a set of three planet gears, held by pins in a ring-like planet carrier, meshing with both the sun gear and the outer gear. Either the outer gear or the sun gear may be held stationary, providing more than one possible torque multiplication factor for each set of gears. Also, if all three gears are forced to rotate at the same speed, the gearset forms, in effect, a solid shaft.

Most automatics use the planetary gears to provide various reductions ratios. Bands and clutches are used to hold various portions of the gearsets to the transaxle case or to the shaft on which they are mounted. Shifting is accomplished, then, by changing the portion of each planetary gearset which is held to the transaxle case or to the shaft.

SERVOS AND ACCUMULATORS

See Figure 5

The servos are hydraulic pistons and cylinders. They resemble the hydraulic actuators used on many other machines, such as bulldozers. Hydraulic fluid enters the cylinder, under pressure, and forces the piston to move to engage the band or clutches.

The accumulators are used to cushion the engagement of the servos. The transaxle fluid must pass through the accumulator on the way to the servo. The accumulator housing contains a thin piston which is sprung away from the discharge passage of the accumulator. When fluid passes through the accumulator on the way to the servo, it must move the piston against spring pressure, and this action smooths out the action of the servo.

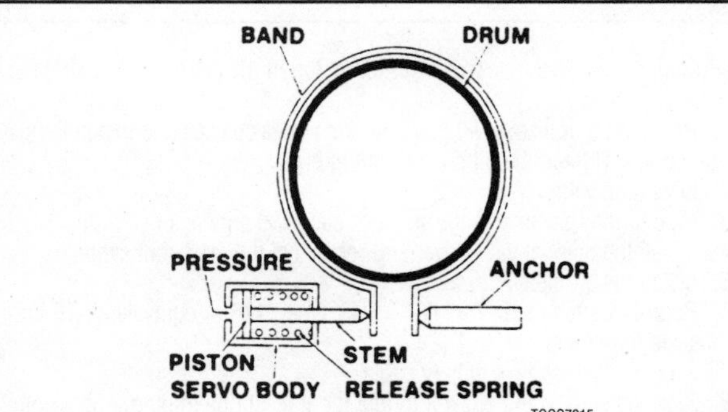

Fig. 5 Servos, operated by pressure, are used to apply or release the bands, to either hold the ring gear or allow it to rotate

HYDRAULIC CONTROL SYSTEM

The hydraulic pressure used to operate the servos comes from the main transaxle oil pump. This fluid is channeled to the various servos through the shift valves. There is generally a manual shift valve which is operated by the transaxle selector lever and an automatic shift valve for each automatic upshift the transaxle provides.

➡Many new transaxles are electronically controlled. On these models, electrical solenoids are used to better control the hydraulic fluid. Usually, the solenoids are regulated by an electronic control module.

There are two pressures which affect the operation of these valves. One is the governor pressure which is effected by vehicle speed. The other is the modulator pressure which is effected by intake manifold vacuum or throttle position. Governor pressure rises with an increase in vehicle speed, and modulator pressure rises as the throttle is opened wider. By responding to these two pressures, the shift valves cause the upshift points to be delayed with increased throttle opening to make the best use of the engine's power output.Most transaxles also make use of an auxiliary circuit for downshifting. This circuit may be actuated by the throttle linkage the vacuum line which actuates the modulator, by a cable or by a solenoid. It applies pressure to a special downshift surface on the shift valve or valves.The modulator also governs the line pressure, used to actuate the servos. In this way, the clutches and bands will be actuated with a force matching the torque output of the engine.

Fluid Pan

For fluid pan (and filter) service, refer to Section 1.

Neutral Starting/Back-up Light Switch

REMOVAL & INSTALLATION

31TH Automatic Transaxle

See Figure 6

1. Disconnect the negative battery cable.
2. Raise and safely support the vehicle. Position a drain pan under the switch.
3. Disconnect the switch electrical connector.
4. Remove the switch from the case.

To install:

5. Verify that the switch operating lever fingers are centered in the switch opening in the case when in **P** and **N**.
6. Install a new seal and screw the switch on the case. Tighten to 24 ft. lbs. (33 Nm). Be sure the new seal has seated properly between the switch and the transaxle housing or a fluid leak could result.
7. Check the continuity of the switch, at the 2 outer terminal pins, for proper operation. Reconnect the electrical connector.
8. Lower the vehicle and check the transmission fluid level. Add if necessary.
9. Reconnect the negative battery cable and check the switch for proper operation.

Fig. 6 Neutral/back-up light switch—31TH models

41TE Automatic Transaxle

See Figures 7, 8 and 9

Vehicles equipped with this transaxle do not utilize a conventional neutral safety switch or back-up light switch. Instead, this automatic transaxle is equipped with a Transaxle Range Sensor (TRS), which is located on top of the valve body, within the transaxle assembly. This sensor performs the functions of the neutral safety and back-up light switches. To remove the sensor, the transaxle fluid pan and valve body must be removed.

The TRS, if defective, must be removed with the transaxle's valve body as an assembly. The TRS is mounted on the top side of the valve body.

1. Disconnect the negative battery cable.
2. Remove the air cleaner assembly.
3. Disconnect the gear shift cable.
4. Remove the manual valve lever.
5. Unplug the transaxle range sensor's electrical connector.
6. Raise and safely support the vehicle.
7. Place a drain pan, with a large opening, under the transaxle oil pan. Loosen the transaxle oil pan mounting bolts and tap the oil pan at one corner to break it loose, allowing the fluid to drain. After the fluid has drained, remove the transaxle oil pan.
8. Remove the transaxle oil filter while allowing the residual transaxle fluid to fully drain.
9. Remove the mounting bolts for the valve body.
10. Separate the Park rod from the guide bracket and remove the valve body assembly from the transaxle.
11. Place the valve body assembly on a workbench.
12. Remove the TRS attaching screw.
13. Remove the manual shaft seal and slide the TRS up the manual shaft to remove it from the valve body.

To install:

14. Install the TRS by sliding it down onto the manual shaft.
15. Install the manual shaft seal halfway down onto the manual shaft, and seat it in the shaft seal groove.
16. Install and tighten the TRS retaining screw to 45 inch lbs. (5 Nm).
17. Install the valve body assembly up into the transaxle. Engage the Park rod into the guide bracket.
18. Install and tighten the valve body mounting bolts to 105 inch lbs. (12 Nm).
19. Install a new transaxle oil filter and O-ring.
20. Before installing the transaxle oil pan, be sure to thoroughly clean the gasket mating surfaces of the transaxle case and transaxle oil pan, as well as the pan magnet. Then, place a light bead of RTV sealer on the oil pan gasket surface. Properly position the new pan gasket on top of the pan gasket mating surface.
21. Position the transaxle oil pan onto the transaxle case and install the pan mounting bolts. Tighten the oil pan mounting bolts.
22. Lower the vehicle.
23. Plug in the transaxle range sensor's electrical connector.
24. Install the manual valve lever and reconnect the gear shift cable.
25. Install the air cleaner assembly.
26. Pour 4 quarts of MOPAR® ATF PLUS Type 7176 or equivalent ATF into the transaxle filler tube.
27. Connect the negative battery cable.
28. Start the engine and allow it to idle for at least one minute. Apply both the parking and service brakes. Move the gear shift selector momentarily through each gear position, ending up in the **P** or **N** position.
29. Check the fluid level, while the engine is running and, if necessary, add sufficient fluid to bring to the correct level.
30. Road test the vehicle.

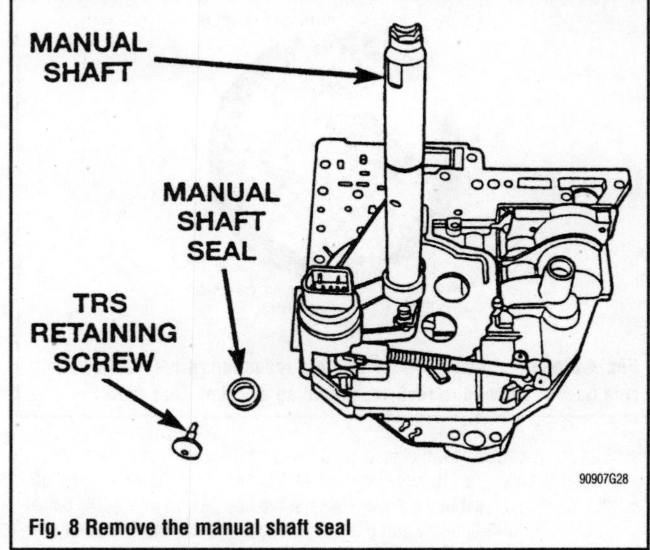

Fig. 8 Remove the manual shaft seal

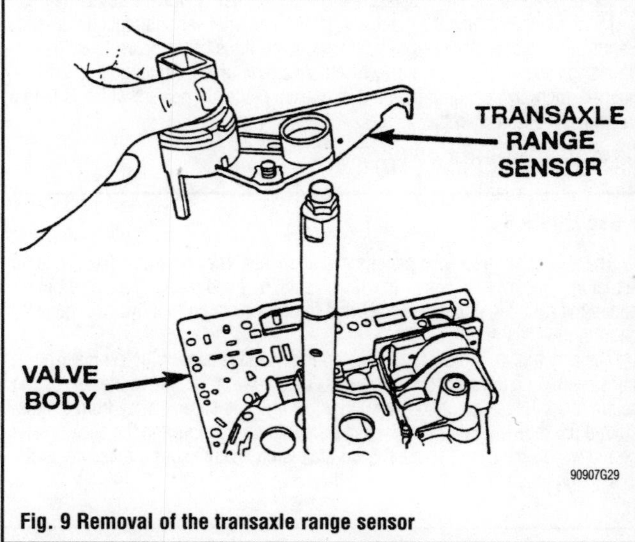

Fig. 9 Removal of the transaxle range sensor

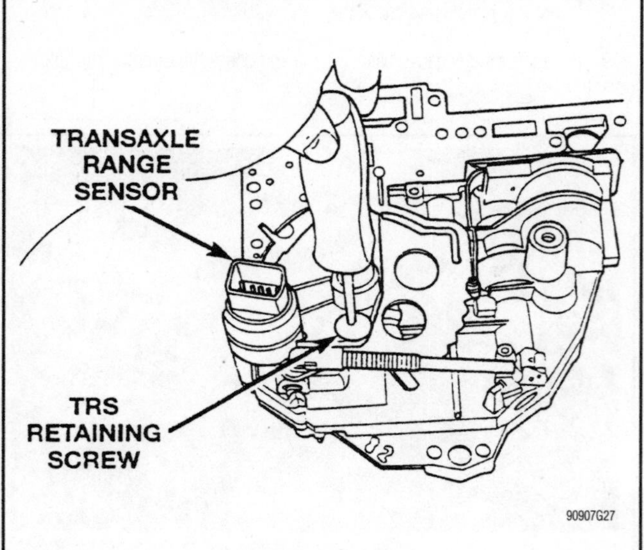

Fig. 7 Remove the TRS retaining screw

ADJUSTMENT

The neutral starting/back-up light switch and the transaxle range sensor are both non-adjustable components.

Automatic Transaxle Assembly

REMOVAL & INSTALLATION

▶ See Figures 10 thru 16

WARNING

If the vehicle is going to be rolled on its own wheels while the transaxle is out of the vehicle, obtain two outer CV-joints to install to the hubs. If the vehicle is rolled without the proper torque applied to the front wheel bearings, the bearings will be destroyed.

1. Disconnect the negative battery cable. If equipped with the 3.0L engine, drain the coolant.
2. Use an engine support fixture to support the engine.
3. Remove the air cleaner assembly if preventing access to the upper bell housing bolts.
4. Disconnect the transaxle shift linkage at the manual valve lever.
5. Squeeze the grommet clips to disconnect the cable at the transaxle bracket.
6. Remove the transaxle oil dipstick tube.
7. Disconnect and plug the transaxle fluid cooler lines.
8. Remove the input and output speed sensors.
9. Remove the upper bell housing mounting bolts.
10. Raise and safely support the vehicle. Remove the front wheels.
11. Position a drain pan under the transaxle where the halfshafts enter the differential or extension housing. Remove the right and left halfshaft assemblies.
12. Drain the transaxle fluid.
13. Remove the torque converter dust shield (inspection cover), matchmark the torque converter to the flexplate and rotate the engine clockwise to remove the torque converter bolts.
14. Detach the wiring harness connections to the transaxle range switch and the Park/Neutral position switch.
15. Remove the front motor mount insulator and bracket.
16. If equipped with Distributorless (DIS) ignition system, remove the crankshaft position sensor from the bell housing.
17. Remove the starter motor mounting bolts and set the starter motor aside. Do not allow the starter motor to hang suspended from the battery cable.
18. Position a transmission jack under the transaxle.
19. With the transaxle mount firmly in position, remove the left transaxle mount.
20. Remove the lower bell housing bolts.
21. Pull the transaxle completely away from the engine and carefully lower it from the vehicle.
22. To prepare the vehicle for rolling, secure the engine with a suitable support or reinstall the front motor mount to the engine. Then, reinstall the ball joints to the steering knuckle and install the retaining bolt. Install the obtained outer CV-joints to the hubs, install the washers and tighten the axle nuts to 180 ft. lbs. (244 Nm). The vehicle may now be safely rolled.

To install:

23. Install the transaxle securely on the transmission jack. Rotate the converter so it will align with the positioning of the flexplate.

WARNING

If the torque converter has been replaced, a torque converter clutch break-in procedure must be performed. This procedure will reset the transaxle control module break-in status. Failure to perform this procedure may cause transaxle shutter. To properly do this, a DRB or equivalent scan tool, is required to read or reset the break-in status.

24. Apply a coating of high temperature grease to the torque converter pilot hub.

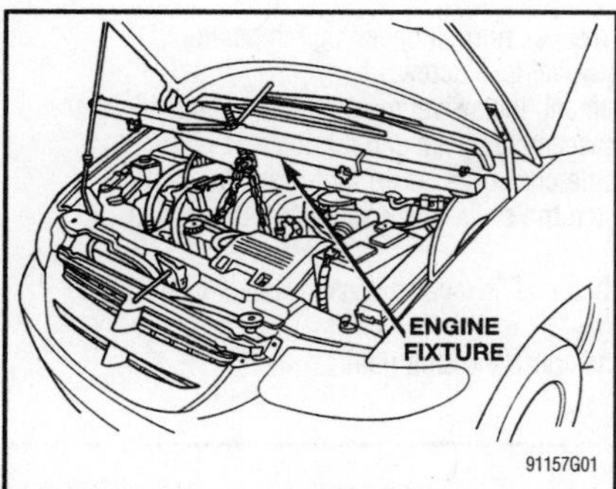

Fig. 10 In order for the transaxle to be removed from the vehicle, an engine support must be used

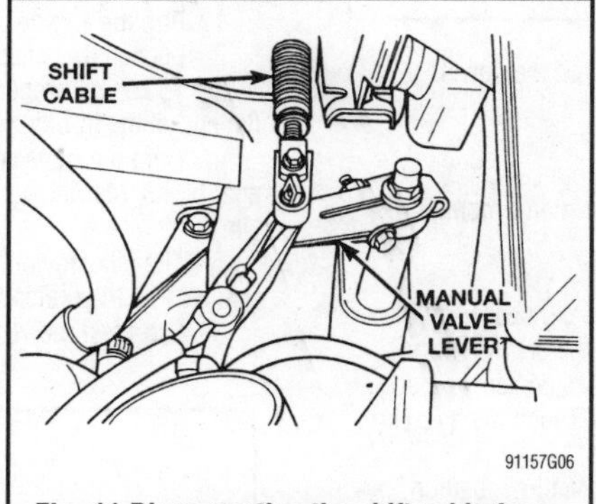

Fig. 11 Disconnecting the shift cable from the manual valve lever

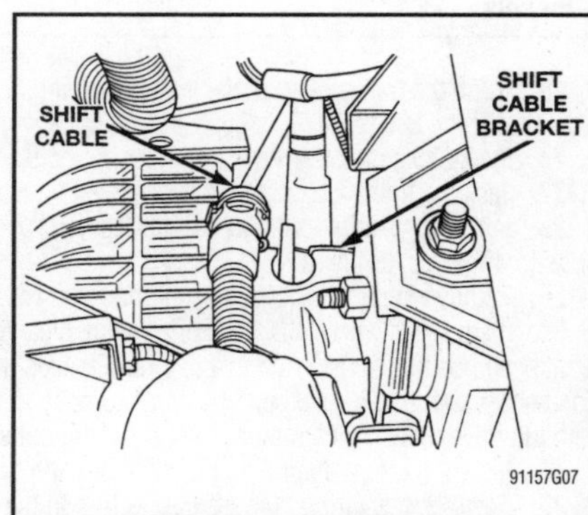

Fig. 12 After the cable is disconnected, remove it from the bracket

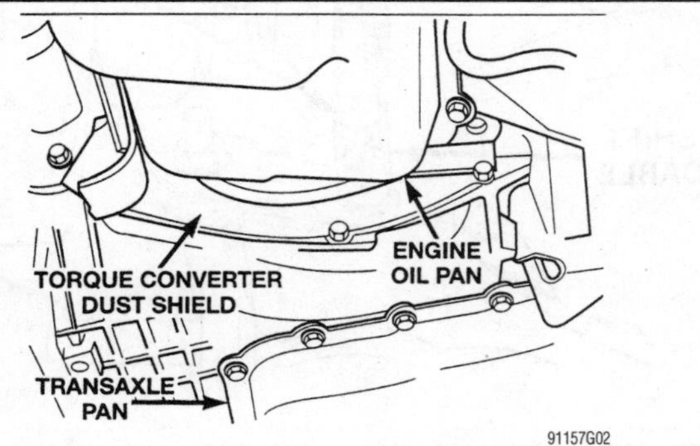

Fig. 13 To access the torque converter bolts, remove the torque converter dust shield

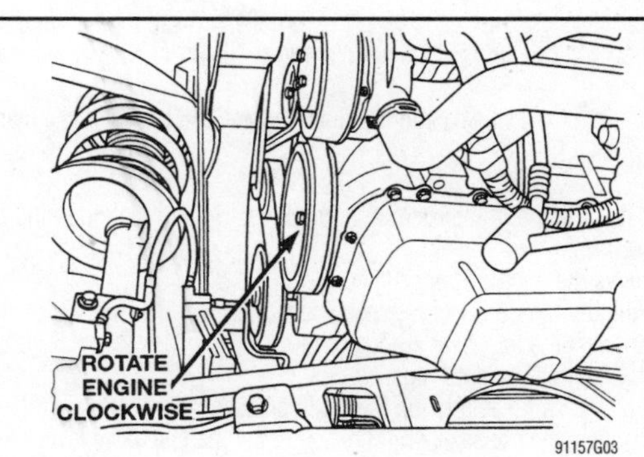

Fig. 14 Use the crankshaft damper nut to rotate the engine clockwise to access the torque converter bolts

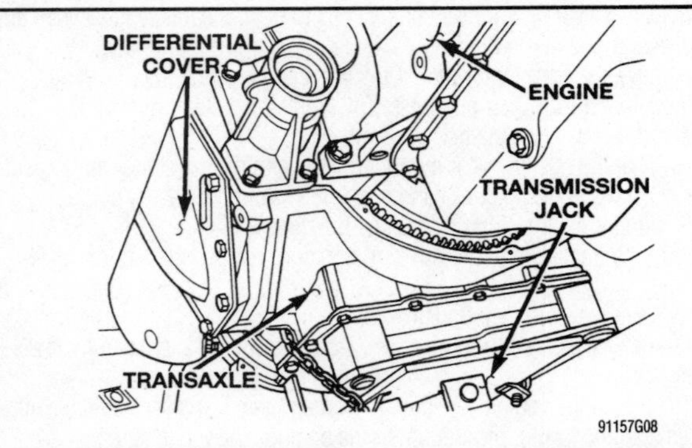

Fig. 15 A transmission/transaxle jack should be used to remove the transaxle from the vehicle

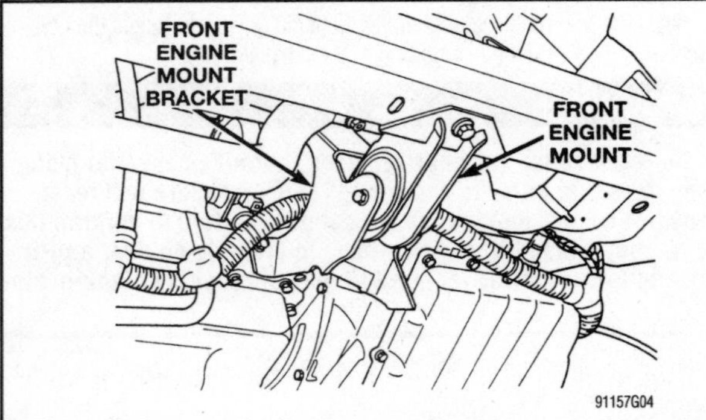

Fig. 16 With the transaxle secured to the jack, remove the engine mounts

25. Raise the transaxle into place and push it forward until the dowels engage and the bell housing is flush with the block.
26. Install the lower transaxle bell housing bolts.
27. Jack the transaxle up and install the left transaxle mount.
28. Install the starter to the transaxle. Tighten the starter motor mounting bolts to 40 ft. lbs. (54 Nm).
29. Remove the transaxle jack from under the vehicle.
30. If equipped with D.I.S. ignition system, clean off the old spacer on the crankshaft position sensor and install a new spacer. Install the crankshaft position sensor to the transaxle bell housing and push down until contact is made with the drive plate. Tighten the sensor retaining bolts to 105 inch lbs. (12 Nm).
31. Install the front engine mount insulator and bracket.
32. Reattach the wiring harness connectors to the Park/Neutral position switch and the transaxle range switch.
33. Align the torque converter to the flexplate mounting bolt holes. Install the torque converter bolts and tighten to 55 ft. lbs. (75 Nm). Install the torque converter inspection cover.
34. Install the right and left halfshaft assemblies. Install the ball joints to the steering knuckles. Tighten the axle nuts to 180 ft. lbs. (244 Nm) and install new cotter pins.
35. Install the front wheels and lug nuts. Tighten the lug nuts in a star pattern to 95 ft. lbs. (129 Nm).
36. Lower the vehicle.
37. Install the upper transaxle mounting bolts. Tighten the mounting bolts to 70 ft. lbs. (95 Nm).
38. Remove the engine support fixture.
39. Install the input and output speed sensors.
40. Reconnect the transaxle oil cooler lines.
41. Install the transaxle oil dipstick tube.
42. Attach the shift cable to the transaxle bracket.
43. Reconnect the transaxle shift linkage to the manual valve lever.
44. Install the air cleaner assembly. Fill the transaxle with the proper amount of clean, fresh MOPAR® ATF Plus 7176 automatic transmission fluid.
45. If equipped with the 3.0L engine, refill the cooling system to the correct level with a 50/50 mix of clean, ethylene glycol antifreeze and water. Bleed the cooling system.
46. Ensure all linkages, electrical connectors and fluid lines have been reattached.
47. Reconnect the negative battery cable and check the transaxle for proper operation. Perform the transaxle quick learn and torque converter clutch break-in procedures.

ADJUSTMENTS

Gearshift Cable Adjustment

See Figure 17

Normal operation of the Park/Neutral position switch provides a quick check to confirm proper linkage adjustment.

Move the gear selector lever slowly forward until it clicks into the Park position. The starter should operate when the ignition switch is turned to the **START** position.

After checking the Park position, move the selector slowly toward the Neutral position, until the lever drops into the **N** position. If the starter will also operate at this point, the gear shift linkage is properly adjusted. If the starter fails to operate in either position, linkage adjustment is necessary, as follows:

1. Park the vehicle on level ground and set the parking brake.
2. Place the gear shift lever in the **PARK** position and remove the key.
3. Loosen the cable adjuster screw at the transaxle operating lever.
4. Move the transaxle operating lever fully forward to the Park position.
5. Release the parking brake, then rock the vehicle to assure that it is in park lock. Reset the parking brake.
6. Tighten the cable adjustment screw to 70 inch lbs. (8 Nm). The gear shift cable should now be correctly adjusted.
7. Verify **PRNDL** indicator still displays the corresponding gear

Throttle Pressure Linkage

1. Run the engine until it reaches normal operating temperature.
2. Loosen the adjustment swivel lock screw.
3. To ensure proper adjustment, the swivel must be free to slide along the flat end of the throttle rod. Disassemble, clean and lubricate as required.
4. Hold the transaxle throttle control lever firmly toward the engine, against its internal stop. Tighten the swivel lock screw to 100 inch lbs. (11 Nm).
5. The adjustment is finished and linkage backlash was automatically removed by the preload spring.
6. Road test the vehicle and check the shift points.

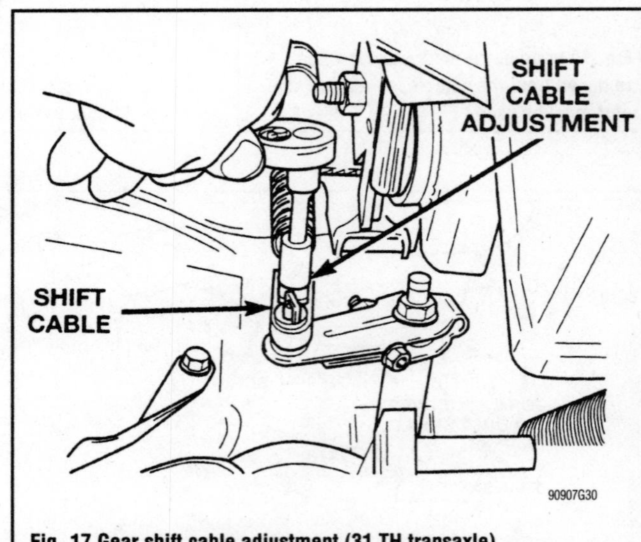

Fig. 17 Gear shift cable adjustment (31 TH transaxle)

Halfshafts

REMOVAL & INSTALLATION

Front

➧ **See Figures 18 thru 28**

On vehicles with Anti-Lock Brakes (ABS), each outer CV-joint will be equipped with an ABS speed sensor tone wheel, which is utilized to determine vehicle speed for ABS brake operation.

1. Disconnect the negative battery cable.
2. Remove the cotter pin from the end of the stub axle. Remove the nut lock and spring washer. With the brakes applied, loosen, but do NOT remove, the axle nut and washer with the vehicle still on the ground, or damage to the wheel bearing will result.
3. Raise and safely support the vehicle. Remove the wheel.
4. Remove the front brake caliper assembly from the steering knuckle assembly and support from the strut assembly using a strong piece of wire.
5. Remove the front brake rotor from the hub/bearing assembly.
6. Remove the retaining nut and washer from the halfshaft stub axle.
7. Separate the outer tie rod from the steering knuckle.
8. If equipped, remove the ABS wheel speed sensor from the steering knuckle.
9. Remove the wheel stop from the steering knuckle, if equipped.
10. Remove the nut and bolt that clamps the steering knuckle to the ball joint stud. Using a prybar, pry the control arm down to release the ball stud from the steering knuckle. Be careful not to tear the ball joint grease seal when prying down from the steering knuckle.
11. Separate the outer CV-joint splined shaft from the hub and bearing assembly by holding the CV-joint housing and pulling the steering knuckle away. Be careful not to damage the outer CV-joint wear sleeve or separate the inner CV-joint.
12. Support the halfshaft assembly at the CV-joint housing. Install a prybar between the transaxle housing and the inner tripod joint (CV-joint). Pry against the inner tripod joint until the retainer snapring on the tripod joint disengages from the transaxle side gear.
13. Remove the halfshaft assembly from the vehicle by holding the inner tripod joint and interconnecting shaft and pulling it straight out of the transaxle side gear. Do not allow the splines or the snapring of the shaft to drag across the sealing lip of the transaxle-to-tripod joint oil seal.

To install:

14. Thoroughly clean the tripod joint shaft splines and oil seal contact surface. Apply a light coating of clean transaxle lubricant to the oil seal sealing surface of the tripod joint.
15. Hold the halfshaft assembly by the tripod joint and interconnecting shaft and install the halfshaft assembly into the transaxle, being careful not to damage the oil seal. Be sure the inner joint clicks into place inside the differential. Check that the snapring is fully engaged by attempting to pull the halfshaft assembly out by hand. If it cannot be removed by hand, the snapring is engaged.
16. Thoroughly clean the steering knuckle and hub/bearing area of all debris and moisture, where the CV-joint will be installed into the steering knuckle. Also, thoroughly clean the bearing shield of the outer CV-joint.
17. Pull the front strut out and insert the splined outer CV-joint into the front hub.
18. Insert the ball joint stud into the steering knuckle clamp. Install a **new** steering knuckle-to-ball joint stud clamping nut and bolt. Be sure to use an exact replacement nut and bolt during installation. Tighten the bolt to 105 ft. lbs. (145 Nm).
19. Install the tie rod end into the steering knuckle. Tighten the tie rod end-to-steering knuckle nut to 45 ft. lbs. (61 Nm).
20. Install the disc brake rotor.
21. Install the brake caliper assembly onto the steering knuckle.
22. Install the axle washer and nut. Tighten the nut to about 45 ft. lbs. (61 Nm) temporarily.
23. If removed, install the ABS wheel speed sensor.

91157P03

Fig. 18 The axle nut should be loosened before jacking the car

91157P02

Fig. 19 To loosen the nut, remove the cotter pin, nut lock, and spring washer

91157P01

Fig. 20 With the vehicle on the ground, loosen the axle nut with an appropriately sized socket and a breaker bar

91157P04

Fig. 21 Remove the axle nut and washer, and discard the nut. (A new axle nut should be used each time the axle is removed)

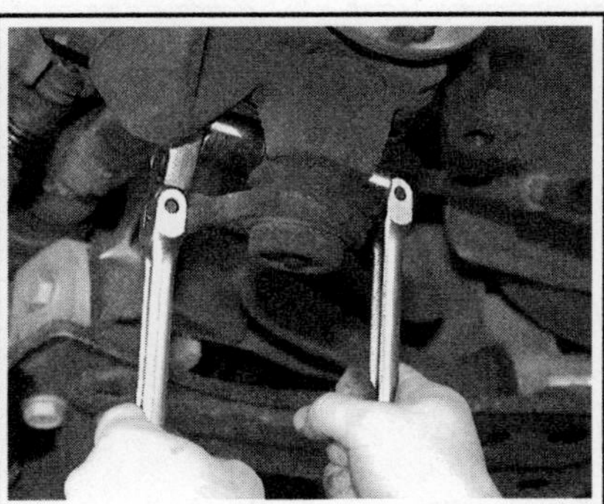

91157P06

Fig. 22 Using a breaker bar and a ratchet . . .

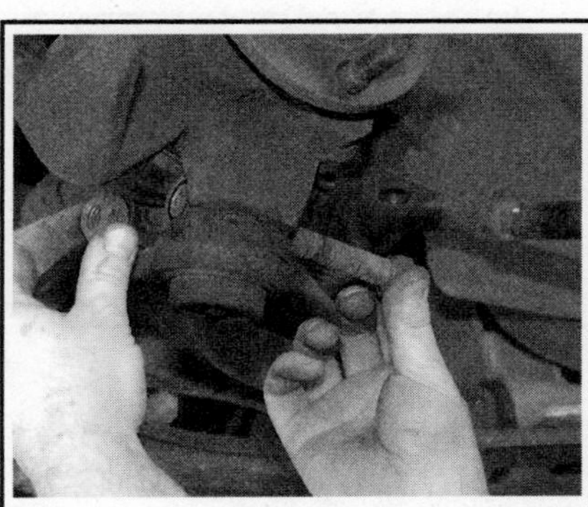

91157P05

Fig. 23 . . . remove the ball joint pinch bolt and nut

Fig. 24 Using a prybar, CAREFULLY separate the ball joint from the steering knuckle (Be careful not to damage the speed sensor wheel or ball joint boot)

Fig. 25 Once the ball joint is separated from the knuckle, pull the knuckle away from the axle and rotate it sideways

Fig. 26 It may be necessary to LIGHTLY pry outward on the inner CV joint to disengage the lock ring on the inner CV joint shaft

Fig. 27 Carefully remove the axle; do NOT let the inner splines drag on the transaxle seal during removal

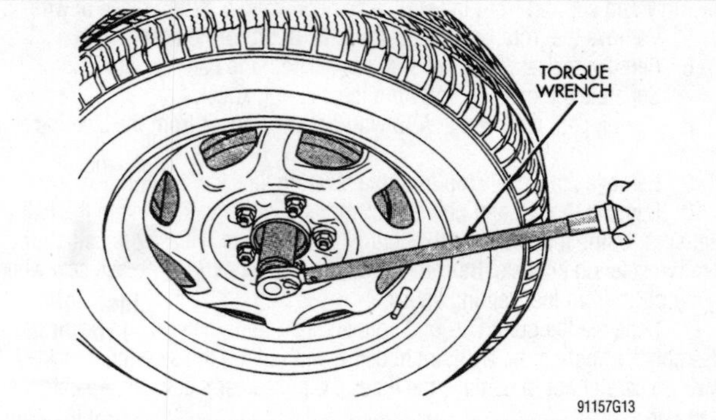

Fig. 28 Make sure to tighten the outer axle nut to the proper torque specification to prevent damage to the wheel bearing

24. Install the wheel and lug nuts. Tighten the lug nuts in a star pattern, to 95 ft. lbs. (129 Nm).
25. Lower the vehicle. Do NOT roll the vehicle until the axle nut has been properly tightened or damage to the front wheel bearings will result.
26. With the vehicle's brakes applied, tighten the axle nut to 180 ft. lbs. (244 Nm). Install the spring washer, nut lock and a new cotter pin. Wrap the cotter pin prongs tightly around the axle nut lock.
27. Reconnect the negative battery cable. Road test the vehicle.

Rear

See Figures 18, 19, 21, 29 and 30

1. Disconnect the negative battery cable.
2. Raise and safely support the vehicle.
3. Remove the rear wheel.
4. Remove the cotter pin from the end of the halfshaft. Remove the nut lock, spring washer, axle nut and washer.
5. Remove the inner shaft retaining bolts. The halfshaft is spring loaded. Compress the inner halfshaft joint slightly and pull downward to clear the differential.
6. Remove the halfshaft.

To install:

7. Install the halfshaft.
8. Install and tighten the inner shaft retaining bolts to 45 ft. lbs. (61 Nm).
9. Install the washer and nut on the axle shaft. Tighten the nut to 180 ft. lbs. (244 Nm). Install the spring washer, nut lock and a new cotter pin.
10. Install the wheel and lug nuts. Tighten the lug nuts to 95 ft. lbs. (129 Nm).
11. Lower the vehicle and reconnect the negative battery cable.

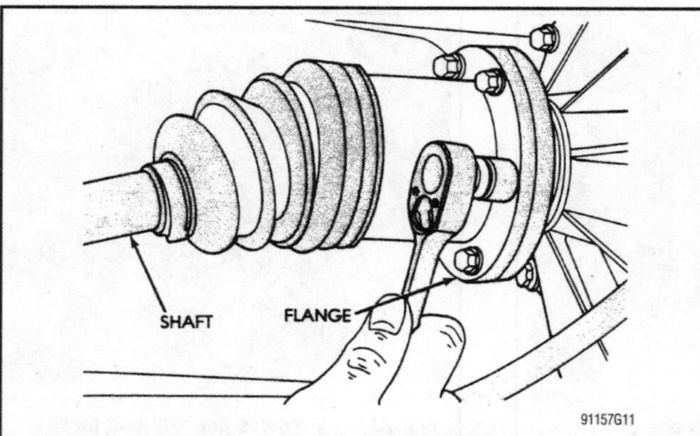

Fig. 29 Disconnecting the rear halfshaft at the differential

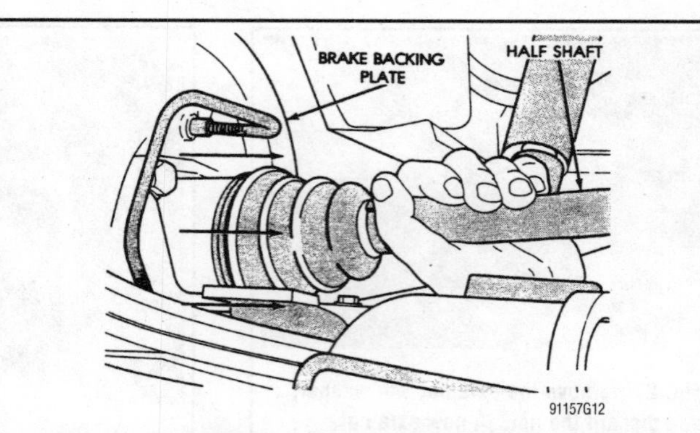

Fig. 30 Once the outer axle nut is removed, pull the axle from the vehicle

OVERHAUL

➡On some models, the only service that can be performed on the halfshaft assemblies is to replace the driveshaft seal boot on the inner tripod joint.

If any failure to the internal halfshaft components is found, the halfshaft must be replaced as an assembly.

➡The lubricant type and amount necessary for the inner joints is different than that for the outer joints. Use only the recommended lubricants in the specified amounts when servicing the halfshafts.

Inner Tripod Joint Seal Boot

See Figures 31 thru 38

The inner tripod joints do not use any internal retainers in the tripod housing to hold the spider assembly in the housing. Therefore, do not pull on the interconnecting shaft to detach the tripod housing from the transaxle stub shaft. Removing them in this way will damage the inboard joint sealing boots.

1. Remove the halfshaft requiring boot replacement from the vehicle, as outlined earlier in this section.
2. Remove the large boot clamp that holds the inner tripod joint sealing boot to the tripod joint housing. Discard the clamp. Then, remove the small clamp that holds the inner tripod joint sealing boot to the interconnecting shaft and discard. Remove the sealing boot from the tripod housing and slide it down the interconnecting shaft.

✲✲ WARNING

When removing the tripod joint housing from the spider joint, hold the rollers in place on the spider trunions to keep the roller and needle bearings from falling off.

3. Slide the interconnecting shaft and spider assembly out of the tripod joint housing.
4. Remove the snapring that holds the spider assembly to the interconnecting shaft. Remove the spider assembly from the interconnecting shaft. If the spider won't come off by hand, you can remove it by tapping the spider with a brass drift. Do NOT hit the outer tripod bearings trying to remove the spider assembly from the interconnecting shaft.
5. Slide the sealing boot off the interconnecting shaft.
6. Thoroughly clean and inspect the spider assembly, tripod joint housing, and interconnecting shaft for any signs of excessive wear. If any parts show extreme wear, the halfshaft must be replaced.

To install:

➡The inner tripod joint sealing boots are made from two different types of material. High temperature applications use silicone rubber, whereas standard temperature applications use Hytrel® plastic. The silicone sealing boots are soft and pliable. The Hytrel® sealing boots are stiff and rigid. The replacement sealing boot MUST BE the same type of material as the sealing boot that was removed.

7. Slide the inner tripod joint sealing boot retaining clamp onto the interconnecting shaft. Then, slide the replacement inner tripod joint sealing boot onto the interconnecting shaft. The inner tripod joint sealing boot MUST be positioned on the interconnecting shaft, so the raised bead on the inside of the seal boot is in the groove on the interconnecting shaft.
8. Install the spider assembly onto the interconnecting shaft with the chamfer on the spider assembly toward the interconnecting shaft. The spider must be positioned on the interconnecting shaft far enough to fully install the retaining snapring. If the spider assembly will not fully install by hand, you can tap the spider body with a brass drift. Do NOT hit the outer tripod bearings trying to install the spider on the interconnecting shaft.
9. Install the spider assembly-to-interconnecting shaft retaining snapring into the groove on the end of the interconnecting shaft. Be sure the snapring is fully seated in the groove on the interconnecting shaft.
10. Distribute ½ the amount of the grease provided in the seal boot service package (DO NOT USE ANY OTHER TYPE OF GREASE) into the tripod housing. Put the remaining amount into the sealing boot.
11. Align the tripod housing with the spider assembly, then slide the tripod housing over the spider assembly and interconnecting shaft.
12. Install the inner tripod joint seal boot-to-interconnecting shaft clamp evenly on the sealing boot.
13. Clamp the sealing boot onto the interconnecting shaft using a suitable crimper. Place the crimping tool over the bridge of the clamp. Tighten the nut on the tool until the jaws of the tool are closed completely together, face-to-face.

➡The seal must not be dimpled, stretched or out-of-shape in any way. If the seal is NOT correctly shaped, equalize the pressure in the seal and shape it by hand.

14. Position the sealing boot into the tripod housing retaining groove. Install the seal boot retaining clamp evenly on the sealing boot.

✲✲ WARNING

The following positioning procedure determines the correct air pressure inside the inner tripod joint assembly before clamping the sealing boot to the inner tripod joint housing. If this procedure is not performed before clamping the sealing boot to the tripod joint housing, boot durability can be adversely affected. When venting the inner tripod joint, be careful so the inner tripod sealing boot does not get punctured or damaged in any other way. If the sealing boot is punctured or damaged while being vented, it cannot be used.

15. Insert a small prytool or equivalent tool between the tripod joint and sealing boot to vent the inner tripod joint assembly. When inserting the prytool between the tripod housing and the sealing boot, make sure the tool is held flat and firmly against the tripod housing. If this is not done, damage to the sealing boot can occur. If the inner tripod joint has a Hytrel® (hard plastic) boot, make sure the tool is placed between the soft rubber insert and the tripod housing, and not the hard plastic sealing boot and soft rubber insert.
16. With the tool inserted between the sealing boot and the tripod joint housing, position the inner tripod joint on the driveshaft until the correct sealing boot edge-to-edge length is attained for the type of sealing boot material being used. Then remove the tool.

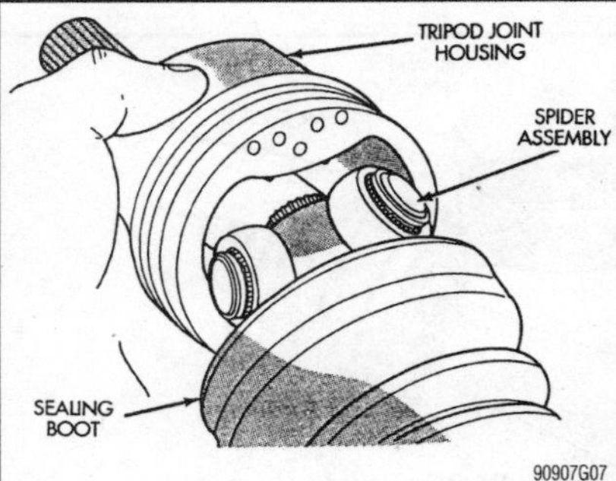

Fig. 31 After discarding the boot clamps, remove the tripod joint housing from the interconnecting shaft and spider assembly

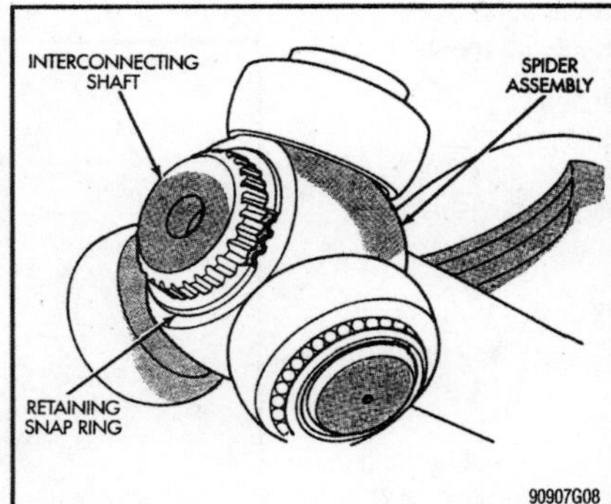

Fig. 32 Location of the spider assembly's retaining snapring

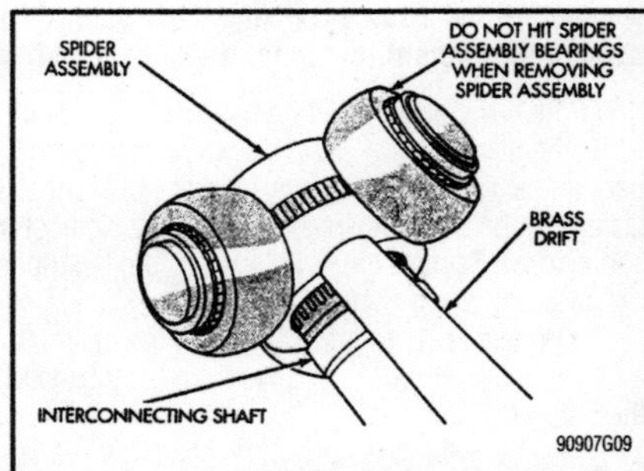

Fig. 33 If you encounter difficulty removing the spider assembly from the interconnecting shaft, use a brass drift to tap the spider

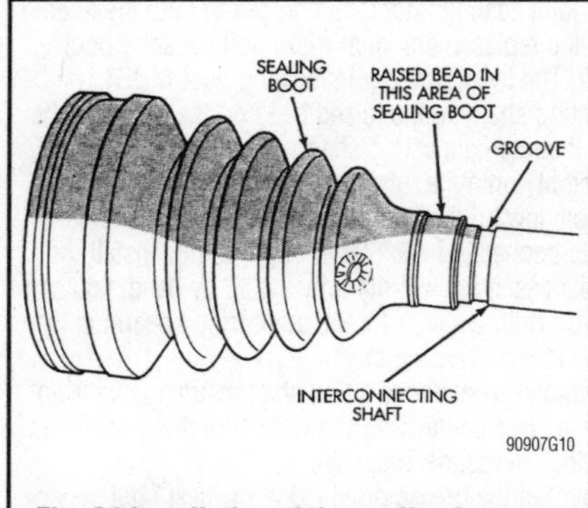

Fig. 34 Installation of the sealing boot on the interconnecting shaft

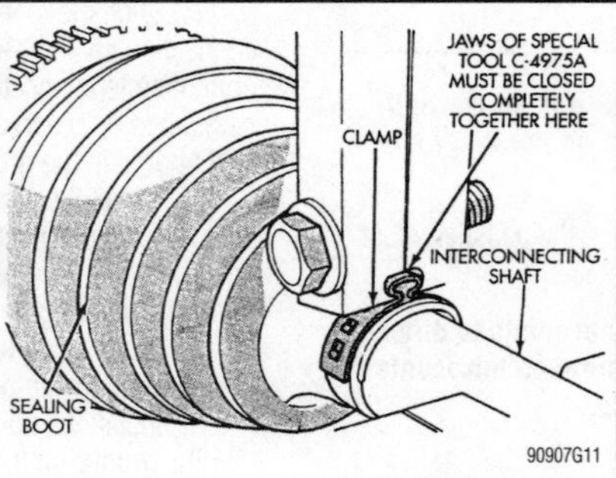

Fig. 35 Tighten the nut on the crimping tool until the jaws are completely closed, face-to-face

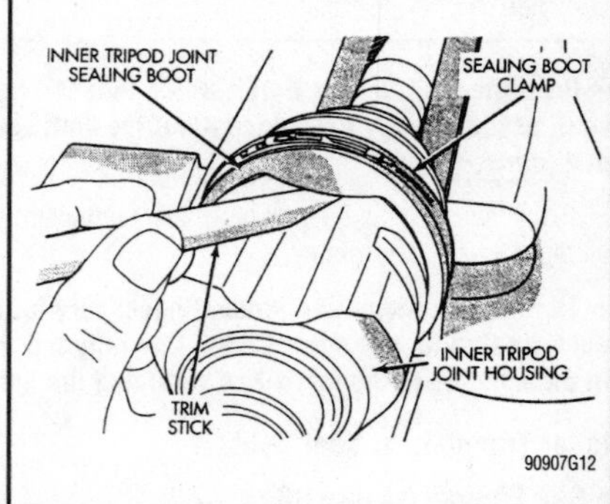

Fig. 36 Carefully insert a small prytool or trim stick to vent the tripod joint

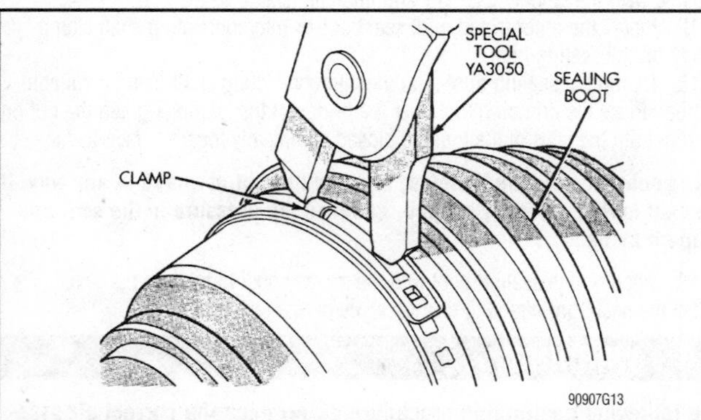

Fig. 37 When installing a latching-type boot clamp, position a suitable clamp locking tool on the clamp as shown . . .

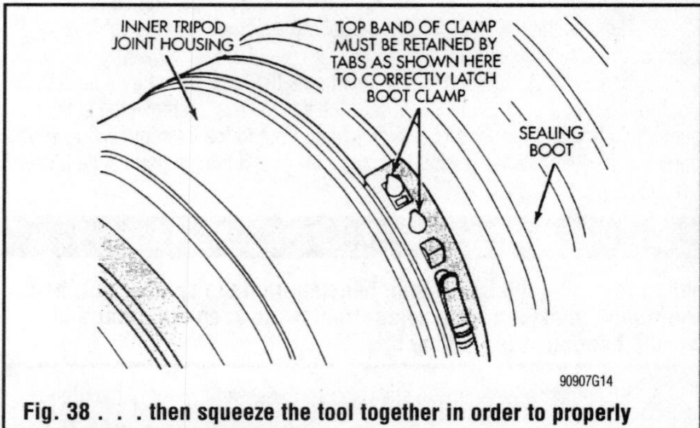

Fig. 38 . . . then squeeze the tool together in order to properly install the latching-type clamp

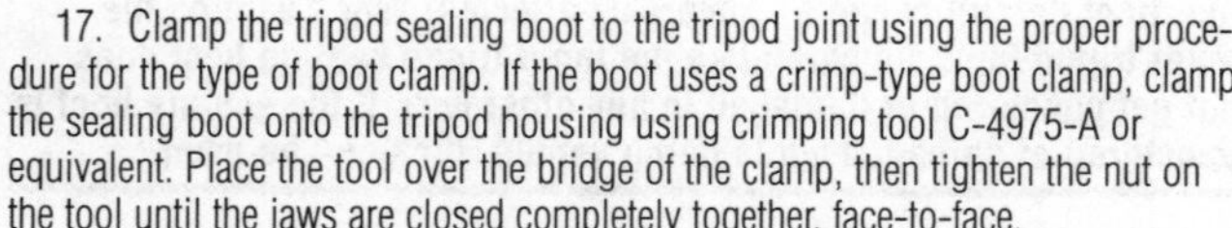

17. Clamp the tripod sealing boot to the tripod joint using the proper procedure for the type of boot clamp. If the boot uses a crimp-type boot clamp, clamp the sealing boot onto the tripod housing using crimping tool C-4975-A or equivalent. Place the tool over the bridge of the clamp, then tighten the nut on the tool until the jaws are closed completely together, face-to-face.
18. If the boot uses low profile, latching type boot clamps, clamp the sealing boot onto the tripod housing using clamp locking tool YA3050 or equivalent, as shown in the accompanying figure. Place the prongs of the clamp locking tool in the holes of the clamp. Squeeze the tool together until the top band of the clamp is latched behind the 2 tabs on the lower band of the clamp.
19. Install the halfshaft in the vehicle, as outlined earlier in this section.

Outer CV-Joint Seal Boot

See Figures 39, 40, 41, 42 and 43

This procedure only applies to vehicles equipped with removable outer CV joints. Some 1997 and later models use a different type of axle which does not allow servicing of the outer CV joint. If the outer boot needs replacement, the inner tripod assembly will need to be removed.

1. Remove the halfshaft from the vehicle, as outlined earlier in this section.
2. Remove the large boot clamp that holds the inner tripod joint sealing boot to the tripod joint housing. Discard the clamp. Then, remove the small clamp that holds the inner tripod joint sealing boot to the interconnecting shaft and discard. Remove the sealing boot from the tripod housing and slide it down the interconnecting shaft.
3. Wipe away the grease to expose the outer CV-joint.
4. Remove the outer CV-joint from the interconnecting shaft by performing the following:
   a. Place the interconnecting shaft in a soft jawed vise.
   b. Using a soft-faced hammer, sharply hit the end of the CV-joint housing to dislodge the housing from the internal circlip on the interconnecting shaft.
   c. Slide the outer CV-joint off the end of the interconnecting shaft; the joint may have to be tapped off using a soft-faced hammer.

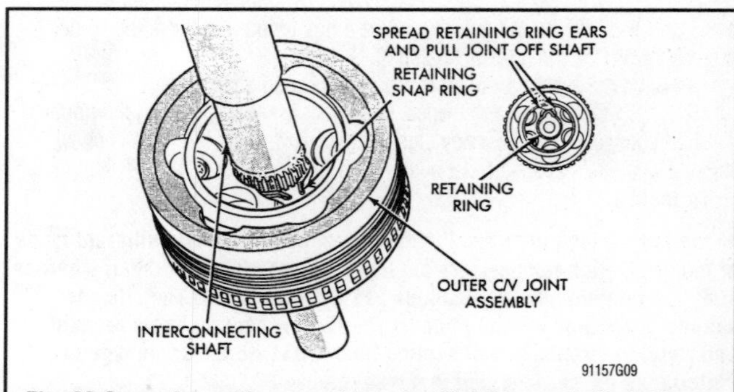

Fig. 39 On models with removable outer CV joints, a circlip holds the joint to the shaft

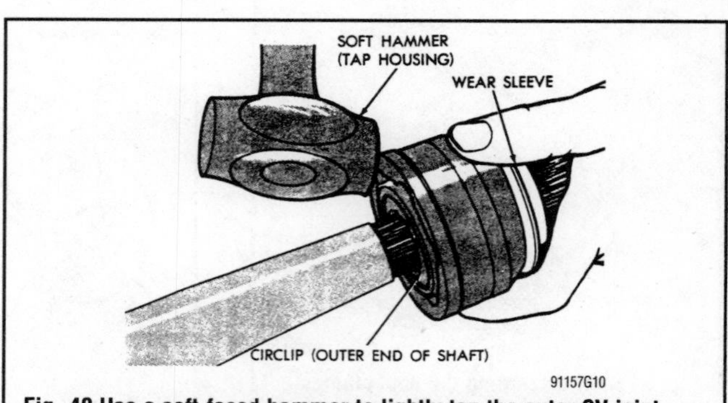

Fig. 40 Use a soft-faced hammer to lightly tap the outer CV joint from the shaft

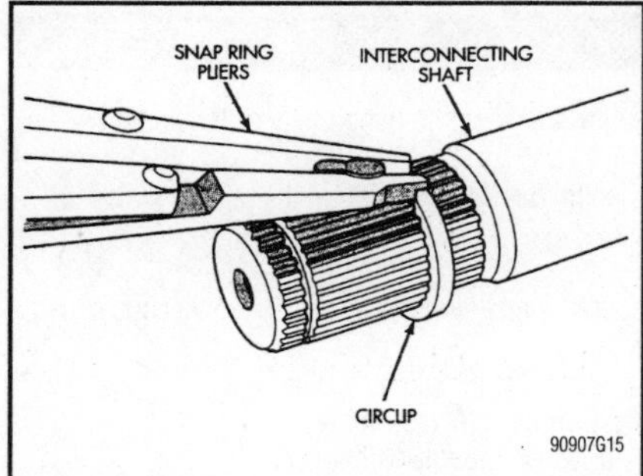

Fig. 41 Remove the circlip from the shaft using a pair of snapring pliers before removing the boot

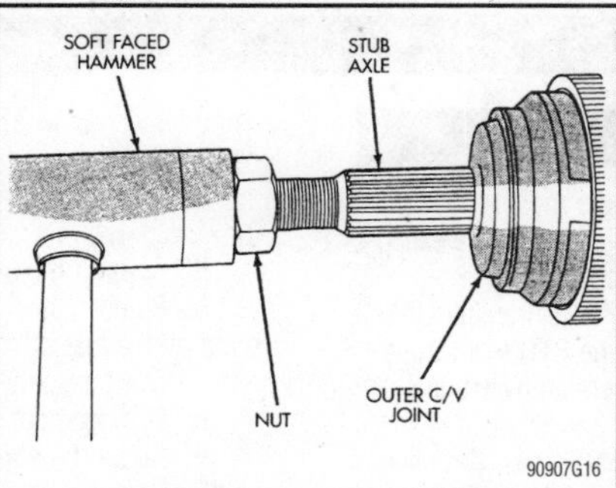

Fig. 42 If necessary, use a soft faced hammer to install the outer C/V joint to the interconnecting shaft

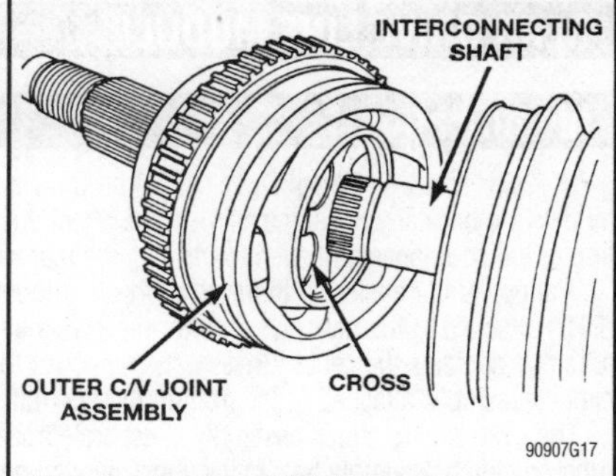

Fig. 43 The outer CV-joint must be installed until the cross of the joint is seated against the shaft circlip

5. Use a pair of snapring pliers to remove the large circlip from the interconnecting shaft before trying to remove the outer CV-joint sealing boot.
6. Slide the faulty boot off the interconnecting shaft.
7. Throughly clean and inspect the outer CV-joint and interconnecting joint for signs of excessive wear. If any parts show extreme wear, the halfshaft must be replaced.

To install:

8. Slide the new boot-to-interconnecting shaft retaining clamp onto the interconnecting shaft. Slide the outer CV-joint assembly boot onto the interconnecting shaft. The boot must be positioned on the interconnecting shaft so the raised bead of the inside of the seal boot is in the groove on the interconnecting shaft.
9. Align the splines on the interconnecting shaft with the splines on the cross of the outer CV-joint and start the outer CV-joint onto the interconnecting shaft.
10. Install the outer CV-joint onto the interconnecting shaft by using a soft-faced hammer and tapping the end of the stub axle (with the nut installed) until the outer CV-joint is fully seated on the shaft.
11. The outer CV-joint must be installed on the interconnecting shaft until the cross of the CV-joint is seated against the circlip on the shaft.
12. Place ½ of the grease provided with the boot service package (DO NOT USE ANY OTHER TYPE OF GREASE) into the outer CV-joint housing. Place the remaining grease into the boot.
13. Install the outer CV-joint boot-to-interconnecting shaft clamp evenly on the sealing boot.
14. Clamp the boot onto the interconnecting shaft using C-4975-A or an equivalent crimping tool, as follows:
    a. Place the crimping tool over the bridge of the clamp.
    b. Tighten the nut on the crimping tool until the jaws on the tool are closed completely together, face-to-face.
15. Position the outer CV-joint boot into its retaining groove on the outer CV-joint housing. Install the boot-to-housing clamp evenly on the housing. Install the sealing boot-to-outer CV-joint retaining clamp evenly on the sealing boot.
16. Clamp the boot onto the outer CV-joint housing using a suitable crimping tool. Place the crimping tool over the bridge of the clamp, then tighten the nut on the crimping tool until the jaws on the tool are closed completely together, face-to-face.
17. Install the halfshaft in the vehicle, as outlined earlier in this section.

POWER TRANSFER UNIT

Power Transfer Unit Assembly

REMOVAL & INSTALLATION

See Figures 44, 45 and 46

1. Raise and safely support the vehicle.
2. Remove the front wheels.
3. Remove the right front halfshaft and plug the seal hole.
4. Matchmark the front driveshaft flange and remove the driveshaft from the Power Transfer Unit (PTU). Suspend the driveshaft with wire.
5. Remove the cradle plate.
6. Remove the PTU mounting bracket bolts at the rear of the unit.
7. Remove the right outboard support bracket near the right halfshaft.
8. Remove the mounting bolts and the PTU from the vehicle.

To install:

9. Position the PTU on the transaxle and install the mounting bolts. Tighten the bolts to 30 ft. lbs. (41 Nm).
10. Install the right outboard support bracket. Tighten the bolts to 37 ft. lbs. (50 Nm).
11. Install the rear mounting bracket. Tighten the bolts to 37 ft. lbs. (50 Nm).
12. Install the cradle plate. Tighten the bolts to 38 ft. lbs. (51 Nm).
13. Align the matchmark and install the driveshaft.
14. Install the right front halfshaft.
15. Install the front wheels and lower the vehicle to the floor.

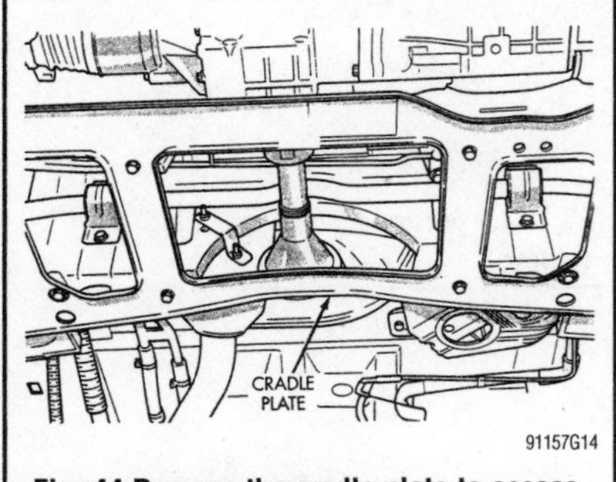

Fig. 44 Remove the cradle plate to access the power transfer unit

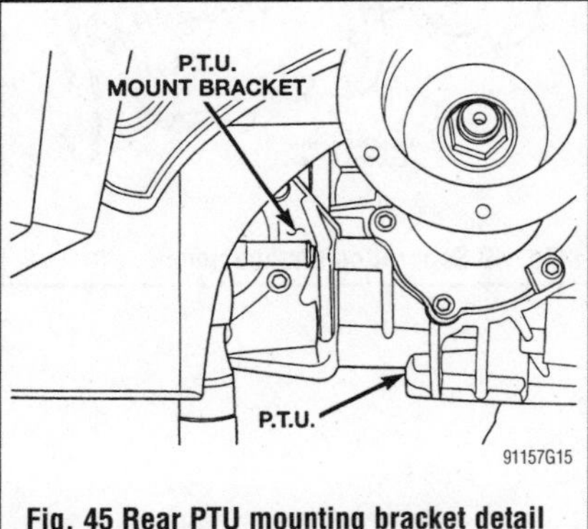

Fig. 45 Rear PTU mounting bracket detail

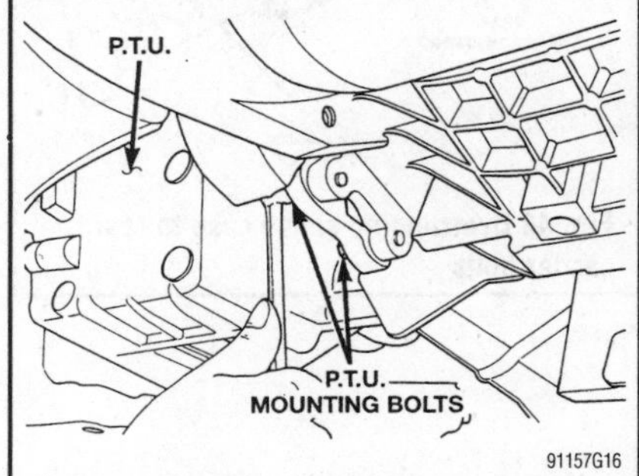

Fig. 46 Lower mounting bracket detail for the PTU

REAR DRIVE LINE MODULE

Identification

Chrysler offers All Wheel Drive (AWD) on Caravan/Voyager models. These models are basically the same as the front wheel drive versions, with the exception of the components needed for driving the rear wheels as well.

The power is transferred to the rear wheels through the Power Transfer Unit (PTU) attached to the transaxle. The power travels through the PTU to a torque tube that contains the center driveshaft. The power then enters an overrunning clutch assembly, attached to the front of the rear differential carrier.

The overrunning clutch assembly is separate from the rear carrier. The overrunning clutch assembly has an vacuum operated dog clutch, it is lubricated with Mopar ATF type 7176. The rear carrier is lubricated with SAE 85W-90 gear lube.

Rear Drive Line Assembly Module

See Figure 47

REMOVAL &INSTALLATION

1. Raise and safely support the rear of the vehicle.
2. Remove the right and left inner halfshaft joint mounting bolts.
3. Support the inner side of the halfshaft, by hanging it from the frame

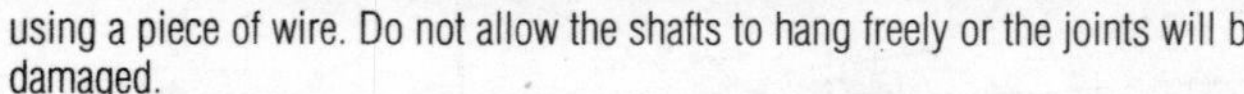

using a piece of wire. Do not allow the shafts to hang freely or the joints will be damaged.

4. Remove the mounting bolts from the rear side of the propeller shaft at, the rear carrier.
5. Support the propeller shaft.
6. Remove the viscous coupling retaining nut and slide the viscous coupling off the rear driveline assembly.
7. Disengage the vacuum line at the driveline module.
8. Disengage the electrical lead from the assembly.
9. Support the rear of the driveline module with a jack.
10. Remove the rear driveline module front mounting bolts. Partially lower the unit from the vehicle.
11. Remove the rear driveline module from the vehicle.

To install:

12. Position the driveline module in the vehicle. Install the front mounting bolts and tighten to 40 ft. lbs. (54 Nm).
13. Reconnect the vacuum line and electrical lead. Install the viscous coupling and nut. Tighten the nut to 120 ft. lbs. (162 Nm).
14. Connect the propeller shaft to the driveline module, tighten to 21 ft. lbs. (28 Nm).
15. Connect the rear halfshafts to the rear driveline module. Tighten the bolt to 45 ft. lbs. (61 Nm).
16. Lower the vehicle. Check the operation of the drive train.

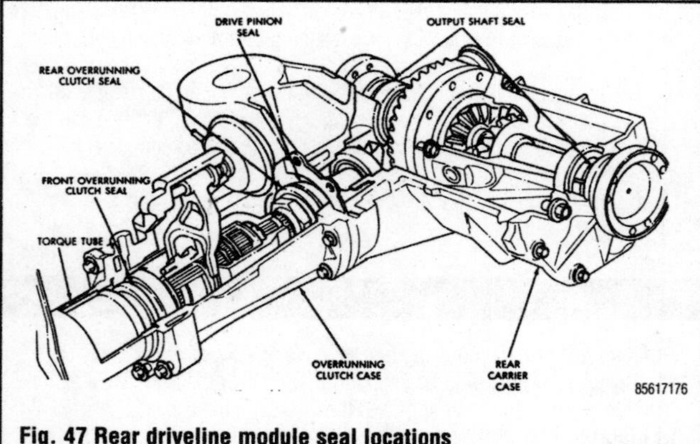

Fig. 47 Rear driveline module seal locations

Drive Pinion

REMOVAL & INSTALLATION

See Figures 48 thru 54

1. Raise and safely support the vehicle.
2. Remove the rear driveline module from the vehicle.
3. Remove the overrunning clutch case-to-rear carrier bolts. Separate the overrunning clutch case from the rear carrier.
4. Remove the overrunning clutch outer race snapring and slide the clutch race off of the shaft.
5. Using a spline socket and a wrench, remove the pinion nut.
6. Unfasten the front carrier cover retaining bolts and remove the carrier cover.
7. Place a block of wood under the end of the pinion shaft. Tap the end of the pinion against the wood to remove the spacer from the shaft.

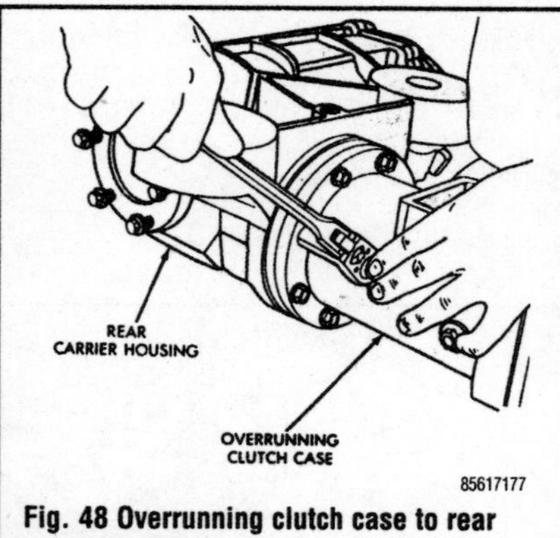

Fig. 48 Overrunning clutch case to rear carrier bolts

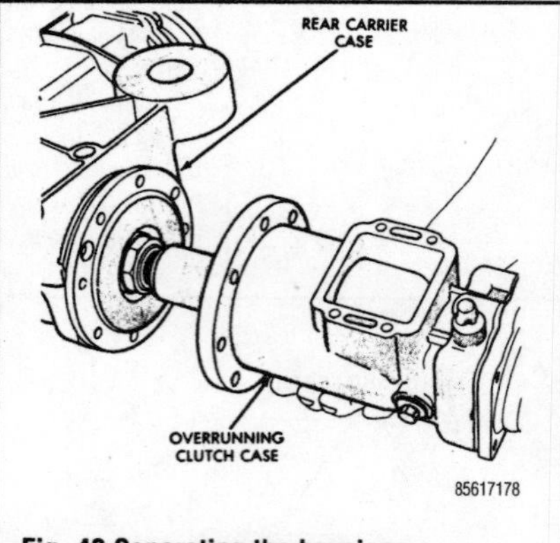

Fig. 49 Separating the housings

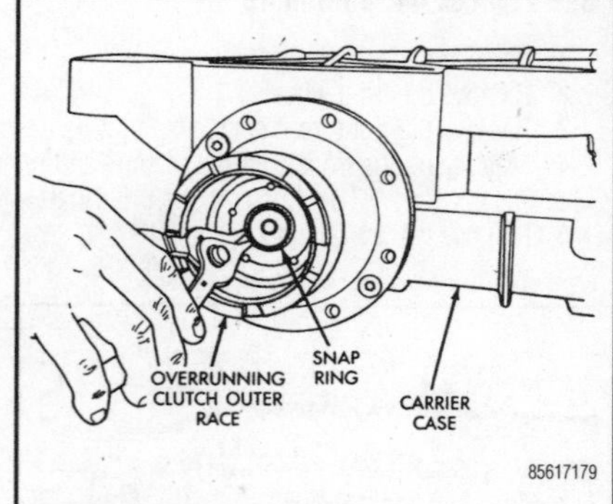

Fig. 50 Overruning clutch snapring removal

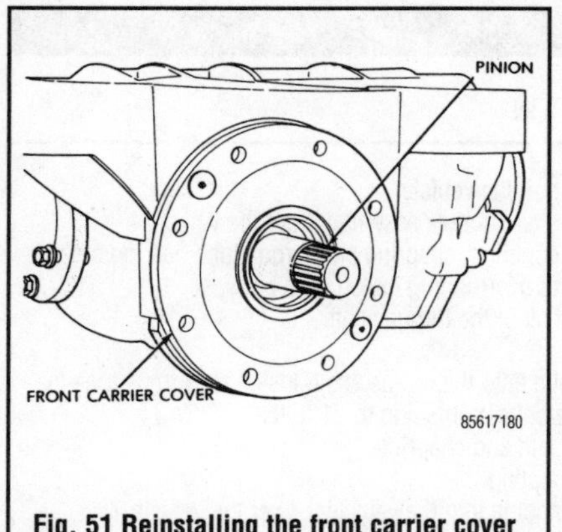

Fig. 51 Reinstalling the front carrier cover

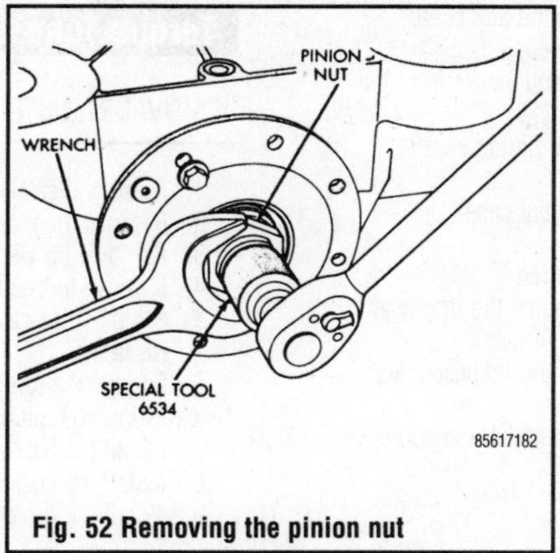

Fig. 52 Removing the pinion nut

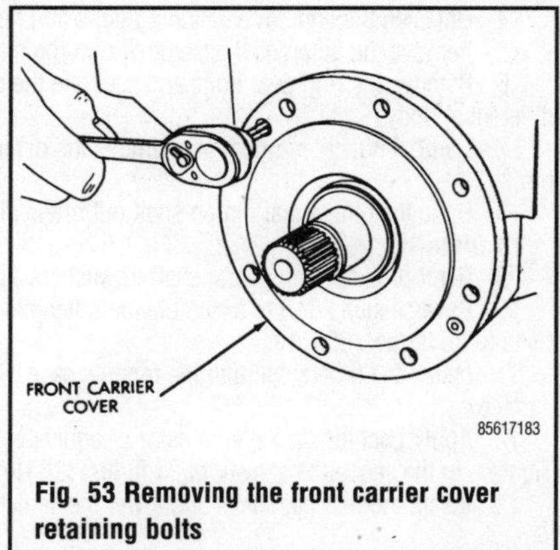

Fig. 53 Removing the front carrier cover retaining bolts

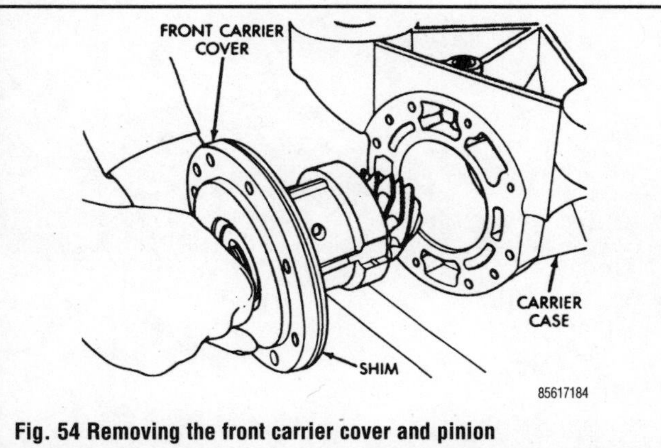

Fig. 54 Removing the front carrier cover and pinion

To install:

8. Install the front carrier onto the case and tighten the retaining nuts to 105 inch lbs. (12 Nm).
9. Clean and inspect the seal area, apply a light coat of oil to the drive pinion seal.
10. Install the seal using a seal installer. The seal must be installed with the spring towards the rear of the case.
11. Apply a light coat of oil onto the drive pinion spacer and slide it onto the pinion shaft with the tapered side facing out.
12. Apply a light coat of oil to the overrunning clutch seal and install with a seal installer, the seal must be installed with the spring facing outward.
13. Install the pinion nut and tighten to 150 ft. lbs. (203 Nm).
14. Install the overrunning clutch outer race and snapring.
15. Apply Loctite® sealer to the overrunning clutch sealing surface and install the clutch case to the rear carrier. Tighten to 21 ft. lbs. (28 Nm).
16. Install the rear driveline module into the vehicle. Check and fill the fluid as required.

Differential Side Gears

REMOVAL & INSTALLATION

See Figures 55 and 56

1. Raise and safely support the rear of the vehicle.
2. Disconnect both rear halfshafts from the axle carrier assembly.
3. Using 2 prybars, remove the output shaft.

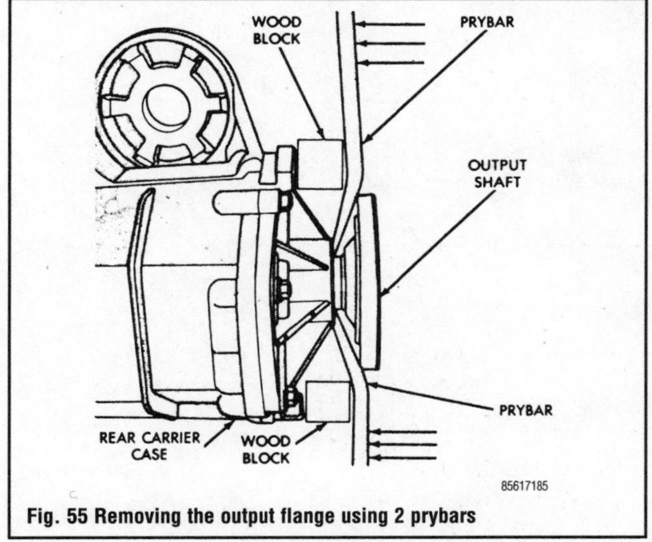

Fig. 55 Removing the output flange using 2 prybars

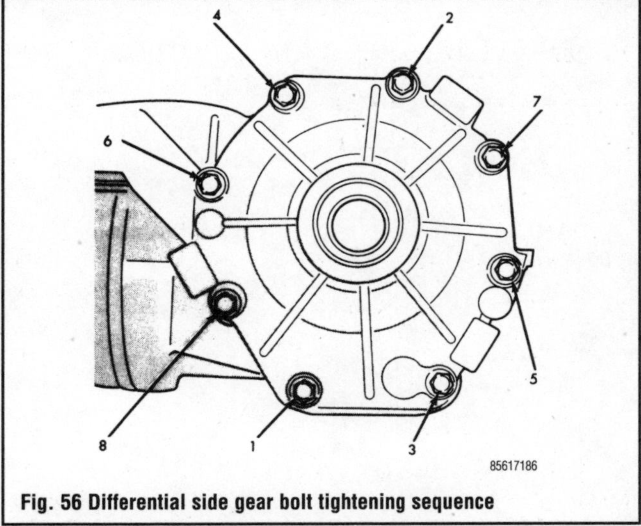

Fig. 56 Differential side gear bolt tightening sequence

4. Unfasten the end cover retaining bolts and remove the end cover.
5. Remove the differential assembly from the rear driveline case.
6. Remove the ring gear bolts and separate the differential case from the differential body.
7. Using a punch and hammer, remove the differential pinion shaft pin.
8. Slide the differential pinion shaft out of the differential case.

To install:

9. Replace the pinion gears, shaft or washers as required.
10. Reverse steps 8–5 to assemble the differential. Tighten the ring gear bolts to 70 ft. lbs. (95 Nm).
11. Install the differential into the module case. Clean and inspect sealer surfaces.
12. Apply Loctite® gasket eliminator or equivalent, and install the end cover. Tighten, in the sequence shown, to 21 ft. lbs. (28 Nm).
13. Install the rear halfshafts and lower the vehicle.

Torque Tube

REMOVAL & INSTALLATION

1. Raise and safely support the vehicle.
2. Remove the rear driveline module assembly from the vehicle.
3. Remove the viscous coupling, snapring and torque tube bearing shield.
4. Remove torque tube to overrunning clutch case bolts.
5. Slide the torque tube off of the torque shaft.

To install:

6. Engage the torque tube onto the torque shaft. Install the torque tube to the overrunning clutch case bolts, tightening to 21 ft. lbs. (28 Nm).
7. Install the bearing shield and snapring.
8. Install the viscous coupling.
9. Install the driveline module into the vehicle. Lower the vehicle.

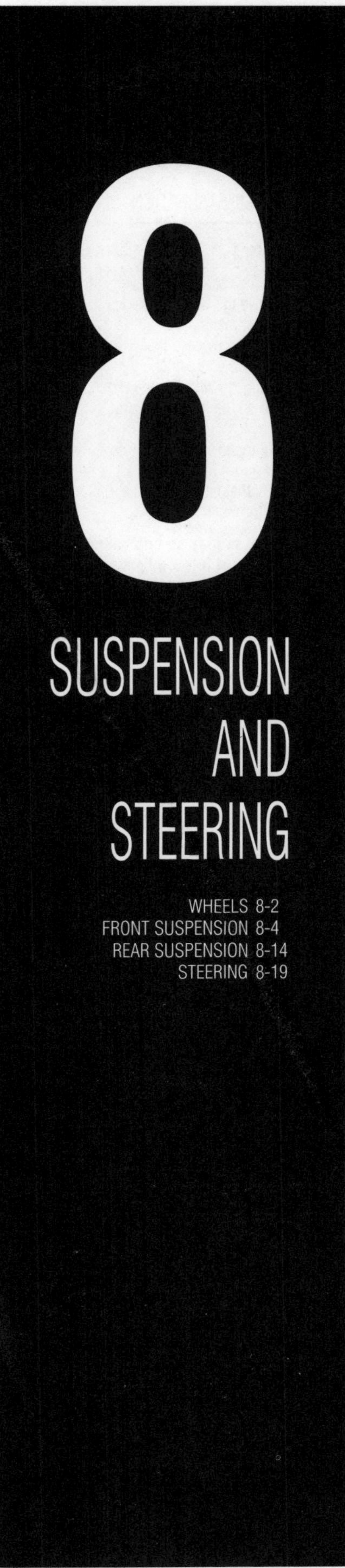
8
SUSPENSION
AND
STEERING
WHEELS 8-2
FRONT SUSPENSION 8-4
REAR SUSPENSION 8-14
STEERING 8-19

WHEELS

Wheel Assembly

REMOVAL & INSTALLATION

See Figure 1

1. Park the vehicle on a level surface.
2. Remove the jack, tire iron and, if necessary, the spare tire from their storage compartments.
3. Check the owner's manual or refer to Section 1 of this manual for the jacking points on your vehicle. Then, place the jack in the proper position.
4. If equipped with lug nut trim caps, remove them by either unscrewing or pulling them off the lug nuts, as appropriate. Consult the owner's manual, if necessary.
5. If equipped with a wheel cover or hub cap, insert the tapered or small end of the tire iron in the groove and pry off the cover.
6. Apply the parking brake and block the diagonally opposite wheel with a wheel chock or two.

➡Wheel chocks may be purchased at your local auto parts store, or a block of wood cut into wedges may be used. If possible, keep one or two of the chocks in your tire storage compartment, in case any of the tires has to be removed on the side of the road.

7. Place the selector lever in **P** or Park.
8. With the tires still on the ground, use the tire iron/wrench to break the lug nuts loose.

➡If a nut is stuck, never use heat to loosen it or damage to the wheel and bearings may occur. If the nuts are seized, one or two heavy hammer blows directly on the end of the bolt usually loosens the rust. Be careful, as continued pounding will likely damage the brake drum or rotor.

9. Using the jack, raise the vehicle until the tire is clear of the ground. Support the vehicle safely using jackstands.
10. Remove the lug nuts, then remove the tire and wheel assembly.

To install:

11. Make sure the wheel and hub mating surfaces, as well as the wheel lug studs, are clean and free of all foreign material. Always remove rust from the wheel mounting surface and the brake rotor or drum. Failure to do so may cause the lug nuts to loosen in service.
12. Install the tire and wheel assembly and hand-tighten the lug nuts.
13. Using the tire wrench, tighten all the lug nuts, in a crisscross pattern, until they are snug.
14. Raise the vehicle and withdraw the jackstand, then lower the vehicle.
15. Using a torque wrench, tighten the lug nuts in a crisscross pattern to 95 ft. lbs. (129 Nm). Check your owner's manual or refer to Section 1 of this manual for the proper tightening sequence.

⁂ WARNING

Do not overtighten the lug nuts, as this may cause the wheel studs to stretch or the brake disc (rotor) to warp.

16. If so equipped, install the wheel cover or hub cap. Make sure the valve stem protrudes through the proper opening before tapping the wheel cover into position.
17. If equipped, install the lug nut trim caps by pushing them or screwing them on, as applicable.
18. Remove the jack from under the vehicle, and place the jack and tire iron/wrench in their storage compartments. Remove the wheel chock(s).
19. If you have removed a flat or damaged tire, place it in the storage compartment of the vehicle and take it to your local repair station to have it fixed or replaced as soon as possible.

INSPECTION

Inspect the tires for lacerations, puncture marks, nails and other sharp objects. Repair or replace as necessary. Also check the tires for treadwear and air pressure as outlined in Check the wheel assemblies for dents, cracks, rust and metal fatigue. Repair or replace as necessary.

Wheel Lug Studs

REPLACEMENT

With Disc Brakes

See Figures 2 and 3

1. Raise and support the appropriate end of the vehicle safely using jackstands, then remove the wheel.

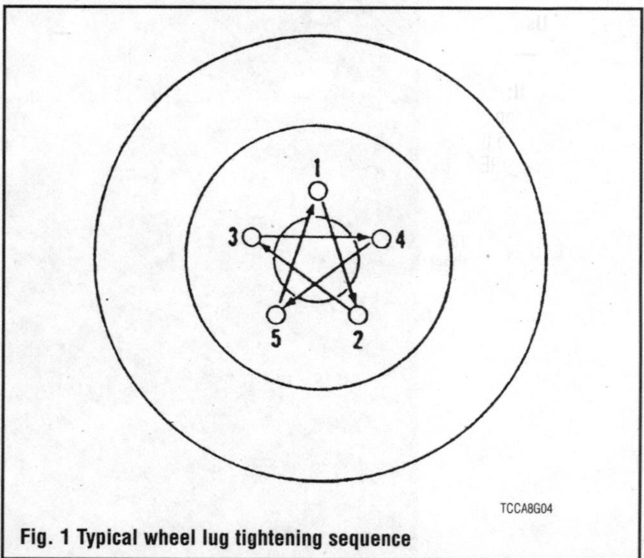

Fig. 1 Typical wheel lug tightening sequence

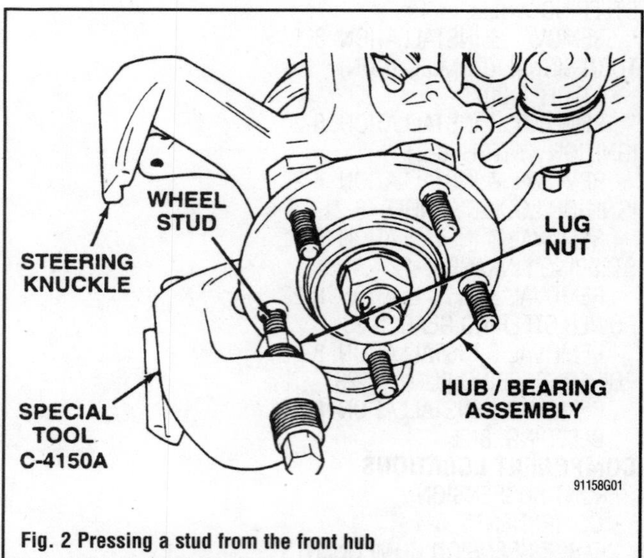

Fig. 2 Pressing a stud from the front hub

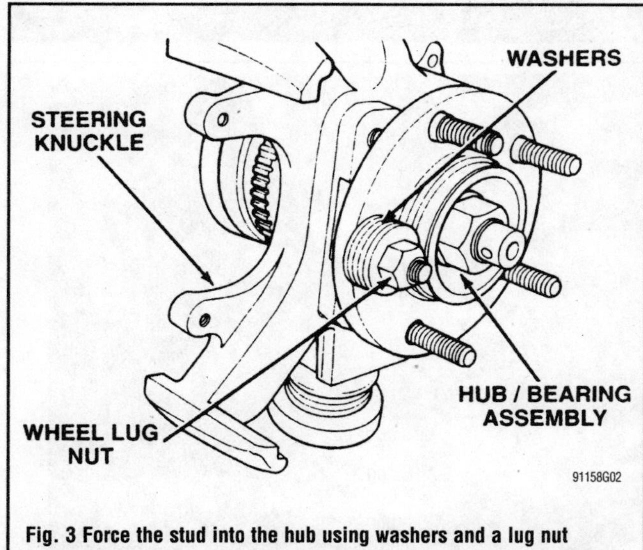

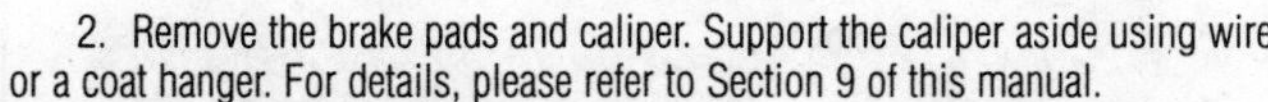
Fig. 3 Force the stud into the hub using washers and a lug nut

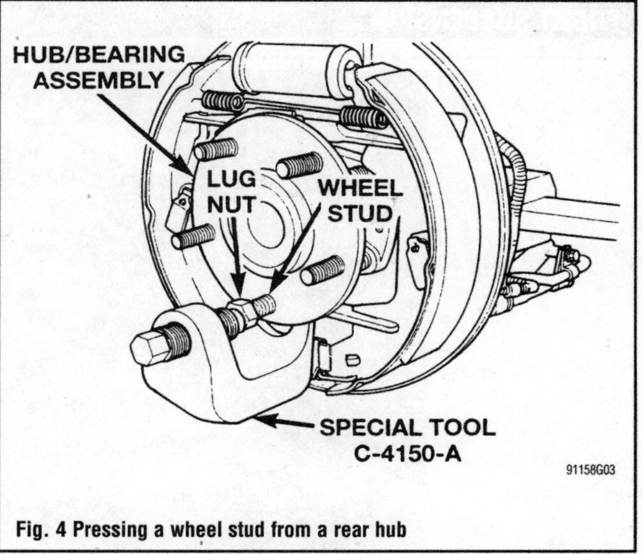

Fig. 4 Pressing a wheel stud from a rear hub

2. Remove the brake pads and caliper. Support the caliper aside using wire or a coat hanger. For details, please refer to Section 9 of this manual.
3. Remove the brake rotor. If equipped with rear disc brakes, remove the parking brake shoe assembly.
4. Install a lug nut on the end of the stud to be removed from the hub/bearing assembly. Turn the hub so that the stud being removed is lined up with the notch cast into the front of the steering knuckle. Install special stud removal tool C-4150, or equivalent, on the hub/bearing flange and wheel stud.
5. Tighten down on the special tool; this will push the stud out from behind the hub/bearing flange.

To install:

6. Clean the stud hole with a wire brush.
7. Install the new lug stud through the hole in the hub/bearing flange, then position about 4 flat washers over the stud and thread the lug nut. Hold the hub/rotor while tightening the lug nut, and the stud should be drawn into position. MAKE SURE THE STUD IS FULLY SEATED, then remove the lug nut and washers.
8. Install the brake rotor. If equipped with rear disc brakes, install the parking brake shoe assembly.
9. Install the brake caliper and pads.
10. Install the wheel, then remove the jackstands and carefully lower the vehicle.
11. Tighten the lug nuts to the proper torque.

With Drum Brakes

➧ See Figures 4 and 5

1. Raise the vehicle and safely support it with jackstands, then remove the wheel.
2. Remove the brake drum.
3. If necessary to provide clearance, remove the brake shoes, as outlined in Section 9 of this manual.
4. Using a large C-clamp and socket, press the stud from the axle flange.
5. Coat the serrated part of the stud with liquid soap and place it into the hole.

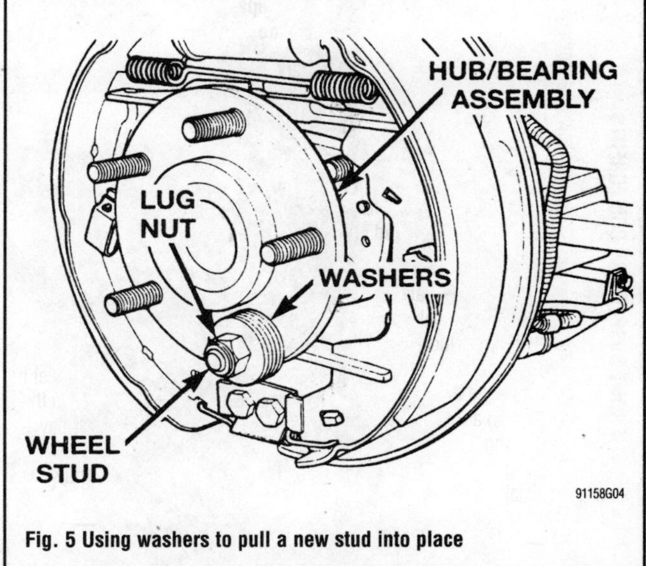

Fig. 5 Using washers to pull a new stud into place

To install:

6. Position about 4 flat washers over the stud and thread the lug nut. Hold the flange while tightening the lug nut, and the stud should be drawn into position. MAKE SURE THE STUD IS FULLY SEATED, then remove the lug nut and washers.
7. If applicable, install the brake shoes.
8. Install the brake drum.
9. Install the wheel, then remove the jackstands and carefully lower the vehicle.
10. Tighten the lug nuts to the proper torque.

FRONT SUSPENSION

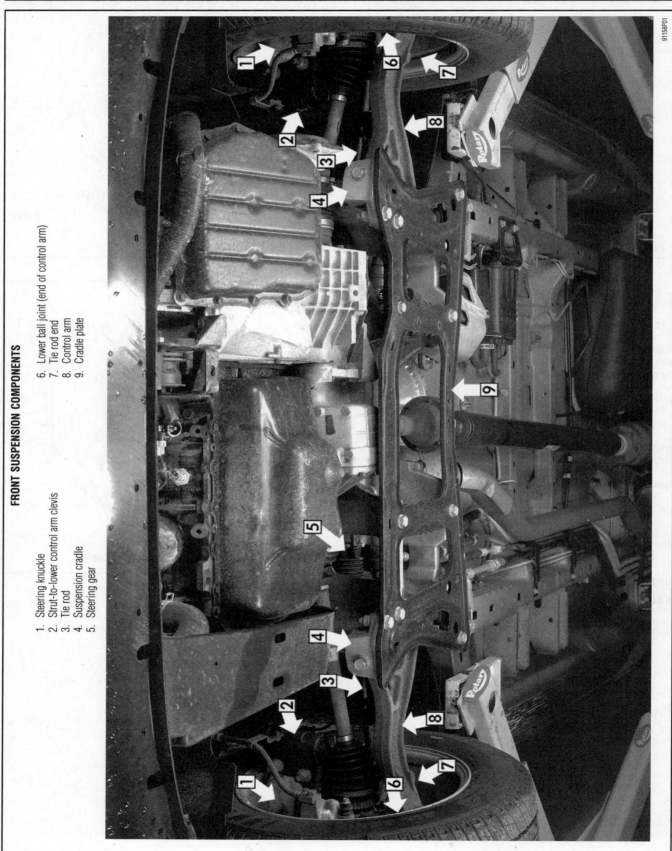

FRONT SUSPENSION COMPONENTS

1. Steering knuckle
2. Strut-to-lower control arm clevis
3. Tie rod
4. Suspension cradle
5. Steering gear
6. Lower ball joint (end of control arm)
7. Tie rod end
8. Control arm
9. Cradle plate

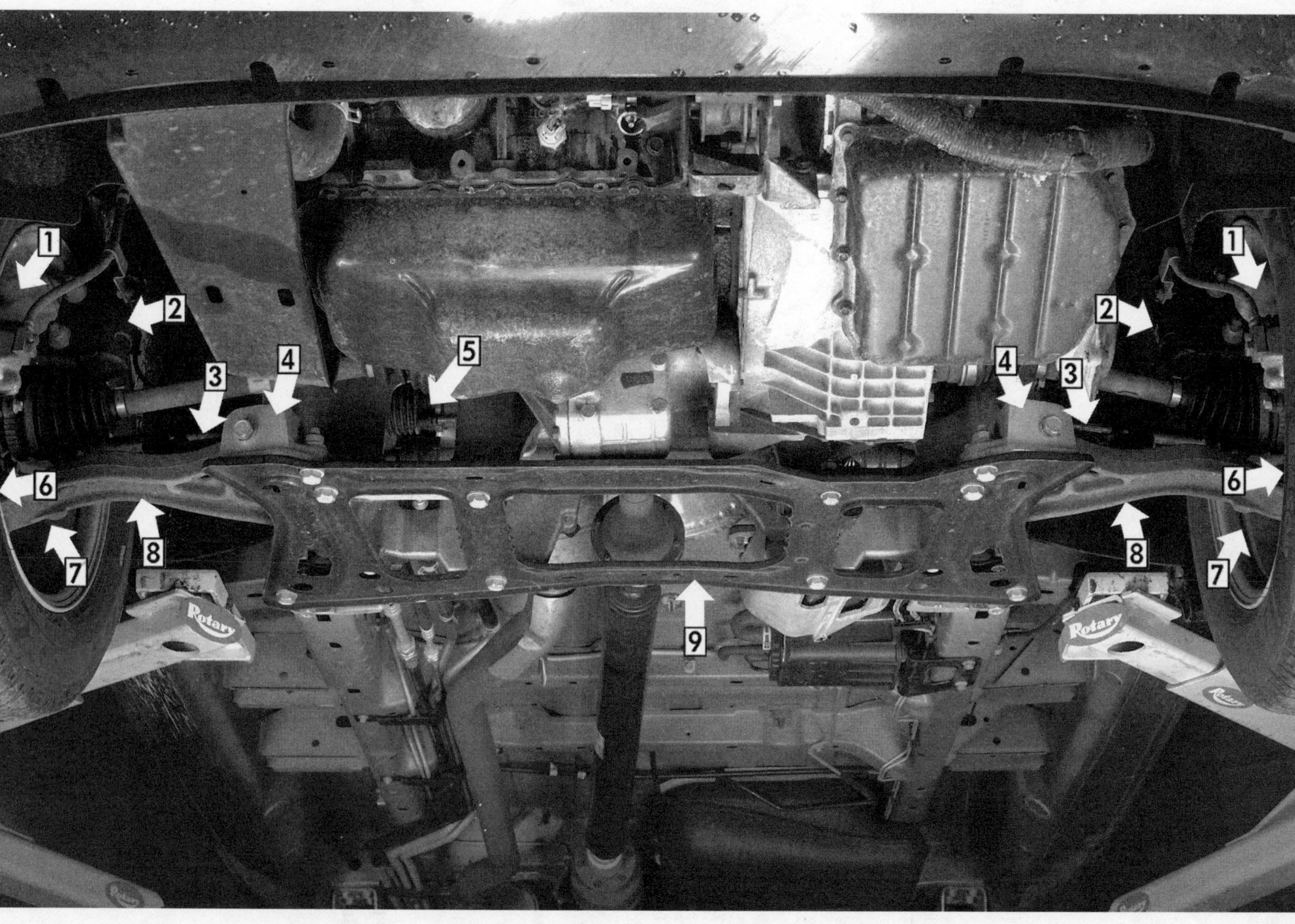

Struts

REMOVAL & INSTALLATION

See Figures 6 thru 11

1. Raise and safely support the vehicle.
2. Remove the front wheel.
3. If equipped, remove the brake hose routing bracket and ABS speed sensor cable routing bracket from the strut damper brackets.
4. If equipped, remove the sway bar attaching link from the mounting bracket on the strut assembly. Hold the sway bar attaching link stud using a 6mm hex bit while removing the retaining nut with a box wrench.

WARNING

The steering knuckle-to-strut assembly attaching bolts are of the serrated type and, therefore, cannot be turned during the removal procedure. Hold the bolts stationary in the steering knuckle while removing the nuts.

5. Remove the steering knuckle-to-strut assembly attaching bolts.
6. Remove the three nuts securing the strut assembly upper mount to the strut tower. Remove the strut assembly from the vehicle.

To install:

7. Position the strut assembly into the strut tower and loosely install the upper washers and nuts. Tighten the three attaching upper mount nuts to 21 ft. lbs. (28 Nm).
8. Position the lower mount over the steering knuckle and loosely install the attaching bolts and nuts. If one of the attaching bolts is a cam bolt, the cam bolt must be installed in the lower slotted hole of the strut clevis bracket. Be sure that the attaching nuts face the front of the vehicle. Tighten the attaching nuts to 65 ft. lbs. (88 Nm) plus an additional 1/4 turn.
9. If equipped, install the sway bar attaching link to the bracket on the strut assembly. Using a 6mm hex bit and crowfoot, tighten the sway bar link bracket attaching nut to 65 ft. lbs. (88 Nm).
10. If equipped, install the brake hose retaining bracket and ABS speed sensor cable routing bracket onto the strut assembly bracket. Tighten the mounting bolts to 10 ft. lbs. (13 Nm).
11. Install the front wheels and lug nuts. Tighten the lug nuts, in a star pattern sequence, to 95 ft. lbs. (129 Nm). Lower the vehicle and check the wheel alignment. Adjust, if necessary.

OVERHAUL

See Figures 12 thru 17

1. Remove the strut assembly from the vehicle.
2. Secure the strut assembly into a bench vise. Mount the strut assembly in the vertical position, clamping the strut assembly at the strut clevis bracket ONLY.
3. Using a coil spring compressor, compress the coil spring. It is required that the upper spring seat and second spring coil from the bottom be secured within the jaws of the spring compressor tool.
4. Using a wrench, hold the end of the strut shaft from rotating and remove the strut shaft nut.
5. Remove the upper strut mount from the strut assembly. Carefully remove the coil spring compressor tool from the coil spring.
6. Remove the upper spring seat and pivot bearing assembly from the coil spring.
7. Remove the coil spring from the strut. If the coil spring is being reused, mark the coil spring for correct reinstallation position.

To install:

8. With the strut assembly mounted firmly in the bench vise, install the coil spring on the strut assembly. Be sure the end of the coil spring's bottom coil aligns with the strut clevis bracket.
9. Install the upper spring seat onto the coil spring. Position the notch on the top of the spring seat in alignment with the strut clevis bracket.

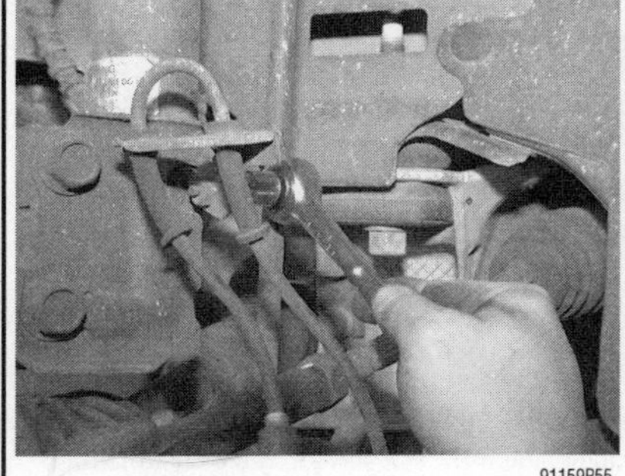

Fig. 6 Unbolting the brake hose and ABS speed sensor bracket from the strut

Fig. 7 Removing the sway bar link

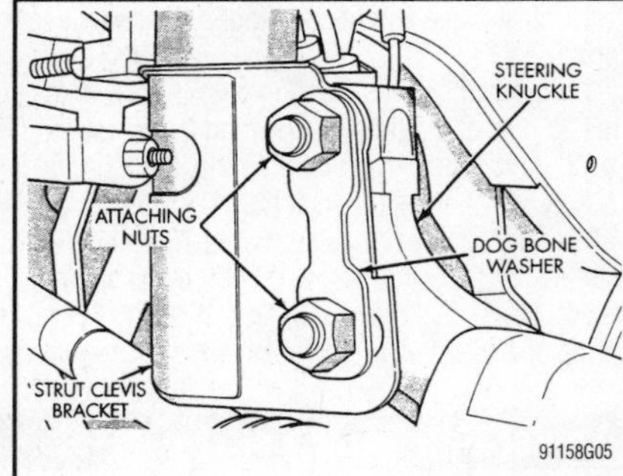

Fig. 8 The strut is attached to the steering knuckle with two bolts. Hold the bolts stationary while removing the nuts

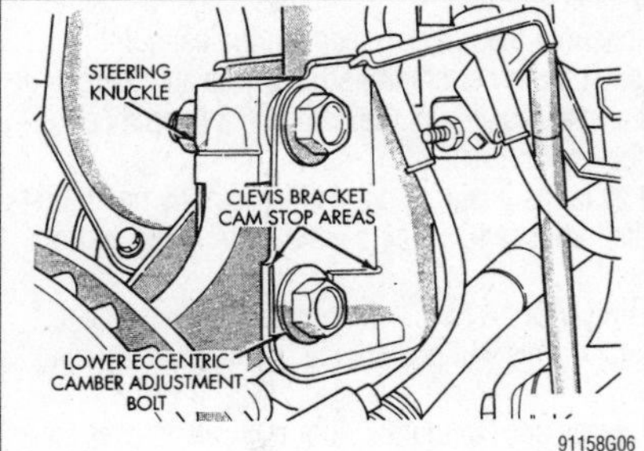

Fig. 9 Some models may be fitted with an eccentric bolt; make sure to mark its position before removal to retain the alignment settings

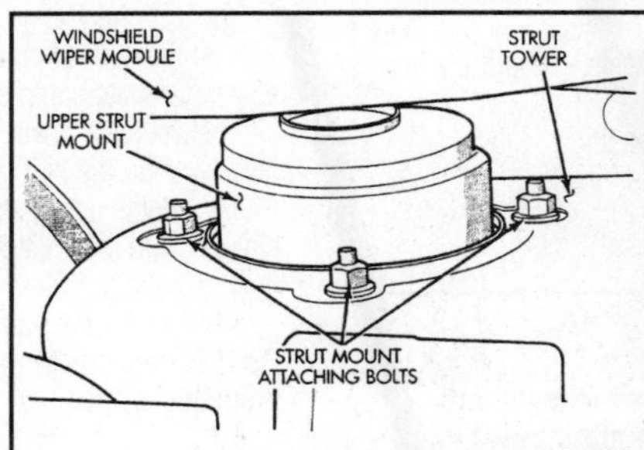

Fig. 10 After the strut is detached from the steering knuckle, remove the three bolts that secure the upper strut to the strut tower

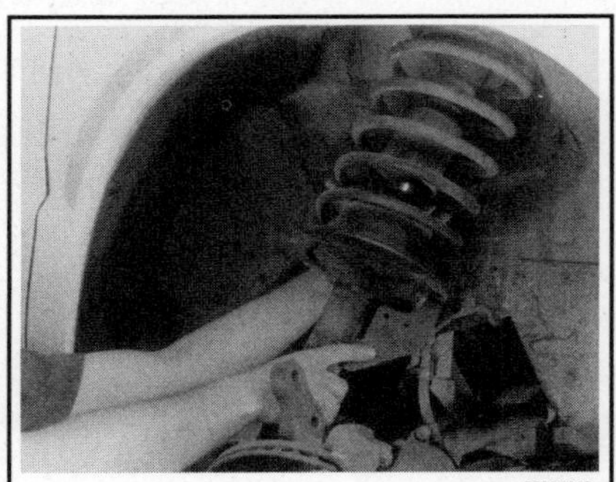

Fig. 11 Now the strut can be removed from the vehicle

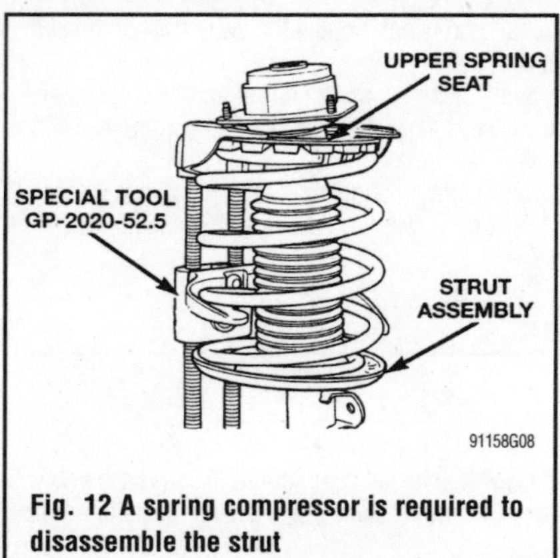

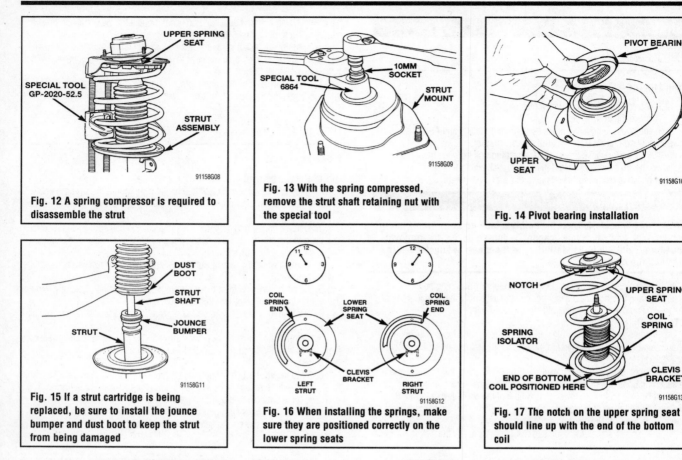

Fig. 12 A spring compressor is required to disassemble the strut

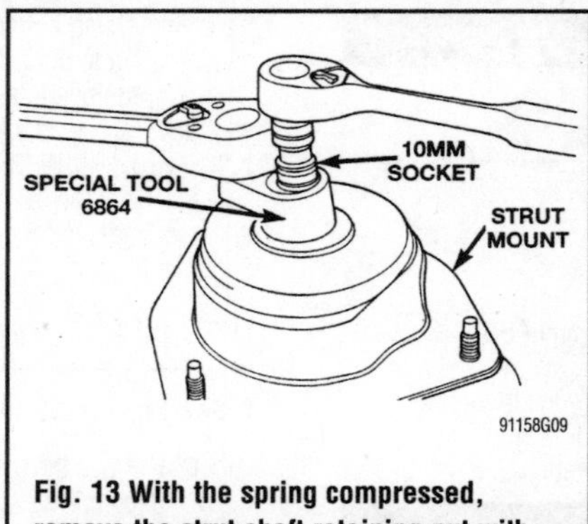

Fig. 13 With the spring compressed, remove the strut shaft retaining nut with the special tool

Fig. 14 Pivot bearing installation

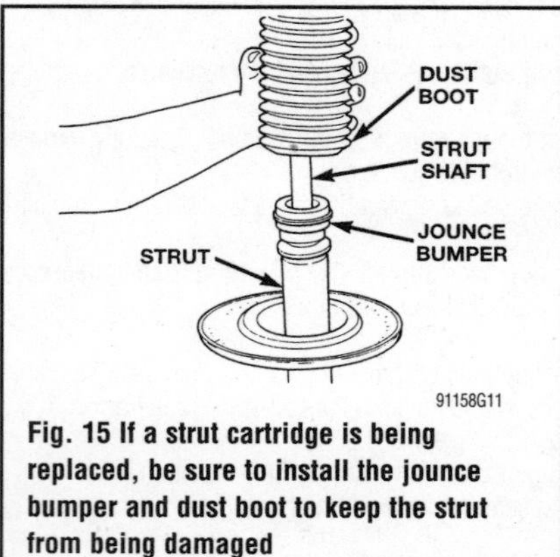

Fig. 15 If a strut cartridge is being replaced, be sure to install the jounce bumper and dust boot to keep the strut from being damaged

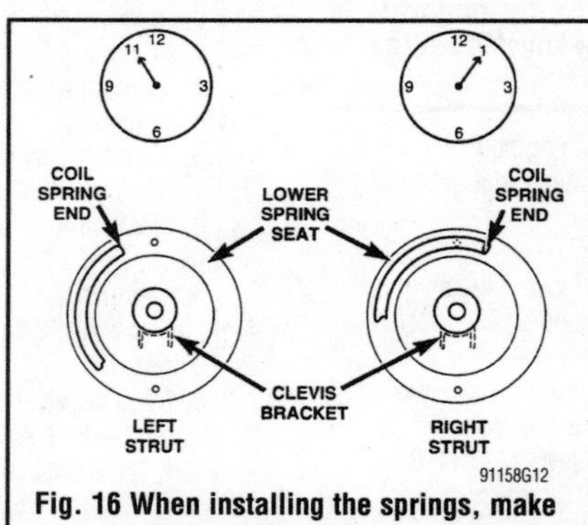

Fig. 16 When installing the springs, make sure they are positioned correctly on the lower spring seats

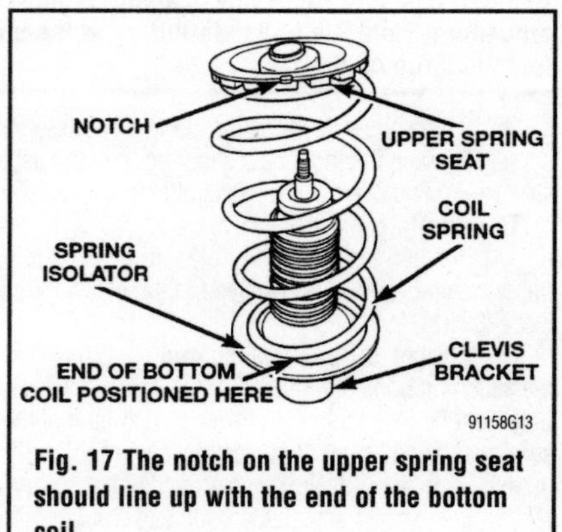

Fig. 17 The notch on the upper spring seat should line up with the end of the bottom coil

10. Install the compressor tool onto the coil spring, and compress the spring.
11. Install the pivot bearing onto the top of the upper spring seat with the smaller diameter side of the bearing facing toward the spring seat.
12. Install the strut mount on the upper spring seat of the strut assembly. Loosely install the strut shaft nut.
13. Tighten the strut shaft nut to 70 ft. lbs. (94 Nm). This step is performed with the spring compressor tool still installed on the spring.
14. Check that the top of the coil spring is seated correctly against the upper spring seat. Carefully remove the spring compressor tool.

Lower Ball Joint

INSPECTION

Inspect the ball joint dust cover for cracks and damage by pushing on it with your finger. If the dust cover is cracked or damaged, the component must be replaced, or damage to the ball joint will result.

1. With the weight of the vehicle resting on the road wheels, grasp the ball joint grease fitting.
2. If the ball joint is worn, the grease fitting will rotate easily.
3. Replace the lower control arm ball joint if movement is evident.

REMOVAL & INSTALLATION

See Figures 18, 19 and 20

Special Chrysler Tools 6758, 6908–4 and 6919 or equivalents, are required to remove and install the lower ball joint. An arbor press is also required to remove and install the ball joint.

1. Raise and safely support the vehicle. Remove the front wheel.
2. Remove the lower control arm. Using a flat blade tool, pry off the seal from the ball joint.
3. Position a receiving cup, special tool 6758 or its equivalent, to support the lower control arm.
4. Install remover, special tool 6919 or its equivalent, over the stud and against the joint upper housing.
5. Using an arbor press, press the joint assembly from the lower control arm.

To install:

6. Position the ball joint housing into the control arm cavity. Be sure the ball joint is not cocked in the control arm bore, or this will cause the ball joint to bind. The notch in the ball joint stud must face inward to the control arm to allow for clearance of the ball joint-to-steering knuckle clamp bolt.
7. Position the assembly in a press with special tool 6758 or its equivalent, supporting the control arm.
8. Position the ball joint installer special tool 6908–4 or its equivalent, on the bottom of the ball joint.
9. Carefully align the ball joint assembly. Using a press, apply pressure against the control arm assembly until the housing ledge of the ball joint assembly seats completely against the lower control arm surface and there is no gap between the lower control arm and ball joint. Be careful not to apply excessive force on the ball joint or the control arm.
10. Install a new seal boot as far as it will go on the ball joint by hand, first making sure the shield of the ball joint seal is facing outward from the end of the control arm.
11. Grease the ball joint using MOPAR® Multi-Mile grease, or equivalent. Do NOT over grease the ball joint or this will prevent the seal boot from being properly installed.
12. To install the new seal, place special tool 6758 or equivalent, over the seal boot and align it squarely with the bottom edge of the seal boot. Apply

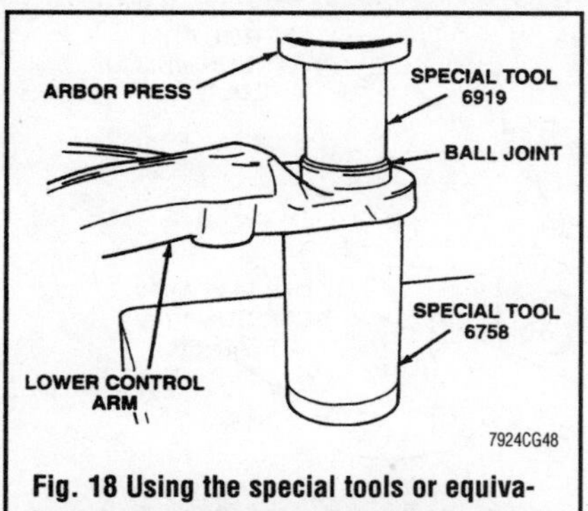

Fig. 18 Using the special tools or equivalent size sockets, press the ball joint from the lower control arm—1996–99 models

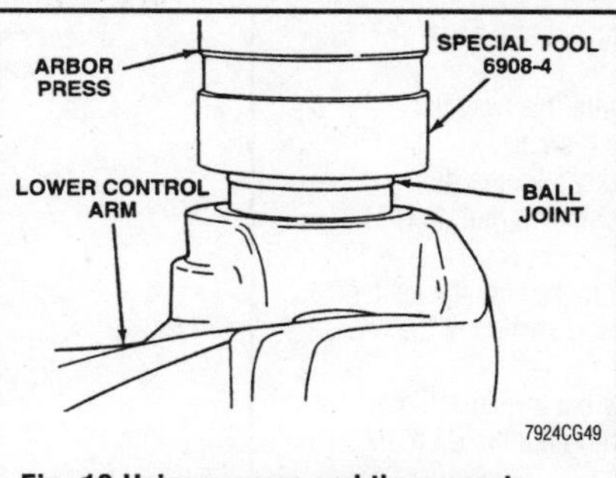

Fig. 19 Using a press and the correct adapters, carefully press the new ball joint into the lower control arm—1996–99 models

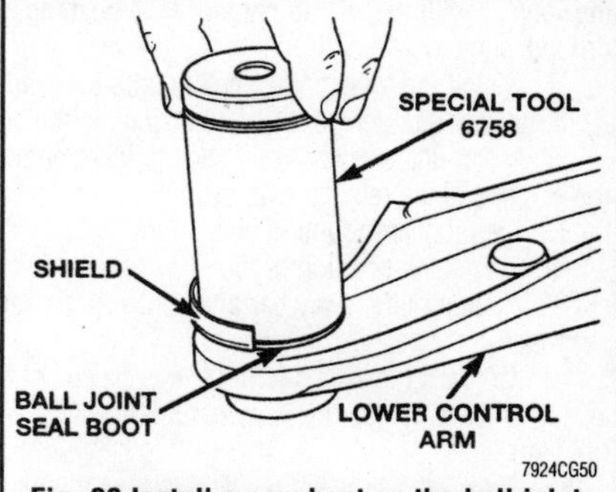

Fig. 20 Install a new boot on the ball joint using tool No. 6758 or an equivalent socket—1996–99 models

hand pressure only, until the new seal boot is against the top surface of the control arm.

13. Install the control arm in the vehicle.
14. Install the front wheel and lug nuts. Tighten the lug nuts to 95 ft. lbs. (129 Nm).
15. Lower the vehicle. Check the wheel alignment.
16. Road test the vehicle.

Sway Bar

REMOVAL & INSTALLATION

See Figures 21, 22, 23 and 24

1. Raise and safely support the front of the vehicle on jack stands or a frame contact hoist.
2. Remove the 10 mounting bolts securing the cradle plate to the front suspension cradle. Remove the cradle plate from the vehicle.
3. Remove the nuts connecting the sway bar connecting links to each end of the sway bar. Disconnect the links from the ends of the sway bar.
4. Remove the sway bar bushing retainers from the front suspension cradle and remove the sway bar and bushings as an assembly from the vehicle.
5. Inspect the bushings for wear. Replace as necessary. Center bushings are split, and are removed by opening the split and sliding from the sway bar.

To install:

6. If required, install the new sway bar-to-crossmember bushings on the sway bar with the split in the replacement bushing positioned toward the rear of

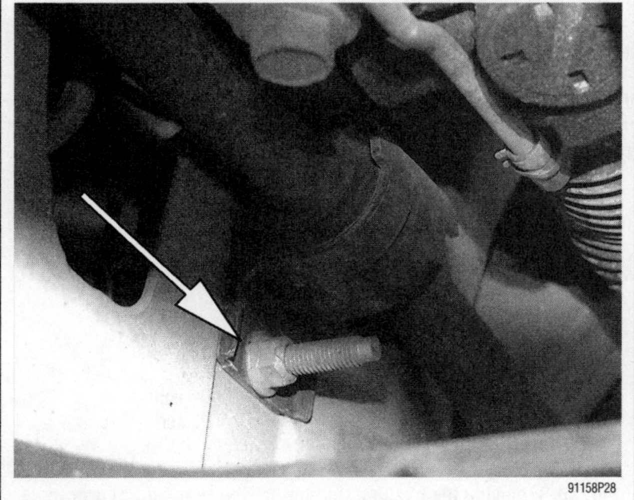

Fig. 21 Remove the front sway bar bushing retainer nuts

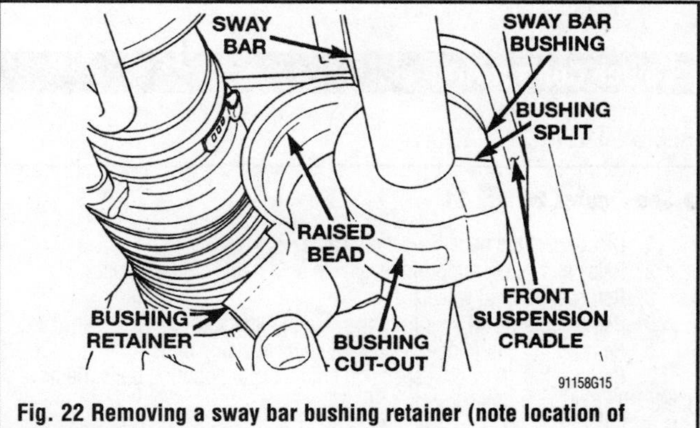

Fig. 22 Removing a sway bar bushing retainer (note location of bushing)

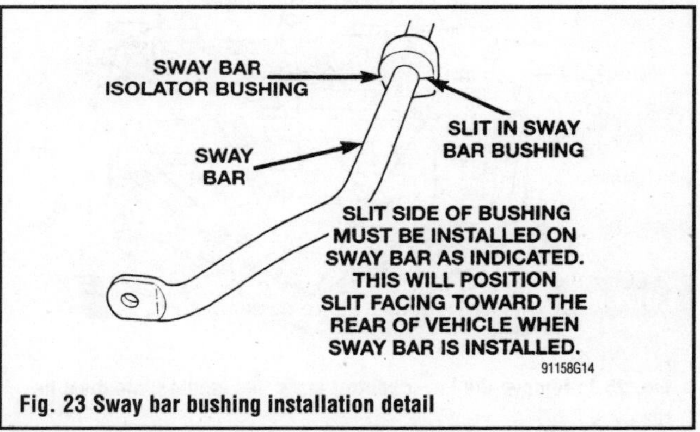

Fig. 23 Sway bar bushing installation detail

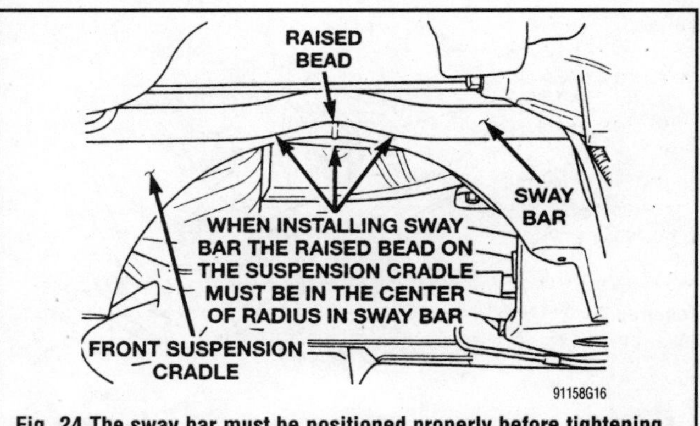

Fig. 24 The sway bar must be positioned properly before tightening the bushing retainers

the vehicle, with the square corner of the bushing facing down toward the ground when installed.

7. Install the sway bar assembly onto the cradle. Be sure the sway bar bushings are aligned with the depressions in the suspension cradle.

8. Install the sway bar bushing retainers onto the cradle, aligning the raised bead of the retainer with the cutouts in the bushings. Install, but do NOT tighten the retainer mounting bolts at this time.

9. Check the position of the sway bar at this time and make sure the center curved section of the sway bar lines up with the center curved section of the suspension cradle.

10. Connect the sway bar links to each end of the sway bar and install the attaching nuts. Torque the sway bar link-to-sway bar attaching nuts to 65 ft. lbs. (88 Nm).

11. Torque the sway bar bushing retainer mounting bolts to 50 ft. lbs. (68 Nm).

12. Install the front suspension cradle plate to the front suspension cradle and install the mounting bolts. Torque the 10 cradle plate mounting bolts to 123 ft. lbs. (165 Nm).

13. Lower the vehicle.

14. Check the wheel alignment.

Lower Control Arm

REMOVAL & INSTALLATION

See Figures 25 thru 31

1. Disconnect the negative battery cable.
2. Raise and safely support the vehicle on a frame contact hoist.
3. Remove the front wheels.
4. Remove the wheel stop from the steering knuckle.
5. Remove the ball joint–to–steering knuckle clamp bolts.
6. Remove the 10 front suspension cradle plate mounting bolts. Remove the cradle plate from the vehicle.

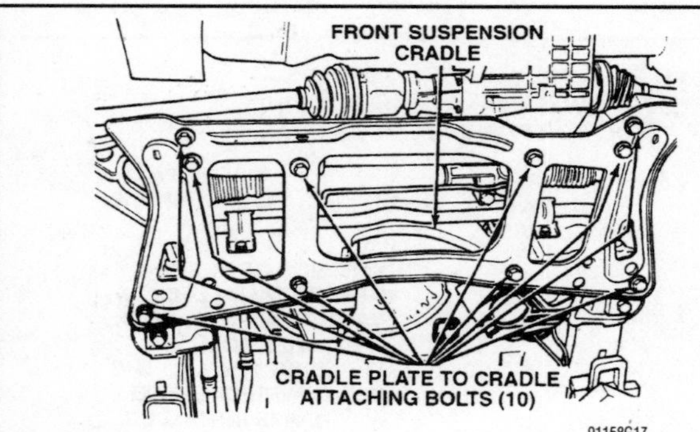

Fig. 25 To remove the lower control arms, the cradle plate must be removed

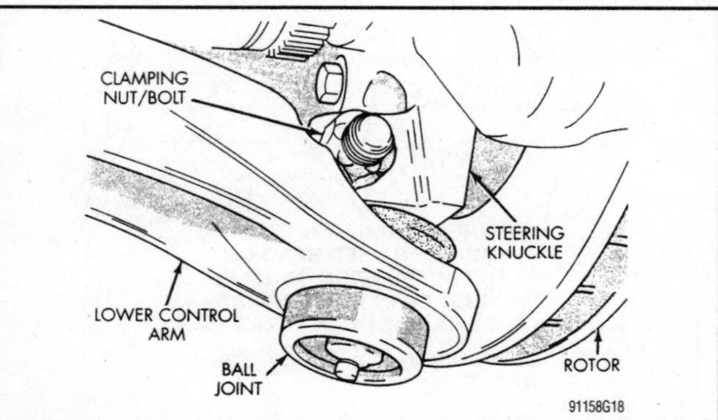

Fig. 26 Remove the steering knuckle clamping bolt and nut, then separate the ball joint

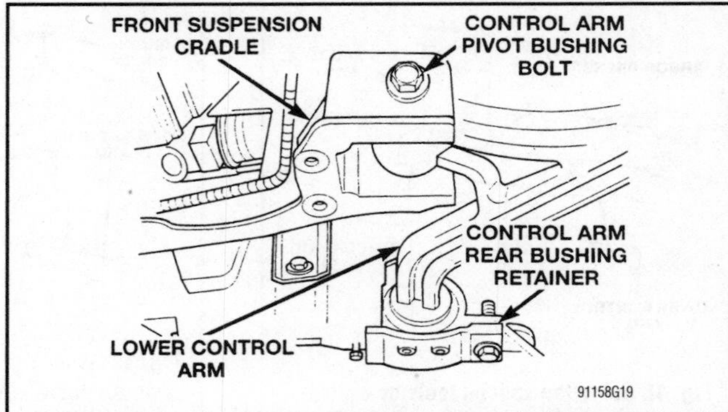

Fig. 27 With the cradle plate removed, the control arm rear bushing retainer bolts can be accessed, as well as the cradle mounting bolts

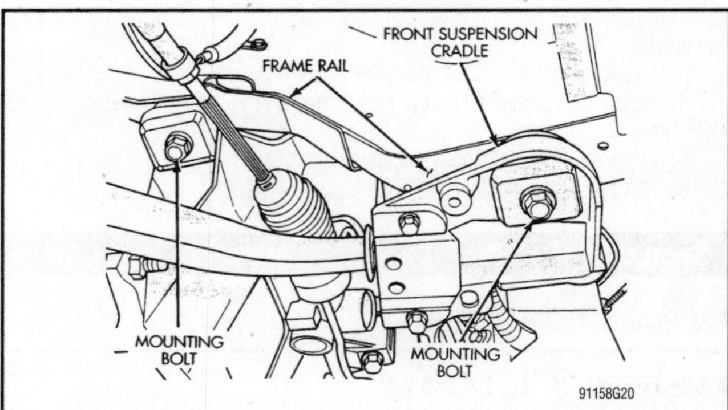

Fig. 28 To allow the control arm pivot bolts to be removed, loosen (but do NOT remove) the cradle-to-frame rail mounting bolts

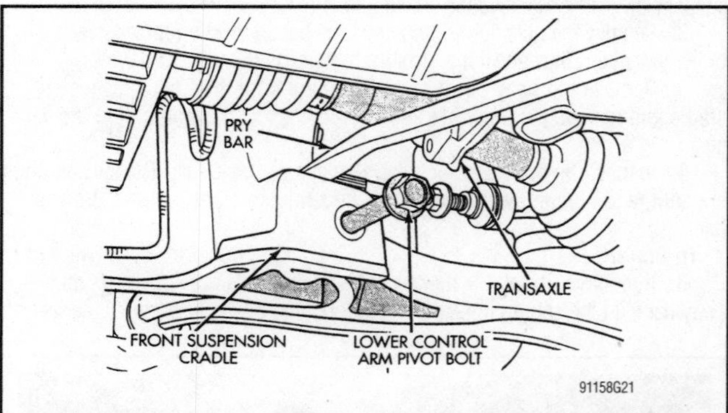

Fig. 29 Carefully pry the cradle downward to allow the pivot bolt to be removed

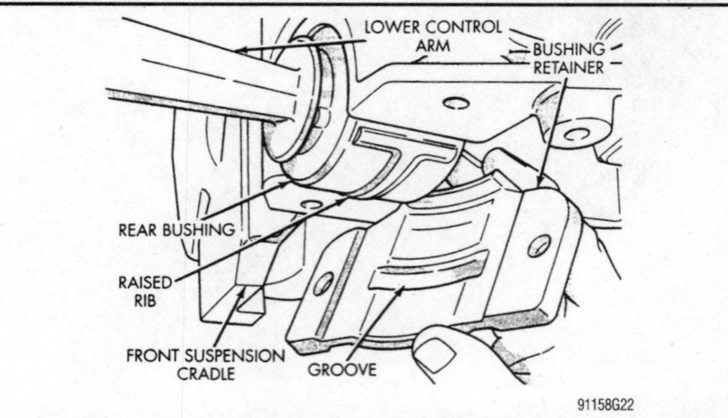

Fig. 30 Removing the bushing retainer for the rear control arm (note groove in the retainer that aligns with bushing)

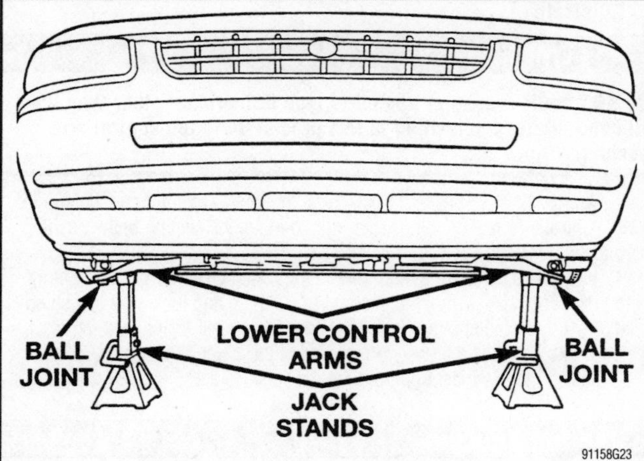

Fig. 31 The full weight of the vehicle must be on the control arms before the pivot bolts are tightened; the bushings will prematurely fail if this is not performed

***** WARNING**

Pulling the steering knuckle out from the vehicle after releasing it from the ball joint can separate the inner CV-Joint. Use care NOT to allow the inner CV-Joint to separate. In addition, DO NOT use substitute fasteners of a lower grade (strength) than those originally used.

7. Separate the ball joint stud from the steering knuckle by prying between the ball stud at the knuckle and the lower control arm. Be careful not to tear the ball joint seal.
8. Loosen, but **do not** remove the front lower control arm-to-suspension cradle pivot bolt.
9. Remove the retainer that secures the rear lower control arm bushing to the front suspension cradle.

➡If the left side lower control arm requires removal, lower the front suspension cradle to allow the pivot bolt to clear the transaxle.

10. Loosen, but **do not** fully remove the 2 left side suspension cradle mounting bolts and lower the cradle.
11. Lower the left front corner of the suspension cradle until the lower control arm pivot bolt clears the transaxle. Remove the pivot bolt and lower control arm from the vehicle. Inspect the lower control arm for distortion and bushings for excessive deterioration. Replace if necessary.

To install:

12. Place the lower control arm into the front suspension cradle and install the front lower control arm-to-suspension cradle pivot bolt. **Do not** tighten or torque the pivot bolt at this time.
13. If installing the left side lower control arm, pry down on the left front corner of the suspension cradle to allow the pivot bolt to clear the end of the transaxle. Install the pivot bolt into the suspension cradle and lower control arm.
14. Install the lower control arm rear bushing retainer. Be sure the raised rib of the rear bushing is correctly seated in the groove of the bushing retainer. **Do not** torque the retainer mounting bolts at this time.
15. Insert the ball joint stud into the steering knuckle and install the clamp bolt. Torque the clamp bolt to 105 ft. lbs. (145 Nm).
16. Install the front suspension cradle plate to the suspension cradle and install the 10 mounting bolts. Torque the cradle plate mounting bolts to 123 ft. lbs. (165 Nm).
17. Place jack stands underneath the lower control arms **as close to, but not on**, the ball joints as possible.
18. Lower the vehicle onto the jack stands until the vehicle's total weight is supported by the jack stands.
19. Torque the front lower control arm pivot bolt to 120 ft. lbs. (163 Nm).
20. Torque the lower control arm rear bushing retainer mounting bolts to 50 ft. lbs. (68 Nm).
21. Install the front wheels and lug nuts. Torque the lug nuts, in a star pattern, to 95 ft. lbs. (129 Nm).
22. Remove the jack stands and lower the vehicle to the ground.
23. Reconnect the negative battery cable. Inspect wheel alignment and adjust, if necessary.
24. Road test the vehicle.

CONTROL ARM BUSHING REPLACEMENT

➡Special Chrysler Tools 6908–1, 6908–2, 6908–3, 6908–4 and 6908–5 or equivalents, are required to remove and install the control arm bushings.

Front Bushing

▸ See Figures 32, 33 and 34

1. Remove the lower control arm.
2. Mount the control arm in a vise without using excessive clamping force.
3. Assemble for removal of the front bushing, the bushing reciever special tool 6908–2, bushing remover special tool 6908–1, nut special tool 6908–3 thrust washer, threaded rod and small nut.
4. To remove the front bushing from the lower control arm, hold the threaded rod stationary and tighten the nut special tool 6908–3. This will force the front bushing out of the lower control arm and into the bushing reciever tool.

To install:

5. Mount the control arm in a vise.
6. Position the front bushing into the lower control arm so that the 2 rubber blocks on the bushing are positioned horizontally.
7. Assemble for installation of the front bushing, the bushing reciever special tool 6908–5, bushing installer special tool 6908–4, nut special tool 6908–3 thrust washer, threaded rod and small nut onto the control arm and front bushing.
8. To install the front bushing into the lower control arm, hold the threaded

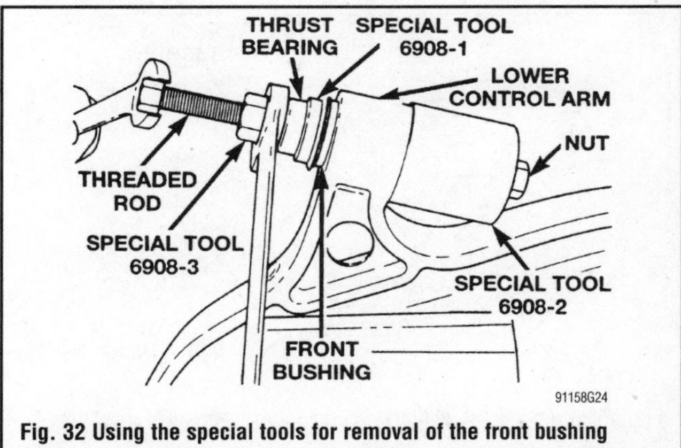

Fig. 32 Using the special tools for removal of the front bushing

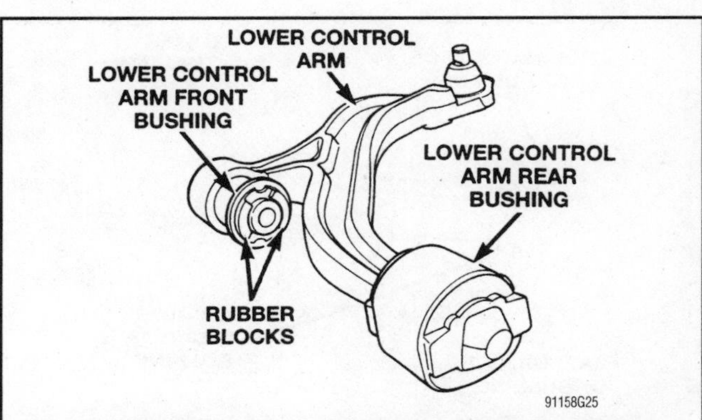

Fig. 33 Positioning the new bushing for installation into the control arm

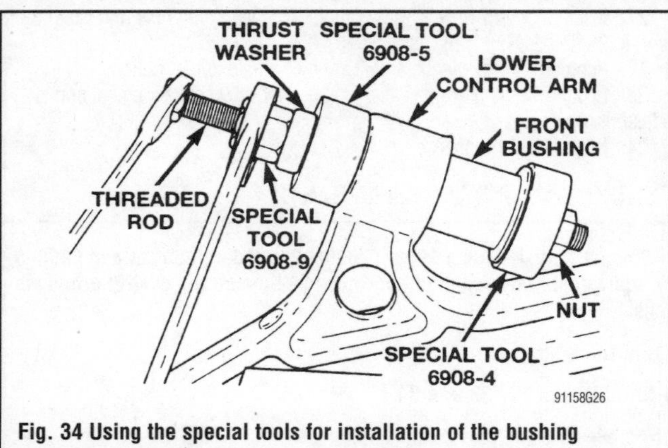

Fig. 34 Using the special tools for installation of the bushing

rod stationary and tighten the nut special tool 6908–3. This will pull the front bushing into the lower control arm.

9. Continue pulling the front bushing into the control arm until it seats squarely against the control arm and there is no gap between the bushing and control arm.
10. Install the lower control arm onto the vehicle.

Rear Bushing

➧ **See Figures 35 and 36**

1. Remove the lower control arm.
2. Mount the control arm in a vise without using excessive clamping force.
3. Using a sharp cutting tool (such as a razor), slit the rear bushing lengthwise to allow its removal from the control arm.
4. Remove the bushing from the control arm.

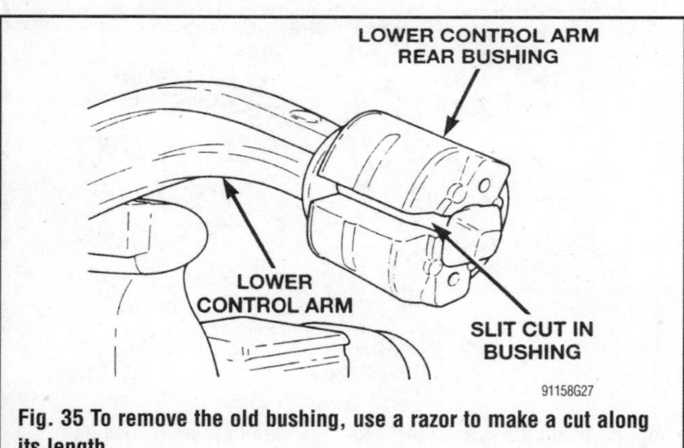

Fig. 35 To remove the old bushing, use a razor to make a cut along its length

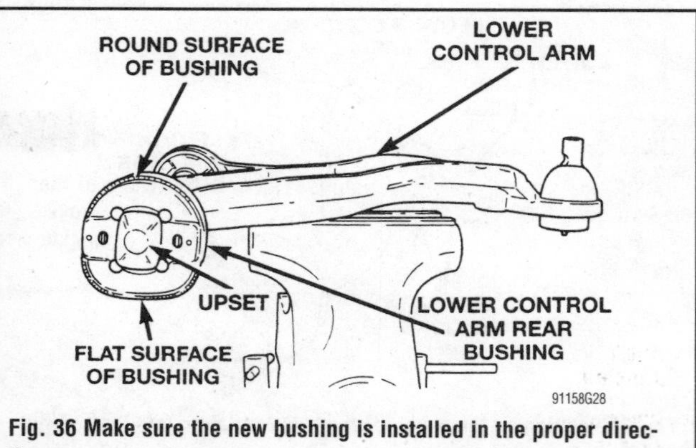

Fig. 36 Make sure the new bushing is installed in the proper direction

To install:

✲✲ WARNING

Do NOT apply grease or any other type of lubricant other than the silicone lubricant specified in this procedure to the control arm bushing.

5. Apply MOPAR® Silicone Spray Lube, or an equivalent, to the hole in the lower control arm rear bushing. This will aid in the installation of the bushing onto the control arm.
6. With the control arm held firmly in the bench vise, install the bushing onto the control arm. Install the bushing by pushing and rocking the bushing until it is fully installed onto the control arm. Be sure when the bushing is installed that it is past the upset on the end of the lower control arm.
7. Install the lower control arm onto the vehicle.

Steering Knuckle

REMOVAL & INSTALLATION

➧ **See Figures 37 thru 44**

1. Disconnect the negative battery cable.
2. Remove the cotter pin from the end of the stub axle. Remove the nut lock and spring washer. With the brakes applied, loosen, but do NOT remove the axle nut and washer with the vehicle still on the ground or damage to the wheel bearing will result.
3. Raise and safely support the vehicle. Remove the wheel.
4. Remove the front brake caliper assembly from the steering knuckle assembly and support from the strut assembly using a strong piece of wire.
5. Remove the front brake rotor from the hub/bearing assembly.
6. Remove the retaining nut and washer from the halfshaft stub axle.

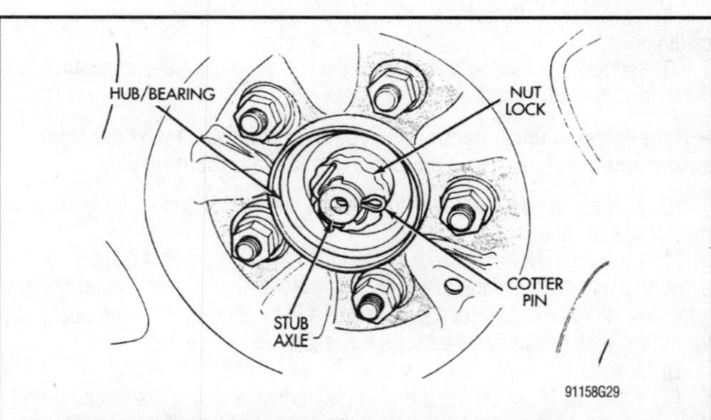

Fig. 37 Before raising the vehicle, remove the cotter pin and nut lock, and slightly loosen the axle nut

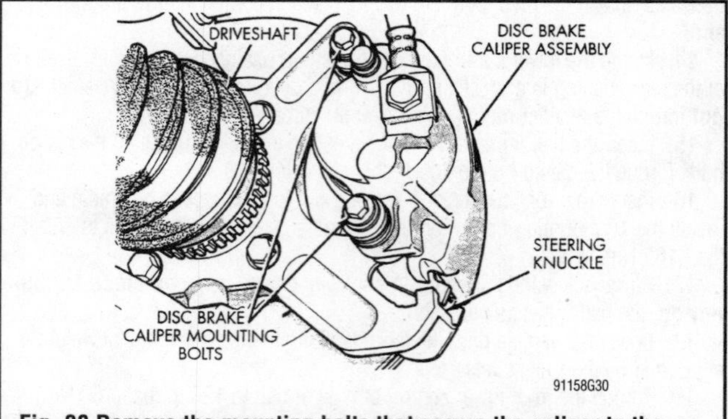

Fig. 38 Remove the mounting bolts that secure the caliper to the steering knuckle

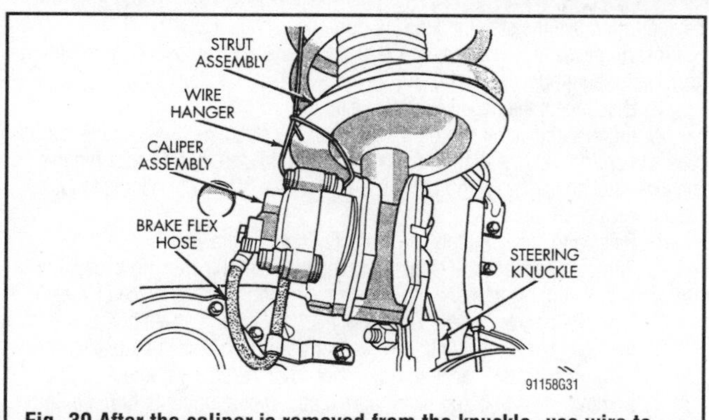

Fig. 39 After the caliper is removed from the knuckle, use wire to suspend it from the strut

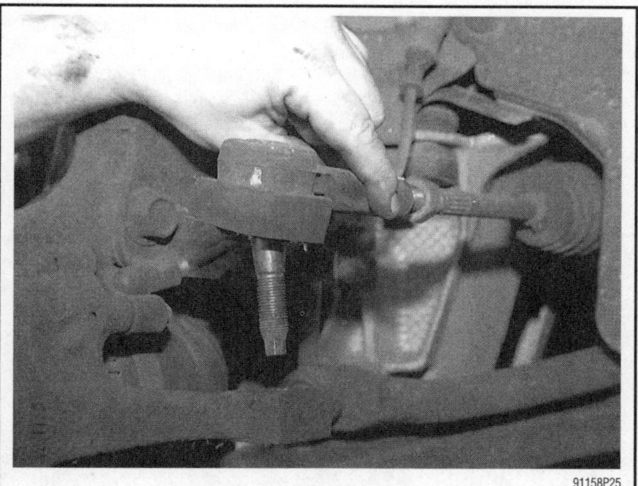

Fig. 40 Next, remove the tie rod from the steering knuckle

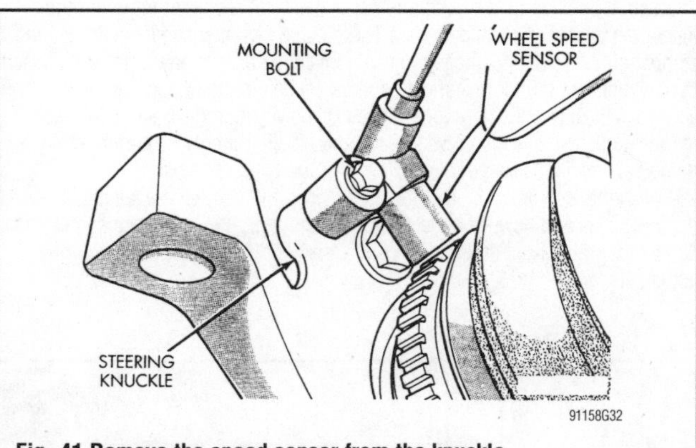

Fig. 41 Remove the speed sensor from the knuckle

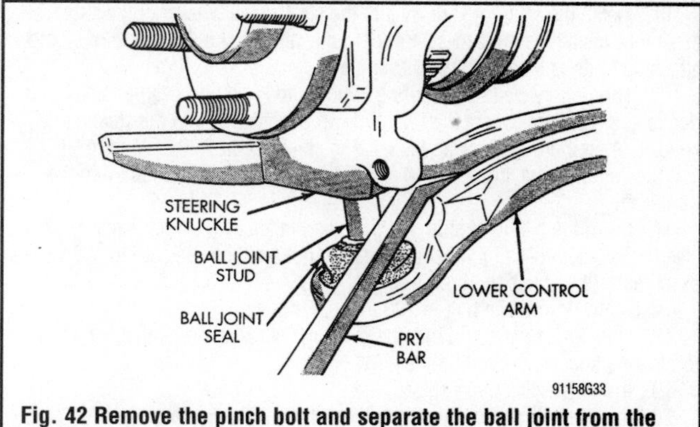

Fig. 42 Remove the pinch bolt and separate the ball joint from the knuckle

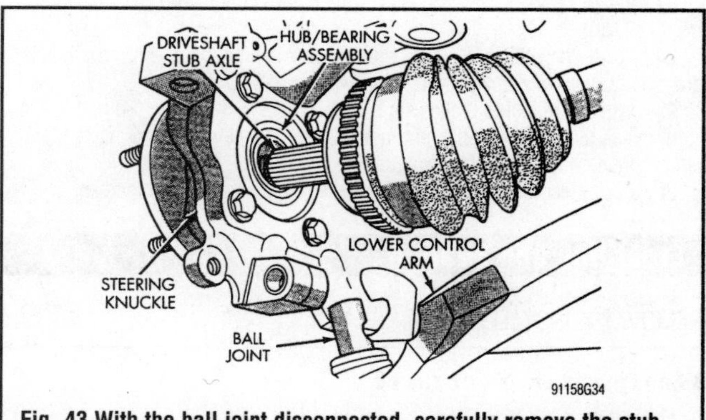

Fig. 43 With the ball joint disconnected, carefully remove the stub axle from the hub

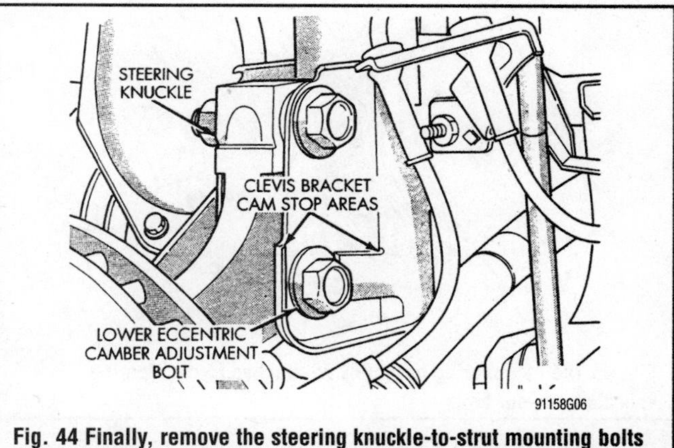

Fig. 44 Finally, remove the steering knuckle-to-strut mounting bolts

7. Separate the outer tie rod from the steering knuckle.
8. Remove the ABS wheel speed sensor from the steering knuckle.
9. Remove the wheel stop from the steering knuckle, if equipped.
10. Remove the nut and bolt that clamps the steering knuckle to the ball joint stud. Using a prybar, pry the control arm down to release the ball stud from the steering knuckle. Be careful not to tear the ball joint grease seal when prying down from the steering knuckle.
11. Separate the outer CV-joint splined shaft from the hub and bearing assembly by holding the CV-joint housing and pulling the steering knuckle away. Be careful not to damage the outer CV-joint wear sleeve or separate the inner CV-joint.
12. Support the halfshaft assembly at the CV-joint housing. Pull the knuckle assembly away from the halfshaft. Take care not separate the halfshaft inner CV-Joint, or damage to the CV-Joint will occur. Support the halfshaft.

**** WARNING**

The steering knuckle-to-strut assembly attaching bolts are of the serrated type and must NOT be turned during the removal procedure. Be sure to hold the bolts stationary in the steering knuckle while removing the nuts

13. Remove the 2 steering knuckle-to-strut clevis bracket mounting bolts and remove the steering knuckle from the vehicle.

To install:

➡If equipped with eccentric strut assembly attaching bolts, it must be installed in the bottom (slotted) hole of the strut clevis bracket.

14. Install the steering knuckle into the strut clevis bracket of the strut assembly. Install the strut-to-steering knuckle attaching bolts and torque both attaching bolts to 65 ft. lbs. (90 Nm) plus an additional 1/4 turn.
15. Thoroughly clean the steering knuckle and hub and bearing area of all debris and moisture, where the CV-joint will be installed into the steering knuckle. Also thoroughly clean the bearing shield of the outer CV-joint.
16. Pull the front strut out and insert the splined outer CV-joint into the front hub.
17. Insert the ball joint stud into the steering knuckle clamp. Install a **new** steering knuckle-to-ball joint stud clamping nut and bolt. Be sure to use an exact replacement nut and bolt during installation. Torque the bolt to 105 ft. lbs. (145 Nm).
18. Install the tie rod end into the steering knuckle. Torque the tie rod end-to-steering knuckle nut to 45 ft. lbs. (61 Nm).
19. Install the disc brake rotor.
20. Install the brake caliper assembly onto the steering knuckle.
21. Install the axle washer and nut. Tighten but do not torque.
22. Install the ABS wheel speed sensor.
23. Install the wheel and lug nuts. Torque the lug nuts, in sequence, to 95 ft. lbs. (129 Nm).
24. Lower the vehicle. Do NOT roll the vehicle until the axle nut has been properly torqued or damage to the front wheel bearings will result.
25. With the vehicle's brakes applied, torque the axle nut to 180 ft. lbs. (244 Nm). Install the spring washer, nut lock and a new cotter pin. Wrap the cotter pin prongs tightly around the axle nut lock.
26. Reconnect the negative battery cable. Check the wheel alignment.

Front Hub and Bearing

REMOVAL & INSTALLATION

See Figures 45, 46, 47 and 48

The hub and wheel bearing unit is serviced as a complete assembly. Replacement of the front drive hub and bearing assembly can be done without having to remove the steering knuckle from the vehicle. However, if the hub/bearing assembly is frozen to the steering knuckle, removal of the steering knuckle is required.

1. Disconnect the negative battery cable.
2. Remove the cotter pin from the end of the stub axle. Remove the nut lock and spring washer. With the brakes applied, loosen, but do NOT remove the axle nut and washer with the vehicle still on the ground or damage to the wheel bearing will result.
3. Raise and safely support the vehicle. Remove the wheel.
4. Remove the front brake caliper assembly from the steering knuckle assembly and support from the strut assembly using a strong piece of wire.
5. Remove the front brake rotor from the hub/bearing assembly.
6. Remove the retaining nut and washer from the halfshaft stub axle.
7. Remove the ABS wheel speed sensor from the steering knuckle.
8. Remove the 4 hub and bearing assembly mounting bolts from behind the steering knuckle.
9. Remove the hub and bearing assembly from the steering knuckle.

To install:

10. Thoroughly clean the mating surfaces of the steering knuckle and the hub and bearing assembly of any foreign material or nicks so the surfaces are clean and smooth.
11. Install the new hub and bearing assembly and tighten the mounting bolts in a crisscross pattern to 45 ft. lbs. (65 Nm). Be sure the hub and bearing assembly is seated squarely against the front steering knuckle.
12. Install the disc brake rotor.
13. Install the brake caliper assembly onto the steering knuckle.
14. Install the axle washer and nut. Tighten but do not torque.
15. Install the ABS wheel speed sensor.
16. Install the wheel and lug nuts. Torque the lug nuts, in sequence, to 95 ft. lbs. (129 Nm).
17. Lower the vehicle. Do NOT roll the vehicle until the axle nut has been properly torqued or damage to the front wheel bearings will result.
18. With the vehicle's brakes applied, torque the axle nut to 180 ft. lbs. (244 Nm). Install the spring washer, nut lock and a new cotter pin. Wrap the cotter pin prongs tightly around the axle nut lock.
19. Reconnect the negative battery cable. Check the wheel alignment.

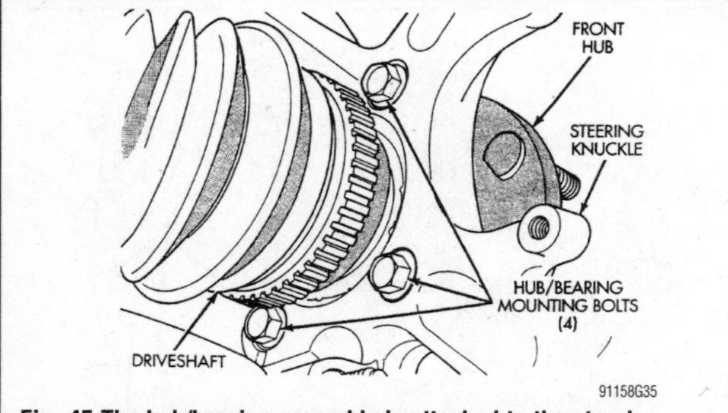

Fig. 45 The hub/bearing assembly is attached to the steering knuckle with four bolts

Wheel Alignment

If the tires are worn unevenly, if the vehicle is not stable on the highway or if the handling seems uneven in spirited driving, the wheel alignment should be checked. If an alignment problem is suspected, first check for improper tire inflation and other possible causes. These can be worn suspension or steering components, accident damage or even unmatched tires. If any worn or damaged components are found, they must be replaced before the wheels can be properly aligned. Wheel alignment requires very expensive equipment and involves minute adjustments which must be accurate; it should only be performed by a trained technician. Take your vehicle to a properly equipped shop.

Following is a description of the alignment angles which are adjustable on most vehicles and how they affect vehicle handling. Although these angles can apply to both the front and rear wheels, usually only the front suspension is adjustable.

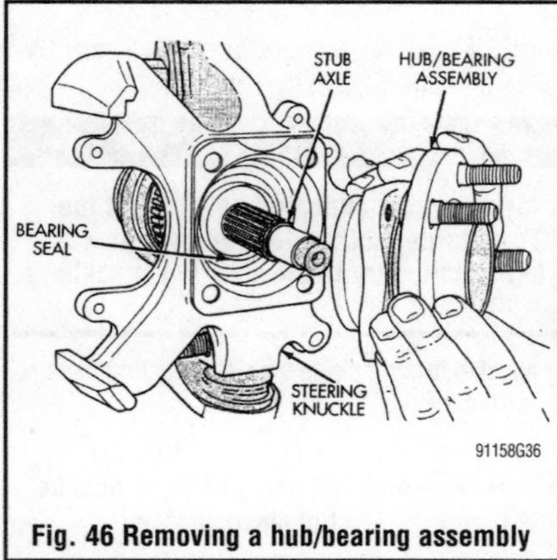

Fig. 46 Removing a hub/bearing assembly

Fig. 47 If the hub/bearing is "frozen" to the steering knuckle, separate the ball joint and lightly tap on the hub/bearing from behind

Fig. 48 The hub/bearing assembly should free itself from the steering knuckle

CASTER

➧ See Figure 49

Looking at a vehicle from the side, caster angle describes the steering axis rather than a wheel angle. The steering knuckle is attached to a control arm or strut at the top and a control arm at the bottom. The wheel pivots around the line between these points to steer the vehicle. When the upper point is tilted back, this is described as positive caster. Having a positive caster tends to make the wheels self-centering, increasing directional stability. Excessive positive caster makes the wheels hard to steer, while an uneven caster will cause a pull to one side. Overloading the vehicle or sagging rear springs will affect caster, as will raising the rear of the vehicle. If the rear of the vehicle is lower than normal, the caster becomes more positive.

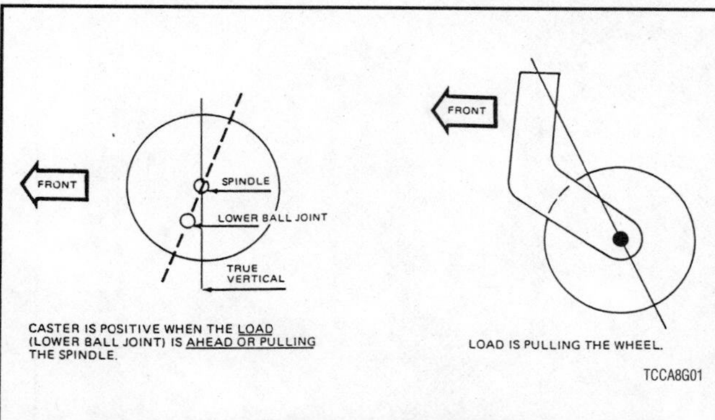

Fig. 49 Caster affects straight-line stability. Caster wheels used on shopping carts, for example, employ positive caster

CAMBER

➧ See Figures 50, 51 and 52

Looking from the front of the vehicle, camber is the inward or outward tilt of the top of wheels. When the tops of the wheels are tilted in, this is negative camber; if they are tilted out, it is positive. In a turn, a slight amount of negative camber helps maximize contact of the tire with the road. However, too much negative camber compromises straight-line stability, increases bump steer and torque steer.

TOE

➧ See Figures 53 and 54

Looking down at the wheels from above the vehicle, toe angle is the distance between the front of the wheels, relative to the distance between the back of the wheels. If the wheels are closer at the front, they are said to be toed-in or to have negative toe. A small amount of negative toe enhances directional stability and provides a smoother ride on the highway.

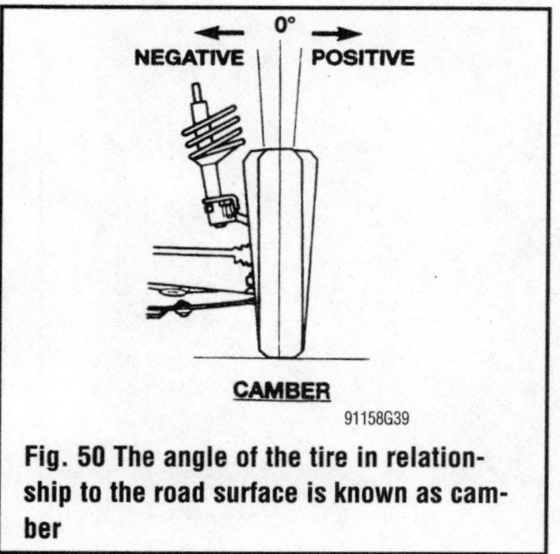

Fig. 50 The angle of the tire in relationship to the road surface is known as camber

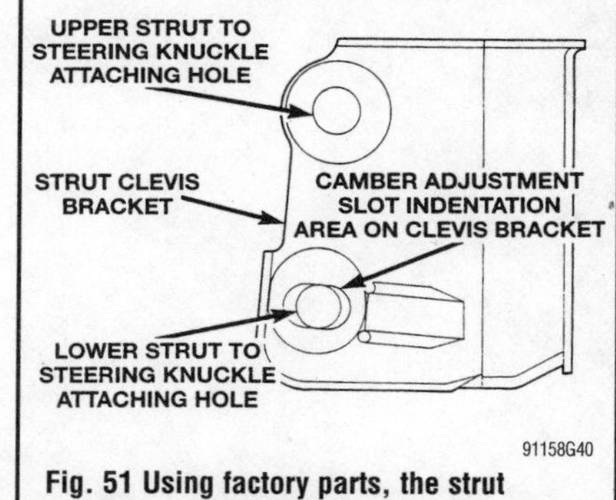

Fig. 51 Using factory parts, the strut mounts can be modified to allow for camber adjustment

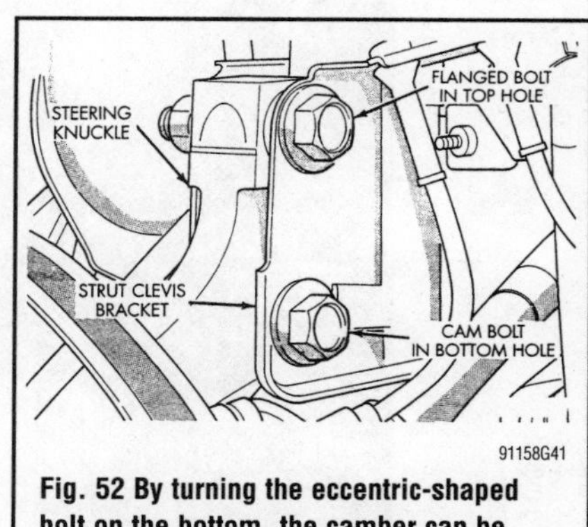

Fig. 52 By turning the eccentric-shaped bolt on the bottom, the camber can be changed

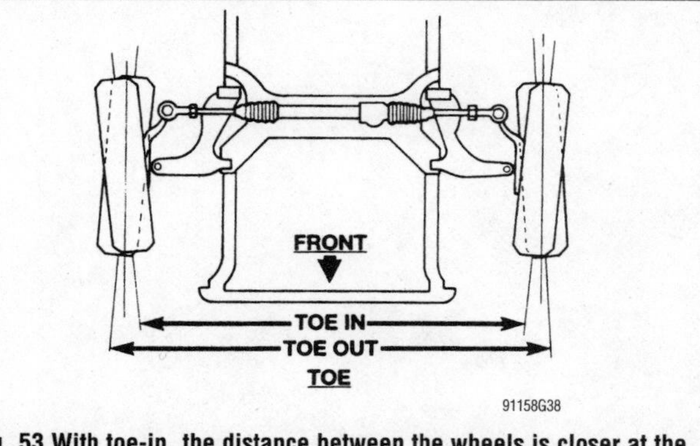

Fig. 53 With toe-in, the distance between the wheels is closer at the front than at the rear

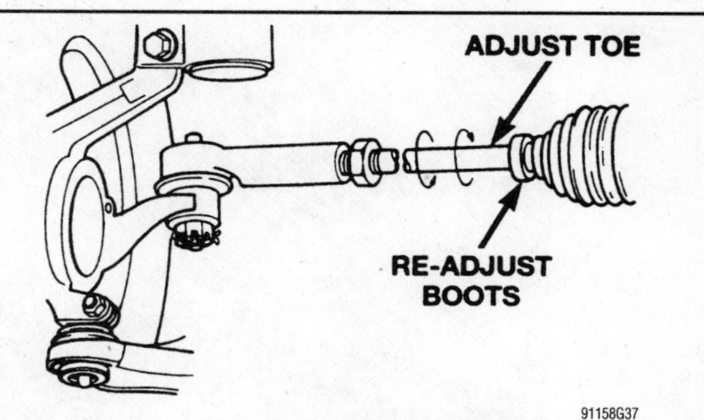

Fig. 54 By adjusting the length of the tie rods, the toe can be changed

REAR SUSPENSION

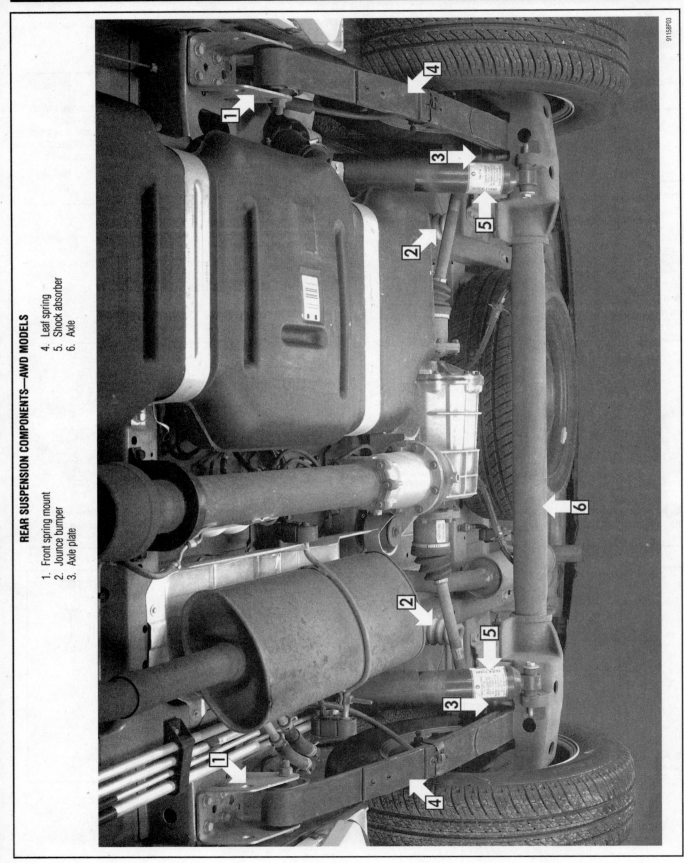

REAR SUSPENSION COMPONENTS—AWD MODELS

1. Front spring mount
2. Jounce bumper
3. Axle plate
4. Leaf spring
5. Shock absorber
6. Axle

91158P03

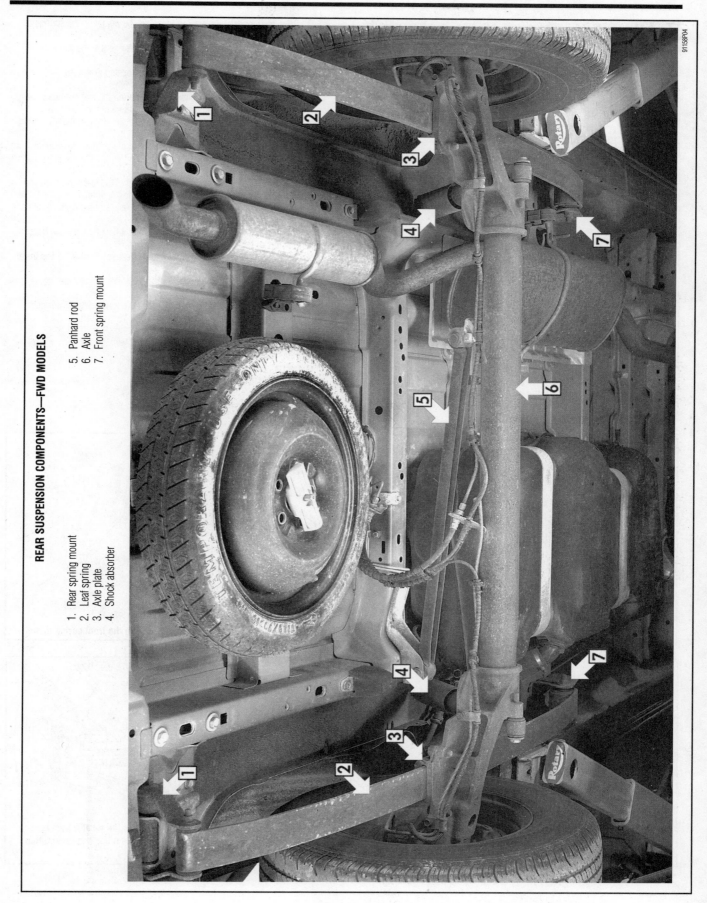

REAR SUSPENSION COMPONENTS—FWD MODELS

1. Rear spring mount
2. Leaf spring
3. Axle plate
4. Shock absorber
5. Panhard rod
6. Axle
7. Front spring mount

Leaf Springs

REMOVAL & INSTALLATION

See Figures 55 thru 61

1. Raise and safely support the rear of the vehicle on safety stands. Locate the safety stands under the frame contact points to a comfortable working position.

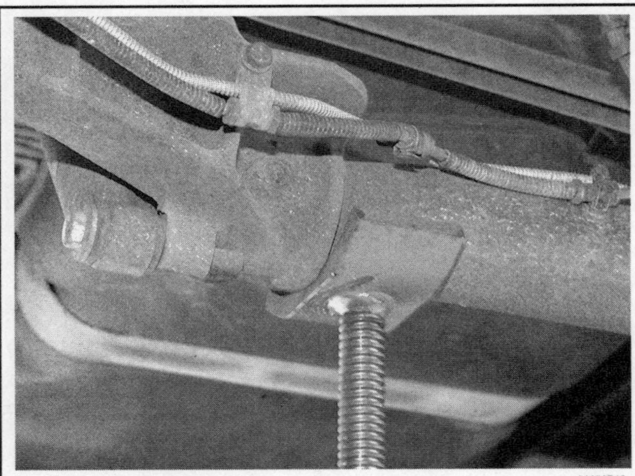

Fig. 55 Make sure to support the axle before loosening the axle plate bolts

2. Raise the rear axle just enough to relieve the weight on the springs and support on safety stands.
3. Disconnect the lower ends of the shock absorbers at the rear axle bracket.
4. Loosen and remove the axle plate bolts located at the leaf springs.
5. Lower the rear axle assembly slightly to permit the rear springs to hang free. Support the spring and remove the 4 bolts that mount the front spring hanger. Remove the rear spring shackle nuts and plate. Remove the leaf spring from the shackle.
6. Remove the rear leaf spring assembly from the vehicle. Remove the front pivot bolt from the front leaf spring mount.

To install:

7. Install the front spring mount onto the front of the leaf spring eye and install pivot bolt and nut. Start the pivot nuts but do not tighten completely. Be sure to install the the pivot bolt so it is facing inboard to prevent structural damage.
8. Raise the front of the spring and install the 4 hanger mounting bolts. Tighten the mounting bolts to 45 ft. lbs. (61 Nm).
9. Install the rear of the leaf spring onto the rear spring shackle and install the shackle plate, but do not tighten.
10. Check to be sure the lower leaf spring isolator is in proper position.
11. Raise the axle assembly and align under the leaf spring locator post. Install the rear axle plate bolts and torque to 80 ft. lbs. (108 Nm).
12. Install the rear shock absorber to the lower brackets.
13. Lower the vehicle to the ground so the full weight is on the springs. Tighten the mounting components as follows:
    a. Front pivot bolt: 115 ft. lbs. (156 Nm)
    b. Shackle nuts: 45 ft. lbs. (61 Nm)
    c. Shock absorber bolts: 75 ft. lbs. (101 Nm)
14. Road test the vehicle.

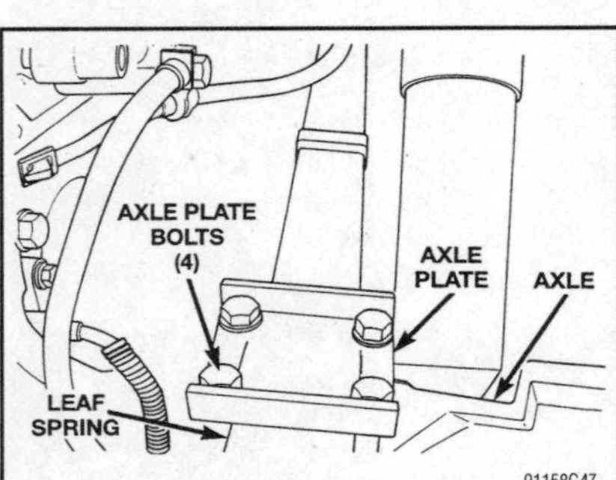

Fig. 56 To disconnect the leaf spring from the axle, the four axle plate bolts need to be removed

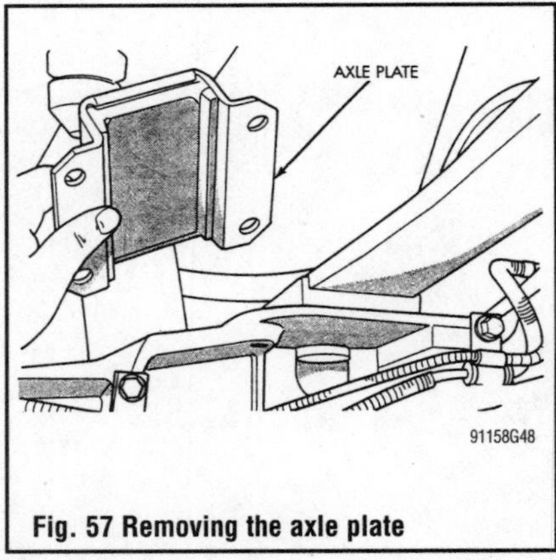

Fig. 57 Removing the axle plate

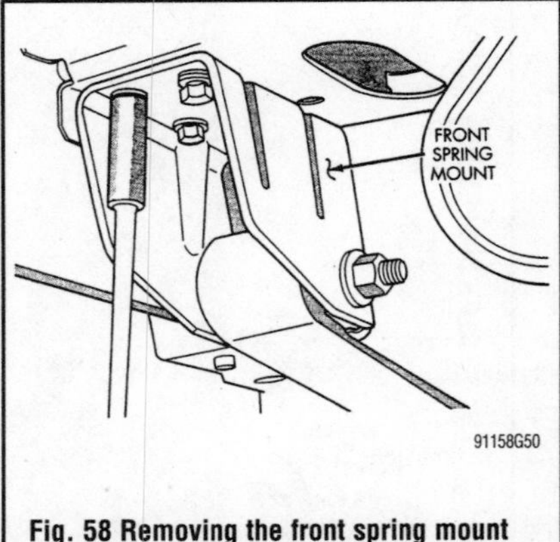

Fig. 58 Removing the front spring mount

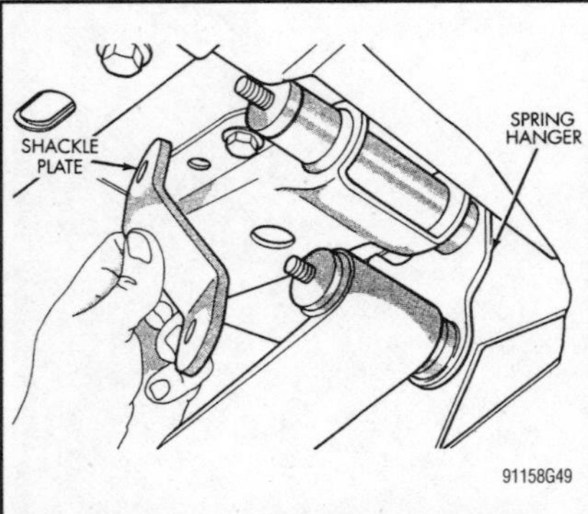

Fig. 59 Removing the rear spring from the hanger

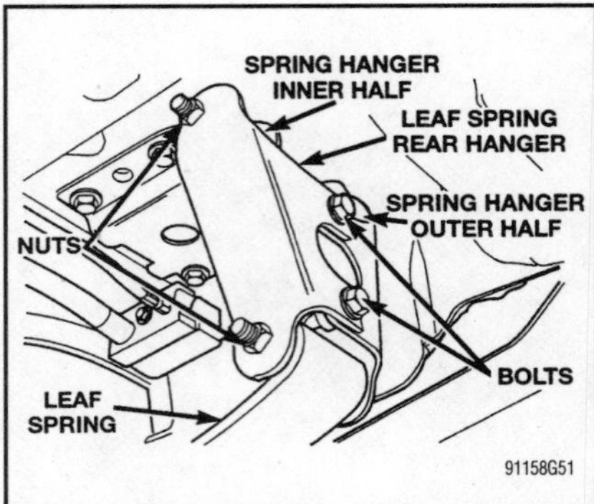

Fig. 60 The rear spring mount on AWD vehicles is slightly different

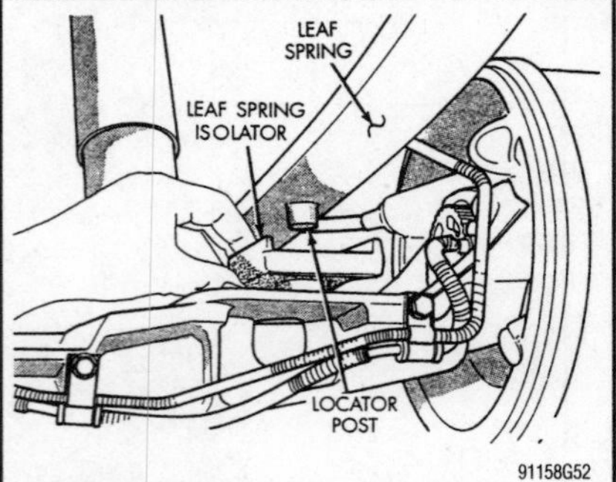

Fig. 61 Make sure the locator post is aligned with the isolator and indentation in the axle

Shock Absorbers

REMOVAL & INSTALLATION

See Figure 62

1. Raise and safely support the vehicle with safety stands.
2. Support the rear axle with a floor jack.
3. Remove the top and bottom shock absorber bolts.
4. Remove the shock absorbers.

To install:

5. Place the new shock in position and install the mounting bolts. For 1993–95, tighten to 80 ft. lbs. (108 Nm) for the lower bolts and 85 ft. lbs (115 Nm) for the upper bolts. For 1996–97, torque the shock absorber mounting bolts to 75 ft. lbs. (101 Nm).
6. Remove the floor jack supporting the rear axle and lower the vehicle to the ground.

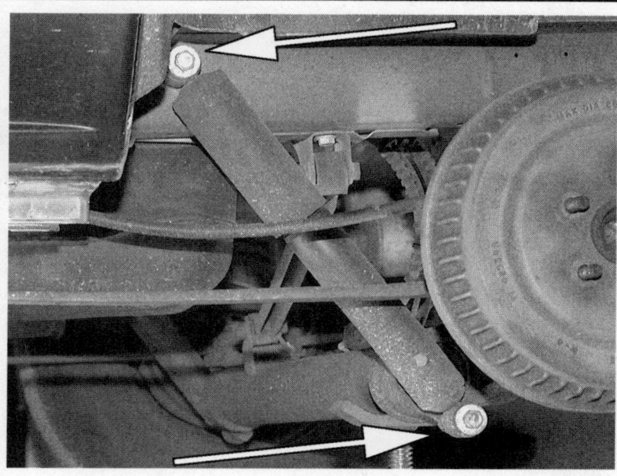

91158P17

Fig. 62 The rear shock absorbers are attached with two bolts

TESTING

See Figure 63

The purpose of the shock absorber is simply to limit the motion of the spring during compression and rebound cycles. If the vehicle is not equipped with these motion dampers, the up and down motion would multiply until the vehicle was alternately trying to leap off the ground and to pound itself into the pavement.

Contrary to popular rumor, the shocks do not affect the ride height of the vehicle. This is controlled by other suspension components such as springs and tires. Worn shock absorbers can affect handling; if the front of the vehicle is rising or falling excessively, the "footprint" of the tires changes on the pavement and steering is affected.

The simplest test of the shock absorber is simply push down on one corner of the unladen vehicle and release it. Observe the motion of the body as it is released. In most cases, it will come up beyond it original rest position, dip back below it and settle quickly to rest. This shows that the damper is controlling the spring action. Any tendency to excessive pitch (up-and-down) motion or failure to return to rest within 2–3 cycles is a sign of poor function within the shock absorber. Oil-filled shocks may have a light film of oil around the seal, resulting from normal breathing and air exchange. This should NOT be taken as a sign of failure, but any sign of thick or running oil definitely indicates failure. Gas filled shocks may also show some film at the shaft; if the gas has leaked out, the shock will have almost no resistance to motion.

While each shock absorber can be replaced individually, it is recommended that they be changed as a pair (both front or both rear) to maintain equal response on both sides of the vehicle. Chances are quite good that if one has failed, its mate is weak also.

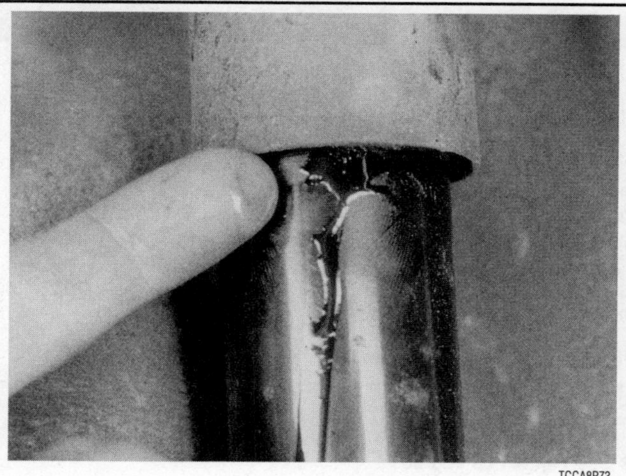

TCCA8P73

Fig. 63 When fluid is seeping out of the shock absorber, it's time to replace it

Sway Bar

REMOVAL & INSTALLATION

See Figure 64

1. Raise and safely support the vehicle.
2. Remove the 2 lower bolts which hold the sway bar to the link arm on each side of the vehicle.
3. Loosen, but do not remove, the bolts that attach the sway bar bushing retainers to the rear axle housing.
4. While holding the sway bar in place, remove the 4 bushing retaining bolts and remove the sway bar from the axle.
5. If the sway bar links need to be replaced, remove the upper link arm-to-bracket bolt, then remove the link arm from the frame rail mounting bracket.

To install:

6. Inspect the clamps, retainers and bushings, and replace any that are damaged or severely worn.
7. Install the sway bar to the rear axle. The slits in the bushing should face up in the installed position. Do not tighten the bolts.
8. Install the 2 lower link bolts, do not tighten these.
9. Lower the vehicle so all the weight is on the wheels. With the vehicle at its curb height, torque all of the bolts as follows:
   a. Bushing-to-axle bracket—45 ft. lbs. (61 Nm)
   b. Link arm-to-frame rail bracket—45 ft. lbs. (61 Nm)
   c. Sway bar-to-link arm—45 ft. lbs. (61 Nm)
   d. Link arm bracket-to-frame rail—290 inch lbs. (33 Nm)

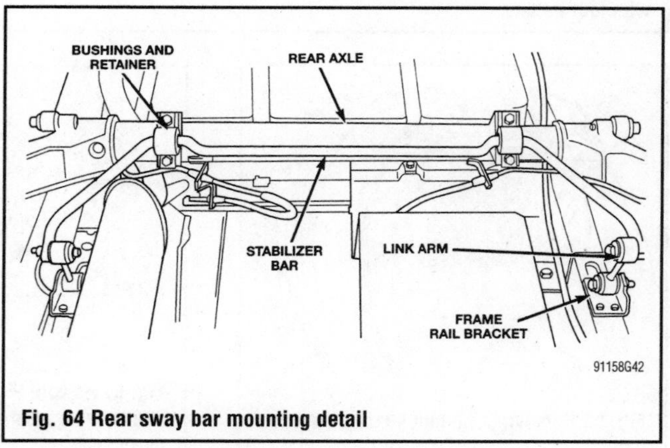

91158G42

Fig. 64 Rear sway bar mounting detail

Hub and Bearings

The rear wheel bearing is designed for the life of the vehicle and requires no type of adjustment or periodic maintenance. The bearing is a sealed unit with the wheel hub and can only be removed and/or replaced as an assembly.

If the wheel bearing is worn or damaged, the vehicle will produce vibration or growl noise. With the transaxle shifted into **N** and the vehicle coasting, the noise should continue. Road test the vehicle on a smooth, level road surface to determine the location of the worn/damaged bearing. The road test will also determine if the noise is the rear wheel bearing or differential gear noise. Accelerate the vehicle to a constant speed. Once the vehicle has reached a constant speed, swerve the vehicle back and forth from left to right. This will change the noise level by loading and unloading the wheel bearings.

REMOVAL & INSTALLATION

FWD Vehicles

➧ **See Figures 65 and 66**

1. Raise and safely support the vehicle. Remove the rear wheel.
2. Remove the rear brake drum.
3. Disconnect the parking brake cable from the parking brake cable actuating lever.
4. Remove the rear wheel speed sensor from the rear wheel hub/bearing flange.

✲✲ WARNING

During removal of the hub/bearing assembly, be sure not to damage any of the teeth on the ABS tone wheel. Damage to the tone wheel teeth will result in false ABS cycling and corrosion of the ABS tone wheel.

5. Remove the 4 wheel hub and bearing assembly mounting bolts.
6. Remove the wheel hub and bearing assembly from the vehicle.

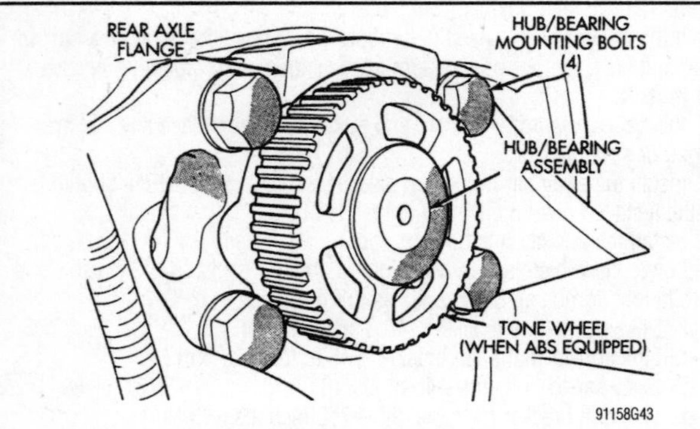

Fig. 65 The rear hub/bearing assembly is secured to the axle flange with four bolts

To install:

7. Install the 4 hub and bearing assembly mounting bolts into the 4 mounting holes in the rear axle flange.
8. Align the rear wheel hub and bearing assembly to the 4 mounting bolts. Start the mounting bolts into the bearing assembly and tighten the mounting bolts in a criss-cross pattern until the brake support plate and hub and bearing assembly are both squarely seated onto the rear axle flange.
9. Torque the wheel hub and bearing assembly mounting bolts to 95 ft. lbs. (129 Nm).
10. Install the rear wheel ABS speed sensor into the hub and bearing flange. Torque the speed sensor attaching bolt to 105 inch lbs. (12 Nm).
11. Reconnect the parking brake cable to the cable actuating lever.
12. Install the brake drum.
13. Install the rear wheels and lug nuts. Torque the wheel lug nuts, in a star sequence, to 95 ft. lbs. (129 Nm).
14. Lower the vehicle. Road test the vehicle.

AWD Vehicles

➧ **See Figures 67 and 68**

1. Set the parking brake to keep the rear axle from turning when loosening the hub nut.
2. Remove the cotter pin and nut retainer, and **slightly** loosen the hub nut.

✲✲ WARNING

Completely loosening the hub nut can cause damage to the bearing.

3. Raise and safely support the rear of the vehicle securely on jackstands.
4. Remove the wheel.
5. Remove the speed sensor to prevent it from being damaged when removing the halfshaft.
6. Remove the halfshaft.
7. Remove the disc brake caliper and hang it from the inner fender with safety wire.
8. Release the handbrake and remove the rotor.
9. Remove the four bolts that secure the hub/bearing assembly and remove it from the axle.

To install:

10. Install the hub/bearing to the axle and torque the bolts to 95 ft. lbs. (129 Nm)
11. Install the disc brake rotor.
12. Install the caliper.
13. Install the halfshaft. Tighten the hub nut as much as possible by using the handbrake to prevent the axle from turning.
14. Install the speed sensor into the hub and bearing flange. Torque the speed sensor attaching bolt to 105 inch lbs. (12 Nm).
15. Place the wheel onto the hub. Install the lug nuts and tighten them securely.
16. Lower the vehicle.
17. Install the rear wheels and lug nuts. Torque the wheel lug nuts, in a star sequence, to 95 ft. lbs. (129 Nm).
18. Torque the hub nut to 180 ft. lbs. (244 Nm) Install the spring washer, nut retainer and a new cotter pin.
19. Road test vehicle.

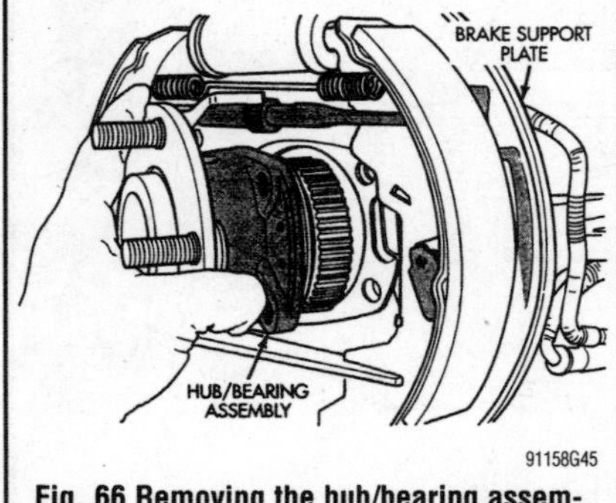

Fig. 66 Removing the hub/bearing assembly

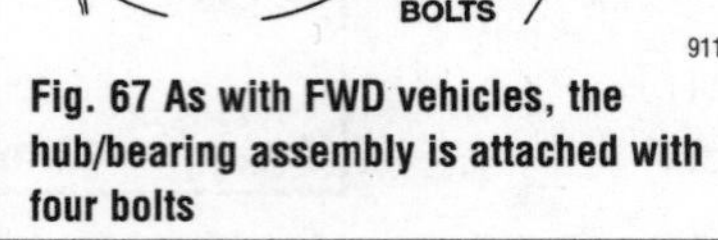

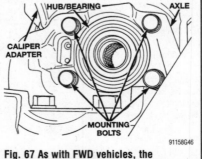

Fig. 67 As with FWD vehicles, the hub/bearing assembly is attached with four bolts

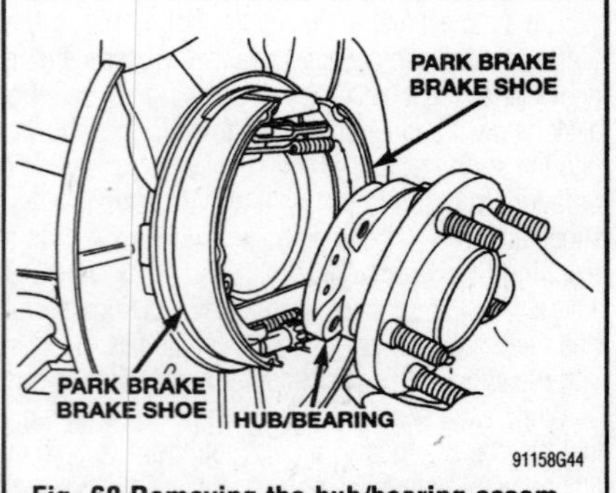

Fig. 68 Removing the hub/bearing assembly on an AWD vehicle

STEERING

➧ See Figure 69

Steering Wheel

REMOVAL & INSTALLATION

➧ See Figures 70 thru 78

✻✻ CAUTION

The Supplemental Inflatable Restraint (SIR) system must be disarmed before removing the steering wheel. Failure to do so may cause accidental deployment of the air bag, resulting in unnecessary SIR system repairs and/or personal injury.

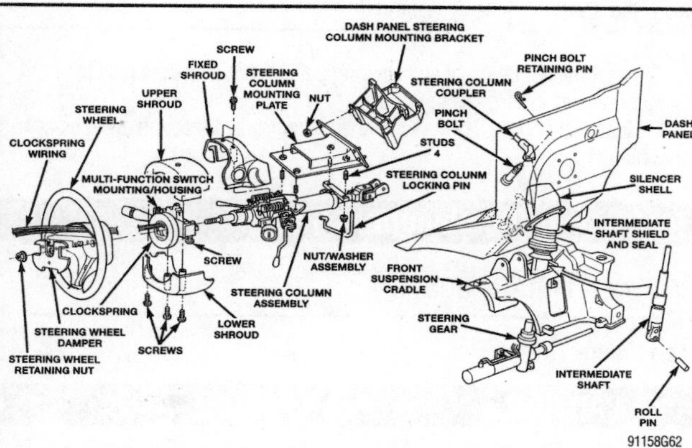

Fig. 69 Exploded view of the steering column and related components

1. Disconnect and isolate the negative (ground) battery cable. Allow the system capacitor to discharge for at least 2 minutes before continuing with the removal procedure. This will disable the air bag system.
2. Make sure the front wheels are in the straight-ahead position.
3. Turn the ignition key cylinder to the **LOCK** position and remove the key. Turn the steering wheel a ½ turn toward the left until the steering column becomes locked in position.
4. Remove the 3 bolts attaching the air bag module to the steering wheel. Remove the air bag module.

✻✻ CAUTION

When carrying a live air bag, make sure the bag and trim cover are pointed away from the body. In the unlikely event of an accidental deployment, the bag will then deploy with minimal chance of injury. When placing a live air bag on a bench or other surface, always face the bag and trim cover up, away from the surface. This will reduce the motion of the module if accidentally deployed.

5. Disconnect the wiring connectors from the air bag module, horn switch and speed control switches.
6. Remove the routing clip for the wiring harness from the air bag module studs.
7. Remove the steering wheel mounting nut from the steering column shaft and remove the steering wheel damper from the steering wheel.
8. Using a steering wheel puller tool, remove the steering wheel from the steering column shaft. Do not thread the steering wheel puller tool bolts into the steering wheel more than a ½ in. or damage to the SRS clockspring will result. Do not hammer or bump the steering column or shaft when removing the steering wheel.

Fig. 70 The airbag is attached to the steering wheel by three fasteners

Fig. 71 After the airbag is unbolted from the steering wheel . . .

Fig. 72 . . . reach behind and unplug the electrical connections

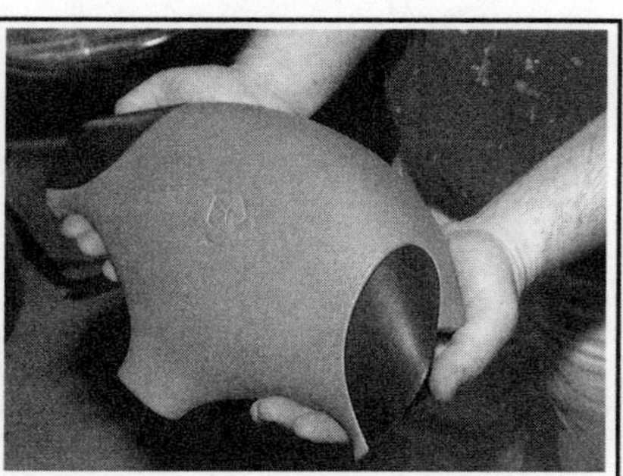

Fig. 73 Always hold the airbag away from your body when transporting it to a storage area

Fig. 74 With the airbag removed, the steering wheel retaining nut can be removed

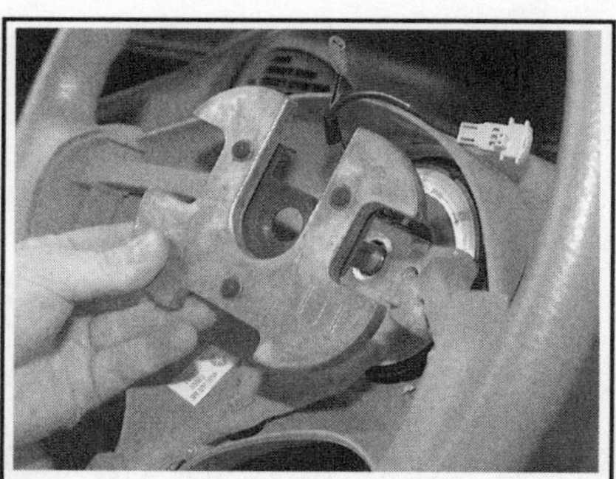

Fig. 75 After the nut is removed, set aside the damper plate . . .

91158P07

Fig. 76 . . . and use a paint marker to matchmark the steering wheel shaft with the wheel

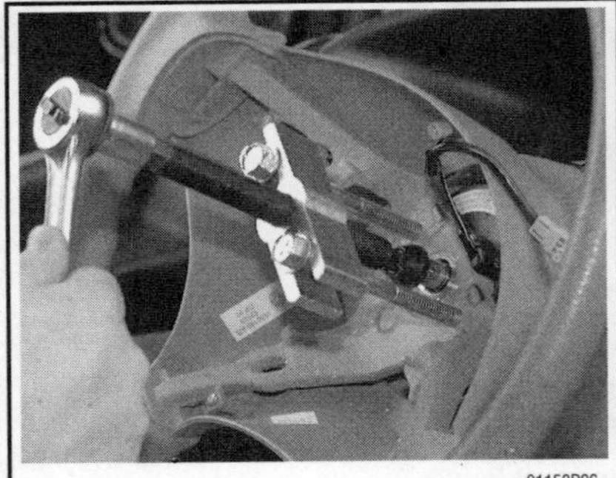

91158P06

Fig. 77 A steering wheel puller must be used to remove the wheel from the shaft

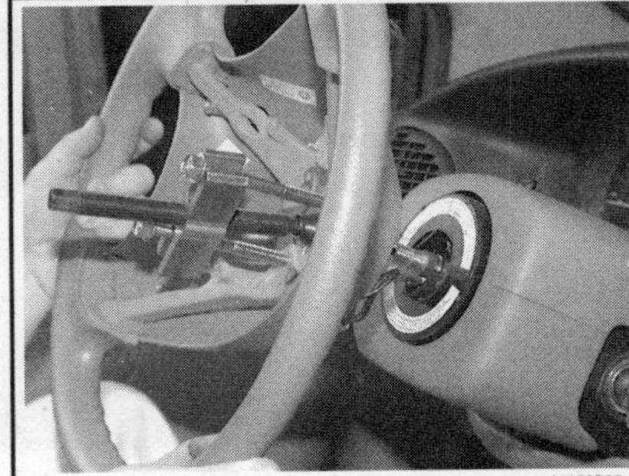

91158P05

Fig. 78 Once the wheel is free of the shaft, carefully route the wires through the wheel

To install:

9. Before installing the steering wheel, the clockspring **must be centered.** Center the clockspring as follows:

a. Disengage the lock mechanism by depressing the 2 plastic locking pins.

b. Turn the clockspring rotor clockwise until it stops, while the lock mechanism is disengaged. Do not use excessive force.

c. From the end of the clockwise travel, turn the clockspring rotor counter-clockwise. The clockspring wires should be at the top. Engage the clockspring locking pins.

d. Turn the clockspring a ½ additional rotation counter-clockwise from the center locked position. This should put the clockspring wiring at the bottom.

e. The clockspring is now correctly positioned for installation of the steering wheel.

10. Install the steering wheel onto the steering column shaft. Make sure the master splines of the steering wheel and steering shaft are in correct alignment. Be sure the flats on the steering wheel align with the formations on the clockspring. All wiring leads from the clockspring must be routed correctly.

11. Install the steering wheel damper onto the steering wheel in its original position.

12. Install the steering wheel-to-steering shaft retaining nut. Torque the retaining nut to 45 ft. lbs. (61 Nm).

13. Reconnect the horn switch wiring lead from the clockspring, onto the steering wheel horn switch wiring.

14. If equipped with speed control, reconnect the speed control wiring from the clockspring onto the speed control switch.

15. Install the wiring lead from the clockspring onto the air bag module. Make the wiring connection onto the air bag module, by pressing straight in on the connector. Be sure it is fully seated.

16. Install the air bag module to the steering wheel and then install the 3 air bag module attaching nuts. Torque all 3 air bag module attaching nuts to 100 inch lbs. (11 Nm).

17. When reconnecting the battery on a vehicle that has had the air bag removed, the following procedure should be used:

a. Connect the DRB or equivalent scan tool, to the ASDM diagnostic 6-way connector.

b. Turn the ignition key to the **ON** position. Exit the vehicle with the DRB, and install the latest version of the proper diagnostic cartridge into the DRB.

c. Make sure there are no occupants in the vehicle and reconnect the negative battery cable.

d. Using the DRB, read and record active or stored fault codes. Take appropriate actions to correct any faults.

e. Erase stored fault codes. If problems remain, fault codes will not erase.

f. From the passenger side of the vehicle, turn the ignition key to **OFF** and then **ON**, observing the instrument cluster air bag lamp. It should go ON for 6–8 seconds, then go out. This will indicate that the air bag system is functioning normally.

**** WARNING**

If the air bag warning lamp fails to light, blinks ON and OFF or goes ON and stays ON, there is an air bag system malfunction.

g. Test the operation of any steering column functions such as the horn, lights or speed control system.

18. Road test vehicle. Be sure the speed control and steering systems are functioning properly.

Turn Signal (Combination) Switch

REMOVAL & INSTALLATION

See Figure 79

**** CAUTION**

The Supplemental Inflatable Restraint (SIR) system must be disarmed before working around the air bag or SIR system wiring. Failure to do so may cause accidental deployment of the air bag, resulting in unnecessary SIR system repairs and/or personal injury.

1. Disconnect and isolate the negative battery cable from the battery.
2. In order to disarm the air bag system, allow the system capacitor to discharge for at least 2 minutes, before performing any removal procedures.
3. Remove the upper and lower steering column shrouds.
4. Disconnect the electrical connector from behind the combination switch.
5. Remove the mounting screws securing the combination switch to the steering column adapter collar.
6. Remove the combination switch from the vehicle.

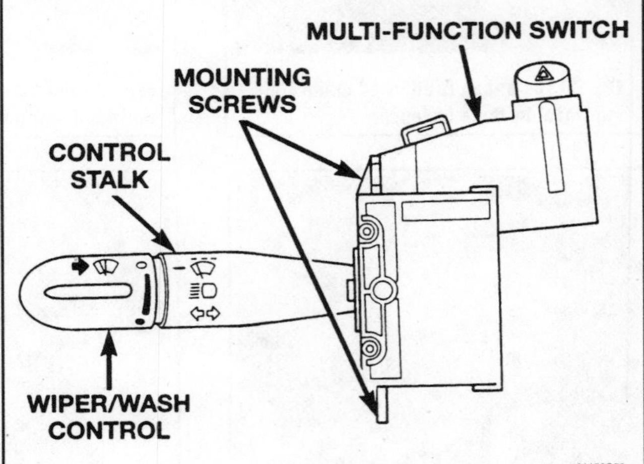

91158G53

Fig. 79 The turn signal (multi-function) switch is attached to the steering column by two screws

To install:

7. Install the combination switch to the steering column adapter collar. Tighten the combination switch mounting screws.
8. Reconnect the electrical connector to the combination switch.
9. Install the upper and lower steering column shrouds and tighten the retaining screws.
10. Reconnect the negative battery cable and check all functions of the combination switch for proper operation.

Ignition Switch

REMOVAL & INSTALLATION

➧ **See Figures 80, 81, 82 and 83**

✲✲ CAUTION

The Supplemental Inflatable Restraint (SIR) system must be disarmed before removing any components in the area of the air bag system. Failure to do so may cause accidental deployment of the air bag, resulting in unnecessary SIR system repairs and/or personal injury.

1. Disconnect and isolate the negative battery cable from the battery.
2. Allow the SIR system capacitor to discharge for at least 2 minutes, before performing any removal procedures. The air bag system is now disabled.
3. Remove the key cylinder (ignition lock).
4. Using a No. 10 Torx® tamper proof bit, remove the ignition switch mounting screw.
5. Depress the ignition switch retaining tab and carefully pry the ignition switch from the steering column.
6. Disconnect the electrical connectors from the ignition switch and remove the switch from the vehicle.

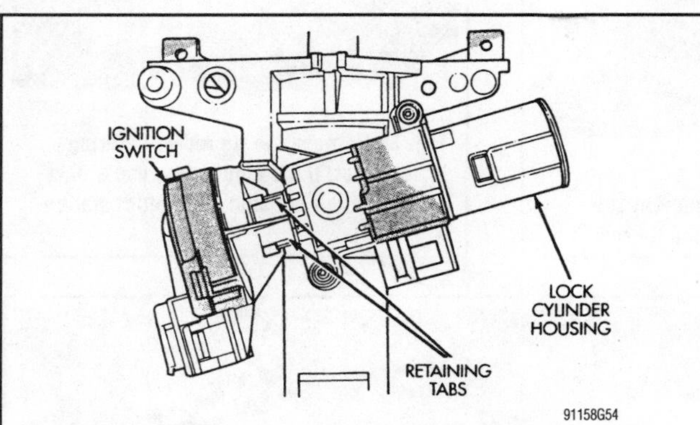

Fig. 80 The ignition switch is attached to the lock cylinder housing by two retaining clips and a single tamper-resistant screw

To install:

7. Be sure the ignition switch is in the **RUN** position and the actuator shaft in the ignition lock housing is in the **RUN** position.
8. Reconnect the electrical connectors to the ignition switch.
9. Carefully install the ignition switch, making sure the ignition switch snaps over the retaining tabs.
10. Install and tighten the ignition switch mounting screw.
11. Install the key cylinder (ignition lock). Complete the installation by reversing the removal procedures.
12. Reconnect the negative battery cable.
13. Check switch operation.

Ignition Lock Cylinder

REMOVAL & INSTALLATION

➧ **See Figure 81**

✲✲ CAUTION

The Supplemental Inflatable Restraint (SIR) system must be disarmed before working around the air bag or SIR wiring. Failure to do so may cause accidental deployment of the air bag, resulting in unnecessary SIR system repairs and/or personal injury.

1. Disconnect and isolate the negative battery cable from the battery.
2. In order to disarm the air bag system, allow the SIR system capacitor to discharge for at least 2 minutes, before performing any removal procedures.
3. Remove the screws that secure the parking brake release handle to the instrument panel.
4. Remove the screws that secure the bottom of the lower steering column cover to the instrument panel.
5. Disengage the retaining clip that holds the right side of the lower steering column cover to the instrument panel.
6. Remove the lower steering column cover from the vehicle.
7. Remove the mounting screws that hold the upper and lower steering column shrouds and remove the lower steering column shroud.
8. Install the ignition key and turn the key cylinder to the **RUN** position. This is important because it will not only aid in removal of the ignition lock, but will also place the socket (in the lock cylinder housing) in proper alignment for the installation of the replacement ignition lock.
9. Press in the lock cylinder retaining tab and remove the key cylinder (ignition lock).

To install:

10. Install the ignition key into the replacement ignition lock key cylinder. Turn the key to the **RUN** position. Depress the ignition lock key cylinder retaining tab.
11. Align the shaft at the end of the ignition lock cylinder with the socket in the end of the ignition lock cylinder housing.
12. Align the ignition lock cylinder with the grooves in the lock cylinder

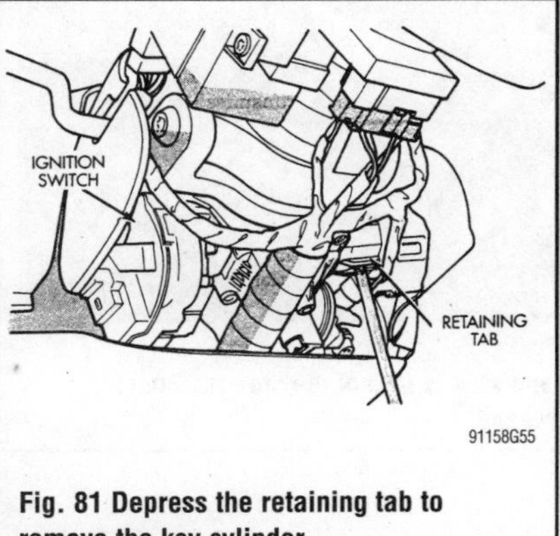

Fig. 81 Depress the retaining tab to remove the key cylinder

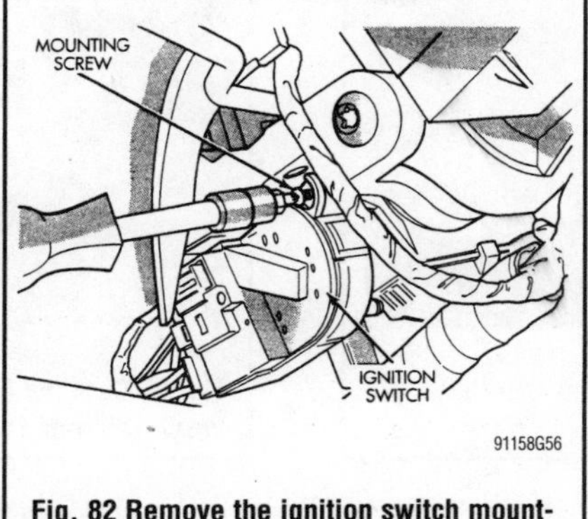

Fig. 82 Remove the ignition switch mounting screw . . .

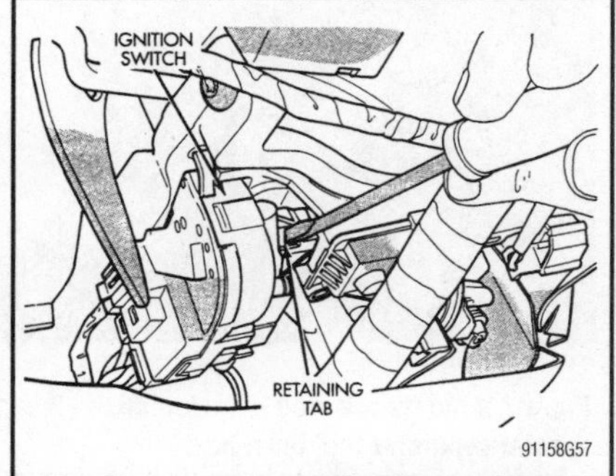

Fig. 83 . . . and carefully depress the retaining tabs while separating the switch from the lock cylinder housing

housing. Push the ignition lock cylinder into the housing until the retaining tab sticks through the opening in the lock cylinder housing.

13. Turn the ignition key to the **OFF** position and remove the key.
14. Install the lower steering column shroud and install the mounting screws.
15. Place the lower steering column cover into correct position on the lower instrument panel and engage the clip that secures the right side of the cover to the instrument panel.
16. Install the lower steering column mounting screws.
17. Install the mounting screws that hold the parking brake release handle to the instrument panel.
18. Reconnect the negative battery cable.

Steering Linkage

REMOVAL & INSTALLATION

Tie Rod Ends

See Figures 84, 85, 86, 87 and 88

1. Raise and safely support the front of the vehicle on safety stands. Remove the front wheels.
2. Wire brush the tie rod threads and liberally soak with penetrating oil. Loosen the inner tie rod-to-outer tie rod jam nut.
3. Mark the tie rod position on the inner tie rod threads.
4. Remove the tie rod-to-steering knuckle nut by holding the tie rod end stud with an $^{11}/_{32}$ socket while loosening and removing the nut with a box wrench.
5. Using a puller tool, separate the tie rod end from the steering knuckle. If the joint is to be reused, do not use a wedge-type tool to hammer the connection apart or the outer tie rod end will be damaged.

Count the number of turns when removing tie rod end. Install the new tie rod end the same amount of turns.

6. Unscrew the outer tie rod end from the rack inner tie rod.

To install:

7. Thread the new tie rod end onto the inner tie rod, the same number of turns as was required for removal.
8. Install the tie rod end to the steering knuckle. Install the outer tie rod-to-steering knuckle nut. Torque the nut, using a crowfoot and $^{11}/_{32}$ socket, to 40 ft. lbs. (54 Nm). Install a new cotter pin.
9. Check the toe setting. Adjust the toe setting to the correct specifications by turning the inner tie rod, taking care not to twist the boot.
10. Tighten the jam nut to 55 ft. lbs. (75 Nm).
11. Install the front wheels and lug nuts. Torque the lug nuts to 95 ft. lbs. (129 Nm).
12. Lower the vehicle.
13. Re-check the wheel alignment and make any adjustments, if necessary. Road test the vehicle.

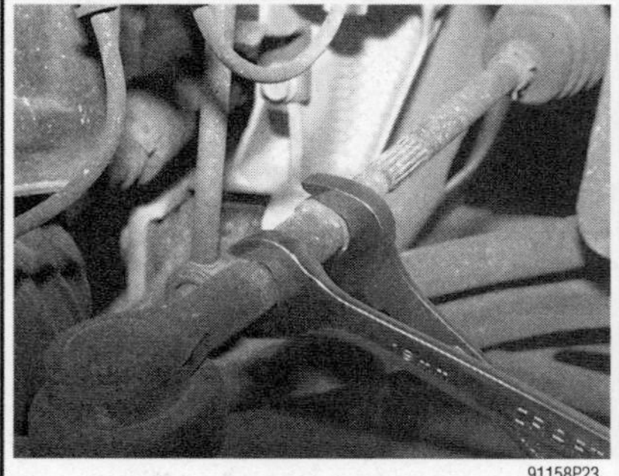

91158P23

Fig. 84 Before removing the tie rod end from the steering knuckle, loosen the tie rod jam nut

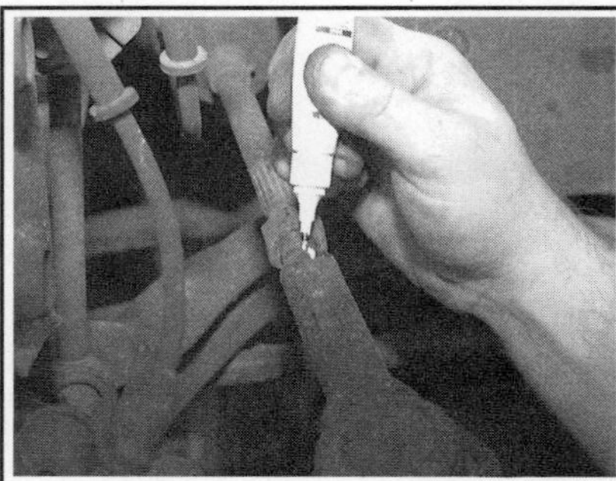

91158P22

Fig. 85 To preserve the alignment settings, mark the threads on the tie rod

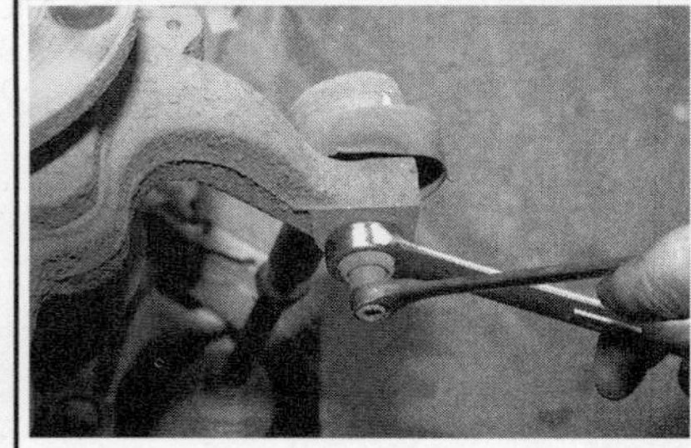

91158P20

Fig. 86 Remove the tie rod-to-steering knuckle nut; if the stud spins, use a back-up wrench on the stud and hold it stationary

91158P19

Fig. 87 If the tie rod stud is frozen inside the steering knuckle, a special separator tool must be used

91158P24

Fig. 88 Once the tie rod end stud is free of the steering knuckle, unscrew it from the tie rod end

Power Steering Gear

REMOVAL & INSTALLATION

See Figures 89, 90, 91 and 92

WARNING

Position the steering column in the locked position to prevent the SRS clockspring from becoming accidentally over-extended, when the steering column is disconnected from the intermediate coupler.

1. With the ignition key in the locked position, turn the steering wheel to the left until the steering wheel locks itself in position.
2. Disconnect the negative battery cable.
3. Disconnect the steering column shaft coupler from the steering gear intermediate coupler.
4. Raise and safely support the vehicle.
5. Remove the front wheels.
6. Place a drain pan under the power steering fluid lines and disconnect the fluid hose from the metal tube portion of the power steering fluid return line and allow the steering fluid to drain into the pan.
7. Remove the tie rod ends from the steering knuckles.
8. Remove the 2 bolts and loosen the third, mounting the ABS Hydraulic Control Unit (HCU) to the front suspension cradle. Rotate the HCU rearward to allow access to the cradle plate mounting nut and bolt just ahead of the HCU.
9. Remove the front suspension cradle plate from the front suspension cradle.
10. Remove the retaining bracket attaching the power steering fluid lines to the front suspension cradle.
11. Using an 18mm crowfoot, disconnect the power steering fluid pressure and return lines from the power steering gear.
12. Remove the 3 bolts and nuts mounting the rack and pinion steering gear to the suspension cradle.
13. Lower the steering gear from the suspension cradle enough to allow access to the steering column intermediate coupler roll pin. Remove the roll pin and separate the intermediate coupler from the steering gear shaft.
14. Remove the rack and pinion steering gear assembly from the front suspension cradle.

To install:

15. Install the rack and pinion steering gear assembly into the front suspension cradle, providing enough room to install the intermediate coupler.
16. Connect the steering gear shaft to the intermediate coupler and secure with roll pin.
17. Place the steering gear assembly in correct position on the suspension cradle and install the 3 steering gear mounting bolts and nuts. Torque the bolts and nuts to 100 ft. lbs. (136 Nm).
18. Connect the power steering fluid pressure and return lines to the correct fittings on the steering gear. Torque the power steering fluid line tube fittings to 275 inch lbs. (31 Nm).
19. Install the outer tie rod ends to the steering knuckles. Torque the tie rod end-to-steering knuckle nuts to 40 ft. lbs. (54 Nm).
20. Install the front suspension cradle plate to the front suspension cradle. Torque the 10 mounting bolts and nuts to 123 ft. lbs. (165 Nm).
21. Install the bracket mounting the power steering fluid lines to the suspension cradle. Be sure the protective heat shields cover the entire rubber hose hose-to-tube connection of both power steering fluid hoses.
22. Install the hose onto the metal tube portion of the power steering fluid return line. Install hose clamp on the return hose. Be sure the hose clamp is installed past the upset bead on the tube.
23. Install the front wheels and lug nuts. Torque the lug nuts, in a star sequence, to 95 ft. lbs. (129 Nm).
24. Lower the vehicle just enough to access the interior of the vehicle.
25. Using the intermediate coupler, turn the front wheels to the left until the intermediate coupler shaft is correctly aligned with the steering column coupler. Connect the steering column shaft coupler to the steering gear intermediate coupler. Install the steering column coupler-to-intermediate shaft retaining pinch bolt. Torque the pinch bolt nut to 250 inch lbs. (28 Nm).
26. Reconnect the negative battery cable.
27. Refill power steering reservoir, with the correct amount of clean, fresh MOPAR® Power Steering Fluid or equivalent, and bleed the system.
28. Check the toe setting and adjust, if necessary. Road test the vehicle and check steering operation.

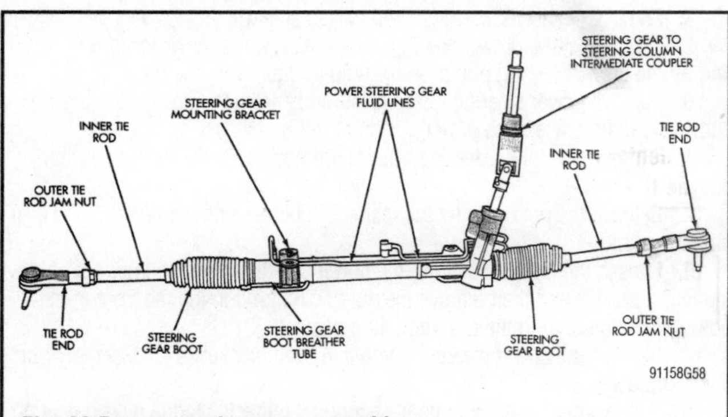

Fig. 89 Power steering gear assembly

Power Steering Pump

REMOVAL & INSTALLATION

2.4L (VIN B) Engine

See Figures 93 thru 99

1. Disconnect and isolate the negative battery cable from the battery.
2. Remove the power steering drive belt. It is not necessary to remove the belt from the engine.
3. Loosen, but do not remove the nut securing the front bracket for the power steering pump to the aluminum mounting bracket.

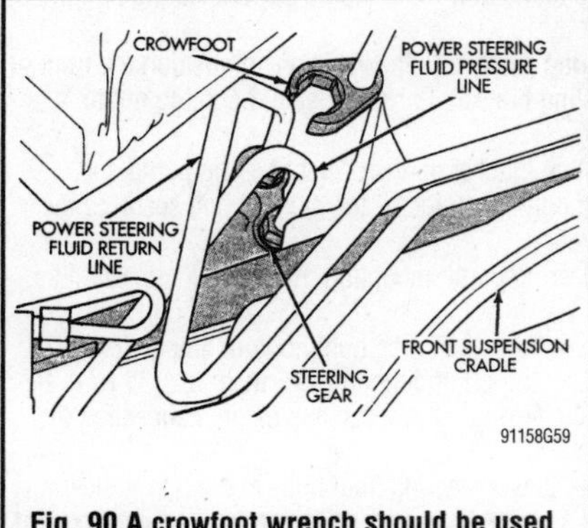

Fig. 90 A crowfoot wrench should be used to remove the power steering lines

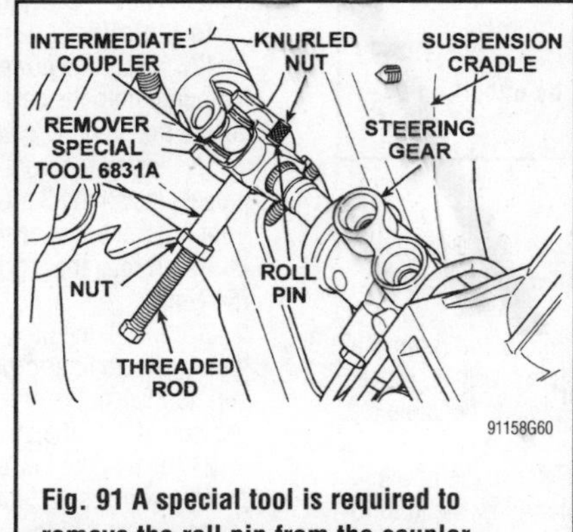

Fig. 91 A special tool is required to remove the roll pin from the coupler

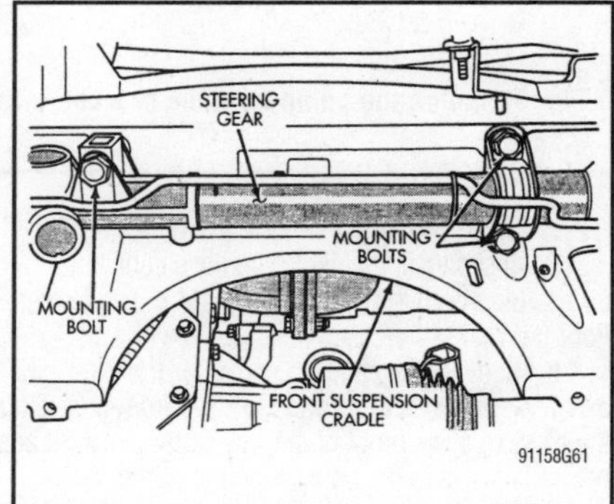

Fig. 92 The steering gear is mounted to the front suspension cradle by three bolts

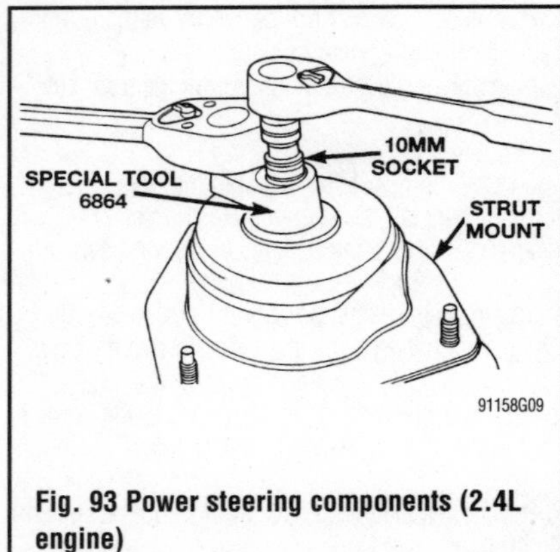

Fig. 93 Power steering components (2.4L engine)

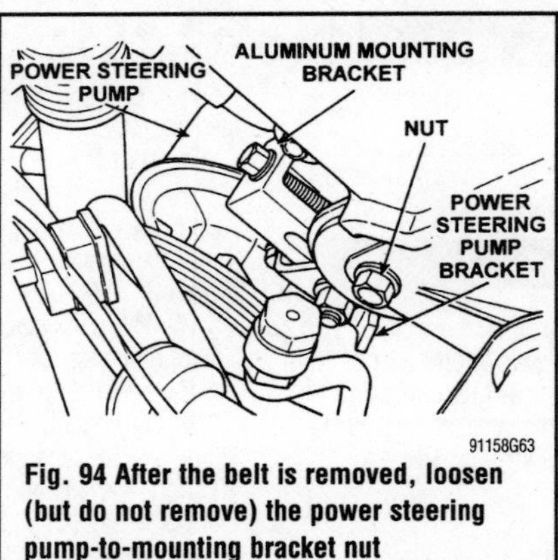

Fig. 94 After the belt is removed, loosen (but do not remove) the power steering pump-to-mounting bracket nut

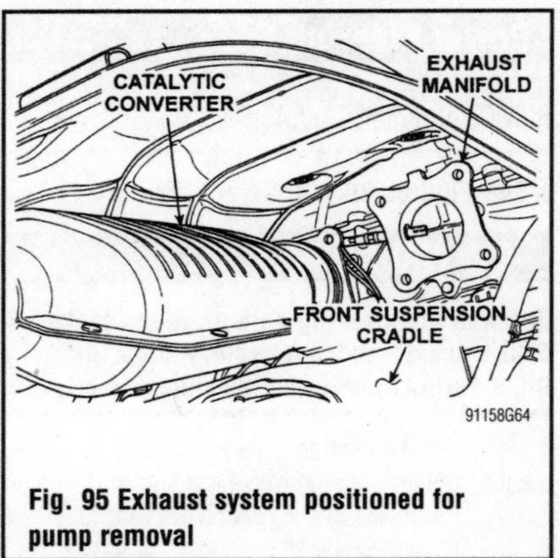

Fig. 95 Exhaust system positioned for pump removal

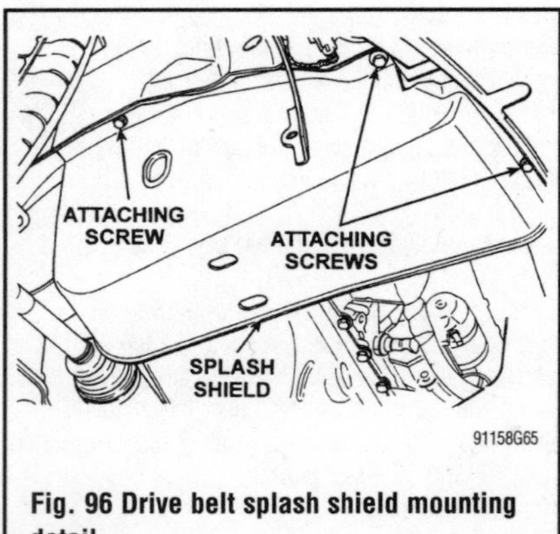

Fig. 96 Drive belt splash shield mounting detail

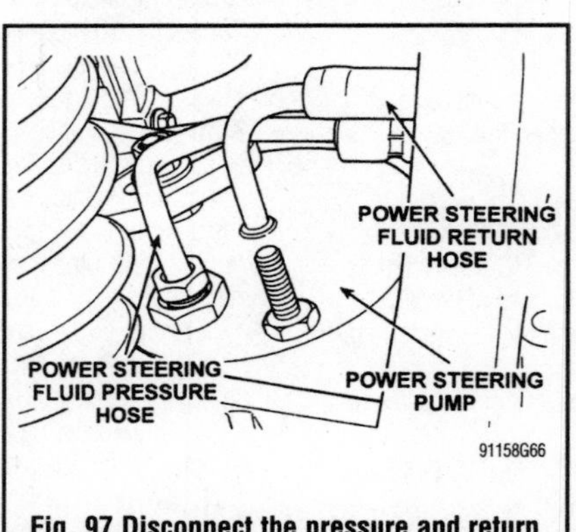

Fig. 97 Disconnect the pressure and return lines from the pump

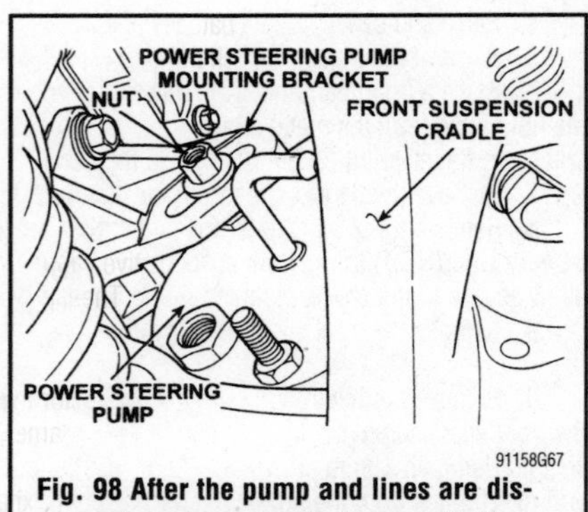

Fig. 98 After the pump and lines are disconnected and drained of excess fluid, remove the adjustment bracket nut

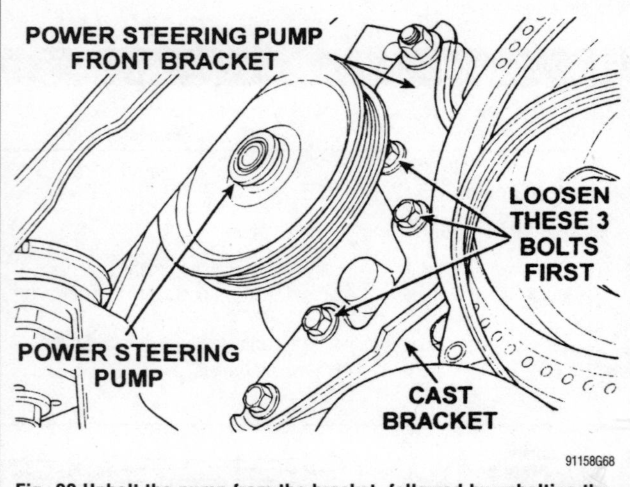

Fig. 99 Unbolt the pump from the bracket, followed by unbolting the bracket

4. Raise and safely support the vehicle.
5. Disconnect the wiring harness connector to the oxygen sensor which is accessible through the oxygen sensor wiring harness grommet in the vehicle floor pan.
6. Remove the catalytic converter from the exhaust manifold and remove all exhaust system hangers and isolators from the exhaust system brackets. Move the exhaust system out of the way as far rearward and to the left as possible to provide access to the power steering pump.
7. Place a drain pan under the power steering pump. Remove the power steering fluid return line hose on the front suspension cradle. Allow the fluid to drain from the pump and hose.
8. Remove the accessory drive belt splash shield.
9. Disconnect the power steering remote reservoir supply hose from the fitting on the power steering pump. Allow fluid to drain from the hose.
10. Remove power steering fluid pressure line from the power steering pump and drain any excess power steering fluid.
11. Remove the power steering fluid return hose from the power steering pump.
12. Remove the nut securing the rear of the power steering pump to the cast mounting bracket.
13. Loosen the 3 bolts securing the power steering pump to the front mounting bracket and then remove the nut and bolt mounting the front of the power steering pump to the cast mounting bracket.
14. Remove the power steering pump and front bracket as an assembly from the cast bracket.
15. Remove the 3 mounting bolts securing the bracket to the power steering pump and separate the bracket from the power steering pump.
16. Remove the power steering pump from the vehicle. Transfer any parts from the power steering pump to the new replacement power steering pump.

To install:

17. Install the power steering pump into the vehicle and position the front of the pump onto the cast mounting bracket. Loosely install mounting nut to secure the pump in place.
18. Install the front mounting bracket on the power steering pump and loosely install the 3 mounting bolts, then install the nut and bolt securing the front bracket to the cast bracket.
19. Torque the 3 power steering pump mounting bracket bolts to 40 ft. lbs. (54 Nm).
20. Install the high pressure fluid line to the pump output fitting. Torque the high pressure line-to-power steering pump fitting to 275 inch lbs. (31 Nm). Be sure to inspect the pressure line O-ring for any damage before connecting the pressure line to the steering pump.
21. Install the low pressure power steering fluid hose to the power steering pump low pressure fitting. Be sure the hose clamps are properly reinstalled and hoses are clear of the accessory drive belts.

22. Install the power steering fluid reservoir supply hose to the power steering pump fluid fitting. Be sure all hoses are clear of any accessory drive belts and hose clamps correctly installed.
23. Install the power steering drive belt.
24. Install the accessory drive belt splash shield.
25. Install the hose on the power steering fluid return line on the front suspension cradle. Be sure the hose clamps and heat shield tubes are correctly reinstalled.
26. Reconnect the exhaust pipe to the exhaust manifold. Install the hangers and isolators onto the exhaust system brackets. Torque the nuts and bolts to 250 inch lbs. (28 Nm).
27. Reconnect the wiring harness connectors to the oxygen sensor. Install the wiring harness grommet into the vehicle floor pan.
28. Remove the drain pan and lower the vehicle.
29. Torque the top mounting nut and bottom mounting bolt on the power steering pump front mounting bracket to 40 ft. lbs. (54 Nm).
30. Refill the power steering pump reservoir with the correct amount of clean power steering fluid.
31. Reconnect the negative battery cable. Bleed the power steering system.
32. Run the engine and check the system for leaks and proper steering operation.

3.0L (VIN 3) Engine

See Figures 95, 96 and 100

1. Disconnect and isolate the negative battery cable.
2. Remove the accessory drive belt. The belt does not have to be removed from the engine.
3. Raise and safely support the vehicle.
4. Disconnect the wiring harness connector to the oxygen sensor which is accessible through the oxygen sensor wiring harness grommet in the vehicle floor pan.
5. Remove the catalytic converter from the exhaust manifold and remove all exhaust system hangers and isolators from the exhaust system brackets. Move exhaust system out of the way as far rearward and to the left as possible to provide access to the power steering pump.
6. Place a drain pan under the power steering pump. Remove the power steering fluid return line hose on the front suspension cradle. Allow the fluid to drain from the pump and hose.
7. Remove the accessory drive belt splash shield.
8. Disconnect the power steering remote reservoir supply hose from the fitting on the power steering pump. Allow fluid to drain from the hose.
9. Remove power steering fluid pressure line from the power steering pump and drain any excess power steering fluid.
10. Remove the power steering fluid return hose from the power steering pump.
11. Remove the rear support bracket mounted behind the power steering pump to the engine block.
12. Remove the 2 mounting bolts that secure the pump to the alternator/power steering pump and belt tensioner mounting bracket.
13. Remove the power steering pump and pulley assembly out from the vehicle. Transfer all required parts from the pump to the new replacement pump before installation.

To install:

14. Position the front of the power steering pump up onto the mounting bracket. Torque the 2 power steering pump-to-mounting bracket bolts to 40 ft. lbs. (54 Nm).
15. Install the rear power steering pump-to-engine block support bracket. Torque the 2 support bracket mounting bolts to 40 ft. lbs. (54 Nm). Install the nut to the mounting stud behind the pump and torque to 40 ft. lbs. (54 Nm).
16. Install the high pressure fluid line to the pump output fitting. Torque the high pressure line-to-power steering pump fitting to 275 inch lbs. (31 Nm). Be sure to inspect the pressure line O-ring for any damage before connecting the pressure line to the steering pump.
17. Install the low pressure power steering fluid hose to the power steering pump low pressure fitting. Be sure the hose clamps are properly reinstalled and hoses are clear of the accessory drive belts.
18. Install the accessory drive belt.
19. Install the hose on the power steering fluid return line on the front suspension cradle. Be sure the hose clamps and heat shield tubes are correctly reinstalled.
20. Reconnect the exhaust pipe to the exhaust manifold. Install the hangers and isolators onto the exhaust system brackets. torque the nuts and bolts to 250 inch lbs. (28 Nm).
21. Reconnect the wiring harness connectors to the oxygen sensor. Install the wiring harness grommet into the vehicle floor pan.
22. Install the accessory drive belt splash shield.
23. Remove the drain pan and lower the vehicle.
24. Refill the power steering pump reservoir with the correct amount of clean power steering fluid.
25. Reconnect the negative battery cable. Bleed the power steering system.
26. Run the engine and check the system for leaks and proper steering operation.

3.3L (VIN R) and 3.8L (VIN L) Engines

See Figures 101 and 102

1. Remove and isolate the negative battery cable.
2. Raise and safely support the vehicle. Place a drain pan under the power steering pump.
3. Disconnect the wiring harness connector to the oxygen sensor which is accessible through the oxygen sensor wiring harness grommet in the vehicle floor pan.
4. Remove the catalytic converter from the exhaust manifold and remove all exhaust system hangers and isolators from the exhaust system brackets. Move exhaust system out of the way as far rearward and to the left as possible to provide access to the power steering pump.
5. Remove the power steering fluid return line hose on the front suspension cradle. Allow the fluid to drain from the pump and hose.
6. Remove the accessory drive belt splash shield.
7. Remove accessory drive belt.
8. Disconnect the power steering remote reservoir supply hose from the fitting on the power steering pump. Allow fluid to drain from the hose.
9. Remove power steering fluid pressure line from the power steering pump and drain any excess power steering fluid.

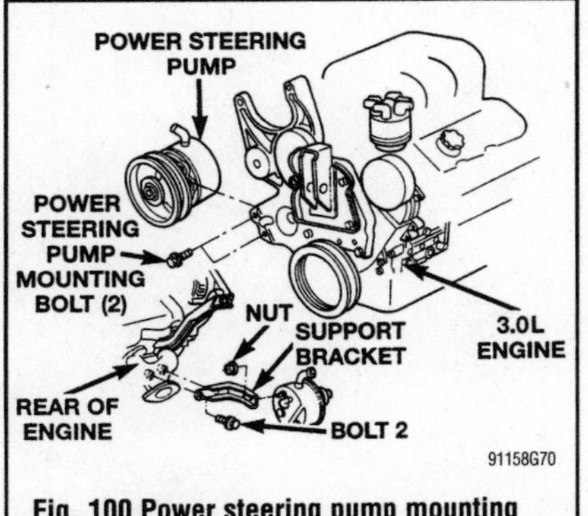

Fig. 100 Power steering pump mounting detail (3.0L engine)

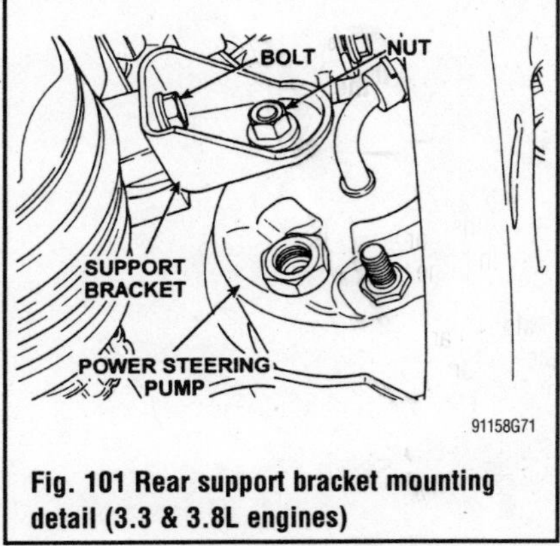

Fig. 101 Rear support bracket mounting detail (3.3 & 3.8L engines)

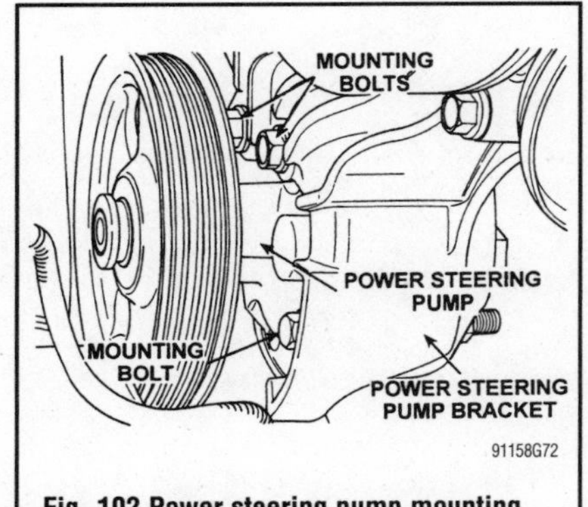

Fig. 102 Power steering pump mounting detail (3.3 & 3.8L engines)

10. Remove the power steering fluid return hose from the power steering pump.

11. Remove the rear support bracket mounted behind the power steering pump to the engine block.

12. Remove the 3 mounting bolts that secure the pump to the alternator/power steering pump and belt tensioner mounting bracket.

13. Remove the power steering pump and pulley assembly from the vehicle. Transfer all required parts from the pump to the new replacement pump before installation.

To install:

14. Position the front of the power steering pump up onto the mounting bracket. Torque the 3 power steering pump-to-mounting bracket bolts to 40 ft. lbs. (54 Nm).

15. Install the rear power steering pump-to-engine block support bracket. Torque the support bracket mounting bolts to 40 ft. lbs. (54 Nm). Install the nut to the mounting stud behind the pump and torque to 40 ft. lbs. (54 Nm).

16. Install the high pressure fluid line to the pump output fitting. Torque the high pressure line-to-power steering pump fitting to 275 inch lbs. (31 Nm). Be sure to inspect the pressure line O-ring for any damage before connecting the pressure line to the steering pump.

17. Install the low pressure power steering fluid hose to the power steering pump low pressure fitting. Be sure the hose clamps are properly reinstalled and hoses are clear of the accessory drive belts.

18. Install the accessory drive belt.

19. Install the hose on the power steering fluid return line on the front suspension cradle. Be sure the hose clamps and heat shield tubes are correctly reinstalled.

20. Reconnect the exhaust pipe to the exhaust manifold. Install the hangers and isolators onto the exhaust system brackets. Torque the nuts and bolts to 250 inch lbs. (28 Nm).

21. Reconnect the wiring harness connectors to the oxygen sensor. Install the wiring harness grommet into the vehicle floor pan.

22. Install the accessory drive belt splash shield.

23. Remove the drain pan and lower the vehicle.

24. Refill the power steering pump reservoir with the correct amount of clean power steering fluid.

25. Reconnect the negative battery cable. Bleed the power steering system.

26. Run the engine and check the system for leaks and proper steering operation.

BLEEDING

CAUTION

The power steering fluid level should be checked with the engine OFF to prevent injury from moving components. Power steering oil, engine components and exhaust system may be extremely hot if the engine has been running. Do not start the engine with any loose or disconnected hoses or allow hoses to touch a hot exhaust manifold or catalyst.

➡In all power steering pumps, use only MOPAR® Power Steering Fluid or equivalent. DO NOT use any type of automatic transmission fluid in the power steering system.

Wipe the filler cap clean, then check the fluid level. The dipstick should indicate FULL COLD when the fluid is at normal room temperature of approximately 70–80°F.

1. Fill the power steering pump fluid reservoir to the proper level. Allow the fluid to settle for at least 2 minutes.
2. Start the engine and let run for a few seconds. Turn the engine OFF.
3. Add fluid if necessary. Repeat this procedure until the fluid level remains constant after running the engine.
4. Raise and safely support the vehicle so the front wheels of the vehicle are off the ground.
5. Start the engine. Slowly turn the steering wheel right and left, lightly contacting the wheel stops. Then turn the engine OFF.
6. Add power steering fluid if necessary.
7. Lower the vehicle and turn the steering wheel slowly from lock to lock.
8. Turn OFF the engine. Check the fluid level and refill as required.
9. If the fluid is extremely foamy, allow the vehicle to stand a few minutes and repeat the above procedure.

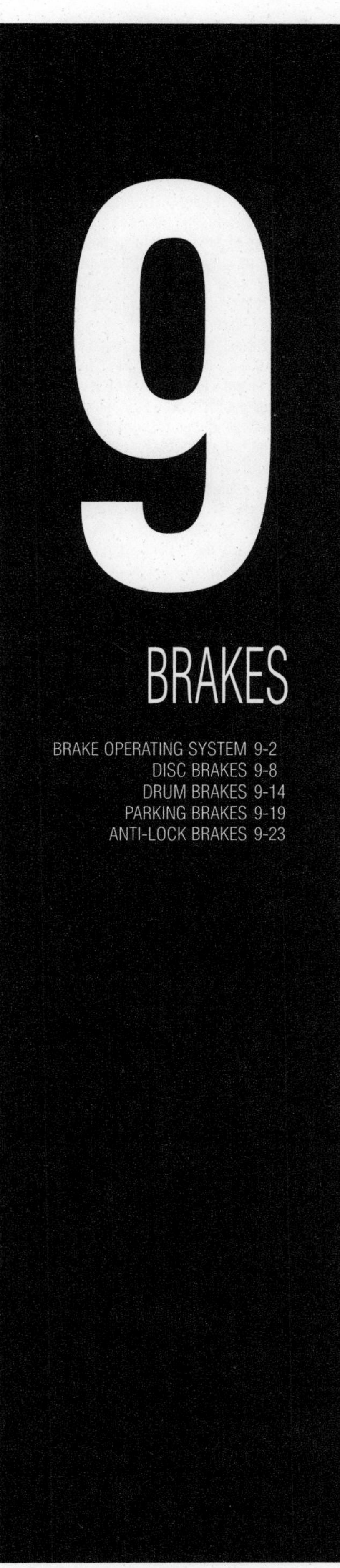
9
BRAKES
BRAKE OPERATING SYSTEM 9-2
DISC BRAKES 9-8
DRUM BRAKES 9-14
PARKING BRAKES 9-19
ANTI-LOCK BRAKES 9-23

BRAKE OPERATING SYSTEM

Basic Operating Principles

Hydraulic systems are used to actuate the brakes of all modern automobiles. The system transports the power required to force the frictional surfaces of the braking system together from the pedal to the individual brake units at each wheel. A hydraulic system is used for two reasons.

First, fluid under pressure can be carried to all parts of an automobile by small pipes and flexible hoses without taking up a significant amount of room or posing routing problems.

Second, a great mechanical advantage can be given to the brake pedal end of the system, and the foot pressure required to actuate the brakes can be reduced by making the surface area of the master cylinder pistons smaller than that of any of the pistons in the wheel cylinders or calipers.

The master cylinder consists of a fluid reservoir along with a double cylinder and piston assembly. Double type master cylinders are designed to separate the front and rear braking systems hydraulically in case of a leak. The master cylinder coverts mechanical motion from the pedal into hydraulic pressure within the lines. This pressure is translated back into mechanical motion at the wheels by either the wheel cylinder (drum brakes) or the caliper (disc brakes).

Steel lines carry the brake fluid to a point on the vehicle's frame near each of the vehicle's wheels. The fluid is then carried to the calipers and wheel cylinders by flexible tubes in order to allow for suspension and steering movements.

In drum brake systems, each wheel cylinder contains two pistons, one at either end, which push outward in opposite directions and force the brake shoe into contact with the drum.

In disc brake systems, the cylinders are part of the calipers. At least one cylinder in each caliper is used to force the brake pads against the disc.

All pistons employ some type of seal, usually made of rubber, to minimize fluid leakage. A rubber dust boot seals the outer end of the cylinder against dust and dirt. The boot fits around the outer end of the piston on disc brake calipers, and around the brake actuating rod on wheel cylinders.

The hydraulic system operates as follows: When at rest, the entire system, from the piston(s) in the master cylinder to those in the wheel cylinders or calipers, is full of brake fluid. Upon application of the brake pedal, fluid trapped in front of the master cylinder piston(s) is forced through the lines to the wheel cylinders. Here, it forces the pistons outward, in the case of drum brakes, and inward toward the disc, in the case of disc brakes. The motion of the pistons is opposed by return springs mounted outside the cylinders in drum brakes, and by spring seals, in disc brakes.

Upon release of the brake pedal, a spring located inside the master cylinder immediately returns the master cylinder pistons to the normal position. The pistons contain check valves and the master cylinder has compensating ports drilled in it. These are uncovered as the pistons reach their normal position. The piston check valves allow fluid to flow toward the wheel cylinders or calipers as the pistons withdraw. Then, as the return springs force the brake pads or shoes into the released position, the excess fluid reservoir through the compensating ports. It is during the time the pedal is in the released position that any fluid that has leaked out of the system will be replaced through the compensating ports.

Dual circuit master cylinders employ two pistons, located one behind the other, in the same cylinder. The primary piston is actuated directly by mechanical linkage from the brake pedal through the power booster. The secondary piston is actuated by fluid trapped between the two pistons. If a leak develops in front of the secondary piston, it moves forward until it bottoms against the front of the master cylinder, and the fluid trapped between the pistons will operate the rear brakes. If the rear brakes develop a leak, the primary piston will move forward until direct contact with the secondary piston takes place, and it will force the secondary piston to actuate the front brakes. In either case, the brake pedal moves farther when the brakes are applied, and less braking power is available.

All dual circuit systems use a switch to warn the driver when only half of the brake system is operational. This switch is usually located in a valve body which is mounted on the firewall or the frame below the master cylinder. A hydraulic piston receives pressure from both circuits, each circuit's pressure being applied to one end of the piston. When the pressures are in balance, the piston remains stationary. When one circuit has a leak, however, the greater pressure in that circuit during application of the brakes will push the piston to one side, closing the switch and activating the brake warning light.

In disc brake systems, this valve body also contains a metering valve and, in some cases, a proportioning valve. The metering valve keeps pressure from traveling to the disc brakes on the front wheels until the brake shoes on the rear wheels have contacted the drums, ensuring that the front brakes will never be used alone. The proportioning valve controls the pressure to the rear brakes to lessen the chance of rear wheel lock-up during very hard braking.

Warning lights may be tested by depressing the brake pedal and holding it while opening one of the wheel cylinder bleeder screws. If this does not cause the light to go on, substitute a new lamp, make continuity checks, and, finally, replace the switch as necessary.

The hydraulic system may be checked for leaks by applying pressure to the pedal gradually and steadily. If the pedal sinks very slowly to the floor, the system has a leak. This is not to be confused with a springy or spongy feel due to the compression of air within the lines. If the system leaks, there will be a gradual change in the position of the pedal with a constant pressure.

Check for leaks along all lines and at wheel cylinders. If no external leaks are apparent, the problem is inside the master cylinder.

DISC BRAKES

Instead of the traditional expanding brakes that press outward against a circular drum, disc brake systems utilize a disc (rotor) with brake pads positioned on either side of it. An easily-seen analogy is the hand brake arrangement on a bicycle. The pads squeeze onto the rim of the bike wheel, slowing its motion. Automobile disc brakes use the identical principle but apply the braking effort to a separate disc instead of the wheel.

The disc (rotor) is a casting, usually equipped with cooling fins between the two braking surfaces. This enables air to circulate between the braking surfaces making them less sensitive to heat buildup and more resistant to fade. Dirt and water do not drastically affect braking action since contaminants are thrown off by the centrifugal action of the rotor or scraped off the by the pads. Also, the equal clamping action of the two brake pads tends to ensure uniform, straight line stops. Disc brakes are inherently self-adjusting. There are three general types of disc brake:

1. A fixed caliper.
2. A floating caliper.
3. A sliding caliper.

The fixed caliper design uses two pistons mounted on either side of the rotor (in each side of the caliper). The caliper is mounted rigidly and does not move.

The sliding and floating designs are quite similar. In fact, these two types are often lumped together. In both designs, the pad on the inside of the rotor is moved into contact with the rotor by hydraulic force. The caliper, which is not held in a fixed position, moves slightly, bringing the outside pad into contact with the rotor. There are various methods of attaching floating calipers. Some pivot at the bottom or top, and some slide on mounting bolts. In any event, the end result is the same.

DRUM BRAKES

Drum brakes employ two brake shoes mounted on a stationary backing plate. These shoes are positioned inside a circular drum which rotates with the wheel assembly. The shoes are held in place by springs. This allows them to slide toward the drums (when they are applied) while keeping the linings and drums in alignment. The shoes are actuated by a wheel cylinder which is mounted at the top of the backing plate. When the brakes are applied, hydraulic pressure forces the wheel cylinder's actuating links outward. Since these links bear directly against the top of the brake shoes, the tops of the shoes are then forced against the inner side of the drum. This action forces the bottoms of the two shoes to contact the brake drum by rotating the entire assembly slightly (known as servo action). When pressure within the wheel cylinder is relaxed, return springs pull the shoes back away from the drum.

Most modern drum brakes are designed to self-adjust themselves during application when the vehicle is moving in reverse. This motion causes both shoes to rotate very slightly with the drum, rocking an adjusting lever, thereby causing rotation of the adjusting screw. Some drum brake systems are designed to self-adjust during application whenever the brakes are applied. This on-board adjustment system reduces the need for maintenance adjustments and keeps both the brake function and pedal feel satisfactory.

POWER BOOSTERS

Virtually all modern vehicles use a vacuum assisted power brake system to multiply the braking force and reduce pedal effort. Since vacuum is always available when the engine is operating, the system is simple and efficient. A vacuum diaphragm is located on the front of the master cylinder and assists the driver in applying the brakes, reducing both the effort and travel he must put into moving the brake pedal.

The vacuum diaphragm housing is normally connected to the intake manifold by a vacuum hose. A check valve is placed at the point where the hose enters the diaphragm housing, so that during periods of low manifold vacuum brakes assist will not be lost.

Depressing the brake pedal closes off the vacuum source and allows atmospheric pressure to enter on one side of the diaphragm. This causes the master cylinder pistons to move and apply the brakes. When the brake pedal is released, vacuum is applied to both sides of the diaphragm and springs return the diaphragm and master cylinder pistons to the released position.

If the vacuum supply fails, the brake pedal rod will contact the end of the master cylinder actuator rod and the system will apply the brakes without any power assistance. The driver will notice that much higher pedal effort is needed to stop the car and that the pedal feels harder than usual.

Vacuum Leak Test

1. Operate the engine at idle without touching the brake pedal for at least one minute.
2. Turn off the engine and wait one minute.
3. Test for the presence of assist vacuum by depressing the brake pedal and releasing it several times. If vacuum is present in the system, light application will produce less and less pedal travel. If there is no vacuum, air is leaking into the system.

System Operation Test

1. With the engine **OFF**, pump the brake pedal until the supply vacuum is entirely gone.
2. Put light, steady pressure on the brake pedal.
3. Start the engine and let it idle. If the system is operating correctly, the brake pedal should fall toward the floor if the constant pressure is maintained.

Power brake systems may be tested for hydraulic leaks just as ordinary systems are tested.

***** WARNING**

Clean, high quality brake fluid is essential to the safe and proper operation of the brake system. You should always buy the highest quality brake fluid that is available. If the brake fluid becomes contaminated, drain and flush the system, then refill the master cylinder with new fluid. Never reuse any brake fluid. Any brake fluid that is removed from the system should be discarded.

Brake Light Switch

REMOVAL & INSTALLATION

See Figures 1 and 2

1. Disconnect the negative battery cable.
2. Depress and hold the brake pedal while rotating the brake light switch in a counterclockwise direction, about 30 degrees.
3. Pull the switch rearward, then remove it from its mounting bracket.
4. Detach the electrical connector from the brake light switch, then remove the switch from the vehicle.

To install:

➡Before installing the switch, you must move the plunger into its fully extended position, as described in the following step.

5. Hold the brake light switch firmly in one hand. Use your other hand to pull outward on the plunger of the switch until it has ratcheted out to its fully extended position.
6. Attach the electrical connector to the brake light switch.
7. Mount the brake light switch into the bracket as follows:
   a. Depress the brake pedal as far down as possible, then install the switch in the bracket by aligning the index key on the switch with the slot at the top of the square hole in the mounting bracket.
   b. When the switch is fully installed in the bracket, rotate the switch clockwise about 30 degrees in order to lock the switch into the bracket.

***** WARNING**

Don't use extreme force when you pull on the brake pedal to adjust the switch. If too much force is used, you can damage the brake light switch or striker.

8. Gently pull back on the brake pedal until the pedal stops moving. This causes the switch plunger to ratchet backward to the proper position.
9. Connect the negative battery cable.

Master Cylinder

REMOVAL & INSTALLATION

See Figures 3, 4 and 5

➡It is very important to understand that different types of master cylinders are used on this vehicle. Vehicles equipped with traction control utilize a center port master cylinder, while vehicles not equipped with traction control utilize a compensating port master cylinder. Be sure to verify if the vehicle being worked on is equipped with traction control or not equipped with traction control and that the correct master cylinder is

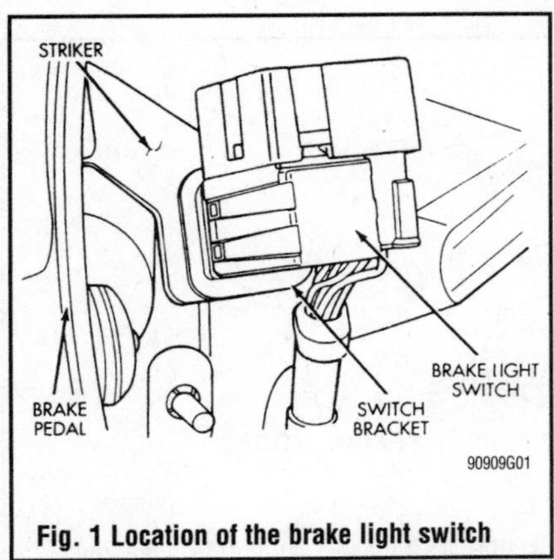

Fig. 1 Location of the brake light switch

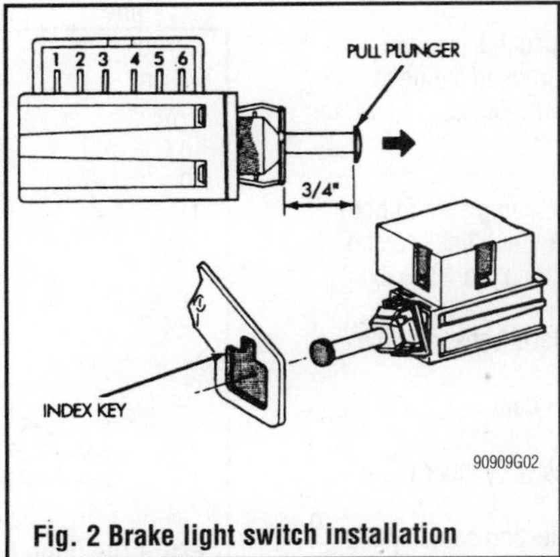

Fig. 2 Brake light switch installation

Fig. 3 The master cylinder uses a special filler tube to allow easier filling of the reservoir

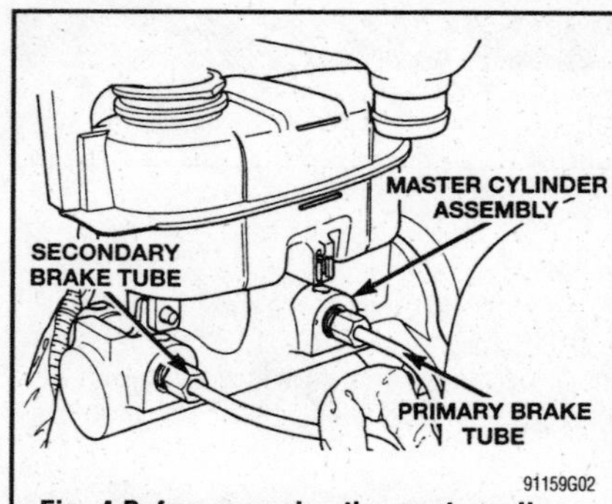

Fig. 4 Before removing the master cylinder from the booster, disconnect the brake tubes

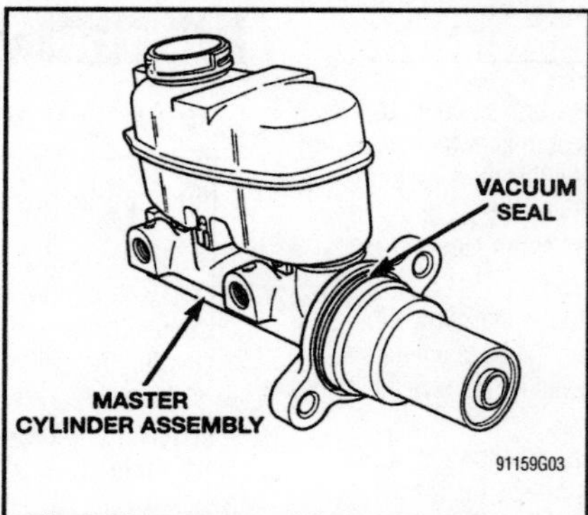

Fig. 5 The vacuum seal must be replaced each time the master cylinder is removed

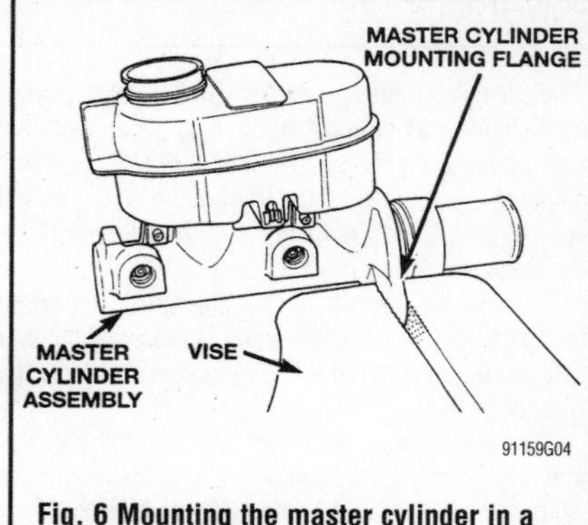

Fig. 6 Mounting the master cylinder in a vise for bleeding

installed. Also, vehicles equipped with four wheel disc brakes use a master cylinder with a different piston bore than the other master cylinders. Be sure to install the correct master cylinder for the type of brake system that the vehicle is equipped with.

1. With the engine turned OFF, pump the brake pedal several times until a firm brake pedal is achieved.
2. Disconnect the negative battery cable.
3. To prevent possible hydraulic system contamination, thoroughly clean all surfaces of the brake fluid reservoir, filler neck and master cylinder. Use MOPAR® Brake Parts Cleaner, or an equivalent solvent.
4. Remove the brake fluid reservoir filler tube by pushing down and turning. Remove the cap from the removed filler tube and install it on the brake fluid reservoir.
5. Disconnect the brake fluid level sensor wiring connector from the side of the brake fluid reservoir.
6. Disconnect the brake lines from the master cylinder. Plug the outlet ports and brake lines to prevent fluid loss and dirt entry.
7. To prevent any dirt particles from falling into the vacuum booster, thoroughly clean the master cylinder and power brake booster using MOPAR® Brake Parts Cleaner, or equivalent. Remove the master cylinder attaching nuts and remove the master cylinder.
8. Remove the vacuum seal located on the mounting flange of the master cylinder by carefully pulling it away from the master cylinder. Discard the old vacuum seal.

To install:

9. Bench bleed the replacement master cylinder.
10. Install a new vacuum seal onto the master cylinder. Be sure the new seal is seated squarely in the groove of the master cylinder casting.
11. Position the master cylinder on the booster studs, aligning the booster pushrod with the master cylinder piston. Secure the master cylinder with the mounting nuts. Torque the mounting nuts to 18 ft. lbs. (25 Nm).
12. Reconnect the primary and secondary brake lines to the primary and secondary ports in the master cylinder. Make sure the fluid in the reservoir is at the proper level.
13. Have an assistant apply the brake pedal. With the pedal depressed, loosen the forward brake line fitting until the brake pedal drops to the floor. Tighten the fitting before the brake pedal is allowed to return. Repeat until no more air bubbles are released.
14. Repeat the previous Step at the rear brake line.
15. Final tighten the brake lines at the master cylinder, being sure to hold the brake lines securely during the tightening of the brake line fittings to control orientation of the flex section. Torque the brake line fittings to 13 ft. lbs. (17 Nm).
16. Reconnect the wiring connector to the brake fluid level sensor on the side of the master cylinder.
17. Install the filler tube onto the master cylinder brake fluid reservoir.
18. Reconnect the negative battery cable. Refill the master cylinder brake fluid reservoir and bleed the brake system.
19. Road test the vehicle using extreme caution while testing brake system operation. Check the brake fluid level and top off if necessary.

BENCH BLEEDING

See Figures 6 and 7

WARNING

All new master cylinders should be bench bled prior to installation. Bleeding a new master cylinder on the vehicle is not a good idea. With air trapped inside, the master cylinder piston may bottom in the bore and possibly cause internal damage.

1. Secure the master cylinder in a bench vise using only the master cylinder mounting flange.
2. Remove the master cylinder reservoir cap.
3. Manufacture or purchase bleeding tubes and install them on the master cylinder as illustrated.
4. Fill the master cylinder reservoir with clean, fresh brake fluid until the level is within 0.25 in. of the reservoir top.

Ensure the bleeding tubes are below the level of the brake fluid, otherwise air may get into the system making your bleeding efforts ineffective.

5. Use a blunt tipped rod (a long socket extension works well) to slowly depress the master cylinder piston. Make sure the piston travels full its full stroke.
6. As the piston is depressed, bubbles will come out of the bleeding tubes. Continue depressing and releasing the piston until all bubbles are expelled from the master cylinder.
7. Refill the master cylinder with fluid.
8. Remove the bleeding tubes.
9. Install the master cylinder reservoir cap.
10. Install the master cylinder on the vehicle.

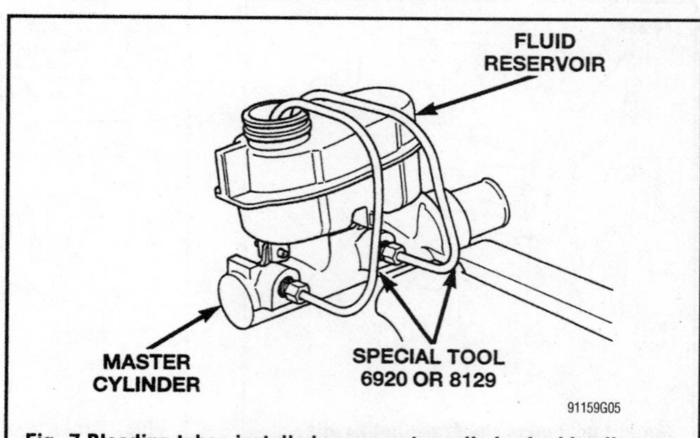

Fig. 7 Bleeding tubes installed on a master cylinder for bleeding

Power Brake Booster

REMOVAL & INSTALLATION

➧ See Figures 8 thru 15

1. Disconnect the negative battery cable.
2. With the engine not running, pump the brake pedal until a firm pedal is achieved (approximately 4–5 strokes).
3. Remove the battery from the vehicle.
4. Remove the air inlet resonator/air cleaner assembly from the engine compartment.
5. If equipped with speed control, disengage the wiring harness connector from the speed control servo. Disconnect the vacuum lines from the speed control servo and vacuum reservoir on the battery tray.
6. Remove the bolt securing the speed control servo bracket to the battery tray. Move the bracket forward to unhook it from the battery tray and remove.
7. Remove the battery tray from the vehicle.
8. On 3.3L and 3.8L engines, perform the following:
   a. Remove the EGR valve and vacuum transducer as an assembly from the intake manifold.
   b. Remove the 2 bolts mounting the throttle body to the intake manifold and the clip securing the wiring harness to the throttle cable bracket. Then remove the throttle body and throttle cable bracket as an assembly from the intake manifold.
9. Disengage the wiring harness connector from the brake fluid level sensor in the master cylinder fluid reservoir.
10. To prevent any dirt particles from falling into the vacuum booster, thoroughly clean the master cylinder and power brake booster using MOPAR® Brake Parts Cleaner, or equivalent.

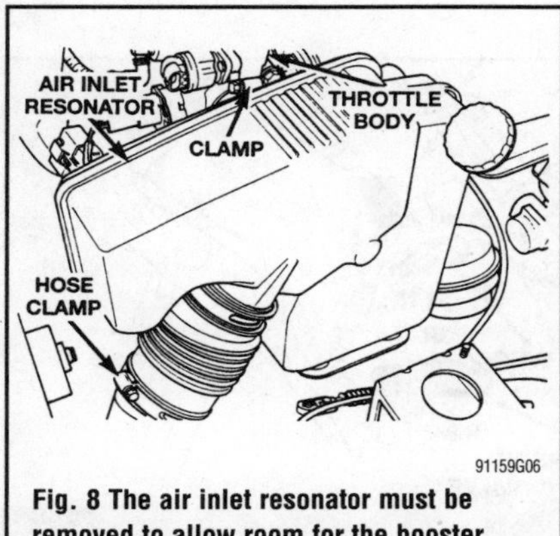

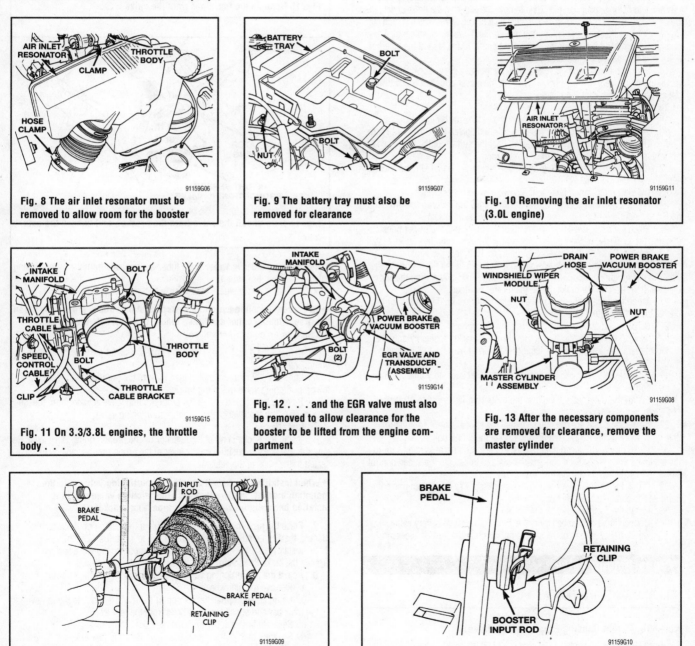

Fig. 8 The air inlet resonator must be removed to allow room for the booster

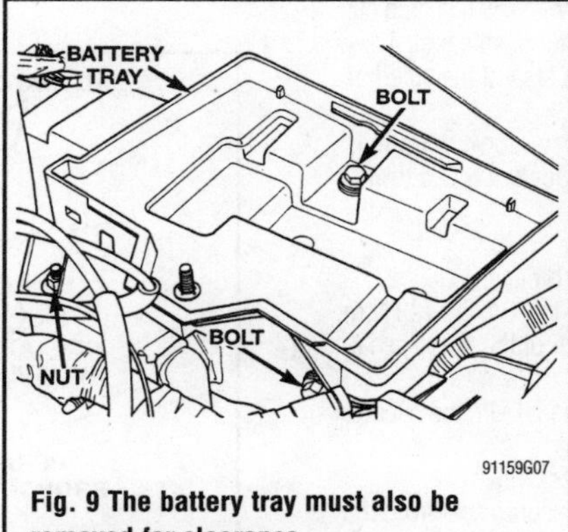

Fig. 9 The battery tray must also be removed for clearance

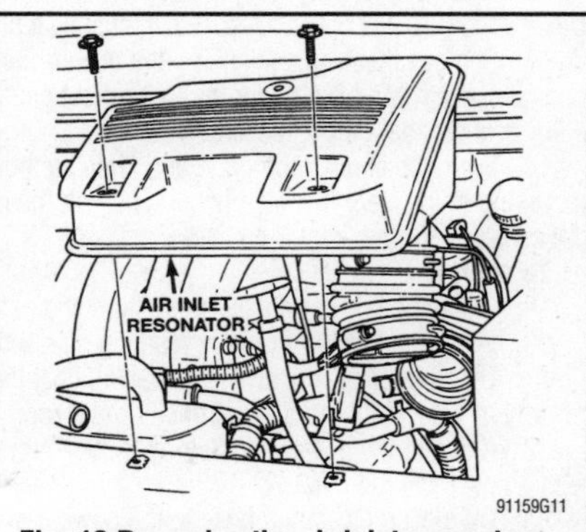

Fig. 10 Removing the air inlet resonator (3.0L engine)

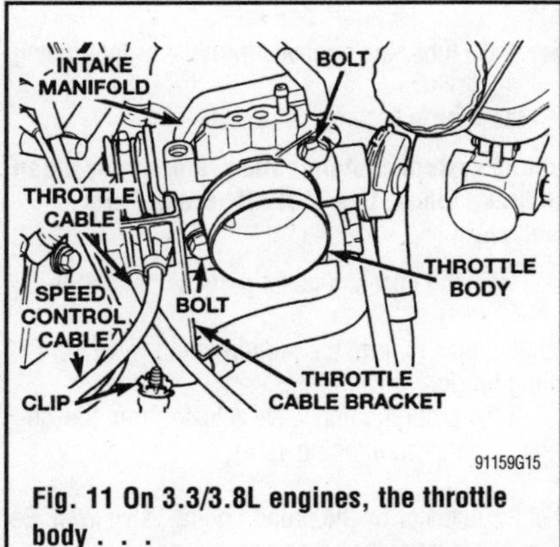

Fig. 11 On 3.3/3.8L engines, the throttle body . . .

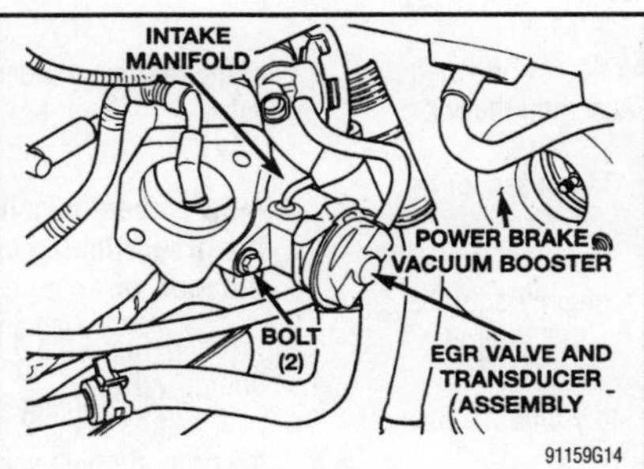

Fig. 12 . . . and the EGR valve must also be removed to allow clearance for the booster to be lifted from the engine compartment

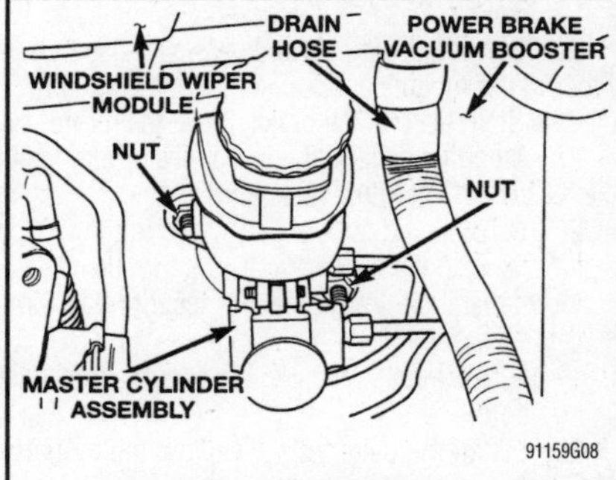

Fig. 13 After the necessary components are removed for clearance, remove the master cylinder

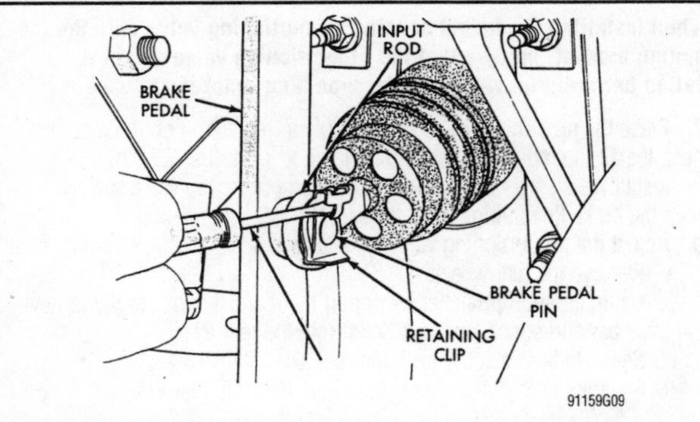

Fig. 14 Disconnect the booster from the pedal by removing the retaining clip from the pin

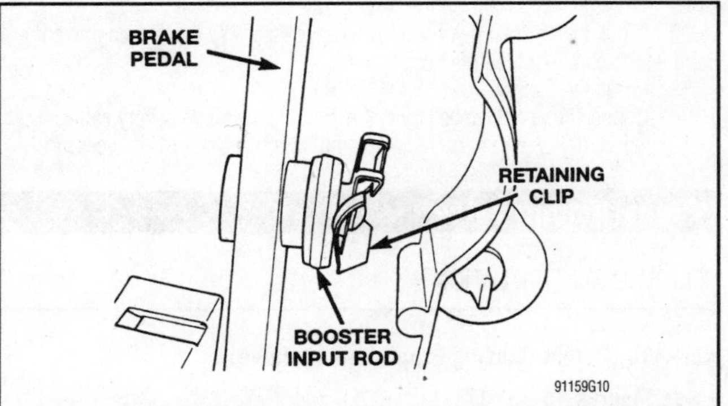

Fig. 15 The retaining clip can be removed by lifting the curved tab with your thumb and pushing sideways

11. Remove the clip attaching the drain hose for wiper module to the brake tube at the master cylinder. Remove the drain hose from the windshield wiper/motor module assembly.

➡It is not necessary to disconnect the brake lines from the master cylinder when removing the master cylinder from the vacuum booster.

12. Remove the 2 nuts that secure the master cylinder to the power booster.
13. Remove the master cylinder and brake tubes as an assembly from the vacuum booster. When the master cylinder is removed, lay it out of the way on top of the left motor mount.
14. Disconnect the vacuum hose from the check valve located on the power booster. Do not remove the check valve.
15. Locate the vacuum booster input rod-to-brake pedal attachment under the instrument panel. Position a small, flat-bladed prying tool between the center tang on the power booster input rod-to-brake pedal pin retaining clip.
16. Rotate the pry tool enough to allow the retaining clip center tang to pass over the end of the brake pedal pin. Then remove the clip from the brake pedal pin. Discard the clip, it is not to be reused. It must be replaced with a new retaining clip.
17. Remove the 4 nuts attaching the power booster to the dash panel. These nuts are accessible from under the instrument panel, in the area of the steering column and pedal bracket assembly.
18. From the engine compartment, slide the power booster forward until its mounting studs clear the dash panel. Then tilt the power booster up and toward the center of the vehicle to remove.

To install:

19. Place the power booster in position against the dash panel.
20. Install the 4 power booster mounting nuts and tighten to 21 ft. lbs. (29 Nm).
21. Using Lubriplate®, or an equivalent, coat the surface of the brake pedal pin where it contacts the power booster input rod.
22. Connect the power booster input rod to the brake pedal pin and secure with a new retaining clip.
23. Connect the vacuum hose to the power booster check valve.
24. Using a soft tool such as a trim stick, remove the vacuum seal from the master cylinder mounting flange and install a NEW vacuum seal.
25. Place the master cylinder back into position against the power booster, aligning the push rod of the booster unit with the master cylinder piston. Install and tighten the master cylinder mounting nuts to 18 ft. lbs. (25 Nm).
26. Connect the wiper module drain hose to the bottom of the windshield wiper/motor module assembly. Loosely install the tie strap attaching the wiper module drain hose to the brake line at the master cylinder.
27. Plug the wiring harness connector into the brake fluid level sensor on the master cylinder fluid reservoir.
28. On 3.3L and 3.8L engines, perform the following:
    a. Install the throttle body and throttle cable bracket assembly onto the intake manifold. Install the clip securing the wiring harness to the throttle cable bracket.
    b. Install the EGR valve and vacuum transducer assembly onto the intake manifold.
29. Install the battery tray. Tighten the mounting fasteners to 10 ft. lbs. (14 Nm).
30. If equipped with speed control, install the speed control servo and bracket onto the battery tray. Tighten the bracket mounting bolt.
31. If equipped with speed control, install the wiring harness connector to the speed control servo. Then connect the vacuum lines onto the speed control servo and vacuum reservoir on the battery tray.
32. Install the air inlet resonator/air cleaner assembly into the engine compartment. Securely tighten the hose clamps.
33. Install the battery.
34. Connect the positive battery cable, then the negative battery cable.
35. Check the operation of the stop lamp switch and adjust, if necessary.

Proportioning Valve

REMOVAL & INSTALLATION

Non-ABS (Height Sensing Proportioning Valve)

See Figures 16 and 17

1. Using a brake pedal depressor, move and lock the brake pedal to a position past its first 1 inch of travel. This will prevent brake fluid from draining out of the master cylinder when the brake tubes are removed from the proportioning valve.

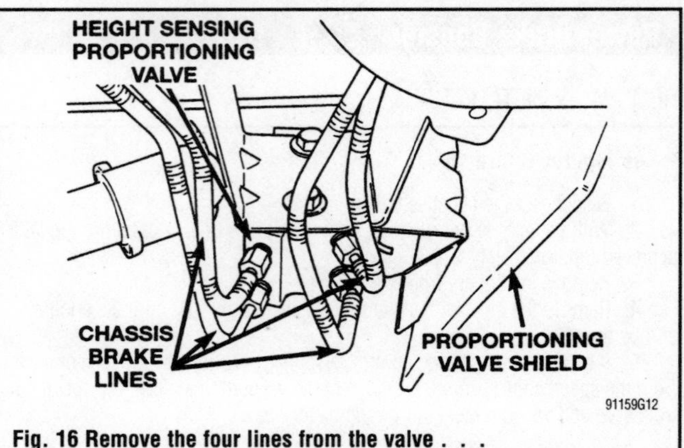

Fig. 16 Remove the four lines from the valve . . .

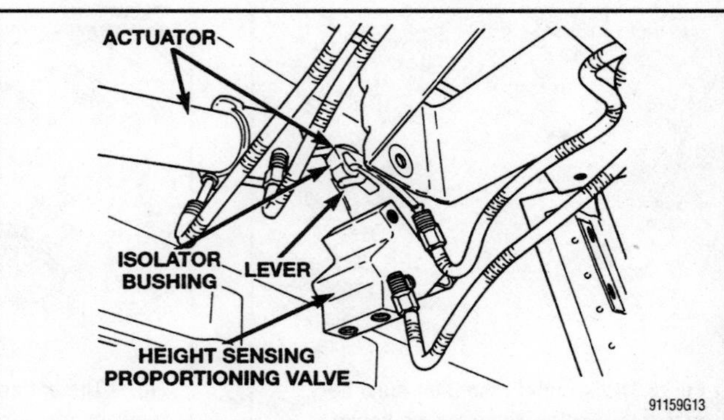

Fig. 17 . . . unbolt the valve from the bracket, and unhook the actuator

2. Raise and safely support the vehicle securely on jackstands.

➡To prevent possible hydraulic system contamination, thoroughly clean the proportioning valve and brake tubes. Use MOPAR® Brake Parts Cleaner, or an equivalent solvent.

3. Remove the 4 brake lines from the inlet and outlet ports of the proportioning valve.
4. Loosen the 2 retaining bolts, then remove the proportioning valve from the proportioning valve mounting bracket.
5. Remove the hooked end of the proportioning valve actuator from the isolator bushing on the lever of the height proportioning valve.

To install:

6. Install the hooked end of the actuator on the proportioning valve lever. Be sure that the isolator bushing on the lever of the proportioning valve is fully seated in the hook of the actuator.

➡When installing the height sensing proportioning valve onto the mounting bracket, be sure that the proportioning valve shield is installed between the valve and the mounting bracket.

7. Place the proportioning valve assembly into position on the mounting bracket. Install the mounting bolts and tighten to 17 ft. lbs. (23 Nm).
8. Install the chassis brake lines into the proportioning valve assembly. Tighten the brake line fittings to 12 ft. lbs. (16 Nm).
9. Adjust the proportioning valve actuator according to the following steps:
    a. Remove the rear wheels.
    b. Using an appropriate jack, support the rear axle prior to the removal of the track bar and shock absorber bolts from the rear axle.
    c. Separate the track bar from the rear axle.
    d. Separate both of the shock absorbers from the rear axle.

➡When lowering the rear axle, be sure that the leaf springs do not make contact with the hoist, which will limit the downward movement of the axle. If this happens, an improper adjustment of the actuator may result.

e. Loosen, but do not remove, both of the leaf spring-to-front spring hanger pivot bolts.

f. Lower the rear axle so it is at its farthest point of downward movement.

g. Loosen the adjustment nut on the actuator.

h. Be sure that the hooked end of the actuator is correctly seated in the clip on the proportioning valve lever and that the clip is positioned correctly on the lever of the proportioning valve.

i. Pull the proportioning valve actuator housing toward the spring hanger until the proportioning valve lever bottoms on the proportioning valve body. Hold the proportioning valve actuator in this position while tightening the adjusting nut to 45 inch lbs. (5 Nm). Proportioning valve adjustment is now complete.

j. Connect the shock absorbers and track bar to the rear axle. Install, but do not tighten any of these mounting bolts at this time.

k. Install the wheels.

10. Bleed the brake system.
11. Lower the vehicle. Be sure that the suspension is supporting the full weight of the vehicle.
12. Tighten the following bolts to these specifications:
- Spring-to-front hanger pivot bolts—115 ft. lbs. (156 Nm)
- Shock absorber mounting bolts—75 ft. lbs. (101 Nm)
- Track bar mounting bolt—70 ft. lbs. (95 Nm)

13. Carefully road test the vehicle to verify proper brake system operation.

Brake Hoses and Lines

Metal lines and rubber brake hoses should be checked frequently for leaks and external damage. Metal lines are particularly prone to crushing and kinking under the vehicle. Any such deformation can restrict the proper flow of fluid and therefore impair braking at the wheels. Rubber hoses should be checked for cracking or scraping; such damage can create a weak spot in the hose and it could fail under pressure.

Any time the lines are removed or disconnected, extreme cleanliness must be observed. Clean all joints and connections before disassembly (use a stiff bristle brush and clean brake fluid); be sure to plug the lines and ports as soon as they are opened. New lines and hoses should be flushed clean with brake fluid before installation to remove any contamination.

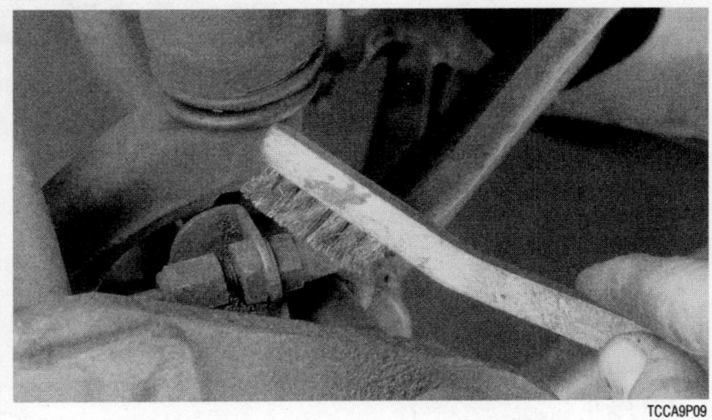

TCCA9P09

Fig. 18 Use a brush to clean the fittings of any debris

REMOVAL & INSTALLATION

See Figures 18, 19, 20 and 21

1. Disconnect the negative battery cable.
2. Raise and safely support the vehicle on jackstands.
3. Remove any wheel and tire assemblies necessary for access to the particular line you are removing.
4. Thoroughly clean the surrounding area at the joints to be disconnected.
5. Place a suitable catch pan under the joint to be disconnected.
6. Using two wrenches (one to hold the joint and one to turn the fitting), disconnect the hose or line to be replaced.
7. Disconnect the other end of the line or hose, moving the drain pan if necessary. Always use a back-up wrench to avoid damaging the fitting.
8. Disconnect any retaining clips or brackets holding the line and remove the line from the vehicle.

➡If the brake system is to remain open for more time than it takes to swap lines, tape or plug each remaining clip and port to keep contaminants out and fluid in.

To install:

9. Install the new line or hose, starting with the end farthest from the master cylinder. Connect the other end, then confirm that both fittings are correctly threaded and turn smoothly using finger pressure. Make sure the new line will not rub against any other part. Brake lines must be at least 1/2 in. (13mm) from the steering column and other moving parts. Any protective shielding or insulators must be reinstalled in the original location.

✲✲ WARNING

Make sure the hose is NOT kinked or touching any part of the frame or suspension after installation. These conditions may cause the hose to fail prematurely.

10. Using two wrenches as before, tighten each fitting.
11. Install any retaining clips or brackets on the lines.
12. If removed, install the wheel and tire assemblies, then carefully lower the vehicle to the ground.
13. Refill the brake master cylinder reservoir with clean, fresh brake fluid, meeting DOT 3 specifications. Properly bleed the brake system.
14. Connect the negative battery cable.

Bleeding The Brake System

See Figures 22, 23 and 24

When any part of the hydraulic system has been disconnected for repair or replacement, air may get into the lines and cause spongy pedal action (because air can be compressed and brake fluid cannot). To correct this condition, it is necessary to bleed the hydraulic system so to be sure all air is purged.

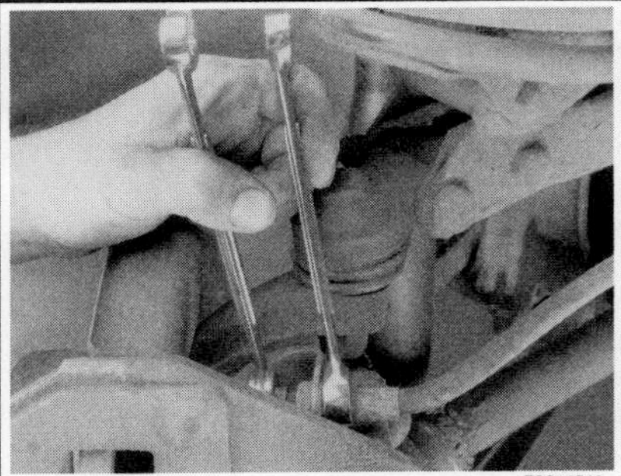

TCCA9P10

Fig. 19 Use two wrenches to loosen the fitting. If available, use flare nut type wrenches

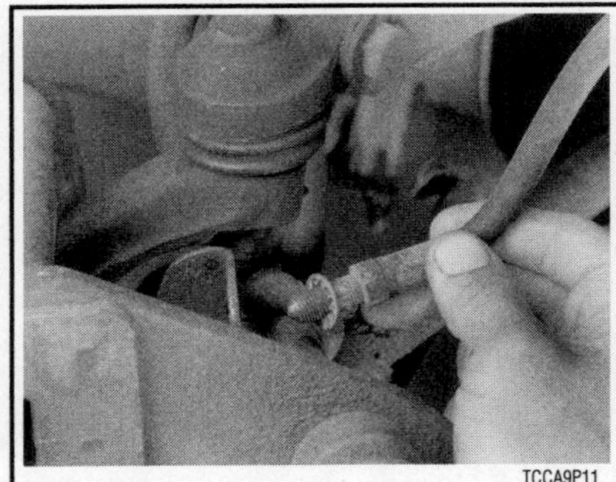

TCCA9P11

Fig. 20 Any gaskets/crush washers should be replaced with new ones during installation

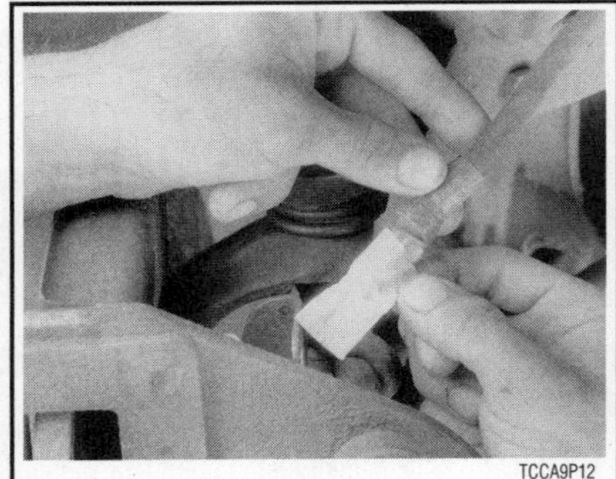

TCCA9P12

Fig. 21 Tape or plug the line to prevent contamination

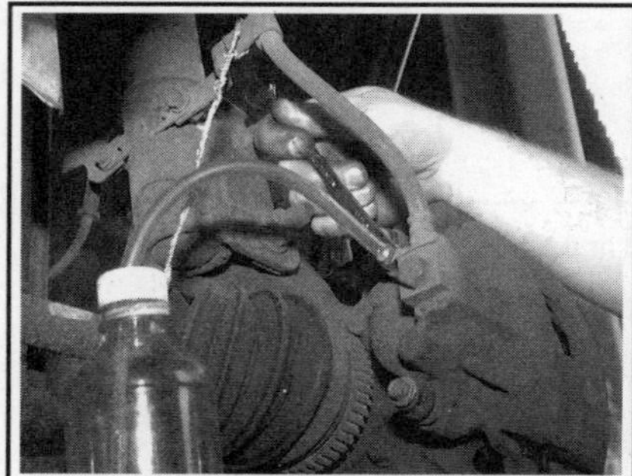

91159P37

Fig. 22 With a clear plastic hose in a container of clean brake fluid, open the bleeder screw at least one full turn

91159P22

Fig. 23 A vacuum bleeding kit can also be used to bleed the brakes

91159P38

Fig. 24 Make sure to replace the bleeder screw caps after bleeding the brakes

When bleeding the brake system, bleed one brake cylinder at a time, beginning with the left rear wheel cylinder first. ALWAYS Keep the master cylinder reservoir filled with brake fluid during the bleeding operation. Never use brake fluid that has been drained from the hydraulic system, no matter how clean it is.

The primary and secondary hydraulic brake systems are separate and are bled independently. During the bleeding operation, do not allow the reservoir to run dry. Keep the master cylinder reservoir filled with brake fluid.

1. Clean all dirt from around the master cylinder fill cap, remove the cap and fill the master cylinder with brake fluid until the level is within ¼ in. (6mm) of the top edge of the reservoir.
2. Clean the bleeder screws at all 4 wheels. The bleeder screws are located on the back of the brake backing plate (drum brakes) and on the top of the brake calipers (disc brakes).
3. Attach a length of rubber hose over the bleeder screw and place the other end of the hose in a glass jar, submerged in brake fluid.
4. Open the bleeder screw at least 1 full turn. Have an assistant slowly depress the brake pedal.
5. Close the bleeder screw and tell your assistant to allow the brake pedal to return slowly. Continue this process to purge all air from the system.
6. When bubbles cease to appear at the end of the bleeder hose, close the bleeder screw and remove the hose. Tighten the disc brake caliper bleeder screw to 11 ft. lbs. (15 Nm) and the drum brake wheel cylinder bleeder screw to 80 inch lbs. (10 Nm).
7. The correct brake system bleeding sequence is:
   - Left rear wheel
   - Right front wheel
   - Right rear wheel
   - Left front wheel
8. Check the master cylinder fluid level and add fluid accordingly. Do this after bleeding each wheel.
9. Repeat the bleeding operation at the remaining 3 wheels, ending with the one closet to the master cylinder.
10. Fill the master cylinder reservoir to the proper level.

DISC BRAKES

⁂ CAUTION

Older brake pads or shoes may contain asbestos, which has been determined to be cancer causing agent. Never clean the brake surfaces with compressed air! Avoid inhaling any dust from any brake surface! When cleaning brake surfaces, use a commercially available brake cleaning fluid.

Brake Pads

REMOVAL & INSTALLATION

➧ See Figures 25, 26, 27, 28 and 29

1. Remove brake fluid from the master cylinder brake fluid reservoir until the reservoir is approximately ½ full. Discard the removed fluid.
2. Raise and safely support the of the vehicle. Remove the wheels.
3. Remove the brake caliper assembly that requires brake pad replacement.
4. Support the caliper out of the way with a strong piece of wire. Do not let the caliper hang by the brake hose or damage to the brake hose will result.
5. If necessary, compress the caliper piston into the bore using a C-clamp. Insert a suitable piece of wood between the C-clamp and caliper piston to protect the piston.
6. Remove the outboard disc brake pad from the caliper by prying the brake pad retaining clip over the raised area on the caliper. Slide the brake pad down and off the caliper.
7. Remove the inboard disc brake pad from the caliper by pulling the brake pad away from the caliper piston until the retaining clip on the pad is free from the caliper piston cavity.

To install:

8. Be sure the caliper piston has been completely retracted into the piston bore of the caliper assembly. This is required when installing the brake caliper equipped with new brake pads.
9. If equipped, remove the protective paper from the noise suppression gaskets on the new disc brake pads.
10. Install the new inboard disc brake pad into the caliper piston by pressing the pad firmly into the cavity of the caliper piston. Be sure the new inboard brake pad is seated squarely against the face of the brake caliper piston.
11. Install the outboard disc brake pad by sliding it onto the caliper assembly.
12. Install the brake caliper assembly.
13. Install the wheels and lug nuts. Torque the lug nuts, in a star pattern sequence, to 95 ft. lbs. (129 Nm). Apply the brake pedal several times until a firm pedal is obtained.
14. Check the fluid level in the master cylinder and add fluid as necessary. Road test the vehicle.

INSPECTION

➧ See Figure 30

1. If you can't accurately determine the condition of the brake pads by visual inspection, you must remove the caliper, then remove the brake pads.
2. Measure the thickness of the brake pad's lining material at the thinnest portion of the assembly. Do not include the pad's metal backing plate in the measurement.
3. When a set of brake pads are worn to a total thickness of 0.313 inch (7.95mm) for front brakes, or 0.280 inch (7.0mm) for rear brakes, they should be replaced.
4. Replace both brake shoe assemblies (inboard and outboard). It is necessary that both wheel sets be replaced whenever the brake shoe assemblies on either side are replaced.
5. If the brake shoes do not require replacement, reinstall the assemblies making sure each brake shoe is returned to the original position.

91159P33

Fig. 25 Once the two bolts are removed, the caliper can be lifted from the disc and steering knuckle

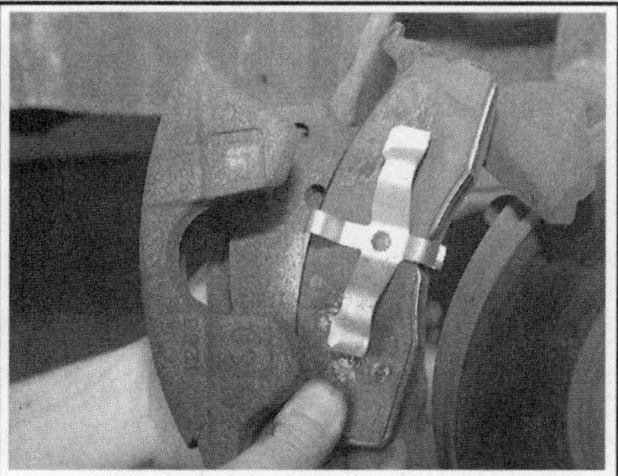

91159P32

Fig. 26 The outside brake pad is held in place by a spring clip that is riveted to the pad

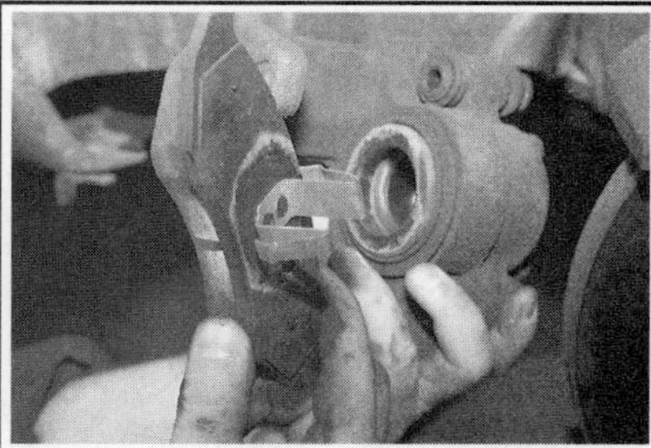

91159P31

Fig. 27 The inside pad is also retained by a spring clip; it can be removed after the outside pad has been removed from the caliper

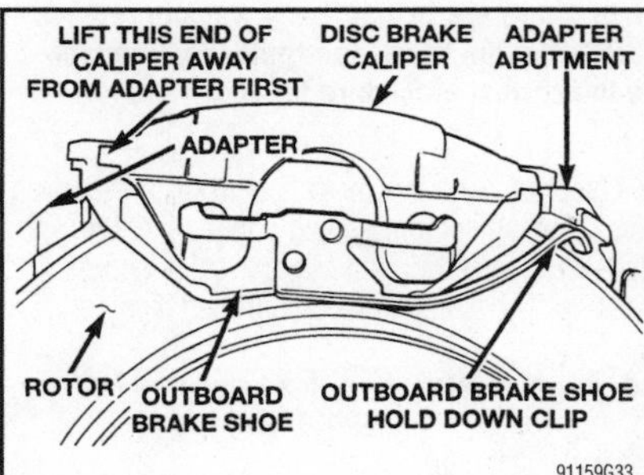

Fig. 28 The brake pads on rear calipers are removed in a similar manner as front pads, with the exception of a slightly different spring clip on the outboard shoe

91159P42

Fig. 29 Before installing new pads, the piston needs to be recessed into the bore

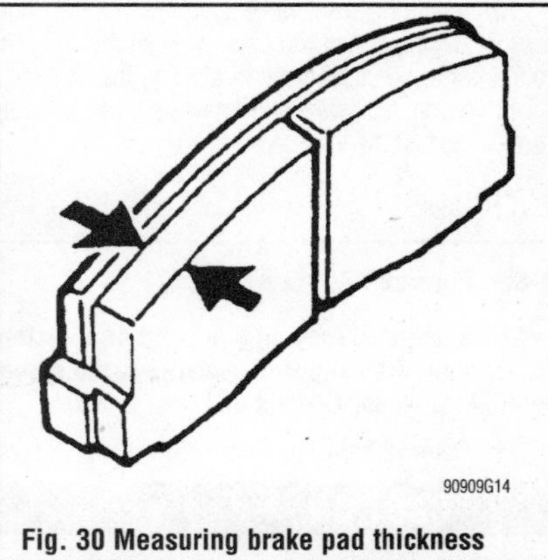

90909G14

Fig. 30 Measuring brake pad thickness

Brake Caliper

REMOVAL & INSTALLATION

See Figures 31 thru 36

1. Raise and safely support the vehicle. Remove the wheels.
2. If the caliper is only being removed from the bracket (as for a brake pad change), move to Step 3. If the caliper is being removed from the vehicle (as for replacement or an overhaul and reseal), remove the brake hose attaching bolt from the caliper. Remove the hose from the caliper and discard the washers. New seal washers will be required at assembly. Plug the brake hose to prevent fluid leakage.
3. Remove the caliper guide pin bolts that secure the caliper to the steering knuckle.
4. Remove the caliper by slowly sliding it away from the steering knuckle. Slide the opposite end of the brake caliper out from under the machined abutment on the steering knuckle.
5. Using a strong piece of wire, support the brake caliper assembly off the strut unit. Do NOT allow the caliper to hang from the brake fluid flex hose or damage to the hose will result.

To install:

6. Clean both steering knuckle abutment surfaces of any dirt, grease or corrosion. Then lubricate the abutment surfaces with a liberal amount of MOPAR® Multipurpose Lubricant, or equivalent.
7. Properly position the brake caliper over the brake pads and disc rotor. Be careful not to allow the caliper seals or guide pin bushings to get damaged by the steering knuckle bosses. Install the caliper guide pin bolts and torque to 16 ft. lbs. (22 Nm). Be careful not to cross thread the guide pin bolts.
8. If removed, attach the brake hose to the caliper using new washers. Tighten the banjo bolt to 35 ft. lbs. (47 Nm).
9. Bleed the brake system.

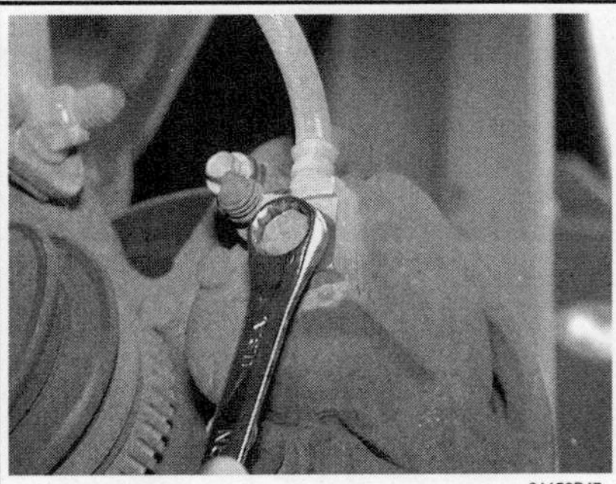

91159P47

Fig. 31 If the caliper is going to be removed for overhaul, remove the brake hose

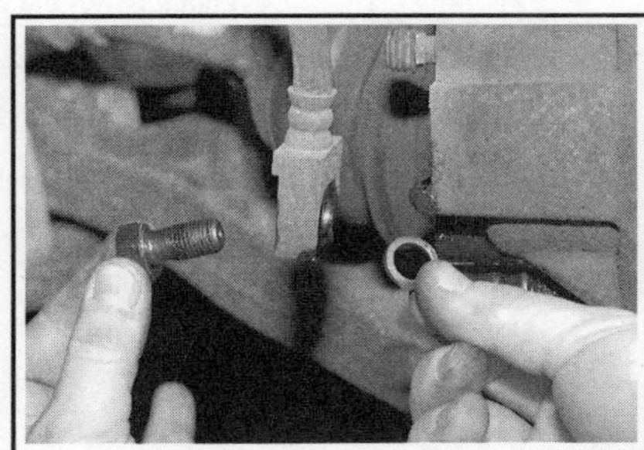

91159P46

Fig. 32 The banjo bolt uses copper gaskets on each side of the hose fitting; they should be replaced whenever the bolt is removed

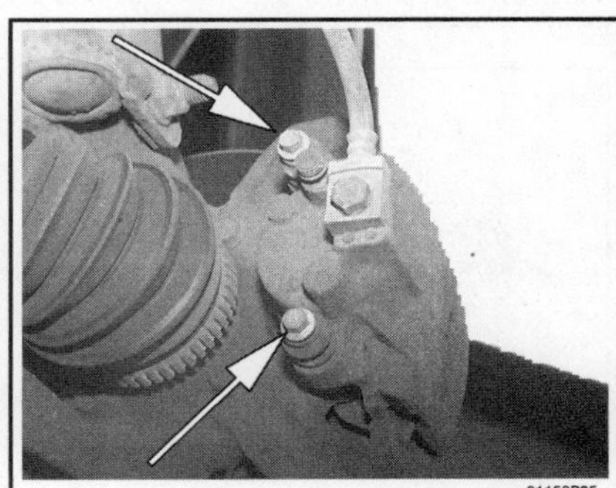

91159P35

Fig. 33 The caliper is attached to the steering knuckle with two bolts

91159P34

Fig. 34 The bolts secure the sliding pins to the steering knuckle

91159P33

Fig. 35 Once the two bolts are removed, the caliper can be lifted from the disc and steering knuckle

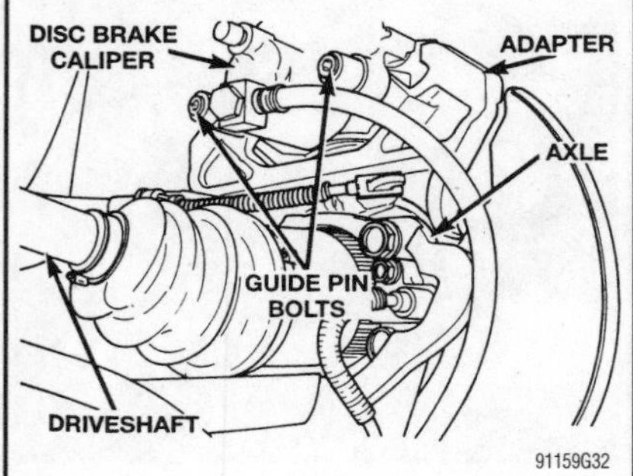

91159G32

Fig. 36 Rear disc brake calipers are mounted in the same manner as front calipers

10. Install the front wheels and lug nuts. Torque the lug nuts, in a star pattern sequence, to half torque specifications. Then repeat the tightening sequence to the full torque specification of 95 ft. lbs. (129 Nm). Lower the vehicle.

11. Pump the brake pedal several times to insure that the brake pedal is firm. Road test the vehicle.

OVERHAUL

See Figures 37 thru 47

Some vehicles may be equipped dual piston calipers. The procedure to overhaul the caliper is essentially the same with the exception of multiple pistons, O-rings and dust boots.

1. Remove the caliper from the vehicle and place on a clean workbench.

CAUTION

NEVER place your fingers in front of the pistons in an attempt to catch or protect the pistons when applying compressed air. This could result in personal injury!

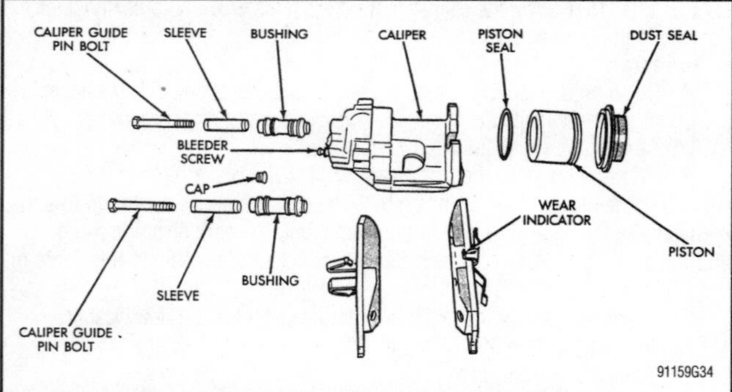

91159G34

Fig. 37 Exploded view of a front disc brake caliper assembly

Depending upon the vehicle, there are two different ways to remove the piston from the caliper. Refer to the brake pad replacement procedure to make sure you have the correct procedure for your vehicle.

2. The first method is as follows:
   a. Stuff a shop towel or a block of wood into the caliper to catch the piston.
   b. Remove the caliper piston using compressed air applied into the caliper inlet hole. Inspect the piston for scoring, nicks, corrosion and/or worn or damaged chrome plating. The piston must be replaced if any of these conditions are found.

3. For the second method, you must rotate the piston to retract it from the caliper.

4. If equipped, remove the anti-rattle clip.

5. Use a prytool to remove the caliper boot, being careful not to scratch the housing bore.

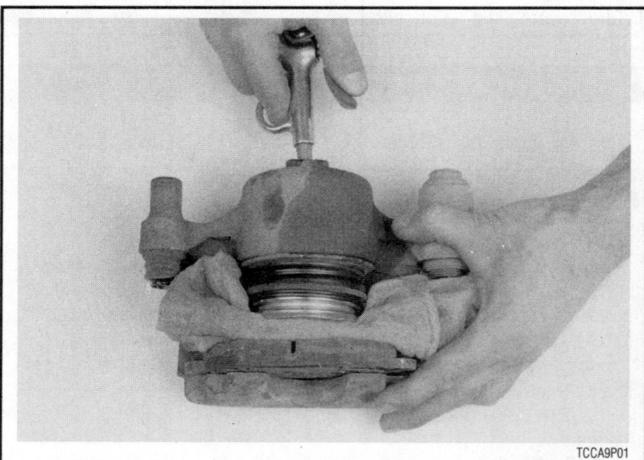
TCCA9P01

Fig. 38 For some types of calipers, use compressed air to drive the piston out of the caliper, but make sure to keep your fingers clear

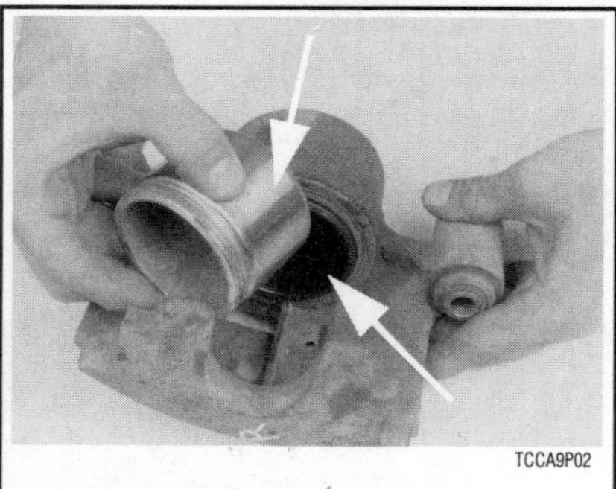
TCCA9P02

Fig. 39 Withdraw the piston from the caliper bore

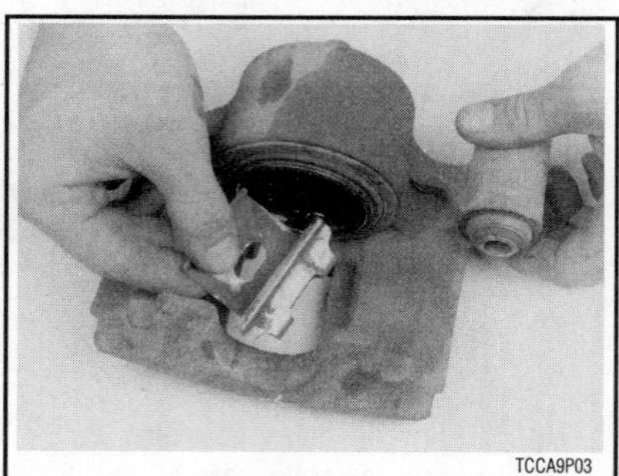
TCCA9P03

Fig. 40 On some vehicles, you must remove the anti-rattle clip

TCCSA9P04

Fig. 41 Use a prytool to carefully pry around the edge of the boot . . .

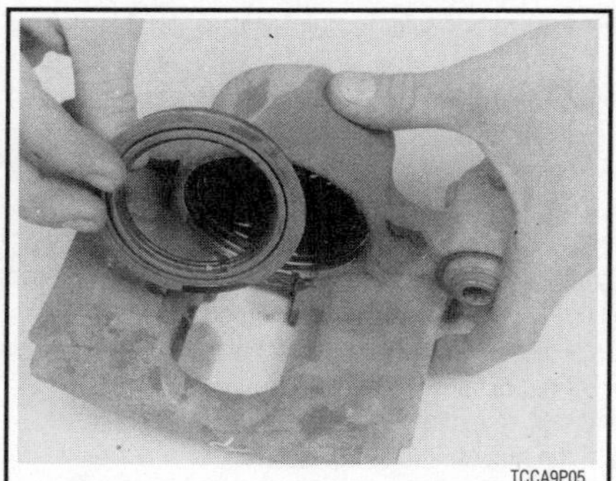
TCCA9P05

Fig. 42 . . . then remove the boot from the caliper housing, taking care not to score or damage the bore

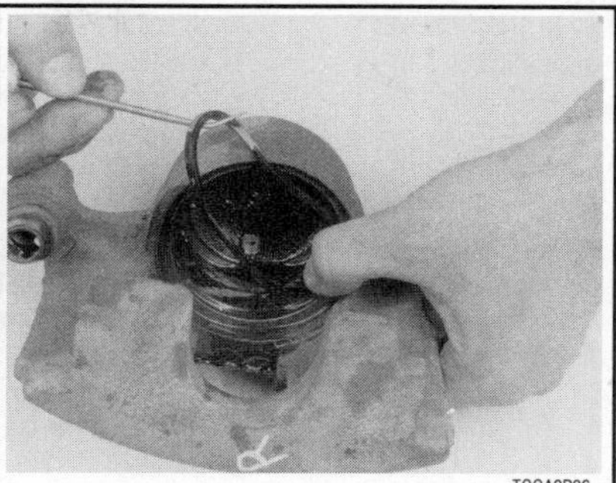
TCCA9P06

Fig. 43 Use extreme caution when removing the piston seal; DO NOT scratch the caliper bore

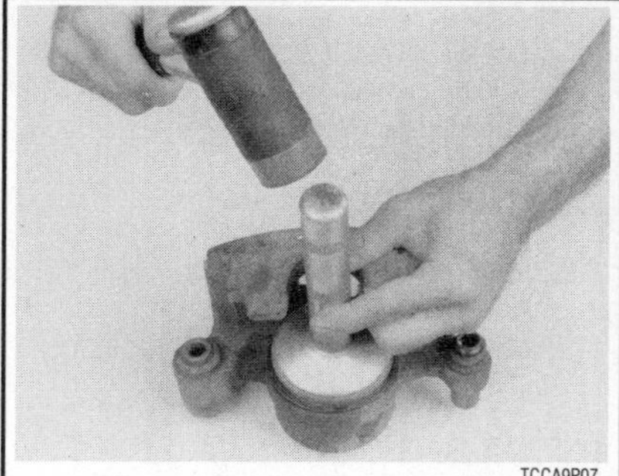
TCCA9P07

Fig. 44 Use the proper size driving tool and a mallet to properly seal the boots in the caliper housing

91159P41

Fig. 45 Before mounting the caliper onto the steering knuckle, remove the sliding pins . . .

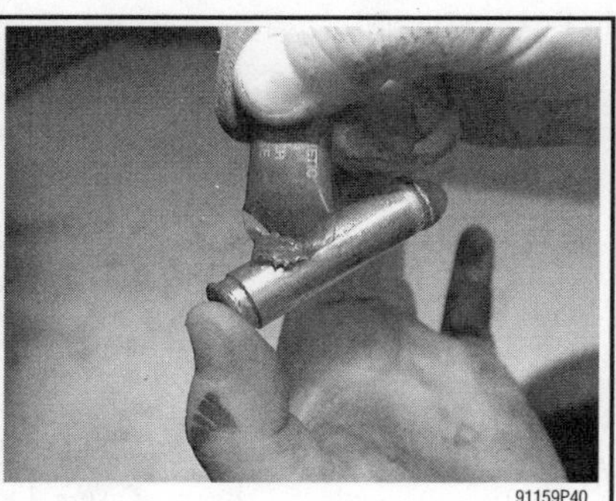
91159P40

Fig. 46 . . . and lubricate them with the grease supplied with the rebuild kit

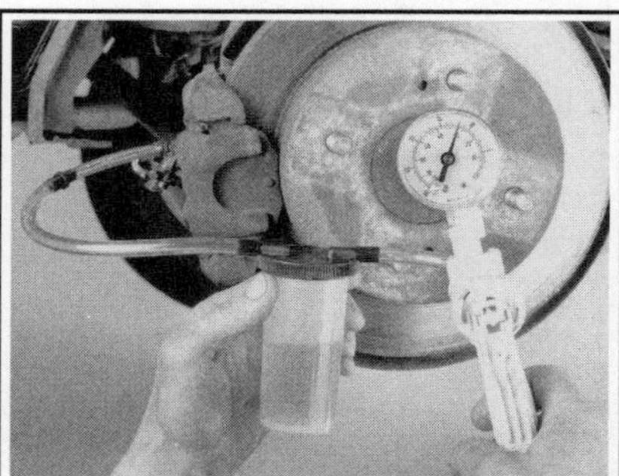
TCCA9P08

Fig. 47 There are tools, such as this Mighty-Vac, available to assist in proper brake system bleeding

6. Remove the piston seals from the groove in the caliper bore.
7. Carefully loosen the brake bleeder valve cap and valve from the caliper housing.
8. Inspect the caliper bores, pistons and mounting threads for scoring or excessive wear.
9. Use crocus cloth to polish out light corrosion from the piston and bore.
10. Clean all parts with denatured alcohol and dry with compressed air.

To assemble:

11. Lubricate and install the bleeder valve and cap.
12. Install the new seals into the caliper bore grooves, making sure they are not twisted.
13. Lubricate the piston bore.
14. Install the pistons and boots into the bores of the calipers and push to the bottom of the bores.
15. Use a suitable driving tool to seat the boots in the housing.
16. Install the caliper in the vehicle.
17. Install the wheel and tire assembly, then carefully lower the vehicle.
18. Properly bleed the brake system.

Brake Disc (Rotor)

REMOVAL & INSTALLATION

See Figures 48, 49 and 50

1. Raise and safely support the vehicle.
2. Remove the wheel.
3. Remove the caliper and brake pads. Do not disconnect the brake hose from the caliper. Support the caliper from the strut using a strong piece of wire; do not let the caliper hang from the brake hose.
4. Remove the factory installed clips, if equipped, from the wheel studs. It is not necessary to reinstall these clips.

91159P51

Fig. 48 Support the caliper with wire as shown to prevent damage to the flexible hose

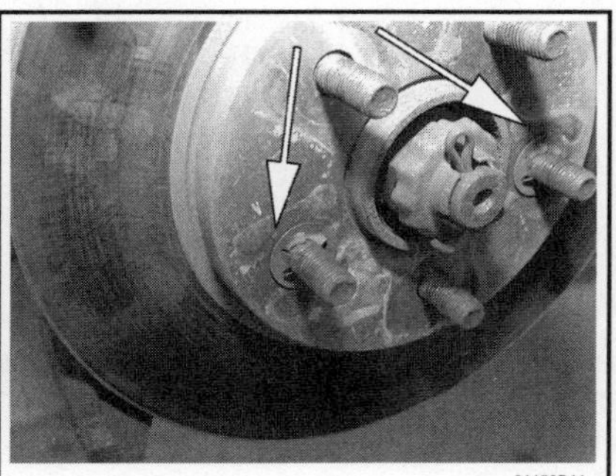
91159P44

Fig. 49 The rotor is held in place by spring clips

91159P49

Fig. 50 Once the caliper is removed, the rotor can be taken off the hub

5. Chalk an index mark on the brake rotor before removal to show its exact installation on the hub. Remove the rotor from the hub. Be sure to clean the mating surface between the hub and the rotor of any dirt, grease or debris before installing the rotor.

To install:

6. Install the rotor on the hub.
7. Install the caliper and brake pads.
8. Install the wheel and lug nuts. Torque the lug nuts, in a star pattern sequence, to 95 ft. lbs. (129 Nm).
9. Lower the vehicle and depress the brake pedal several times to position the caliper piston. Road test the vehicle.

INSPECTION

See Figures 51, 52, 53 and 54

Whenever the brake calipers or pads are removed, inspect the rotors for defects. The brake rotor is an extremely important component of the brake system. Cracks, large scratches or warpage can adversely affect the braking system, at times to the point of becoming very dangerous.

Light scoring is acceptable. Heavy scoring or warping will necessitate refinishing or replacement of the disc. The brake disc must be replaced if cracks or burned marks are evident.

Check the thickness of the disc using a micrometer. Measure the thickness at 12 equally spaced points 1 in. (25mm) from the edge of the disc. If thickness varies more than 0.0005 in. (0.013mm), the disc should be refinished, provided equal amounts are cut from each side and the thickness does not fall below 0.843 in. (21.4mm). Be sure to remove as little as necessary from each rotor side.

Check the run-out (warpage) of the disc using a dial indicator. Total run-out of the disc installed on the car should not exceed 0.005 in. (0.013mm). The disc can be resurfaced to correct minor variations, as long as equal amounts are cut from each side and the thickness is at least 0.882 inch (22.4mm) on the front rotors, or 0.443 in. (11.25mm) on the rear rotors, after resurfacing.

Check the run-out of the hub (disc removed). It should not be more than 0.0012 inch (0.030mm). If so, the hub should be replaced.

All rotors have markings for MINIMUM allowable thickness cast on an unmachined surface or an alternate surface. Always use this specification as the **minimum** allowable thickness or refinishing limit. Refer to a local auto parts store or machine shop, if necessary, where rotors are resurfaced.

If the rotor needs to be replaced with a new part, the protective coating on the braking surface of the rotor must be removed with an appropriate solvent before installing the rotor to the vehicle.

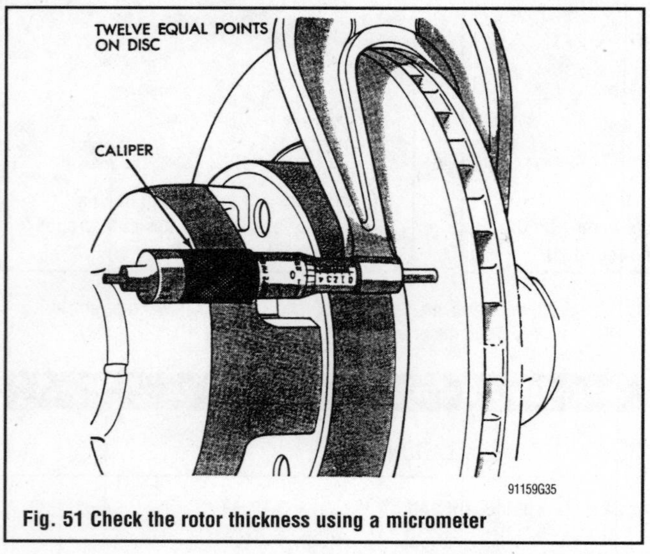

Fig. 51 Check the rotor thickness using a micrometer

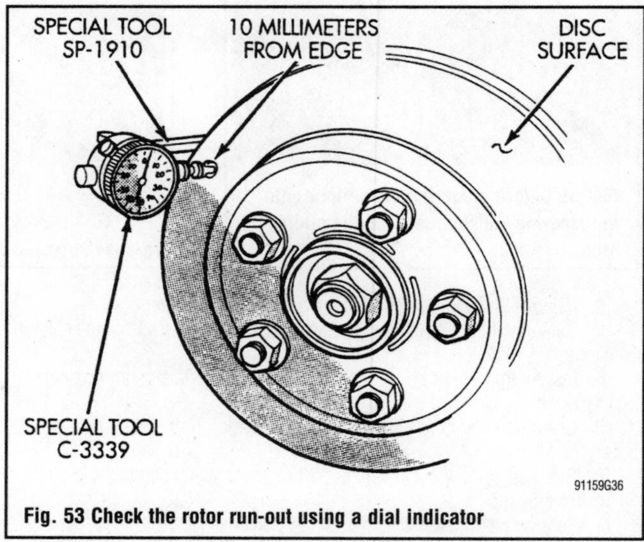

Fig. 53 Check the rotor run-out using a dial indicator

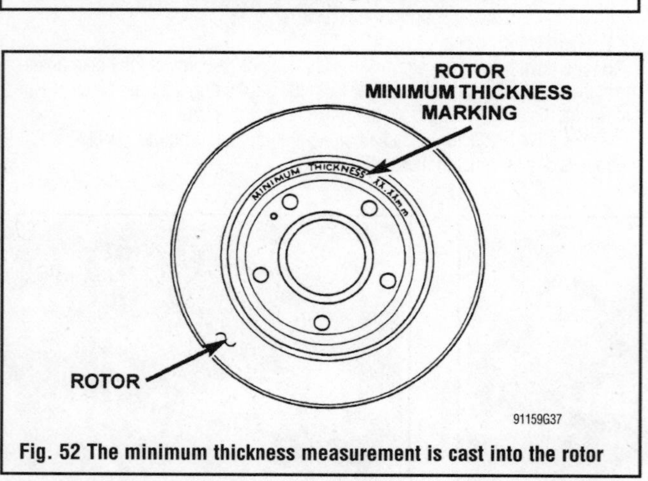

Fig. 52 The minimum thickness measurement is cast into the rotor

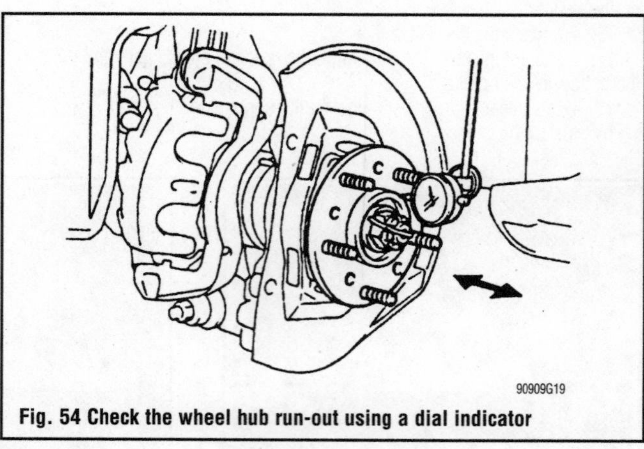

Fig. 54 Check the wheel hub run-out using a dial indicator

DRUM BRAKES

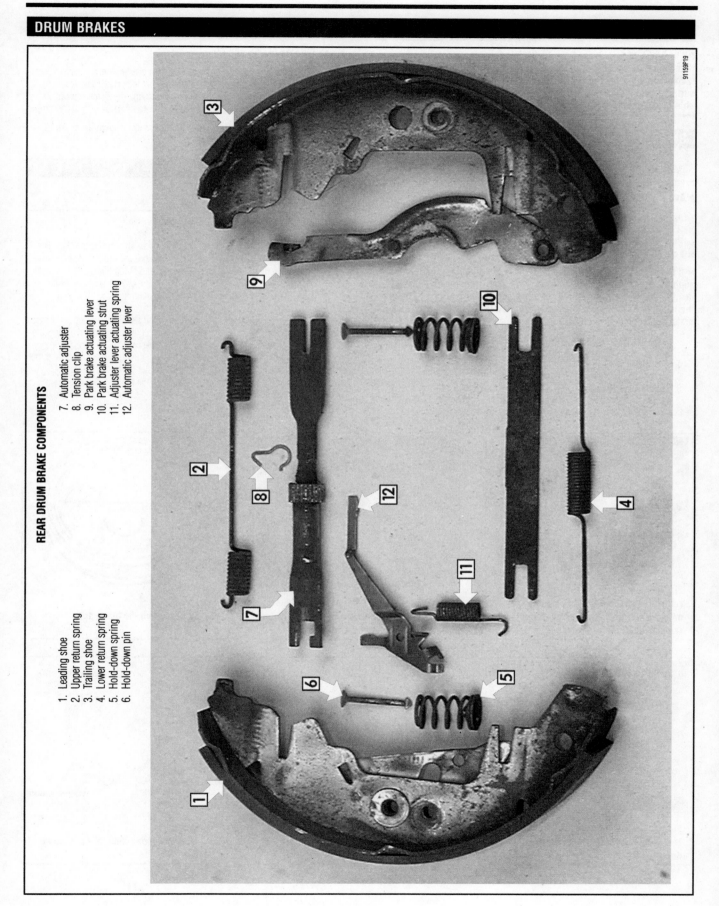

REAR DRUM BRAKE COMPONENTS

1. Leading shoe
2. Upper return spring
3. Trailing shoe
4. Lower return spring
5. Hold-down spring
6. Hold-down pin
7. Automatic adjuster
8. Tension clip
9. Park brake actuating lever
10. Park brake actuating strut
11. Adjuster lever actuating spring
12. Automatic adjuster lever

91159P19

⁂ CAUTION

Older brake pads or shoes may contain asbestos, which has been determined to be cancer causing agent. Never clean the brake surfaces with compressed air! Avoid inhaling any dust from any brake surface! When cleaning brake surfaces, use a commercially available brake cleaning fluid.

Brake Drums

REMOVAL & INSTALLATION

See Figures 55 and 56

1. Raise and safely support the vehicle.
2. Remove the rear wheels.
3. Remove the brake drum from the hub assembly by pulling the drum straight off the wheel studs.

➡If the drum is difficult to remove, remove the plug from the rear brake support plate. Push the self adjuster lever away from the star wheel using a thin screwdriver. The lever and star wheel are accessed through the hole on the rear brake support plate. Rotate the star wheel using a brake adjusting tool to retract the shoes.

4. Inspect the brake drum for thickness and runout. Replace or machine as necessary.

To install:

5. Install the brake drum to the hub assembly.
6. Adjust the brake shoes.
7. Install the rear wheel and lug nuts. Torque the lug nuts, in a star pattern sequence, to 95 ft. lbs. (129 Nm). Lower the vehicle.

INSPECTION

See Figures 57, 58 and 59

1. Inspect the brake drums for cracks, signs of overheating or excessive wear.
2. Measure the drum run-out and diameter. If not to specification, resurface the drum. Run-out should not exceed 0.006 inch (0.15mm). The diameter variation (oval shape) of the drum braking surface must not exceed 0.004 inch (0.090mm).

➡All brake drums are marked with the maximum allowable brake drum diameter on the face of the drum.

Brake Shoes

INSPECTION

See Figure 60

1. Measure the combined thickness of the brake shoe rim and lining. The minimum leading brake shoe rim and lining thickness specification is 1/8 inch (3.0mm). The minimum trailing brake shoe rim and lining thickness specification is 7/64 inch (2.8mm).
2. If any of the measurements fall below the minimum specifications, replace the brake shoes.
3. Thoroughly clean all parts. The brake lining should show contact across the entire width and from heel to toe; otherwise, replace. Clean and inspect the brake support plate and the automatic adjuster mechanism. Be sure that the adjuster mechanism has full movement throughout it adjustment range and that its teeth should be in good condition. If the adjuster is worn or damaged, replace it. If the adjuster is serviceable, lubricate the moving parts with high-temperature grease. Check the brake springs. Overheating indications are paint discoloration or distorted end coils. Replace parts as required.

91159P24

Fig. 55 Many times it is necessary to retract the shoes slightly by turning the adjuster star (inside the brake drum) to remove the drum for inspection

91159P01

Fig. 56 The brake drum is removed by pulling it straight off the wheel studs

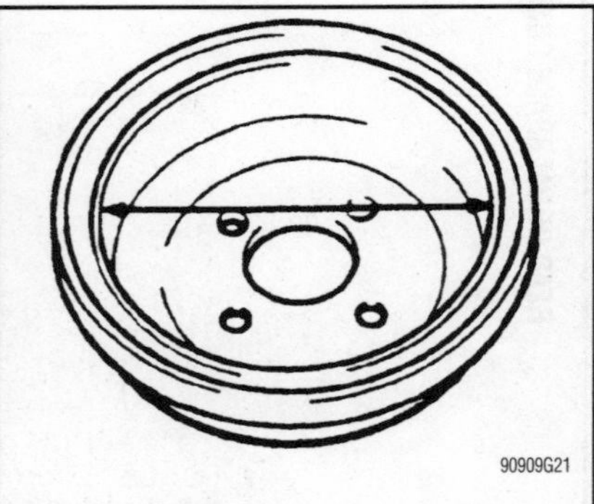

90909G21

Fig. 57 Inspecting the brake drum inside diameter

91159P03

Fig. 58 The maximum machining diameter is cast into the outer rim of the brake drum

91159P02

Fig. 59 Use a wire brush to clean the outside of the brake drum to find the maximum diameter

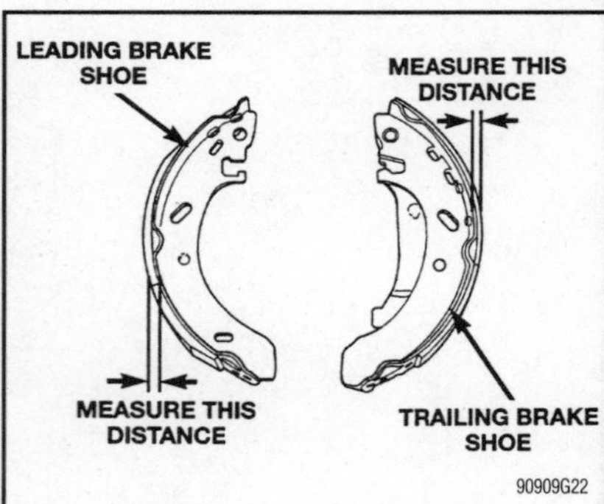

90909G22

Fig. 60 Brake shoe lining thickness measurement

REMOVAL & INSTALLATION

See Figures 61 thru 75

1. Raise and safely support the vehicle.
2. Remove the rear wheels and the brake drums.
3. Be sure the parking brake pedal is in the released position. Create slack in the rear parking brake cables by grasping an exposed section of the front parking brake cable, pulling it down and rearward. Maintain the slack in the brake cable by installing a pair of locking pliers onto the parking brake cable just rearward of **only the rear** body outrigger bracket.
4. Remove the adjustment lever spring from the automatic adjustment lever and front brake shoe (leading brake shoe).
5. Remove the automatic adjustment lever from the front brake shoe (leading brake shoe).
6. Remove the brake shoe-to-brake shoe lower return spring.
7. Remove the tension clip that secures the upper return spring to the automatic adjuster assembly.
8. Remove the brake shoe-to-brake shoe upper return spring.
9. Remove the rear brake shoe (trailing brake shoe) hold-down clip and pin.
10. Remove the trailing brake shoe, parking brake actuating lever and parking brake actuating strut from the brake support plate.
11. Remove the automatic adjuster assembly from the leading brake shoe.
12. Remove the leading brake shoe hold-down clip and pin. Remove the leading brake shoe.
13. Remove the parking brake actuator plate from the leading brake shoe and install onto the replacement brake shoe.

To install:

14. Thoroughly clean and dry the backing plate. To prepare the backing plate, lubricate the 8 brake shoe contact areas and brake shoe anchor, using suitable grease.

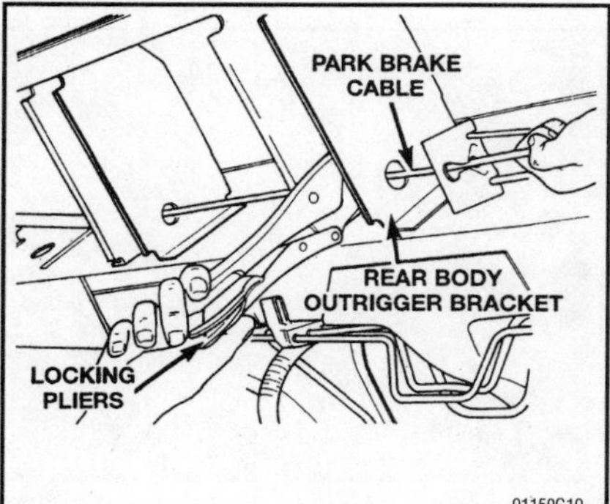

Fig. 61 Creating slack in the parking brake cables

Fig. 62 Begin the brake shoe removal procedure by disconnecting the adjuster lever actuator spring

Fig. 63 Once the spring is removed, the automatic adjuster lever can be removed

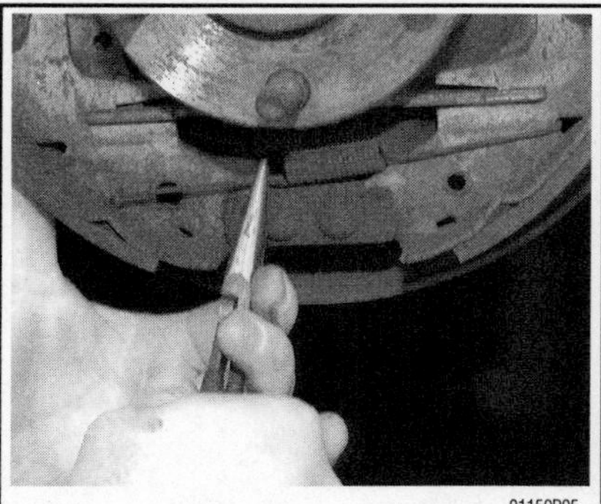

Fig. 64 Next, remove the lower brake shoe return spring(s)

Fig. 65 The upper brake shoe return spring has a small clip that secures the adjuster to the spring

Fig. 66 A brake service tool makes removal of the return springs easier

Fig. 67 Remove the upper return spring

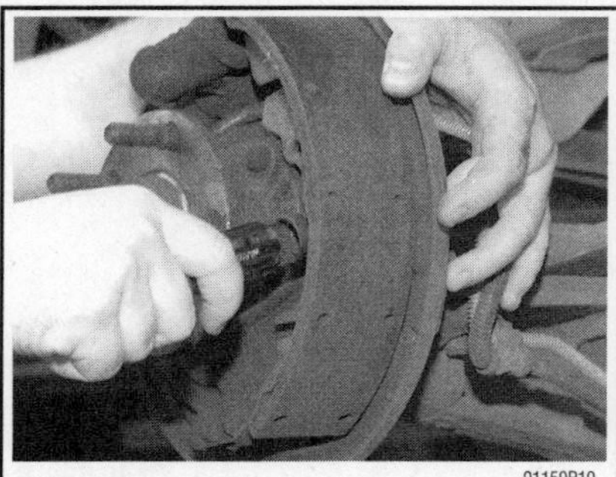

Fig. 68 Next, remove the hold-down springs and pins; a special tool makes this job easier

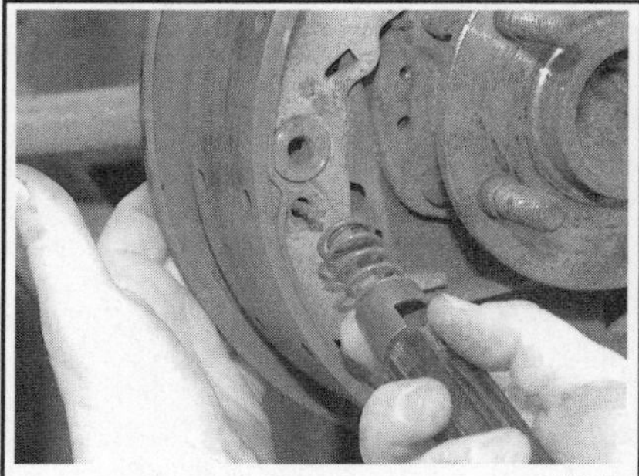

Fig. 69 Use a finger to hold the pin in place when twisting the spring cap with the special tool

91159P12
Fig. 70 The leading shoe can now be removed from the backing plate . . .

91159P11
Fig. 71 . . . followed by the adjuster mechanism . . .

91159P27
Fig. 72 . . . and the park brake actuating strut

91159P21
Fig. 73 Separate the park brake actuating lever from the rear shoe

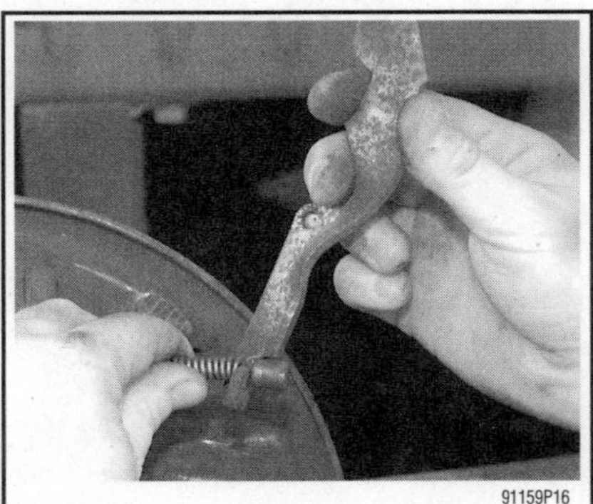
91159P16
Fig. 74 Finally, remove the park brake actuating lever from the cable

91159P18
Fig. 75 Before installing the new shoes and hardware, apply lubricant to the shoe contact areas (arrows)

15. Install the leading brake shoe into position on the brake shoe support plate. Secure the leading brake shoe by installing the brake shoe hold-down clip and pin.
16. Install the parking brake actuating strut onto the leading brake shoe and then install the parking brake actuating lever onto the strut.
17. Lubricate the shaft threads of the automatic adjuster screw assembly with anti-seize lubricant. Install the automatic adjuster screw assembly onto the leading brake shoe.
18. Install the trailing brake shoe onto the parking brake actuating lever and parking brake actuating strut.
19. Place the trailing brake shoe into position on the brake support plate and install the brake shoe hold-down clip and pin.
20. Install the brake shoe-to-brake shoe upper return spring.
21. Install the tension clip that secures the upper return spring to the automatic adjuster assembly. Be sure the tension clip is positioned on the threaded area of the adjuster assembly or the function of the automatic adjuster will be affected.
22. Install the brake shoe-to-brake shoe lower return spring.
23. Install the automatic adjustment lever onto the leading brake shoe.
24. Install the actuating spring onto the automatic adjustment lever and leading brake shoe. Check to be sure the automatic adjustment lever makes positive contact with the star wheel on the automatic adjuster assembly.
25. Once the brake shoes and all other brake system components are fully and correctly installed, remove the locking pliers from the front parking brake cable. This will remove the slack and correctly adjust the parking brake cables.
26. Make sure there is no grease on the brake shoe linings, then install the brake drums.
27. Adjust the rear brakes, then lower the vehicle and check the brakes for proper operation.
28. Install the wheel and lug nuts. Torque the lug nuts, in a star pattern sequence, to 95 ft. lbs. (129 Nm).
29. Road test the vehicle. The automatic adjuster will continue to adjust the brake shoes during the road test.

ADJUSTMENTS

See Figures 76 and 77

➡Normally, self-adjusting drum brakes will not require manual brake shoe adjustment. However, in the event of brake shoe replacement, it is advisable to make the initial adjustment manually to speed up the adjusting time.

91159P25
Fig. 76 To adjust the rear drum brakes, remove the rubber cap . . .

91159P24

Fig. 77 . . . and use an adjuster tool to rotate the adjustment star wheel

1. Raise and safely support the rear of the vehicle securely on jackstands.
2. Disconnect the parking brake cable (for the wheel that is being serviced) from the parking brake cable equalizer. This step is necessary to gain access to the star wheel adjuster. If this is not done, the cable and spring inside of the brake drum will be in the way of the star wheel.
3. Remove the rubber plug from the rear brake adjusting hole, in the back of the rear brake backing plate.
4. Make sure that the parking brake lever is fully released.
5. Insert Special Brake Adjusting Tool C-3784 or equivalent, into the adjusting hole on the backing plate and against the star wheel of the adjusting screw. Move the tool handle upward until a slight drag is felt when the vehicle's road wheel is turned.
6. Insert a small (but strong) thin rod through the adjusting hole. Push the adjusting lever out of engagement with the star wheel. Be careful not to bend or distort the lever or spring. While holding the lever out of engagement, back off the star wheel just enough to ensure a free wheel with no brake shoe drag.
7. Repeat this procedure on the other rear wheel.
8. Install the rubber plug back into the adjusting hole.
9. Connect the parking brake cable(s) to the equalizer.
10. Lower the vehicle.
11. Carefully road test the vehicle and check for proper brake system operation.

Wheel Cylinders

REMOVAL & INSTALLATION

➧ See Figures 78

1. Raise and safely support the vehicle.
2. Remove the wheel, brake drum and brake shoes.
3. Using a line wrench, remove the brake line from the wheel cylinder. Use care to keep brake fluid off any painted surfaces which will be damaged by the brake fluid. Plug the brake line opening to prevent fluid spillage and/or system contamination.
4. Remove the wheel cylinder bolts and remove the cylinder from the backing plate.

To install:

5. Apply a small bead of silicone sealant around the wheel cylinder mounting surface of the backing plate.
6. Start the brake line into the wheel cylinder. Use care not to cross-thread the fitting.
7. Install the wheel cylinder on the backing plate and tighten the retaining bolts. Torque the retaining bolts to 75 inch lbs. (8 Nm).
8. Tighten the brake line. Torque the brake line fitting to 145 inch lbs. (17 Nm).
9. Install the brake shoes and brake drum. Install the wheel and lug nuts. Torque the lug nuts, in a star pattern sequence, to 95 ft. lbs. (129 Nm). Adjust the brakes.
10. Bleed the brake system using DOT 3 brake fluid. Lower the vehicle.
11. Road test the vehicle and check the brakes for proper operation.

OVERHAUL

➧ See Figures 79 thru 88

Wheel cylinder overhaul kits may be available, but often at little or no savings over a reconditioned wheel cylinder. It often makes sense with these components to substitute a new or reconditioned part instead of attempting an overhaul.

If no replacement is available, or you would prefer to overhaul your wheel cylinders, the following procedure may be used. When rebuilding and installing wheel cylinders, avoid getting any contaminants into the system. Always use clean, new, high quality brake fluid. If dirty or improper fluid has been used, it will be necessary to drain the entire system, flush the system with proper brake fluid, replace all rubber components, then refill and bleed the system.

1. Remove the wheel cylinder from the vehicle and place on a clean workbench.
2. First remove and discard the old rubber boots, then withdraw the pistons. Piston cylinders are equipped with seals and a spring assembly, all located behind the pistons in the cylinder bore.
3 Remove the remaining inner components, seals and spring assembly. Compressed air may be useful in removing these components. If no compressed air is available, be VERY careful not to score the wheel cylinder bore when removing parts from it. Discard all components for which replacements were supplied in the rebuild kit.
4. Wash the cylinder and metal parts in denatured alcohol or clean brake fluid.

⁂ WARNING

Never use a mineral-based solvent such as gasoline, kerosene or paint thinner for cleaning purposes. These solvents will swell rubber components and quickly deteriorate them.

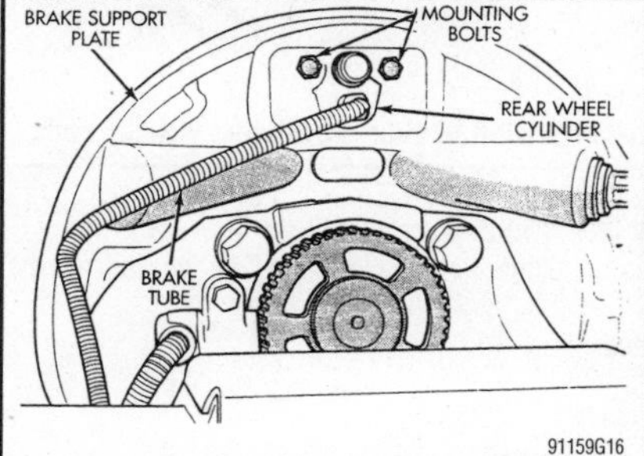

91159G16

Fig. 78 The wheel cylinder is mounted to the support plate by two bolts; disconnect the hydraulic line from the cylinder and remove the bolts

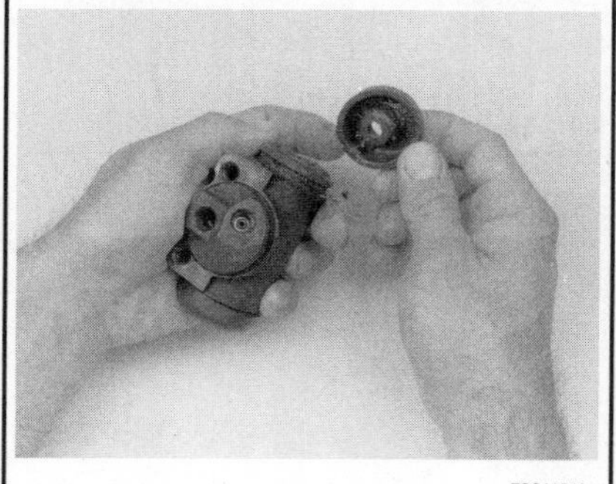
TCCA9P13

Fig. 79 Remove the outer boots from the wheel cylinder

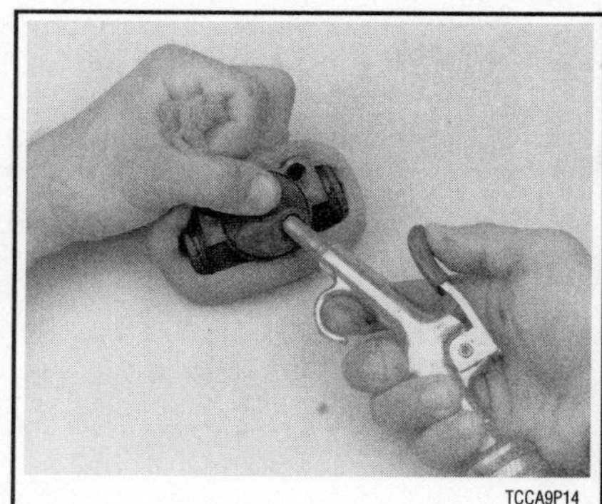
TCCA9P14

Fig. 80 Compressed air can be used to remove the pistons and seals

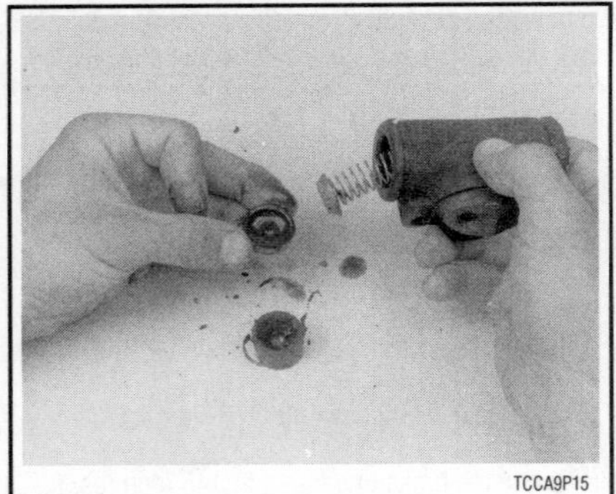

TCCA9P15

Fig. 81 Remove the pistons, cup seals and spring from the cylinder

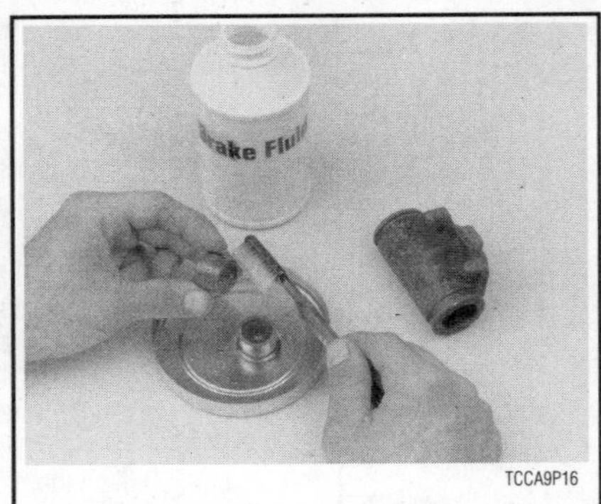

TCCA9P16

Fig. 82 Use brake fluid and a soft brush to clean the pistons . . .

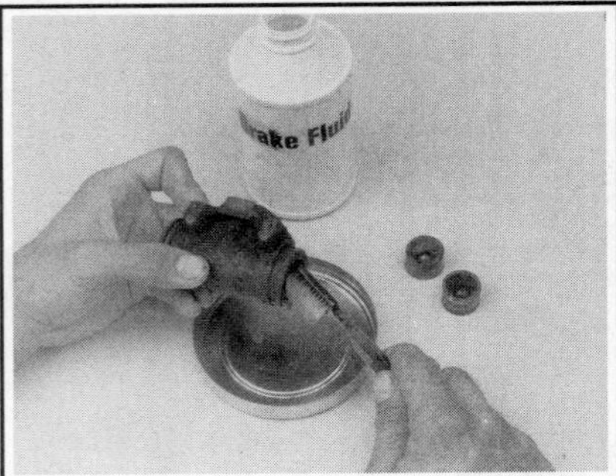

TCCA9P17

Fig. 83 . . . and the bore of the wheel cylinder

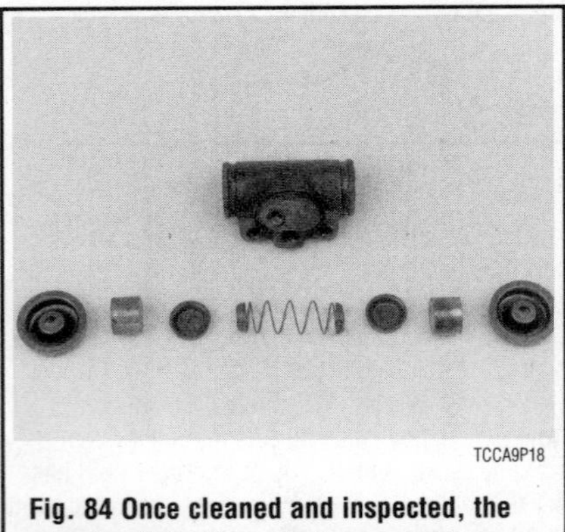

TCCA9P18

Fig. 84 Once cleaned and inspected, the wheel cylinder is ready for assembly

TCCA9P19

Fig. 85 Lubricate the cup seals with brake fluid

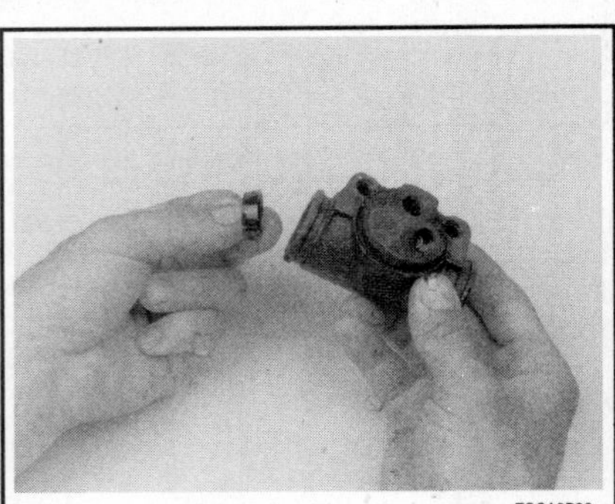

TCCA9P20

Fig. 86 Install the spring, then the cup seals in the bore

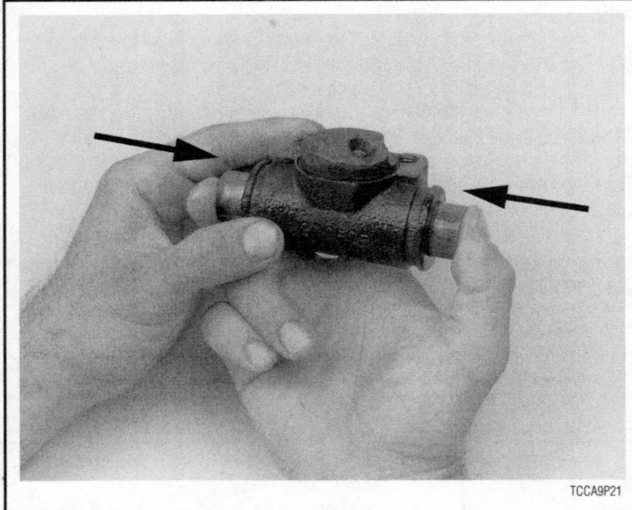

TCCA9P21

Fig. 87 Lightly lubricate the pistons, then install them

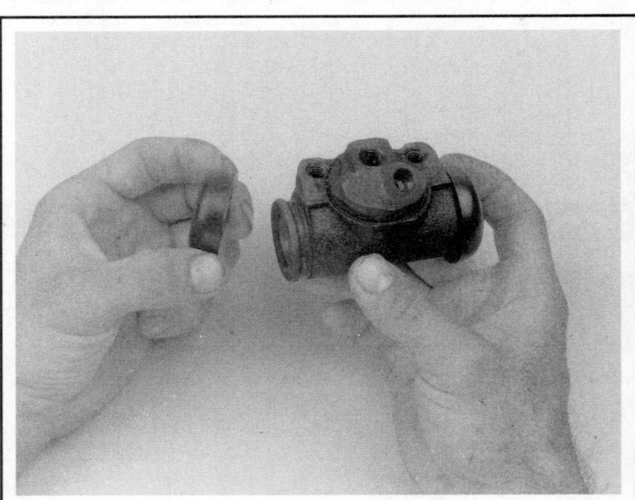

TCCA9P22

Fig. 88 The boots can now be installed over the wheel cylinder ends

5. Allow the parts to air dry or use compressed air. Do not use rags for cleaning, since lint will remain in the cylinder bore.
6. Inspect the piston and replace it if it shows scratches.
7. Lubricate the cylinder bore and seals using clean brake fluid.
8. Position the spring assembly.
9. Install the inner seals, then the pistons.
10. Insert the new boots into the counterbores by hand. Do not lubricate the boots.
11. Install the wheel cylinder.

PARKING BRAKE

Cables

REMOVAL & INSTALLATION

Front Cable

See Figures 89, 90 and 91

1. Raise and safely support the vehicle.
2. Manually lock out the automatic self-adjuster mechanism of the parking brake pedal assembly.
3. Remove the intermediate brake cable and the left rear parking brake cable from the parking brake cable equalizer.
4. Remove the front parking brake cable housing retainer from the body outrigger bracket. Use a hose clamp or a 14mm box wrench to compress the fingers of the cable housing retainer.
5. Lower the vehicle to the ground.
6. Remove the left front door sill molding from the vehicle.
7. Remove the left front kick panel for access to the parking brake cable and parking brake pedal assembly.
8. Lift the floor mat/carpet for access to the parking brake cable and vehicle floor pan. Remove the seal and the cable from the floor pan.
9. Pull the cable forward and disconnect from the lever clevis. Tap the cable housing end fitting out of the pedal assembly bracket.
10. Remove the parking brake cable retainer from the parking brake pedal assembly bracket.

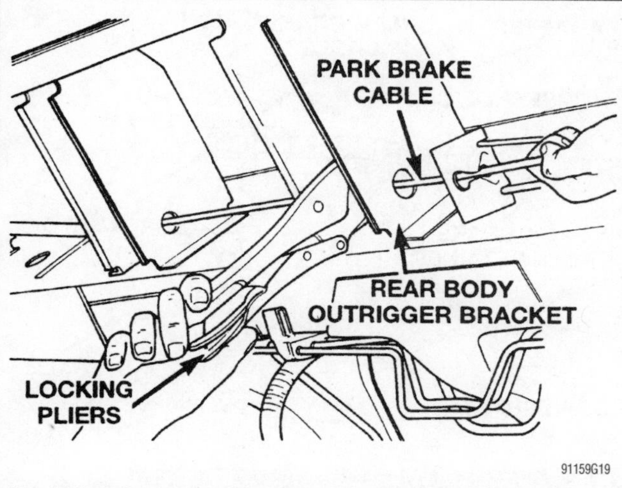

Fig. 89 Before removing the park brake cable, lock out the self-adjusting mechanism

11. Pull the cable assembly out of the vehicle through the floor pan hole.

To install:

12. Feed the new cable through the floor pan hole.
13. Route the brake cable end button through the hole in the parking brake pedal assembly bracket.
14. Install the brake cable retainer onto the parking brake cable. Install the parking brake cable retainer into the park brake pedal assembly bracket.
15. Install the parking brake cable end into the retainer previously installed into the parking brake pedal bracket.
16. Install the front parking brake cable end button into the clevis of the parking brake pedal mechanism.
17. Install the floor pan seal into the hole in the floor pan. Install the seal so the flange on the seal is flush with the floor pan. Place the floor mat/carpet back down on the floor.
18. Raise and safely support the vehicle.
19. Install the cable and housing into the body outrigger bracket. Be sure the housing retainer fingers lock the housing firmly into position.
20. Connect the parking brake cables to the parking brake cable equalizer.
21. Lower the vehicle to the ground.
22. Engage the automatic self-adjusting mechanism.
23. Apply and release the parking brake pedal one time only. This will correctly seat the parking brake cables.
24. Road test the vehicle and check for proper brake operation.

Intermediate Parking Brake Cable

See Figures 89, 90 and 92

1. Raise and safely support the vehicle.
2. Manually lock out the automatic self-adjuster mechanism of the parking brake pedal assembly.
3. Remove the intermediate brake cable and the left rear parking brake cable from the parking brake cable equalizer.
4. Disconnect the intermediate parking brake cable from the cable connector attaching it to the right rear parking brake cable.
5. Remove the intermediate parking brake cable from the cable guides on the vehicle frame rail.

To install:

6. Install the ends of the parking brake cables through the parking brake cable guides.
7. Connect the intermediate parking brake cable to the cable connector at the right rear parking brake cable.
8. Connect the intermediate parking brake cable to the parking brake cable equalizer.
9. Engage the automatic self-adjusting mechanism.
10. If equipped, install and properly position the foam collar on the parking brake cable to prevent the brake cable from rattling against the floor of the vehicle.
11. Lower the vehicle to the ground.
12. Apply and release the parking brake pedal one time only. This will correctly seat the parking brake cables.
13. Road test the vehicle and check for proper brake operation.

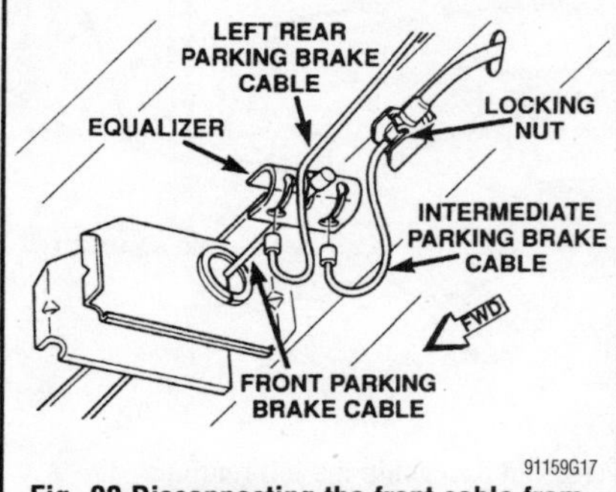

Fig. 90 Disconnecting the front cable from the intermediate and left rear parking brake cables

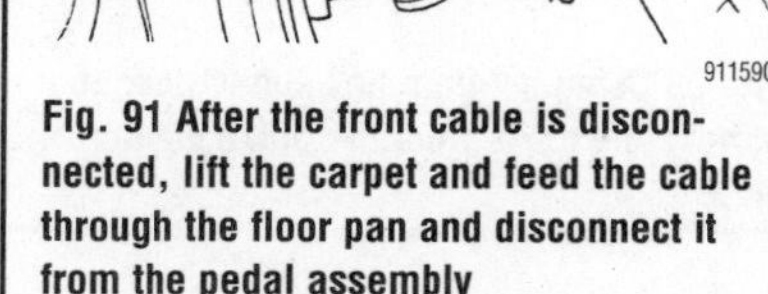

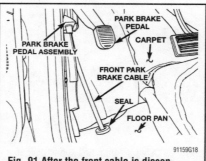

Fig. 91 After the front cable is disconnected, lift the carpet and feed the cable through the floor pan and disconnect it from the pedal assembly

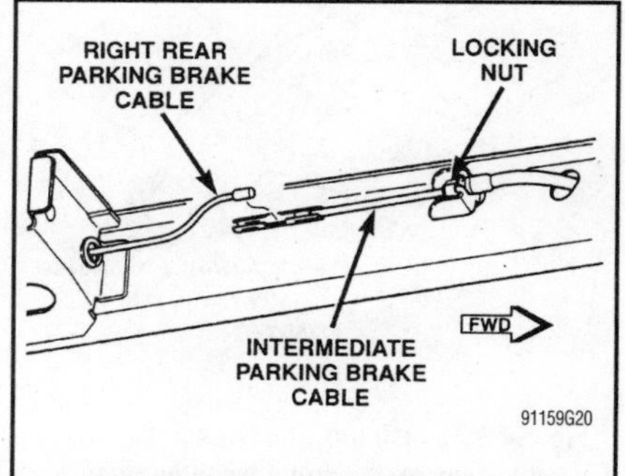

Fig. 92 Disconnecting the intermediate cable from the right rear parking brake cable

Right Rear Parking Brake Cable

➧ See Figures 89 and 90, 92, 93, 94 and 95

1. Raise and safely support the vehicle. Remove the right rear wheel.
2. Remove the right rear wheel brake drum.
3. Manually lock out the automatic self-adjuster mechanism of the parking brake pedal assembly as follows:
   a. Position the park brake pedal in the fully released position.
   b. From below the vehicle, firmly grasp the exposed section of the front parking brake cable and pull downward until all free movement is removed from the parking brake cable.
   c. Install a pair of locking pliers onto the parking brake cable just rearward of the second body outrigger bracket.
4. Disconnect the right rear parking brake cable from the connector on the intermediate parking brake cable.
5. Remove the right parking brake cable housing from the body bracket by slipping a 14mm box wrench over the end of the brake cable retainer to compress the retaining fingers.
6. Remove the brake shoes from the brake support plate.
7. Disconnect the cable from the parking brake actuator lever in the brake shoe assembly. Compress the cable housing retainer lock with a mini-hose clamp or 14mm box wrench and pull the cable from the brake support plate.

To install:

8. Install the new cable through the brake support plate. Engage the cable housing retainer fingers until they lock the cable housing firmly into place.
9. Attach the cable to the parking brake actuator lever on the brake shoe assembly. Install the brake shoes, brake drum, and rear wheel. Torque the lug nuts, in sequence, to 95 ft. lbs. (129 Nm).
10. Install the brake cable housing retainer into the body bracket, making sure cable housing retainer fingers lock the cable housing firmly into place.
11. Connect the right rear parking brake cable to the connector on the end of the intermediate parking brake cable.
12. Remove the locking pliers from the front parking brake cable. The parking brake cables will automatically adjust.
13. Lower the vehicle.
14. Apply and release the parking brake pedal one time only. This will correctly seat the parking brake cables.
15. Road test the vehicle and check for proper brake operation.

Left Rear Parking Brake Cable

➧ See Figures 89 and 90, 93, 94, 95 and 96

1. Raise and safely support the vehicle. Remove the left rear wheel.
2. Remove the left rear wheel brake drum.
3. Manually lock out the automatic self-adjuster mechanism of the parking brake pedal assembly as follows:
   a. Position the park brake pedal in the fully released position.
   b. From below the vehicle, firmly grasp the exposed section of the front parking brake cable and pull downward until all free movement is removed from the parking brake cable.
   c. Install a pair of locking pliers onto the parking brake cable just rearward of the second body outrigger bracket.
4. Disconnect the left rear parking brake cable from the parking brake cable equalizer.
5. Remove the left parking brake cable housing from the body bracket by slipping a 14mm box wrench over the end of the brake cable retainer to compress the retaining fingers. A small aircraft type hose clamp can also be used.
6. Remove the brake shoes from the brake support plate.
7. Disconnect the cable from the parking brake actuator lever in the brake shoe assembly. Compress the cable housing retainer lock with a mini-hose clamp or 14mm box wrench and pull the cable from the brake support plate.

To install:

8. Install the new cable through the brake support plate. Engage the cable housing retainer fingers until they lock the cable housing firmly into place.
9. Attach the cable to the parking brake actuator lever on the brake shoe assembly. Install the brake shoes, brake drum, and rear wheel. Torque the lug nuts, in sequence, to 95 ft. lbs. (129 Nm).
10. Install the brake cable housing retainer into the body bracket, making sure cable housing retainer fingers lock the cable housing firmly into place.
11. Connect the left rear parking brake cable end to the parking brake cable equalizer bracket.
12. Remove the locking pliers from the front parking brake cable. The parking brake cables will automatically adjust.
13. Lower the vehicle.
14. Apply and release the parking brake pedal one time only. This will correctly seat the parking brake cables.
15. Road test the vehicle and check for proper brake operation.

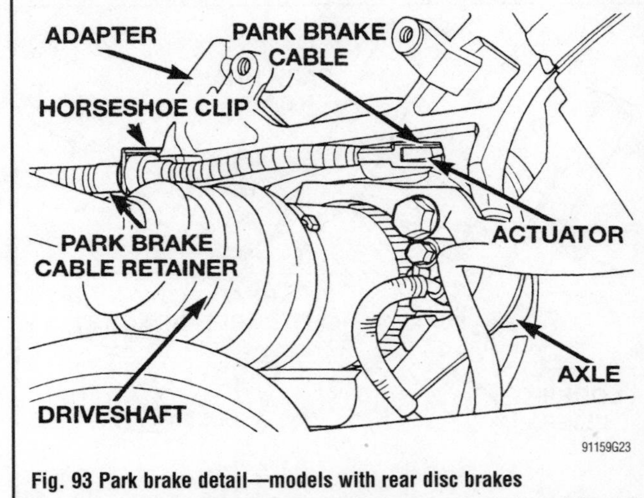

Fig. 93 Park brake detail—models with rear disc brakes

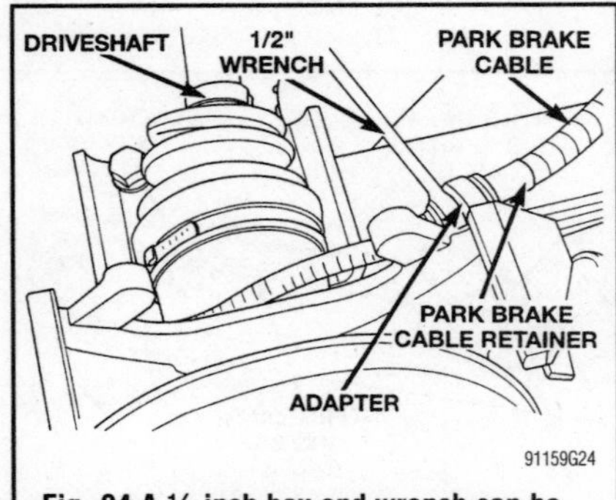

Fig. 94 A ½ inch box end wrench can be used to remove the cable from the adapter on models equipped with disc brakes

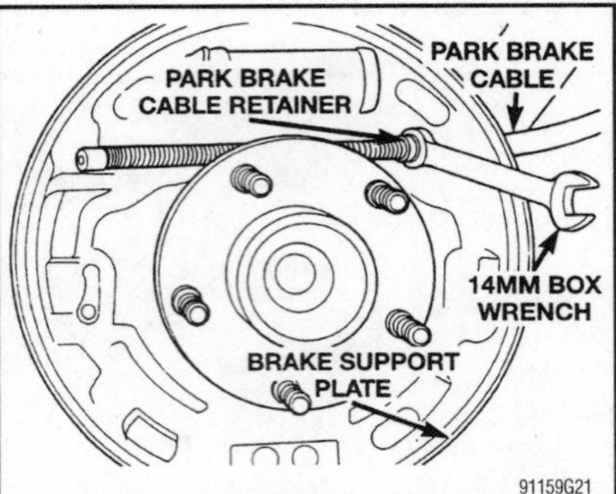

Fig. 95 Using a 14mm box end wrench to remove the cable from the brake support plate

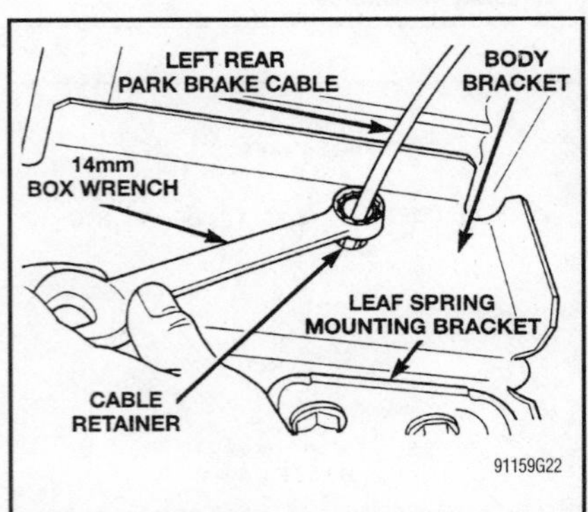

Fig. 96 Removing the left rear parking brake cable from the body bracket

ADJUSTMENT

1996–97 Models

CAUTION

The self-adjusting feature of this parking brake lever assembly contains a clockspring loaded to approximately 8 pounds. Care must be taken to prevent excessive jarring of the assembly. Do not release the self-adjuster lockout device before installing cables into the equalizer. Keep hands out of the self-adjuster sector and pawl area. Failure to observe this warning in handling this mechanism could lead to serious injury.

MANUAL LOCK-OUT OF AUTOMATIC SELF-ADJUSTER

1. Be sure the parking brake pedal (system) is in the fully released position.
2. From underneath the vehicle, have an assistant grasp the exposed section of the front parking brake cable and pull downward until all free movement is eliminated from the cable.
3. Install a 3/16 in. drill bit into the clockspring and position against the parking brake pedal arm.

ENGAGING THE AUTOMATIC SELF-ADJUSTER

1. Be sure all the parking brake cables are correctly installed, clipped as required and properly connected.
2. Using a pair of pliers, firmly grasp the lock pin previously installed in the parking brake pedal mechanism.
3. Remove the lock pin from the parking brake pedal mechanism by pulling it firmly and rapidly from the park brake mechanism. This will allow the mechanism to correctly adjust the parking brake cables.
4. Apply and release the parking brake pedal one time. This will seat the parking brake cables. The rear wheels should rotate freely without dragging.

1998–99 Models

The parking brake pedal mechanism utilized in this vehicle is designed so that the automatic adjuster is not required to be locked out when servicing the parking brake pedal or cables.

This mechanism is designed so that the adjuster mechanism will rotate only ½ turn when the tension is released from the parking brake cable. This eliminates the need to lock out the automatic adjuster when servicing the parking brake pedal mechanism and cables.

Use the following procedures to release the tension from the parking brake cables and the automatic adjuster in the pedal mechanism.

LOCK-OUT OF AUTOMATIC ADJUSTER

1. From underneath the vehicle, have an assistant grasp the exposed section of the front parking brake cable and pull rearward on it. While holding the cable in this position, install a pair of locking pliers on the front parking brake cable just rearward of the second body outrigger bracket.
2. Disconnect the left rear and intermediate parking brake cables from the parking brake cable equalizer.
3. Remove the equalizer from the front parking brake cable.
4. Remove the locking pliers from the front parking brake cable. This will enable the adjuster in the parking brake pedal mechanism to rotate around to its stop. This will relieve the tension from the adjuster and front parking brake cable.

ENGAGING THE AUTOMATIC ADJUSTER RESET

1. From underneath the vehicle, have an assistant grasp the exposed section of the front parking brake cable and pull rearward on it. While holding the cable in this position, install a pair of locking pliers on the front parking brake cable just rearward of the second body outrigger bracket.
2. Install the equalizer onto the front parking brake cable.
3. Connect the left rear and intermediate parking brake cables into the correct locations on the parking brake cable equalizer.
4. Remove the locking pliers from the front parking brake cable. This will enable the adjuster in the parking brake pedal mechanism to tension the parking brake cables.
5. Apply and release the parking brake pedal one time. This will seat the parking brake cables and enable the automatic adjuster in the parking brake pedal mechanism to correctly tension the parking brake cables.

Parking Brake Shoes

REMOVAL & INSTALLATION

See Figures 97 thru 103

On models with rear disc brakes, the parking brake shoes are located inside the rotor.

1. Set the parking brake. This will keep the hub/bearing and axle shaft from rotating while loosening the hub nut.
2. Raise and safely support the vehicle securely on jackstands.
3. Remove the rear wheel.
4. Remove the following components from the stub shaft of the outer C/V joint:
   - Cotter pin
   - Nut retainer
   - Spring washer
   - Hub nut and washer
5. Release the parking brake.
6. Create slack in the rear parking brake cables by grasping the exposed section of the front parking brake cable and pulling rearward on it. While holding the cable in this position, install a pair of locking pliers on the front parking brake cable just rearward of the second body outrigger bracket.
7. Remove the rear disc brake rotor.
8. Remove the horseshoe clip from the retainer on the end of the parking brake cable, then disconnect the end of the cable from the actuator lever on the adapter.
9. Remove the cable end from the adapter. Utilize a ½ inch wrench slipped over the parking brake cable retainer to compress the locking tabs on the cable retainer.
10. Remove the wheel speed sensor from the hub/bearing and adapter.

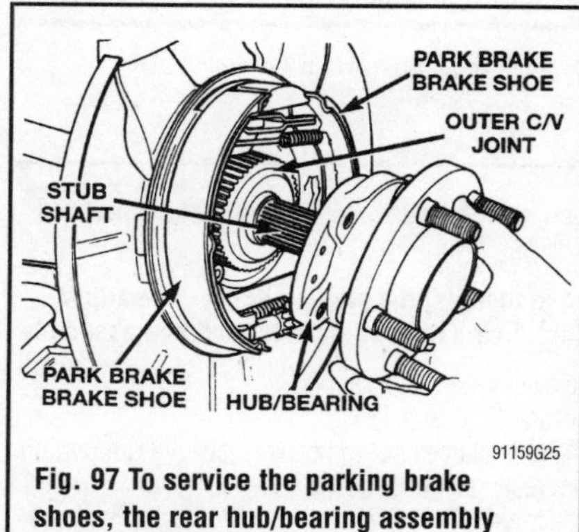

Fig. 97 To service the parking brake shoes, the rear hub/bearing assembly needs to be removed

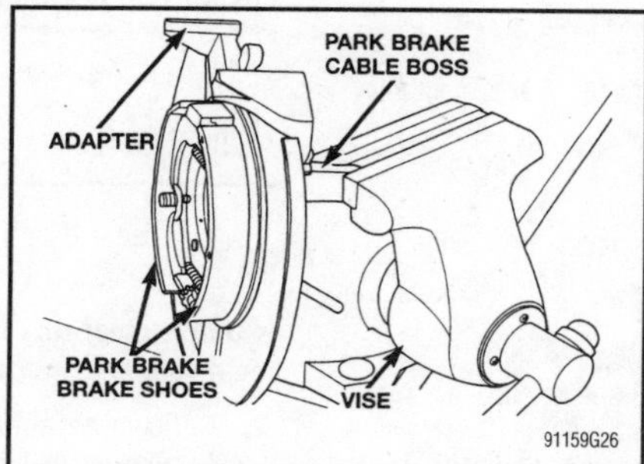

Fig. 98 After removing the hub/bearing assembly, remove the disc adapter and park brake backing plate from the rear axle and mount it in a vise for service

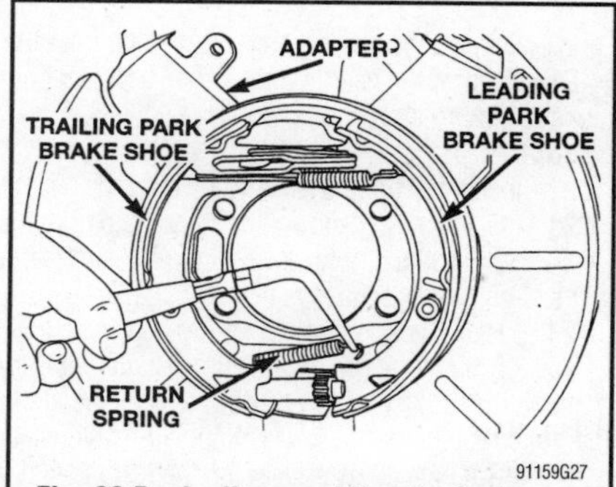

Fig. 99 Begin disassembling the brake shoe assembly be removing the lower return spring

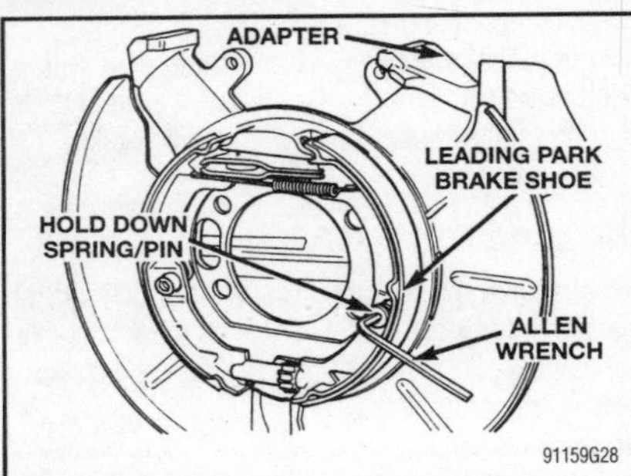

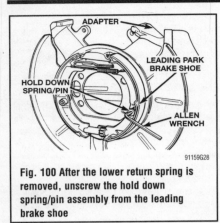

Fig. 100 After the lower return spring is removed, unscrew the hold down spring/pin assembly from the leading brake shoe

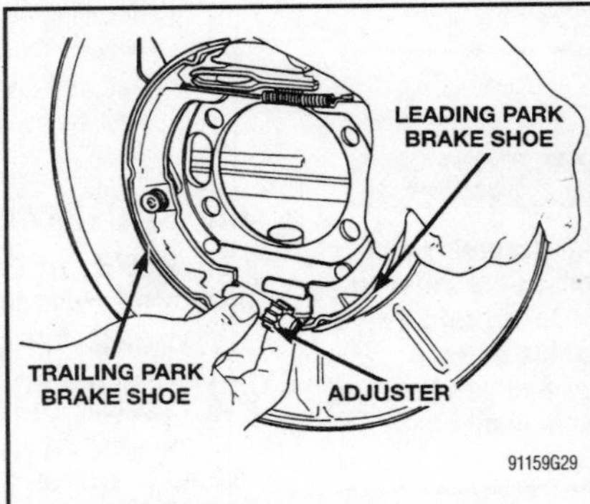

Fig. 101 Next, unhook the leading shoe from the adjuster mechanism . . .

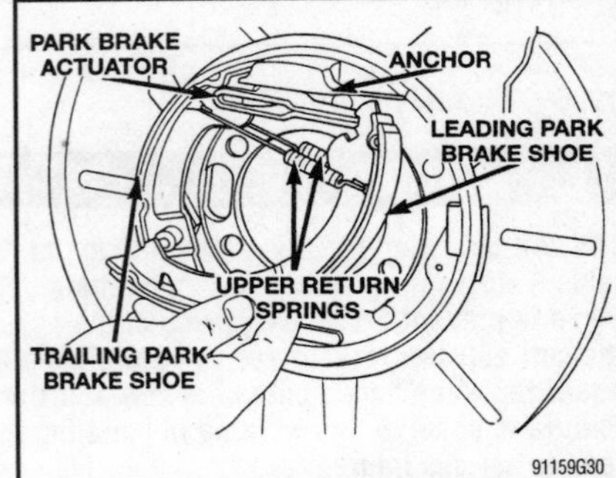

Fig. 102 . . . and relax the tension on the upper return springs; them unhook them from the leading shoe

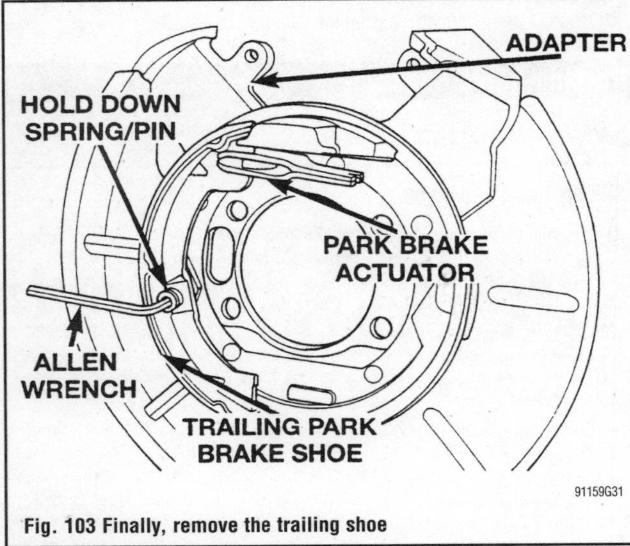

Fig. 103 Finally, remove the trailing shoe

11. Remove the hub/bearing assembly.
12. Remove the adapter from the rear axle.
13. Mount the adapter in a vise using the anchor boss for the park brake cable.
14. Remove the lower return spring from the leading and trailing arm brake shoes.
15. Remove the hold-down spring and pin from the leading park brake shoe.
16. Remove the adjuster from the leading and trailing park brake shoe.
17. Remove the leading parking brake shoe from the adapter. The leading brake shoe is removed by rotating the bottom of the brake shoe inward until the top of the brake shoe can be removed from the brake shoe anchor. Then remove the upper return springs from the leading brake shoe.
18. Remove the upper return springs from the trailing park brake shoe.
19. Remove the hold-down spring and pin from the trailing park brake shoe.
20. Remove the trailing park brake shoe from the adapter.
21. Remove the parking brake shoe actuator from the adapter and inspect for signs of abnormal wear and binding at the pivot point.

To install:

22. Install the trailing brake shoe onto the adapter.
23. Install the hold-down spring and pin onto the trailing park brake shoe. Be sure to install the hold-down pin in the straight up and down position. This will ensure proper engagement with the adapter.
24. Install the upper return springs onto the trailing park brake shoe.
25. Install the upper return springs onto the leading park brake shoe. Then position the top of the leading park brake shoe at the upper anchor and rotate the bottom of the shoe outward until correctly installed on the adapter.
26. Install the adjuster between the leading and trailing park brake shoe.
27. Install the hold-down spring and pin onto the leading park brake shoe. Be sure to install the hold-down pin in the straight up and down position. This will ensure proper engagement with the adapter.
28. Install the lower return spring onto the leading and trailing park brake shoes. When installing the hold-down spring, it is to be installed behind the shoes.
29. Install the 4 mounting bolts for the adapter and hub/bearing into the bolt holes in the axle.
30. Position the adapter on the 4 mounting bolts installed in the rear axle.
31. Install the hub/bearing assembly.
32. Install the wheel speed sensor onto the hub/bearing and adapter.
33. Install the parking brake cable into its mounting hole in the adapter. Be sure that all of the locking tabs of the cable retainer are expanded out to ensure the cable will not pull out of the adapter.
34. Connect the end of the parking brake cable onto the end of the parking brake actuator lever.
35. Install a new horseshoe clip onto the parking brake cable retainer. The horseshoe clip is installed between the retainer for the park brake cable and the adapter. Horseshoe clip must be installed with the curved end of the clip pointing straight up and the edge of the curved end facing toward the rear of the vehicle.
36. Remove the locking pliers from the front parking brake cable.
37. Adjust the parking brake shoes.
38. Install the rear disc brake rotor and caliper assemblies.
39. Set the parking brake.
40. Clean all foreign material off of the threads of the outer C/V joint stub shaft. Then perform the following:
    - Install the washer and hub nut. Tighten the hub nut to 180 ft. lbs. (244 Nm)
    - Install the spring washer
    - Install nut retainer and a new cotter pin
41. Install the rear wheel.
42. Lower the vehicle.
43. Fully apply and release the parking brake pedal one time only. This will correctly seat and adjust the parking brake cables.

CAUTION

Before moving the vehicle, pump the brake pedal several times to ensure that the vehicle has a firm enough pedal to stop the vehicle.

44. Road test the vehicle and check for proper brake operation.

ADJUSTMENT

1. Raise and safely support the rear of the vehicle. Remove the wheel and tire assemblies.

➡Unlike other rear disc brake models, the parking brake shoe adjustment cannot be performed through a hole in the rotor and hub assembly.

2. Remove the rear brake caliper and rotor.
3. Remove the hub and bearing assembly.
4. Check the brake shoe inside diameter of the parking brake drum portion of the rotor using a brake drum reset gauge, or equivalent.
5. Using a ruler that reads in 64th of an inch, accurately read the measurement of the inside diameter of the parking brake drum.

6. Reduce the inside diameter measurement of the brake drum that was taken, using the reset gauge, by 1/64 inch.
7. Reset the gauge so that the outside measurement jaws are set to the reduced measurement.
8. Place the gauge over the parking brake shoes. This tool must be located diagonally across at the top of one shoe and bottom of the opposite shoe (widest point) of the parking brake shoes.
9. Utilizing the star wheel adjuster, adjust the parking brake shoes until the brake shoe linings are just touching the jaws of the gauge tool.
10. Repeat step 8, measuring shoes in both directions.
11. Install the hub and bearing assembly.
12. Install brake rotor and rotate to verify that the parking brake shoes are not dragging. If dragging is evident, remove the rotor and back off the star wheel adjuster one notch and recheck. Continue with the previous step until there is no more brake shoe dragging against the drum.
13. Install the brake caliper.
14. Install the wheel and tire assembly.
15. Lower the vehicle.
16. Apply and release the parking brake pedal one time. This will seat and correctly adjust the parking brake cables.

⁂ CAUTION

Before moving the vehicle, pump the brake pedal several times to ensure that the vehicle has a firm enough pedal to stop the vehicle.

17. Road test the vehicle.

ANTI-LOCK BRAKE SYSTEM

General Information

The Teves Mark IV-g Anti-lock Brake System (ABS) was an option on the 1996 Chrysler Minivan models. Beginning in 1997, these same models are equipped with the Teves Mark 20 ABS system. Both of these ABS systems operate in basically the same manner, however, they may use some different components.

When conventional brakes are applied in an emergency stop or on ice, one or more wheels may lock. This may result in loss of steering control and vehicle stability. The purpose of the Anti-lock Brake System (ABS) is to prevent lock up under heavy braking conditions. This system offers the driver increased safety and control during braking. Anti-lock braking operates only at speeds above 3 mph (5 km/h).

Under normal braking conditions, the ABS functions the same as a standard brake system with a diagonally split master cylinder and conventional vacuum assist.

If wheel locking tendency is detected during application, the system will enter anti-lock mode. During anti-lock mode, hydraulic pressure in the four wheel circuits is modulated to prevent any wheel from locking. Each wheel circuit is designed with a set of electrical valves and hydraulic line to provide modulation, although for vehicle stability, both rear wheel valves receive the same electrical signal. The system can build or reduce pressure at each wheel, depending on signals generated by the Wheel Speed Sensors (WSS) at each wheel and received at the Controller Anti-lock Brake (CAB).

PRECAUTIONS

Failure to observe the following precautions may result in system damage:

- Before performing electric arc welding on the vehicle, disconnect the control module and the hydraulic unit connectors.
- When performing painting work on the vehicle, do not expose the control module to temperatures in excess of 185°F (85°C) for longer than 2 hours. The system may be exposed to temperatures up to 200°F (95°C) for less than 15 minutes.
- Never disconnect or connect the control module or hydraulic modulator connectors with the ignition switch ON.
- Never disassemble any component of the Anti-Lock Brake System (ABS) which is designated unserviceable; the component must be replaced as an assembly.
- When filling the master cylinder, always use brake fluid which meets DOT-3 specifications; petroleum-based fluid will destroy the rubber parts.
- Working on ABS system requires extreme amount of mechanical ability, training and special tools. If you are not familiar have your vehicle repaired by a certified mechanic or refer to a more advanced publication on this subject.

Diagnosis and Testing

For the proper diagnostic procedure for either the entire ABS system or a single component of the system, a scan tool (DRB or equivalent) is necessary. Because of the complexity of the ABS system and the importance of correct system functioning, it is a good idea to have a qualified automotive mechanic test the system if any problems have been detected.

The self-diagnostic ABS start up cycle begins when the ignition switch is turned to the **ON** position. An electrical check is completed on the ABS components, such as the wheel speed sensor continuity and other relay continuity. During this check the amber anti-lock light is turned on for approximately 1–2 seconds.

Further functional testing is accomplished once the vehicle is set in motion.

- The solenoid valves and the pump/motor are activated briefly to verify function
- The voltage output from the wheel speed sensors is verified to be within the correct operating range

If the vehicle is not set in motion within 3 minutes from the time the ignition switch is set in the **ON** position, the solenoid test is bypassed, but the pump/motor is activated briefly to verify that it is operating correctly.

For the Teves Mark IV-g system fault codes are kept in a non-volatile memory until either erased by the DRB or erased automatically after 50 ignition cycles (key **ON-OFF** cycles). The only fault that will not be erased after the 50 ignition cycles is the CAB fault. On the Teves Mark 20 system, DTCs are kept in the controller's memory until erased with the DRB scan tool, or they are erased automatically after 3,500 miles or 255 key cycles which ever occurs first. A CAB fault can only be erased by the DRB scan tool. More than one fault can be stored at a time. The number of key cycles since the most recent fault was stored is also displayed. Most functions of the CAB and ABS system can be accessed by the DRB scan tool for testing and diagnostic purposes.

To read the Diagnostic Trouble Codes (DTC's) perform the following:

1. Inspect the ABS components and connectors for damage and/or proper connections. Keep in mind that the brake light circuit also provides an input to to the ABS system. If the brake lights do not work, they must be fixed before proceeding.
2. Connect a DRB or equivalent scan tool to the Data Link Connector (located under the driver's side instrument panel). A scan tool must be used to access these codes.
3. Turn the ignition to the **ON** position. Wtih the scan tool, select "ABS".
4. Use the scan tool to select "Inputs/Outputs", and read the brake switch status. While pressing on the brake pedal, check the scan tool display. Select "Read DTC" and record any trouble codes which may appear. Sometimes, the cause of one trouble code may trigger additional codes to be set. If more than one code appear, a certain sequence of tests may be necessary. The beginning of each test will indicate if another test should be performed first.
5. Once the problem is corrected, use the scan tool to erase the trouble code(s).

Trouble Code Displays

The following is a list of the Teves Mark IVg Anti-lock Brake System (ABS) trouble codes that the DRB (or equivalent) scan tool may display for 1996 Chrysler minivan models:

- Diagnostic compare
- Left front inlet valve
- Left front outlet valve
- Left front sensor circuit failure
- Left front sensor continuity < > 25 MPH
- Left front sensor continuity > 25 MPH
- Left front sensor signal missing
- Left front sensor speed comparison
- Left rear inlet valve
- Left rear outlet valve

- Left rear sensor circuit failure
- Left rear sensor continuity < 25 MPH
- Left rear sensor continuity > 25 MPH
- Left rear sensor signal missing
- Left rear sensor speed comparison
- Pump motor circuit not working properly
- Pump motor not running
- Right front inlet valve
- Right front outlet valve
- Right front sensor circuit failure
- Right front sensor continuity < 25 MPH
- Right front sensor continuity > 25 MPH
- Right front sensor signal missing
- Right front sensor speed comparison
- Right rear inlet valve
- Right rear outlet valve
- Right rear sensor circuit failure
- Right rear sensor continuity < 25 MPH
- Right rear sensor continuity > 25 MPH
- Right rear sensor signal missing
- Right rear sensor speed comparison
- System overvoltage
- System undervoltage
- Valve block feed failure
- Valve power feed circuit

The following is a list of the Teves Mark-20 Anti-lock Brake System (ABS) trouble codes that the DRB (or equivalent) scan tool may display for 1997–99 Chrysler minivan models:

- CAB power feed circuit
- CCD communication
- Controller failure
- Left front sensor circuit failure
- Left front sensor signal failure
- Left rear sensor circuit failure
- Left rear sensor signal failure
- Pump motor circuit not working properly
- Right front sensor circuit failure
- Right front sensor signal failure
- Right rear sensor circuit failure
- Right rear sensor signal failure
- System overvoltage
- System undervoltage

Wheel Speed Sensors

REMOVAL & INSTALLATION

One of the primary inputs to the ABS system is from the wheel speed sensors. There is a sensor at each wheel that reads magnetic impulses from a toothed gear-like tone wheel. The sensors are easily damaged and must be handled with care. Make sure the wheel sensor surfaces are clean since they are magnetic and attract metal chips and debris. Use care when removing, installing and routing the sensor wiring. The wiring must be correctly installed to avoid ABS problems later.

Front Wheel Sensor

See Figures 104 thru 109

1. Disconnect negative battery cable.
2. Carefully raise and safely support the vehicle. Remove the front wheel.
3. Remove the 2 mounting screws that attach the front channel bracket and grommet retainer to the outer vehicle frame rail.
4. Pull the speed sensor cable grommet and wiring connector through the hole in the strut tower. Disconnect the vehicle wiring harness connector from the speed sensor connector. Be careful not to damage the pins on the connector.
5. Remove the bolt that mounts the speed sensor head to the steering knuckle.
6. Gently remove the speed sensor head from the steering knuckle.

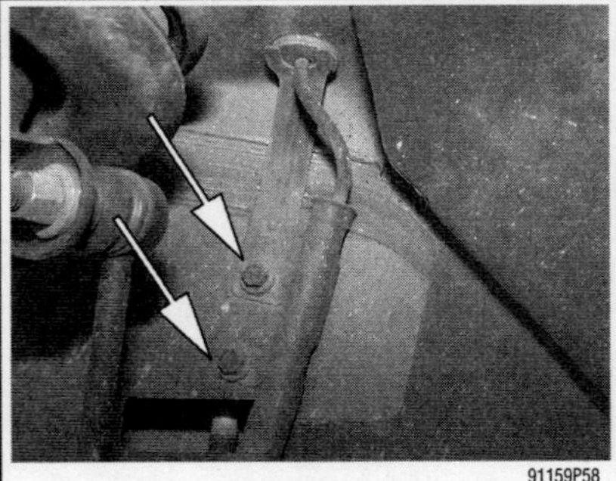

91159P58

Fig. 104 Remove the two screws that secure the mounting bracket and grommet retainer . . .

91159P57

Fig. 105 . . . then pull the grommet down . . .

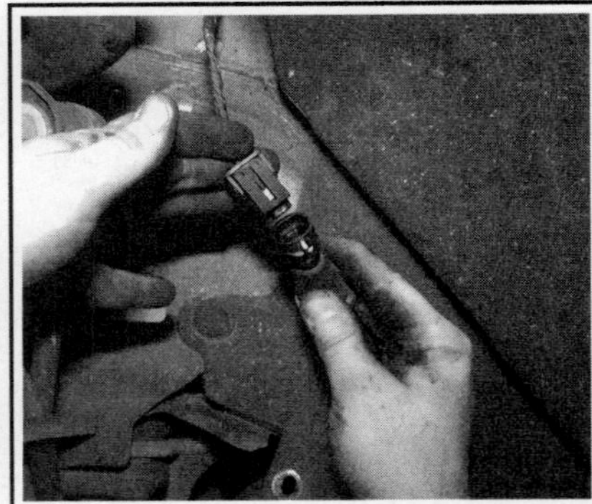

91159P56

Fig. 106 . . . and unplug the connector

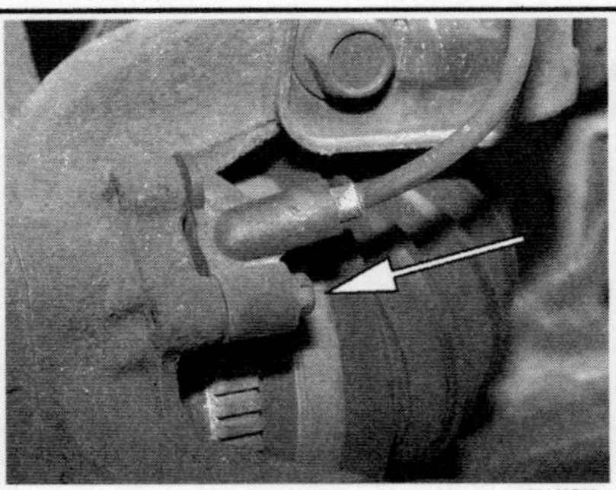

91159P53

Fig. 107 Next, remove the bolt that secures the wheel sensor . . .

91159P52

Fig. 108 . . . and carefully remove it from the steering knuckle

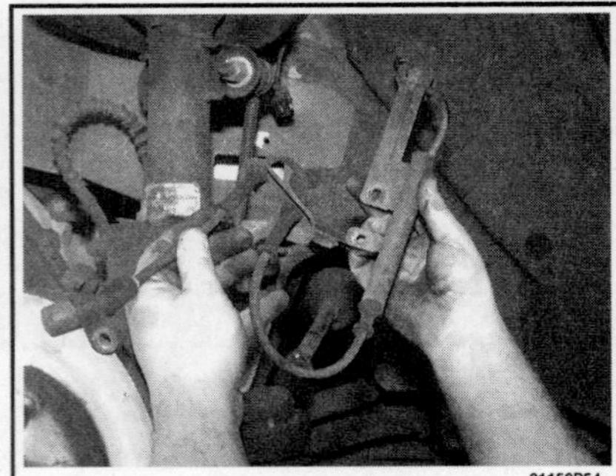

91159P54

Fig. 109 The wheel sensor assembly can now be removed from the vehicle

WARNING

Do not remove the speed sensor with pliers for any reason. If the speed sensor has seized, due to corrosion, remove it with a small mallet and punch. Lightly tap the edge of the sensor ear, rocking the sensor from side to side until it is free.

7. Remove the speed sensor cable grommets from the retaining bracket.
8. Remove the wheel speed sensor from the vehicle.

To install:

9. Install the speed sensor head into the steering knuckle. Install the mounting screw and torque to 105 inch lbs. (12 Nm).
10. Inspect the air gap between the face of the wheel speed sensor and the top surface of the tone wheel. The air gap must be less than the maximum allowable tolerance of 0.047 inch (1.2mm).

➡Correct system operation depends on the wheel speed sensor cables being installed properly. Be sure the sensor cables are installed in the retainers. Failure to do this could result in cable over extension and/or contact with moving parts. This could result in an open circuit and/or false sensor readings.

11. Install the speed sensor wiring grommets into the intermediate retaining bracket on the strut assembly. Be sure the sensor cable is routed correctly to the strut assembly on the rearward side of the stabilizer bar link.
12. Install the 2 mounting bolts that attach the channel bracket to the vehicle frame. Torque the 2 bolts to 95 inch lbs. (11 Nm).
13. Install the channel bracket and grommet retainer onto the vehicle frame rail. Be careful not to pinch the speed sensor cable under the channel bracket.
14. Connect the wheel speed sensor connector to the vehicle wiring harness connector. Be sure to securely latch the connector locking tab and seat the connector properly.
15. Insert the sensor cable and cable grommet into the hole in the strut tower.
16. Install the front wheel and lug nuts. Tighten the wheel lug nuts in a star pattern sequence and torque the nuts to half specification. Then repeat the lug nut torquing sequence to full specified torque of 95 ft. lbs. (129 Nm).
17. Lower the vehicle. Reconnect the negative battery cable.
18. Road test the vehicle to check the operation of the ABS and base brake systems.

Rear Wheel Sensor

See Figures 110, 111, 112 and 113

1. Disconnect the negative battery cable.
2. Carefully raise and safely support the vehicle. Remove the rear wheel.
3. Remove the speed sensor cable grommet, then the wiring harness through the hole in the vehicle floor pan. Do NOT pull on the speed sensor wiring when removing the grommet from the underbody.
4. Disconnect the speed sensor wiring connector from the vehicle wiring harness. Be careful not to damage the pins of the wiring connectors. Also inspect the connectors for any signs of previous damage.
5. Remove the speed sensor wiring from the rear brake flex hose routing clips. Be careful to NOT damage the routing clips on the rear brake flex hose. The routing clips are molded to the brake hoses and if they are damaged, the brake flex hoses will require replacement.
6. If removing the right side rear speed sensor, remove the speed sensor cable grommet from the axle flange, brake tube clip and routing clip from the track bar bracket on the axle.
7. Remove the 2 rear speed sensor cable/brake tube routing clips and then unclip the speed sensor cable from the routing clips on the rear brake tube.
8. Remove the speed sensor head mounting bolt from the rear bearing. Remove the wheel speed sensor head from the rear bearing assembly.

WARNING

Do not remove the wheel speed sensor with pliers for any reason. If the speed sensor has seized, due to corrosion, remove it with a hammer and punch. Lightly tap the edge of the sensor ear, rocking the sensor from side to side until it is free.

9. Remove the wheel speed sensor from the vehicle.

To install:

10. Install the wheel speed sensor head into the rear wheel bearing assembly. Be sure the plastic, anti-rotation pin is fully seated in wheel bearing flange before installing the mounting bolt. Install the mounting bolt and torque to 105 inch lbs. (12 Nm).
11. Inspect the air gap between the face of the wheel speed sensor and the top surface of the tone wheel. The air gap must be less than the maximum allowable tolerance of 0.047 inch (1.2mm).
12. Install the 2 routing brackets that secure the speed sensor cable and brake tube to the rear axle. The speed sensor cable must be routed underneath the brake tube. Be careful not to damage the brake hose routing clips.
13. Install the speed sensor cable into the rear brake flex hose routing clips.
14. If installing the right rear speed sensor cable, install the cable grommet onto the rear axle brake flex hose bracket.

WARNING

The left and right rear wheel speed sensor connectors are keyed differently. Therefore, when connecting a speed sensor cable to a vehicle wiring harness, do NOT force the connectors together, or damage to the connectors will result.

15. Connect the speed sensor wiring connector to the vehicle wiring harness and install the sensor cable grommet back into the wiring access hole on the vehicle underbody. Be sure the speed sensor connector is fully seated and locked into the vehicle wiring harness. Be sure the speed sensor cable grommet is fully seated into the vehicle underbody wiring access hole.
16. Install the wheel and lug nuts. Tighten the wheel lug nuts in a star pat-

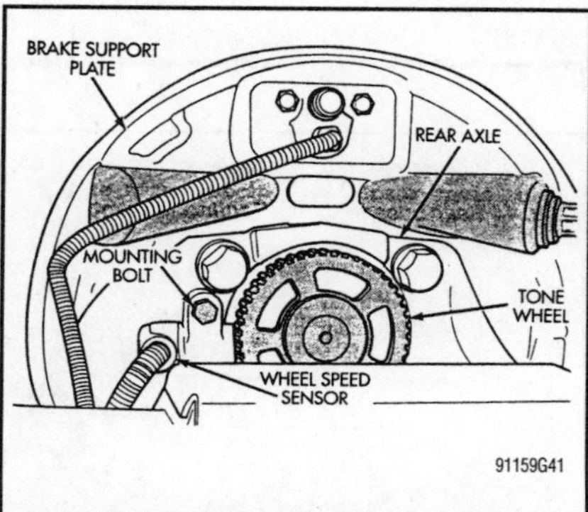

Fig. 110 Rear wheel speed sensor location (vehicles with drum brakes)

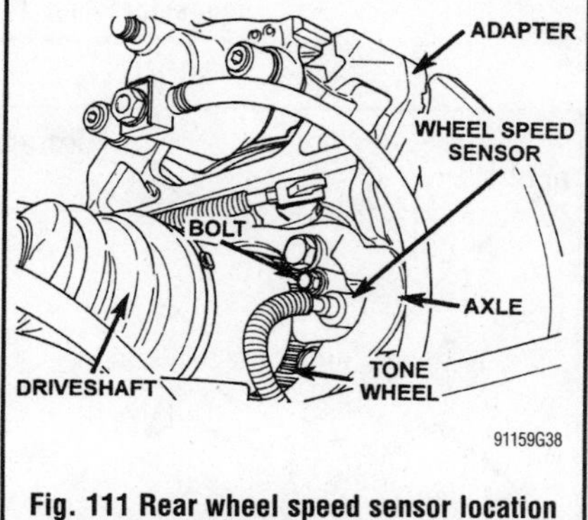

Fig. 111 Rear wheel speed sensor location (vehicles with disc brakes)

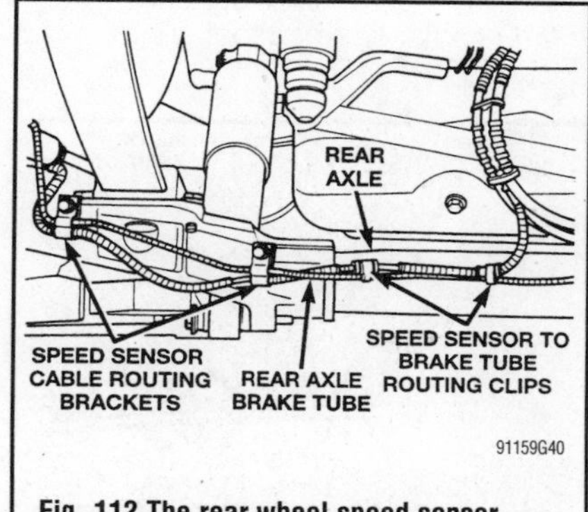

Fig. 112 The rear wheel speed sensor cable routing detail

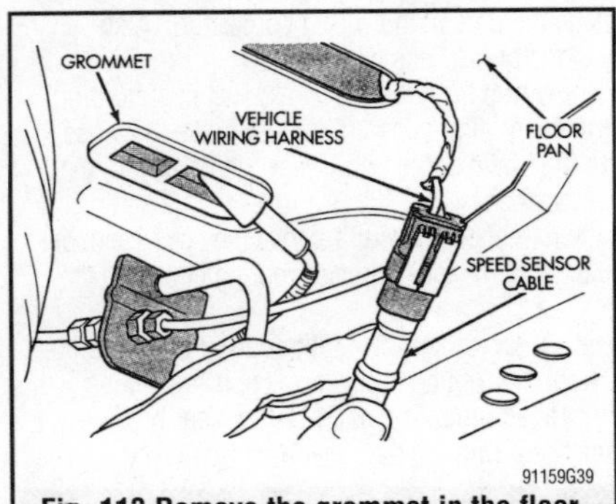

Fig. 113 Remove the grommet in the floor pan to access the speed sensor cable connector

Fig. 114 On 1996 vehicles, the CAB unit is located under the instrument panel near the heater A/C duct

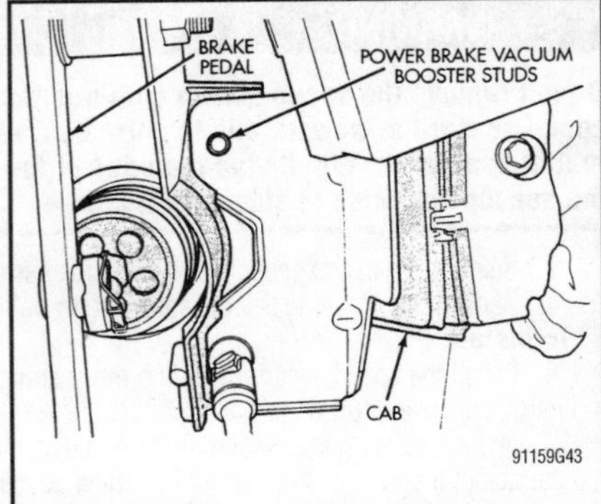

Fig. 115 The CAB bracket is held in place by two nuts

tern sequence and torque the nuts to half specification. Then repeat the lug nut tightening sequence to full specified torque of 95 ft. lbs. (129 Nm).

17. Lower the vehicle to the ground.
18. Reconnect the negative battery cable. Road test the vehicle and check for proper base and ABS braking system operation.

TESTING

1. Inspect the sensor and its connector. If the sensor looks damaged or connector looks disengaged, repair it as necessary.
2. With the ignition key turned **OFF**, disengage the wheel speed sensor connector. Inspect the condition of the terminals and repair as necessary.
3. Using an ohmmeter, measure the resistance between the wheel speed sensor connector terminals on the sensor side.
4. The resistance should measure 900–1300 ohms. If the resistance measures outside this value, replace the wheel speed sensor.
5. Then, measure the resistance between either one of the wheel speed sensor pins and ground on the sensor side.
6. If the resistance measures below 15k ohms, replace the wheel speed sensor.

Controller Anti-lock Brakes (CAB)

REMOVAL & INSTALLATION

1996 Vehicles

See Figures 114 and 115

➡The CAB is mounted under the instrument panel on the side of the brake pedal bracket toward the center of the vehicle.

1. Turn the ignition switch **OFF**.
2. Disconnect the negative battery cable.
3. Loosen the retaining bolt, then unplug the 60-pin wiring harness connector from the CAB.
4. Remove the 2 nuts attaching the CAB mounting bracket to the brake pedal bracket, then remove the CAB from the vehicle.

To install:

5. Install the CAB module and bracket assembly onto the brake pedal bracket. Secure the CAB in place with the 2 mounting nuts. Tighten the mounting nuts to 21 ft. lbs. (28 Nm).
6. Attach the 60-way connector to the CAB by hand as far as possible, then use the CAB connector retaining bolt to fully seat the wiring harness connector into the CAB.
7. Tighten the 60-way connector retaining bolt and tighten to 35 inch lbs. (4 Nm).
8. Connect the negative battery cable.

1997–99 Vehicles

See Figures 116, 117 and 118

➡The CAB is mounted to the bottom of the Hydraulic Control Unit (HCU).

1. Disconnect the negative battery cable.
2. Using a brake pedal depressor, move and lock the brake pedal to a position past its first 1 inch of travel. This will prevent brake fluid from draining out of the master cylinder when the brake tubes are removed from the proportioning valve.
3. Raise and safely support the vehicle securely on jackstands.
4. Disengage the 25-way wiring harness connector from the CAB by grasping the lock on the connector and pulling it out from the connector as far as it will go. This will remove the connector out from the CAB socket.

**** WARNING**

Do not apply a 12 volt power source to any terminals of the 25-way connector when it is disengaged.

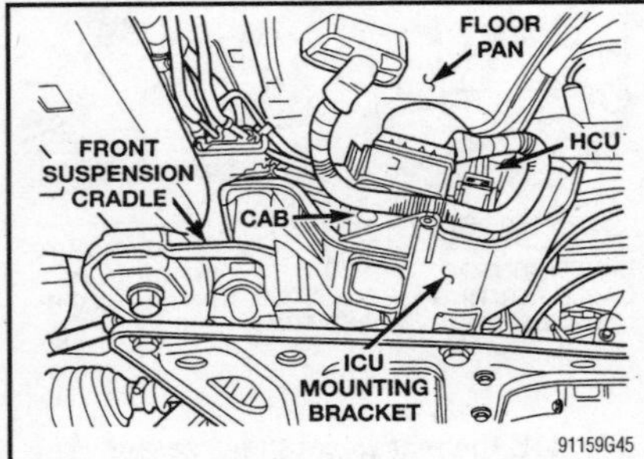

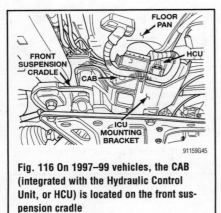

Fig. 116 On 1997–99 vehicles, the CAB (integrated with the Hydraulic Control Unit, or HCU) is located on the front suspension cradle

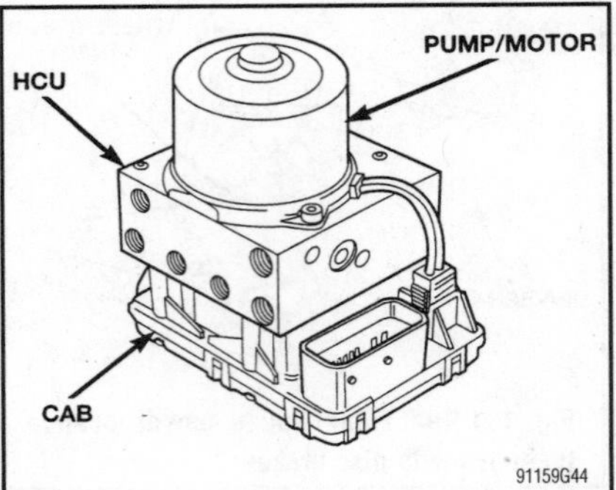

Fig. 117 Once the HCU is removed, the CAB can be removed

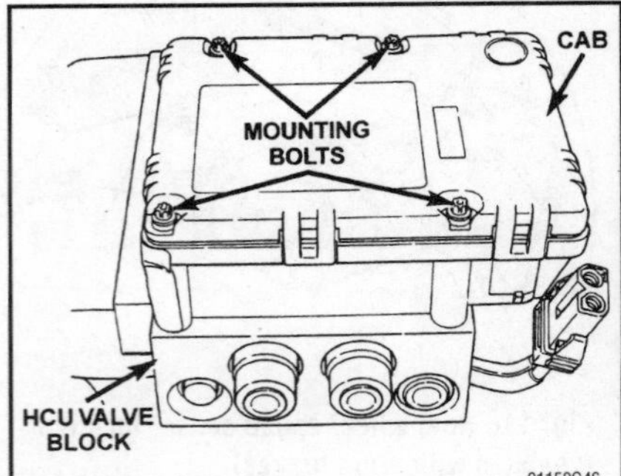

Fig. 118 The CAB can be separated from the HCU by removing the 4 mounting screws

5. To prevent possible hydraulic system contamination, thoroughly clean the HCU and brake tubes. Use MOPAR® Brake Parts Cleaner, or an equivalent solvent.
6. Label and disconnect the chassis brake tubes from the inlet and outlet ports of the HCU.
7. Remove the 3 bolts attaching the HCU mounting bracket to the front suspension crossmember.
8. Remove the HCU and the mounting bracket as a unit from the vehicle.
9. Remove the 3 bolts mounting the HCU to the mounting bracket. Separate the HCU from the mounting bracket.
10. Unplug the pump motor wiring harness from the CAB.
11. Loosen the 4 mounting bolts, then separate the CAB from the valve block of the HCU.

To install:

12. Place the CAB in position against the valve block of the HCU. Install and tighten the 4 mounting bolts to 17 inch lbs. (2 Nm).
13. Plug the pump motor wiring harness into the CAB.
14. Install the HCU onto the mounting bracket and tighten the 3 mounting bolts to 97 inch lbs. (11 Nm).
15. Place the HCU and mounting bracket assembly into position on the front suspension crossmember and tighten the mounting bolts to 21 ft. lbs. (28 Nm).
16. Install the chassis brake tubes into their correct port locations on the HCU valve block. Tighten the brake tube fittings to 13 ft. lbs. (17 Nm).
17. Install the 25-way connector into the CAB socket. Install the connector in the following manner:
    a. Position the connector into the CAB socket and carefully push it down as far as it will go.
    b. Once the connector is fully seated into the socket, push in the connector lock as far as it will go. This pulls the connector into the socket which locks it in the installed position.
18. Install the routing clips onto the brake tubes.
19. Lower the vehicle.
20. Connect the negative battery cable.
21. Remove the brake pedal positioning tool from the vehicle.
22. Bleed the base brake system and the ABS hydraulic system.
23. Road test the vehicle to ensure proper operation of the base and ABS systems.

Hydraulic Control Unit (HCU)

REMOVAL & INSTALLATION

1996 Vehicles

➧ See Figure 119

➡The Hydraulic Control Unit (HCU) is located on the driver's side of the vehicle, mounted onto the front suspension crossmember.

1. Disconnect and isolate the negative battery cable.
2. Disengage the HCU 10-way and 2-way connectors from the retaining bracket. Then disengage the HCU 10-way and 2-way connectors from the vehicle wiring harness located on the driver's side strut tower.
3. Disconnect the HCU wiring pigtail retaining straps from the master cylinder brake tubes. There are 2 retaining straps, one above and one below, the steel braid on the master cylinder tubes.
4. Using a brake pedal positioning tool, or equivalent, depress the brake pedal past the first 1 inch of travel and hold in this position. This will isolate the master cylinder reservoir from the brake hydraulic system, which will prevent the brake fluid from draining out of the reservoir.
5. Raise and safely support the vehicle securely on jackstands.
6. Using Brake Parts Cleaner, thoroughly clean all surfaces, brake line fittings and connections to the HCU.
7. Label and disconnect the chassis brake tubes from the inlet and outlet ports of the HCU.
8. Remove the 3 bolts attaching the HCU mounting bracket to the front suspension crossmember.
9. Remove the HCU and the mounting bracket as a unit from the vehicle, pulling the HCU wiring pigtail through the opened master cylinder tube clip retaining straps.

Fig. 119 The HCU is located on the front suspension crossmember

To install:

10. Locate and lock the HCU wiring pigtail into the routing clips located on the primary and secondary master cylinder-to-HCU brake tubes. When the wiring pigtail is installed in the routing clips, be sure that the brake tubes and wiring harness do not touch any other components.
11. Place the HCU and mounting bracket assembly into position on the front suspension crossmember and tighten the mounting bolts to 21 ft. lbs. (28 Nm).
12. Install the chassis brake tubes into their correct port locations on the HCU valve block. Tighten the brake tube fittings to 13 ft. lbs. (17 Nm).
13. Lower the vehicle.
14. Engage the HCU 10-way and 2-way connectors into the vehicle wiring harness connectors.
15. Install the HCU 10-way and 2-way connectors back into the bracket located on the driver's side strut tower.
16. Connect the negative battery cable.
17. Remove the brake pedal positioning tool from the vehicle.
18. Bleed the base brake system and the ABS hydraulic system.
19. Road test the vehicle to ensure proper operation of the base and ABS systems.

1997–99 Vehicles

➡Refer to the removal and installation procedures outlined under Controller Anti-lock Brakes (CAB), earlier in this section.

Proportioning Valve

REMOVAL & INSTALLATION

➧ See Figure 120

1. Using a brake pedal depressor, move and lock the brake pedal to a position past its first 1 inch of travel. This will prevent brake fluid from draining out of the master cylinder when the brake tubes are removed from the proportioning valve.
2. Raise and safely support the vehicle securely on jackstands.

➡To prevent possible hydraulic system contamination, thoroughly clean the proportioning valve and brake tubes. Use MOPAR® Brake Parts Cleaner, or an equivalent solvent.

3. Remove the 4 brake lines from the inlet and outlet ports of the proportioning valve.
4. Remove the bolts securing the proportioning valve bracket to the vehicle frame rail. Remove the proportioning valve assembly from the vehicle.

To install:

5. Place the proportioning valve assembly into position on the frame rail. Install the mounting bolts and tighten to 10 ft. lbs. (14 Nm).

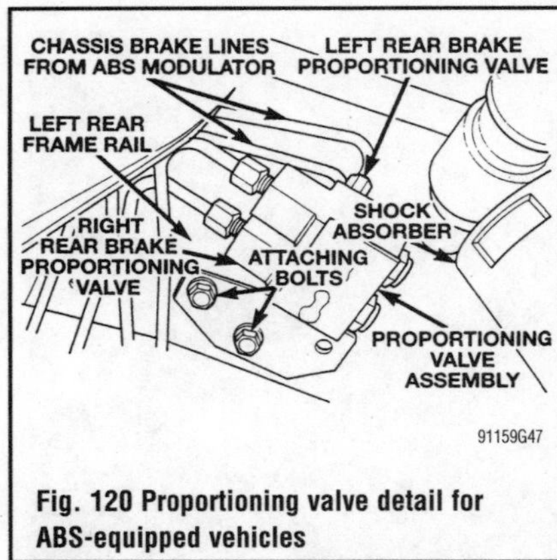

Fig. 120 Proportioning valve detail for ABS-equipped vehicles

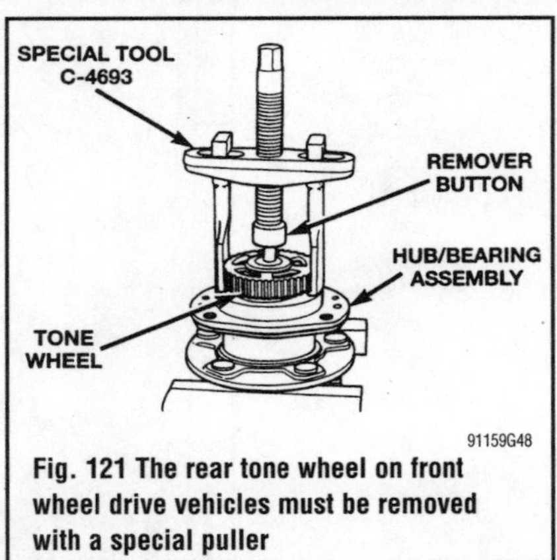

Fig. 121 The rear tone wheel on front wheel drive vehicles must be removed with a special puller

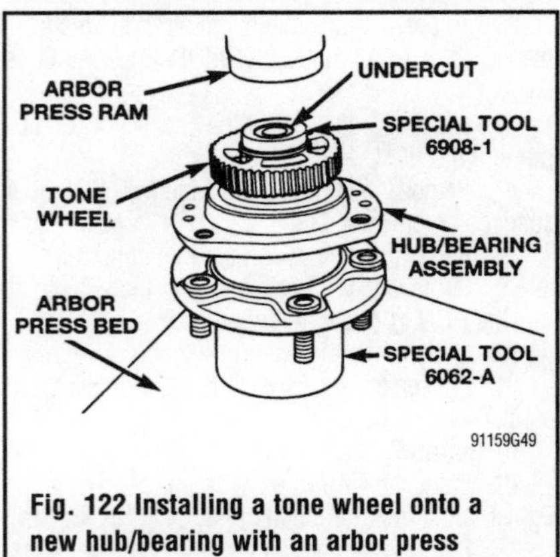

Fig. 122 Installing a tone wheel onto a new hub/bearing with an arbor press

6. Install the chassis brake lines into the proportioning valve assembly. Tighten the brake line fittings to 12 ft. lbs. (16 Nm).
7. Bleed the brake system.
8. Lower the vehicle.
9. Carefully road test the vehicle to verify proper brake system operation.

Tone (Exciter) Ring

REMOVAL & INSTALLATION

Rear Wheel (All Wheel Drive Only) and Front Wheel Tone Rings

The front ABS tone ring and rear ABS tone ring (All Wheel Drive only) are integral components of the halfshaft assemblies and therefore, cannot be serviced separately. If any of these tone rings require service, the halfshaft assembly must be replaced.

However, the rear ABS tone ring on front wheel drive vehicles can be serviced separately.

Rear Wheel (Front Wheel Drive Only)

See Figures 121 and 122

1. Remove the rear wheel speed sensor from the rear hub/bearing flange.
2. Remove the rear wheel hub/bearing assembly from the vehicle.
3. Install 3 lug nuts on 3 of the wheel mounting studs to prevent possible thread damage while installing the assembly in a bench vise. Using Puller Special Tool C-4693, or equivalent, remove the tone wheel from the back of the hub/bearing assembly.

To install:

4. Position the hub/bearing assembly in an arbor press supported by Receiver Special Tool 6062A-3. Position Driver Special Tool 6908-1 with the undercut side facing up on top of the tone wheel.
5. Press the tone wheel onto the hub/bearing assembly until it fits flush with the end of the hub shaft.
6. Install the hub/bearing assembly onto the vehicle.
7. Install the rear wheel speed sensor onto the rear hub/bearing flange.
8. Inspect the air gap between the face of the wheel speed sensor and the top surface of the tone wheel. The air gap must be less than the maximum allowable tolerance of 0.047 inch (1.2mm).
9. Install the brake drum/rotor.
10. Install rear wheel(s).
11. Adjust the rear brakes.

Bleeding the ABS System

See Figures 22, 23 and 24

The bleeding procedure is a 2-step process, one of which will require use of the DRB scan tool or its equivalent. Bleed the system as follows:

1. Locate the diagnostic connector under the dash panel to the left of the steering column cover.
2. Connect the DRB scan tool to the connector. Install the correct cartridge for the Anti-Lock Brake systems. Check to make sure the CAB (Controller Anti-lock Brakes) does not have any fault codes stored in it. If it does, remove them using the DRB scan tool.

CAUTION

Be sure to always wear safety glasses when bleeding the brake system. This will prevent personal injury to your eyes in case fluid squirts out at high pressure.

3. Bleed the base brake system using the non-ABS manual bleeding method as outlined earlier in this section. Be sure to bleed the brake system in the correct sequence.
4. Utilizing the scan tool, go to the "Bleed ABS" routine. Firmly apply the brake pedal to initiate the "Bleed ABS" cycle one time. Release the brake pedal.
5. Using the scan tool, go on to bleed the Anti-Lock Brake System according to the scan tool literature.
6. Once bleeding with the scan tool is complete, repeat the conventional bleed procedure for the base brake system.
7. Perform this procedure until the brake fluid flows clear and free of air bubbles. Check brake fluid level periodically to prevent the reservoir from running low on fluid. Top off the master cylinder reservoir to the proper level with DOT 3 type brake fluid only.
8. Road test the vehicle to check for proper brake system operation.

BRAKE SPECIFICATIONS

All measurements in inches unless noted

Year	Model	Master Cylinder Bore	Brake Disc Original Thickness	Brake Disc Minimum Thickness	Brake Disc Maximum Run-out	Brake Drum Diameter Original Inside Diameter	Brake Drum Diameter Max. Wear Limit	Brake Drum Diameter Maximum Machine Diameter	Minimum Lining Thickness Front	Minimum Lining Thickness Rear
1996	Caravan	0.940	0.940	0.880	0.005	9.00	9.09	9.06	0.060	0.060 ①
	Town & Country	0.937	0.940	0.881	0.005	9.84	9.93	9.90	0.062	0.062 ①
	Voyager	0.937	0.939	0.881	0.005	9.84	9.93	9.90	0.060	0.060 ①
1997	Caravan	0.937	②	③	0.005	9.84	9.93	9.90	0.313	④
	Town & Country	0.937	②	③	0.005	9.84	9.93	9.90	0.313	④
	Voyager	0.937	②	③	0.005	9.84	9.93	9.90	0.313	④
1998	Caravan	⑤	⑥	⑦	0.005	9.84	9.93	9.90	0.313	④
	Town & Country	⑤	⑥	⑦	0.005	9.84	9.93	9.90	0.313	④
	Voyager	⑤	⑥	⑦	0.005	9.84	9.93	9.90	0.313	④
1999	Caravan	⑤	⑥	⑦	0.005	9.84	9.93	9.90	0.313	④
	Town & Country	⑤	⑥	⑦	0.005	9.84	9.93	9.90	0.313	④
	Voyager	⑤	⑥	⑦	0.005	9.84	9.93	9.90	0.313	④

① For riveted brake shoes: 0.031
② Front rotor: 0.939-0.949
Rear rotor: 0.458-0.478
③ Front rotor: 0.881
Rear rotor: 0.409
④ Rear drum brake shoes: 0.031
Rear disc brake pads: 0.281
⑤ FWD models: 0.937
AWD models: 1.000
⑥ Front rotor: 0.939-0.949
Rear rotor: 0.482-0.502
⑦ Front rotor: 0.881
Rear rotor: 0.443

91159C01

Troubleshooting the Brake System

Problem	Cause	Solution
Low brake pedal (excessive pedal travel required for braking action.)	· Excessive clearance between rear linings and drums caused by inoperative automatic adjusters	· Make 10 to 15 alternate forward and reverse brake stops to adjust brakes. If brake pedal does not come up, repair or replace adjuster parts as necessary.
	· Worn rear brakelining	· Inspect and replace lining if worn beyond minimum thickness specification
	· Bent, distorted brakeshoes, front or rear	· Replace brakeshoes in axle sets
	· Air in hydraulic system	· Remove air from system. Refer to Brake Bleeding.
Low brake pedal (pedal may go to floor with steady pressure applied.)	· Fluid leak in hydraulic system	· Fill master cylinder to fill line; have helper apply brakes and check calipers, wheel cylinders, differential valve tubes, hoses and fittings for leaks. Repair or replace as necessary.
	· Air in hydraulic system	· Remove air from system. Refer to Brake Bleeding.
	· Incorrect or non-recommended brake fluid (fluid evaporates at below normal temp).	· Flush hydraulic system with clean brake fluid. Refill with correct-type fluid.
	· Master cylinder piston seals worn, or master cylinder bore is scored, worn or corroded	· Repair or replace master cylinder
Low brake pedal (pedal goes to floor on first application—o.k. on subsequent applications.)	· Disc brake pads sticking on abutment surfaces of anchor plate. Caused by a build-up of dirt, rust, or corrosion on abutment surfaces	· Clean abutment surfaces
Fading brake pedal (pedal height decreases with steady pressure applied.)	· Fluid leak in hydraulic system	· Fill master cylinder reservoirs to fill mark, have helper apply brakes, check calipers, wheel cylinders, differential valve, tubes, hoses, and fittings for fluid leaks. Repair or replace parts as necessary.
	· Master cylinder piston seals worn, or master cylinder bore is scored, worn or corroded	· Repair or replace master cylinder
Decreasing brake pedal travel (pedal travel required for braking action decreases and may be accompanied by a hard pedal.)	· Caliper or wheel cylinder pistons sticking or seized	· Repair or replace the calipers, or wheel cylinders
	· Master cylinder compensator ports blocked (preventing fluid return to reservoirs) or pistons sticking or seized in master cylinder bore	· Repair or replace the master cylinder
	· Power brake unit binding internally	· Test unit according to the following procedure: (a) Shift transmission into neutral and start engine (b) Increase engine speed to 1500 rpm, close throttle and fully depress brake pedal (c) Slow release brake pedal and stop engine (d) Have helper remove vacuum check valve and hose from power unit. Observe for backward movement of brake pedal. (e) If the pedal moves backward, the power unit has an internal bind—replace power unit

TCCA9C01

Troubleshooting the Brake System (cont.)

Problem	Cause	Solution
Spongy brake pedal (pedal has abnormally soft, springy, spongy feel when depressed.)	• Air in hydraulic system	• Remove air from system. Refer to Brake Bleeding.
	• Brakeshoes bent or distorted	• Replace brakeshoes
	• Brakelining not yet seated with drums and rotors	• Burnish brakes
	• Rear drum brakes not properly adjusted	• Adjust brakes
Hard brake pedal (excessive pedal pressure required to stop vehicle. May be accompanied by brake fade.)	• Loose or leaking power brake unit vacuum hose	• Tighten connections or replace leaking hose
	• Incorrect or poor quality brake-lining	• Replace with lining in axle sets
	• Bent, broken, distorted brakeshoes	• Replace brakeshoes
	• Calipers binding or dragging on mounting pins. Rear brakeshoes dragging on support plate.	• Replace mounting pins and bushings. Clean rust or burrs from rear brake support plate ledges and lubricate ledges with molydisulfide grease. **NOTE:** If ledges are deeply grooved or scored, do not attempt to sand or grind them smooth—replace support plate.
	• Caliper, wheel cylinder, or master cylinder pistons sticking or seized	• Repair or replace parts as necessary
	• Power brake unit vacuum check valve malfunction	• Test valve according to the following procedure: (a) Start engine, increase engine speed to 1500 rpm, close throttle and immediately stop engine (b) Wait at least 90 seconds then depress brake pedal (c) If brakes are not vacuum assisted for 2 or more applications, check valve is faulty
	• Power brake unit has internal bind	• Test unit according to the following procedure: (a) With engine stopped, apply brakes several times to exhaust all vacuum in system (b) Shift transmission into neutral, depress brake pedal and start engine (c) If pedal height decreases with foot pressure and less pressure is required to hold pedal in applied position, power unit vacuum system is operating normally. Test power unit. If power unit exhibits a bind condition, replace the power unit.
	• Master cylinder compensator ports (at bottom of reservoirs) blocked by dirt, scale, rust, or have small burrs (blocked ports prevent fluid return to reservoirs).	• Repair or replace master cylinder **CAUTION:** Do not attempt to clean blocked ports with wire, pencils, or similar implements. Use compressed air only.
	• Brake hoses, tubes, fittings clogged or restricted	• Use compressed air to check or unclog parts. Replace any damaged parts.
	• Brake fluid contaminated with improper fluids (motor oil, transmission fluid, causing rubber components to swell and stick in bores	• Replace all rubber components, combination valve and hoses. Flush entire brake system with DOT 3 brake fluid or equivalent.
	• Low engine vacuum	• Adjust or repair engine

TCCA9C02

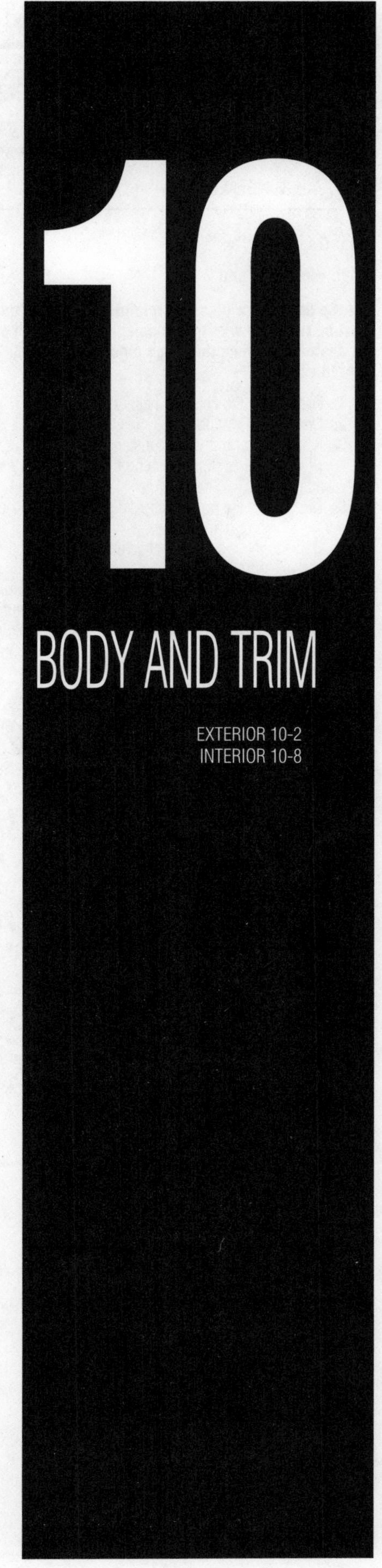

10 BODY AND TRIM

EXTERIOR

Doors

REMOVAL & INSTALLATION

Front Door

See Figures 1 and 2

If the door hinge pins and retaining clips are being removed, they must be replaced with new pins and clips, which can be purchased at the dealership. Once the hinge pins are removed, they lose their structural integrity.

1. Disconnect the negative battery cable.
2. Open the front door.
3. Remove the front wheelhouse splash shield.
4. Disengage the clips attaching the door wiring harness connector to the inner fender brace.
5. Disconnect the positive lock slide located on the side of the wiring connectors.
6. Depress the locking tab attaching the wiring harness connector halves together.
7. Disconnect the door harness from the body wiring harness.
8. Remove the door check strap-to-A pillar mounting bolts.
9. Support the weight of the door on a suitable lifting device.
10. Remove the lower hinge-to-door end frame mounting bolts.

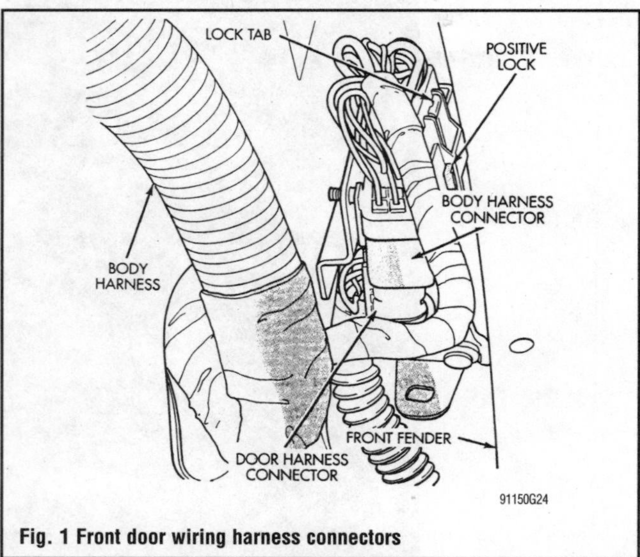

Fig. 1 Front door wiring harness connectors

11. While holding the door steady on the lifting device, remove the upper hinge-to-door end frame mounting bolts.
12. Remove the door from the vehicle.

To install:

13. Support the weight of the door on a suitable lifting device.
14. Position the door to the vehicle. While holding the door steady on the lifting device, install the upper hinge-to-door end frame mounting bolts. Tighten the bolts to 105 inch lbs. (12 Nm).
15. Install the door check strap to the A pillar and tighten the mounting bolts to 105 inch lbs. (12 Nm).
16. Install the lower hinge-to-door end frame mounting bolts and tighten to 25 ft. lbs. (34 Nm). Be sure to align the door to achieve equal spacing to the surrounding body panels. These panels should be flush across all gaps.
17. Connect the door harness to the body wiring harness.
18. Connect the positive lock slide on the side of the wiring connectors.
19. Connect the clips attaching the door wiring harness connector to the inner fender brace.
20. Install the front wheelhouse splash shield.
21. Connect the negative battery cable.
22. Verify door operation and alignment. Adjust as necessary.

Sliding Door

See Figures 3 thru 8

To avoid damaging the body paint, apply several layers of masking tape to the body around the rear end of the upper roller channel and the forward edge of the quarter panel.

1. Disconnect the negative battery cable.
2. Open the door.
3. Apply masking tape to the door jamb area.
4. Remove the screw holding the upper roller arm stop bumper to upper roller arm.
5. Remove the stop bumper from the upper roller arm.
6. Remove the center stop bumper trim cover from the sliding door.
7. Remove the center stop from the sliding door.
8. Remove the sliding door sill plate.
9. Remove the hold open latch striker.
10. Open the quarter glass.
11. Remove the center roller channel end cover.

WARNING

Do not allow the center hinge roller to contact the quarter glass. This glass can break.

12. Support the sliding door on a suitable lifting device with a padded upper surface. The door must be moveable with the lifting device in position.
13. Roll the door rearward until the lower rollers disengage from the lower channel.

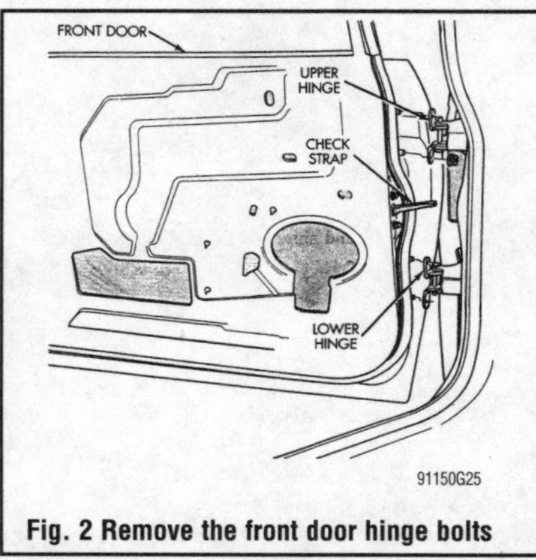

Fig. 2 Remove the front door hinge bolts

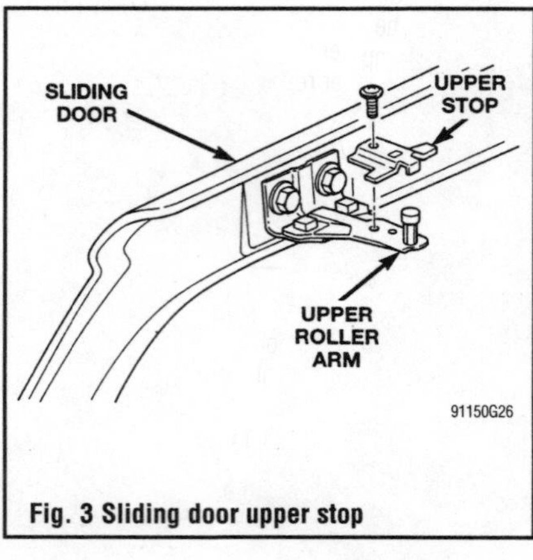

Fig. 3 Sliding door upper stop

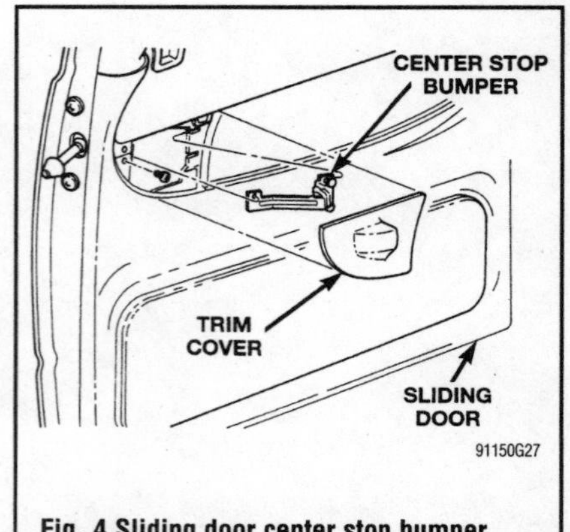

Fig. 4 Sliding door center stop bumper

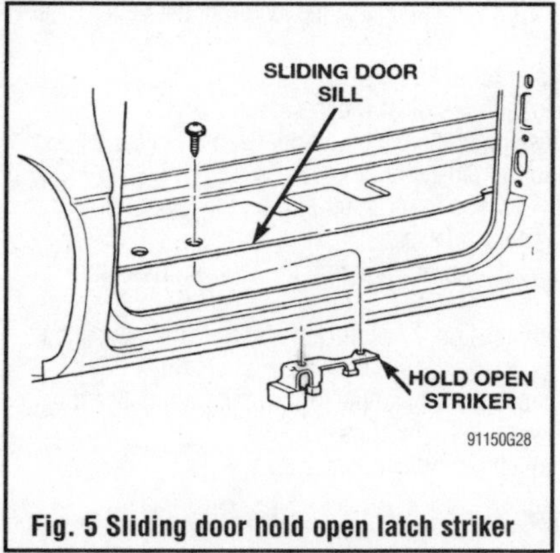

Fig. 5 Sliding door hold open latch striker

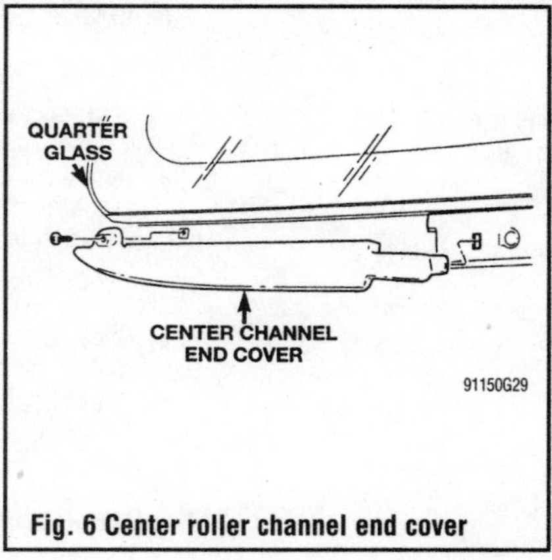

Fig. 6 Center roller channel end cover

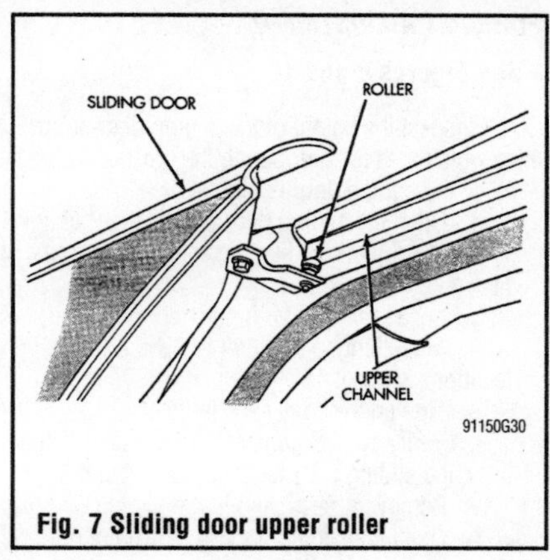

Fig. 7 Sliding door upper roller

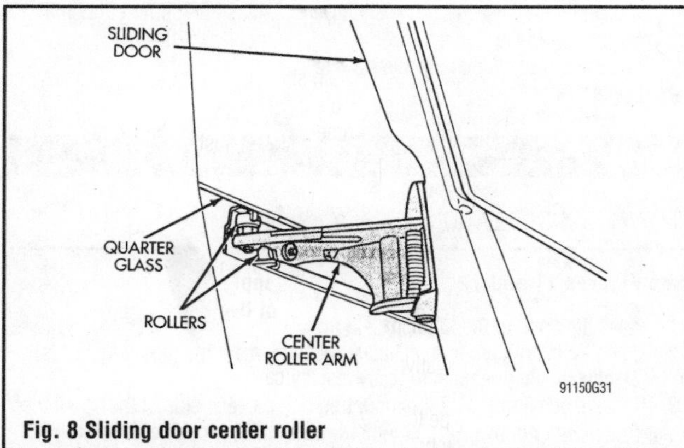

Fig. 8 Sliding door center roller

14. Roll the door rearward until the upper and center hinge rollers disengage from the upper and center channels.
15. Remove the sliding door from the vehicle.

To install:

16. Place the sliding door in position on a lifting device.
17. Position the door rearward of the sliding door opening.

WARNING

Do NOT allow the center hinge roller to contact the quarter glass. The glass can break.

18. Engage the center hinge rollers into the center channels.
19. Roll door forward until lower rollers engage into rear of lower channel.
20. Engage the upper hinge into the upper channels.
21. Install the hold open latch striker.
22. Install the sliding door sill plate.
23. Install the center roller channel end cover.
24. Install the center stop on the sliding door.
25. Install the center stop bumper trim cover on the sliding door.
26. Place the upper roller stop bumper in position on the upper roller arm.
27. Install screw to secure the upper roller arm stop bumper to upper roller arm.
28. Remove masking tape from body surfaces.
29. Verify sliding door operation and fit. Adjust if necessary.

ADJUSTMENT

Front Door

1. With the door fully closed, check the flush and gaps of the door.
2. The door should be aligned to 0.20 inch (5mm) gap to the front fenders and rear door. The door should fit flush across all of the gaps.
3. If necessary, loosen the bolts to reposition the door, then tighten the bolts to 105 inch lbs. (12 Nm).

Sliding Door

PRELIMINARY CHECKS

1. Close the sliding door, visually inspecting the C-post striker alignment entry into latch. The striker at this point must not affect alignment.
2. On vehicles equipped with a left side sliding door, inspect the fuel door blocker striker entry into latch. The striker at this point must not affect alignment.
3. Inspect the C-post and B-post for door-to-aperture gaps and door-to-door gaps. All gaps should measure 0.160–0.240 inch (4–6mm).
4. Inspect the door for height using character lines as a reference, as well as the roof contour as a controlling factor.

UP/DOWN ADJUSTMENT

See Figure 9

1. Visually inspect the sliding door for fitting low at the rear of the door by checking the alignment of the belt line of the door to quarter panel.
2. Fully open the sliding door.
3. Check to be sure that all of the center hinge bolts are tight.
4. Adjust the rear of the sliding door up by rotating the center hinge bolts clockwise.
5. Close the door and inspect the alignment.
6. Re-adjust the center hinge if necessary to obtain alignment between the belt line of the sliding door and quarter panel.
7. Fully open the sliding door and install a locknut to the center hinge bolt. Tighten the locknut until it butts up against the welded nut on the center hinge. Tighten the nut to 11 ft. lbs. (15 Nm). It may be necessary to use a backup wrench to hold the center hinge bolt to prevent it from turning while tightening the nut.
8. Verify door alignment and re-adjust if necessary.

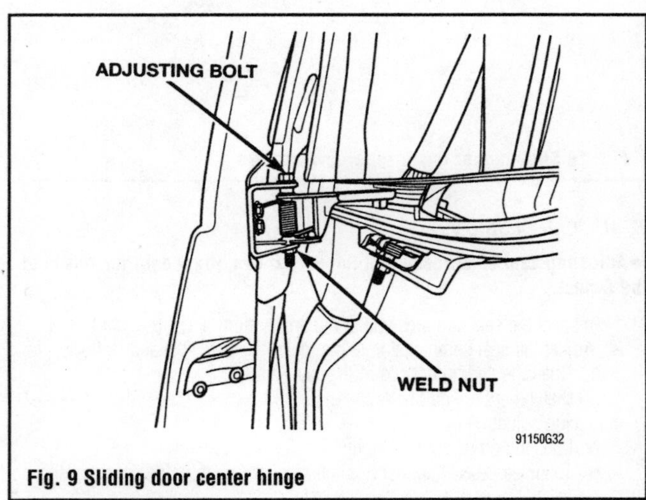

Fig. 9 Sliding door center hinge

FORE/AFT ADJUSTMENT

See Figures 9 and 10

1. Inspect the height of the sliding door at the B-post and C-post to determine which area is contributing the greatest to the incorrect gaps.
2. If the sliding door is high at the C-post;
   a. Open the sliding door to mid-point of travel.
   b. Matchmark outline of center hinge on the sliding door to assist in making adjustments.
   c. Loosen the center hinge bolts.
   d. Move hinge fore or aft to position the sliding door into the correct location.
   e. Tighten the center hinge bolts.
   f. Verify door alignment and re-adjust if necessary.
3. If the sliding door is low at the B-post;
   a. Remove access plug in the sliding door trim panel.
   b. Open the sliding door to mid-point of travel.
   c. Matchmark outline of the lower roller arm bracket on the sliding door to assist in making adjustments.
   d. Loosen the lower roller arm bracket bolts.
   e. Move the hinge downward to raise the door.
   f. Tighten the lower roller arm bracket bolts.
   g. Verify door alignment and re-adjust if necessary.
4. If the sliding door is low at the C-post;
   a. Open the sliding door to mid-point of travel.
   b. Matchmark outline of center hinge on the sliding door to assist in making adjustments.
   c. Rotate the adjustment bolt up or down to move the door position.
   d. Move the hinge downward to raise the door.
   e. Tighten the center hinge bolts.
   f. Verify door alignment and re-adjust if necessary.
5. If the sliding door is high at the B-post;
   a. Remove access plug in the sliding door trim panel.
   b. Open the sliding door to mid-point of travel.
   c. Matchmark outline of lower roller arm bracket on the sliding door to assist in making adjustments.
   d. Loosen the lower roller arm bracket bolts.
   e. Move the hinge upward to raise the door.
   f. Tighten the lower roller arm bracket bolts.
   g. Verify door alignment and re-adjust if necessary.

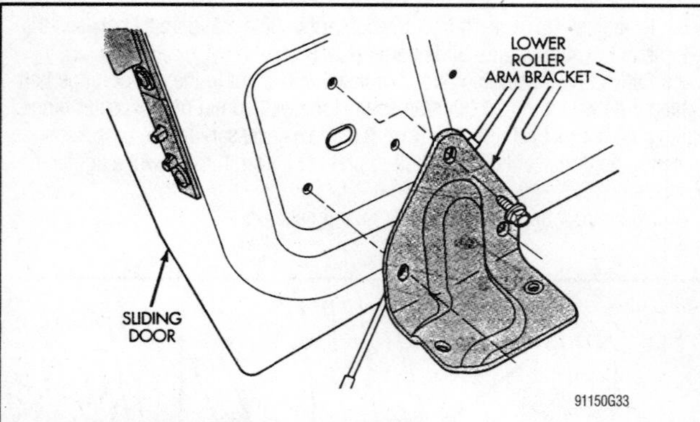

Fig. 10 Sliding door lower roller arm bracket

SEAL COMPRESSION

Adjusting seal compression at the B-post can affect door flushness at the C-post.

1. Inspect the seal compression at top and bottom of B-post seal.
2. Adjust the seal compression at the top of the B-post seal as follows:
   a. Open the sliding door to mid-point of travel.
   b. Matchmark the outline of the upper roller arm on the bracket to assist in making adjustments.
   c. Loosen bolts securing the upper roller arm to the bracket.
   d. To increase seal compression, shorten the length of the upper roller arm.
   e. To decrease seal compression, increase the length of the upper roller arm.
   f. Tighten all of the upper roller arm bolts.
   g. Verify door alignment and re-adjust if necessary.
3. Adjust the seal compression at the bottom of the B-post seal as follows:
   a. Open the sliding door to mid-point of travel.
   b. Matchmark the outline of the lower roller arm on the lower roller arm bracket to assist in making adjustments.
   c. Loosen bolts securing the lower roller arm to the lower roller arm bracket.
   d. To decrease seal compression, pivot the lower roller arm toward the center of the vehicle.
   e. To increase seal compression, pivot the lower roller arm outward.
   f. Tighten all of the lower roller arm bolts.
   g. Verify door alignment and re-adjust if necessary.

STABILIZER ADJUSTMENT

1. Open sliding door.
2. Loosen the bolts securing the stabilizers to the sliding door enough that the stabilizers can move with some effort.
3. Close and then reopen the sliding door.
4. Tighten all bolts.

Hood

REMOVAL & INSTALLATION

See Figures 11 and 12

1. Raise the hood to the full up position.
2. Using an instrument to matchmark location, mark the mounting bolt(s) and hinge attachment positions for easy installation.
3. Remove one hood-to-hinge mounting bolt on each side of the hood, then loosen (but do not remove, yet) the other bolts until they can be removed by hand.
4. With assistance from a helper supporting the other side of the hood, remove the second mounting bolts on each side of the hood.
5. Carefully remove the hood from the vehicle. Be careful not to scratch the hood when placing it away from the vehicle.

To install:

6. With assistance from a helper supporting the other side of the hood, place the hood into correct position on the vehicle and install mounting bolts finger tight.
7. Be sure to line up the hood with the marks made for the hinge locations then tighten the bolts to 10 ft. lbs. (14 Nm).
8. Verify hood operation and inspect the hood alignment.

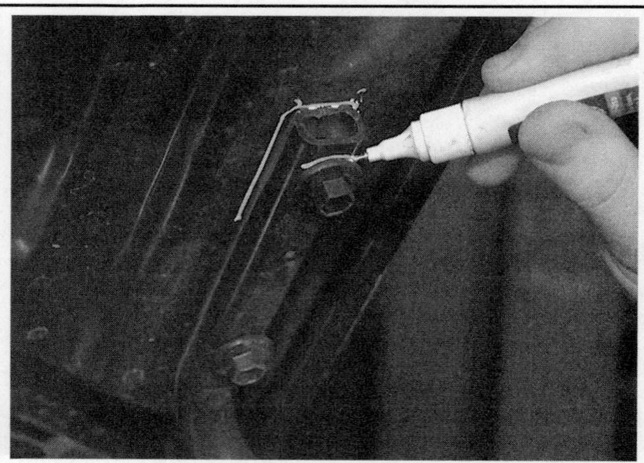

Fig. 11 Using a good paint pen, matchmark the hood hinge and mounting bolt locations before removing the hood. This will be extremely helpful when trying to align the hood during installation

91150P08

Fig. 12 After marking the hood hinges, loosen the hood mounting bolts, then remove

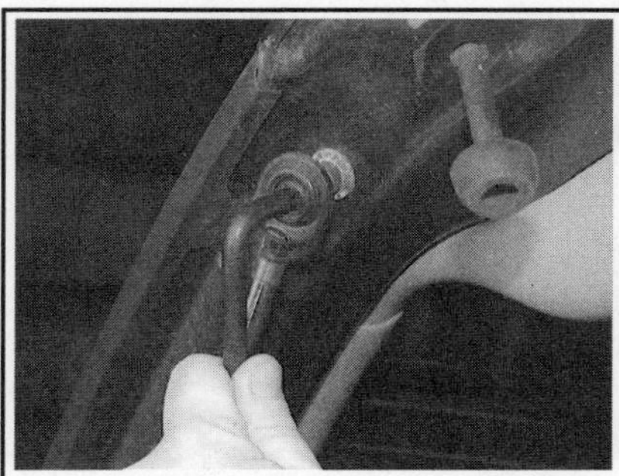
91150P05

Fig. 13 Remove the support cylinder mounting screw using a Torx® end wrench tool

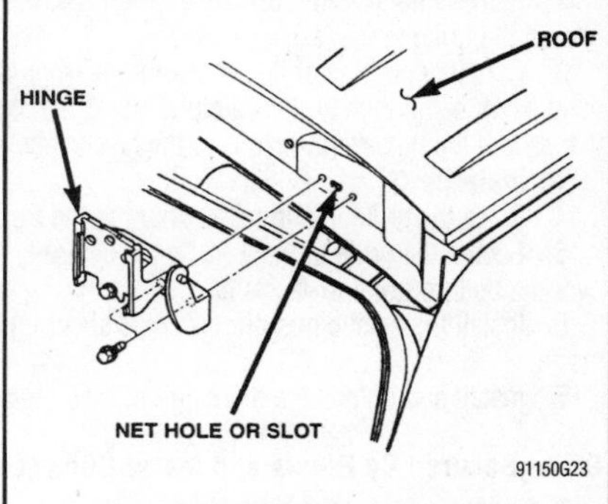

91150G23

Fig. 14 Remove the liftgate hinge-to-roof mounting bolts

ALIGNMENT

1. Check to make sure that the hood bolts are positioned correctly at the matchmarks and tighten.
2. With the hood fully closed, check the flush and gaps of the hood.
3. The hood should be aligned to 0.160 inch (4mm) gap to the front fenders and flush across the top surfaces along the fenders.
4. If necessary, loosen the bolts to reposition the hood, then tighten the bolts to 10 ft. lbs. (14 Nm).

Liftgate

REMOVAL & INSTALLATION

➧ **See Figures 13 and 14**

1. Open the liftgate.
2. Remove screws securing the liftgate wiring connector to the rear header panel.
3. Disconnect the liftgate wiring harness from the body wiring harness.
4. Remove the liftgate upper window frame molding.
5. Disconnect the rear window washer hose from the spray nozzle.
6. Support the liftgate in the open position using a suitable lifting device.
7. Remove the screws holding the support cylinders to the liftgate.
8. Remove the liftgate hinge-to-roof header mounting bolts.
9. With assistance, remove the liftgate from the vehicle.

To install:

10. With assistance, place the liftgate into position on the vehicle.
11. Install the liftgate hinge-to-roof header mounting bolts and tighten to 24 ft. lbs. (33 Nm).
12. Install the screws securing the support cylinders to the liftgate and tighten to 21 ft. lbs. (28 Nm).
13. Remove the support device from under the liftgate.
14. Connect the liftgate wiring harness to the body wiring harness.
15. Install the liftgate wiring connector-to-rear header panel screws.
16. Connect the rear window washer hose to the spray nozzle.
17. Install the liftgate upper window frame molding.
18. Align the liftgate to the vehicle.

ALIGNMENT

After the liftgate is installed, verify the alignment. The liftgate should have gaps to all adjacent panels as well as fit flush across the gaps.

1. The liftgate gaps should measure out as follows:
   - 0.280 inch (7mm) to the rear fascia
   - 0.240 inch (6mm) to the roof
   - 0.160 inch (4mm) to the taillights
2. If necessary, loosen the bolts to reposition the liftgate.

Grille

REMOVAL & INSTALLATION

➡If the front grille assembly is held in place by metal clips only, refer to the short procedure. If the grille is secured by rivets and metal clips, refer to the long procedure. To determined this, remove the mounting fasteners that secure the front fascia to the radiator closure panel, (located along the top edge of the front grille) then place your hand down to feel where the lower grille tabs meet the fascia panel. You should feel either just metal clips, or rivets and clips.

Grille Secured By Metal Clips (Short Procedure)

➧ **See Figures 15, 16 and 17**

1. Remove the mounting screws, holding the grille to the front fascia and radiator closure panel, along the top of the grille.

91150P06

Fig. 15 At the top of the grille assembly, remove the mounting screws and the push pin fasteners

91150P17

Fig. 16 Removing the grille assembly from the vehicle (notice the 7 tabs on the fascia where the metal clips attach)

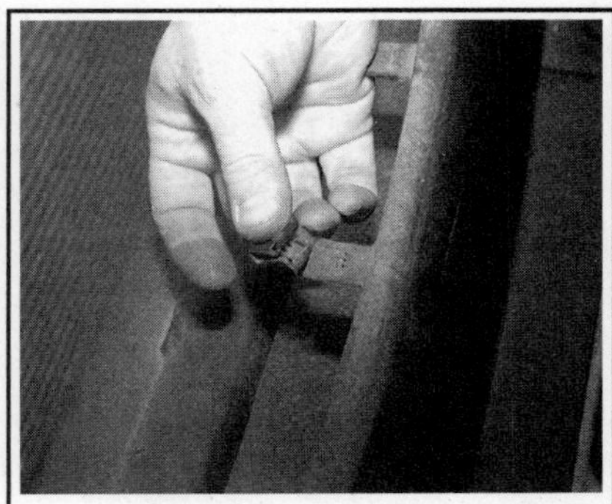
91150P07

Fig. 17 Example of what the lower grille-to-fascia tab retaining clips look like

2. Remove the plastic push-in fasteners securing the top right and left corners of the grille to the fascia.
3. Carefully pull the grille away from the front of the vehicle and place your hand down behind the grille. Carefully and firmly disengage the 7 metal clips that secure the bottom grille tabs to the fascia tabs.

To install:

4. Place the grille in correct position on the front fascia.
5. Secure the grille to the front fascia by firmly pushing the 7 metal clips over the bottom grille-to-fascia tabs.
6. Install the plastic push-in fasteners securing the top of the grille to the fascia.
7. Install and tighten the mounting screws.

Grille Secured By Rivets and Metal Clips (Long Procedure)

➧ See Figures 17, 18, 19 and 20

1. Disconnect the negative battery cable.
2. From inside the engine compartment, remove the nuts securing the headlamp modules to the radiator closure panel.
3. Remove the screw securing the top of the headlamp module to the closure panel.
4. Separate the headlamp module from the radiator closure panel.
5. Disengage wire connectors from back of the headlamp module.
6. Separate the headlamp module from the vehicle.
7. Remove the mounting bolts, holding the front fascia to the radiator closure panel, located on each side of the front grille and through the headlamp module openings
8. Raise and safely support the vehicle.
9. Remove the front wheels.
10. Remove the plastic push-in fasteners securing the right and left front wheelhouse splash shields to the frame rails.
11. Remove the mounting screws securing the wheelhouse splash shields to the front fenders, then remove from the vehicle.
12. Remove the bolts securing the front fascia to the bottom of the front fenders.
13. Remove the mounting bolts that secure the bottom of the fascia to the radiator closure panel.
14. Disengage the fog lamp/parking and turn signal lamp wiring harness connector, if necessary.
15. Remove the front bumper fascia from the vehicle.
16. Disengage the clips that secure each side of the grille to the front fascia.
17. Using a 0.250 inch drill bit, remove the rivets that secure the bottom of the grille to the front fascia and remove.

To install:

18. Place the grille in correct position on the front fascia.
19. If you are experienced in the use of a pop riveter, secure the bottom of the grille to the front fascia, using the correct size rivets. If a pop riveter is not being used, secure the bottom of the grille to the front fascia using correct size washers, nuts and bolts.
20. Install the clips securing each side of the grille to the front fascia.
21. Place the front fascia/grille assembly in position on the front of the vehicle and engage the fog lamp/parking and turn signal lamp wiring harness connector (if necessary). Install the mounting bolts securing the bottom of the fascia to the radiator closure panel.
22. Install and tighten the mounting bolts securing the fascia to the bottom of the front fenders.
23. Install the front wheelhouse splash shields onto the vehicle and secure with the mounting screws and push-in fasteners.
24. Install the front wheels and lower the vehicle to the ground.
25. Install and tighten the mounting bolts, holding the front fascia to the radiator closure panel, located on each side of the front grille and through the headlamp module openings
26. Place the headlamp module in position on the front of the vehicle.
27. Plug in the wiring harness connectors into the back of the headlamp module, then install in position against the radiator closure panel.
28. Install and tighten the headlamp module mounting screw and nuts.
29. Connect the negative battery cable.
30. Verify the operation of the headlamps and check alignment.

Outside Mirrors

REMOVAL & INSTALLATION

➧ See Figures 21, 22, 23 and 24

1. Open the door.
2. Remove the screw securing the molding at the lower portion of the side view mirror.
3. Remove the lower molding.
4. Remove the bolt securing the top side of the mirror assembly to the A pillar.
5. Remove the bottom side view mirror-to-A pillar mounting bolts.
6. If equipped, unplug the power side view mirror wiring harness connector.
7. Remove the side view mirror assembly from the vehicle.

To install:

8. If equipped, plug in the power side view mirror wiring harness connector.
9. Place the side view mirror assembly into position on the vehicle and install the top mounting bolt.
10. Install the bottom mirror assembly mounting bolts. Carefully tighten the mounting bolts.
11. Install the lower molding and secure with the mounting screw.

Antenna

REPLACEMENT

➧ See Figures 25, 26 and 27

1. Disconnect the negative battery cable.
2. Remove the glove box from the instrument panel.
3. Disengage the antenna cable connector from the extension cable.

91150P02

Fig. 18 Remove the rear mounting nuts for the headlamp module assembly

91150P03

Fig. 19 Remove the headlamp module assembly top mounting bolt

91150P01

Fig. 20 Carefully pull out the headlamp module assembly

4. Remove the right side trim kick panel.
5. Using a small prying tool, carefully remove the rubber grommet insulator from the door hinge pillar.
6. Route the antenna cable through the hinge pillar into the opening between the door hinges.
7. Safely raise and support the vehicle on safety stands.
8. Remove the front wheel.
9. Remove the inner fender splash shield.

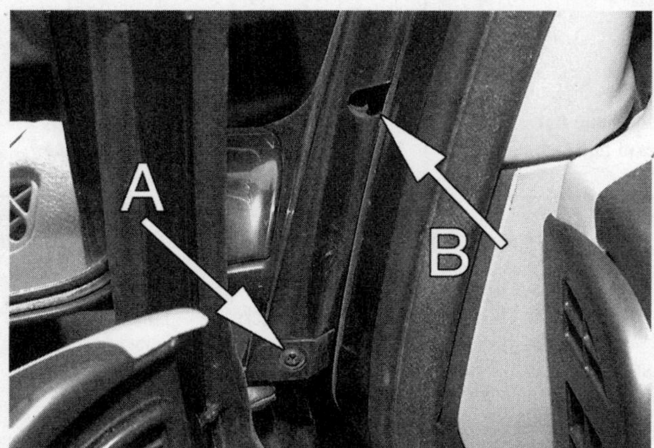

Fig. 21 Remove the lower molding retaining screw (A) from the side of the side view mirror assembly. After removing the lower molding, remove the top side view mirror mounting screw (B)

10. If equipped, slide the plastic sleeve on the antenna mast for access to the mast nut. Remove the antenna mast from the base.
11. Remove the plastic cap from the cap nut. Using a cap nut tool, remove the cap nut securing the antenna base to the front fender.
12. Remove the antenna base from under the front fender.

To install:

13. Place the antenna base assembly into position on the vehicle.
14. Secure the antenna base to the fender by installing the cap nut. Using the special cap nut tool and a torque wrench, tighten the cap nut to 28–32 inch lbs. (3–4 Nm). Install the plastic cap onto the cap nut.
15. Install and tighten the antenna mast to the antenna base. If equipped, slide the plastic sleeve back into place over the mast nut.
16. Install the inner fender splash shield.
17. Install the front wheel.
18. Lower the vehicle.
19. Route the antenna cable through the hinge pillar into the vehicle and secure the rubber grommet insulator back in place on the hinge pillar.
20. Plug the antenna cable connector into the extension cable.
21. Install the right side trim kick panel.
22. Install the glove box into the instrument panel.
23. Connect the negative battery cable.

Fenders

REMOVAL & INSTALLATION

➧ **See Figure 28**

1. Remove the side view mirror assembly.
2. Remove the headlamp housing.

Fig. 22 Remove the lower molding from below the side view mirror

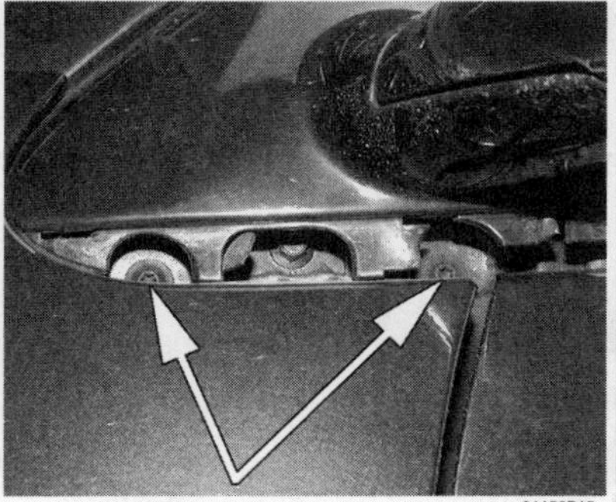

Fig. 23 Remove the 2 lower side view mirror assembly mounting bolts

Fig. 24 Pull the side view mirror assembly away from the vehicle

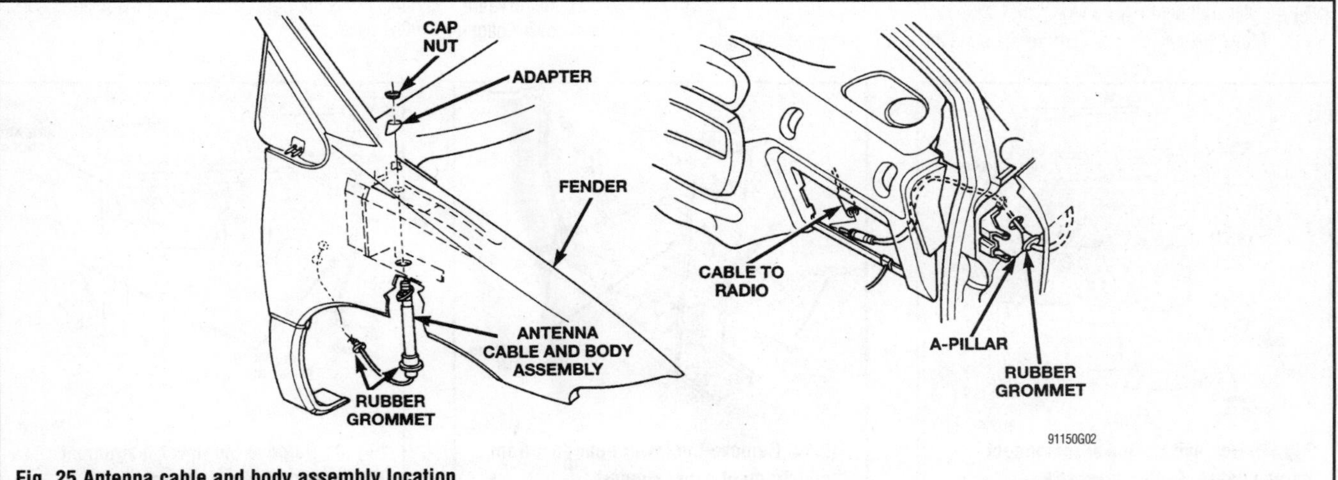

Fig. 25 Antenna cable and body assembly location

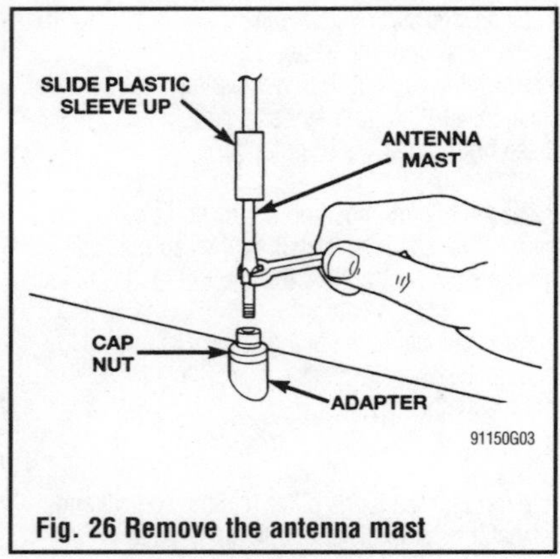

Fig. 26 Remove the antenna mast

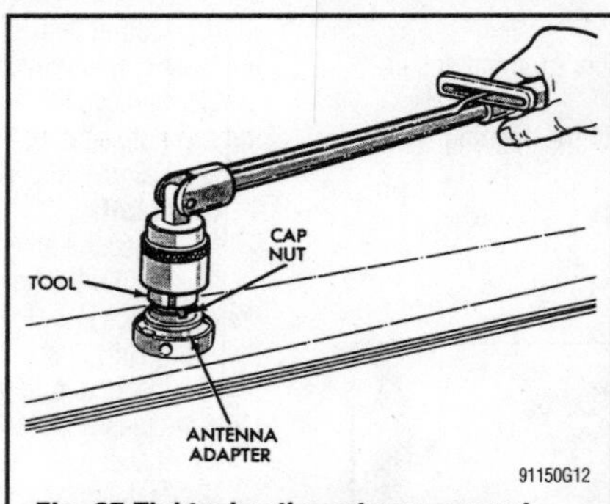

Fig. 27 Tightening the antenna cap nut using a special cap nut socket and torque wrench

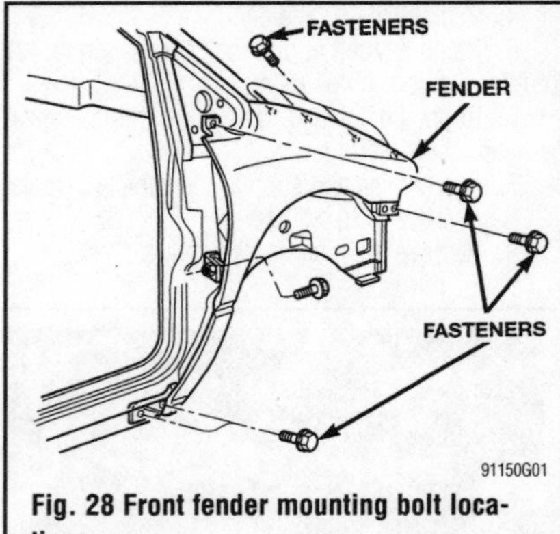

Fig. 28 Front fender mounting bolt locations

3. Remove the mud guard.
4. Remove the inner fender splash shield.
5. Remove the front fender-to-fascia retaining nuts.
6. Remove the fender-to-lower rocker panel bolt.
7. Remove the fender-to-lower cowl panel mounting bolt.
8. Carefully pull the side of the front fascia away from the fender and remove the fender-to-upper rail mounting bolts.
9. Remove the fender from the vehicle.

To install:

10. Place the fender into position on the vehicle and start the center upper rail mounting bolt.
11. From inside the engine compartment, install all of the bolts attaching the fender to the upper rail and tighten.
12. Install and tighten the fender-to-lower cowl panel mounting bolt.
13. Install and tighten the fender-to-lower rocker panel bolt.
14. Place the fascia back into position and install the fender-to-fascia nuts.
15. Install the inner fender splash shield and mud guard.
16. Install the headlamp housing assembly.
17. Install the side view mirror assembly.
18. Check the fender for flush and gap.

INTERIOR

Instrument Panel and Pad

REMOVAL & INSTALLATION

➧ **See Figures 29 thru 36**

1. Disconnect the negative battery cable.

⁂ CAUTION

The vehicles covered by this manual are all equipped with a Supplemental Restraint System (SRS), which uses an air bag. Whenever working near any of the SRS components, such as the impact sensors, the air bag module, steering column and instrument panel, disable the SRS, as described in Section 6.

2. Disable the air bag system.
3. Remove the screws that hold the lower instrument panel console to the floor bracket and instrument panel.
4. Move the console rearward from around the instrument panel supports.
5. Remove the lower instrument panel console.
6. Remove the screw that secures the lower heat duct to the instrument panel support.
7. Remove the heat duct from the vehicle.
8. Remove the bolts securing the lower supports to the instrument panel frame and floor.
9. Remove the right instrument panel end cover by performing the following;
   a. Open the passenger side door.
   b. Disengage the retaining clips securing the cover to the instrument panel.
   c. Remove the foam pad covering the A/C inlet projection of the end cover, if equipped.
10. Remove the left instrument panel end cover by performing the following;
   a. Open the driver side door.
   b. Remove screws holding the parking brake release handle to the instrument panel.
   c. Remove the screws that hold the bottom of the lower steering column cover to the instrument panel.
   d. Remove the screw that holds the right side of the lower steering column cover to the instrument panel.

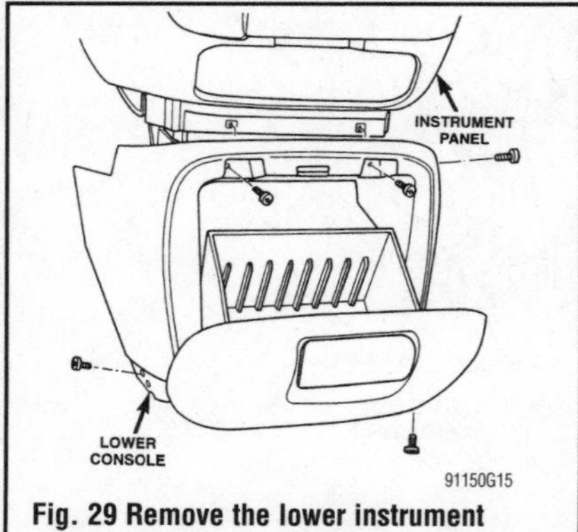

Fig. 29 Remove the lower instrument panel console from the vehicle

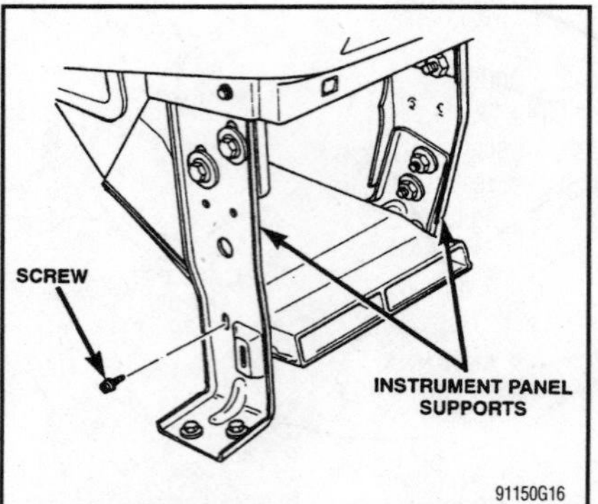

Fig. 30 Remove the lower heat duct from the instrument panel support

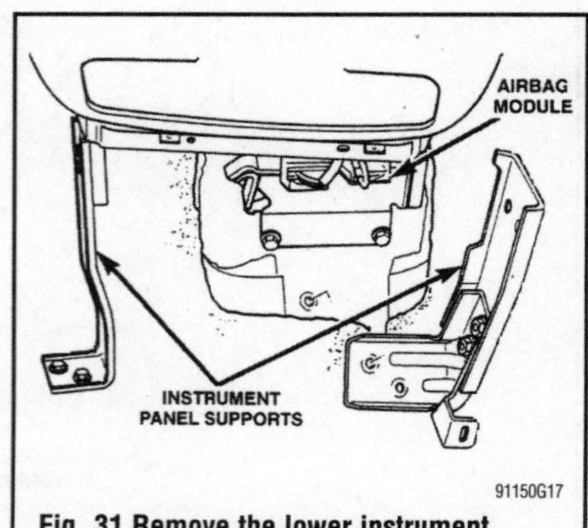

Fig. 31 Remove the lower instrument panel supports from the vehicle

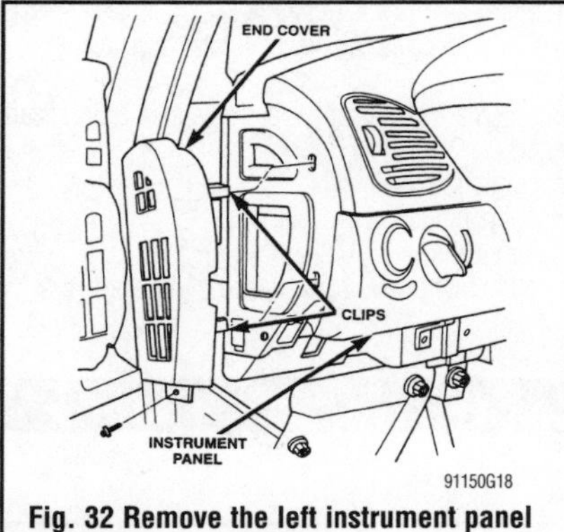

Fig. 32 Remove the left instrument panel end cover

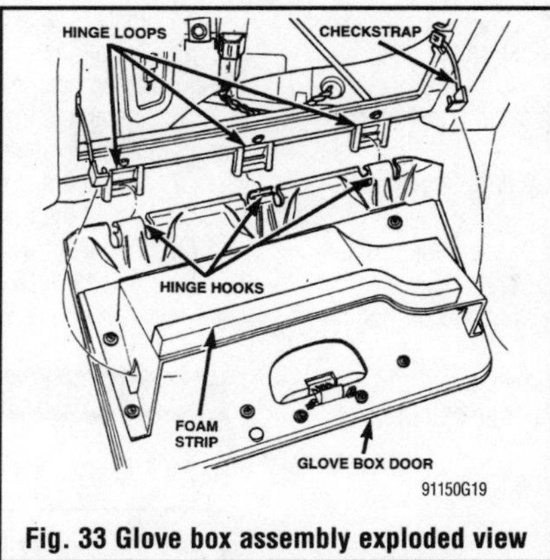

Fig. 33 Glove box assembly exploded view

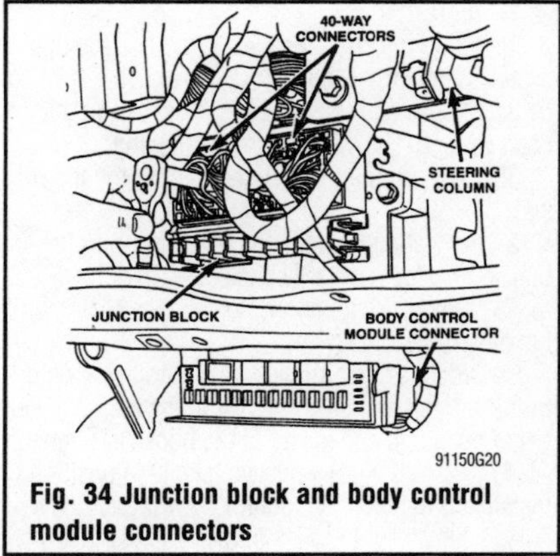

Fig. 34 Junction block and body control module connectors

e. Disengage the parking brake release cable case from the groove on the end of the parking brake release handle, then disengage the cable end pivot from the slot on the release handle.

f. Disengage the retaining clips securing the end cover to the instrument panel.

11. Disengage the wiring harness connector from the passenger air bag module.

12. Disengage the hidden retaining clips that secure the door sill plate from the door sill. Remove the left and right side door sill plates from the vehicle.

13. Disengage the hidden retaining clips that secure the interior cowl trim from the cowl panel. Remove the left and right side interior cowl trim from the vehicle.

14. Remove the A-pillar trim covers.

15. Remove the glove box.

16. Unplug the antenna lead connector from behind the glove box.

17. Remove the knee blocker reinforcement panel from under the steering column.

18. Unplug the lower two, 40-pin wiring harness connectors from the main junction block near the left side cowl panel.

19. Unplug the instrument panel wiring harness connector from the bottom of the body control module.

20. Unplug the two, 40-pin wiring harness connectors from the right of the steering column.

21. Remove the clinch bolt securing the upper steering column shaft to the lower steering column shaft. Separate the upper and lower shaft.

22. Remove the nuts securing the instrument panel frame to the metal brake pedal support on each side of the steering column.

23. If equipped with a mechanical transmission range indicator, perform the following;

a. Remove the indicator cable loop.

b. Remove the clip securing the gear shift cable end to the gear selector adapter.

c. Pull the cable end from the gear selector.

d. Disconnect the clip for the indicator cable and guide tube from the shift cable bracket and move out of the way.

24. Remove the nut securing the gear shift cable bracket to the instrument panel frame.

25. Remove the bracket from the instrument panel.

26. Remove the screw and bolt holding the hood release handle to the instrument panel, then set the handle out of the way.

27. Using a very flat pry tool wrapped in a towel to prevent scuffing or damaging the instrument panel pad, disengage the clips holding the rear edge of the instrument panel top cover. Pull up on the cover enough to unplug the wiring harness connector from the message center.

28. Pull the top cover rearward to disengage the hooks that secure the front of the cover to the instrument panel. Remove the instrument panel top cover from the vehicle.

29. Unplug the wire connector from the HVAC wiring harness connector behind the glove box area.

30. Remove the bolts securing the instrument panel frame to the brackets on the cowl side panels.

31. Loosen, but do not remove, the pivot bolts holding the instrument panel to the cowl panels.

32. Remove the bolts securing the instrument panel frame to the dash panel below the windshield opening.

33. With the help of an assistant, remove the instrument panel assembly from the vehicle.

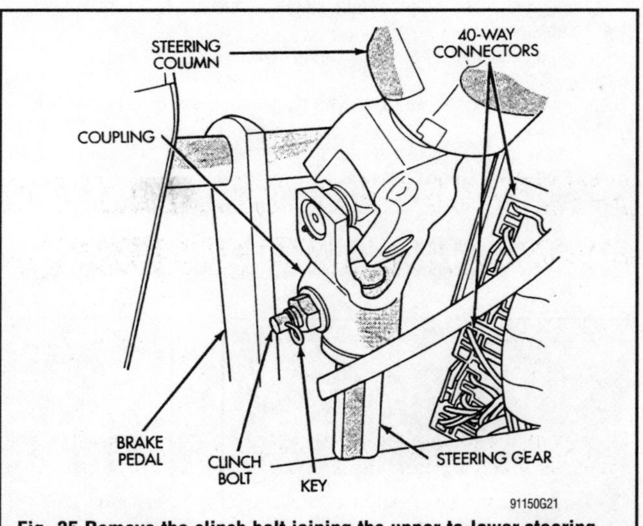

Fig. 35 Remove the clinch bolt joining the upper-to-lower steering column shafts

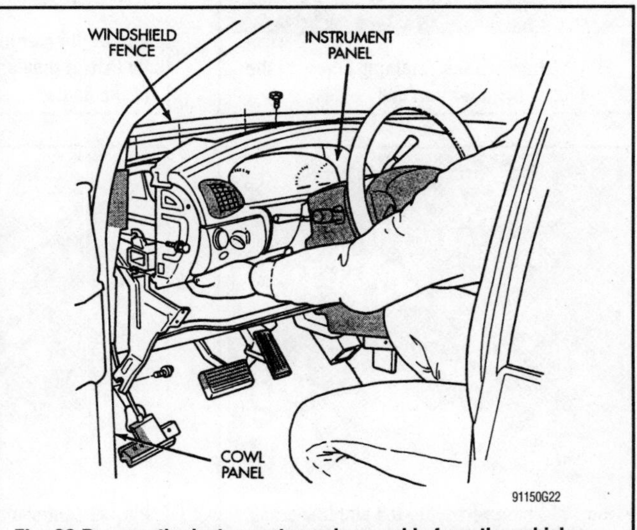

Fig. 36 Remove the instrument panel assembly from the vehicle

To install:

34. With the help of an assistant, correctly position the instrument panel assembly into the vehicle.
35. Install and tighten the bolts securing the instrument panel frame to the dash panel below the windshield opening.
36. Tighten the pivot bolts holding the instrument panel to the cowl panels.
37. Install and tighten the bolts securing the instrument panel frame to the brackets on the cowl side panels.
38. Plug the wire connector into the HVAC wiring harness connector behind the glove box area.
39. Place the instrument panel top cover onto the instrument panel and plug in the wiring harness connector to the message center. Install the top cover being certain to engage all of the hooks and retaining clips.
40. Place the hood release handle in position on the instrument panel. Install and tighten the mounting screw and bolt.
41. Install the gear shift bracket to the instrument panel.
42. If equipped with a mechanical transmission range indicator, install the indicator cable and guide tube. Install the cable retaining clips.
43. Install and tighten the nuts securing the instrument panel frame to the metal brake pedal support on each side of the steering column.
44. Join the upper steering column shaft to the lower steering column shaft and secure with the clinch bolt.
45. Plug in the two, 40-pin wiring harness connectors to the right of the steering column.
46. Plug in the instrument panel wiring harness connector to body control module.
47. Plug in the lower two, 40-pin wiring harness connectors to the main junction block.
48. Install the knee blocker reinforcement panel.
49. Plug in the antenna lead connector.
50. Install the glove box.
51. Install the A-pillar trim covers.
52. Install the cowl trim covers door sill plates
53. Plug in the wiring harness connector to the passenger air bag module.
54. Install the left and right instrument panel end covers.
55. Install the lower steering column cover. Be sure to install the parking brake release handle.
56. Install the lower supports to the instrument panel frame and floor. Install and tighten the mounting fasteners.
57. Install the lower heat duct into the vehicle.
58. Install the lower instrument panel console assembly.
59. Connect the negative battery cable.
60. Test all the instrument on the instrument panel assembly to verify that they operate properly.

Door Panels

REMOVAL & INSTALLATION

See Figures 37 thru 47

1. Disconnect the negative battery cable.
2. If equipped, use a small flat bladed tool to pry out the courtesy lamp from the door trim panel and disconnect the lamp wiring harness.
3. If equipped, remove screws mounting the door assist handle to the inner door panel.
4. If equipped, remove screw mounting the door pull cup to the inner door panel.
5. If equipped, remove screws mounting the trim panel to the door from underneath the map pocket.
6. If equipped with a window crank, perform the following;
   a. Using a special tool for this purpose, remove the clip that retains the window crank to the regulator shaft.
   b. Remove the window crank. Be careful not to lose the plastic trim washer(s).
7. If equipped with power windows, perform the following;
   a. Use a small prying tool to remove the screw cover from the power switch panel.

91150P13
Fig. 37 Remove the retaining screw at the bottom of the door pull cup

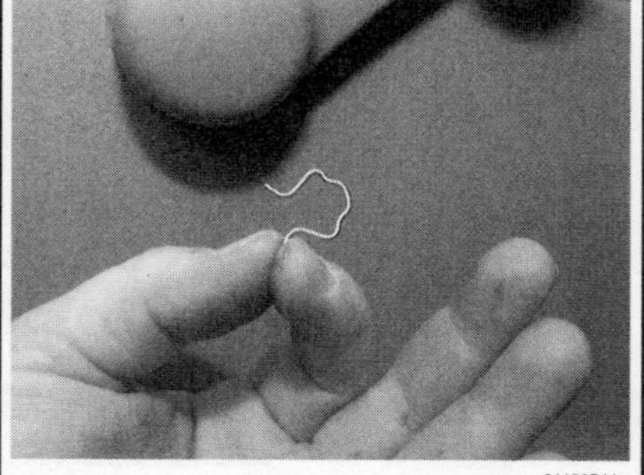
91150P11
Fig. 38 Be careful, these clips can be easily lost. If they are lost, they are available at the dealer

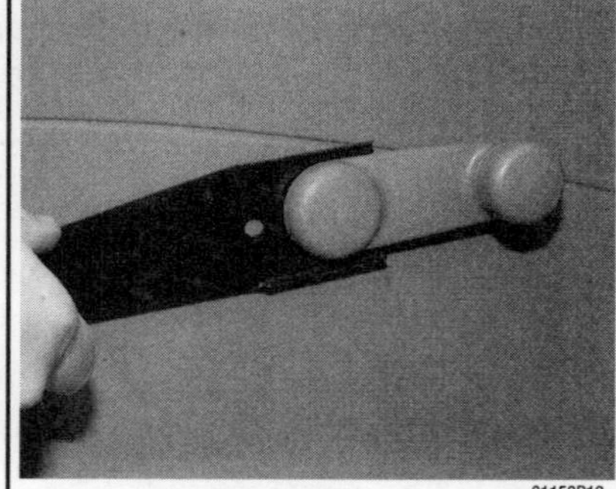
91150P12
Fig. 39 Using a special tool, remove the window crank handle retaining clip

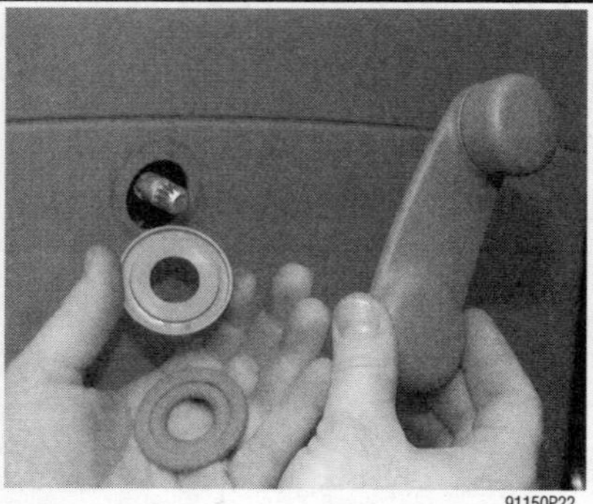
91150P22
Fig. 40 When removing the window crank, be sure not to lose these trim washers

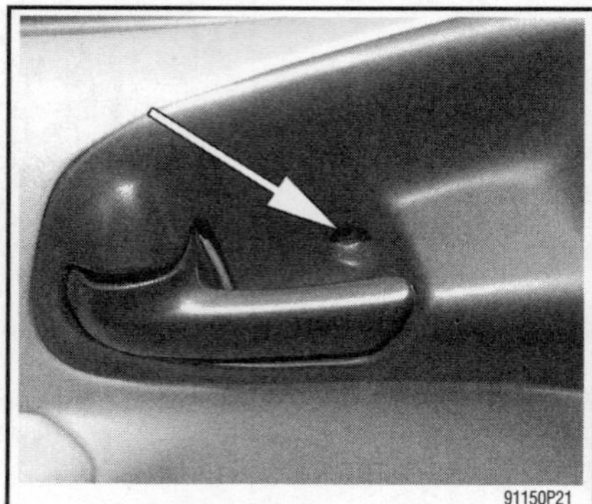
91150P21
Fig. 41 Remove the retaining screw located behind the latch release handle

91150P25
Fig. 42 Using a special trim removal tool, carefully pry the door panel clips away from the door itself

91150P20
Fig. 43 Carefully pull the door trim panel away from the door . . .

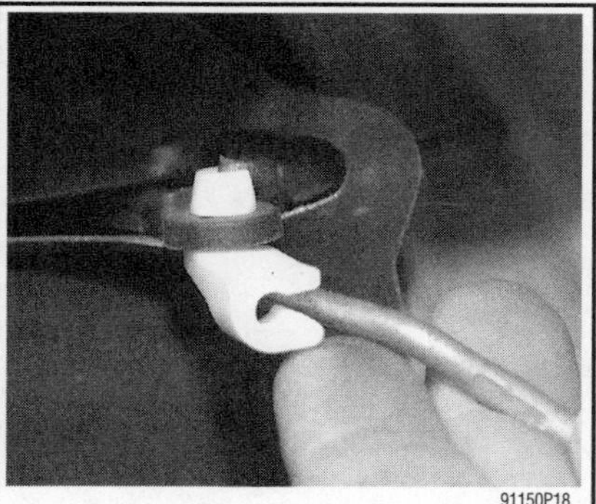
91150P18
Fig. 44 . . . then disengage the retaining clip from the linkage rod . . .

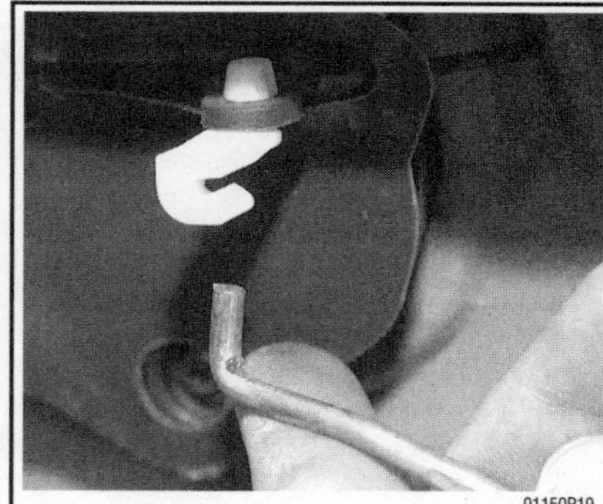
91150P19
Fig. 45 . . . then remove the linkage rod from the latch handle clip

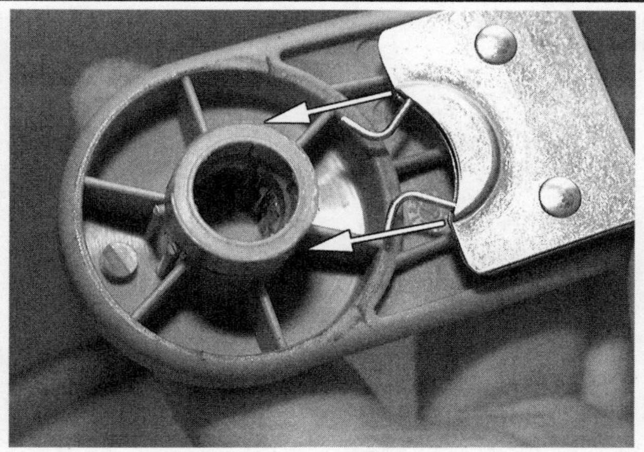
91150P24
Fig. 46 Install the window crank handle retaining clip in place behind the crank handle. A special tool such as this one can be a great help when installing this clip

91150P23
Fig. 47 This is what the retaining clip looks like once it is installed in the back of the crank handle. Now the handle can be installed onto the regulator shaft

b. Remove the power switch panel retaining screws. Remove the power switch panel from the door trim panel.

c. Disengage the wiring harness connector from the switch assembly.

8. If equipped, remove the memory seat/mirror switch, using a small prying tool, and unplug the wiring connector.

9. If equipped, remove the screw holding the door trim to the door panel from behind inside latch release handle.

10. Using a special trim removal tool, disengage the clips retaining the door trim to the door frame around perimeter of the panel.

11. Lift the trim panel upward to disengage the flange from the inner belt molding at the top of the door.

12. Tilt the top of the trim panel away from the door to gain access to the latch linkage.

13. Disengage the clip attaching the linkage rod to the inside latch release handle. Separate the linkage rod from the latch handle.

14. Remove the door trim panel from the vehicle.

To install:

15. Support the top of the door trim panel away from the door enough to gain access to the latch linkage.

16. Insert the linkage rod into the latch handle. Engage the clip that holds the linkage rod secured to the latch handle.

17. Place the door trim panel in position against the door and install into the inner belt molding at the top of the door.

18. Firmly push the trim panel against the door to engage the retaining clips around the perimeter of the door.

19. If equipped, install and tighten the screw holding the door trim to the door panel from behind inside latch release handle.

20. If equipped, install the memory seat/mirror switch.

21. If equipped with power windows, install the power switch panel assembly.

22. If equipped with a window crank, perform the following;

a. Install the retaining clip into the groove on the back of the window crank handle.

b. Hold the plastic trim washer(s) over the regulator shaft or on the window crank.

c. Position the window crank on the regulator shaft and push the crank firmly onto the regulator shaft to engage the retaining clip.

23. If equipped, install the screws mounting the trim panel to the door from underneath the map pocket.

24. If equipped, install the screw mounting the door pull cup to the inner door panel.

25. If equipped, install the screws mounting the door assist handle to the inner door panel.

26. If equipped, install the courtesy lamp into the door trim panel.

27. Connect the negative battery cable.

Door Locks

REMOVAL & INSTALLATION

See Figures 48 and 49

1. Disconnect the negative battery cable.

2. Remove the interior door panel and peel away the plastic sound shield to gain access to the door handle.

3. Roll up the door glass.
4. Through the access hole at the rear of the inner door panel, disengage the Vehicle Theft Security System (VTSS) switch connector from the door harness, if equipped.
5. Remove the push pin fasteners securing the VTSS switch harness to the inner door reinforcement bar, if equipped.
6. Disconnect the clip that retains the door latch linkage to the door latch.
7. Separate the latch linkage from the latch.
8. Disengage the clip retaining the door lock linkage to the door latch.
9. Remove the lock linkage from the latch.
10. Remove the nuts attaching the outside door handle to the door outer panel.
11. Remove the outside door handle from the vehicle.
12. Disengage the clip holding the lock cylinder into the outside handle.
13. Remove the door lock from the door handle.

To inside:

14. Engage the clip into the outside handle to hold the door lock cylinder.
15. With the link arm positioned toward the rear of the vehicle, push the lock cylinder into the door handle until the clip snaps into place.
16. Insert the lock linkage into the door latch.
17. Engage the clip to hold door lock linkage to latch.
18. Insert the latch linkage into door latch.
19. Engage clip to hold door latch linkage to latch.
20. Insert push pin fasteners attaching the VTSS switch harness to the inner door reinforcement bar, if equipped.
21. Plug the VTSS switch connector into the door harness, if equipped.
22. Verify door latch operation.
23. Install the plastic sound shield and interior door panel.
24. Connect the negative battery cable.

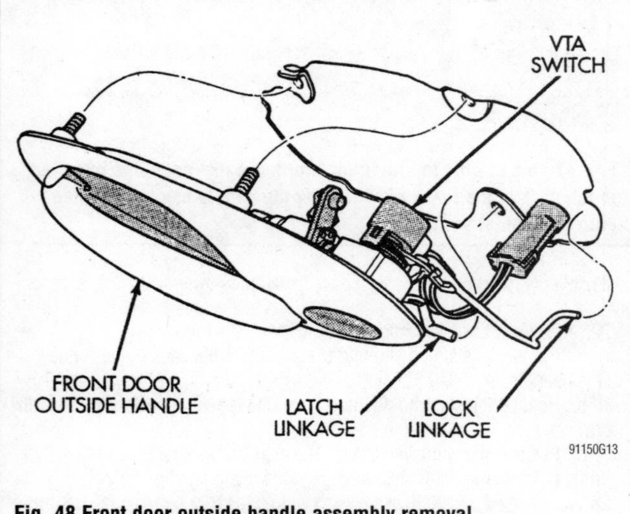

Fig. 48 Front door outside handle assembly removal

Liftgate Lock

REMOVAL & INSTALLATION

➧ **See Figures 50 and 51**

1. Remove the liftgate interior trim panel.
2. Remove the power lock motor.
3. Disengage the outside handle link from the clip on the liftgate latch.
4. Disconnect the Vehicle Theft Security System (VTSS) switch from the wiring harness, if equipped.
5. If equipped, disconnect the VTSS switch from the back of the lock cylinder.
6. Disengage lock link, if equipped.
7. Remove the nut attaching the outside liftgate handle to the liftgate.
8. Disengage the retaining groove holding the handle to the liftgate.
9. Remove the outside liftgate handle and links from the vehicle.
10. Remove the lock cylinder retaining clipfrom the door handle.
11. Remove the door lock cylinder and arm from the handle. Do not remove the E-clip.

To install:

12. Engage the retaining clip into the liftgate handle.
13. Push the lock cylinder into the handle until the clip engages the lock cylinder groove with an audible click.
14. Position the outside liftgate handle and links onto the liftgate.
15. Engage the retaining groove to hold handle to the liftgate by pushing the handle to the right for centering.
16. Install nut to mount the outside liftgate handle to the liftgate.
17. Connect the VTSS switch to the back of the lock cylinder and plug in wiring harness, if equipped.
18. Engage the outside handle link to the clip on the liftgate latch.
19. If equipped, install the lock link.
20. Install the power lock motor.
21. Verify lock cylinder and liftgate operation.
22. Install the liftgate trim panel.
23. Connect the negative battery cable.

Door Glass and Regulator (Manual and Electric)

REMOVAL & INSTALLATION

➧ **See Figures 52 thru 57**

1. Disconnect the negative battery cable.
2. Remove the door trim panel and plastic sound shield.
3. Remove the inner belt molding as follows:
   a. Peel the upper corner seals away from the inner belt molding.
   b. Pull the inner belt molding upward to disengage the retaining channel in bottom of molding from the door panel flange.
4. Remove the outer belt molding as follows:
   a. Roll down the door glass.

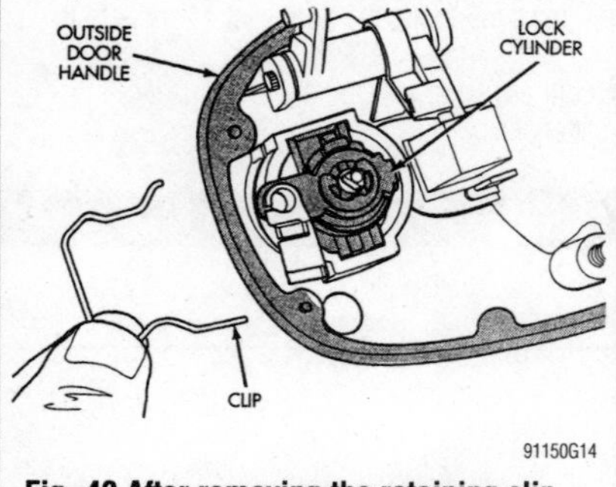

Fig. 49 After removing the retaining clip, pull the lock cylinder straight out from behind the handle assembly

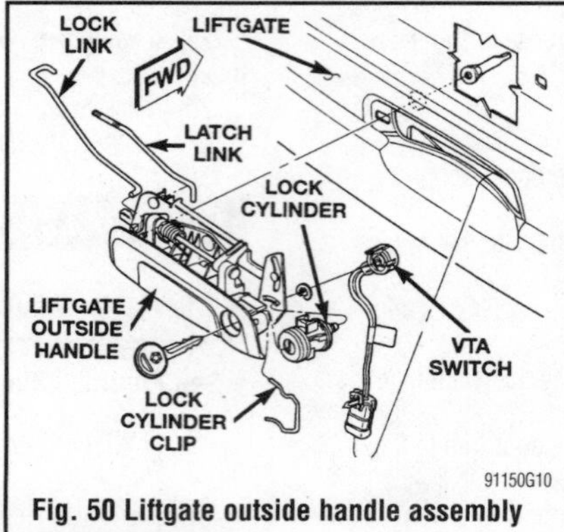

Fig. 50 Liftgate outside handle assembly exploded view

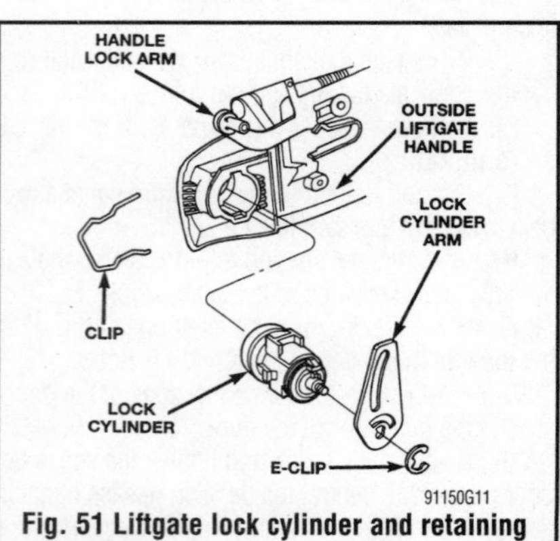

Fig. 51 Liftgate lock cylinder and retaining clip removal

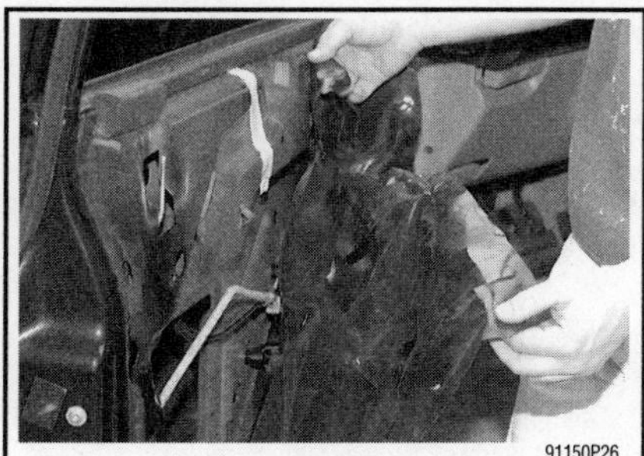

Fig. 52 Carefully peel the protective plastic sheet away from the inner door assembly. This will expose the location of the window regulator

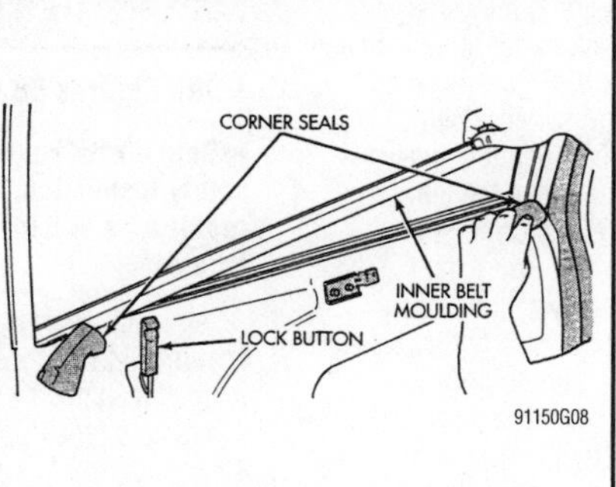

Fig. 53 Front door inner belt molding removal

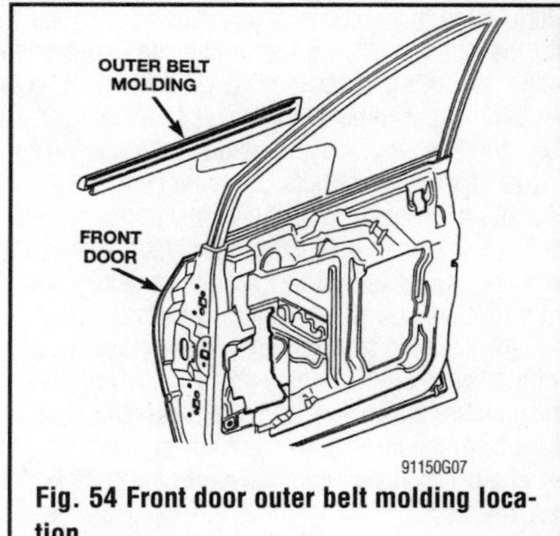

Fig. 54 Front door outer belt molding location

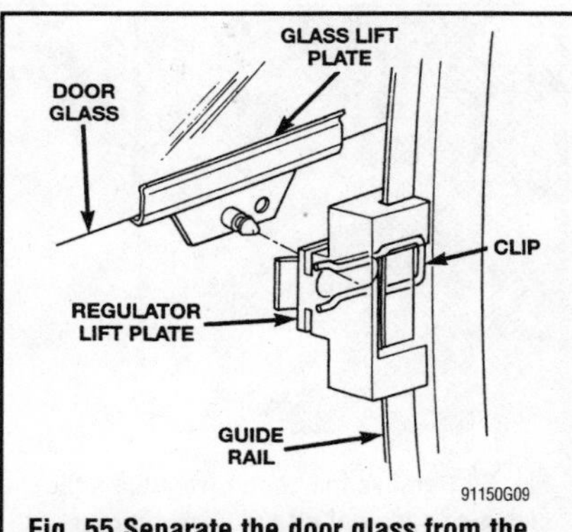

Fig. 55 Separate the door glass from the regulator lift plate by disengaging clip

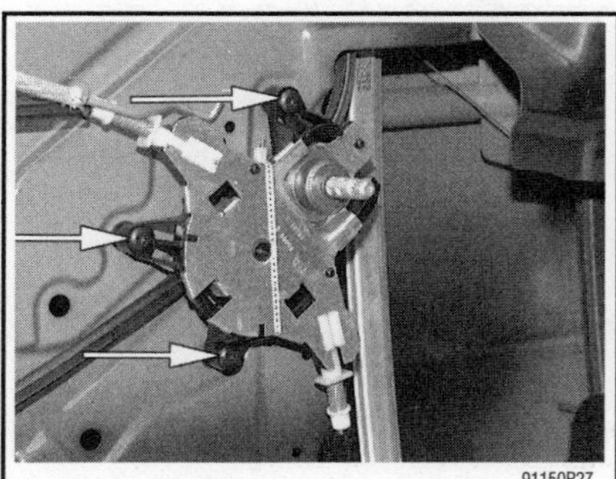

Fig. 56 Window regulator mechanism mounting screws—manual window regulator shown

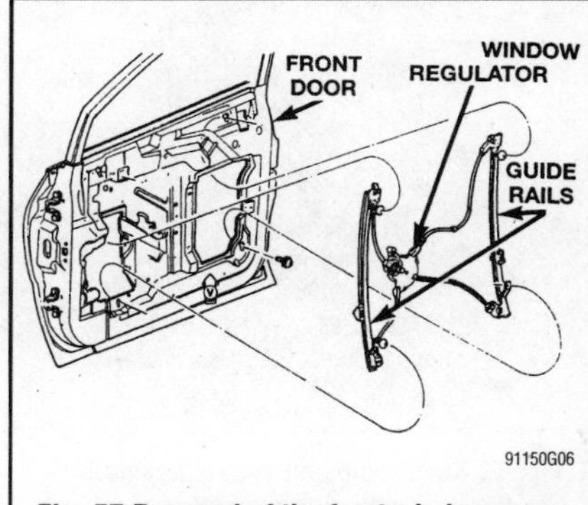

Fig. 57 Removal of the front window regulator and guide rail mechanism

b. Using a hook tool, disengage the interlocking lip at the base of the inward edge of the belt molding. Remove the molding from the door.

5. If equipped, remove the radio speaker.
6. Position the glass to gain access to the front and rear regulator lift plates through the front and rear door panel access holes.
7. Remove the clips securing the door glass to the regulator lift plates.
8. Separate the glass from the regulator lift plates and from the glass run weatherstrip.
9. Insert the front of the glass between the glass run channel and outer door panel.
10. Remove the glass from the vehicle by lifting the glass upward and out of the exterior side of the opening at the top of the door.
11. Disengage the wiring connector from the power window motor, if equipped.
12. Loosen screws attaching the front and rear window guide rails to the inner door panel.
13. Remove screw heads on the guide rails from key hole slots in inner door panel.
14. Loosen screws attaching regulator to inner door panel.
15. Remove the regulator from the inner door panel.
16. Extract the front and rear guide rails through the front and rear access holes.

To install:

17. Insert the front and rear guide rails through the front and rear access holes.
18. Position the window regulator in place against the inner door panel.
19. Place screw heads on guide rails in position through key hole slots in inner door panel.
20. Tighten the screws to attach front and rear guide rails to inner door panel.
21. Engage the wiring connector to the power window motor, if equipped.
22. Install clips that attach the door glass to the window regulator lift plates.
23. Install the glass through the window opening with the front inserted between the run channel and outer door panel.
24. Lower the glass downward into the door.
25. Install the ends of the glass into the glass run weatherstrip channels at the front and rear of door.
26. Place the glass in position on regulator lift plates.
27. Snap the glass mounting studs into clips on the regulator lift plates.
28. If equipped, install the radio speaker.
29. Install the inner and outer belt moldings.
30. Verify door glass operation and fit.
31. Install the plastic sound shield and door trim panel.
32. Connect the negative battery cable.

Windshield and Fixed Glass

REMOVAL & INSTALLATION

If your windshield, or other fixed window, is cracked or chipped, you may decide to replace it with a new one yourself. However, there are two main reasons why replacement windshields and other window glass should be installed only by a professional automotive glass technician: safety and cost.

The most important reason a professional should install automotive glass is for safety. The glass in the vehicle, especially the windshield, is designed with safety in mind in case of a collision. The windshield is specially manufactured from two panes of specially-tempered glass with a thin layer of transparent plastic between them. This construction allows the glass to "give" in the event that a part of your body hits the windshield during the collision, and prevents the glass from shattering, which could cause lacerations, blinding and other harm to passengers of the vehicle. The other fixed windows are designed to be tempered so that if they break during a collision, they shatter in such a way that there are no large pointed glass pieces. The professional automotive glass technician knows how to install the glass in a vehicle so that it will function optimally during a collision. Without the proper experience, knowledge and tools, installing a piece of automotive glass yourself could lead to additional harm if an accident should ever occur.

Cost is also a factor when deciding to install automotive glass yourself.

Performing this could cost you much more than a professional may charge for the same job. Since the windshield is designed to break under stress, an often life saving characteristic, windshields tend to break VERY easily when an inexperienced person attempts to install one. Do-it-yourselfers buying two, three or even four windshields from a salvage yard because they have broken them during installation are common stories. Also, since the automotive glass is designed to prevent the outside elements from entering your vehicle, improper installation can lead to water and air leaks. Annoying whining noises at highway speeds from air leaks or inside body panel rusting from water leaks can add to your stress level and subtract from your wallet. After buying two or three windshields, installing them and ending up with a leak that produces a noise while driving and water damage during rainstorms, the cost of having a professional do it correctly the first time may be much more alluring. We here at Chilton, therefore, advise that you have a professional automotive glass technician service any broken glass on your vehicle.

WINDSHIELD CHIP REPAIR

See Figures 58 thru 72

➡Check with your state and local authorities on the laws for state safety inspection. Some states or municipalities may not allow chip repair as a viable option for correcting stone damage to your windshield.

Although severely cracked or damaged windshields must be replaced, there is something that you can do to prolong or even prevent the need for replacement of a chipped windshield. There are many companies which offer windshield chip repair products, such as Loctite's® Bullseye™ windshield repair kit. These kits usually consist of a syringe, pedestal and a sealing adhesive. The syringe is mounted on the pedestal and is used to create a vacuum which pulls the plastic layer against the glass. This helps make the chip transparent. The adhesive is then injected which seals the chip and helps to prevent further

TCCA0P00

Fig. 58 Small chips on your windshield can be fixed with an aftermarket repair kit, such as the one from Loctite®

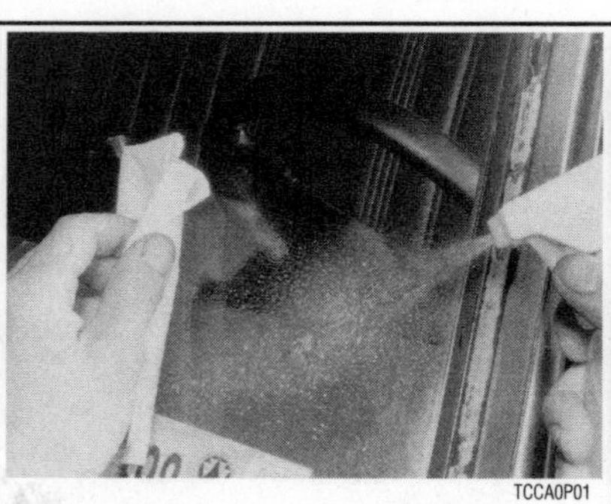

TCCA0P01

Fig. 59 To repair a chip, clean the windshield with glass cleaner and dry it completely

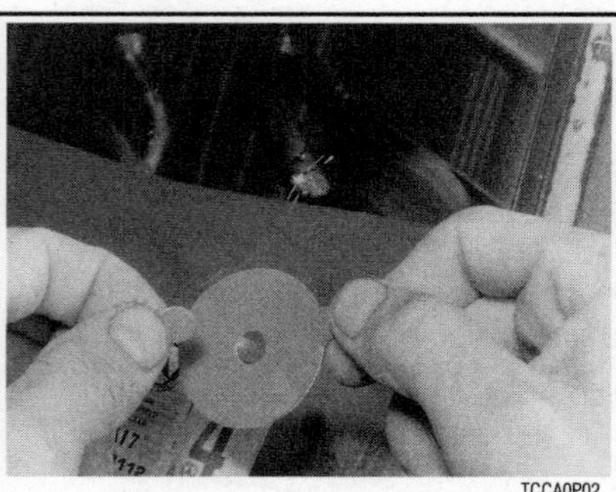

TCCA0P02

Fig. 60 Remove the center from the adhesive disc and peel off the backing from one side of the disc . . .

TCCA0P03

Fig. 61 . . . then press it on the windshield so that the chip is centered in the hole

TCCA0P04

Fig. 62 Be sure that the tab points upward on the windshield

TCCA0P05

Fig. 63 Peel the backing off the exposed side of the adhesive disc . . .

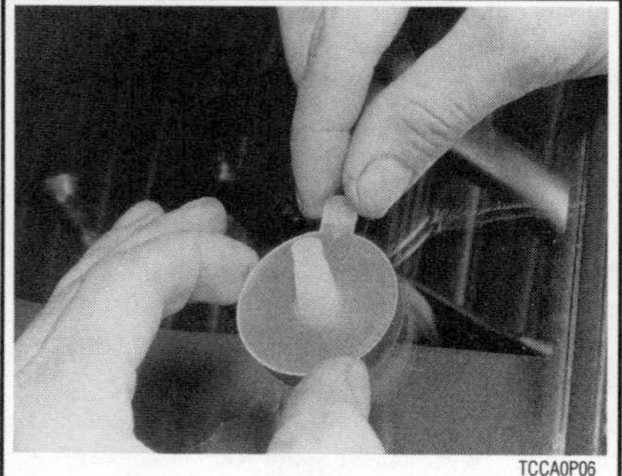

TCCA0P06

Fig. 64 . . . then position the plastic pedestal on the adhesive disc, ensuring that the tabs are aligned

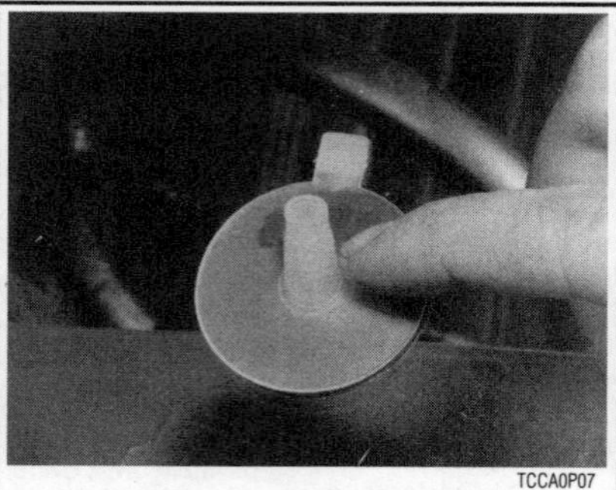

TCCA0P07

Fig. 65 Press the pedestal firmly on the adhesive disc to create an adequate seal . . .

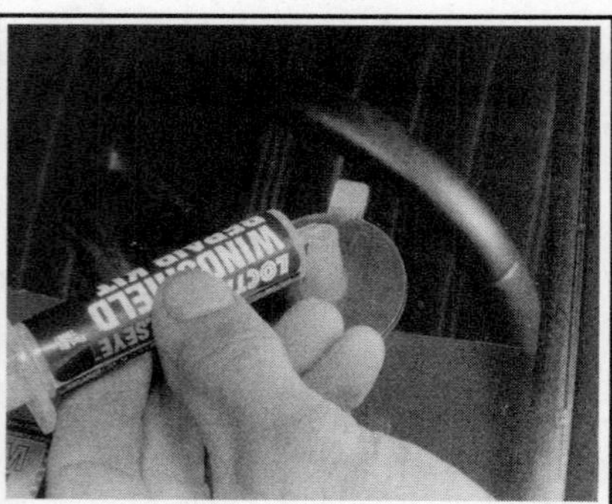

TCCA0P08

Fig. 66 . . . then install the applicator syringe nipple in the pedestal's hole

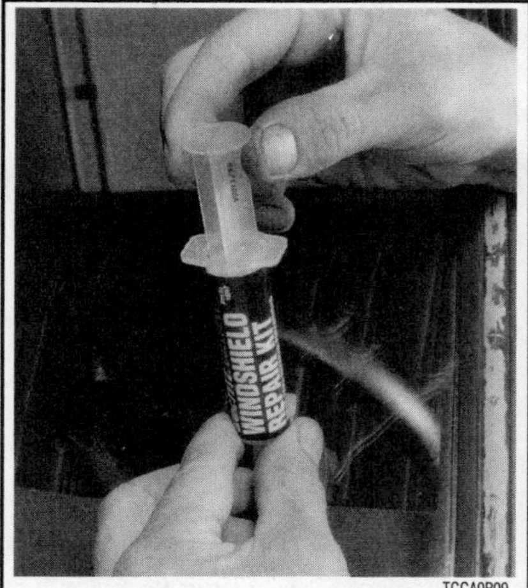

Fig. 67 Hold the syringe with one hand while pulling the plunger back with the other hand

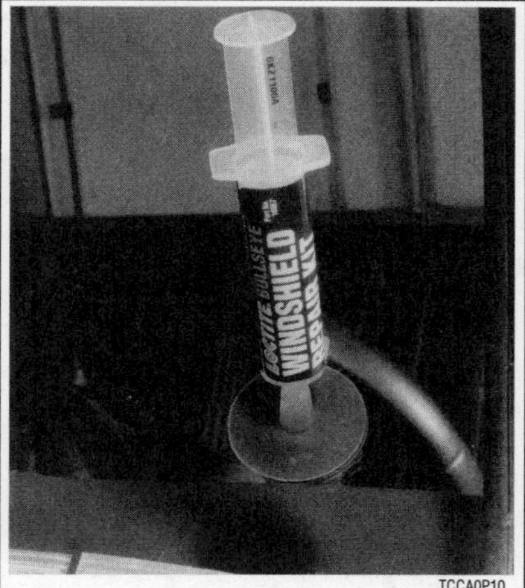

Fig. 68 After applying the solution, allow the entire assembly to sit until it has set completely

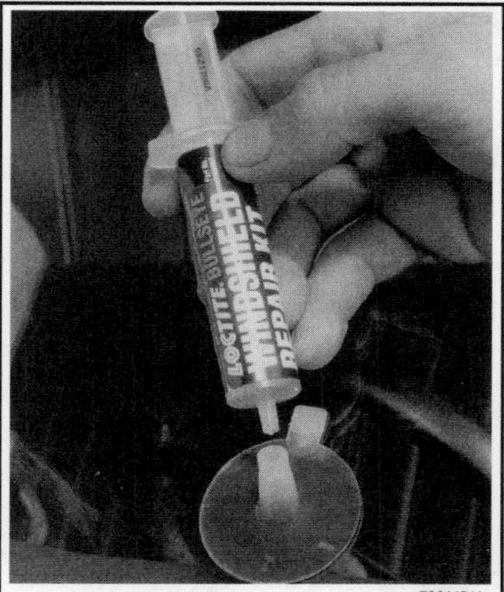

Fig. 69 After the solution has set, remove the syringe from the pedestal . . .

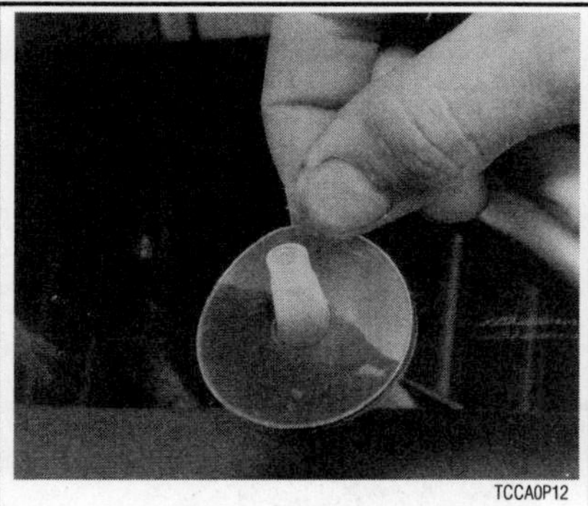

Fig. 70 . . . then peel the pedestal off of the adhesive disc . . .

Fig. 71 . . . and peel the adhesive disc off of the windshield

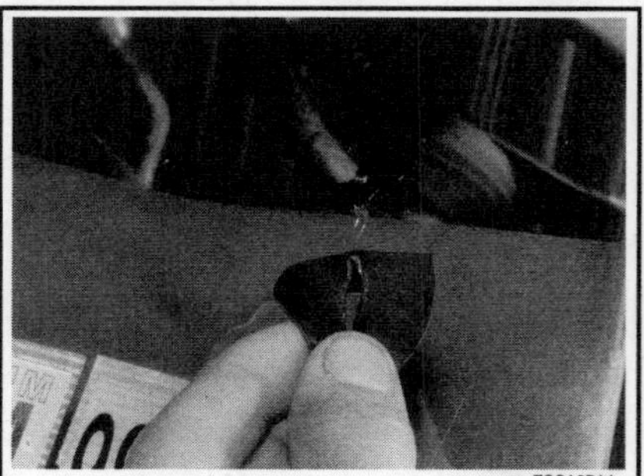

Fig. 72 The chip will still be slightly visible, but it should be filled with the hardened solution

stress cracks from developing. Refer to the sequence of photos to get a general idea of what windshield chip repair involves.

➡**Always follow the specific manufacturer's instructions.**

Inside Rear View Mirror

REPLACEMENT

1. Disconnect the negative battery cable.
2. Loosen the mirror setscrew.
3. Lift the mirror from the mounting bottom.
4. Installation is the reverse of the removal procedure.

Seats

REMOVAL & INSTALLATION

Front Seats

➧ **See Figure 73**

1. Disconnect the negative battery cable.
2. From under the vehicle, remove the nuts securing the front seat risers to the floor.
3. Remove the seat and riser from the floor.

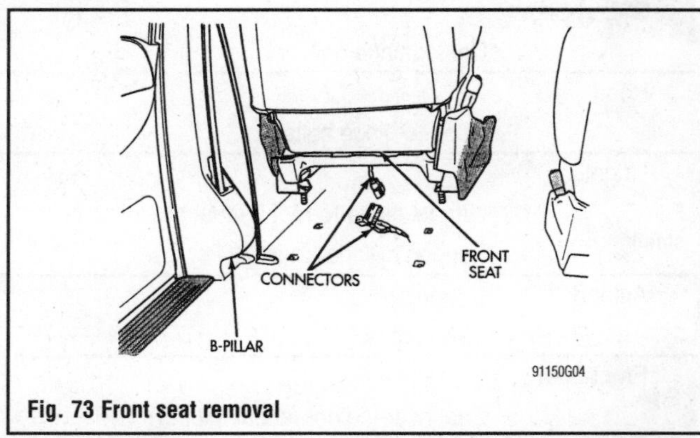

Fig. 73 Front seat removal

4. If equipped, tip the seat rearward and disengage the wiring connectors from the body harness.
5. Remove the seat from the vehicle.

To install:

6. Place the seat into position in the vehicle.
7. If equipped, tip the seat rearward and plug the wiring connectors into the body harness.
8. Position the seat and riser into the floor.
9. From under the vehicle, install the nuts securing the front seat risers to the floor. Tighten the retaining nuts to 44 ft. lbs. (60 Nm).
10. Connect the negative battery cable.

Rear Seats

➧ See Figure 74

Release levers are located on the rear leg assemblies, near the floor.

1. Squeeze each release handle and rotate downwards to deploy the wheels. A lock indicator button pops up when the seat is unlocked.
2. Remove the seat(s) from the vehicle.

To install:

3. Roll the seat into position over the strikers in the floor.
4. Squeeze the release handle and rotate upward until the lock indicator button returns into the handle. If not properly latched, the seats could become loose, possibly resulting in personal injury.
5. After installing the seats, be sure the red indicator button on the release handles return into the handles.

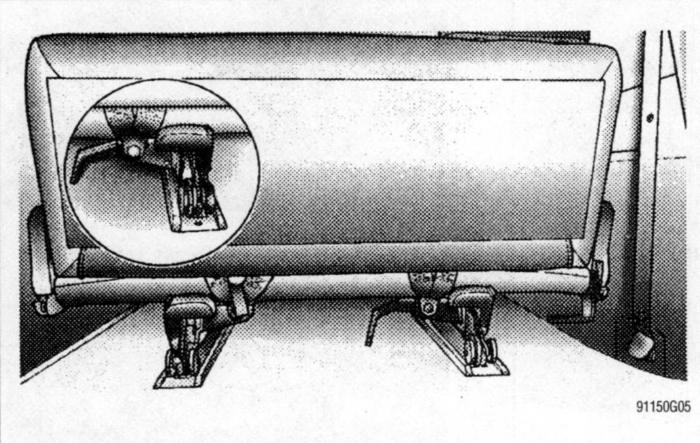

Fig. 74 Location of rear seat release levers

Power Seat Motor

The power seat track and motors are serviced as an assembly.

REMOVAL & INSTALLATION

1. Disconnect the negative battery cable.
2. Remove the seat from the vehicle.
3. Remove seat cushion.
4. Remove the nut attaching the recliner to the seat back frame.
5. Remove bolts attaching seat back frame to seat track.
6. Remove stud on seat back frame from recliner.
7. Remove the seat back.
8. If the power seat track is being replaced, transfer the power recliner, wire harness and trim covers to replacement seat track.

To install:

9. Install the wiring harness.
10. Place the seat back in position.
11. Insert stud on seat back frame into recliner.
12. Install bolts to hold seat back frame to seat track.
13. Install the nut attaching recliner to seat back frame.
14. Install the seat cushion.
15. Install the seat into the vehicle.
16. Connect the negative battery cable.

TORQUE SPECIFICATIONS

Components		Ft. Lbs.	Nm
Front Door			
	Upper hinge-to-door end frame mounting bolts	105 inch lbs.	12
	Door check strap-to-A pillar bolts	105 inch lbs.	12
	Lower hinge-to-door end frame mounting bolts	25	34
Sliding Door			
	Center hinge bolt locknut	11	15
Hood			
	Hood-to-hinge bolts	10	14
Liftgate			
	Liftgate hinge-to-roof header mounting bolts	24	33
	Support cylinder-to-liftgate screw	21	28
Antenna			
	Base cap nut	28-32 inch lbs.	3-4
Front Seat			
	Seat riser-to-floor retaining nuts	44	60

91150C01

GLOSSARY

AIR/FUEL RATIO: The ratio of air-to-gasoline by weight in the fuel mixture drawn into the engine.

AIR INJECTION: One method of reducing harmful exhaust emissions by injecting air into each of the exhaust ports of an engine. The fresh air entering the hot exhaust manifold causes any remaining fuel to be burned before it can exit the tailpipe.

ALTERNATOR: A device used for converting mechanical energy into electrical energy.

AMMETER: An instrument, calibrated in amperes, used to measure the flow of an electrical current in a circuit. Ammeters are always connected in series with the circuit being tested.

AMPERE: The rate of flow of electrical current present when one volt of electrical pressure is applied against one ohm of electrical resistance.

ANALOG COMPUTER: Any microprocessor that uses similar (analogous) electrical signals to make its calculations.

ARMATURE: A laminated, soft iron core wrapped by a wire that converts electrical energy to mechanical energy as in a motor or relay. When rotated in a magnetic field, it changes mechanical energy into electrical energy as in a generator.

ATMOSPHERIC PRESSURE: The pressure on the Earth's surface caused by the weight of the air in the atmosphere. At sea level, this pressure is 14.7 psi at 32°F (101 kPa at 0°C).

ATOMIZATION: The breaking down of a liquid into a fine mist that can be suspended in air.

AXIAL PLAY: Movement parallel to a shaft or bearing bore.

BACKFIRE: The sudden combustion of gases in the intake or exhaust system that results in a loud explosion.

BACKLASH: The clearance or play between two parts, such as meshed gears.

BACKPRESSURE: Restrictions in the exhaust system that slow the exit of exhaust gases from the combustion chamber.

BAKELITE: A heat resistant, plastic insulator material commonly used in printed circuit boards and transistorized components.

BALL BEARING: A bearing made up of hardened inner and outer races between which hardened steel balls roll.

BALLAST RESISTOR: A resistor in the primary ignition circuit that lowers voltage after the engine is started to reduce wear on ignition components.

BEARING: A friction reducing, supportive device usually located between a stationary part and a moving part.

BIMETAL TEMPERATURE SENSOR: Any sensor or switch made of two dissimilar types of metal that bend when heated or cooled due to the different expansion rates of the alloys. These types of sensors usually function as an on/off switch.

BLOWBY: Combustion gases, composed of water vapor and unburned fuel, that leak past the piston rings into the crankcase during normal engine operation. These gases are removed by the PCV system to prevent the buildup of harmful acids in the crankcase.

BRAKE PAD: A brake shoe and lining assembly used with disc brakes.

BRAKE SHOE: The backing for the brake lining. The term is, however, usually applied to the assembly of the brake backing and lining.

BUSHING: A liner, usually removable, for a bearing; an anti-friction liner used in place of a bearing.

CALIPER: A hydraulically activated device in a disc brake system, which is mounted straddling the brake rotor (disc). The caliper contains at least one piston and two brake pads. Hydraulic pressure on the piston(s) forces the pads against the rotor.

CAMSHAFT: A shaft in the engine on which are the lobes (cams) which operate the valves. The camshaft is driven by the crankshaft, via a belt, chain or gears, at one half the crankshaft speed.

CAPACITOR: A device which stores an electrical charge.

CARBON MONOXIDE (CO): A colorless, odorless gas given off as a normal byproduct of combustion. It is poisonous and extremely dangerous in confined areas, building up slowly to toxic levels without warning if adequate ventilation is not available.

CARBURETOR: A device, usually mounted on the intake manifold of an engine, which mixes the air and fuel in the proper proportion to allow even combustion.

CATALYTIC CONVERTER: A device installed in the exhaust system, like a muffler, that converts harmful byproducts of combustion into carbon dioxide and water vapor by means of a heat-producing chemical reaction.

CENTRIFUGAL ADVANCE: A mechanical method of advancing the spark timing by using flyweights in the distributor that react to centrifugal force generated by the distributor shaft rotation.

CHECK VALVE: Any one-way valve installed to permit the flow of air, fuel or vacuum in one direction only.

CHOKE: A device, usually a moveable valve, placed in the intake path of a carburetor to restrict the flow of air.

CIRCUIT: Any unbroken path through which an electrical current can flow. Also used to describe fuel flow in some instances.

CIRCUIT BREAKER: A switch which protects an electrical circuit from overload by opening the circuit when the current flow exceeds a predetermined level. Some circuit breakers must be reset manually, while most reset automatically.

COIL (IGNITION): A transformer in the ignition circuit which steps up the voltage provided to the spark plugs.

COMBINATION MANIFOLD: An assembly which includes both the intake and exhaust manifolds in one casting.

COMBINATION VALVE: A device used in some fuel systems that routes fuel vapors to a charcoal storage canister instead of venting them into the atmosphere. The valve relieves fuel tank pressure and allows fresh air into the tank as the fuel level drops to prevent a vapor lock situation.

COMPRESSION RATIO: The comparison of the total volume of the cylinder and combustion chamber with the piston at BDC and the piston at TDC.

CONDENSER: 1. An electrical device which acts to store an electrical charge, preventing voltage surges. 2. A radiator-like device in the air conditioning system in which refrigerant gas condenses into a liquid, giving off heat.

CONDUCTOR: Any material through which an electrical current can be transmitted easily.

CONTINUITY: Continuous or complete circuit. Can be checked with an ohmmeter.

COUNTERSHAFT: An intermediate shaft which is rotated by a mainshaft and transmits, in turn, that rotation to a working part.

CRANKCASE: The lower part of an engine in which the crankshaft and related parts operate.

CRANKSHAFT: The main driving shaft of an engine which receives reciprocating motion from the pistons and converts it to rotary motion.

CYLINDER: In an engine, the round hole in the engine block in which the piston(s) ride.

CYLINDER BLOCK: The main structural member of an engine in which is found the cylinders, crankshaft and other principal parts.

CYLINDER HEAD: The detachable portion of the engine, usually fastened to the top of the cylinder block and containing all or most of the combustion chambers. On overhead valve engines, it contains the valves and their operating parts. On overhead cam engines, it contains the camshaft as well.

DEAD CENTER: The extreme top or bottom of the piston stroke.

DETONATION: An unwanted explosion of the air/fuel mixture in the combustion chamber caused by excess heat and compression, advanced timing, or an overly lean mixture. Also referred to as "ping".

DIAPHRAGM: A thin, flexible wall separating two cavities, such as in a vacuum advance unit.

DIESELING: A condition in which hot spots in the combustion chamber cause the engine to run on after the key is turned off.

DIFFERENTIAL: A geared assembly which allows the transmission of motion between drive axles, giving one axle the ability to turn faster than the other.

DIODE: An electrical device that will allow current to flow in one direction only.

DISC BRAKE: A hydraulic braking assembly consisting of a brake disc, or rotor, mounted on an axle, and a caliper assembly containing, usually two brake pads which are activated by hydraulic pressure. The pads are forced against the sides of the disc, creating friction which slows the vehicle.

DISTRIBUTOR: A mechanically driven device on an engine which is responsible for electrically firing the spark plug at a predetermined point of the piston stroke.

DOWEL PIN: A pin, inserted in mating holes in two different parts allowing those parts to maintain a fixed relationship.

DRUM BRAKE: A braking system which consists of two brake shoes and one or two wheel cylinders, mounted on a fixed backing plate, and a brake drum, mounted on an axle, which revolves around the assembly.

DWELL: The rate, measured in degrees of shaft rotation, at which an electrical circuit cycles on and off.

ELECTRONIC CONTROL UNIT (ECU): Ignition module, module, amplifier or igniter. See Module for definition.

ELECTRONIC IGNITION: A system in which the timing and firing of the spark plugs is controlled by an electronic control unit, usually called a module. These systems have no points or condenser.

END-PLAY: The measured amount of axial movement in a shaft.

ENGINE: A device that converts heat into mechanical energy.

EXHAUST MANIFOLD: A set of cast passages or pipes which conduct exhaust gases from the engine.

FEELER GAUGE: A blade, usually metal, or precisely predetermined thickness, used to measure the clearance between two parts.

FIRING ORDER: The order in which combustion occurs in the cylinders of an engine. Also the order in which spark is distributed to the plugs by the distributor.

FLOODING: The presence of too much fuel in the intake manifold and combustion chamber which prevents the air/fuel mixture from firing, thereby causing a no-start situation.

FLYWHEEL: A disc shaped part bolted to the rear end of the crankshaft. Around the outer perimeter is affixed the ring gear. The starter drive engages the ring gear, turning the flywheel, which rotates the crankshaft, imparting the initial starting motion to the engine.

FOOT POUND (ft. lbs. or sometimes, ft.lb.): The amount of energy or work needed to raise an item weighing one pound, a distance of one foot.

FUSE: A protective device in a circuit which prevents circuit overload by breaking the circuit when a specific amperage is present. The device is constructed around a strip or wire of a lower amperage rating than the circuit it is designed to protect. When an amperage higher than that stamped on the fuse is present in the circuit, the strip or wire melts, opening the circuit.

GEAR RATIO: The ratio between the number of teeth on meshing gears.

GENERATOR: A device which converts mechanical energy into electrical energy.

HEAT RANGE: The measure of a spark plug's ability to dissipate heat from its firing end. The higher the heat range, the hotter the plug fires.

HUB: The center part of a wheel or gear.

HYDROCARBON (HC): Any chemical compound made up of hydrogen and carbon. A major pollutant formed by the engine as a byproduct of combustion.

HYDROMETER: An instrument used to measure the specific gravity of a solution.

INCH POUND (inch lbs.; sometimes in.lb. or in. lbs.): One twelfth of a foot pound.

INDUCTION: A means of transferring electrical energy in the form of a magnetic field. Principle used in the ignition coil to increase voltage.

INJECTOR: A device which receives metered fuel under relatively low pressure and is activated to inject the fuel into the engine under relatively high pressure at a predetermined time.

INPUT SHAFT: The shaft to which torque is applied, usually carrying the driving gear or gears.

INTAKE MANIFOLD: A casting of passages or pipes used to conduct air or a fuel/air mixture to the cylinders.

JOURNAL: The bearing surface within which a shaft operates.

KEY: A small block usually fitted in a notch between a shaft and a hub to prevent slippage of the two parts.

MANIFOLD: A casting of passages or set of pipes which connect the cylinders to an inlet or outlet source.

MANIFOLD VACUUM: Low pressure in an engine intake manifold formed just below the throttle plates. Manifold vacuum is highest at idle and drops under acceleration.

MASTER CYLINDER: The primary fluid pressurizing device in a hydraulic system. In automotive use, it is found in brake and hydraulic clutch systems and is pedal activated, either directly or, in a power brake system, through the power booster.

MODULE: Electronic control unit, amplifier or igniter of solid state or integrated design which controls the current flow in the ignition primary circuit based on input from the pick-up coil. When the module opens the primary circuit, high secondary voltage is induced in the coil.

NEEDLE BEARING: A bearing which consists of a number (usually a large number) of long, thin rollers.

OHM: (Ω) The unit used to measure the resistance of conductor-to-electrical flow. One ohm is the amount of resistance that limits current flow to one ampere in a circuit with one volt of pressure.

OHMMETER: An instrument used for measuring the resistance, in ohms, in an electrical circuit.

OUTPUT SHAFT: The shaft which transmits torque from a device, such as a transmission.

OVERDRIVE: A gear assembly which produces more shaft revolutions than that transmitted to it.

OVERHEAD CAMSHAFT (OHC): An engine configuration in which the camshaft is mounted on top of the cylinder head and operates the valve either directly or by means of rocker arms.

OVERHEAD VALVE (OHV): An engine configuration in which all of the valves are located in the cylinder head and the camshaft is located in the cylinder block. The camshaft operates the valves via lifters and pushrods.

OXIDES OF NITROGEN (NOx): Chemical compounds of nitrogen produced as a byproduct of combustion. They combine with hydrocarbons to produce smog.

OXYGEN SENSOR: Use with the feedback system to sense the presence of oxygen in the exhaust gas and signal the computer which can reference the voltage signal to an air/fuel ratio.

PINION: The smaller of two meshing gears.

PISTON RING: An open-ended ring with fits into a groove on the outer diameter of the piston. Its chief function is to form a seal between the piston and cylinder wall. Most automotive pistons have three rings: two for compression sealing; one for oil sealing.

PRELOAD: A predetermined load placed on a bearing during assembly or by adjustment.

PRIMARY CIRCUIT: the low voltage side of the ignition system which consists of the ignition switch, ballast resistor or resistance wire, bypass, coil, electronic control unit and pick-up coil as well as the connecting wires and harnesses.

PRESS FIT: The mating of two parts under pressure, due to the inner diameter of one being smaller than the outer diameter of the other, or vice versa; an interference fit.

RACE: The surface on the inner or outer ring of a bearing on which the balls, needles or rollers move.

REGULATOR: A device which maintains the amperage and/or voltage levels of a circuit at predetermined values.

RELAY: A switch which automatically opens and/or closes a circuit.

RESISTANCE: The opposition to the flow of current through a circuit or electrical device, and is measured in ohms. Resistance is equal to the voltage divided by the amperage.

RESISTOR: A device, usually made of wire, which offers a preset amount of resistance in an electrical circuit.

RING GEAR: The name given to a ring-shaped gear attached to a differential case, or affixed to a flywheel or as part of a planetary gear set.

ROLLER BEARING: A bearing made up of hardened inner and outer races between which hardened steel rollers move.

ROTOR: 1. The disc-shaped part of a disc brake assembly, upon which the brake pads bear; also called, brake disc. 2. The device mounted atop the distributor shaft, which passes current to the distributor cap tower contacts.

SECONDARY CIRCUIT: The high voltage side of the ignition system, usually above 20,000 volts. The secondary includes the ignition coil, coil wire, distributor cap and rotor, spark plug wires and spark plugs.

SENDING UNIT: A mechanical, electrical, hydraulic or electro-magnetic device which transmits information to a gauge.

SENSOR: Any device designed to measure engine operating conditions or ambient pressures and temperatures. Usually electronic in nature and designed to send a voltage signal to an on-board computer, some sensors may operate as a simple on/off switch or they may provide a variable voltage signal (like a potentiometer) as conditions or measured parameters change.

SHIM: Spacers of precise, predetermined thickness used between parts to establish a proper working relationship.

SLAVE CYLINDER: In automotive use, a device in the hydraulic clutch system which is activated by hydraulic force, disengaging the clutch.

SOLENOID: A coil used to produce a magnetic field, the effect of which is to produce work.

SPARK PLUG: A device screwed into the combustion chamber of a spark ignition engine. The basic construction is a conductive core inside of a ceramic insulator, mounted in an outer conductive base. An electrical charge from the spark plug wire travels along the conductive core and jumps a preset air gap to a grounding point or points at the end of the conductive base. The resultant spark ignites the fuel/air mixture in the combustion chamber.

SPLINES: Ridges machined or cast onto the outer diameter of a shaft or inner diameter of a bore to enable parts to mate without rotation.

TACHOMETER: A device used to measure the rotary speed of an engine, shaft, gear, etc., usually in rotations per minute.

THERMOSTAT: A valve, located in the cooling system of an engine, which is closed when cold and opens gradually in response to engine heating, controlling the temperature of the coolant and rate of coolant flow.

TOP DEAD CENTER (TDC): The point at which the piston reaches the top of its travel on the compression stroke.

TORQUE: The twisting force applied to an object.

TORQUE CONVERTER: A turbine used to transmit power from a driving member to a driven member via hydraulic action, providing changes in drive ratio and torque. In automotive use, it links the driveplate at the rear of the engine to the automatic transmission.

TRANSDUCER: A device used to change a force into an electrical signal.

TRANSISTOR: A semi-conductor component which can be actuated by a small voltage to perform an electrical switching function.

TUNE-UP: A regular maintenance function, usually associated with the replacement and adjustment of parts and components in the electrical and fuel systems of a vehicle for the purpose of attaining optimum performance.

TURBOCHARGER: An exhaust driven pump which compresses intake air and forces it into the combustion chambers at higher than atmospheric pressures. The increased air pressure allows more fuel to be burned and results in increased horsepower being produced.

VACUUM ADVANCE: A device which advances the ignition timing in response to increased engine vacuum.

VACUUM GAUGE: An instrument used to measure the presence of vacuum in a chamber.

VALVE: A device which control the pressure, direction of flow or rate of flow of a liquid or gas.

VALVE CLEARANCE: The measured gap between the end of the valve stem and the rocker arm, cam lobe or follower that activates the valve.

VISCOSITY: The rating of a liquid's internal resistance to flow.

VOLTMETER: An instrument used for measuring electrical force in units called volts. Voltmeters are always connected parallel with the circuit being tested.

WHEEL CYLINDER: Found in the automotive drum brake assembly, it is a device, actuated by hydraulic pressure, which, through internal pistons, pushes the brake shoes outward against the drums.

MASTER INDEX

Total Car Care, continued

Sentra/Pulsar/NX 1982-96
PART NO. 8263/52700
Stanza/200SX/240SX 1982-92
PART NO. 8262/52750
240SX/Altima 1993-98
PART NO. 52752
Datsun/Nissan Z and ZX 1970-88
PART NO. 8846/52800

RENAULT
Coupes/Sedans/Wagons 1975-85
PART NO. 58300

SATURN
Coupes/Sedans/Wagons 1991-98
PART NO. 8419/62300

SUBARU
Coupes/Sedan/Wagons 1970-84
PART NO. 8790/64300
Coupes/Sedans/Wagons 1985-96
PART NO. 8259/64302

SUZUKI
Samurai/Sidekick/Tracker 1986-98
PART NO. 66500

TOYOTA
Camry 1983-96
PART NO. 8265/68200
Celica/Supra 1971-85
PART NO. 68250
Celica 1986-93
PART NO. 8413/68252
Celica 1994-98
PART NO. 68254
Corolla 1970-87
PART NO. 8586/68300
Corolla 1988-97
PART NO. 8414/68302
Cressida/Corona/Crown/MkII 1970-82
PART NO. 68350
Cressida/Van 1983-90
PART NO. 68352
Pick-ups/Land Cruiser/4Runner 1970-88
PART NO. 8578/68600
Pick-ups/Land Cruiser/4Runner 1989-98
PART NO. 8163/68602
Previa 1991-97
PART NO. 68640
Tercel 1984-94
PART NO. 8595/68700

VOLKSWAGEN
Air-Cooled 1949-69
PART NO. 70200
Air-Cooled 1970-81
PART NO. 70202
Front Wheel Drive 1974-89
PART NO. 8663/70400
Golf/Jetta/Cabriolet 1990-93
PART NO. 8429/70402

VOLVO
Coupes/Sedans/Wagons 1970-89
PART NO. 8786/72300
Coupes/Sedans/Wagons 1990-98
PART NO. 8428/72302

SELOC MARINE MANUALS

OUTBOARDS
Chrysler Outboards, All Engines 1962-84
PART NO. 018-7(1000)
Force Outboards, All Engines 1984-96
PART NO. 024-1(1100)
Honda Outboards, All Engines 1988-98
PART NO. 1200
Johnson/Evinrude Outboards, 1.5-40HP, 2-Stroke 1956-70
PART NO. 007-1(1300)
Johnson/Evinrude Outboards, 1.25-60HP, 2-Stroke 1971-89
PART NO. 008-X(1302)
Johnson/Evinrude Outboards, 1-50 HP, 2-Stroke 1990-95
PART NO. 026-8(1304)
Johnson/Evinrude Outboards, 50-125 HP, 2-Stroke 1958-72
PART NO. 009-8(1306)
Johnson/Evinrude Outboards, 60-235 HP, 2-Stroke 1973-91
PART NO. 010-1(1308)
Johnson/Evinrude Outboards, 80-300 HP, 2-Stroke 1992-96
PART NO. 040-3(1310)
Mariner Outboards, 2-60 HP, 2-Stroke 1977-89
PART NO. 015-2(1400)
Mariner Outboards, 45-220 HP, 2 Stroke 1977-89
PART NO. 016-0(1402)
Mercury Outboards, 2-40 HP, 2-Stroke 1965-91
PART NO. 012-8(1404)
Mercury Outboards, 40-115 HP, 2-Stroke 1965-92
PART NO. 013-6(1406)
Mercury Outboards, 90-300 HP, 2-Stroke 1965-91
PART NO. 014-4(1408)
Mercury/Mariner Outboards, 2.5-25 HP, 2-Stroke 1990-94
PART NO. 035-7(1410)
Mercury/Mariner Outboards, 40-125 HP, 2-Stroke 1990-94
PART NO. 036-5(1412)
Mercury/Mariner Outboards, 135-275 HP, 2-Stroke 1990-94
PART NO. 037-3(1414)
Mercury/Mariner Outboards, All Engines 1995-99
PART NO. 1416
Suzuki Outboards, All Engines 1985-99
PART NO. 1600
Yamaha Outboards, 2-25 HP, 2-Stroke and 9.9 HP, 4-Stroke 1984-91
PART NO. 021-7(1700)
Yamaha Outboards, 30-90 HP, 2-Stroke 1984-91
PART NO. 022-5(1702)
Yamaha Outboards, 115-225 HP, 2-Stroke 1984-91
PART NO. 023-3(1704)
Yamaha Outboards, All Engines 1992-98
PART NO. 1706

STERN DRIVES
Marine Jet Drive 1961-96
PART NO. 029-2(3000)
Mercruiser Stern Drive Type 1, Alpha, Bravo I, II, 1964-92
PART NO. 005-5(3200)
Mercruiser Stern Drive Alpha 1 Generation II 1992-96
PART NO. 039-X(3202)
Mercruiser Stern Drive Bravo I, II, III 1992-96
PART NO. 046-2(3204)
OMC Stern Drive 1964-86
PART NO. 004-7(3400)
OMC Cobra Stern Drive 1985-95
PART NO. 025-X(3402)
Volvo/Penta Stern Drives 1968-91
PART NO. 011-X(3600)
Volvo/Penta Stern Drives 1992-93
PART NO. 038-1(3602)
Volvo/Penta Stern Drives 1992-95
PART NO. 041-1(3604)

INBOARDS
Yanmar Inboard Diesels 1988-91
PART NO. 7400

PERSONAL WATERCRAFT
Kawasaki 1973-91
PART NO. 032-2(9200)
Kawasaki 1992-97
PART NO. 042-X(9202)
Polaris 1992-97
PART NO. 045-4(9400)
Sea Doo/Bombardier 1988-91
PART NO. 033-0(9000)
Sea Doo/Bombardier 1992-97
PART NO. 043-8(9002)
Yamaha 1987-91
PART NO. 034-9(9600)
Yamaha 1992-97
PART NO. 044-6(9602)

"...and even more from CHILTON"

General Interest / Recreational Books

ATV Handbook
PART NO. 9123
Auto Detailing
PART NO. 8394
Auto Body Repair
PART NO. 7898
Briggs & Stratton Vertical Crankshaft Engine
PART NO. 61-1-2
Briggs & Stratton Horizontal Crankshaft Engine
PART NO. 61-0-4
Briggs & Stratton Overhead Valve (OHV) Engine
PART NO. 61-2-0
Easy Car Care
PART NO. 8042
Motorcycle Handbook
PART NO. 9099
Snowmobile Handbook
PART NO. 9124
Small Engine Repair (Up to 20 Hp)
PART NO. 8325

Total Service Series

Automatic Transmissions/Transaxles Diagnosis and Repair
PART NO. 8944
Brake System Diagnosis and Repair
PART NO. 8945
Chevrolet Engine Overhaul Manual
PART NO. 8794
Engine Code Manual
PART NO. 8851
Ford Engine Overhaul Manual
PART NO. 8793
Fuel Injection Diagnosis and Repair
PART NO. 8946

COLLECTOR'S SERIES HARD-COVER MANUALS

Chilton's Collector's Editions are perfect for enthusiasts of vintage or rare cars. These hard-cover manuals contain repair and maintenance information for all major systems that might not be available elsewhere. Included are repair and overhaul procedures using thousands of illustrations. These manuals offer a range of coverage from as far back as 1940 and as recent as 1997, so you don't need an antique car or truck to be a collector.

MULTI-VEHICLE SPANISH LANGUAGE MANUALS

Chilton's Spanish language manuals offer some of our most popular titles in Spanish. Each is as complete and easy to use as the English-language counterpart and offers the same maintenance, repair and overhaul information along with specifications charts and tons of illustrations.

TOTAL SERVICE SERIES / SYSTEM SPECIFIC MANUALS

These innovative books offer repair, maintenance and service procedures for automotive related systems. They cover today's complex vehicles in a user-friendly format, which places even the most difficult automotive topic well within the reach of every Do-It-Yourselfer. Each title covers a specific subject from Brakes and Engine Rebuilding to Fuel Injection Systems, Automatic Transmissions and even Engine Trouble Codes.

For the titles listed, visit your local Chilton® Retailer

For a Catalog, for information, or to order call toll-free: 877-4CHILTON.

1020 Andrew Drive, Suite 200 • West Chester, PA 19380-4291
www.chiltonsonline.com

2P2VerB